BUSINESS AND SOCIETY TODAY:
MANAGING SOCIAL ISSUES

BUSINESS AND SOCIETY TODAY:
MANAGING SOCIAL ISSUES

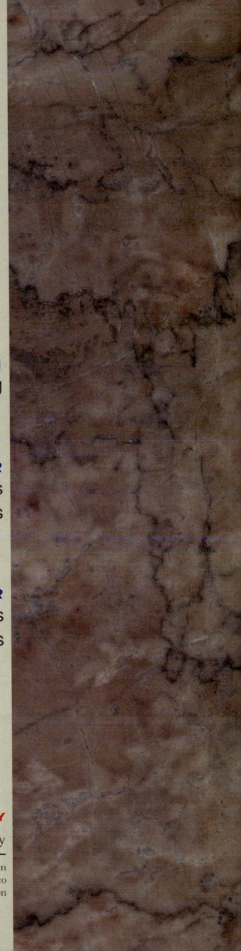

JOHN H. JACKSON
University of Wyoming

ROGER LeROY MILLER
Institute for University Studies
Arlington, Texas

SHAWN G. MILLER
Institute for University Studies
Arlington, Texas

WEST PUBLISHING COMPANY
I(T)P® An International Thomson Publishing Company

Pacific Grove • Albany • Belmont • Bonn • Boston • Cincinnati • Detroit • Johannesburg • London
Los Angeles • Madrid • Melbourne • Mexico City • New York • Paris • San Francisco
Singapore • St. Paul/Minneapolis • Tokyo • Toronto • Washington

Text Copyediting: Mary Berry and Beverly Peavler
Text Proofreader: Suzie Franklin Defazio
Indexer: Margaret Jarpey
Composition: Parkwood Composition Service, Inc.
Interior Art: Mary Anderson—Parkwood Composition Service, Inc.

British Library Cataloguing-in-Publication Data. A catalogue record for this book is available from the British Library.

COPYRIGHT ©1997   By WEST PUBLISHING COMPANY
An International Thomson Publishing Company
ᴵ⒯ᴾ® The ITP logo is a trademark under license.

04 03 02 01 00 99   8 7 6 5 4 3 2

Library of Congress Cataloging-in-Publication Data

Jackson, John H.
    Business and society today: managing social issues/John H. Jackson,
Roger LeRoy Miller, Shawn G. Miller.
        p.   cm.
    Includes index.
    ISBN 0-314-20386-9 (alk. paper)
    1. Social responsibility of business—United States.   2. Industrial policy—
United States.   3. Business ethics—United States.   I. Miller, Roger LeRoy.
II. Miller, Shawn G.   III. Title.
HD60.5.U5J33 1997
658.4 '08—dc21   96–46393
                                                                            CIP

CONTENTS IN BRIEF

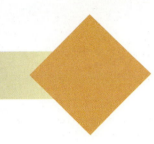

CONTENTS

◆◆ Part II
BUSINESS ETHICS AND CORPORATE
SOCIAL RESPONSIBILITY   79

Chapter 4: The Fundamentals of Business Ethics   81

Chapter 5: Managerial Values and the Corporate
Culture   107

Chapter 6: Corporate Social Responsibility   141

Chapter 7: Ethical Decisions in a Global
Environment   169

COMPANY FOCUS

COMPANY FOCUS (CONTINUED)

Ⓖ MANAGING SOCIAL ISSUES

PREFACE TO THE INSTRUCTOR

It is ironic that America's corporate world is under so much scrutiny today, probably even more than at any other time in our history. The irony exists because only a few short years ago, a system that completely denied the legal and moral underpinnings of our free enterprise system—including, of course, corporations—completely disintegrated after seventy-four years. When the Soviet Empire finally called it quits, many believed that the message was clear: Capitalism is the only viable system that can guarantee long-run economic growth and improvement in the material well-being of the world's citizens. The euphoria of the proponents of capitalism did not last long. Economic growth rates slowed in the European Union as well as in the United States. Japan faced a major recession. Then questions about income inequality within the United States arose. At the same time, the press reported "scandals" about corporate misadventures. Finally, an increasing number of corporate executives were and continue to be subjected to criminal prosecution for what used to only be violations of civil law.

It is within the above-described context that we decided to develop a new text that would place American business in an appropriate setting. The manager of tomorrow can no longer simply learn the "nuts and bolts" of business activities, such as business law, accounting, finance, and the like. Rather, tomorrow's manager must also learn what society, and perhaps more specifically, government, wants and expects.

Knowledge is power and, in this case, students' knowledge of the new changing role of business in America and the global society will give them the power to prepare and to act in a way that is ethical, legal, and conducive to the long-run best interests of the business entities for which they work.

THOROUGHLY MODERN AND FORWARD LOOKING

We have had one great advantage over our competitors—we started this text from scratch several years ago. Consequently, we have been able to focus on the most modern aspects of business and society relationships. We have also made sure that all of the text is forward looking. Hence, students will come away from this course with a strong base on which to build the skills they will need next year, the year after, and for many years to come. We have consistently sought out the most up-to-date research results, the most recent case studies, and the latest federal and state statutes and regulations. We believe that students will appreciate the contemporary feeling that this new text generates.

PEDAGOGY WITH A PURPOSE

Every chapter in this text includes pedagogical devices that we believe will strongly aid students in (1) understanding the material, (2) retaining the material, and (3) actually wanting to read about the subject matter.

VOCABULARY

To make sure that students master important vocabulary, we have created a four-pronged vocabulary enhancement system, which consists of the following:

1. Vocabulary terms are boldfaced in the text. An explanation is then given.
2. *Terms and Concepts for Review* are found at the end of each chapter with appropriate page numbers in case the student does not understand the word. He or she can then go back to the appropriate page and look up how it is used in context.
3. A *Glossary* at the back of the book provides an easy alphabetical review of the vocabulary.

MANAGING SOCIAL ISSUES

This in-text feature provides your students with a variety of important examples taken from the business world about how different companies and managers have responded to social issues. There are eight types of these features:

▶ Barriers to Success
▶ Global/International
▶ Ethical/Social Responsibility
▶ Making a Difference
▶ Multicultural/Tolerance
▶ Information/Technology
▶ Small Business/Entrepreneurial
▶ Forging New Alliances (Partnerships)

For Critical Analysis—to make sure that students don't simply read and forget the features just mentioned, we end each one with a critical-thinking question.

COMPANY FOCUS

Every chapter has one to three mini-case studies entitled *Company Focus*. These mini-cases present a wide variety of different company settings.

The New Bottom Line—at the end of every *Company Focus*, we present what we call *The New Bottom Line*, in which we offer to your students a forward-looking view of where management must go in order to succeed in the new business/society environment.

THE DELICATE BALANCE

Every chapter ends with a section called *The Delicate Balance* in which we take the chapter's main focus and present it in terms of the trade-offs that management must make today and in the future.

Chapter Summary

Every chapter ends with a ten-to fifteen-statement point-by-point summary providing students with a helpful self-test system. If they don't understand a summary point, they can go back to the appropriate place in the chapter and review the material.

Exercises

Rather than simply providing students with rote questions at the end of each chapter, we have developed what we believe to be the best set of exercises available. Specifically, these exercises require, among other things, reexamination of charts, tables, and exhibits; critical analysis of the same; and so on. We also ask your students to develop short speeches on particular topics as well as other communication-oriented activities.

Selected References

Each chapter ends with a manageable set of references for further reading.

Internet: The Future Is Now

Because the Internet has become an increasingly important part of our lives, we devote small sections at the end of each chapter to Internet addresses that will allow students to peruse more information on specific topics. This section is entitled *Resources on the Internet*.

CHAPTER-ENDING CASE STUDIES

Every chapter ends with an in-depth case study, most of which are taken from recent corporate events in America. These case studies, when appropriate, are thoroughly footnoted to aid students who wish to pursue particular aspects of each case.

Critical Thinking Again

At the end of each case study, there are three to five *Critical Thinking Questions*. We believe these will help students have a better understanding of the case studies.

SUPPLEMENTS

Business and Society Today: Managing Social Issues comes with an extensive supplements package aimed at making the course more accessible to your students and more easily taught by you. The supplements are as follows:

Instructor's Manual with Test Bank

The *Instructor's Manual* includes chapter outlines, suggested answers for the chapter features, end-of-chapter cases, and twenty-five multiple-choice test questions per chapter.

Supplemental Case Booklet

The booklet, which includes an additional case for each chapter in the text, is free with each new book.

Videos

Video topics include ethics and corporate social responsibility.

Introduction to the Internet

For more information on how to access legal and other sources on the Internet, students can refer to a new printed supplement accompanying *Business and Society Today*, entitled *Understanding and Using the Internet*, by Bruce J. McLaren. This booklet, which is approximately 170 pages in length, includes an *Instructor's Manual*.

Overhead Transparencies

This package will include selected figures from the text.

ACKNOWLEDGMENTS

A group of extremely hard-working reviewers helped us improve our manuscript at all stages of the numerous drafts that we have gone through in the past five years. We thank these reviewers profusely for the time that they put in to help us make this a better text for both students and professors.

ERIC J. AKERS
Ashland University

HARVEY L. BAUMAN
Appalachian State University

FRANK J. CAVALIERE
Lamar University

JAMES H. CONLEY
Eastern Michigan University

CYNTHIA L. CORDES
SUNY Brighamton University

GEORGE C. DAVIS
Jacksonville State University

KATHLEEN A. GETZ
The American University

DAVID HOCH
University of Southwest Louisiana

MICHAEL H. HOGG
Tulane University

THOMAS A. KLEIN
University of Toledo

KENNETH R. MAYER
Cleveland State University

DIANE S. MCNULTY
The University of Texas at Dallas

DINAH PAYNE
University of New Orleans

MARTIN SCHNITZER
Virginia Tech

MARTA SZABO WHITE
Georgia State University

JUDY WILES
Southeast Missouri State University

No textbook project is ever done in a vacuum. We have our editor, Clyde Perlee, Jr., to thank for encouraging us to develop this project and for all of his help in guiding us along the path to publication. In addition, we also had the benefit of Jan Lamar's expert guidance as we developed the manuscript. She also took on the responsibility of overseeing the production of the supplements. We thank her for her unrelenting enthusiasm and professionalism. The design of this book was undertaken by Lee Anne Storey, while its production was coordinated by Regan Stilo. We wish to express our unending gratitude to them. We benefited from the expert copyediting of Mary Berry and Beverly Peavler. Among the proofreaders, we can single out Suzie Franklin DeFazio, to whom we express our appreciation. Also, we were fortunate to have the indexing services of Margaret Jarpey and benefited from the typing, editorial, and management services of Suzanne Jasin of K&M Consulting who, as usual, never faltered under an overwhelming workload.

We plan to revise this text for many years to come. Consequently, we welcome any and all comments and criticism from you or your students. It is only by taking your views to heart that we can ever hope to improve our product.

J.H.J.
R.L.M.
S.G.M.

DEDICATION

To Linda, Jeff, Jodie, and Cody who
know of both the grumpiness and pride
associated with writing textbooks.
J.H.J.

To Pierre Emmanuel,
You are living proof that computer
experts and music can mix well together,
provided of course that other essential
ingredients are present.
R.L.M.

To my parents and Sabine.
S.G.M.

PART 1

BUSINESS AND SOCIETY

CHAPTER 1

THE RELATIONSHIP BETWEEN BUSINESS AND SOCIETY

CHAPTER OUTLINE

- Ethical Perspectives
- Political Perspectives
- Social Perspectives
- Cultural and Demographic Perspectives
- Environmental Perspectives
- Technological Perspectives
- Global Perspectives

INTRODUCTION

From as far back as anyone could remember, the chief industry of the small French town of Montreuil-sur-Mer had been the production of imitation English jet beads and German black glass trinkets. In 1815, a stranger settled in the city and struck on the idea of substituting shellac for resin in the manufacturing process of these products. This change, as an observer described it,

> caused a revolution. It had in fact reduced the price of the raw material enormously, and this had made it possible, first to raise the wages of the workers—a benefit to the district; secondly, to improve the quality of the goods—an advantage to the consumer; and third, to sell them at a lower price even while making three times the profit—a gain for the manufacturer.

The stranger who brought about this revolution became rich, "which was good," and made those around him rich, "which was better." He gave his name as Father Madeleine, and he used his wealth for the benefit of the community, building a rest home for old and disabled workers, two schools, a health-care facility for the poor, and an extra wing in the local hospital. Before his arrival, again according to the observer,

> the whole region was stagnant; now it was alive with the healthy strength of labor . . . Unemployment and misery were unknown. There was no pocket so dark that it did not contain a little money and no dwelling so poor that it did not contain some joy.

If Father Madeleine sounds too good to be true, there is a reason. He is a fictional character, the creation of Victor Hugo (1820–1885) in his classic novel *Les Misérables* (1862).[1] A great critic of business in general in his time, Hugo endowed Father Madeleine—also known as Jean Valjean—with the aspects of his ideal businessperson, one who benefits society to a greater extent than he benefits himself through economic activity. Hugo was not the first social commentator, and will not be the last, to present a negative view of businesses' motives. In his fiction he provided what he believed to be the appropriate blueprint for corporate values.

Recently, Hugo's ideas have become mainstream. The past few decades have seen a dramatic shift in what has traditionally been the acceptable basic **incentive structure** for the American capitalist market system. The "bottom line" was once unquestioned as the basis for the decision-making process of American business. Today, however, there are some alternatives clamoring for space and attention:

▼ Simply put, business is expected to be as concerned with the well-being of society as it is with its own profit margins.[2]

One goal of this textbook is to put the profit motive in its proper perspective. Making money is still the only way a business can survive, but the modern market-

---

1. Victor Hugo, *Les Misérables*, trans. L. Fahnestock and N. MacAfee (New York: Signet Classics, 1987), pp. 159–160.
2. D. P. Quinn and T. M. Jones, "An Agent Morality View of Business Policy," *Academy of Management Review*, January 1995, p. 22.

place demands that businesses also pay attention to the rights of employees and minorities, the well-being of local and global communities, the natural environment, and other social concerns.

Another goal of this textbook is to provide the theoretical and practical knowledge needed in today's business environment. In this opening chapter, we introduce many of the issues that will form the basis for our later discussions. We start with a short look at the changing ethical perspectives of business.

ETHICAL PERSPECTIVES

People often complain that politicians, business leaders, and other influential individuals are less honest than before. Whether this perception is substantiated by reality cannot be proved. Nevertheless, the perception that the leaders of our nation are less honorable or moral than their predecessors were continues to be a popular view among many Americans.

Why do businesspeople have an image problem among some? Part of the issue may stem from the fact that virtually all persons are purchasers of services or goods sold by businesses. Consumers are always worried about whether they are paying too much for a particular product or service or whether the quality is as good as the seller claims. In effect, buyers can at times have an adversarial relationship with sellers. Given this potential antipathy, it is sometimes not difficult to convince the American public that businesspeople act in unethical ways.

BUSINESS ETHICS YESTERDAY AND TODAY

The ethical issues facing businesses today are often more complicated and more in the public eye than they were a hundred years ago. This situation stems from the availability of virtually instantaneous news reporting and a concurrent increased public awareness of ethical issues (in addition, some people believe that members of the mass media go out of their way to look for bad things to relate about businesspeople).[3] Assuming that the press gives people what they want, why, one might ask, was the public less concerned about such issues a century ago?

One of the main reasons is that we were a financially poorer society a century ago. When people are struggling to make ends meet, they are not likely to be concerned about ethics, or lack of them, in the business world. We can surmise that in the world today with so many countries that are much poorer than America, what may seem unethical to Americans might actually have to be "business as usual" in those countries. Ethics and a country's standard of living are intimately tied together. In other words, we, as a nation, can be more concerned about ethical issues in business because we are less concerned about simple material survival.[4]

Furthermore, technology has enhanced our ability to communicate the unethical behavior of others to all parts of the country, and even the world. If a politician is caught accepting a bribe, or a corporate vice president is found embezzling funds, chances are good that the story will be featured on the six o'clock news. If the Italian government collapses under the weight of its own corruption, Cable News Network (CNN) is there

---

3. R. E. Smith, "Ethics in an Interactive World," *Business and Society Review*, Fall 1994, p. 48.
4. A. B. Carroll, "Social Issues in Management Research: Experts' View, Analysis, and Commentary," *Business and Society*, April 1994, p. 5.

to lead us through each step of the process. The indiscretions of community leaders, which thirty years ago might have been overlooked, are reported on the nightly news and featured in news magazine cover stories. So business ethics can be put in a practical light:

▼ Today, more than ever before, if you are an unethical business leader, there is a good chance you are going to get caught.

CORPORATE AMERICA'S COMMITMENT TO ETHICS

You will discover when you read Chapters 4 to 7—which are devoted exclusively to business ethics—that many companies are responding to the public awareness of this issue by promoting ethics within their ranks. The Ethics Resource Center in Washington, D.C., estimates that three out of every five American companies have codes of ethics in place. These codes are meant to instill in employees a commitment to ethical activity above and beyond the letter of the law, as well as to reassure consumers, employees, and investors that a company is trustworthy.

Ethical Trade-Offs Most corporate executives are well aware that ethical issues, just like other business issues, involve **trade-offs**. The difficulty lies in deciding just how to make those trade-offs. Do you trade improved ethical behavior on the part of managers for corporate profits? Do you trade the costs of overall improved worker safety, worker security, and worker health care for the possible loss of jobs? Can you afford to maintain an inefficient, obsolete plant, thereby saving jobs at the expense of streamlining operations and becoming more competitive with foreign companies? These are not rhetorical questions but problems that managers deal with every day.

Ethical Breakdowns Given the pressure on managers to show profits, it is not surprising that they may be reluctant to accept the trade-offs implicit in ethical issues. In fact, a survey of middle-level managers by Joseph Badaracco of Harvard Business School and consultant Allen Webb showed that in most companies, "behaving ethically" was measured by performance and loyalty, not ethics. These managers were not encouraged by their seniors to "overinvest" in ethical behavior, and a third of those polled did not feel upper management respected those who notified authorities of unethical activity within the corporation.[5]

This attitude goes far in explaining the reaction of many companies—even those with **ethics codes**—toward whistleblowers. In 1995, Prudential Insurance, whose ethics code encourages employees to help customers "achieve financial security and peace of mind," was the target of a $12.4 million lawsuit by Rich Martin, a former salesperson. Martin claimed the company fired him after he reported deceptive sales practices. This seeming disparity between an ethics code and actual unethical behavior lingers in corporate America. In *Exhibit 1–1*, you can read about a number of companies that may not have lived up to their own ethical guidelines. Note that our assessment here is highly subjective. The companies involved may disagree with the interpretations presented in *Exhibit 1–1*.

---

5. J. Badaracco and A. Webb, "Business Ethics: The View from the Trenches," *California Management Review*, Winter 1995, pp. 8–28.

▼ **EXHIBIT 1–1 "Do What I Say, Not What I Do"**—Companies That May Not Have Lived Up to Their Own Ethical Guidelines

Company	Ethical Guidelines	Corporate Behavior
Dow Corning	This giant corporation was one of the first American companies to install an internal ethics program, and its process of ethics training is still widely respected. The Dow Corning ethics system includes a Business Conduct Committee staffed by managers, constant ethical audits of business operations, and a code of ethics that encourages employees to raise ethical issues with superiors.	The same year Dow Corning began its ethics program—1976—an engineer quit the company in protest of safety questions concerning the company's silicone breast implants. A memo the next year noted that 52 of 400 test implant procedures had resulted in ruptures. Despite these warning signals, the company placed the breast implants on the market. Fifteen years later, Dow Corning was the main target of a class-action lawsuit brought by 65,000 breast implant recipients. The suit contended that the women had incurred a number of health problems resulting from silicone leaks in the implants. Dow Corning settled for $2 billion.
General Electric	This giant corporation, the sixth largest in the United States, has an ethics program "as good as any in the United States," according to one legal expert. Its written ethics policy is supplemented by fourteen toll-free ethics help lines for employees.	In the 1990s alone, General Electric and its subsidiaries have paid fines and settlement fees in sixteen cases of abuse, fraud, and waste in contracts with the federal government.
Intel	In its written mission statement, this computer chip company states that it strives to "listen to our customers" and "communicate mutual intentions and expectations."	In 1994, a math professor noticed that Intel's Pentium microchip was flawed. When he called the company to report the flaw, Intel told him that it was aware of the problem but did not plan to do anything about it. As news of the flaw spread, Intel insisted that the "bug" would affect only those computer programmers doing highly complex mathematical equations. Therefore, Intel refused to offer consumers a replacement chip. Within two weeks, this perceived arrogance on Intel's part sparked a public relations disaster. Industry insiders, consumers, and the media had been given the impression that Intel was trying to cover up the flawed chip.
Body Shop International	This British company, which offers a variety of beauty and soap products, prides itself on being one of the world's most socially and environmentally conscious corporations. One of the company's selling points has been a refusal to sell products tested on animals. In fact, its products originally bore labels that read "Not Tested on Animals."	In 1989, Body Shop quietly stopped labeling its products "Not Tested on Animals." The new labels read "Against Animal Testing." It turns out that Body Shop suppliers had been using ingredients that had been tested on animals, even as Body Shop had been telling its customers that the opposite was true.

POLITICAL PERSPECTIVES

When confronted with certain behavior on the part of business, the public will often turn to government to keep business in line. As government is usually willing to comply, companies must necessarily become involved in the political process.

BUSINESS INFLUENCE IN POLITICS

Businesses have their own political agendas that may include keeping cheaper foreign products out of the United States. To be globally competitive today takes hard work and sometimes many years. A few businesses might want to take a short cut by lobbying government agencies and politicians in order to obtain a competitive advantage, particularly over foreign competitors. (Businesses, however, often also seek to change those specific government rules that actually harm consumers.)

Short-Term Influence A company may use government protection to maximize short-run profits. One of the most notorious examples occurred in the 1980s, when the U.S. government, at the corporate community's urging, convinced Japan to impose voluntary export restraints on its automobiles. The American car makers were presented with a unique opportunity to increase their market share substantially through price advantage, but they chose instead to increase car prices to maximize **short-term profits**. Although this approach may have pleased some stockholders, it did not help the companies become more efficient producers. Consequently, the car makers were not prepared to weather the 1990–1992 recession and were forced to close down dozens of plants and lay off tens of thousands of workers. Furthermore, the automakers alienated many in Congress who felt betrayed by what they considered an example of excessive self-interest. In contrast, Harley-Davidson—after a management buyout in 1981—used import protection to retool its manufacturing facilities and improve its motorcycles, and it became internationally competitive.

WHERE DOES BUSINESS DRAW THE LINE?

Some analysts might argue that business should not be involved in politics at all, but should focus its efforts on producing the goods and services desired by American consumers. Others take the opposite approach, arguing that it is in the best interests of stockholders for their businesses to lobby for beneficial legislation, or against detrimental legislation.[6]

The problem—even for those who favor intensive lobbying efforts—is where to draw the line. When does a business's attempt to influence legislation leave the realm of good business behavior and enter the realm of unethical activity? To what extent is a business's contribution to political campaigns motivated by a desire to increase the power and prestige of upper management rather than to benefit the shareholders in general? We discuss the proper (and improper) role of business in the political arena in Chapter 11.

THE POLITICS OF REGULATORY AGENCIES

Much of the legal and regulatory environment of business is determined by rules made within government regulatory bodies. These rules are not created in a vacuum. In the past, agencies were oriented toward a specific industry, as in the case of the (now defunct)

6. B. Avishai, "What Is Business's Social Compact?" *Harvard Business Review,* January–February 1994, p. 38.

Interstate Commerce Commission, which was originally created to regulate railroad rates and routes "in the public interest." In recent decades, the approach has changed and agencies have been created to implement reforms across industries, to regulate specific functions of all businesses, and to regulate areas such as worker safety and environmental protection. The Environmental Protection Agency, for example, was created to ensure protection of the environment by controlling polluters, in whatever business the polluters might be. The Equal Employment Opportunity Commission was created to end discrimination in employment, whoever the employer might be.

THE ECONOMIC EFFECTS OF REGULATION—SHORT RUN VERSUS LONG RUN

Managers are aware that there is an economic impact every time legislation is passed that creates a new regulatory environment for business. Some regulatory legislation specifically requires that the economic costs and benefits associated with certain actions be estimated. For example, the National Environmental Policy Act of 1969 requires that all federal agencies contemplating actions that might affect the environment prepare an **environmental impact statement**. This statement must give numerical estimates of both the costs and the benefits of a proposed federal action.

In general, though, the regulatory acts passed by Congress do not require government agencies to make a complete analysis of total costs and benefits to the nation. Furthermore, some costs may not show up in the short run. They become apparent only after industry has had time to react to the new legislation.[7] Under the current law initiated in the 1970s, for example, the entire fleet of cars manufactured by each automaker must average 27.5 miles per gallon of gasoline. This is the corporate average fuel economy, which companies must attain or else face government fines. This requirement for **fleet mileage standards** may be altered only with the consent of the National Highway Traffic Safety Administration.

In meeting these government standards, the car companies found that one of the best ways to increase gas mileage was to reduce the weight of the cars they sold. Reducing the weight of cars was generally accomplished by shrinking the size of the car itself and replacing heavier materials, such as steel, with lighter materials, such as plastic. From a fuel-economy point of view, downsizing made sense; smaller cars travel farther on a gallon of gas. But they also offer less protection to their occupants in the case of a crash. The lower the weight of the car, generally the higher the probability of injury or death when the car is involved in an accident. It has been estimated that the occupants of small cars are twice as likely to die in an accident as the occupants of large cars. One of the net effects of the government-sponsored downsizing of U.S. automobiles, then, may be greater numbers of highway fatalities.[8] This is a prime example of the intricacies of the business-government-society relationship.

The perception in the 1970s that the world was running out of oil provided the original impetus for fleet mileage standards. But times have changed, and the inflation-corrected price of gas has fallen over the years. Many people (politicians included) see little reason to continue insisting that fleet mileage standards be revised upward periodically. Consequently, the rationale for these standards is now shifting from energy

7. B. Shaffer, "Firm-Level Responses to Government Regulation: Theoretical and Research Approaches," *Journal of Management*, Fall 1995, p. 495.
8. R. L. Miller and F. B. Cross, *The Legal and Regulatory Environment Today* (St. Paul: West Publishing Co., 1993), p. 41.

conservation to environmental preservation. Some argue that these standards should be kept in place, because the United States must help reduce emissions from internal combustion engines and thereby minimize global warming.

SOCIAL PERSPECTIVES

Changes in society and changes in the way society views the role of business affect how businesses operate. We have already pointed out that businesses are vulnerable to the political constraints often imposed by societal pressures. Similarly, the social issues of the day, such as civil rights, can often change the way in which businesspersons are expected to act.[9] These expectations, though not necessarily carrying any legal authority, may alter the way in which people conduct commercial activities: We will be discussing many social issues throughout this textbook, for example, education, the homeless, and acquired immune deficiency syndrome (AIDS).

Consider, for example, the issue of quality in education, which is generally perceived to be on the decline in America. Businesses complain that they are forced to add additional on-the-job-training programs because of poorly educated workers. Businesses have also been called on to contribute directly to public education in low-income neighborhoods. With respect to the important issue of what to do about the homeless in America, businesses find that they are in a controversial situation if a homeless shelter is built in their geographic location. Owners of restaurants, retail stores, and other establishments generally perceive the presence of homeless people as a negative, and therefore bad for business. Here again, businesses, especially large ones, are expected to financially participate in solving the problems of the homeless.

Finally, the problems associated with the spread of AIDS have reached the business community. Businesses must be aware of the implications of the Americans with Disabilities Act

---

9. L. S. Paine, "Managing for Organizational Integrity," *Harvard Business Review*, March–April 1994, p. 106.

of 1990 when they are dealing with employees or potential employees who suffer from AIDS. Many businesses have started AIDS education programs.

All in all, business and the problems of society are intimately linked, as you will see throughout the rest of this textbook.

CULTURAL AND DEMOGRAPHIC PERSPECTIVES

The nation's increased cultural and demographic diversity—not only in the work force but in the population as a whole—is having a tremendous impact on business organizations. An increasing percentage of school-age children in many states were not born in the United States. The problems faced by school districts that have students from many different countries, such as in Los Angeles, are precursors of the problems that many businesses will face.

MANAGING DIVERSITY

The U.S. work force has always included a wide variety of workers from many cultural backgrounds, and the challenges of this situation are not new. Ways of handling a culturally diverse group of workers have changed, however. For example, managers often oversee assembly line workers who speak languages other than English. In the past, a manager would have expected the workers to learn English. Today, a more realistic and ethical approach—and sometimes the only legal approach—is for managers to help workers learn English or to learn at least a few words of the foreign language themselves.

Human resources management today is indelibly linked to Title VII of the 1964 Civil Rights Act. In 1971 the Supreme Court clearly stated the intent of Congress in enacting Title VII: "to achieve quality of employment opportunities and remove barriers that have operated in the past to favor an identifiable group of white employees over other employees."[10]

The practical effect of Title VII can be seen in affirmative action programs. Although affirmative action has recently come under question in a number of state legislatures and even in the halls of the U.S. Congress, as we discuss in Chapter 14, it has offered minority groups a greater chance at equal employment opportunities. Some businesses have opposed affirmative action like other regulatory legislation, on the ground that it is overly intrusive in the hiring process. There is a strong argument, however, that properly managing diversity can provide a competitive advantage. With a well-designed scheme of **diversity management**—the process of adapting to employees from different cultures— a company can benefit from the greater adaptability and problem-solving capabilities of a culturally diverse work force (see *Exhibit 1–2* on page 12).

Managers must also accept diversity among customers, as state and federal regulations protect consumers from being discriminated against because of race, gender, age, or disability. Not only is serving the widest variety of customers in the best interest of any business; discriminatory action also can bring negative publicity and costly legal action against a company (see the *Case—Discrimination at Denny's*—at the end of this chapter).

---

10. *Griggs v. Duke Power Co.*, 401 U.S. 424 (1971).

▼ **EXHIBIT 1–2 Managing Cultural Diversity**

Higher Career Involvement of Women
- Dual-care couples accepted
- Sexism and sexual harassment not tolerated
- Work/family conflict accommodated

Is There Bias in
- Recruitment?
- Training and development?
- Compensation and benefits?
- Promotion?

Does the Organization Stress
- Accepting and valuing differences among employees?
- Including different cultural symbols in the office environment?

Managing Cultural Diversity

Perception of Diversity
- Problem or opportunity?
- Resistance or support from the majority workplace culture?
- Challenge met or barely addressed?

Heterogeneity in Race, Ethnicity, and Nationality
- Monitor effect on cohesiveness, communications, conflict resolution, and morale
- Monitor effects of group identity on employee interaction (such as stereotypes)
- Prejudice (racism, ethnocentricity) not tolerated

SOURCE: Adapted from T. Cox and S. Blake, "Managing Cultural Diversity: Implications for Organizational Competitiveness," *The Executive,* August 1991, pp. 45–56.

WOMEN IN THE BUSINESS COMMUNITY

Given a boost by affirmative action and a redefinition of "a woman's role," women have become a significant force in the U.S. economy. Some statistics purport to show that more than a third of the new small businesses formed in the United States during the 1990s have been founded by women, and more than two-thirds of the employees at these companies are also female.

Although there are exceptions (see *Managing Social Issues—The World of the Small-Business Entrepreneur: A Man's World?*), for the most part female entrepreneurs have branched out in service-oriented industries: 36 percent of female-operated businesses are in the caring and curing industry; 32 percent dress, beautify, and feed people; 19 percent deal in computers, electronics, and manufacturing; and 13 percent offer entertainment or novelty services. One reason for this orientation is that many of these areas allow women to address the needs of other women, but another is that women, compared with male entrepreneurs, still have trouble attracting start-up capital. Therefore, women tend to substitute labor for capital and to start businesses in which the customer pays before receiving the product or services.

It is interesting to note that despite their growing presence on the management scene, almost no women are currently serving prison time for business fraud. This has led one commentator to conclude that "the woman entrepreneur is scrupulously honest; perhaps more so than her male equivalent."[11]

ENVIRONMENTAL PERSPECTIVES

Another issue that has changed the business landscape is concern over the well-being of the environment. Every businessperson can now expect to deal with environmental rules and regulations at some point during his or her career.[12] Virtually every aspect of business is now covered by a host of local, state, and federal environmental rules and regulations. Most of these rules are comparatively recent in origin, the majority of them having been passed in the past twenty years. In any case, environmental awareness is now firmly ingrained in the U.S. consciousness:

▼ **Even if environmental regulations did not exist, many businesses would still feel compelled to act in an environmentally sound manner because that is the "socially responsible thing to do."**

For a few businesses selling recyclable and biodegradable consumer products, the "green" revolution means more "green" in the cash register. The sale of ecologically sound products is on the rise as consumers become more aware of their desirability.

THE APPLICATION OF CRIMINAL LAW TO ENVIRONMENTALLY HARMFUL ACTIONS

There are incentives other than profits for a corporation to be eco-friendly. A current change in the regulatory environment of business is the seriousness with which environmentally destructive actions are viewed by the legislatures and courts. A few years ago, for example, three officers of the Everett Steel Companies were sentenced to prison for one year each as part of a plea agreement entered into with the Environmental Protection Agency (EPA) and the Department of Justice. The three men were charged with

---

11. A. D. Silver, "The New American Hero," *Wall Street Journal Europe,* May 25, 1994, p. 6.
12. R. Benton, Jr., "Environmental Knowledge and Attitudes of Undergraduate Business Students Compared to Non-Business Students," *Business and Society,* August 1994, p. 191.

MANAGING SOCIAL ISSUES

THE WORLD OF THE SMALL-BUSINESS ENTREPRENEUR: A MAN'S WORLD?

Although women now make up over 40 percent of the work force and an increasing number of women own their own businesses, there are still areas of the corporate world that are considered "for men only." When was the last time, for example, that you came across a woman who owned and operated a construction company, an engine repair shop, or a car and truck dealership? The percentage of these companies owned by women is still relatively low, but the numbers show this to be changing.

Challenging Perception

According to the U.S. Small Business Administration, in the last decade, women's share of sole proprietorships in agriculture, fishing, and forestry rose from 10 percent to more than 17 percent. In that same period, the percentage of women who owned mining, manufacturing, and construction businesses rose from 6 percent to 9 percent. Even more dramatic is the fact that public utility, transportation, and communication companies owned by women jumped to 14.6 percent from 6.8 percent.

Beyond the numbers, the female owners themselves say they face a number of challenges. The most common is gaining credibility from customers and competitors. "You have to prove yourself maybe five times more [than a man], and after you prove yourself five times more, you're only equal," said Barbara Kavovit, who owns a commercial construction company in Mount Vernon, New York. Victoria Rosellini, who operates her own ambulance company in Baltimore, Maryland, senses that customers do not think she can do the heavy lifting associated with the business and doubt she has the technical ability to keep her trucks running. Arden Haddox, who founded a company that rebuilds rack-and-pinion automobile steering mechanisms in North Ridgeville, Ohio, has developed a strategy to deal with the "sigh-and-eye-rolling" men who frequent her business. "I purposely talk over their heads a lot of the time," she says.

Rules for Success

Women who have established themselves in male-dominated industries have suggestions for those who might follow in their footsteps:

1. Know your stuff. As Haddox has learned, once men find out she knows what she is talking about, they are more inclined to accept her. Although this legitimacy deals more with perceptions than reality, such acceptance can make the job easier and help business.

2. Don't take offense. If male customers refuse to accept a female owner, or they slight her in some way, it is particularly important that she not take the insult personally. "If you worry about whether people like you, you won't make it," said a woman who owns a hazardous waste clean-up and disposal service. "You've got to know where you're going and who you are and have a good sense of self or you'll get real confused."

3. Set the tone. A common complaint of women proprietors is that male employees do not want to take orders from them. The wrong tactic in the face of such insubordination is to become angry and start yelling. Kavovit says in these situations she takes a low-key approach so employees see she is not a threat and respond in a like manner.

4. Develop your self-confidence. Because the pressures of being a woman in a male-dominated field can be overwhelming, self-confidence can go a long way in reducing the stress. Kavovit says, "You have to build yourself up—your inner self and your outer self." Self-confidence can be developed by educating yourself about every aspect of your particular field and joining "all the networking groups you can because that's the biggest support you can have."

For Critical Analysis:

Some female entrepreneurs feel they have a competitive advantage by bringing a "woman's touch" to male-dominated fields. Rosellini, who runs an ambulance company, gives as an example the fact that her employees cover a patient's head if it is raining—something, presumably, that an employee of a male-dominated ambulance company would not do. Do you find this reasoning compelling? Explain your answer.

SOURCE: S. Nelton, "No Longer for Men Only," *Nation's Business*, July 1994, pp. 64–65.

conspiring to violate the Resource Conservation and Recovery Act (RCRA) by illegally transporting and disposing of hazardous waste. The RCRA requires the EPA to issue regulations to monitor and control hazardous waste disposal. In addition to the prison terms, the Everett Steel Companies were ordered to pay more than $500,000 to the EPA and the Washington Department of Ecology for clean-up of the hazardous waste.

In Ohio, the owner of Herbert Orr Company pleaded guilty to a charge of illegal storage of hazardous waste and was ordered by the court to join the Sierra Club for three years. The corporate officer was also sentenced to 120 days of home incarceration, ordered to perform 16.5 hours of community service, and fined $10,000. Herbert Orr Company was fined $75,000.

To avoid such penalties, many companies are conducting "environmental audits" as a protective measure. The audits—which include surveys, assessments, and inspections—can provide a snapshot of a corporation's environmentally related activities. The goal of an audit is to evaluate whether the company is keeping up with environmental statutes. In 1995 the EPA provided companies with further incentive to conduct environmental audits. That year, the government agency issued a policy statement to the effect that it would deal less harshly with violations discovered during a self-audit. The EPA also said it would allow companies to correct the problems themselves before it would bring criminal charges.[13]

---

13. L. L. Raclin, "Environmental Audits: Risks and Rewards," *Kirkpatrick & Lockhart Business Law Update,* Summer 1995, pp. 4–6.

THE FUTURE

Many businesses view current environmental regulations as a nuisance. Others realize that such regulations are necessary to ensure the high quality of life to which most Americans are accustomed. If anything can be said with certainty about the future of environmental regulation, it is that laws relating to the storage and disposal of waste materials will become increasingly complex. New laws and regulations are being written and put into effect in every jurisdiction in the United States. These regulations affect almost all businesses, from major industries, such as automobile manufacturers and electric utilities, to small family-owned service businesses, such as dry cleaners.

An understanding of environmental issues and laws is essential for anyone who wishes to function in the world of business. The increasingly complex technical and legal issues related to environmental concerns necessitate an awareness that a problem may require something more than a few technological fixes before it can be resolved. Likewise, the social conflicts that arise around many controversial ecological issues further complicate the role of businesses in the proceedings (see *Managing Social Issues—Barriers to Success: Losing Paradise*).

TECHNOLOGICAL PERSPECTIVES

In the early 1960s, many social and economic commentators argued that all of the obvious inventions had been made and that the percentage of resources devoted to research and development in the United States would likely fall. This attitude was fostered by the sense that few truly revolutionary devices would be invented in the future. But the experts were soon proved wrong by the mass production of the silicon chip and the computer. Because computers themselves have brought about so many changes in the way we use and exchange information, the technological complacency of the 1960s has given way to a more positive attitude about the potential for future improvement in technology.

The computer provides a good example of the rate at which technological innovations are continuing to occur. The first computers built in the 1940s and 1950s were crude, bulky machines that required vast quantities of electricity and huge air conditioners to cool their many vacuum tubes. Today, the equivalent of a large room full of computers from that time can be held in the palm of your hand. *Exhibit 1–3* shows that the estimated reduction of the

▼ **EXHIBIT 1–3**
The Falling Costs of Computer Technology
In less than two decades, the price per unit of speed (1 million instructions per second) has fallen from about $1,100 to 50 cents. Costs today are less than .04 percent of what they were in 1978.

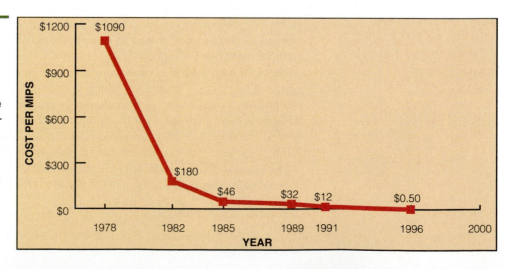

MANAGING SOCIAL ISSUES

BARRIERS TO SUCCESS: LOSING PARADISE

It is almost impossible to overstate the value of Ecuador's Galápagos Islands to the international science community. The archipelago's 15 main and 106 smaller islands, located roughly 600 miles off the South American coast, contain a treasure trove of unique plant and animal life—95 percent of the reptiles, 50 percent of the birds, 42 percent of the flora, 70 to 80 percent of the insect life, and 17 percent of the fish found in the protected wildlife area are found nowhere else in the world. Since the HMS *Beagle* delivered Charles Darwin to the Galápagos in 1835, scientists have considered the islands "a rare window on evolution—a place to look at the world evolving without the heavy hand of man."

But the Galápagos Islands also offer a wealth of natural resources to Ecuador's population, one of the poorest in South America. Many Ecuadorians have begun to "mine" these resources, which has led to warnings from ecologists that the sanctuary and its nonhuman inhabitants are in great danger. Just as the islands have offered scientists a microcosm of evolution, they now provide businesspersons and environmentalists alike an isolated lesson on the challenges of balancing economy and ecology.

Tourism

Although tourism generates as much as $60 million annually in revenue, its effects on the islands have not been entirely positive. In 1970 the population of the Galápagos was 2,000; by 1995, the number swelled to 15,000 to accommodate 50,000 visitors a year, and it is rising at an 8 percent annual rate. The influx has introduced prostitution and drug use to the islands, along with alien animal life, touching off an environmental catastrophe. Goats and burros are destroying the habitat of the rare Galápagos tortoise; dogs are eating land iguanas; and these animals, along with pigs, cows, and rats, are decimating plant life.

Demand for Sea Cucumbers

People have also flocked to the islands to harvest the bottom-dwelling sea cucumber, which is prized as an aphrodisiac in many Asian countries. In an attempt to reduce the black market for the sea cucumber, in October 1994 the Ecuadorian government allowed for a limited annual catch of 550,000. Nonetheless, within two months, more than seven million sea cucumbers had been harvested. Moreover, the *pepineros*, as the sea cucumber harvesters are called, killed nearly 100 endangered tortoises for meat and burned protected mangrove areas to provide drying space for their haul.

Locals React

Under pressure from the scientific community, the government banned further sea cucumber fishing several months after its "limited test" began. Angry *pepineros* responded by holding scientists and their families hostage and blocking the entrance to the Charles Darwin Research Center. Almost a year later, the research station, along with the airport in the provincial capital of Puerto Baquerizo Moreno, was occupied for two weeks as residents demanded greater local control. The Ecuadorian government, though eager to retain the profits from eco-tourism, does not have the will or the finances to control activities on the island. Conservationists fear that unless the international community steps in, the Galápagos will lose many of the characteristics that make it an ecological wonder.

For Critical Analysis:

Before the sea cucumber boom in the early 1990s, the pepineros *rarely made more than $71 a month. By harvesting sea cucumbers, they can earn as much as $100 a day. To what extent should such economic details be factored into environmental decisions, not only in the Galápagos but also in other ecologically threatened areas, such as the Brazilian rain forests?*

SOURCE: Information from Michael D. Lemonick, "Can the Galápagos Survive?" *Time*, October 30, 1995, pp. 81–82; and Esther Schrader, "Sea Cucumber Mania Threatens Galápagos Islands," *Portland Oregonian*, April 9, 1995, p. A6.

cost of computing power has declined from $1,090 per measured unit (millions of instructions per second) to about 50 cents per measured unit today. Furthermore, it has been estimated that children's computer video games in the year 2002 will have the same speed and computing power as some of today's multimillion-dollar supercomputers.

TECHNOLOGY'S IMPACT

Computers and telecommunications networks, like the combustion engine and electricity before them, are greatly changing the economy. Because consumers and suppliers can be linked more directly, inefficient intermediaries are finding themselves without a role in the service chain (see *Company Focus: SoundScan Inc.*). On the whole, however, the business community has prospered greatly from the technological revolution. Entire new industries, from personal computers to compact discs to the Internet, have been created, bringing thousands of new jobs with them. The fax machine, cellular phone, and on-line services have freed executives and employees from the restrictions of the desk at the office and the 9-to-5 workday. This freedom has led many to increased productivity and efficiency, not to mention more time at home. (On the negative side, technology can lead to longer working hours, because work is no longer confined to the office. For example, it is becoming common for people to take computers and beepers on their vacations.)

REGULATION AND THE INFORMATION SUPERHIGHWAY

Technology has introduced to both the corporate community and government the challenge of regulating the information superhighway. On the Internet, information is virtually unlimited and available to anyone with access to a computer with a modem. Using digitization—the process by which data (video, sound, or text) is transformed into a binary code in which a single stream of 0s and 1s can be decoded by electronic hardware—the ability to transfer information is almost limitless. This technology, in theory, can allow an infinite number of copies of a book or movie to be distributed through telephone lines at minimal cost. Although this is appealing to consumers, it is a frightening scenario for authors, producers, and publishers.

In April 1994 a 20-year-old student at the Massachusetts Institute of Technology was indicted for distributing $1 million worth of software on an electronic bulletin board (BBS) that he operated. The student's lawyer claims that his client is not liable for the manner in which others used the information on his BBS. In another case that raises similar questions, Frank Music Corporation sued the on-line service CompuServe for the unauthorized use of recordings, including "Unchained Melody," on its bulletin board.[14] With over fifty million people around the world having Internet access, these issues will continue to inspire debate on the ramifications of an "information democracy."

GLOBAL PERSPECTIVES

Linked to the information technology revolution, which is "making the world smaller," as the cliché goes, is a concurrent change in the global perspectives of the business community.[15] It is clear that American businesses face worldwide competition in a growing number of key industries, such as automobiles, steel, computers, and consumer electronics.

---

14. B. Kantrowitz, "My Info Is NOT Your Info," *Newsweek*, July 18, 1994, p. 54.
15. M. A. Hilt, B. B. Tyler, C. Hardee, and D. Park, "Understanding Strategic Intent in the Global Marketplace," *Academy of Management Executive*, May 1995, p. 12.

COMPANY FOCUS: SOUNDSCAN, INC.
REVOLUTIONIZING THE MUSIC BUSINESS

What do country music's favorite son Garth Brooks and the hard-core rap group N.W.A. have in common? Musically, not much, but the careers of both were given a critical boost from information technology introduced into the recording industry by SoundScan, Inc.

Flawed Data

Since the early 1960s, *Billboard* has provided the music industry with weekly charts to indicate the rate at which various products are selling. For most of that time, the methods the magazine used to create the charts were unscientific at best, relying on telephone surveys of store owners. It was an open secret in the industry that the system was flawed: not only were the store owners less than accurate in their reporting, but record companies attempted to influence the charts.

In 1991, Mike Shallet and Mike Fine, two marketing analysts with knowledge of *Billboard*'s weaknesses, started SoundScan with the goal of tracking compact disc, cassette, and record album sales electronically. The process, already in use in other industries such as clothing and groceries, involved a computerized system that registers every time an album is passed through a scanner at the checkout stand. The information is tabulated each week at SoundScan's headquarters and then sold to subscribers, including *Billboard* and major distributors such as Sony Music and the Polygram Group.

Transforming the Industry

The impact that accurate reporting had on the music business was startling. Genres such as country and rap were selling many more units than anybody had previously thought, and the resultant increased industry attention moved acts such as Garth Brooks and N.W.A. from the fringes into the mainstream. Record stores would purchase their stock based on *Billboard*'s sales forecasts. The former faulty information had caused these stores to misjudge the market, and many times left them stuck with extra copies of a product they assumed would sell in greater quantities. According to one distributor, SoundScan "totally changed the industry" by allowing performers' popularity to be determined by sales, not record companies.

In 1995, SoundScan licensed its technology to Victor Company of Japan, Ltd. The company will add to its dominance in the American market—SoundScan equipment functions in more than 15,000 outlets—the ability to track 40 percent of the music and videos sold in the world.

The New Bottom Line

Information technology has the power to transform billion-dollar industries. The companies that take advantage of it, such as SoundScan, will be rewarded accordingly. Companies that do not will suffer. Although major record distributors initially balked at SoundScan's services, they soon found they needed the unbiased information that only SoundScan could offer. One of the company's harshest critics finally "caved in" and signed on because "all [his] competitors [would] have access to these numbers," and he did not want to be "left out in the cold."

SOURCE: Information from Z. Schiller, "Making the Middleman an Endangered Species," *Business Week*, June 6, 1994, pp. 114–115; "SoundScan, Inc.: Sales Data Tracking System Is Licensed to Japan's Victor," *Wall Street Journal*, March 24, 1995, p. B3, and C. Phillips, "Rock n' Roll Revolutionaries," *Los Angeles Times*, December 8, 1991, p. 6.

Although Japan and Germany will continue to be the major trading rivals of the United States into the next century, they will doubtless be pushed aside to varying degrees by emerging industrialized powers, such as South Korea, China, Thailand, and Mexico.

The competition for the loyalty of the U.S. consumer will become only more pronounced in the future as other countries with low labor costs continue exporting their goods to the United States. Similarly, U.S. exporters will find themselves competing with more and more rivals in foreign markets around the world. Thus, the international aspects of doing business are increasingly important for American managers. After all, the percentage of total domestic output accounted for by international trade (imports and exports) has tripled since World War II, to over 20 percent. The need to be globally competitive is a reality for an increasing number of American businesses.[16]

FACING FOREIGN COMPETITION

The European Union (EU) consists of fifteen countries. It is an area of relatively free trade—no tariffs (taxes on imports) or other restrictions. The EU has many problems, not the least of which is an inability to agree on a common form of currency. In any case, however, the more than 360 million European consumers are going to challenge the business leadership role of the United States around the world.

American companies must learn how to deal with the various rules under which businesses in Europe are operating. Many of those rules were designed specifically to keep out American (and other non-European) businesses. Some EU policymakers continue to be more concerned with maintaining employment than with providing European consumers access to lowest-cost products. This concern is well illustrated by the French government's decree a few years ago that all imported videocassette recorders (VCRs) be approved by one single customs inspector. The anti-import slant of this requirement was evident to even the most nationalistic citizens, and the requirement was later dropped.

The VCR example illustrates the inherent trade-off in attempting to boost local employment by enacting laws to exclude foreign products. Although the exclusions may protect domestic employment in the short term, the long-term benefits are not so clear. Such barriers to trade mean that consumers will suffer a drop in living standards because they can no longer acquire low-cost imported products. In essence, all consumers will be subsidizing a small subset of domestic workers in industries that are unable to compete effectively with low-cost imports.

THE CHALLENGES OF THE MULTINATIONAL CORPORATION

One aspect of the highly competitive nature of our global economy is the blurring of nationalities in the business world. When a Japanese company such as Sony builds a plant in the United States, it becomes unclear whether the company is American or Japanese. For example, many American-made automobiles are built from parts manufactured in other countries. In fact, the 1993 Ford Crown Victoria was classified as an import by the U.S. Customs Service. All of the major American automobile manufacturers are involved in joint ventures with Japanese automobile companies, which means that their fortunes are increasingly tied to each other.

It is also sometimes difficult for a corporation to decide to what country it owes its allegiance. In fact, many **multinational companies** are spread around the globe to the point where they would be hard pressed to argue that their allegiance is to their specific country of origin—the place where the company was first formed.

Managing a Multinational Corporation (MNC) The globalization of business has led to a relatively new challenge for managers: managing abroad. Successfully integrating a

---

16. M. W. Hordes, F. A. Clancy, and J. Baddaley, "A Primer for Global Start-ups," *Academy of Management Executive,* May 1995, p. 7.

U.S.–based company in a foreign country is an immensely difficult undertaking, and it requires managers to expand the parameters of their performance (see *Company Focus: General Electric Medical Systems Group*). In most cases, it is necessary that the manager relocate to the site of the MNC. Even advances in technology cannot replace the value of interpersonal employee-management relationships. The manager must also battle against the attitude that "it worked back home, so it will work here."

Despite reports (and criticisms) of the "Americanization" of the globe, underlying cultural differences will hamper any attempts to blindly export American attitudes and

COMPANY FOCUS: GENERAL ELECTRIC MEDICAL SYSTEMS GROUP

THINKING GLOBALLY

For General Electric Medical Systems Group (GEMS), the 1990s have been a decade of global expansion. The company manufactures diagnostic imaging equipment—computerized axial tomography (CAT) scan and X-ray equipment, magnetic resonance systems, and so on—in Paris, Tokyo, and Milwaukee, with sales and service departments spread from Italy to China to Russia. Technology has facilitated much of this global spread, as electronic mail and a global videoconferencing facility that links more than 100 operational sites allow for the rapid transfer of information. But the overseas success of GEMS can also be attributed to its Global Leadership Program (GLP), administered by the company's human resources department.

The Global Leadership Program

The GLP is geared toward coordinating the various cultures that make up the GEMS "family." Managers from Europe, Asia, and the Americas are gathered together for training and brainstorming sessions from which comes the backbone of the company's global strategy. These sessions have resulted in relatively simple suggestions (such as translating the GEMS newsletter, *The World*, into a variety of languages) as well as more complex ones (such as the organization of the videoconferencing facilities).

As the GLP is a multiyear process that often involves relocation, GEMS provides a support package for managers and their families who have been uprooted and placed in a foreign culture. This preparation includes predeparture counseling, host-country support, and cross-cultural and language guidance. The company also provides resources for the education of the transferred employees' children. The assumption behind these human resource provisions is relatively straightforward: the better adjusted managers are in their new surroundings, the more effective they will be on the job.

The Domestic Application of Multicultural Standards

Those employees who remain in the United States are not exempt from the GEMS multicultural standards. Reflecting the company's status in the global market, the GEMS Milwaukee headquarters are frequently visited by administrators, salespersons, technicians, and other representatives from different countries. For this reason, almost a third of the Milwaukee-based staff members have received training in a foreign language, cross-cultural training, or both.

The New Bottom Line

Although GEMS has earned plaudits for its GLP, the company is not unique when it comes to its global awareness and training. Any company with multinational concerns will find that the steps GEMS has taken, or variations on them, are absolutely necessary to compete in the global market.

SOURCE: "GE Medical Systems," *Personnel Journal*, January 1992, p. 55.

products. Understanding a foreign culture is critical in making wise decisions about business operations, from marketing to finance to personnel to anything else.

As far as business attitudes are concerned, the United States differs from other countries in many key ways (see *Exhibit 1–4.*). A businessperson who does not understand these differences is at an extreme disadvantage. Take *feng shui*, for example, a practice followed in China, Hong Kong, Singapore, Japan, and Vietnam. In *feng shui*, a practitioner recommends the most favorable conditions for a business venture by studying factors such as the placement of buildings and furniture. For example, a building should face the water and be flanked by mountains, yet not block the view of positive mountain spirits. For that reason, many office buildings in Hong Kong have see-through lobbies. Furthermore, elevators are placed diagonally in the front of the building to keep the structure's own positive spirits from leaving. Sharp angles, in contrast, are avoided. Needless to say, a foreign contractor who is unaware of *feng shui* is likely to offend locals—a mistake the well-known architect I. M. Pei made in designing the Bank of China building in Hong Kong. He apparently placed certain windows facing the "wrong" direction, and violated a number of other *feng shui* dictates.[17]

Exporting U.S. Law Unfortunately for many American businesses, even if they become experts in foreign cultures, they may be at a disadvantage in overseas business deals. A glaring example of this concerns bribery, a common business practice in many parts of the world, yet illegal under U.S. law, specifically the 1977 Foreign Corrupt Practices Act.[18] The three most attractive Asian countries for foreign investment—China, India, and Indonesia—are also the three most "corrupt" by American standards. Payoffs to government officials add as much as 5 percent to the cost of operating a business in China; Indonesian tax officials have been known to demand bribes from foreign companies even when tax returns are in perfect order.[19]

▼ **EXHIBIT 1–4**
Values That Differ by Nation

In the United States	In many other countries
Time is to be controlled	Time is fluid, malleable
Change is encouraged	Tradition is valued
Individualism is encouraged	Group orientation is favored
Informality is allowed	Formality is expected
Individual competition within the organization is encouraged	Cooperation is encouraged
Equality/egalitarianism is valued	Hierarchy/authority is emphasized
Work is emphasized: "one lives to work"	Leisure is valued: "one works to live"
Direct/explicit communications style is preferred	Indirect/implicit communications style is preferred
Emphasis is on action	Emphasis is on planning and preparation

SOURCE: International Orientation Resources.

17. B. H. Shmitt and Y. Pang, "In Asia, the Supernatural Means Sales," *New York Times*, February 19, 1995, p. F11.
18. B. Ettorre, "Why Overseas Bribery Won't Last," *Management Review*, June 1994, p. 20.
19. L. Kraar, "How Corrupt Is Asia?" *Fortune*, August 21, 1995, p. 26.

Business environments that accept bribery hurt American companies. The situation in which a U.S. power-generator company lost a $320 million bid to a Japanese company in the Middle East after government officials demanded a $3 million "fee" is not uncommon.[20] When the U.S. government tracked a sample of one hundred international deals worth a total of $45 billion, it found that most American companies were undercut by offers that included bribes, allowing foreign rivals to win 80 percent of the deals.[21]

How can American companies compete under these circumstances? Some, no doubt, try to beat foreign competition by joining them in "greasing palms." But the penalties for those caught are severe. In October 1995, a former vice president at Lockheed Martin Corporation was fined $125,000 and sentenced to 18 months in prison for bribing a member of the Egyptian Parliament in order to win a contract for cargo planes. Some companies use a certain measure of disguise: In China, Hewlett-Packard subscribes to local custom by providing journalists with the equivalent of $12 for cab fare to attend the company's news conferences. The most ethical path, however, seems to be to invest through legal channels and hope for the best. Boeing Company, for example, spends $100 million a year to train Chinese workers to use its technology, and the company recently donated $25 million in hardware and software to 20 Chinese universities.[22] The hope that philanthropy-inspired goodwill can supersede bribery may be idealistic, but until the situation changes, it is a U.S.–based MNC's best strategy.

---

20. D. Mikbank and M. W. Brauchli, "Greasing Wheels: How U.S. Concerns Compete in Countries Where Bribes Flourish," *Wall Street Journal*, October 2, 1995, p. 1.
21. A. Borrus, "A World of Greased Palms," *Business Week*, November 6, 1995, p. 36.
22. Mikbank and Brauchli, *op. cit.*, p. 6.

THE DELICATE BALANCE

As the United States enters the twenty-first century, business finds itself sometimes walking a tightrope. Increased competition from all parts of the globe is forcing corporate downsizing, cost cutting, and in general increased attempts at more efficiency. At the same time, Congress, as well as state legislatures and state, federal, and local regulators, is imposing an increasingly heavy social burden on corporate America. "Only the strong shall survive" seems to be a fitting maxim in today's business environment. *Strong*, however, does not mean what it used to mean. Aggressively going after a good rate of return on investment now involves being strong politically and ethically. Bottom-line calculations are more complex than ever before. The delicate balance involves weighing political, moral, ethical, and social considerations along with profit considerations at all times.

TERMS AND CONCEPTS FOR REVIEW

Diversity management 11
Environmental impact statement 9
Ethics codes 6

Fleet mileage standards 9
Incentive structure 4
Multinational companies 20

Short-term profits 8
Trade-offs 6

SUMMARY

1. Because we as a nation were poorer a hundred years ago, we did not have the luxury to consider many of the ethical issues that face businesses today. Moreover, virtually instantaneous news reporting has put most ethical issues in the public eye, and therefore ethics questions are more complicated today than in the past.

2. The majority of major U.S. corporations have codes of ethics, but because trade-offs often exist between ethical behavior and profitability, ethical breakdowns have occurred.

3. Corporate America attempts to influence politics in order to further its interests. Such influence can either be indirect or direct, but in all cases it requires resources—money and people. Today, corporations must deal with the politics of regulatory agencies.

4. Businesses have to deal with (a) declining educational quality, (b) the problem of the homeless, and (c) some workers who are infected with the AIDS virus.

5. Corporations today have an increasingly diverse labor force. How they deal with this situation is called "diversity management." Corporations are also changing as the percentage of the labor force that is female grows.

6. Although many environmental problems facing corporations may involve ethics, today they also involve potential criminal liability. Increasingly, corporate officers are being fined and jailed for the environmental wrongs committed by their corporations.

7. The great technological surge forward with the advent of the silicon chip and the computer has created both problems and opportunities for today's corporations. The telecommunications revolution, and especially the Internet, has created opportunities and problems, particularly for government regulators. Telecommunications improvements have also increased the amount of global competition for U.S. business.

8. Corporations must deal with foreign competition. Some do so by becoming multinational corporations (MNCs).

EXERCISES

1. Reread the two quotations from Victor Hugo's novel that were given at the beginning of this chapter. Why do these quotations represent an idealized view of "socially conscious" capitalists? In what respect did Hugo's vision conform to what successful capitalists actually do for an economy?

2. Why is the ethics issue today more complicated for business than it was in the past?

3. What does it mean to say that there are ethical trade-offs?

4. Reexamine *Exhibit 1–1*. Which example of an ethical breakdown do you think was the most serious? Why?

5. "The business of business is business. Businesses should stay out of politics." Do you agree with this statement? If you disagree, indicate why.

6. What trade-off has been involved in increasing the gas mileage of automobiles?

7. To what extent does business have responsibility for halting the decline in the quality of public education?
8. To what extent does business have responsibility to help the homeless?
9. Reexamine *Exhibit 1–2*. Choose one cluster. Write an outline of a short speech explaining the elements of that particular cluster as part of a diversity management scheme.
10. Look at the four rules for women who wish to establish themselves in a male-dominated industry outlined in *Managing Social Issues—The World of the Small-Business Entrepreneur: A Man's World?* Which rule, in your opinion, is the most important? Defend your answer.
11. In what way is an environmental audit a protective measure?
12. To what extent has technological progress helped the business community? To what extent has it harmed the business community?
13. How does the information technology revolution affect the global view of business?

SELECTED REFERENCES

▶ Cotchett, Joseph W., and Stephen P. Pizzo. *The Ethics Gap: The Erosion of Ethics in Our Professions, Business and Government.* Carlsbad, Calif.: Parker & Son Publications, 1991.

▶ Danley, John R. *The Role of the Modern Corporation in a Free Society.* Notre Dame, University of Notre Dame Press, 1994.

▶ McRae, Hamish. *The World in 2020: Power, Culture, and Prosperity.* Boston: Harvard Business School Press, 1995.

▶ Naisbitt, John. *Global Paradox: The Bigger the World Economy, the More Powerful Its Smallest Players.* New York: Morrow, 1994.

▶ Sethi, S. Prakash, and Cecilia M. Falbe, eds. *Business and Society: Dimensions of Conflict and Cooperation.* Lexington, Mass: Lexington Books, 1987.

▶ Voich, Dan Jr., and Lee P. Stapina, eds. *Cross-cultural Analysis of Values and Political Economy Issues.* Westport, Conn.: Preager, 1994.

RESOURCES ON THE INTERNET

▼ The Internet is a web of educational, corporate, and research computer networks around the world. Today, over 50 million people are using it, and over 70,000 networks are connected to it. Perhaps the most interesting part of the Internet is the World Wide Web, commonly called the Web, which is a vast interlinked network of computer files all over the world. You can use the Internet to find discussion groups, news groups, and electronic publications. The most common use of the Internet is for electronic mail (E-mail).

▼ At many colleges and universities, you can get an E-mail address and a password. Your address is like a mailbox at which you will receive electronic information. Many of the chapters of *Business and Society Today* end with Internet addresses and activities that you will find helpful in your study of the relationship among business, society, and government. You might want to get an Internet address now. Then you could pick up a copy of the new users' handbook and start using E-mail.

▼ The user-friendly **gopher** menus can help you roam in the Internet. You first open your connection the way you would in order to send or receive E-mail. Then you type **gopher** (we boldfaced what you will type in to operate your computer) and hit the return key. You will then be presented with a first-level menu of choices. Choose one by moving the cursor (arrow) up or down to the item you want to open (at the blinking cursor, type in the number of your choice). When you are done playing around, type in Q. The largest gopher site is at the University of Minnesota. To reach it, type gopher and then type **tc.umn.edu.**

CASE

DISCRIMINATION AT DENNY'S

Background

"We were told we should take whatever measure we could to keep A-A's to a minimum," explained a former employee at a Denny's restaurant in San Jose, California. "You could seat white customers ahead of A-A's. You could put A-A's in the rear and stall in serving them. You could ask A-A's to pay before eating. Or, if you really wanted to get the job done, you could lock them out." The point of these strategies was to keep "A-A's"—in-house code for African Americans—from feeling welcome at the franchise. "You were to eliminate them from your restaurant," added the employee, who was hired in 1990. "No questions asked, just get it done."

The employee's words add credence to the perception that racism was endemic in the corporate culture at Denny's and its parent company, Flagstar Companies. In 1993, Flagstar had no senior African American managers, and no minority officers or directors. Of 163 Denny's franchises, only one was owned by an African American. There was also strong evidence of the kind of discriminatory activity toward African Americans described by the San Jose employee. As a result, a number of customers, along with the U.S. Justice Department, had filed lawsuits against the restaurant chain.

Jerry Richardson, chief executive officer (CEO) of Flagstar, denies that the problems were institutional. "It makes no sense that we would condone racism," he said in 1993. "We're $2 billion in debt. Denny's needs all the customers it can get." But Denny's management appears to have made an error common in corporate America. It based its antidiscrimination safeguards on amorphous policies rather than on active monitoring and sensitivity training. Furthermore, some of the policies that Denny's headquarters did promote allowed individual managers to act out personal racist tendencies.

The Lawsuits

National attention was first brought to possible racism at Denny's as the result of an incident on December 30, 1991, in San Jose, California. Eighteen African American college and high school students entered the franchise after attending a "College Forum Night" cosponsored by the National Association for the Advancement of Colored People (NAACP). An initial group of six of the students was told that groups of that size would have to pay $2 per person to be seated and were required to make full payments upon ordering. The students then offered to break into groups of four, but they were still told they must pay in advance. While the debate was taking place, one of the students learned that white classmates sitting in a group of six had not been asked to prepay. The African American students left the restaurant and later presented the company with a discrimination lawsuit.

A similar incident occurred nearly two years later. Six African American officers of the Uniformed Secret Service stopped at a Denny's in Annapolis, Maryland, en route to the U.S. Naval Academy to screen potential attendees for a speech by President Bill Clinton. The officers, who were part of a twenty-one-person contingent and had less than an hour to finish their meal, sat at a table together, while their supervisor—also African American—was seated with a group of white agents. The African American officers noticed that their companions had been served, and they asked the waitress about the delay. They were told that the meals were on the way. The group at the table proceeded to watch as other customers were seated and served, but their own meals did not arrive. Finally, as the other Secret Service members had finished, the group was forced to leave without eating. They also filed a discrimination lawsuit.

These two occurrences served as the backdrop for a civil suit brought by thirty-two plaintiffs in California. The suit describes a case in which an African American child was denied a Denny's "Birthday Meal" and numerous instances in which African American customers were refused orders, forced to prepay, and forcibly ejected from restaurants by police. The suit also describes the company policy of "blackout," in which managers instructed employees to discourage African American customers from patronizing particular franchises.

Questionable Policies

The company's practices were given heavy coverage by the national media. *CBS Evening News* anchor Dan Rather commented that the African American Secret Service agents "put their lives on the line every day, but they can't get served at Denny's." The negative publicity was hurting sales, especially in African American neighborhoods, as some consumers boycotted Denny's in protest. One franchise manager noted that in the weeks immediately following the Annapolis incident, business in his southern California Denny's was down 18 percent. Meanwhile, Flagstar's management continued to deny that racism was promoted or tolerated in its corporate culture. One spokesperson insisted that the company's problems were with service, not race. Admitting that some African Americans may have been poorly treated, she added, "Unfortunately, others have had lengthy waits, too."

Clearly, however, some Denny's policies did give managers the discretion to apply certain "house rules" selectively. A computerized network installed in 1988 gave the company's executives a means to determine which franchises suffered the highest incidents of customer "walk-outs," or eating without paying. Thirty specific franchises, including the one in San Jose, were targeted as having high rates of walk-outs, and regulations were designed to control the problem. These unposted regulations included prepayment by late-night groups of 10 or more and $2-per-person minimum tabs to discourage loitering.

Within the regulations, managers were given free reign to apply the walk-out and loitering rules at their discretion, as well as the opportunity to implement "additional operating procedures which improve the operation at an individual restaurant." One analyst, noting the risks of offending individuals or classes of people inherent in such general rules, called them "a prescription for calamity."

Making Amends

In the wake of the controversy, Denny's discontinued the $2 fee—though leaving the prepayment policy in effect—and promised to discipline personnel who may have misapplied the policies. The restaurant chain also took a number of more significant steps to try to improve its image. On April 1, 1993, the company entered into a consent agreement with the Justice Department in which it agreed to "reinforce policies of equitable treatment [for all customers] and to communicate guidelines to all employees." As part of the agreement, Denny's appointed a civil rights monitor, Joseph D. Russell, to oversee sensitivity training for employees and to oversee random testing for bias in the company. Russell developed an eight-hour voluntary program for Denny's management to explore the economic issues related to diversity awareness.

Two months later, CEO Richardson signed a "Fair Share" contract with the national NAACP. Under the agreement, Flagstar would earmark more than $1 billion to increase the number of minority vendors and employees at Denny's and

the corporation's three other restaurant chains—Hardee's, Quincy's, and El Pollo Loco. A "management employment" provision of Fair Share called for 325 African American managers to be hired at Flagstar operations by 2001. The agreement also provides that $96 million be made available to minority purchasing agents.

Finally, on August 1, 1993, a federal judge in Baltimore, Maryland, approved a settlement of $55.4 million to resolve the class-action lawsuits. Under its terms, each Secret Service member would receive $35,000, and the San Jose students were awarded $25,000 apiece. It was the largest settlement since the Public Accommodation Act was adopted in 1964 to deal with racial discrimination suits.

Flagstar took other steps to improve its image. It produced a television commercial entitled "You Are Welcome" in which a racially diverse group of employees promises that everyone will be treated well at the chain. In the ad, one employee says, "I am human," and another adds, "I will make mistakes."

CEO Richardson still denies institutional bias, and he insisted on a clause in the consent agreement that allowed Denny's to avoid admitting to any wrongdoing. But the company has lived up to its agreements. In the first year after signing "Fair Share," Flagstar hired 103 new minority managers, and in November 1994 the company signed a deal with African American–owned NDI to operate 47 Denny's franchises in the Northeast.

Critical Thinking Questions

1. Consider the original intent of the rules to discourage walk-outs and loitering. Are these rules inherently unethical? In other words, did the problems of Denny's stem more from racist policies or from a failure to monitor its practices properly? Explain your answer.

2. In this case, it was noted that some Denny's stores suffered financially because of the negative publicity. In what other ways does Denny's—or any other business involved in a high-visibility discrimination controversy—"pay" in the wake of such incidents?

3. How effective would encouraging other employees to report discrimination in the workplace be as a step in changing the corporate culture at Denny's and at other service organizations?

4. Consider Denny's "Fair Share" agreement with the NAACP. These kinds of agreements are often criticized as being publicity stunts on the part of the offending company.

CASE (CONTINUED)

They are also labeled "payoffs" accepted by special interest groups in exchange for easing off the offending company. Discuss the pros and cons of these sorts of agreements. How, in this case, could it be argued that the ends justify the means?

5. What is your opinion of the television advertisement Denny's ran in the wake of the controversy? Why might Denny's have been better off not running the television spots?

SOURCE: Information from H. Kohn, "Service with a Sneer," *New York Times Magazine*, November 6, 1994, pp. 44, 78; A. E. Serwer, "What to Do When Race Charges Fly," *Forbes*, July 12, 1993, p. 95; R. Martin, "Prepayment Policy at Denny's Sparks Civil-Rights Uproar," *Nation's Restaurant News*, January 27, 1992, p. 3; L. Duke, "Secret Service Agents Allege Racial Bias at Denny's," *Washington Post*, May 24, 1993, p. A4; C. Hawkins, "Denny's: The Stain That Isn't Coming Out," *Business Week*, June 28, 1993, pp. 98–99; L. Bird, "D'Arcy TV Ad for Denny's Seeks to Mend Image Amid Bias Suits," *Wall Street Journal*, June 21, 1993, p. B3; "Trendy 'Empowerment' Ethic Carries Risks, Obligations," *Nation's Restaurant News*, February 10, 1992, p. 31; G. Johnson, "Rights Monitor to Serve Up Some Sensitivity at Denny's Chain," *Los Angeles Times*, August 12, 1993, p. A17; B. A. Holden, "Parent of Denny's Restaurant, NAACP Agree on Plan to Boost Minorities' Role," *Wall Street Journal*, July 1, 1993, p. A3; B. Carlino, "Denny's TV Ad Rolls Out Welcome Mat for All Races," *Nation's Restaurant News*, July 19, 1993, p. 12; E. de Lisser and B. A. Holden, "Denny's Begins Repairing Its Image—and Its Attitude," *Wall Street Journal*, March 11, 1994, p. B1; B. Carlino, "Denny's Pays $54 Million to Settle Bias Suits," *Nation's Restaurant News*, June 6, 1994, p. 1; and "Making Amends at Denny's," *Business Week*, November 21, 1994, p. 47.

CHAPTER 2

CORPORATE LEGITIMACY AND CRITICISMS OF BUSINESS

CHAPTER OUTLINE

INTRODUCTION

Returning for a moment to the travails of Victor Hugo's Father Madeleine from the beginning of Chapter 1, after he has established himself as the best possible kind of businessperson, his past comes back to haunt him. Another man has been charged with crimes he committed, and he must decide whether or not to reveal himself as Jean Valjean. In agonizing self-debate with his conscience, Valjean appeals to the good he has done as a businessperson, and the consequences for the French town of Montreuil-sur-Mer:

> I have created all this! I keep it all alive; wherever a chimney is smoking, I have put the fuel in the fire and meat in the pot; I have produced comfort, circulation, credit; before me there was nothing; I have enlivened, animated, quickened, stimulated, enriched, the whole region. . . . What I am doing is not for myself. Everyone's prosperity goes on increasing, industry is quickened and grows, factories and workshops multiply, families—a hundred families, a thousand families—are happy; the population grows, villages spring up where there were only farms, farms spring up where there was nothing; poverty disappears, and with poverty disappear debauchery, prostitution, theft, murder, all vices and crimes. And the poor mother raises her child! And the whole country is rich and honest![1]

Again, Hugo presents a vision of the good a businessperson can do in society. In doing so, he touches on a question that is fundamental to this textbook and will be the basis of this second introductory chapter: Is business activity in and of itself a worthy function in society?[2] Hugo thought that business can enliven, animate, quicken, stimulate, and enrich—all worthy results.

The basic economic concept of mutually beneficial exchange—an exchange of goods and services that makes both parties better off—is generally accepted as the basis of all transactions in society. It is the manner in which these economic actions can be carried out that has raised criticism about the inherent positive qualities of any economic activity. The discussion of the function of business in society has intensified in the late 1990s. Recent political upheavals have led many commentators to label capitalism the preferred economic system of free peoples around the globe. Consequently, we begin our examination of business with a review of the principles of capitalism—a system, ironically, with which Victor Hugo, over 100 years ago, rarely found favor.

CAPITALISM, COMPETITION, AND PROFIT PERCEPTIONS

The day McDonald's opened in Beijing, 40,000 customers went through its doors, setting a one-day sales record for any McDonald's restaurant in the world. The previous record holders were two McDonald's outlets on the Chinese border city of Schenchen, not far from Hong Kong. The Beijing McDonald's has 700 seats and 29 cash registers

---

1. Victor Hugo, *Les Misérables,* trans. L. Fahnestock and N. MacAfee (New York: Signet Classics, 1987), p. 230.
2. S. P. Sethi and P. Steidlmeier, "The Evolution of Business' Role in Society," *Business and Society Review,* Summer 1995, p. 9.

and boasts 1,000 employees selected from 22,000 applicants. Just a few years earlier, the biggest McDonald's in the world was in Moscow. It still serves over 20,000 customers a day.

The fact that the most successful branches of the world's most successful fast-food chain are found in Russia and China, the past and present bastions of communism, has not gone unnoticed. Some commentators have gone so far as to assert that the United States "won" the Cold War not because of its nuclear arsenal but because American corporations such as McDonald's and Coca-Cola spread the precepts of free market capitalism behind "enemy lines." But as capitalism has gained global ascendancy, questions about its merits continue to be raised. Before we delve into the free market's relative worth as a setting for the business-government-society relationship, let us establish a clear definition of capitalism and other relevant economic systems.

THREE BASIC ECONOMIC QUESTIONS

In every nation, no matter what the form of government, there are three questions to be answered: *what and how much*, *how*, and *for whom* goods and services will be produced.

1. What and how much will be produced? Literally billions of different things could be produced with a society's scarce resources. Some mechanism must exist that causes some things to be produced and others to remain as either investors' pipe dreams or individuals' unfulfilled desires.

2. How will it be produced? There are many ways to produce a desired item. It is possible to use more labor and less capital, or vice versa. It is possible to use more unskilled labor and fewer units of skilled labor. Somehow, in some way, a decision must be made as to the particular mix of inputs, the way they should be organized, and how they are brought together at a particular place.

3. For whom will it be produced? Once a commodity is produced, who should get it? In a market economy, individuals and businesses purchase commodities with money income. The question, then, is what mechanism is there to distribute income, which then determines how commodities are distributed throughout the economy.[3]

Although this textbook will generally steer clear of economic theories, you should be aware of two economic "laws." These laws help answer the questions listed above:

▼ The *law of demand* states that, holding all other things constant, as the price of goods and services rises, the quantity demanded of those goods and services will fall. As the price of goods and services falls, the quantity demanded will rise.

▼ The *law of supply* basically states that, holding all other things constant, as the price of goods and services goes up, so does the quantity supplied—and, correspondingly, as these prices go down, so does the quantity supplied.

Consider compact discs. Because of the law of demand, given a limited income, a person will buy more compact discs each week when the per-unit price is low than when the per-unit price is high. The company that manufactures compact discs, however, makes a greater profit when the per-unit price is higher, for any given quantity sold. In fact, according to the law of supply, the higher the per-unit price, the more compact discs

---

3. R. L. Miller, *Economics Today*, 9th ed. (Redding, Mass.: Addison-Wesley, 1997), p. 117.

that manufacturer will produce for sale. When you combine the incentives of the buyer and the seller, you have the law of supply and demand.

ECONOMIC SYSTEMS

The three basic economic questions stated in the previous section are answered according to which economic system is in place in any given society. The rules of an economic system are embedded in a framework of formal institutions, such as laws, and informal institutions, such as customs. It is important to remember that though theoretical in nature, economic systems are created by humans and can be changed by humans (see *Managing Social Issues—International Issues: Vietnam's Doi Moi*). Therefore, although the three systems listed in *Exhibit 2–1* represent specific models of **capitalism, communism,** and **socialism,** most real-world societies are an amalgam of these three systems.

Some researchers prefer to classify economic systems according to whether they are market systems or command systems. A market system is one in which decision making is decentralized. A command system is one in which most decision making is centralized.

THE NEED FOR ENLIGHTENED CAPITALISM

With the fall of the Soviet Union in the early 1990s, the limitations of a pure communist command economic system were exposed in dramatic fashion. The utopian ideals that form the philosophical basis for communism—that a society can not only function but also flourish with communal ownership of goods and services—were shown to bear little relationship to reality. "Communism was essentially about restricting the ability of

▼ **EXHIBIT 2–1
Three Economic
Systems**

Capitalism	Socialism	Communism
▶ Individuals hold government-protected property rights to most resources, including those used in production and their own labor.	▶ Individuals typically have exclusive rights to consumption goods (consumer goods) such as stereos and books, which they can buy and sell.	▶ The concept that people will be motivated to contribute to community service and the public sector rather than to work out of mere self-interest forms the basis of the system.
▶ Within the legal framework of society, individuals (and, as we shall see, corporations) can use their resources in whatever manner they choose.	▶ Individuals have restricted rights to income-producing goods, such as machinery and often their own labor.	▶ Pure communism would see the absence of economic class distinctions.
	▶ The rights to income-producing resources are usually assigned and enforced by government employees.	▶ In practice, nations that designated themselves communist had centrally planned (command) economies in which the state also extended its control to the choice of jobs for all workers.

▣ MANAGING SOCIAL ISSUES

INTERNATIONAL ISSUES: VIETNAM'S *DOI MOI*

Early on the morning of April 30, 1975, in the garden of the American embassy in Saigon, U.S. Marines burned millions of cash dollars deemed too heavy to transport out of the besieged city. Later that day, the North Vietnamese army occupied the southern capital, renaming it Ho Chi Minh City, and installed communism as the economic system for a reunited Vietnam. On April 30, 1995, the city celebrated the twentieth anniversary of the U.S. embassy's capture, and buildings were draped with banners bearing the hammer and sickle and Ho Chi Minh's portrait. Alongside these traditional communist symbols flew a red, white, and blue insignia familiar to most Americans—the logo of Pepsi Cola. The soft-drink giant was the official sponsor of the celebrations.

Capitalist corporations sponsoring communist holidays? What has happened in Vietnam?

The New Socialist Capitalist

In 1986 Vietnam began an economic liberalization process officially called *"Doi Moi,"* or "economic renewal." The Vietnamese government felt compelled to adopt *Doi Moi* after observing the success of capitalist Asian nations such as Thailand and Taiwan. Some observers have labeled it an experiment in state-controlled free markets, a contradiction in terms in many economists' minds.

Vietnamese businesspersons are unlikely to argue over semantics as they take advantage of the new policies. Le Ve Kiem, for example, tried to start an animal feed business before *Doi Moi,* and though the business was profitable, the political environment forced him to shut it down. In those days, "officials would accuse you of exploiting people if you employed more than twenty workers," remembers Kiem. But when the new policies were announced, Kiem started again and now runs a conglomerate, called Huy Hoang, that does business in garment manufacturing, construction and property development, tourism, banking, and investment. Kiem operates Huy Hoang in a partnership with the communist government. "I'm considered to be a socialist capitalist," Kiem says proudly.

Communist Markets

Foreign investors are not as optimistic about *Doi Moi* as Kiem is. Despite economic reforms, the Vietnamese government does not allow private ownership of land and has not widened its tolerance of political dissent. Paul Nazer, who runs a branch of France's Christian Bernard Ltd. in Ho Chi Minh City, complains that the government taps his phone lines and intercepts fax transmissions. Nazer and other foreign businesspersons relate that corruption is rampant, and economic decisions are made based on cronyism and graft rather than financial considerations.

Still, even a socialist capitalist Vietnam offers a wealth of opportunity for entrepreneurs. Ho Chi Minh City's 6.6 million inhabitants are embracing one aspect of capitalism—consumerism—with enthusiasm. Television penetration in the city is 93 percent of all households, 68 percent of families own videocassette recorders, and 85 percent own a motorbike. The average income is only $70 a month (American dollars are an unauthorized but an accepted form of currency in Vietnam), but citizens spend almost half of that on consumer items.

"Sure, the risks are here," said one foreign investor. "But this market is ready to explode and you need to be here when it does." For many, the "explosion" occurred in the summer of 1995, when President Bill Clinton lifted the 19-year U.S. embargo against Vietnam. Within a month, Coca-Cola opened the first American factory in that country.

For Critical Analysis:

Over the past decade, China, with a form of government similar to Vietnam's, has also embraced some free market reforms. When asked whether these reforms represented a rejection of communist doctrine, one Chinese official stated, "It does not matter whether a cat is black or white, only that it catch mice." How does this pragmatic approach strike you? Can a socialist capitalist exist? Was President Clinton correct in lifting the embargo even though Vietnam operates a form of government that many Americans feel is antithetical to personal freedom?

SOURCE: Information from K. Cooke, "Vietnam Slips Uneasily into Capitalism," *Financial Times,* January 13, 1995, p. 25; R. E. Yates, "U.S. Investors Enter Vietnam at Own Peril," *Chicago Tribune,* May 8, 1995, p. 1; and F. Warner, "Marketers Are Reaping Benefits of Vietnam's Rising Consumerism," *Wall Street Journal,* November 7, 1995, p. B9.

individuals to accumulate wealth," noted one observer, "and in the process, of course, it failed to generate much wealth for anyone."[4]

The noneconomic principles inherent to communism, however, were not so quickly dismissed. Although Americans—liberal, conservative, and in between—argue about methods and definitions, they tend to demand that an economic system provide not just financial contentment but also social justice. Businessman James A. Autry concisely captured public sentiment when he proclaimed, "If we define capitalism as the application of capital to doing commerce with the intention of *giving a fair return* to investors, then I think capitalism has a bright future. If, on the other hand, we modify that intention to be one of *unrestrained pursuit of profits and increased owner value by doing whatever it takes*, rather than *giving a fair return*, then capitalism is headed for trouble."[5] In other words, Autry offers a vision of an **enlightened capitalism** in which business has a positive intent in addition to maximizing its returns. Free market economists often scoff at such notions, but as we see throughout this textbook, the public does not.

QUESTIONS OF COMPETITION

Every year since 1982, the state of Oregon has hosted the Hood to Coast running race, in which twelve-member relay teams compete over a course of 195 miles that spans the distance from Mount Hood to the Pacific Ocean. Although the race was conceived as a purely recreational event, it has evolved into the stage for a bitter rivalry between shoe manufacturers Nike and Adidas. Both companies sponsor elite teams of runners (one Nike team was captained by Olympic marathon world record holder Alberto Salazar) and place a great deal of importance on an event that has not been shown to have any effect on the bottom line. After Nike's team beat Adidas's team one year, Phil Knight, chairman and chief executive of Nike, ordered all 2,500 employees at the company's Portland plant to cease work and attend an awards ceremony, at which he made derogatory remarks about a recently deceased Adidas executive. In response, Adidas considered clothing its next team in jackets emblazoned with "Up Yours, Phil."[6]

All of this activity has not been lost on the thousands of runners who participate in Hood to Coast for no other reason than pure fun. Race director Bob Foote received a number of complaints that the behavior of Nike and Adidas was obscuring the spirit of the race.[7] Essentially, the companies were "doing whatever it takes" to win the race, thereby ruining the event itself. Many Americans would agree that similar competition sours the fruits of capitalism as well.

Competition and Ethics   According to classic capitalist theory, as espoused by Adam Smith (1723–1790) in *The Wealth of Nations* (1776) and by countless economists since, competition is a key—even an integral—component of a market capitalist system. By providing individuals with an **incentive structure** that rewards efficiency and punishes inefficiency (a system called the "free market"), competition makes capitalism work. Competition causes resources to be allocated efficiently and assures the lowest prices for goods.

A more cynical view of free market capitalism asserts that competition has turned the marketplace into a Darwinian jungle in which ethics are dictated not by rules of fair play

---

4. C. Rosen, "Justice in the Marketplace," *Business Ethics*, July–August 1992, pp. 21–22.
5. J. A. Autry, "The Coming of Enlightened Capitalism," *Business Ethics*, July–August 1992, p. 20.
6. J. Manning, "Nike vs. Adidas," *Portland Oregonian*, April 20, 1995, pp. G1–G2.
7. J. Manning, "Some Think Relay Is Running the Wrong Way," *Portland Oregonian*, April 20, 1995, p. G1.

Berliners sing and dance on top of the Berlin wall in front of the Brandenburg Gate to celebrate the opening of the East-West German borders.

but by "survival of the fittest." (English naturalist Charles Darwin [1809–1882] popularized the theory that plant and animal species evolved by adapting to their natural environments through the natural selection of those individuals who are "fittest" to survive.) The concern is that excessive competition leads to continual ethical breakdowns in the business community. As these breakdowns have received more attention from the public, so has the idea that our competitive nature is somehow to blame (see *Managing Social Issues—Ethics/Social Responsibility: Gunning for Sales* on page 36).

Five Questions Concerning the Free Market In light of the modern business environment, five questions can be used to reassess Adam Smith's theories. The questions are not primarily economic but "macroethical questions about the values of the free enterprise system as such."[8]

1. Is true competition possible? Smith argued that government regulation was unnecessary in true capitalism because market forces would eventually punish those companies that transgressed against society's rules. Today, others urge business theorists to examine whether or not this is a realistic theory, given that "competition becomes so keen, then so vicious, that many, and on occasion all, of the competitors are forced out of business, doing no good either for them or for the society they serve."

2. Does capitalism require a divorce between work and life? In other words, does the intense nature of competition necessarily create a division between what one does for a living and one's life, leading to alienation and depression? Is there a difference between business ethics and personal ethics?

3. Does capitalism create, rather than just supply, its own demand? Is the sovereignty of consumer demand—that consumers make their choices based on free will—

---

8. R. C. Solomon, *Above the Bottom Line: An Introduction to Business Ethics*, 2d ed. (Fort Worth, Tex.: Harcourt Brace College Publishers, 1994), pp. 193–197. The remaining quotes in this section are from this source.

MANAGING SOCIAL ISSUES

ETHICS/SOCIAL RESPONSIBILITY: GUNNING FOR SALES

Representatives of American National Insurance Company have found an effective method of drumming up business in the high-crime neighborhoods of Southern California. They scan local newspapers for mentions of drive-by shootings and other violent crimes, and visit the area in which the incident occurred. Using newspaper clippings about the violence as a "sales prop," they then try to persuade residents with family members who are vulnerable to such crimes to purchase life insurance before it is too late.

A Profitable Business

A spokesperson for the California Association of Life Underwriters called such efforts "a sad commentary on our times," denouncing the procedure for playing "on people's fears" in order to sell insurance. But Peter Groom, legal counsel for the California Department of Insurance, points out that there is nothing illegal about the practice, as his department does not—and cannot—legislate standards of good taste. "At what point does it become inappropriate to frighten people into buying insurance?" he asks. "I don't have the answer."

Magdy Barsoum, a regional director at American National Insurance, says that his company is simply filling a market need that is being ignored by competitors. Most of the policies sold in this manner are relatively small, ranging from $5,000 to $10,000, with monthly premiums of $10. Even while paying out $70,000 to $80,000 in claims a month on violent deaths, Barsoum says, "We are doing fantastic business."

The Consumer's Perspective

Barsoum also insists that his clients do not feel as though they are being unfairly treated. In fact, he says, his agents do not fear for their safety when entering high-risk zones, because "the people in these areas need us so they protect us." One American National agent claims that he does not need to use newspaper clippings to get business, as most of his policies are sold through referrals from relatives of clients.

Evelyn Martin, a resident of a federal housing project in the Los Angeles area, believes the life insurance policies have become a necessity. She owns one on herself and hopes to be able to cover her twenty-one-year-old son similarly, because "sooner or later, kids around here will be shot at or shot, or stabbed or something." She has seen neighboring families who have had "to go around with a cup in their hands" to cover the costs of funerals, and she does not want to suffer that fate.

For Critical Analysis:

The tone of this feature may seem biased. On what grounds are insurance company sales tactics defensible? Also, consider the people who purchase the insurance under these circumstances. What is their role in determining whether the practice is ethical or not? Should their needs be taken into consideration when judging the morality, or lack thereof, of the insurance companies?

SOURCE: L. Sahagun, "In Wake of Gang Violence, Insurers Come Knocking," *Los Angeles Times*, October 5, 1990, p. 1.

threatened by competitive activities such as advertising? Do some companies create demand against the interests of consumers, as with Saturday morning television advertisements that entice children to demand sugary breakfast cereals? (See *Company Focus: Calvin Klein, Inc.* on page 38.)

4. Does capitalism in fact serve those who are least well off in society? One of the unfulfilled promises of communism was a society in which poverty was unknown. In fact, the opposite occurred as tens of millions of Chinese and Soviet citizens died of starvation at various times in the past seventy years. Capitalism's record on poverty is also flawed; although the free market offers opportunities for successful entrepreneurs, success is out of reach for some. (Some economists may think this a moot question, as capitalist theory does not promise the eradication of poverty.)

5. Can business regulate itself, or is government regulation a necessity? Can business regulate itself, and is allowing it to do so in the best interests of society? "If a business enterprise causes sickness or suffering or destroys public land," asks writer Robert Solomon, is society willing to allow Smith's "invisible hand" to enact its self-correcting properties? The extent to which government regulation influences business activity is a major political issue of the 1990s, and this no doubt will continue. This textbook will address many of the issues of that debate.

PROFITS AND HOW THEY ARE PERCEIVED

Autry's vision for enlightened capitalism mentioned earlier denigrates another aspect of free market systems that many economists consider sacrosanct: the pursuit of profits.

The Role of Profits According to economists, profits and losses perform a basic function in a market economy—they direct resources to their highest-valued uses. In effect, profits provide the major instrument of consumer control over producers. Variations in profits often result from a major shift in consumer demand for one product relative to others. Profits are also considered the bait that induces entrepreneurs to take more risk— the greater the risk, the greater the rewards:

▼ **If the inducement of profits were ever eliminated, risk taking would be reduced, and society would suffer.**

In many cases, businesses are motivated as much by the fear of losing money as they are by the desire to make money. The existence of losses, or *negative profits*, indicates that resources in the particular industry are not as highly valued as those same resources might be in another industry. Capital therefore moves away from that industry, or, at a minimum, no further capital is invested in it.

Michael Eisner, Chairman of The Walt Disney Company, addresses shareholders during a meeting regarding the purchase of Capital Cities/ABC, Inc. in New York on January 4, 1996.

COMPANY FOCUS: CALVIN KLEIN, INC.
ADVERTISING AND SOCIAL VALUES

I f advertising has a single overriding theme, it seems to be that "sex sells." Whether it's perfume, cigarettes, or dish-washing detergent, Madison Avenue believes that if it can get our attention, it has won half the battle in getting us to buy the advertised products. What is a better eye-catcher, the logic follows, than sexual innuendo or suggestive images? Although there is a widespread opinion that the preponderance of sex in advertising underscores a continuing crisis of morals, most advertisers insist their work simply reflects society's values. And, as Calvin Klein, Inc., learned, when an ad campaign does violate these values, society's response can be swift and decisive.

The Campaign and the Criticism

The clothing designer Calvin Klein and the company that bears his name have been testing the limits of sexuality in advertising since 1980, when a fifteen-year-old Brooke Shields asked television viewers, "You know what comes between me and my Calvins?" in a jeans commercial. The answer: "Nothing at all." A few local television stations refused to run the ad, which was a muted response compared with the outcry that met the company's advertising efforts in the mid-1990s.

The more recent campaign, for a line of high-priced jeans, featured television commercials, magazine ads, bus posters, and billboards with teen-age models in a variety of poses. In some versions, the models were wearing denim shorts that clearly showed their underwear. In others, young men were shirtless. In one particularly criticized television ad, a partly undressed male model listened to an off-screen voice comment on his body. In another, a young female model's miniskirt clearly showed her underwear.

Immediate criticism met the campaign. One nationally syndicated columnist raged that the models were "posed in what looked like opening scenes from a porn movie" and attacked businesses such as Calvin Klein that are "busy financing our social meltdown." The ads also drew censure from child welfare authorities, leaders of the Catholic League, and the American Family Association, which called for a boycott of stores selling the jeans. Calvin Klein employees, asserted a social commentator, "ought to be ashamed of themselves."

Calvin Klein's Response

A month after launching the campaign, Calvin Klein ran an advertisement announcing that the company had been "taken aback" by the criticism, and that because the message of the advertising "has been misunderstood by some," the "remainder of this campaign" would cease "as soon as possible." The ad also defended the campaign, claiming that it offered a "positive message" about "the spirit, independence, and inner worth of today's young people."

Barbara Lippert, a critic for *Adweek*, believes Calvin Klein ultimately misjudged how far he could take sex in advertising. "It's one thing to show different combinations of adults doing different things to each other," she says. "[E]roticizing children," however, is a line that cannot be crossed.

The New Bottom Line

In a perfect world, perhaps the moral of this story would be something along the lines of "today's media-savvy consumers will remember when a particular company has offended their sense of morals." In reality, however, Calvin Klein's profits did not suffer because of the controversy. One explanation is that the consumers who actually buy Calvin Klein products were not nearly as offended by the ads as their parents were. Another, even more cynical, is that any publicity is good publicity. In the end, each individual company must decide how far it is willing to test society's norms in order to sell its product.

SOURCE: S. Elliott, "Calvin Klein to Withdraw Child Jean Ads," *New York Times*, August 28, 1995, pp. C1, C6.

Perceptions of Profits   In economic theory, the concept of making "too much" profit is contradictory. High profits indicate that people are placing a relatively high value on the product or service whose production is generating the high profits. In the long run, relatively high profits attract more competitors, who force prices lower and thereby lower profits.

Many societies throughout history, however, have embraced the concept of **"obscene" profits** and made it a political issue. Profits garnered by any individual or corporation that are so great as to cause harm to society might be considered "obscene"; by extension, the profit maker is seen as greedy, which is usually a socially undesirable characteristic. In much of Christian and Islamic theology, any profit is considered obscene. Both the Bible and the Koran warn against profiteering business activities. Both making a profit by charging what "the market will bear" and "usury," or collecting interest, were prohibited in the Bible. It is still illegal today to charge interest in some Islamic nations.

More recently, the label *obscene* has been reserved for particular multibillion-dollar industries. In the 1970s and 1980s, following several embargoes imposed on the United States by oil-producing countries in the Middle East, gasoline prices skyrocketed, leading to a consumer outcry against oil companies. In response, Senator Henry Jackson, a Democrat from Washington, called the executives of seven of the largest oil companies before his subcommittee for a probe of "obscene profits."[9] During his first term in office, President Bill Clinton criticized both health-care and pharmaceutical corporations for excessive profits.

The idea of excessive profits is tied to another concept that we address throughout this textbook: no longer is self-interest or profit accepted as the only goal of a business. In fact, companies are expected by some to surrender profits for the good of society. A beer company, for example, is often expected to produce costly public service announcements that warn of the dangers of minors' drinking and of drinking and driving. Some economists believe this places an unfair burden on corporations, whose function, they say, is to make profits, not solve society's ills. A more popular theory is that a corporation is a part of society, and therefore has a responsibility to act not only in its own, but also in society's, best interests.

THE CORPORATION

The latter argument makes an interesting assumption: it personifies business, assigning it a responsibility as if it were an individual. Is this a reasonable assumption? To answer that question, one must have a better understanding of the characteristics of a common business form: the corporation.

WHAT IS A CORPORATION?

A **corporation** is an artificial person, with its own corporate name, owned by individual shareholders. It is a legal entity with rights and responsibilities. The corporation substitutes itself for shareholders in conducting corporate business and incurring liability, yet its authority to act and the liability for its actions are separate and apart from the individuals who own it.[10] Responsibility for the overall management of the corporation is entrusted to a board of directors, which is elected by the shareholders. Corporate officers are hired by the board of directors to run the daily business operations of the corporation.

---

9. G. Karey, "Regulation & the Environment," *Platt's Oilgram News*, April 11, 1994, p. 3.

10. P. Jeffcut, "The Interpretation of Organization: A Contemporary Analysis and Critique," *Journal of Management Studies*, March 1994, p. 225.

A decision in 1819 by the U.S. Supreme Court assured that the property rights of private corporations would have the same protection afforded to other forms of property.[11] This decision gave a corporation the same right as an individual to use its resources in whatever manner it chooses within legal restrictions.[12]

THE CORPORATE "BEING"

Although legally a corporation is an "artificial person," in reality it is a community of persons working toward a similar goal of offering a product or service to the larger community. The individuals that make up a corporate entity are not fixed; most large corporations experience constant turnover of personnel on all levels and sometimes re-engineer the basic structure of the entity. Even so, as a legal artificial person, the corporation remains unchanged. Consequently, it is sometimes difficult to regard a corporation as anything but the sum of its parts, which makes assigning responsibility for corporate actions a frustrating task. Such frustration is evident in the rhetorical question put forth by the English jurist Edward Thurow (1731–1806): "Did you expect a corporation to have a conscience, when it has no soul to be damned and no body to be kicked?"

If we are to discuss the social impact of corporations, however, we will, in a sense, need to find the "being" within a corporation. Chapters in this textbook on corporate culture (Chapter 5), corporate social responsibility (Chapter 6), and corporate governance (Chapter 12) will help in the search. For now, however, it is important to understand that despite its ethereal reputation, the corporation is not a mysterious amalgam of suspicious forces. Each corporation has a chain of command with individuals who are responsible, and answerable, for individual decisions.

Because of their economic power, as Adolph A. Berle and Gardiner C. Means wrote, "Corporations have ceased to be merely legal devices through which the private business transactions of individuals may be carried on . . . . [The corporation] has accrued to it a combination of attributes and powers and has attained a degree of prominence entitling it to be dealt with as a major social institution."[13] These attributes and powers have subjected the fictitious person of the corporation to a great deal of scrutiny.

CORPORATE POWER AND LEGITIMACY

If popular culture hints at popular opinion, then the film *Demolition Man* offers insight into the concern of some about the power of business in its corporate form. The futuristic Sylvester Stallone movie, set in the year 2032 in the city of San Angeles, presents a scenario in which giant corporations have complete influence over the government. The result is a bland fascist society that forbids smoking, alcohol, red meat, salt, and sex. The society is dominated by omnipresent computers that watch over the population and give out tickets for the unauthorized use of obscene language. Corporations have broken into violent confrontation, with Taco Bell's winning the "fast-food wars." Stallone's character, a frozen rugged twentieth-century hero thawed out to combat a dangerous twenty-first-century criminal, is presented as the antithesis of the corporate conformity and profit motive that threaten society.

---

11. *The Trustees of Dartmouth College v. Woodward*, 17 U.S. (4 Wheaton) 518 (1819).
12. R. L. Miller and G. A. Jentz, *Business Law Today: Text & Summarized Cases—Legal, Ethical, Regulatory and International Environment*, 3rd ed. (St. Paul: West Publishing Co., 1994), pp. 626–627.
13. A. A. Berle and G. C. Means, *The Modern Corporation and Private Property*, rev. ed. (New York: Harcourt Brace Jovanovich, 1967), p. 3.

Corporate Power and the Supercorporation

The producers of *Demolition Man* were going for comic effect by suggesting that, in the future, all restaurants would be called Taco Bell. But PepsiCo, the owner of Taco Bell, along with sister chains Pizza Hut and KFC, has been described as having a "take no prisoners" attitude toward the food service business. In the 1990s, PepsiCo, desiring entry into the Italian and Mexican midscale markets, bought California Pizza Kitchen, East Side Marios, and Chevys. To join the drive-through restaurant resurgence in the 1990s, PepsiCo rapidly purchased two such chains, Hot n' Now and Checkers Drive-In.[14] No industry watcher would predict that PepsiCo will control all, or even a majority, of the fast-food business in 2032, but the company is certainly positioning itself for growth in that market.

Corporate Power Americans still love the idea of the "mom and pop" corner shop, so some people are slightly uneasy with the idea of a single corporation such as PepsiCo controlling such a large number of assets. Combine this with another American characteristic, mistrust of power—seen in the separation of powers among the president, Congress, and the Supreme Court—and the result in some places is a concern about the extent to which business manipulates or otherwise influences society. On the one hand is the view that corporations have a right to some power because of their stewardship of the economic functions in society. On the other hand is the concern that corporations can become *too* powerful.

As we see in *Exhibit 2–2*, business can assert its influence in a number of different areas. In economic theory, each one of these powers is counterbalanced by the need to make profits, which in turn dictates that corporations use their power in keeping with the wishes of consumers and, therefore, society.

The Supercorporation Size alone does not account for the relative power of any single corporation, but it does stand to reason that the more resources a business controls,

▼ **EXHIBIT 2–2**
The Powers of Today's Large Businesses

Power	Definitions
1. Economic	A corporation can keep prices artificially high if it is able to keep out competitors (for example, maintain a monopoly).
2. Political	A corporation can influence legislators through lobbying, campaign contributions, and gifts.
3. Social	A corporation can influence the way employees dress, exercise, diet, date, and go to church.
4. Technological	A corporation can determine which innovations and inventions go into production.
5. Environmental	A corporation can add pollutants to the air and water or, conversely, can add pollution-abatement equipment to the production process.
6. Employment	A corporation can hire and fire citizens, as well as set safety and other workplace standards. Also, it can open and close plants in communities, bringing or taking away prosperity.

14. "Is Life Imitating Art?" *Nation's Restaurant News*, November 29, 1993, p. 17.

the more influence it will wield. Although the American legal and political system contains a number of safeguards against individual businesses becoming powerful enough to offset competitive balance (see Chapter 10), the largest companies are magnificent in their scale (see *Exhibit 2–3*). Furthermore, the trend toward the merging—or the combining of assets and resources—of smaller companies to form larger ones (or of large companies to form huge ones) is on the upswing. In one recent nine-month period, the value of all announced mergers reached $248.5 billion, more than any other entire year on record.[15]

With these larger and more powerful companies comes the worry that they will practice undue control over our everyday lives—from selecting the products we choose on grocery shelves to selecting the politicians we choose on the election ballot. A spate of mergers in the telecommunications industry during the mid-1990s particularly raises questions about who will control what some consider a critical resource: information.

CORPORATE LEGITIMACY

Many observers view the trend toward mergers and larger corporations as a trend toward greater efficiency. When companies merge, they often eliminate inefficient resources, producing a more proficient business entity. In contrast to the mergers of the 1980s, which were often characterized as being motivated by greed, the 1990s mergers are said to be more legitimate, in a business sense. In July 1995, for example, IBM paid $3.5 billion—about twice the expected price—to purchase Lotus Development Corporation. The parent company's stated goal was to gain ownership of Lotus's successful Notes groupware program, giving it an edge in the high-growth market for networked software.[16]

▼ **EXHIBIT 2–3 America's Ten Largest Corporations**

Company	Revenues ($ in millions)	Profits ($ in millions)	Number of Employees
1. General Motors	168,828.6	6,880.7	709,000
2. Ford Motor	137,137.0	4,139.0	346,990
3. Exxon	110,009.0	6,470.0	82,000
4. Wal-Mart Stores	93,627.0	2,740.0	675,000
5. AT&T	79,609.0	139.0	299,300
6. IBM	71,940.0	4,178.0	252,215
7. General Electric	70,028.0	6,573.0	222,000
8. Mobil	66,724.0	2,376.0	52,000
9. Chrysler	53,195.0	2,025.0	126,000
10. Philip Morris	53,139.0	5,450.0	151,000

SOURCE: "The Fortune 500," *Fortune*, April 29, 1996, p. F1.

---

15. P. L. Zweig, "The Case against Mergers," *Business Week*, October 30, 1995, p. 122.
16. A. Cortese, "Clicking on *Merge* Isn't Enough," *Business Week*, October 30, 1995, p. 126.

Turner Broadcasting's Chairman and President Ted Turner (left) and Time Warner Chairman and CEO Gerald Levin (right) prior to a news conference at the Time Life Building in New York on September 22, 1995.

How, then, is the legitimacy of a business measured? If a company's legitimacy is determined by its profit-making ability, then the defenders of mergers such as the one carried out by IBM and Lotus are on solid ground. Although nobody can absolutely predict whether the merger will prove beneficial, the intent is evident. By definition, however, legitimacy is the possession of power through recognized standards of acceptance.[17] Historically, the term has been applied to regimes or governments; for example, Henry VIII was the *legitimate* monarch of England. We consider our presidents to be legitimate because, even if we do not agree with their policies, they achieved power through the accepted rules of our form of government.

Whereas capitalism is unchallenged as the legitimate economic system in the United States, the legitimacy of some business practices is coming under increased scrutiny. Mergers, for example, may have social costs that cause many observers to question their legitimacy. The measures to eliminate inefficiencies almost always lead to job loss for large numbers of employees. Merging companies may close operational centers in the streamlining process, negatively affecting the communities in which the factories or office branches were located. Consumer advocates also argue that because mergers often involve companies that offer the same products and services, each merger further reduces consumer choice (see the *Case—The Super Bank*—at the end of this chapter).

CAN CORPORATIONS COMMIT CRIMES?

As we have established, a corporation is not a living person and therefore must act through the will of human beings. Hence, any crime committed in the corporate name must be

17. M. B. Meznar and D. Nigh, "Managing Corporate Legitimacy: Public Affairs Activities, Strategies, and Effectiveness," *Business and Society,* Spring 1993, p. 30.

committed by one or more persons in control of the corporation's affairs or in the employment of the corporation.[18]

Because a criminal act requires intent, the law stated that a corporation, because it has no mind of its own, could not be guilty of a crime. Today, this common law view does not always prevail. Corporations may be charged with many types of crimes.

When the law requires intent as an element of crime, the agent's or employee's intent may be imputed to the corporation. An important factor is how high in the corporate hierarchy the individual stands. Is the employee high enough in the management structure that his or her conduct can be interpreted as a corporate act? If so, then the corporation can be held liable for the actions of that employee. This test is known as the "high managerial agent" rule.[19] Crimes for which corporations have been indicted or convicted include manslaughter, homicide, arson, and grand theft. (For examples of different corporate crimes, see *Exhibit 2–4.*)

Liability of Officers and Directors Although an officer of a corporation generally cannot be held personally liable for crimes of the corporation or of corporate employees simply because he or she is an officer, if that officer was in a position to prevent the crime, he or she may be held liable. Normally, the court must show that the crimes were committed at the officer's direction with his or her permission.

This does not mean that it must be proved that the officer had criminal intent. In some instances, when employees under a corporate officer's supervision commit crimes, criminal liability may be imposed on the officer for his or her negligent failure to supervise the employees (see *Company Focus: Union Carbide Corporation* on page 46).

Worker safety is another area of potential officer and director liability. The Occupational Safety and Health Act of 1970 established specific regulations concerning safety in the workplace. Criminal penalties for willful violations of the act, however, are limited. Until very recently, even blatant violations of federal workplace guidelines often did not meet with serious penalties. The Justice Department, in 1988, stated that the existence of criminal penalties in the Occupational Safety and Health Act did not preempt state and local criminal laws. Since then, states have successfully prosecuted individuals for criminal violations of worker safety standards.

"Vicarious" Liability Corporate criminal liability is vicarious. That is, one person can be punished for the acts of another. Thus, the corporation that is found to be criminally responsible for an act committed by an employee can be fined for that offense. Through the fine, stockholders and employees suffer. The justification for such vicarious criminal liability involves a showing that the corporation could have exercised control and precluded the act or that persons in supervisory positions within the corporation authorized, consented to, or knew of the act.

CRIMINAL PENALTIES

In 1984, a seven-member U.S. Sentencing Commission was charged with the task of standardizing the sentences for corporate crimes.[20] The commission established sentencing

18. B. S. Roberts, A. J. Chaset, L. Haac, and H. M. O'Neill, "Preventative Medicine for Corporate Culture," *Business and Society Review*, Summer 1995, p. 34.

19. A. J. Dahoub, A. M. A. Rasheed, R. L. Priem, and D. A. Gray, "Top Management Team Characteristics and Corporate Illegal Activity," *Academy of Management Review*, January 1995, p. 138.

20. D. R. Dalton, M. B. Metzger, and J. W. Hill, "The New U.S. Corporate Sentencing Guidelines: A Wake-up Call for Corporate America," *Academy of Management Executive*, February 1994, p. 7.

▼ EXHIBIT 2–4 Some Reported Corporate Crimes in the 1990s

Company	Crime	Circumstances
Imperial Food Products	Involuntary manslaughter	On September 3, 1991, a fire at the Imperial poultry-processing factory in Hamlet, North Carolina, killed twenty-five employees and injured another fifty-six. The owner of the plant, Emmett Roe, had ordered the emergency exit doors to be locked from the outside to discourage the theft of chicken nuggets, leaving the employees trapped in the fire. Roe was found guilty of two charges of involuntary manslaughter and was sentenced to almost twenty years in prison.
Rexon Technology	Illegally selling arms to Iraq	The U.S. Arms Control Act forbids American companies to sell artillery components to certain unfriendly countries, including Iraq. In 1995, the New Jersey munitions company pleaded guilty to selling 300,000 sets of weapons components to Iraq. These components were utilized as part of 155-millimeter shells used against American troops in the Gulf War of 1991. As punishment, the company voluntarily went out of business and was fined $500,000.
C. R. Bard	Concealing information	One of the products manufactured by this health-care company is the heart catheter, a device that allows blood to flow to the heart more easily. Between 1987 and 1990, 22,000 of Bard's catheters were inserted into patients. In fifty instances, these catheters broke in the patients' arteries—twenty-two of these patients required emergency surgery, and two of them died. Bard pleaded guilty to 391 counts involving various federal crimes and paid a $61 million fine. Three Bard executives were found guilty of lying to the Food and Drug Administration about the design of catheters and of concealing a series of malfunctions that tests had proved common in the catheters. Each executive could face a maximum prison sentence of five years and a $250,000 fine.
Durex Industries	Wrongful death	In 1992, nine-year-old Daniel Perez and his friend Anthony Storman died after breathing toluene fumes in an unfenced and unlocked Durex Industries trash bin in Tampa, Florida. Not only should the area have been locked off, but also, the chemicals had been dumped illegally according to environmental laws. In 1995, a court awarded the family of Perez $50 million in damages.
Georgia-Pacific	Tax evasion	In 1981, the forest products company purchased the Santa Fe Swamp near Gainesville, Florida, for around $2 million. Three years later, the company valued the land at $24 million for tax reduction purposes. In 1991, after paying $16 million in back payments to the Internal Revenue Service, Georgia-Pacific paid a criminal fine of $5 million for its actions.

guidelines for thirty-two levels of offenses. The punishment for each offense was to depend on such factors as the seriousness of the charge, the amount of money involved, and the extent to which top company officials were involved. Under the new sentencing guidelines, corporate lawbreakers face sanctions and fines that can be as high as hundreds of millions of dollars.

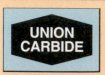

COMPANY FOCUS: UNION CARBIDE CORPORATION
THE QUESTION OF EXECUTIVE RESPONSIBILITY

In December 1984, a leak at the Union Carbide Corporation's plant in Bhopal, India, emitted poisonous methyl isocyanate gas fumes into the environment, causing the worst industrial disaster in history. About 1,500 people died within three days of the incident, and in the intervening decade another 2,500 died from the fumes inhaled at the time. Almost eleven years after it occurred, the disaster is still haunting Warren Anderson, who was Union Carbide's chairman at the time of the disaster.

Assigning the Blame

Immediately following the leak, Anderson flew to Bhopal, where he was arrested by Indian officials. He was soon released, and he returned to the United States and retired the following year at the age of sixty-five. Five years later, Union Carbide reached a settlement with the Indian government to pay $470 million to the victims of the leak and their families.

Union Carbide's internal investigation, along with an independent study, concluded that the disaster occurred because of a deliberate act by a disgruntled Indian employee. Furthermore, the Bhopal plant was owned and operated by an Indian company of which Union Carbide owned 50.9 percent of the stock. The Indian manager had made some bad decisions and provided poor maintenance for the plants. Nevertheless, Anderson has been blamed for the continuing plight of Bhopal's victims, two-thirds of whose claims against the company have not been processed. Those who are receiving compensation get only 200 rupees ($7) a month, a quarter of India's average monthly income.

The attention has earned Anderson the enmity of many human rights and consumers groups. In 1995, *Covert Action Quarterly* published his photo with an article entitled "Arrest This Man: Accused Corporate Killer of Bhopal Found," and it made public his address in the retirement community of Vero Beach, Florida. On the tenth anniversary of the event, protesters waved banners that read "Hang Anderson! Killer Carbide go back."

India's Response

In January 1992, India's magistrates court charged Anderson with "culpable homicide amounting to murder" and ordered him to appear in court that February 1. After Anderson failed to appear, the court requested that he be extradited to face the charges. Union Carbide reacted to the request by reasserting that Anderson had "no involvement with the operations of the Indian company" and stated that "to persist in continued harassment of Anderson . . . would send a signal to the world that the Indian government is permitting those who favor local political expediency to dominate its policymaking."

The implied threat appears to have accomplished its goals. India's government has resisted formally passing the extradition request on to the U.S. State Department for fear of harming U.S.–Indian relations and frightening off potential multinational corporations otherwise attracted by the country's free market reforms. Another possible legal avenue—seizing Union Carbide's assets in India until Anderson appeared before the court—was closed after a determination that such a move would negatively affect the Indian stock market.

The New Bottom Line

Although little proof has been offered connecting Anderson with the Bhopal disaster, his name continues to be linked to the incident. Anderson's experience heralded an environment in which senior management is deemed ultimately responsible for company policy and action. A number of chief executive officers, lacking the shield of international politics, have been held accountable for a subordinate's actions.

SOURCE: Information from P. Chatterjee, "Bhopal Chief Retires to Beach Resort in Florida," *Inter Press Service*, March 14, 1995; and M. Ullah, "Indian Court Seeks Extradition of Former Union Carbide Chairman," *San Diego Union-Tribune*, March 28, 1992, p. D5.

Adding to the codified changes in punishment for corporate crime is the fact that the attitude of enforcement agencies has undergone an adjustment. In 1993, Alfred B. Saroni was convicted on charges that he instructed his employees to dump 126,000 gallons of poisoned waste into storm drains that led to the Oakland Estuary and San Francisco Bay. Saroni became the first person in northern California ever sent to federal prison for an environmental crime. "In the past, it's more likely that we would have gone after the corporation by seeking fines and restitution," admitted a U.S. attorney. "Now, we'll try to put someone in jail, if that person was overseeing the whole operation."[21]

Public Criticism of Business

"The only thing corporations seem to be interested in is making money." Although some economists and stockholders would see this Gallup survey statement as a compliment, it was clearly issued as an indictment. Does this difference in perceptions mirror a gap between the perceptions of corporate America and those of the public? According to an extensive survey carried out by Gallup, Inc., and the Center for Ethics Studies at Marquette University, it does.[22] After interviewing 1,053 adult consumers and 100 chief executive officers (CEOs) at large companies, the surveyors found the following results:

▶ Of the CEOs surveyed, 44 percent viewed business ethics as having improved in the 1990s. Only 16 percent of the consumers agreed with this statement.
▶ In contrast, 56 percent of the consumers felt business ethics had deteriorated in the 1990s, whereas only 28 percent of the executives were willing to go so far.
▶ Of the 727 responding consumers who were employed, only 27 percent were willing to label their place of employment as "highly ethical." Sixty-four percent of the CEOs, however, would make that statement about their own companies.
▶ Ninety-two percent of the CEOs felt that, as head of the company, they could insert "strong influence" on the ethics of their employees. Only 57 percent of consumers were willing to grant the CEO that degree of moral influence.
▶ Within their own organizations, 63 percent of the CEOs felt that employees would report ethical or legal breaches within the company to authorities. Only 36 percent of the consumers felt this was the case, and a substantially higher number (46 percent) thought the probable response of employees would be to "mind their own business." (For other survey results, see *Exhibit 2–5* on page 48.)

The authors of the survey had a number of theories about the discrepancies between CEOs and consumers. First, they postulated that consumers may rely too heavily on the news media for their opinions of corporate America. The media's view is skewed by a propensity to emphasize spectacular cases of purported unethical business behavior while ignoring the more routine aspects of corporate life. Second, the authors said it is possible that consumers have raised their ethical expectations of business to unrealistic heights and are determined to accept nothing less than perfect performance. With such expectations, consumers would tend to ignore the organizational pressures placed on managers and might fail to appreciate how intense competition could occasionally lead

21. J. Doyle, "Jail Terms for Corporate Crime," *San Francisco Chronicle*, April 22, 1993, p. A1.
22. G. R. Laczniak, M. W. Berkowitz, R. G. Brooker, and J. P. Hale, "The Ethics of Business: Improving or Deteriorating?" *Business Horizons*, January 1, 1995, pp. 39–59.

▼ **EXHIBIT 2–5 Consumer and CEO Views on Corporate Ethics**

Management Practices Always Considered Unethical	Consumers	Executives
Misleading advertising or labeling	87%	91%
Causing environmental harm	86%	76%
Lack of equal opportunity for minorities and women	77%	85%
Insider trading	78%	95%
Poor product safety	84%	85%
Using nonunion labor in a unionized company	35%	11%
Padding expense accounts	79%	98%
Overpricing	65%	46%
Hostile takeovers	52%	19%
Moving jobs overseas	45%	2%
Closing a plant	25%	1%

SOURCE: G. R. Laczniak, M.W. Berkowitz, R. G. Brooker, and J. P. Hale, "The Ethics of Business: Improving or Deteriorating?" *Business Horizons*, January 1, 1995, p. 39.

to "questionable" ethics. Finally, say the authors, CEOs may have exaggerated their own beliefs in ethics because they wanted the poll to shed a positive light on their profession.

REDUCING THE PERCEPTION GAP

There is some temptation to debate the two sides of the equation—to try to determine who is right. Are consumers too cynical? Are the CEOs blind to ethical violations, or are they lying? To establish a "reality" with which to measure the results of the poll would be an interesting academic undertaking, but pointless from a business perspective. According to the authors of the Gallup/Center for Ethics Study survey, in this case "perception is reality," and business must move to change the perception. The failure to reverse public distrust could have severe consequences for business, because

> ultimately business is granted license by society to perform its economic function [and] when business accountability is not in balance with business power, the public can intervene to make structural changes that will affect the very strictures under which firms operate. Admittedly, such adjustments take a fair amount of time to unfold. But when they do, the changes in ground rules are often of major proportions. One need only look at the current restructuring—some would say reinventing—of the American health-care system to find a clear example of society's having found the performance of a particular sector of the economy to be unsatisfactory.[23]

Such issues, combined with public discontent, led to tighter government regulation in a variety of areas in the 1990s, from the banking and securities industry to labeling

---

23. *Ibid.*, p. 44.

requirements for alcohol, food, and drug products to stricter standards for environmental advertising claims. Each new round of regulation adds greater costs to doing business, costs that can hardly be afforded in the ultracompetitive—and often less regulated—global economy.

The authors of the survey offer a number of suggestions concerning what steps business should take to improve the perception and reality of unethical business practices. These include communicating more effectively with consumers through the media, cultivating higher ethical expectations, and conducting internal ethics audits to assure that those expectations are realized.

These suggestions have merit but fail to address the overwhelming challenges of doing business in the 1990s. Corporations need to take a comprehensive strategic approach to their social responsibility, as we explore in the next chapter by introducing the concept of the management of stakeholder issues.

THE DELICATE BALANCE

There remains little doubt that capitalism is the most efficient system for improving the material well-being of humans. The failure of centralized planning within the command systems of the former Soviet Union and its satellite countries can leave even less doubt that the three *Ps* of capitalism—prices, private property, and profits—will remain the basis of economic systems for many years to come. At the same time, though, the most significant business form in the capitalist system—the corporation—comes under scrutiny and criticism. Corporate decision makers today are expected to bring better products to market at lower prices while at the same time making sure that their rewards are not excessive. Those rewards, of course, are profits. For corporations, the delicate balance involves incorporating goals such as giving the consumer fair value in addition to making profits.

TERMS AND CONCEPTS FOR REVIEW

Capitalism 32

Communism 32

Corporation 39

Enlightened capitalism 34

Incentive structure 34

Law of demand 31

Law of supply 31

"Obscene" profits 39

Socialism 32

SUMMARY

1. The three basic questions that every society must answer are (a) What and how much will be produced? (b) How will it be produced? and (c) For whom will it be produced?

2. Under the law of demand, higher prices yield smaller quantities demanded, and vice versa. Under the law of supply, higher prices yield larger quantities supplied, and vice versa.

3. The trilogy of economic systems involves capitalism, communism, and socialism. In principle, all economic systems are a combination of some capitalism (market system) and some centrally planned command system.

4. Although command socialism and communism clearly failed in the Soviet Union, unbridled capitalism has not been the alternative sought by some observers. Rather, they argue in favor of enlightened capitalism in which businesses have goals beyond simply maximizing profits.

5. The backbone of capitalism is an incentive structure that rewards efficiency and punishes inefficiency. This system, also called the free market, appears desirable in theory, but at least one critic, Robert C. Solomon, asked the following questions: (a) Is true competition possible? (b) Does capitalism require a divorce between work and life? (c) Does capitalism create, rather than just supply, its own demand? (d) Does capitalism in fact serve those who are the least well off in society? and (e) Can business regulate itself, or is government regulation a necessity?

6. The changing profitability of business investment reflects changing supplies and demands for particular products. Profits offer the positive inducement to increase investment in a particular area. Losses offer the negative inducement to disinvest in that area. The definition of obscene profits varies from person to person and society to society, but the concept is widely discussed today.

7. A corporation is an artificial person owned by shareholders and operated by a board of directors that hires officers, who then create an organizational structure with employees. Corporations have become major social institutions with the power to affect political outcomes.

8. The so-called supercorporation involves billions of dollars of assets and yearly sales. Size alone, though, does not always indicate power. Giant corporations have been broken up, gone bankrupt, and altered themselves in the face of global competition.

9. Although capitalism appears to be the legitimate economic system in the United States, the legitimacy of some corporate practices have been increasingly scrutinized. In particular, plant closings, downsizing, and the like—all in the name of efficiency—have been criticized in recent years.

10. Increasingly, the government has imposed criminal liability on corporations for the actions of its agents and employees. Additionally, officers of corporations have begun to be fined and put in jail for the actions of corporate employees. In particular, the U.S. Sentencing Commission has created thirty-two levels of corporate criminal offenses for which corporate officers can be jailed and fined.

11. There is a definite gap between CEOs' perceptions and those of the public about many issues. Consumers have perhaps unrealistically high ethical expectations of business, whereas many CEOs have not raised their expectations to match.

EXERCISES

1. "All exchange is mutually beneficial. If it weren't, the exchange would not take place." Analyze this statement.

2. Explain the law of demand and why you believe it is an accurate predictor of the way individuals respond to changing prices.

3. Under an economic system in which private property rights do not exist, there still must be some mechanism used to determine how resources are allocated. Outline such a mechanism.

4. What is the difference between capitalism and enlightened capitalism?

5. Describe the incentive structure that exists within a capitalist system as opposed to a noncapitalist system.

6. Reread the five macroethical questions starting on page 35 about the values of a free enterprise system. Which of those five questions is the most relevant for you? Explain your answer.

7. What is the difference between profits and "obscene" profits?

8. What is the difference between a corporation and a supercorporation?

9. "Corporations are the basis of an effective system of capitalism. Because we accept the legitimacy of capitalism, we therefore must accept the legitimacy of the corporate form of business organization." Indicate whether you agree or disagree with this quotation. Explain your answer.

10. Reexamine *Exhibit 2–2*. Is the technological power of the corporation more important today than it was, say, fifty years ago? Why or why not?

11. How can a corporation be responsible for a crime?

12. Look at *Exhibit 2–4*. Explain which corporate crime you believe could most easily have been avoided and exactly how it could have been avoided by the corporation's officers and directors.

13. Is it fair that a corporate officer, who has no knowledge of an illegal act by a corporation employee, can be put in jail for that action if it is determined to be criminal?

14. "The only thing corporations seem to be interested in is making money." What else could corporations be expected to do, and why?

SELECTED REFERENCES

▶ Craypo, Charles, and Bruce Nissen, eds. *Grand Designs: The Impact of Corporate Strategies on Workers, Unions, and Communities*. Ithaca, N.Y.: ILR Press, 1993.

▶ Harrison, Bennett. *Lean and Mean: The Changing Landscape of Corporate Power in the Age of Flexibility*. New York: Basic Books, 1994.

▶ Jones, Bryan D., and Lynn W. Bachelor. *The Sustaining Hand: Community Leadership and Corporate Power*. Lawrence, Kans.: University of Kansas Press, 1993.

▶ Korten, David C. *When Corporations Rule the World*. San Francisco: Barrett-Koehler Publishers, 1995.

▶ Ross, Robert J., and Kent C. Trachte. *Global Capitalism: The New Leviathan*. Albany, N.Y.: State University of New York Press, 1990.

RESOURCES ON THE INTERNET

▼ Because of its wealth of information on corporations in the United States, Hoover's Online is an invaluable resource. For the List of Lists, the Top Ten Business News Stories of the week, and data on more than 1,500 corporations, access Hoover's Online at

http://www.hoovers.com

or

gopher://gopher.hoovers.com

▼ For daily news on the world of business and corporations, you can access Money Online at

http://pathfinder.com:80/ @d6YEsCc@wAAQDqr/time/daily/ money/1997/latest.html

C A S E

The Super Bank

Background

In the summer of 1995, Chemical Banking Corporation announced a planned merger with rival Chase Manhattan Corporation. The combination of Chemical, the nation's fourth largest bank in terms of assets, and Chase, the nation's sixth largest, created a single entity with $20 billion in assets, the largest banking company in the United States and the fourth largest in the world.

The Chemical-Chase entity dominates the market in a number of areas. It ranks first in global loan syndications, global custody of pension fund investments, international electronic money transfers, and overseas trading revenue. It is the premier New York area bank, leads domestic middle-market banking, and ranks first among banks in mortgages for wealthier individuals in the United States. The two banks combined are second only to Citicorp in credit-card balances outstanding.

Judging by the jump in stock prices for both companies when the merger was announced, investors were optimistic about the prospects of the merged superbank. Many of the 75,000 employees of the two organizations in 51 countries and 39 states were less enthusiastic about the proposed transaction, however, and consumer groups warned that a Chemical-Chase combination was not in the best interests of banking customers.

A Former Leader

Named after former secretary of the treasury Salmon P. Chase, the Chase National Bank of the City of New York was founded in 1877. The bank attained early success in financing imports and exports, and after a 1930 merger with Equitable Trust became the largest bank in the world.

Chase National solidified its position as a preeminent international franchise by opening branches overseas in the early part of the twentieth century. It also gained in reputation by lending to sovereign nations and large U.S. corporations. Another merger, with the Bank of Manhattan in 1955, gave the newly named Chase Manhattan a strong presence in the retail industry of New York City.

Chase Manhattan, however, had lost its status as the nation's premier bank because of a series of unprofitable real estate dealings in the 1970s and the failure of New York City to pay its debts in 1975. The bank was also hurt by a strategy of lending to developing countries—which caused millions of dollars in losses when these countries defaulted throughout the 1980s—and another real estate market collapse in the early 1990s. Although it was recovering somewhat through securities-underwriting gains, Chase Manhattan still lagged well behind Citicorp and Chemical, making a merger with the latter attractive.

The Competitive Pressures of the Industry

The prospect was also appealing to Chemical during a year that the banking industry that would undergo 600 mergers, readjusting to technological innovations that were changing the nature of the business. In 1995, more than $250 billion in U.S. bank and thrift assets were involved in the mergers, up from $190 billion in 1994. By 1996, there would be fewer than 10,000 commercial banks in the United States—down from 14,500 in 1984—and some experts believe the industry will shrink by another 6,000 before stabilizing. In an environment permeated with credit-card terminals and automatic teller machines (ATMs), the demand for a large number of banks no longer exists. Furthermore, this demand will continue to shrink as electronic home banking from personal computers becomes more widespread.

One of the motivating factors behind the banking industry mergers is a desire to spread the costs of acquiring and implementing the technological features that will dominate banking in the future. Another is an opportunity to remain competitive while closing down a number of branch networks that will become obsolete as consumers do their banking from home. Finally, a strengthening financial atmosphere—the New York Stock Exchange financial stock index was up 27 percent at the time of the Chemical-Chase deal, and the NASDAQ financial stock index was up 34 percent—brought with it higher bank share prices, making acquisitions more affordable.

Reactions to the Merger

Principals of the Chemical-Chase deal announced that the new bank planned to cut $1.5 billion in annual costs by 1997, with most of the savings coming from the closure of "redundant" operations. The cuts were expected to increase the value of the combined banks' per-share earnings by more than $2, from $5.65 to $8. Predictably, investors responded employees and close 100 branches in the New York area. For consumers, the merger would cause a certain amount of inconvenience, as branches were closed, accounts were transferred, and new credit cards and ATM cards were issued.

Some consumer analysts thought the merger's effects would go far beyond temporary annoyance. "The big concern is that whenever we see banks with a huge presence merging, we see fees increased and fees for things that used to be free," said a research analyst at the Center for Study of Responsive Law. (In fact, the fees for an ATM transaction did rise.) That Washington-based consumer interest group co-authored a study of three hundred banks that showed that the fees for checking and savings accounts increased at nearly twice the rate of inflation, with the largest banks charging the highest fees. This follows a theory that as the number of banks decreases, the competitive nature of the market will change, allowing the institutions to raise the price of their services.

Social activists also criticized the merger on the ground that as branches closed, lending in poor neighborhoods would be cut. The Reverend Jesse Jackson called the Chemical-Chase merger another round of "economic violence" that would benefit relatively few shareholders while harming employees and members of the community. Jackson promised to try to block approval of the merger by federal regulators through "litigation, legislation and demonstrations."

Community Loans and Grants

Bank officials moved quickly to head off the criticism. Maintaining that the merger would allow Chemical-Chase to provide improved products and services, Walter V. Shipley, chief executive officer of the new bank, denied that consumers would suffer. "We still have to remain competitive. We don't want to price ourselves out of the market," he said.

helent amounts in the areas where they....... Accordingly, community activists have the power to hold up billion-dollar deals.

To further avoid possible bottlenecks in the political process, the banks sent questionnaires to 375 community groups, asking what grants they would require from the multibillion-dollar pledge. "We don't want to submit to what has been seen in the past as CRA blackmail," said a Chemical reinvestment officer. "There will be some unhappy people who don't get what they want. But we don't want to be in the position where we have one group that holds us hostage while 350 groups sign on."

Some of the groups called the effort a public relations stunt conceived to smooth the government approval process. "You don't wave an $18 billion magic wand and click your heels three times" to quiet lending concerns, said Nelson Antonio Denis, representing an East Harlem, New York, community group. Describing a Chemical branch in a Hispanic neighborhood in the middle of 40 vacant buildings, Denis noted that the bank loaned 3½ cents in the community for each $1 in deposits it accepted in 1993 and 1994. "It is presiding over housing rot and then lends its money elsewhere," he told regulators in a meeting of government officials and community activists.

Future Strategy

Ironically, Chemical received a top grade from regulators concerning its community lending records when the bank merged with Manufacturers' Hanover in 1992. In 1994, Chemical provided $502 million in community investment loans and $6.1 million in grants to nonprofit and community groups. The political pressure, said one activist, aims to ensure "their commitment level after the merger goes up, not down."

CASE (CONTINUED)

It was unlikely that the efforts of community groups would cause approval of the merger to be blocked, but a prolonged process could have cost the new bank revenues and hurt investor confidence. Chemical-Chase's strategy of pledging grants and loans was ultimately successful, and the tactic will undoubtedly be used in the continued mass of mergers that experts predict will revolutionize the banking industry in the near future. These grants and loans may benefit community groups and citizens of low-income neighborhoods, but analysts warn that there will be casualties in the consolidation trend: bank employees. A study by one research firm predicted the loss of half a million bank jobs in the second half of the 1990s.

Critical Thinking Questions

1. To be sure, any large merger in any industry will almost by definition result in some job losses. After all, one of the reasons to merge is to become more efficient, often by cutting costs through layoffs. Are workers as a group therefore worse off because of huge mergers? Under what circumstances could workers be better off in the short run if such mergers were prevented, but worse off in the long run?

2. How is the consumer helped by mergers in the banking industry? How is the consumer hurt by these mergers? In the end, is the consumer better or worse off with fewer, but larger, banks in the United States?

3. If this is a classic stockholder-driven merger, what is your opinion of the ethics of stockholder-driven mergers?

4. Examine the role that community activists played in the Chemical-Chase merger process. In what way are they a positive force in the process? If you owned stock in Chase or Chemical, what would be your opinion of the community activists?

5. In what way does a bank or any other business have a responsibility to the community in which it operates? Why would banks in low-income neighborhoods be tempted to lend to clients outside the neighborhood? Is this an unethical practice or simply a smart business strategy?

SOURCE: Information from J. Mathews, "Case, Chemical to Merge, Creating Largest U.S. Bank," *Washington Post*, August 29, 1995, p. A1; S. Lipin, "Joining Fortunes: Chemical and Chase Set $10 Billion Merger, Forming Largest Bank," August 29, 1995, pp. A1, A10; C. Kraul, "Bank Merger Mania," *Los Angeles Times*, August 29, 1995, p. 1; S. Pullian, "'Synergy Fever Fuels Surge in Chemical, Chase Stock," *Wall Street Journal*, August 29, 1995, p. C1; "Consumer Groups Fault Chase-Chemical Deal," *Los Angeles Times*, August 29, 1995, p. 3; "Jackson Says He'll Oppose Merger of Chemical, Chase," *Wall Street Journal*, August 29, 1995, p. A6; M. T. Prenon, "Local Workers' Fate Uncertain in Wake of Chase, Chemical Merger," *Westchester County Business Journal*, September 4, 1995, p. 7; S. Hansell, "2 Big Banks in Merger Set Aid for Poor," *New York Times*, November 1, 1995, pp. D1, D4; and "Community Activists against Chemical-Chase Merger," *State Journal Register*, November 17, 1995, p. 39.

BUSINESS AND STAKEHOLDERS TODAY

INTRODUCTION

T he public, it seems, would like business to exemplify the values of Jean Valjean, as described in the introductions to Chapters 1 and 2. People are disappointed when business does not live up to such standards. Even Victor Hugo, however, would approve of Coca-Cola Company's effect on living standards in Romania (see *Company Focus: Coca-Cola Company*) or of the culture that former chairman Arnold Hiatt created at Stride Rite Corporation.

In 1971, Stride Rite became the first U.S. corporation to open an on-site day care center, at its Massachusetts headquarters. Since then, the shoe manufacturing and retail company has committed itself to improving the quality of life for employees and community members. Among Stride Rite's programs are the following:

▶ A *scholarship program* awards educational scholarships each year to two high school seniors who are dependents of company employees.
▶ *Child- and elder-care services* have been expanded for more than twenty years to provide care for children and elderly dependents of employees and community members at the Stride Rite Integrational Center.
▶ After working for Stride Rite for three months, employees are eligible for *tuition assistance*, including an 80 percent reimbursement for those who complete preapproved courses with a C average or better.
▶ Employees can take part in fitness, cholesterol information, weight control, blood pressure screening, nutrition, and stress management programs at a *wellness center* at the company's Cambridge, Massachusetts, headquarters.
▶ An *employee volunteer program* allows employees to volunteer two hours a week at one of two Cambridge public schools. While helping students with academic, athletic, and career awareness skills, employees receive full pay for their efforts.

Stride Rite also offers employees generous family leave time, stock-purchasing plans, and retirement and capital accumulation plans, along with a matching gifts program that replicates money given by workers to charitable foundations with a limit of $2,000 per employee per year.[1]

"[Hiatt's] original impetus behind all this wasn't business," says a human resources executive who worked under the former CEO. "It just seemed like the right thing to do."[2] Business has not suffered from doing the "right thing." Stride Rite management believes the company's reputation and policies allow it to choose from a more qualified pool of prospective employees, inspire loyalty and efficiency among the existing work force, and lessen profit-draining practices such as absenteeism.

In this final introductory chapter, we introduce management theories that Stride Rite and other companies have incorporated into the profit-making process. Although the individual strategies vary from organization to organization, each one is based on a similar foundation: the interests of the corporation and of society are not mutually exclusive, and it is bad business practice to treat them as such.[3]

---

1. J. J. Laabs, "Stride Rite's Benefits Mirror Its Commitment to Individual, Family and Community-Service Goals," *Personnel Journal*, July 1993, p. 55.
2. J. J. Laabs, "Family Issues Are a Priority at Stride Rite," *Personnel Journal*, July 1993, p. 49.
3. S. P. Sethi and P. Steidlmeier, "The Evolution of Business' Role in Society," *Business and Society Review*, Summer 1995, p. 55.

COMPANY FOCUS: COCA-COLA COMPANY

COCA-COLA REVITALIZES A NATION

Often, a company can help a community by simply conducting normal business activities there. An extreme but instructive example is that of Coca-Cola Company's presence in Romania. Until the 1989 overthrow of Communist dictator Nicolae Ceausescu, the 23 million inhabitants of the country were the poorest, most repressed populace in Eastern Europe. In the 1990s, the country has struggled to erect a modern economy, and a great deal of its success in doing so can be attributed to the efforts of Coca-Cola.

The Multiplier Effect

By 1996, the soft-drink giant had eight bottling plants in Romania, employing 2,500 workers and reaching annual sales of $120 million. In the five years since it formed a joint venture with Romania's largest bottler of soft drinks, Ci-So S.A., Coca-Cola has poured $150 million into the country, part of a total of $1.5 billion it invested in Eastern Europe over that time. The implications of Coca-Cola's efforts in Romania, however, reach far beyond these numbers. Because it had almost no foreign investors before CocaCola,

Romania has provided economists with an ideal opportunity to measure the multiplier effect of business operations in a developing country by tracing the creation of employment and wealth, as well as the transfer of modern technology and management methods.

According to a study at the University of South Carolina College of Business Administration, Coca-Cola has helped create a class of microentrepreneurs in Romania by making its product available to small retailers and kiosk owners. The report on the study states that by the mid-1990s as many as 25,000 small shops "started or maintained business because of Coca-Cola. . . . Many also sold soap, cigarettes, and other high turnover products, but would have gone bankrupt without Coca-Cola." The economists estimated that for every Romanian the company directly employed, eleven other jobs were created elsewhere.

Other Companies Follow Coca-Cola

Coca-Cola's influence has not been lost among Romanians themselves. "[Under communism] our system always guaranteed that we got second-rate products, so there was no pride in what we sold," said one general store owner in downtown Bucharest. "Then Coke comes in with its new trucks and new bottles and its drivers in new uniforms. Everything is high quality. That makes us feel better about ourselves."

Other companies have followed Coca-Cola's lead into Romania. A small advertising business owned by Bogdan Ennou, for example, allied itself with the soft-drink company in 1993. It has since been able to sign contracts with Xerox, Gillette, Nestlé, Texaco, and Samsung, which have all opened operations in Romania. "If you're accepted by Coke, it's like a blank check," says Ennou.

The New Bottom Line

Every business has a multiplier effect in the community in which it functions, though the effect may not be as marked as that of Coca-Cola in Romania. Indeed, it is the web of these multiplier effects that forms the basis of local, national, and global economies. It follows that business, by its very nature, has a responsibility to the society it supports and by which it is supported.

SOURCE: N. C. Nash, "Coke's Great Romanian Adventure," *New York Times*, February 26, 1995, Section 3, pp. 1, 10.

THE CORPORATION'S SOCIAL RESPONSIBILITY

Stride Rite—as well as virtually all corporations—bases its ideas about the role of the corporation on four areas of corporate responsibility:

1. Responsibility to shareholders.
2. Responsibility to employees.
3. Responsibility to the community.
4. Responsibility to customers.[4]

The first responsibility has always been a cornerstone of management strategy:

▼ **If a corporation cannot produce an acceptable rate of return to its investors, in most instances it will cease to exist.**

The other three responsibilities involve social issues. The idea of a corporation's having social responsibility represents a broadening of the corporation's implied contract with the environment in which it operates. Although organizations today are expected, and even encouraged, to realize profits, they must do so within the boundaries of ethical behavior as decided by society.[5]

THE SOCIAL CONTRACT

The economic goals of a corporation can be seen as inherently concurrent with those of society as a whole. Noted economists suggest that business furthers the interests of society by furthering its own interests and maximizing its rate of return to investors. Business presents society with an environment in which to earn and spend money income. It supplies the U.S. gross domestic profit (GDP)[6] and shares technological innovations. These benefits improve the quality of life for Americans. Side effects such as damage to the environment were at one time felt to be acceptable trade-offs for economic progress.

Beginning in the 1950s, however, a new, implicit contract began to be formed between business and society. Concerns were voiced about employee safety and health, disclosure to the consumer, the health of the environment, and equal opportunities for minorities. Under the terms of this new **social contract**, business is obligated to operate within the boundaries of the *social* environment.[7]

A Counterproductive Contract?   A number of analysts disagree with the basic idea of corporate social responsibility. Economist Milton Friedman asserts that a company has

---

4. Laabs, "Family Issues Are a Priority at Stride Rite."
5. H. J. Van Buren, "Competitiveness, Wages, and Corporate Responsibility," *Business and Society Review*, Summer 1995, p. 63.
6. GDP represents the total market value of all final goods and services produced within a nation's borders each year. This method of measuring a nation's income replaced gross national product (GNP), which measures the market value of all final goods and services produced by a nation's residents, even when the production takes place *outside* national borders.
7. M. Anshen, "Changing the Social Contract," in *Ethical Theory in Business*, 2d ed., eds. T. L. Beauchamp and N. E. Bowie (Englewood Cliffs, N.J.: Prentice Hall, 1983), pp. 99–103.

only one responsibility to society: "to use its resources and engage in activities designed to increase its profits so long as it stays within the rules of the game, which is to say, engages in open and free competition without deception or fraud." Friedman further believes that the marketplace will punish those organizations that do not stay within "the rules of the game," and any corporate funds used toward social ends come from the pocket of shareholders and are, as such, antithetical to the corporation's purpose.[8]

Another argument against corporate social responsibility is marked by a refusal to assign the attributes of a moral or immoral person to the corporation. As we discussed in Chapter 2, although the corporation is a legal person, there are numerous roadblocks to treating it as a person. John R. Danley argues that a corporation is more like a machine, and he therefore logically resists any attempt to place moral responsibilities on it. Just as one cannot blame the automobile in a drunk driving accident, Danley says, "to ascribe responsibility to such machines [as corporations] . . . is tantamount to mistaking the created for the creator."[9]

Accepting the Social Contract Proponents of corporate social responsibility argue that the corporation is not separate from society; it is part of society and enjoys a reciprocal relationship with its environment. This case has been put bluntly with statements such as "It is hard to do business when the town is burning down." Joseph R. Desjardins makes the argument more eloquently by pointing out that corporations exist only

> because individuals come together to carry out jointly the business of producing goods and services. The particular form of that joint activity in any society is determined by social norms. For example, in contemporary American society, corporations are enterprises with explicit state charters, and they must function according to the positive laws of the society. At a deeper level, the particular form of the contemporary American corporation is the product of socially evolved conceptions of property rights. The powers those property rights confer and the limits on the exercise of those powers are defined by norms that develop over time through the pull and tug of forces within the society. . . . A given corporate structure will naturally lead to specifically defined duties and responsibilities for the people who inhabit that institution. The norms that define these duties, when internalized by corporate employees, help shape the values and behavior of those employees. Given all this, we reach the inescapable conclusion that the corporation is social by its very nature.[10]

The Responsibilities of the Powerful Arguments for and against the social contract notwithstanding, corporate executives and managers are accepting social responsibilities on a widespread scale (see *Exhibit 3–1* on page 60). We spend an entire chapter discussing corporate social responsibility (Chapter 6), but it is important at this time to understand that business social responsibility is in many ways an extension of business power. In the past, government was expected to support social goals, and the business of business was business. This responsibility is shifting:

---

8. M. Friedman, "The Social Responsibility of Business Is to Increase Its Profits," in *Ethical Theory in Business,* 2d ed., eds. T. L. Beauchamp and N. E. Bowie (Englewood Cliffs, N.J.: Prentice Hall, 1983), pp. 81–83.
9. J. R. Danley, "Corporation Moral Agency: The Case for Anthropological Bigotry," in *Business Ethics: Reading and Cases in Corporate Morality,* eds. W. M. Hoffman and J. M. Moore (New York: McGraw-Hill, 1990), pp. 165–170.
10. J. R. Desjardins, "Virtue and Business Ethics," in *Contemporary Issues in Business Ethics,* eds. J. R. Desjardins and J. J. McCalls (Belmont, Calif.: Wadsworth, 1990), pp. 54–59.

▼ **EXHIBIT 3–1 Ten Trends toward Social Responsibility in the 1990s**

Trend 1.	**The Pursuit of Happiness.** American workers spend more hours on the job than do those of any other industrialized nation. Although this fact is not likely to change any time soon, more American workers do appear to be adjusting their lifestyles to allow for more leisure. More than 5 million Americans work at home full-time or part-time, giving themselves more freedom to balance work and relaxation. In light of this trend, companies are offering more flexible schedules, work-at-home opportunities, and sabbaticals to valued employees.
Trend 2.	**The Greening of the Corporation.** Businesses are becoming more sensitive to environmental concerns. This includes recycling products, managing waste, and working to keep air and water free from pollution.
Trend 3.	**Volunteering.** Employees from every level of the corporation are donating their time and skills to help the less privileged. Companies are encouraging this trend by providing different kinds of volunteer opportunities, such as mentoring programs for local school students.
Trend 4.	**The Peace Conversion.** Since the end of the Cold War in the early 1990s, the federal government has drastically cut defense spending. As a result, companies that relied on making weapons and other instruments of war have had to diversify to survive.
Trend 5.	**Cause Marketing.** More and more companies are basing marketing campaigns around their corporate social responsibility. For example, when Burger King began using recycled paper in its packaging, the fast-food chain included this information in its advertising.
Trend 6.	**The Family-Friendly Workplace.** Companies are beginning to realize that employees worried about a problem at home are less effective at work. Furthermore, more women are in the workplace than ever before. Consequently, on-site day-care centers, provisions for elderly care, parental leave, and even company-sponsored summer camps are becoming more common.
Trend 7.	**Cooperation with Government.** The late 1980s and early 1990s saw the passage of a number of sweeping laws dealing with the social responsibility of corporations (the Civil Rights Act, the Americans with Disabilities Act, the Clean Air Act, and so on.). Many companies are trying to stay within the law with codes of conduct and other methods of self-regulation.
Trend 8.	**Diversity in the Workplace.** The American work force today looks nothing like the work force of twenty years ago. The workplace has more women and nonwhite employees. Furthermore, gay and lesbian workers are more visible than in the past. Companies are responding with a variety of programs to "value differences" in the new work force.
Trend 9.	**Improving the Consumer-Business Relationship.** Today's consumers want to know what's in a product, how it was tested, who produced it, and under what working conditions it was made. They also want to know where the package will go once the product is discarded. Companies are responding with toll-free consumer hot lines, increased labeling, marketing campaigns, and other devices to give the consumer insight into their practices.
Trend 10.	**Technological Breakthroughs.** Technology has made the American workplace a much more efficient environment. Fax machines and E-mail have made communications infinitely less time consuming. Portable computers and modems give employees more freedom from their offices. Satellite conference meetings save the time and expense of travel.

SOURCE: C. Cox, "Is Business Waking Up?" *Business Ethics*, January–February 1992, pp. 20–22.

▼ As companies have gained more power in society, they have been assigned rising expectations.

Society now relies on business to improve the quality of education, alleviate world hunger and poverty, reduce unemployment, support the arts and medical research, and resolve urban social problems.[11] Furthermore, the Iron Law of Responsibility—if you abuse your power, you lose your power—is becoming an adage of the modern marketplace.

THE STAKEHOLDER CONCEPT

If you recall, Stride Rite saw itself as having responsibilities to four distinct groups: shareholders, employees, the community, and customers. This suggests that the shoe company is taking a stakeholder approach to management. The **stakeholder concept** is an outgrowth of the concept of corporate social responsibility; it suggests that a corporation has a responsibility to all groups or entities that have a stake, or interest, in the corporation's operations.[12]

Traditionally, the most important stakeholders of a corporation have been the stockholders; indeed, the term *stakeholder* is sort of a play on the word *stockholder*. The stakeholder approach does not deny that the corporation has responsibilities to its stockholders, but it does imply that those responsibilities do not give the company the right to ignore the interests of other groups, such as employees or consumers. Under the stakeholder perspective, for example, an automobile manufacturer would not deny workers eye shields simply because the costs of purchasing the safety equipment would cut into the value of the company's stock.

There are a number of groups with whom business is intricately linked. The most important groups include owners, employees, consumers, the environment, local and global communities, and the government.

OWNER STAKEHOLDERS

Individual owners (including owners of some small corporations and unincorporated entities) have an intimate relationship with their operations: they must pay with their own money any debts piled up because of bad management, bad luck, or any other reason. In many large corporations, where legally the stockholders are the owners, this is not the case: an individual stockholder's share in any of the debts or damages incurred by the firm is limited to the value of his or her shares in the firm.

In large, publicly held corporations, the trade-off for this limited liability exposure is the inability to participate in the day-to-day running of the corporation. Although theoretically stockholders control the firm and can vote out directors who allow improper management, in reality the stockholders' power is limited. In most large corporations, no stockholder owns more than a small fraction of the total, or outstanding, stock, and any one stockholder is unlikely to rally enough support to challenge the board of directors' control of the firm.

Shareholder Activists The individual stockholder's limited power has recently undergone a change. Investors are beginning to pressure corporations with tactics such as media exposure and government attention. Some have formed a class of corporate owners called *shareholder activists*. These groups of shareholders pressure companies to boost profits and dividends, link executive pay to performance, and oust inefficient

---

11. R. C. Solomon, *The New World of Business: Ethics and Free Enterprise in the Global 1990s* (Lanham, Md.: Littlefield Adams Quality Paperbacks, 1994), p. 206.
12. M. B. E. Clarkson, "A Stakeholder Framework for Analyzing and Evaluating Corporate Social Performance," *Academy of Management Review*, January 1995, p. 92.

management. Consequently, executives and managers are giving more weight to the concerns of owner stakeholders in the decision-making process. For example, shareholders of the giant pharmaceutical company Pfizer, Inc., forced the company to stop selling flavoring agents to tobacco-products companies. In the 1990s, a number of CEOs from major corporations—General Motors, IBM, Apple, and Eastman Kodak, to name a few—have been expelled by dissatisfied stockholders.[13]

Social Investing Shareholders who want to tie their personal values directly to their investments are turning in greater numbers to social investing. These investors consider social factors, as well as financial ones, when making investment decisions. In the 1970s, social investing was primarily identified with South Africa, as investors opposed to the South African government's policy of apartheid pressured American firms to divest themselves of business interests in that country. Today, social investors avoid manufacturers of alcohol or tobacco products, weapons, or nuclear energy; companies involved in promoting gambling; and companies with poor pollution or discrimination records. By investing only in so-called social mutual funds, shareholders can make sure their dollars are being invested in politically correct corporations.

EMPLOYEE STAKEHOLDERS

Historically, employees have had one basic right: to be paid for work they have been hired to perform. But after thirty years of legislation, employees today enjoy many other rights.[14] These include limited rights to privacy, the right to object to immoral or illegal work requirements, and the right to freedom of choice in decisions made outside the workplace. Employees also have the right not to be discriminated against on the basis of race, color, gender, age, national origin, or disability. In addition, today's employees enjoy many privileges and services unavailable to earlier generations (see *Exhibit 3–2*).

Despite the extensive legislation and union collective bargaining agreements to protect employees, employers in most states have retained one key right: employment at will. This right allows employers to remove workers for any legal reason when necessary.

Employee Attitudes The growing lack of job security is fostering a sense among some employees that their concerns are disregarded by management. In the past, employees drew power from organized labor.[15] But in 1996, only 11 percent of the nation's private sector work force was represented by a union, compared with 36 percent in 1953.

No single force has emerged to take the place of unions in regaining the balance. A recent study of employee attitudes by economist Richard Freeman of Harvard University and law professor Joel Rogers of the University of Wisconsin at Madison suggests that millions of low- and middle-level American workers feel ignored by company management but do not speak up because they worry about keeping their positions.[16] Another recent study by the Council of Communication Management found that of 705 employees at 70 companies, 64 percent did not always believe what they were told by management, 61 percent felt they were not well informed of management plans, and 54 percent said decisions were not explained well.[17]

---

13. G. Fabrikant, "Battling for Hearts and Minds at Time Warner," *New York Times*, February 26, 1995, p. 9.
14. E. S. Stanton, "Employee Participation: A Critical Evaluation and Suggestions for Management Practice," *SAM Advanced Management Journal*, Autumn 1993, p. 18.
15. R. C. Ford and M. D. Fottler, "Empowerment: A Matter of Degree," *Academy of Management Executive*, August 1995, p. 21.
16. S. Dentzer, "Anti-Union, But Not Anti-Unity," *U.S. News and World Report*, July 17, 1995, p. 47.
17. "Hello . . . ?" *Business Week*, May 16, 1994, p. 8.

▼ **EXHIBIT 3–2**
Counseling Services Provided in American Companies
Among large and medium-sized U.S. companies, almost 80 percent offer counseling and social services to their employees.

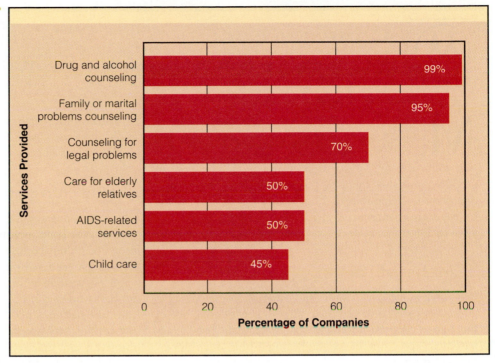

SOURCE: *Business Week,* July 10, 1995, p. 8.

Providing Empowerment "Why doesn't management," one worker wondered, "have the sense [to understand that] if workers love to get up in the morning and come to work, they're going to produce like hell?"[18] Companies that practice theories of stakeholder management do understand this, and their policies reflect that understanding (see *Company Focus: Motorola, Inc.* on page 64). As competitive practices have forced many American companies to downsize, management is realizing that a smaller work force must compensate with higher efficiency. Consequently, in corporate strategy sessions the issue of human resources is receiving as much attention as the traditionally major issues of financial performance and product and service quality. "We are becoming proactive partners in the business," said a human resources executive at Sony Music Entertainment, Inc. "The only acknowledgment of the people aspect used to be, 'What is the head count?' Now they say, 'Let's take each one of these strategic issues and look through the lens of human resources.' "[19]

There are a number of ways to empower employees. One that has been popular is a Japanese concept called the **quality circle**, in which representatives of the work force regularly meet with management to discuss corporate decisions. Some companies give employees a greater stake in the performance of the company through gain-sharing methods such as linking pay to performance, stock contributions, and retirement plans. The Seattle-based coffee chain Starbucks, Inc., designates employees who work more than twenty hours a week as "partners," and offers them benefits such as low-cost health insurance and stock options. Starbucks management gives partial credit for its rapid growth (a sixfold increase in net profit since 1985, to over $300 million in 1996) to employees who

18. Dentzer, *op. cit.*
19. B. P. Noble, "Retooling the 'People Skills' of Corporate America," *New York Times,* May 22, 1994, p. 8.

COMPANY FOCUS: MOTOROLA, INC.

A NEW TASK FOR EMPLOYEES: SETTING WAGES

Many corporate executives would be alarmed at the concept of allowing workers to dictate pay. But since 1992, Motorola, Inc., has been experimenting with just that process in a unique application of employee empowerment. At the company's manufacturing operation in Schaumburg, Illinois, a policy of peer review for pay requires employees to vote on one another's performance to determine salaries.

Team-Based Pay

Peer review for pay is only one facet of the cooperative efforts between labor and management at Motorola, one of the nation's largest nonunion manufacturers. The "team-based pay" program focuses on distinguishing superior performers from average and below average co-workers, and paying them accordingly. The program also claims to eliminate subjectivity—a constant criticism of pay-for-performance systems—from the process.

At the Shaumburg plant, each worker achieves a maximum base pay after thirty-nine weeks on the job. Afterwards, an individual worker's wages are determined on two levels: the team's performance and the individual's performance. First, team members and management set performance goals for each team as a group at the start of any particular year. These goals incorporate numerical targets based on costs, quality, production times, percentage of scrap, and other performance measures for whatever product is being manufactured. At the end of the year, the per-

formance of each team is measured against its projections, and Motorola sets aside a pool of money for merit pay based on that performance.

The Incentive Structure

Although management determines the amount in the merit pool, it is the team members who vote on each others' performance. After bonuses are awarded on a team basis according to team performance, individual compensation is granted according to the results of the voting. Because even the best worker can be punished if he or she is part of a team that performs poorly, Motorola hopes that peer pressure can help increase overall productivity. The company's ultimate goal is to have maximum guaranteed base pay correspond with the wages of what Motorola describes as a "consistently good, solid performer."

The New Bottom Line

As union influence declines in the nongovernment sectors of the American economy, companies are turning to other methods of involving employee stakeholders in executive-level decisions, such as determining wages. Many companies are finding that employee empowerment can be profitable. Since 1987, Motorola has raised productivity more than 125 percent with its experimental attitude toward peer review pay and other programs to include employees in the management process.

SOURCE: F. Swoboda, "Motorola Empowers Peers," *International Herald Tribune*, May 26, 1994, p. 11.

take a personal interest in the company's well-being.[20] Other companies allow employees to become part or full owners; this policy provides the employees with the ultimate incentive to succeed but raises another set of questions in the process (see the *Case—An Employee Takeover at United Airlines—*at the end of this chapter).

Whereas the traditional social contract between companies and employees was founded on ideas such as loyalty and job security, today's stakeholder contract between

20. D. L. Boroughs, "The Bottom Line on Ethics," *Business Week*, March 20, 1995, pp. 62–63.

the two parties offers a different bargain: "There will never be job security. You will be employed by us as long as you add value to the organization, and *you* are continuously responsible for finding ways to add value. In return, you have the right to demand interesting and important work, the freedom and resources to perform it well, pay that reflects your contribution, and the experience and training needed to be employable here or elsewhere."[21]

CONSUMER STAKEHOLDERS

In the economic atmosphere of the 1950s, sellers rushed to mass manufacture consumer products perhaps with less concern than we have today for product quality or safety. Competitive pressures from foreign manufacturers forced U.S. companies to emphasize quality in the manufacturing of their products, leading to a movement called total quality management, or TQM (see Chapter 18).

Businesses were also forced to deal with a growing consumer movement. By the 1970s, consumers, led by activists such as Ralph Nader, began to demand information and feedback on product manufacture and quality on an unprecedented scale. Companies began to discontinue activities if perceived as socially undesirable by a large enough group of consumers. Since 1980, for example, consumer pressure has protected some old-growth forests from the timber industry's chainsaws, forced cigarette manufacturers to discontinue advertising on television, and propelled international guidelines to reduce the production of ozone layer–depleting chlorofluorocarbons. Today, almost no domestic airline flights allow smoking, which is a direct result of complaints from individual consumers and consumer groups.

21. B. O'Reilly, "The New Deal: What Companies and Employees Owe One Another," *Fortune*, June 13, 1994, p. 44.

Consumers wield their power through activities ranging from information campaigns to boycotts, and they have found that in many cases corporations are willing to respond to their concerns (see *Exhibit 3–3* on pages 68–69). Consumers also have the power to demand government protection if a business does not correct a perceived injustice on its own.

In any event, the ultimate stakeholder in a corporation is the consumer. If consumers don't get what they want, they will allow the corporation to die.

THE ENVIRONMENT AS STAKEHOLDER

Consumer environmentalists have provided a voice for the "silent" stakeholder: the environment. Although the environment does not have an actual voice in the debate, it often speaks eloquently enough. By the 1970s, carbon monoxide emissions from automobiles had rendered the air in many metropolitan areas almost unbreathable. Toxic wastes released into rivers, streams, and oceans sometimes rendered water unswimmable and undrinkable for humans, as well as unlivable for many forms of aquatic life. Other emissions of pollutants into the atmosphere have threatened the balance of nature to an extent that is not yet fully understood. Not all of these problems have been solved, but legislation brought on by public pressure has improved the environment to a certain extent. Some argue that at times the costs outweigh the benefits to society.

COMMUNITY STAKEHOLDERS

In an analysis of stakeholder relationships between business and society, the community—in a local, national, and global sense—may be overlooked. The fact that a business provides a community's citizens with essentials such as employment, goods and services, and tax dollars for public programs is usually taken for granted, at least until that business closes. In return, however, communities have traditionally been expected to shoulder the burden of corporate irresponsibility. For example, when a tire factory dumps its waste in a river, the company itself will not directly pay for the right to pollute. It is often the community that does pay in a variety of ways: the loss of recreational activities in the polluted river, the possible tainting of underground water reservoirs that may lead to health problems, the destruction of the aesthetic beauty of the river, and so on.

Local and National Community Concerns of the Corporation   Government regulations have forced businesses to assume some of these social costs, but many corporations are also independently deciding that the community is an important stakeholder. Corning, Inc., for example, a company located in Corning, New York, has made a point of acting responsibly toward its namesake. When the company built a new headquarters in the early 1990s, it deliberately kept the height of the structure at a minimum to avoid overshadowing the town. The corporation also distributes leaflets warning of the dangers of smoking, bulimia, anorexia nervosa, and herpes to its employees, who represent half of the town's twelve thousand inhabitants.[22]

Corporations can also influence a community positively by simply locating themselves there. Following a series of destructive riots in 1968, the Glenville neighborhood of Cleveland was abandoned by the corporate community. In fact, residents had an 8-mile bus ride to the nearest grocery store. In 1990, Finast Supermarkets opened a

---

22. "Re-engineering, with Love," *Economist*, September 8, 1995, p. 69.

73,000-square-foot superstore in Glenville. Other retail stores, including a Rite Aid, quickly followed, as did a condominium development. By the mid-1990s, seventy-five new homes had been constructed in the area, with plans for fifty more.[23]

Finally, businesses have attempted to benefit the national community—people throughout the United States—and have incorporated such programs into their marketing strategies (see *Managing Social Issues—Making a Difference: The President's Project* on page 70). In 1990, for example, Adolph Coors Company launched a five-year, $40 million national program to promote literacy. (Coors, like any business involved in cause-related marketing, has not lost sight of its profit-maximizing goals. As we see in Chapter 19, the key to community stakeholder management is finding a balance between the needs of the community and the goals of the corporation.)

The Global Community Whereas Corning and Finast targeted local communities and Coors aimed at a national one, the business community is coming to recognize that it has a responsibility to the global community as well. Multinational corporations are under increasing pressure to recognize human rights abuses in overseas communities. In the mid-1990s, Federated Department Stores announced it would follow the example of Liz Claiborne, Inc., and Eddie Bauer, Inc., by ceasing operations in Myanmar (formerly Burma) because of the Southeast Asian country's unacceptable treatment of its citizens. Other corporations have attempted to improve the working conditions of employees in foreign production facilities[24] (see *Managing Social Issues—International Issues: Business's Burden* on page 71). It seems clear that as international economic activity increases, so will scrutiny of its effect on the global community.[25]

GOVERNMENT AS STAKEHOLDER

Governments at all levels—local, state, and federal—are stakeholders of the corporate world. After all, governments buy hundreds of billions of dollars of goods and services from corporations in the private sector. Governments also set standards for many of the goods they purchase and regulate all aspects of corporate activity. Consequently, corporations must take account of the effects of their actions on governments. There is another side to the story, however: corporate taxes finance a large part of all government activity. Thus, corporations and governments have a symbiotic relationship.

STAKEHOLDER ANALYSIS

The process by which a business communicates, negotiates, and carries out relationships with the various stakeholder groups is known as **stakeholder management**. It is an integral part of the strategic management process we examine in great detail in the final chapter of this textbook.

A company must do some preliminary research before it can undertake stakeholder management:

---

23. Boroughs, *op. cit.*, pp. 65–66.
24. J. Manakkalathil and E. Rudolf, "Corporate Social Responsibility in a Globalizing Market," *SAM Advanced Management Journal*, Winter 1995, p. 29.
25. D. M. Schilling and R. Rosenbaum, "Principles for Global Corporate Responsibility," *Business and Society Review*, Summer 1995, p. 55.

▼ **EXHIBIT 3–3 Boycotts of the 1990s**

Target	Boycott Called by	Reasons for Boycott	Outcome
PepsiCo	A nationwide coalition of college students	PepsiCo and a number of other major companies are criticized for business operations in Myanmar (formerly Burma). The government of that Southeast Asian country has consistently repressed the free speech of its citizens and has repeatedly failed to deliver promised democratic elections.	Pressure from students forced Harvard University to cancel plans to switch from Coca-Cola to Pepsi in its dining halls. Other companies, such as Levi Strauss, Liz Claiborne, and Reebok International, did stop doing business in Myanmar. PepsiCo— which earns almost $8 million per year in the country—continued its business operations there.
The City of Miami, Florida	African American community leaders in Miami	When South African activist Nelson Mandela visited the city of Miami in 1990, he was not given a warm welcome by Cuban American and Jewish officials. Those groups were angered by Mandela's support of Cuban president Fidel Castro and Palestine Liberation Organization leader Yasir Arafat, respectively. Angered in turn by the treatment of Mandela, local African American leaders called for a boycott of the city by African American tourists.	The boycott lasted until 1993, when it was called off in return for agreements by the city to improve business opportunities for local African Americans. Due to the boycott, 25 conventions in the city were canceled, causing a loss of $17 million to local businesses.
Time Warner	Police groups across the nation	In 1992, Time Warner recording artist and rapper Ice-T released a song entitled "Cop Killer." Many police officers were outraged by the lyrics of the song, which they felt encouraged violence against the police.	At Ice-T's request, Time Warner pulled "Cop Killer" from the stores. Eventually, Ice-T left Time Warner, and the boycott ended.
L'Oreal	People for the Ethical Treatment for Animals (PETA)	PETA has targeted L'Oreal and other cosmetics companies for testing their products on animals.	After four years of its boycott, in 1994 PETA received a pledge from L'Oreal promising that the company would no longer conduct animal testing.

▼ Before a company can manage its stakeholders, it must identify the ones that have the greatest effect on the organization.[26]

This process of **stakeholder analysis,** as defined by Jeffrey S. Harrison and Caron St. John, involves "identifying and prioritizing key stakeholders, assessing their needs, collecting ideas from them, and integrating this knowledge" into the management process.[27] According to Harrison and St. John, the three steps in stakeholder analysis include iden-

---

26. L. D. Lerner and G. E. Fryxell, "CEO Stakeholder Attitudes and Corporate Social Activity in the Fortune 500," *Business and Society,* April 1994, p. 58.

27. J. S. Harrison and C. St. John, *Strategic Management of Organizations and Stakeholders: Theory and Cases* (St. Paul: West Publishing Co., 1994), p. 17.

▼ **EXHIBIT 3–3** *continued*

Target	Boycott Called by	Reasons for Boycott	Outcome
Florida Citrus Commission	National Organization for Women (NOW) and National Education Association (NEA)	In 1994, the Florida Citrus Commission hired conservative talk-show host Rush Limbaugh to help sell Florida orange juice. NOW protested because of what it called Limbaugh's negative attitude toward women, whereas the NEA disagreed with Limbaugh's statements about teachers' unions. Both groups asked consumers to boycott Florida orange juice.	The boycott seemed to have no effect on sales of Florida orange juice. In fact, rallies held by NOW and the NEA to publicize their boycott were consistently attended by more Limbaugh supporters than boycott supporters.
H. J. Heinz/ Starkist Tuna	Earth Island Institute	For decades, the methods used by tuna harvesters also killed large numbers of dolphins. In the late 1980s, the San Francisco–based Earth Island Institute began bringing attention to this issue by calling for a boycott of tuna fish companies.	In 1990, H. J. Heinz, the parent company of Starkist Tuna, agreed to use "dolphin-safe" methods to catch tuna. Today, other tuna brands, such as Chicken of the Sea, Deep Sea Tongol Tuna, and Ocean Light Tuna, proudly display "dolphin-safe" on their packaging.
Nestlé	A number of church groups nationwide	Nestlé has traditionally sold large amounts of infant baby formula in developing nations. Leaders of this boycott contend that new mothers in these countries cannot afford the formula, do not know how to sterilize bottles, and do not have clean water with which to mix the formula. The use of infant baby formula, they insist, has caused the sickness and death of thousands of babies.	Nestlé denies these charges. Church groups called for a boycott in 1977 that is still in effect today.

tifying, classifying, and prioritizing stakeholder groups.[28] We have already identified many, though not all, of the key stakeholders, so we jump ahead to the second step: classification.

CLASSIFICATION OF STAKEHOLDERS

Once stakeholders have been identified, managers will find it helpful to classify them according to specific criteria. Each stakeholder or stakeholder group makes different demands on a corporation, and each one has different levels of power over that corporation. An understanding of these factors is integral to stakeholder analysis. As shown in *Exhibit 3–4*

---

28. *Ibid.*, pp. 17–23.

MANAGING SOCIAL ISSUES

MAKING A DIFFERENCE: THE PRESIDENT'S PROJECT

In the years since his presidency (1977–1981), Jimmy Carter has established a reputation as an inveterate activist. His self-imposed duties have taken him from Haiti to the Middle East, but in 1991 he turned to the problems facing his own state, Georgia, with The Atlanta Project (TAP). Carter's plan was to establish a consortium of business, civic, and government forces to alleviate the social ills that plague Atlanta. The former president's vision included a five-year period in which an army of a hundred thousand volunteers would link the "two Atlantas"—the mostly African American urban areas and the mostly white suburbs—for the public good. Area businesses have been enthusiastic in their support for TAP, but as the first "term" came to a close, their participation raised questions about the nature of their social responsibility.

Corporate Involvement

TAP is an amalgamation of 20 "clusters" coordinated by a central office. Each cluster represents a distinct neighborhood or area and is supervised by a coordinator and assistant coordinator, who live in that cluster. The thinking behind the system is that the coordinators and assistant coordinators will address the specific needs of their own resident areas, thereby cutting down on bureaucratic inefficiency.

Each cluster has a corporate sponsor from the Atlanta business community, and each corporate sponsor assigns an executive to work full-time on-site with the cluster's coordinator. Corporate sponsors include the Coca-Cola Company, Sprint, Marriot Corporation, AT&T Trust Company, Turner Broadcasting Systems, Inc., Prudential Life Insurance Company, and BellSouth. These companies and their fellow participants have donated close to $35 million to TAP.

When surveyed, almost all of the companies participating said they expect to improve or heighten their image as a good corporate citizen. The banks involved hope to deflect some of the criticism concerning investment in the inner cities that has plagued their industry. The companies also noted benefits in improved employee morale, as workers have found a convenient system in which to channel their volunteer and community service energies.

Reinventing TAP

The most persistent criticism of TAP was that its participants were more interested in publicity than in problem solving. Although he noted the project's successes in a report commissioned by TAP, Emory University political science professor Michael W. Giles questioned its emphasis on "feel good" events, such as health fairs, that do little to further TAP's long-term goals. Community leaders have been even harsher in their assessment, calling TAP "a public relations entity" that forces projects on local citizens, rather than empowering them to make their own decisions.

Former president Carter has taken the criticism seriously, and TAP has promised to work more closely with community groups. A first step may be the discontinuation of the hierarchical cluster system. But TAP will continue, and an offspring group called the America Project is working to construct similar business-community consortiums in other metropolitan areas without repeating Atlanta's mistakes.

For Critical Analysis:

Corporations generally will not donate large sums of money without retaining some sense of control over how it is to be spent. How does this fact conflict with the concept of community empowerment?

SOURCE: Information from A. B. Carroll and G. T. Horton, "Do Joint Corporate Social Responsibility Programs Work?" *Business and Society Review,* Summer 1994, pp. 24–28; J. Vejnoska, "The Atlanta Project Group Has Abandoned Mission, Report Finds," *Atlanta Constitution,* February 16, 1995, p. E3; and J. Blake, "Social Service Agencies Change Tune, Sing Atlanta Project's Praises," *Atlanta Constitution,* October 22, 1995, p. H5.

on page 72, three "slots" into which individual and group stakeholders can be fitted are (1) those with an ownership stake in the corporation, (2) those with economic dependence on the corporation, and (3) those with social interests in the corporation. These roles are not

▣ MANAGING SOCIAL ISSUES

INTERNATIONAL ISSUES: BUSINESS'S BURDEN

At a time when it was receiving considerable criticism for a weak stance on China's human rights record, the Clinton administration released a set of "model business principles" for U.S. companies operating overseas. The voluntary practices suggested by the government include the development of codes that avoid child labor, forced labor, and discrimination; reject bribes; and promote a safe and healthful workplace. The administration also announced plans to sponsor a "best practices award" to recognize good corporate citizenship by U.S. companies abroad. The principles were immediately dismissed by analysts as shortsighted and unenforceable. If such principles were to be enacted, it was agreed, individual companies would have to take the initiative themselves.

The public's reception was much warmer for Seattle-based Starbucks Coffee Company's guidelines geared toward improving working conditions for its foreign coffee suppliers. The Starbucks guidelines call for suppliers to employ child labor only when it does not "interfere with mandated education." The company also urges suppliers to help workers gain "access to safe housing, clean water, and health facilities and services," endorses freedom of association, and stresses the right of workers to "work because they want to or need to, but not because they are forced to do so." In general, Starbucks wants its suppliers to offer wages that at least "address the basic needs of workers and their families."

Although retail companies such as Nike, Inc., Levi Strauss Associates, and Reebok International, Ltd., have taken steps to address the working conditions of overseas laborers, Starbucks is the first company dealing with agriculture to do so. Near-sustenance wages, child labor, and poor sanitary conditions are common problems for agricultural workers in developing countries, and the coffee company was lauded by global human rights activists for its code. Robert Dunn, president of the trade group Business for Social Responsibility, called the Starbucks guidelines a "benchmark for a lot of importers of agricultural commodities" and said that Starbucks had "drawn a roadmap that will make it easier for other companies to assess whether what they currently do is adequate."

For Critical Analysis:

Like the Clinton administration's code, the Starbucks guidelines do not contain provisions that specifically punish violators. "The last thing I want is for people to start shaking in their boots when they see me coming," said a Starbucks vice president for coffee. Why would a company shy away from taking firmer steps to control foreign suppliers? What control mechanisms could be put in place if a company wanted to do so?

SOURCE: Information from R. S. Greenberg, "U.S. Quietly Unveils Code for Firms Working Abroad," *Wall Street Journal Europe,* May 30, 1995, p. 10; and G. P. Zachary, "Starbucks Adopts Guidelines to Help Non-U.S. Workers," *Wall Street Europe,* October 23, 1995, p. 6.

mutually exclusive. They will be explored in much more depth in Chapters 12 through 19, but for now they provide a good introduction to stakeholder issues.

Identifying the Needs of Stakeholders *Exhibit 3–4* on page 72 reinforces many of the ideas noted earlier in the chapter. Stockholders are not the only stakeholder group with a financial interest in the corporation. Employees rely on the corporation for wages and benefits, governments and local communities rely on the corporation for tax receipts, and suppliers (some of whom are also customers) rely on the corporation for the revenues necessary for their own livelihood.

Within an industry, there is a certain amount of economic interdependence among competitors, as each must act and react to strategies implemented by the others. Furthermore, many foreign governments depend on corporate investment to bring goods

▼ EXHIBIT 3–4 The Stakes of Various Stakeholders

Ownership:	The value of the organization has a direct impact on the wealth of these stakeholders.	▶ Managers who own stock in the organization ▶ Directors who own stock in the corporation ▶ All other stockholders
Economic Dependence:	Stakeholders can be economically dependent without having ownership. Each one of these stakeholders relies on the corporation in some way for financial well-being.	▶ All salaried managers ▶ Creditors ▶ Internal Revenue Service ▶ Employees ▶ Customers ▶ Suppliers ▶ Competitors ▶ Local communities ▶ Regulatory agencies
Social Interests:	These stakeholders are not directly linked to the organization but have an interest in making sure the organization acts in a socially responsible manner.	▶ Special interest and activist groups ▶ Government leaders ▶ The media

SOURCE: Adapted from R. E. Freeman, *Strategic Management: A Stakeholder Approach* (Boston: Pitman, 1984).

and services into their country. Social stakeholders, though lacking a formal connection with the corporation, still rely on the organization to uphold society's values and expectations. It is this economic, social, political, and technological interdependence among and between stakeholders that makes the study of the business/society/government triangle so fascinating.

Identifying the Influences of Stakeholders Harrison and St. John recognize three areas in which stakeholders influence the corporation: formal, economic, and political.

Formal influence comes from contractual or legislative rights to make decisions on issues concerning the corporation. The Environmental Protection Agency, for example, has the right to dictate emission standards to corporations, and each government agency has a set of powers through which it can control business activity. Owner stakeholders also have power over the corporation through agreements signed at the time the individuals or groups obtained their ownership stakes.

Economic influence comes from the threat of withholding products, capital, services, revenues, or other business transactions from the corporation. Consumers, when organized in an interest group, for example, have the economic power that comes from the threat of a boycott.

Political influence is derived from the ability to influence lawmakers, society, or regulatory agencies to change the environment in which a corporation functions. Recent efforts by antismoking groups, for example, have severely limited the freedom of organizations to establish their own smoking policies, and these efforts may yet severely limit the freedom of tobacco companies to sell cigarettes.

THE FULL RANGE OF STAKEHOLDERS

Stakeholder analysis also involves identifying the extent to which an organization depends on each stakeholder for its survival.[29] The organization should prioritize its stakeholders:

▼ **In most for-profit organizations, customers, employees, and owners are the three most important stakeholder groups.**

If a tennis shoe manufacturer cannot produce a product desired by consumers, it does not matter if that company's rubber production center keeps in line with environmental regulations—the company will fail. Similarly, if the company cannot motivate its employees or maximize profits to the satisfaction of owners, then its practice of providing free tennis shoes to inner-city schools will not keep it operating.

INFORMATION GATHERING

Managers have been given one advantage in the stakeholder analysis process: stakeholders are generally more than willing to give their opinions to management. Employees, shareholders, government officials, and community and consumer groups are usually eager to make their views known. The challenge for managers comes in limiting meetings with stakeholders to those that are essential, as well as in disseminating the information gathered efficiently.

In fact, the amount of information available to managers is staggering. Marketing departments provide sales patterns and consumer responses. Formal surveys—conducted by the corporation itself, the media, or members of the academic community—may contain crucial data. The media, through print outlets such as the *Wall Street Journal* and *Business Week*, as well as numerous business programs offered on cable television, offer a mountain of business news each day. Representatives from internal and external stakeholder groups on the boards of directors of large corporations also represent an information source. Finally, because of technological innovations, companies are getting information more easily and more quickly than ever before; this trend is sure to continue.

---

29. T. Donaldson and L. E. Preston, "The Stakeholder Theory of the Corporation: Concepts, Evidence, and Implications," *Academy of Management Review*, January 1995, p. 65.

The Delicate Balance

The view that a company has to take account of all of the various stakeholders—owners, employees, the community, customers, and government—can be confusing at best for a decision maker. The delicate balance involves weighing the demands of all stakeholder groups at each point in time without being overwhelmed. Most businesses have a hard enough time simply keeping one step ahead of the competition. In other words, the time and energy needed for business survival often overshadows the time and energy that might be devoted to analyzing various stakeholder issues. Nonetheless, managers of today, and particularly of tomorrow, will have to understand how their corporations fit into the community, how employees as a group must be treated, and how their companies can deal with the expanding role of government.

Terms and Concepts for Review

Quality circle 63

Social contract 58

Stakeholder analysis 68

Stakeholder concept 61

Stakeholder management 67

Summary

1. The four areas of corporate responsibility are responsibility to shareholders, employees, the community, and customers. Nonetheless, if a corporation cannot produce a competitive rate of return, it will fail.

2. There is an implied social contract that requires a business to further the interests of society while at the same time maximizing its rate of return to investors. Not all view this social contract/social responsibility concept in a positive light. (Critics argue that there is little way for corporate managers to know what is in fact socially responsible behavior.)

3. Ten trends toward corporate social responsibility in the 1990s are (a) the pursuit of happiness, (b) the greening of the corporation, (c) volunteering, (d) the peace conversion, (e) cause marketing, (f) the family-friendly workplace, (g) cooperation with government, (h) diversity in the workplace, (i) improving the consumer-business relationship, and (j) technological breakthroughs.

4. The stakeholder concept is based on the idea that it is not only investors who have a stake, or interest, in the corporation. Employees, consumers, the environment, local and global communities, and the government are also stakeholders.

5. Even shareholders with a very small percentage of the total shares outstanding of a corporation can directly influence the corporation's behavior if they become shareholder activists. Other shareholders can invest in corporations that demonstrate values that are socially aligned with their own. One way they can do this is by buying shares in so-called social mutual funds.

6. Employees today have limited rights to privacy, freedom of choice on how to live outside the workplace, and so on. They have the right to be free of discrimination based on race, color, gender, age, national origin, or disability. Job security is not a right they have obtained, however, and therefore some say employees lack empowerment. Quality circles, in which employees are able to give suggestions to management, may give workers a greater sense of empowerment.

7. The ultimate stakeholder in a corporation is the consumer, because consumers, through their dollar votes, decide which products and services survive and which do not. Additionally, consumers form pressure groups to impose increased regulation of the marketplace. Finally, consumers get involved in group boycotts in order to get corporations to change their behavior.

8. One might consider the environment as a stakeholder that speaks through environmentalists. Public pressures have forced corporations to work to solve environmental problems.

9. The community, including businesses in areas surrounding a corporation and people in the entire nation, can be considered another stakeholder. Each corporation also has, as a stakeholder, the global community.

10. Governments at all levels are stakeholders of corporations, because governments depend on corporations for taxes while at the same time being important customers and imposing regulations on businesses.

11. To undertake stakeholder management, corporations first have to engage in stakeholder analysis. This necessitates identifying, classifying, and prioritizing stakeholder groups. For most corporations, customers, employees, and owners are the most important stakeholder groups.

EXERCISES

1. Analyze the employee programs that Stride Rite Corporation offers, all listed at the beginning of this chapter. Which ones do you think yield the highest benefit per dollar spent? Why?
2. Explain the so-called multiplier effect of a large corporation's starting a new plant in an isolated community.
3. What forces a corporation to earn an acceptable rate of return on invested capital?
4. In what way is the concept of a social contract related to the concept of any contract? In what way is it not related?
5. Milton Friedman was quoted in the section "A Counterproductive Contract?" Offer an opposing view to that of Friedman.
6. Examine *Exhibit 3–1* carefully. Which trend toward social responsibility is the most obvious, in your mind? Why?
7. Draw a schematic showing how each stakeholder group affects each of the other stakeholder groups. Label your arrows.
8. Explain the concept of social investing.
9. *Exhibit 3–2* shows the types of counseling services provided by American corporations. List some of the costs of those counseling services.
10. How would increased job security give employees more empowerment?
11. Look at the boycotts of the 1990s listed in *Exhibit 3–3*. Pick one boycott, and relate how such a boycott could effectively change a corporation's behavior.
12. How can the environment be a stakeholder, when the environment is not human?
13. How can a corporation possibly take account of the global community?
14. No government typically owns any shares in a private for-profit corporation in the United States. Therefore, how can the government be considered a stakeholder?
15. Why is stakeholder analysis necessary before stakeholder management principles can be developed?
16. "The customer is always right." How does this statement relate to the issue of stakeholder analysis?
17. Imagine that you are the head of a CD-ROM development company in a major U.S. city. Prioritize your stakeholders, and give reasons for your decisions.

SELECTED REFERENCES

▶ Ackoff, Russell L. *The Democratic Corporation: A Radical Prescription for Recreating Corporate America and Rediscovering Success.* New York: Oxford University Press, 1994.

▶ Braybooke, David. *Ethics in the World of Business.* Savage, Md.: Rowman & Littlefield, 1983.

▶ Freeman, R. Edward. *Strategic Management: A Stakeholder Approach.* Boston, Mass.: Pitman, 1984.

▶ Freeman, R. Edward, and Daniel R. Gilbert, Jr. *Corporate Strategy and the Search for Ethics.* Upper Saddle River, N.J.: Prentice Hall, 1988.

▶ Yavitz, Boris, and William H. Newman. *Strategy in Action.* New York: Free Press, 1982.

CASE

AN EMPLOYEE TAKEOVER AT UNITED AIRLINES

Background

On July 24, 1994, management and labor at United Airlines Corporation (UAL) finalized an agreement that made the airline company the largest employee-owned firm in the world. By trading wage cuts and work-rule concessions for guaranteed job security, 48,000 of UAL's 76,000 workers accepted an Employee Stock Ownership Plan (ESOP) that gave them a 55 percent equity stake in the company.

Negotiators hailed the ESOP as essential for the troubled company, which had lost $50 million the year before. The employees' nearly $5 billion in concessions over six years would allow the company to become more competitive, and some analysts predicted that employee ownership would increase employee incentives to maximize profits. Other industry watchers were not as positive concerning the deal. Internal dissension among unions assured that the agreement was not supported by all UAL employees, and a troubling question remained: Would employee owners make decisions that benefited themselves and not necessarily the company's other stakeholders?

Problems at United

UAL's recent history has been one of turmoil. Since 1985, the company has had to deal with a twenty-nine-day pilot strike, infighting between employee groups, hostile takeover attempts—from, among others, Donald Trump—and four previous employee buyout attempts. Rumors of takeovers, mergers, and mass layoffs left UAL at a competitive disadvantage in the struggling airline industry; in the two years before 1993's $50 million deficit, the company lost almost $1.4 billion. As one United executive remarked, "For too long, this company has been anything but united."

A number of factors contributed to the situation. United and other major airline carriers were being hurt by smaller, more streamlined rivals; in 1993, Southwest Airline Company was able to carry passengers for 7.1 cents per mile, which was 25 percent below similar costs for United. Other costs, such as fuel and travel agency commissions, were also on the rise, and executives found themselves unable to contain industry-wide fare wars. Although no executive would blame the employees for the company's troubles, cutting labor costs seemed to be the only means to stay competitive.

During negotiations for a new labor contract, UAL's chairman, Stephen M. Wolf, gave his unions an ultimatum: unless they would agree to trade wage cuts and other concessions for an ownership stake, he would be forced to proceed with plans to reengineer the airline and drop thousands of jobs. To place more pressure on the unions, Wolf began taking bids to outsource work done by 2,800 mechanics in San Francisco and work crews in New York City.

Problems within the Union

United's Union Coalition, which represents the Air Line Pilots Association (ALPA) and the International Association of Machinists (IAM), was having its own difficulties. Although the coalition's leaders were willing to accept Wolf's offer with a few changes, many of its rank-and-file members were not. In fact, 7,500 of the 26,000 employees represented by IAM gave formal notice that they wanted to be represented by another union. Furthermore, the flight attendants, who make up more than 25 percent of UAL's work force, refused to consider the offered terms and had little role in the negotiations.

Nevertheless, the deal was completed long before Wolf's November 13 deadline. In return for the $4.9 billion cut in labor costs, employees gained not only an equity stake in the company but also the guarantee that more than 70 percent of them—including pilots, machinists, and salaried employees—would be protected from layoffs during the six-year length of the contract. Employees would also be able to place three members on the 12-member UAL Board of Directors, as well as replace Wolf with their own choice for the chairman and CEO, Gerald Greenwald. The buyout agreement also contained provisions for UAL's plan to start a low-cost "airline within an airline," named United Shuttle.

Although more than 70 percent of shareholders voted in favor of the new labor contract, the deal was less popular among employees. Among IAM members, the deal was barely ratified—only 56 percent of its members gave a yes vote. The disaffected members hired a lawyer and strongly considered filing a lawsuit against their union to block the agreement. The flight attendants never agreed to the contract and consequently were scheduled to get an 8 percent pay raise, compared with a 23.5 percent salary cut for the pilots and a 15.7 percent cut for the machinists. Asked if this would not sour relations between flight attendants and other union workers, an executive with the Association of Flight Attendants

CASE (CONTINUED)

replied, "Our view was that this was not something mandatory. . . . If somebody wants to have hard feelings about it, that is their choice."

Finally, the 28,000 employees who held management or nonunion jobs were given an 8.25 percent pay cut—not as large as some of their co-workers but still large enough to cause resentment, especially because, unlike their union peers, they had not been given the opportunity to vote on the contract. Neither the flight attendants nor the nonunion, nonsalaried employees were protected from layoffs.

The Power of Empowerment

After taking control of UAL, Greenwald toured the United States in an attempt to sell the divided work force on the concept of employee ownership. The employee buyout, he told an audience in the Washington, D.C., area, "is not simply an end in itself. It is a beginning, a point of departure for a qualitatively new kind of company; a company in which the economic interests of shareholders, management and labor—so often at odds—are, for once, brought together." Greenwald emphasized the new "empowerment" at UAL, or as an observer noted, the necessary attitude among union members that "it's not us versus them anymore, because now we are them."

Greenwald has instituted a number of symbolic changes to reflect the idea of employee power and responsibility. A glass partition outside the executive suite has been taken down; the company's new president, John Edwardson, offers coffee and bagels to employees in his office on Friday mornings; and the corporate slogan "Come Fly the Friendly Skies" has been corrected to read, "Come Fly *Our* Friendly Skies."

As one insider remarked, however, "taking down a glass wall doesn't run an airline." Investors worry that the unions' tendencies toward job preservation might handicap the company's ability to make the cost-cutting decisions that are inevitable. Furthermore, what would occur if the interests of the various unions came in conflict with one another? One major stockholder fears the possibility that the dissenting flight attendants will walk off the job, leaving "the untenable prospect of a union going on strike against a union-owned company."

A cross-section of opinions from various UAL employees underscores the different agendas competing within the work force:

▶ "Mechanics and pilots have always had a rift between them. You go to the airport, and right away there's an argument about who's responsible for the latest job—me breaking the airplane so you have to fix it or you keeping it fixed so I can fly it," says a captain, who also called management "dinosaurs."

▶ "This is the kind of place where management usually thinks they are way up there and the rest of us are way down here," says a mechanic. "They want to make sure the shareholders get what they want, but they don't care much about employees. All that's got to change."

▶ "The idea that you'll have labor unions running the company suggests that perhaps not the best business decisions will be made," says a nonunion crew schedules planner. The same person asks, "Why are you taking 8.25 percent of my pay, when I didn't contribute to this high-cost operation?" and points out that there are "clearly" union members saying, "Wait 'till we take over."

▶ "We're managed differently from other groups," says a flight attendant. "When it comes to the boys in the cockpit, things are different. The pilots stay in downtown hotels, and we are stuck out at the airport. . . . The irony, of course, is that the bosses ought to think a lot harder about how we feel if they want to keep the passengers happy. We're the people who spend all the time with the passengers."

How can this divisiveness be overcome? Greenwald, for one, was confident that the principle of ownership would keep unions from making decisions based on personal goals rather than on the good of the company.

Early Failure and Success

UAL's first year as an employee-owned company gave the company's shareholders reasons to question Greenwald's assertion. During that time, the company planned to hire 1,000 new flight attendants, 500 pilots, 200 mechanics, and 1,200 clerical workers. It constructed two new hangers at a cost of $117 million and increased by 13 percent the routes run by a new, low-fare West Coast shuttle. Furthermore, the company seemed to justify the concerns of a director who worried that employee owners would "[go] out and buy new planes" when the company announced plans to expand overseas service. Despite the fact that the buyout deal had been based on a desire to cut costs, costs actually rose during Greenwald's first year.

Consequently, approval of UAL's performance among Wall Street investors was lacking. In the seven months after the buyout, UAL's stock value increased only 3.5 percent, compared with jumps of 64 percent for Northwest and 21 percent for Delta. Because employee owner compensation is directly tied to stock prices, this was a particularly important development.

Employee infighting also continued. In December 1993, the six thousand dissident machinists tried to split off from the IAM and failed only after a bitter election marked by fist-fights and racial slurs. A month later, six nonunion reservations clerks sued in a federal court to try to overturn the agreement. Even the pilots threatened to boycott some of Greenwald's improvement measures unless their demands to fire disliked upper managers were met.

Greenwald can, however, point to successes under his rule. Employee sick leave declined 12 percent in May 1995 from a year earlier, which was taken as a sign that employee owners are more eager to come to work than before. UAL also enjoyed first-quarter profits for the first time in six years in 1995. But the performance has not been strong enough to alleviate questions about whether UAL will survive its five-year labor agreement without financial disaster. The company was fortunate in that the mid-1990s were an unusually strong period for the airline industry. What will happen, observers wonder, when the industry has a slump, and UAL needs to lay off pilots, mechanics, flight attendants, and other employees? Layoffs are difficult enough for management when employee stakeholders are not also owner stakeholders.

Critical Thinking Questions

1. In small businesses, the owners often perform "employee" tasks; for example, the owner of a family restaurant might do the cooking herself. In fact, the small-business owner is often held up as a good example of the motivated capitalist. Why, then, in a large corporation such as United, are there so many questions concerning sharing the owner and employee stakeholder roles?

2. If you owned stock in United, how would you view the employee ownership of the company?

3. As a consumer of United's services, in what ways could employee ownership of UAL affect your relationship with the company?

4. Consider the animosity between management, pilots, mechanics, and flight attendants at United. How could the employee ownership situation help restore trust among the different groups?

5. The federal government actively encouraged the United employee ownership plan. Why would government stakeholders back the idea of employee ownership, both in United's case and in general?

SOURCE: Information from K. Labich, "Will United Fly?" *Fortune*, August 22, 1994, pp. 72–77; "Wolf Turns Employee-Owned United Over to Greenwald, New Board," *Aviation Daily*, July 13, 1994, p. 61; K. Kelly and W. Zellner, "The Airlines to Labor: Buy In—Or Get Bashed," *Business Week*, November 1, 1993, p. 40; M. Veverka, "Union Revolt Spreads: Labor Leaders Push for Vote as Ranks Unravel," *Crain's Chicago Business*, May 23, 1994, p. 1; M. H. Cimini, "Developments in Industrial Relations," *Compensation and Working Conditions*, October 1994, p. 31; J. Ward, "United Front," *Financial World*, September 1, 1994, p. 26; R. M. Weintraub, "The Gospel According to Greenwald," *Washington Post*, August 9, 1994, p. D10; J. A. Donaghue, "United We Fly," *Air Transport World*, October 1, 1994, p. 5; M. M. McCarthy, "Risky Flight Plan: Unlike Rival Airlines, United Is Setting Off on Costly Expansion," *Wall Street Journal*, March 6, 1995, p. A1; P. Flint, "The Buck Stops Lower," *Air Transport World*, September 1, 1995, p. 28; and M. Veverka, "United Buyout's First Year: It Won't Get Any Better Than This," *Crain's Chicago Business*, July 3, 1995, p. 1.

PART II

BUSINESS ETHICS AND CORPORATE SOCIAL RESPONSIBILITY

CHAPTER 4

THE FUNDAMENTALS OF BUSINESS ETHICS

CHAPTER OUTLINE

▶ The Nature of Ethics and Business Ethics
▶ Morals and Ethics
▶ Business Ethics and Values

INTRODUCTION

L ife involves trade-offs. Life in the world of business does also. Some argue that those in business must sometimes accept unpleasant trade-offs:

How you cling to your purity, young man! How afraid you are to soil your hands! All right, stay pure! What good will it do? Why did you join us? Purity is an idea for a yogi or a monk. . . . To do nothing, to remain motionless, arms at your sides, wearing kid gloves. Well, I have dirty hands. Right up to the elbows. I've plunged them in filth and blood.[1]

The debate as to whether a business and its employees can be successful without having "dirty hands" is central in defining the role business plays in society. The so-called father of capitalism, Scottish economist Adam Smith (1723–1790), suggested that the ultimate goal of a free enterprise system is to produce quality goods at reasonable prices.[2] To what extent does society accept actions that deviate from those of a yogi or a monk to achieve that goal?

Over the past thirty years, the pendulum of public opinion has taken a definite swing toward the monkish ideal. Previously, any discussion of ethical behavior in the business world would have been rejected out of hand. Like Jean-Paul Sartre's character quoted above, the businessperson was allowed to—indeed, was almost expected to—have disdain for anyone who chose to wear kid gloves. The "whatever it takes" or "dog eat dog" nature of the free market was accepted, and often celebrated, by American society. When quintessential capitalist John D. Rockefeller (1839–1937) was asked if he would pay an employee $1 million a year, the tycoon answered that he certainly would, if the person knew how to glide over every moral restraint with childlike disregard.

Times have certainly changed. American society today is fighting what it perceives to be a weakening of its ethical standards. Some have scrutinized the business community's activities and found them lacking at the ethical level. Press accounts of insider-trading fraud, product tampering, massive industrial pollution, and a host of other scandals have focused public attention on the questionable ethical philosophies behind the "whatever it takes" attitude (see *Exhibit 4–1*).

Robert Solomon of the University of Texas at Austin thinks public scrutiny of business ethics will only increase in the late 1990s. "Deprived of a [military] global antagonist [at the end of the Cold War], we defenders of free enterprise have been forced to look inward, to ask ourselves hard questions that go beyond the usual slogans about freedom, prosperity, and the evils of communism," says Solomon. "The problems, the possibilities, and the preconditions that we call 'the free enterprise system' have themselves been called into question."[3]

Consequently, a relatively new task for all businesspersons is to *integrate* ethics with their business activities. No longer does society accept the business practice of putting ethical concerns aside in the name of expediency. In a capitalist system, every businessperson faces one major ethical issue:

---

1. Jean-Paul Sartre, *Dirty Hands*, in *No Exit and Other Plays*, trans. Lionel Abel (New York: Vintage International, 1989), p. 218.
2. Adam Smith, *An Inquiry into the Nature and Causes of the Wealth of Nations*, 1776.
3. R. Solomon, *The New World of Business* (Lanham, Md.: Littlefield Adams Quality Paperbacks, 1994), p. 1.

▼ **EXHIBIT 4–1**
Company Limits in the Pursuit of Profits

Respondents who were asked, "Which of the following things do you think business would do in order to obtain greater profits?" answered as follows:	
Harm the environment	47%
Endanger public health	38%
Sell unsafe products	37%
Knowingly sell inferior products	44%
Deliberately charge inflated prices	62%
Put its workers' safety at risk	42%

SOURCE: Business Week/Harris Poll, "The Public Is Willing to Take Business On," *Business Week*, May 29, 1989, p. 29.

▼ **How can those in the business world act in an ethically responsible manner and at the same time make profits for their owners?**

The ultimate goal of this chapter, and of the three that follow, is to provide you with the basic tools necessary for analyzing ethical issues in business contexts. These chapters cannot tell you how to decide ethical issues, but they can help you establish your own ethical standards and understand those of others. Although you can never be fully prepared for the task of ethical decision making—because no two situations are ever exactly alike—the more you analyze current ethical issues (and some past issues), the better prepared you will be to make any ethical decisions you may face in the future.

THE NATURE OF ETHICS AND BUSINESS ETHICS

Before we can talk about ethics, we need to define it. **Ethics** can be defined as the study of what constitutes right or wrong behavior. It is the branch of philosophy that focuses on morality and the way in which moral principles are applied to daily life (the next section focuses on morals and ethics). Ethics has to do with fundamental questions about the fairness, justice, rightness, or wrongness of an action. Often, ethical questions or statements contain the words *ought* or *should*. When we say that someone *ought* to do something, we are not saying that he or she is required to do it. We are saying that the person *should* do it because it is the fair, just, or right thing to do, or because it is "expected" by society.

Many social critics have observed that the terms *business* and *ethics* are mutually exclusive.[4] Some are halfway joking; others are quite serious. Nonetheless, because business is a set of interactions between individuals and groups of individuals, it is as subject to the dictates of ethics as is a personal relationship or a tennis match. **Business ethics** focuses on what constitutes right or wrong behavior in the world of business and on how moral

---

4. D. Vogel, "Business Ethics: New Perspectives on Old Problems," *California Management Review*, Summer 1991, p. 101.

principles are applied by businesspersons to situations that arise in their daily work and during their careers.[5]

It is important to remember that business ethics is not a separate *kind* of ethics. Businesspersons should not necessarily adopt one set of ethical principles to guide them in their business decisions and another set to guide them in their personal lives. The ethical standards that we set up for our behavior as, say, mothers, fathers, or students apply equally well to our activities as businesspersons. Business activities are just one part of the human enterprise, and business ethics as a subset of ethics relates specifically to the kinds of situations that arise in the everyday world of business.

MORALS AND ETHICS

In the sense that ethics relies on an inner sense of right and wrong, ethical principles are linked with morality. Although **morals** encompass a wide variety of behavior patterns based on shared values, the concept can be generally defined as a universal set of guidelines or rules that determine our actions and character. (Remember, however, that determinations of "right" and "wrong" may vary over time as society decides what is acceptable [and unacceptable] behavior at any given point in time. As will become clear throughout the course of this textbook, businesspersons must constantly monitor these changes in society in order to judge public expectations of how individuals and corporations "should" act.)

Probably the best-known example of a moral charter in Western Judeo-Christian thought is the Ten Commandments, from the Old Testament of the Bible, which provides society with a basis for moral actions. That tradition also provided the Golden Rule: "Always treat others as you would like them to treat you." Because other religions have similar versions of these orders and precepts—such as the teachings of the Koran for Muslims—many feel that religion dictates morality.

STAGES OF MORAL DEVELOPMENT

The premise that religion dictates morality has been amended by a generation of psychologists who insist that religion is only *one* of the societal factors that shape moral development. Lawrence Kohlberg, perhaps the best-known scholar on the psychology of morals and ethics, believed that an individual's direct sensory experience, intuition, and logic combine with the influence of authority figures in religion, law, and business to create moral reasoning.[6] Kohlberg also postulated that an individual's moral development takes place in a series of sequential stages that follow intellectual development. In other words, as people grow, they use different inputs in their moral reasoning and will progressively make different moral judgments.

The "Heinz Test" Kohlberg "measured" an individual's moral reasoning by presenting the person with a hypothetical moral dilemma. One of the more common problems concerns the plight of Heinz, a poor man whose wife, Wilma, is dying from a rare disease. A chemist has developed a drug that will save Wilma, but he is demanding $2,000 for a single dose. Heinz has only $1,000, and he has no hope of raising the remainder of the fee

---

5. J. M. Gustafson, "The Booming Business of Business Ethics," *Business and Society Review*, Spring 1992, p. 84.
6. D. E. Kirrane, "Managing Values: A Systematic Approach to Business Ethics," *Training and Development*, November 1, 1990, p. 52.

before his wife dies. The chemist, who believes he has a right to profit from his drug, refuses to lower the price or to allow Heinz to pay the balance at a later date. The question Kohlberg poses is, "Should Heinz steal the money to pay for the drug?"[7]

Changes in Moral Reasoning By observing responses to the above and similar problems—including responses in a research project in which he followed the progress of seventy-five boys as they grew up over a period of twenty years—Kohlberg discovered what he believed to be a *pattern* in the development of moral reasoning. At the earlier stages, the relative goodness or badness of an action is highly dependent on the action itself. For example, in the case of Heinz, it would be immoral to obtain the money illegally, because it is "wrong to steal." In the later stages, in which subjects have aged and became more intellectually sophisticated, other moral criteria enter the equation—Heinz would be morally *obligated* to steal the money, because the right to life supersedes all other considerations.

Kohlberg believed these patterns evolve as each individual moves from a state of self-interest to a state of caring to a state of principle. In self-interest, we concern ourselves only with the maximization of our own well-being. In caring (which we refer to as *utilitarianism* later in the chapter), we are aware of the interests of others, as well as our own. In our principled state, we are motivated by what is "right," regardless of the consequences. As a result, moral reasoning progresses from a desire to avoid punishment, to a concern for people one knows or can imagine, to an interest in universal standards of fairness and justice.[8] (For the results of Kohlberg's study, see *Exhibit 4–2* on page 86.)

Kohlberg's work has received its share of criticism. The subject pool for his research was predominantly male and white, which raises questions about the applicability of the findings to a culturally diverse society. He considered morals to be universal and absolute, a line of thinking that has fallen out of favor. Nevertheless, Kohlberg's research does offer an explored theory as to how we shape our moral reasoning.

PHILOSOPHICAL DISCUSSIONS OF ETHICS

Whatever intellectual stimulation Kohlberg may provide on the question of morals (a universal set of guidelines for our behavior), for many he is not as satisfying on the question of ethics—the study of right and wrong behavior. Although moral principles serve as the guiding force in an individual's personal ethics system, they do not provide any quantifiable steps or stages of ethical development. In fact, Kohlberg predicts that people in different stages of moral reasoning will have distinct ethical personalities. Consider, for example, a stockbroker who is illegally offered a "hot tip" from a friend. If the stockbroker is in the "caring" state, he will likely pretend that he did not hear the tip and counsel his friend on the dangers of violating federal securities laws. In the "principled" state, however, the stockbroker could conceivably report his friend to the authorities, despite any personal hardship that act might entail.[9]

The question of what constitutes an ethical existence has been debated almost since the beginning of recorded history. For the ancient Greeks, the key to an ethical existence rested in "the good life." For the majority to attain "the good life," all participants—from

---

7. J. Rest, *Moral Development Advances in Research and Theory* (Minneapolis: University of Minneapolis Press, 1986), p. 184.
8. J. B. Cullen, B. Victor, and C. Stephens, "An Ethical Weather Report: Assessing the Organization's Ethical Climate," *Organizational Dynamics*, September 22, 1989, p. 50.
9. *Ibid.*

▼ **EXHIBIT 4–2**
Kohlberg's Six Stages of Moral Development

In following the progress of seventy-five boys for twenty years during the middle of the twentieth century, Lawrence Kohlberg formulated the theory that there are six sequential stages of moral development. Each stage provides a different motivation for following the established rules and ethical parameters of society:

1. To avoid punishment.

2. To satisfy self-centered needs and elicit a positive external response.

3. To conform to the group interest to please others in the group.

4. To accept legal restrictions as being in the best interests of society.

5. To accept legal restrictions balanced with individual rights as being in the best interests of society and the individual.

6. To find satisfaction in being ethical and moral for personal reasons.

Kohlberg's research suggests that children rely on external guidelines for moral direction, and as they grow older, they turn internally for guidelines of proper moral behavior. The psychologist also pointed out that most of his subjects achieved Stages 4 and 5, with very few of them reaching Stage 6. If this is correct, then, businesspersons, like other members of society, may respond to different situations with different ethical responses, depending on which stage of moral development they have reached.

SOURCE: Lawrence Kohlberg, "State and Sequence: The Cognitive Developmental Approach to Socialization," in *Handbook of Socialization Theory and Research*, ed. D. A. Gosline (Chicago: Rand McNally, 1969).

the warrior to the shepherd to the merchant—must discharge their duties and their roles for the benefit of society.

Socrates In the eyes of Socrates (469–399 B.C.E.), ethical behavior was a direct result of the quest for knowledge. He believed that there existed a moral law that was higher than the law of human beings. His student, Plato (428–348 B.C.E.), extrapolated that justice was also an absolute concept that existed independent of human definition.

Aristotle Plato's pupil and successor, Aristotle (384–322 B.C.E.), proved to be the most resilient proponent of "the good life." In his *Nicomachean Ethics* (written around 330 B.C.E.), the philosopher wrote that to achieve *eudaimonia*, roughly translated as "happiness" or "living well," one had to live an active life of practical virtue based on the philosophical consideration of moral virtue. Aristotle believed "the good life" requires a great deal of contemplation and practice (see *Exhibit 4–3*).

Aristotle believed that the study of ethics offered the knowledge that was necessary for people to act properly and live contentedly. The philosopher felt that our ultimate goal is happiness, and that to achieve happiness each person must find his or her function. Because Aristotle saw the human being as "the rational animal," he felt that a person's primary function is to reason. Using this logic, the philosopher concluded that for a man or a woman to be happy, he or she must act rationally.

Aristotle believed that because ethics and rationality go hand in hand, the ideal person *practiced* acting ethically and rationally until he or she could do so naturally. To do so, one must exist in the *mean*, or middle, and thus avoid extreme behavior. For example, courage is the ideal mean between cowardice and foolhardiness, and as such represents a virtue (moral excellence) that all humans must strive to attain. Aristotle took this **doctrine of the mean** into the realm of social commentary, using it as a basis for his belief that

▼ **EXHIBIT 4–3
"The Good Life,"
According to
Aristotle**

> What a man has to do, then, is to live actively in accordance with reason (or not without reason). But what an *x* and a good *x* have to do is the same in kind—for example, a lyre player and a good lyre player, and so in general in all cases, superiority in excellence being added to what he has to do: what a lyre-player does is to play the lyre, what a good one does is to play it well. A man's good, therefore, turns out to be active living in accordance with excellence—in accordance with the best and most perfect excellence. Moreover, in a complete life. For one swallow does not make a summer, nor does one day; and similarly a man is not made blessed and *eudaimon* by one day or by a short period of time.

"middle people" were society's best hope. Being neither rich (and therefore prideful and unwilling to be ruled) nor poor (and therefore envious with a servile mentality), such people were ideal citizens. This aspect of Aristotelianism has found its way into modern political discourse with its focus on the "middle class."

Aristotle and his fellow Greeks have had a profound influence on ethics and morals. Led by Aristotle, the Greeks were also instrumental in establishing the study and teaching of ethics as a necessity in a civilized culture.

Religious Ethics in Western Civilization After the rise of Christianity in the Western World, the focus moved from philosophy to scripture for ethical teaching. The Western religious tradition—more specifically, the Judeo-Christian religious tradition—is rooted in the belief that certain absolute truths have been revealed through the prophets, the Bible, and religious institutions. These teachings establish, for all who believe in them, an *absolute ethical duty* to act in accordance with them. It is not the consequences of an act that determine how ethical the act is, but the nature of the act itself. For example, if, like Robin Hood, an individual decides to rob the rich to help the poor, that individual's benevolent motive does not alter the fact that he or she has acted unethically ("sinned"), because stealing violates the Seventh Commandment, "Thou shalt not steal."

The preeminent early Christian philosopher was Saint Augustine (354–430 C.E.). Although he did not disagree with the Greeks, Saint Augustine faulted their methods. That is, he applauded their ideas about a just and ethical society, but he lamented their inability to provide any practical means to achieve it. He believed that a just society could only be delivered by God, and that a person's happiness and morality were based on that person's obedience to God and the church.

Kant and Duty-Based Ethics After the eighteenth-century philosophical movement known as the Enlightenment discredited many of the traditional sources of philosophy, many philosophers supplemented religion with logic as the basis for ethical theory. Immanuel Kant (1724–1804) identified some guiding principles for moral behavior based on what he believed to be the fundamental nature of human beings. Kant held that it is rational to assume that human beings are endowed with moral integrity and the capacity to reason and conduct their affairs rationally; therefore, their thoughts and actions should be respected. It is assumed that believers accept that they have certain ethical *duties*, such as not to lie or cheat. In America, the dominant duty-based ethical standard derives from religious sources, such as the previously mentioned Golden Rule of the ancients.

A central postulate in Kantian ethics is that one ought never act unless one is willing to have the rule of conduct on which one acts become universal law. This **categorical imperative** asks us to apply our own morals to society. Thus, we could ask ourselves whether we want to live in a society in which everyone lied when it was in his or her best

MANAGING SOCIAL ISSUES

INTERNATIONAL ISSUES: KANT AND THE CITY OF KALININGRAD

Many of the ethical philosophers you are studying in this chapter are from past centuries and millenniums. Are they and their ideas relevant and viable in the modern world?

Many residents of Kaliningrad, a Russian city with a population of just under one million, would answer "of course." In rediscovering their culture and roots since the breakup of the Soviet Union at the end of 1991, the citizens of Kaliningrad have turned to Immanuel Kant for guidance and inspiration.

Background

When Kant was born in Kaliningrad in 1724, the city was part of Germany and known as Koenigsberg. Kant lived his whole life without venturing outside the province, then called East Prussia.

Near the end of World War II, the Red Army overran Nazi forces in East Prussia. Three years later, Joseph Stalin expelled the German population from the area and renamed both the city and the province Kaliningrad. Tens of thousands of Soviet citizens, many from Gulag labor camps, were forcibly settled in Kaliningrad to replace the ousted Germans.

Since regaining its ideological freedom in 1991, the region has turned to its German history for a heritage other than that supplied by Soviet-style communism—even though the population is almost completely Russian. German has eclipsed English as the most popular foreign language in schools, and German language courses for businesspersons are oversubscribed.

Kant, a German, is now treated by the Russian populace as a local hero. An international Kant society has relocated to the city, and a new Kant museum is in the works. The city art gallery presents a show called "Artists Honor Kant."

"Kant is eternal," insists a local art official, who is gathering works from artists in twenty-six countries for a large retrospective in the future.

Kant is not just the darling of the art community. "Our schoolchildren learn Kant," says Irinia Kuznetsova, the territory's top official for education and welfare. "Not just the categorical imperative," she proudly notes, but "all the problems of Kant's ethics." German schools, she adds, have "no such courses."

Toward a New Self-Identity

Professor Vladimir Gilmanov, who teaches philosophy at the local university, has been tracking what he calls the "unexpected, really incomprehensible" changes in the self-identity of the people in Kaliningrad since the fall of communism. "Cultural phenomena like Kant are concrete points of contact in this land," he theorizes. "They become part of our self-consciousness."

Ultimately, Gilmanov believes, the reverence for Kant springs out of a revulsion for Soviet culture, which was based on the subservience of the individual to the state. Kant, who emphasizes the importance of free will, offers an attractive, even rebellious, alternative. "Lots of kids, rock fans, pop-culture fans, visit Kant's grave," he remarks.

Kaliningraders, who are pushing to return the region's name to Koenigsberg, find nothing contradictory about their interest in Kant and all things German. "This is our tradition too," says a young resident, "and we want to continue it."

For Critical Analysis:

Tradition aside, how could the teachings of Kant help Kaliningrad's policymakers bring a modern economy to the region?

SOURCE: D. Benjamin, "A Russian Enclave Smitten with Kant Also Loves Germany," *Wall Street Journal*, August 19, 1994, p. A1.

interests. If we would not want to live in such a society, then, according to the categorical imperative, we must consider lying an unethical activity.

Kant's thinking also lends itself to the **denteological perspective** of ethical choice. This theory supposes that the moral worth of a decision cannot be dependent on the results of the decision, but instead must depend on the intentions of the decision makers (see *Managing Social Issues—International Issues: Kant and the City of Kaliningrad*).

Problems with Duty-Based Ethics Sometimes, applying religious or Kantian ethics can pose difficulties. This is especially true in the business context. For example, a business executive negotiating with another firm's representatives may feel it necessary to "stretch the truth" or "hold back" information to obtain the best "deal" for his or her employer. Is this a violation of religious precepts or Kant's categorical imperative? In an absolute sense it is, for it is unethical in both religious and Kantian terms. Remember, though, that the executive also owes an ethical duty to his or her employer (not to mention other stakeholders) to make decisions that are in the best interests of the firm. Furthermore, what if the executive knows that unless the deal is struck, the employer will have to lay off a large number of longtime employees who depend on the firm for their economic welfare? Would "stretching the truth" in negotiating the deal then be consistent with the religious ethical duty to be compassionate toward others, or with the Kantian imperative to act only as we would have all others act?

You can see how, in the business context, ethical decision making may involve fulfilling not just one ethical responsibility but a number of ethical responsibilities simultaneously.[10] When one ethical duty conflicts with another, the businessperson has to decide which duty is the most fundamental and then act accordingly. In the situation here, the executive may conclude that the ethical duty to be fully honest with others is more fundamental than the duty owed to the firm (even though the cost of this decision may include a personal cost, such as not obtaining a future promotion or pay raise, which will affect not only the executive but also his or her family). Alternatively, the executive might decide that the ethical duty owed to the firm and its employees (and possibly to his or her family) is more fundamental than, and thus overrides, the duty to be fully honest with the other negotiators. As this example illustrates, frequently the ethical decisions faced by businesspersons are not clear-cut; that is, the decisions involve choices not between good and bad alternatives but between good and *less* good alternatives, or between poor and less poor ones.[11]

JUSTICE: THE FAIRNESS QUESTION

One method of ethical reasoning that we often use to make decisions concerns **justice**, or the concept of what is fair according to the prevailing standards of society. "Who said life is fair?" has become the common cry of the resigned, but the truth is that we do expect life to be reasonably fair. We expect our wages to be fair, commensurate with our work. We expect our taxes to be fair, commensurate with the services provided and the burden on our fellow citizens. We expect the rule of law to be fair, treating each individual equally under its precepts.

In the twentieth century, we have taken *justice* to mean an equitable distribution of the burdens and rewards that society has to offer. The distributive process varies from society to society. Those in a democratic society believe in the "equal pay for equal work" doctrine, in which individuals are rewarded for the sweat of their brows according to what value the free market places on their services. Because the market places different values on different occupations, the rewards, such as wages, are not necessarily equal.[12] Nonetheless, the rewards are seen by many as being just. A politician who argued that a

---

10. D. J. Gritzsche, "Emerging Ethical Issues in International Management," SAM *Advanced Management Journal*, Autumn 1990, p. 42.

11. J. L. Badaracco, Jr., and A. Webb, "Business Ethics: A View from the Trenches," *California Management Review*, Winter 1995, p. 8.

12. D. P. Hanson, "Managing for Ethics: Some Implications of Research on the Prisoner's Dilemma Game," SAM *Advanced Management Journal*, Winter 1991, p. 16.

supermarket clerk should receive the same pay as a physician, for example, would not receive many votes from the American people. At the other extreme, communist theorists have argued that justice would be served by a society in which burdens and rewards were distributed respectively to each individual according to their abilities and their needs.

Degrees of Justice Most modern societies have mixed systems, which has led to a never-ending controversy concerning what is just and what is unjust. Every political debate, whether it be over health care, crime, or taxes, centers on the idea of justice. The American Revolution (1775–1783), the French Revolution (1789–1799), and the fall of the Soviet Union (1991) were each precipitated by a feeling among the general public that the prevailing system was not fair.

There are different types of justice by which any society attempts to create fairness. *Distributive justice* refers to how burdens and benefits are distributed, and it is at the heart of the debate over equal pay for equal work. *Procedural justice*, on which legal systems are based, refers to a decision-making process by judgments, mediation, and agreement. *Compensatory justice* refers to decisions made to compensate one group or an individual who has been wronged by another group or individual. (Compensatory justice is the major justification for affirmative actions programs, which we discuss in Chapter 14).

Rawls and the Principle of Justice Moral theorist John Rawls based his theories of justice on what he called the "veil of ignorance." In short, Rawls believed that a test of whether a principle or practice is fair or just would be to ask whether the principle or practice would be chosen by a society whose collective eyes were "veiled" to wealth, class, color, and the like. "This ensures that no one is advantaged or disadvantaged in the choice of principles by the outcome of natural chance or the contingency of social circumstances," Rawls has written.[13]

---

13. J. Rawls, *A Theory of Justice* (Cambridge, Mass.: Harvard University Press, 1971), p. 12.

PriceCostco Background

PriceCostco was formed on October 21, 1993, by merging The Price Company and the Costco Wholesale Corporation, two of the top three membership discount retailers in the United States.

PriceCostco operates a chain of cash-and-carry membership warehouses that sell high-quality, nationally branded, and selected private-label merchandise at low prices. Its target markets include both businesses that buy goods for commercial use or resale and individuals who are employees of specific organizations. The company tries to reach high sales volume and fast inventory turnover by offering a limited choice of merchandise in many product groups at competitive prices.

The company takes a strong position on behaving ethically in all transactions and relationships. It expects employees to behave ethically. For example, no one can accept gratuities from vendors. The company also expects to behave ethically, according to domestic ethical standards, in any country in which it operates.

CODE OF ETHICS

By Jim Sinegal

OBEY THE LAW

The law is irrefutable! Absent a moral imperative to challenge a law, we must conduct our business in total compliance with the laws of every community where we do business.

- Comply with all statutes.

- Cooperate with authorities.

- Respect all public officials and their positions.

- Avoid all conflict of interest issues with public officials.

- Comply with all disclosure and reporting requirements.

- Comply with safety and security standards for all products sold.

TAKE CARE OF OUR EMPLOYEES

To claim "people are our most important asset" is true and an understatement. Each employee has been hired for a very important job. Jobs such as stocking the shelves, ringing members' orders, buying products, and paying our bills are jobs we would all choose to perform because of their importance. The employees hired to perform these jobs are performing as management's "alter egos." Every employee, whether they are in a Price Club or Costco warehouse, or whether they work in the regional or corporate offices, is a PriceCostco ambassador trained to give our members professional, courteous treatment.

Today we have warehouse managers who were once stockers and callers, and vice presidents who were once in clerical positions for PriceCosta. We believe that PriceCosta's future executive officers are currently working in our warehouses, depots, buying offices, and accounting department, as well as in our home offices.

To that end, we are committed to these principles:

- Provide a safe work environment.

- Exceed ecological standards required in every community where we do business.

- Comply with all applicable wage and hour laws.

- Comply with all applicable anti-trust laws.

- Protect "inside information" that has not been released to the general public.

TAKE CARE OF OUR MEMBERS

The member is our key to success. If we don't keep our members happy, little else that we do will make a difference.

- Provide top-quality products at the best prices in the market.

- Provide a safe shopping environment in our warehouses.

- Provide only products that meet applicable safety and health standards.

- Sell only products from manufacturers who comply with "truth in advertising/packaging" standards.

- Provide our members with a 100% satisfaction guaranteed warranty on every product and service we sell, including their membership fee.

- Assure our members that every product we sell is authentic in make and in representation of performance.

- Make our shopping environment a pleasant experience by making our members feel welcome as our guests.

- Provide products to our members that will be ecologically sensitive.

TAKE CARE OF OUR MEMBERS

Our member is our reason for being. If they fail to show up, we cannot survive. Our members have extended a "trust" to PriceCostco by virtue of paying a fee to shop with us. We can't let them down or they will simply go away. We must always operate in the following manner when dealing with our members:

Rule #1 – The member is always right.
Rule #2 – In the event the member is ever wrong, refer to rule #1.

There are plenty of shopping alternatives for our members. We will succeed only if we do not violate the trust they have extended to us. We must be committed at every level of our company, with every ounce of energy and grain of creativity we have, to constantly strive to "bring goods to market at a lower price."

- Pay a fair wage.

- Make every job challenging, but make it fun!

- Consider the loss of any employee as a failure on the part of the company and a loss to the organization.

- Teach our people how to do their jobs and how to improve personally and professionally.

- Promote from within the company to achieve the goal of a minimum of 80% of management positions being filled by current employees.

- Create an "open door" attitude at all levels of the company that is dedicated to "fairness and listening."

RESPECT OUR VENDORS

Our vendors are our partners in business and for us to prosper as a company, they must prosper with us. It is important that our vendors understand that we will be tough negotiators, but fair in our treatment of them.

- Treat all vendors and their representatives as you would expect to be treated if visiting their places of business.

- Pay all bills within the allocated time frame.

- Honor all commitments.

- Protect all vendor property assigned to PriceCostco as though it were our own.

- Always be thoughtful and candid in negotiations.

- Provide a careful review process with at least two levels of authorization before terminating business with an existing vendor of more than two years.

- Do not accept gratuities of any kind from a vendor

RESPECT OUR VENDORS

These guidelines are exactly that - guidelines, some common sense rules for the conduct of our business. Intended to simplify our jobs, not complicate our lives, these guidelines will not answer every question or solve every problem. At the core of our philosophy as a company must be the implicit understanding that not one of us is required to lie or cheat on behalf of PriceCostco. In fact, dishonest conduct will not be tolerated. To do any less would be unfair to the overwhelming majority of our employees who support and respect PriceCostco's commitment to ethical business conduct.

If you are ever in doubt as to what course of action to take on a business matter that is open to varying ethical interpretations, take the high road and do what is right.

If you want our help, we are always available for advice and counsel. That's our job and we welcome your questions or comments.

Our continued success depends on you. We thank each of you for your contribution to our past success and for the high standards you have insisted upon in our company.

If we do these four things throughout our organization, we will realize our ultimate goal, which is to REWARD OUR SHAREHOLDERS.

Rawls developed a comprehensive theory of the distribution of justice, or what is called distributive justice. Rawls then asked how, within a society whose rules are designed through a "veil of ignorance," one should then distribute the costs and benefits of all actions. To arrive at a set of rules that would maximize fairness, Rawls suggested that several principles had to be followed. First, each and every individual within an institution or affected by it must have an equal right to the most extensive liberty that is compatible with a like liberty for all. Second, any inequalities, both social and economic, that are defined by an institutional structure or fostered by it must be considered arbitrary unless they are at the same time (1) arranged so that the least advantaged individuals obtain the greatest benefits and (2) the outgrowth of each individual's innate fair and equal chance to reach any social position.

Under a perfect system of distributive justice, all individuals have equal access to the training necessary for advancement, all basic human rights are protected, and the most disadvantaged members of society are not unfairly taken advantage of.

UTILITARIANISM

"People should act so as to generate the greatest good for the greatest number." This is a paraphrase of the major premise of utilitarian theory. **Utilitarianism** is a philosophical theory first developed by Jeremy Bentham (1748–1832) and then advanced, with some modifications, by John Stuart Mill (1806–1873)—both British philosophers. In contrast to duty-based ethics and Kant's moral theory, utilitarianism is *outcome oriented*. It focuses on the consequences of an action, not on the nature of the action itself or on any set of preestablished laws. Utilitarian thinking, therefore, is said to correspond to a **teleological perspective** of ethics, which places the greater importance on the outcome of an ethical decision than on the intent of the decision maker.

Right and Wrong in Utilitarianism Under a utilitarian model of ethics, an action is morally right when, among the people it affects, it produces the greatest amount of good for the greatest number. When an action affects the majority adversely, it is morally wrong. Applying the utilitarian theory thus requires (1) a determination of what individuals will be affected by the action in question; (2) an assessment, or **cost-benefit analysis,** of the negative and positive effects of alternative actions on these individuals; and (3) a choice among alternative actions that will produce maximum societal utility—or, in other words, the greatest positive benefits for the greatest number of individuals.

How does a utilitarian determine what constitutes the general welfare or happiness of individuals? Bentham's approach to this question was to define happiness strictly in terms of physical pleasure or pain. By thus quantifying happiness, he felt it would be possible to calculate scientifically, by a kind of moral mathematics, the human costs and benefits of any legislative decision. Mill argued that qualitative factors, such as psychological and spiritual well-being, also play a significant role in creating happiness and need to be considered in calculations of the positive and negative effects of a decision. For Mill and later followers of the utilitarian school of thought, what constitutes happiness is individually determined. Therefore, the successful application of the utilitarian welfare maximization principle depends on the freedom—and the physical, mental, social, and financial ability—of all individuals to make and express their choices.

For the businessperson, utilitarianism is linked strongly to the concept of stakeholder analysis, which basically assesses the negative and positive affects of alternative actions on the corporation's different stakeholders. This can become problematic, especially when the greatest amount of good for the greatest numbers of citizens is in contrast to corporate self-interest. In this context, managers must also consider the short-term versus the long-term ramifications of their decisions, as well as the relative importance of those directly and indirectly affected by their actions.

Problems with Utilitarianism As you have probably noted, utilitarianism is no panacea for ethical dilemmas in business. Although interesting in principle, the philosophy suffers from a major problem: Any true calculation of overall welfare, happiness, or utility requires a knowledge of what the *actual* consequences, both negative and positive, of a given decision will be. Rarely, if ever, can all possible ramifications of a decision be predicted with total accuracy. This is especially true with decisions that may affect millions of people.

Another problem with utilitarianism is that it always involves both winners and losers; that is, it is impossible to satisfy everybody with a policy action based on the principle of maximum total utility. Consider the following example: Smith, a manufacturer, owns many plants. One of the plants is much older than the others. Equipment at the old plant is outdated and inefficient, and the costs of production at that plant are now twice what they are at any of Smith's other plants. The price of the product cannot be increased because of competition, both domestic and international. What should Smith do?

A utilitarian analysis of the problem would weigh the costs of closing the plant (the financial insecurity of those who would be laid off) against the benefits of closing the plant (the future financial security of the firm and of those workers who would retain their jobs at the other plants). If Smith decides the issue from a utilitarian perspective, he will very likely close the plant, because closing the plant will yield the greatest benefit for the greatest number of people. The winners are the majority, who will be aided by the decision; the losers are the workers at the old plant, now without jobs. Furthermore, stakeholder analysis instructs us that Smith's decision also affects other interests. The community surrounding the closed plant is certainly hurt, because it loses tax revenues, and the other businesses feel the "trickle-down effect" of the workers' lost incomes. The environment, however, may benefit by the elimination of the plant's waste products. The challenge of balancing the various interests can leave little room for utilitarian-based reasoning.

Utilitarianism is often criticized because its objective, calculated approach to problems tends to reduce the welfare of human beings to plus and minus signs on a cost-benefit worksheet. Furthermore, how does one quantify the social costs and benefits of a corporation's actions, such as producing violent video games for children? Finally, utilitarian reasoning has been used to justify certain human costs that some segments of society find unacceptable. Some private in vitro fertilization centers, for example, conduct research on human embryos, a practice that many people find morally unjust despite its possible widespread medical benefits.

RIGHTS

Another problem with utilitarianism is that it tends to downplay the idea of rights, or the idea that each individual or group is entitled to exist under certain conditions regardless of any external circumstances. The term *human rights* implies that certain rights—to life, to freedom, to the pursuit of happiness—are conveyed on birth and cannot be arbitrarily taken away. Denying the rights of an individual or group is considered to be unethical and illegal in most, though not all, parts of the world.

For example, from a utilitarian standpoint, the decision to test drugs or medicine on a human being might be an acceptable ethical decision for a medical company, because presumably a majority of the population would benefit from the experimentation. According to the **principle of rights**, however, there can be no justification to put even a

single life in danger in order to test drugs for the well-being of society. The rights principle, in effect, focuses only on the individual, whereas the utilitarian principle focuses on society as a whole.[14] When the principle of rights is utilized, no amount of cost-benefit analysis can be used to justify an action that harms an individual. The principle of rights underlies not only the civil rights movement but also senior citizens' rights, the rights of persons with disabilities, privacy rights, children's rights, fetal rights, animals' rights, women's rights, and rights for gay men and lesbians.

Ideally, a person's rights can be overridden only by a more basic right. Consider the example of the rights outlined in the Americans with Disabilities Act (1990). One of the goals of this act was to eliminate discriminatory hiring and firing practices that prevented otherwise qualified disabled workers from fully participating in the national labor force. The rights of workers with disabilities, nonetheless, can in a sense be overridden by an employer's inability to make a (financially) reasonable accommodation for such workers. In other words, there are limits to the employer's obligation to accommodate a worker under this federal law.

Legal Rights Certain rights are guaranteed by the government and its laws, and these are considered *legal rights*. The U.S. Constitution and its amendments, as well as state and federal statutes, lay out the rights of American citizens. Those rights can be disregarded only in extreme circumstances, such as during wartime. Legal rights include the freedom of religion, speech, and assembly; protection from improper arrest and searches and seizures; and proper access to counsel, confrontation of witnesses, and cross-examination in criminal prosecutions. Also held to be fundamental is the right to privacy in many matters. Legal rights are to be applied without regard to race, color, creed, gender, or ability.

---

14. D. P. Quinn and T. A. Jones, "An Agent Morality View of Business Policy," *Academy of Management Review*, January 1995, p. 22.

Moral Rights *Moral rights* exist without the need for legal fortification, though laws often strengthen and protect rights we would consider moral, such as the right not to be killed. The philosopher Jean-Jacques Rousseau (1712–1788) ascribed to the "social contract" theory that moral rights were derived from an individual's participation in the life of society. A citizen is morally obligated to live by the laws of the city, state, or country, and in return, the government is morally obligated to protect the citizen's rights.

BUSINESS ETHICS AND VALUES

One additional concept needs to be contemplated to complete our discussion of the fundamental ethical ideas: **values**—a belief structure governing one's personal conduct. There has been a great deal of discussion about values in recent years; "values in transition" has become a catchphrase used in discussing modern culture, or the decline thereof.[15] Political election campaigns debate "family values" as the competing candidates and political parties give their opinions on what constitutes our cultural traditions. In a business sense, *value* is defined using the consumer terms of price and quality. The thousands of business decisions made daily, in business entities from General Motors to the corner bait and tackle shop, are largely dictated by calculations of competing values (see *Company Focus: PepsiCo* on pages 96–97).

VALUES AND MORALS

Milton Rokeach, a twentieth-century scholar on the subject, called values *the enduring beliefs that a specific mode of conduct is personally or socially preferable to the opposite mode of conduct.*[16] In other words, values help us define good from bad. Rokeach also differentiated between instrumental and terminal values. We use *instrumental values* as a means of achieving goals; they represent the mode of conduct that we find acceptable in order to reach an end. Examples of instrumental values include honesty, self-control, independence, and rationality. *Terminal values* represent the end to be reached. According to Rokeach, happiness, freedom, prosperity, and inner peace are terminal values.[17]

The combination of instrumental and terminal values provides individuals and businesses with goals to strive for and acceptable means by which to achieve them. As such, they suggest another definition of values: *the criteria upon which important decisions are made.*[18] Critical in understanding the concept of values is the comprehension that they are not the same as morals, which we defined earlier in the chapter as a universal set of principles. Values are not universal; in fact, they can vary dramatically from individual to individual or from group to group.

BUSINESS VALUES AND THE CORPORATE CULTURE

As the emphasis on business ethics has increased, so too has the scrutiny of values in the business community. Values reflect general beliefs of right and wrong, and as such they are needed in order to form the basis of ethical decision making within a business.

---

15. B. Z. Postner and W. H. Schmidt, "Values and the American Manager: An Update Updated," *California Management Review*, Spring 1992, p. 80.
16. Milton Rokeach, *The Nature of Human Values* (New York: Free Press, 1973).
17. *Ibid.*
18. G. F. Cavanagh, *American Business Values in Transition* (Upper Saddle River, N.J.: Prentice Hall, 1976), p. 1.

The levels of organization and personal interaction that exist within any given business correspond, if only loosely, to the same characteristics sociologists use to define cultures in an anthropological sense. Therefore, the term **corporate culture** can be regarded as a pattern of basic assumptions and values that are considered valid and that are taught to new members as the proper way to perceive, think, and feel in the organization.[19]

A corporate culture can be created in various ways. We address this in detail in Chapter 5. For now it is important to understand that a corporate culture reflects the specific values system of the given business. Organizations have a number of outlets through which they can articulate these values, including pronouncements from company officials and other forms of mission statements. These articulations—what the members of the corporate culture say they value—are the company's **espoused values**. The values reflected in the way the corporation and its members actually behave are its **enacted values**.[20] When a firm's enacted values are not in accordance with its espoused values, that firm's corporate culture is often open to criticism and, in some cases, legal action. (For an example, see *Managing Social Issues—Barriers to Success: Conflicting Values* on page 98.)

CORPORATE VALUES VERSUS SOCIETAL VALUES

John D. Rockefeller once said that the growth of a business is "merely a survival of the fittest." This statement reflects a certain set of values that many of us do not use in daily life. Indeed, the values that are celebrated by society as a whole—charity, honesty, kindness, and so forth—have little to do with a Darwinian jungle in which only the strong survive. In fact, many businesspersons admit that they operate under a different values system while on the job.

Do a businessperson's values change the minute he or she walks through the doors into the workplace? *Should* they change? Although in a number of instances society's values have influenced organizational strategy (see the *Case—Taking the Rap for Corporate Values*—at the end of this chapter), some members of the business community do not think society's values necessarily have a place in the competitive playing field of corporate survival. PriceCostco, however, is one company that stresses both legal and ethical duties. (See the foldout exhibit in this chapter for PriceCostco's Code of Ethics.)

The Poker Analogy In his often-cited article for the *Harvard Business Review*, "Is Business Bluffing Ethical?" Albert Carr compared the ethics of business to those of a poker game.[21] Carr quotes the British statesman Henry Taylor to make his point: "Falsehood ceases to be falsehood when it is understood on all sides that the truth is expected to be broken." According to Carr, business, like poker, has its own "special ethics" that differ from the "ethical ideals of civilized human relationships." Business, like poker, "calls for the distrust of the other fellow." In business, as in poker, "cunning deception and concealment of one's strength and intentions, not kindness and openheartedness," are necessary.

In telling the story of a man who dyes his hair as a precept to lying about his age on a job application, Carr is unapologetic in his defense. "This was a lie, yet within the accepted rules of the business game," he writes. "No one should think any the worse of the game of business because its standards of right and wrong differ from the prevailing traditions of morality in our society."

19. E. H. Schein, *Organizational Culture and Leadership* (San Francisco: Jossey-Bass, 1985), p. 9.
20. C. Argyris and D. A. Schon, *Organizational Learning* (Reading, Mass.: Addison-Wesley, 1978).
21. A. Z. Carr, "Is Business Bluffing Ethical?" *Harvard Business Review*, January–February 1968, pp. 143–150.

COMPANY FOCUS: PEPSICO
THE WORTH OF CORPORATE VALUES

How much is a corporate value system worth to the image of the company? Or perhaps the question should be, How much is the appearance of corporate values worth to a corporation? PepsiCo, Inc., faced that question in the spring of 1989 and swallowed a $5 million product endorsement with pop star Madonna.

"The Choice for a New Generation"

When rival Coca-Cola's launching of New Coke failed spectacularly in 1985, Pepsi saw a golden opportunity to solidify its position as the preferred soft drink of American youth. Between 1985 and 1987, the company increased its U.S. advertising budget from $116.7 million to $135.8 million. With stars such as Tina Turner, Lionel Richie, and most spectacularly, Michael Jackson in its advertising stable, Pepsi was establishing itself as "the choice for a new generation." The strategy seemed to be working: in 1988, for the first time ever, Pepsi passed Coke in supermarket retail sales.

Pepsi's Madonna Advertisement

Madonna seemed like a perfect choice for Pepsi's next big advertising campaign. Despite her carefully structured "bad girl" persona, the twenty-eight-year-old singer and actress was a dominant figure in pop culture: a study released by Marketing Evaluations TVQ at the time found that Madonna was recognized by 88 percent of respondents.

In one of the largest single-day media buys in history, Pepsi aired Madonna's two-minute "Make A Wish" advertisement on March 2, 1989. The commercial, which was aired in the United States during the popular *Cosby Show* and in forty other countries around the world, is believed to have been viewed by approximately 250 million people. The advertisement consisted of the pop star watching a home movie of herself at eight years old having a birthday party. As the spot comes to an end, the modern Madonna watches her younger self blow out her birthday candles, and she advises the girl, "Go ahead, make a wish." The advertisement was set to "Like a Prayer," a song from Madonna's latest album.

The next day, the cable television station MTV aired Madonna's "Like A Prayer" music video for the first time. The video depicts Madonna wearing a black negligée while receiving the sacrament of Christ, a scene filled with sexual innuendo involving an animated statue of Christ.

The Law and Corporate Values Of course, the prevailing values of society can be imposed on business, through legislation passed by elected officials of the society. Ethics involves an active process of applying values, which may range from religious principles to customs and traditions. A **social ethic** expresses the dominant ethical values, or shared beliefs, of society in general. Indeed, it is the sharing of beliefs and the desire to spread these beliefs that cause people to organize as groups — pressure groups lobbying Congress to create or amend a law, social groups urging Americans to be for or against abortion, and so on. When enough people are convinced, say, that a certain law is wrong, sufficient pressure will be exerted on government to change that law so that it more effectively represents the social ethic.

All ethical decisions in the workplace cannot be made by the law, however. Our laws force us to behave ethically or face undesirable consequences—a fine or even imprisonment. In the interest of preserving personal freedom, as well as for practical reasons, the law does not, and cannot, codify all ethical requirements. No law says, for example, that it is *illegal* to lie to one's family, but it may be *unethical* to do so. Similarly, in the business world, numerous actions might be unethical but not necessarily illegal:

COMPANY FOCUS: (CONTINUED)

Reactions of Consumers and PepsiCo

The reaction of religious groups was immediate and pointed. The Reverend Donald Wildmon, director of the American Family Association, called the Madonna video "one of the most offensive things I've ever seen." As head of a Christian advocacy group with approximately 380,000 members and hundreds of local chapters, Wildmon was in a position to do more than just complain about the video. He called for a boycott of PepsiCo and its products until the "Make A Wish" commercial was pulled. A few days after Wildmon's announcement, PepsiCo announced "a temporary hold on the commercial until we see a reaction to the video." More religious groups joined the boycott, and PepsiCo's offices were flooded with letters and phone calls from angry consumers. PepsiCo pulled the ad and ended its affiliation with Madonna.

PepsiCo executives claimed they had not seen the video before it aired and had not been told that it would air so quickly after the introduction of the commercial. "We knew she was making a video with a church and a choir," one of them told the *Wall Street Journal*. "We didn't know the video featured burning crosses, priests, and religious figures."

The New Bottom Line

PepsiCo subjected itself to a great deal of criticism for "caving in" to religious groups—for allowing the values of a relatively small group of consumers to dictate company policy. But PepsiCo executives realized that a boycott of their products in protest of their pulling the Madonna spot was highly unlikely, whereas the image of PepsiCo as insensitive to religious values could do the company great harm. Today, corporations must realize that the values of even a small part of the community should be respected, even if that means incurring high costs in the short run.

SOURCE: "PepsiCo and Madonna," Harvard Business School Case No. 49-590-038, 1990.

▼ **Mere compliance with the law does not always equate with ethical behavior.**

At times, a corporation's compliance with the law may be unethical, or at the least not in keeping with the values of the corporation. There have been instances when a private organization has deemed a law ethically unacceptable, and used its business power to change that law (see *Company Focus: National Football League* on page 100).

BEN FRANKLIN AND AMERICAN VALUES: CAPITALISM

If laws reflect the values of society, then it stands to reason that different societies will have different laws. That premise holds especially true in business. For example, Chinese businesspersons have a tradition of giving bribes to establish *guanxi* ("connections") to secure contracts. In contrast, many Western societies, especially in the United States, do not approve of bribes.

Benjamin Franklin, one of the framers of the Constitution, attempted to delineate what he believed to be American values in his *Autobiography*, published between 1771 and 1788.

◰ MANAGING SOCIAL ISSUES

BARRIERS TO SUCCESS: CONFLICTING VALUES

The cover of the January 1992 *Playboy* featured the "Swedish Bikini Team," five women in bathing suits who starred in a series of Old Milwaukee beer commercials on television. Executives of the Stroh Brewing Company hoped the blonde quintet would help recapture their beer's rapidly dwindling share of the twenty-five- to thirty-five-year-old male consumer market. Many workers at the company, however, were less than thrilled with the idea. In fact, the Swedish Bikini Team concept kicked off the first lawsuit linking a company's advertising to its treatment of female employees.

Employee Complaints about the Ad

That winter, five female employees at Stroh filed lawsuits against the brewery. In their complaints, the women described repeated instances of sexual harassment, including lewd, sexist comments with physical intimidation and abuse from male employees at the company's bottling plant in St. Paul, Minnesota. The women contended that this atmosphere was propagated by Stroh's "sexist, degrading" promotional and advertising campaigns, including the Swedish Bikini Team commercial.

In a letter to the company's three thousand employees, Stroh president William L. Henry said the advertising was meant "to be a humorous parody of competitors' advertising and at the same time to capitalize on the equity the company has in the slogan, 'It doesn't get any better than this.'" (That slogan had been an Old Milwaukee standby for years, often coming up in a commercial just as a group of male friends were enjoying the great outdoors. In the newer commercials, things would get "even better" when the Swedish Bikini Team mysteriously showed up from out of the wilderness.)

In defense, George E. Kuhn, general counsel for Stroh, pointed to the company's decade-old policy against sexual harassment. He mentioned that employees had been disciplined and even fired for violating the policy.

That explanation, however, didn't sit well with Jeanne Keopple, one of the women who sued Stroh and the only female machinist at the St. Paul plant. "When the company, as a whole, is treating women as body parts, it pretty much sends a message to the employees," she said. "What I want Stroh's to do is to take a look at that and understand that they are giving a big stamp of approval." Another plaintiff, Dianne Novotny Young, added that pulling the ads "would send a very clear message to the workers that this kind of attitude and treatment of women isn't acceptable."

Stroh's Compromise

Partly because the Stroh employees' lawsuit came in the wake of law professor Anita Hill's testimony of sexual harassment by Supreme Court nominee Clarence Thomas in 1991, Stroh and its employees found themselves part of a nationwide debate. Roy Grace, a New York advertising guru, called the lawsuit "insane" for trying "to build a case that the way men interrelate with women is based on what they see on television commercials." The lawsuit also raised questions about beer commercials as a genre and prompted Lori Peterson, attorney for the Stroh employees, to comment, "Cleavage has been done to death. Let's try something new."

For its part, Stroh promised to give its employees a "sensitivity training course in diversity and sexual harassment." But Kuhn also said that "there are no current plans to withdraw the commercials."

For Critical Analysis:

This is a classic case of conflicting values and as such raises questions all managers have to face at some point in their careers: Whose values count? Whose values should be reflected when such conflicts occur? Is one set of values "better" than another? How do you decide?

His theories were unique, if only because they espoused an idea that had not yet gained popularity: the idea that morality was an integral part of good business. For Franklin, leading a moral life, in business as well as elsewhere, came down to following thirteen rules, or "virtues" (see *Exhibit 4–4*).

▼ **EXHIBIT 4–4 Benjamin Franklin's Thirteen Virtues**

Virtue	Interpretation
1. Temperance	Eat not to dullness; drink not to elevation.
2. Silence	Speak not but what may benefit others or yourself; avoid trifling conversation.
3. Order	Let all your things have their places; let each part of your business have its time.
4. Resolution	Resolve to perform what you ought; perform without fail what you resolve.
5. Frugality	Make no expense but to do good to others or yourself; i.e., waste nothing.
6. Industry	Lose no time; be always employ'd in something useful; cut off all unnecessary actions.
7. Sincerity	Use no hurtful deceit; think innocently and justly, and, if you speak, speak accordingly.
8. Justice	Wrong none by doing injuries, or omitting the benefits that are your duty.
9. Moderation	Avoid extremes; forbear resenting injuries so much as you think they deserve.
10. Cleanliness	Tolerate no uncleanliness in body, clothes, or habitation.
11. Tranquility	Be not disturbed at trifles, or at accidents common or unavoidable.
12. Chastity	Rarely use venery but for health or offspring, never to dullness, weakness, or the injury of your own or another's peace or reputation.
13. Humility	Imitate Jesus and Socrates.

Ever the pragmatist, Franklin suggested that his readers write the thirteen virtues in a little book and mark down a black mark every time they violated one of them. This comparison to a business ledger is not far-fetched, for Franklin also saw the thirteen virtues as being necessary for good business practice. In his autobiography he wrote of his days working for the *Pennsylvania Gazette*: "In order to secure my credit and character . . . I took care not only to be in reality industrious and frugal but to avoid all appearance to the contrary. I dressed plainly; I was seen at no places of idle diversion. I never went a-fishing or shooting; a book, indeed, sometimes debauched me from my work, but that was seldom, snug, and gave no scandal; and, to show that I was not above my business, I sometimes brought home the paper I purchased at the stores through the streets in a wheelbarrow."[22]

Franklin had his share of critics, most of whom echo contemporary concerns that American values are too deeply rooted in the idea that people can live on bread alone.

22. *The Autobiography of Benjamin Franklin*, ed. L. W. Labaree et al. (New Haven: Conn.: Yale University Press, 1975), pp. 125–126.

COMPANY FOCUS: NATIONAL FOOTBALL LEAGUE
NFL'S KING DAY ULTIMATUM

Shortly after being sworn in as governor of Arizona in 1987, Evan Meacham rescinded a paid holiday for state workers honoring the late civil rights leader Dr. Martin Luther King, Jr. Meacham's action caused a storm of criticism across the country, and many members of the business community decided to show their displeasure in financial terms. From 1987 to 1992, the Phoenix downtown area alone lost 166 conventions that had promised 165,000 hotel attendees and approximately $190 million in business. It is estimated that the state as a whole suffered more than $250 million in lost profits because of Meacham's action, not including the incalculable amount from those organizations that refused to consider Arizona at all. The most telling blow came from the National Football League (NFL) in 1990, citing the insult to King's memory as the reason the league decided against holding the 1993 Super Bowl in Phoenix.

The NFL's Value Judgment

When the NFL granted Phoenix the 1993 Super Bowl, the city's business community was ecstatic. Estimated revenues from the championship game were expected to be approximately $200 million, spread out among hotel proprietors, retailers, and restaurateurs. The NFL had one condition on its final acceptance of Sun Devil Stadium in the suburb of Tempe, however: King's birthday would have to be reinstated as a holiday.

On November 6, 1989, Arizona voters defeated an initiative for the King holiday by less than 1 percent of all of the votes cast. NFL Commissioner Paul Tagliabue immediately urged football team owners to pull the game out of Arizona. Four months later, they did so, moving the site of the game to the Rose Bowl in Pasadena, California.

Arizona's Reaction

Another wave of criticism swept over the state. State tourism official Maggie Wilson said she was bombarded with questions from potential visitors such as "Are we all racists here [in Arizona]? Aren't we ashamed of ourselves? And what are we going to do about it?" The answer was a huge voter registration drive among the state's travel industry workers—including hotel, airline, and car rental employees—by a tourism industry group called Hospitality Employees for Arizona's Future. The efforts paid off in November 1992, when another measure to enact the King holiday passed with 61 percent of the vote. Although half of those who voted in favor of the measure did so because of their opinion of King, 14 percent did so because of the loss of the football game and the economic impact of the loss on the state. These voters were no doubt pleased when, in 1993, Commissioner Tagliabue announced Phoenix as the site of the 1996 Super Bowl.

The New Bottom Line

Along with the hundreds of business organizations that withheld business from Arizona, the NFL showed that industry is not helpless in the face of undesired political actions. Although the football league has been criticized for lack of minority representation in management positions, it is certainly in keeping with the values of the NFL to take a stand on the King holiday issue. With almost 60 percent of its players being African American, the league felt a responsibility that went beyond the obvious public relations concerns.

SOURCE: Information from L. Del Russo, "Arizona Officials Hail Passage of Bill Establishing Dr. King Holiday," *Travel Weekly*, October 16, 1992, p. 1; S. Bergsmen, "Holiday Flap Still Haunts Arizona," *Hotel and Motel Management*, October 17, 1988, pp. 37–38; and A. Stevens, "Arizonians Grapple with the Problems Created by Vote against Holiday for Martin Luther King," *Wall Street Journal*, January 21, 1991, p. B5.

THE DELICATE BALANCE

Certain "standard" views of morality and ethics have been around for literally hundreds of years. There are, nonetheless, conflicting views about what is and is not ethical. For example, assume the vice president of a medium-size company has to make a managerial decision that will adversely affect certain employees. By definition, the opposite decision will forcibly affect others—perhaps another group of employees, or the shareholders, or the community. The vice president may reach one conclusion if following the duty-based ethics of Kant, and a different conclusion if following the utilitarian theory developed by Bentham.

When making corporate decisions, managers may wish to follow the principle of rights. If so, they might argue for major increases in expenditures for product testing. They might argue for much greater expenditures for whatever is necessary to improve worker safety. The delicate balance here involves the trade-off between never putting a single life in danger on the one hand and getting products to market at competitive prices so that the firm itself can survive on the other hand. After all, if a firm overspends on product testing and worker safety, all workers in the company may find themselves out of a job should the company go bankrupt.

TERMS AND CONCEPTS FOR REVIEW

Business ethics 83
Categorical imperative 87
Corporate culture 95
Cost-benefit analysis 91
Denteological perspective 88
Doctrine of the mean 86

Enacted values 95
Espoused values 95
Ethics 83
Justice 89
Morals 84
Principle of rights 92

Social ethic 96
Teleological perspective 91
Utilitarianism 91
Values 94

SUMMARY

1. In a capitalist system, perhaps the one major ethical issue facing managers is how to act in an ethically responsible manner while simultaneously making profits for shareholders.

2. Even though ethics can be simply defined as the study of what constitutes right or wrong behavior, the application of this definition involves myriad interpretations of ethical behavior. (Business ethics is perhaps more complicated than personal ethics, because business decisions can affect so many different individuals and groups.)

3. According to Lawrence Kohlberg, there are six stages of moral development, which start at avoiding punishment and end with finding satisfaction in being ethical and moral for simply personal reasons. He believed that few individuals reach the last stage.

4. Whereas Socrates argued that there exists a moral law higher than the law of human beings, Aristotle argued that individuals should practice acting ethically until such behavior becomes natural. Aristotle said that one must exist in the mean, or middle, and thus avoid extreme behavior (the doctrine of the mean).

5. Many ethical principles in Western civilization are derived from the Judeo-Christian religious traditions, such as "Thou shall not steal."

6. The philosopher Immanuel Kant argued that one ought never act unless one is willing to have the maxim on which one acts become universal law. He called this the categorical imperative. The belief that the moral worth of a decision is a function of the intention of the decision maker is the denteological perspective.

7. Although justice is the concept of what is fair according to society's prevailing standards, it does not mean everyone should, for example, be paid the exact same amount no matter what type of work he or she does.

8. John Rawls argued in favor of a system of distributive justice (how the burdens and benefits of living are distributed) developed through a set of rules designed with a "veil of ignorance" in mind. He thus argued in favor of the individual's having an equal right to the most extensive liberty compatible with a like liberty for all. Under Rawls's system of distributive justice, all individuals have equal access to the necessary training for advancement.

9. Outcome-based theories of ethics are often derived from utilitarianism, a philosophy developed by Jeremy Bentham. A teleological perspective places great importance on the outcome of any ethical decision (as opposed to the intent of the decision maker). The application of a utilitarian view of ethical decision making requires (a) a determination of who will be affected, then (b) making a cost-benefit analysis, and finally (c) choosing the action that leads to the maximum utility for society.

10. If one accepts the principle of rights, one can never justify putting lives in danger. People in the United States have certain legal rights guaranteed by the Constitution and by state and federal statutes. According to Jean-Jacques Rousseau, we also have moral rights, which exist without the need for legal fortification.

11. Values are derived from long-held beliefs about the "right" ways to conduct oneself. Values help us define good and bad. We use instrumental values as a way of achieving our goals and have terminal values that represent the end to be reached.

12. Values of managers are often reflected in the corporate culture within an organization. Company pronouncements and mission statements show the organization's espoused values. What actually happens within the organization reflects the corporation's enacted values.

EXERCISES

1. Write out a clear statement of the distinction between ethics and business ethics.

2. Reexamine *Exhibit 4–2*, where you read about Lawrence Kohlberg's six stages of moral development. Develop one example of how a person in each stage would respond to a given moral dilemma.

3. Explain how you could apply Aristotle's "doctrine of the mean" to current political discourse concerning the issue of "taxing the rich."

4. Imagine the following scenario: Your company is on the verge of bankruptcy. It currently employs 250 individuals in a very small community. During your negotiations for a new contract that could save the company, another bidder enters the picture. You hear about the outrageous claims that this competitive bidder is making with respect to its ability to satisfy the contract. You are preparing for the final negotiation session tomorrow.
    a. If you simply speak the truth, without stretching it, what ethical precepts will you be following, and who developed those precepts?
    b. To whom is your duty based—yourself, the shareholders of the corporation, the community, the employees of the corporation, or some other group?
    c. Because you know for certain that the competitive bidder could not perform the contract as well as your company could, are you justified in "stretching the truth" during your final negotiations?
    d. Develop a stakeholder effects chart that shows how your decision will affect different stakeholders.

5. Assume that you wish to follow John Rawls's concept of using the veil of ignorance to develop a perfect system of distributive justice. Describe the experiment you could use with, say, one thousand people, all of whom would be allowed to help create society's rules.

6. You have been asked to decide whether tobacco companies should be made illegal, because it is well known that smoking causes lung cancer, among other illnesses. Write down two columns, one for costs and one for benefits, of this policy decision. Would Jeremy Bentham have been for or against this policy? Why?

7. Now make a list of the difficulties involved in actually carrying out the cost-benefit analysis in *Exercise 6* in terms of placing real dollar values on the costs and on the benefits. Do these difficulties matter for your analysis?

8. When carrying out a cost-benefit analysis, should you worry about which individuals or groups suffer the costs of a particular policy action, and which individuals or groups reap the benefits? Why or why not?

9. In this chapter, we gave one example of when one person's rights have been overridden by a more basic right; it related to the Americans with Disabilities Act. Develop two more examples showing how an individual's rights have been overridden by another right.

10. What is the relationship between ethics, values, and morals?

11. "All ethical decisions in the workplace cannot be made by the law." Do you agree? If so, what does determine those ethical decisions that are not made by the law?

12. Pick any three of Benjamin Franklin's thirteen virtues outlined in *Exhibit 4–4*, and create a managerial equivalent that would be beneficial to a corporation.

13. Should the government do more to control television programs that some individuals find offensive, either because of too much violence, too much sex, or too much plain stupidity? If your answer is yes, on what ethical theory is it based? If your answer is no, on what ethical theory is it based?

14. Richard Green, executive vice president of Blistex, Inc., once said, "The creation and maintenance of a profitable company means that stable employment and a good working environment can exist for a number of people. This can only be accomplished by utilizing the profit motive and the free market economy. Being a Christian and a good manager are not mutually exclusive." Green was responding to a statement by Pope John Paul II, who had urged an organization of Catholics who are chief executive officers to apply "the teachings of the Church to the business world." Make a list of how certain Judeo-Christian teachings might be applied to the business world.

SELECTED REFERENCES

▶ Buchholz, R. A. *Fundamental Concepts and Problems in Business Ethics*. Upper Saddle River, N.J.: Prentice Hall, 1989.

▶ Glover, Jonathan. *Responsibility*. New York: Humanities Press, 1970.

▶ Hart, H. L. A. *Law, Liberty, and Morality*. Stanford, Calif.: Stanford University Press, 1963.

▶ Hoffman, W. M. and J. M. Moore. *Business Ethics: Readings and Cases in Corporate Morality*. 2d ed. New York: McGraw-Hill, 1990.

RESOURCES ON THE INTERNET

▼ Certain groups believe that corporations should not use animals for testing. If you are interested in animal rights, you can access the House of Representatives Web site at

http://www.house.gov/

You can also access the Personal Library Software site at

http://www.pls.com:8001

▼ You can research the affiliates of a particular corporation with the help of the Corporate Affiliates Research Center database (for a fee). You do so by using the commercial on-line service GEnie. Select

Research & Reference Services

When there, select

Corporate affiliate center

CASE

TAKING THE RAP FOR CORPORATE VALUES

Background

In March 1992, Warner Brothers Records, a division of the conglomerate Time Warner, Inc., released the fifth album of recording artist Tracy Morrow, better known as Ice-T. Although Ice-T had built his reputation as a rapper, *Body Count* was not a rap album; it leaned more toward heavy metal, a loud subgenre of rock 'n' roll.

Sales of *Body Count* were steady, if not spectacular, but the release did not garner much attention in the national media until the lyrics to one of its songs were published in the June edition of a Dallas police association newsletter. The song, called "Cop Killer," includes the following lines:

I got my 12 gauge sawed off
I got my headlights turned off
I'm 'bout to bust some shots off
I'm 'bout to dust some cops off . . .
Die, die, die, Pig. Die!

In response, the Combined Law Enforcement Association of Texas (CLEAT), which represents about twelve thousand of that state's police officers, called for a boycott of Time Warner's products. CLEAT's efforts got an unexpected boost when Vice President Dan Quayle, in the middle of a reelection campaign in which "family values" were a major theme for his Republican party, attacked the song and its distributor. "I am outraged at the fact that Time Warner, a major corporation, is making money off a record . . . that suggests it is OK to kill cops," said Quayle.

Reactions

Quayle's comments, quickly echoed by President George Bush, who called the lyrics "sick," catapulted Ice-T and "Cop Killer" into the national spotlight. Sixty members of Congress sent a letter to Time Warner expressing a "deep sense of outrage" that the corporation continued to distribute *Body Count*.

The National Sheriff's Association and the Fraternal Order of Police joined CLEAT in calling for a boycott. Police groups in Boston and New York took more forceful action, initiating proceedings toward divesting their pension funds' stock in the company. The New York Patrolmen's Benevolent Association was thought to have owned Time Warner stock worth approximately $100 million at the time.

Tempers boiled over at Time Warner's shareholders' meeting on July 16. Actor Charlton Heston set the tone for the event by reading the lyrics of the song out loud before asking Gerald Levin, Time Warner co–chief executive officer and president, "Were that song entitled 'Fag Killer,' or if the lyrics read 'Die, die, die, kike, die,' would you still sell that album?" Heston also chastised the company for sending copies of the compact disc to radio stations in miniature body bags.

CLEAT president Ron DeLord compared Time Warner executives to Nazi propagandist Joseph Goebbels. A member of the National Organization of Police Organizations called Levin "a sick mind running a sick company." Time Warner's business partners also expressed their displeasure at the song. The Chrysler Corporation decided not to renew its cross-media marketing program with the company, a move that cost Time Warner as much as $57 million. "Where we have the opportunity to choose, we as a company will not support the escalation of sex and violence in the media," said John Damoose, Chrysler's vice president of marketing.

Time Warner's Early Resistance

In defending the song and the company's decision to continue distributing the album, Time Warner concentrated on Ice-T's freedom of expression. After the acrimonious stockholders' meeting, the Recording Industry Association of America placed full-page ads in the *New York Times*, the *Los Angeles Times*, and other publications urging "the resistance of censorship."

"Is it our responsibility to limit the views of artists, writers, journalists, musicians, and film makers so that they don't offend corporate executives as well as society at large?" Levin asked in a letter to the *Wall Street Journal*. "We stand for creative freedom. . . . We believe that the worth of what a journalist or an artist has to say does not depend on preapproval from a government official or a corporate sponsor or a cultural elite of the right or of the left."

There were also charges that the negative reaction to "Cop Killer" was based on racism. Ice-T, who is African American, said, "I think by [the album] being rock it infiltrated into homes of a lot of parents not used to having their kids play records by rappers [and] by saying the word *rap* they

CASE (CONTINUED)

can get a lot of people who think 'rap-black, rap-black-ghetto,' and don't like it."

Some observers mentioned that there have been songs by white artists whose themes echoed that of "Cop Killer" with no comparable national controversy. For example, Eric Clapton's version of Bob Marley's "I Shot the Sheriff" was one of the most popular songs in the United States in 1974, and Lou Reed escaped criticism for the following 1989 lyrics: "This cop who died in Harlem/You'd think they'd got the warning/I was dancing when his brains ran down the street."

Time Warner's Social Responsibility.

Other observers saw the incident as a reflection of Time Warner's social responsibility, or lack thereof. "Of course Ice-T has the right to say whatever he wants," wrote syndicated columnist Michael Kinsley. "But that doesn't require any company to provide him an outlet. And it doesn't relieve a company of responsibility for the messages it chooses to promote." In other words, if Time Warner had decided not to release "Cop Killer," it would have been making a judgment on its image as a corporation, not censoring a controversial voice. When discussing why Chrysler chose not to renew its marketing contract with Time Warner, the auto-making company spoke of protecting the "integrity and quality" of "how we communicate [our] products."

Disturbed by Time Warner's actions, Richard Day, the editor in chief of *Industry Week*, came up with three questions that he felt top-level managers at any company should ask themselves about their firm's actions:

▶ What kind of behavior do we want to encourage?
▶ What kind of behavior do we want to discourage?
▶ What are the values that our management holds dear and wants its employees to embrace?

In his defense of his company's actions, Levin said he believed that Time Warner was upholding the behavior and values of a "democratic society" by giving voice to a song "rooted in the reality of the streets" of American inner cities. In contrast, his critics attributed Time Warner's actions to another value: greed. In their letter to the company, some members of Congress charged, "It appears you have chosen potential profit over any reasonable sense of public responsibility." Protesters at the stockholders' meeting carried signs that read, "Time

Warner Puts Profits Over Police Lives." The *New York Times* wondered, "Are [Time Warner's] profits and principles on a collision course?"

Profits or Principles?

The controversy was not a financial windfall for Time Warner. The week after the stockholders' meeting, the company's stock fell from $116 a share to $104 a share. Company officials worried that the boycott would adversely affect the economic performance of the conglomerate's other products, from *Sports Illustrated* to the Six Flags theme parks to the motion picture *Batman Returns*. Furthermore, the police union pension funds threatened to divest millions of dollars of Time Warner stock.

Ironically, the company's only financial benefit came as a direct result of the publicity of the boycott. Weekly sales of *Body Count* immediately doubled, and in the first week after the boycott, the album rose thirteen places on *Billboard* magazine's chart of the top two hundred albums.

New Policies at Time Warner

During the last week of July, five months after the release of the album, Warner Brothers began releasing *Body Count* without the "Cop Killer" track. Ice-T said the move was a reaction to bomb threats received at Warner Brothers offices. "It's not a Warner Bros. fight, it's my fight," said the singer. "Warner Bros. is taking the sweat for me, and the cops feel that this record was done for the money. So I'm going to pull the song off the record just to prove to them that it ain't about that."

Within a week, Time Warner stock had recovered, and the sales of *Body Count* had dropped dramatically. CLEAT declared a "cease fire" in its fight with Time Warner, and it decided to purchase, rather than divest, the company's stock so that "we can watch them . . . and become involved in [the conglomerate's] governance," explained CLEAT president DeLord. "Then we can really have an impact on what Time Warner does."

Six months later, Time Warner let Ice-T go from his contract and canceled the release of his album *Home Invasion*. Both Time Warner and Ice-T cited "creative differences," but a Warner Brothers insider said that the parent company had gone "gun shy" after the "Cop Killer" controversy: "They've gone from being the most liberal company to going over everything with a fine-toothed comb."

CASE (CONTINUED)

Other Time Warner artists were also influenced by this change in policy. The rapper Tragedy, also known as Intelligent Hoodlum, was forced to remove the song "Bullet" from his album *Black Rage*. The song contained these lyrics: "If you ever, ever put a nightstick to my head, I'm going to shoot your . . . ass dead." The rap group Boo-Ya-Tribe was asked to edit the song "Shoot 'Em Down" from its album, and the company dropped the rap group Almighty RSO after the Boston Police Patrolman's Association denounced one of the band's releases.

Warner Brothers spokesman Bob Merlis denied that these actions were specifically related to the "Cop Killer" controversy: "There's increased sensitivity throughout the industry. . . . We've always imparted a cautionary note when we've thought that the marketability of a given record was dubious because of content."

Critical Thinking Questions

1. This case clearly shows how subjective values can be. Rejecting, for argument's sake, the possibility that Ice-T was merely looking for shock value in the song "Cop Killer," what values does his music represent? Compare them with the so-called family values espoused by Vice President Quayle.

2. Do you agree with Levin's arguments? What are the strong and weak points of his reasoning with regard to the values of a "democratic society"?

3. Does the moral responsibility of Time Warner, and indeed of any company that would find itself in a similar situation, lie with key stakeholder groups or with broader concepts such as censorship or artistic freedom?

4. Did Time Warner ultimately make the right decision? How would you have handled the controversy if you were in a position of power at that corporation?

5. Although *Body Count* benefited from the attention, the album was not a breakthrough commercial success. How do you feel the entire controversy would have played itself out if *Body Count* had topped national sales charts and sold five million copies?

SOURCE: Information from B. D. Brown, "Quayle Boosts 'Cop Killer' Boycott Campaign," *Washington Post*, June 20, 1992, p. B1; D. Jehl, "Bush Attacks Hollywood's 'Sick' Anti-Police Themes," *Los Angeles Times*, June 30, 1992, p. A1; A. T. Lester and M. Tousignant, "Reaction to Ice-T Song Heats Up," *Washington Post*, June 25, 1992, p. C1; C. Morris, "Police, Time Warner Face Off over 'Cop Killer,' " *Billboard*, July 25, 1992, p. 1; S. Donanton and R. Serafin, "Chrysler Won't Renew Deal with Time Warner," *Automotive News*, September 28, 1992, p. 11; J. Ressner, "'Cop Killer' Is Iced," *Rolling Stone*, September 3, 1992, p. 16; G. M. Levin, "Why We Won't Withdraw 'Cop Killer,'" *Wall Street Journal*, June 24, 1992, p. A20; A. Light, "Ice-T: The Rolling Stone Interview," *Rolling Stone*, August 20, 1992, p. 30; M. Kinsley, "Ice-T: Is the Issue Social Responsibility . . . ," *Time*, July 20, 1992, p. 88; C. R. Day, Jr., "Just What *Are* Our Values?" *Industry Week*, August 17, 1992, p. 7; R. Clurman, "Pushing All the Hot Buttons," *New York Times*, November 29, 1992, section. 2, p. 2; K. Zimmerman, "All Claiming Victory in 'Cop Killer' Battle," *Variety*, August 3, 1992, p. 48; G. Reibman, "Boston Police Union Planning Suit against Time, Ice-T, Almighty RSO," *Billboard*, August 15, 1992, p. 84; J. L. Roberts, "Time Warner Releases Ice-T from Contract," *Wall Street Journal*, January 29, 1993, p. B1; and K. Neely, "'Cop Killer' Aftershocks," *Rolling Stone*, October 29, 1992, p. 32.

CHAPTER 5

MANAGERIAL VALUES AND THE CORPORATE CULTURE

CHAPTER OUTLINE

INTRODUCTION

Aristotle might not have completely agreed, but most Americans would have said that Stanley James Cardiges appeared to be living the good life. The American Honda Motor Company senior vice president had a six-figure income and a $770,000 mansion in Laguna Hills, California. His home was filled with the fruits of his labor: Oriental rugs, a baby grand piano, a laser karaoke machine, an extensive art collection, and air-conditioned garages for his expensive cars.

Cardiges was good at what he did—determining which dealerships would get exclusive rights to sell Hondas. One of his colleagues said that the showrooms and service departments under Cardiges's control were "a monument to the Honda."[1] With all of this going for him, why, in 1992, did Cardiges quit his job?

The answer came out in the spring and summer of 1994, when Cardiges and sixteen other former Honda officials were indicted on charges of illegally accepting millions of dollars in bribes from Honda dealers. Cardiges, who pleaded not guilty on all counts, was charged with racketeering, mail fraud, and conspiracy.

American Honda itself has not been charged with any wrongdoing, and the company has taken pains to distance itself from the indictments. "Importantly, the illegal actions perpetrated by a few former employees were not and are not a reflection of American Honda's corporate culture," a company spokesperson said in a statement.[2] American Honda's ethics policies instituted in 1986 do not allow employees to "seek or accept . . . payments, fees, services, or loans from any person or business entity that does nor seeks to do business with American Honda," unless the transaction is fully disclosed in writing. Even then, the policy prohibits employees from accepting gifts over $50.

All individuals are responsible for their own actions, but can a business be faulted for ethical breaches by its employees? For all its protestations of innocence, American Honda must have been aware of the potential for the conflict of interest that its relationship with its dealerships invited. The company defended itself with its corporate ethics policy.

In this chapter, we examine the components involved in creating an atmosphere of strong ethical values within a business environment. At American Honda, as at any company, an unenforced ethics policy or a limit on the cash value of gifts alone is not sufficient. It takes a concerted effort by executives, managers, and other employees to create a corporate culture in which ethical decision making is not just a policy but a reality.

VALUES AND ETHICAL DECISION MAKING

The previous chapter discussed Kant's categorical imperative and Aristotle's doctrine of the mean as guideposts in ethical decision making. The truth is that philosophy can provide useful intellectual materials, but most of us, as Lawrence Kohlberg suggested in Chapter 4, base our ethical blueprints on the stimuli we receive from our environments. Indeed, some psychologists claim that people today suffer from **cognitive overload,** meaning that there are too many factors to process mentally in deciding what is ethical behav-

---

1. S. Walsh, "A Top Honda Executive's Rise to Wealth," *Washington Post*, August 7, 1994, p. H1.
2. *Ibid.*, p. H14.

ior and what is not. It is almost impossible to avoid **cognitive dissonance,** or inconsistency between one's moral beliefs and one's actions. For example, one might oppose the slaughter of animals in principle but nonetheless eat meat or wear leather shoes and belts.

NORMATIVE ETHICS

To help deal with cognitive overload, individuals often practice *selective perception* by making conscious or subconscious decisions as to which facets of society on which they are going to base their ethical behavior. For example, even if we find the practice by which young cattle are raised to be somewhat distasteful, through selective perception many of us can still eat veal, because society's message against the practice is not strong enough for much dissuasion.

The menu from which we select is provided by *normative ethics*, through which we justify the moral principles on which we base our actions. **Ethical norms**—distinct sets of social rules for behavior—are provided for us from various sources, including family and friends, the local community, national beliefs, religious beliefs, the workplace, and, of course, the law.

In the context of ethical norms in the workplace, a manager's decision-making process can present ethical dilemmas. According to LaRue Tone Hosmer, this is because the decision-making process often includes a conflict between an organization's economic performance (measured by growth in revenues and profits) and its social performance (stated in terms of obligations to persons within and outside of the organization).[3] How a manager deals with these dilemmas depends on his or her values—the personal values the manager brings to work—as well as the values of the corporate culture.[4] In other words, a manager's values affect the decisions that he or she makes in the individual business niche.

For example, Mark Small, a seal hunter, was criticized for his actions because the Chinese were buying entire seal carcasses just to get the male sex organs for use as aphrodisiacs. Small gave a rebuttal that reflected his values: "This deal with China is not about sex organs. Seals are a renewable resource, and we have found a market for them."[5] Within his own limited corporate culture, Small's values allow him to make business decisions that might seem ethically or morally questionable to others.

DECISION PRINCIPLES OF ETHICAL MANAGEMENT

In discussing the individual manager's responsibilities "in the game," business writer Albert Carr brings up the example of a produce manager in a supermarket who finds a number of half-rotten tomatoes among a crop of good ones. It would be relatively simple to expose only the good side of the fetid tomatoes and, by spreading them equally in plastic-wrapped six-packs, effectively conceal them from the eyes of the consumer.

We read about Carr's poker analogy in Chapter 4, so we should not be surprised by his advice to the produce manager: Don't waste product by throwing it away when you can legally, if not ethically, sell it. "If an executive allows himself to be torn between a decision based on business considerations and one based on his private ethical code, he exposes himself to a grave psychological strain," Carr says.[6] Can you, as a future business manager, accept Carr's reasoning?

---

3. L. T. Hosmer, *The Ethics of Management* (Homewood, Ill.: Irwin, 1991), p. 3.
4. A. L. Balazs, "Value Congruency: The Case of the Socially Responsible Firm," *Journal of Business Research,* March 1990, p. 171.
5. "Now Hear This," *Fortune,* June 27, 1994, p. 16.
6. A. Z. Carr, "Is Business Bluffing Ethical?" *Harvard Business Review,* January–February 1968, p. 148.

Complexity of Managerial Decisions In his writings on the ethics of management, Hosmer finds managerial decision making more complex than simply deciding between personal and economic ethics. Hosmer urges managers to understand the "behavioral implications" of their decision making. He has reached some conclusions about the complexity of this process by managers to back his point:

1. **Most ethical decisions have extended consequences.** Besides its immediate results, a decision can have a much greater effect on an organization and consequently, on society. The extended consequences of the produce manager, for example, could be unwanted. What if a customer suffered a bacterial infection after accidentally eating one of the rotten tomatoes? The negative publicity from such an incident would damage the reputation of the supermarket, and customers would move on to a competitor.
2. **Most ethical decisions have multiple alternatives.** There is rarely a decision-making situation with only two choices. Perhaps the produce manager could work out a deal with the supplier that limits the amount of rotten fruit for which the supermarket has to pay, therefore solving the economic dilemma of lost revenue. It is often easier to consider only the two most obvious options—in this case, throw away the fruit or sell it—but it is not always in the best ethical interests of either the individual or the organization to do so.
3. **Most ethical decisions have uncertain consequences.** Managers often like to think that their decisions lead to measurable financial rewards or debts. Again, this deterministic model—without probabilities—makes decision making easier, but it can be a risky way to run a business. Not only must the social benefits and costs be factored into decision making, but the *unintended* results must also be included. If the victim of the bacterial infection decided to sue the supermarket, whatever costs the produce manager might have initially saved by selling the rotten tomatoes would be dwarfed by the settlement of the lawsuit.
4. **Most ethical decisions have personal implications.** Carr believes that ethical issues in management are impersonal, but Hosmer points out that they can have profound effects on a manager's life. If a job applicant falsifies a résumé, that person must understand that if the deception is discovered, the result will indeed be personal: loss of the job. The supermarket produce manager could face a similar fate as another unintended consequence of the spoiled fruit.[7]

Analysis of Ethical Problems in Management In the face of a myriad of consequences from the seemingly harmless act of hiding a few half-rotten tomatoes, how is a manager supposed to make even the simplest of decisions? Considering that ethical decisions often need to be made on the spur of the moment, who has time for consequences?

The answer is found in values and moral principles. If the produce manager's values don't allow him to cheat the customers, then he doesn't have to think twice before tossing the half-rotten tomatoes into the garbage. In balancing values in the workplace, Hosmer suggests three different forms of analysis: economic, legal, and philosophical.

The *economic analysis* relies on the values of the marketplace. Hosmer presents, as an example, the unpleasant task of laying off employees, which all managers must face at one time or another. Any ethical qualms can be eased by knowledge that there is a well-functioning labor market in the United States, and if the workers can adjust to the changing demands of this marketplace, they will find employment. Economic theory is simple, sometimes deceptively so: society has a limited quantity of resources, and when con-

---

7. Hosmer, *op. cit.*, pp. 13–15.

sumers are provided with the highest-quality goods at the lowest possible prices, then these resources are being used as efficiently as possible. As long as managers help this process evolve, managers are acting ethically, as far as economics is concerned.[8]

The *legal analysis* makes the decisions even easier for the manager. As long as something is not illegal—that is, as long as society has not decided that it should be prohibited—it is usually an acceptable business practice.

The shortcomings of both the legal and economic analyses become evident in the face of the *philosophical analysis*, which recognizes notions of right and wrong and often relies on conscience instead of law or simple managerial math. When AT&T Corporation announced in 1996 that it would lay off forty thousand workers over a three-year period, it may have been on solid ground economically and legally. But how ethical was the decision, according to some of the philosophies we discussed in Chapter 4? Teleologically, does the move result in the greatest amount of good for the greatest number of people? Denteologically, is this a morally worthy decision that meets the categorical imperative? Of course, AT&T officials may argue that the layoffs were philosophically justifiable because its remaining seventy thousand employees and society in general will benefit from a stronger, more efficient company.

Trade-Offs and Ethical Decision Making

The point remains that the tension between economic, legal, and philosophical values is necessary to help a manager solve ethical problems. Frequently, to ensure that a decision or action is at once profitable, legal, and ethical, some profitability or some ethical considerations must be sacrificed—or *traded off*—in the decision-making process. Thus, the concept of **trade-off** is intimately involved in ethical decision making.

Trade-Offs Always Exist No matter what your approach to ethics in the business world or in your personal life, you will need to make trade-offs between desirable goals:

▼ Recognizing the nature of the trade-offs required to resolve an ethical conflict is the primary step in the ethical decision-making process.

After you have identified the trade-offs, you must bring your own—or your firm's—ethical standards to bear on the decision. You must decide whether one goal is more important or fundamental than one or more other goals, and you must minimize, as much as possible, any modification or sacrificing of that goal.

The ethical trade-offs that businesspersons normally face are not clear-cut between "good" and "bad" alternatives, but often have costs and benefits that can be assessed. By definition, ethical dilemmas arise only when two or more *ethical* goals come into conflict. In many cases, the trade-off will concern social versus economic goals of an organization. For example, assume that a corporate executive has to decide whether to approve the sale of a new product that would be beneficial for most consumers but that might have undesirable side effects for a small percentage of its users. In this situation, the trade-off is obvious: on the one hand, to expose an unknown but extremely small number of individuals to possible harm while allowing all other consumers to enjoy the benefits of the new product (and, in the process, allowing the company to make higher profits) or, on the other hand, to protect that small number of individuals from possible harm and prevent all other consumers from enjoying the benefits of the new product.

8. R. M. Kanter, "Values and Economics," *Harvard Business Review*, May–June 1990, p. 4.

Type I versus Type II Errors In statistics, the trade-off in the sale of the new product is known as a trade-off between Type I and Type II errors. A **Type I error** occurs because of the sin of *commission*. When the new product is sold and there is an undesirable side effect—a customer becomes sick or is injured—the harm occurs because of the sin of commission. In contrast, if the product is not introduced in the marketplace, a **Type II error** will occur. Type II errors result from the sin of *omission*. All of the benefits that people would have derived had the product been introduced do not exist if the product is not marketed.

Let us take a specific example that involves a pharmaceutical company. The firm has developed a new medication that is very effective in the treatment of high blood pressure. The only problem is that the company estimates that one user in a million may have a violent allergic reaction to the drug, which might result in death. The trade-off here is between the Type I error (the one-in-a-million chance that someone will suffer or even die as a result of using the medication) and the Type II error (that people may die from cardiovascular disease or other problems resulting from high blood pressure if the new medication is never introduced into the marketplace).

Because, in this case, Type I errors can be observed and linked directly to the new medication, they are usually the ones that make the headlines. In contrast, Type II errors resulting from the nonintroduction of the new medication into the marketplace are not easily calculated. There have been estimates of Type II errors for nonintroductions of similar medications. One estimate claimed that a delay in government approval of beta-blockers that treat hypertension and other cardiovascular disease between 1967 and 1976 could be blamed for more than ten thousand deaths annually.[9] Because it is difficult to predict what would have happened accurately, however, there is simply no widely acceptable way to measure how much suffering and dying occur because a new medication is withheld from the marketplace.

WHY MANAGERS MAKE INCORRECT ETHICAL DECISIONS

As Kohlberg's theory of the six stages of moral development suggested (see Chapter 4), a number of different factors influence how any individual manager approaches a trade-off situation. The values we accumulate—from family and friends, cultural traditions, educational and religious experiences, and legal and governmental decree—all affect our decision-making process in any situation. Businesspersons must also deal with the value systems imposed on them by stakeholder groups, including owners, customers, suppliers, employees, the community, activist groups, unions, government agencies, and even the natural environment.

With all the various pressures, internal and external, it is not surprising that managers make some incorrect ethical decisions. It happens all the time; just look at the business section of your local newspaper. It would be rash to assume that managers don't know when they are acting unethically, yet it would also be overly cynical to assume that all businesspersons are inherently unethical and will choose profits over morals every time.

Ethical Self-Testing Saul Gellerman, former dean of the University of Dallas Graduate School of Management, has tried to explain why "good" managers stray from the ethical path. His basic theory rests on four common rationalizations used to excuse misconduct:

---

9. P. Brimelow and L. Spencer, "Food and Drugs and Politics," *Forbes*, November 22, 1993, p. 115.

1. A belief that the activity is within reasonable ethical and legal limits—that it is not "really" illegal or immoral.
2. A belief that the activity is in the individual's or the corporation's best interests—that the individual would somehow be expected to undertake the activity.
3. A belief that the activity is "safe" because it will never be found out or publicized.
4. A belief that because the activity helps the company, the company will condone it and even protect the person who engages in it.[10]

By using the term *rationalizations*, Gellerman broadly hints that managers do know when they make an unethical decision but convince themselves to the contrary. His advice to fight the temptation to make such decisions is simple: when in doubt, don't.

If it were that simple, however, there wouldn't be a need in this textbook for four chapters on business ethics and corporate social responsibility. There are other, more involved methods of arguing with oneself about the ethics of a business decision. They revolve around a set of tests to help managers steer clear of actions they may later regret:

▶ **Publicity test.** How would you feel if your decision or the results of your decision were to make it onto the front page of the newspaper or the local television news?
▶ **Trusted friend test.** How would a spouse, family member, or friend with the courage to give you an honest answer react if you explained your decision to one of them?
▶ **Reciprocity test.** How would you feel if you were one of the parties affected by this decision? (Notice the influence of Kant.)

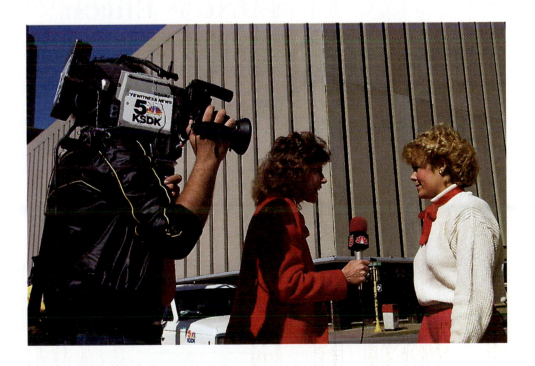

10. S. W. Gellerman, "Why 'Good' Managers Make Bad Ethical Choices," *Harvard Business Review*, July–August 1986, p. 88.

▶ **Universality test.** What would be the result if everyone made the same decision? (Again, notice Kant's influence.)

▶ **Obituary test.** How would you feel about leaving behind the results of this decision as a legacy?[11]

Again, these kinds of ethical self-tests rely on individual values. There will always be a small number of businesspersons who do not care that a close friend will tell them that defrauding customers is wrong, or who are unconcerned that they may leave behind a legacy as an embezzler. These individuals will not be helped by Gellerman's tests, at least as he envisioned them.

Organizational Values In the end, there is one test of values on which every manager can rely: his or her continued employment. Every business has its own set of organizational values, and almost by definition an employee must, at a minimum, perform according to those values to keep drawing a paycheck. The very fact that a manager is able to rise to that position on the corporate ladder indicates that he or she has acquired, or at least accepted, a set of value norms from the organization. (Whether those organizational values are in keeping with those of society as a whole is, of course, another question, as is whether those values lead to "bad" decisions by the organization's managers.) In the second part of this chapter, we examine just how an organizational, or corporate, culture is formed, and what part ethics plays in its formation.

CREATING AN ETHICAL CORPORATE CULTURE

Fortune has noted a new trend in corporate offices around the country: an easing of strict business dress codes. Large corporations such as General Dynamics, H. J. Heinz, Allstate Insurance, and PepsiCo have instituted "dress down" days. Over twelve thousand companies participated in the fourth annual Casual Day fund raiser for United Cerebral Palsy Associates. The market research firm NPD Group found that morale increases in 61 percent of workers who are allowed to trade in suits for jeans.[12]

Creating an ethical corporate culture is not as simple as changing dress codes, but the need in today's world to create such an environment is greater than even the need for a drastic increase in staff morale.[13] The corporation cannot dictate the values of its employees outside the office, but it can take steps to influence those values in managers who are making business decisions. In short,

▼ **You can take two managers with the same core values and place them in different corporate cultures, and there is no guaranty they will react the same way to a given ethical challenge. A corporation's success will ultimately be reflected in the overall ethical standards of the culture it has created.**[14]

---

11. *Integrity and Management*, Harvard Business School Case No. 9-392-005, 1992.

12. E. Schonfeld, "Dress Codes Unravel," *Fortune*, June 27, 1994, p. 16.

13. M. Hatch, "The Dynamics of Organizational Culture," *Academy of Management Review*, October 1993, p. 657.

14. P. Flanagan, "The ABCs of Changing Corporate Culture," *Management Review*, July 1995, p. 57.

THE NEED FOR ETHICAL MANAGERS

Police departments that are understaffed have been known to play a sort of trick on motorists. A department will place an empty police car at an intersection or stretch of highway. Unsuspecting drivers automatically slow down at the first glimpse of the car, responding to the sight of authority even though no actual authority exists; they could fly by the empty police car at 100 miles per hour with no legal consequences.

Business executives need to create the same sense of authority as the empty police car; they cannot be watching over their employees every minute of the business day, but their ethical presence needs to be ubiquitous. The ethical and moral tone for a corporate culture is modeled on the principles of upper-level management (see *Exhibit 5–1* on page 116).

HOW EXECUTIVES SHAPE THE CORPORATE CULTURE

A leader in any institution is important. A leader in a business organization is important for obvious reasons, not the least of which is the way in which he or she influences the corporate culture. Organizational behavior specialists Debra L. Nelson and James Campbell Quick have presented five ways in which corporate leaders influence those who work with them:

1. By the issues that leaders show are the most important.
2. By the way in which leaders react to crises.
3. By the general behavior of leaders.
4. By the reward system that leaders use.
5. By the hiring and firing practices of leaders.[15]

Issues That Leaders Show Are Most Important If the leader of a business organization focuses on cost cutting, others will take notice. If a leader focuses on seeking out new markets abroad, others will take notice. If a business leader focuses on weeding out product buyers who take "gifts" (that is, kickbacks) from sellers, others will take notice. For example, although they were eventually forced to soften their stance, the founders of Ben and Jerry's Homemade, Inc., an ice cream company, set a standard of egalitarianism by limiting executive salaries (see *Managing Social Issues—Culture Shock at Ben and Jerry's* on page 117).

Similarly, the examples set by Leo Burnett, founder of the largest advertising agency in the United States, still dominate that company's corporate culture, even though Burnett retired in 1967. During staff meetings at Leo Burnett Company, disputes are often solved by invoking the phrase, "What would Leo think?" Employees still use the black pencils favored by Burnett, and a small book expounding the founder's wisdom, called *The 100 Leos*, has been published. In fact, when forming the company's *Operating Principles* in 1988, executives used quotations from Burnett's surviving memos. Hence, Burnett's ideals—such as employing "only talented, idea-oriented people with high standards" and striving to "be recognized as the best advertising agency in every market where we do business"—have been codified in operating principles that hang in every employee's

---

15. Debra L. Nelson and James Campbell Quick, *Organizational Behavior: Foundations, Realities, and Challenges* (St. Paul: West Publishing Co., 1994), pp. 497–499.

▼ **EXHIBIT 5–1**
Ethical Principles for Business Executives

Principle	Behavior
1. Honesty	Ethical executives never deliberately mislead or deceive others by partial truths, misrepresentations, selective omissions, or overstatements.
2. Integrity	Ethical executives always do what they think is right, even when circumstances might dictate otherwise. Not only will they stick to their beliefs but they also will fight for them.
3. Promise keeping and trustworthiness	Ethical executives fulfill not only the letter but the spirit of their promises. They can be trusted always to apply relevant information and to correct misunderstandings of fact.
4. Loyalty	Ethical executives remain loyal to individuals and institutions even through adverse times. They never reveal confidential information for personal advantage. If they choose to accept alternative employment, they give their current employer sufficient notice and never utilize confidential trade secrets in their new employment.
5. Fairness	Ethical executives never exercise power arbitrarily. They have a commitment to justice and equal treatment for all. They are tolerant and open minded.
6. Concern for others	Ethical executives live by the Golden Rule—"Do unto others as you would have them do unto you." They help those in need. They achieve business objectives in a way that causes the least harm and the most good.
7. Respect for others	Ethical executives respect the interests, rights, and privacy of those who have an interest in a business decision. They treat everyone with equal dignity regardless of national origin, race, creed, or religion.
8. Law abidance	Ethical executives follow the law.
9. Commitment to excellence	Ethical executives actively seek excellence and attempt to improve their productivity at all times.
10. Leadership	Ethical executives know that they are in a position of leadership and wish always to create a positive ethical role for others.
11. Reputation and morale	Ethical executives actively pursue the development of their organization's good reputation. They engage in conduct that promotes the high morale of that organization's employees.
12. Accountability	Ethical executives accept personal responsibility for the ethical quality of their decisions.

SOURCE: *Ethics: Easier Said Than Done,* Vol. 2, No. 1, 1989, published by Josephon Institute of Ethics.

▣ MANAGING SOCIAL ISSUES

CULTURE SHOCK AT BEN AND JERRY'S

In the business world, a corporate culture ultimately relies on profits for growth. In the mid-1990s, this fact caught up with Ben and Jerry's Homemade, Inc., the ice cream company whose growth during the 1980s was made even more impressive by a corporate culture that based itself on social responsibility and egalitarianism in the workplace.

Corporate Culture at Ben and Jerry's

Ben Cohen and Jerry Greenfield started Ben and Jerry's in a Burlington, Vermont, storefront in 1977. The company, which offers its customers unusual flavors such as Heath Bar Crunch and Cherry Garcia, has gained a reputation as the paragon of the socially minded corporation.

Cohen, as CEO, and Greenfield, as vice chairperson, developed a corporate culture based on service to their community and the environment. Ben and Jerry's buys milk only from Vermont companies. It refuses to use milk from cows fed bovine growth hormone because of the belief that such agricultural technology hurts family farms and may be unhealthful.

The company also spurned the trend of ever-escalating upper-management salaries. In the company's first sixteen years of existence, the highest-paid officer was not allowed to make more than seven times the wages of the lowest-paid full-time worker.

Policy Change

In its seventeenth year, however, that policy changed. Despite more than a hundred franchises and $140 million in sales, by the mid-1990s the company's performance was flagging. Sales slowed, and the company was losing market shares to Haagen-Dazs Company, which sold the best-selling brand of gourmet ice cream in the United States.

In the summer of 1994, Cohen responded to these difficulties by resigning as CEO. He told the *Wall Street Journal*, "In the future, we'll have sales of $200 million or $300 million. I don't think I have the skills to lead our company in that direction."

And, he announced, in its attempt to lure in someone with those skills, the company would be abandoning its seven-to-one pay ratio rules. Based on the $19,000 salary of an ice cream scooper, the new CEO, under the old rules, would not be able to make more than Cohen's 1993 salary of $133,212. The average salary of CEOs at major corporations the previous year was over $1 million. "This decision was the hardest one that the board has ever made and is very hard for [the] Ben and Jerry's staff to hear," Cohen admitted.

The company was careful to make clear that this change in salary structure would have little, if any, effect on its populist corporate culture. The new CEO would, Cohen insisted, be someone who "has the skills and vision to see around the corners of our future business development and has always wanted to wear jeans to work."

For Critical Analysis:

Why couldn't Ben and Jerry's lure a high-powered, effective new CEO with the same salary structure, but in addition, a generous stock option plan that would allow the new CEO to benefit monetarily from future growth in sales and profits?

SOURCE: Information from W. M. Bulkeley, "Ben & Jerry's Is Looking for Ben's Successor," *Wall Street Journal*, June 14, 1994, p. B10; and J. Mathews, "Ben & Jerry's Melting Social Charter," *Washington Post*, June 14, 1994, p. D3.

office. In fact, the last principle states, "We will operate, at all times, in an ethical and moral manner *as if Leo were looking over our shoulders.*"[16] [Emphasis added.]

How Leaders React to Crises The corporate culture is truly put to the test when a crisis strikes. The way an organization's leader reacts during a crisis time transmits immediate

16. P. Jones and L. Kahaner, *Say It and Live It* (New York: Currency/Doubleday, 1995), pp. 44–47.

information about the corporate culture to all those who work around him or her.[17] At no other time is learning so intense.

Consider two different types of reactions to a crisis. When the Food and Drug Administration (FDA) claimed that there might be excessive levels of a potentially dangerous chemical in Perrier mineral water, the leaders of the parent company in France, Source Perrier, S.A., could have turned a deaf ear or fought the FDA. Instead, in 1990 they recalled all existing Perrier supplies, thereby incurring millions of dollars in losses. They then shipped new bottles throughout the world and engaged in a massive advertising campaign stressing their commitment to safety. Perrier's sales rebounded remarkably, showing that the company's customers had kept faith in the safety of its products.

In 1994, when word began filtering into the Intel Corporation that its Pentium computer chip had a bug that caused errors in mathematical calculations, Intel Chairman Andrew S. Grove reacted quite differently. He insisted publicly that the imperfection would affect only highly complex mathematical functions, and that most customers would only experience a problem from it once in every 27,000 years.[18] Intel initially refused to replace the flawed chips unless customers could prove that they were directly affected by the bug. It wasn't until IBM refused to ship any more PCs with the allegedly flawed Pentium chip that Intel was forced to come forth with more information about the problem. (Ultimately, Intel offered to replace any Pentium chips that customers wanted replaced, free of charge.)

Clearly, the reactions of the leaders of Perrier and Intel when faced with a crisis were quite different. How they reacted sent quite different signals to all of the employees in their organizations.[19]

The General Behavior of Leaders Employees look to their organizations' leaders for ideas about appropriate behavior. Leaders, through their teaching, coaching, and role-playing, create the values of their organization (see the *Case—Herbert D. Kelleher and Southwest Airlines*—at the end of this chapter). For example, Joseph P. Sullivan, chairman of Vigoro Corporation, a Chicago-based fertilizer and farm supply company, gives $500,000 to charitable causes a year, the equivalent of his annual salary. He is a major donor to programs ranging from the American Refugee Committee, which sends American doctors and nurses to refugee camps around the world, to a theater troupe from Santa Fe, New Mexico, composed of teenagers whose families have been shattered by substance abuse. Sullivan applies the same principles to Vigoro. He routinely offers incentive bonuses to employees who work at the company's rural farm-center stores, and also offers free counseling for workers with emotional and substance abuse problems.[20]

The Reward System That Leaders Use Do leaders simply give salary increases based on years of performance? Or do they give salary increases based solely on merit? The answers to these questions will elucidate, to some extent, the corporate culture. If leaders pay people only according to years of service, then employees have little incentive to "put out 110 percent." In contrast, if leaders reward only through merit, then employees are basically forced to be productive and innovative, or their salaries will fall behind

---

17. A. A. Marcus and R. S. Goodman, "Victims and Shareholders: The Dilemmas of Presenting Corporate Policy during a Crisis," *Academy of Management Journal*, June 1991, p. 281.

18. D. S. Jackson and J. Van Tassel, "When the Chips Are Down," *Time*, December 26, 1994–January 2, 1995, p. 126.

19. P. F. Mahoney, "It's an Emergency—Do We Have a Plan? (Crisis Management Techniques for Business)," *Management Review*, January 1993, p. 45.

20. R. A. Melcher, "A Rainmaker for Human Rights," *Business Week*, May 16, 1994, p. 122.

those of their colleagues. A reward system, however, can work against ethical behavior in a corporate culture. Frequently, emphasis on meeting sales targets can drive managers to unethical, and even illegal, measures.

Also important is whether employees perceive the reward system as being used randomly or unfairly versus consistently and fairly. Employees who believe that reward standards are applied consistently and fairly will usually react positively to a corporate culture—even if they disagree with the basis for the rewards. However, nepotism or any other form of favoritism in a corporate culture that does not seem to reward merit will negatively affect employee morale and performance. In short,

▼ **Leaders manage best when they give clear signals about how employees are rewarded and follow through on those signals.**

Exhibit 5–2 summarizes the strengths and weaknesses of the three reward systems most commonly used in corporations today.

▼ **EXHIBIT 5–2 Strengths and Weaknesses of Contemporary Reward Systems**

Reward System	Aspects	Strengths	Weaknesses
Flexible benefits plan	A flexible benefits plan allows employees to choose what benefits they want, rather than having management choose for them. For example, an employee can choose to take benefits entirely in cash, partly in health insurance, partly in retirement plans, or partly in stock.	Plans are tailored to fit employee needs, so this system improves morale and performance.	Tailoring plans to employee needs can be complicated and therefore costly.
Banking time off	Given that time off with pay is very attractive to many employees, in this system good performance is rewarded by time off. Employees can "bank" this time off—save it over a period of time—for accumulated use.	Being contingent on an employee's performance, this system should improve that performance.	This system requires that an organization give more time off to its best performers.
Skill-based pay	Provides increased compensation for employees who improve their work-related skills while on the job.	Employees must learn and use new skills to increase their pay, thereby increasing the overall skill level in the corporation.	Training costs to improve employee skills can be high. Furthermore, labor costs will increase with a more skilled work force.

SOURCE: E. E. Lawler III, *Strategic Pay* (San Francisco: Jossey-Bass, 1990).

Hiring and Firing Practices of Leaders If a business organization's leaders always go outside to fill openings for top management positions, it generates a particular type of organizational culture.[21] Managers then realize that the positions at the top of the organization chart may never be available to them. They may always think, consciously or not, in terms of where else they will go to work when they have reached the "end of the line."

If, in contrast, an organization has a history of promoting from within to fill upper-level management positions, it creates a very different culture. Typically, it tends to foster a more creative and productive environment, because managers know they always have the chance of moving up the ladder of managerial success.

How, why, and when employees and managers are fired within an organization are also important in creating a caring corporate culture. When managers are allowed to fire people just before important holidays, such as Christmas, it generates a signal to other members of the organization. When corporate firings seem capricious and arbitrary, that too generates a set of signals and fosters a climate of fear and anxiety—which is not conducive to high productivity. When firings are carried out fairly, according to well-established guidelines for warning individual employees and managers about their performance problems—and when these guidelines are followed consistently—it will foster a particular type of business organization culture.

Fairness is the watchword here: Are the firing practices of the organization fair to everyone concerned?

SOCIALIZATION OF THE CORPORATE CULTURE

Despite the importance of the executive in a corporate culture, there are limits to a leader's influence. A strong corporate culture needs an underlying ethical atmosphere that can exist independently of top management. This is achieved through **socialization,** or the process in which people are taught the values and rules of a society or business. "Socialized" motorists will slow down at the sight of a police car, even an empty one, because since they were small children, they have been taught that if you speed past a police car, you will get a ticket. The power of the empty police car is only reinforced by the fact that a significant percentage of motorists have received speeding tickets at some point in their driving experience.

Corporate socialization relies upon similar principles of learning and reinforcement. A particular manager may have a reputation for being extremely displeased with any subordinate who arrives at the office later than the manager. Through a process of socialization, which may include warnings from co-workers and a few stern lectures from the manager, new employees will learn at what time they should be sure to make their appearance.

There are numerous stages in the socialization process within a corporate culture. Nelson and Quick have developed three stages of such a process: (1) anticipatory socialization, (2) encounter, and (3) change and acquisition.[22]

Anticipatory Socialization Stage The first stage of the socialization process occurs before a new employee's first day on the job. Anticipatory socialization encompasses the preconceived notions and expectations that a newcomer receives from contact with a personnel officer and others in the organization. According to Nelson and Quick, the two key aspects of anticipatory socialization are *realism* and *congruence.*

---

21. C. M. Pearson and I. I. Mitroff, "From Crisis Prone to Crisis Prepared: A Framework for Crisis Management," *Academy of Management Executive,* February 1993, p. 48.
22. Nelson and Quick, *op. cit.,* pp. 500–502.

Realism is the degree to which the new employee has realistic expectations concerning the corporate culture he or she is entering. Information concerning the organizational values should be passed on during anticipatory socialization in order to help the new employee prepare for the employment situation. Obviously, the person will acquire a deeper understanding of the corporate culture the longer he or she is on the job.

Congruence has two parts. First, there must be congruence between the new employee's abilities and the demands of the upcoming employment. Secondly, the values of the organization and the values of the newcomer must harmonize. It is important that the latter concern be given equal weight with the former, because a new employee who does not fit into the corporate culture can be a disruptive influence. In some cultures, such as in South Korea, personal values are a determining factor in employment. The Hanjin group, which includes Korean Airlines (KAL), for example, requires patriotism and professionalism in its new employees. At KAL, employees are expected to act as civilian diplomats, with polished manners, refined speech, and a mastery of at least one foreign language. Female employees are forbidden to wear jeans even off duty.[23]

Encounter Stage The instant the new employee starts a job, he or she enters the encounter stage of socialization. It typically lasts six to nine months, or even a year. During this period, the values of the corporate culture are instilled in the employee. New employees face three basic demands that will determine their success on the job:

1. Role demands. New employees may not know exactly where they fit in, and therefore they may suffer role uncertainty. They may be told one thing by one worker and other things by another worker, and therefore might experience role conflict. In any event, during the encounter stage, they will sort out conflicting ideas about their roles until they settle into the roles that the corporate culture expects of them.

2. Task demands. Every new employee has a job to do—a set of tasks. Because of on-the-job learning, new employees will overcome any problems with their task demands during the second stage of socialization. (If not, they may either quit or be fired.)

3. Interpersonal demands. All new employees find themselves in one or more interpersonal relationships at work. These include relationships with equals; subordinates; superiors; and employees in other departments whom they meet casually in social settings, such as in the lunchroom. How well a new employee is able to handle interpersonal demands may determine whether he or she advances within the corporate organization.

Change and Acquisition Stage At the end of the encounter stage, a third and final stage of socialization begins—change and acquisition. Now new employees are no longer considered new but rather have mastered the demands of their jobs. They have negotiated and clarified their roles and do well at the required tasks. At this point, they are also expected to have incorporated the values of the corporate culture, and perhaps imparted some of their own values to the organization (see *Exhibit 5–3* on page 122).

Organizational Rites and Rituals Just as motorists who do not speed are remunerated by not getting speeding tickets and by eventually receiving lower insurance rates, employees who comply with the values of a corporate culture usually receive rewards.

---

23. S. M. Lee, S. Yoo, and T. M. Lee, "Korean Chaebols: Corporate Values and Strategies," *Organizational Dynamics*, 1991, pp. 36–50.

▼ **EXHIBIT 5–3**
The Organizational Socialization Process: Stages and Outcomes

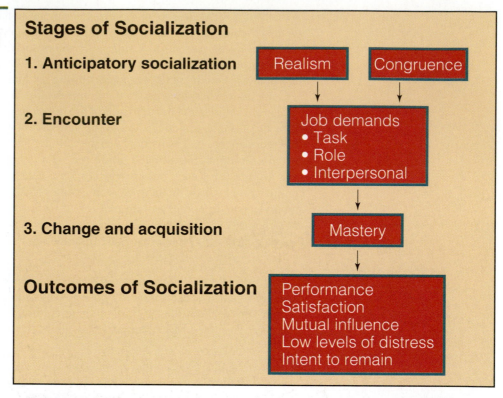

Stages of Socialization

1. **Anticipatory socialization** — Realism / Congruence

2. **Encounter** — Job demands
   • Task
   • Role
   • Interpersonal

3. **Change and acquisition** — Mastery

Outcomes of Socialization
Performance
Satisfaction
Mutual influence
Low levels of distress
Intent to remain

SOURCE: Debra L. Nelson and James Campbell Quick, *Organizational Behavior: Foundations, Realities, and Challenges* (St. Paul: West Publishing Co., 1994), p. 501, Figure 16.2. (Reprinted with permission.)

The most obvious form of reward is continued employment and increased salary, but for the sake of socialization, many businesses use rites and rituals to show appreciation for exemplary behavior. There are at least six types of organizational rites:

1. *Rites of passage*, such as promotion, show that an employee's status has changed.

2. *Rites of enhancement*, such as the awarding of a valued corner office, show that an employee has been properly rewarded for adherence to the values of the corporation.

3. *Rites of renewal* celebrate growth and change in an organization. Recognition dinners or office parties in honor of particular employees are popular rites of renewal.

4. *Rites of integration* gather together the diverse units of a corporate culture to emphasize a sense of shared commitment within an organization. Organizations are now attempting to promote this integration through management retreats or seminars that attempt to bring together employees outside the confines of the workplace.

5. *Rites of conflict reduction* help deal with the conflicts or disagreements that inevitably occur in corporate cultures. Again, corporations are increasingly turning outside the normal organizational setting for management retreats or seminars that focus on conflict resolution.

6. *Rites of degradation*, such as demotion or the retraction of duties, show punishment for persons who fail to respect the values of the corporate culture.[24]

How well a company can succeed in establishing these rites as an integral part of the corporate culture can have a measurable effect on its profitability. Some companies, such

---

24. H. M. Trice and J. M. Beyer, "Studying Organizational Cultures through Rites and Ceremonials," *Academy of Management Review*, Vol. 9, 1984, pp. 653–669.

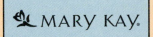

COMPANY FOCUS: MARY KAY COSMETICS
A RITUAL OF SUCCESS AT MARY KAY COSMETICS

For Mary Kay Ash, founder and chair emeritus of Mary Kay Cosmetics—a Fortune 500 company with over $1.5 billion in annual profits—it all started with Stanley Home Products in the 1940s. As a struggling salesperson, Ash was inspired toward success by a particular Stanley ritual. "Sitting in the back of the room during my first seminar," remembers Ash, "I saw this tall, skinny, pretty, successful woman made queen as a reward for being the best in a company contest and I determined to be that queen the following year." She succeeded in that goal, and her memories of the event have led to one of the most spectacular organizational rituals in the business community.

Seminars

Every summer, nearly forty thousand Mary Kay sales representatives pay a $125 registration fee and their own travel expenses to attend Seminar in Dallas. Each Seminar is elaborately scripted to focus on and enhance the corporation's core values; it is, in Ash's words, "a combination of the Academy Awards, the Miss America pageant, and a Broadway opening." The pomp and circumstance of Seminar is geared toward emphasizing the rewards of hard work and success as a Mary Kay sales representative.

The process of becoming successful begins with a single day of training and a case filled with cosmetics, after which a representative can sell the company's product. Then, if a sales representative recruits another sales representative, she receives a commission on whatever that person is able to sell. If a sales representative brings in thirty recruits and her commissions reach $16,000 over a period of four months, she becomes a director. When she reaches higher goals, she becomes eligible for a number of rewards, including a pink Cadillac. The top sales representatives become national directors and earn an average salary of $279,000.

Rewarding Top Performers

At Seminar, the most successful sales representatives are presented as examples. Each year during Awards Night, Ash distributes $38 million worth of Cadillacs, furs, diamonds, and other awards to the company's top performers of the previous year. The recipients parade on a lighted stage, escorted by males (known as "token men") who work at Mary Kay offices. With a band playing in the background, Ash seats each woman on a throne and places a crown on her head.

Although Ash is traditional in her approach—basing the company, she says, on the Golden Rule and the motto "God first, family second, career third"—Seminar reflects a corporate culture that celebrates the strength and earning power of women. The gathering provides a chance for individual sales representatives to give personal testimonials on how selling Mary Kay products gave them economic freedom and personal liberation from former underpaid jobs. In fact, spouses who accompany sales representatives to Seminar attend "husbands' seminars" for instruction on how to support their wives and deal with the fact that their wives may make more money than they do.

The New Bottom Line

With her Seminar and rewards, Ash has recognized a set of organizational rites that enhance company goals of sales performance, customer satisfaction, and creating a corporate culture in which every employee is given a chance to excel. Ash is aware that in many sectors of the business community, some of her practices are perceived as being ostentatious. She points to her expanding profits in rebuttal. "So you think pink Cadillacs are tacky?" asks a magazine cover on display in the Mary Kay Museum. "What color was the car your company gave you?"

SOURCE: Information from M. K. Ash, *Mary Kay* (New York: Harper & Row, 1981); S. Hollandsworth, "Hostile Makeover," *Texas Monthly*, November 1, 1995, p. 128; T. Dunkel, "The Tupperware Lady Is an M.B.A.," *Working Woman*, April 1, 1995, p. 44; and N. Kruh, "In the Pink," *Atlanta Constitution*, August 29, 1993, p. M1.

as Mary Kay Cosmetics, are defined to some extent by their organizational rites and rituals (see *Company Focus: Mary Kay Cosmetics*).

CORPORATE ETHICS PROGRAMS

Rites and rituals serve a socialization purpose, but a corporation also needs concrete ethics programs to provide its employees with a substantive ethics policy. Three possible parts of an ethics program are the ethics committee, ethics training, and the corporate code of ethics.

The Ethics Committee   A company's ethics committee can have several functions: to establish or recommend policy, to interpret policy, to enforce policy, to serve as an appeals board, or to investigate employees. Usually, the most difficult task of an ethics committee is deciding who will serve on it. The committee must be made up of a mixture of top, middle, and lower management, as well as other employees.

Nancy McReady Higgins, director of corporate ethics policies for Boeing Company in Seattle, warns that there are pros and cons to the inclusion of senior executives on an ethics committee. On the pro side, members of top management lend visibility and credibility to the committee, and their inclusion reinforces the idea that ethics is an important part of the company's policy. The cons focus around the fact that many top executives lack the time to contribute much to an ethics committee and may thus be seen as mere window dressing. Furthermore, the presence of senior management might cause others on the committee to be less than totally honest in criticizing internal ethics.

Higgins proposes three guidelines for forming an ethics committee: (1) decide the committee's specific purpose, which will suggest its membership; (2) choose a structure that will work within the particular company; and (3) choose members who are dedicated to ethics.[25]

Ethics Training   Many companies have found that the best alternative to simply telling an employee to "do the right thing" is an ethics training program. Various surveys show that by the mid-1990s, 30 to 40 percent of American companies were engaged in some sort of ethics training.[26]

The Problem with Ethical "Rules"   According to ethics specialists Dan Rice and Craig Dreilinger, many ethics training programs are doomed to be insufficient because "they easily lend themselves to a focus on the 'thou shalt nots.'" When management provides strict rules, employees tend to learn what they should and should not do in specific situations. However, in the actual business world, situations are rarely as specific as anybody would predict. Rice and Dreilinger believe that ethics training programs should focus on providing broader guidelines that can be applied in situations not covered by "rules."

These two researchers also see flaws in such popular corporate practices as having company ethicists, ethics hot lines, and company officials responsible for handling ethics violations. Although helpful at times, these practices lead to the problem of transferring the ethical responsibility from the employee to some "higher" source, thereby defeating

---

25. *Prevention of Corporate Liability Current Report*, Vol. 2, No. 4 (May 16, 1994), p. 10.
26. L. A. Berger, "Train All Employees to Solve Ethical Dilemmas," *Life-Health Insurance Edition*, March 1, 1995, p. 70.

their purpose. The aim of ethics programs, say Rice and Dreilinger, should be "to provide employees with the tools they need to identify ethical issues and to work out how to resolve them."[27]

Situational Ethics Training Consultant Lawrence Berger believes that the most effective form of ethics training is to give employees a "simple set of procedures" to guide ethical decision making (see *Exhibit 5–4*). An employee who follows these guidelines can apply the precepts of ethical decision making to whatever situation arises.

There are a number of methods for training employees to use guidelines such as those in *Exhibit 5–4*. Berger suggests providing trainees with case studies of ethically challenging situations that have occurred within their particular industry, and then having them apply the guidelines in other environments.[28] Unisys Corporation has developed a *Handbook of Ethical Business Practices* that focuses not only on specific rules but also on "rules of thumb" to handle the "gray areas" of consulting for the federal government. All employees to whom the rules are relevant are required to review the handbook through a series of small-group discussions.[29]

▼ **EXHIBIT 5–4**
An Ethical Decision-Making Model

Steps	Considerations
1. Identify the problem.	What makes it an ethical problem? Think in terms of rights, obligations, fairness, relationships, and integrity. How would you define the problem if you stood on the other side of the fence?
2. Identify the stakeholders.	Who has been hurt? Who could be hurt? Who could be helped? Are they willing players, or are they victims? Can you negotiate with them?
3. Diagnose the situation.	How did it happen in the first place? What could have prevented it? Is it going to get worse or better? Can the damage be undone?
4. Analyze your options.	Imagine the range of possibilities. Limit yourself to the two or three most manageable. What are the likely outcomes of each? What are the likely costs?
5. Make your choice.	What is your intention in making this decision? How does it compare with the probable results? Can you discuss the problem with the affected parties before you act? Could you disclose without qualms your decision to your boss, the CEO, the board of directors, your family, or society as a whole?
6. Act.	Do what you have to do. Don't be afraid to admit errors. Be as bold in confronting a problem as you were in causing it (if that is indeed the case).

SOURCE: L. A. Berger, "Train All Employees to Solve Ethical Dilemmas," *Life-Health Insurance Edition*, March 1, 1995, p. 70.

27. D. Rice and C. Dreilinger, "Rights and Wrongs of Ethics Training," *Training and Development*, May 1, 1990, p. 103.
28. Berger, *op. cit.*
29. W. N. Hunter, "Ethics Training Program Builds Credibility for Unisys," *Government Computer News*, August 21, 1989, p. 83.

Other organizations have tried to add some levity to their ethics training programs by presenting them in the form of games. Citicorp, Inc., for example, has created The Work Ethic, a board game in which participants strive to correctly solve legal, regulatory, policy-related, and judgment ethics questions. Martin Marietta has its own version of a role-playing ethics contest with Gray Matters (see *Managing Social Issues—Making a Difference: Playing Games at Martin Marietta*).

Corporate Ethical Codes Another integral part of a corporate ethics program, and a way for everyone in a company to be aware of the ethical standards expected of employees, is for that company to create, print, and distribute a **code of ethics**.[30] In 1968, about a third of companies polled had ethical codes. By 1970, about three-fourths had such codes, and today well over 90 percent of the Fortune 500 companies have ethical codes of conduct. Indeed, such codes have become a permanent fixture in the business policymaking landscape. (See the foldout of the PriceCostco Code of Ethics for an example.)

In general, ethical codes provide employees with the knowledge of what their firm expects in terms of their responsibilities and behavior. Relationships that are covered include employee-employee, employee-manager, employee-consumer, and employee-supplier relationships. Some ethical codes offer a lengthy and detailed set of guidelines for employees. Others are not really codes at all but rather summary statements of goals, policies, and priorities. Some companies have their codes framed and hung on office walls or printed on sets of cards to be carried at all times by executives.

Do Ethical Codes Work? Do ethical codes really result in more ethical behavior on the part of employees? Many believe that they do. Johnson & Johnson has a widely lauded code of ethics, which was given much of the credit for the company's praiseworthy reaction to the Tylenol disaster of 1982 (see *Exhibit 5–5* on page 128). The crisis arose when some bottles of the company's popular nonaspirin pain reliever were tampered with and the product was contaminated with cyanide, which caused the deaths of several persons in Chicago. When top managers at J&J were informed of the problem, they immediately formed a committee to handle the crisis. Following the company's credo, the committee created a set of priorities, the first one being to assure the safety of its customers. To this end, the committee recalled Tylenol from the market until the company could develop tamper-resistant packaging for its product.

The second priority was to communicate openly with the buying public about what had happened and why it had happened. This was done through numerous press releases, press conferences, and printed statements, as well as television and radio interviews. The third priority was to maintain the company's goodwill and reputation.

Some thought, at the time, that J&J would never recover its former lead in the pain-reliever market. The doubters were wrong. J&J was profitable again by 1987. In 1990, eight years after the disaster, Tylenol products made up 31 percent of the domestic market for painkillers,[31] thanks in no small part to an adherence to the company's ethics code. J&J's credo is specific enough to provide guidance, yet general enough to apply to a wide range of situations and crises. Furthermore, it reflects values that seem to have been clearly instilled in upper management. Chairman James Burke said, "After the crisis was

---

30. G. R. Weaver, "Corporate Codes of Ethics: Purpose, Process, and Content Issues," *Business and Society*, Spring 1993, p. 44.
31. K. Deveny, "Painkiller Ads Strive to Give Foes Headaches," *Wall Street Journal*, January 23, 1990, p. B1.

MANAGING SOCIAL ISSUES

MAKING A DIFFERENCE: PLAYING GAMES AT MARTIN MARIETTA

Consider the following scenario: On Sunday, you host an anniversary party for your brother and sister-in-law. The celebration runs well into the early morning and causes you to oversleep and miss the next morning at work. When confronted by your superior after lunch, do you (1) claim illness; (2) invent an emergency; or (3) tell the truth, however embarrassing it may be?

If you chose Number 3—the most important ethical value, after all, is honesty—then you would be on your way up the career ladder to success in the board game Gray Matters. Designed by the ethics office at the defense industry giant Martin Marietta, the game is aimed at giving employees an enjoyable manner in which to deal with a serious concern in their industry.

The Challenges of the Game

In the summer of 1992, Martin Marietta spent $10,000 to produce five hundred copies of Gray Matters and made the game available to employees either through a lending program or a $25 purchase. The game consists of fifty-five ethically challenging scenarios; it deducts or awards points to players according to their answers. Some of the situations in Gray Matters, such as the oversleeping example offered above, are industry neutral. Other conundrums along a similar vein ask players how they would react to their boss's spending too much office time on personal affairs, or to discovering that a co-worker is using drugs while on the job. (The boss is to be confronted and reported to the company's ethics office, whereas the drug user is to be steered to the company's employee assistance program.)

Gray Matters also contains scenarios that are specific to the defense industry and therefore are more likely to occur during the career of a Martin Marietta employee. How would an employee respond, for example, if a U.S. Army program manager offered the use of a new beach home "with no strings attached"? The player who accepts the offer, even if he or she made rental payments, is deducted points for activity that could be construed as unethical. The player who politely refuses by saying it "just wouldn't look right" is awarded ten points. The score of the player who chooses to refuse but gives no reason is not affected.

Finding "Something Different"

George Sammet, vice president of Martin Marietta's ethics office, envisioned the game as "Gershwinian, not Wagnerian—something that people would want to play, that they'd want to take home to their families." The game did prove popular with employees. One said that when colleagues played, there were "a lot of heated discussions when we didn't agree on what was the right answer." The game was also popular with other members of the business community. Martin Marietta shipped thirty-five copies of the Gray Matters game to other corporations, and even ten universities requested a copy. Sammet does not foresee any more production runs of the game, however. "Who knows what I might do tomorrow," he says. "When you're doing ethics training, you've got to do something different."

For Critical Analysis:

If establishing an ethical corporate culture is so important for Martin Marietta, shouldn't the company have given away the game rather than charging employees $25?

SOURCE: R. N. Meyers, "At Martin Marietta, This Board Game Is Lesson in Ethics," *Wall Street Journal*, September 25, 1992, p. A5E.

over we realized that no meeting had been called to make the first critical decision. Everyone of us knew what we had to do. We had the *Credo* to guide us."[32]

32. Jones and Kahaner, *op. cit.*, p. 137.

▼ **EXHIBIT 5–5**
Johnson and Johnson's *Credo*

We believe our first responsibility is to the doctors, nurses and patients, to mothers and fathers and all others who use our products and services. In meeting their needs everything we do must be of high quality. We must constantly strive to reduce our costs in order to maintain reasonable prices. Customers' orders must be serviced promptly and accurately. Our suppliers and distributors must have an opportunity to make a fair profit.

We are responsible to our employees, the men and women who work with us throughout the world. Everyone must be considered as an individual. We must respect their dignity and recognize their merit. They must have a sense of security in their jobs. Compensation must be fair and adequate, and working conditions clean, orderly and appropriate. We must be mindful of ways to help our employees fulfill their family responsibilities. Employees must feel free to make suggestions and complaints. There must be equal employment, development and advancement for those qualified. We must provide competent management and their actions must be just and ethical.

We are responsible to the communities in which we live and work and to the world community as well. We must be good citizens—support good works and charities and bear our fair share of taxes. We must encourage civic improvements and better health and education. We must maintain in good order the property we are privileged to use, protecting the environment and natural resources.

Our final responsibility is to our stockholders. Business must make a sound profit. We must experiment with new ideas. Research must be carried on, innovative programs developed and mistakes paid for. New equipment must be purchased, new facilities provided and new products launched. Reserves must be created to provide for adverse time. When we operate according to these principles, the stockholders should realize a fair return.

SOURCE: Johnson & Johnson.

Codes Have Their Critics Of course, the mere existence of a code of ethics does not ensure ethical behavior. Dow Corning had been applauded in the business community for its dedication to ethics as represented by a strong code, yet the company suffered huge monetary losses because of what many saw as a collapse of internal ethics concerning its silicone breast implant manufacture and distribution.

Critics of ethical codes point to examples provided by companies like Dow Corning and claim that many codes are simply legalistic documents that forbid specific actions rather than create an ethical atmosphere. Critics say that the codes often include little more than legalistic rules and platitudes instead of truly important ethical guidelines, because the latter may touch on sensitive issues.

Other critics contend that no matter how good an ethics code is, the code itself has little effect on the ethical attitudes and behavioral patterns of the company's employees. Rather, as we have discussed,

▼ **It is the example set by top management that promotes ethical (or unethical) conduct by other members of the corporate culture. Employees learn what acceptable norms of conduct are by observing top management's behavior.**

A company sends even stronger messages by its rites of passage, such as rewards and punishments. Finally, in most cases, an ethics code is most effective when combined with a thorough ethical training program.

CORPORATE DISCIPLINARY POLICY

As Dow Corning's experience shows, even the best ethics policy can't ensure that a corporate culture will be free of unethical, or even illegal, activities. Where an ethics policy fails, a disciplinary policy must succeed if a business is going to survive.

Companies do not view unethical behavior as being as serious as illegal behavior, so they tend to be more lenient toward employees when questions of ethics are involved. Management consultant N. Elizabeth Fried researched the question of disciplining workplace "cheats" and found that many managers tend to look the other way.

One example Fried uncovered concerned a salesman named Kashra, who did everything in his power to keep his boss, Doug, from traveling with him to visit a zero-sales territory. When the pair got into a company car to make the trip, Kashra faked a heart attack. When that failed to convince Doug not to make the trip, Kashra proceeded to drive the car into a guardrail, nearly killing them both. Unfortunately for Kashra, the impact of the crash popped open the trunk crammed with four months' worth of undelivered customer samples Kashra had been selling at retail. Kashra was fired for "unauthorized use of company property" and "poor performance," but Doug never filed theft charges against him.

In another case, a custodian was allowed to file five workers' compensation claims within two years for a back injury he allegedly suffered while changing a company lightbulb. Management finally investigated the matter when another employee informed the company's manager that the custodian, while on sick leave, was performing on a bucking bronco in a rodeo. [33]

Strict Disciplinary Policy   In many cases, companies try to avoid disciplining employees for unethical behavior because managers see only two possible punishments—demotion or firing—which may seem overly harsh under the circumstances. Michael J. Denton, a lawyer for Allied Signal, Inc., in Petersboro, New Jersey, believes disciplinary policy must go far beyond those two alternatives to be effective.[34] Denton thinks that, after establishing organizational sentencing guidelines, managers must ask three basic questions when involved in any disciplinary situation:

1. Did the employee violate the law, a regulation, or company policy?
2. Was the conduct intentional or negligent?
3. Was there a failure of management responsibility?

Denton also suggests that managers must consider whether the employee admitted to unprompted, unethical conduct and any harm the conduct caused.

After managers have answered these questions, they may choose to fire or demote the employee. Denton, however, offers other, less severe possible punishments. Offenders might be fined, or ordered to study the very guidelines they have broken in order to serve as "ethical facilitators" on the same issues for other employees.

Some observers might find Denton's policy subjective, and it is:

▼ **For a disciplinary policy to be effective, it must be based on the organizational value system that has been accepted by management and employees.**

Without this cultural consensus, a strict disciplinary policy can cause more problems concerning morale than it solves concerning misconduct.

---

33. "Workplace Cheats Get Off Easy, Author Says," *Los Angeles Times*, May 17, 1994, p. D9.
34. *Prevention of Corporate Liability Current Report*, Vol. 2, No. 4 (May 16, 1994), pp. 11–12.

Legal Disciplinary Policy According to Denton, in extreme cases, employees breaking the law must obviously be turned over to authorities for treatment in the justice system. An expert panel that reviewed Fried's research asserted that both Kashra and the custodian should have been handed over to the appropriate authorities. "Prosecution . . . clearly signals to other employees that the company will not tolerate criminal misconduct [and] that employees who engage in such activities will not only lose their jobs but also face the criminal justice system," the panel said.

Self-Policing Many companies with internal ethics violations have found it better to police themselves than be left open to more damaging punishments from state or federal authorities. Self-policing companies routinely receive more lenient treatment from prosecutors than do those who are less vigilant in that area.

Sometimes, the authorities will actually reward self-policing businesses. In North Dakota, for example, environmental prosecutors promise not to use incriminating information against companies that come forward of their own accord. In Illinois, state officials indicate they are willing to drop criminal prosecutions against a company if it voluntarily reports violations.[35]

The most effective tool to promote self-policing is a compliance program. Such a program contains internal audits, surprise inspections, and an outlet for whistleblowing (discussed below), thus providing a quick and effective solution to ethical breakdowns. Fifteen of sixteen state attorney general offices surveyed by the *Wall Street Journal* said that companies with compliance programs are more likely to receive lighter penalties for a wide range of environmental, antitrust, securities, and public-health law violations.[36] Federal sentencing guidelines on white-collar crime reflect similar thinking.

---

35. J. Woo, "Self-Policing Can Pay Off for Companies," *Wall Street Journal*, September 8, 1993, p. B9.
36. *Ibid.*

Executive Liability The legal system is not silent with respect to executive liability for the wrongful acts of employees. Under state law and the Revised Model Business Corporations Act, officers and directors have specified duties of care and loyalty. With those duties are certain liabilities of directors and officers. Those liabilities may indeed, and increasingly do, include responsibility for the wrongful actions of employees who are not properly supervised. Executives can also find themselves liable for employees' actions under what is known as the **law of agency**. An agency is created any time a subordinate is given the right to act on behalf of the superior. In this situation, the executive is the superior, and the employee is the agent. It is well established in the law that the executive is always responsible for any harm caused to a third party by an employee operating in the scope of his or her employment. This is known as the **doctrine of vicarious liability**—liability is without regard to the personal fault of the executive for the wrongs committed by an employee in the course or scope of employment. Liability is imposed on employers because they are deemed to be in a better financial position to bear the loss. The superior financial position carries with it the duty to be responsible for damages.

Executives may find themselves liable even for intentional wrongs that their employees commit while on the job. An executive may find himself or herself liable when an employee commits assault and battery while acting within the scope of employment. An executive who knows or should have known that an employee has the propensity for committing wrongful acts generally is liable for the employee's acts even if they would not ordinarily be considered within the scope of employment. For example, assume that the Blue Moon Bar employs Arnold Muensch as a bouncer, even though the employer is aware that Muensch has a history of arrest for assault and battery. While working one night, and within the scope of his employment, he viciously attacks a patron who "looks at him funny." The Blue Moon Bar will bear the responsibility for Muensch's acts, because the employer knew of this propensity for committing such wrongful acts.

An executive will normally be liable for permitting an employee to engage in reckless acts that could injure others. For example, an employer observes an employee smoking while filling containerized trucks with a highly flammable liquid. Failure to stop the employee will cause the employer to be liable for any injuries that result.

More specifically, Emmett Roe, the owner of an Imperial Food Products poultry plant in Hamlet, North Carolina, was sentenced to twenty years in prison for involuntary manslaughter after the death of twenty-five of his workers. To prevent employees from stealing chicken parts, Roe had ordered emergency exits in the plant to be locked. When a fire broke out in the plant, the employees were unable to escape the building.[37]

WHISTLEBLOWING

If businesses today are more willing to turn in their employees, employees are also more willing to disclose wrongdoing in their companies. **Whistleblowing** occurs when a company employee goes outside the corporate chain of command to upper-level executives within the company to complain about the unethical conduct of other workers or immediate supervisors.[38] Whistleblowing may also take place when an employee reveals his or

---

37. "Poultry Producer Gets 20 Years in Deaths of 25 Workers in Fire," *Washington Post*, September 15, 1992, p. A9.
38. M. P. Miceli and J. P. Near, "Relationships among Value Congruence, Perceived Victimization, and Retaliation against Whistle-Blowers," *Journal of Management*, Winter 1994, p. 773.

her concerns to persons outside the company, such as those in the media or government. In some instances, the government rewards whistleblowers with cash payments. We think of whistleblowers as courageous employees who risk their careers to disclose nefarious practices by their employers. The conduct of whistleblowers is not always desirable or praiseworthy, however; some are motivated by unfounded personal grievances.[39]

Although whistleblowing may occur in the public sector, such as when a Pentagon employee reveals that a particular weapons system has failed to perform satisfactorily, we are concerned here with whistleblowing by employees of private firms (see *Company Focus: General Electric*). The most notorious incidences of whistleblowing in the private sector typically involve revelations by an employee that his or her company consciously overlooked design or manufacturing defects that rendered a particular product unnecessarily dangerous to consumers. For example, if an automobile is defectively designed so that its engine sometimes emits carbon monoxide through the air-conditioning ducts of the dashboard, an employee might feel compelled to reveal the potential hazards to the media or to the appropriate consumer protection agency.

CAREER PROSPECTS FOR WHISTLEBLOWERS

Even the most principled employee would have to consider the potentially adverse consequences that might result from a decision to blow the whistle on a company's product.[40] Whistleblowing employees are often treated as outsiders by their immediate supervisors, as well as by their fellow employees. Furthermore, they may lose their jobs and any hope for a job in the field. For example, a worker who reveals that his company's new jet engine sometimes stalls during takeoff may find not only that his career at the company is over but also that he cannot get a job anywhere else in that industry. Companies are understandably reluctant to hire persons known for "making waves" or publicizing product flaws. Even the most ethical company may fear that such an employee will blow the whistle on a nonexistent or relatively minor product flaw and thus cause the firm to suffer adverse publicity, as well as government investigations and fines.

What happens to the whistleblower who, for whatever reason, is not fired by the company? In general, this person will not be welcomed back by immediate supervisors, because they will consider the employee a traitor who pointed the finger of blame at them by disclosing the shortcomings of a product or policy. They may believe that the disclosure itself inferred that the whistleblower's immediate supervisors were uninterested in the complaint or that they tried to prevent the employee from revealing the problems.

Some employees may resent the whistleblower because of their own guilty feelings about their failure to reveal the flaws in the product or policy, or because they believe that the adverse publicity will affect the company's fortunes and hence the security of their own jobs. Other employees may share the same feelings of betrayal as the whistleblower's immediate supervisors have. The whistleblower, though still employed, may be relegated to less important tasks or transferred to a less important position. Moreover, the frequency of company promotions may slow down considerably.

WHISTLEBLOWING AND LOYALTY

Much of the ostracism whistleblowers face stems from the fact that their revelations, no matter how well intentioned or beneficial to society, may be seen as a breach of loyalty to

---

39. M. P. Miceli and J. P. Near, "Whistleblowing: Reaping the Benefits," *Academy of Management Executive,* August 1994, p. 65.
40. T. Barnett, "Why Your Company Should Have a Whistleblowing Policy," *SAM Advanced Management Journal,* Autumn 1992, p. 37.

COMPANY FOCUS: GENERAL ELECTRIC
THE WHISTLEBLOWER—BOUNTY HUNTER OR PATRIOT?

Chester Walsh learned firsthand a fact about the False Claims Act that critics had long decried: its "carrot and stick" approach to whistleblowing. By bringing evidence to the U.S. Justice Department about the fraudulent behavior of his employer, General Electric Company, Walsh stood to enjoy the carrot of 15 to 25 percent of any financial recovery won by the government. But after GE settled with the government for $69 million, the Justice Department tried to give Walsh a smaller share of the settlement than the law required.

Findings and Reactions

From 1986 to 1990, Walsh gathered information on a scam being orchestrated by GE and Israeli general Rami Dotan, in which high-level GE employees had used phony invoices to divert U.S. aid to Israel into their own, and Dotan's, pockets. The scheme allegedly defrauded the U.S. government of $42 million, and it might have continued had not Walsh smuggled numerous boxes of documents from Tel Aviv to his home in the United States.

Even as GE admitted the wrongdoing, the company tried to paint Walsh as a bounty hunter who had waited until the time was ripe to go public with his information. When Walsh first began to see evidence of the fraud, "only" $15 million had been diverted; by the time he reported the scandal, another $27 million was gone, which increased his share of the ensuing lawsuit. Furthermore, GE officials stated, if only Walsh had come to them with the information first, they would have rectified the situation themselves.

The Justice Department also began casting aspersions on Walsh's character as soon as the government had secured the $69 million from GE. Government lawyers asked a federal judge to decrease Walsh's reward, which could have been as high as $14.9 million under the law, to $4.5 million. The government argued that a reduced amount would "send a strong message that whistle-blowers may not manipulate"

the False Claims Act. The Justice Department went on to claim that an Israeli government investigation "ultimately would have led" U.S. investigators to uncover GE's fraud.

The Ruling of the Court

"The government's position is shocking," countered John R. Phillips, one of Walsh's attorneys. "It will send a scary message to all those who want to expose fraud." For his part, Walsh dismissed charges that he had waited for his own personal gain: "You don't just wake up one morning and take on GE."

Federal judge Carl B. Rubin agreed. In his written order, he said it "would have been difficult, if not impossible, to sustain a case against GE" without Walsh's efforts. He pointed out that not only had another GE employee been reassigned after reporting his suspicions to the corporation, but also that the Federal Bureau of Investigation believed that GE had known about the Israeli fraud for two years without doing anything to stop it.

"This is not the first case where this Court has noted antagonism of the Justice Department to a whistle-blower," wrote Judge Rubin. Whistleblowing "should be encouraged by monetary rewards." He backed up his words by rewarding Walsh with $13.4 million, the largest sum ever given under the False Claims Act.

The New Bottom Line

In rebuttal to General Electric's vilification of Walsh, it could be pointed out that no matter what the financial reward, it must have been difficult for Walsh to decide to give up his career and his corporate friends when he was not even sure he would prevail legally. However, the monetary reward included in the False Claims Act certainly must have affected his decision to blow the whistle, and this reward will continue to offer an incentive for employees to report fraudulent dealings with the government.

SOURCE: Information from A. K. Naj, "Justice Department Seeking to Reduce Reward for Whistle-Blower at GE Unit," *Wall Street Journal*, November 4, 1992, p. A4; and A. K. Naj, "Federal Judge Awards Ex-GE Staffer Record Amount in Whistle-Blower Case," *Wall Street Journal*, December 7, 1992, p. A5.

their employer. Whistleblowing represents a conscious decision by the employee to reveal something believed to be immoral or illegal about the company's products or practices. It forces the employee to step outside the corporate family and essentially renounce membership in the company.

It may be argued, however, that whistleblowing is in fact an act of loyalty, as it is an attempt to improve product quality or avert future liability for the company. In any case, the duty of loyalty owed by an employee can be overstated. The company does provide the worker with a job, but the employment relationship does not require that employees give up their freedom of speech. Employees are free to express opinions that may not be favorably received by their employers.

TRADE-OFFS AND WHISTLEBLOWING

The would-be whistleblower must weigh the costs and benefits of disclosure. Such decisions necessarily involve trade-offs, which in turn depend on the individual's own goals, objectives, and beliefs. Because the decision of the whistleblower to come forward may affect the lives of many people, particularly those who work for the same employer, it is a decision that must be carefully considered. The revelation that the employer has defrauded the government of millions of dollars, for example, will not only affect the whistleblower's own career opportunities but may also result in the discharge of other employees if the disclosures cause the employer's business to drop off significantly. Yet the employee's failure to reveal the fraud might allow it to be continued indefinitely, thereby imposing a hidden—but real—cost on society and, by implication, its taxpayers.

Although people are inclined to support laws that encourage whistleblowers to come forward and disclose the marketing of dangerous or defective products, there are trade-offs associated with tightening up the existing laws. If both the rewards available to whistleblowers and the prohibitions against retaliatory actions by employers were bolstered, then we would expect more people to come forth with revelations about undesirable conduct by their employers. Some whistleblowers might be motivated by monetary considerations, whereas others might disclose problems because of a deep sense of moral duty. The increase in whistleblowing, however, could lead to greater disruptions of workplace productivity. It could also encourage persons harboring grudges or personal vendettas to come forward, even though their claims might be without foundation. If the laws were weakened, these problems would be reduced, but the harm caused to society by the conduct of employers would continue.

In terms of the statistical nomenclature discussed earlier, we would view stronger whistleblowing laws as leading to a Type I error (increasing numbers of false claims), whereas the weakening or complete elimination of whistleblower laws would lead to a Type II error (the reduced likelihood that the undesirable conduct would be revealed at all). The protection currently offered to whistleblowers has undoubtedly been shaped out of recognition by legislators for the need to discourage people from making disclosures without adequate evidence.

THE DELICATE BALANCE

Every corporation should establish a set of ethical norms in both an explicit and an implicit manner. Explicitly, the company can promulgate a code of ethics. Implicitly, it can create a corporate culture, through its managers' actions that creates an environment for ethical decision making. There is a delicate and complex balance between the creation of an ethical corporate environment and actual managerial decision making. Ultimately, every ethical decision has extended consequences, and these are often uncertain. This uncertainty impinges on every ethical decision, because in the real world, trade-offs exist all the time. Nonetheless, it is the awareness and recognition of such trade-offs that allow corporations to walk the fine line necessary to resolve ethical conflicts.

More specifically, the delicate balance involves trading off between Type I and Type II errors, or errors in commission versus errors in omission. Because Type I errors are what the public and government officials can see and measure, they tend to get the most attention both in the press and in corporate decision-making situations. Society's welfare, though, is also involved in Type II errors, even if the costs of these errors are less easily measured. A corporate decision maker thus has a commitment to society; for example, to fight for the introduction of a new drug that may save thousands of lives and reduce the suffering of millions of people, even if there is a slight chance of a Type I error (bad side effects for a limited number of people).

TERMS AND CONCEPTS FOR REVIEW

Code of ethics 126
Cognitive dissonance 109
Cognitive overload 108
Doctrine of vicarious liability 131

Ethical norms 109
Law of agency 130
Socialization 120
Trade-off 111

Type I error 112
Type II error 112
Whistleblowing 131

SUMMARY

1. Because we receive so much stimuli from our environment, most people today suffer from cognitive overload and cognitive dissonance. The establishment of ethical norms both in and out of the corporate culture can help avoid these problems.

2. Managers face a complex job in which ethical decisions have extended and uncertain consequences. Most ethical decisions have multiple alternatives, as well as personal implications.

3. Managers must subject each of their actions to economic, legal, and philosophical analyses. Ultimately, trade-offs between desirable goals are involved and must be recognized in order to resolve ethical conflicts. There is rarely, if ever, a clear-cut trade-off between what is good and what is bad.

4. Most decisions have Type I errors (errors of commission), as well as Type II errors (errors of omission). When an action is not undertaken, such as not introducing a new product, all the benefits that would have been derived from the introduction of the new product are forfeited (a Type II error). The costs of Type II errors are difficult to measure, whereas the costs of Type I errors—such as the bad side effects of a newly introduced drug—are easier to measure and consequently get more media review.

5. One way to determine whether one's corporate decision is "right" is to subject oneself to the publicity, trusted friend, reciprocity, universality, and obituary self-tests.

6. An important way to establish an ethical corporate culture is to have ethical managers who subscribe to honesty, integrity, promise keeping and trustworthiness, loyalty, fairness, concern for others, respect for others, and accountability, among other attributes.

7. Ethical bosses create an ethical corporate culture (a) by explicitly demonstrating which issues are most important, (b) by the way in which they react to crises, (c) by their general behavior, (d) by the reward system that they use, and (e) by their hiring and firing practices.

8. Within a corporate culture, a socialization process occurs in at least three stages: (a) the hiring process (anticipatory socialization stage); (b) the first six to nine months, when new employees find out what their roles, tasks, and interpersonal demands are (encounter stage); and (c) when the person is no longer considered a new employee (change and acquisition stage).

9. Ethically correct and desirable behavior can be socialized by certain organizational rites, including promotion (the rite of passage) and recognition dinners (the rite of renewal).

10. Ethics committees and ethics training are ways to establish ethical norms within a corporation. A corporate code of ethics may also be valuable in establishing an ethical corporate culture. If members of top management do not follow the corporate code in a time of crisis, though, the code will have little value.

11. Corporate disciplinary policies sometimes allow managers to turn a blind eye to illegal activities of employees; guilty employees are not turned over to the authorities. However, because liability is placed on corporate executives with increasing frequency due to the doctrine of vicarious liability, most companies now have more stringent disciplinary policies.

12. Increasingly, employees are blowing the whistle on inappropriate or illegal activities of their employers. Federal laws provide whistleblowers with significant cash rewards. Some believe that whistleblowing is a breach of loyalty to the corporation. In any case, every whistleblower faces a potential trade-off—the possibility of benefiting society through the whistleblowing activity versus the possibility of being fired and being unable to get a job in the same industry.

EXERCISES

1. Virtually all automobile manufactures face the situation that Honda faced in the introductory example in this chapter. Outline the steps that an auto manufacturer could take to avoid kickbacks to those people responsible for allocating not only new dealerships but also the limited supplies of popular new models.

2. Develop a hypothetical situation in which a modern corporate manager might suffer from cognitive overload.

3. Explain what forces in the marketplace prevent managers from consistently cheating their customers.

4. Pick one hypothetical ethical decision-making example in which multiple alternatives are available. List the alternatives. Then list the uncertain consequences of each potential decision.

5. Make a diagram with simple circles to demonstrate where the intersections of economic, legal, and philosophical analyses of ethical problems may occur.

6. Write a short speech that you would give to a class to explain the difference between Type I and Type II errors. Include sufficient examples to make your point clear.

7. You have just been asked by the board of directors to create a division within your company that will purchase manufactured goods from the People's Republic of China. The directors tell you that in so doing, you will bring lower-priced products into the United States, thereby not only increasing your corporation's own business but also benefiting American consumers. You are also told that workers in China will benefit by your company's purchases. You now read in a national newspaper that the Chinese government has been accused of using prison laborers to produce certain low-priced products for export to the United States and elsewhere. It is up to you to test yourself using the publicity, trusted friend, reciprocity, universality, and obituary self-tests outlined in this chapter. Write down how you would fare in applying each self-test if you agreed to carry out the assignment of the board of directors.

8. Some politicians have argued that values can be taught only within the family structure. Does this mean that business itself cannot teach ethical corporate behavior? Explain your answer.

9. As an effective corporate manager, you have succeeded in establishing a long-term collaborative relationship with a single supplier of one of your main inputs. In so doing, you have, by definition, effectively locked out the possibility of doing business with any other suppliers of that critical input, at least for a few years. Explain whether such behavior is consistent with ethical decision making. Who benefits and who loses?

10. *Exhibit 5–1* lists twelve ethical principles for business executives. Is it possible that some of these ethical principles are inconsistent, or at least at odds, with others? If your answer is yes, give two examples.

11. The chapter gave an example concerning Perrier mineral water in which the parent company in France decided to recall all existing bottles. At the time there was evidence that the substance supposedly tainting the bottled mineral water was not harmful to humans in the amount that was found in the tested bottles. Also, there was a rumor that it was one of Perrier's competitors that actually "tipped off" the FDA. If you were part of upper management at Perrier, would you have aggressively used this information? If so, how? If not, why not?

12. You learned about the six types of organizational rites as outlined by Trice and Beyer in this chapter. Explain which of those six rites are the most important in the socialization process within the corporate culture.

13. Take the position of a critic of corporate ethical codes. Assume you are giving a short speech on the subject, and write an outline of that speech.

14. Assume you are a proponent of corporate codes of ethical behavior. Write an outline of the speech you would make in favor of such codes.

15. Why do many corporations not turn in to the police those employees who have committed illegal acts?

16. Make a list of potential employee actions that could expose an executive to personal liability because of the doctrine of vicarious liability.

17. Is whistleblowing inconsistent with loyalty to the corporation? Explain your answer.

SELECTED REFERENCES

▶ Anthony, Peter. *Managing Culture*. Philadelphia: Open University Press, 1994.

▶ Eells, Richard. *The Government of Corporations*. New York: Free Press, 1962.

▶ Frederick, William Crittenden. *Values, Nature, and Culture in the American Corporation*. New York: Oxford University Press, 1995.

▶ Maris, Robin. *The Economic Theory of "Managerial" Capitalism*. New York: Basic Books, 1964.

▶ Ott, J. *The Organizational Cultural Perspective*. Pacific Grove, Calif.: Brooks-Cole, 1989.

▶ Schultz, Majken. *On Studying Organizational Culture: Diagnosis and Understanding*. New York: W. de Gruyter, 1995.

▶ Stein, Howard F. *Listening Deeply: An Approach to Understanding and Consulting in Organizational Culture*. Boulder, Colo.: Westview Press, 1994.

▶ Trompenaars, Fons. *Riding the Waves of Culture: Understanding Diversity in Global Business*. Burr Ridge, Ill.: Irwin Professional Publishing, 1994.

RESOURCES ON THE INTERNET

▼ For information on management ethics, a good source is Academy of Management (AM) On-Line. AM can be accessed at
http://hsb.baylor.edu/html/fuller/am/am home.htm

▼ The Foundation for Enterprise Development (FED) is an organization dedicated to fostering highly productive and competitive corporate cultures. FED's activities focus on providing practical information and assistance to companies so they can integrate employees into business decisions through a variety of means. You can access FED's home page at
http:/www.fed.org/fed/

▼ If you want to obtain other people's ideas about some ethical issues in biotechnology, you can access, either directly through your Internet gateway or through a commercial on-line service, the news group set up just for biotechnology:
BIT.LISTSERVE.BIOTECH

▼ If you want to join a news group that involves itself with the risk to society of computer use, you can access one at
COMP.RISKS

CASE

HERBERT D. KELLEHER AND SOUTHWEST AIRLINES

Background

Since its deregulation in 1978, the airlines industry in the United States has been highly competitive, and consequently highly unstable. Without government control of factors such as rates and schedules, those airlines unable to adjust became victims of the new realities of fare wars, fluctuating fuel prices, and hub control. The traditional carriers Eastern, TWA, and Pan American fell into bankruptcy as the entire industry lost a total of nearly $7.5 billion from 1989 to 1992.

The single exception in this bleak landscape is Southwest Airlines (SWA), which not only survived the uncertainties of deregulation but has even prospered. SWA began as a regional Texas carrier with three planes in 1971, and by 1996 the airline was operating more than two thousand flights a day. In the quarter-century since its inception, the company has been profitable in every year but two. Much of SWA's success has been attributed to founder and chairman Herbert D. Kelleher and the unique corporate culture he has carefully structured.

Many analysts dismiss the idea that organizational culture can have as profound an effect on a company's profitability as can the organization's financial decisions or other corporate-level strategies. But SWA's performance in a struggling industry (compared by Kelleher to "being the tallest guy in a tribe of dwarfs") belies that assumption. SWA's code of ethics, based on values such as customer satisfaction, employee empowerment, cost control, and a strong dose of organizational humor, is now universally recognized as giving the company a competitive advantage over the more traditionally structured airlines.

The No-Frills Approach at Southwest Air

SWA was born out of Kelleher's perception of the need for a low-cost carrier in Texas to compete with Braniff and Texas International Airlines in the 1960s. A commitment to fares low enough to compete with those offered by bus companies has characterized SWA's corporate strategy in the years since. The resulting no-frills approach to service gives the airline's customers a different experience then they would find on larger airlines. SWA passengers, for example, are not offered a first-class section, do not receive assigned seats, and are offered no food on board except peanuts or crackers. They must also recheck their own baggage during transfer stops, even if they are continuing on with SWA.

Given the loyalty of frequent SWA flyers, these "extras" are not missed. The airline's flights average only fifty-five minutes—not long enough for most passengers to miss a full meal. Furthermore, without the time demands of baggage transfer or food loading, SWA ground crews can turn around an aircraft at the gate in about fifteen minutes, compared with nearly an hour at other airlines. This allows Southwest planes to complete ten flights in a single day—double the industry average—and the ultraefficient use of capital assets brings down the per-unit costs across the system.

Another key cost-saving measure is SWA's ticket distribution system. Other airlines rely on independent travel agencies to book 90 percent of their tickets. SWA, however, for many years refused to link up with the computerized systems that travel agents use, forcing travel agents to use the telephone when customers wanted an SWA flight. The negative side of this was that many travel agents openly dissuaded customers from flying SWA; the positive side was that nearly half the airline's tickets were sold directly to passengers, providing the airline with nearly $30 million in annual savings. These cost reductions allowed the average fare of an SWA flight to be in the $60 range, seemingly low enough for flyers to forgive the lack of frills. "Sure you get herded on the plane, and sure you only get peanuts and a drink," said one customer. "But Southwest does everything they can to get you to the right place at the right time, and that's most important."

Kelleher's Corporate Values

Under the influence of Kelleher, what SWA lacks in perks it makes up in a corporate culture that appears to bring the best out in employees and customers. Described by a peer as "shrewd, sharp, and focused; a raving lunatic having fun," Kelleher's irreverence is legendary. He has appeared at company parties dressed as Elvis Presley or Roy Orbison and singing "Jailhouse Rock" and "Pretty Woman," respectively. At speaking engagements he has been known to tell audiences that the accomplishments he is most proud of include being "very good at projectile vomiting" and never having contracted a serious venereal disease.

Kelleher's sense of humor permeates the organizational culture at SWA. It plays a major part in the three basic values that Kelleher promotes at the airline, according to

James Campbell Quick, professor at the University of Texas at Arlington:

> **Value 1:** Work should be fun . . . it can be play . . . enjoy it.
> **Value 2:** Work is important . . . don't spoil it with seriousness.
> **Value 3:** People are important . . . each one makes a difference.

For example, the company's people department (as opposed to the more common term, *personnel department*) is instructed by Kelleher to use sense of humor as part of the criteria for hiring. This does not mean the airline is looking for people who make jokes at the expense of others, but it does mean the company seeks employees who have an attitude, or a set of values, that is not too rigid or restrictive to operate in SWA's dynamic culture. As Kelleher explains,

> We can train people to do things where skills are concerned. But there is one capability we do not have and that is to change a person's attitude. So, we prefer an unskilled person with a good attitude rather than a highly skilled person with a bad attitude. We take people who come out of highly structured, hierarchical, dictatorial corporate environments if they have the attitude potential. They may have just molded their mannerisms to conform to that rigid environment. When we have them here for a while, they learn they can relax . . . and let their real selves come out.

Employee Reaction

These "relaxed" employees provide passengers with attention they would not receive on other airlines. During delays at the gate, flight attendants have been known to award prizes to the passengers with the largest holes in their socks. These employees also use the intercom in a nontraditional manner, announcing, "Good morning, ladies and gentlemen. Those of you who wish to smoke will please file out to our lounge on the wing where you can enjoy our feature film, 'Gone With the Wind.'"

By allowing employees to enjoy their work and develop a relationship with the company that goes beyond payment for service, Kelleher embodies Quick's third organizational value. Despite the fact that the wages of SWA employees are on par with, if not below, industry standards, the airline has been almost completely free of the labor problems that have plagued its competitors. SWA has experienced only one strike in its history, a six-day walkout by the machinists union in 1984.

In financial reports, employees are described as "heroines and heroes" and "wondrous and valorous people," and they are characterized as having "wonderful hearts and souls." The workers respond to this atmosphere of praise by showing a willingness to perform beyond the call of their duties. It is not uncommon for SWA ticket agents to help unload luggage or pilots to assist at the boarding gate. In 1984, maintenance supervisors in Kansas City felt so underutilized that they formed the Boredom Club and petitioned management to increase the number of flights to the city per day.

An end result of this *esprit de corps* is that SWA employees see work as a series of challenges rather than as a burden. Consequently, the airline's organizational culture has been adept at turning environmental threats into opportunities. During the U.S. government's military preparations for the war in the Persian Gulf from August to November 1990, for example, jet fuel prices doubled. The situation forced carriers to raise ticket prices to compensate, which drove away passengers and hurt the industry. At SWA, approximately one-quarter of the employees created the "Fuel from the Heart" program; each employee donated a specified number of gallons of fuel back to the company from each paycheck, with the price set at $1.10 per gallon. The program was eventually structured as a payroll deduction plan and continued until the end of the war in the winter of 1991.

Growth and the Continuing Culture

As SWA's corporate culture continues to be celebrated and Kelleher attains a stature that is rare among corporate chairpersons, industry analysts have one question: Will the company be able to hold on to its values as it expands? For its first quarter-century of existence, SWA limited itself to 375-mile flights. But by the mid-1990s, 15 percent of the routes exceeded 800 miles, reaching distances as great as 1,400 miles and flying to sites such as Nashville, Tennessee. In 1996, SWA expanded into Florida. Furthermore, the company doubled its number of aircraft to 226 between 1990 and 1995; in the same period it also had a 100 percent increase in the employee roster, to 20,000.

A prevailing view is that Kelleher's unique culture will not survive expansion. "Southwest will develop a bureaucracy," predicts one observer, using a term Kelleher disdains. Leaders within SWA, however, say they are committed to keeping their values. Executive Vice President Colleen Barrett created

CASE (CONTINUED)

a forty-four member "culture committee" to ensure that those values were not lost in growth, and the company is devising new means, such as "ticketless" travel—which saved $25 million in 1995 alone—to keep fares down.

There is also concern that if and when Kelleher leaves his post, he will take the driving force behind the company's values and culture with him, a concept the chairman dismisses. "I think fundamentally Southwest will retain its same culture," Kelleher says, after joking that the question is irrelevant because he is immortal. "The organization . . . is stronger than any individual who's part of the organization."

Critical Thinking Questions

1. If Kelleher's corporate values ("work should be fun," "work is important . . . don't spoil it with seriousness") have worked such wonders at SWA, why do you think they have not been adopted by many large companies?

2. What are the risks of a corporate culture based on humor?

3. Why would growth, in the minds of some analysts, necessarily force SWA to change its corporate culture? Do you agree that large companies must have a culture that is more bureaucratic and, in this case, more subdued?

4. Why would the SWA corporate culture be conducive to positive management-employee relations?

5. Consider the following scenario: An SWA flight attendant jumps out of a baggage compartment in order to surprise the passengers. One passenger is so startled that he falls backward and hits his head on a wall, causing serious health damage. What would be the ramifications for Kelleher's values and the airline's corporate culture?

SOURCE: Information from B. O'Brian, "Flying on the Cheap: Southwest Airlines Is a Rare Carrier: It Still Makes Money," *Wall Street Journal*, October 26, 1992, p. A1; K. Labich, "Is Herb Kelleher America's Best CEO?" *Fortune*, May 2, 1994, p. 44; A. Reed, "Southwest Style in Europe," *Air Transport World*, August 1, 1995, p. 63; J. C. Quick, "Crafting an Organizational Culture: Herb's Hand at Southwest Airlines," *Organizational Dynamics*, September 22, 1992, pp. 45–56; J. M. Feldman, "Seriously Successful," *Air Transport World*, January 1, 1994, p. 60; S. McCartney, "Southwest Airlines May Be Heading into Calmer Skies," *Wall Street Journal*, July 17, 1995, p. B4; J. M. Feldman, "Attacking Traditional Management Structure," *Air Transport World*, November 1, 1994, p. 30; and "Southwest Airlines General Ready for Fare Wars," *Business Journal–Portland*, May 5, 1995, p. 10.

CHAPTER 6

CORPORATE SOCIAL RESPONSIBILITY

CHAPTER OUTLINE

- Individual and Corporate Responsibility
- The Argument against Corporate Social Responsibility
- The Argument for Corporate Social Responsibility
- Optimizing Profits

INTRODUCTION

"Time is short," began Anita Roddick. "I have only a few minutes to begin a process of glasnost . . . so I'll be blunt." The managing director of Body Shop International was about to address the 31st Congress of the International Chamber of Commerce in Cancun, Mexico, on October 21, 1993. Most of the speeches preceding Roddick's had celebrated the new opportunities for business in world markets that were becoming increasingly open, but Roddick was taking a different approach to the situation:

> Listening to much of the debate over [international] trade, I wonder if we come from the same world. I've heard much about increased rates of growth in trade, but little about stronger communities of healthier children. I have heard much about the march of progress, but little about the people and cultures who are being trampled underfoot. . . . We all agree on one important thing: business is now entering the center stage. It is faster, more creative, it's more wealthy than government. However, if it comes with no moral sympathy, or honorable code of behavior, God help us all. . . . Business can and must be a force for positive social change. It must not only avoid hideous evil—it must actively do good.[1]

Roddick was calling for "corporate responsibility—plain and simple," which she defined as "changing our basic notion of what motivates us as business people" by considering factors "other than financial profits." She closed her speech by urging her colleagues to practice a "gentler, kinder way of business" with core values of community, social justice, and environmental awareness that would give them a "vital, driving sense of responsibility to people and the planet."

Roddick may have been exaggerating a bit in claiming to "begin a process of glasnost," and her fervor has left her open to criticism for supposed ethical violations within her own company. Yet she is not the first to criticize corporations for being overly concerned with company profits and comparatively indifferent to what we call social concerns. After all, the concept of corporate social responsibility has existed since the first corporation was created. Roddick's speech, however, to an audience not used to being lectured on such issues, does reflect a concern with "actively doing good" that is growing within and without the business community.

According to classic capitalist theory, the primary function of corporate directors and officers is to make those decisions that will maximize the rate of return to the company's owners—the shareholders. The shareholders of IBM, for example, expect the company's board of directors to hire officers who can manage the day-to-day affairs of the company in a way that will maximize the return to the shareholders. Certain economists therefore consider the idea of corporate social objectives absurd; they believe that business enterprises should concern themselves only with generating profits. These theorists postulate that social welfare then would be improved indirectly, because self-interested entrepreneurs would take whatever steps were necessary to operate in the most efficient manner possible in the competitive market. The "invisible hand" that Adam Smith imagined would maximize social welfare because of the self-interested actions of business enterprises—not because of any conscious social agendas. In other words, Adam Smith would expect any benefits to society

---

1. A. Roddick, speech presented at the 31st Congress of the International Chamber of Commerce, Cancun, Mexico, October 21, 1993.

resulting from IBM's development of new products to follow from that company's efforts to maximize its profits, not from its conscious attempts to improve the welfare of society as a whole.

INDIVIDUAL AND CORPORATE RESPONSIBILITY

A contrasting theory was paraphrased by the American industrialist Henry Ford when he said, "A business that makes nothing but money is a poor kind of business." Along that line of thought, legitimacy is conferred on a business not by satisfied shareholders but by a society that allows that business to exist in the first place. Society allows a business to serve its economic function so long as that business does not abuse its power with respect to the central values of that society—which in the case of the United States would be democracy, freedom, justice, and the sanctity of individual rights. In fact, it is the responsibility of business to uphold and protect these values.

DEFINITION OF INDIVIDUAL RESPONSIBILITY

What exactly do we mean when we speak of responsibility? For individual responsibility to exist, three requirements are necessary: (1) someone is to be praised or blamed; (2) something has to be done; or (3) some kind of trustworthiness can be expected.[2]

When someone is to be praised or blamed, we are dealing with the causal sense of responsibility, in which we make a legal or moral judgment on an action taken in the past. By holding individuals accountable for their actions, we try to determine their intentions, free will, degree of participation, and appropriate reward or punishment in a given situation.

When responsibility means that something has to be done, we are concerned with following established guidelines or those associated with societal norms. For example, people in our society have expectations of the responsibilities of parents to children, teachers to students, doctors to patients, and citizens to the law. If an individual does not act in the way society has deemed proper, he or she will face the punishment of society.

When responsibility infers that some kind of trustworthiness is to be expected, we are saying that a person's independent thought processes justify an attitude of trust in those who interact with that person. This kind of responsibility concerns whether an individual can make responsible decisions.

At each of the three levels, the individual's sense of responsibility is entrenched in his or her rationality; to be responsible, one must act according to reason, with clear goals and purposes. Responsibility also hinges on respect—respect for the needs and rights of society and of other individuals. Responsible individuals do not look on either society or other people as mere resources to be used for personal gain or satisfaction.

DOES A CORPORATION AS AN ENTITY HAVE RESPONSIBILITY?

Any discussion of corporate responsibility brings up issues we first addressed in Chapter 2: Can we speak of the corporation in the same terms as we do an individual? Does it

---

2. K. E. Goodpaster and J. B. Matthews, Jr., "Can a Corporation Have a Conscience?" *Harvard Business Review*, January–February 1992, pp. 133–134.

make sense to speak of moral or immoral companies? Are corporations constrained by the same ethical considerations that apply to individuals? The collective nature of the corporate entity admittedly poses some philosophical difficulties for those who wish to evaluate the morality or ethics of corporate behavior. Many prominent German companies, for example, profited from the sale of their goods to Adolf Hitler's military organization and arguably contributed to the devastation of World War II. It seems strange, however, to view the companies themselves as immoral. We usually think of morals and ethics as applying only to individuals.

The study of ethics and morality usually presupposes that the actor is able to distinguish between right and wrong. Even though corporations are often viewed as being little more than bureaucratic amalgamations of human beings, they are still artificial entities. The actions a corporation takes are not usually directly attributable to a single person but to groups of employees, so any discussion of corporate intent may be imprecise. Corporations, however, are concerned with being perceived as "ethical" organizations, because consumers may be less willing to purchase the products of companies that engage in what the consumers believe to be unethical or immoral behavior.

Philosopher John Ladd, to a certain extent echoing Albert Carr and his poker analogy outlined in Chapter 4, dismisses the idea that corporations should be held to individual standards. "It is improper to expect organizational conduct to conform to the ordinary principles of morality," Ladd says. "We cannot and must not expect formal organizations, or their representatives acting in their official capacities, to be honest, courageous, considerate, sympathetic, or to have any kind of moral integrity. Such concepts are not in the vocabulary, so to speak, of the organizational language game."[3]

Robert Solomon disagrees with Ladd's philosophy because it does not take into account the realities of the organizational structure and corporate culture.[4] Solomon points to the classic example of the *Exxon Valdez*, the huge oil tanker that spilled eleven million gallons of oil into Alaska's Prince William Sound in 1989 after going aground, allegedly because the captain was intoxicated. At first glance, one would say that the responsibility obviously lies with Joseph Hazlewood, captain of the *Valdez*, an individual who had been drinking and decided to "sleep it off" instead of doing his duty and piloting the tanker.

Solomon points out, however, that there are many other levels of both responsibility and blame within the company. First of all, if Hazlewood was not steering the tanker, who was? The answer is the first mate, who apparently was not proficient at the task. Shouldn't every tanker have a reserve pilot, in case of emergency? Who in the corporation would make that decision? Furthermore, Hazlewood had a history of drinking problems. Who in the corporation had the responsibility of deciding that this history was not relevant in determining Hazlewood's ability to be an effective captain?

Then there was the fact that the *Valdez* was not double hulled, as many tankers are. Finally, Exxon's own emergency measures, which were supposed to minimize the damage in such situations, were painfully slow, allowing the damage from the spill to be far more widespread than it could have been.

There are many levels of blame in the *Valdez* case, but if we go back to our definition of responsibility for the individual, we see there is a basic argument for corporate responsibility. Hazlewood is certainly to be held accountable for the spill, but so is Exxon, whose leadership failed to provide safety measures against such a disaster. By not providing those measures, Exxon "broke the rules" by disregarding its responsibility to the Prince William

---

3. *Ibid.*, p. 134.

4. R. Solomon, *The New World of Business* (Lanham, Md.: Littlefield Adams Quality Paperbacks, 1994), pp. 220–223.

Sound community—not to damage its pristine beauty. In the end, Exxon showed that through its internal decision-making process, it did not act responsibly, and the company was punished accordingly—by fines, lawsuits, and the cost of clean-up.

DEFINITION OF CORPORATE SOCIAL RESPONSIBILITY

If we expect Exxon not to spill oil into our waterways, we thus expect the corporation to live up to its social responsibility. What exactly does that mean? Despite greater recognition of the basic concept, there has been little overall agreement on an exact definition. Keith Davis and Robert Blomstrom define **corporate social responsibility** as the obligation of the internal corporate decision makers to "take actions which protect and improve the welfare of society as a whole along with their own interests."[5] This definition is helpful, because it introduces the idea of balance within corporate responsibility—the balance of improving society and protecting the company's own interests. Implicit in this definition are the moral and ethical obligations a company has with regard to its employees, the community, and other stakeholders we have discussed. From the moral standpoint, the definition of corporate social responsibility could be the actions taken by corporate decision makers to help society without contributing to the direct profits of the corporation.

Another definition, from Milton Friedman, is actually an antidefinition; Friedman refutes the idea of corporate social responsibility by turning back to Adam Smith. Friedman sees "one and only one" social responsibility of business: "to use its resources and engage in activities designed to increase its profits, so long as it stays within the rules of the game."[6] This is not to say that Friedman advocates an economic free-for-all but rather fair, rule-abiding, responsible behavior in a market free of deceit, coercion, and

5. K. Davis and R. L. Blomstrom, *Business and Society: Environment and Responsibility*, 3d ed. (New York: McGraw-Hill, 1975), p. 6.

6. M. Friedman, *Capitalism and Freedom* (Chicago: University of Chicago Press, 1962), p. 133.

other unethical activities. Many observers dismiss Friedman's vision as hopelessly utopian. Friedman's definition has earned him the derision of many adherents of corporate social responsibility—including a number of CEOs.

RIGHTS AND RESPONSIBILITIES

In *Politics*, Aristotle argues that any political system relies on a blurring of the distinction between the rulers and the ruled—that a stable society relies on its citizens "ruling and being ruled in turn."[7] The American experience has boiled this concept down to the old Puritan saying, "With rights come responsibilities." Americans today like to believe that the rights conferred on those of us living in a modern democratic society demand responsibilities to uphold the ideals of that society.

American corporations have not historically been held to such a high standard. Businesses were allowed, and even expected, to use cost-benefit analysis as an ethical decision-making tool. Most experts believe this attitude began to change after World War II, when the United States became the dominant economic power in the world, and American companies began making enough profits to start thinking about social issues. Attention began to be turned to externalities, or those factors of production and distribution that were not reflected in a cost-benefit analysis. Externalities include the effect of a business's actions on the community and the environment. For the "right" that businesses had to make large profits, they were given the "responsibility" of not harming society. In a sense, businesses were asked to act like individuals, and this gave rise to the concept of corporate citizenship.

The Pyramid Theory In economic terms, the idea of corporate citizenship relies on conciliating the drive for profit with the public welfare.[8] This involves the idea of **Pareto optimality,** a condition in microeconomic theory in which the scarce resources of society are being used so efficiently by the producing firms, and the goods and services are being distributed so effectively by the competitive markets, that it would be impossible to make any single person better off without harming some other person.[9] Pareto optimality will probably never be realized, but it does offer the goal, as well as the incentive, for a business to balance its economic and social demands.

Archie Carroll uses a pyramid theory to explain how each business can be in the best position to contribute to Pareto optimality for the entire economy. At the base of the pyramid are economic responsibilities. The organization has to be profitable, or it will cease to exist, and any other discussion of its social responsibility will be academic. Therefore, economic responsibilities are the foundation on which all other responsibilities lie. At the second level of the pyramid are the legal responsibilities of those involved in the organization. They must obey the law, for the law is society's codification of what is right and what is wrong. At the next higher level in the pyramid are ethical responsibilities, which involve the obligation of each actor to do what is fair, just, and right. Finally, at the top of the pyramid is a set of philanthropic responsibilities that make the corporation a good corporate citizen[10] (see *Exhibit 6–1*).

---

7. L. Strauss and J. Cropsey, eds., *History of Political Philosophy*, 3d ed. (Chicago: University of Chicago Press, 1987), pp. 138–139.
8. C. Smith, "The New Corporate Philosophy," *Harvard Business Review*, May–June 1994, p. 107.
9. L. T. Hosmer, *The Ethics of Management* (Homewood, Ill.: Irwin, 1991), p. 36.
10. A. B. Carroll, "The Pyramid of Corporate Social Responsibility: Toward the Moral Management of Organizational Stakeholders," *Business Horizons*, July–August 1991, pp. 39–48.

▼ **EXHIBIT 6–1 The Pyramid Theory**

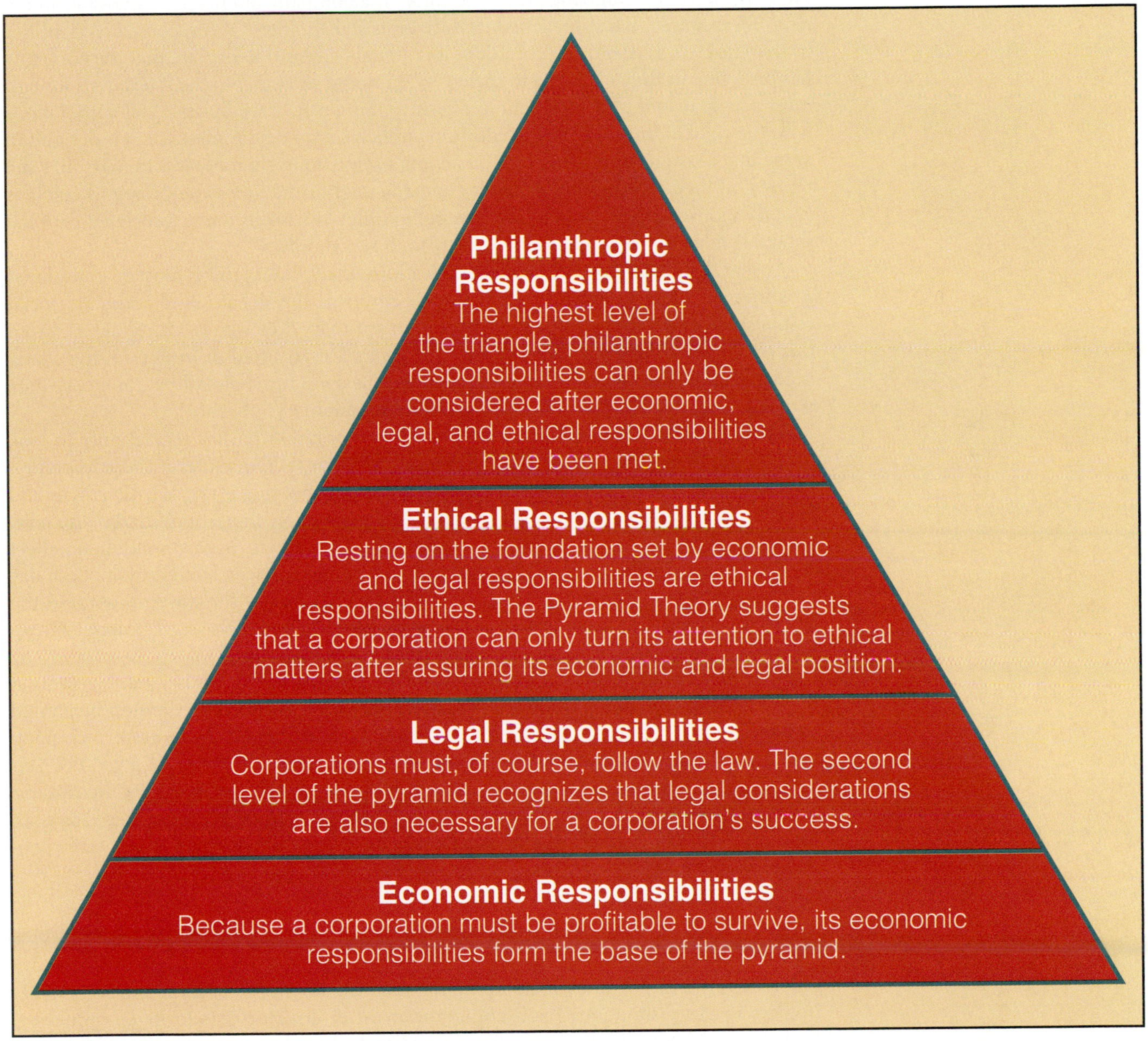

Philanthropic Responsibilities
The highest level of the triangle, philanthropic responsibilities can only be considered after economic, legal, and ethical responsibilities have been met.

Ethical Responsibilities
Resting on the foundation set by economic and legal responsibilities are ethical responsibilities. The Pyramid Theory suggests that a corporation can only turn its attention to ethical matters after assuring its economic and legal position.

Legal Responsibilities
Corporations must, of course, follow the law. The second level of the pyramid recognizes that legal considerations are also necessary for a corporation's success.

Economic Responsibilities
Because a corporation must be profitable to survive, its economic responsibilities form the base of the pyramid.

Conflicting Corporate Duties Building a pyramid of corporate social responsibilities may seem straightforward, but it ignores several problems. First, many companies have internal conflicts about what their own duties are:

▼ Because corporations may be subject to conflicting loyalties, they must make trade-offs in deciding whether to pursue a particular course of action. Furthermore, even a corporation's decision to be socially responsible can lead to disagreements over where the finite social dollars should go.

The second problem with the pyramid is that any characterization of a corporation as socially responsible or irresponsible depends on an identification of its stakeholders—those to whom the company owes allegiance. If a company discharges wastewater into a river, for example, has it breached its duty to its stakeholders? If the company identifies its shareholders as its only stakeholders, it is arguably absurd to declare that the company has breached its duty of loyalty to society by dumping sewage into the river, even though most people would find such actions offensive. Similarly, if we believe that corporations have the right to fund advertising efforts to publicize a particular message, it is difficult to argue that a corporation doing so is breaching its duty to its shareholders to maximize the returns on their investments. Another company might fund television programs (such as Mobil's sponsorship of *Masterpiece Theatre*) in order to have its name associated with the shows. Is that company upholding its duty to its stakeholders?

As we noted in Chapter 3, the needs of various stakeholder groups must be considered in corporate strategy. At one end of the spectrum in the debate over corporate social responsibility is the notion that the corporation's primary duty is to its shareholders. From this perspective, directors and corporate managers are regarded as trustees of the shareholders' funds. The owners of any corporate business are the shareholders, and corporate directors and officers have a duty to act in the shareholders' interest.

Then there are those who contend that the corporation has an ethical duty to look beyond profit maximization to the welfare of consumers. Therefore, if the corporation produces a baby food that babies like and mothers buy, but that is not nutritionally sound because of a high sodium or sugar content, the corporation should not market the baby food. Many people believe that they, as individual consumers, have absolutely no effect on the pricing, quality, and nature of the products and services offered by modern-day giant corporations. They feel that only through regulation by the government and the courts can consumers be protected from unsafe or faulty products (see *Company Focus: Larami Corporation*).

In addition to its duty to consumers of its products, each business has an obligation to its own employees. Some of this duty is backed by federal and state statutes, but much of it relies on the ethical status of executives and management. Furthermore, a corporation is part of a particular community, and thus has a responsibility to be a good citizen and neighbor. Finally, many stress that the corporation has a duty to society. Because so much of the wealth and power of this country is controlled by business, they contend, business in turn has a responsibility to society to use that wealth and power in socially beneficial ways.

THE CORPORATE BALANCING ACT

Obviously, it is impossible for a corporation to satisfy the needs of each one of its stakeholders in every situation. Each corporate board of directors has to make numerous trade-offs in determining corporate goals. Directors do have an ethical—and even a legal—responsibility to shareholders, because they control the shareholders' wealth. Society has also deemed that corporate directors and officers have an ethical duty not to market defective or unreasonably dangerous products; this social ethic is written into warranty and product-liability laws. Similarly, they have a duty to provide safe working conditions for their employees, and this also is written into law. But there is no law stating which of these duties should come first—or, more realistically, how much weight each duty should be given on the balancing scales beyond the minimum prescribed by law.

The trade-offs are even more complicated because these duties overlap considerably. For example, for a corporation to run smoothly and productively, it must recruit qualified

COMPANY FOCUS: LARAMI CORPORATION

CORPORATE SOCIAL RESPONSIBILITY AND THE WELFARE OF THE CONSUMER

The Larami Corporation found itself in the center of a gun control controversy—water gun control, that is. The main issue wasn't so much a ten-year-old's right to bear squirt guns but a manufacturer's responsibility for the way its product is used.

The Super Soaker

By 1992, Larami had taken the toy market by storm with its Super Soaker, a squirt gun with a unique air propulsion system that shoots water as much as 50 feet away. The company's biggest profit maker, the Super Soaker had cornered 70 percent of the squirt gun market; in fact, it was the top-selling toy of any brand as summer rolled around.

Consumer complaints about the product were also increasing. Reports of youths using their Super Soakers as actual weapons were flooding police stations around the nation, including cases where the guns had been filled with ammonia, urine, and bleach. Improper use of the squirt gun had been blamed for the death of one victim and the serious wounding of two others.

A backlash against the Super Soaker quickly took shape. Boston mayor Raymond Flynn urged retailers in his city to stop selling the product, and a state senator in Michigan introduced a bill to outlaw the toy. Robert Frederick, a researcher at the Center for Business Ethics at Bentley College in Waltham, Massachusetts, suggested that Larami declare "a moratorium on production as a goodwill gesture."

Company Reactions

Some retailers—most notably Woolworth's and Bradlee's—pulled the squirt guns from their shelves, but Larami showed no such inclinations. The Philadelphia-based company released a statement of sympathy for the family of the boy who was killed, while at the same time disclaiming any liability for the way the toy was being used.

"If this is [Larami's] only horse, they're going to have to weather the storm and hope the problem just goes away," said one industry watcher of the controversy. But Robert Frederick disagreed: "Companies typically lie low to avoid blame, but in so doing show a lack of concern in the public eye," he claimed. "To me, that's not good business."

Another industry analyst pointed out that all the attention would do more to help sales of the Super Soaker than to hurt them: "Slapping a 'Banned in Boston' on the gun is the best way to make sure that every kid in America gets one this summer."

The New Bottom Line

In today's consumer environment—with politicians, interest groups, and the media vying for quick publicity— no company with a controversial product is going to escape public scrutiny. Unfortunately, however, those groups sometimes exhibit a short attention span. If a company waits for a controversy to slip out of public attention, the results sometimes can be less than disastrous: in 1994, the Super Soaker was again the most popular summer toy on the market.

SOURCE: J. Pereira, "Toy Market Faces Dilemma As Water Gun Spurs Violence," *Wall Street Journal*, June 11, 1992, p. B1; and S. D. Coolidge, "A Totally Tubular Summer Fad," *Christian Science Monitor*, August 4, 1995, p. 1.

personnel. To attract qualified personnel in a competitive marketplace, the firm must offer a competitive salary, a good benefits package, and desirable working conditions. If this is done and the corporation is well managed by the qualified personnel, ideally profits will increase, and both shareholders and employees will benefit.

This ideal result is not a certainty, however. What is certain is that such expenses will mean reduced profits for shareholders in the short run. Similarly, corporate philanthropic activities that receive wide publicity may benefit shareholders in the long run—if the enhanced public image of the corporation entices more consumers to purchase its product—but such long-run benefits are difficult to calculate.

In sum, acting responsibly toward each stakeholder group in the corporate context is not easy. Ideally, each corporate decision would provide equal benefits for all individuals affected by that decision, but this is rarely possible. When it is not, the company must make difficult trade-offs. Sometimes, the trade-off is between economic and social goals; sometimes, it is between competing social goals. Because no single company has the luxury of being all things to all stakeholders, managers must be well versed in the relative costs and benefits of any socially responsible action taken by their corporations.

RESPONSIBILITY VERSUS RESPONSIVENESS

The concept of corporate social responsibility is sometimes confused with the responsiveness of the corporate entity in a particular crisis. Researchers Robert Akerman and Raymond Bauer have developed what they call the *action-oriented view* of this distinction. They believe that the term *social responsibility* is not dynamic enough to describe the willingness of a business to react and respond to the demands of society at any point in time. They point out that the term *responsibility* itself implies the assumption of an obligation. It therefore places the emphasis on motivation "rather than on performance."[11] Akerman and Bauer place more emphasis on what corporations actually do than on what corporations say they are going to do. Thus, the researchers like to use the term *corporate social responsiveness*, or simply just **responsiveness**. The term notes an action-oriented environment in a business organization.

Another researcher, S. Prakash Sethi, also believes that responsiveness is a more appropriate term and concept. Sethi has provided an analytical framework for classifying organizational behavior when the organization responds to a societal need.[12] He identifies three stages of corporate behavior: (1) social obligation, (2) social responsibility, and (3) social responsiveness.

Sethi starts his analysis by recognizing that when the market or the law forces a corporation to act in a certain way, that corporation faces a social obligation. This is similar to the bottom two levels on Carroll's pyramid of corporate social responsibility. Next, Sethi offers a stage of corporate social responsibility in which corporate managers act in such a way that their actions are consistent with society's expectations and values. Finally, the third stage of behavior is more preventive and anticipatory. It involves the organization's social responsiveness and places the organization in its long-run role in a dynamic social system. (For insight on how these stages affect managerial behavior, see *Exhibit 6–2*.)

THE ARGUMENT AGAINST CORPORATE SOCIAL RESPONSIBILITY

Most arguments against corporate social responsibility today dispute degree instead of validity, but some people find fault with the idea of placing the burdens of social concerns

---

11. R. Akerman and R. Bauer, *Corporate Social Responsiveness: The Modern Dilemma* (Reston, Va.: Reston, 1976), p. 7.
12. S. P. Sethi, "Dimensions of Corporate Social Performance: An Analytical Framework," *California Management Review*, Spring 1975, pp. 58–64.

▼ **EXHIBIT 6–2 Sethi's Stages and Corporate Behavior**

Dimensions of Corporate Behavior	Stage One Social Obligation	Stage Two Social Responsibility	Stage Three Social Responsiveness
Ethical norms	Considers business value-neutral; managers expected to behave according to their own ethical standards.	Defines norms in community terms, for example, good corporate citizen. Avoids taking moral stand on issues that may harm its economic interests or go against prevailing social norms.	Takes definite stand on issues of public concern; advocates institutional ethical norms even though they may be detrimental to its immediate economic interest or
Social accountability for corporate actions	Construes narrowly as limited to stockholders; jealously guards its prerogatives against outsiders.	Construes narrowly for legal purposes, but broadened to include groups affected by its actions; management more outward looking.	Willing to account for its actions to other groups, even those not directly affected by its actions.
Response to social pressures	Maintains low public profile, but if attacked, uses PR methods to upgrade its public image, denies any deficiencies; discloses information only where legally required.	Accepts responsibility for solving current problems; will admit deficiencies in former practices and attempt to persuade public that its current practices meet social norms; attitude toward critics conciliatory; freer information disclosures Stage One.	Willingly discusses activities with outside groups; makes information freely available to public; accepts formal and informal inputs from outside groups in decision making. Is willing to be publicly evaluated for its various activities.
Philanthropy	Contributes only when direct benefit to it clearly shown; otherwise, views contributions as responsibility of individual employees.	Contributes to noncontroversial and established causes; matches employee contributions.	Activities of Stage Two, in addition to support and contributions to new, controversial groups whose needs it sees as unfulfilled and increasingly important.
Activities pertaining in governmental actions	Strongly resists any regulation of its activities except when it needs help to protect its market position; avoids contact; resists any demands for information only where legally required.	Preserves management discretion in corporate decisions, but cooperates with government in research to improve industry-wide standards; participates in political process and encourages employees to do likewise.	Openly communicates with government; assists in enforcing existing laws and developing evaluations of business practices; objects publicly to governmental activities that it feels are detrimental to the public good.

SOURCE: S. P. Sethi, *California Management Review,* Spring, 1975, p. 63.

on business. Some economists protest the economic principles behind corporate social responsibility. Further dissent is found among those who do not feel that business, in its present form, is equipped to handle social problems.

MILTON FRIEDMAN AND THE "INVISIBLE HAND"

Milton Friedman, as we discussed earlier, has continued the tradition of Adam Smith, who wrote in 1776 that individuals acting in their own self-interest would be guided, as if by an "invisible hand," to maximize social welfare. Friedman argues that the only social obligations of business are to maximize profits and obey the law. According to Friedman, corporate social responsibility as it is now widely regarded is a "fundamentally subversive doctrine."[13] Friedman does not approve of businesspersons who: "believe that they are defending free enterprise when they declaim that business is not concerned 'merely' with profit but also with promoting desirable 'social' ends; that business has a 'social conscience' and takes seriously its responsibilities for providing employment, eliminating discrimination, avoiding pollution and whatever else may be the catchwords of the contemporary crop of reformers. In fact they are . . . preaching pure and unadulterated socialism."[14]

Friedman points out that the United States has elected officials to make social policy. No one elects top management in U.S. corporations. Thus, no one, according to Friedman, really wants corporate officers to make social policy. They should therefore think and act only in terms of their duty to their ultimate bosses—the shareholders. In so doing they will find that they must create an employment atmosphere that keeps workers satisfied and therefore productive. In so doing they also must create products that customers want to buy in large enough quantities to generate profits. Those, according to Friedman, are the duties of today's managers—nothing more and nothing less. He finds it preposterous that shareholder funds (that is, profits) are used to promote philanthropic endeavors favored by corporate executives (see *Company Focus: Consumers United Insurance Company*).

CORPORATE SOCIAL RESPONSIBILITY AS OUTMODED

R. E. Freeman and Jeanne Liedka could not be further from Friedman on the ideological spectrum, but they too reject the traditional concept of corporate social responsibility. In doing so, they embrace a version of corporate social responsibility that goes far beyond what most businesspeople would be willing to accept.

Freeman and Liedka feel that Friedman and his proponents have succeeded in making the focus of the debate whether or not a corporation's primary purpose is to maximize profits.[15] The two economists see the standard idea of corporate social responsibility as "inherently conservative—it starts with the standard received wisdom and then attempts to 'fix' its unintended consequences." In their minds, it promotes a view of business and society as separate entities, linked solely by a set of responsibilities. Only by making corporations part of a larger social mosaic in which "'caring' has primary significance" can business free itself from the constraints of corporate social responsibility. Freeman and Liedka have come up with what they believe forms a platform for a "new conversation"— a new view—about corporate social responsibility (see *Exhibit 6–3* on page 154).

OTHER LIMITATIONS OF CORPORATE SOCIAL RESPONSIBILITY

Many other arguments against corporate social responsibility have been offered. These focus mainly on costs and efficiency, a fear of monolithic business, the complexity of making the socially responsible decision, and accountability.

Costs and Efficiency Some argue that by directing capital toward a social goal instead of within the corporation, a decision maker is effectively making the business operation

---

13. Freidman, *op. cit.*, p. 133.

14. M. Freidman, "The Social Responsibility of Business Is to Increase Profit," *New York Times Magazine*, September 13, 1970, pp. 32–33, 122–126.

15. R. E. Freeman and J. Liedka, "Corporate Social Responsibility: A Critical Approach," *Business Horizons*, July–August 1991, pp. 92–98.

COMPANY FOCUS: CONSUMERS UNITED INSURANCE COMPANY

THE DANGERS OF CORPORATE SOCIAL RESPONSIBILITY

The businessperson who takes his or her social responsibility seriously must continually balance social goals and profits. The rewards and satisfactions of maintaining balance in these two areas can be great. The temptation to place too much emphasis on social goals can be dangerous, however.

A Pioneering Company

In 1969, Jim Gibbons started Consumers United Insurance Company in Washington, D.C. He vowed that his company would serve as a "model for American business." (Many of his innovative management strategies, in fact, have recently become popular in the business community.) Almost immediately, Gibbons turned full ownership of Consumers United over to his employees and allowed them to set their own work schedules.

As an insurance company, Consumers United was also a pioneer. It began insuring domestic household partners in the mid-1980s. It was one of the few insurance companies in the country not to test its applicants for human immunodeficiency virus (HIV) infection when the acquired immune-deficiency syndrome (AIDS) epidemic hit. In fact, Gibbons tried to set up a special insurance policy specifically for people who were HIV-positive, only to have the idea rejected by the Delaware Insurance Department. (Consumers United is regulated in Delaware because it was incorporated in that state.)

Good Intentions

By the late 1970s, Consumers United was collecting more than $80 million in premiums per year; in 1986, the company oversaw approximately $47 million in investments. Like some insurance companies, however, it was always a few bad investments away from disaster, and Gibbons's passion for social investing finally caught up with him.

In 1985, Consumers United spent $7 million on a twenty-six-acre parcel of vacant land in Washington, D.C. The neighborhood was known as Parkside-Paradise, but in reality it was neither. Gibbons, with the help of the D.C. government, was going to build a complex of townhouses and apartments on the site. "Parkside," he says, "was my dream."

It turned into a nightmare. When the city failed to follow through with its promises to build the complex and pave the surrounding streets, illegal dumpers took advantage of the empty lots by filling them with refuse. The Delaware Insurance Department was appalled and classified the $7 million investment as a "nonperforming loan."

There were other mistakes, as Gibbons fell prey to a series of con artists. For example, to support a plan to feed inner-city poor with "French intensive gardening," Consumers United bought a two-hundred-acre farm in Virginia. When the farmer disappeared, along with any hope of a miracle crop, so did the company's investment.

Finally, in 1992, with Consumers United struggling under a $2.5 million lawsuit from its landlord, Delaware regulators placed the company in receivership. By February 1993, Gibbons no longer had control of the company, and its employee owners had lost everything.

The Legacy of Consumers United

Gibbons's legacy is still felt in Parkside, where many inner-city students were able to attend college thanks to Consumers United's funding of a program called Young People on the Rise. As commendable as its goals have been, said an official from the Delaware Insurance Department, "Would you want him to [invest] . . . your insurance money?"

The New Bottom Line

The real victims of Gibbons's poor (but well-intentioned) investing were the two hundred employee owners of Consumers United, who lost everything, and groups such as Young People on the Rise, who might have ultimately benefited from a more fiscally sound investment strategy. Like any other aspect of a corporation, social responsibility must be approached with good business sense.

SOURCE: B. Gifford, "Too Much of a Good Thing," *Business Ethics*, November–December 1993, pp. 21–24.

▼ **EXHIBIT 6–3**
Three Propositions for a New Conversation about Corporate Social Responsibility

Proposition #1:	Corporations are connected networks of stakeholder interests.
Proposition #2:	Corporations are places in which individual human beings and human communities engage in caring activities that are aimed at mutual support and unparalleled human achievement.
Proposition #3:	Corporations are merely the means through which human beings are able to either create and recreate or describe and redescribe their visions of self and community.

SOURCE: R. E. Freeman and J. Liedka, "Corporate Social Responsibility: A Critical Approach," *Business Horizons,* July–August 1991, p. 96.

less efficient. Although it may satisfy an automobile company's social goals to contribute $1 million annually to the United Way, for example, that contribution represents $1 million not reinvested in making better cars.

Monolithic Business Some theorists worry that big business already has enough power and should not be trusted to be society's conscience as well. The basic values of business—efficiency and materialism—are not the basic values of society. By saddling corporations with social responsibility, we are giving them an avenue through which to impose their values in an area in which these values are not appropriate.

Complexity Some critics suggest that businesspeople are not trained to handle social problems and asking them to do so is akin to asking a taxi driver to pilot a jet plane. Social ills, such as discrimination against minorities and women, are so deep-seated and multifarious that even experts in the field often can't begin to solve them. What chance, then, does an executive with an MBA or an advertising expert have? (See the *Case—Benetton and Responsive Advertising*—at the end of this chapter.)

Accountability Because social involvement by business is commonly seen as an unquestionable good, there is little scrutiny of the results. Some critics point out that because there is no legislation concerning the matter, society has no control over a business's social activities. For example, companies are often lauded for contributing to the construction of cultural landmarks, such as a new classical music concert hall or a performing arts center. When a new concert hall is built, however, it inevitably leads to the end of economic viability for the old one. The business community in which the old concert hall exists—restaurants, cafés, shops, and parking garages—suffers a loss of customers, who now flock to the location of the new establishment. By contributing to the new concert hall, the participating companies are essentially choosing the well-being of one community over another, a choice for which they cannot be held legally accountable.

THE ARGUMENT FOR CORPORATE SOCIAL RESPONSIBILITY

It is important to note that the above arguments against corporate social responsibility are not currently popular among some academicians and economists. Most proponents of corporate social responsibility base their views on a combination of ethical and practical considerations. They feel that business has a moral duty to consider society's well-being when making decisions. Accompanying this attitude is the practical wisdom that "you can't do business with your house on fire."

TRADITIONAL CORPORATE SOCIAL RESPONSIBILITY: NOBLESSE OBLIGE

The idea of corporate social responsibility in the United States started with the leaders of the industrial revolution. Steel magnate Andrew Carnegie (1835–1919) gave $350 million (which is equivalent to a sum considerably higher than $2 billion in today's dollars) for philanthropic causes. He founded the Carnegie Corporation of New York to fund education; the Carnegie Endowment for International Peace; the Carnegie Foundation for the Endowment of Teaching; and the Carnegie Institution of Washington, which conducts scientific research. Over $56 million of Carnegie's charitable funds went to build 2,500 libraries in the United States, Great Britain, Canada, and other English-speaking countries.[16] When he retired, Carnegie wrote an article, called "Wealth," which outlined how large personal fortunes should be used to better society.

Henry Ford (1863–1947), founder of the Ford Motor Company, created the Ford Foundation, the world's largest philanthropic organization. Oil tycoon John D. Rockefeller gave $183 million to start the Rockefeller Foundation in 1913.

Of course, much of this philanthropic activity had a public relations motive. In the early part of the twentieth century, big business was criticized for antisocial behavior. But there was also a sense of **noblesse oblige**, "the obligations of nobility." This concept goes back to ancient times; in many civilizations the upper classes felt a responsibility to aid the unfortunate. As the concept became preeminent in the Western hemisphere, the different religious groups prodded the upper classes to redistribute some of their wealth to the poor.

The Charity Principle Notions of philanthropy, for the most part, are based on the **charity principle**—the expectation of giving to the poor. A sense of charity is as old as the differences in income and wealth among segments of society. Royalty has consistently been expected to give to the poor. Passages in the Koran dictate that Muslims always be charitable to those in need. The Bible has many passages about charity. Throughout the history of business in the United States, corporate leaders have always engaged in some charitable actions.

As can be expected, private charitable activity has been the highest when public charitable activity has been the lowest. Until the twentieth century, government was not expected to provide much of a safety net for those in need. Consequently, the private sector, particularly in the late 1800s, engaged in commensurately high levels of charitable activities. Today, those in need can turn to Social Security, Aid to Families with Dependent Children, and unemployment insurance, to name just a few public sources of financial help. It is not surprising, therefore, that wealthy businesspersons today funnel their charitable activities in other directions—museums, opera, and the other arts, for example.[17] Today there are many quasi-public organizations, such as the Community Chest and the United Way, to which businesses and wealthy individuals donate large sums of money.

---

16. *World Book Encyclopedia*, 1979, s.v. "Carnegie, Andrew."
17. These public entities receive public subsidies, too, however.

Trusteeship Some say that charity is not the only principle on which corporate philanthropy is based. Rather, they believe that today's corporate executives must view themselves as trustees for the public welfare. In other words, in spite of the fact that corporations are privately owned, their leaders often believe they have an obligation to the general public. This trusteeship view of corporate philanthropy was developed more than thirty years ago by Frank W. Abrams, when he put forth the then-revolutionary concept that business managers should have their own version of the physicians' Hippocratic Oath:

> Business firms are man-made instruments of society. They can be made to achieve their greatest social usefulness—and thus their future can be best assured—when management succeeds in finding a harmonious balance amongst the claims of the various interested groups. . . . Management, as a good citizen, and because it cannot properly function in an acrimonious and contentious atmosphere, has the positive duty to work for peaceful relations and understanding among men—for a restoration of men in each other in all walks of life.[18]

It is not surprising that the trusteeship principle of corporate social philanthropy forms the basis of the modern stakeholder view of how managers should act. The public at large—Abrams's "various interested groups"—is broken up into various stakeholders: shareholders, employees, consumers, and the community, for example. Well-intentioned business executives take account of the effects of their actions on all stakeholders, not just the effects on the shareholders.

Questions of Paternalism The attitude of **paternalism**—the idea that some other person knows what is best for the individual better than the individual knows for himself

---

18. F. W. Abrams, "Management's Responsibilities in a Complex World," *Harvard Business Review*, May 1951, pp. 29–35.

or herself—in the actions of Carnegie, Ford, and others is obvious; in fact, these entrepreneurs probably would have been proud to have themselves perceived as wise and kind parents to their workers or the impoverished masses. This attitude may have been admired in the early part of the century, but it is not today. For the most part, today's resistance to paternalism has focused on the government and its attempts to regulate such activities as smoking and health care. Programs such as welfare have also come under public attack by some people for being paternalistic.

As far as business is concerned, the idea of paternalism provides another balancing act. There is certainly the widespread belief that a corporation "owes" its employees certain benefits, such as workers' compensation, health insurance, and child-care facilities. Corporations are also expected to show concern for other stakeholders, such as the community and the environment. There is a line, though, that business should not cross in its efforts to be socially responsible—a line that managers must learn to recognize.

The Boston billboard company Ackerly Communications, for example, no doubt felt it was doing the right thing when it announced in 1994 that it would no longer post movie advertisements featuring guns in high-crime areas. Some local activists, however, were not pleased with what they felt was a "paternalistic" pattern—the gun ban only covered African American neighborhoods. "If it's bad for the black community, maybe it's bad for everyone," said John Roberts, head of the Massachusetts Civil Liberties Union.[19]

MODERN CORPORATE SOCIAL RESPONSIBILITY: ENLIGHTENED SELF-INTEREST

In response to Roberts's criticism, Ackerly Communications CEO Lou Nickinello said he was only acting on the "community's concern."[20] Besides, he added, if he canceled all his billboards that included guns, he would go out of business.

Nickinello's defense underlies a trend in corporate social responsibility today. Because of a growing distrust of business, the idea of *noblesse oblige* has lost some of its luster; it has become difficult for the public to trust a company that claims to be giving something for nothing. In addition, in the economic slowdown of the late 1980s and early 1990s, companies could no longer justify giving money away for philanthropic reasons alone. (See *Managing Social Issues—Forging New Alliances: Honda and Giving for Education* on page 158.)

The more popular view of corporate social responsibility today is **enlightened self-interest**, or the marriage between economic and social concerns. If a company can explain that its social responsibility has an economic motive, it will satisfy both a mistrustful public and its shareholders. There are several key aspects of enlightened self-interest, as noted by experts on corporate social responsibility, and we examine them now.

Positive Publicity If society expects corporations to have social concerns, then it is certainly within a company's best interests to be socially active, and to trumpet that fact. Often—as is the case with the Ford Foundation, the Ronald McDonald House, and other foundations—the name of the corporation features prominently in the name of the philanthropic organization.

---

19. "Self-Banned in Boston," *Newsweek*, July 25, 1994, p. 6.
20. *Ibid.*

⊡ MANAGING SOCIAL ISSUES

FORGING NEW ALLIANCES: HONDA AND GIVING FOR EDUCATION

Honda, Inc., may be a Japanese corporation, but it has a significant presence in the United States. After all, the company builds more cars in this country than in Japan. Thus, it is no surprise that Honda is at the vanguard of a new wave of social responsibility among Japanese corporations toward Americans. One of the company's more ambitious projects could help its host country in a vital area: education.

Eagle Rock School

The American Honda Education Corporation (AHEC), a nonprofit spin-off from the giant parent corporation, is committed to donating $40 million over a ten-year period to launch and support the Eagle Rock School in Estes Park, Colorado. The school and educator training center, which opened in the summer of 1994, gives preference to students who have not been able to succeed in the rigid, highly structured public school system.

The hope is that troubled students will benefit from the atmosphere of living in the crest of the Rockies, and will flourish in a curriculum that not only stresses education but also builds self-esteem through a series of Outward Bound–style activities. Honda has set a budget of $15,000 per student to cover needed expenses, an amount in line with annual tuition at many colleges and universities.

Eagle Rock plans to publicize its successes by inviting educators from public schools around the country to watch its work in progress. "There is no reason why anything that American Honda is going to do could not be done in a large school district," pointed out Rex Brown, senior fellow at the Education Commission, a school reform think tank based in Denver. "[Eagle Rock] goes way beyond Band-aids like Adopt-a-School, and way beyond most business partnerships."

Motives beyond Philanthropy

American Honda's affiliation with Eagle Rock was no happenstance. The corporation sent two of its employees, Tom Dean and Makato Itabashi, to spend a year studying the social problems that plague the United States. Eventually, education reform was targeted as an area in which Honda could make a difference, and AHEC was founded.

Shinsaqku Sogo, president of the Inter-Pacific Institute for Communication in Denver, thinks that more Japanese companies will follow American Honda's lead. He noted that historically, Japanese multinational corporations have stuck with "high-brow" philanthropy—giving to Japanese-related programs, prestigious universities, and cultural institutions. As these companies become more comfortable with the often dizzying mosaic of American culture, Sogo believes, their social responsibility will diversify accordingly.

For Critical Analysis:

How does the concept of enlightened self-interest apply to Honda's desire to diversify its philanthropic activities in the United States?

SOURCE: B. Warren, "At the Head of Its Class," *Business Ethics*, July–August 1993, p. 17.

Fear of Government Regulation It is widely accepted among the business community that self-regulation is preferable to government regulation. The proponent of enlightened self-interest can argue that companies must act in a socially responsible manner before public outcry forces the government to make them socially responsible. In 1969, for example, the Motion Picture Association of America created a Classification and Rating Administration board to rate motion pictures based on content, and in 1990 the Recording Industry Association of America started to place warning labels on compact discs with sexually explicit lyrics—both actions designed to head off a movement within federal and state government to regulate those industries.

OPTIMIZING PROFITS

Proponents of enlightened self-interest can defend their position by pointing to polls like the one conducted by Roper Starch Worldwide. Based on interviews with almost two thousand individuals, the pollsters found that when choosing between products of equal price and quality, 78 percent of the respondents would choose the product from the company with the better philanthropic record.[21] The poll also showed that two-thirds would switch brands to a manufacturer that supported a social cause they liked, and one-third of those surveyed said they were more influenced by a company's social activism than by its advertising.

The headline of a short article in *Fortune* describing the poll read, "Good Citizenship Is Good Business." The headline jumps to conclusions, however, as do some proponents of enlightened self-interest. Nowhere does the poll give the reader a quantitative study of how a positive public image might financially benefit a company. It would be very difficult for any polling organization or research firm to supply this information; as this textbook goes to press, no absolutely reliable formula for equating corporate social responsibility and profits exists. Furthermore, polls like this one may in fact reflect people's attitudes or intentions rather than their actual behavior. Also, people are not always honest in answering the interviewers' questions.

Companies can only make strong assumptions about the profit-enhancing effects of a public relations-minded social responsibility campaign. As is true in the preceding section with the idea of long-term best interest, most of the incentive for enlightened self-interest is negative. The corporate executive worries, if we *don't* do it, something bad will happen.

MAXIMUM PROFITS AND OPTIMUM PROFITS

Executives who accept the idea of enlightened self-interest today must be willing to accept **optimum profits** rather than **maximum profits**. In most annual reports, a CEO tells the company's stockholders that every measure is being taken to ensure maximum profits. In the planning session with managers, however, the same CEO may accept optimum profits, which is a satisfactory level of profits considering external pressures, such as government regulation. Executives who make social responsibility decisions based on long-run goals are trading maximum short-run profits (the most that could be made this quarter) for optimum profits (what they are willing to make this quarter in light of other developments).

ETHICAL INVESTING

During the 1970s, so-called **ethical investing mutual funds** were started. The founders of these mutual funds guaranteed to the purchasers of their shares that they would invest only in companies that were ethical. They would not invest in the Dow Chemical Company, for example, because it produced napalm that was used in the Vietnam War. They would not invest in corporations that had any dealings with South Africa, because at that time South Africa practiced *apartheid*, or complete separation of the races. Today, there are various types of ethical investing mutual funds that specifically invest money in corporations that are "environmentally kind."

The popularity of ethical investment funds has definitely been increasing, climbing from $40 billion in 1984 to an estimated $75 billion in 1996. The money managers of these ethical funds scan the universe of over 8,500 publicly held companies to determine

---

21. J. Martin, "Good Citizenship is Good Business," *Fortune*, March 21, 1992, pp. 15–16.

these ethical funds scan the universe of over 8,500 publicly held companies to determine which ones meet their ethical standards. *Exhibit 6–4* gives a sampling of ethical funds.

The funds vary widely in where they will or will not invest. In some cases, the determining factor may be a firm's involvement in defense contracts or in nuclear power plants. In other cases, it may be the extent to which a firm is concerned with consumer protection.

Ethical funds sometimes must face trade-offs between optimum profits and maximum profits. A study comparing 1990 returns on ethical investments to the Dow Jones Industrial Average (DJIA) showed that although some funds gained higher returns than the DJIA, the ethical funds lagged behind in overall rate of return. As the Parnassus Fund's returns show, however, the study's findings are not true for all ethical investing mutual funds (see *Managing Social Issues—Parnassus Fund: Socially Successful Investing*).

STRATEGIC CORPORATE PHILANTHROPY

Corporate philanthropy can be strategic when decision makers undertake it in a consistent, well-planned manner, with specific concrete goals in mind. More specifically, this occurs when the corporate gift givers actively work with the recipient. Craig Smith, president of Corporate Citizen, a Seattle think tank, disagrees that corporate social responsibility precludes maximum profits, and he warns of how that line of thinking can hurt a

▼ **EXHIBIT 6–4**
"Ethical" Funds

Fund Name & Telephone	Sales Charge	1990–1991 Return*	1991–1992 Return*	Portfolio
Pax World 800-767-1729	None	22.4%	2.4%	Avoids liquor, tobacco, gambling industries; Department of Defense contractors
New Alternatives 516-466-0808	5.66%	12.4%	−4.0%	Purchases stock in firms involved in conservation and recycling
Calvert-Ariel Appreciation 800-368-2748	4.75%	21.6%	10.9%	Avoids investments in South Africa
Dreyfus Third Century 800-645-6561	None	21.5%	0.8%	Invests in companies with policies on the environment, employment, and consumer protection
Parnassus 800-999-3505	3.50%	17.3%	3.2%	Invests in companies sensitive to employees, customers, and communities

*Returns are from July 1 to June 31 of each year.

SOURCE: Roger LeRoy Miller and Alan D. Stafford, *Economic Issues for Consumers,* 7th ed. (St. Paul: West Publishing Co., 1994), p. 24.

▣ MANAGING SOCIAL ISSUES

PARNASSUS FUND: SOCIALLY SUCCESSFUL INVESTING

The investment community generally has a low opinion of ethical investing mutual funds, but its criticisms do not hit the mark in the case of the Parnassus Fund. In an industry in which profits are valued above all other performance considerations, Parnassus and its president, Jerome L. Dodson, have prospered by making decisions to invest in companies based on their treatment of the environment as well as their potential profit margins. In the process, Dodson has proved that, as he puts it, "You don't need to suck wind because you're a social investor."

The Investment Balancing Act

With a 150 percent cumulative five-year return for its investors from 1990 to 1995, Parnassus has hardly been standing still. Not only does its success more than double the performance of any other socially motivated mutual fund in the same time period, but it also ranks tenth among *all* long-term growth funds. The secret to his success, says Dodson, lies in balancing the social and economic prospects of any company the fund considers.

This balancing act is restricted by a set of guidelines. The social guidelines will not allow Parnassus to invest in industries involved with gambling, alcohol, tobacco, nuclear power, or weapons. The fund favors companies that show ethical treatment of employees, equal employment opportunity, environmental protection, and ethical business practices. Financially, Dodson focuses on one major factor: potential growth.

Mentor Graphics typifies the type of company that attracts Dodson's interest. By producing advanced software that allows engineers to design specialized semiconductors, Mentor satisfied the criteria of operating in a growing market. On the social side, the company was highly rated in its employee relations, offering benefits such as on-site health care. To find such companies, Dodson admits that "you have to look a little harder, but there are more than enough to choose from."

Rationale for the Parnassus Philosophy

Why add the social component to a mutual fund business, which is difficult enough without more restrictions? Simply put, Parnassus's shareholders "like to invest in companies that are good corporate citizens." Dodson dismisses the notion that socially responsible investing necessarily limits a fund's effectiveness. He credits his own success to in-depth knowledge of two hundred companies, from which he chooses to invest Parnassus's $150 million. "Clearly, [other social funds] need to get better at financial analysis, and then they'll do well."

For Critical Analysis:

Parnassus will invest in a company that experiments with animals in order to save human lives, but it does not consider companies that conduct animal experiments for cosmetics research. Do you find this stance to be consistent with the fund's stated social goals?

SOURCE: Information from F. W. Frailey, "Jerome Dodson: Insider Interview," *Kiplinger's Personal Finance*, October 1, 1995, p. 90; and J. Wyatt, "A Fund That Does Well by Doing Good," *Fortune*, December 13, 1993, p. 40.

corporation dearly.[22] As an example, Smith offers the Exxon Education Foundation, long regarded as a paragon of social responsibility. Because the foundation has outside directors, it is not linked with the business leaders of Exxon, beyond a huge endowment. In essence, Exxon was willing to accept what it considered to be optimum profits by funding

22. C. Smith, "The New Corporate Philosophy," *Harvard Business Review*, May–June 1994, p. 107.

a philanthropic organization with little or no direct ties to profits. Consequently, the foundation proceeded in its social funding without considering the interests of Exxon itself, including good relations with environmental groups.

This strategy proved disastrous after the *Exxon Valdez* oil spill in 1989. Exxon's chairman, Lawrence G. Rawl, had no contact with environmental groups through his company's foundation, and he had nowhere to turn for advice. Exxon was forced to take a defensive stance against the outrage of the Audubon Society, the Sierra Club, the National Wildlife Federation, and other environmental organizations. Had Rawl established relationships with his corporation's "natural" enemies in the political-environmental-business landscape, his corporation might have had an easier time in the years of litigation that followed the spill.

The McDonald's Corporation took a different approach. Long the target of environmentalists because of the huge amount of waste generated by the corporation's international chain of fast-food restaurants, McDonald's decided to take a conciliatory stance. In 1990, the corporation entered a nonfinancial agreement with the Environmental Defense Fund (EDF). A joint EDF–McDonald's Solid Waste Task Force (SWTF) was created, and by the summer of 1994, twenty-three of the forty-two SWTF initiatives to reduce waste had been completed. Thanks to the alliance, McDonald's changed its packaging from polystyrene foam to paper, and the negative publicity from environmental groups lessened considerably.[23]

---

23. T. A. Hemphill, "Strange Bedfellows Cozy Up for a Clean Environment," *Business and Society Review,* Summer, 1994, p. 40.

THE DELICATE BALANCE

There is no doubt that the age of the so-called unenlightened corporate manager is over. For one thing, there is always the threat that an investigative journalist will uncover a corporation's wrongdoing. Also, those who argue against even the concept of corporate social responsibility seem to be part of a dwindling minority. For the most part today, all major corporations accept that they must act in a socially responsible manner.

Furthermore, the way in which corporations engage in socially responsible behavior is changing. Global competition, a subject you will read more about in the next chapter, is forcing many corporations to cut costs and become more efficient. One such cost-cutting maneuver by major corporations involves reducing the size and number of contributions given out each year. Today's corporation is constantly reexamining the delicate balance between keeping its good name in the community through corporate contributions and other socially responsible acts as well as keeping its products low priced through effective cost cutting everywhere in the organization.

TERMS AND CONCEPTS FOR REVIEW

Charity principle 155
Corporate social responsibility 145
Enlightened self-interest 157
Ethical investing mutual fund 159

Maximum profits 159
Noblesse oblige 155
Optimum profits 159
Pareto optimality 146

Paternalism 156
Responsiveness 150

SUMMARY

1. In order for an individual in a corporate organization to be held responsible for his or her actions, there must be within the organization (a) someone to praise or blame, (b) something that has to be done, and (c) some kind of trustworthiness that can be expected from the individual.
2. The idea of the responsibility of a corporation includes the fact that the corporation is a legal fiction. Consequently, the actions of a corporation can only be attributed to some individuals within that corporate structure.
3. One definition of corporate social responsibility involves the obligation of corporate decision makers to take actions that protect and improve the welfare of society as a whole.
4. Pareto optimality, a microeconomics concept, occurs when firms are using resources and producing goods in such a way that it would be impossible to make one person better off without harming another person. This is an ideal, or goal, of an efficient business.
5. According to Archie Carroll, a pyramid theory is useful in explaining how each individual business can contribute to Pareto optimality for the entire economy. At the base of the pyramid, the organization must be profitable, or it will not exist. At the second level, all actions must be legal. At the next level, individual actors within the business community must act ethically. At the top, corporations should undertake some philanthropic responsibilities.
6. Because corporations are subject to conflicting loyalties, they must constantly make trade-offs, particularly in deciding where "social" funds should go. Some of the trade-offs involve safer working conditions, safer products, higher-quality products, lower prices, increased or decreased employment within a community, and so on.
7. Some researchers, including Robert Akerman and Raymond Bauer, argue in favor of an action-oriented view of corporate social responsibility. They believe it should be called corporate social responsiveness.
8. According to researcher S. Prakash Sethi, there are three critical stages of corporate behavior: (a) social obligation, (b) social responsibility, and (c) social responsiveness.
9. Some free market economists, such as Milton Friedman, follow the tradition of Adam Smith, who wrote in 1776 that individuals acting in their own self-interest would be guided, as if by an invisible hand, to maximize total social welfare. Consequently, Friedman and others argue that the entire concept of corporate social responsibility is to be questioned. According to these critics, we in the United States have elected leaders to make social policy. Since corporate directors and managers are not elected, they should not be making social policy.
10. Researchers R. E. Freeman and Jeanne Liedka argue that corporations should become part of a larger social mosaic in which caring has primary significance. Thus, they see corporations as needing to care for all stakeholders, including employees, consumers, and the community.
11. Proponents of traditional corporate responsibility included Andrew Carnegie, Henry Ford, and John D. Rockefeller. They set up numerous philanthropic foundations and were governed by a sense of "the obligations of nobility," or *noblesse oblige*.

12. The idea that corporations should engage in philanthropic activities is based on the charity principle. Charitable giving from all sectors of the economy, however, has declined as the government has assumed more of the role of helping those in need in our society.

13. The trusteeship theory says that corporate executives must engage in philanthropy because they are trustees for the public welfare.

14. Today, the most prevalent theory of corporate social responsibility relates to enlightened self-interest, or the marriage between economic and social concerns. Being a good corporate citizen generates (a) long-term benefits, (b) positive publicity, and (c) perhaps less government regulation.

15. Today, many modern corporations engage in strategic corporate philanthropy, in which they have an active role in dealing with the recipients of any corporate contributions.

EXERCISES

1. Explain the inherent conflict between the *laissez-faire* ("let it alone") theories of free market economists such as Milton Friedman and the general concept of corporate social responsibility.

2. This chapter listed three basic concepts that relate to individual responsibility. The first one requires that someone be praised or blamed. Why is this important?

3. We often say that corporations should be held criminally responsible for corporate actions, but how can a court criminally prosecute a corporation?

4. Review the *Exxon Valdez* oil spill information contained near the beginning of this chapter. Write down a series of steps that Exxon could have taken to avoid that disaster.

5. Reexamine *Exhibit 6–1*, which illustrates the pyramid theory of Archie Carroll. Make an outline of a short speech that you might give in which you explain which of the four levels of the pyramid is most important for the corporation and which level is most important for society.

6. How does the marketplace punish corporations that tend to ignore the welfare of all stakeholders? Give examples.

7. What is the difference between corporate social responsibility and corporate social responsiveness? Is the difference significant, in your view? If so, why?

8. Researchers R. E. Freeman and Jeanne Liedka provide three propositions for a new conversation about corporate social responsibility, presented in *Exhibit 6–3*. Choose one proposition, and find an example of an actual corporation and how a "new conversation" concerning that corporation's activities could result.

9. Corporate officials in charge of charitable contributions by a corporation are responsible to whom?

10. Explain why traditional corporate social responsibility has sometimes been called the doctrine of *noblesse oblige*.

11. How might you criticize the concept of corporate trusteeship by using arguments against paternalism?

12. What is the difference between the enlightened self-interest of a corporation and the profit-maximizing method of business operation?

13. Give examples of how corporate philanthropy can lead to positive publicity. Explain how a corporation might quantify the benefits of this positive publicity.

14. What guidelines would you give to the new head of your corporation's department regarding the distribution of money to various charities? Include at least six points.

SELECTED REFERENCES

▶ Baron, David P. *Business and Its Environment.* Upper Saddle River, N.J.: Prentice Hall, 1996.

▶ Buchholz, R. A. *Fundamental Concepts and Problems in Business Ethics.* Upper Saddle River, N.J.: Prentice Hall, 1989.

▶ Chamberlain, Neil W. *The Limits of Corporate Responsibility.* New York: Basic Books, 1973.

▶ Donaldson, R. "The Social Contract: Norms for a Corporate Conscience." In *Business Ethics: Readings and Cases in Corporate Morality*, 2d ed., eds. W. M. Hoffman and J. M. Moore. New York: McGraw-Hill, 1990.

▶ Estes, Ralph W. *Tyranny of the Bottom Line: Why Corporations Make Good People Do Bad Things.* San Francisco: Berret-Koehler, 1996.

▶ Pava, Moses L. *Corporate Responsibility and Financial Performance: The Paradox of Social Cost.* Westport, Conn.: Quorum Books, 1995.

▶ *Social Responsibilities of Business Corporations.* New York: Committee for Economic Development, 1971.

▶ Walton, Clarence C. *Corporate Social Responsibilities.* Belmont, Calif.: Wadsworth, 1967.

▶ Weber, D. Edward. *Stories of Virtue in Business.* Lanham, Md.: University Press of America, 1995.

RESOURCES ON THE INTERNET

▼ A number of socially responsible corporations have taken up residence on the Internet. The Progressive Business Web Pages is a valuable source of information concerning these businesses. This site can be accessed at

http://envirolink.org.products

▼ For a wealth of information on philanthropic organizations in the United States, you can access the Internet Non-Profit Center, a project of the American Institute of Philanthropy, at

http://human.com/inc/indext.html

or at the following gopher site:

gopher.human.com/11/inc

▼ You can obtain a great deal of information about corporations from the Dunn & Bradstreet databases. If you use the commercial on-line service GEnie, select

Research & Reference Services

Then select

Dunn & Bradstreet (D&B) database

There is a charge for using this service.

▼ From the same on-line commercial service, you can access Dow Jones News Retrieval (for a fee). Do the same as above, but finally select

DowJonesNews/Retrieval

BENETTON AND RESPONSIBLE ADVERTISING

Background

When Luciano Benetton formed Fratelli Benetton near Treviso, Italy, in 1965 with three family members, his initial goal was to establish a small business to sell colorful sweaters. Three decades later, Benetton Group, S.p.A., has more than 7,000 stores in over 110 countries.

Industry watchers have attributed Benetton's success in no small part to the company's various advertising campaigns. In 1984, Benetton hired award-winning photographer Oliviero Toscani to create a new line of advertisements. Given free reign, Toscani came up with a series of ads that showed racially and culturally diverse youths frolicking in bright Benetton clothing. The photographer's idealistic vision of a racially harmonious world was so successful that in 1990 the firm adopted the slogan "United Colors of Benetton" as a catchphrase in its ideological advertising.

Corporate Social Responsibility and Advertising

Despite the success of the current ad campaign, in 1991 Toscani began a new campaign that removed all Benetton products from the company's advertising. Instead, journalistic photographs of thought-provoking or disturbing events, with the green and white United Colors of Benetton logo located in the margins, began showing up in magazines and billboards around the world. Toscani's goal, as Penn State education professor Henry Giroux notes, was to shift Benetton's "emphasis from selling a product to selling an image of corporate social responsibility."

In the campaign's first year, the images in Benetton ads included multicolored condoms floating like balloons through the air, a priest kissing a nun on the lips, and a row of test tubes filled with blood. As the campaign continued, the photos became more editorial in their content: a duck covered with oil symbolized environmental concerns; a photo of a terrorist car bombing protested political violence; and a depiction of former President Ronald Reagan as an AIDS patient appeared in objection to U.S. government policies regarding the disease. Luciano Benetton even appeared nude in one advertisement to urge consumers to give their old clothes to charity.

Peter Fressola, Benetton's director of communication in North America, believes his company's ads have a higher value to society than does most advertising. "We're doing cor-porate communication. We're sponsoring these images in order to change people's minds and create compassion around social issues. We think of it as art with a message." As director of advertising, Toscani says he chooses his images based on their social and political content, not on their effect on the firm's sales: "I am responsible for the company's communication; I am not really responsible for its economics."

Those at Benetton who are responsible for the company's economics see the campaign as a way to both promote social change and sell sweaters. The firm's advertising campaign literature explains: "Among the various means available to achieve the brand recognition that every company must have, we at Benetton believe our strategy for communication to be more effective for the company and more useful for society than would be yet another series of ads showing pretty girls wearing pretty clothes." This belief has been forged through research done by the company, which claims that in the 1990s, "consumers are as concerned by what a company stands for as they are about the price/value of that product."

The strategy appears to be working. Despite recessions in several major markets, Benetton's worldwide sales have doubled since 1988, and in 1996 the firm's net income increased 16 percent from the previous year. David Roberts, an analyst with Nomura International London, says that the firm's global "name recognition is approaching that of Coca-Cola."

Negative Reactions

Acclaim for Benetton's advertising strategy has not been universal, however. Ronald Reagan, for example, was not pleased with the ad in *Colors*, Benetton's quarterly magazine, which showed a picture of his face covered with lesions and included a fictitious obituary saying the ex-president had recently died from AIDS. "Benetton apparently believes that offensiveness and bad taste will sell its products to the American people," said a Reagan spokesperson.

Toscani defended the ad to an Italian magazine, saying Reagan deserved the criticism because he "did nothing to spread the use of condoms, he did nothing to sensitize the people to the risk of contracting" AIDS. But criticism of the ad did not come only from Reagan supporters. Columnist Joseph Perkins called the tactic "simple" and added, "The Italian clothier ought to stick to making halter tops and T-shirts and leave politics to those who know what they are talking about."

CASE (CONTINUED)

Benetton sometimes even draws criticism from the communities whose causes the firm claims to espouse. In 1993, the French nonprofit organization Arcat Sida, or Association for Research Against AIDS, called for a boycott of Benetton products in response to an ad that showed photographs of various body parts with tattoos that read "HIV Positive."

Pierre Bergé, who heads Arcat Sida, remarked, "It is a shame to create this sort of publicity based on the suffering of AIDS." The group took out a "United Boycott" ad in several French journals. The text, a letter to Luciano Benetton, reads, in part, "Mr. Benetton, during the agony, the sales continue."

Another ad, which portrayed an AIDS patient named David Kirby in a hospital room shortly before he would die from the disease, also brought an onslaught of criticism on Benetton. The Kirby image, said one observer, only served to strengthen the stereotype of people with AIDS: "that they are ravaged, disfigured, and debilitated by the syndrome (and that) they are generally . . . desperate, but resigned to their inevitable deaths." In other words, by relying on "clichés enforced through dominant images and their social effects, the Benetton ad reproduces rather than challenges conventional representations that portray people with AIDS as helpless victims."

Benetton ads have even drawn the attention of some federal governments. An advertisement featuring a newborn baby covered in blood was banned in Germany, France, Italy, and the United Kingdom at the urging of the Advertising Standards Authority (ASA). After the firm ran a photo showing the blood-soaked uniform of a Croatian soldier killed in the war in Bosnia, Lucette Michaux-Chévry, France's minister for humanitarian affairs, decried the exploitation of war for business and urged the French people to boycott Benetton products and "to pull them off people who are going to wear them."

Success of the Ad Campaign

In answer to the protests against the ads concerning AIDS issues, Benetton's Peter Fressola said, "The greatest foe in the fight against AIDS is invisibility. It takes a shocking image sometimes to jar people out of complacency. The purpose of the ads is not to sell clothing, but the caveat is that Benetton is in business to sell apparel. The ads are designed, at the same time as they raise awareness of a serious issue, to make awareness of our label."

Giroux bristles at this "moral high ground" that he feels Benetton takes regarding its controversial ads. He focuses on the presence of the firm's logo in each of the photographs. He believes the logo asserts that "the purpose of advertising is to subordinate all values to the imperative of profit." For Giroux, a statement by a Benetton official, "We want anyone who has seen the logotype, even fleetingly, to never forget it, or at least to forget it slowly," offers a "powerful indictment" of the firm's rationale. Giroux says, "Isolated from historical and social contexts, Benetton's images are stripped of their political possibilities and reduced to a spectacle of fascination, horror, and terror. . . . The logo produces a 'zone of comfort' confirming a playfulness which allows the viewer to displace any ethical or political understanding of the images contained in the Benetton ads."

Giroux also points to the powerful commercial potential of "shock, sensationalism, and voyeurism." After the ASA called for a ban on the ad with the blood-covered baby, an Adwatch survey showed that 12 percent of people polled spontaneously recalled the advertisement—up 400 percent from the week before, when no ban had been mentioned. An Adwatch analyst marveled that such recall was "outrageous—in terms of value for money, [the ad] is way ahead of the field."

Critical Thinking Questions

1. Do you think that Benetton is crossing boundaries of ethics and good taste with its politically tinged advertising campaign? Do you agree with Henry Giroux that "the purpose of advertising is to subordinate all values to the imperative of profit"?

2. How does Benetton's advertising campaign affect your attitude toward purchasing its products? Would you take part in a Benetton boycott?

3. Whether you agree or disagree with the content of Benetton's ads, should they be subject to government regulation for moral content?

4. Oliviero Toscani says, "I am responsible for the company's communication; I am not really responsible for its economics." Do you accept this statement? How are communications and economics linked in advertising?

5. Could Benetton do more for causes such as AIDS prevention by donating money and providing volunteers to organizations that deal with the social issue instead of by making it the centerpiece of an advertising campaign?

SOURCE: Information from A. M. Spindler, "French Ad Urges Boycott of Benetton," *New York Times*, November 23, 1993, p. B11; P. Gumbel, "Benetton Is Stung by Backlash over Ad," *Wall Street Journal*, March 4, 1994, p. A4; H. A. Giroux, "Benetton: Buying Social Change," *Business and Society Review*, Spring 1994, p. 7–10; "A Blast at Benetton," *Washington Post*, June 29, 1994, p. D3; R. Crain, "Social Marketing Misses the Mark," *Advertising Age*, September 26, 1994, p. 22; and "Banned Baby Ad Breaks Adwatch Recall Record," *Marketing*, September 19, 1991, p. 8.

CHAPTER 7

ETHICAL DECISIONS IN A GLOBAL ENVIRONMENT

CHAPTER OUTLINE

- The Global Economy
- Regulating Global Ethics
- Further Issues in Global Ethics

INTRODUCTION

*I*n the 1940s, Republican presidential candidate Wendell Wilkie spoke optimistically of "one world" in which all the countries around the globe would be linked by a single market. His prophecy has not yet come true, but just how close are we toward a unified world economy? According to some, the new "global" economy is more myth than reality. Paul Krugman, a professor at the Massachusetts Institute of Technology, says, "We are living in a world which is about as integrated, give or take a few measures, as the world of the 19th century."[1]

Krugman points to a variety of statistics to back his claim. As a percentage of gross world production, trade in goods and services is only marginally larger now than it was in the years before World War I. Measured against gross domestic product, U.S. imports in 1880 were 8 percent; by the mid-1990s, that number had risen to only 11 percent.[2] Because of greater restrictions on immigration, international labor mobility is also lower than it was at the turn of the century. In Asian corporations, noted one observer, "foreign board members are as rare as British sumo wrestlers."[3]

Today's executives and managers may appreciate Krugman's argument on an intellectual level, but statistics also show that more of them are involved in international business transactions than ever before. As of the mid-1990s, researchers at the United Nations counted 35,000 different companies doing business overseas, totaling 170,000 foreign affiliates among them.[4] Even those companies concerned primarily with domestic trade must deal with the global economy in deciding where to secure raw materials, services, supplies, and even human resources.

Managers in the nineteenth century would have been amazed by the global decisions that now go into the production of a consumer good such as the Mazda sports car. The MX-5 Miata was designed in California; its prototype was produced in England and assembled in Michigan and Mexico using electronic components invented in New Jersey—all financed by funds from New York and Tokyo.[5]

The free market seems to be everywhere. One symbol is the Tiananmen Square intersection in Beijing, where a lone Chinese dissident stopped a row of tanks for a brief instant during the bloody pro-democracy demonstrations in June 1989; soon after, that intersection became home to the world's largest McDonald's.[6]

With new business opportunities comes a new set of ethical considerations for the global manager. If the management of a successful Florida supermarket chain decides to expand into Georgia and Alabama, it has a completely different set of challenges than a California television manufacturer opening a plant in Mexico. In this chapter, we examine the ethics of global business—the ethics of a world economy that, if not unified according to Krugman's definition, has indeed been transformed by financial, political, and technological earthquakes.

---

1. A. Farnham, "Global—Or Just Globaloney?" *Fortune,* June 27, 1994, p. 98.
2. *Ibid.*
3. *Ibid.*
4. "Multinationals: Back in Fashion," *Economist,* March 27, 1993, Survey 1.
5. R. Reich, "Who Is Them?" *Harvard Business Review,* March–April 1991, p. 79.
6. T. Friedman "The Buck Doesn't Stop for Human Rights in China," *Pittsburgh Gazette,* May 24, 1994, p. A5. It is also interesting to note that this particular McDonald's was forced to move to another location to make way for a shopping mall.

THE GLOBAL ECONOMY

The communications revolution has made business, particularly finance, a global activity. Seldom does anything occur in one part of the world that remains unknown in another part of it. A political event that causes businesses to rethink investing in one country may instantaneously cause financial capital to flow out of that country into other countries. It is not surprising that the globalization of business in the world today has created dramatic changes in our business culture.

GLOBALIZATION OF BUSINESS CULTURE

Most experts agree that our global economy is rooted in the economic dominance of the United States during the postwar years of World War II. Richard D. Robinson sees the *postwar decade* (the years immediately following the end of World War II) as the first of four distinct eras of international business development.[7] During that decade, as the United States gave aid to its former foes in West Germany and Japan, American companies began to take advantage of the low-cost resources (such as labor) that were available in these and other foreign countries. Indeed, cheap resources and labor have historically been among the primary incentives for doing business outside one's home country.

The second era, the *growth years* (1955–1970), focuses on the resurgence of Western Europe and Japan on the international economic scene. Fueled by the Vietnam War, the American economy was very strong during the 1960s. During the growth years, the possibility of high profits in foreign markets was realized through the development of international communications systems and technology such as jet air travel.

In the *time of trouble*, the third era, lasting throughout the 1970s, the United States started to fall from its lofty economic position. The value of the dollar relative to gold plummeted as a series of policy decisions by the Nixon administration (1969–1974) led to the abandonment of the Bretton Woods agreement of 1945. It was this agreement that kept the price of gold, in terms of dollars, fixed for many years. Although the United States maintained a dominant economic position, the other industrialized countries were catching up, which in itself favored the trend toward globalization.

The relative decline (until the mid-1990s) of the United States is the focal point of the fourth era, the *new international order*, which runs from 1980 to the present. Japan and Germany, along with newly developed industrial nations such as South Korea and Taiwan, have taken their places as economic powers on the world stage, often dealing from positions of strength with regard to the United States.

The new international order also involves the growth of political pressures around the globe. Without strong government control in many regions, religious, ethnic, and nationalistic differences are leading to disastrous situations. These pressures have already exploded in the Baltic states and in African countries such as Somalia, Burundi, and Rwanda and may yet surface in other areas within the former Soviet Union.

THE MULTINATIONAL OR GLOBAL CORPORATION

The representatives of U.S. businesses in foreign countries most often come in the form of a **multinational corporation (MNC)**, now often called a **global corporation**. (A global

---

7. R. D. Robinson, "Background Concepts and Philosophy of International Business from World War II to the Present," in *International Business Knowledge: Managing International Functions in the 1990s*, eds. W. A. Dymsza and R. G. Vamberry (New York: Praeger, 1987), pp. 3–4.

corporation is a more loosely associated group of large domestic corporations from around the world.) Very simply, the MNC is a corporation that has business operations in two or more countries. It is a manifestation of the growth years; as domestic economies expanded, so did the incentive for companies to move branches of operation outside the home country in the form of subsidiaries. By the mid-1990s, companies based in the United States had nearly twenty thousand affiliates around the world. (For an idea of the extent of U.S. multinational corporations, see *Exhibit 7–1*.)

▼ EXHIBIT 7–1 U.S. Multinational Corporations

By the mid-1990s, corporations based in the United States either wholly owned or partially owned 18,698 businesses around the globe. The map below shows in which countries these American affiliates were based.

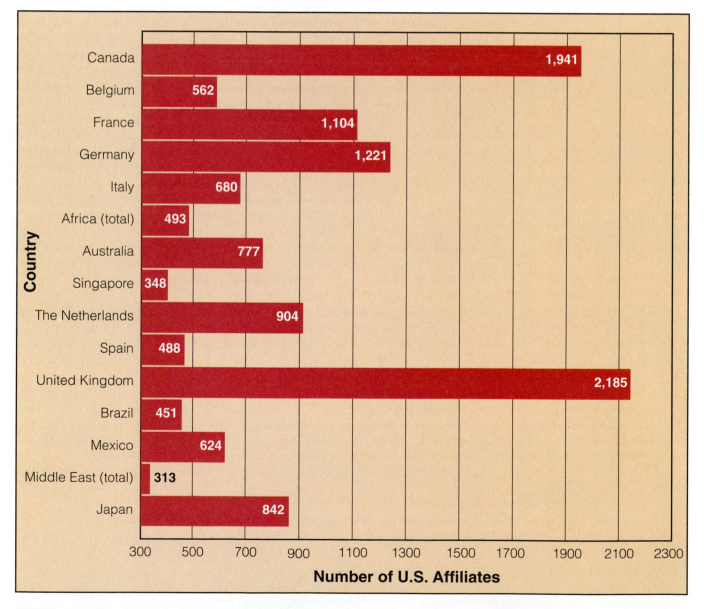

SOURCE: *Survey of Current Business*, June 1995, p. 35.

A BRIEF HISTORY OF MNCs[8]

The international trading company has a long history that includes England's East India Company, established during the reign of Elizabeth I (1533–1603), as well as the American and European companies of the nineteenth century that mined the rich natural resources of Africa, South America, and Asia. But those companies were separate entities that were rarely in contact with any sort of centralized control from home. For our purposes, the precursor to the modern multinational corporation made its first appearance at the end of the 1800s, when communications technology, as limited as it was, made contact between a headquarters and its foreign subsidiaries possible.

Singer and Early MNCs In 1851, Bostonian I. M. Singer invented the first sewing machine; in 1867, the Singer Sewing Machine Company became the first American international business when it built a factory in Glasgow, Scotland. By the end of the 1880s, the company had become an international conglomerate with branches from Montreal to Russia to Australia. Essentially, Singer discovered an economic truism that multinational corporations still rely on today: it is often more profitable to manufacture a product in a foreign market than to manufacture it in a home country for export. The sewing machine company's incentive to open the Glasgow branch was provided by the end of the American Civil War (1861–1865); as U.S. currency rebounded, premiums on foreign exchange were cut, and local wages increased. The foreign-based manufacturing strategy worked so well, in fact, that by 1874 Singer was selling more than half its machines in foreign markets: 126,694 out of 241,679 total sold. Such figures convinced George B. Woodruff, the company's British representative, that "we can never make our business solid except by Branches at all great centers."[9]

Standard Oil, General Electric, International Harvester, and a number of other American companies came to the same conclusion. The improvement in travel and communications via steamship, railway, and telegraph made the control of overseas branches logistically possible. Companies also began to discover that placing local managers, with their understanding of local customs and culture, in charge of subsidiaries improved profits. Furthermore, the spread of protectionism solidified the need for expansion. Many economic historians believe that this was the most important factor for early MNC growth: as governments introduced tariffs to boost local manufacturing and limit imports, it simply became necessary for foreign companies to "go local."

There were a number of European multinational corporations, but U.S. companies were the most dominant by the early 1900s. In 1901, for example, the American Westinghouse factory was the largest industrial plant in Great Britain. Standard Oil was the largest company in all of Europe at the turn of the century, and in 1914 the Ford Motor Company was responsible for a quarter of the automobiles on that continent. The response has been echoed in countries all over the world ever since: "America has invaded Europe not with armed men, but with manufactured goods," complained one British politician. "Its leaders have been captains of industry and skilled financiers whose conquests are having a profound effect on the lives of the masses from Madrid to St. Petersburg."

MNCs and the World Wars In the years between World War I (1914–1918) and World War II (1939–1945), the development of international trade and multinational activity slowed. A number of factors contributed to this situation; an important one was the

---

8. This section is adapted from C. Tugendhat, *The Multinationals* (New York: Random House, 1972), pp. 9–35.
9. M. Wilkins, *The Emergence of Multinational Enterprise* (Cambridge, Mass.: Harvard University Press, 1970), pp. 41–43.

pessimistic feeling that the Great War, as World War I was then known, would not be the end of aggressively nationalistic behavior in the world. With further hostilities expected, some companies were wary of investing abroad, and others were swept up in a fervor to discriminate against foreigners. Inflation also took its toll; with currency in countries such as Germany and Austria nearly worthless, foreign investment was not to be expected. Finally, the Great Depression of 1929 bankrupted thousands of companies and severely limited the resources of the many that survived.

Following World War II, a strong dollar and restored international political stability led to a golden era of U.S. multinational activity. In addition, technological advances made it possible for executives at home to control overseas subsidiaries to a much larger extent. The United States was producing a great many of these advanced technologies, which further benefited the country's corporations. By the end of the 1960s, U.S. companies accounted for an estimated 65 percent of all foreign direct investment in the world. From 1955 to 1970, U.S. direct investment abroad actually grew faster than the U.S. economy as a whole.[10]

The Modern Multinational Corporation Even in its period of rapid growth, U.S. economic activity abroad was dominated by the larger companies. In 1967, nearly half of all American direct investments abroad belonged to three companies: Standard Oil, General Motors, and Ford. In the three decades since, that situation has changed significantly. Rising economic powers such as Japan and Germany have matched the level of the United States in terms of international business activity. Also, a weak dollar has made the United States an attractive site for foreign investment. Furthermore, continual improvements in communications technology have made it much easier to run a business overseas, and this has allowed increased involvement from smaller companies. Finally, important international trade agreements such as the General Agreement on Tariffs and Trade (GATT), the World Trade Organization (WTO), and the North American Free Trade Agreement (NAFTA) have removed the trade barriers that previously limited such activity.

The high levels of international business activity have led some observers to suggest that the very idea of the multinational corporation is outdated. Robert Reich, U.S. secretary of labor under President Bill Clinton, proposed that companies that function internationally are part of a series of "global webs" that make the nationality of a corporation irrelevant. Reich wrote that there is little functional difference between "an American corporation that makes or buys abroad much of what it sells around the world and a 'foreign' corporation that makes or buys in the U.S. what it sells."[11]

The Evolution of the Multinational Corporation Some observers suggest that international businesses evolve, both on an individual level and as a corporate genre. Perhaps the first step occurs when a company such as Singer discovers a need to sell its product in a foreign market for any number of reasons, the most important of which we discuss in the next section. Eventually,

> it becomes necessary to establish a headquarters-based international sales division to coordinate sales to customers in several market countries. Then, as a natural outgrowth, it becomes necessary to establish sales organizations abroad, with all of them reporting to the central international sales division. The next step is the crucial decision to set up

---

10. M. Wilkins, *The Maturing of Multinational Enterprise* (Cambridge, Mass.: Harvard University Press, 1970), p. 375.

11. A. Brummer, "Clintonomics and the Class of MIT," *Guardian* (London), February 6, 1993, p. 27.

manufacturing facilities in market countries and link them to the local marketing and sales organizations. Gradually, the management of these foreign-based facilities becomes staffed by foreign nationals. At this point, the progression from the national company that exports overseas to the multinational company with complete operations in several countries is complete.[12]

This is not, however, the end of the development. The company described is still controlled by the home-based corporate headquarters, and it rarely interacts with affiliates in other countries. The multinational corporation becomes global, or multidomestic, when each separate affiliate functions as a partner in a business confederation. "Instead of a single tree with many branches," writes one businessperson, "there are several corporate trees corresponding to several home country markets which are coequal at least in principle."[13] This multidomestic company has naturally progressed to a form in which overall corporate strategy is designed globally while production and sales decisions are made locally. To avoid confusion, we continue to refer to companies that have reached this state as multinational, but be aware that the definition has been somewhat broadened in recent years.

ECONOMIC BENEFITS OF MNCs

An MNC has the same goal as any other business: to maximize the profits of the company by enlarging its market share and boosting the price of its stocks. At times, the business activity can provide other rewards as well. Karl M. Topp, president and CEO of Die Welt Development Company (DWDC), speaks in glowing terms of his company's joint venture in Kaliningrad, Russia, "a city that is suffering a severe energy shortage, among other

---

12. K. E. Agthe, "Managing the Mixed Marriage," *Business Horizons*, January 1, 1990, p. 37.
13. *Ibid.*

hardships."[14] "Stories of global warming do not help the people living there," Topp says, "but U.S. businesses creating new enterprises can." Noting that the city never had energy problems until Joseph Stalin came along, Topp believes it is "up to U.S. citizens to share their knowledge with the Russians so they can help themselves."

From an ethical viewpoint, Topp's statements are praiseworthy. Companies, however, do not live on ethics alone, and DWDC's investment in rebuilding hydroelectric power plants and other energy-producing facilities in Kaliningrad goes beyond goodwill. "The needs of [Russia's] huge population are enormous," says Topp, "and those considering investing in Russia have a good chance of [building] a sound business foundation."

In the end, whatever side benefits they may receive, MNCs are looking for that sound business foundation. When Topp and DWDC were considering investment in Russia, they gave the competitive advantages of the region equal, if not more, weight than the suffering of the people. A company must understand the competitive advantages of the global corporation before considering the ethical challenges it provides. These advantages are summarized in *Exhibit 7–2*.

ECONOMIC CHALLENGES FOR THE MNC

Not all business ventures in foreign lands end in positive results. Marshall I. Goldman, a professor of Russian economics at Wellesley College, warns of the "hazards and uncertainties" of doing business in Russia.[15] For one thing, Russia "does not yet have a commercial code that governs in practice as well as theory," and that situation exposes assets invested in joint ventures to a constant risk.

Even more alarming, says Goldman, is the Russian Mafia. When Coca-Cola initially refused to pay protection money, a bottling plant that the company was building in Moscow was firebombed. A different Mafia group regularly hijacks Pepsi trucks and sells whatever merchandise they happen to be transporting. This kind of violence often makes it difficult for an MNC to convince employees to relocate and work in Russia. Even if an employee were willing to do so and accept the risks, the cost of maintaining an expatriate in Russia for a year would be between $300,000 and $400,000—more than enough to make the home company think twice.

An unstable government, with the accompanying lack of law and order, is only one of the risks MNCs face; not every country offers the danger of firebombing, but each one has its own challenges:

▼ A country might have a prohibitively high tax rate, a sluggish economy, an inadequately trained work force, or an inadequate transportation system—each of which can divert funds from the MNC's primary motive of making a profit.

MNCs AND HOST COUNTRIES

During the most recent colonial period in international business, international companies enjoyed a significant advantage: they were able to bring their domestic systems of laws with them. At the turn of the century in Peking (Beijing today), for example, the Western powers set up zones of influence, leaving the "foreign" section of the city a hodgepodge of different rules and regulations. The goal of this legal partitioning was not

---

14. "Do the Risks of Starting Joint-Ventures in Russia Outweigh the Benefits?" *Harvard Business Review*, May–June 1994, p. 41.

15. *Ibid.*, p. 36.

▼ **EXHIBIT 7–2 Competitive Advantages of Multinational Corporations**

Cost Advantages	Cost Benefits	Product Differentiation	Product Benefits
Cost reductions via foreign assembly and manufacturing	Because labor costs are lower in other countries, the shipment of parts to those countries may result in lower costs for the MNC. MNCs in the United States have been doing this in Mexico for many years. Some are starting to do it with the formerly closed economies in Eastern Europe, such as Poland, Hungary, and the Czech Republic.	Foreign product distribution in the United States	An MNC can be a distributor for premium foreign products that are highly valued in the United States relative to domestic products. French champagne, Swiss and Belgian chocolates, and luxury German and English automobiles come to mind. Premium foreign-brand and foreign-produced products often give an American MNC an advantage over competitors, particularly if the MNC has signed an exclusive-dealing contract with the foreign manufacturer.
Branding subcontracted finished products from low-cost foreign sources	Many MNCs place their brand names on products that are wholly manufactured in developing countries. Nike has been doing this for many years, as has Benetton.	Selling abroad	The same argument can be used in foreign countries. Often American-made products are considered premium products in other countries. Coca-Cola has maintained a competitive advantage abroad and has obtained higher profits abroad than in the United States because of its American brand premium. Levi's products sell for more elsewhere than they do in the United States.
Global sourcing	This practice has become widespread within corporations that sell small appliances. The companies may end up sourcing parts and subassemblies in the People's Republic of China, Singapore, Hong Kong, Thailand, and elsewhere. These MNCs often quickly switch their source for a component to a neighboring country where they can get it for a lower cost.		
Market expansion abroad resulting in economies of scale	To enjoy the lowest per-unit cost, some MNCs require larger markets and hence larger total demand for their products. They do so not in their home country, in which the market may be saturated, but rather abroad. They are able to move down a declining per-unit cost curve.	Joint ventures as a way to increase product quality	In addition to learning cost-reduction technologies, MNCs in the United States can learn product differentiation and quality improvement methodologies.
The transfer of technology through joint ventures	Many MNCs form joint ventures with efficient foreign producers in order to obtain technological know-how. Such new knowledge can lead to lower costs.	Product licensing in the United States	Many beer companies have licensed famous foreign brands for American markets. The same is true elsewhere. Coors is brewed by Asahi in Japan and by Molsen in Canada. Budweiser is brewed by Guinness in Ireland, Oriental in Korea, and Suntory in Japan. Heineken is brewed by Kirin in Japan and Whitehead in Great Britain.

to ensure that "superior" Western values prevailed in "less civilized" countries; for the most part, the trading powers used their influence to ignore local law and culture. (This exploitation in Peking drove a secret society called the Harmonious Fists to start the Boxer Rebellion in 1898–1900, which was a strong antiforeign movement in China.)

MNCs today have a different relationship with countries in which they do business. The **host government** now has a great deal of regulatory power over any MNC that does business in its jurisdiction, and dealing with that power is a major challenge of international business. Although the host government will often use its power to attract global corporations, it also can act counter to an MNC's interests. Coca-Cola, for example, was expelled from India in 1977 because the company refused to turn over the formula for its soft drink to its Indian business partners, as was then required by law. (Coca-Cola reentered the country in 1993.) In 1995, India took further steps to protect its interests from MNCs; it launched a project to develop and record genetic "profiles" of local flora to keep international drug companies from seeking patents on potentially useful by-products of the plants.[16] Similarly, the South Korean government has moved to prevent international music companies, such as Sony Music and Warner Music, from handling domestic recording acts.[17] An MNC can also experience problems with a host government if the latter's bureaucracy is unstable or inefficient. For example, although the opportunities for global corporations in Russia appear almost limitless, many foreign investors are unwilling to brave the unpredictable government infrastructure to do business in that country. In March 1995, the Russian government presented foreign companies with an "excess wage" tax of 38 percent on all their Russian employees, retroactive to January 1, 1994. Because Russian law allows penalties on retroactive taxes—despite the fact that the companies could not have paid taxes that did not then exist—the fines can be quite heavy. For example, Coca-Cola paid a total of $1.4 million in taxes and fines.[18]

Foreign Corrupt Practices Act At least one piece of U.S. legislation extends American law—and, in this case, business ethics—across international borders. In the 1970s, the U.S. press, and government officials as well, uncovered a number of business scandals involving large side payments by American corporations—such as Lockheed Aircraft—to foreign representatives for the purpose of securing advantageous international trade contracts. In response to this unethical behavior, Congress passed the **Foreign Corrupt Practices Act (FCPA)** in 1977.

The act is divided into two major parts. The first part, which applies to all U.S. companies and their directors, officers, shareholders, employees, or agents, prohibits giving bribes (or anything of value) to foreign government officials if the purpose of the payments is to obtain or retain business for the U.S. company. The second part of the act is directed toward accountants, because bribes had often been concealed in corporations' financial records. The act requires all companies to keep detailed records that "accurately and fairly" reflect the company's financial activities, as well as to have an accounting system that provides "reasonable assurance" that all transactions entered into by the company are accounted for and legal.

Cultural Distance Even under the best of circumstances, MNCs will have to deal with the problem of **cultural distance;** that is, the psychological and sociological distance between the society of the home country and the host country. Cultural distance directly affects a company's efficiency and thus its profitability:

16. "Indian Project Will Safeguard Genetic Value of Plants," *Nature*, May 18, 1995, p. 173.
17. B. H. Suh, "South Korea Moves against Majors," *Billboard*, November 20, 1993, p. 48.
18. P. Galuszka, "And You Think You've Got Tax Problems," *Business Week*, May 29, 1995, p. 50.

▼ The greater the cultural distance, the longer it will take for an employee to adjust to life in the host country and, consequently, the longer it will take for the MNC to operate at peak efficiency.

The potential for culturally based miscommunication in different countries is seemingly overwhelming. A manager working in a Buddhist culture, for example, must never touch a co-worker's head, which is held as a sacred part of the body. In a Muslim culture, the left hand is considered unclean. In many African, Asian, and South American cultures, it is rude to point using the index finger. Crossing your ankle over your knees will insult business associates in Southeast Asia and the Middle East. Managers must avoid placing an open hand over a closed fist in France and whistling in India.[19]

To help lessen cultural distance, many companies provide cultural training for employees and their families who are going abroad. General Motors spends nearly $1 million a year on such training; the company uses consultants such as Moran, Stahl & Boyer International to prepare expatriates for the business and personal challenges of a foreign country. GM's general director of international personnel credits this program with the organization's premature employee return rate of only 1 percent, compared with as high as 25 percent for competitors. By the mid-1990s, nearly half of the major U.S. corporations that send personnel abroad had some form of preparatory training, up from only 10 percent a decade earlier.[20]

Corporate Imperialism An MNC that ignores the rights of the home country in order to exploit its human and natural resources can be labeled imperialist. In 1952, Jacobo Arbenz, the head of the democratically elected government in Guatemala, expropriated some of the United Fruit Company's land in that country for the use of local families. Two years later, at the behest of United Fruit and its business interest, the U.S. Central Intelligence Agency (CIA) orchestrated the overthrow of the Arbenz administration. *El pulpo*, or "the octopus," as United Fruit was known in Central America, continued to immerse itself in local politics and wars into the 1970s.[21]

Complaints of Host Countries Imperialism is only one of the complaints that host countries have about "invading" MNCs. Some of the more common complaints are listed here, but be aware that a complaint is not necessarily a perfectly accurate reflection of reality in all circumstances:

1. **The destruction of the environment.** Large-scale manufacturing and mining operations can lead to environmental destruction (see *Company Focus: Texaco* on page 180). Host countries complain that MNCs are more worried about profits than about protecting the environment. Although it is true that many MNCs in the past showed little respect for the host country's ecological settings, today more and more host countries are passing laws and regulations that put many of the same restrictions on MNCs that those MNCs face in the United States.

2. **National sovereignty challenges.** Large, powerful MNCs may have a disquieting influence in the governments of developing countries, according to those governments'

19. M. Munter, "Cross-Cultural Communication for Managers," *Business Horizons*, May 1, 1993, p. 69.

20. S. Lublin, "Companies Use Cross-Cultural Training to Help Their Employees Adjust Abroad," *Wall Street Journal*, August 4, 1992, p. B1.

21. R. Solomon, *The New World of Business* (Lanham, Md.: Littlefield Adams Quality Paperbacks, 1994), p. 322.

Company Focus: Texaco

The Multinational Corporation's Responsibility to Its Host Community

Consider the following situation: The Indigo Company buys up a vacant lot in your neighborhood and builds a purple dye factory. Within a couple of months, you and your neighbors start to notice that the tap water in your sinks and showers has turned decidedly purple. Within a year, the situation has become intolerable. Everyone's clothes have a purple hue, thanks to discolored washing machine water, and one of the neighborhood children has had a nasty allergic reaction to a substance in the dye.

What do you and your neighbors do? Being Americans, you probably form a coalition and sue the Indigo Company for tainting the water supply. It's a lawsuit you would probably win, as Indigo had clearly acted irresponsibly toward the community.

A community of Ecuadoran Indians has a similar problem with Texaco, and it is seeking a similar solution. Increasingly, lawsuits have become the last refuge for native populations seeking redress from MNCs that have been less than good guests.

The Lawsuit

Elias Piyague, a leader of the six-hundred-member Secoya tribe, addressed reporters in the board room of the New York County Lawyers Association. Dressed in traditional garb— bright pink shirts and shorts—he told the gathered reporters: "Our rivers have been poisoned. We cannot drink. We cannot bathe. We cannot believe in the future of our existence."

Piyague was one of a number of Ecuadoran Indians who had left the rain forests of their home country to come to New York to announce the lawsuit against Texaco. The Indians charge the giant oil company with having dumped three thousand gallons of oil a day into the lagoons that provide them with water. They seek more than $1 billion in damages.

Ecuador's Dilemma

The lawsuit typifies a growing conflict being faced by many South and Central American countries: What balance should be made between a need to harvest rich natural resources and environmental concerns? In the case of Ecuador and Texaco, the conflict is particularly difficult. The oil company first came to the country twenty-six years ago at the invitation of the government. Texaco built a pipeline through the country, and oil became a major source of revenue for Ecuador. Currently, about half of the country's export earnings rely on oil. Oil is Ecuador's primary, and some say solitary, hope of ever paying off its large national debt.

The Indians' lawsuit claims, however, that for all its benefits, Texaco's presence is placing an untenable burden on living conditions. The discharge of oil into rivers and lagoons not only affects the Indians' drinking and bathing water but also kills off many of the fish that they rely on for their diet. Furthermore, settling basins have overflowed onto many of the roads around the oil fields, and the slick overflow makes driving and walking hazardous for the estimated thirty thousand residents of the area.

Texaco's Defense

Ricardo Viega, a lawyer with Texaco's Latin America and West African division, told the *New York Times* that the company never disposed of any oil in the Indians' water supply. He admitted that some oil probably had seeped onto the roads but dismissed the notion that this was grounds for a lawsuit. He further stated, "We have studies that oil on the skin does not cause disease as claimed by [the Ecuadoran Indians'] lawyers."

Viega also pointed out that the suit should have been brought in Ecuador against the state oil company, Petroecuador. Texaco sold its 37.5 percent share in the industry in 1991 and had not directly operated any of the old fields since its contract with the Ecuadoran government ran out in 1990.

The New Bottom Line

Multinational corporations can no longer assume, as used to be the case, that environmental irresponsibility in their developing host countries would go unnoticed. In the spring of 1994, the Ecuadoran Indians won a major victory when a New York judge ruled that their over $1 billion suit could go forward if the plaintiffs could prove that company decisions affecting their habitat were made in the United States.

SOURCE: A. Salplucas, "Ecuadorian Indians Suing Texaco," *New York Times*, November 4, 1993, p. D3.

officials. In particular, large MNCs have been seen as a threat to the sovereignty of these governments, which in the past have sometimes been relatively weak. A classic case occurred in the early 1970s, when John McCone, a director at International Telephone and Telegraph, offered the CIA $1 million and a plan to overthrow Salvador Allende, a Marxist, to prevent Allende from taking control of the Chilean government. At the same time, a Brazilian minister complained that MNC involvement had made "the result of [his country's] prosperity less and less Brazilian."[22]

3. The disruption of social patterns. MNCs bring with them the values and customs of their countries of origin. When an American MNC, for example, establishes itself in a Muslim country, the customs and values of its American employees may be quite different from those of the host country. Social disruption can occur as locals observe behavior by the MNC employees that is inconsistent with their own.

4. Perceived inequities. Host countries claim that MNCs are able to purchase raw materials from them at low prices, but that the price of imported goods from industrial countries is relatively high. According to host countries, this creates an inequity.

5. Pressure on the legal system. According to host countries, some MNCs force host governments to change their legal systems in order to receive MNC investments. Specifically, host countries may be forced to develop laws of contracting and sales that are similar to those of the United States, and they see this as an imposition.

Any public airing of these complaints, whether by representatives of the host country or by public-interest groups in the home country, is certain to bring a defensive response from the accused MNC.

However, the complaints may be justified. Often a host government has provided an MNC with extensive enticements for its business, but these inducements are not acceptable to a segment of the local community. To use an example of an MNC in the United States, in 1993 the Alabama government was able to entice Mercedes-Benz AG to make that state the site of the company's first U.S. auto plant. To accomplish this, state officials promised to (1) build a $35 million training center at the new plant, (2) pay the salaries of the workers as they were being trained, (3) purchase 2,500 Mercedes vehicles for state use, and (4) exempt the automobile company from a number of local and state taxes in what came to be called Alabama's Mercedes Law. In total, these concessions cost Alabama state taxpayers well over $300 million, which took funds away from pressing social issues such as the state's troubled public education system. "There are a lot of people in Alabama who think we gave the farm away," said one disgruntled member of the state legislature.[23]

Benefits to the Host Government Often, MNCs are very good guests and provide the host country with a number of benefits. *Exhibit 7–3* on page 182 lists some of the advantages a host company can derive from an MNC.

The idea that global corporations can be agents of social and economic change in host countries, especially in countries with developing economies, is summed up by one multinational manager who claims that his mission is based on the concept that "good quality toilet paper is a part of modern life."[24] As such, the responsibility of providing modern essential benefits lies with the global manager.

---

22. R. J. Barnett and R. E. Muller, *The Power of Multinational Corporations* (New York: Touchstone, 1974), p. 191.
23. E. S. Browning and H. Cooper, "Ante Up: State's Bidding War over Mercedes Plant Made for Costly Chase," *Wall Street Journal*, November 24, 1993, p. A1.
24. *Ibid.*, p. 31.

▼ **EXHIBIT 7–3**
Benefits of MNCs for the Host Country

- Improve the host country's productivity.
- Increase the host country's gross domestic product and therefore raise living standards.
- Allow the host country greater access to international markets.
- Foster new product development in the host country.
- Teach the host country's employees new skills.
- Allow for the training of a management class.
- Introduce new organizational techniques.
- Provide a model for host country businesses in terms of quality standards and even ethical standards.
- Create investment opportunities for host country businesses.
- Provide a market for host country service industries.
- Cause host country capital to flow to more productive uses (for example, higher rate of return).

MANAGEMENT STRATEGY FOR RUNNING AN ETHICAL MNC

The multicultural view of global business is infinitely more complicated than the imperialistic view. Running an MNC today involves the economic, legal, and philosophical tensions of ethical decision making that we discussed in Chapter 5.

Guidelines for MNCs Trade-offs between social and economic goals are inevitable. We cannot offer golden rules for global managers to follow in every situation, but these managers can follow certain guidelines relating to the responsibilities of MNCs abroad. MNCs have a duty to protect and respect human rights in all countries, even if the host country's government does not do so itself. Furthermore, MNCs have the obligation to create a healthful working environment for the host country's employees and to create adequate standards of employee safety.

MNCs must respect local practices and customs, even at the expense of profits. MNCs cannot simply ignore local customs that seem out of place, ridiculous, meaningless, or trivial. The responsible MNC is run in such a way that there is harmony among its staff and the host population. MNCs, when they make investments elsewhere, must commit to a long-term relationship. That means involving all stakeholders in the host country in decision making. It also means providing quality goods and services in order to reach long-term profitability, rather than simply focusing on short-term profits.

Because of the stresses inherent in any situation in which the values and customs of different cultures come in contact, a key decision-making skill for managers abroad is conflict resolution. (For four stances toward conflict resolution for global managers, see *Exhibit 7–4*.) Finally, the responsible MNC must implement ethical guidelines within the organization in the host country. It must provide management leadership and develop a cadre of local managers who will be a credit to their community. In so doing, the MNC will foster respect for both local and international laws.

▼ **EXHIBIT 7–4**
A Guide to Conflict Resolution for Global Managers
According to Robert Solomon, global managers should assume four stances toward conflict resolution:

1. The **absolute stance**, or the "moral" position, in which any alternative is intolerable.

2. The **hypothetical stance**, or the empathetic approach, in which the manager asks himself or herself, "What if I were in their position?"

3. The **procedural stance**, in which no substantive principles are involved, but a fair dispute resolution process takes place.

4. The **local agreement stance,** in which no principles or procedures interfere with consensus, which is to be reached by negotiation.

SOURCE: R. Solomon, *Above the Bottom Line* (Fort Worth, Tex.: Harcourt Brace College, 1994), p. 363.

The Ethical Algorithm To help the global manager deal with the intricacies of running an ethical MNC, Tom Donaldson offers an "ethical algorithm" as a decision-making tool in dilemmas that involve cultural differences.[25] This method distinguishes between questions in which host-country economic development is involved and questions in which it is not.

When economic development is involved, the question becomes a matter of common sense: If the same business practice were considered at home, what would the decision be? If we do not accept slave labor in Detroit, says Donaldson, we should not accept it in the People's Republic of China. When economic development is not involved, Donaldson turns to two more questions: (1) Is it possible to conduct business without the practice in question? (2) Does the practice in question violate a "fundamental international right?"

Of course, individual managers might have different opinions as to what is a fundamental international right. Donaldson, considered a pioneer in the field of international ethics, has his own list of fundamental international rights:

1. The right to freedom of physical movement.
2. The right to ownership of property.
3. The right to freedom from torture.
4. The right to a fair trial.
5. The right to nondiscriminatory treatment.
6. The right to physical security.
7. The right to freedom of speech and association.
8. The right to minimal education.
9. The right to political participation.
10. The right to sustenance.[26]

Donaldson's list is a good starting point for any global manager, but as we have stressed a number of times, real-life situations are rarely as simple as printed lists of suggestions. For example,

25. T. Donaldson, *The Ethics of International Business* (New York: Oxford University Press, 1989), p. 80.
26. *Ibid.*, p. 81.

▼ Just because a manager does not accept slave labor in Detroit, there is no guarantee that he or she, or the MNC, is going to be able to have any effect on how it is viewed in China or any other country.

Many global corporations are answering—or, some would say, avoiding—the question of rights infringements in host countries by taking an ethically neutral stance. When the Shell Oil Company was criticized for continuing a new natural gas project in Nigeria despite that country's execution of activist Ken Saro-Wira, the company responded that it had no options. Shell said that the only form of social protest that the Nigerian government was capable of responding to was force, and Shell was not prepared to sponsor an insurrection.[27] It could be argued that Shell also was not prepared to give up potential profits.

The heavy criticism Shell received across the globe for its actions in Nigeria has spurred other companies to consider various means of ensuring that they do not negatively affect the citizens of host countries. In 1995, the Gap clothing company—charged with improprieties during a labor struggle in El Salvador—agreed to independent monitoring of its Mandarin International contractor by a human rights representative. "The Gap's move will have a profound impact on the [retail] industry," predicted one observer. "The message is clear. If you [or your contractor violates human rights], you are responsible."[28]

REGULATING GLOBAL ETHICS

Few Americans would disagree with Donaldson's international rights list, as it mirrors the Bill of Rights (the first ten amendments to the U.S. Constitution). In that sense it offers a limited perspective on fundamental rights—one that reflects the legal and cultural system of Donaldson's home country. This brings up an important question: How much should the ethics of one country influence another, and what steps should each government of the world take to ensure its country's ethical independence?

THE TRIUMPH OF CAPITALISM

Because the Cold War was more a battle of economic theory than of missiles and bullets, when the United States "won" the Cold War at the end of the 1980s, many observers saw it as a victory of capitalism over communism and state-controlled socialism. In the years following the breakup of the Soviet Union, more and more former Communist countries turned, at least rhetorically, to capitalism to save their moribund economies. Thus, many feel that the values of Adam Smith are winning out over the values of Karl Marx. Other capitalist values, such as the privatization of government-owned companies or industries, have also swept the globe, as we discuss in Chapter 8.

However, the American way of using the market economy and capitalism may not be best for all countries. Americans certainly tend to be **ethnocentric**—centered on one's own race or culture—as well as **geocentric**—centered on one's own physical location in the world—in their perspectives of business. Although our kind of capitalism may lead to high economic growth rates for the entire world in the long run, it may not be best in the

---

27. M. Woollacott, "A World Forced to Keep Bad Company," *Guardian* (London), November 18, 1995, p. 27.
28. F. Haq, "El Salvador–Labor: Union, Gap Agreement Resolves Clothing Battle," *Inter Press Service*, December 20, 1995.

short run. A country that has lived through decades of centralized planning with limited incentives for workers to be productive cannot change overnight into what we might view as the most appropriate capitalist system. It takes time for workers and managers to be trained in a new system. It takes time to privatize what used to be vast state sectors in all of these formerly centrally planned economies.

Just because some former Communist countries are moving slowly toward a market economy does not mean that they are acting improperly. Americans do not have all the answers. American businesspersons can offer advice, but not certainty or truth. Our truth in the business world may not be valid elsewhere (see *Managing Social Issues—Barriers to Success: Capitalism in Russia* on page 186).

DIFFERENT CULTURES, DIFFERENT VALUES

Ethnocentric businesspersons view capitalism as they do a slice of pizza, to use a rather frivolous analogy. Nothing, except perhaps Mom, baseball, and apple pie, is more American than pizza. Still, it would be a mistake to assume that all cultures appreciate pizza—or capitalism—in the same way Americans do.

For Pizza Hut, the pizza analogy is anything but frivolous. The fast-food organization plans to open a hundred new outlets in China before the year 2000, and any assumptions that ours is the only way to make pizza would lead to disaster. First of all, cheese is not popular in China. If Pizza Hut served pizzas there using the same amounts of cheese as it does in the United States, very few people would be interested. Furthermore, unlike Americans, the Chinese prefer very sweet pizza. Again, a reluctance to change the basic pizza design would be bad business.

Luckily for the stockholders of PepsiCo, which runs Pizza Hut, the company does not have an ethnocentric perspective. Very little cheese is used on Pizza Hut pizzas in China, and the fast-food chain gives its customers laminated tabletop cards with information about how cheese is made. Also, Pizza Hut of China substitutes pineapple chunks for olives on its menu to satisfy the population's sweet tooth. The result: the restaurant franchise in Guangzhou sells between five thousand and six thousand pizzas a day.[29]

Japan and Bribery Just as an American teenager might find a pizza with pineapples and little or no cheese distasteful, so might an American businessperson find the idea of bribery morally and ethically reprehensible. That does not change the fact that forms of bribery are accepted by communities throughout the world, including our important trading partner and home to many American MNCs—Japan. Private businesses in Japan retain as a "counselor" a Japanese government official who has retired into private business. These counselors often use their former contacts to steer government business to the company that has hired their services, a practice that American business standards label as bribery and therefore unethical. Furthermore, the practice is forbidden by U.S. law.

In Japan, in stark contrast, this American view is itself considered highly unethical. Japanese society sees two benefits of business's "taking care" of retired civil servants. First, once government officials turn forty-five, they are expected to retire as soon as they are outranked by anyone younger than they are. Early retirement would be financially untenable without the help of private business. Second, Japanese citizens expect the salaries and pensions of civil servants to be kept low in order to control taxes and minimize bureaucracy. The difference between what a civil servant could have made in private business versus civil service is expected to be offset by the "counselor fees" he or she

---

29. S. D. Goll, "Pizza Hut Tosses Its Pies into the Ring," *Wall Street Journal*, May 27, 1994, p. B1.

MANAGING SOCIAL ISSUES

BARRIERS TO SUCCESS: CAPITALISM IN RUSSIA

A year before the fall of the Soviet Union, American journalist David Remnick happened on a showing of the film *Wall Street* in Moscow's Lenin Hall. "If I hadn't known then that Communist ideology was dead, I knew it by the closing credits," he writes of the experience. Remnick recalls a reaction by the mostly young crowd of Russians that would have made "poor Oliver Stone weep." Instead of taking the movie as an indictment of weak morals in American big business, as Stone, the film's director, had intended, the audience behaved as if it was watching a utopian fantasy. When Michael Douglas's character, Gordon Gekko, delivered his infamous line "Zhadnost—eto khorosho!" ("Greed is good!"), the crowd went wild. "There were whoops of approval," Remnick remembers. "Unironic whoops."

After the fall of the Communist regime in the fall of 1991, capitalism did triumph in many of the fifteen newly formed states. It was Gordon Gekko's brand of capitalism, however, which has little, if any, resemblance to the moral brand of the free market that Ben Franklin had envisioned.

Russian Ethics

Indeed, nothing was sacred. A Russian entrepreneur planned to take the chemically preserved body of Lenin on a tour around the world, where anybody who wanted could see the remains of the Communist leader—for a price. The KGB offers tourists the opportunity, for thirty dollars, to tour the police force's headquarters and, as a bonus, to sit in former chief Yuri Andropov's chair.

Capitalism in Russia today is characterized by corruption in many forms: bribes, kickbacks, Mafia payoffs, and other scams so numerous that they run, in the words of Russia's chief state inspector, Yuri Boldyrev, "beyond the limits of the imagination." Ethics is simply not yet part of the Russian business transaction. "There isn't a single major transaction that takes place on the level," Tad Wolff, a co-founder of United Farm Technologies, told *Business Ethics*. In working to build a dairy farm, Wolff admits that he has a "suspended code of ethics, precisely because I know the environment in which I am operating. Our whole multi-million dollar project in Kazakhstan would not have happened if I didn't wake up to the fact that certain key government officials had to be paid under the table for their help."

Corporate social responsibility is also a foreign concept in Russia's form of capitalism. Vladimir Preobrazhensky tried twice to set up a nonprofit organization to help charities, and twice he failed. "You know, in Russian to call someone an 'idealist' means he is a fool," says Preobrazhensky of the experience.

The Cultural Basis of Ethics

Some economists have theorized that Russia's seeming lack of ethics may only be a different set of ethics. For many Russians, business is not something practiced in office buildings with the help of lawyers and accountants; it is the result of personal relations in which all parties benefit. Legal contracts are almost unheard of, and even when they do exist, there is almost no way to enforce them. As the Russian proverb goes, "It is better to have one hundred friends than one hundred rubles."

Many Russians may feel that they don't have the luxury to consider ethics. A poll in the newspaper *Izvestia* revealed that 63 percent of Muscovites feared civil war, chaos, impoverishment, or hunger in the near future. With the nation's economy in flux—inflation was running at a peak of 2,400 percent a few years ago—a pragmatic view tends to dominate talks of morality. One Russian police officer directing traffic explained, "If I received a normal salary, I wouldn't take bribes. But without taking bribes, I wouldn't be able to feed my wife, who is pregnant. We do it in order to survive, not to play in the casino."

For Critical Analysis:

These kinds of reports from former Communist countries have led some commentators to muse that citizens there were better off under the old system than under capitalism today. Is this a valid comment?

SOURCE: C. Scharf, "The Wild, Wild East," *Business Ethics*, November–December 1992, pp. 20–23.

earns after retirement. In fact, the Japanese feel that the promise of these fees will keep civil servants incorruptible when in office, because the civil servants thus know that their financial future is secure.[30] Although the abolition of bribery as an accepted practice might be good for business on a multinational scale, it would be difficult to eradicate it from cultures where it has a niche (see *Managing Social Issues—Making a Difference: Transparency International Tackles Bribery* on page 188).

Ethical Relativism Who is right when the ethical systems of different countries clash? This is a difficult question to answer. Take as an example the Japanese-American disagreement over the propriety of "counselors." It is hard to fault the Japanese for a system that they do not see as dishonorable, yet Americans have reason to be wary of "counselors." In the United States, such a system has led to the abuse of billions of dollars of taxpayer money and has prompted a law that prohibits top congressional aides from lobbying in Congress for a year after leaving a position on Capitol Hill. One of President Bill Clinton's first actions after taking office in 1992 was to install a rule barring top federal officials from lobbying their old offices for five years following the end of their government employment.

In the end, businesses must consider **ethical relativism**, or the question of whether ethical principles should be defined only by what one particular society or one particular individual considers to be ethical at any given moment. As businesses run into more and more situations like the Japanese "counselors" or the murder of dissidents by the Algerian government, they will have to decide how ethically relative they are willing to be. Just as an imperialist can be faulted for disregarding local sovereignty, so can a relativist be criticized for giving too much credence to it.

One does not have to travel to Japan or Algeria to find examples of ethical relativism. A number of Amish communities in the United States take their ethical underpinnings directly from biblical dictates such as "Be not conformed to this world" and those requiring them to live apart from "unbelievers." Consequently, Amish people refuse to accept any form of government assistance and rely on themselves to provide for all members of the community. This includes establishing nonprofit savings and loan associations to provide funds for young couples to purchase homes and a variant of workers' compensation in which the community, not the government, provides for those injured on the job. Successful Amish people also offer seed money for start-up companies, and the business community feels a responsibility to staff its positions with fellow Amish.[31] This ethical relativism has not hurt the Amish economically. In many instances, Amish businesses in Lancaster County, Pennsylvania, have had to take steps such as limiting advertising in order to curtail their success, in keeping with biblical proscriptions against becoming too wealthy and prideful.[32]

International Codes of Conduct As is true within any domestic business, the ethical relativism of an MNC is strongly affected by its corporate culture. Many global businesses are taking the path of "higher standards" in solving the question of ethical relativism. That is, through conduct codes much like those we discussed in Chapter 5, they are setting levels of conduct for subsidiaries that respect, but do not necessarily rely on, the culture in

---

30. P. Drucker, "Business Ethics," *Public Interest*, September 17, 1995, p. 27.
31. B. Ingersoll, "Old Order: GOP's Plans to Curtail Government Benefits Bring No Pain to Amish," *Wall Street Journal*, December 22, 1995, p. A1.
32. J. Eckhoff, "Amish Business Owners' Problem: Too Much Success," *Central Pennsylvania Business Journal*, November 10, 1995, p. 11.

Managing Social Issues

Making a Difference:
Transparency International Tackles Bribery

In Mexico, it's called *la mordida*. In France, it's *un pot de vin*. The English word is *bribery*, and Peter Eigen would like to put a stop to it, though he's not holding his breath.

Eigen, a former official at the World Bank, found himself demoralized and disgusted by the corruption he witnessed in Africa and Latin America. To improve the situation, Eigen has started Transparency International (TI), a nonprofit group based on the human rights organization Amnesty International. The group held its inaugural meeting in Berlin on May 4, 1993, and previewed plans to promote "transparency" in corporate halls and public offices around the world. Eigen says that TI will promote "standards of conduct," and try to create "islands of integrity," or countries where businesspersons and government officials will promise to maintain ethical standards.

Advantages for the United States

One country that should jump to embrace TI's efforts is the United States; indeed, American-based multinational corporations such as General Electric Company and Boeing Company pledged their support immediately. Since the 1977 passage of the U.S. Foreign Corrupt Practices Act, which forbids payments to foreign officials when seeking overseas contracts, American companies have complained that they face a competitive disadvantage in relation to corporations from other countries that lack such restrictions. In fact, a German, Dutch, or Japanese company can write off the value of a bribe given to secure a contract before calculating corporate tax liabilities; the bribe is considered just another cost of business.

The U.S. government, under heavy pressure from its home business interests, has tried periodically to influence other countries. "The U.S. has taken a step no one else has, and it puts our business people, regarding illicit payments, in a difficult position," moaned U.S. trade negotiator Mickey Cantor in 1993.

The U.S. government has had only limited success. Companies from other countries are not eager to give up their competitive advantage over their American counterparts. Eigen admits that the German companies from which he has asked for help expressed "no real enthusiasm" for TI; a few months earlier, an attempt in that country to abolish tax credits for foreign bribes was handily defeated in the Bundestag (the lower house in the German Parliament).

Advantages for Developing Countries

Any success TI might have would benefit not only the United States but also developing nations, which cannot afford the social costs of bribery. According to one estimate, African leaders have approximately $20 billion in Swiss bank accounts; Eigen speculates that phony projects used to hide bribes may account for up to a third of the debt in developing countries. In China, state assets have fallen by more than $50 billion since 1983 because of corruption by government officials.

Eigen admits that at first, TI will be forced to accept into its fold governments and companies that are participating in the very activity they will be pledging to end; TI "will not be a club of angels," he says. He believes he can have a positive effect, however, if he can get the proverbial foot in the door.

For Critical Analysis:

Although there is only limited proof that the U.S. Foreign Corrupt Practices Act has had a significantly negative impact on American competitiveness, many international businesspeople complain that the law hurts American companies in specific countries and instances. Should the federal government consider repealing the act?

SOURCE: Information from R. Keately, "U.S. Campaign against Bribery Faces Resistance from Foreign Governments," *Wall Street Journal*, December 24, 1993, p. B7; "Clean, Not Laundered," *The Economist*, May 8, 1993, pp. 7, 78; and K. Pennar, "The Destructive Costs of Greasing Palms," *Business Week*, December 6, 1993, p. 134.

which they exist. (See *Exhibit 7–5* for an excerpt from the Caterpillar Tractor Company's applauded international code.)

TOOLS OF GLOBAL REGULATION

As anybody who watches the daily deliberations of the United Nations can attest, it is very difficult for the sovereign nations of the world to come to a conclusion on any specific issue. For the most part, this has held true when it comes to regulating global ethics. The three codes that do exist, which are described in the following text, were formed primarily from a desire to protect developing countries from "greedy" MNCs.

International Chamber of Commerce Like domestic chambers of commerce, the International Chamber of Commerce (ICC) is primarily concerned with promoting trade and the free market. The ICC issued its first code for MNCs in 1972. This code, made up of nonobligatory recommendations, made an effort to turn the MNC–host country relationship into more of a partnership than a rental of resources. The ICC urged MNCs to provide the host country with the vital statistics of their business operations, and it advised MNCs to hire local labor and take on local partners in joint business operations. In turn, the ICC urged host countries to allow MNCs to function without a strenuous regulatory burden.

▼ **EXHIBIT 7–5 Caterpillar's Principles for International Business**

Differing Business Practices	Understandably, there are differences in business practices and economic philosophies from country to country. Some of these differences are a matter of pluralism—there isn't necessarily "one best way." Other differences, however, may conflict with proven, well-accepted, fair business procedures. Such differences may be a source of continuing dispute. And they may inhibit rather than promote fair competition.
	Examples of the latter include varying views regarding competitive practices, boycotts, information disclosure, international mergers, accounting procedures, tax systems, intercompany pricing, national content requirements, product labeling, product safety standards . . . and industrial property and industrial trademark laws. In such areas, we favor more uniform practices among countries and encourage multilateral efforts to harmonize business practices and procedures.
Observance of Local Laws	A basic requirement of any business enterprise is that it know and obey the law. This is rightfully required by those who govern, and it is well understood by business managers. However, a corporation operating on a global scale inevitably encounters laws which vary widely from country to country. They may even conflict. And laws in some countries encourage or require business practices which—based on experience elsewhere in the world—are believed to be wasteful or unfair.
	We are guided by the belief that the law is not an end but a means to an end—the end presumably being order, justice, and, not infrequently, strengthening of the governmental unit involved. If it is to achieve these ends in changing times and circumstances, the laws must be clear and uniformly applied, and cannot be insusceptible to change or free of criticism. The law can benefit from both.
	Therefore, in a world characterized by a multiplicity of divergent laws at international, national, state, and local levels, Caterpillar's intentions fall into two parts: (1) to obey the law; and (2) to offer, where appropriate, constructive ideas for change in the law.

SOURCE: Caterpillar Code of Worldwide Business Conduct and Operating Principles, revised August 1, 1992.

Organization for Economic Cooperation and Development The Organization for Economic Cooperation and Development (OECD) is a Paris-based group representing government, industry, and union interests in industrialized countries. The guidelines of the OECD are based on a simple premise: MNCs are supposed to follow the rules and regulations of the host and member countries, and the member countries are supposed to treat MNCs as they would domestic companies. When it formed in 1976, the organization also offered a range of voluntary guidelines in the areas of competition, transfer of technology, financing, taxation, and disclosure of information.

United Nations Code for MNCs The United Nations code for MNCs focuses attention on the ethical problems concerning MNCs and developing countries. The code attempts to convince MNCs from industrial countries not to take advantage of countries with more vulnerable economies. For example, under the code, MNCs should not sell products to developing countries that have been banned in developed countries for health reasons. The code also takes into consideration other consumer, human rights, and environmental issues.

It is important to note that none of the above codes has any legally binding power. Currently, aside from the Foreign Corrupt Practices Act, there is no significant American rule of law regulating a U.S.–based MNC's activities abroad (see *Company Focus: Nike*).

FURTHER ISSUES IN GLOBAL ETHICS

If a giant multinational corporation, Corporation X, offered to pay $10 million to dump toxic waste in your backyard, what would you do? As with many other decisions concerning money, it would depend on the circumstances. It would depend on your yearly income; the more you made, the less incentive you would have to lose your backyard to toxic waste. It would depend on how much Corporation X was offering; if it was enough that you could leave the neighborhood, the offer might be more tempting.

Many developing countries and their citizens find themselves in just that situation. For decades, the former Soviet Union used its Eastern Bloc countries as dumping grounds. When East Germany had exhausted its own natural resources, it found new revenue by allowing West Germany to dump toxic waste within its borders. Brazil and other South American countries come under constant criticism for selling the lumber from their rain forests, even though the buyers are usually from the same country as the critics.

We talked about paternalism in Chapter 6 with regard to corporate social responsibility, and the term springs up again with regard to ethical relativism:

▼ **When one country assumes that it has higher ethical standards than another country and tries to force ethics across borders, the offended country inevitably accuses the other country of paternalism.**

The paternalism controversy is brought up most often with regard to U.S. treatment of developing nations. In some cases, however, the issue has been raised even between developed nations. In this final section, we look at the complications involved in exporting ethics, as well as some of the negative effects that such an apparently noble activity can have for exporters.

COMPANY FOCUS: NIKE
APPLYING THE LAWS OF HOME ABROAD

Consider this ugly picture of conditions for laborers in Nike production facilities in Indonesia: "Amid the glue and paint fumes, workers without protective clothing operate hot molds, presses, and cutting machines," reported the *Portland Oregonian*. For their troubles, the article continued, the workers made fifteen cents an hour. Is there a law to prevent such practices by U.S. multinational corporations?

The Legal Environment for MNCs

Almost countless government regulations have outlawed unsafe labor conditions in the United States, but not much U.S. legislation has concerned itself with the rights of workers abroad. A law has been on the books since 1930 that banned the importation of goods made with slave labor, but the fines for violating the law amount to $1,000 or less, which is not even a slap on the wrist for most businesses; indeed, it is more like a peck on the cheek. It would be naïve to think that U.S. companies have stayed completely clear of slave labor; in China alone, it is estimated that ten million to fifteen million people work in forced labor shops making electronics equipment (much of which the U.S. imports).

There are no federal guidelines to dictate how American MNCs treat their employees overseas or to keep MNCs from buying products produced by slave labor in one country for production and sale in another. As foreign and domestic competition for U.S. companies grows, so will the pressure to find inexpensive labor and raw materials abroad, beyond the scope of U.S. labor laws.

Nike's Response

What if fifteen cents an hour is a good wage in economically depressed Indonesia? In disputing the *Oregonian*'s article, Nike chairman and CEO Philip Knight claimed that "Nike's foreign factories generally offer the highest pay and the best work conditions of any athletic shoe factories in the particular country. In China, a worker in a Nike factory makes higher wages than a professor at Beijing University."

The New Bottom Line

Knight's defense may say more about the average salary of a Chinese professor than about Nike's generosity, but it does bring up the following question: Should American companies take American attitudes on human rights along with them when they do business abroad, or should they let the Indonesian worker decide if fifteen cents an hour constitutes a good living? Because government regulation of this area is almost impossible, each company must make its own decisions on how to treat overseas workers. But managers should be aware that media outlets like the Oregonian *often discover these types of stories, and the resulting negative publicity is never good for business.*

SOURCE: Information from "Emancipation Proclamation," *Business Ethics*, September–October 1993, p. 10; and "If the Shoe Fits . . . ," *Business Ethics*, November–December 1992, p. 10.

HUMAN RIGHTS AND THE MNC

Corporate leaders, who avoid the political and bureaucratic entanglements that often handicap government, must make their own decisions about MNCs and human rights. Again, it is a question of maximum versus optimum profits. MNCs obviously enjoy maximum profits when they branch into a country that offers cheap labor. Increasingly, however, MNCs are accepting their social responsibilities and thus are willing to settle for optimum profits. In 1993, for example, General Motors stockholders cast twenty-eight million votes in favor of a resolution advising GM management not to buy any "slave-made" goods for use in any country in the world, and not to sell any GM products to "slave-labor" facilities[33] (see the *Case—Levi Strauss and the Values-Based Approach to Business Abroad*—at the end of this chapter).

The Republic of South Africa is a good place to analyze the reactions of MNCs to human rights violations. The first biracial elections were held in South Africa in 1994. Prior to that, the officially supported system of racial segregation, apartheid, prevented black South Africans from participating in the political process. Racial segregation and the supremacy of whites had been traditionally accepted in South Africa even prior to the passage of the legal basis for apartheid in 1948. Throughout the 1970s and 1980s, unions, churches, and students organized protests against apartheid. In 1991, President Frederick de Klerk announced a repeal of the acts that were the legal basis for apartheid. In March 1992, South African whites voted to end their minority rule. When Nelson Mandela was elected president of South Africa in 1994, it signaled not only a new beginning for South African society but for global business as well.

Prior to the end of apartheid and the granting to blacks of full citizenship rights, MNCs operating in South Africa were criticized for operating in an environment of human rights violations. The Sullivan Principles were created in 1977 by the Reverend Leon Sullivan, an African American minister and member of the board of directors for General Motors. When his internal pressures to convince GM to withdraw business concerns from South Africa failed, Reverend Sullivan formulated the principles as a guideline for U.S. businesses that were active in South Africa and wished to behave socially and morally (see *Exhibit 7–6*). Initially, twelve corporations signed on to the principles: General Motors, Union Carbide, Ford, Otis Elevator, 3M, IBM, International Harvester, American Cyanamid, Citibank, Burroughs, Mobil, and Caltex. By 1983, the number reached 183.

The political and social landscape in South Africa has changed dramatically since the Sullivan Principles were formulated, but forty-five years of apartheid does not disappear overnight. Many social issues still need to be resolved in the country, and socially conscious investors will continue to monitor the situation carefully. After Mandela called for reinvestment in his country, the South African Council of

---

33. "Emancipation Proclamation," *Business Ethics*, September–October 1993, p. 10.

▼ **EXHIBIT 7–6**
The Sullivan Principles

1. Allow no segregation of the races in work facilities.

2. Treat all employees equally and fairly.

3. Provide equal pay for equal work for all employees.

4. Initiate and develop training programs that will prepare substantial numbers of nonwhites for supervisory, administrative, clerical, and technical jobs.

5. Increase the number of nonwhites in management and supervisory decisions.

6. Improve the quality of employees' lives outside the workplace in such areas as housing, transportation, health facilities, and recreation.

SOURCE: K. Paul, "Corporate Social Monitoring in South Africa: A Decade of Achievement, An Uncertain Future," *Journal of Business Ethics*, Vol. 8 (1989), pp. 463–469.

▼ EXHIBIT 7–7 South Africa's New Code of Business Conduct

Code	Conduct
• Equal opportunity	Companies should ensure that their operations are free from discrimination based on race, sex, religion, political opinion, or physical handicap, and they should implement affirmative action programs designed to protect the historically disadvantaged.
• Training and education	Companies should develop and implement training and education programs to increase the productive capacities of their South African employees.
• Workers' rights	Companies should recognize representative unions and uphold their employees' rights to organize openly, bargain collectively, picket peacefully, and strike without intimidation and harassment.
• Working and living conditions	Companies should maintain safe and healthy work environments.
• Job creation and security	Companies should strive to maintain productive employment opportunities and create new jobs for South Africans.
• Community relations	Companies should share information about their practices and projected plans with communities affected by their operations.
• Consumer protection	Companies should inform consumers of any possible dangers associated with their products and develop and uphold appropriate safety and quality standards.
• Environmental protection	Companies should utilize environmentally sound practices and technologies, disclose how and in what amounts they dispose of their waste products, and seek to minimize hazardous waste.
• Empowerment of black businesses	Companies should strive to improve the development of black-owned South African businesses by purchasing from and subcontracting to such firms.
• Implementation	Companies should cooperate with monitors established to implement these standards by disclosing relevant information in a timely fashion.

SOURCE: C. Cox, "Welcome to South Africa," *Business Ethics,* November–December 1993, p. 40.

Churches released its "new" Sullivan Principles, designed to reflect the political reality (see *Exhibit 7–7*).

There is no doubt that many investors and MNCs will wish to take advantage of the new political situation in South Africa. Despite its social problems, the country has maintained a strong economic infrastructure and will thus attract investment. "Our hope is that the social investment community will not, in a sense, put South Africa behind them and say that it's a past issue," explained Tim Smith, executive director of the Interfaith Center on Corporate Responsibility (a coalition of 250 religious organizations with investment portfolios worth a combined $35 million), as he called for reinvestment in South Africa. "But [it is our hope that they] take the skills, knowledge, and energy they've developed and help create a new phase of nation building in a democratic South Africa."[34]

---

34. C. Cox, "Welcome to South Africa," *Business Ethics,* November–December 1993, p. 39.

ETHICS OF EMPLOYMENT FLOW

When American companies decide to go abroad for assembly, manufacturing, or both, they often benefit the workers of the host countries. In so doing, these MNCs may hurt employees and their families in the United States: unrestrained competition from other countries may eliminate some American jobs, because other countries have lower-cost labor than we do. This is a compelling argument for a politician from an area that might be threatened by foreign competition. For example, a representative from an area whose local economy relies heavily on a shoe factory would certainly be upset about the possibility of constituents losing their jobs because of competition from lower-priced shoe manufacturers in Brazil.

The Cost of Saving American Automobile Jobs We must realize, though, that every time we attempt to protect the jobs of American workers by putting restrictions on imports, that protection costs the American public money. Consider an example in the automobile industry. To protect American automobile workers, the United States forced Japan to enter into a "voluntary" agreement to restrict U.S. sales of Japanese cars to 1.68 million units per year. That agreement started in April 1981 and has continued into the 1990s in various forms.

Robert W. Crandall, a researcher with the Brookings Institution, has estimated how much this voluntary trade restriction has cost American consumers in terms of higher car prices. According to his estimates, the reduced supply of Japanese cars pushed their prices up by $1,000 apiece. The higher price of Japanese imports in turn enabled domestic producers to raise their prices an average of $400 a car. This price increase in 1983 alone totaled $4.3 billion—and it shows few signs of shrinking in the 1990s. Crandall also estimated that about 26,000 jobs in auto-related industries were saved by the voluntary import restrictions. Dividing $4.3 billion by 26,000 jobs yields a cost to consumers of more than $160,000 *per year* for every job saved in the auto industry. The federal government could have saved American consumers over $2 billion on their car purchases in

1996 if, instead of implicitly agreeing to import restrictions, it had simply given $100,000 to every autoworker whose job was to be preserved by the voluntary import restraints.

Saving Jobs in Other Industries The above numbers for the auto industry are no fluke. The same sort of calculations have been made for other industries. Tariffs in the apparel industry, for example, were increased between 1977 and 1981, saving the jobs of about 116,000 U.S. apparel workers—at a cost of $45,000 per job each year. The producers of citizens band (CB) radios also managed to get tariffs raised between 1978 and 1981. About 600 workers in the industry kept their jobs as a result, but at an annual cost to consumers of over $85,000 per job. The cost of protectionism has been even higher in other industries. Every job preserved in the glassware industry due to trade restrictions costs $200,000 each year. In the maritime industry, the yearly cost of trade protections is $270,000 per job. In the steel industry, the cost of preserving a job has been estimated at an astounding $750,000 per year. If free trade were permitted, each worker losing a job could be given a cash payment of even half that amount each year, and the consumer would still save a good deal of money.

INTELLECTUAL PROPERTY INFRINGEMENT

Another significant issue in today's global environment is the protection of **intellectual property rights**. Although *intellectual property* is an abstract term for an abstract concept, it is nonetheless familiar to virtually everyone. Trademarks, copyrights, and patents are all forms of intellectual property. The book you are reading is copyrighted. The personal computer you use at home or school is trademarked. Some of the resident software within that computer might be copyrighted. You see advertisements for trademarked items everyday—Xerox, IBM, and the like.

Within the United States, the framers of the Constitution over two hundred years ago knew that there had to be protection for creative works. Article I, Section 8, of the Constitution authorizes Congress "to promote the Progress of Science and useful Arts, by securing for limited Times the Authors and Inventors the exclusive Right to their respective Writings and Discoveries." Laws protecting patents, trademarks, and copyrights are explicitly designed to protect and reward inventive and artistic creativity. In the United States we have both statutory and common law that protect trademarks, service marks, collective marks, trade names, patents, and copyrights.

What about the protection of American intellectual property abroad, however? Intellectual property rights infringement has been one of the greatest problems for MNCs. Until recently, very little worldwide protection for intellectual property has existed. There has been an almost wholesale pirating of American videos, compact discs, and cassettes abroad. American computer and software companies have seen their products copied and sold without the payment of royalties throughout the world. In certain situations, the United States has been able to pressure trading partners into controlling pirated intellectual property within their borders. In 1995, the United States and China resolved a bitter dispute when the latter agreed to establish at least twenty-two task forces to oversee an antipiracy campaign. That same year, however, experts estimated that 95 percent of all software sold in Russia had been illegally duplicated.

One of the major benefits of the passage of the last round of GATT in late 1994 was the increased worldwide protection for American intellectual property. Consider the excerpts from GATT in *Exhibit 7–8* on page 197. Furthermore, NAFTA specifically included a part on intellectual property that had articles relating to copyright, sound

recordings, trademarks, patents, trade secrets, and the enforcement of intellectual property rights.

Today the WTO is in the process of developing ways to enforce intellectual property rights vigorously throughout the world. Although it is just a first step, American MNCs now have a world organization providing a channel through which they can pursue those countries that violate their intellectual property rights.

EXPORTING CORPORATE SOCIAL RESPONSIBILITY

Some American MNCs are discovering the economic benefits of exporting corporate social responsibility abroad:

▼ **Socially responsible MNCs are finding that they have a competitive advantage in countries where the idea of philanthropic business actions is relatively new and exciting to managers.**

More than half of the Fortune 500 companies are starting or increasing overseas philanthropy.[35]

After underwriting a study that found that the public's expectation of corporate social responsibility is as high in some Asian countries as it is in the United States, IBM has been actively encouraging social programs in its host countries. For example, in Japan, IBM set up a product development team to build devices to help people with disabilities and a profit center that sells specialized hardware to Japanese citizens with disabilities.[36] The company has donated money to disabled rights groups and instituted a hiring program for people with disabilities that has been accepted by local businesses throughout the country. These actions have not gone unnoticed. In a recent poll of Japanese citizens, IBM

---

35. C. Smith, "The New Corporate Philosophy," *Harvard Business Review,* May–June 1994, p. 112.
36. *Ibid.*, p. 113.

▼ **EXHIBIT 7–8**
**General Agreement
on Tariffs and Trade
(1994) with Regard
to Intellectual
Property Rights**

1. Members shall ensure that enforcement procedures are available under their national laws so as to permit effective action against any act of infringement of intellectual property rights covered by this Agreement, including expeditious remedies to prevent infringements and remedies which constitute a deterrent to further infringements. These procedures shall be applied in such a manner as to avoid the creation of barriers to legitimate trade and to provide for safeguards against their abuse.

2. Procedures concerning the enforcement of intellectual property rights shall be fair and equitable. They shall not be unnecessarily complicated or costly, or entail unreasonable time-limits or unwarranted delays.

ranked second only to Sony in its reputation for corporate social responsibility. This prestige has given IBM a unique position in the tightly knit Japanese business community.

For American Express, cause marketing provided the impetus for opening a branch in Budapest, Hungary, in 1991.[37] The American Express Foundation has been helping the former Communist country establish a tourism industry by sponsoring research on how a local museum could attract tourists and by setting up an education program in more than twenty Hungarian secondary schools. By 1994, the program was preparing five hundred young Hungarians, many from depressed areas, for careers in the tourism industry. The program will be a boon for Hungary, a country that desperately needs tourist income. (Of course, American Express now has an advantage over its competitors in serving the credit-card needs of those future tourists.)

INTERNATIONAL COMPETITION AND CORPORATE SOCIAL RESPONSIBILITY

How long corporate social responsibility will remain a net export for the United States is questionable. Corporate giving in the United States declined by 1 percent from 1992 to 1993, the first decline since the Great Depression, and estimates for the mid-1990s predicted a further drop-off.[38] It has leveled off through 1997.

The recession of the early 1990s may explain some of the decline, but experts think it can be attributed in large part to the fact that U.S. companies are losing market share to foreign competitors that do not spend nearly the same amount on corporate philanthropy. These foreign competitors, which have reaped the benefits of this advantage, now have the funds to act socially responsible, whereas many American companies are finding that they can no longer do so.

Japanese corporations, in particular, have been moving aggressively to establish a philanthropic foothold in the United States. More than two hundred Japanese companies—including giants such as Hitachi, Sony, Matsushita, and Toyota—have established foundations in the United States.[39] These foundations have contributed in areas ranging from educational programs to minority rights organizations to cultural concerns.

Foreign philanthropy will not reach the level of domestic giving in the United States for many years. The greater challenge is overseas, where MNCs have to compete with

---

37. *Ibid.*
38. *Ibid.*
39. *Ibid.*, p. 114.

local companies in the arena of social responsibility. One of the most impressive examples of such a local company is King Kar, a Taiwanese soft-drink producer.[40] King Kar has recently gone on the offensive against the two dominant soft-drink producers in its market, Coca-Cola and PepsiCo, with dramatic results. Morgan Sun, the executive director of King Kar's charitable foundation, decided to sponsor a campaign to help victims of floods in China, a country in which many Taiwanese citizens have roots. Instead of just donating money, he set up a program that asked the Taiwanese people to help. Under King Kar's auspices, more than 10 percent of the island's twenty-two million people pledged monthly donations for flood relief, and ten thousand of them volunteered to collect the money. Next, King Kar turned its attention to Somalia, and in three years it raised over $100 million, putting the company on par with the United Nations International Children's Emergency Fund (UNICEF) as a charitable force in the region. The results have been tangible. Thanks to increased name recognition from the charity campaign, King Kar surplanted Pepsi as the number two soft drink in Taiwan.[41]

---

40. *Ibid.*
41. *Ibid.*, p. 115.

THE DELICATE BALANCE

If the global expansion fervor did not affect all U.S. corporations in the 1990s, in the twenty-first century it certainly will. The number of companies exploring the possibility of setting up subsidiaries abroad, or at least having products assembled or manufactured abroad, is increasing. At the forefront of such activities, of course, are multinational corporations, many of which are based in the United States. These world-ranging giants, now sometimes called global corporations because they consist of a series of domestic corporations loosely linked together, face increasing scrutiny from the public, the press, and politicians not only at home but also abroad.

Here the delicate balance has become a tightrope walk for some of these companies. As ethical standards for business reach higher levels in the United States, there is an outcry that such standards should be placed on global corporations' activities in developing countries. Several problems arise when attempts are made to impose these standards, however. For example, a U.S. corporation's activities in some countries with respect to gender equality in the workplace may run up against serious moral, religious, and even legal constraints. The idea of profitability reveals other dilemmas. The reason why many global corporations seek production sites in developing countries is because of the cost advantage in so doing. If American standards for worker safety, wages, and the like were applied in these production sites, the cost advantages would disappear. Would it be ethical, then, simply to pull out of these countries? The people who were benefiting—particularly the workers in the production facilities—would be hurt.

Whatever delicate balance a global corporation figures out today may not be appropriate tomorrow. Consequently, U.S. corporate leaders have to monitor the social, economic, political, moral, and ethical situations in developing countries constantly to make the most appropriate decisions today.

TERMS AND CONCEPTS FOR REVIEW

Cultural distance 178
Ethical relativism 187
Ethnocentric 184
Foreign Corrupt Practices Act
  (FCPA) 178

Geocentric 184
Global corporation 171
Host government 178

Intellectual property rights 195
Multinational corporation (MNC)
  171

SUMMARY

1. There have been four distinct eras of international business development: (a) the postwar decade; (b) the growth years, from 1955 to 1970, during which Western Europe and Japan came on the international economic scene; (c) the time of trouble during the 1970s, when the United States abandoned the Bretton Woods agreement of 1945 (and allowed the price of gold to float); and (d) the new international order, which began in 1980 and runs through the present, during which Germany, Japan, and the newly industrialized nations of Southeast Asia have become world powers.

2. International trading companies have a long history, dating at least back to the East India Company of the late 1500s. The first American multinational business was the Singer Sewing Machine Company, which built a factory in Glasgow, Scotland, in 1867. By the early 1900s, U.S. companies had become the most dominant multinational corporations throughout the world. In 1967, about half of all American direct investments abroad belonged to Standard Oil, General Motors, and Ford. Today the United States is the leader in international investing, but it does not have hegemony.

3. A multinational corporation becomes a global, or multidomestic, corporation when each separate affiliate functions as a partner in a business confederation rather than simply as a branch of a central organization in the home country.

4. Multinational corporations have the following competitive advantages: (a) cost reductions via foreign assembly and manufacturing, (b) the ability to brand subcontracted finished products from low-cost foreign sources, (c) the ability to utilize global sourcing to find the cheapest parts and subassemblies, (d) market expansion abroad that results in economies of scale and hence lower per-unit costs, and (e) the transfer of technology through joint ventures.

5. Multinational corporations also have the benefit of being able to distribute foreign products in the United States, which allows for product differentiation. The same benefit occurs when a multinational corporation sells an American-made product abroad. Additionally, multinational corporations can use joint ventures as a way to increase product quality.

6. Today, most host governments have a great deal of regulatory power over any multinational corporation doing business within their jurisdictions. When host governments are inefficient or unstable, multinational corporations can experience severe problems. Such is the case in Russia today, and consequently there has been less investment from multinational corporations in that country than would otherwise have occurred.

7. In 1977, Congress passed the Foreign Corrupt Practices Act, which makes it illegal for U.S. companies to give bribes to foreign government officials in order to obtain business.

8. When multinational corporations are set up in other countries, they have to deal with the problem of cultural distance, which includes sociological and psychological differences between the society of the home country and that of the host country. Employees from the home country may take relatively long periods of time to adjust to the cultural differences in the host country, and miscommunications are almost inevitable.

9. Host countries have the following complaints about multinational corporations (not all of which necessarily reflect reality): (a) the destruction of the environment, (b) challenges to the host country's national sovereignty, (c) the disruptions of social patterns in the host country, (d) perceived inequities, and (e) pressure on the host country's legal system.

10. According to those who support the proliferation of multinational corporations, these companies provide the following benefits: (a) they improve the host country's productivity, (b) they increase the host country's living standards, (c) they foster new product development in the host country, (d) they upgrade the skills of the host country's employees, (e) they introduce new organizational techniques, and (f) they cause the host country's capital to flow to more productive uses.

11. A multinational corporation must implement ethical guidelines within the organization in the host country. Such ethical guidelines can, at least in part, follow the ethical algorithm developed by Tom Donaldson, which includes the rights to freedom of physical movement, ownership of property, a fair trial, nondiscriminatory treatment, political participation, and sustenance, among others.

12. American managers tend to believe that the American capitalist way of doing business is best for all countries. This ethnocentric perspective may not be appropriate in countries that for decades had centrally planned economic systems and are now trying to make the transition to market economies.

13. American-based multinational corporations must accept different cultural environments in order to succeed elsewhere. For example, food chains must recognize the differences in food preferences throughout the world in order to market their products elsewhere. Also, a number of countries accept bribery much more readily than the United States does. When we judge other countries according to our own ethics, we are in effect taking an imperialist ethical stand. Some argue for ethical relativism; that is, that the ethical practices of other countries should be judged in terms of the ethical standards of those countries.

14. At present, international codes of ethics have been developed by (a) the International Chamber of Commerce, (b) the Organization for Economic Cooperation and Development, and (c) the United Nations. None of these codes has the force of law, however.

15. Today, American multinational corporations are expected, to some extent, to export U.S. views of business ethics. In particular, American corporations using manufacturing facilities abroad are increasingly being asked by shareholders, American-based employees, unions, and the public at large to do business only in those countries that provide basic freedoms and safe working conditions for their workers.

16. One of the first codes of business conduct for multinational corporations has become known as the Sullivan Principles. It is based on the Reverend Leon Sullivan's six basic principles for companies doing business in South Africa prior to the end of apartheid.

17. Some argue that American corporations have the ethical responsibility to American workers not to go abroad in search of low-cost labor. Rather, it is argued, these companies should employ American workers and keep jobs at home in the United States. The favoring of protectionism over free trade can be very costly. Virtually all import restrictions imposed by the federal government have turned out to be extremely expensive in terms of annual dollars per job saved.

18. Because so much of the world's wealth is in intellectual property, the issue of intellectual property rights infringement abroad has become very important. The last round of the General Agreement on Tariffs and Trade included several procedures to safeguard intellectual property rights throughout the world.

19. Because corporate giving in the United States has been declining in the 1990s, the marketing benefits of corporate giving by foreign-based multinational corporations have become more evident. In particular, foreign-based multinational corporations have used charitable giving and other corporate citizenship activities to garner a good deal of positive publicity in the U.S. marketplace.

EXERCISES

1. Make a list of manufactured products that are supposedly American made but that nonetheless contain foreign-manufactured parts. (Hint: Think of cars, computers, and so forth.)

2. In the introduction to the chapter, Paul Krugman is quoted as saying that the United States is no more globally integrated today than it was in the nineteenth century. If he is correct, why is there so much emphasis today on the globalization of business?

3. Richard D. Robinson has outlined four eras of international business development, the last of which is the new international order, from 1980 to the present. Robinson contends that Germany and Japan have taken their places as economic powers on the world stage. Today, however, Germany is suffering from 10 percent unemployment, and Japan is facing a monumental banking crisis. Will those two countries therefore lose their predominant places in the international economic order? Explain your answer.

4. Why might the term *global corporation* be more appropriate than *multinational corporation*?

5. Why did the years between World War I and World War II see a slowing down in the development of international trade and multinational activity?

6. What has been the effect of such international trade agreements as the North American Free Trade Agreement (NAFTA) and the passage of the final round of the General Agreement on Tariffs and Trade (GATT)?

7. In at least two paragraphs, develop an argument in favor of the view that a corporation's home nationality is currently irrelevant and may become even more so in the future.

8. Present a definition of a multidomestic corporation, and relate it to the argument you just made in *Exercise 7*.

9. In the chapter, you read about five types of cost advantages of a multinational corporation. Create a hypothetical business that chooses to become a multinational corporation. Use examples of that business and its products to demonstrate each of the five potential cost advantages outlined in the chapter.

10. Make your own list of all the possible advantages of a company's becoming multinational. Alongside each advantage, write a possible disadvantage (particularly the disadvantage "if things don't go right").

11. You are head of a company that manufactures state-of-the-art small appliances. One of your directors claims that your company is not taking advantage of global outsourcing. He specifically knows that you could take many of the development and production stages of your business overseas, particularly to the Southeast Asian countries of China, South Korea, Singapore, Malaysia, Taiwan, and Thailand. He gives the example of the man-ufacturing cost of a small plastic component used in many of your products. If outsourced to the People's Republic of China, the component could be built for 6 cents each, whereas your costs at home are 10.5 cents. You are requested to prepare a report for the next board of directors meeting on what you plan to do about global outsourcing. Outline the benefits of global outsourcing. Then outline its costs. Specifically, make sure you address the issue of the low wages that are being paid to workers in Southeast Asia, as well as the potential job loss to workers in the United States.

12. "Since 1977, when the Foreign Corrupt Practices Act was passed, American-owned and American-based multi-nationals have been at a decided disadvantage in obtaining foreign contracts." Do you agree with this statement? Explain why you agree or disagree.

13. What alternatives do American companies have to sending American workers to foreign subsidiaries? What are the costs and benefits of these alternatives relative to sending Americans abroad to work?

14. In this chapter, you read about five possible complaints of host countries in regard to multinational corporations. Write a response to each complaint that gives a counter-argument.

15. Assume that you are head of a large multinational corporation. Make a list of the ways in which you can attempt to manage the ethical standards utilized by managers in your foreign subsidiaries.

16. The chapter listed ten fundamental international rights developed by Tom Donaldson. Get a copy of the U.S. Constitution, and relate each of the ten fundamental rights to a right presented in the Bill of Rights.

17. In Europe today, some intellectuals and politicians claim that the failure of communism, socialism, and centrally planned economies in general is not equivalent to the triumph of capitalism. Do you agree with them? Explain.

18. You are asked to be a consultant for the government in a small country that has recently switched from a centrally planned, state-controlled economy to an increasingly free market–based economy. Take two different points of view—an ethnocentric one and a geocentric one—and develop two separate paragraphs outlining what you think should be done in the immediate future to help the economy and its people.

19. In many countries, forms of bribery are considered an acceptable way of doing business. Except for payments to facilitate the handling of officially required papers and so on, the Foreign Corrupt Practices Act makes bribery by American companies abroad a criminal offense. Are there still ways for American companies either to skirt

the existing law or to obtain new business without bribery? Explain.

20. If international codes of business conduct do not have the force of law, why are they beneficial nonetheless?

21. In spite of the fact that apartheid no longer exists in South Africa, do you think that the Sullivan Principles, listed in *Exhibit 7–6*, are useful and meaningful for all businesses? If so, which ones are still useful, and why?

22. The new code of conduct for business activities in South Africa, as presented in *Exhibit 7–7*, seems to be all-encompassing. Explain what impediments South Africa faces with respect to implementing all the recommendations contained in *Exhibit 7–7*. Give reasons for your answers.

23. Why is intellectual property infringement more important today than it was, say, fifty years ago?

SELECTED REFERENCES

▶ Brown, Noel J., and Pierre Quiblier, eds. *Ethics and Agenda 21: The Moral Implications of a Global Consensus.* New York: United Nations Environment Programme, 1994.

▶ Desai, Meghnad, and Paul Redfern, eds. *Global Governance: Ethics and Economics of the World Order.* New York: Pinter, 1995.

▶ Fisher, Roger. *Points of Choice.* New York: Oxford University Press, 1978.

▶ Folsom, Ralph H., Michael Wallace Gordon, and John A. Spanogle, Jr. *International Business Transactions.* St. Paul: West Publishing Co., 1988.

▶ Henkin, Louis. *How Nations Behave.* 2d ed. New York: Columbia University Press, 1979.

▶ Hoffman, W. Michael, ed. *Emerging Global Business Ethics.* Westport, Conn.: Quorum Books, 1994.

▶ Jennings, Marianne Moody. *Business: Its Legal, Ethical, and Global Environment.* Belmont, Calif.: Wadsworth, 1994.

▶ Solomon, Robert C. *The New World of Business: Ethics and Free Enterprise in the Global 1990s.* Lanham, Md.: Littlefield Adams Quality Paperbacks, 1994.

RESOURCES ON THE INTERNET

▼ You can access the original 1947 General Agreement on Tariffs and Trade (GATT) by going to
gopher://gopher.law.cornell.edu:70/ 00/0/foreign/flectcher/BH209.txt

The gopher address is
Gopher.law.cornell.edu

Then you should select
Foreign and International Law: Primary Documents and Commentary

Next, select
Multilateral treaties by category

Then you should select
Trade and Commercial Relations

Finally, you should select
The General Agreement on Tariffs and Trade

▼ For information on the 1994 GATT, access
http://ananse.irv.uit.no/trade_law/gatt

▼ For the full text of the North American Free Trade Agreement (NAFTA), including daily dispatches from the White House, access
http://the-tech.mid.edu/Bulletins/ nafta.html

The gopher address is
gopher://niord.shsu.edu/

▼ If you use the commercial service CompuServe, you can obtain the legal aspects of importing and exporting goods by doing the following. Type in
Go itforum

From your library menu, you should choose
Browse

Then select
IT Practices

Then you should select
Legal Aspects of U.S. Importing

─── RESOURCES ON THE INTERNET (CONTINUED) ───

or

Legal Aspects of U.S. Exporting

▼ You can get information about NAFTA and the text of the agreement at the following Web site:

**http://the-tech.mit.edu/Bulletins/
nafta.html**

▼ If you want to know more about international trade law, the best place to go is probably the following Web site:

**http://ananse.irv.uit.no/trade_law/
nav/trade.html**

▼ The World Bank is an international financial organization that lends billions of dollars to many of the world's poorest nations. In many cases, the World Bank provides aid (in the form of cash, industry, and jobs) to countries that have been overlooked by the world's wealthier nations. You can access data on any of the World Bank's programs by accessing

**http://www.worldbank/org.html/
extdr/about.html**

▼ If you are interested in how another country views business ethics, you should explore Ethical Business, originating in Great Britain, at

**http://www.bath.ac.uk/Centres/
Ethical/**

CASE

LEVI STRAUSS AND THE VALUES-BASED APPROACH TO BUSINESS ABROAD

Background

During the 1980s, Levi Strauss & Company, the world's largest supplier of brand name clotheswear, began relocating its manufacturing facilities overseas. By the end of the decade, about half of the company's product came from hired factories abroad.

For the most part, Levi Strauss ignored working conditions at these foreign plants. In late 1991, however, one of its contractors in Saipan, a U.S. possession in the Mariana Islands chain of the western Pacific, was accused of using Chinese women as virtual slaves. A lawsuit by the U.S. Labor Department charged that the plant owners, the Tan family, had illegally taken kickbacks from the Chinese workers brought to the island under contract from China, and also owed over 1,300 workers more than $10 million in back pay.

Levi Strauss ran its own investigation of the Tan family operation and found that it paid its workers wages below the legal minimum. Levi Strauss subsequently fired the contractor.

Values-Based Approach

Levi Strauss's lack of awareness about the working conditions imposed by its contractors overseas was disturbing to company chairman and chief executive Robert Haas, the great-great-grandnephew of founder Levi Strauss. Haas had made a name for himself as a maverick in the business world for his concept of "responsible commercial success"—the belief that the corporation can be an ethical entity that is as concerned with its social responsibility as its profits.

Under Haas, Levi Strauss spent the 1980s restructuring with this idea of responsible success as its goal. For example, the company's Diversity Council offers a link between senior management and groups representing Hispanic Americans, African Americans, Asian Americans, gay men and lesbians, and all women. Haas also oversaw the development of the Levi Strauss Aspiration Statement, a corporate credo that spells out the company's values-based approach and commitment to ethics, which is to guide all business decisions. Each Levi Strauss employee is expected to take part in the Core Curriculum, a series of training programs that deals with issues of ethics, empowerment, and diversity.

The company has been willing to take these values beyond the walls of its corporate headquarters. In 1992, Levi Strauss revoked its contributions to the Boy Scouts of America after the organization refused to accept homosexuals as scouts or allow them to serve as scoutmasters.

This approach has its critics in the business community. "The company has the P.C. mindset," says apparel consultant Alan G. Millstein. "The Haases think that they talk to God." The results of the so-called politically correct mindset, however, have proved tangible. The company has doubled the number of minority managers to 36 percent since Haas became CEO in 1984, and women have climbed from 32 percent of management to 54 percent in that same time period. According to federal labor statistics, both numbers are well above average for U.S. businesses. Furthermore, the company generated over $6 billion in revenues in 1995, up from $2 billion in 1979.

Global Source Guidelines

To ensure that the values at Levi Strauss's overseas contractors matched those of the company at home, after the Saipan incident Haas decided to come up with a set of guidelines for contractors abroad. He formed a working group of fifteen employees who spent nine months researching the issue.

The task force interviewed various stakeholder groups—from sewing machine operators to plant managers to shareholders—and applied the results to an ethical decision-making model in order to come up with Levi Strauss's Global Sourcing Guidelines. These guidelines state that the company will not initiate or renew contractual relationships in countries with the following conditions:

▶ Where sourcing would have an adverse affect on our global brand image.
▶ Where there is evidence that Company employees or representatives would be exposed to unreasonable risks.
▶ Where there are pervasive violations of basic human rights.
▶ Where political or social turmoil unreasonably threatens our commercial interests.

The task force also devised Terms of Engagements, which covered environmental, ethical, health and safety, and labor requirements for overseas business partners. Once the various guidelines were established, the company held training sessions for one hundred U.S.–based managers, who would then enforce them with Levi Strauss's seven hundred contractors worldwide.

In its initial audit, the company severed ties with thirty contractors based on their failure to comply with the sourcing guidelines. In other situations, the company demanded that contractors add safety features such as emergency exits and stairways, reduce crowding, and invest in water treatment systems.

The company continues to monitor its contractors in this way. In 1994, the company learned that a contractor in Indonesia was strip-searching its female workers to determine whether or not they were menstruating, and therefore entitled to time off without pay, according to the Muslim laws of that country. Levi Strauss immediately canceled its contract with the factory.

China

The most controversial action taken as a result of the Global Sourcing Guidelines came in 1993, when Levi Strauss decided to discontinue investments in the Chinese market and phase out $40 million worth of contracts with Chinese manufacturers. The company had annually purchased about five million shirts and pants from China, representing 2 percent of the company's total output. The determination came from the dictates of the sourcing guidelines concerning human rights.

At the time Levi Strauss announced these intentions, the U.S. Congress was debating whether or not to allow China to keep its most-favored-nation trade status in light of the country's many human rights violations. Critics saw the timing of Levi Strauss's pullout as more than mere coincidence. "You could make a very cynical case that Levi is getting good PR out of this," said Richard Brecher, director of business advisory services at the U.S.–China Business Council. "It's very easy to thump your chest and condemn China. I would argue that some of the harshest critics of China are doing little to promote human rights in China."

Stakeholder Concerns

Reaction in China to Levi Strauss's pullout was muted, at best. An official of the Chinese Foreign Ministry remarked, "At present there are tens of thousands of foreign companies investing in China. If one or two want to withdraw, please do."

Other countries in which Levi Strauss operates have expressed their displeasure with the company's methods. Choy Ming Bill, who heads the Malaysian Textile Manufacturers, calls Levi Strauss's constant inspections "irritating" and charges that the company is "splitting hairs" when it examines wage records. "They're looked at as crackpots in Asia," notes a source who has worked with the company in the region.

To a certain extent, some Levi Strauss board members agree. Noting the huge potential for profits in China, they have questioned Haas's strategy and have forced a review of the sourcing guidelines. Because Levi Strauss's competitors have not shown a commensurate concern for the social welfare of their overseas workers, the worry is that the company is placing itself at a competitive disadvantage. "High-minded efforts usually evaporate because people with far less scruples decide to low-ball labor, and dictates of the market eliminate these ethical assays," says Larry Byrnes, director of the Council on Hemispheric Affairs.

Haas explains the company's actions as follows: "We are not doing this because it makes us feel good—although it does. We are not doing this because it is politically correct." The CEO believes that unethical business practices abroad could hurt his company's image—and consequently its sales. "Consumers are looking more and more to the company behind the product," he says. "Companies have to wake up to the fact that they are more than a product on a shelf. They're behavior as well."

Haas adds that there are other incentives for responsible corporate social behavior. "In today's world, a TV exposé on working conditions can undo years of effort to build brand name loyalty. Why squander your investment when, with commitment, reputational problems can be prevented?"

Bangladesh

Levi Strauss's reaction to child labor problems with overseas contractors underlines Haas's position. In 1994, the company discovered that manufacturing contractors in Bangladesh and Turkey were employing underage female workers. As this was a clear violation of the sourcing guidelines, the company ordered the contractors to discontinue the practice.

The Bangladeshi contractors agreed to fire the girls, some of whom were as young as eleven years old, but noted that such an action would have disastrous effects on the young workers' families. Making the equivalent of $384 a month, the girls—the oldest children in large, single-parent families—were the sole economic support for their families.

The intention of the sourcing guidelines is "not to have a devastating effect on families," so the company worked out a compromise. The contractors would continue paying the underage workers their salaries until they reached legal age, and until that time Levi Strauss would cover the costs of

CASE (CONTINUED)

tuition, uniforms, and supplies to allow the girls to attend the local school. If the girls did not wish to return to work once they reached the legal age, they would not be required to do so.

Under the program, fourteen children are attending school in Bangladesh and six in Turkey. Haas sees the situation as a shining example of the values of the Global Sourcing Guidelines: "We were able to retain three quality contractors [and] at the same time, our values and brand image were protected."

The company has realized other, more fiscally substantial dividends from its guidelines. After an NBC exposé disclosed that the discount chain Wal-Mart—a major customer of Levi Strauss—was benefiting from child labor in Bangladesh, Wal-Mart decided to stop purchasing goods produced in that country, including those produced by Levi Strauss. By pointing to its sourcing guidelines, Levi Strauss was able to gain an exemption and keep Wal-Mart's business.

Haas readily admits that the Global Sourcing Guidelines "limit our options and squeeze profit margins." He adds, however, that "over the years, we have found that decisions that emphasize cost to the exclusion of all other factors do not best serve a company's—or its shareholders'—long-term

interests. Our five straight years of record sales and earnings, and a doubling of the size of our business in as many years, support our conclusion."

Critical Thinking Questions

1. Do you agree with Levi Strauss's approach toward taking responsibility for the actions of its contractors? Is such a stand always in the best interests of the people whose rights Levi Strauss is endeavoring to protect?

2. Would knowledge of human rights abuses by contractors to an American company prevent you from purchasing that company's product?

3. Despite its intentions, Levi Strauss has been accused of being overly paternalistic—even culturally imperialistic. Do you agree with these accusations? Should American companies, and ultimately American consumers, dictate cultural practices in other countries, even if they find these practices abhorrent?

4. How can a company's policy with regard to foreign subsidiaries affect its corporate culture at home?

5. What difficulties might Levi Strauss encounter in implementing its Global Sourcing Guidelines?

SOURCE: Information from "Exporting Jobs and Ethics," *Fortune*, October 5, 1992, p. 10; F. Swoboda, "Levi Strauss to Drop Suppliers Violating Its Worker Rights Rules," *Washington Post*, March 13, 1992, p. D1; R. Mitchell, "Managing by Values," *Business Week*, August 1, 1994, pp. 46, 49, 51, 52; J. Impoco, "Working for Mr. Clean Jeans," *U.S. News and World Report*, August 2, 1993, pp. 49–50; "Levi Strauss & Co. Business Partner Terms of Engagement and Guidelines for Country Selection"; R. D. Haas, "Ethics in the Trenches," *Across the Board*, May 1994, pp. 12, 13; G. Pascal Zachary, "Levi Tries to Make Sure Contract Plants in Asia Treat Workers Well," *Wall Street Journal*, August 1, 1994, p. A8; C. Miller, "Levi to Sever Link with China," *Marketing News*, June 7, 1993, p. 10; "No More Dockers," *Time*, May 17, 1993, p. 21; and M. Clifford, "Levi's Law," *Far Eastern Economic Review*, April 14, 1993, p. 60.

PART

PART **III**

BUSINESS AND GOVERNMENT

CHAPTER 8

AN INTRODUCTION TO GOVERNMENT REGULATION OF BUSINESS

CHAPTER OUTLINE

▶ History of Government Regulation

▶ Government Influence on Business

▶ Regulatory Agencies: The "Fourth Branch of Government"

▶ The Public Speaks: To Regulate or Not to Regulate

INTRODUCTION

The *Federal Register* is not light reading. This daily publication of the executive branch prints government orders, rules, and regulations and is filled with sentences such as "CFR part 1320 sets forth procedures for agencies to follow in obtaining OMB clearing for information collection requirements under the Paperwork Reduction Act of 1980, 44 U.S.C. 3501 et seq."[1]

The number of pages in the *Register* is an indication of the amount of regulatory activity by the federal government over the past thirty years. During the 1970s, a decade that witnessed an explosion of new regulations, the *Register* reached almost 100,000 pages each year. After President Ronald Reagan was elected in 1980 on a platform that promised to limit the size of the federal bureaucracy, his administration oversaw a series of rules that to some extent restrained government agencies from issuing new regulations and implementing old ones. The result was a leaner *Register*. In the late 1980s and early 1990s, the pendulum swung again toward increased government regulatory action, and by 1996 the *Register* was almost 70,000 pages strong.

Is a thick *Federal Register* "good" for the United States? Are greater amounts of government influence on daily life good for any country or community? How you answer this question depends on your opinion of the government's ability to lead. The Chinese statesman Sun Yat-sen (1867–1925) believed that "the foundation of the government of a nation must be built upon the rights of the people, but the administration must be trusted to the experts." An earlier counterpart, the Swedish statesman Axel Oxenstierna (1583–1654), counseled, "Do you not know, my son, with how little wisdom the world is governed?"

Regulation can be broadly defined as a government's direct influence on the social and economic activity of a society through its ability to pass rules and make laws. A government's overriding ideology—often provided by the political party in power—usually dictates its regulatory policies with regard to business; however, if one were to ask businesspersons what they think of regulation, most would answer more along the lines of Oxenstierna than Sun Yat-sen. Many proponents of the free market believe that Adam Smith's "invisible hand" does a better job of allocating society's resources than could any government official or agency. They see excessive government regulation as placing an unacceptable burden on business.[2]

There are those, however, who are in favor of regulation. Consumer advocacy groups such as Ralph Nader's Public Citizen keep the public aware of the quality of goods and services, as well as push the government for regulatory curbs on business and guidelines for the quality and safety of products. "Green" watchdog organizations, such as the Audubon Society and the Sierra Club, have led a movement to increase the number of environmental regulations. Furthermore, the Civil Rights Acts of 1964 and 1991 and the Americans with Disabilities Act of 1990, which included myriad new rules and regulations, came as the result of grassroots activity by minorities, women, and persons with disabilities who felt they were being discriminated against by underregulated American businesses.

Chapters 8 through 11 address the factors behind the somewhat unstable relationship between government, business, and society. The issues discussed are at the heart of a debate central to businesspersons, politicians, and economists: What is the proper role of government in business?

---

1. "Rules and Regulations," *Federal Register*, December 6, 1991, p. 64004.
2. K. P. Phillips, "U.S. Industrial Policy: Inevitable and Ineffective," *Harvard Business Review*, July–August 1992, p. 104.

HISTORY OF GOVERNMENT REGULATION

The seeds for government regulation in the United States were planted by the framers of the Constitution, though it is doubtful that they planned or envisioned for the federal government to encompass as much it does today. Article I, Section 8, of the Constitution expressly permits Congress "to regulate Commerce with foreign Nations, and among the several States, and with the Indian tribes." This clause, referred to as the **commerce clause**, has had a greater impact on business than has any other provision in the Constitution. The power it delegates to the federal government ensures the uniformity of rules governing the movement of goods through the states.

For some time, the commerce clause was interpreted as being limited to *interstate* (between-state) commerce and not as being applicable to *intrastate* (within-state) trade. In 1824, however, the U.S. Supreme Court held that Congress has the power to regulate any activity—interstate or intrastate—that "affects" interstate commerce. A farmer's wheat production intended wholly for consumption on his or her own farm, for example, was held to be subject to federal regulation, because that home consumption reduced the demand for wheat in the market and thus may have had a substantial economic effect on interstate commerce.[3]

Federal regulation remained almost nonexistent during the early years of the United States. U.S. citizens, still smarting from memories of King George III's colonial meddling, resisted (not entirely successfully) the idea of government interference in private affairs until after the Civil War (1861–1865). When the industrial revolution changed the economy and the "Robber Barons" (John D. Rockefeller, Andrew Carnegie, and Henry Ford, among others) began to assert more, and frequently unwelcome, influence over the daily lives of the people, those attitudes changed. The ensuing populist movement, driven by agrarian and labor groups, reflected mistrust by the "common people" of this new elite class of "big business" people.

In the 1880s, the government began to react to the public's desire to rein in big business. A study of how the government "regulated" the railroad industry—then the nation's most powerful private sector—shows the beginnings of the modern regulatory environment. (For an overview of regulation in the United States, see *Exhibit 8–1* on pp. 214–15.)

NINETEENTH-CENTURY REGULATORY BEGINNINGS— THE RAILROADS

Many industries flourished during the second half of the nineteenth century, but the railroads were the epitome of this capitalist golden age. Because this industry was the focal point of interstate commerce, its growth matched, in a sense, the growth of the country. From 1830 to 1890, the total number of miles of railway track in the United States nearly doubled every decade. After the first transcontinental railway was finished in 1869, the railroads became the dominant transport mechanism in the country: within five years, 90 percent of trade between the two coasts was by rail.[4]

Market Pressure As the railroads' profits escalated, so did competitiveness within the industry. Railroads face extremely high fixed costs. To do business, the early railroads had to lay miles and miles of track before they could put the first locomotive in service. The

---

3. *Wickard v. Filburn*, 317 U.S. 111, 63 S.Ct. 82, 87 L.Ed. 122 (1942).
4. "Note on Railroad and Trucking Regulation," Harvard Business School Case No. 9-793-041, August 3, 1994, p. 2.

costs of the locomotives and railcars themselves also were high. Once a railroad had incurred these fixed costs, they were unrecoverable, with little or no alternative use for track or hardware. Thus, their opportunity cost became close to zero.

These high fixed costs made the strategy of lowering rates to attract more business an extremely risky one for the railroad industry. Following the Panic of 1873, which drove the rail companies to "excess competition" for scarce business, Albert Fink, president of the Louisville and Nashville Railroad, tried to create a type of monopoly, called a pool, to set rates and allocate traffic among its members. Although these efforts to contain "excess competition" ultimately failed because the individual railroads kept breaking the rules, the obvious price fixing enraged those interests that relied on the railroads for the transport of goods. Angered by the railroads' practice of charging much higher rates for short hauls than longer ones—a practice also brought on by high fixed costs—owners of small businesses, shippers, farmers, and passengers began to pressure their local governments to "do something" about the railroads.

The Interstate Commerce Act The first reaction to this outcry came in the early 1870s, when many midwestern states passed legislation that controlled railroad rates within their borders. The railroad industry resisted these so-called Granger Laws (named after the farmers' organization known as the National Grange of the Patrons of Husbandry, which pushed for the laws), arguing that they restricted the railroads' right to be free of state interference without due process of law under the Fourteenth Amendment. After almost fifteen years of legal wrangling, in 1886 the Supreme Court ruled in *Wabash v. Illinois* that states had no jurisdiction to regulate *interstate* commerce, effectively putting an end to the Granger Laws. As a result, Congress passed the Interstate Commerce Act in 1887, which established federal control over the railroad industry. Under the auspices of the act, the nation's first federal regulatory agency, the Interstate Commerce Commission (ICC), was formed. The ICC was charged with enforcing the act's mandate that all rates be "reasonable and just" by prohibiting rate discrimination, pooling, and differences in short- and long-haul rates, except under certain circumstances.

At the time, the Interstate Commerce Act represented a significant foray into regulation by the federal government. Its limited power during its early years, however, showed that the courts were not quite ready for an activist federal government. Of the sixteen ICC-related appeals heard by the Supreme Court from 1887 to 1905, only one was not decided in favor of the railroads.[5]

REGULATORY MOMENTUM IN THE TWENTIETH CENTURY

With the turn of the century came the Progressive Era in American politics. The public's hostility toward big business was at a high point, fueled by writers such as Upton Sinclair, whose *The Jungle* (1906), a harshly critical exposé of the nation's meat-packing industry, was either muckraking "yellow" journalism or the first example of investigative journalism, depending on one's point of view. Fledgling grassroots organizations such as the National Consumers' League began questioning whether the prices of products were fair and the products being offered were of the highest quality possible.

The national leaders of the time, Presidents Theodore Roosevelt (1901–1909), William Howard Taft (1909–1913), and Woodrow Wilson (1913–1921), echoed these concerns and oversaw a number of new regulatory developments. The Pure Food and

---

5. *Ibid.*, p. 4.

Drug Act of 1906 and the Sherley Amendment (1912) attempted to protect consumers from fraudulent or unsafe food and drugs. The Clayton Act of 1914 and the Federal Trade Commission Act of 1914, both of which will be discussed in more detail in Chapter 10, strengthened federal laws that prohibited monopolies and the restraint of trade.

The railroad industry did not escape the Progressive Era free of further regulatory burdens. The Elkins Act (1903), the Hepburn Act (1906), and the Mann-Elkins Act (1910) reinforced the power of the ICC and reduced the power of the railroad companies to control routes and pricing.

During World War I (1914–1918), some industries were nationalized. The U.S. Railway Administration, created at the end of 1917, operated the railroads as a single, integrated system until the end of the war. Congress was so impressed by the efficient manner in which this federal board ran the railroads that it considered making the situation permanent. In the end, however, Congress settled on the Transportation Act of 1920, which increased the ICC's power by various means, including giving the agency control of minimum rates and the ability to regulate entry and exit from regional and national markets.

The Great Depression and the New Deal The 1920s were a prosperous time for the railroads, as well as for the entire nation. Regulatory activity was minimal. The decade saw only one significant regulatory act for the railroad industry: the Railway Labor Act of 1926, which established guidelines for collective bargaining in the industry.

After the start of the Great Depression in 1929, the railroads found themselves without enough freight to fill the 2.6 million railroad cars to which the industry had expanded during the 1920s. By 1932, in the depths of the Great Depression, the railroads failed to cover the fixed costs for nearly three-quarters of the miles run.[6] The railroads were kept out of bankruptcy only by President Franklin D. Roosevelt (in office from 1932–1948) and his era of regulation known as the New Deal.

Roosevelt's plan to spur the nation's recovery from the Great Depression centered on direct involvement by the federal government in business. The Securities Act of 1933 and the Securities and Exchange Act of 1934 increased federal regulation of the stock market and restored investor confidence. The Banking Act of 1933 created the Federal Deposit Insurance Corporation (FDIC) to protect most depositors by insuring their deposits. The decade also saw significant labor legislation with the Norris-LaGuardia Act (1932) and the Wagner Act (1935), which permitted employees to organize unions and engage in collective bargaining, respectively.

Ironically, Roosevelt's New Deal provided the railroad industry with a boost by encouraging the very pooling activities that the Granger Laws of the 1870s had once tried to prevent. Passage of the Emergency Railroad Transportation Act in 1934 allowed railroad companies to share equipment, tracks, and terminals.

Regulation and Deregulation since World War II In the second half of the twentieth century, the power and influence of the railroads declined as other industries, such as trucking and the airlines, evolved into the country's main transporters. In fact, rail business declined so drastically that the industry became one of the few to ask consistently for protective regulation.

After World War II (1939–1945), the U.S. economy was strengthened to the point where big business complained of being restricted by untoward government intrusion. The rise and fall of regulation since that time has been cyclical and has depended as much on public attitudes as on economic necessity. The *laissez-faire* attitude of the prosperous, postwar

---

6. *Ibid.*, p. 7.

▼ EXHIBIT 8–1 A Time Line of Regulation in the United States

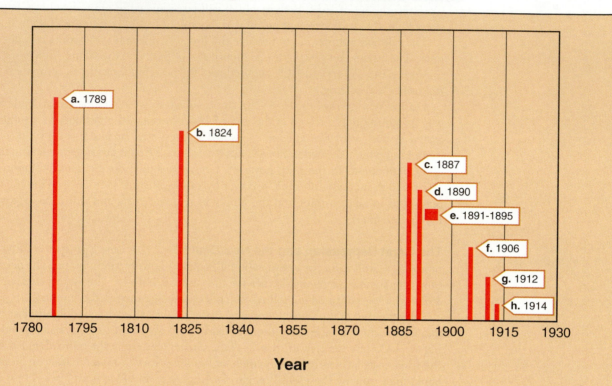

Year

Description:

a. The U.S. Constitution is ratified. Article I, Section 8, of the Constitution—the commerce clause—provides the legal basis for regulation.

b. The U.S. Supreme Court rules that the commerce clause gives the Congress the power to regulate any business activity that affects both interstate and intrastate trade. This broad interpretation paves the way for much of the federal legislation to follow.

c. Passage of the Interstate Commerce Act. This act establishes the control of the federal government over the railroad industry. Congress forms the nation's first federal regulatory agency, the Interstate Commerce Commission (ICC).

d. Passage of the Sherman Antitrust Act, the first major law to protect consumers from anticompetitive practices by business.

e. The populist movement reaches its peak. Farmer and labor groups voice mistrust of "big business" barons born of the Industrial Revolution. Populism makes early demands that government protect the people from business.

f. Passage of the Pure Food and Drug Act, the first major law to protect consumers from fraudulent or unsafe food and drugs.

g. Passage of the Sherley Amendment, which reinforces the Pure Food and Drug Act.

h. Passage of the Clayton Act and the Federal Trade Commission Act. Both laws strengthen the Sherman Antitrust Act.

1950s gave way to the idealistic policies of the 1960s and 1970s, during which much social legislation was passed—for example, the Civil Rights Act of 1964, the Water Quality Act of 1965, the Occupational Safety and Health Act of 1970, and the Consumer Product Safety Act of 1972.

▼ **EXHIBIT 8–1 A Time Line of Regulation in the United States** *continued*

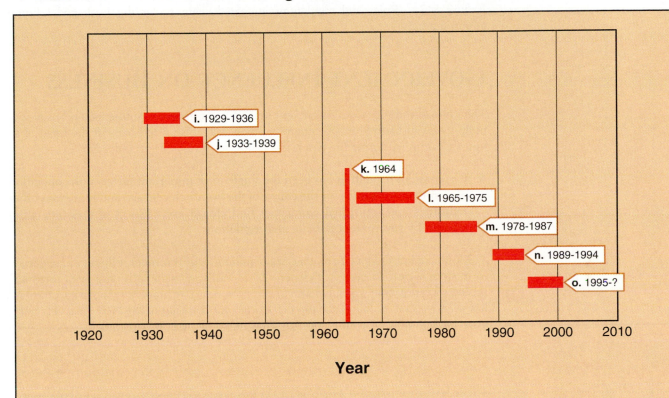

Description:

i.   The Great Depression. Economic hardships led many Americans to question business practices of the preceding decade.

j.   The New Deal, a legislative program adopted by President Franklin D. Roosevelt to alleviate the effects of the Great Depression. The Securities Act of 1933 and the Securities and Exchange Act of 1934 increase regulation of the stock market in order to restore investor confidence. The Banking Act of 1933 forms the Federal Deposit Insurance Corporation to protect depositors in the nation's banks. The Norris-LaGuardia Act of 1932 and the Wagner Act of 1935 strengthen the nation's labor unions.

k.   Passage of the Civil Rights Act. This act moves to protect Americans from being discriminated against on the basis of race, creed, or religion.

l.   A decade of increased social legislation along the line of the Civil Rights Act. Legislation passed during this period strengthens the rights of workers and

consumers, provides financial assistance for poor Americans, and moves to protect the environment.

m.   Deregulation. In reaction to the regulation explosion of the late 1960s and early 1970s, this period of deregulation sees the removal of regulatory restraints on certain industries. Under Presidents Jimmy Carter (1977–1981) and Ronald Reagan (1981–1989), the airline, trucking, and communications industries are heavily deregulated.

n.   Reregulation. Under Presidents George Bush and Bill Clinton, the trend of deregulation is reversed. A number of new regulations are placed on the banking and telecommunications industries, as well as many other sectors of the economy.

o.   "Re"-deregulation. As Congress becomes more conservative, political pressure is rising to eliminate many regulations pertaining to the environment, workers' rights, and international trade.

A backlash against this regulatory atmosphere began in 1978, when President Jimmy Carter instigated the **deregulation** of the airline and trucking industries. Deregulation is the opposite of regulation; it involves the removal of regulatory restraints on business. Ronald Reagan continued the process; during his two terms as president (1981–1989),

Reagan struck down regulatory controls of the telephone and bus industries. President Reagan, in fact, pushed deregulation as one of the central tenets of his presidency (see *Exhibit 8–2*).[7] Rules and regulations increased again under the Bush and Clinton administrations.

GOVERNMENT INFLUENCE ON BUSINESS

The railroad industry—as just one example of a government's influence on business—underscores just why the government-business relationship has been at the heart of so much controversy during the past few decades (see *Exhibit 8–3*). Indeed,

▼ **Government regulation has been the single most important factor in the operation of a railroad company over the course of the twentieth century, and numerous other industries and individual companies find almost every aspect of their operation affected by government policies and regulations.**

Most people would agree that a certain amount of government influence is necessary in modern society to protect a citizen's basic rights, set standards, and keep unethical business interests from causing harm to communities. The modern scope of government, however, goes beyond any scenario that existed at the height of the New Deal. This situation has naturally raised the question, How much regulation is too much?

GOVERNMENT'S NONREGULATORY EFFECT ON BUSINESS

The federal government is a daily player in the nation's economic scene. The government buys and sells goods, hires and fires employees, plans a budget, and so on, just as a private company does. Unlike a private company, however, the federal government has a budget of more than $1½ trillion and approximately two million employees. Consequently, decisions

▼ **EXHIBIT 8–2 Principles of Ronald Reagan's Deregulation**

▶ Support "sunset" legislation requiring that Congress periodically reassess the viability of regulatory laws.

▶ Carry out cost-benefit analyses of regulatory laws, and impose regulations only when benefits exceed costs.

▶ Choose the least expensive methods to achieve regulatory goals.

▶ Consider the size of a company when passing regulatory laws.

▶ Shift regulatory rules to the states.

▶ Reduce unnecessary paperwork and regulatory delays.

▶ Eliminate rigid compliance rules by relying on economic incentives and penalties to encourage companies to meet standards.

SOURCE: "Deregulation: A Fast Start for the Reagan Strategy," *Business Week,* March 9, 1981, p. 63.

7. D. Bandow, "Is Business Drowning in a Regulatory Tide?" *Business and Society Review,* Summer 1992, p. 45.

▼ **EXHIBIT 8–3 Government Influences on Corporations in the United States**

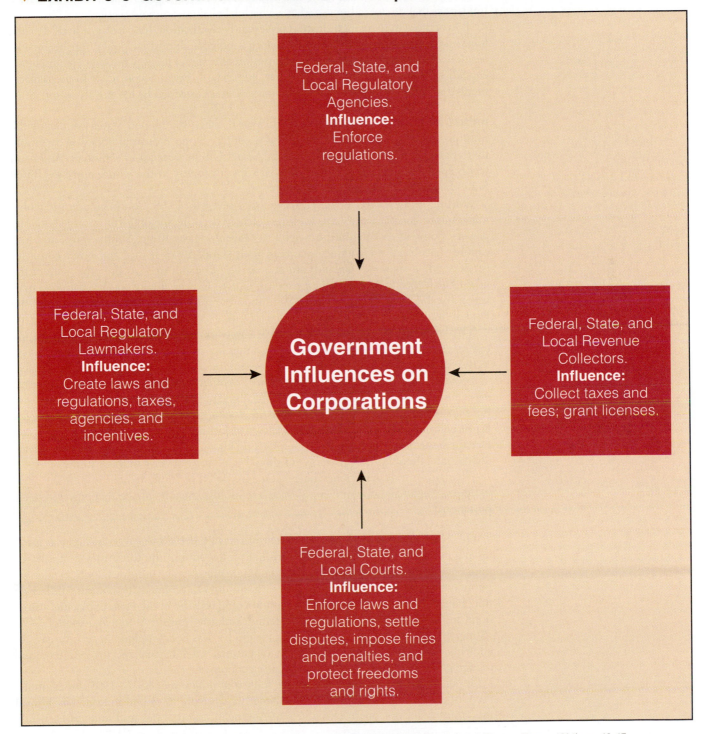

SOURCE: Based on information contained in R. E. Freeman, *Strategic Management: A Stakeholder Approach* (Boston: Pitman, 1984), pp. 13–17.

made by federal government decision makers tend to ripple through the entire national economy. Its almost unimaginable size means that the federal government is bound to have influences that do not fall under what we have labeled government regulation.

Two of those influences, **industrial policy** and **privatization**, have become hotly debated topics among both the electorate and elected officials. Industrial policy can be broadly defined as any systematic attempt by a government to direct the way resources are used in a capitalist economy (such as that of the United States). Privatization refers to the replacement of government services with those same services provided by the private sector.

Industrial Policy At the close of World War II, when the United States was clearly the most powerful nation on earth, there was no outcry for an industrial policy. Why should there have been? Japan, Europe, and the Soviet Union were all in shambles. American technology and craftsmanship were by far superior to any in the world, and the United States had ready markets for its products.

Starting in the 1970s, however, there was a reversal of U.S. dominance in the global marketplace. Japan rose from its wartime defeat to become one of the top world economic powers. Some of its Pacific Rim neighbors (Taiwan, Hong Kong, South Korea, and Singapore) have seen astronomical gains in their standards of living, and other countries (such as Malaysia and Thailand) are also starting to catch up. On the other side of the world, the fifteen countries of the European Union (EU) gradually became a unified market in the 1990s. With more than 380 million consumers, the EU hopes to surpass the United States in the world market.

The key to global competitiveness today is maximizing human resources—not natural resources, as was the case in the past. Thus, a number of economists have argued for a new industrial policy.[8] Some U.S. businesspersons and economists, for example, want the federal government to match the "helping hands" of other governments, industry by industry. These businesspersons argue that when the European governments subsidize the large airliner made by Airbus, we should subsidize the Boeing Company and McDonnell Douglas. If our cellular phone industry faces obstacles in Japan, then Japanese equipment should face the same obstacles here. If the German and Japanese economies have a higher private savings rate, then the U.S. government should encourage savings in this country.

Changes in industrial policy have been considered or implemented in four key areas to help U.S. global competitiveness: trade, technology, health care, and energy and transportation.[9]

Trade The Omnibus Trade and Competitiveness Act of 1988 was seen by many as introducing congressionally mandated government intervention into the business of international trade. Section 301 of the act requires a presidential administration to identify publicly those countries practicing "unfair trade" and to threaten "retribution" if they do not change their policies. Federal retribution could only be in the form of placing restrictions on those countries believed to be acting "unfairly" toward American exporters. The "Super 301," as the clause is known in trade circles, has been credited in recent years for allowing American semiconductor manufacturers, satellite makers, toy retailers, and orange growers to gain a foothold in Japan's economy.

Super 301, however, does not ensure industrial policy success. In 1995, for example, the Clinton administration quietly threatened Japan with $6 billion in trade sanctions if the country did not open its markets to American automobiles and auto parts, which

---

8. S. Evans, K. Ewing, and P. Nolan, "Industrial Relations and the British Economy in the 1990s: Mrs. Thatcher's Legacy," *Journal of Management Studies*, September 1992, p. 571.
9. Phillips, *op. cit.*, pp. 106–107.

President Clinton signs Security Agreement with Japan's Prime Minister Hashimoto Ryutaro at Akasaka Palace, Japan in April, 1996.

account for 60 percent of the U.S. trade deficit with that country.[10] Japan, however, was secure in the knowledge that such sanctions would ignite a trade war, with disastrous results for the American economy. Even hints of a Super 301 action in this dispute sent the dollar plunging against the yen, drove U.S. interest rates up, and shook international bond markets—a situation politically untenable for any American president.[11] Consequently, the two countries averted a trade war with an agreement that left Japan's policy toward U.S. automobiles and auto parts virtually unchanged.[12] The stand-off demonstrates the important fact that industrial policy with regard to international trade is limited by political reality.

Technology Concern that the United States not fall behind other countries, especially Japan, in producing new technology has led to specific industrial policy decisions to spur American research and development. In 1991, President Bush approved federal assistance for the development of the world's fastest "tearflop" computer, which was considered critical in helping U.S. companies maintain the upper hand in global competitiveness. President Clinton continued a program of federal support for "manufacturing technology centers" designed to integrate new technology into private business (see *Managing Social Issues— Forging New Alliances:* Kohsetsushi *American Style* on page 220).

Health Care "Few people think of the national debate about health care in terms of industrial policy," says one business writer. "But proposals for fixing the health-care system are in fact proposals for an industrial policy in an important economic sector." How

---

10. B. Davis, "Auto Trade Disputes Suggest Some Lessons," *Wall Street Journal*, July 3, 1995, p. A1.
11. D. Harbrecht, "Why Washington Backed Down at the Midnight Hour," *Business Week*, October 17, 1994, p. 46.
12. H. Cooper, "U.S., Japan Sign Agreement on Autos, But Comments Hint at Long Struggle," *Wall Street Journal*, August 24, 1995, p. A2.

⬚ Managing Social Issues

Forging New Alliances: Kohsetsushi American Style

In Japan, companies with fewer than 300 employees have an important business partner—the government. Through a network of 172 technology centers known as *kohsetsushi*, the government offers these small businesses assistance, training, and other services connected with cutting-edge technology. Philip Shapira of the Georgia Institute of Technology calls the *kohsetsushi* "a key factor in Japan's [economic] success." He credits them with creating an environment in which Japanese small businesses are much more likely to be using advanced technology than are their American counterparts.

American *Kohsetsushi*

Many politicians and businesspersons in the United States have been looking at *kohsetsushi* with an eye toward a similar system on their own shores. The Omnibus Trade and Competitiveness Act of 1988 authorized the U.S. Commerce Department's National Institute of Standards and Technology to set up seven manufacturing technology centers (MTCs)—in Cleveland, Ohio; Columbia, South Carolina; Troy, New York; Ann Arbor, Michigan; Overland Park, Kansas; Minneapolis, Minnesota; and Torrance, California. Each is financed by a combination of federal, state, and private funds.

During his 1992 election campaign and in the months after he took office, President Bill Clinton showed himself to be a proponent of *kohsetsushi*. He proposed adding an additional 163 MTCs at a cost of around $500 million a year by 1996. Like the Japanese model, Clinton's MTCs would share technological advances with manufacturers with less than 500 employees, offer training sessions, and help the companies choose the most appropriate equipment.

Kohsetsushi as Industrial Policy

Not all the experts are convinced that such a program would be in the country's best interests. Alan Blinder, a professor of economics at Princeton University, warns that it "does not follow axiomatically that what works for [Japan] would work in our country." He points out that the federal system of government in the United States is likely to foster a different type of competitiveness than is found in Japan: politicians from 50 states and 435 congressional districts would be competing against one another for federal manufacturing centers.

There is also a lingering mistrust in the United States of an industrial policy in which the government essentially picks winners and losers by guiding tax dollars toward one industry or company and not another. "What makes anybody think that bureaucrats can do a better job targeting capital investment than the private sector?" asks one analyst.

MTC Successes

George Sutherland, director of the Cleveland MTC, refutes such charges. With MTCs, he insists, all customers receive help if they want it. The National Institute for Standards and Technology estimates that some 3,500 small- and medium-sized manufacturers have benefited from the technology centers with an approximate total of $200 million in increased sales and savings in productions costs.

A suggestion from an employee at the Northeast MTC in Troy, New York, for example, allowed Newburgh Molded Products in Newburgh, New York, to increase its output of plastic bottle caps by 66 percent a day. Sutherland's center helped the Accu-Spray Company of Bedford Heights, Ohio, increase the efficiency of its low-pressure paint-spraying systems by 50 percent, helping the company to realize a 57 percent increase in sales from 1990 to 1991. Through the MTC in California, Lawrence Livermore Laboratory has an outlet to assist small businesses in switching from defense technology to aerospace, medical technology, plastic, and other areas. "We don't have any losers," says Sutherland, "only winners."

For Critical Analysis:

The primary objection to MTCs comes from those who do not believe that tax dollars should directly subsidize businesses. As a manager, what problems do you see accompanying assistance from an MTC?

SOURCE: S. Miller, "High Tech, High Cost—and Hype?" *Insight*, November 2, 1992, pp. 6–9, 30–31.

important is that economic sector? In 1997, health-care costs accounted for an estimated 15 percent of the U.S. gross domestic product, a situation that places pressure on families and businesses that must purchase insurance for themselves and their employees. General Motors, for example, estimates that it costs about $1,000 per car sold to pay its health-care bill, compared with about $200 per car for Japanese car companies.[13] Such high health outlays caused many large businesses to lobby for health-care reform during the first two years of the Clinton administration. In fact, before he was forced to drop it from his national agenda in 1994 (greatly influenced by pressure from *small* businesses), President Clinton's proposal for a national health-care system envisioned the creation of fifty-nine new federal programs and the expansion of twenty others.[14]

Energy and Transportation The perceived deterioration of the country's transportation infrastructure and the increase in oil imports have led the Departments of Energy and Transportation to consider national strategies in these areas. President Clinton promised a national energy policy for the United States to cut back on the high use of oil and other sources of energy. However, a focus on specific technologies has taken the place of an overall strategy. The federal government, for example, gives $65 million annually toward developing an advanced light water nuclear reactor. Furthermore, with almost $100 billion in highway and mass transit programs to distribute, Congress has an enormous effect on transportation policy.

Privatization For at least a decade, privatization has been offered as a cure for some of the nation's social ills. In the mid-1990s, the Republican-dominated Congress increased pressure to turn state control of businesses, land, and buildings over to private ownership. Supporters of privatization argue that some services could be provided more efficiently by the marketplace. For example, there has been a growing movement to force the federal government to contract with private firms to operate prisons. Another privatization idea has cropped up in the debate over reforming the welfare system. It has been proposed that instead of federally supported housing assistance, the government should offer vouchers that recipients could use to pay for housing in privately owned buildings. Public school privatization and roadside maintenance privatization have also garnered a number of supporters in state and federal legislatures.

Other Nonregulatory Effects on Business by Government Government does not have to regulate actively in order to influence the way business operates. After all, federal, state, and local governments control, according to some calculations, over 40 percent of the annual national output in the United States, and these governments purchase over 25 percent of the annual national output. By the very virtue of its size, government influences business. Government is the largest employer in the nation, accounting for twenty million workers. Many of those workers learn how to do their jobs in specific ways when they work for local, state, or federal governments. If they then go into the private sector, they bring with them some of those habits and procedures—good and bad—which then influence private-sector workers around them.

In the process of purchasing so many goods and services, the government sets standards that influence the way private businesses have to operate in order to be competitive. Those who agree to sell goods and services to government, especially the federal government, often are faced with an array of requirements. Building contractors, for example,

---

13. Thanks to reviewer F. Calviere for this information.
14. D. Armey, "Your Future Health Plan," *Wall Street Journal*, October 13, 1993, p. A22.

who wish to work on federal government projects are required to pay "prevailing wages" as required by the Davis-Bacon Act and the Walsh-Healy Act. Some government contracts cannot be obtained unless the bidders agree to hire a certain percentage of minorities. In some cases, because government can set requirements for private-sector bidders, it influences them without *directly* imposing regulations on their behavior.[15]

Furthermore, in many instances the government competes with the private sector and thus influences it. The U.S. Postal Service, for example, competes with private delivery services such as United Parcel Service, FedEx, Airborne, DHL, and even newspaper delivery services, which now handle magazine deliveries. It could even be argued that the U.S. Postal Service has helped foster an entirely new technology—the fax machine—because of its monopoly on first-class letters and historically uneven service.

The government has a number of other effects on business. For example, it influences the private sector by granting subsidies, or payments to producers or users of specific goods and services, such as agricultural products and operas. The government also affects the private sector's behavior by how it taxes different businesses and business activities. Finally, it guides the private sector with its monetary policy—the Federal Reserve Board's decisions to raise or lower interest rates.

TYPES OF REGULATION

It would be a mistake to try to gather all government regulation under one heading. Different regulations have different methods and different goals. Some regulation is drafted with a specific industry in mind, whereas some covers the entire spectrum of the business world. Some regulation purports to control industry, and some claims to assist it.

Generally, however, there are two types of government regulation. One is **economic regulation** which covers the regulation of natural monopolies and inherently noncompetitive industries. **Social regulation** tries to protect the public welfare across all industries.[16] (See *Exhibit 8–4* for examples of both kinds of regulation.)

Economic Regulation Earlier in the chapter we saw an example of economic regulation with regard to the Interstate Commerce Commission (ICC), which was finally shut down in 1996. Other economic regulatory bodies, such as the Federal Communications Commission (FCC), control industries by setting maximum and minimum prices, restricting entry of new companies, and controlling services that companies may offer. The FCC was established in 1935 to regulate interstate communications and later covered the radio, telegraph, and telephone industries. After cable television companies were allowed to set their own rates in 1986, cable rates rose at three times the rate of inflation. Because cable operators hold a near 100 percent monopoly in cable-wired cities, consumer interest groups pressured the regulatory authorities to restrain costs. The result was the Cable TV Reregulation Act of 1992, which allowed the FCC to order a 10 to 15 percent cutback in cable rates. (Cable rates were again deregulated in 1996 with the new telecommunications act.)

The concept of "obscene" profits, which we discussed in Chapter 2, contributes to a strong argument for economic regulation (see the *Case—Merck and Drug Company Profits*—at the end of this chapter).

---

15. T. A. Kochan, J. C. Wells, and M. Smith, "Consequences of a Failed IR System: Contract Workers in the Petrochemical Industry," *Sloan Management Review*, Summer 1992, p. 79.
16. D. R. Wholey and S. M. Sanchez, "The Effects of Regulatory Tools on Organizational Population," *Academy of Management Review*, October 1991, p. 743.

▼ **EXHIBIT 8–4**
Examples of Economic and Social Regulation and Corresponding Agencies

Agency	Type of Regulation
Product Markets	
Federal Communications Commission (FCC)	Economic
Federal Trade Commission (FTC)	Social and economic
Labor Markets	
Equal Employment Opportunity Commission (EEOC)	Social
Financial Markets	
Securities and Exchange Commission (SEC)	Social
Energy and Environment	
Environmental Protection Agency (EPA)	Social
Federal Energy Regulatory Commission	Economic
Health and Safety	
Occupational Safety and Health Administration (OSHA)	Social and economic

Social Regulation Social regulation reflects concern for public welfare across all industries. In other words, social regulation focuses on the impact of production and services on the environment and society, on the working conditions under which goods and services are produced, and sometimes on the physical attributes of goods. The aim of social regulation is a better quality of life for all through a less polluted environment, better working conditions, and safer and better products. For example, the Food and Drug Administration (FDA) attempts to protect against impure and unsafe food, drugs, cosmetics, and other potentially hazardous products; the Consumer Product Safety Commission (CPSC) specifies minimum standards for consumer products in an attempt to reduce "unreasonable" risks of injury; the Environmental Protection Agency (EPA) watches over the amount of pollutants released into the environment; the Occupational Safety and Health Administration (OSHA) attempts to protect workers against work-related injuries and illnesses; and the Equal Employment Opportunity Commission (EEOC) seeks to provide fair access to jobs.

INTERNATIONAL REGULATION

In its early days, the most the U.S. government did with respect to international business activities was impose taxes on goods imported into the United States. At times, the government banned outright both imports and exports to certain countries because of wars or other reasons. Today, the story is quite different. The federal government heavily regulates imports into the United States. Also, to a lesser extent, it regulates what products are exported. In the last several decades, the federal government also has attempted to influence the behavior of U.S. corporations abroad. Even more recently, the federal government has put pressure on other countries in an attempt to change the behavior of the domestic corporations that are operating in their own countries.[17] For example, the U.S. government has complained about the use of prison labor in the People's Republic of China.

Export Control The U.S. Constitution provides in Article I, Section 9, that "No Tax or Duty shall be laid on Articles exported from any State." Thus, Congress cannot impose any export taxes. Congress can, however, use a variety of other devices to control exports. Congress may set export quotas on various items, such as grain being sold abroad. Under the Export Administration Act of 1979, restrictions can be imposed on the flow of technologically advanced products and technical data.

Devices to stimulate exports and thereby aid domestic businesses include export incentives and subsidies. The Revenue Act of 1971, for example, gave tax benefits to firms marketing their products overseas through certain foreign sales corporations, by exempting income produced by the exports. Under the Export Trading Company Act of 1982, U.S. banks were encouraged to invest in export trading companies (exporting firms that have joined to export a line of goods). The Export-Import Bank provides financial assistance, consisting primarily of credit guaranties given to commercial banks that in turn loan funds to U.S. exporting companies.

Import Control All nations have restrictions on imports, and the United States is no exception. Restrictions include strict prohibitions, quotas, and tariffs. Under the Trading with the Enemy Act of 1917, for example, no goods may be imported from nations that have been designated enemies of the United States. Other laws prohibit the importation of illegal drugs, books that urge insurrection against the United States, and agricultural products that pose dangers to domestic crops or animals.

Quotas are limits on the amounts of goods that can be imported. Sometimes quotas are "voluntary"—there is no legislation creating them—as they have been since 1981 for the numbers of automobiles that can be imported to the United States from Japan. Currently, Japan "voluntarily" limits the numbers of automobiles it exports to the United States. **Tariffs** are taxes on imports. A tariff is usually a percentage of the value of the import, but it can be a flat rate per unit (such as per barrel of oil). Tariffs raise the prices of imported goods, which causes some consumers to purchase less expensive, domestically manufactured goods.

The United States has specific laws directed at what it sees as unfair international trade practices. **Dumping**, for example, is the sale of imported goods at "less than fair value." *Fair value* is usually determined by the price of those goods in the exporting country. Dumping is designed to obtain a larger share of the U.S. market. To prevent this practice, an extra tariff—known as an *antidumping duty* (extra tax)—may be assessed on the imports (see *Company Focus: Eastman Kodak Corporation* on pp. 226–27).

The procedure for imposing antidumping duties involves two U.S. government agencies: the International Trade Commission (ITC) and the International Trade Administration (ITA). The ITC is an independent agency that makes recommendations to the president concerning temporary import restrictions. The ITC assesses the effects of dumping on domestic businesses. The ITA is part of the Department of Commerce and decides whether import sales are at less than fair market value. The ITA's determination establishes the amount of antidumping duties to be imposed, which are set to equal the difference between the price charged in the United States and the price charged in the exporting country. A duty may be enacted retroactively to cover past dumping.

---

17. J. A. Mello, "The Environmental Cost of Free Trade," *Business and Society Review*, Fall 1994, p. 15.

Multinational Trade Agreements To minimize trade barriers among nations, most of the world's leading trading nations are signatories to the General Agreement on Tariffs and Trade (GATT). GATT—and now its permanent successor, the World Trade Organization (WTO)—became the principal instrument for regulating international trade. Originally negotiated in 1947, GATT went through seven major tariff and trade renegotiations. Between 1964 and 1967, for example, forty-eight countries negotiated tariff reductions of 50 percent on a broad range of products. Between 1973 and 1979, one hundred countries negotiated nearly a dozen agreements relating to other trade barriers. An eighth and final round of negotiations (called the Uruguay Round) between 1986 and 1993 resulted in agreements relating to intellectual property rights, investment policies, dispute resolution, and other topics.

Under Article I of GATT, each member country agreed to grant **most-favored-nation status** to other member countries. This article obligated each GATT member to treat other GATT members at least as well as the country that received its most favorable treatment with regard to imports or exports.

In 1994, the United States, Canada, and Mexico signed the North American Free Trade Agreement (NAFTA), creating a virtual North American free trade zone. Opponents of NAFTA argued that opening the economic borders would result in a large number of American and Canadian jobs being exported to Mexico because of that country's lower wages and environmental regulatory climate. Proponents countered that consumers in all three countries would benefit from an increased choice of lower-cost imported items.

REGULATING EXTERNALITIES

When a paper mill dumps its waste products in a nearby river, pollution obviously results. The paper company does not pay the "cost" of the pollution, and therefore neither do its primary customers. But that pollution does represent a cost, and possibly a very high one, to the surrounding community. The quality of life for those who live on the banks of the river declines—perhaps it is now unsafe for their children to swim in the river, or perhaps tainted groundwater has seeped into their underground wells. There is definitely a cost to the environment of the river, as the fauna and flora that live in it suffer from the effects of the pollution.

The private cost to the paper company for the pollution differs from the social cost being paid by the community. When this occurs, we term the situation an *externality*, because individual decision makers in the company are not paying all the costs. Rather, some of the costs remain external to the company's decision-making process. **Negative externalities,** such as pollution, are often cited as reasons why government regulation is needed. After all, the full cost of using a scarce resource such as water, air, or the ozone layer is borne one way or the other by all those who live in a society. When a firm that is producing a negative externality and the customers buying that firm's product do not take into consideration the external costs in their decision-making processes, society suffers.

Correcting for negative externalities is often expensive, and few firms are willing to shoulder the burden voluntarily and alone. Without government intervention, there would be no mandatory reason for the paper mill mentioned above to stop its polluting; voluntary discontinuation of the activity would necessitate finding a more costly alternative, which would lead to higher prices for the paper, which would cut into the company's profits. Simply forbidding the paper mill to dump waste into the river, however, is not as attractive an alternative as it would seem at first glance. The costs of finding another method of disposing of the pollution might be so great that the paper mill could not afford

COMPANY FOCUS: EASTMAN KODAK CORPORATION
ANTIDUMPING LAWS AND INTERNATIONAL COMPETITION

Rick Bachelder, president of Filmet, a Pittsburgh photofinishing store, had always been a loyal customer of the Eastman Kodak Corporation. After all, Kodak representatives had helped him get back on his feet when his store burned down many years before. But business is business, and it was with some guilt that Bachelder admitted he was thinking of buying the paper he used to print photos from a source other than Kodak. "We're getting prices from . . . Fuji lower than we've had [from Kodak], period," the store owner explained.

Kodak in Trouble

To be precise, Japan's Fuji Photo Film Company was offering entrepreneurs like Bachelder 25 percent off Kodak's prices for photographic paper. Competition from Fuji and other private production companies was adding to Kodak's overall sinking fortunes in 1993. The company's 1988 earnings of $1.4 billion had not been approached since that time. Christopher J. Steffen, "the white knight" who had been hired at the beginning of 1993 as chief financial officer to turn Kodak's fortunes around, abruptly quit in April of that year after a dispute with Kodak's chairman of the board, Kay R. Whitmore.

The news sent Kodak's stock reeling, knocking more than $5 off the worth of a share and reducing the company's market value by $1.7 billion. Wall Street analysts grumbled that "the wrong guy resigned," and one said, "Either the board members get Whitmore to deliver results or they deliver Whitmore's head."

Attacking the Japanese Company

In August Whitmore was replaced by George M. C. Fisher. The new chairman and chief executive officer immediately targeted Fuji for attack and vowed "to go right at the Japanese." Within days of that remark, Kodak had filed a petition with the U.S. Department of Commerce and the International Trade Commission (ITC) charging Fuji with selling photographic paper in the United States for as low as one-fourth its prices in Japan. Kodak's experts alleged that Fuji was dumping—selling billions of dollars of product below cost—in the United States in order to discourage Kodak from investing in new technology. Once Kodak slipped in research and development, these experts told the federal government, Fuji would take advantage of its stronger market position by raising prices. Kodak added that Fuji was able to swallow the losses from underpricing

to stay in business. The river might be cleaner, but would that be worth the unemployment of the mill's workers and the subsequent ripple effect through the community?[18]

Solving the Problem of Negative Externalities Some argue that the signals in the economy must be changed so that decision makers will take into account *all* the costs of their actions. In the case of automobile pollution, for example, we might devise some method whereby motorists are taxed according to the amount of pollution they cause. In the case of a firm, we might devise a system whereby businesses are taxed according to the amount of pollution for which they are responsible. This, theoretically, would not close the paper mill but would give it an economic incentive to install pollution-abatement equipment.

The problems of dealing with negative externalities become even more complicated when not just a single paper mill but an entire industry is involved. Furthermore,

---

18. T. A. Hemphill, "Can New Environmental Laws Overcome Old Flaws?" *Business and Society Review*, Fall 1992, p. 46.

COMPANY FOCUS: (CONTINUED)

the U.S. market because it held a hugely profitable, "monopoly-like" position in its home market.

The ITC Ruling

Fuji responded that because Kodak held a dominant position in the U.S. market, the American company was the pricing leader for photographic paper. Fuji, therefore, offered consumers "alternatives, in both quality and price."

The ITC sided with Kodak; it ruled in October 1993 that Fuji was selling its products at less than fair market value. To level the playing field, the U.S. Commerce Department proposed a 360 percent tariff on the paper, one of the highest tariffs ever proposed on a Japanese product. Fuji balked at such immense import duties and signed an agreement with the Commerce Department in which it agreed to raise prices voluntarily instead of suffering the tariffs. Under the agreement, the Commerce Department would determine the "foreign market value" of the paper, and Fuji would sell the product at or above that price.

The value turned out to be about 10 cents more per square foot of paper than many domestic purchasers were willing to pay. The Nashua Corporation—Fuji's largest mail-order customer—switched a $14 million account to Kodak. Within days other customers, including Wal-Mart, Moto Foto, and Genovese Drug Stores, were considering similar moves. In response, Fuji started building a $250 million paper plant in Greenwood, South Carolina. The plant will qualify Fuji as a domestic producer and free it from international pricing regulations on items produced domestically.

The New Bottom Line

Corporations must see regulation for what it is: a strategic factor. In this case, Kodak used antidumping laws to gain a competitive advantage over a major foreign rival, and it forced Fuji to change its strategy.

SOURCE: Information from J. E. Rigdon, "Kodak Quietly Offers Discounts of 10% to 20% to Some Big Customers, " *Wall Street Journal*, August 17, 1993, p. B6; J. E. Rigdon and G. Naik, "Steffen's Move, after Clash over Strategy, Prompts Nose Dive in Stock Price," *Wall Street Journal*, April 29, 1993, p. A3; J. E. Rigdon, "New Focus: Hiring Fisher, Kodak Gambles on a Future in Multimedia World," *Wall Street Journal*, October 29, 1993, p. A1; "Kodak Announces It Won a Round over Fuji Paper," *Wall Street Journal*, October 13, 1993, p. A4; and W. Bounds, "Japanese Firms Will Raise Charges on Color Pattern," *Wall Street Journal*, August 22, 1994, p. A4.

▼ Few of us would argue that cleaner air is a just and desirable goal. But who is going to pay for it?

In 1971, the federal government mandated that new automobiles must have engines that run on unleaded gasoline instead of the more highly polluting leaded models. More recently, in the winter of 1994, drivers in fifty of the country's most polluted cities were required to use a cleaner but more expensive blend of reformulated gasoline. (It must be noted that scientific evidence showed that the blend actually created more pollution, because it was less efficient.) Few automobile companies would have voluntarily changed their engine designs, and few consumers would have voluntarily spent 10 cents more a gallon in order to obtain cleaner air. In these cases, as in many others concerning air pollution, water pollution, affirmative action, or product safety, government regulation has been the primary way to control negative externalities.

Regulation Changes Incentives Regulation often requires firms to innovate in order to find new ways to deal with increased regulation costs. Consider the example of pollution credits. In an industry in which each stationary polluter is allowed credit for a certain

amount of pollution, a market for excess pollution credits develops. Manufacturers that devise ways to produce their products with less pollution end up being able to sell their pollution credits to other manufacturers in the same area. This can create an economic incentive for manufacturers to innovate ways in which they can manufacture the same amount of product with lower pollution rates. (Opponents of this system insist that it allows polluters to avoid making necessary improvements, because they can instead wait for pollution credits to become available.)

Unfortunately, pollution regulation has created tremendous costs for much of American industry. Additionally, though, it has created an entirely new industry—the pollution-control industry. Numerous companies that cater to industry's need to control pollution have sprung up. This situation has created a booming market for engineers and consultants in the private as well as the public sector.

REGULATORY AGENCIES: THE "FOURTH BRANCH OF GOVERNMENT"

Regulatory agencies have been on the American political scene since the last stages of the industrial revolution, but their golden age came during the regulatory explosion of the 1960s and 1970s. Congress itself could not have overseen the actual implementation of all the laws—concerning pollution and a number of other social problems—that it was enacting at the time. It therefore chose, and still chooses, to delegate these tasks to others, particularly when the issues relate to highly technical areas, such as, for example, the benefits of trench walls on construction sites, to name just one. By creating and delegating some of its authority to an administrative agency, Congress may indirectly monitor a particular area in which it has passed legislation without becoming bogged down in the details relating to enforcement—details best left to specialists.

As we head into the next century, the government has been hiring increasing numbers of specialists to oversee its legislation. In fiscal year 1996, the 56 federal regulatory agencies reached an all-time high by spending over $16 billion to administer their regulations, and they employed over 133,000 federal workers to do so.[19] Before deciding whether these numbers represent the natural outgrowth of a capitalist country with over 265 million citizens and 15 million different businesses or a regulatory process gone mad, it is helpful to understand the background of the regulatory agencies and their specific responsibilities.

THE CHARACTERISTICS OF REGULATORY AGENCIES

Simply stated, the fifty-six federal regulatory agencies are government bodies that are created to enforce laws and regulations. (See *Exhibit* 8–5 on page 230 for a selected list of regulatory agencies.) In 1977 the Senate Governmental Affairs Committee went beyond that basic description and gave the federal regulatory agency its present form. According to the committee, such an agency has at a minimum the following characteristics:

1. It is required to be governed by the Administrative Procedures Act of 1945.
2. It deals mainly with business activity in the United States.
3. Its leadership is appointed by the president.
4. It can make decisions that are then carried out.
5. It establishes rules that create both benefits and costs to businesses.[20]

Constitutional Basis for Agencies   Most U.S. government textbooks speak of the system of checks and balances of the three branches of the U.S. federal government—executive, legislative, and judicial. Recent history, however, shows that it may be time to regard the regulatory agencies as a fourth branch of the government. Although there is no mention of regulatory agencies at any point in the U.S. Constitution, they can and do make **legislative rules**, or *substantive rules*, that are as legally binding as laws passed by Congress. With such powers, this administrative branch has an influence on the nation's businesses that rivals that of the president, Congress, and the courts.

The constitutional authority for delegating congressional powers to administrative agencies—and the basis of all administrative law—is generally held to be implied by Article I of the Constitution. Section 1 of that article grants all legislative powers to Congress to oversee the implementation of all laws. Article I, Section 8, gives Congress the power to make all laws necessary for executing its specified powers. These passages have been construed by the courts, under what is known as the **delegation doctrine**, as granting Congress the power to establish administrative agencies that can create rules and regulations for implementing those laws.

Enabling Legislation   To create an administrative agency, Congress passes **enabling legislation**, which specifies the name, composition, and powers of the agency being created. The Federal Trade Commission, for example, was created in 1914 by the Federal Trade Commission Act. The act prohibits unfair and deceptive trade practices. It also describes the procedures that the agency must follow to charge persons or organizations with violations of the act, and it provides for judicial review of agency orders. Other portions of the act grant the agency powers to "make rules and regulations for the purpose of

---

19. M. Warren, *Reforming the Federal Regulatory Process: Rhetoric or Reality?* (St. Louis, Mo.: Washington University, Center for the Study of American Business, June 1994), p. 1; and *Regulation*, 1996, No. 3, p. 26.
20. *Congressional Quarterly's Federal Regulatory Directory*, 5th ed. (Washington, D.C.: Government Printing Office, 1985–1986), p. 2.

▼ EXHIBIT 8–5 Selected Regulatory Agencies

Name	Date Formed	Principal Duties
Federal Reserve System Board of Governors (Fed)	1913	Determines policy with respect to interest rates, credit availability, and the money supply.
Federal Trade Commission (FTC)	1914	Prevents business from engaging in unfair trade practices; stops formation of monopolies in the business sector; protects consumer rights.
Securities and Exchange Commission (SEC)	1934	Regulates the nation's stock exchanges, in which shares of stocks are bought and sold; requires full disclosure of the financial profiles of companies that wish to sell stocks and bonds to the public.
Federal Communications Commission (FCC)	1934	Regulates all communications by telegraph, cable, telephone, radio, and television.
National Labor Relations Board (NLRB)	1935	Protects employees' rights to join unions and bargain collectively with employers; attempts to prevent unfair labor practices by both employers and unions.
Equal Employment Opportunity Commission (EEOC)	1964	Works to eliminate discrimination based on religion, sex, race, color, national origin, age, or disability; examines claims of discrimination.
Environmental Protection Agency (EPA)	1970	Undertakes programs aimed at reducing air and water pollution; works with state and local agencies to help reduce environmental hazards.
Occupational Safety and Health Administration (OSHA)	1970	Creates and enforces safety and health standards for U.S. workplaces; carries out inspections of workplaces to ensure compliance with standards.
Nuclear Regulatory Commission (NRC)	1974	Ensures that electricity-generating nuclear reactors in the United States are built and operated safely; regularly inspects the operations of such reactors.

carrying out the Act," to conduct investigations of business practices, to obtain reports from interstate corporations concerning their business practices, to investigate possible violations of federal antitrust statutes, to publish findings of its investigations, and to recommend new legislation. The act also empowers the FTC to hold trial-like hearings and to adjudicate certain kinds of trade disputes that involve FTC regulations or federal antitrust laws.

THE OPERATION OF REGULATORY AGENCIES

Enabling legislation makes the regulatory agency a potent organization, and knowledge of its operation is a necessity for business managers. The Securities and Exchange Commission, for example, imposes rules regarding what disclosure must be made in a stock prospectus. Under the SEC's enforcement authority, its staff also prosecutes alleged violations of these regulations. Finally, it sits as judge and jury in deciding whether its rules have been violated and if so, what punishment to impose on the offender (although the judgment may be appealed in federal court). These three operations—rulemaking, enforcement, and adjudication—are the basic functions of most regulatory agencies. Taken together, and supplemented by broad investigative powers, these three functions may be termed the **administrative process.**

Rulemaking The first major function of a regulatory agency is the formulation of new regulations—the so-called rulemaking function. The power that an agency has to make rules is conferred on it by Congress in the agency's enabling legislation. Enabling legislation is almost always written in very broad terms, but Congress is constitutionally limited in how much power it can delegate to a regulatory agency.

There are three types of rules that an agency may create. We have already mentioned the first, *legislative rules.* The other two are interpretative rules and procedural rules. *Interpretative rules* are statements and opinions issued by an agency explaining how that agency interprets and intends to apply the statutes it enforces. Because interpretative rules do not have the force of rules of law, they are not automatically binding on private individuals or organizations (see *Company Focus: Infinity Broadcasting Corporation*).

Procedural rules describe an agency's methods of operation. They also establish procedures for dealings with the agency in and through hearings, negotiations, settlements, presentation of evidence, and other activities.

The rulemaking process begins with a notice of the proposed regulation in the *Federal Register*, following which there is a predetermined period of time during which private parties may comment on the regulation either in writing or in hearings on the proposed rule (if any are held). After the public has been given an opportunity to comment on the proposed rule, the agency reviews this information and publishes a final rule in the *Federal Register*.

Enforcement The first aspect of the enforcement function of an agency concerns investigative power. Virtually every phase of the administrative process requires that regulatory agencies obtain a wide array of information concerning the activities of organizations that they are charged with overseeing. Although the agencies by nature have a wide knowledge of facts pertinent to any regulatory circumstance, there are often instances in which the enforcement of rules will rely on further investigation. The two most important investigative tools available to a regulatory agency are subpoenas and searches and seizures.

A **subpoena** is a writ, or order, compelling an individual or organization to hand over specified books, papers, records, or documents during the course of an agency investigation. In a search and seizure, the agency gathers information through on-site inspections of a home, office, or factory. The agency can also do on-site physical testing, such as safety inspections of underground coal mines or environmental monitoring of factory emissions. Because of the intrusive nature of such actions, there are several safeguards against an agency's abuse of its investigatory powers (see *Exhibit 8–6* on page 234).

Having undertaken and concluded an investigation, an agency may begin an administrative action against an individual or organization by issuing a complaint. Complaints are brought by private citizens and organizations but are prosecuted by the agency having authority over the particular subject matter. The majority of these actions are resolved at their initial stage, without the need for a formal adjudicatory process. Settlement is an appealing option to firms, because (1) regulated industries often do not want to appear uncooperative with the regulating agency, (2) regulators are likely to have acquired pertinent—and damaging—information over a prolonged period of investigation, and (3) litigation is costly. Because settlements also conserve agency resources, agencies devote a great deal of effort to advising and negotiating so as to avoid formal actions.

COMPANY FOCUS: INFINITY BROADCASTING CORPORATION

THE FCC AND INTERPRETING INDECENCY

Infinity Broadcasting Corporation is one of the success stories of the airwaves. By 1996, the company owned eighteen AM and FM radio stations in the top markets around the country, including Los Angeles, New York, Philadelphia, Boston, and Chicago. With annual revenues of more than $150 million, Infinity found itself the fourth most successful broadcasting corporation in the country, behind only industry giants such as CBS and ABC. The future growth of the company, however, was far from assured, thanks to an employee's personal battle with the Federal Communications Commission (FCC).

Infinity and Howard Stern

Infinity president Mel Karmazin's operating formula is relatively simple. With an eye for high profit margins, he purchases stations in major markets only. His corporate staff consists of seven people, resulting in an operating margin of 45 percent. In fact, Karmazin's only real extravagances are the high-priced, high-visibility personalities who work at his radio stations. The highest-priced, most visible of these stars is Howard Stern, the "shock-jock" whose success in dozens of markets is crowned by his being the top-rated morning personality in both New York and Los Angeles.

Stern and the FCC

The FCC, which was created in 1934 to consolidate federal control of interstate communications, is a classic economic regulatory agency. Its primary purpose is to control the exit and entry of television and radio stations into the market. The agency is also involved in interpretive social regulation, because it is required to act in society's best interests by regulating—and, when necessary, banning—"indecent" material on the nation's airwaves.

It is the latter duty that involved the FCC with Stern, whose scatological language has raised questions about the appropriateness of his entertainment style on a medium easily accessible by young children. In 1994, the FCC fined Infinity stations in Baltimore, New York, Philadelphia, and Manassas, Virginia, a total of $200,000 for airing "language [by Stern] that describes sexual activities and organs in patently offensive terms." Combined with earlier fines for similar offenses, that brought to Infinity fines totaling $1,706,000 because of Stern.

Adjudication When formal actions cannot be avoided, a regulatory agency may try to prosecute alleged offenders of agency rules in trial-like proceedings before an administrative law judge (ALJ) or, in some instances, before the appointed heads of the agency, its board of commissioners. Thus, the agency acts as a police officer, prosecutor, judge, and jury in regulatory agency **adjudication**. Procedures differ among the various agencies, but a typical scenario of adjudication might proceed as follows.

In the initial investigatory phase, one of the agency's staff attorneys might take statements under oath. Alternatively, the agency might request documents or records of some kind. In most instances, the agency's requests are enforceable by a federal court order; failure to comply with the court order can result in fines or even jail sentences for contempt of court.

During this phase of the process, the agency may offer to negotiate and reach some settlement or agreement concerning the actions with which the agency is concerned. If no settlement between the agency and the party under investigation is reached, then the agency staff can seek the approval of the agency head or the commissioners to issue a formal complaint. The complaint is issued as a public document and may be accompanied by a press release. The party charged in the complaint responds by filing an answer. The case is then presented before an ALJ in an administrative hearing. If the case is settled

COMPANY FOCUS: (CONTINUED)

Although he complains of being unfairly persecuted by the government, Stern gets a good deal of publicity from the fines. For his part, Karmazin had remained relatively silent concerning Stern, and at no time had Infinity publicly asked the disc jockey to tone down his act.

Infinity and the FCC

In 1994, the FCC added a new tactic in its efforts to restrict Stern. Combining its economic regulatory powers with its social regulatory goals, the agency made it be known that it was holding up approval of Infinity's purchase of one radio station in Los Angeles and two more in Washington, D.C., because of indecency complaints against Stern. FCC commissioner James H. Quello said that he was concerned that granting Infinity the licenses would be "condoning [Stern's] conduct."[a]

Stern's earning power was huge, so the almost $2 million in fines could be written off as business expenses, albeit painfully. Karmazin, however, could not so easily dismiss FCC threats to block Infinity's pending deals, which were worth almost $200 million. After the *New York Times* reported that the FCC was delaying, and considering block-ing, the purchases of the radio stations, Infinity's stock dropped 9 percent, to $30.25 a share, and investor confidence was wavering. Karmazin said publicly that his company was "not looking to thumb our nose at the FCC" but refused to censor Stern—"that's why they make on-off buttons," he said.

The FCC approved the sale of all three stations, although grudgingly, by May 1994. FCC commissioners told the press that they would have tried to block the sales had it not been for the difficulties such an action would have had standing up in court. Instead, the agency levied another $800,000 fine on Infinity for Stern's language, which the parent company is contesting.

The New Bottom Line

Infinity was able to resist the FCC's attempt to tone down Stern's act. Many corporations are dissuaded from taking such issues to court because of the costs. In a case where something as legally vague as "indecency" is at issue, however, the odds of successfully resisting a regulatory agency are in the company's favor.

a. D. Pearl, "Infinity Acquisition Is Delayed as FCC Weighs Protest against Howard Stern," *Wall Street Journal*, January 3, 1994, p. A12.

before the hearing, a consent order is issued (this order is agreed to voluntarily by both parties). If not, the ALJ renders an initial order, which may compel the charged party to pay damages or forbid the party from carrying on a specified activity. Either side may appeal the ALJ's initial order. An appeal is usually taken to a federal appellate court, though some decisions may be appealed to a federal district court. If no appeal is taken, or if the case is not reviewed or considered anew by the agency commission, the ALJ's initial order becomes the final order of the agency. Otherwise, the final order may come from the commission's decision or from that of the reviewing court.

THE PUBLIC SPEAKS: TO REGULATE OR NOT TO REGULATE

Obviously, the public plays a large role in the regulatory relationship between government and business. The public casts its approval or disapproval of a politician's policies—including his or her stand on regulation—through its votes. Special interest groups—which represent interests as diverse as those of all women or as specific as migrant farm workers in

▼ **EXHIBIT 8–6 Requirements for the Use of Agency Investigatory Methods**

1. Investigative demands must be specific and not unreasonably burdensome.	The Fourth Amendment stricture on unreasonable searches and seizures is also a barrier to the abuse of agency investigative powers. It has been modified in the context of the regulatory process, however. The U.S. Supreme Court has held that although the regulatory subpoena must adequately describe the material sought, "the sufficiency of the specifications is variable in relation to the nature, purposes, and scope of [the agency's] inquiry."
2. Information sought must be relevant.	Also according to the Fourth Amendment, even if an investigation is carried out with legal authorization and for a legitimate purpose, any information sought must be relevant to that purpose.
3. The privilege against self-incrimination may be available.	The protection against compelled, self-incriminating testimony afforded by the Fifth Amendment is limited in the context of the regulatory process. First, an agency has fairly broad powers to require that certain records be kept by an individual or organization and that the records be made available to the agency on demand as part of a regulatory program. Second, the privilege against self-incrimination is available only to the person asserting it; it cannot be asserted on behalf of another individual or on behalf of an organization, such as a corporation.
4. The warrant requirement provides protection.	The Fourth Amendment protects against unreasonable searches and seizures by requiring that in most cases, a physical search for evidence must be conducted under the authority of a warrant.

Dade County, Florida—can also affect the government's regulatory policies, especially those concerning negative externalities such as pollution, by seeking hearings before regulatory agencies.

The public influences business even more directly—through the marketplace:

▼ **Free market devotees such as Milton Friedman argue against regulation in general, saying that a well-informed public will punish companies that produce negative externalities such as unsafe products. Consumers, insists Friedman, will take their dollars elsewhere, forcing the offending company to either behave responsibly or go out of business.**

Sometimes, as is the case with the changeover to the metric system, public indifference to proposed legislation can squelch regulation, at least temporarily (see *Managing Social Issues—Barriers to Success: Saying No to the Metric System*). The public also has the power to influence business through boycotts and support of special interest groups, such as the American Civil Liberties Union or the American Association of Retired Persons.

It is not that government and business are helpless in the face of an overly active public. Both institutions routinely use the mass media to influence the public's outlook. In the case of politicians, this becomes especially obvious during election campaigns. And every January, during the State of the Union address, the president explains policy decisions and presses for further support in the upcoming year. The government also has less partisan methods of reaching the public, such as public service announcements detailing the dangers of smoking or the need for community efforts to control crime. Recently, with

MANAGING SOCIAL ISSUES

BARRIERS TO SUCCESS: SAYING NO TO THE METRIC SYSTEM

What do Liberia, Myanmar, and the United States have in common? They are the only three countries in the world that have resisted the metric system as an official form of weights and measures. Advocates of metrication in the United States have argued for years that the country's stubborn resistance toward making the change has hurt American companies in the global marketplace and will continue to do so. Many businesspeople, however, have staunchly resisted regulatory attempts to force the metric system on an obviously unwilling public.

Reason for Regulatory Change

As early as 1790, Thomas Jefferson was pushing for a change in the way the United States went about weighing and measuring. Five years later, a French government decree on the metric system was published in the New World. Based on the number 10, the French creation used the gram (0.0022046 pounds), the meter (39.37 inches), and the liter (61.25 cubic inches) as the basic units of weight, length, and capacity, respectively. The French decree was widely ignored by Americans at the time and has been treated with suspicion ever since.

Proponents of the metric system lament U.S. shortsightedness. Gary P. Carver, head of the federal metric program at the National Institute of Standards, warns that the country's international competitiveness is hurt by its insistence on yards and gallons instead of meters and liters. Carver points out that the European Union has vowed to stop accepting nonmetric products at the end of the century, and the Japanese government has highlighted the lack of metrication as an impediment for American goods in that country.

The first regulatory attempt to align the United States with the rest of the world came in 1975, with the Metric Conversion Act. The bill basically asked the public to switch to the metric system voluntarily. Not surprisingly, it had little effect, because Americans were not enthusiastic about learning a new form of weights and measures. In 1988, Congress decided to toughen its regulation and passed the 1988 Omnibus Trade and Competitiveness Act, which mandated that the federal government conduct all its economic activity in metric units by October 1, 1992. In addition, an amendment to the Fair Packaging

and Labeling Act of 1966 required the metric system to be the primary means of listing contents on packages in American stores.

The Metric Backlash

In spite of these regulatory dictates, the United States had hardly moved to the metric system by the mid-1990s. The government has not been stringent in enforcing its own rules. In 1994, the General Accounting Office (GAO), a government watchdog agency, reported that although many government branches have plans to convert to the metric system, very few have actually done so. "Generally speaking," noted the GAO, "the more directly a proposed conversion affects the private sector or the public, the greater the resistance."

Business has had a strong hand in opposing the regulations, which many believe impose unnecessary costs on products sold only in the United States. The argument is simple: U.S. customers do not want to see kilograms and centimeters on their products, so why should we be forced to put them there? Intense lobbying (see Chapter 11) by the Food Marketing Institute, a group that represents food retailers and wholesalers, weakened the Fair Packaging and Labeling Act. In a revamped state, the act allowed for traditional American weights and measurements to be most prominent on labels as long as metric units are displayed in some fashion. Foods that are packaged at the retail level—such as produce and meat—do not need metric labels at all.

Change for Business

Still, individual companies not packaging food at the retail level will have to adjust. At Stewart Brothers Paint Company in Alliance, Ohio, managers have to make a choice between two methods of compliance: either reprogram the in-house computer to produce labels with metric conversions or have employees stencil the changes on every can of paint. Neither option is particularly appealing; the former will cost money—about $5,000—and the latter, time. "We deal in gallons and quarts and pints," lamented Ronald Lyons, the company president. "We always have. It's easiest for us."

MANAGING SOCIAL ISSUES: (CONTINUED)

For Critical Analysis:

What reasons would a business have for converting to the metric system without government regulation? Does your answer help you decide whether the American public is being shortsighted in resisting a change to that system?

SOURCE: Information from H. Martin, "A Mania for Metric," *Los Angeles Times*, October 19, 1992, p. B3; and L. M. Litvan, "Sizing Up Metric Labeling Rules," *Nation's Business*, November 1994, p. 62.

improvements in the information superhighway and the proliferation of the home computer, government officials have been holding on-line town hall meetings, in which they directly interact with the public. Many corporations have large public relations budgets to help them communicate their views to consumers, and every business, no matter how large or small, uses advertising to try to influence how the public makes its choices.

THE DELICATE BALANCE

In the middle to late 1990s, popular sentiment against the federal government was running high. There has been a great deal of complaining about the paternalistic attitude that many people find in federal, state, and local governmental attempts to influence social change. Sixty-seven percent of the Americans who responded to a *Reader's Digest* survey a few years ago picked big government over big business and big labor as a threat to the nation's future.[21] When it comes to regulation, however, it would be safe to say that the general public is *reactive* rather than *proactive*. In other words, most of us think about or try to fight regulation only when it applies to our daily lives.

A majority of Americans, for example, may disagree with the federal government's policy of spending billions a year to subsidize American farmers. Relatively few, however, are willing to give up their time to lobby against the practice, nor will many provide financial support for politicians who promise to end agricultural subsidies. The National Association of Concerned Farmers, in contrast, has a strong incentive not only to lobby but also to spend millions of dollars to ensure that the farm subsidies continue.

As another example, before seven people died as a result of someone tampering with Tylenol bottles in 1982 in Chicago, few Americans saw the need for plastic sealing of bottled products. After the Tylenol incident, however, that need became apparent. If Johnson & Johnson had not taken its own steps to protect its product, the government, under pressure from the public, would surely have forced the company to do so. Fifteen years later, not only pain relievers but also virtually any health-care product in a bottle are protected by a tamper-resistant device.

One of the most dramatic examples of the effect that a single incident can have on the public's view of an entire industry—and consequently on that industry's regulatory future—is the accident at the Three Mile Island (TMI) nuclear power plant near Middletown, Pennsylvania, on March 28, 1979. On that day, TMI's nuclear reactor began emitting "puffs" of radiation as a result of a stuck valve and inadequately trained personnel. Although nobody was hurt in the incident, it caused panic among members of the public who suddenly questioned whether nuclear energy was the wonderful power alternative they had previously thought it to be. In an effort to reassure consumers, the Nuclear Regulatory Commission enacted hundreds of new regulations over the next five years, causing, as one observer stated, "the balance of decision-making [shifted] sharply from the utilities to the regulatory." Unable to keep up with the changes, the U.S. nuclear power program collapsed. In the five years following the TMI incident, construction of seventy-five plants was canceled, including twenty-eight already under construction.[22] Today, despite the fact that nuclear power provides a cheap source of energy and is widely used in Europe, no nuclear power plants are in the planning stage in the United States.

---

21. R. L. Bartley, "Resuming the Revolution," *Wall Street Journal*, December 16, 1994, p. A14.

22. J. Cook, "Nuclear Follies," *Forbes*, February 11, 1985, pp. 82–100.

TERMS AND CONCEPTS FOR REVIEW

Adjudication 232
Administrative process 231
Commerce clause 211
Delegation doctrine 229
Deregulation 215
Dumping 224

Economic regulation 222
Enabling legislation 229
Industrial policy 218
Legislative rule 229
Most-favored-nation status 225
Negative externality 225

Privatization 218
Quota 224
Regulation 210
Social regulation 222
Subpoena 231
Tariff 224

SUMMARY

1. Regulation is the government's direct influence on the social and economic activity of society through the rules and laws that it passes. In the United States, regulation is legally based on the commerce clause of the Constitution, which allows Congress to regulate commerce between and among states.

2. Some of the first regulations concerned the railroads in the 1800s. The first regulatory agency was the Interstate Commerce Commission, which was created by the Interstate Commerce Act of 1887. Regulation continued in the early 1900s with the Pure Food and Drug Act of 1906, the Clayton Act of 1914, and the Federal Trade Commission Act of 1914.

3. During the Great Depression, the New Deal set the stage for active regulation of business through the enactment of the Securities Act of 1933, the Securities and Exchange

Act of 1934, the Banking Act of 1933, the Norris-LaGuardia Act of 1932, and the Wagner Act of 1935.

4. A burst of regulatory activity occurred in the 1960s and 1970s only to be followed by a certain amount of deregulation in the late 1970s and the 1980s. The Clinton administration reversed that trend during its first two years, from 1993 to 1995. Starting in 1995, the Republican-controlled Congress tried to reduce the amount of regulation on business.

5. Government can affect the business community by its industrial policy and by the amount of privatization it undertakes. With respect to industrial policy, the Omnibus Trade and Competitiveness Act of 1988 allowed the federal government to intervene in international business transactions by forcing countries practicing "unfair trade" to change their ways. During the late 1980s and early 1990s, some industrial policy that favored technology was enacted. There have also been attempts by the government to influence business activities in health care, energy, and transportation.

6. There are two types of regulation: economic and social. The former attempts to regulate natural monopolies and inherently noncompetitive industries, whereas the latter tries to protect the public welfare across all industries. For example, the Federal Communications Commission is involved in economic regulation. The Consumer Product Safety Commission is involved in social regulation. The Federal Trade Commission is involved in both economic and social regulation.

7. The federal government regulates international business activities through export controls and certain restrictions on imports via quotas, tariffs, and laws against dumping (selling imported goods at less than fair value).

8. The participation of the United States in multinational trade agreements, such as the General Agreement on Tariffs and Trade (GATT), the World Trade Organization (WTO), and the North American Free Trade Agreement (NAFTA), affects the way U.S. businesses can engage in international activities.

9. Regulation is justified when common property resources are concerned and business generates negative externalities. A common negative externality is increased pollution. The government can regulate businesses to avoid or minimize negative externalities through taxation and specific regulations, such as the amount of pollution that automobiles may generate.

10. The regulatory agencies, of which there are dozens, have been labeled by some political scientists as a fourth branch of government. The Constitution does not mention regulatory agencies. Through the delegation doctrine, however, the federal government determined that because Congress has the power to make all laws necessary for executing its specified powers (Article I, Section 8), it can delegate those powers to agencies.

11. Federal agencies cannot come into existence until there is enabling legislation. Once an agency comes into being, it is able to undertake three operations: rulemaking, enforcement, and adjudication. An agency's rules have the force of law. It is able to enforce them through subpoenas, fines, and orders to do or refrain from doing some act. Alleged offenders of agency rules can be called before an administrative law judge in a courtlike setting.

12. The public can influence regulation through special interest groups that seek hearings before regulatory agencies.

EXERCISES

1. Some countries have very little regulation concerning the way businesses run their affairs. Indeed, there was very little regulation in the United States prior to the nineteenth century. Make a list of ways in which today's businesses might act differently if there were no regulations whatsoever.

2. Try to envision a situation in which a business's activities could not be construed to involve interstate commerce. Write a detailed explanation of how you would argue in front of a court why this particular business should not be regulated by the federal government, because the federal government can regulate only interstate commerce.

3. The chapter pointed out that railroads face very high fixed costs. Explain why an industry facing high fixed costs might engage in extensive price cutting for certain products or services it sells in order to prevent potential competitors from entering the industry.

4. Research the program known as the New Deal. Write a list of all the federal statutes passed that ultimately involved increased regulation of American businesses.

5. Reexamine *Exhibit 8–2*, which shows the principles of President Ronald Reagan's deregulation philosophy in the 1980s. Translate those principles into an action plan that you would give to an existing regulatory agency.

6. Imagine that you are the chief executive officer of a large consumer electronics manufacturer. Make a list of how government influences your business through nonregulatory means.

7. Prepare a one-minute speech outlining why you are in favor of manufacturing technology centers (MTCs). Then create a one-minute speech opposing MTCs.

8. Argue in favor of the privatization of such government-owned and government-run activities as (a) the U.S. Postal Service, (b) municipal garbage collection, (c) municipal and county fire departments, (d) public education, and (e) public housing.

9. Give an example of regulation that could be viewed as both economic and social.

10. Under what circumstances would you be in favor of import quotas? Make a detailed list of your reasons.

11. Why would a foreign company ever wish to sell its products in the United States at less than fair value?

12. There is no mention of regulatory agencies in the Constitution. What, therefore, is the constitutional basis for regulatory agencies?

13. What is the difference between an interpretative agency rule and a procedural agency rule?

14. Assume that the Occupational Safety and Health Administration (OSHA) has decided to impose a new rule on your business, the manufacture of ladders for household use. OSHA wants you to reinforce those ladders so that they will not fail under the weight of a three-hundred-pound person. How would you argue in front of OSHA to make your point that such a new rule is not appropriate?

SELECTED REFERENCES

▸ Bos, Dieter. *Pricing and Price Regulation: An Economic Theory for Public Enterprises and Public Utilities.* New York: Elsevier, 1994.

▸ Cary, William L. *Politics and the Regulatory Agencies.* New York: McGraw-Hill, 1967.

▸ Himmelberg, Robert F., ed. *Antitrust and Business Regulation in the Postwar Era, 1946–1964.* New York: Garland Publishing, 1994.

▸ Himmelberg, Robert F., ed. *New Issues in Government-Business Relations since 1964: Consumerist and Safety Regulation, and the Debate over Industrial Policy.* New York: Garland Publishing, 1994.

▸ Jones, L. R. *Corporate Environmental Policy and Government Regulation.* Greenwich, Conn.: JAI Press, 1994.

▸ McChesney, Fred S., and William F. Shughart II, eds. *The Causes and Consequences of Antitrust: The Public-Choice Perspective.* Chicago: University of Chicago Press, 1995.

▸ Mitnick, Barry. *The Political Economy of Regulation.* New York: Columbia University Press, 1980.

RESOURCES ON THE INTERNET

▽ For access to the *Federal Register* and other government regulations, CLIO is a useful gopher site. CLIO is the name of an information system that contains data from a number of government sources, including the U.S. National Archives and Records Administrations (NARA). Through this site, you can also order a number of government publications for your own use. CLIO can be accessed at

http://www.nara.gov/

or, on gopher at

gopher://gopher.nara.gov/

▽ A number of regulatory agencies have their own home pages on the Internet. For information on Environmental Protection Agency standards, guidelines, and regulations, you can access

http://www.epa.gov/

▽ For information on the Food and Drug Administration, you can access
http://vm.cfsan.fda.gov/index/html

▽ For information on the Occupational Safety and Health Act, you can access the Office of Environment, Safety, and Health at
gopher://dewet.tis.inel.gov:2019/

▽ For information on a citizen watchdog group trying to influence the policies of the Federal Communications Commission, access
gopher://gopher.cpsr.org:70/00/
taxpayer__assets/

Action__Needed__on__Cable

CASE

MERCK AND DRUG COMPANY PROFITS

Background

Bill Clinton gave a hint of his feelings toward the drug industry during a 1992 presidential debate with George Bush and Ross Perot when he said, "I think you have to tell the pharmaceutical companies they can't keep raising drug prices at three times the rate of inflation." Once in office, President Clinton continued to speak out on the subject, castigating the vaccine industry for making a "profit at the expense of our children" and calling vaccine prices "shocking." First Lady Hillary Clinton, who was deeply involved in health-care reform, further criticized drug companies for "price gouging, cost shifting and unconscionable profiteering."

For Dr. P. Roy Vagelos, chairman and chief executive officer of the pharmaceutical giant Merck & Company, such statements constituted "a tremendous slam" to the drug industry. In response, he wrote an open letter that appeared as a three-quarter-page ad in the *New York Times, Washington Post, Philadelphia Inquirer, Wall Street Journal*, and *USA Today*. In the letter, Vagelos said that the problem of high drug costs was complex and could not be alleviated by hasty government action. "We need a search for the truth," he wrote, "not scapegoats."

Vagelos knew, however, that the Clintons were not isolated in their criticisms of his industry, and that good public relations alone were not going to save his company from the widespread belief that drug prices were too high. Vagelos had set into motion a plan to hold off the government regulation of drug prices three years before Clinton became president, and much of Merck's corporate strategy during the Clinton administration was heavily influenced by the realities and threats of federal intervention spurred on by public outrage.

Price Controls in the Drug Industry

Before President Franklin D. Roosevelt's New Deal (1933–1939), federal drug policy could be summed up by two Latin words: *caveat emptor*, or "let the buyer beware." Drugs could and did contain ingredients ranging from petroleum by-products to arsenic. Even after the Pure Food and Drug Act of 1906, government policy was more interested with fair labeling than consumer safety. In other words, drug manufacturers could still use arsenic in their products, as long as the products were not mislabeled.

That situation changed in the mid-1930s in the wake of a grievous error by the Massengill Company of Bristol, Tennessee. The company wanted to market a liquid form of sulfanilamide, an antibacterial drug. Massengill's scientists used diethylene glycol to dissolve the sulfanilamide, apparently without testing the agent for toxicity. The newly formed Food and Drug Administration (FDA) seized all shipments of the drug after initial reports of its harm, but 107 people ultimately died from the effects of Massengill's Elixir Sulfanilamide. Because of restrictions placed on its prosecutorial power, the FDA had no course of action but to fine Massengill $26,000 for mislabeling.

The resulting public uproar led to the Federal Food, Drug, and Cosmetic Act of 1938 (FFD&C Act), which banned interstate commerce of harmful substances and specified that new drugs must be approved by the FDA. This added a new—and expensive—step to the manufacture of drugs, as pharmaceutical companies had to invest heavily in research and development (R&D) to ensure that their products would meet with FDA approval. Although the financial returns for the industry have remained well above average in the postwar years (19 percent, by some estimates), drug companies have insisted that strong profits are necessary to counter the high cost and speculative nature of creating and testing new drugs.

The public first became aware of the large profits being made on prescription drugs in 1959, when Senator Estes Kefauver held hearings on competition in the pharmaceutical industry. Until that time, consumers had generally been more concerned with their health than with the costs of drugs; cost was often dismissed by prescribing physicians as being of secondary importance. Kefauver's hearings led to more stringent control of drug manufacturing and marketing by the FDA through the Kefauver-Harris Amendments to the FFD&C Act in 1962, but the senator did not get the price controls for which he had asked.

Ironically, those amendments had the effect of raising drug prices even higher as the costs of R&D increased with the regulations. By the early 1970s, the development costs for a new drug were estimated at $16 million, up from $1 million or $2 million a decade before. By the mid-1990s, development costs had skyrocketed to over $250 million per drug. These costs were being passed on to the consumer at an alarming rate. Health-care expenditures now account for about 15 percent of each year's total national income.

The drug industry's single largest customer—the government—decided that these costs were too high; Medicaid payments for brand name drugs rose 85 percent from 1984 to 1989. In the early 1990s Congress passed legislation requiring drug companies to offer rebates to state governments. When President Clinton made his remarks about the "shocking" prices of drugs, the atmosphere seemed ripe for Senator Kefauver's thirty-year-old cry for price controls in the drug industry to become reality.

Merck's Voluntary Price Restraints

Vagelos and other executives at Merck moved to fend off regulatory price controls well before President Clinton took the issue to the public. While arguing that the existing profit incentives had resulted in the most innovative and progressive medical system in the world, in 1990 Merck—the world's largest prescription drug manufacturer, with almost $10 billion in yearly sales—promised not to raise the price of its products by more than the rate of inflation for consumer goods. In 1991, Vagelos criticized his industry rivals for not taking the same path. Noting the continuing annual 10 to 12 percent rise in drug prices, he warned, "I detest regulation, but it may be brought about by my colleagues. . . . Drug prices are such an obvious target."

Vagelos's fears were confirmed when a task force formed by President Clinton began speaking openly of congressionally imposed price controls on health-care products and services. The president also questioned Merck's policy of self-restraint, noting that although the company's aggregate drug prices rose only 3.1 percent in 1992, the prices of its more popular products rose well above the inflation rate. The list price of a daily dose of Merck's popular heart medicine Vasotec (enalapril maleate), for example, went up 6.3 percent, and the cost of the company's Prilosec (omeprazole) ulcer medicine rose 7.2 percent. To many in the Clinton administration, this proved that drug companies could not be trusted to restrain costs without a government watchdog.

In 1993, Merck offered a more stringent voluntary price restraint program. Under Merck's plan, drug manufacturers would limit price increases for any one product to one percentage point above the inflation rate. Independent auditors would monitor these policies and order penalties on any pricing that was deemed excessive. These "rollbacks" would go into a government fund to improve access to health care. Merck calculated that the proposal, if adopted industry-wide, would save consumers between $7 billion and $9 billion in

three years. Because the proposal hinged on individual drug prices instead of average prices, it was greeted with initial resistance by other pharmaceutical companies. Eventually, however, after positive reviews from the Clinton administration, seventeen other drug companies agreed to follow Merck's lead.

Merck's Marketing Strategy

Vagelos and Merck were not going to rely on the ever-shifting political winds to ensure the company's continued health in a changing market. In July 1993, Merck paid $6 billion to acquire Medco Containment Services, Inc., one of the biggest drug distributors in the United States. Medco had been a pioneer in the ever-growing business of mail-order drug delivery; when purchased by Merck, it was dealing with 90 percent of the country's pharmacies and delivering products to 33 million Americans. With the merger, Merck was able to eliminate the intermediary between itself and drug purchasers, giving itself a built-in competitive advantage in terms of lower costs should price controls be put into effect.

Armed with its new acquisition, Merck took another step toward expanding its reach into the new health-care environment. In 1994, the company lobbied Congress and the president to allow entities such as Medco to manage the Clinton administration's proposed Medicare drug plan. Under the Clinton plan, drug costs for Medicare would be forced down by a 17 percent rebate that drug manufacturers would be required to pay back to government. Merck believes Medco could cut costs by 5 percent over the government plan, without requiring the rebate. The potential for Merck if its proposal is accepted is overwhelming: Medicare beneficiaries spend about $40 billion a year on drugs.

Epilogue

In March 1995, Families USA, a health-care consumer group, released a study showing that the prices of the twenty top-selling prescription drugs rose 4.3 percent in the prior year, compared with a 2.7 percent inflation rate over the same time period. Indeed, as the Clinton administration's health-care reform plan fizzled, so did pressure on drug companies to keep their promises about holding down drug costs. Nonetheless, Merck's strategies seem to have paid off. The company's earnings rose 12 percent in 1994, and industry analysts credit the success in large part to the Merck-Medco managed health-care business.

CASE (CONTINUED)

Critical Thinking Questions

1. Should government-imposed price controls be placed on drug industry products? Using other regulated industries as a model, name some of the possible consequences for both the drug industry and consumers.

2. Given what you know concerning the concept of "obscene profits," is Hillary Clinton's charge of "unconscionable profiteering" justified? Is there a moral responsibility to keep prescription drug prices as low as possible?

3. You are the chief executive officer of a pharmaceutical company that has raised the price of its best-selling ulcer medicine 7.2 percent over the past year. How do you justify your company's actions, both economically and ethically?

4. What would be some of the benefits of agreeing to price controls for Merck and other large pharmaceutical companies?

5. Does the Merck-Medco merger and its proposed effect on Merck's costs provide any useful information on the debate over drug prices? How might a free market economist use the merger in an argument against price controls?

SOURCE: Information from M. Waldholz, "Clinton Attack 'Disappoints' Merck Chief," *Wall Street Journal*, February 19, 1993, p. B2; *Note on Pharmaceutical Industry Regulation* (Boston: Harvard Business School Publishing, 1994); D. Kreutzer, "Merck, a Lesson in Industrial Policy," *Wall Street Journal*, August 4, 1993, p. A8; M. Waldholz, "Merck's Chairman Blames Price Rises on Industry Rivals," *Wall Street Journal*, November 8, 1991, p. B2A; M. Waldholz, "Drug Firms Propose Voluntary Program Limiting Price Rises to Inflation Rate," *Wall Street Journal*, March 15, 1993, p. A3; D. R. Olmos, "Merck to Buy Marketer of Drugs for $6 Billion," *Los Angeles Times*, July 29, 1993, p. A1; E. Tanouye, "Merck Campaigns for Management of Medicare Drugs," *Wall Street Journal*, May 3, 1994, p. B5; and L. Bongiorno, "Hot Damn, What a Year!" *Business Week*, March 6, 1995, p. 98.

CHAPTER 9

REFORM IN THE REGULATORY ARENA

CHAPTER OUTLINE

INTRODUCTION

Frank Cremeans, a freshman member of the new Republican majority in the 104th Congress, had run for office for four reasons. "It was the EPA, OSHA, the health department, and the mine-inspection agency," said Cremeans, owner of Cremeans Concrete & Supply Company in Gallipolis, Ohio. Those four state and federal regulatory agencies arrived at his business unannounced at the same time a few years before his election and made quite an impression on Cremeans, who had to spend that whole day dealing with the government officials. "They all showed up, one after the other. I couldn't believe it," said Cremeans, who vowed that one of his major goals in the House of Representatives will be to attack "overregulation."[1]

Cremeans was not the only businessperson to attain public office during the 1994 elections on the basis of concern over regulation; the perception that the Clinton administration had unreasonably increased the federal government's role in regulating business pervaded electoral activity in 1994. Maine's new independent governor, Angus King, who ran an energy conservation company before taking office, remarked that the U.S. political system had become "estranged from Economics 101."[2]

Entrepreneurs' complaints about government are hardly a recent phenomenon. But dissatisfaction—especially in the small-business community—with the Clinton administration's efforts to achieve the goals of repeated promises to "reinvent government" reinvigorated calls for regulatory reform.[3] Despite presidential initiatives such as the "National Performance Review," which, if fully implemented, would save the government $108 billion over five years and reduce the civilian federal work force by 252,000 (about 12 percent),[4] the business community in general did not believe the president was committed to reforming the regulatory process.

Melinda Warren, assistant director of the Center for the Study of American Business at Washington University in St. Louis, thinks President Clinton's regulatory policies were both good and bad for American business. The increases in real spending for regulations were going down (from 6.6 percent in 1992 to 0.5 percent in 1996), as were staff increases (from 6 percent in 1992 to 1 percent in 1996). However, real growth was still occurring, and by 1996 both spending and staffing for regulation reached record levels—almost $17 billion and 132,690 employees, respectively (see *Exhibit 9–1*).[5]

The regulatory agencies that oversee social regulations, such as those concerning job safety and the environment, are poised to increase their spending to much higher levels than agencies charged with economic regulations (see *Exhibit 9–2* on page 246). This pattern guarantees that business complaints concerning intrusive government will continue into the new century. Business managers will have to understand the basis for, and the consequences of, regulatory reform in their particular industry or business and resist blindly accepting the general preconceptions of regulatory issues. Although undoubtedly in need of some reform, the regulatory process is rarely as bad as the heads of various business associations, or as good as the director of OSHA, would have one believe.

---

1. B. Bowers and U. N. Gupta, "To Fight Big Government, Some Join It," *Wall Street Journal*, November 11, 1994, p. B1.
2. *Ibid.*
3. *Ibid.*
4. H. Birnbaum and P. Thomas, "Clinton Moves to Streamline Government," *Wall Street Journal*, September 8, 1993, p. A2.
5. M. Warren, *Reforming the Federal Regulatory Process: Rhetoric or Reality?* (St. Louis: Washington University, Center for the Study of American Business, June 1994), pp. 1–3.

▼ **EXHIBIT 9–1   Regulatory Trends in Spending, 1970–Present**

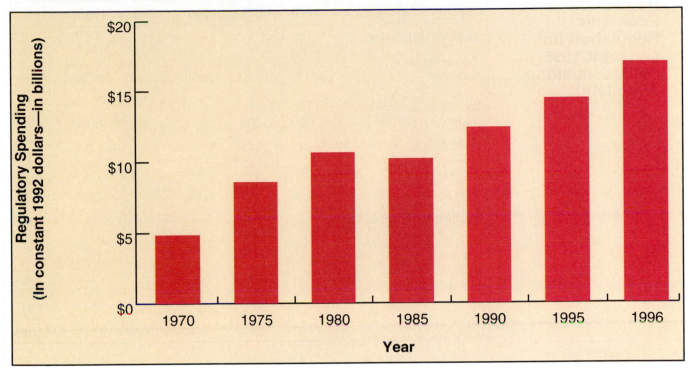

SOURCE: Washington University, Center for the Study of American Business, St. Louis, Missouri; and authors' estimates.

REGULATORY TRADE-OFFS

When we discussed trade-offs in Chapter 5, we were referring to the decisions a company or individual makes regarding the balance of ethics versus profits when those two (not completely incompatible) forces were in opposition. In the regulatory arena, trade-offs concern the good a regulation brings to society versus the harm it does, in the form of lost profits and jobs, to an industry or business. In other words, regulations reflect trade-offs between social and economic goals.[6]

Regulatory agencies traditionally assess the trade-offs involved in new regulations. OSHA, for example, predicted that its new rules governing electrical equipment would cost business $21.7 billion annually but would save 60 lives and eliminate 1,600 worker injuries a year. The agency also estimated that its safety equipment regulations for manufacturing workers would cost $52.4 billion, save 4 lives, and prevent 712,000 lost workdays because of injuries each year.[7] Disagreement between business and government often occurs when the two parties dispute whether such trade-offs are justified. As a group, regulatory reformers often believe that the trade-offs do not measure up.

6. R. Banham, "Market in Need of Self-Regulation," *Journal of Commerce and Commercial Affairs*, October 7, 1991, p. 11A.
7. R. B. Slater, "OSHA Goes on the Offensive," *Business and Society Review*, Spring 1994, p. 45.

▼ **EXHIBIT 9–2 Social Regulation versus Economic Regulation (in constant 1995 dollars; millions of dollars)**

	Fiscal Year					
	1970	**1975**	**1980**	**1985**	**1990**	**1995**
Social Regulation						
Consumer safety and health	$ 710	$1,491	$2,349	$2,689	$3,796	$ 5,330
Job safety and other working conditions	128	359	753	862	1,002	1,235
Environment	214	841	1,651	2,495	4,164	5,424
Energy	64	275	550	481	462	582
Total social regulation	1,116	2,966	5,303	6,527	9,424	12,571
Economic Regulation						
Finance and banking	86	151	362	624	1,080	1,337
Industry-specific regulation	91	160	279	289	320	468
General business	115	206	355	507	743	1,230
Total economic regulation	292	517	996	1,420	2,143	3,035

SOURCE: Washington University, Center for the Study of American Business, St. Louis, Missouri.

BENEFITS OF REGULATION

Chapter 8 discussed the potential benefits of regulation, such as controlling negative externalities, without any quantitative analysis of such benefits. Attempts at such analysis are relatively rare, as it is often difficult to estimate these benefits.[8] In 1980, the Center for Policy Alternatives at MIT conducted a study that asserted that federal regulation of the environment and workplace saved billions of dollars in decreased medical costs and avoidance of employee accidents.

It is often easier to look at the benefits of regulation in terms of simple statistical evidence instead of actual dollar values. For most of the 1970s and 1980s, for example, an average of 3.4 million gallons of oil were spilled by business each year. After a regulatory crackdown in the late 1980s, that number had dropped to 55,000 gallons in 1991.[9] By requiring new standards for workers in the manufacturing industry, OSHA estimated that it was preventing 4 deaths and over 60,000 injuries a year.[10] The Food and Drug Administration (FDA) points to drugs that have had disastrous results in Europe that it kept off the shelves in the United States: the pain reliever Indomethancin caused 36 deaths in Great Britain and Germany; the pain reliever Fenclofenac caused 7 deaths in

---

8. L. N. Gerston, "No Competition at 35,000 Feet (Effects of Deregulation in the Airline Industry)," *Journal of Commerce and Commercial Affairs*, August 26, 1991, p. 4A.
9. "Slants & Trends," *Air Water Pollution Report*, August 31, 1992, p. 2.
10. "52.4M Costs Seen by OSHA," *American Metal Market*, August 3, 1994, p. 10.

Great Britain; and a drug to prevent urinary problems, Terodilence, was responsible for numerous cases of heart trouble and 14 deaths in Great Britain and Germany.[11]

ECONOMIC COSTS OF REGULATION

It is much simpler to predict the costs of regulation than its benefits, and business has not been reluctant to do so (see *Exhibit 9–3* on page 248). Business, after all, has an incentive to understand such costs in order to reduce them. Often when the federal government announces plans for a new set of regulations, the affected industry objects on the basis of the associated costs. For example, in 1995, the Agriculture Department presented a food safety plan that would guard against contamination of meat and poultry. The affected industries immediately protested the $734 million start-up cost of the regulation.[12]

Murray Weidenbaum, director of the Center for the Study of American Business, divides the economic costs of regulation into two basic categories: direct and indirect.[13]

Direct Costs   When the government hires an individual to work for a regulatory agency, it pays that individual a salary plus benefits that include health-care insurance and retirement plans. Every time a regulatory agency employee uses the telephone, there is a direct cost involved. Every time a regulatory agency employee makes an examination of a private manufacturing site, there is a direct cost involved. Every time a regulatory agency lawyer goes to court to sue a private company, there is a direct cost. All these **direct costs of regulation** have grown through the years, even correcting for inflation. After all, at the beginning of this century there were virtually no regulatory agencies, and today there are almost sixty.

Indirect Costs   The **indirect costs of regulation** are its hidden costs. They usually show up in a higher price for goods and services. Consider an example. Government regulation requires that when you have a new house built you must use a certain amount of insulation in the attic, whether you want to or not. Your house will in fact cost more because of that government regulation. Estimates of such "hidden taxes" that are due to building regulations on new dwellings run as high as one-third the price of the house. In other words, if one compares a house in a jurisdiction with relatively few building code requirements with a house of similar quality in a jurisdiction that has an extreme number of requirements, the latter home might cost at least 30 percent more.

Every business affected by government regulation faces indirect costs, and these are substantial:

▼ **According to some estimates, every dollar spent on direct regulatory costs generates at least $20 in indirect costs.**[14]

One of the most obvious indirect costs involves the expense of the additional paperwork burden that American businesses must process because of increased regulation.

---

11. D. Levy, "Group: FDA's Tough Drug Rules Save Lives," *USA Today*, February 3, 1995, p. A1.

12. B. Ingersoll, "Food Fight Seen as U.S. Offers Safety Program," *Wall Street Journal*, February 1, 1995, p. B1.

13. M. Weidenbaum, *Costs of Regulation and Benefits of Reform* (St. Louis: Washington University, Center for the Study of American Business, November 1980), p. 3.

14. *Ibid.*

▼ **EXHIBIT 9–3 Costs to Business of Regulation**

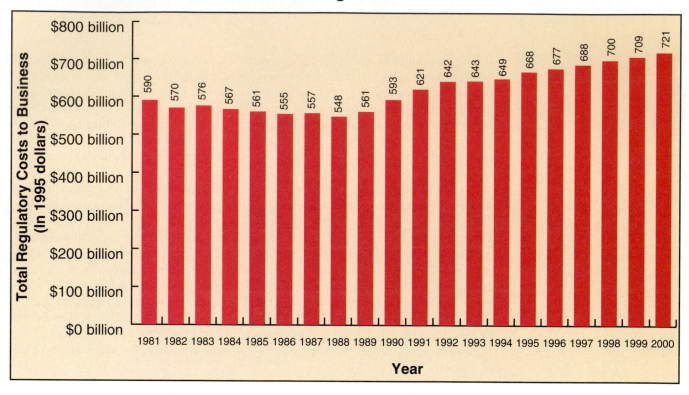

SOURCE: T. D. Hopkins, *Profiles of Regulatory Costs,* SBA Contract No. SBAHQ-95-M-0298, Draft Final Report, 1995, Table A-1.

INDUCED COSTS OF REGULATION

Weidenbaum's analysis of the economic costs of regulation also includes the **induced costs of regulation**. These are economic costs that will not show up directly on a firm's, or its customers', balance sheet, but that are nonetheless induced, or caused, by regulatory activity.[15] Two of these induced costs are connected with employee stress and technological and medical innovations.

Cost of Greater Employee Stress Can you remember the first time you decided to fill out your income tax return yourself? For most people this is not a fond memory. If you are unfamiliar with the tax code and the language of the Internal Revenue Service, even the simplest tax form is complicated. If you are like most Americans, you experienced stress as you tried to wade through the explanations and calculations to fill out your first tax return. Government paperwork can and does create stress.

Now multiply the stress that you may have experienced (and perhaps still do every April) by thousands and thousands for all the individuals working in the private sector who are required by law to comply with as many as hundreds of local, state, and federal paperwork requirements. Managers may have to fill out forms for dozens of different regulatory agencies at the three different levels of government. They may have to prove that they have complied with up to hundreds of regulations that apply to their various businesses.

---

15. *Ibid.*

Often, if the paperwork is not completed on time, substantial fines can be imposed on the employer's business. The threat of these fines and perhaps even of job loss creates additional stress on the employees responsible for filling out regulatory paperwork. This induced cost becomes a direct cost when firms are forced to hire extra employees or temporary help to cope with the paperwork generated by regulation.

The Cost to Technological and Medical Innovation Funds that an industry or individual company are forced to use to ensure that new products meet regulatory requirements are funds that cannot be used on further innovation. These are called **opportunity costs**: if you spend money on A, those funds are not available to spend on B. Furthermore, the realities or prospects of regulatory burdens often discourage an industry from expanding in certain fields (see *Company Focus: Inventive Products* on pp. 250–51). For these and other reasons, the biotechnology industry has been increasingly outspoken in its criticism of the regulatory burden from the Environmental Protection Agency (EPA) and the FDA.

In the fall of 1994, the EPA announced a new policy concerning pesticides that has particularly annoyed the biotechnology industry. Biotechnicians complain that the new regulations on genetically engineered microorganisms (such as pest-eating bacteria) and plants that are genetically engineered to resist pests are so burdensome that they could possibly keep innovations off the market.[16] Henry Miller, who worked on biotechnology policy at the FDA from 1979 to 1993, noted that the agency took four years in the 1990s to review Flavr Savr, a genetically engineered tomato, whereas reviews of human insulin and human growth hormone in the early 1980s took only five and eleven months, respectively.[17]

COST-BENEFIT ANALYSES OF REGULATION

Although most people, and even most business executives, would agree that some government review of new medicines or biotechnology innovations is necessary, disagreement centers on whether the costs to business are greater than the benefits received by society.[18] Going back to Jeremy Bentham's utilitarian theories in Chapter 4, would-be reformers of the regulatory process often point to cost-benefit analysis of all regulation to show that the projected costs of many individual regulations indeed outweigh their benefits. One of the first unsuccessful bills to come out of the Republican-dominated House of Representatives in 1995 would have required regulatory agencies to conduct a cost-benefit analysis for regulations with a cost exceeding $25 million. In response to complaints that such a law goes too far and would paralyze the regulatory process, Representative Greg Ganske said, "If it's acceptable to place a regulatory burden on the public, why not place it on the federal agencies?"[19]

The Cost of a Life "Try to put a dollar value on, say, drinking water in a community," said one proponent of environmental protection regulation.[20] This statement brings up one aspect of regulatory risk assessment that troubles observers on both sides of the regulatory debate. The fact is, cost-benefit analysis requires that a monetary value be placed

---

16. H. I. Miller, "You Call This a Pro-Technology Policy?" *Wall Street Journal*, September 13, 1994, p. A18.
17. *Ibid.*
18. A. Etzioni, "Corporate Behavior: Fewer Flaws Mean Fewer Laws," *Business and Society Review*, Spring 1992, p. 13.
19. T. Noah, "Five Agency Officials Attack GOP Bill to Require Added Study of New Rules," *Wall Street Journal*, February 3, 1995, p. B4.
20. "Weighing the Risks," *Nation's Business*, December 1994, p. 40.

COMPANY FOCUS: INVENTIVE PRODUCTS

THE SENSOR PAD AND FDA ENFORCEMENT

Glen Wright, the president of Inventive Products, had to fire his own brother and reduce his work force to two from a peak of twenty-eight in 1988. He says he now spends his days on the telephone telling physicians that he cannot send them samples of the Sensor Pad, a breast cancer home detection device that has entangled his company in a nine-year battle with the Food and Drug Administration (FDA). Wright, who claims that his struggle is proof of how the federal government stifles small-business innovation, disagrees with those who applaud the FDA for having the strictest guidelines for medical product safety in the world.

An Aid to Early Detection

Breast cancer, the second leading cancer killer of women, causes about 46,000 deaths annually. Medical practitioners stress that early detection reduces to a large degree the risk of death, and the federal government has sponsored numerous public awareness programs to inform women of the need for regular breast cancer testing and self-examination. Because the friction of fingers on dry skin makes self-detection difficult, women are advised to examine themselves in the bathtub or shower.

Wright, an inventor whose products range from a blood serum filter to nonaerosal foaming pumps, created the Sensor Pad in 1985 and set up Inventive Products to make and market the product. He then placed his son in charge of the new corporation. The Sensor Pad—a 9½-inch dual layer of latexlike plastic filled with liquid silicone—was designed to overcome the friction problem in breast examination. The lower pad clings to the skin while the upper pad "floats" on the liquid silicone, eliminating friction and allowing the user to detect more easily the small lumps that may signify breast cancer.

FDA Reservations

The Sensor Pad has been approved in Japan, Singapore, Korea, Thailand, and many Western European countries, but the FDA has not yet granted permission for the pad to be marketed and sold in the United States. The agency has several worries about the Sensor Pad, not the least being that it could either mask abnormalities or cause women to feel something that was not there, which would result in undue stress and unneeded medical examinations. There is also the concern by the FDA that women would rely completely on the sensor pad and ignore traditional breast-testing methods, such as mammograms and examinations by physicians.

Wright counters that the Sensor Pad is meant to enhance existing breast-testing methods, not to replace them.

---

on items the humanist in each of us would rather not appraise—for example, health, safety, and in extreme cases, life.

Nonetheless, whether explicitly or implicitly, we must appraise these things, in spite of the old saying "You can't put a price on human life." Regulators cannot simply say that all risk in society from automobile accidents, poisonous food products, flammable clothes, and so on must be zero. That is impossible. We will never be able to live in a risk-free society. The reason is *scarcity of resources*:

▼ **Virtually every time the risk of something bad happening is reduced, a cost is involved.**

Adding air bags to cars, for example, is not free, even though it benefits society by reducing the risk of serious injury and loss of life in a collision. Why, one might ask, weren't air bags on cars in the 1950s, 1960s, or 1970s? They were technologically impossible to make in the 1950s and 1960s. Even when automobile safety engineers were able

COMPANY FOCUS: (CONTINUED)

Initially, he said, the FDA's response was positive, and the agency's concerns were primarily that the Sensor Pad be properly labeled. Then, because the pad did not have a "substantially equivalent" product already on the market, the FDA decided that the Sensor Pad would have to go through a long and expensive "premarket approval process," which required that studies be conducted in professional settings using data comparing the pad with other detection methods.

After a series of tests was deemed insufficient by the FDA, in 1988 the Wrights decided to place the Sensor Pad on the market anyway, gambling that the courts would not see the product as a medical device as defined by medical law. Over the next 15 months, Inventive Products sold 250,000 pads to almost 200 hospitals. In April 1989, however, federal agents seized a large number of pads from the company's plant in Decatur, Illinois, as well as from some hospitals. In 1992, the FDA seized another $1,000 worth of the pads from the Decatur plant.

Controversial Restrictions

Many members of the medical community believe the FDA's actions in the case of the Sensor Pad to be inappro-priate for a noninvasive product. John Wither, a surgeon at the Maui Clinic in Hawaii, says the pad twice helped him find lumps that otherwise would have gone unnoticed. "There is no question that the Sensor Pad increases my tactile ability," he says. Other sources believe that the FDA is influenced by potential lawsuits should the Sensor Pad fail to detect breast cancer. The FDA, in turn, claims that the Wrights have made the process more difficult for themselves by refusing to follow federal guidelines. "The thing that amazes me," says Wright, "is that the research spending on breast cancer keeps going up and I can't get this simple $7 product in the hands of women who want it."

The New Bottom Line

The power of federal regulators can never be taken lightly. They have the legal ability to shut down any operation that they deem is in violation of federal rules and regulations. Any manufacturer, especially those in the medical field, must work closely with attorneys who have had extensive experience working with the individuals on the regulatory staff who can decide whether a product can enter or remain on the market.

SOURCE: Information from M. Cimons, "Federal Panel Withholds Approval of Breast Exam Device," *Los Angeles Times*, September 2, 1994, p. A21; B. Bowers, "Safety First: How a Device to Aid in Breast Self-Exams is Kept off the Market," *Wall Street Journal*, April 12, 1994, p. A1; "Seizure Actions Filed," *FDA Enforcement Report*, May 27, 1992, p. 21.

to develop them, however, their costs were prohibitive. Human life may be priceless, but our resources are not without limit. If consumers were given the choice between reducing the probability of dying in an automobile accident by spending $5,000 more per car, many would choose not to spend the additional money. We each place an implicit value on our own lives, and it is not infinity.

Virtually none of us buys life insurance that values our own life at $100 million. Thus, when a regulatory agency passes a rule that imposes costs on manufacturers (and hence consumers) to the extent that the implicit value placed on a human life is $100 million, the agency is probably using society's resources inefficiently. Regulators must decide on the value of a human life. If they do not, they may pass regulations that impose costs on manufacturers and consumers that generate implicit human life values in the hundreds of millions of dollars.

In monetary terms, the regulatory costs of saving a life have increased greatly in recent years. A study by the Center for Risk Analysis, a branch of the Harvard University School of Public Health, underscored this point by giving examples of what the median cost of saving one year of life through environmental protection has been (see *Exhibit 9–4*). Another study, by the World Bank, discovered that the value per cancer case avoided under the U.S. Clean Air Act has risen from approximately $15 million in 1987 to $194 million in 1994.[21]

The Cost of Employee Rights The issue of appraising employee rights is not as morally unsettling as is placing a value on human life, but it brings up some of the same problems when subjected to a cost-benefit analysis. It is almost always easier to place a value on the costs than it is to quantify the benefits.[22] For example, the concept behind workers' compensation laws seems just: if an employee is injured on the job, the employer should shoulder the expenses of rehabilitation. It is difficult, if not impossible, to come up with a dollar figure to represent the benefits of workers' compensation, but numerical values can be found for the costs. Jonathan Gruber of the Massachusetts Institute of Technology and Alan B. Kreuger of Princeton University conducted a study that found that 86 percent of the average increase in employer workers' compensation costs for ten job classifications resulted in reduced wages between 1979 and 1988.[23]

Opponents of government regulation of work force issues often paraphrase the University of Chicago's Sam Peltzman, who declared, "People who say there is no trade-off between regulation and employment are smoking something."[24] Some of the measures by which regulation reduces the demand for labor are self-explanatory. The Family and Medical Leave Act of 1993, for example, which allows employees to take up to twelve weeks of unpaid leave a year for family and medical reasons, applies only to companies with fifty or more permanent workers. Therefore, small businesses have an incentive not

▼ **EXHIBIT 9–4 The Costs of Saving a Year of Life**

These numbers reflect the estimated cost of saving *one year of life*—first by type of preventive measure and then by selected federal agency. They are median *net* costs, meaning that direct costs have been reduced by any offsetting savings that may result from the regulatory efforts. The first two preventive measures have a cost of less than zero because the costs of childhood immunizations and drug and alcohol treatment are outweighed by savings to society.

Preventive Measure	Net Cost per One Year of Life Saved
Childhood immunizations	Less than zero
Drug and alcohol treatment	Less than zero
Helmet protection	$ 2,000
Water chlorination	$ 4,000
Highway improvements	$ 64,000
Asbestos controls	$ 1,865,000
Pollution control at paper mills	$ 7,522,000
Radiation controls (at industrial sites and for radiologists)	$27,386,000

Regulatory Agency	Net Cost per One Year of Life Saved
Federal Aviation Administration	$ 23,000
Consumer Product Safety Commission	$ 68,000
National Highway and Traffic Safety Administration	$ 78,000
Occupational Safety and Health Administration	$ 88,000
Environmental Protection Agency	$7,629,000

SOURCE: Harvard University School of Public Health, Center for Risk Analysis.

---

21. "Is Saving a Life Too Costly?" *Haznews*, August 1, 1994, p. 2.
22. C. A. B. Osigweh, Jr., "Elements of an Employee Responsibilities and Rights Paradigm," *Journal of Management*, December 1990, p. 835.
23. C. Farrell, "The Scary Math of New Hires," *Business Week*, February 22, 1993, p. 70.
24. *Ibid.*

to hire any more permanent workers after their payroll has reached forty-nine. The General Accounting Office estimated the outlay for maintaining health-insurance coverage for employees on leave, another obvious cost of the act, at $674 million annually.[25]

THE COMPETITIVE ADVANTAGES OF REGULATION

If you were to ask business executives what the federal government could do that would best help their companies, most would say the government should reduce regulation (see *Exhibit 9–5*). Many economists and businesspersons, however, see this one-sided repudiation of regulation as being not only simplistic but also financially counterproductive. Those who study business attitudes toward regulation from an economic perspective insist that industries and corporations actively use regulation to gain competitive advantages over both domestic and international rivals. Despite perceptions to the contrary, there are reasons for some businesses to welcome regulators.

CREATION OF NEW MARKETS

Although new regulation may increase the short-term operating costs of the targeted business or industry, it can also create demand for a previously nonexistent product. We discuss this in more detail in Chapter 16 with regard to environmental regulation, but the concept is straightforward. If the government requires all automobiles to be equipped with air bags, for example, then the companies that produce air bag materials and components are presented with a huge increase in demand for their product. There are many similar examples (see *Managing Social Issues—Information/Technology: The Business of Noise Laws*).

THE ADVANTAGES OF SIZE

"For small businesses, there is indeed a lot to fear from Washington."[26] These words were spoken during the debate over President Clinton's health-care reform plan in 1993

▼ **EXHIBIT 9–5
An Executive's
Wish List**
The following are answers of the top executives of 250 midsize manufacturing companies when asked what a top priority for the federal government with regard to business should be.[a]

a. Figures represent multiple responses.

Priority	Percentage
Less regulation	81
More tax incentives	68
Greater access to capital	66
Improved employee math and reading skills	48
Employee retraining	42
Establishment of an official U.S. industrial policy	36

SOURCE: *Wall Street Journal*, October 15, 1993, p. R16.

25. G. Klotz, "Regulatory Chokehold: The High Cost of 'Employees' Rights,'" *Wall Street Journal*, August 3, 1993, p. A14.
26. R. Wartzman and J. Sadler, "Motley's Crew: A Fervent Lobbyist Rallies Small Business to Battle Health Plan," *Wall Street Journal*, January 5, 1994, p. A1.

MANAGING SOCIAL ISSUES

INFORMATION/TECHNOLOGY: THE BUSINESS OF NOISE LAWS

The year 1993 was not a good one for the Big Three, the world's leading commercial aircraft manufacturers. Boeing Company, Airbus Industries, and McDonnell Douglas Corporation had no net new orders that year. In fact, because commercial airlines were struggling financially, the entire airplane construction industry had only seventy-five net orders in 1993, one of its worst years in history. There was hope on the horizon, however, as the industry was about to get a boost from an unexpected source: regulation.

The Airport Noise and Capacity Act

At the beginning of the 1990s, 2.7 million people were exposed to an average of 65 decibels or higher over a 24-hour period by being in the proximity of landing or departing airplanes. Because exposure to that kind of noise can lead to a variety of health and stress problems, Congress passed the Airport Noise and Capacity Act of 1990. Under the legislation, noisier airplanes designated as Stage 2 versions, which include the Boeing 727, will have to be phased out in favor of quieter Stage 3 versions by December 31, 1999. At the time the bill was passed, there were about 2,300 Stage 2 planes in the U.S. domestic fleet. Although

some of these were slated for replacement or upgrading, many airlines had hoped to keep their planes in use well into the next century.

Compliance with the Airport Noise and Capacity Act will not be inexpensive. The Federal Aviation Administration (FAA) pointed out in a report to the Environmental Protection Agency, "Aviation technology is among the most expensive and complex in the U.S. economy." The FAA estimates that the noise-control rules will cost airlines $4 billion by 2000.

Confident Predictions

Such numbers please airline manufacturers. As the deadline for FAA compliance nears, orders of new airplanes will be going up. Boeing, which has developed a new, quieter model, called the 777, forecasts the worldwide market for new aircraft seating between 70 and 170 passengers at around 3,000 planes before 2000, enough to keep profits up at all the major manufacturers. McDonnell Douglas chief financial officer Herbert Janese said more proposals had come across his desk in April 1994 than had in the previous two years combined. Adam Brown, director of planning for

and 1994; they specifically refer to a measure in the proposal that would require all businesses to help pay for their employees' medical-insurance coverage. The speaker was referring to the fact that the proposal would burden small businesses much more than large ones. Even though a new regulation such as the employer health-care mandate could have wound up costing General Motors—with its 500,000 employees—millions of dollars, it would have been an even heavier burden on a construction company with only 30 workers.

As *Exhibit 9–6* on page 256 shows, the smaller a business is, the more it will have to pay per employee and per dollar of sales to comply with government regulations. A small business does not have the financial resources to spread these costs over a number of different business operations. It usually cannot afford to hire another employee to handle the paperwork that comes with regulations, and therefore must use someone from its existing staff. Furthermore, in the smaller business, each employee normally represents a larger percentage of the operating costs; thus, paying for each individual's medical coverage costs proportionately more for a small company than for a large one. One critic of the ill-fated 1994 Clinton health-care plan claimed the employer mandate would have put 1.5 million small-business employees out of work.[27]

27. *Ibid.*

MANAGING SOCIAL ISSUES: (CONTINUED)

Airbus, estimates that new orders for all jet manufacturers will hit a level of 800 in 1998.

A Side Bargain: Noise-Reduction Kits

There are signs, however, that such optimism is unwarranted. Although the regulation forces airlines to modernize their fleets, it does not require that they purchase new planes to do so. In the mid-1990s, the commercial airline industry was not in a position to begin purchasing new fleets. From 1991 to 1994, the nation's carriers lost a combined $10 billion, so they were not eager to purchase a new 777-class jet for $50 million.

Many airlines are turning to a less expensive means of compliance with the act: the jet engine noise-reduction kit developed by Federal Express Aviation Services, Inc. (FEASI). A subsidiary of Federal Express Corporation, FEASI began developing the original Boeing 727 "hush kits" to meet its own noise-reduction requirements. News of the kit's success quickly spread throughout the industry, and by 1992 FEASI

had sold kits to Trump Shuttle, European Air Transport, Polaris Leasing, and Pan American World Airways. By retrofitting the engines of old planes with the kits, which cost between $1.65 million and $2.45 million, an airline could bring its fleet to Stage 3 standards at a fraction of the cost of purchasing new planes.

In 1995, instead of buying new aircraft, Delta Airlines ordered forty-six hush kits from FEASI with an option for fifty-two more. Air New Zealand delayed an order of six new 737s from Boeing in order to install hush kits in older models of the plane. It appears that the airline manufacturers were correct in their assumption that the new noise regulations would be good for business, but just which business will ultimately reap the most benefits is uncertain.

For Critical Analysis:

Where did the managers of the Big Three airplane manufacturers err in predicting the consequences of the new noise regulations?

SOURCE: Information from R. M. Weintraub, "An Industry's Quiet Turnaround," *Washington Post*, May 24, 1994, p. D1; M. Cone, "Airliners Remain above Battle on Southland Smog Pollution," *Los Angeles Times*, February 20, 1995, p. A1; D. Yawn, "Hush, Hush, Sweet 727s," *Memphis Business Journal*, March 30, 1992, p. 1; "Delta Orders 46 Hush Kits for Boeing 727-200s," *Airport*, January 3, 1995, p. 4; and B. O'Brian, "Delta Will Buy Nine Airbus Jets for $600 Million," *Wall Street Journal*, March 6, 1992, p. A4.

Of course, the regulatory burden of small businesses can give larger corporations a competitive advantage. A large company, which has more resources with which to handle the effects of regulation—including increased paperwork and higher costs for technological improvements and mandated programs—may push for regulatory measures if it believes they might force some of its smaller competitors out of business. Consider three examples: pharmaceutical drug regulation, the regulation of service station underground gasoline storage tanks, and affirmative action programs.

Pharmaceutical Drug Regulation The *Case—Merck and Drug Company Profits—* in Chapter 8 contained a prime example of the benefits that size confers on a corporation. Merck & Company was able to push for government regulations on drug prices because, with $10 billion annually in sales, it could respond to price competition more easily than its smaller competitors.

As a hypothetical example, consider a new Food and Drug Administration regulation that ends up requiring the purchase of a $10 million testing machine that has to be upgraded each year at a cost of $10 million. One pharmaceutical company produces 10 million pills a year, so its additional cost for the new regulation is $1 per pill. A larger pharmaceutical company produces 100 million pills per year, so its additional cost for the regulation is $.10 per pill. Which company will have the competitive advantage after the new regulation is instituted?

▼ **EXHIBIT 9–6 Average Regulatory Costs per Employee and per Dollar of Sales, by Size of Firm**

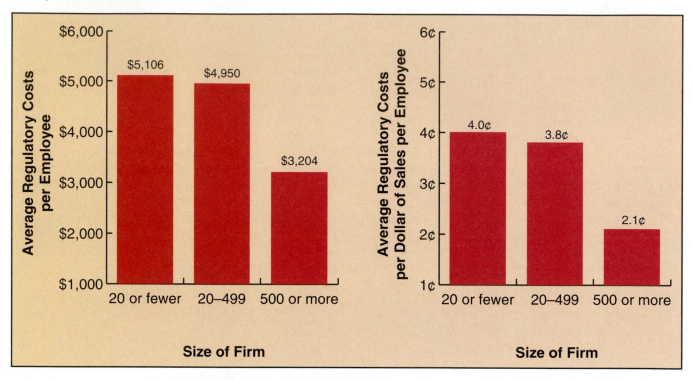

SOURCE: U.S. Small Business Administration, Office of Advocacy. (In 1996 dollars.)

Service Station Underground Gasoline Storage Tanks In some cities in the United States, local regulations have required that underground gasoline storage tanks at service stations all be made of a certain type of fiberglass. The goal is to reduce underground seepage of gasoline. When such regulations are passed, they require that a service station shut down completely for a period of time—as long as a month or two—while the old underground metal tanks are removed and the new fiberglass tanks are installed. A small, independent service station owner with only one service station typically cannot survive being out of business for so long, whereas a chain of service stations can. It is not surprising that in some cities where such regulations have been created, virtually all small, independent service station owners ended up selling their businesses to larger chains.

Affirmative Action Programs To comply with the federal government's affirmative action programs, companies hiring new employees have had to make sure that they comply with all explicit and implicit regulations.[28] Large corporations quickly realized that they needed to establish foolproof procedures so that they would not be sued because of a violation of federal affirmative action laws and regulations. Their legal staffs, often in conjunction with federal lawyers and regulators, devised sophisticated hiring practices that made sure they were in full compliance with affirmative action programs. The addi-

---

28. T. R. Roosevelt, "From Affirmative Action to Affirming Diversity," *Harvard Business Review*, March 1, 1990, p. 107.

tional cost of the labor power and time could be spread out over literally thousands of hires over the years.

Now consider the impact of affirmative action programs on small businesses. These businesses do not have in-house lawyers, and hire so few employees that it takes a long time to establish the procedures needed for compliance with affirmative action programs. Consequently, the cost of affirmative action programs is much higher per new hire for small businesses than for large ones. Indeed, this analysis can be applied to any federal government regulation that requires new procedures, particularly with respect to employment.

REGULATORY HARASSMENT

As businesses have come to accept a certain amount of government regulation, they have used it in their competitive strategies: individual firms or even entire industries may use regulation to adversely affect potential competitors or small firms. In the early 1990s, for example, the trucking industry was in the process of trying to win government approval for larger vehicles, including hundred-foot triple-trailer rigs, when a commercial began to appear regularly on U.S. television sets.[29] The ad—produced and paid for by the Association of American Railroads—showed a woman and her two young children almost run off the road by a triple-trailer truck.[30] Congress subsequently passed legislation prohibiting the large trucks in states that did not already do so.

LEVELING THE PLAYING FIELD

By making all the companies in an industry share the same rules, government regulation can indirectly benefit those firms that are already in a position to comply. Gordon Crane, the president of Apple & Eve, Inc., was very pleased to see the National Labeling and Education Act of 1990 go into effect in the spring of 1994. The act requires juice makers to state on their labels exactly how much real juice, as compared with sugar and water, is contained in their products. Apple & Eve makes only 100 percent juice products and was now in a position to take greater advantage of recent consumer trends that favor real juice over other juice drinks. Other companies, such as Seagram Company and Ocean Spray Cranberries, Inc. (whose juice products contain less than half real juice), were not enthusiastic about the new labeling requirements. As Crane noted, his competitors could no longer hide "behind . . . a cocktail, a montage, or whatever other fanciful name they come up with."[31]

CONTROL OF ENTRY

For businesses or individuals that are already established in their fields, government control of new entrants into a field is a positive benefit of regulation. The fewer competitors a business entity has to contend with, the greater the likelihood of higher-than-normal profits. Local cable television companies, for example, certainly benefited from their government-sanctioned monopolies for years, because any competition was illegal. Other examples abound: Through licensing and other entry requirements, state govern-

---

29. G. S. Johnson, "Truckers Put the Pedal to the Metal as Deregulation Sparks Expansion," *Journal of Commerce and Commercial Affairs*, April 19, 1995, p. 1A.

30. D. Machalaba, "Truckers, Smarting from Negative Ads, Unveil Campaign to Polish Their Image," *Wall Street Journal*, September 13, 1991, p. A7.

31. L. Bird, "New Labels Will Tell Real Story on Juice Drinks," *Wall Street Journal*, May 3, 1994, p. B1.

ments often restrict entry into fields such as law, medicine, accounting, taxi driving, and hairdressing.

SUBSIDIES

Industries are sometimes willing to give up decision-making control in order to reap the benefits of government subsidies—direct payments. During the late 1980s and early 1990s, for example, government agricultural programs were subsidizing American farmers at a rate of $25 billion a year[32]—a strong incentive indeed for the industry to allow regulations such as federal control of acreage in production. In a pure economic sense, a subsidy is a government-sponsored competitive advantage.[33] Subsidies are often biased; for example, a government may be interested in granting subsidies to attain political objectives (such as keeping a low unemployment rate) or to protect an obsolete but popular industry (as some critics have charged in the case of agricultural subsidies in the United States).

Other subsidies may be based on performance standards. In 1994, for example, the European Union gave £11.2 million ($16.8 million) in investment subsidies to Jaguar Cars, a subsidiary of Ford Motor Company, with provisions for withholding or taking back the money "if there is underachievement."[34]

"CORPORATE WELFARE"

Businesses have been known to use government intervention to directly increase their competitive capabilities. This practice is known, somewhat derisively, as "corporate

---

32. R. L. Miller, *Economics Today*, updated 8th ed. (New York: HarperCollins College Publishers, 1996), p. 630.
33. M. Atkins, "Rice Subsidies Have to Go?" *Business Review*, January 1, 1994, p. 28.
34. "Ford Motor Co: EU Panel Clears Subsidies for Jaguar's New Car Line," *Wall Street Journal*, March 30, 1994, p. A1.

welfare" and is strongly linked to the capture theory of regulation in which the industry "captures" the regulators so they help the industry. In many of these cases, business is seen as taking advantage of government at the expense of the taxpayer. In 1995, for example, when the defense firms Lockheed Corporation and Martin Marietta merged to form Lockheed Martin, the federal government reimbursed the new company about $1 billion to cover the costs of related plant shutdowns and employee relocations. This payment was made despite the facts that thirty thousand workers lost their jobs anyway and the new company will generate nearly $12 billion in annual military sales.

As another example, the U.S. Agricultural Department's Market Promotion Program (MPP) provides more than $100 million each year for companies to promote themselves through activities such as advertising and market research overseas. In 1993, Sunkist Growers, Inc., received $6.6 million from MPP, E. & J. Gallo Winery received $4.3 million, and Sunsweet Growers received $2.4 million. The Corporate Welfare Project in Washington, D.C. (certainly not an unbiased observer), estimated that U.S. companies were given over $167 billion in taxpayer funds for "corporate welfare" in fiscal year 1995.[35]

DEREGULATION AND REREGULATION

The past few decades have seen a backlash against the unreasonable and unnecessarily high costs of compliance, as well as the unacceptable influence of corporations in the regulatory bureaucracy. This dissatisfaction has manifested itself in the reform movement known as deregulation. As we noted in the previous chapter, deregulation is the opposite of regulation and refers to the elimination or phasing out of regulations on economic activity.

Deregulation has been as much a political activity as an economic one. Consequently, it is difficult to say whether deregulation has been successful in the United States. It can be stated with certainty only that deregulation has been a volatile policy, and one with often explosive consequences for the industries and companies it has targeted.

THE DEREGULATORY IMPULSE

Not surprisingly, the 1980s have been called the era of deregulation, and the deregulatory impulse has been intricately linked to the Reagan administration (1981–1989). The truth is, however, that although President Reagan enthusiastically carried out his promise to reduce the regulation of American business (during his first term at least), the deregulation movement actually had already begun (see *Exhibit 9–7* on page 260).

Pre-Reagan Deregulation The public mood concerning government intervention in the market system, which had been positive starting with the idealistic Kennedy years (1961–1963) and had continued through President Lyndon B. Johnson's "Great Society" (1963–1969), began to sour in the mid-1970s. First of all, the Watergate scandal in 1974 changed the public's view of the federal government as an instrument of high morality and pure motives. Also, and perhaps more important, in the aftermath of the Organization of Petroleum Exporting Countries (OPEC) oil embargo, the economy hit a rough period during the Ford administration (1974–1977) and the Carter administration

---

35. J. Shields, "Getting Corporations Off the Public Dole," *Business & Society Review*, Summer 1995, pp. 4–8.

▼ **EXHIBIT 9–7**
Some Milestones in Deregulation Legislation

Law	Year	Effects
Airline Regulation Act	1978	Eliminated the Civil Aeronautics Board; gave airlines control over fares charged and routes flown.
Natural Gas Policy Act	1978	Decontrolled interstate natural gas prices but allowed states to control such prices within their boundaries.
Depository Institutions and Monetary Control Act	1980	Deregulated interest rates offered on deposits; also allowed savings and loans and banks to expand the services they offered.
Motor Carriers Act	1980	Reduced control of the Interstate Commerce Commission over interstate trucking rates and routes.
Staggers Rail Act	1980	Gave railroads more flexibility in setting rates and in dropping unprofitable routes.
Bus Regulatory Reform Act	1982	Allowed intercity bus lines to operate without applying for federal licenses in most circumstances.
Cable Communications Policy Act	1984	Deregulated 90 percent of cable TV rates by the end of 1986.

(1977–1981). Interest rates and inflation skyrocketed concurrently and were matched by a rise in unemployment—a situation known as stagflation. The federal budget deficit reached levels that, although quite acceptable by 1990s standards, caused a great deal of concern at the time. Business organizations began to blame the nation's economic problems on ten years of arbitrary, and perhaps frivolous, federal government intervention.

In reaction, during the second half of his term, President Carter began deregulating various industries. Carter pushed for, and obtained, several economic regulatory reform measures. In 1978, he supported the Airline Deregulation Act, which dismantled the Civil Aeronautics Board and gave airlines control over fares charged and routes flown.[36] His administration also favored the Motor Carriers Act of 1980. Prior to that act, the Interstate Commerce Commission (ICC) stringently regulated interstate trucking rates and routes. After the act was passed, trucking companies were gradually allowed to determine their own routes, as well as to determine the rates they charged companies and individuals that wanted to truck goods across state lines. In 1978, the Federal Communications Commission (FCC) effectively completed the deregulation of the television broadcast industry, which freed up cable companies to compete directly with the three biggest networks—ABC, NBC, and CBS—and in a sense led to the existence of the multiple television channels that we enjoy today.

The Reagan Deregulatory Revolution The Carter administration's efforts at deregulation evidently did not go far enough, as Reagan was elected in a landslide in 1980, partly for promising to "get the government off the people's backs." Although President

---

36. M. B. Solomon, "Pro-Regulation Forces in U.S. See Chance to Alter Air Policy," *Journal of Commerce and Commercial Affairs*, September 16, 1992, p. 8A.

Reagan did produce a good deal of deregulatory legislation, his most effective reform strategy was to cut funding for the various regulatory agencies, in essence tying their hands. First, he appointed agency heads deemed sympathetic to the changes. Then his administration required all the agencies to perform cost-benefit analyses on new regulation proposals and withdrew its backing for any of these rules that it felt would be too costly to business.

According to some estimates, during Reagan's eight years in office, the Department of Energy reduced its paperwork demands on the private sector by over 800,000 hours.[37] In the 1970s, the National Highway Traffic Safety Administration made about fifteen investigations into auto defects a year. During the first year of the Reagan administration, it undertook fewer than six. Activities at the EPA changed similarly: during the Carter administration the EPA referred about two hundred cases a year to the Justice Department, whereas in the first year of the Reagan administration the EPA referred fewer than thirty. The EPA during the Reagan administration literally shut down its office of enforcement and reduced its enforcement legal staff by over 80 percent.

THE LEGACY OF DEREGULATION

By the mid-1990s the shine of deregulation had worn off for many, particularly as an instrument for regulatory reform. Deregulation, like any other regulatory action, appeared to have both costs and benefits.

Benefits of Deregulation Some argue that consumers of airline, trucking, and telephone services were better off after deregulation. Many airline passengers and firms using interstate trucking companies paid lower prices. Both businesses and consumers paid less for long-distance phone service.[38]

Costs of Deregulation Deregulation, however, has a number of costs, many of them social. For example, it initially had allowed the creation of numerous airline companies, but a wave of mergers and acquisitions (as well as bankruptcies) then occurred and seemed to reduce competition. In the banking industry, deregulation similarly has allowed for fewer, but larger, banking institutions.

Prior to deregulation, furthermore, regulated airlines used **cross-subsidization**. They charged airline passengers in popular markets more in order to subsidize good service to small communities. After deregulation occurred, no further cross-subsidization was possible because of intense competition. Consequently, airline passengers flying to and from small cities saw the frequency and quality of service decline.[39] Specifically, they ended up having to fly in smaller propeller planes with a slightly higher chance of being involved in an accident (not to speak of higher noise levels) and faced a reduction in route and destination choices.[40]

Deregulation in the Airline Industry As of 1993, 18 percent of the airline industry was in Chapter 11 bankruptcy, and one industry observer noted that the airlines had lost more than twice the accumulated profit they had earned since they began commercial

37. R. L. Miller and F. B. Cross, *The Legal and Regulatory Environment Today: Changing Perspectives for Business* (St. Paul: West Publishing Co., 1993), Chapter 8.
38. R. L. Miller, *Economics Today*, 7th ed. (New York: HarperCollins College Publishers, 1994), p. 342.
39. *Ibid.*, p. 343.
40. A. Barnett, T. Curtis, J. Goranson, and A. Patrick, "Better Than Ever: Nonstop Jet Service in an Era of Hubs and Spokes," *Sloan Management Review*, Winter 1992, p. 49.

service in the 1920s.[41] Major carriers such as Braniff, Pan Am, Eastern, Continental, and TWA have either been forced into bankruptcy or been liquidated. The airlines are perceived to be waging constant price wars, which have helped consumers but have cut into the airlines' profits and hampered some technological, safety, and rehabilitative services. By the mid-1990s, U.S. commercial airlines had an older fleet of airplanes than did Italy, France, Great Britain, Japan, Canada, or Germany.[42]

These perceptions, however, may not accurately reflect what has happened (see *Exhibit 9–8*). The number of airline passengers has almost doubled since 1987. Revenues per passenger mile have fallen by more than 25 percent. Complaints have fallen by more than 50 percent. Surprisingly for most observers, fatal accidents per 100,000 departures have decreased almost 75 percent. During the nine years before deregulation, total fatalities were 1,459. In the nine years after deregulation, total fatalities dropped to 1,036, despite an enormous increase in passenger miles traveled. This is a dramatic improvement. In terms of fatal accidents per million miles traveled, there was a decline of almost 60 percent during the nine years after deregulation.

Deregulation in the Trucking Industry A clear example of how employees fare in deregulated industries can be found in the trucking business. By letting any carrier operate on any route and make rate changes on short notice, the Motor Carriers Act of 1980 led to a sharp increase in the number of independent trucking companies. Within five years, the number of trucking companies almost doubled, and by the mid-1990s, 30,000 independent carriers had increased competitive pressures on the industry. Shipping prices plummeted, with some independent companies offering "discounts" of as much as 50 percent to capture business in the highly competitive market.

41. P. S. Dempsey, "The Bitter Fruits of Airline Deregulation," *Wall Street Journal*, April 8, 1993, p. A15. (Note, though, that these numbers are uncorrected for inflation and are therefore grossly exaggerated.)
42. *Ibid.*

▼ **EXHIBIT 9-8 Effects of Deregulation on the Air Travel Industry**

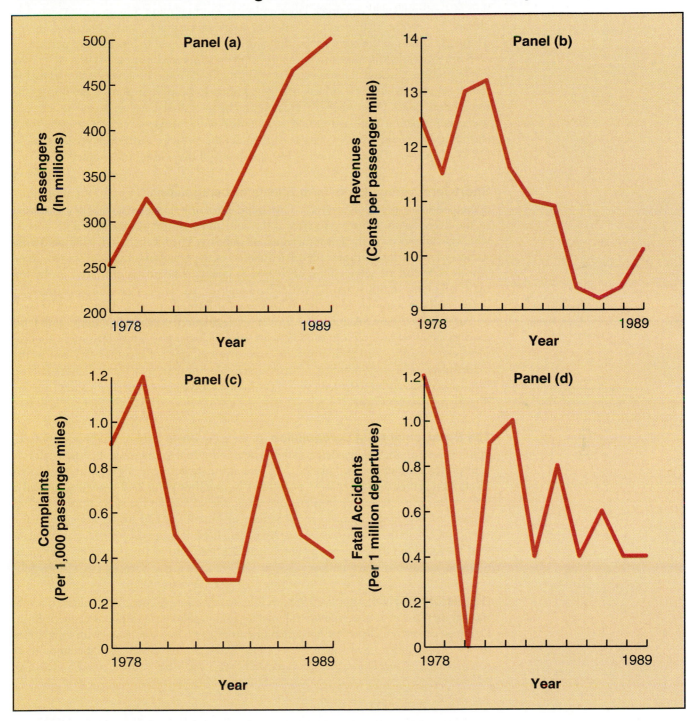

SOURCE: R. L. Miller, *Economics Today*, 7th ed. (New York: HarperCollins College Publishers, 1994), p. 684.

Before deregulation there were 900,000 trucking jobs; since deregulation, that number has grown to nearly 1.5 million. Almost all of the new carriers, not wanting the burden of work rules that dominate labor contracts, are nonunion. Consequently, whereas almost 90 percent of the nation's intercity trucking contracts were controlled by the Teamsters Union in the early 1960s, that number has dropped to less than 10 percent.[43]

Some worry that the pressure on small companies to keep business has placed a heavy burden on the truckers themselves to stay on the road; some observers estimate that as many as one-third of these drivers use illegal drugs to help them stay awake during the extra hours behind the wheel.[44] Trucking companies that have managed to succeed under deregulation have had to find ways to deal with intense price competition and a shrinking number of drivers willing to work under the new circumstances (see the *Case— CRST Maneuvers Through Trucking Deregulation*—at the end of this chapter).

Short-Term versus Long-Term Effects of Deregulation Thus, in the short term, deregulation has predictable effects. One is the inevitable shakedown of some companies in the deregulated industry. Another is the sometimes drastic displacement of workers who were employed in the formerly regulated industry. The level of service for many consumers may fall; for example, after deregulation of the telephone industry started, some aspects of telephone service have decreased in quality. The power of unions in the formerly regulated industry may decrease. Bankruptcies may cause disruptions, particularly in the local economy where the headquarters of the formerly regulated firm were located.

Proponents of deregulation, or at least of less regulation, contend that these short-term tremors are offset by long-run, solid benefits, such as lower prices for consumers. Indeed, some even see the market fluctuations as positive examples of social Darwinism in the marketplace. The high numbers of bankruptcies do not represent deregulation's failure, these observers say, but rather show that the industries are becoming "razor sharp" by cutting away inefficient firms.[45]

The Backlash against Deregulation In the early 1990s, public, and hence political, opinion was turning against deregulation where individual safety was concerned, such as with prescription drugs, workplace safety, and airline travel. One survey of the Air Lines Pilots Association showed that 43 percent of its member pilots said deregulation had a "greatly adverse" effect on commercial aviation safety.[46] Along the same lines, a Gallup telephone poll showed that nearly two-thirds of Americans had lost confidence in the safety and efficiency of airlines.[47] As we have seen, these feelings do not necessarily square with the facts, but the perceptions have opened a floodgate of questions about deregulation and, eventually, reregulation.

Regulatory Revival After the 1988 presidential election, George Bush allowed a substantial increase in both regulatory rulemaking and expenditures. Under President Bush, Congress passed the Clean Air Act Amendments of 1990, the Americans with Disabilities Act of 1990, and the Civil Rights Act of 1991. These acts have increased the amounts of rulemaking and regulation that affect virtually every business in the United States. The

---

43. H. Bernstein, "Truckers Feel the Burn of Deregulation," *Los Angeles Times*, May 1, 1994, p. M5.
44. K. Labich, "The Scandal of Killer Trucks," *Fortune*, March 30, 1987, pp. 85–87.
45. T. Ferguson, "Deregulation Delivers the Goods," *Wall Street Journal*, June 29, 1993, p. A19.
46. R. E. Dallos, "Sky-High Airline Debt Feeds Air Safety Debate," *Los Angeles Times*, October 22, 1989, p. D1.
47. "The Nation," *Los Angeles Times*, August 30, 1989, p. A2.

Cable Reregulation Act of 1992 also was evidence of a regulatory revival during the Bush administration, though the president did not favor that particular legislation.

Reregulation A sure sign of the backlash against deregulation has been the call for reregulation emanating from industry insiders and concerned consumer groups. A number of formerly regulated industries talk of **reregulation**. Usually, the issue is raised when deregulatory policies lead to unintended results. The most strident calls for reregulation are typically from heads of companies in formerly regulated industries. For example, the president of USAir asked for reregulation of the airline industry as far back as 1987.

Why would the heads of firms in previously regulated industries ask for reregulation? Some argue that the lives of managers in a regulated industry are much easier than in a deregulated one. Prior to deregulation in the airline industry in 1978, rates and schedules were controlled by the government. Consequently, there was virtually no competition for routes or fare wars—torturous strategies for airlines but celebrated by consumers. Before deregulation, most airlines were almost practically guaranteed profits, an enviable position for any industry.

Ironically, the one intended effect of deregulation—open competition—has not necessarily taken place. In 1996, six airlines controlled 85 percent of U.S. air traffic. The reason lies in barriers to entry in the industry, which, if anything, are more stringent now than they were before deregulation. There are two basic reasons for these entry obstacles:

1. Gates and landing slots have been in short supply because deregulation spawned the hub-and-spoke system, which funnels most traffic through large, now overcrowded airports in such places as Atlanta, Chicago, and New York. Any potential newcomer airline can get gates only if an incumbent rival makes them available.

2. Frequent flyer bonus systems make it increasingly difficult for newcomer airlines to compete with established carriers. Business travelers, for example, would not necessarily switch to a lower-cost airline to save their companies money, because doing so would eliminate the benefit of the frequent flyer miles they personally retain.

These and other barriers to entry may be substantial enough to prevent the emergence of new airlines. Hence, Congress is giving more attention to reregulation. We will probably not see a return to the requirements of government approval for every airline schedule and rate, as was the case prior to 1978. Reregulation, however, would mean that the days of aggressive deregulation were over.

REGULATORY EFFICIENCY

In a mid-1990s survey by the Associated Press, 95 percent of American adults indicated that they believed the government wasted "a great deal" or "quite a lot" of money.[48] This concern underlies one of the catchwords that came out of the global economic slowdown in the late 1980s and early 1990s: *efficiency*. Our search for more efficiency was in part based on global competition:

▼ **In the United States, the realization that the country might never again be the dominating economic giant it was in the post–World War II era caused a reassessment of policy both within and without private industry.**

48. D. E. Rosebaum, "Remaking Government," *New York Times*, September 8, 1993, p. A1.

The effect of this line of thinking on regulatory reform was twofold. First, the emphasis shifted from reforming an *oversized* government to reforming a *wasteful* government. In introducing his "National Performance Review," President Clinton called the regulatory arrangement "old fashioned, outdated. . . . It's government using a quill pen in the age of WordPerfect."[49] Many business leaders echo this desire for greater efficiency in their relationship with government: "Business is not seeking less regulation. It is seeking smarter regulation," says Mary Bernhard, manager of environmental policy for the U.S. Chamber of Commerce.[50]

LIMITS TO THE BENEFITS OF REGULATION

One of the prerequisites for "smarter regulation" seems to be an application of basic economic theory. There is a point at which the marginal costs of a regulation exceed the marginal benefits of that regulation; this is the **law of diminishing marginal returns**—after some point the additional return from an activity grows smaller and smaller. Many critics believe that the regulatory establishment in general, and the regulatory agencies in particular, ignore this law and instead often push the costs of their activity past the maximum net benefits (benefits minus costs) limit. The purpose of each individual regulator is to create regulations; for obvious reasons, it is hardly in the regulator's best interests to inform his or her superiors that no further regulations are needed. Consequently, regulators have turned their budgets and bureaucracies into, as one observer put it, "a restaurant where the more the customer eats the hungrier he becomes."[51]

Environmental risk manager Michael Markels, Jr., explains what happens when the law of diminishing marginal returns is applied to regulation: "We cannot achieve better than perfection. If we promulgate regulations to take selenium out of the drinking water, we cannot reduce the concentration below zero. Long experience teaches that the benefits of regulation per unit of cost are greatest when the costs are low, but fall off rapidly as the benefits move towards perfection. Getting the last few atoms of selenium out of drinking water may cost as much as all the prior benefits."[52]

Markels further points out that in "the real world," people adjust their behavior to the costs that regulate it. Taken to its logical end, this tendency means that as regulation increases, a growing number of individuals will opt out of the regulatory process. When the costs of regulation are low, the effect will be minimal; but as those costs expand, so will the consequences. Often, these consequences are distributed throughout society with some disturbing effects (see *Managing Social Issues—Ethics and Social Responsibility: Hazardous Waste and Native Americans*).

If this trend is unchecked, the results can be worse than a case in which no regulation existed at all. As a historical example, Markels offers the Eighteenth Amendment to the U.S. Constitution, which made the production and consumption of alcohol illegal in the United States in 1920. Initially, this policy (known as Prohibition) was successful in its goal of decreasing the alcohol consumption of people in the United States. The point was quickly reached, however, at which the maximum net benefits of the policy had been attained; that is, the percentage of the population willing to follow the law had done so. The costs to the government of enforcing the compliance of those individuals who refused to give up alcohol grew out of proportion to the initial benefits of Prohibition to society.

---

49. Birnbaum and Thomas, *op. cit.*
50. "Weighing the Risks," p. 40.
51. M. Markels, Jr., "Benefits of Regulation Have Their Limits," *Wall Street Journal*, November 27, 1987, p. A18.
52. *Ibid.*

Managing Social Issues

Ethics and Social Responsibility: Hazardous Waste and Native Americans

When Boston Edison Company needed to find someplace to store spent fuel from its Pilgrim Nuclear Power Station in 1995, it did not even consider an in-state storage site. Massachusetts law restricts the storage not only of nuclear leftovers but also of any kind of hazardous or toxic waste to the point at which there are no options for companies such as Boston Edison but to search elsewhere. In this case, Boston Edison's hunt led it to the state of New Mexico, where the company offered the Mescalero Apache tribe $250 million over forty years to store the nuclear waste on its reservation.

As stringent state environmental laws shrink the hazardous waste options for firms such as Boston Edison, more of them are looking toward Native American–owned land for solutions. Consequently, regulations that benefit many communities—which no longer have to worry about 900 million annual tons of toxic waste winding up in their backyards—may be having the opposite effect on Native Americans. Strict regulations have raised the value of potential waste sites to the point at which tribal leaders are having a difficult time turning down the millions of dollars corporations offer them, despite the possible environmental drawbacks.

Semisovereignty and Poverty

Because Native American reservations are semisovereign and somewhat disassociated from state regulations and political pressures, tribal leaders can accommodate incinerators, hazardous waste dumps, landfills, and nuclear storage facilities. Furthermore, as a representative from a Pittsburgh waste-disposal company wrote, "The regulatory environment has grown increasingly complex and even when technically approved, public hysteria has stopped construction of environmentally sound processing and disposal facilities." He continued, "Because the American Indian has many aspects of self-government over their reservation, they possess an opportunity to bypass the barriers to state-of-the-art waste disposal."

The destruction of traditional cultures and natural resources has led to unemployment, alcoholism, and attendant difficulties in many Native American communities. Along with legal gambling, hazardous waste disposal offers many tribal communities help in combating their economic problems.

"We Do Not Want to Harm Mother Earth"

Many Native American communities, seeing the damage that industrial waste has done to the New York Mohawks' once pristine reservation and other tribal lands, have resisted these opportunities. The Mescalero Apaches, for example, decided not to accept Boston Edison's nuclear waste. The Ogala Sioux of South Dakota's Pine Ridge, where the annual per-capita income averages $2,000 and unemployment is nearly 80 percent, resisted the garbage business and at least $30 million in potential royalties. "We do not want to harm Mother Earth," explained Rinard Yellow Boy, the tribe's director of solid waste.

Other tribes have chosen a different path. In the early 1990s, southern California's Kumeyyay Indian Campo Band—who said it did not want to offer "a playground for non-Indians" and would "starve before we'd sell beads or pose for pictures"—made a deal with Mid-American Waste Systems, Inc., that would bring the tribe revenues of $50 million over twenty years. In return, the waste management company would operate an eight-hundred-acre landfill on Campo land that could handle 40 percent of San Diego County's trash needs. Mid-American also plans to give the Campo preferential treatment in job hiring for the landfill.

The Future Use of Reservations

In spite of Mid-American's claims of environmental safety, many ranchers and other nearby neighbors worried that the landfill would contaminate the area's groundwater. Local assemblyman Steve Peace blasted "sleaze merchants" such as Mid-American, which took advantage of the sovereignty of Native Americans to avoid California's strict environmental standards and high fees. Peace even introduced a bill that would require the state to oversee any landfills or hazardous waste dumps built on tribal reservations.

Tribal chairman Ralph Goff of the Campo called Peace's bill "an insult to us" and added, "He's making it seem like

MANAGING SOCIAL ISSUES: (CONTINUED)

we are unable to govern ourselves." Eventually, the Campo's sovereignty won out over Peace's objections, and within a few years the U.S. Congress had passed legislation reaffirming tribal powers over their own lands. The use of reservations as waste sites will increase in 1999 when the Department of Energy is responsible for forty-two thousand tons of deadly poisonous radioactive wastes that are temporarily being stored in underwater reactor pools or by commercial power plants such as Boston Edison. By the

mid-1990s, sixteen tribes had applied for or received federal grants to become depositories for this waste.

For Critical Analysis:

Should the federal government restrict or take away the sovereignty of Native American tribes to keep them from causing environmental damage to reservation land? In other words, which side has the ethical high ground in this case?

SOURCE: Information from C. J. Prince, "Apache Tribe Says No to Nuclear Waste Site," *Boston Business Journal*, February 10, 1995, p. 12; R. Tomsho, "Dumping Grounds: Indian Tribes Contend with Some of Worst of America's Pollution," *Wall Street Journal*, November 29, 1990, p. A1; M. Satchell, "Trashing the Reservations," *U.S. News and World Report*, January 11, 1993, p. 24; B. Sutherland, "Early Building Start Planned for Campo Landfill," *San Diego Business Journal*, July 11, 1994, p. 7; and R. Frammolino, "Bill Would Curb Dumps on Reservation Indians," *Los Angeles Times*, April 3, 1991, p. B10.

Eventually, the situation became clearly "much worse than the previous, unregulated condition. More people were drinking more than before, and the deleterious health effects of alcohol consumption skyrocketed."[53] This argument doesn't even take account of the deleterious health effects to the nondrinking population, who suffered from the rise of crime brought on by Al Capone and his bootlegging gangster contemporaries. Nationwide, the murder rate set records during Prohibition, rising to a level 25 percent above the years preceding 1920. When the Eighteenth Amendment was repealed in 1933, the murder rate declined for eleven consecutive years.[54]

SELF-REGULATION: AN ALTERNATIVE TO REGULATION

The problem for those who decry any sort of regulation and therefore want deregulation, or at least regulatory streamlining, is that they must come up with an alternative. Furthermore,

▼ **Even the most stringent critic of government intervention in the market must realize that modern society will not accept completely unregulated business.**

An idea gaining more credence in the business world is **self-regulation**, in which an industry or firm that understands society's requirements takes the responsibility of implementing regulations itself.[55] There is an undeniable strain of idealism inherent in self-regulation, as the publisher of the magazine *Business Ethics*, Marjorie Kelly, noted in an editorial on the subject:

---

53. *Ibid.*

54. D. K. Benjamin and R. L. Miller, *Undoing Drugs* (New York: Basic Books, 1993), p. 21.

55. S. J. Ashford and A. S. Tsui, "Self-Regulation for Managerial Effectiveness: The Role of Active Feedback Seeking," *Academy of Management Journal*, June 1991, p. 251.

COMPANY FOCUS: SEGA OF AMERICA
STOPPING THE VIOLENCE

The victim: a scantily clad woman. The stalkers: dark-hooded zombies with blood-sucking devices. The scene: a deserted bathroom. Is this the plot of the latest B-grade vampire movie down at the corner theater? No, it is the setting for Sega of America's video game Night Trap. Marketing violent merchandise like this game and others has helped Sega gain a foothold in the highly competitive video game trade, but it has also left the company open to consumer scorn and retail outlet revolt. For Sega, and indeed the entire video game industry, the compromise rests in self-regulation.

Catching Up with Nintendo

In 1989, Nintendo of America held 80 percent of the video game market. Four years later, Sega was challenging the industry giant and even pulling ahead of it in some markets, such as in the sales of sixteen-bit video game players. When the dust cleared in 1993, Sega had $3 billion in sales to Nintendo's $4.3 billion, and Sega announced a line of interactive movie games on CD-ROM that its executives hoped would push the company well ahead of its main competitor.

Industry experts attribute Sega's quick rise in part to the popularity of its "blood-and-guts approach" compared with Nintendo's more family-oriented products. Besides Night Trap, Sega owners also have access to Mortal Kombat, in which participants vicariously rip the heads off their opponents. Sega's marketers played up their company's "hipness" with television advertisements that portrayed a dim-witted family sitting on a porch watching an electric bug zapper at work; one of the family members was playing a Nintendo game with equal enthusiasm.

First Steps in Self-Regulation

As Sega was gaining market share, it was also fielding criticism concerning the violence of some of its products, especially Night Trap and Mortal Kombat. Fearing federal intervention, in June 1993 Sega created a "Videogame Rating Council" consisting of experts in the fields of sociology, education, and psychology (all appointed by the company). This council set up three categories: GA for general audiences, MA-13 for mature audiences, and MA-17 for adults. "We believe in self-regulation, not government regulation," said William White, Jr., marketing director for Sega.

As the concept of self-regulation evolves, what's at work is really a maturation process—a passage from a lower to a higher level of ethical maturity, akin to passing from adolescence into adulthood. . . . And we don't need the government to tell us to clean up the environment. We accept that there is a world out there beyond our own ego, or beyond our own balance sheet, and we recognize our duty to be responsible to that broader world. We mature as individuals for many of the same reasons that capitalism is maturing today: because of social pressure, fear of punishment, good role models, personal values, or simply the passage of time.[56]

In our previous discussions of business ethics, we saw that some companies do seem to follow this maturation process into self-regulation.[57] At least according to some of its stakeholders and business observers, Levi Strauss was not seeking profitability when it decided to pull its manufacturing out of China because of that country's human rights abuses. In any event, in the past decade, numerous alliances of groups espousing social initiatives have sprung up in the self-regulatory spirit.

56. M. Kelly, "Capitalism Grows Up," *Business Ethics*, January–February 1995, p. 9.
57. A. S. Tsui and S. J. Ashford, "Adaptive Self-Regulation: A Process View of Managerial Effectiveness," *Journal of Management*, Spring 1994, p. 93.

COMPANY FOCUS: (CONTINUED)

Nintendo Retaliates

Nintendo reacted to Sega's self-regulation with a mixture of skepticism and scorn, calling it "a smokescreen for more violent games." It rejected adopting such a rating system itself, it said, because its own products were "acceptable to the whole family." Verbal attacks were only part of Nintendo's strategy. First, the company provided Seattle television station KOMO a chance to film Night Trap's more violent scenes. KOMO then showed the clips to the local chapter of the National Organization for Women and taped the responses. Next, Nintendo gave the Senate Subcommittee on Juvenile Justice videotapes of scenes from Night Trap and Mortal Kombat. The scenes were presented to the public at a congressional press conference and then found their way onto national television news shows.

The publicity produced the strongest antiviolence movement on Capitol Hill to date, as Senators Joseph I. Lieberman and Herbert Kohl began holding hearings on the possibility of government regulation of video games. Soon afterward, in December 1993, toy store chains Toys "Я" Us and FAO Schwartz pulled Night Trap from their shelves. Within two months, Sega—abandoning the argument that the game was suitable entertainment for adults—withdrew Night Trap from sale with promises to rerelease a toned-down version.

Further Self-Regulation

Nintendo's attempts to cast Sega in the role of villain wound up having some unintended results. Forced to defend themselves, Sega executives began telling Congress and consumers that they were not the only video game company that produced violent games. The spotlight turned from Sega to the entire industry, including Nintendo, which had its own version of Mortal Kombat to defend. Eventually, to head off swelling support for regulation in Congress, in April 1994, twelve game companies—including Sega and Nintendo—formed the Interactive Digital Software Association (IDSA), which in turn announced the Entertainment Industry Ratings System Committee. IDSA promised Congress that the committee would have a ratings system in place for the holiday season, a move that won its members at least a temporary reprieve from the efforts of Senators Lieberman and Kohl.

The New Bottom Line

Fledgling industries such as the home video game business often experience a short period in which regulation is lax. Once this grace period comes to an end, however, members of the industry sometimes must choose between self-regulation and government regulation. In most cases, as Sega decided, the former is far more desirable.

SOURCE: Information from T. Davey, "Sega Pulls Ahead of Nintendo in Video Wars," *San Francisco Business Times*, January 7, 1994, p. 9; "Nintendo Rejects Video Game Rating Scheme," Newsbyte News Network, May 27, 1993; J. Burgess, "Video Game Rivals United to Create Ratings System," *Washington Post*, March 5, 1994, p. C1; and "Videogame Makers Form IDSA, New Trade Group," *Consumer Electronics*, April 11, 1994, p. 44.

Skeptics often claim, as was the case with regard to Levi Strauss in China, that such steps are ultimately self-serving and are taken to gain positive publicity or to propitiate special interest groups. Thus, perhaps some forms of self-regulation are not so much ethically enhancing as they are a response to the fear of punishment posed by Kelly or, as the case may be, the fear of harmful regulation. Consider the Motion Picture Association of America and the Recording Industry Association of America. They have provided rating systems for feature films and warning stickers for explicit lyrics, respectively, to avoid more stringent government regulation of their products. In 1994, in response to complaints that computer video games were excessively violent, a consortium of video companies introduced a system for rating their games; similar criticism of network television shows could lead to self-regulation in the near future (see *Company Focus: Sega of America*).

In a sense, the question of whether self-regulation is altruistic or is the result of more self-serving intentions is moot. If we accept that the ends justify the means, and the ends are industries and firms that are more in tune with societal demands in a nonregulatory environment, then the motivation behind self-regulation is incidental.[58]

---

58. J. P. Guthrie, C. M. Grimm, and K. G. Smith, "Environmental Change and Management Staffing: A Reply," *Journal of Management*, Winter 1993, p. 889.

THE DELICATE BALANCE

As you have read in this chapter, waves of regulation, deregulation, and reregulation have been the rule rather than the exception in the United States. Some groups are still convinced that more regulation is almost always better than less. After all, according to these regulation proponents, American businesses, because they seek to increase profits, cannot be trusted to do what is best for society and, in particular, the consumer. At the opposite extreme are avid proponents of deregulation, most of whom argue that in general, regulation has had more costs than benefits. They do not claim that regulation *per se* is necessarily wrong but rather that in practice, regulators have imposed costs that far outstrip any benefits to the American economy.

It appears that the antiregulation mood apparent in the early days of the Republican-dominated Congress in 1995 is quickly coming to an end. Two years later, no significant deregulation or antiregulation legislation had been passed (although the federal Interstate Commerce Commission was finally shut down). The promise to force regulatory agencies to subject every new rule and regulation to a cost-benefit analysis never became law. The number of pages in the *Federal Register* did not significantly drop in 1995 or 1996. Additionally, increased regulation of the Internet was inserted into the 1996 Telecommunications Act (although that section of the act was immediately attacked as unconstitutional and was deemed so by federal courts.

It is clear that a delicate balancing act is at play. Some people can be made better off through regulation. Others may be made worse off. Congress (and to a lesser extent, state lawmakers) is ultimately responsible for legislation that allows for more or less regulation. Business, nonetheless, can behave in an ethically responsible way to avoid government regulation.

TERMS AND CONCEPTS FOR REVIEW

Cross-subsidization 261
Direct costs of regulation 247
Indirect costs of regulation 247

Induced costs of regulation 248
Law of diminishing marginal
   returns 266

Opportunity cost 249
Reregulation 265
Self-regulation 268

SUMMARY

1. Regulatory spending in constant dollars has more than tripled since 1970. Social regulation has increased at a much more rapid rate than has economic regulation.

2. Some of the economic benefits of regulation include a cleaner environment and a workplace in which there are decreased medical costs because of fewer employee accidents. Regulation of the pharmaceutical industry, in addition, has reduced the number of undesired side effects of drugs.

3. The economic costs of regulation include the costs for businesses (passed on to consumers) of complying with regulations. These indirect costs must be added to the direct costs of running the regulatory agencies. According to Murray Weidenbaum, every dollar spent on direct regulatory costs generates at least $20 in indirect costs. There are also induced costs of regulatory activity, such as the costs of greater employee stress and a reduction in technological and medical innovation (recall Type II error from Chapter 5).

4. To undertake a cost-benefit analysis of regulation, one has to place a value on saving a human life (or on saving one year of human life). The reason is that regulations that reduce risk normally are costly—they use scarce resources. A study by the Center for Risk Analysis at the Harvard University School of Public Health estimated that asbestos controls have a net cost per year of life saved of almost $2 million, and the net cost per year of life saved for radiation controls (at industrial sites and for radiologists) is over $27 million. The study further estimated that the Environmental Protection Agency, through its regulations, implicitly costs Americans almost $8 million per year of life saved.

5. Although executives, when queried, often ask for less regulation, some regulation can be beneficial to certain businesses. In particular, regulation can create new markets for safety and pollution-abatement equipment. Furthermore, much regulation favors large companies at the expense of small companies, because the former can spread out a fixed cost of regulation over a larger number of units sold. Also, increased regulation can help certain firms by forcing competitors in an industry to follow the same rules.

6. The period of deregulation began during the Carter administration (1977–1981) and increased in intensity during the Reagan years (1981–1989). Deregulation made its mark in the airline and trucking industries. In both industries, in spite of numerous problems caused by deregulation, consumers are paying lower prices today than they

did during the 1970s. In the trucking industry, consumers also have a much wider choice of service suppliers.

7. During the Bush administration (1989–1993), significant legislation was passed that once again increased regulation, including the Americans with Disabilities Act of 1990, the Civil Rights Act of 1991, and the Cable Reregulation Act of 1992. Calls for reregulation were especially loud in the airline industry. Deregulation of the airline industry had actually reduced the number of carriers. Also, the public mistakenly perceived that airline travel had become less safe, when in fact it had become increasingly safer on a per-passenger-mile basis.

8. At the beginning of the Clinton administration in 1993, there was an emphasis on reforming wasteful, as opposed to oversized, government. Regulatory activities were to become more efficient. Little was done to change the actual nature of regulatory agencies, however. After all, regulators have a vested interest in increasing their budgets and bureaucracies, so they are not likely to tell Congress that they should no longer make new rules. Regulators also ignore the law of diminishing marginal returns: at some point the benefits of additional regulations are less than the costs of the regulations.

9. One alternative to government regulation is industry self-regulation, which has occurred in the motion picture industry, the video game industry, and the recording industry.

EXERCISES

1. Look again at *Exhibit 9–1*. Does it appear that the trend in regulatory spending has changed over time?

2. Reexamine *Exhibit 9–2*. According to the figures, was the percentage increase in the cost of social regulation greater, about the same as, or less than the percentage increase in the cost of economic regulation?

3. Murray Weidenbaum argues that for every dollar of direct regulatory agency expenditures, industry spends at least $20 in response. Choose an actual or hypothetical regulation. Write down a list of every new activity that a business might have to engage in pursuant to the regulation. Order the list in terms of which new activities would cost the business the most.

4. Of the two induced costs of regulation mentioned in the chapter, which one do you think is more important to society? Defend your answer.

5. "No monetary value can be put on saving a human life. This is what humanism is all about." Do you agree with this viewpoint? In an essay of several paragraphs, support your opinion.

6. You have just discovered statistics that show that a new OSHA standard for workers in a particular industry has kept at least 5 people from dying and 26,000 people from being injured in that industry. Was the new standard therefore a success? Explain your answer.

7. How can the concept of trade-offs be applied to risk reduction?

8. Make a list of new markets that you think have been created because of increased government regulation.

9. This chapter gave three examples of how increased regulation might benefit larger firms in a given industry. Develop another example with a detailed analysis of exactly how established larger firms might benefit from a new actual or hypothetical regulation.

10. How do licensing and other entry requirements benefit those already in the legal and medical professions?

11. Pick one of the deregulation acts listed in *Exhibit 9–7*. Do research to find out specifically how firms in the industry were affected by the act. Did the majority of firms benefit or lose? In what way did they do so?

12. The statistics clearly show that the probability of dying in an airline accident is lower today than it was twenty-five years ago. Nonetheless, many consumers believe that airline safety has been compromised since deregulation. Can you explain why the public generally has an incorrect view of the trend in airline safety?

13. Explain why certain groups may suffer when an industry is initially deregulated. Explain which of these groups will suffer, and how.

14. At the beginning of the Clinton administration in 1993, the emphasis shifted from complaints about oversized government to complaints about a wasteful government. How would suggested reforms differ depending on which view of the problem one held? Make a list of government reform proposals that you would argue for if you believed that government was oversized. Make another list of government reform proposals that you would suggest if you believed that government was simply wasteful.

15. Present several examples of business activities that follow the law of diminishing marginal returns.

16. A number of examples of industry self-regulation were given in the chapter. Find three other examples that are currently in effect.

SELECTED REFERENCES

▶ Armstrong, Mark. *Regulatory Reform: Economic Analysis and British Experience.* Cambridge, Mass.: MIT Press, 1994.

▶ Burnham, David. *A Law unto Itself: The IRS and the Abuse of Power.* New York: Random House, 1990.

▶ Crandall, Robert W. *Talk Is Cheap: The Promise of Regulatory Reform in North American Communications.* Washington, D.C.: Brookings Institution, 1995.

▶ Eisner, Marc Allen. *Regulatory Politics in Transition.* Baltimore, Md.: Johns Hopkins University Press, 1993.

▶ Himmelberg, Robert F., ed. *Regulatory Issues since 1964: The Rise of the Deregulation Movement.* New York: Garland Publishing, 1994.

▶ Mieczkowski, Bogdan. *Dysfunctional Bureaucracy.* Lanham, MD.: University Press of America, 1991.

▶ Robinson, Glen. *American Bureaucracy.* Ann Arbor: University of Michigan Press, 1991.

▶ Schmidt, S. W., et al. *American Government and Politics Today.* 1997–1998 ed. St. Paul: West Publishing Co., 1997, Chapter 14.

▶ Schoenbrod, David. *Power without Responsibility.* New Haven, Conn.: Yale University Press, 1993.

▶ United States Congress. *Hearing on the Need for Regulatory Reform.* Washington, D.C.: Government Printing Office, 1995.

RESOURCES ON THE INTERNET

▼ The U.S. Small Business Administration (SBA) is dedicated to helping the owners of small businesses understand and meet the challenges of operating a business— including how to deal with regulation. The SBA can be accessed at

http://www.sbaonline.sba.gov/

or

gopher://www.sbaonline.sba.gov./

or

ftp://www.sbaonline.sba.gov/

▼ The Library of Congress is an excellent source for information on federal government regulatory agencies. To use this source, access

gopher://riceinfo.rice.edu:70/11/ Subject/Government

and go to

Federal Government Information from Library of Congress

▼ To find information about the numerous agencies of the federal government, go to

United States Federal Register

▼ Every year, the government publishes thousands of reports on virtually every topic imaginable. To look up government information researched and produced by government agencies and departments, use the University of Minnesota gopher at

gopher.micro.umn.edu

and choose

Libraries/Information from US Federal Government

▼ If you want to find out what is going on in our government agencies, you may want to look into the following service:

clari.news.gov.agency

▼ When members of Congress want a particular regulation or regulatory agency investigated, they turn to the General Accounting Office (GAO). For GAO reports on virtually every area of the government, try an anonymous FTP at

ftp.cu.nih.gov

and take the following Path:

/gao reports

or try the following gopher address:

wiretap.spies.com

and choose

GAO Transition Reports

▼ For information on Intellectual Property law, access

http://www.legal.net/intellct.htm

CASE

CRST MANEUVERS THROUGH TRUCKING DEREGULATION

Background

Harold Smith, chairman of the trucking company CRST International, has sour memories of the days before the industry was deregulated by the Motor Carriers Act of 1980. Like its competitors, the Cedar Rapids, Iowa–based company was restricted as to what freight it could carry, where in the country it could carry it, and what price it could charge for the service. The Interstate Commerce Commission (ICC) determined these regulations, and Smith remembers spending a great deal of time fighting the agency for new routes "instead of running a trucking company." In one instance, he was chastised by the agency for transporting *red* farm-tractor blades, when CRST was only authorized to carry *yellow* farm-tractor blades, identical in every way except for their color. It was "22 years of hell" under regulation, according to Smith.

However, it was these "early lessons that helped prepare us for deregulation," says one of the company's employees. "We became a task-force oriented company, with an opportunistic bent, so deregulation was just another problem to be dealt with." For most of the trucking industry, the years following deregulation were indeed problematic. In the first five years, nearly 10,000 new companies entered the business, which drastically increased the competitive pressures on firms that had never had to compete in a free market before. By 1987, trucking companies were going out of business at four times the annual rate of the 1970s. More than 100,000 truck drivers lost their jobs within four years. CRST prospered, however, rising from 134th in industry revenues the year before deregulation to 65th two years after. The company concentrated on improving its efficiency, which lowered its prices—the prototypical strategy for a deregulated business.

CRST's Early Strategic Response to Deregulation

In fact, deregulation immediately improved the efficiency of the entire industry. In May 1981, when Smith applied for nationwide, all-commodity trucking authority, he received almost immediate approval and a 40-word sentence delineating CRST's new rights. Before deregulation, the firm's operating guidelines from the ICC for the transportation of one commodity between two cities consisted of 164 pages of complex details covering route and price rules.

With the new nationwide authority and freedom from price restrictions, CRST immediately began offering shippers package deals of services and reduced rates. The company's goal was to eliminate, as much as possible, "deadheading," or returning with empty, unpaid capacity after a delivery was made. Under deregulation, the key to profitable trucking is keeping empty trips to a minimum, and CRST believed it had found a competitive advantage in its ability to do so. Most companies, said one CRST executive, were unaware of how much deadheading they had had under ICC route regulation.

By structuring routes so that they eliminated empty trips, CRST was able to offer large manufacturers and retailers such as General Mills, Inc., and Du Pont Company significantly lower rates than its competitors offered. General Mills, for example, saved 50 to 60 percent off the single haul rate by working out delivery schedules with CRST that eliminated deadheading. A typical CRST haul for the food manufacturer would carry cereal boxes from St. Paul, Minnesota, to Cedar Rapids, Iowa, and then to distribution centers in South Chicago, Illinois, and Kingston, Pennsylvania. After unloading its goods, the truck would reload at nearby Hershey, Pennsylvania, to carry Hershey Food Corporation chocolate products back to Cedar Rapids.

Du Pont, which had previously used "hundreds" of trucking companies to deliver its products, switched to forty small carriers like CRST after deregulation. Du Pont's logistics director calls CRST "very cost effective," a statement backed by increased transactions between the two companies. When deregulation went into effect, CRST revenues from Du Pont were $518,000; two years later, they increased to about $6 million.

CRST was also one of the first companies to pick up on a new line of business called "piggybacking," in which shipments are hauled part of their distance by truck and the rest of the way by train, using the railroad as a subcontractor. By 1983, CRST had seventy-five refrigerated trailers that could be connected to trains, and the company was doing piggyback business with General Foods, Iowa Beef Processor, and Arco Polymers.

To procure this new business, even with the improvements in efficiency, CRST, like most trucking companies, had to endure rate cuts of up to 20 percent in the early days of deregulation. Consequently, CRST is placed in the position of turning down contracts if they are not cost efficient. When Ford Motor Company demanded bigger rate reductions on Michigan-Virginia hauls, CRST dropped the business. The company will also charge uncompetitive high rates on routes involving areas with scarce backhauls, because it cannot afford excessive deadheading.

The only mechanism by which CRST can offer discounts without severely damaging profits is the close control of operations. Tight schedules dictate delivery times, loading times, and return times. Because most of CRST's drivers are nonunion and therefore not subject to rigid Teamsters Union work rule restrictions, the company is usually able to meet its time deadlines. In fact, many trucking companies are finding that they need the flexibility of nonunion drivers to stay competitive: by 1997, only around 5 percent of the commercial drivers in the United States were members of the union.

Marketing Success

Deregulation also gave trucking companies the latitude to tailor services to individual customers, a freedom CRST incorporated as part of its marketing strategy. Previously, ICC regulations had spared trucking companies from the need to advertise. Consequently, there was little advertising expertise in the industry; one 1981 survey of shippers described the marketing efforts of trucking companies as ranging from "horrible" to "dismal." CRST took advantage of this vacuum in the years immediately following deregulation to offer tailor-made delivery plans based on a customer's particular delivery needs. Swift Independent Packing Company, a meat-packing firm, increased its business with CRST sevenfold to $2 million because of the trucking firm's marketing acumen. "They were ahead of the pack," noted Swift's transportation director.

"Value-Added" Technology

CRST continued its innovations by embracing the "value-added" trend of trucking in the 1990s. As competition became more fierce, trucking companies began offering customers value-added service, meaning they offered some feature that was unavailable from other companies for the same price. In the 1980s, CRST's personalized service was its primary value-added component. In the 1990s, the company moved to electronic data interchange, or mobile communications.

In the highly competitive deregulated trucking industry, carriers have been forced to make themselves more responsive to consumer demands for fast service calls and last-minute pickups and deliveries. In 1992, CRST became the first carrier to upgrade its mobile communications system by venturing into satellite tracking. That year, Rockwell International installed its Mobile Communications Satellite Service (MCSS) in 950 CRST trucks. MCSS gave the company a number of value-added features. Customers were provided with computer terminals that granted them instant status information on trucks hauling their products. No longer would truckers have to "call in" their positions, because the satellite tracking performs that task automatically. MCSS can also be used to transmit messages from CRST bases to the drivers, and managers can use that capability to convey instructions on where to buy fuel and how much to buy at each stop. This allows CRST to purchase gas strategically based on differences in fuel prices and tax rates among different states.

Challenges of Deregulation

Critics of trucking deregulation argue that it has transformed the industry into an unstable amalgam of companies and employees at the mercy of cutthroat competition. CRST would not agree with that antideregulation statement, but it has experienced the uncertainties of the unregulated market. With intense price competition—nonexistent under the ICC's previous rate-setting policies—any change in the market can have a major effect on individual companies.

In reaction to increased competition from trucking firms, in the late 1980s railroad companies began turning to double-stack container trains to improve their freight position. By carrying one container loaded above another, double-stack container trains could double their capacities with little relative rise in operating costs. Consequently, double-stack shippers between Los Angeles and Chicago were able to lower rates 15 percent from 1988 to 1989. Forced to drop its own rates to stay competitive, CRST had to cancel plans to buy fifty more trucks. "We're barely making money," said CRST's president John Smith at the time. "We're doing everything we can to keep costs down."

Price competition also leaves the industry vulnerable to external events, such as Iraq's invasion of Kuwait in the summer of 1990. The event drove the price of crude oil to a record high of $40 a barrel. Trucking companies were able to pass some of the higher fuel costs on to shippers, but not all. "[Trucking companies] are taking it on the chin," said one industry analyst at the time. "Most carriers are recouping only 70 to 80 percent of their rising fuel costs."

CASE (CONTINUED)

The Driver Shortage

But Michael Wood, an executive vice president of CRST, does not believe that fuel costs represent the most intense pressure on rates. That distinction goes to higher wages stemming from a shortage of available drivers. "We've done everything we can to improve the lifestyle of a truckload driver," he says. "The only thing we can do now is pay higher wages."

Paradoxically, as deregulation was increasing the efficiency of trucking companies and the demand for their services, it was forcing some truck drivers out of the business. After the passage of the Motor Carriers Act, carriers started seeking the services of cheaper, nonunion drivers. Excess capacity and rate pressures on trucking companies forced them to push their drivers to levels of performance that many of the employees found unacceptable. CRST may advertise its ability to go across the country in sixty hours as a value-added bonus for shippers, but that is an excruciating task for the two-person team doing the driving.

"Pre-regulation, companies had very precise, defined lines, and drivers got into a pattern that was regular and redundant," says one industry expert. After deregulation, though, the companies "got better truck utilization, but drivers found themselves going anywhere and on any day of the week." In return for a demanding schedule, drivers have seen their wages drop compared with wages for factory jobs, for example, which allow a more stable personal life. Before 1980, drivers "accepted the difference in lifestyle because of the [high wages]," says CRST's Smith. "That's not the case today."

Consequently, by 1994, CRST was facing an annual driver turnover of more than 100 percent per year, and the company's recruiting staff had a higher budget than its marketing division. Like its competitors, the company has tried a variety of ways to make the driver's lifestyle more bearable, such as allowing husband-and-wife teams and offering family support groups and counseling. With 10 to 12 percent of the industry's rigs sitting idle for lack of drivers, however, most companies realize they are going to have to raise wages to attract more recruits. Smith predicted that freight rates would rise 3 to 5 percent to cover some of the costs of higher wages and that, as with fuel, most of the increase would be covered by the trucking companies and not their customers—thanks to the competitive pressures of deregulation.

Critical Thinking Questions

1. Imagine a discussion between a free market economist and a union leader on the relative benefits of trucking deregulation. What points would each make? With whom do you agree? Why?

2. Explore the "triangle" relationship between trucking companies, consumers, and employees that has occurred since deregulation of the trucking industry. What trade-offs are involved with each stakeholder group?

3. What characteristics of CRST allowed it to welcome deregulation? What might be the profile of a trucking company that did not look forward to lessening government influence?

4. What is the effect of deregulation on value-added technology? Would CRST still have made those technological improvements in a regulated environment? Would the timetable for such improvements have been different?

5. What ethics-based argument for reregulation of the trucking industry can be made? Do you agree with this argument?

SOURCE: Information from A. R. Karr, "On the Rise: Iowa Trucker Prospers after Deregulation Eases Rules on Routes," *Wall Street Journal*, February 13, 1984, p. A1; T. W. Ferguson, "Deregulation Delivers the Goods," *Wall Street Journal*, June 29, 1993, p. A19; R. Bowman, "It's Not Just Bells and Whistles," *Chilton's Distribution*, February 1, 1993, p. 30; "Rockwell Lands First Customer for Mobile Satellite Service," *Inside IVHS Waters Information Service*, June 22, 1992; D. Machalaba, "Trains Double Up to Get Truck Business," *Wall Street Journal*, July 28, 1989, p. A3A; J. A. Cooke, "Freight Rates: How High Will They Go?" *Traffic Management*, January 1, 1991, p. 34; D. Machalaba, "Long Haul: Trucking Firms Find It a Struggle to Hire and Retain Drivers," *Wall Street Journal*, December 28, 1993, p. A1; and H. L. Richardson, "Can We Afford the Driver Shortage?" *Transportation & Distribution*, August 1, 1994, p. 30.

CHAPTER 10

ANTITRUST LAW AND BUSINESS

CHAPTER OUTLINE

INTRODUCTION

Many purists cringe at the idea that the sport of baseball should be considered a business—or at least they did until the strike of 1994–1995—but major league baseball has enjoyed a business advantage of which any other industry would be jealous. For more than seventy years, baseball has been exempted from antitrust laws. In 1922, the United States Supreme Court held that professional baseball was not within the reach of federal antitrust laws because it was not "interstate commerce."[1] Under modern interpretations of the U.S. Constitution's commerce clause, this decision is clearly wrong. Nonetheless, professional baseball retains its antitrust exemption (this exemption applies only to baseball, not to other professional sports).

Most other industries and firms have not been so lucky. Today's far-reaching antitrust laws—direct descendants of fifteenth-century English common law actions intended to limit restraints on trade—recognize that it has always been in the best interest of some firms to limit competition or to seek special protection from government.

In the United States, concern over anticompetitive practices arose soon after the Civil War with the growth of large corporations and their attempts to reduce or eliminate competition. They did this legally by tying themselves together in a **trust,** or a legal entity in which a trustee holds title to property for the benefit of another. The participants in the most famous trust, Standard Oil, transferred their stock to a trustee and received trust certificates in exchange. The trustee then made decisions with respect to setting prices, controlling production, and determining the control of exclusive geographical markets for all of the oil companies that were in the Standard Oil trust. It became apparent that the trust wielded so much economic power that corporations outside the trust could not compete effectively.

Many states attempted to control such monopolistic behavior by enacting statutes outlawing the use of trusts, or **antitrust laws**. At the national level, the government recognized the problem and in 1887 passed the Interstate Commerce Act, followed by the Sherman Antitrust Act in 1890. Later, Congress passed the Clayton Act (1914) and the Federal Trade Commission Act (1914) to curb further anticompetitive or unfair business practices. Since their passage, some of these acts have been amended numerous times by Congress to broaden and strengthen their coverage. (See *Exhibit 10–1* on page 280 for major antitrust laws.)

We now examine these major antitrust statutes, focusing particularly on the Sherman Antitrust Act and the Clayton Act. Remember in reading this chapter that the basis of antitrust legislation is the desire to foster competition. Antitrust legislation was initially created, and continues to be enforced, because of the belief that competition leads to lower prices, more product information, and a better distribution of wealth between consumers and producers. In recent years, American antitrust law has also been used as a tool to promote these benefits on a global level, with varying degrees of acceptance by the governments of other nations.

THE SHERMAN ANTITRUST ACT

The author of the Sherman Antitrust Act of 1890, Senator John Sherman—brother of the famed Civil War general and a recognized financial authority—had been concerned for

---

1. *Federal Baseball Club of Baltimore, Inc. v. National League of Professional Baseball Clubs* (1922).

years about diminishing competition within American industry. This concern led him to introduce into Congress in 1888, in 1889, and again in 1890 bills designed to destroy the large combinations of capital that were, he felt, creating a lack of balance within the nation's economy. He told Congress that the Sherman Antitrust Act "does not announce a new principle of law, but applies old and well-recognized principles of the common law."[2] Certainly, common law trade regulation was not very familiar to the legislators in the Fifty-first Congress of the United States. The public concern over large-business integration and trusts was familiar, however, and in 1890, Congress passed "An Act to Protect Trade and Commerce and Unlawful Restraints and Monopolies"—more commonly known as the Sherman Antitrust Act or the Sherman Act.

The Sherman Act applies only to restraints that have a significant impact on commerce. Because Congress can regulate only interstate commerce, in principle only interstate commerce is affected by this act. State regulation of anticompetitive practices addresses purely local restraints on competition. Courts have construed the meaning of *interstate* commerce more and more broadly (except in the case of professional baseball), however, bringing even local activities within the purview of the Sherman Act if they have a significant anticompetitive effect on interstate commerce. The Sherman Act also extends to U.S. nationals abroad who are engaged in activities that have an effect on U.S. foreign commerce.

MAJOR PROVISIONS OF THE SHERMAN ACT

Sections 1 and 2 contain the main provisions of the Sherman Act:

Section 1: Every contract, combination in the form of a trust or otherwise, or conspiracy, in restraint of trade or commerce among the several States, or with foreign nations, is hereby declared to be illegal [and is a felony punishable by fine and/or imprisonment].

Section 2: Every person who shall monopolize, or attempt to monopolize, or combine or conspire with any other person or persons, to monopolize any part of the trade or commerce among the several States, or with foreign nations, shall be deemed guilty of a felony [and is similarly punishable].

These two sections of the Sherman Act are quite different. Section 1 requires two or more persons, because a person cannot contract, combine, or conspire alone.

▼ Thus, the essence of the illegal activity in Section 1 of the Sherman Act is the *act of joining together* to restrain trade or commerce.

Section 2 applies both to an individual person and to several people, because it uses the words *every person*. Thus, unilateral conduct can result in a violation of Section 2. The cases brought to court under Section 1 of the Sherman Act differ from those brought under Section 2. Section 1 cases are often concerned with finding an agreement (written or oral) that leads to a restraint of trade. Section 2 cases deal with the structure of a monopoly in the marketplace.

Whereas Section 1 focuses on agreements that are restrictive—that is, agreements that have a wrongful purpose—Section 2 looks at the so-called misuse of monopoly power in the marketplace. Both sections seek to curtail market practices that result in undesired monopoly pricing and output behavior. Any case brought under Section 2, however, must

2. 21 Congressional Record 2456 (1890).

▼ EXHIBIT 10–1 Major U.S. Antitrust Legislation

Legislation

Sherman Antitrust Act (1890)	**1. Major Provisions:**
	  a. Section 1—Prohibits contracts, combinations, and conspiracies in restraint of trade.
	    (1) Horizontal restraints subject to Section 1 include price-fixing arrangements, group boycotts (joint refusals to deal), horizontal trade association agreements, and joint ventures.
	    (2) Vertical restraints subject to Section 1 include territorial or customer restrictions, resale price maintenance agreements, and refusals to deal.
	  b. Section 2—Prohibits monopolies and attempts or conspiracies to monopolize.
	2. Interpretive Rules:
	  a. Rule of reason—Applied when an anticompetitive agreement may be justified by legitimate benefits. Under the rule of reason, the lawfulness of a trade restraint will be determined by the purpose and effects of the restraints.
	  b. *Per se* rule—Applied to restraints on trade that are so inherently anticompetitive that they cannot be justified and are deemed illegal as a matter of law.
	3. Jurisdictional Requirements—The Sherman Act applies only to activities that have a significant impact on interstate commerce.

Clayton Act (1914)	**Major Provisions:**
	1. Section 2—As amended in 1936 by the Robinson-Patman Act, prohibits price discrimination that substantially lessens competition and prohibits a seller engaged in interstate commerce from selling two or more buyers goods of similar grade and quality at different prices when the result is a substantial lessening of competition or the creation of a competitive injury.
	2. Section 3—Prohibits exclusionary practices, such as exclusive-dealing contracts and tying arrangements, when the effect may be to substantially lessen competition.
	3. Section 7—Prohibits mergers when the effect may be to substantially lessen competition or tend to create a monopoly.
	  a. Horizontal merger—The acquisition by merger or consolidation of a competing firm engaged in the same relevant market. Will be unlawful only if a merger results in the merging firms' holding a disproportionate share of the market, resulting in a substantial lessening of competition, and if the merger does not enhance consumer welfare by increasing efficiency of production or marketing.
	  b. Vertical merger—The acquisition by a seller of one of its buyers or vice versa. Will be unlawful if the merger prevents either merging firm from competing in a segment of the market that otherwise would be open to it, resulting in a substantial lessening of competition.

Federal Trade Commission Act (1914)	Prohibits unfair methods of competition; established and defined the powers of the Federal Trade Commission.

Enforcement of Antitrust Laws

Antitrust laws are enforced by the Department of Justice; by the Federal Trade Commission; and in some cases by private parties, who may be awarded treble damages and attorneys' fees.

Exemptions from Antitrust Laws

1. Labor unions (under Section 6 of the Clayton Act of 1914).
2. Agricultural associations (under Section 6 of the Clayton Act of 1914, the Capper-Volstead Act of 1922, and the Fisheries Cooperative Marketing Act of 1976).
3. Insurance—when state regulation exists (under the McCarran-Ferguson Act of 1945, as amended).
4. Export trading companies (under the Webb-Pomerane Act of 1918 and the Export Trading Act of 1982).
5. Professional baseball (by 1922 judicial decision).
6. Oil marketing (under the Interstate Oil Compact of 1935).
7. Other activities, including certain national defense actions, special research consortiums, state actions, and actions of certain regulated industries.

be one in which the "threshold" or "necessary" amount of monopoly power already exists. We will look at these two sections and the types of activities that they prohibit in greater detail when we discuss the enforcement of the Sherman Act.

Note that the Sherman Act does not tell businesses how they should act. It tells them how they should *not* act. In this sense, the act is *proscriptive* rather than *prescriptive*. It is the basis for *policing* rather than for *regulating* business conduct.

COURT RESPONSE TO THE SHERMAN ACT

Initially, the Sherman Act was stripped of any effectiveness as the courts interpreted it narrowly and refused to apply it to activities that today would constitute violations of Section 1 of the Sherman Act.[3] Then, in 1897, the United States Supreme Court swung the other way and declared illegal certain price-fixing agreements and territorial divisions on the ground that without exception, *every* restraint of trade was forbidden by Section 1 of the act. This absolutist position clearly could not hold for long. The Court retreated once again, first condemning only direct restraints in an 1898 case and then concluding twenty years later that restraints held lawful by common law should not be prohibited by the Sherman Act.

This change in the Court's view—from condemning every restraint of trade to making some exceptions—was expressed in the case against Standard Oil Company of New Jersey (1911). Beginning with this decision, a *rule of reason* was applied to certain types of anticompetitive agreements.

Rule of Reason Under the **rule of reason**, anticompetitive agreements are analyzed with the view that they may, in fact, constitute reasonable restraints of trade. When applying this rule, the court considers the purpose of the arrangement, the powers of the parties, and the effect of their actions in restraining trade. If the court deems that legitimate competitive benefits outweigh the anticompetitive effects of the agreement, the agreement will be held lawful (see *Managing Social Issues—Multicultural/Tolerance: Social Engineering at MIT* on pp. 282–83).

The need for the rule of reason is obvious. If the rule of reason had not been developed, virtually any business agreement conceivably could violate the Sherman Act. Justice Louis Brandeis effectively phrased this sentiment in *Chicago Board of Trade v. United States*, a case decided in 1918: "Every agreement concerning trade, every regulation of trade, restrains. To bind, to restrain is of their very essence. The true test of legality is whether the restraint imposed is such as merely regulates and perhaps thereby promotes competition or whether it is such as may suppress or even destroy competition."

Per Se Rule Certain kinds of restrictive contracts will not be judged under the rule of reason. Instead, they will be presumed illegal *per se*. *Per se* means "in itself" or "inherently," and *per se* **violations** are those that are deemed so inherently anticompetitive as to constitute unreasonable restraints of trade as a *matter of law*. Under the *per se* rule, there is no need to examine any other facts or evidence.

The *per se* standard was set forth in the classic case *United States v. Socony-Vacuum Oil Co.* (1940), in which the United States Supreme Court condemned all **price-fixing agreements** as unlawful *per se*. In footnote 59 of the opinion, which became the most famous footnote in antitrust law, Justice William O. Douglas wrote:

---

3. R. L. Miller and F. B. Cross, *The Legal and Regulatory Environment Today* (St. Paul: West Publishing Co., 1993), p. 580.

MANAGING SOCIAL ISSUES

MULTICULTURAL/TOLERANCE: SOCIAL ENGINEERING AT MIT

In 1989, the Department of Justice (DOJ) undertook an investigation of alleged price-fixing behavior among a group of the nation's most prestigious colleges and universities. The schools involved included the eight Ivy League institutions (Brown, Columbia, Cornell, Dartmouth, Harvard, Princeton, Yale, and the University of Pennsylvania) and the Massachusetts Institute of Technology (MIT). The DOJ learned that since 1958, these schools had met twice a year to trade information on the financial aid packages they would offer to incoming students and their families.

The Ivy Overlap Group

This so-called "Ivy Overlap Group" developed methods for analyzing students' financial needs; agreed not to award any merit scholarships; and compared and adjusted proposed "family contributions," or net tuition prices. The goal of each review meeting was to make sure that each of the ten thousand or so students who applied to more than one of the schools in the group would be offered the same basic financial aid package.

The Ivy Overlap Group also shared information about proposed tuition increases. Throughout a year, the universities exchanged data on proposed tuition increases for the following year and adjusted their tuition rates accordingly. They also discussed prices for room and board, which resulted in

similar rates being charged at a wide variety of universities. Room and board at Harvard, for example, which is located in very expensive Cambridge, Massachusetts, was the same as at Brown, which is in much less expensive Providence, Rhode Island.

The Ivy League schools and MIT argued that such meetings were necessary to prevent schools from engaging in a bidding war for talented students. According to the Ivy Overlap Group, because each school offered similar financial aid, students were free to choose a college based on academic, rather than financial, considerations. The DOJ refused to apply the rule of reason to the case and disagreed. After a two-year investigation, the DOJ charged the colleges with price fixing in violation of Section 1 of the Sherman Act..

MIT Stands Alone

In 1991 the Ivy League schools, citing the high costs of a prolonged court battle, entered into a consent decree with the DOJ in which they agreed that they would no longer discuss current financial aid information among themselves. MIT, however, confident of the integrity of its financial aid process, refused to give in and went to trial. The school argued that it had to keep its admission policies "need-blind" in order to continue upholding the social

[A] conspiracy to fix prices violates Section 1 of the Act though no overt act is shown, though it is not established that the conspirators had the means available for accomplishment of their objective, and though the conspiracy embraced but a part of the interstate or foreign commerce in the commodity. . . . Price-fixing agreements may or may not be aimed at complete elimination of price competition. The group making those agreements may or may not have the power to control the market. But the fact that the group cannot control the market prices does not necessarily mean that the agreement as to prices had no utility to the members of the combination. The effectiveness of price-fixing agreements is dependent on many factors, such as competitive tactics, position in the industry, the formula underlying price policies. Whatever economic justification particular price-fixing agreements may be thought to have, the law does not permit an inquiry into their reasonableness. They are all banned because of their actual potential threat to the central nervous system of the economy.

In addition to price-fixing arrangements, other types of activities discussed in the following sections—such as group boycotts, horizontal market divisions, and resale price maintenance agreements—are normally considered illegal *per se* under Section 1 of the Sherman Act.

MANAGING SOCIAL ISSUES: (CONTINUED)

ideal of equal opportunity to higher education. MIT believed that the Ivy Overlap Group, by promoting the socioeconomic diversity of its members, improved the overall quality of the schools and was acceptable under rule of reason standards. MIT also pointed out that by giving university access to the widest number of talented but needy students, the Ivy Overlap Group had actually increased consumer choice in the matter.

MIT lost at trial, as U.S. district court judge Louis C. Bechtle of Philadelphia ruled the Ivy Overlap Group "plainly anticompetitive." The court found that the agreements "created a horizontal restraint which interfered with the natural functioning of the marketplace by eliminating the student's ability to consider price differences when choosing a school and by depriving students of the ability to receive financial incentives which competition between those schools may have generated." A year later, however, the court of appeals reversed Bechtle's decision, stating that the lower court erred in its truncated rule of reason analysis by failing to "more fully investigate the procompetitive and noneconomic justifications proffered by MIT."

Eventually, in 1994, MIT and the DOJ settled the case. Under the agreement, MIT is not allowed to restore the Ivy Overlap Group process, but it can exchange limited information about financial aid policies with other need-blind institutions. Both sides declared victory. The Justice Department said it had received what it had strived for all along in discontinuing the Ivy Overlap Group process, which it believed cost entering students $1,000 to $2,000 more than if it had not existed. But MIT president Charles M. Vest said the settlement gave the school "98 percent" of what it had sought and would allow for a "more modern system to replace the overlap process."

For Critical Analysis:

After they signed the consent decrees, the Ivy League schools found that financial aid offers varied as much as $5,000 from school to school, and university officials were complaining about prospective students' haggling for the best aid package. Given MIT's arguments concerning the social benefits of the Ivy Overlap Group, does this result justify or contradict the institution's rule of reason defense?

SOURCE: Information from "MIT Held to Violate Antitrust Law with Scholarship Policies," *Liability Week*, September 8, 1992, p. 24; "Government, MIT Settle Ivies Price-Fix Case," *FTC Watch*, January 17, 1994, p. 11; and S. Stecklow and W. M. Bulkley, "Antitrust Case against MIT Is Dropped Allowing Limited Exchange of Aid Data," *Wall Street Journal*, December 23, 1993, p. A 12.

ENFORCEMENT OF THE SHERMAN ACT

The Sherman Act is enforced by the Justice Department, and in some cases private parties can also sue for damages or other remedies. The courts have determined that the test of ability to sue depends on the directness of the injury suffered by the would-be plaintiff.

▼ **Therefore, a person wishing to sue under the Sherman Act must prove (1) that the antitrust violation either directly caused or was at least a substantial factor in causing the injury that was suffered and (2) that the unlawful actions of the accused party affected business activities of the plaintiff that were protected by antitrust laws.**

One of the unique features of the Sherman Antitrust Act is that it allows any person injured as a result of violations of the act to bring a suit for treble damages against the defendants, in addition to reasonable attorneys' fees.

Any person found guilty of violating the Sherman Act is subject to criminal prosecution for a felony. Currently, if convicted, a person can be fined up to $350,000, imprisoned for three years, or both. A corporation can be fined a maximum $10 million, which was the record penalty U.S. West paid in 1991 for violating antitrust law in the telephone industry. The Department of Justice can simultaneously institute civil proceedings to restrain the conduct that is in violation of the act. The various remedies that the Justice Department has asked the courts to impose include **divestiture** (making a company give up one or more of its operating functions) and dissolution.[4]

Generally, anticompetitive actions fall into two broad categories: horizontal trade restraints and vertical trade restraints.

SECTION 1 VIOLATIONS—HORIZONTAL RESTRAINTS

Horizontal trade restraints are those resulting from concerted action by direct competitors in the marketplace. Price-fixing agreements, as previously discussed, fall into this category. Other horizontal trade restraints subject to Section 1 include group boycotts, horizontal market divisions, trade association activities, and joint ventures.

Group Boycotts   Any agreement by two or more sellers to refuse to deal with, or to boycott, a particular person or firm is prohibited by the Sherman Act. Such **group boycotts**, or joint refusals to deal, have been held to constitute *per se* violations of Section 1 of the Sherman Act. Section 1 will be violated if it can be demonstrated that the boycott or joint refusal to deal was undertaken with the intent of eliminating competition or preventing entry into a given market. Some boycotts, such as group boycotts against a supplier for political reasons, may be protected under the First Amendment right to freedom of expression.

Horizontal Market Divisions   It is a *per se* violation of Section 1 of the Sherman Act for competitors to divide up territories or customers. For example, manufacturers A, B, and C compete against one another in the states of Kansas, Nebraska, and Iowa. By agreement, A sells products only in Kansas, B sells only in Nebraska, and C sells only in Iowa. This concerted action reduces costs and allows all three (assuming there is no other competition) to raise the price of goods sold in their respective states. It is also a violation of the Sherman Act.

The same violation would take place if A, B, and C had simply agreed that A would sell only to institutional purchasers (school districts, universities, state agencies and departments, cities, and so forth) in the three states, B only to wholesalers, and C only to retailers.

Trade Associations   Businesses within the same general industry or profession frequently organize trade associations to pursue common interests. Their joint activities may provide for exchanges of information, representation of the members' business interests before government bodies, and the setting of regulatory standards to govern their industry or profession. The rule of reason is applied to many of these horizontal actions. For example, if a court finds that a trade association practice or agreement that restrains trade is nonetheless sufficiently beneficial both to the association and to the public, it may deem the restraint reasonable. Other trade association agreements may have such substantially anticompetitive effects that the court will consider them to be in violation of Section 1 of the Sherman Act. In 1978, for example, the United States Supreme Court held that the Society of Professional Engineers' Code of Ethics—which prohibited the discussion of

---

4. G. D. Webster, "Avoiding Antitrust Liability," *Association Management*, January 1995, p. 167.

prices with a potential customer until the customer had chosen an engineer—was a Section 1 violation. The Supreme Court found that this ban on competitive bidding was "nothing less than a frontal assault on the basic policy of the Sherman Act."[5]

Joint Ventures Joint ventures undertaken by competitors are also subject to antitrust laws. A **joint venture** is an (increasingly popular) undertaking by two or more individuals or firms for a specific purpose. In fiscal year 1995, the Department of Justice received eighty-nine petitions for clearance of joint ventures, up from twenty-one a decade earlier. This escalation has been attributed mainly to pressures from foreign competitors. In the past, some American companies so dominated their industries that there was little need for outside help. Now, however, these companies may need to improve technology or generate new products so quickly that they turn to former competitors for assistance. In the 1980s, for example, American automakers formed joint ventures with Japanese counterparts to produce consumer-friendly small, inexpensive automobiles.[6]

The rule of reason applies to these ventures. Whether a joint venture will be considered a violation of the Sherman Act will depend on whether the companies can show a legitimate reason for the enterprise, such as research or innovation, that offsets its anticompetitive effects.

SECTION 1 VIOLATIONS—VERTICAL RESTRAINTS

Vertical trade restraints involve the distribution of goods and arise from agreements made between firms at different levels in the distribution process.[7] Vertical restraints subject to Section 1 of the Sherman Act include territorial or customer restrictions and resale price maintenance agreements.

Territorial or Customer Restrictions In arranging for the distribution of its products, a manufacturer often wishes to insulate dealers from direct competition with other dealers selling the firm's products. In this endeavor, they may institute territorial restrictions, or they may attempt to prohibit wholesalers or retailers from reselling the products to certain classes of buyers, such as competing retailers.[8] For example, distributors for Anheuser-Busch, Miller Brewing, and other domestic brewer franchises are limited in the geographical area to which they can ship their product. Similar situations exist with automobile and mattress distributorships.

Resale Price Maintenance Agreements Resale price maintenance agreements— also known as *fair trade agreements*—arise when manufacturers specify what the minimum retail prices of their products must be. For many years, such vertical agreements were authorized under *fair trade laws*. Today, these vertical agreements are normally considered *per se* violations of Section 1 of the Sherman Act. Although manufacturers are allowed to determine the retail prices of their products when they are sold through their own stores or outlets, they may only *suggest* retail prices for their products when they are sold by independent retailers (see *Company Focus: Saturn* on pp. 286–87).

---

5. Miller and Cross, *op. cit.*, p. 585.
6. N. Templin, "Strange Bedfellows: More and More Firms Enter Joint Ventures with Big Competitors," *Wall Street Journal*, November 1, 1995, p. A1.
7. D. Reiffen and M. Vita, "Comment: Is There New Thinking on Vertical Mergers?" *Antitrust Law Journal*, Spring 1995, p. 917.
8. S. J. Hoch and S. Banerji, "When Do Private Labels Succeed?" *Sloan Management Review*, Summer 1994, p. 431.

COMPANY FOCUS: SATURN

PRICE FIXING IN THE SHOW ROOM?

When Pittsburgh businessman Ty Ballou bought a Nissan Altima automobile in 1994, he found the right price but not the right feeling. "I got a good deal, but I had to exert way too much emotion to get it done," he says. "It left me with a bad taste in my mouth." The experience led Ballou to conclude that he would "rather pay more and know I got a good price, though maybe not the lowest price, than have to go through the anxiety of haggling."

Ballou is hardly unique among automobile consumers. A survey by J. D. Power & Associates in 1992 showed that 68 percent of customers said they dreaded haggling with car salespersons. Many people, furthermore, simply do not want to take the time to bargain for an auto. In 1990, General Motors's independent Saturn unit revamped its sales techniques to respond to this consumer demand and pioneered the "no-haggle" strategy for selling its product. That approach contributed to Saturn's overnight success story and inspired many imitations in the industry. The Justice Department, however, is beginning to think that the no-haggle blueprint is an illegal vertical agreement.

The "No-Haggle" Concept

The concept behind the no-haggle strategy is as simple as the name itself. It likens the pricing of a car to the pricing of a pineapple or a paperback. Just as consumers do not expect to have to bargain for those items, Saturn consumers no longer have to bargain for automobiles. The list price on Saturn's product is not the starting point for future negotiations; it is the price of the car. Saturn trains its managers and salespersons in low-pressure techniques, creating the antithesis of the stereotypical "car shark." Dealers are given relatively large territories, so they find themselves competing against other companies rather than one another.

The "pamper instead of pressure" scheme resulted in an impressive word-of-mouth campaign among consumers, and by the summer of 1993 Saturn was selling twice as many cars per dealer than Toyota Motor Company, the closest competitor. At the same time, dealers were having a hard time keeping up with demand; they had on average a ten-day supply of cars on hand—representing one-sixth normal stock.

The trend was not long in spreading to other divisions of General Motors. The auto giant began using the no-haggle

Refusals to Deal Refusals to deal—group boycotts—were discussed earlier as a prohibited horizontal activity. In vertical trade agreements, even though manufacturers are not permitted to set retail prices for their products, they can refuse to deal with retailers or dealers that cut prices to levels substantially below the manufacturers' suggested retail prices. In 1919, the Supreme Court held that a manufacturer did not violate the Sherman Act by refusing to sell its product to price-cutting retailers. The Court emphasized that a firm can deal with whomever it chooses.[9]

SECTION 2 VIOLATIONS—MONOPOLIZATION

Section 2 of the Sherman Act makes it unlawful to "monopolize or attempt to monopolize." As mentioned earlier, a violation of Section 1 of the Sherman Act requires at least two persons, because the nature of the violation is a contract, a trust arrangement, or a conspiracy to restrain trade. Section 2 can be violated by a single firm if it intentionally obtains or maintains monopoly power.

The Sherman Act does not define **monopoly**. Theoretically, a pure monopoly exists when only one firm controls the market for a particular product or service. In practice,

---

9. Miller and Cross, *op. cit.*, p. 587.

COMPANY FOCUS: (CONTINUED)

strategy in concert with "value pricing" to rescue the ailing Oldsmobile division. In value pricing, the list price of a car includes charges for popular options such as power steering or air conditioning; this strategy offers consumers a lower overall price but requires them to accept all the options. Ford Motor Company began to use the sales methods with its Escort and Thunderbird coupe models, and it found similar success.

Hints of Price Fixing

In 1994, as the no-haggle strategy and value pricing became more popular—practiced in about 5 percent of the nation's dealerships—the Justice Department launched a probe into whether these strategies violated antitrust law. At question was the issue of vertical agreements known as vertical pricing, or the imposition of minimum prices by manufacturers. The law is primarily aimed toward keeping manufacturers from requiring discount stores to charge a comparatively high minimum price for their products. The question is not

whether Saturn and other dealers are fixing prices. The concern at the Justice Department is whether they are doing so at the expense of the consumer. One dealer called the investigation "a giant fishing expedition," but industry analysts note that Saturn outlets do seem to agree not to undercut one another and, as we have seen, are consequently enjoying enormous success.

The New Bottom Line

In 1994, an Oregon consulting group found that the prices at no-haggle dealerships were actually around 3 percent higher than at the "haggling" show rooms. If Saturn customers are willing to pay more for the convenience of the no-haggle approach, then not only does the Department of Justice have a weak case but the technique also will no doubt spread in the future.

SOURCE: Information from R. L. Simpson and N. Templin, "Car Hagglers May Still Drive Best Car Deals," *Wall Street Journal*, October 12, 1994, p. B1; L. Brydoff, "Dealers Try New Strategy: The No-Haggle Price Tag," *San Diego Business Journal*, August 31, 1992, p. 15; D. Woodruff, "Saturn—GM Finally Has a Winner," *Business Week*, August 17, 1992, p. 86; and D. Levin, "U.S. Launches Antitrust Probe of Auto Dealers," *Wall Street Journal*, October 11, 1994, p. A3.

however, a company may be regarded as *monopolizing* a market when it acts aggressively to exclude competitors. In 1966, the United States Supreme Court held that the following two elements are required to establish a Section 2 violation:[10]

1. The *possession of monopoly power* in the relevant market.
2. The *willful acquisition or maintenance of that power* as distinguished from growth or development as a consequence of a superior product, business acumen, or historical accident.

THE CLAYTON ACT

In 1914, Congress attempted to strengthen federal antitrust laws by enacting the Clayton Act. The Clayton Act was aimed at specific monopolistic practices that substantially reduced competition or that could lead to monopoly power but that were not clearly prohibited by the Sherman Act. The Clayton Act is enforced by both the Justice Department

---

10. *United States v. Grinnell Corp.*, 384 U.S. 563, 86 S.Ct. 1698, 16 L.Ed.2d 778 (1966).

and the Federal Trade Commission (FTC). Created in 1914, the FTC is an administrative agency with the authority to conduct investigations relating to alleged violations of antitrust law, to make reports and recommendations to Congress regarding regulations, and most important, to promulgate interpretive rules and general statements of policy with regard to unfair or deceptive acts or practices. Private parties may sue for treble damages and attorneys' fees under the Clayton Act, just as they may under the Sherman Act.

SECTION 2—PRICE DISCRIMINATION

Section 2 of the Clayton Act prohibits **price discrimination**, which occurs when a seller charges different prices to different buyers for the same product. Because some businesses circumvented Section 2, Congress strengthened this section by amending it with the passage of the Robinson-Patman Act in 1936. As amended, Section 2 prohibits price discrimination except in cases in which the differences are due to differences in costs (production, transportation, or promotional costs, for example). To violate Section 2, the price discriminator must be engaged in interstate commerce, and the price discrimination must lessen competition substantially.[11] The Robinson-Patman Act also prohibits sellers from selectively cutting prices to levels substantially below those charged by their competitors, unless such pricing practices can be justified by demonstrating that the lower price in one locality was charged "in good faith to meet an equally low price of a competitor."[12]

SECTION 3—EXCLUSIONARY PRACTICES

Under Section 3 of the Clayton Act, sellers or lessors cannot sell or lease "on the condition, agreement or understanding that the . . . purchaser or lessee thereof shall not use or deal in the goods . . . of a competitor of the seller." In effect, this section prohibits two types of vertical agreements involving exclusionary practices—exclusive-dealing contracts and tying arrangements.

Exclusive-Dealing Contracts **Exclusive-dealing contracts** arise when a seller or manufacturer forbids a buyer to purchase the products of the seller's competitors. An exclusive-dealing contract is prohibited when the effect of the contract is "to substantially lessen competition or tend to create a monopoly." The leading exclusive-dealing contract decision is that of *Standard Oil Co. of California v. United States* (1949). In this case, the largest gasoline seller in the nation made exclusive-dealing contracts with independent service stations in seven western states. These contracts involved 16 percent of all retail outlets, whose sales were approximately 7 percent of all retail sales in that market. The United States Supreme Court found that these contracts were in violation of Section 3 of the Clayton Act.

Tying Arrangements In a **tying arrangement**, the seller of a product conditions the sale of that product on the buyer's agreement to purchase another product manufactured or distributed by the seller. The legality of such arrangements depends on many factors, particularly the business purpose or effect of the arrangement. In 1936, for example, the United States Supreme Court held that International Business Machines's practice of requiring the purchase of punch cards (the tied product) as a condition of leasing its tabulation machines

---

11. L. Ianello and B. Maxey, "Claims of Price-Fixing Nip at Industry's Heels," *Journal of Commerce and Commercial Affairs,* June 20, 1991, p. 8A.
12. Miller and Cross, *op. cit.,* p. 591.

(the tying product) was unlawful. In 1917, however, the Court had ruled in favor of U.S. Steel despite the tie-in between the purchase of prefabricated homes and credit. Because there was no evidence that U.S. Steel had significant economic power in either the prefabricated-home market or the credit market, its arrangement was found to be lawful.

Today, manufacturer-authorized service centers are often required to use only the manufacturer's spare parts when repairing the product in question. The Supreme Court has ruled that in some circumstances, such tying arrangements are illegal. In 1985, Eastman Kodak Company announced that it would no longer sell replacement parts for its photocopiers to customers unless they also agreed *not* to have their equipment serviced by independent companies. Two years later, eighteen of those independent service companies sued Kodak and claimed an illegal tying arrangement. Kodak argued that because it does not dominate the photocopier market, it could not possibly dominate the parts market. The Court ruled in 1992, however, that such practices were *per se* illegal, a view disputed by many economists.

SECTION 7—MERGERS

Under Section 7 of the Clayton Act, a person or business organization cannot hold stock and/or assets in another business "where the effect . . . may be to substantially lessen competition." This section is the statutory authority for preventing mergers that could result in monopoly power or a substantial lessening of competition in the marketplace.

Horizontal Mergers Both the Federal Trade Commission and the Antitrust Division of the U.S. Justice Department have established guidelines to determine the legality of **horizontal mergers**—mergers between competitors. Whether the merger will be legal is based on the degree of concentration of market shares of merging firms, although the United States Supreme Court has indicated that it will look at other potential effects of the merger as well.

Mergers are permitted when they enhance consumer welfare by increasing efficiency, so long as they do not increase the probability of horizontal collusion. Sometimes horizontal mergers are seen as a last refuge for financially troubled corporations. When the Syntex Corporation lost patents on the prescription painkillers Naprosyn (naproxen) and Anaprox (naproxen sodium), the drug company found it could not sustain an acceptable rate of return. In order to survive, it agreed to a horizontal merger with Switzerland's Roche Holding Ltd., which created the world's fourth largest drug company. "[Syntex] couldn't have survived in a very highly competitive health care market by themselves," said an industry analyst.[13]

Vertical Mergers **Vertical mergers** occur when a company at one stage of production acquires a company at a different stage of production. Thus, the acquisition of a tire plant by an automobile manufacturer would constitute a backward vertical integration, whereas the automaker's acquisition of a car rental agency would constitute a forward vertical integration. Similarly, the $16.5 billion merger between Capital Cities/ABC and Walt Disney Company in 1995 created a single production and distribution giant unrivaled in the industry. Just one of the benefits of the merger is that Disney gained control of ABC's cartoon programming division, which provided Disney with a guaranteed outlet for its product.[14]

---

13. D. Olmos, "Roche Will Acquire Syntex for $5.3 Billion," *Los Angeles Times*, May 3, 1994, p. D1.
14. E. Jensen, "'What's Up Doc?' 'Vertical Integration,'" *Wall Street Journal*, October 16, 1995, p. B1.

Michael Eisner (left) shakes hands with Thomas Murphy, Chairman of Capital Cities/ABC, Inc., during a news conference on July 31, 1995 prior to Disney's acquiring Capital Cities/ABC, Inc. in a $19 billion merger.

The FTC's approach to vertical mergers depends on a number of factors, including characteristics identified as impeding competition.[15] For example, the commission will attack any vertical merger that prevents competitors of either party from competing in a segment of the market that would otherwise be open to them. AT&T's planned $12.6 billion acquisition of McCaw Cellular Communications in 1993 drew the attention of the Justice Department because AT&T makes equipment—such as radio towers—that some of McCaw's competitors use in their cellular operations. Government officials worried that AT&T could use its position to charge McCaw's competitors a higher rate and provide them with poor service. The Justice Department eventually approved the merger and issued a consent decree that AT&T's equipment and long-distance divisions would have to be insulated from McCaw's cellular service.

Conglomerate Mergers Conglomerate mergers—mergers between firms in unrelated industries—often extend product lines at the retail level, particularly among products that are complementary (although conglomerate mergers can also occur between firms using similar suppliers). A large number of conglomerate mergers, however, occur when merging firms have no direct functional business link. Such mergers involve no changes in market structure, market shares, or concentration ratios. In many cases, conglomerate mergers reduce overhead costs by spreading them over a larger range of output and reducing advertising and other promotional costs.

The 1960s saw numerous conglomerate mergers. Such mergers presented a special challenge to the courts, because the antitrust laws offered little guidance in regard to these noncompetitive mergers. Rather than formulate a general principle or rule applicable to all conglomerate mergers, the courts have tended to look at the pragmatic, real-world effects of

---

15. S. Chatterjee, "Gains in Vertical Acquisitions and Market Power: Theory and Evidence," *Academy of Management Journal*, June 1991, p. 436.

business conglomerations and make their determinations on a case-by-case basis.[16] A landmark case in the 1960s was *Federal Trade Commission v. Procter & Gamble Co.*

The Procter & Gamble Company had acquired Clorox Chemical Company. At the time of the merger, Clorox was the leading manufacturer of household bleach in a highly concentrated market. Purex, the major competitor, did not sell its product in some markets. Procter & Gamble was a large conglomerate. Its large advertising budget, along with other factors, allowed it to enjoy economic advantages in advertising its products. The FTC brought an antitrust action against Procter & Gamble on the ground that its acquisition of Clorox would substantially lessen competition in the household liquid bleach market. The FTC believed that if Procter & Gamble advertised extensively, Clorox's market share would increase. The federal agency prevailed, and Procter & Gamble had to divest itself of Clorox Chemical Company.

In the 1990s, many corporate conglomerate mergers were "undone"—that is, many conglomerates started selling off unrelated businesses in order to specialize in their major business. For example, Sears, Roebuck spun off its insurance business, Allstate; Eastman Kodak sold Sterling Winthrop, its pharmaceutical subsidiary, to a French company; and General Electric divested itself of its aerospace business for more than $3 billion.

ANTITRUST LAW AND BUSINESS

"People of the same trade," once wrote Adam Smith, "seldom meet together, even for merriment and diversion, but the conversation ends in a conspiracy against the public, or in some contrivance to raise prices." Indeed,

▼ **Mistrust of business, especially big business, has been a driving force behind antitrust law.**

In its infancy, antitrust law had a variety of goals, both economic and social. Economically, its primary intent was to preserve competition and uphold the principles of capitalism inherent in offering the best available goods and services at the best available prices. Socially, antitrust laws were conceived to help the "underdog," a popular American folk hero. Inherent in a democracy is the belief that all citizens have equal access to the means for economic advancement, or as lore would have it, the ability to "pull themselves up by their bootstraps." In this sense, antitrust laws were guardians of democratic principles; they allowed the mom-and-pop corner convenience store to coexist with the supermarket down the street.

In the past century, as Americans have come to take certain aspects of democracy for granted, antitrust law has become less concerned with its social aspects and primarily concerned with its economic duties of preserving optimal competition. The various rules and regulations we have discussed in this chapter are geared toward strengthening the values of the capitalist system by not allowing a single firm or a consortium of firms to hold an improper amount of influence in the marketplace.

ANTITRUST AND THE CONSUMER

Although some free market economists, such as Milton Friedman, would argue that the interests of business and society are the same, government regulation through antitrust

---

16. L. Reynolds, "Merger Mania," *Management Review*, April 1994, p. 30.

law is in large part based on protecting the public from Smith's "conspiracy." Historically, some of the nation's preeminent legal minds have seen antitrust law as a tool to promote consumer welfare. They use the following reasoning: "Competition, the ultimate guarantor of efficiency in a market economy, is, quite simply, price competition. Prices that are fixed, not by competitive market forces but by a monopolist or a cartel, will cause attainable output to be forgone, costs to be higher, and consumer welfare thus to be reduced below some realizable level."[17]

The federal government's commitment to protecting consumer welfare has risen steadily since the heyday of the trustbusters at the turn of the century. During the presidential term of the renowned trustbuster Theodore Roosevelt (1901–1909), there were five lawyers in the Justice Department Antitrust Division; under President Franklin D. Roosevelt (1933–1945), that number grew to several hundred.[18] The Reagan administration slashed antitrust staff by 60 percent, but Reagan's successors have rebuilt the division. The Department of Justice has been more active under Clinton than it was under his two predecessors (see *Exhibit 10–2*).

Although numbers of antitrust suits have been pursued by the government regardless of the political party in power, the target of antitrust law is closely linked to the dominant economic theories in Washington. Theodore Roosevelt called himself a "trustbuster" and reflected the nation's mistrust of concentrated economic power with his administration's successful efforts to "bust" Standard Oil and American Tobacco. Enforcement lagged in the *"laissez-faire"* 1920s and the early years of Franklin D. Roosevelt's New Deal, but antitrust powers were strengthened in the late 1930s and again in the early 1950s. In the 1960s, the federal government focused on horizontal and vertical integration. By the 1970s, increased government intervention led to a very broad definition of what constituted anticompetitive business activities.

During the 1980s, under Ronald Reagan, the Department of Justice was mainly concerned with one aspect of anticompetitive activity: price fixing.[19] The trend of enforcement in the last decade of the twentieth century has been somewhere in the middle: too far reaching in the minds of many businesspersons and too limited for business-watchdog organizations.[20] In the 1990s some companies, such as software giant Microsoft Corporation, believe that the federal government's antitrust division has forgotten the advice of the prominent jurist Learned Hand (1872–1961), who once wrote, "The successful competitor, having been urged to compete, must not be turned upon when he wins."

MONOPOLIES AND THE CONSUMER

Historically, monopolies have often been considered something of a cancer in the free market. The basis for this thinking is fear: What could the business magnate desire beyond a monopoly? With no opposition, he or she could set the conditions under which a product or service could be sold and delivered, as well as set prices based on greed rather than free market competition.

This popularly held view is not completely in keeping with economic theory. For example, if one firm owned the means for production of all oranges in the United States, that firm would not price an orange at $20. Presumably, if the price were too high, consumers

---

17. P. M. Boarman, "Antitrust Laws in a Global Market," *Challenge*, January–February 1993, p. 32.
18. "Antitrust: Perceptions and Reality in Coping with Big Business," Harvard Business School Case No. 9-391-292, June 30, 1992, p. 21.
19. "Antitrust Analgesic," *Wall Street Journal*, September 25, 1991, p. A10.
20. M. P. Sharfman and J. W. Dean, Jr., "Conceptualizing and Measuring the Organizational Environment: A Multidimensional Approach," *Journal of Management*, December 1991, p. 681.

▼ **EXHIBIT 10–2 Number of Federal Antitrust Suits since 1981**

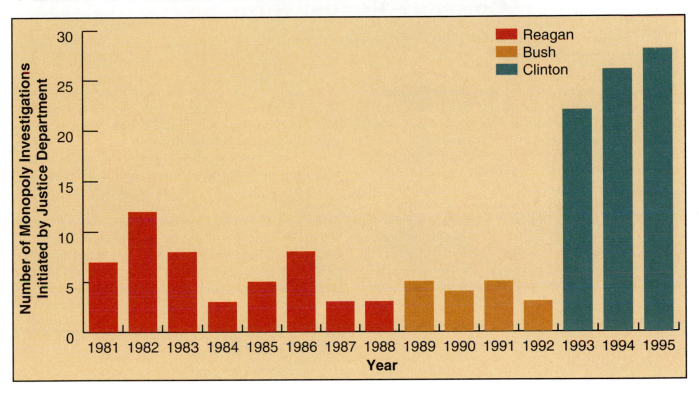

SOURCE: U.S. Department of Justice.

would switch to grapefruits for their citrus intake. Of course, some products, such as a life-saving drug produced by one company, do not have many, if any, **substitutes**, or products that can fill a market gap in a monopolistic situation.

Even with products that have no substitutes, however, a monopolist cannot charge just any price. After all, those who demand the monopolized product with few or no substitutes still have an income constraint. They cannot pay any price at all, because they have income limitations. Thus, even a pure monopolist has a profit-maximizing price, and it is certainly far less than infinite. Although it is true that if one were able magically to transform a pure monopoly into a set of perfect competitors, the price would fall, it would not fall from some astronomical price to some trivial one. We have examples of what happens when a monopoly becomes a more competitive industry. When the airlines were deregulated, prices fell, sometimes dramatically. The same is true for long-distance phone service and for interstate trucking. Prices, however, did not fall by, say, 95 percent. Rather, in some cases they fell by 20 or 30 percent over time. The point is that even pure monopolists are constrained by (1) possible substitutes (however imperfect) and (2) people's limited budgets.

Anticompetitive Behavior Monopoly power is not illegal in and of itself. Recall that there are two elements to the offense of monopolization. In addition to monopoly power, there is the requirement of willful acquisition or maintenance of that power.

▼ A dominant market share may be the result of business acumen or the development of a superior product, or it may simply be the result of a historic accident.

COMPANY FOCUS: NUTRASWEET
THE END OF A MONOPOLY

"From a business standpoint, there's no difference to us between December 14 and December 15 [1992]," said a spokesman for NutraSweet Company. "We are committed to remaining the low-cost producer of aspartame in the U.S. and in other markets in the world."

The spokesman, however, had to know that there was indeed quite a difference for NutraSweet between those two days. On midnight of December 14, the company lost its U.S. patent for aspartame, the sweetener ingredient that launched a revolution in the diet soft-drink industry in the 1980s. The patent had created a decade-long monopoly situation for the company, and how it reacted to competitive pressures would indicate exactly how much different December 15 was to be from the ten preceding years.

Patent Benefits

By the early 1990s, people in the United States were consuming about 8,000 metric tons of aspartame a year, or 80 percent of its world market. The substance—which is almost two hundred times sweeter than sugar—could be found in more than five thousand different products, from Diet Coke and Diet Pepsi to the Equal tabletop sweetener. Thanks to the aspartame patent, NutraSweet and its parent, Monsanto Company, had a virtual lock on the annual $700 million domestic aspartame market.

The most immediate effect of the expired patent would be in the price of aspartame. It previously sold for approximately $45 a pound; the competitive market dropped the price to $30 a pound. NutraSweet officials predicted that the drop would cut the company's annual sales by $250 million in 1993. NutraSweet had other worries as well, such as backlash from customers who had not appreciated the company's classic monopoly practice of charging immoderate prices for aspartame. The company had also insisted that any product using aspartame be emblazoned with the red-and-white NutraSweet swirl. "If we were able to satisfy ourselves that we wouldn't lose any business [by breaking ties with NutraSweet], we would make a change, based on our feelings," said the disgruntled chief executive officer of a New York-based soft-drink bottler.

Filling the Breach

There was no shortage of companies eager to fill the breach. The Holland Sweetener Company (HSC), a joint venture between Dutch and Japanese conglomerates, captured between 35 and 40 percent of the aspartame markets in Europe and Canada when NutraSweet's patent expired in those regions, and HSC planned a similar campaign in the United States.

NutraSweet will also face competition from Johnson & Johnson's sucralose, which is six hundred times sweeter than sugar, and Pfizer, Inc.'s, altamane, which is two thousand times sweeter than sugar. Sucralose was approved for use in Canada during the fall of 1991, and within a year it was the featured sweetener in a number of products, including the soft drinks Orange Crush and Hires Root Beer. Unlike aspartame, sucralose has the benefit of being able to withstand enough heat to be used in baking.

NutraSweet's Strategy

NutraSweet officials dismiss the notion that the patent expiration was a death knell for the company. "One of the nice things about a patent is that the day you get it, you know

COMPANY FOCUS: (CONTINUED)

when it will expire," said Larry Williams, president and chief executive officer of NutraSweet. "So since the day NutraSweet was approved, we've always had a program."

The company accomplished at least part of that program by signing supply agreements with PepsiCo, Inc., and Coca-Cola Company that would keep the two giants using NutraSweet in their products well after the patent ended. This move assured the company dominance in the soft-drink industry, which purchases almost three-quarters of the aspartame sold in the United States. NutraSweet has a new and improved version of aspartame—Sweetener 2000,

which is ten thousand times sweeter than sugar—and the company hopes to have it on the market by the turn of the century.

The New Bottom Line

True monopoly situations for a company are rare, and even when they do exist they are bound to be relatively short lived. Instead of relying on its patent, NutraSweet planned for its expiration. Thus, although the aspartame market will not be as lucrative, the company should continue to prosper.

SOURCE: Information from I. Cintron, "NutraSweet Deadline Nears as HSC Enters US Market," Chemical Marketing Reporter, December 7, 1992, p. 5; A. M. Freedman and R. Gibson, "Monsanto Touts New Sugar Substitute As Sweetest Yet," Wall Street Journal, March 29, 1991, p. B1; "ISO Report Forecasts Sharp Drop in Aspartame Prices in December," Washington Beverage Insight, January 31, 1992, p. 1; A. Naude, "Sweet Dreams," Chemical Marketing Reporter, June 15, 1992, p. 8; and E. DeNitto, "NutraSweet: Refining a Taste for Success," Supermarket News, August 3, 1992, p. 23.

There are many instances in which a patent has given a company *de facto* monopoly control of a market niche (see *Company Focus: NutraSweet*). None of these situations should give rise to antitrust concerns. Indeed, the existence of a **natural monopoly** can sometimes be in the consumer's best interest.

Natural Monopolies A natural monopoly may occur when production rates increase and average per-unit costs fall continuously. A natural monopoly will exist if one firm is able to take advantage of these declining average costs per unit well ahead of any other firm. Once a natural monopoly is established, no other firm at smaller rates of production can come close to competing with the natural monopolist. Consumers might benefit from such a situation and pay much lower prices for the product or service in question as long as the natural monopolist is allowed to produce with minimal government regulation or antitrust scrutiny.

Intent Required Monopoly power, in and of itself, does not constitute the offense of monopolization under Section 2 of the Sherman Act. The offense also requires intent to monopolize. Devising a new low-cost production method and developing and producing better products all hurt rival competitors, but they are not anticompetitive activities. Such actions do not injure competition; they are rather a result of competition.

The intent requirement is, of course, difficult to determine legally. Only from the evidence can the courts infer that a firm had monopoly power and engaged in anticompetitive activities. Even a firm's unilateral refusal to deal with another individual or organization is generally considered permissible. In one instance, however, the Supreme Court declared that it was not allowed.

In the 1970s, the Aspen Ski Company had acquired ownership of three major ski areas in the Aspen, Colorado, area: Ajax (Aspen Mountain), Buttermilk (mainly for beginners), and Snowmass. Another area in the immediate vicinity, Aspen Highlands, was owned by the Aspen Highlands Skiing Corporation. The Aspen Ski Company discontinued its all-

Aspen ticket, which had been usable at all four areas, and replaced it with a three-area ticket that covered only its own facilities. After this occurred, Aspen Highlands's share of the local downhill skiing market declined from over 20 percent in 1976–1977 to 11 percent in 1980–1981. The Aspen Highlands Skiing Corporation filed an antitrust complaint against the Aspen Ski Company alleging that the latter had monopolized the market for downhill skiing service in the Aspen area. It further argued that the discontinuation of the all-Aspen ticket was a purposeful act with intent to monopolize the market. The U.S. district court and the U.S. circuit court of appeals agreed, and finally so did the United States Supreme Court.[21]

Predatory Pricing Among monopolization cases, **predatory pricing**—selling below cost—is one form of conduct that is seen as particularly harmful to the consumer.[22] At first, this reasoning may seem contradictory. Don't consumers benefit from low prices? If a firm sells a valuable product for a price below cost, then isn't it the firm that loses, not the customer? According to antitrust law, the answer to these questions is in many cases yes. Despite the fact that consumers benefit from low prices, however, predatory pricing is still condemned.

Condemnation of predatory pricing is based on the fear that although it may benefit consumers with low prices in the short term, in the longer run it will harm competition. The harm feared is that a rich rival, by pricing below its competitors' costs, could drive competitors out of the market by outlasting them during the phase when prices are below cost. In the subsequent phase, the rich rival would still be in the market but would no longer face any competitors, creating a monopoly. That firm would then be free to reap large profits by raising the price far above what it had been when the firm faced market competition.

Nevertheless, there are procompetitive reasons not only for low prices but even for prices below cost. Such pricing may be, for example, the only way in which a new firm can gain a toehold in a market populated by proven firms, especially if the latter have established brand name recognition in the market. Preventing the entry of new competitors into a market by forbidding them to use low prices, perhaps even prices below cost, would hinder rather than promote competition.

Faced with this uncertainty as to the purpose and effect of firms' pricing decisions, courts have struggled to invent a workable standard for judging predatory pricing. Some courts look at market structure in deciding predatory pricing cases. Under this approach, courts look at the potential for harm to consumers created by a firm's below-cost pricing. If it appears that a firm pricing below cost will be unable to capture monopoly profits at a later time, the courts reject any attempt to discern intent. The essence of the market approach is that if the firm is unlikely to capture monopoly profits through higher prices in the future, intent does not matter. Consumers benefit from the low prices regardless (see the *Case—Wal-Mart: Price Strategy Issues*—at the end of this chapter).

MERGERS AND THE CONSUMER

In the eyes of antitrust law, if a business interest cannot manage a monopoly situation, it will attempt the next best thing—to create a merger, or a union of two or more business entities in which all the property of those entities is held by the resulting firm. Whereas

21. *Aspen Ski Company v. Aspen Highlands Skiing Corporation* (1985).
22. J. B. Baker, "Predatory Pricing after Brooke Group: An Economic Perspective," *Antitrust Law Journal,* Spring 1994, p. 585.

pure monopolies are generally nonexistent, mergers are relatively common in the business world. In fact, the mid-1990s saw a veritable explosion of mergers, which caused one observer to liken the period to "a third industrial revolution"[23] (see *Exhibit 10–3*).

Market Concentration If mergers harm the consumer by decreasing competition, how could antitrust enforcement agencies allow what amounts to a merger explosion? The reason is that the anticompetitive effects of mergers are not as clear-cut as those of monopolies. Remember that under Section 7 of the Clayton Act, a person or business organization cannot hold stock and/or assets in another business "where the effect . . . may be to *substantially* lessen competition" (italics added). In this wording, *substantially* is a subjective term; it is up to antitrust enforcers and the courts to decide whether a merger substantially decreases competition.

We have already seen that vertical, horizontal, and conglomerate mergers can be found to substantially limit competition. Crucial consideration in making this judgment in most merger cases is **market concentration**. Market concentration roughly translates into the allocation of percentage market shares among the various firms in the relevant market. For example, if the four largest grocery stores in Chicago accounted for 90 percent of retail food sales, the market clearly would be concentrated in those four firms. If these four grocery stores decided to merge, it would obviously have a substantial effect on consumers of groceries in the area, as the resulting single business would have almost a monopoly situation, at least initially. If two small grocery stores that only accounted for 3 percent of the market each combined resources, however, the ripple effect would hardly be substantial and probably would not be challenged by local antitrust laws.

Why Businesses Merge The 1980s, like the 1990s, saw a merger binge. The mergers of the 1980s were characterized by some as being unethical and were criticized by some businesspersons and government officials alike. Many market observers, however,

---

▼ **EXHIBIT 10–3 Merger Mania: Selected Mergers and Announced Value of Deals, in the Mid-1990s**

Acquirer	Target	Year	Transaction Value
Disney	Capital Cities/ABC	1995	$19.0 billion
AT&T	McCaw Cellular Communications	1993	$18.9 billion
Chase Manhattan	Chemical Bank	1995	$10 billion
Viacom	Paramount Communications	1994	$9.6 billion
Viacom	Blockbuster Entertainment	1994	$8.0 billion
Time Warner	Turner Broadcasting	1995	$7.5 billion
Merck	Medco Containment Services	1993	$6.2 billion
Westinghouse	CBS	1995	$5.4 billion
Martin Marietta	Lockheed	1994	$5.2 billion

---

23. K. Kelly, "Mergers Today, Trouble Tomorrow?" *Business Week*, September 12, 1994, p. 30.

insist that the mergers of the 1990s have been driven by the market instead of being at odds with it, and that today's mergers will ultimately benefit the consumer by creating more efficient, if larger, firms.[24] *Exhibit 10–4* lists three general points behind this line of reasoning.

The Backlash Despite claims that the new waves of mergers are in the consumer's interest, even the best of business deals can have negative side effects.[25] In the feverishly merging pharmaceutical industry, for example, some of the burden of cutting costs has been borne by its employees. From October 1992 to April 1994, 12,000 pharmaceutical employees lost their jobs; this represented 12 percent of the industry's work force.[26] As we saw in Chapter 2, similar activity in the banking industry has had similar results.

There is also always the possibility that mergers will have anticompetitive effects. On the cusp of the sharp increase in mergers, in the spring of 1992, the Department of Justice and the Federal Trade Commission released new Horizontal Merger Guidelines, which marked the first coordinated regulatory response by the two federal antitrust enforcers. In 1993, two huge announced mergers were withdrawn because of federal concerns: the $29.4 billion Bell-Atlantic/Tele-Communications Inc. merger and the $9.6 billion Viacom/Paramount Communications merger.

ANTITRUST LAW AND FOREIGN TRADE

When the Sherman Act and the Clayton Act were being drawn up, little if any attention was given to how antitrust law would be applied to international business. Indeed, there was scant reason to worry about the competitiveness of U.S. companies abroad, because international economic activity was almost insignificant at the time. As international trade grew, an inconsistency with regard to U.S. antitrust law became unavoidable: foreign sub-sidiaries of U.S. companies often benefited from a lack of enforcement of antitrust laws in other countries. Today the application of U.S. laws to activities elsewhere puts U.S. courts in the position of effectively setting foreign policy (which is the prerogative of the executive, not the judicial, branch).

To clarify the situation, Congress enacted Section 7 of the Sherman Act to delineate when U.S. courts can assert jurisdiction over foreign commerce. In actions brought under the Sherman Act, a U.S. court can decide a case involving purely foreign trade if it has a "direct, substantial, and reasonably foreseeable effect on U.S. domestic trade, U.S. import trade, or the export trade of a person engaged in U.S. export trade."[27] In layperson's terms, this was generally understood as allowing the Department of Justice to challenge activity in foreign markets that directly harmed U.S. consumers. This policy was updated in 1992, when the Bush administration's Justice Department expanded the reach of antitrust legislation to include all firms or individuals who have "a physical presence in the United States."[28]

---

24. D. V. Potter, "Success under Fire: Policies to Prosper in Hostile Times," *California Management Review,* Winter 1991, p. 24.
25. M. H. Riordan and S. C. Salop, "Evaluating Vertical Mergers: Reply to Reiffen and Vita Comment," *Antitrust Law Journal,* Spring 1995, p. 917.
26. J. Greenwald, "Come Together, Right Now," *Time,* August 15, 1994, p. 29.
27. F. B. Cross and R. L. Miller, *West's Legal Environment of Business,* 2d ed. (St. Paul: West Publishing Co., 1995), p. 588.
28. R. J. Ostrow, "U.S. Aims New Antitrust Policy Abroad," *Los Angeles Times,* April 4, 1992, p. D1.

▼ **EXHIBIT 10–4 Economic Reasons for Mergers**

Reason	Example
1. Mergers allow the participating businesses to *save on costs.*	The merger between the Price Club and Costco Wholesale Corporation. These membership club warehouse organizations were in direct competition with each other. Both organizations (and indeed all club warehouses, such as Sam's, a Wal-Mart company) operate on a simple set of principles: locate in relatively low-cost warehouse-type environments, purchase a limited number of items in large quantities in order to force suppliers to give large discounts, and apply a simple 8 percent markup. Both the Price Club and Costco Wholesale were doing well at the beginning of the 1990s and were expanding throughout the United States. Each had a similar administrative and buying system. They decided to merge in the early 1990s, and after several years, the merger was complete. Gradually, PriceCostco (the merged company) was able to eliminate more and more of the overhead in terms of accounting, computerized activities, and buying services. In addition, the merged company represented more than $16 billion of annual buying power after the merger (over $20 billion a few years later). It was able to cut even better deals with its suppliers throughout the world. The end result was lower prices to its customers.
2. Mergers place the resulting firm in a better position to *enter new markets.*	Increased global competition has a dual effect on domestic companies: (1) it has reduced the abilities of companies to set artificially high prices in domestic markets (except perhaps in Japan), and (2) it has provided an incentive to go across borders and overseas in search of profit. When Reliance Electric Co. merged with the $1.39 billion General Signal Corp., in 1994, Reliance's treasurer noted, "It should be easier for a $3.5 billion company to move overseas than a $1.5 billion company."
3. Mergers help businesses consolidate their market positions in the face of *rapid technological change.*	The telecommunications industry, which has been fundamentally changed by wireless communication and a new generation of cable technology dominated by high-capacity fiber-optic lines. With these improvements, cable operators can offer phone conversations and reruns of *Gilligan's Island* on the same system. This so-called Information Superhighway has encouraged a large number of mergers between telephone and cable television companies looking to combine their technologies and operations. Between 1993 and 1994, the telephone giant Sprint Corp. announced a $4 billion joint venture with three of the nation's largest cable operators: Tele-Communications, Inc., Cox Enterprises, and Comcast Corp.; AT&T merged with McCaw Cellular Communications Co.; BellSouth Corp. acquired a 22.5 percent stake in cable company Prime Management Co.; and U.S. West paid $2.5 billion for a piece of the entertainment business of the conglomerate Time Warner, Inc.

SOURCE: R. Smith and G. Steinmetz, "Off to the Races: Mergers Surge as Firms Find a Rising Economy and Cheap Financing," *Wall Street Journal,* March 16, 1994, p. A1; and K. Kelly, "Mergers Today, Trouble Tomorrow?" *Business Week,* September 12, 1994, p. 30.

FOREIGN ANTITRUST ATTITUDES

Not surprisingly, U.S. trade partners were not pleased with the lengthened reach of the Justice Department. The Japanese Foreign Minister, in fact, immediately stated that the move was "not permissible under international law."[29] Japanese and Western European

---

29. *Ibid.*

governments have traditionally looked on government as a positive force in shaping and guiding all facets of an economy, including foreign trade. Consequently, the perceived aggressiveness of U.S. antitrust law is sometimes viewed with a mixture of skepticism and mistrust among foreign trade partners.

Even though emerging economic powers speak of modeling themselves on the American archetype, they often seem unwilling to reign in anticompetitive forces within their economies. In 1994, with great fanfare, Mexico's Federal Competition Commission issued its first-ever finding against companies engaged in monopolistic practices. Twenty companies were named in the commission's sweep—but total fines amounted to only $750,000, which, if actually paid, translates into more of a monopoly fee than a deterrent.[30]

Keiretsu and Japan

Keiretsu, the collaboration of Japanese firms designed to increase overall market efficiency, goes far beyond what any U.S. court would consider being within the boundaries of acceptable horizontal restraints of trade. Roughly translated as "group of companies," *keiretsu* is defined by Professor Patrick Boarman of National University as "cartel-like arrangements . . . in which customers, producers and their suppliers, banks, trading companies, and government agencies are purposefully linked together toward the end that all share in the collective's knowledge base and efficiency gains."[31]

In *keiretsu*, competitors normally join in cooperative ventures, a situation almost unheard of in the American business landscape (see *Managing Social Issues—Forging New Alliances: Computer Giants Come Together*). The Mitsui *keiretsu*, for example, has as its members Toyota, Nissan, Honda, Mitsubishi, Mazda, Subaru, Isuzu, Daihatsu, and Suzuki.[32] A similar situation in the United States would have General Motors, Ford, and Chrysler working together to share some of their secrets, an unlikely scenario (except in the instance of electric-car production, in which the Big Three's cooperation was in fact approved by the Clinton administration).

Enforcement of U.S. Antitrust Law Abroad

In 1994, the Federal Trade Commission and the Justice Department made another attempt to strengthen FTC guidelines to remind companies that "anticompetitive conduct that affects U.S. domestic or foreign commerce may violate the U.S. antitrust laws regardless of where such conduct occurs or the nationality of the parties involved."[33] Among the kind of anticompetitive activity that officials from the two agencies would be required to investigate are the following:

1. "Conduct by foreign firms that has a direct, substantial, and reasonably foreseeable anticompetitive effect on commerce within the United States or on U.S. firms' export business."
2. Mergers of foreign companies with significant sales in the United States.
3. Anticompetitive behavior by foreign companies selling directly to the U.S. government.
4. Anticompetitive activity by importers designed to have a "significant" impact on the United States.[34]

---

30. "Antitrust Wimps," *Business Week*, July 11, 1994, p. 51.
31. Boarman, *op. cit.*, p. 33.
32. *Ibid.*, p. 34.
33. J. Davidson, "Antitrust Guidance for Foreign Trade Proposed By U.S.," *Wall Street Journal*, October 14, 1994, p. B3.
34. *Ibid.*

◫ Managing Social Issues

Forging New Alliances: Computer Giants Come Together

Although U.S. antitrust law has historically frowned upon *cartels*—or arrangements between producers or sellers who band together—some U.S. companies are beginning to experiment with the *keiretsu* approach. A notable example was the efforts at partnership between two fierce competitors, International Business Machines Corporation (IBM) and Apple Computer, Inc.

Taligent and Kaleida

In 1991, IBM and Apple agreed to start two joint ventures, called Taligent and Kaleida, as technology-sharing projects. The plan was to consolidate the two companies' extensive research and development capacities in order to create future software. Taligent was given the task of creating an operating system, code-named "Pink," which would allow programmers to make programs faster and cheaper, and also allow them to customize the programs to the needs of individual clients. Kaleida was to pioneer technologies in multimedia for consumer electronics.

Industry watchers had high hopes for the partnership because of the "tremendous resources" each computer company had at its disposal. Within the business industry, IBM is known for its research teams and computer chip design expertise, whereas Apple has a reputation for consumer-oriented acumen. The two problems some pessimists foresaw were government intervention or a personality clash between IBM's "blue suits" and Apple's "dress-down" corporate style.

Less Than a Partnership

As it turned out, fashion clashes were the least of the two companies' problems. Americans, who lack the Japanese corporate culture to support Japanese-style *keiretsu*, are less likely to cooperate completely in a joint venture. Apple released software in 1992 that enables its users to access IBM programs, but the initial years of the project were hampered by inefficient bureaucracies, inadvisable goals, and lack of cooperation.

In three years, Taligent and Kaleida lost a combined half-billion dollars. Taligent discovered that consumers were not interested in Pink, as a number of similar products had already saturated the market. "They are so out of touch with the marketplace that I think it's unlikely what they produce will be widely accepted," said one program purchaser of Taligent. Kaleida was over two years late in producing its multimedia software, and a handheld CD-ROM player produced by the company was abandoned after eighteen months because "nobody believed in [it]."

Executives from both Apple and IBM had problems agreeing on details of both projects, and Chief Executive A. Nathaniel Goldhaber had trouble working with the managers whom Apple and IBM had recruited to run the venture. Goldhaber remembers a typical incident when he refused to acquiesce to a request for intricate business cards that cost $1 apiece. Instead, he purchased standard boxes of 500 cards for $20 per box. "I can't tell how many points I lost with my staff over that," he said. Another goal of the joint venture, to make inroads in Microsoft Corporation's 80 percent dominance of the personal computer market with its Windows program, fizzled when the two companies refused to share technologies from their existing competing products, Apple's Macintosh approach and IBM's OS/2 system.

On the third anniversary of the official announcement of the Apple-IBM alliance, only one result was considered significant as far as consumers were concerned: the PowerPC chip.

For Critical Analysis:

Is the consumer better served with Apple and IBM combining their knowledge, or by their competing with each other to create new technology?

SOURCE: Information from "An Industry Alliance Bears Fruit," *Byte* August 1, 1993, p. 72; J. Carlton, "Apple-IBM Goal of Universal Computer Faces Hurdles," *Wall Street Journal*, November 9, 1994, p. B4; H. Norr, "Time for Apple, IBM to Get Serious about Partnership," *MacWEEK*, July 11, 1994, p. 28; and E. Schroeder, "'Braun's Charter' Getting Refocused Kaleida on Track," *PC Week*, June 13, 1994, p. 143.

As valid in protecting U.S. consumers as this expanded reach may be, any pronouncement on international enforcement from the U.S. government is bound to be limited by geopolitical reality:

▼ **Whereas the federal government does have influence over U.S. subsidiaries and their actions abroad, it has been historically ineffective in controlling anticompetitive activities of foreign firms.**

Domestic Enforcement When one of the companies involved in what the FTC or the Justice Department considers anticompetitive activity happens to be based in the United States, the government has powerful means of retaliation. Because U.S. companies are under the jurisdiction of U.S. courts, the agencies are backed by the full force of domestic law. Such was the case in 1993, when the Justice Department filed a lawsuit in a Delaware court citing the anticompetitive effects of a proposed sale of a division of General Motors to ZF Freidrichshafen, a German auto parts manufacturer. In its complaint, the Justice Department alleged that the international merger would create a *de facto* monopoly in the business of heavy-duty automatic transmissions, used mostly in garbage trucks and large buses. By blocking the sale, the Justice Department believed ZF Freidrichshafen would be forced to create the needed technology itself—instead of merely inheriting what General Motors had already created—thereby spurring research in the field. In the face of the lawsuit, GM withdrew the sale.[35]

Foreign Enforcement When none of the parties are under the jurisdiction of U.S. courts, the FTC and the Department of Justice find themselves severely hampered in enforcement attempts. Foreign governments react defensively to any American attempt to export the applicability of U.S. antitrust laws. For example, in the 1970s, when U.S. companies tried to prove the existence of a global uranium cartel, many countries—including France, South Africa, Great Britain, Canada, and Australia—enacted laws forbidding their firms and citizens from complying with a U.S. court's requests for information. Even if the Department of Justice is able to acquire incriminating evidence against a foreign company, it is almost impossible to force the offender into a U.S. court unless it has a subsidiary on American soil.

This situation places the enforcement agencies in a frustrating position. In the mid-1990s, U.S. glassmakers complained that a Japanese cartel was effectively shutting them out of a $4.5 billion market by prohibiting Japanese distributors from selling imported glass. The evidence of anticompetitive planning among the cartel would be obvious to any court: the three members of the cartel had kept a constant market share since the end of World War II, with Asahi Glass at 30 percent, Nippon Sheet Glass at 30 percent, and Central Glass at 20 percent.[36] It is unlikely, however, that the Japanese government will allow U.S. courts access to change the situation. Any attempt to do so, in this case or any other, is "contrary to basic principles of international jurisdiction," according to a spokesperson for the Japanese Fair Trade Commission.[37]

A CHANGING FOCUS OF U.S. ANTITRUST POLICY?

In the face of such adamant resistance, the most promising medium for influencing foreign antitrust law may be a bargaining table rather than a U.S. court. Thus, the U.S. gov-

---

35. "Antitrust in Reverse," *Wall Street Journal*, November 29, 1993, p. A12.
36. C. Yang, "Commerce Cops," *Business Week*, December 13, 1993, p. 69.
37. *Ibid.*

ernment consistently pushed for inclusion of global antitrust issues on the agenda of the final round of the General Agreement on Tariffs and Trade (GATT) talks. In the eyes of some antitrust specialists, American efforts in the global community should be limited to such actions. These experts have criticized the United States for being far more preoccupied with the business practices of foreign firms than with arguably anticompetitive practices that continue in the United States (for example, the monopoly power enjoyed by both baseball owners and the baseball players' union, as well as the monopoly position of local public utility companies granted by some state regulatory agencies, which require potential competitors to prove the need for a competing public utility—which is usually impossible).

Others believe that the United States is unreasonable and unwise in its attempts at exporting U.S. antitrust law overseas. MIT professor Lester Thurow underscores what he sees as the fallibility of the American position:

> In March 1990 the two biggest business groups in the world (the Mitsubishi group from Japan and the Daimler Benz–Deutsche Bank group from Germany) held a secret meeting in Singapore to talk about a global alliance. Among other things, both were interested in expanding their market share in civilian aircraft production. From an American perspective, everything about that Singapore meeting was criminally illegal. It violated both antitrust and banking laws. In the United States, banks cannot own industrial firms and businesses cannot sit down behind closed doors to plan joint strategies. . . . Yet in today's world Americans cannot force the world to play the economic game as Americans think it should be played. The game will be played under international, not American rules.[38]

---

38. L. Thurow, *Head to Head* (New York: Morrow, 1992).

THE DELICATE BALANCE

Today, more than ever before, federal antitrust regulators are faced with a dilemma: As the business world becomes more globally interactive, in order for American companies to compete, they must often get bigger. This usually means that mergers are appropriate. But trustbusters in the United States may view such mergers as anticompetitive. In particular, antitrust officials at the Department of Justice and the Federal Trade Commission may be looking only at the *domestic* market to reach those conclusions. In so doing, they may miss the "forest for the trees." That is why some observers argue that antitrust law is currently outdated. They also point out that so much is changing technologically and at such a fast pace that it is meaningless to look at only what is happening today. They cite as an example the Justice Department's effective campaign to prevent Microsoft Corporation from acquiring Intuit, the maker of Quicken personal finance and banking software. The Justice Department's reasoning was that such an acquisition would foreclose future competition in the electronic on-line banking market. Observers of that situation point out that many corporations just as strong as Microsoft could, and have, entered the on-line banking field.

From an international perspective, the attempts of American officials at imposing U.S. views on antitrust law in the rest of the world have not been overly successful. The question remains as to whether we should try to spread our antitrust views abroad or simply allow American companies to get bigger and stronger so that they will be capable of competing worldwide under current conditions.

TERMS AND CONCEPTS FOR REVIEW

Antitrust law 278
Conglomerate merger 290
Divestiture 284
Exclusive-dealing contract 288
Group boycott 284
Horizontal merger 289
Joint venture 285

Market concentration 297
Monopoly 286
Natural monopoly 295
Per se violation 281
Predatory pricing 296
Price discrimination 288
Price-fixing agreement 281

Rule of reason 281
Substitute 293
Trust 278
Tying arrangement 288
Vertical merger 289

SUMMARY

1. The Sherman Antitrust Act was originally introduced in Congress to destroy the large combinations of capital that were thought to distort the nation's economy. The Sherman Act applies only to restraints that have a significant impact on interstate commerce. The states must address purely local restraints on competition.

2. Section 1 of the Sherman Act prohibits persons from conspiring to restrain trade, whereas Section 2 prohibits anticompetitive conduct by individuals or groups in the marketplace.

3. Under the rule of reason, the court must consider all of the circumstances surrounding a case to determine whether the allegedly anticompetitive conduct is a violation of Section 1 of the Sherman Act.

4. The *per se* rule requires that certain kinds of anticompetitive actions not be judged under the rule of reason. *Per se* violations are those that are considered to be so inherently anticompetitive as to constitute unreasonable restraints of trade as a matter of law. When a *per se* violation is involved, there is no need for the courts to examine any other facts or evidence.

5. Private parties may sue for treble damages or other remedies under the antitrust laws. An individual wishing to sue business organizations for antitrust violations must prove (a) that the antitrust violation directly caused, or was at least a substantial factor in causing, the injury that was suffered and (b) that the unlawful actions of the defendant affected the business activities of the plaintiff.

6. A person found guilty of violating the Sherman Act may be fined up to $350,000, imprisoned for three years, or both. A corporation can be fined up to $10 million.

7. Horizontal restraints result from concerted activities by direct competitors and may include price-fixing arrangements, group boycotts, horizontal market divisions, trade association activities, and joint ventures.

8. Vertical restraints—which involve the distribution of goods and arise from agreements made between firms at different levels of the distribution process—include territorial or customer restrictions and resale price maintenance agreements.

9. Resale price maintenance agreements—also known as fair trade agreements—arise when manufacturers specify

minimum prices for their products that must be followed by distributors. These vertical price-fixing agreements are typically considered *per se* violations of Section 1 of the Sherman Act.

10. Section 2 of the Sherman Act makes it unlawful to "monopolize or attempt to monopolize." Unlike Section 1, Section 2 does not require a conspiracy for there to be a violation of the Sherman Act. Section 2 can be violated by a single firm if it intentionally obtains or maintains monopoly power.

11. The Federal Trade Commission (FTC) is an administrative agency created in 1914 that has broad powers to prevent unfair methods of competition and unfair or deceptive acts or practices in commerce. The FTC is empowered to promulgate rules and issue general statements of policy with regard to unfair or deceptive acts or practices.

12. In 1914, Congress passed the Clayton Act to make illegal specific monopolistic practices that could harm competition but that were not clearly prohibited by the Sherman Act. Private parties may sue for treble damages and attorneys' fees under the Clayton Act.

13. Horizontal mergers involve mergers between direct competitors. The legality of a horizontal merger depends in part on the degree of concentration in the industry. Such mergers will not be allowed unless they have significant procompetitive effects. Vertical mergers between firms at different levels of the same industry and conglomerate mergers between firms in unrelated industries may also violate antitrust law.

14. Natural monopolies may arise when production increases and the average per-unit costs fall continuously. If only one firm can take advantage of this situation, it becomes the natural monopolist.

15. U.S. antitrust laws may be applied beyond the borders of the United States. Any conspiracy that has a substantial effect on commerce within the United States may be subject to the Sherman Act, even if the violation occurs outside the United States.

EXERCISES

1. Try to argue the position in favor of exempting professional baseball from federal antitrust laws.

2. Explain in simple language the distinction between Sections 1 and 2 of the Sherman Antitrust Act.

3. The Sherman Antitrust Act makes illegal any agreement that is "in restraint of trade." Some argue that virtually all agreements in effect restrain trade in some small manner. Make a list of common agreements, such as an employment agreement, that in essence restrain trade somehow. Indicate how each agreement does so. (*Hint:* An employment agreement typically prevents the employee from taking a better job at any time during the duration of the agreement.)

4. Super-Tech Industries controls 55 percent of the market in the manufacture and sale of computers. The balance of the market is controlled by five other manufacturers; Alcan Corporation has 25 percent of the market. Alcan's research staff is innovative, but every time Alcan introduces a faster, more powerful, and more efficient computer in the market, Super-Tech immediately informs its customers of the upcoming development of a competing computer that it will sell at 30 percent below the Alcan price. Alcan claims that these activities on the part of Super-Tech are an antitrust violation. Do you think this unilateral action by Super-Tech violates antitrust law? Why or why not?

5. Goodfellows, Inc., is a close corporation with only two shareholders. Goodfellows is engaged in the pizza delivery business. Two other firms serve the same market, but Goodfellows controls 75 percent of the market. The two shareholders agree that one will purchase all of the shares that belong to the other. As a condition of the transaction, the shareholder selling the shares agrees not to open a competing pizza delivery business within a seventy-mile radius or become employed by any rival firm within the same designated area. The covenant is to last five years. Is it an unreasonable restraint of trade?

6. Instant Foto Corporation is a manufacturer of photographic film. At the present time, Instant Foto has approximately 50 percent of the market. Instant Foto advertises that the purchase price for Instant Foto film includes photo processing by Instant Foto Corporation. Instant Foto claims that its film processing is specially designed to improve the quality of the finished photos when using Instant Foto's film. Is Instant Foto's combination of film purchase and film processing an antitrust violation? Explain.

7. Mr. Furniture, Inc., was a company engaged in the wholesale and retail furniture business. Like many other companies in its line of business, Mr. Furniture frequently obtained its furniture products from manufacturers by making purchases on credit. Credit usually was not provided by the manufacturers themselves but rather by institutions engaged in "commercial factoring." These institutions typically purchased the manufacturers' accounts receivable at a discount and assumed direct

responsibility for collecting the outstanding debts. More-over, the factored credit institutions often purchased debt on a nonrecourse basis, meaning that they assumed the entire risk of a debtor's failure to repay. The institutions relied on credit ratings and similar criteria in deciding to which purchasers credit should be extended. Barclays American/Commercial was the dominant factored credit institution in the market in which Mr. Furniture operated. Barclays refused to extend credit for Mr. Furniture's inventory purchases from furniture manufacturers. Mr. Furniture's president, Howard Cassett, asserted that the refusal was based on two elements: (1) Barclays's attempt to monopolize the factored credit market and (2) the personal animosity that Barclays's manager, Jim Stenhouse, harbored toward Cassett. Mr. Furniture sued Barclays, alleging, among other things, violations of the Sherman Act. The trial court ruled that Mr. Furniture lacked standing to bring the antitrust charge; the court held that any alleged monopolization would directly injure other commercial factoring institutions that competed with Barclays, not Mr. Furniture.

a. The court's ruling, affirmed on appeal, was based on the contention that any antitrust violations committed by Barclays would injure its competitors—other credit-factoring institutions—not Mr. Furniture. Should Mr. Furniture have been allowed to complain simply because, as a "consumer" of credit-factoring services, it was harmed by the alleged monopoly over credit extension acquired by Barclays? After all, the antitrust laws are supposed to help consumers, not competitors.

b. The court explicitly held that the alleged personal animosity that the Barclays executive had toward Mr. Furniture's president was irrelevant. There is something to be said for preventing the antitrust laws—because they involve mechanisms of the judicial process—from being used in petty ways, such as to settle personal feuds. Is such abuse any less troubling just because it is done for personal, rather than economic, reasons?

8. The Justice Department was investigating the practice by domestic automobile manufacturers of "value pricing"—not bargaining set-price deals—because its antitrust division suspected price fixing. Given that there are numerous manufacturers of automobiles for sale in the United States (when you include foreign cars), how could consumers be hurt by value pricing?

9. Under what circumstances could you argue that a merger of two large companies would, simply by their combined size, lead to monopolization?

10. Reexamine *Exhibit 10–4*, which lists three economic reasons for mergers. Which reason do you believe is most important today? Substantiate your assertion.

SELECTED REFERENCES

▶ Bork, Robert H. *The Antitrust Paradox: A Policy at War with Itself.* New York: Basic Books, 1978.

▶ Bruckamn, Barbara O., ed. *Predatory Pricing Law: A Circuit-by-Circuit Survey.* Chicago: Section of Antitrust Law, American Bar Association, 1995.

▶ Davidow, Joel. *Antitrust Guide for International Business Transactions.* Washington, D.C.: Bureau of National Affairs, 1995.

▶ Himmelberg, Robert F., ed. *Antitrust and Business Regulation in the Postwar Era, 1946–1964.* New York: Garland Publishing, 1994.

▶ Himmelberg, Robert F., ed. *Evolution of Antitrust Policy from Johnson to Bush.* New York: Garland Publishing, 1994.

▶ Holmes, William C. *Antitrust Law Handbook.* Deerfield, Ill.: Clark, Boardman, Callaghan, 1992.

▶ McChesney, Fred S., and William F. Shughart II, eds. *The Causes and Consequences of Antitrust: The Public Choice Perspective.* Chicago: University of Chicago Press, 1995.

▶ Posner, Richard A. *Antitrust Law: An Economic Perspective.* Chicago: University of Chicago Press, 1976.

▶ Utton, M. A. *Market Dominance and Antitrust Policy.* United Kingdom: Edward Elgar Publishing, 1995; distributed in U.S. by Ashgate Publishing, Brookfield, VT.

RESOURCES ON THE INTERNET

▼ You can find out what the Antitrust Division of the U.S. Department of Justice is doing by addressing
http://www.usdoj.gov/

▼ If you use the Yahoo browser, you can access valuable information about antitrust law. Go to
http://www.yahoo.com/Government/ Law/

RESOURCES ON THE INTERNET (CONTINUED)

▼ If you have any problems with Yahoo, you can get E-mail help at

admin@yahoo.com

▼ For information from the Federal Trade Commission (FTC), access the ConsumerLine at

gopher://consumer.ftc.gov:2416/ 11/ConsumerLine

▼ The law firm Arent, Fox, Kitner, Plotkin, & Kahn provides a general information site on advertising laws. This site includes news of FTC statements and acts, FTC advertising guidelines, and FTC enforcement policy statements. You can access the Advertising Law Internet Site at

http://www.webcom.com/~lewrose/ home.html

▼ For information on a wide variety of legal issues, including antitrust law, access the Federal Legal Research Template at

http://www.netrail.net/~sunburst/

▼ Every country has its own set of business and antitrust laws. For a glimpse at Russian business law, you can access Rules and Regulations in Russia at

http://www.spb.su/rulesreg/

CASE

WAL-MART: PRICE STRATEGY ISSUES

Background

"Let Americans be under no illusion as to the value of price cutting," wrote Louis Brandeis, Supreme Court justice from 1916 to 1939. "It is the most potent weapon of monopoly. Those who succumb to its wiles are thoughtless or weak, but they are selling their birthright for a mess of pottage."

It is logical to infer from this statement that Justice Brandeis would not approve of the methods with which Wal-Mart stores came to dominate the retail business in the 1980s. Pioneering a strategy known simply as "everyday-low-pricing (EDLP)," Wal-Mart procured low prices from suppliers with immense orders and passed the savings on to its customers. The chain's price cutting, which also allowed it to avoid the costs of advertising and promotions, put its competitors at an extreme disadvantage—in 1996 Wal-Mart had combined sales of around $100 billion.

These tactics have long earned Wal-Mart the ire of independent stores that cannot offer EDLP. They accuse the giant chain of predatory pricing, or selling goods below cost to drive other stores out of business with the ultimate goal of raising prices after gaining control of the market. Most legal challenges to Wal-Mart's tactics have failed because judges know that those whom antitrust laws are designed to protect—the consumers—want, and benefit from, lower prices. In 1992, however, three small-store owners in Arkansas played David to Wal-Mart's Goliath, found a sympathetic judge, and threatened to change the way large retailers set prices in the United States.

The Arkansas Lawsuit

Three independent drugstore owners from Conway, Arkansas, brought suit against the local Wal-Mart for violating a state statute called the Arkansas Unfair Trade Practices Act. The plaintiffs claimed that the retailer was selling more than one hundred "highly competitive merchandise" items—including Listerine mouthwash and Crest toothpaste—below cost with the intent of driving them out of business. Sometimes, the suit charges, Wal-Mart would sell the items below their acquisition price. "It's just [become] more and more difficult to compete [with Wal-Mart]," complained Dwayne Goode, owner of American Drugs, Inc., and a plaintiff in the case.

This would be the first test for the Arkansas Unfair Trade Practices Act since it was passed in 1937. The state law prohibits businesses from selling certain items below cost. The statute specifically reads that it is unlawful to advertise or sell "any article or product . . . at less than the cost thereof to the vendor . . . for the purpose of injuring competitors and destroying competition." Because the wording of the law refers almost entirely to the effect of pricing on vendors and does not concern itself with consumers, the plaintiffs saw it as applicable to their case.

Wal-Mart's Response

In its defense, Wal-Mart did not deny its price-cutting strategies; it only denied that they were predatory. Promotional campaigns such as "Let us liberate you from high drug prices" (in which the store offered discounts on medicine and a free prescription of $5) and "meet or beat" (where store managers are allowed to lower prices below those of competitors) were not designed with the specific goal of putting rivals out of business, said Wal-Mart. The given rationale behind Wal-Mart's low-cost sales "is to generate traffic that will purchase other items, offsetting any loss on a particular item sold below cost."

In other words, Wal-Mart said it was taking part in the common practice of loss leaders, or pricing certain items below cost to bring consumers into a store in the hope that they will then purchase other items. Loss leading is considered a legal staple of retailing. Wal-Mart's attorneys argued that the store's prices could be reviewed properly only by analyzing a "basket" representing a wide cross-section of goods, which would offset the low costs of the loss leaders.

Wal-Mart's lawyers also pointed to the fact that the pharmaceutical market in Conway had hardly suffered from Wal-Mart's pricing practices. The three plaintiffs—American Drugs, Baker Drug, and Family Drug—saw their combined margins increase more than 4 percent from 1986 to 1990. Also, of the twelve pharmacies in the town in 1987, all twelve were still in business as the case went to court. (In fact, two more pharmacies had opened.) In an affidavit an expert testified that the local "marketplace seems alive, well, and maximizing consumer welfare through a greater variety of firms and more efficient operations."

CASE (CONTINUED)

State and Federal Pricing Focus

The plaintiffs called these statistics "irrelevant," noting that their case was concerned with the long-term consequences of predatory prices. Had the case been filed in a federal court, they would have had a difficult time proving that such a concern was warranted. Since the mid-1980s, federal judges, taking the lead from a Supreme Court decision in 1986, have been very careful to distinguish between competitive price cutting—"the very essence of competition"—and illegal predatory pricing.

An intent to harm competitors by pricing below cost has not been sufficient to prove predatory pricing in federal courts; the plaintiff must also prove that the defendant could hold monopoly power in the specific market long enough to recoup the losses from predatory actions. This is nearly impossible to predict, and therefore very few predatory pricing suits are even taken to federal court. In fact, while the Wal-Mart case was being argued, a federal court in Texas decided that American Airlines was not using predatory tactics when it drastically cut its air fare prices a year earlier.

The scenario is different in many state legal systems, however. Including Arkansas, twenty-three states have statutes generally forbidding sales below cost. Most of the laws, again like the one in Arkansas, were passed in the wake of the Great Depression in order to protect small stores from having to compete with larger chains. As a result, the focus of state antitrust law is fundamentally different from that of the federal system. Whereas federal antitrust law is designed to protect the consumer and therefore encourage pro-competitive price cutting, the main goal of the states seems to be protecting the small-store owner. In this atmosphere, the Wal-Mart plaintiffs had a much better chance than they would have had if the case had gone to federal court.

The Initial Verdict

Indeed, the initial verdict surprised many legal experts. In October 1993, Judge David L. Reynolds of Chancery Court in Conway ruled in favor of the plaintiffs, saying that Wal-Mart's actions were unlawful under the state statute. The judge rejected the "market basket" defense and found it possible to deduce the retail chain's predatory intent through the following:

▶ The number, frequency, and extent of Wal-Mart's below-cost sales.
▶ Wal-Mart's stated policy to "meet or beat" competitors' prices "without regard for cost."

▶ Wal-Mart's stated policy of aiming to attract a disproportionate number of customers through below-cost sales.
▶ In-store displays that compared Wal-Mart prices of certain products favorably with those of competitors, including the plaintiffs.
▶ Price comparisons that showed that Wal-Mart stores had higher prices in areas with less competition.

Reynolds awarded the plaintiffs $289,000 in lost sales. More important, he also ordered the Conway Wal-Mart to discontinue selling items below cost, which under state law means invoice price plus the "cost of doing business," or overhead.

Reaction

Although Wal-Mart appealed the decision, Judge Reynolds's ruling caused consternation in both legal and business circles. Many pointed out the irony inherent in the judge's ruling: the act of charging low prices is deemed anticompetitive under antitrust laws whose primary function is to limit monopoly power and thereby promote pro-competitive conditions, which manifest themselves through low prices. Furthermore, it was asked, is not the main goal of competition in a free market to obtain a "disproportionate" number of customers, a market strategy that Reynolds used to infer Wal-Mart's guilt? Robert Pitfosky, a Georgetown University law professor, remarked, "If Wal-Mart is more efficient and can sell toothpaste for less, then in the long run, the mom-and-pop businesses may lose out" despite any legal attempts to save them.

To the corporate community, the ruling gave notice that federal antitrust policies were no protection against state statutes such as the one in Arkansas. Retail chains and other businesses would be well served to investigate local laws before attempting below-cost pricing practices. There was also concern that the ruling, if it stood, could have a deleterious effect on the strategy of loss leaders, which are commonly used by other businesses, including grocery stores.

Epilogue

In January 1995, the Arkansas Supreme Court overturned Judge Reynolds's decision. "The loss leader strategy employed by Wal-Mart is readily justifiable as a tool to foster competitiveness and to gain a competitive edge," stated the court's majority, "as opposed to simply being viewed as a stratagem to eliminate rivals altogether." The publicity drawn by the case,

CASE (CONTINUED)

however, ensured that Wal-Mart and other large retail chains would face the issue again. The plaintiffs revealed that they had been contacted by numerous small stores for advice on their own predatory pricing suits, and Wal-Mart faced similar charges in Colorado and Oklahoma.

Critical Thinking Questions

1. Assuming that the ultimate goal of Wal-Mart is to drive smaller competitors out of business, is this ethically acceptable behavior? Explain your answer in utilitarian terms (see Chapter 4).

2. Is it a proper assumption that low prices at chains such as Wal-Mart will eventually drive the mom-and-pop stores out of business? What competitive advantages do the smaller stores have to offset their higher prices?

3. It would appear that many state predatory pricing laws place the interests of small-store owners above those of consumers. What do you believe was the original justification for these laws? How has the situation changed over the intervening time?

4. As a consumer, would you be willing to pay higher prices to keep smaller stores in business? If the answer is yes, do you believe society would be benefited by forcing all consumers to do so?

5. In the case at the end of Chapter 8 we discussed the ramifications of price controls in the drug industry. Are there different ethical considerations in discussing price controls on items such as toothpaste and deodorant as compared with items such as heart medicine? Should there be?

SOURCE: Information from W. Zellner, "Not Everybody Loves Wal-Mart's Low Prices," *Business Week*, October 12, 1992, p. 36; I. Scher and H. J. Gregory, "After *Wal-Mart*, How Low Is Too Low?" *National Law Journal*, November 22, 1993, pp. 19, 20; B. Hunt, "The Irrational Antitrust Case against Wal-Mart," *Wall Street Journal*, October 20, 1993, p. A15; "Wal-Mart Pays $289,000 for Driving Local Stores Out of Business," *Lawyers Weekly USA*, November 8, 1993, p. 554; J. Ramey, "Judge Weights Wal-Mart Pricing," *HFD*, September 13, 1993, p. 10; and "Court Backs Wal-Mart on Pricing," *New York Times*, January 10, 1995, p. D4.

CHAPTER 11

BUSINESS AND PUBLIC POLICY

CHAPTER OUTLINE

◗ Business and Strategic Public Policy
◗ Political Action Committees
◗ Global Business Issues and Public Policy
◗ Strategies for Corporate Influence on Public Policy

INTRODUCTION

The Private Sector Council is a nonprofit business organization whose stated purpose is to "make the Federal Government run more efficiently and improve its productivity." On announcing the recipients of one of its recent Annual Leadership Awards, the organization ran a full-page advertisement in the *Wall Street Journal*. The text of the ad read, in boldfaced and underlined 24-point print,

<u>USUALLY, WE TRY TO KEEP COLLUSION BETWEEN GOVERNMENT AND BUSINESS A SECRET</u>.

The council's joke was that in this case, it wanted everybody to know about a collaboration with business that made government "run more efficiently."[1] The names of the two award recipients, Senator Robert Dole and Tom Labrecque, chief executive officer of the Chase Manhattan Bank, appeared in small print on the bottom of the page while the very idea of a government-business partnership took top billing.

Is the relationship between business and government so adversarial that any sort of partnership feels the need to trumpet itself with full-page ads? Even in the advertisement, cooperation between the two institutions was referred to as "collusion," a term usually used to describe illegal and anticompetitive business actions.

A business, of course, has an individualistic ethical system, whereas government has a collectivist ethical system. Under an individualistic system of ethics, self-interest not only is accepted but also normally ends up benefiting the entire group (particularly if one takes Adam Smith's view, in which an invisible hand of self-interest guides the economy so that the most efficient use of resources results). In addition, such an ethical system inevitably accepts the inequality of individual abilities. Otherwise, it would be difficult to allow those who are better at business to get a reward sufficient to induce them to save, invest, and work hard. Finally, an individualistic ethical system emphasizes that society—that is, government—should impose as few obligations as possible on the individual.

In contrast, the collectivist ethical system of government emphasizes the subordination of individual goals and self-interest to those of the group. Individuals are all considered equal, and much is done to improve the equality of individuals through regulation, legislation, and taxation. Finally, within the government's collectivist ethical system, the individual has numerous obligations to society and is often encouraged (or rather obligated) to forget his or her self-interest.

Because of these disparate ethical systems and incentive structures, some commentators doubt that business and government will ever be partners in the true sense of the word.[2] As this chapter aims to prove, however, that does not mean that a future manager needs to fashion a crash helmet during business school in order to survive a career of bashing heads with opposing government agencies. Managers must

---

1. Advertisement, *Wall Street Journal*, April 20, 1994, p. B3.
2. L. E. Birdsell, "Business and Government: The Walls Between," in *The Business Government Relationship: A Reassessment*, ed. N. H. Jacoby (Santa Monica, Calif.: Goodyear, 1975), pp. 32–34.

learn to regard the government as simply another factor on the market landscape, just as increased foreign competition, rapidly changing technology, or new competing products are factors. Then the manager will be able to make rational strategy decisions that accommodate government regulations, and even use government activity to build and sustain a competitive advantage. To further this end, this chapter explores the different options business has not only for surviving but also for prospering in today's regulatory environment.

BUSINESS AND STRATEGIC PUBLIC POLICY

If we existed in a pure capitalistic system, there would be no such thing as strategic public policy. Firms would succeed or fail based solely on their ingenuity and how they responded to consumer needs. As we have seen, however, the American economy does not function as a pure capitalistic system. In our variation of capitalism, the market economy is under significant influence from **public policy.** There are many possible definitions of public policy, but it can be most simply defined as what the government decides to do or not to do to achieve its purposes.

There is nothing simple, however, about how the public-policy process works and its effect on the "free" market.[3] In fact,

▼ Government intervention can be a crucial factor in the ultimate success or failure of a corporation's drive to maximize its shareholder wealth.

Consequently, it is imperative that business managers understand not only the dynamics of public policy and its implications relative to their particular economic niche but also how they can affect the government's decision-making process. In Chapter 9 we discussed the various ways regulation could be used by an industry or a single company to create and sustain a competitive advantage. In this chapter we explore the means by which a business entity can inject itself into the public policymaking process and affect the outcome of government decisions for its own benefit.

THE POLICYMAKING PROCESS

How does the policymaking process evolve? In the case of the Brady Bill, a law passed in 1993 requiring handgun buyers to wait five days before making a purchase, the process began with a single incident more than a decade earlier. On March 30, 1981, John W. Hinckley, Jr., attempted to assassinate President Ronald Reagan with a handgun. In the process he wounded the president and permanently disabled the president's press secretary, James S. Brady. Although Hinckley had a history of mental illness, he had purchased his handgun easily in Texas by lying on his registration form.

Spurred by the incident, Sarah Brady, James's wife, began a campaign to tighten handgun control laws with stronger federal restrictions. Her efforts were opposed by the handgun-manufacturing industry and its two largest members, Remington Arms, Inc., and Smith & Wesson (which account for almost half the industry's annual $1.1 billion in sales), as well as the powerful National Rifle Association (NRA). With 2.7 million members and an annual budget of more than $75 million, the NRA repre-

---

3. M. A. Glynn, "Strategic Planning in Nigeria versus the U.S.: A Case of Anticipating the (Next) Coup," *Academy of Management Executive,* August 1993, p. 82.

James Brady makes an appearance at an assault weapons ban.

sented the most formidable opposition to efforts by Brady and special interest groups such as Handgun Control, Inc. The NRA based its argument against the Brady Bill on a strict, if somewhat limited, interpretation of the Second Amendment to the U.S. Constitution, which reads, "A well regulated Militia, being necessary to the security of a free State, the right of the people to keep and bear Arms, shall not be infringed."

Spending nearly $20 million a year in lobbying, the NRA was able to keep the Brady Bill off the books for a number of years. Public opinion, however, turned against the NRA as the levels of violence perpetrated by handgun users rose during the 1980s and 1990s. In 1993, according to a Gallup poll, nearly nine out of every ten Americans (88 percent) favored passage of the Brady Bill.[4] The American Medical Health Association, the National Congress of Parents and Teachers, numerous law enforcement organizations, and dozens of other groups openly advocated the five-day waiting period to allow for background checks on handgun purchasers. This pressure eventually proved more powerful than the NRA lobbying power, and the Brady Bill was passed, along with a ban on nineteen different kinds of assault weapons. Proponents of the legislation did not expect it to greatly affect handgun violence—as the NRA often points out, most people who use guns in crimes purchase them on the unregulated black market. These proponents believe, however, that any life saved by the "cooling-off" period was worth the effort. "What is wrong with waiting five days to get a pistol?" asked one congressman.[5]

The passage of the Brady Bill underscores the basic phases of policymaking. First, the issue comes onto the national agenda, in this case beginning with the Reagan assassination attempt and spreading with the concern over escalating handgun violence. Next, various proposals are discussed among government officials and the public; a number of different variations of the Brady Bill were considered before its final passage. Congress then enacts

4. "Brady Bill—Trend," *Gallup Poll Monthly*, March 1993, p. 3.
5. "Congress Responds to Violence: Tackles Guns, Criminals," *Congressional Quarterly*, November 13, 1993, p. 3128.

and implements the legislation, after which its effect on the perceived problem is noted and possible changes in the law are considered. There are a number of variations on this basic process (see *Exhibit 11–1* on page 316), and it is important that any business attempting to influence public policy understand them well before taking action.

MANAGING PUBLIC POLICY

Of course, a businessperson cannot just walk into the Oval Office and confront the president with a list of reasons why public policy should be shaped around his or her interests. Before tackling the public-policy process, a firm must decide which tools are at its disposal and then come up with a strategy to best use them. The first step is to assess the current market conditions. The next step involves assembling the appropriate human resources.

Assessment of Market Conditions A few years ago, the Harvard Business School devised a set of questions that business managers can ask themselves as they prepare to become involved in the public-policy process. According to these guidelines, a firm involved in a particular market should be able to answer the following:

1. How has public policy shaped the market's overall structure?
2. How has the interaction of public policy and the market affected the performance of this firm and that of other relevant firms?
3. What have been the key determinants of public policy in the market?
4. Are public policy and market conditions likely to change in the near future?
5. Would changes in the firm's current strategy be likely to lead to an improvement in performance?[6]

Public policy is constantly changing, so a company seldom has the luxury of formulating a political strategy during a period when its market is untouched by government decisions.[7] For example, a large real estate corporation may have to change its political strategies from month to month as the Federal Reserve Board raises or lowers interest rates. Therefore, the Harvard Business School came up with an additional four questions for firms that have recently been affected by a significant change in public policy:

1. What are the implications of public-policy change for the firm in terms of new opportunities and constraints?
2. How are other firms likely to react to the change?
3. What will happen to this firm's performance if it maintains its current strategy?
4. Given the changes in public policy and their impact on the market, what alternative strategies are consistent with the firm's current objectives and capabilities?[8]

Human Resources Once these questions have been established, a firm needs the human resources to answer them. In the past, business was more reactive in dealing with a less intrusive government, and employees would take time off from their "normal" duties to deal with public policy whenever it happened to affect them. In the past few decades,

---

6. *Public Policy and the Manager: Conceptual Framework*, Note 9-794-028 (Cambridge, Mass.: Harvard Business School, 1993), p. 8.
7. A. Hillman and G. Keim, "International Variation in the Business-Government Interface: Institutional and Organization Considerations," *Academy of Management Review*, January 1985, p. 193.
8. *Public Policy and the Manager: Conceptual Framework*, p. 8.

▼ EXHIBIT 11–1 Selected Models of the Policymaking Process

Models	Process
The Bureaucratic Politics Model	In the bureaucratic politics model, the relative power of the large bureaucracies in Washington, D.C., determines which policies become part of the national agenda and which are implemented. This theory of American politics is based on the struggle among competing interest groups.
The Power Elite, or Elitism, Model	Powerful economic interests determine the outcome of policy struggles, according to the power elite, or elitism, model. The rich and those who know the rich determine what gets done. More important, the power elite decide which items do *not* get on the public agenda and which items get removed if they are already on it.
The Incrementalist Model	Public policy evolves through small changes or adjustments, according to the incrementalist model. Consequently, policymakers examine only a few alternatives in trying to solve national problems. A good public-policy decision is made when contesting interests agree, and agreement is obtained most easily when changes are minimal.
The Rationalist Model	The rationalist model, sometimes thought of as a pure textbook abstraction, hypothesizes a rational policymaker who sets out to maximize his or her own self-interest rather than determining what the public, or collective, interest might be. Rational policymakers will rank goals and objectives according to their benefit to the policymaker. Such a model is often viewed as an alternative to the incrementalist model. This model is also known as the theory of public choice.
The Systems Model	The most general, and perhaps the most ambitious, approach to modeling policy is the systems model, a product of the relationship between the institutions of government and the socioeconomic-political environment. Such a model has (1) inputs from public opinion and crisis; (2) a political process, including legislative hearings, debates, court decisions, party conventions, and so on; (3) a set of policy outputs consisting of legislation, appropriations, and regulations; and (4) policy outcomes, which may provide, for example, more research on the policy.

business has placed more emphasis on professional public-policy "influencers." Many corporations are finding that a government-relations office located in Washington, D.C., or a state capital is a necessary part of running a business.

To understand better how these human resources influence public policy, we examine a fictitious member of one of these Washington staffs, Ms. Harlow, and her role in what has been called the **iron triangle**. The iron triangle represents the three-way alliance among legislators, bureaucrats, and interest groups to make or preserve policies that benefit their respective interests.

Let's say Harlow works for a group of orange farmers in Ocala, Florida, and her job in Washington is to pressure the federal government to keep tariffs on oranges imported from Latin American countries at high levels to protect her employers' product. Harlow occupies the right upper corner of *Exhibit 11–2*, which provides a schematic view of the iron triangle.

Government Relations To her immediate left is the bureaucracy, which as far as Harlow is concerned is the Department of Agriculture. The simple term *bureaucracy* is not adequate to convey the number of levels of federal employees in this branch of the govern-

▼ **EXHIBIT 11–2 The Iron Triangle**

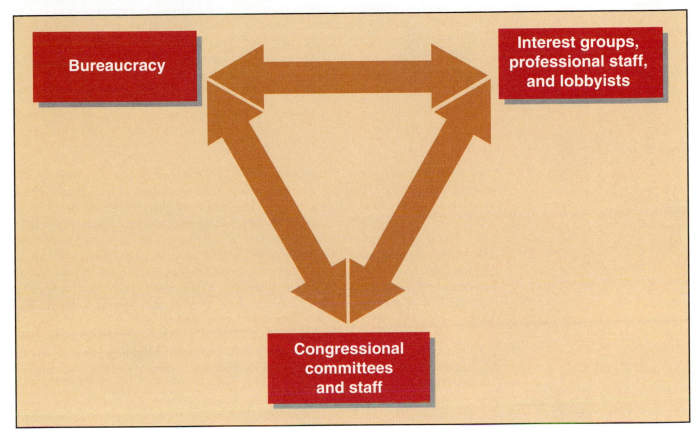

ment. The Department of Agriculture consists of more than 100,000 individuals working directly for the federal government, as well as thousands of other individuals who, directly or indirectly, work as contractors, subcontractors, or consultants to the department. As for legislators, there are two major congressional committees concerned with agriculture—the House Committee on Agriculture and the Senate Committee on Agriculture, Nutrition, and Forestry—each of which has seven subcommittees and large staffs.

Competition Harlow is hardly alone in facing these government entities. Thousands of other employees work for various farm interests doing the same job as she, not to mention still other interest groups that vie for the attention of the Department of Agriculture and Congress. These include the American Farm Bureau Federation, the National Cattleman's Association, the National Milk Producers Association, the Corn Growers Association, the Citrus Growers Association (of which Harlow's employer is a member), and various consumer groups.

Harlow, who has been in Washington for many years, has numerous contacts in government. She does not know the entire staff of the Department of Agriculture, but she knows a sufficient number of the upper-level bureaucrats to get her views heard. In fact, she used to be a business partner with the secretary of agriculture (the head of the department), and she has had several meetings with him to express her (and her employers') views on the importance of high tariffs on imported oranges.

Of course, her friend, the secretary, cannot rescind or approve any tariffs without the approval of Congress. Within Congress, the responsibility for considering import tariffs belongs to the committees and subcommittees in the House of Representatives and the Senate. The ranking members of those committees, most of whom represent farming states, have been on Capitol Hill a long time. They have their own ideas about tariffs on imported oranges, and they keep a close eye on the secretary of agriculture. Consequently, Harlow has cultivated friendships with the congressional committee members and done everything in her power to make sure they appreciate the benefits of high orange tariffs.

LOBBYING

As you may have guessed, Harlow is a lobbyist. She is involved in a tactic of directly influencing public policy known as **lobbying**, which is the process by which organizations or individuals try to induce public officials to pass, defeat, or change the contents of legislation. The art of lobbying has been under some attack in recent years because, by definition, a lobbyist does not act in the **public interest** (for the good of the overall community). He or she is not primarily concerned with the best interests of the community or the national good. The lobbyist is primarily concerned, at least professionally, with the best interests of the organization he or she represents. As **pluralism** (numerous groups competing) in the American political system has become more pronounced, a lobbyist is no longer likely to be representing all business interests. Rather,

▼ **The halls of Congress are now filled with people highlighting labor issues, the environment, ethnic and racial equality, individual property rights, and concerns such as gun ownership.**

Journalist Jeffrey H. Birnbaum points out that despite the ever-growing importance of lobbyists as a political force in the government, they "are almost always the junior players," because "they do not make the decisions." Birnbaum calls them the "underclass" of the halls of power:

> a lower caste that is highly compensated, in part, to make up for their relatively low stature in [Washington, D.C.'s] severely stratified culture. At the top of the hierarchy are members of Congress and Cabinet secretaries. Next come congressional and cabinet staff. And then, at the bottom, come lobbyists. Lobbyists chafe at this. But their status is readily apparent. Frequently they suffer the indignity of standing in hallways or reception areas for hours at a time. Theirs are the first appointments canceled or postponed when other business calls. They do not even like to be called "lobbyists," they prefer "consultants" or "lawyers.". . . One lobbyist put his predicament succinctly: "My mother has never introduced me as 'my son, the lobbyist.' I can't say I blame her."[9]

Despite this negative perception, many lobbyists are highly skilled professionals who reached the top of their fields as lawyers or businesspersons before they began lobbying.

Strategies of Lobbyists No matter who they are, lobbyists have two principal goals: (1) to influence legislation and (2) to gain entry into administrative agencies in order to

---

9. J. H. Birnbaum, *The Lobbyists: How Influence Peddlers Get Their Way in Washington* (New York: Times Books, 1992), pp. 6–7.

obtain the chief prize of the lobbying profession, information.[10] (The latter goal is the primary reason why former cabinet and congressional members and their staffs often make the best lobbyists: access to former colleagues provides these lobbyists with inroads where others would not find them.)

Lobbyists take part in an array of activities to meet these goals:

1. Engaging in private meetings with public officials to make known the interests of the lobbyist's client. Although acting on behalf of clients, lobbyists often furnish needed information to senators and representatives (and government agency appointees) that these officials could not hope to obtain on their own. It is to the advantage of lobbyists to provide accurate information so that the policymaker will rely on them as a source in the future.

2. Testifying before congressional committees for or against proposed legislation.

3. Testifying before executive rulemaking agencies, such as the Federal Trade Commission or the Consumer Product Safety Commission, for or against proposed rules.

4. Assisting legislators or bureaucrats in drafting legislation or prospective regulations. Often, lobbyists can furnish legal advice on the specific details of legislation.

5. Inviting legislators to social occasions such as cocktail parties, boating expeditions, and other events. Most lobbyists feel that contacting legislators in a more relaxed social setting is very effective.

Company Lobbying The best lobbyists offer their employers a variety of services, from public relations advice to direct-mail campaigns. In the modern lobbying environment, however, the most prized possession of a lobbyist or lobbying firm is *access*. All members of Congress and their staffs face time constraints, so when a company hires a lobbyist, what it wants is a chance to make its views heard. In 1993, for example, the defense firm General Dynamics Corporation hired the Washington, D.C., lobbying firm of Cassidy and Associates in a moment of crisis: the Pentagon was on the verge of deciding not to buy Seawolf submarines, sales that were important to General Dynamics. Cassidy's greatest asset was associate Henry K. Guigini, who spent twenty-three years as an administrative assistant for Senator Daniel K. Inouye, the chairman of the defense appropriations subcommittee.[11] Cassidy employees boasted that Guigini "can deliver" Inouye, and by extension the appropriations subcommittee's support for the Seawolf.

Indeed, Inouye made several key speeches in the Senate in support of the Seawolf, and the contract was saved. A spokesperson for Inouye insisted that Guigini had nothing to do with the senator's longtime support for the submarine, but according to insiders, the result cemented the lobbyist's reputation as a "door opener" for defense companies.[12]

Trade Organization Lobbying Businesses in the same general industry or profession frequently organize **trade organizations** to pursue common interests. In the United States today there are well over twenty thousand registered trade organizations. Many of these are classified as business or commercial organizations, and their activities include facilitating the exchange of information, conducting advertising campaigns, setting their own regulatory standards to govern the industry or profession, and lobbying for the business interests of their members.

---

10. V. Novak, "How Drug Companies Operate in the Body Politics," *Business and Society Review*, Winter 1993, p. 58.

11. J. Mintz, "Lobbyists Help Save General Dynamics's Seawolf Sub," *Washington Post*, September 14, 1993, p. C1.

12. *Ibid.*

In general, the trade organizations that are most effective in helping their members represent a narrow interest. For example, when a trade organization representing grocery stores tries to influence legislation about restricting liability claims against grocery stores, it might do well. If that same trade organization lobbies in favor of protecting the environment for all corporations, however, that organization alone probably will not be very effective, because its members will have a variety of views on such a broad issue.

Some trade organizations end up fighting each other because their interests are at opposite ends of the spectrum.[13] A trade organization representing exporters will rarely be in harmony with a trade organization representing domestic producers. After all, domestic producers want to restrict imports that are competing with them. Restrictions on imports, however, ultimately reduce the amount of world trade and therefore have a negative affect on American exporters. Thus, the trade organization representing American exporters will be in favor of lowering all trade restrictions, whereas the trade organization representing domestic producers will want to restrict competing imports into the United States. For an overview of some key trade organizations and their lobbying efforts, see *Exhibit 11–3*.

Grassroots Lobbying Besides using professional lobbyists, corporations and trade organizations use what is called **grassroots lobbying**, or mobilizing employees, customers, and other stakeholders to place pressure on politicians. Sometimes this type of lobbying includes getting the general public involved—the term *grassroots* refers to the members of a community who are directly affected by government's policies and actions.

Grassroots lobbying may have a homespun connotation, but it has evolved into a sophisticated process as more companies and trade organizations recognize the potential of human resources (see *Company Focus: TRW, Inc.* on page 322). After the railroad industry's advertised attack on trucking, for example, the American Trucking Association (ATA) started a grassroots campaign to target six thousand lawmakers, media representatives, shippers, and community leaders.

Some grassroots organizations have grown to a stature that belies their name. The National Federation of Independent Business started in 1943 to represent the interests of small business. Fifty years later it has grown into a force of its own, with over 600,000 members and an annual budget of more than $60 million[14] (see *Managing Social Issues—Small Business/Entrepreneurial: A Strong Voice for Small Business* on page 323).

A company or organization can provide its stakeholders with the incentive to become grassroots activists through a variety of measures. A grassroots program should include regular meetings in which company executives or elected officials discuss political issues that concern the stakeholders. Constant communication via newsletters or E-mail should keep the stakeholder groups informed of relevant issues. A grassroots program should also feature nonpartisan political education courses for stakeholders so they can understand the importance of the legislative issues that affect them and the business organization with which they are affiliated.[15]

Backlash against Lobbyists As the public's discontent with government increased in the mid-1990s, so did its mistrust of so-called influence peddlers. During the 1992 presidential campaign, independent candidate H. Ross Perot increased the scrutiny of lobby-

13. S. A. Lenway and K. Rehbein, "Leaders, Followers, and Free Riders: An Empirical Test of Variation in Corporate Political Involvement," *Academy of Management Journal*, December 1991, p. 893.

14. R. Wartzman and J. Saddler, "Motley's Crew: A Fervent Lobbyist Rallies Small Business to Battle Health Plan," *Wall Street Journal*, January 5, 1994, p. A1.

15. G. D. Keim, "Corporate Grassroots Programs in the 1980s," *California Management Review*, Fall 1985, pp. 111–116.

▼ **EXHIBIT 11–3** Trade Organization Lobbying Activity

Trade Organization	Number of Members	Recent Lobbying Activity
National Association of Wholesalers-Distributors	Approximately 45,000	In favor of product liability reform.
American Trucking Association	Approximately 4,500	Against five-cent-per-gallon fuel tax in Arkansas to raise funds for highway improvements.
Association of American Railroads	Approximately 20	In favor of federal regulation that would have injured railroad workers covered by state workers' compensation funds instead of industry funds.
American Medical Association	Approximately 300,000	In favor of a reduction in federal Medicaid payments (as long as payments to health-care providers are not reduced by regulations).
American Iron and Steel Institute	Approximately 50	In favor of the General Agreement on Tariffs and Trade.
American Bar Association	Approximately 370,000	Against various state court rulings which would forbid law firms from using certain funds to provide free legal services for low-income clients.
Smokeless Tobacco Council	Approximately 5	Against added taxes on tobacco products and regulation of the advertising and sale of tobacco products.
National Turkey Federation	Approximately 5,000	Against "hasty" implementation of federal safe food-handling rules.

ing activity by complaining about "unpatriotic" top Bush administration officials who had resigned their government posts to lobby for foreign governments and companies. Other politicians reacted accordingly. Within ten days of defeating Perot and George Bush—ten weeks before he even took office—Bill Clinton announced that he would be issuing ethical guidelines to tighten restrictions on lobbying activities by top officials of his administration after they leave government.

Under the strictures, Clinton administration appointees would have to wait five years to lobby their old agencies, instead of only one year under the old rules.[16] Beginning January 1, 1996, the Lobbying Disclosure Act placed an annual limit on the value of gifts a lawmaker could receive from any one source ($100), on the value of a single gift ($50), and on the value of charitable contributions accepted in lieu of speaking fees for public appearances ($2,000). The law also requires lobbyists to disclose their salaries and specify the issues they support.

Like many business entities, lobbyists in general have not reacted positively to attempts to regulate their activities. In 1993, after President Clinton proposed to eliminate the tax breaks that allow companies to write off lobbying expenses, lobbyists began lobbying on their own behalf. Six months later, Free Speech Coalition, Inc., an umbrella organization of lobbying interests, was created. As the name implies, the group strives to equate the right to lobby with the constitutional right to free speech.[17]

16. M. Weisskopf, "Clinton to Curb Aides' Future Lobbying," *Washington Post*, November 11, 1992, p. A1.
17. B. McAllister, "From Left to Right, Lobbyists Unite," *Washington Post*, October 5, 1993, p. A12.

COMPANY FOCUS: TRW, INC.
CORPORATE GRASSROOTS LOBBYING

Shirley Hales, a government-relations manager at the Cleveland-based conglomerate TRW, Inc., remembers the dark ages of her company's lobbying information network, before 1993. Lobbyists would use what she calls the "old yell-it-down-the-hall" method. "You'd poke your head out of your cubicle and yell, 'Anybody know if Senator so-and-so is still on this committee or how he feels about a particular bill?'" Not only has the producer of high-tech products and services for the automotive, aerospace, and defense industries dramatically updated its information network; it now uses its advanced technology in the ever-growing field of corporate-fueled grassroots campaigns.

New Focus for Lobbying

For most of its history, TRW's lobbying efforts ran along traditional lines: lots of hours on the phone broken up by frequent fund-raising luncheons and dinners. During the 1992 presidential race, however, independent candidate Ross Perot and his grassroots efforts changed the political landscape. "It's a whole new ballgame now," says Hales. "Legislators don't want just to hear from the lobbyists anymore. They want to hear from the real people—the people they represent."

TRW's government-relations staff knew that it had fifty-five thousand voting employees spread across the nation. It also knew that many of these employees were politically active and could be a powerful grassroots lobbying force if managed appropriately. What the staff did not know was how to manage such a feat; the "old yell-it-down-the-hall" method was clearly not suited to the task.

The CRIS Database

Enter the Constituent Relations Information Systems (CRIS) database, a state-of-the-art computer aid to lobbying that TRW began using in the summer of 1993. CRIS contains updated files on 535 federal and more than 8,000 state government officials. These profiles provide information

vital to TRW's lobbying efforts: on which committees the politicians serve, to which associations they belong, and whether TRW has contributed to their campaign funds. This information is updated constantly at an annual cost of about $20,000 by a Washington, D.C., software company called Capitol Hill Lobbyist.

To supplement this data, CRIS links with some three hundred TRW facilities nationwide, which offer more personalized information on the politicians. At the press of a terminal key, Hales and her staff can know who the legislative representative of any given home district is, whether he or she has visited the firm's local site, and where the government official stands on issues relevant to a particular facility or to TRW as a whole. CRIS also tracks plant "advocates," or politically active managers who make a practice of communicating with local representatives and, in many cases, keep records of their contacts.

Ultimately, CRIS is a tool that allows TRW to run a high-tech grassroots campaign. Using the database's information, the firm's lobbying staff can create the illusion of spontaneous public concern over an issue vital to the company. The methods have been criticized as "Astroturf organizing" by noncorporate local organizers, who point out that a politician's staff members have no way of knowing when there is a corporate hand guiding the TRW employees' actions. But TRW's lobbyists counter that there is a natural incentive for employees to get involved in the political process. After all, the financial welfare of employees is often intricately linked to the financial welfare of the companies for which they work.

The New Bottom Line

Given the effect that government can have on the fortunes of a company, managers would be remiss in not exploring every option when it comes to influencing public policy. TRW has found a valuable lobbying resource in its employees, and other companies may be able to learn from the firm's example.

SOURCE: J. Daly, "TRW Goes to Washington," *Forbes*, December 20, 1993, pp. 27–28.

▣ MANAGING SOCIAL ISSUES

SMALL BUSINESS/ENTREPRENEURIAL: A STRONG VOICE FOR SMALL BUSINESS

The operator of a small business will always complain about the effects of government regulation on profits, but he or she can no longer legitimately claim that the "little person" does not have a voice in Washington, D.C. The 1990s have seen an explosion in the numbers and power of lobbying organizations geared to the concerns of small business. The National Restaurant Association represents 150,000 restaurants nationwide; National Small Business United has 66,000 members; and the National Association of Convenience Stores has a political action committee that gives upward of $100,000 in donations each election cycle. The unrivaled leader in the field is the National Federation of Independent Business (NFIB). With more than 600,000 members and an annual revenue of more than $60 million, the NFIB has significantly increased the influence of small businesses on Capitol Hill.

A Membership-Driven Agenda

Annual dues for the NFIB are $125, for which each member gets a magazine, *Independent Business*; a newsletter, *Capitol Coverage*; and the right to a voice. The NFIB prides itself on allowing its immense membership to set the federation's agenda. Each year members vote on five national political issues—and at least one local issue—and the results directly shape the federation's lobbying efforts.

As a result, legislators know that the NFIB's itinerary is not set by a board of directors but by more than half a million voters. Furthermore, as many small-business owners are well informed when it comes to policy decisions that directly affect them, the NFIB enjoys a highly motivated membership. "When you walk down Main Street, as most members of Congress do, almost every business has an NFIB sticker on the door," notes former representative Mike Synar. John Motley, one of the federation's vice presidents, says that within hours of sending out an "Action Alert" on a specific issue, he can virtually flood a legislator's office with phone calls and letters. "All I need is 20,000 members who want to be involved, and I can turn this town inside out."

The Health-Care Battle

Motley's claims can be substantiated. Intense NFIB opposition helped remove two chairmen of the Senate Small Business Committee during the 1980s. During the Bush administration (1989–1993), the federation was instrumental in killing family leave legislation that would have forced business to give paid leave to employees with a new child or ill family member. (Modified legislation was eventually passed in 1993, however.)

The NFIB truly turned Washington "inside out" by its role in helping defeat President Bill Clinton's health-care plan in 1994. NFIB and its members objected to the proposed "employer mandate" in the plan, which would have required employers to pay for their employees' health insurance. The federation sent out 500,000 letters to members; the letters carried warnings such as, "Because a new plan would stick YOU with the bill for a new health-care system, you need to contact Rep. X RIGHT AWAY." NFIB targeted those legislators with large numbers of small businesses in their district or state, such as Representative Jim Slattery. Slattery was deluged with phone calls and letters, including one from a travel agent who wrote, "If this health plan is [passed], you will have twelve new people on the unemployment rolls in Salina (Kansas) because I will be forced to shut my business down."

Slattery refused to support the employer mandate, and enough of his peers followed suit to gridlock Congress on the issue and effectively kill the president's plan. It was an impressive show of power for the NFIB, which aims to get the small-business owners even more involved in politics—the federation has a goal of one million members by 2000.

For Critical Analysis:

Give some reasons why you might want to join the NFIB. Conversely, why might you not want to join?

SOURCE: Information from R. Wartzman and J. Saddler, "Motley's Crew: A Fervent Lobbyist Rallies Small Business to Battle Health Plan," *Wall Street Journal*, January 5, 1994, p. A1; and S. Headden, "The Little Lobby That Could," *U.S. News and World Report*, September 12, 1994, p. 46.

POLITICAL ACTION COMMITTEES

In the 1994 congressional elections, it cost an average of $3.7 million to run for the Senate and $394,000 to run for the House.[18] It was estimated that any candidate for president in 1996 would have to spend at least $45 million. In short, politicians almost always need money. Consequently, the most important form of direct lobbying from special interest groups clearly has become the political contribution from a group's **political action committee (PAC)**—a group established by and representing the interests of corporations (and labor unions) that raises money and gives donations to campaigns. Most of these contributions take the form of cash donations to the candidate's national reelection committee, which the candidate can use any way he or she pleases.[19]

To avoid limits placed on these direct contributions, there has been a growth in "soft money" donations, in which the contribution goes to the candidate's state-level organizations to be used in efforts to register and attract voters. In the two-year election cycle from 1992 to 1994, the Republican National Committee collected $44 million in these unregulated donations, compared with $39 million for the Democratic National Committee over the same period.[20] More was collected from 1994 to 1996. Therefore,

▼ **As the influence of PACs has grown with each successive election, so has the concern that the electoral process is being captured by the lure of special interest money.[21]**

Politicians have been placed in the awkward position of needing PAC money for their campaigns while at the same time insisting that they are not being "bought" by special interest groups. The balancing act will continue unless drastic reform of the campaign contribution system is initiated. Until that time, PACs will remain an integral part of efforts by the business community to influence public policy.

THE EVOLUTION AND GROWTH OF PACS

Worry about the effect of campaign contributions by business is hardly new to the American political process. As far back as 1894, a progressive Republican named Elihu Root (1845–1937) pushed for a complete ban on corporate contributions to political campaigns.[22] It was not until 1948, however, that the laws that allow for what would later become the PAC were set into place. During that year Congress codified all regulations governing campaign contributions by individuals, corporations, and labor unions. It also noted the Supreme Court's decision in *U.S. v. C.I.O.* that allowed labor unions and corporations to set aside money for contribution to political campaigns.

Federal Election Campaign Acts of 1972 and 1974 It was not until the 1970s that more effective regulation of campaign financing was undertaken. The Federal Election

18. J. Belliveau, "Campaign Spending in '93–'94," *Washington Post*, January 23, 1995, p. A17.
19. E. S. Cabot and K. D. Sheekey, "Let's Send Corporate PACs Packing," *Business and Society Review*, Winter 1990, p. 62.
20. "What's News," *Wall Street Journal*, January 11, 1995, p. A1.
21. G. D. Webster, "PAC Particulars," *Association Management*, June 1995, p. 172.
22. *Political Action Committees and the Financing of Congressional Campaigns*, Note 9-792-080 (Boston, Mass.: Harvard Business School, 1992), p. 3.

Campaign Act of 1972 essentially replaced all past laws and instituted a major reform. The act placed no limit on overall spending but restricted the amount that could be spent on mass media advertising, including television. It also required disclosure of all contributions and expenditures in excess of $100. In principle, the 1972 act limited the role of labor unions and corporations in political campaigns. It also provided for a voluntary $1 checkoff on federal income tax returns for general campaign funds to be used by majority party presidential candidates (this provision first applied in the 1976 presidential campaign).

The act did not go far enough, however. In 1974, Congress passed another act, the Federal Election Campaign Act. It did the following:

1. **Created the Federal Election Commission.** This commission consists of six nonpartisan administrators whose duties are to enforce compliance with the requirements of the act.
2. **Provided public financing for presidential primaries and general elections.** Any candidate running for president who is able to obtain sufficient contributions in at least twenty states can obtain a subsidy from the U.S. Treasury to help pay for primary campaigns. Each major party was given $12.4 million for the national convention in 1996. The major party candidates have federal support for almost all their expenses, provided they are willing to accept campaign-spending limits.
3. **Limited presidential campaign spending.** Any candidate accepting federal support has to agree to limit campaign expenditures to the amount prescribed by federal law.
4. **Limited contributions.** Citizens can contribute up to $1,000 to each candidate in each federal election or primary; the total limit of all contributions from one individual is $25,000 per year. Groups can contribute a maximum of $5,000 to a candidate in any election.
5. **Required disclosure.** Each candidate must file periodic reports with the Federal Election Commission listing who contributed, how much was spent, and for what the money was spent.

The 1974 Act and PACs The 1974 act, as modified by certain amendments in 1976, allows corporations, labor unions, and special interest groups to set up PACs to raise money for candidates. For a PAC to be legitimate, the money must be raised from at least fifty volunteer donors and must be given to at least five candidates in the federal election. Each corporation and each union is limited to one PAC. As you might imagine, corporate PACs obtain funds from executives, employees, and stockholders in their firms, and unions obtain PAC funds from their members. General company funds may *not* be contributed to a PAC.

The Growth of PACs Because of further legislative changes in the late 1970s to encourage political involvement through PACs, their number has grown astronomically, as has the amount of money they spend on elections. There were about six hundred political action committees in 1976; by 1996, there were more than 4,500. The total amount of campaign contributions by PACs grew from $8.5 million in 1972 to an estimated $450 million in 1996 (see *Exhibit 11–4* on page 326). By the 1990s, senators were funding about 30 percent of their campaigns with PAC contributions; for representatives, that number had reached 44 percent.[23]

---

23. "Senate PAC Funds," *Congressional Quarterly Weekly Report,* March 27, 1993, p. 727.

▼ **EXHIBIT 11–4 The Growth of PAC Campaign Contributions, 1972 to Mid-1990s**

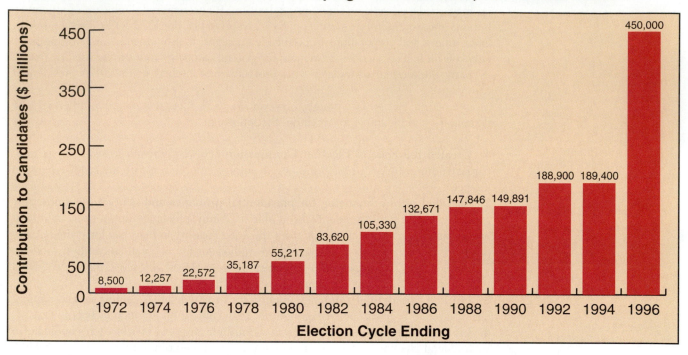

SOURCE: J. E. Cantor, *Campaign Financing in Federal Elections* (Washington, D.C.: Congressional Research Service, 1991), Table 5; and Federal Election Commission.

THE SPENDING PATTERNS OF PACS

It is difficult to know which phenomenon sparked the other: Did the explosion in campaign spending by candidates influence the growing size and number of PACs, or was the reverse true? Between 1972 and 1996, aggregate campaign expenditures by Senate and House candidates rose from $66 million to an estimated $500 million.[24] In the 1993–1994 election cycle, PACs spent more than $380 million influencing politicians.

The first assumption is that the demands of modern campaigning—television and radio commercials, direct-mail campaigns, constant air travel, huge staff—being considerably more expensive than the old railroad whistle stop trips, created a demand for contributions that the PACs were more than happy to fill. More issues exist, however.

Interest groups funnel PAC money to candidates who they think can do the most good for them. Frequently, a PAC will make the maximum contribution of $5,000 to candidates who face little or no opposition. During 1990, the total PAC campaign funds that went to the 79 incumbents who ran unopposed for House seats was $13,277,348. In comparison, the 331 nonincumbent House challengers that same election received only $6,989,631 in PAC money.[25] The great bulk of campaign contributions from 1974 to 1994 went to incumbent candidates rather than to challengers; not coincidentally, during that time the incumbents almost always won.

The link between PAC contributions and incumbents became obvious to some analysts during the 1990 congressional elections, when 96 percent of congressional incum-

---

24. Belliveau, *op. cit.*
25. "A Case in Point: Politics and Skinny Dipping," *Washington Post*, November 3, 1991, p. C2.

bents were reelected, which contradicted a pre-vote poll by the *New York Times* that showed that 63 percent of the public said they disapproved of the job Congress was doing.

Corporations have been as likely to give money to Democrats in Congress as to Republicans, for the simple reason that until the 1994 elections, Democratic incumbents chaired important committees and subcommittees. When the Republicans held committee chairs in the Senate from 1980 to 1986, they reaped benefits in PAC money, as they did in the mid-1990s. Why, you might ask, would business leaders give to Democrats who may be more liberal than themselves? Interest groups see PAC contributions as a way to ensure access to powerful legislators, even if they may disagree with them some of the time. PAC contributions are, in a way, an investment in a relationship. Consequently, a PAC will contribute to unopposed incumbents—who obviously do not need the money to get reelected—to protect and strengthen that relationship.

CONCERNS ABOUT PACs

Is the relationship between politicians and interest groups in the best interests of the American people? Can we assume that a politician who has received PAC money will be more disposed to vote on legislation according to the position of the PAC-backing interest group? Why else would a political action committee give $5,000 to an unopposed candidate?

PACs and Congressional Voting There have been documented links between PAC spending and voting patterns of members of Congress. According to a study by the nonpartisan Center for Public Integrity, between 1985 and 1990, seventeen sugar industry PACs contributed $2.6 million to congressional campaign committees. The study concluded that "the more money a member got from sugar interests, the more likely he or she was to vote in the industry's favor." Eighty-five percent of the twenty-nine senators who received more than $15,000 from the sugar PACs voted to continue foreign-produced sugar quotas, which keep the price for sugar in the United States 11 cents higher per pound than the world average. All the senators who received no contributions from sugar interests, in contrast, voted against the implicit subsidies.[26]

Concern among Legislators Not all politicians welcome political action committee contributions, and some have openly questioned the effect PAC money has had on their profession. To prove their independence from these special interests, ten members of the freshman congressional class of 1994 refused to accept any PAC contributions whatsoever. Senator John F. Kerry stated that even if a politician can "say in all sincerity that he or she is not influenced by tens of thousands of dollars taken in PAC money, the public is fully justified in believing that they have not necessarily elected the best Congress—but merely the best Congress money can buy."[27]

The media is aggressive in its reporting of improprieties in the PAC system, and the public is taking Kerry's words to heart. A 1994 poll by ABC News found that 83 percent of those surveyed felt most members of Congress care more about special interests than about their own constituencies.

---

26. R. L. Miller, *Economics Today*, updated 8th ed. (New York: HarperCollins, 1996), p. 90.

27. J. Kerry, "Should the Boren Amendment Approach to Curtailing PACs Be Adopted?" *Congressional Digest*, February 1987, p. 43, as quoted in *Political Action Committees and the Financing of Congressional Campaigns*, p. 7.

CAMPAIGN FINANCE REFORM

These types of poll results have influenced some politicians. In 1995, two separate bills were introduced in Congress proposing that *all* contributions by PACs be banned. The widespread abuse of contributions led to the complete restructuring of the laws governing state elections in Kentucky (to be discussed shortly).

It is important to recognize, however, that PACs have been important contributors to our pluralistic society. Through PACs, civil rights groups, environmental groups, unions, and other special interest groups have been able to get their opinions heard in state legislatures and in Congress. Many activists and politicians, such as former senator Rudy Boschwitz, disagree with Kerry and see PACs as a vehicle to increase participation in the electoral process. Boschwitz noted that more than twice as many people give to PACs as contribute to individuals. "Somehow," he adds, "the idea of a group of 50 people giving $50 a year to a PAC that then turns around and contributes a thousand dollars a crack to a candidate is viewed as worse than a single contributor writing out a check for a thousand dollars to his favorite candidate."[28]

Perhaps the PACs themselves are not the problem but rather a symptom of a political process that demands too much financially from its participants. This leads to the argument that reform should focus not on PACs but on the system. In fact, popular causes such as term limits for politicians, limits on campaign spending, and public financing for campaigns may deal more directly with the heart of PAC problems. Some states are beginning to experiment with broader reform. During the 1995 Kentucky gubernatorial election, the candidates were not allowed to spend more than $3.6 million on their campaigns, about half of what the previous winner had allocated. The contribution limit was set at $500, down from $4,000. To help keep costs down, candidates were offered $1.2 million in public financing if they agreed to limit their own fund raising to $600,000. The results were more joint appearances by the two candidates to cut down on costs, more debates on public television, and fewer expensive commercials attacking the opposition.[29]

PAC ALTERNATIVES: OTHER MEANS OF ACCESS TO THE PUBLIC-POLICY PROCESS

The lobbying process and PACs are the most obvious ways in which business can enter and have access to the public-policy process, but there are other means of access. Two of them are public opinion formation and lawsuits.

Affecting Public Opinion An effective way in which business can gain access to the public-policy process is by trying to change public opinion so that pro-business candidates will win elections. Additionally, if public opinion can be shaped to favor business interests, current politicians may assess legislative agenda accordingly. Numerous public relations firms have corporations as their clients and attempt to generate or alter public opinion to benefit these clients.

Business can attempt to affect public opinion by advertising on TV, in newspapers (such as the Mobil Oil opinion pieces often found in the *Wall Street Journal*), and on the radio. In the mid-1990s, the tobacco industry was under siege from politicians, state governments, and antismoking special interest groups. These stakeholders were demanding

28. R. Boschwitz, "Should the Boren Amendment Approach to Curtailing PACs Be Adopted?" *Congressional Digest*, February 1987, p. 40, as quoted in *Political Action Committees and the Financing of Congressional Campaigns*, p. 9.
29. J. Harwood, "Kentucky's New Campaign-Finance Law Limits Donations as Well as Interest in Governor's Race," *Wall Street Journal*, October 5, 1995, p. A16.

that tobacco companies take legal and financial responsibility for the costs of their products to society. A particular area of debate was the tobacco industry's advertising, which critics said was aimed at luring young people into a lifelong habit. As can be seen in *Exhibit 11–5* on page 330, tobacco companies such as Philip Morris USA responded with a public relations campaign designed to deflect the negative publicity.

Affecting the Judicial Process Business also can have access to the public-policy process by vigorously pursuing certain types of lawsuits. A number of pro-business public interest law firms pattern themselves after the American Civil Liberties Union (ACLU) and the National Association for the Advancement of Colored People (NAACP). These include the Pacific Legal Foundation, the Washington Legal Foundation, and the Center for Individual Rights. Such public-interest law firms allow businesses access to the public-policy process by vigorously supporting plaintiffs or defendants in lawsuits whose outcomes will have a broad impact on the business community.

For example, businesses have supported public-interest law firms that themselves have supported defendants in lawsuits involving government "taking" of private property. In the 1987 case *Nollan v. California Coastal Commission*, the Pacific Legal Foundation argued that a government agency could not make a building permit contingent on a landowner's agreement to provide a piece of land for public use—in that case a path to the beach. The Supreme Court ruled in the landowner's favor, setting the precedent that there must be an unreasonable burden placed on the community by proposed land development before the government can make such an imposition.

GLOBAL BUSINESS ISSUES AND PUBLIC POLICY

As we saw in Chapter 7, there has been an intense globalization of financial markets in the past few decades, and more American companies are becoming multinational—with subsidiaries abroad—than at any point in history. Each country has a unique regulatory climate, as was discussed in Chapter 10. Some countries, (Germany, for example) are heavily regulated, whereas others (Taiwan and Egypt among them) have comparatively relaxed regulatory controls. Each multinational corporation (MNC) must be aware of the climate for business in whichever foreign nation it enters.

Any American MNC has a *de facto* partner in its business excursions overseas: the U.S. government. The U.S. Constitution gives Congress the power to "regulate Commerce with foreign Nations." Whereas an MNC has a set of economic priorities with its host country, the U.S. government has its own set of foreign policy goals in regard to that same country. Often, these two sets of priorities somewhat mirror each other. Whenever this is not so, industries and corporations must try to influence the foreign policy of the U.S. government, just as they do its domestic actions. We are familiar with the means of influencing public policy—lobbying, PACs, and interest group pressure—but the variables that characterize foreign policy bring their own challenges and difficulties to the private sector.

ECONOMIC POLICY VERSUS FOREIGN POLICY

The historic relations of the United States and other nations cannot be explained in a couple of sentences, but diplomat Henry Kissinger comes close when he discusses the two predominant and contradictory U.S. attitudes toward foreign policy:

▼ "The first" national attitude, notes Kissinger, "is that America serves its values best by perfecting democracy at home, thereby acting as a beacon for the rest of

▼ **EXHIBIT 11–5 Affecting Public Opinion** Among the many proposals in response to charges that the tobacco industry was encouraging underage smoking was the following:

Philip Morris USA proposed a number of changes in various newspaper ads.

▶ **New Federal Age Restriction**
- A federal minimum age of 18 for the sale of tobacco products.

Suggested Prohibitions Against
- The sale of individual cigarettes.
- Cigarette vending machines.
- Tobacco advertising on outward-facing retail window displays within 1,000 feet of schools or playgrounds.
- Mass transit advertising.
- All sales and distribution of tobacco products to consumers through the mail.
- Payments for product placements in movies and television.
- Brand names, logos, characters, or selling messages on non-tobacco-related items, such as caps, tee shirts, jackets, or gym bags.
- All outdoor tobacco product advertising within 1,000 feet of schools or playgrounds.
- Packs of fewer than 20 cigarettes.
- Sampling except in locations where minors are denied access.
- Billboards of less than 225 square feet—the type typically used in urban neighborhoods.
- Advertising in family amusement centers, video arcades, and video games except those located in areas where minors are denied access.
- Permanent brand name advertising in virtually all sports stadiums.

▶ **Suggested Limitations**
- Avoid tobacco advertising in any publication that has more than 15% readership that is under 18.
- Unless sporting and other events are attended by 75% or more spectators who are 18 years or older, all tobacco advertising should be banned.

▶ **Suggested Requirements**
- Retailers and their employees to certify that they understand and will comply with minimum-age laws.
- Minimum-age signage at tobacco retail outlets.
- Tobacco products to be displayed only under the control or within the line of sight of the retailer.
- A tobacco-industry–funded program of $250 million over 5 years to fund retailer compliance and oversight by the Department of Health and Human Services and the Federal Trade Commission.
- Picture ID for those appearing to be under 21.

▶ **Suggested Penalties**
- A system of civil penalties against manufacturers, including fines of up to $50,000 for violations, as well as a system of graduated civil penalties against retailers who sell tobacco products to minors.

mankind; the second, that America's values impose on it an obligation to crusade for them around the world."[30]

Kissinger notes that every U.S. president since Woodrow Wilson (1913–1921) has been governed by these principles, from Wilson's own League of Nations to Jimmy Carter's human rights campaigns to Ronald Reagan's rhetorical (and spending) battles with "the evil empire" of the former Soviet Union.

In 1961, John F. Kennedy declared that the United States was strong enough to "pay any price, bear any burden" to ensure the spread of the concepts of liberty and democracy around the globe. Kennedy's words were appropriate for the rhetoric of the Cold War era, but he was not necessarily speaking for American business interests. The financial goals of American businesses often conflict with the policy aims of the U.S. State Department, though the federal government has the constitutional muscle to prevail when it feels the need to do so (see *Company Focus: Conoco, Inc.* on page 333). When the United States was the world's primary economic power, its industries could afford to allow the government to choose markets for them. As the country lost its dominant position, however, many businesses felt they were bearing too great a burden from foreign policy decisions, and in recent years they have been more active in trying to influence change in this area.[31]

The Question of Embargoes One foreign policy tool that federal governments have traditionally used to punish another country for perceived wrongdoing is the **trade embargo**, which either forbids imports or exports or allows only limited imports or exports between the two nations. In the mid-1990s the United States had four such embargoes in effect—with Fidel Castro's Cuba, Saddam Hussein's Iraq, Muammar Qaddafi's Libya, and Kim Jong Il's North Korea. Cuba and North Korea are under sanction for their communist tendencies, Libya for its terrorist activities, and Iraq as punishment for not complying with the settlement ending the Gulf War of 1991. Also, until South Africa's government lifted its policy of racial apartheid, the United States severely limited trade with that country.[32]

In many cases, companies are reluctant to criticize embargoes. It is poor public relations to speak of trading with a country that represses its citizens along racial lines or shows little regard for human rights. When the political climate shifts enough to allow for dialogue, however, businesses quickly jump to fill the breach.[33] Such was the case regarding the United States and Vietnam.

In 1975, the United States placed a trade embargo on Vietnam in reaction to that country's unwillingness to cooperate with the American government in resolving cases of unaccounted-for soldiers from the Vietnam War. The embargo stood for eighteen years, even as other countries began to take advantage of Vietnam's plentiful national resources, low wages, and burgeoning capitalist economy.

American industry—not wanting to get involved in the prisoner of war/missing in action (POW/MIA) controversy—kept silent until the early 1990s, when the political climate began to change. In December 1992, President George Bush took the initiative toward ending the embargo by permitting U.S. companies to open offices in Vietnam, hire staff, and sign contracts, but not conduct business. Then, in early 1993, a special Senate committee headed by Senator Kerry, who had served in Vietnam during the war,

---

30. H. Kissinger, *Diplomacy* (New York: Simon & Schuster, 1994), p. 18.
31. D. B. Yoffie and H. V. Milner, "An Alternative to Free Trade or Protectionism: Why Corporations Seek Strategic Trade Policy," *California Management Review*, Summer 1989, p. 111.
32. S. P. Sethi, "American Corporations and the Economic Future of South Africa," *Business and Society Review*, Winter 1995, p. 10.
33. P. Belli, "Globalizing the Rest of the World," *Harvard Business Review*, July–August 1991, p. 127.

found no "compelling evidence" that Americans were still being held prisoner in Southeast Asia.[34]

At the same time, a consortium of nations led by France was preparing to provide loans to help Vietnam free itself from its burdensome debt. This act would enable the country to become eligible for millions of dollars in loans from the International Monetary Fund to help develop its economy. If the U.S. embargo was not lifted before this occurred, American companies would be excluded from this market. "Sooner or later the embargo is going to end," said an executive at Caterpillar, Inc. "Our argument is that it should be in time for the U.S. economy to derive some benefit from it."[35]

Firms began directly lobbying the Clinton administration to lift the embargo. During a meeting with administration officials, an executive from United Airlines argued that the airline company was facing massive layoffs at home and was counting on new markets such as those in Vietnam to recover its losses. Within two hours of Clinton's subsequent lifting of the embargo, the airlines announced flights from Los Angeles to Ho Chi Minh City (formerly Saigon).

Free Trade versus Protectionism Mark Twain once said that the free traders win all the arguments and the protectionists get all the votes. What he was referring to was the supporters of the general economic argument in favor of free trade versus the special interest groups that are in favor of protection—that is, restrictions on imports into the United States. From a general economic point of view, the benefits of free trade have been well understood for centuries. In short, maximum overall economic welfare normally occurs in concert with virtually no restrictions on trade, not only among individuals but also among cities, states, and indeed nations. There is little difference between the benefits of free trade among the fifty states in the United States and among the two hundred nations of the world.

---

34. R. S. Greenberger, "Clinton Prepares to Relax Policy on Vietnam as U.S. Business Urges Access to New Market," *Wall Street Journal*, April 12, 1993, p. A12.
35. *Ibid.*

COMPANY FOCUS: CONOCO, INC.
THE CONSEQUENCES OF FOREIGN POLICY ON BUSINESS

When the National Iranian Oil Company (NIOC) announced that it had signed a deal with Conoco Iran NV to develop two offshore oil fields in the Persian Gulf, the global corporation was identified as a Dutch company. Nobody was fooled, however, as it is no secret to the international oil community or the U.S. State Department that Conoco Iran NV is actually a Netherlands-based subsidiary of Conoco, Inc., an oil company located in Houston, Texas. Perhaps NIOC was worried about the anti-American feelings that run rampant through the religious factions in its own country. Alternatively, perhaps NIOC—and Conoco—had a feeling the deal might not be in line with the foreign policy designs of the U.S. executive branch.

Oil Fields and Iranian Politics

Conoco had been a small player in the Iranian oil business until the late 1970s, when the industry was nationalized by Ayatollah Khomeini's Islamic government. All Western oil companies were evicted. Subsequently, Iran faced extreme economic pressures, including a freeze on World Bank loans and a ban on importing Iranian products into the United States, so it was forced to open its oil fields to Western developers. The $1 billion deal with Conoco was just the beginning of a bidding war for Iranian oil reserves, which would include companies from Germany, France, and Great Britain.

United States–Iranian Relations

Conoco followed the letter of the law in its deal with NIOC, as none of the oil or natural gas from the sites would be brought into the United States. It incorrectly predicted the Clinton administration's reaction to the transaction, however. Iran's links to terrorist bombings in Argentina and London, along with the country's intransigent stance in Middle East peace negotiations, had led the administration to view it publicly as a "rogue state." Almost two years before the Conoco deal, the State Department began urging other countries to stop doing business with Tehran.

As an ironic (and embarrassing) twist for the Clinton administration, during that time, the United States overtook Japan and Germany as Iran's leading trading partner. In 1994, U.S. subsidiaries and Iranian firms did almost $5 billion in business, the bulk of which came in the form of U.S. oil companies buying Iranian products and then selling them to a third party. In the eyes of President Clinton and his advisors, Conoco's deal further eroded their credibility in trying to turn other nations against Iran.

The Executive Order

Within a few days of NIOC's announcement, a Clinton statement called the transaction "inconsistent" with U.S. foreign policy, and Secretary of State Warren Christopher criticized Conoco for aiding an "outlaw nation." Within a week, Clinton signed an executive order canceling the business transaction. In explanation, a White House spokesperson said the deal "would dangerously add to [Iran's] economic capacity to do the things that we find objectionable in the world community."

Conoco executives expressed shock at the president's action. During the three years of negotiations, the firm's officials had had as many as thirty meetings with State Department officials to smooth any rough corners. Conoco president and chief executive officer Constantine S. Nicandros said, "We proceeded according to the law, and it was indicated that everything was fine." Industry experts, however, fault the company for not reading the political warning signs concerning Iran coming from the president and Congress. "I can't imagine Conoco going into Iran without both eyes open," said one.

The New Bottom Line

Corporations must understand that foreign policy is not an exact science; politicians can change their opinions on a situation overnight. Even if the U.S. State Department had been giving Conoco a green light for three years, the company had to be aware of the risk it was running by dealing with Iran.

SOURCE: Information from G. McWilliams, "Why Didn't Conoco See This One Coming?" *Business Week*, March 27, 1995, p. 40; and J. Kingston, "Conoco Believed Iran Deal on Course," *Platt's Oilgram News*, April 27, 1995, p. 6.

▼ When free trade is allowed, resources flow to where they have the highest value.

In the process, however, some individuals and industries may suffer, particularly during a time of transition. It is not surprising that the individuals who are negatively affected—whether they be workers, management, or shareholders—will try to protect their own interests. They can do so by lobbying in favor of protection against low-cost imports. Members of the business community (except monopolies) generally favor competition until it appears to harm them or their shareholders and employees. They then become protectionists for their particular industry.

In the United States, special interest groups have succeeded in protecting the following industries: textiles, automobiles, steel, flat-screen panels, citizen's band radios, and certain agricultural products, to name only a few. Often, U.S. negotiations with other countries concerning protectionist policies turn into "trade wars," in which the U.S. government threatens foreign governments with trade sanctions if they do not open their markets to American companies. Sometimes these trade wars become complicated by the differing international interests of domestic companies.

A CLOSER LOOK: THE LOBBYING OF CLINTON AND CHINA

A classic example of the clash between business interests and the federal government's political goals was the controversy in 1994 over whether or not President Clinton should continue the most-favored-nation (MFN) trade status that the United States had granted China as far back as the Nixon administration (1969–1974).[36] During his presidential campaign two years earlier, Clinton had harshly criticized President Bush for continuing to "coddle" China's "dictators" with a policy that was immoral and outdated. Numerous human rights violations in China were cited. Eventually, Clinton decided to continue China's MFN trade status. This decision opened the president to reproach from human rights advocates. It also showed the power of lobbying by business organizations frightened of losing access to the world's largest market for an expanding list of consumer goods, not to mention a market for their many goods made in China.[37]

In 1993, the year before the controversy, the United States was the destination of one-third of China's exports, which left no doubt that the country would suffer mightily from a downsizing of trade with the United States. Business analysts were almost unanimous, however, in their predictions that the long-term pain would also be felt by the United States, which has an integral trade partner in China[38] (see *Exhibit 11–6*).

Without MFN status, many of the goods that China exports to the United States would skyrocket in price. The tax on cotton tank tops, for example, would go from 21 percent to 90 percent; the tax on Chinese-made Barbie dolls and GI Joes would see an increase to 70 percent from 12 percent. In all, according to a study by the International Business and Economic Research Company, American consumers would face $14 billion dollars in higher retail prices from a combination of higher tariffs and more expensive replacements of Chinese goods on store shelves.[39]

A cessation of MFN trade status, and the ensuing trade war, would also hurt a number of American MNCs doing business in China. The following are a few MNCs that would have been affected:

36. J. Maggs, "Clinton Plans Permanent MFN Status for China," *Journal of Commerce and Commercial Affairs*, January 6, 1994, p. 1A.

37. "Clinton's Chinese Lessons," *Economist*, May 21, 1994, p. 13.

38. D. A. Andelman, "Marco Polo Revisited: The Business Opportunities for Western Firms in China Are Colossal—As Are the Myriad Trading Issues," *Management Review*, August 1995, p. 10.

39. L. H. Sun and P. Behr, "Importers, Exporters Depend on China," *Washington Post*, May 22, 1994, p. A28.

▼ **EXHIBIT 11–6 Facets of the U.S.–China Trade Relationship**

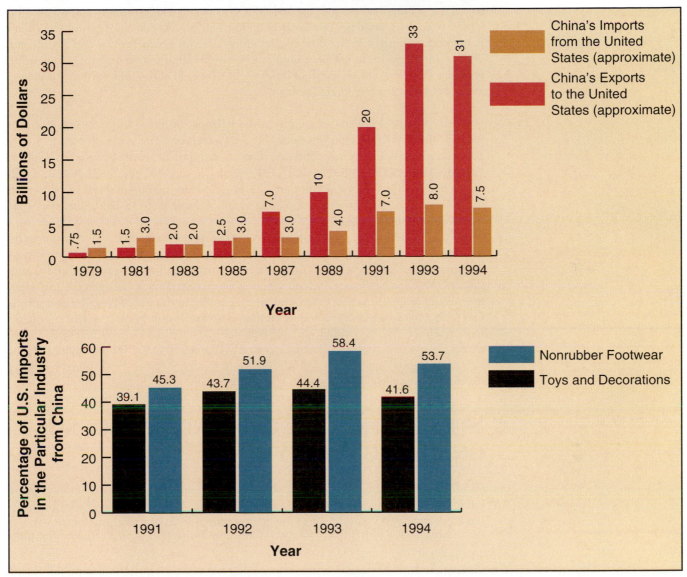

SOURCE: U.S. Commerce Department, State Statistical Bureau.

1. Boeing. On January 1, 1994, the airplane manufacturer had secured orders from China's airlines for sixty-four planes worth $3.9 billion. Boeing vice president John F. Hayden estimated that $2 billion of the order would be canceled with the end of MFN status. Aviation leaders within China had already begun suggesting that the country shift its airplane orders to Europe's Airbus firm, a more stable supplier because the European Union was not pressuring China on the human rights issue. "The threat is real," warned Hayden.

2. Chrysler. The auto manufacturer was in the process of negotiating to build a minivan plant on Chinese soil in 1994. "All things being equal, the Chinese prefer the Chrysler product," Chrysler vice president Thomas Denomme said. "Unfortunately, all things are not equal." A Chinese source confirmed Denomme's fear, saying that if MFN status was revoked, "I don't think Chrysler will have any chance."

3. AT&T. China had recently picked AT&T to create a telecommunications network almost from the ground up, providing an opportunity that AT&T chief executive William J. Warwick compared to the time of Alexander Graham Bell a century ago. By the year 2000, China's goal is to have ten phones per one hundred Chinese people. This would generate some $90 billion worth of business, of which AT&T would get a major piece if it was not hamstrung by foreign policy.[40]

With billions of dollars apparently in the balance, business lobbying was at a fever pitch in the days and weeks preceding Clinton's decision. The chief executives of nine companies—AT&T, Boeing, Chrysler, Digital Equipment, Eastman Kodak, General Electric, Honeywell, Motorola, and TRW—sent Clinton and other administration officials a letter outlining their position on China. The letter highlighted an estimation that the companies' cumulative sales to China would amount to $158 billion over ten years under normal trade relations.

In light of the human rights controversy, the executives were also eager to promote the social benefits of American businesses in China. The lobbying effort included a nine-page document entitled "How U.S. Companies Are Changing the Environment and Conditions of the Chinese People," which argued that increased trade between the two countries would help China's social conditions. According to the executives, the presence of U.S. companies would "accelerate Chinese exposure to the West," "would promote a more open society," and would "provide better employment alternatives for the Chinese." In fact, a representative from Kodak expressed his opinion that "MFN is good for the business community" and "it's good for the human rights issue."[41] (President Clinton renewed China's MFN trade status again in 1995 without much fanfare or discussion.)

STRATEGIES FOR CORPORATE INFLUENCE ON PUBLIC POLICY

For the business manager, the "tools of influence"—political action committees, special interest organizations, and lobbyists—are much more than part of a civics lesson. They represent strategy options for achieving the optimum profits of an industry or firm and, in many cases, for ensuring the very survival of the industry or firm. Reacting to and influencing local, state, and federal governments is often a key element of a manager's job. Consequently, a discussion of the relationship between the private and public sectors requires at least a brief focus on strategy. To be sure, each situation is different and holds countless decisions and options for the business manager. A few general guidelines, however, should help the manager develop a fundamentally stable strategy for dealing with the vagaries of public policy.

THE CORPORATE POLITICAL PROGRAM

The political program on which a corporation embarks should have a specific framework. Numerous frameworks are possible, and each one depends on specific circumstances. To

---

40. *Ibid.*

41. A. Q. Nomani, "U.S. Executives Expect China to Receive Few Trade Penalties for Rights Record," *Wall Street Journal*, May 16, 1994, p. A2.

provide an overview, researchers Carl P. Zeithaml and Gerald D. Keim have developed a five-part framework for a corporate political program. They outline their framework in terms of phases. *Exhibit 11–7* on page 338 presents that five-part framework. One of the weaknesses of this outline, however, is its underlying assumption that all managers understand the workings of the political process, which is not true in too many cases.

POLITICAL ACTION COMMITTEE STRATEGY

In today's political atmosphere, where discussion of lobbying and PACs is laced with derogatory terms such as *influence peddlers* and *vote buying*, the business manager sometimes avoids the use of these forms of influence. While this attitude is understandable— we have seen that even lobbyists themselves are uncomfortable with their roles—it is not entirely realistic. After all,

▼ As long as the law is adhered to, lobbyist and PAC activity by any name is a viable strategic option for businesses.

Favorable Conditions for PAC Action There is always the danger that PAC contributions will not lead to a change in the public-policy process. Clearly, certain conditions must prevail in order for PAC contributions by businesses to be effective. Researcher Larry Sabato of the University of Virginia has developed what he believes to be the optimal conditions that must prevail in order for PAC contributions to be effective.[42] At a minimum, according to Sabato, the issue under concern should be narrow and preferably unopposed. That means that PAC contributions should not target issues that involve broad national concerns, such as further welfare reform. Additionally, if numerous PACs are allied, they work better together. If PACs can be developed at the beginning stages of the legislative process concerning an issue, they will be more effective. Finally, if the issue is not yet visible to the general public, PACs will be more effective.

Favorable Targets for PAC Action Kenneth Gross, a former associate general counsel to the Federal Election Commission, believes that a firm should ask itself certain questions before contributing funds to political targets to ensure responsible and effective use of these dollars. Gross differentiates between incumbents and nonincumbents in this decision-making process. For funds to incumbents, the corporate strategist should ask the following questions:

1. In whose district does the corporation have local offices, divisions, or plans?
2. Which legislators have been particularly accessible and have attempted to understand the problems of the corporation?
3. Which legislators are on the House or Senate committees affecting the corporation?
4. What is the political situation in the district the corporation wants to target? Who especially needs help?
5. Which legislators have voted "correctly" on those issues and concerns affecting the corporation?

Before contributing to nonincumbents, the strategist should ask these questions:

1. What are the electoral chances of the candidate?

---

42. L. J. Sabato, "PAC-Man Goes to Washington," *Across the Board*, October 1984, p. 16.

▼ **EXHIBIT 11–7 A Framework for the Planning, Evaluation, and Integration of Corporate Political Programs**

Phase	Action
Phase 1	In this planning phase, management at all levels must support whatever is being planned. During the planning phase, upper management should require that middle and lower management have input into what the political activity is going to be.
Phase 2	The planned political activity must be assessed. This assessment involves asking why the political action program was planned and what the objectives of the political program are. Managers must be given a chance to comment on both questions. Upper management must identify all the issues, both past and future, that will be involved.
Phase 3	A document is circulated in which the proposed activity and its potential impact are outlined and discussed. Senior management is then allowed to prioritize these effects.
Phase 4	Upper management determines a specific strategy and then attempts to carry it out while realistically assessing the probability of success.
Phase 5	The political action program is implemented and, after the fact, is evaluated. All costs and benefits are examined.

SOURCE: C. P. Zeithaml and G. D. Keim, "How to Implement a Corporate Political Action Program," *Sloan Management Review,* Winter 1985, pp. 23–31.

2. Where does the candidate stand on issues important to the corporation, and how close to the corporation has the candidate been in the past?

3. What do the candidate's poll results say, and how much has he or she raised so far and from what groups?

4. Which House or Senate committee assignments will the candidate seek if elected?

THE CEO AS POLITICAL ENTREPRENEUR

Political entrepreneurs are often perceived as those who enter the political arena to maximize their self-interests. This somewhat cynical view of politicians seems, to many people, to be consistent with the way long-term politicians have acted over the years. They have generally been reelected because of their ability to "bring home the bacon" to their local constituents.

In the 1970s, a new phenomenon arose: the chief executive officer as a political entrepreneur. These political entrepreneurs do not attempt to be elected to public office. Rather, they aggressively get involved in changing the political agenda to favor their companies without necessarily relying completely on company lobbyists or PACs (see the *Case—Dwayne Andreas and the Ethanol Question*—at the end of this chapter). One way they do so is by hiring the most capable people to take charge of political activities on behalf of the corporation. They may also interact socially with influential politicians.

Many chief executive officers require that the top executives of their corporations prepare and give speeches throughout the country in favor of specific political actions. For example, executives of corporations that felt they would benefit from the passage of the Uruguay round of the General Agreement on Tariffs and Trade sent managers to give speeches on the benefits of free trade throughout the country. They became political entrepreneurs, at least with respect to that issue. In a world of increasing communication, active corporate political entrepreneurship probably will be an increasingly useful strategy.

THE DELICATE BALANCE

Today's politicians and their constituents alike are being forced to reexamine some of the traditional roles of government. Most American business leaders feel the need to guide public policy in favor of a leaner government that allows the business community to compete more effectively against global competition while at the same time making sure that business lobbying is not perceived as being simply self-serving. The public tends to believe that any efforts by businesses to change the political system and the amount of government regulation are carried out simply to benefit profitability.

Business leaders have one key fact to help them in this debate: American corporations are no longer owned only by an economic elite. Forty million Americans own stock directly in American corporations, and over 100 million more own stock indirectly through their pension plans. Consequently, one could argue that today what is good for business may in general be good for the average American. Strong, efficient corporations may help the average American enjoy a better retirement.

TERMS AND CONCEPTS FOR REVIEW

Grassroots lobbying 320	Pluralism 318	Public policy 313
Iron triangle 316	Political action committee (PAC) 324	Trade embargo 331
Lobbying 318	Public interest 318	Trade organization 319

SUMMARY

1. The policymaking process typically includes the following steps: (a) the issue comes onto the national agenda; (b) various proposals are discussed among government officials and the public; (c) Congress enacts and implements legislation; and (d) the effects of the legislation are analyzed, and the law is perhaps modified.

2. Before a company in a particular market embarks on an attempt to change public policy, it must be able to answer certain questions, such as the following: (a) How has existing public policy shaped the market's overall structure? (b) What have been the key determinants of past public policy in that market? (c) What changes in the firm's current strategy would be likely to lead to an improvement in performance?

3. Firms that have recently been affected by a significant change in public policy must ask several questions, including these: (a) How are other firms likely to react to the change? (b) What will happen to this firm's performance if it maintains its current strategy?

4. Within the public policymaking process there is an iron triangle that represents the three-way alliance between members of the legislature, bureaucrats, and interest groups. The implicit or explicit goal of iron triangles is to preserve or make policies that benefit the members' respective interests.

5. By definition, most lobbying is not done in the public, or general, interest but rather in the interest of a specific group. Lobbyists have two principal goals: to influence legislation and to gain entry into administrative agencies. Lobbyists perform their jobs by meeting with public officials privately, testifying before both Congress and executive rulemaking agencies, assisting legislators in drafting legislation, meeting with legislators socially, and providing information to legislators.

6. Individual companies may attempt specific lobbying tasks. Trade organizations attempt to obtain benefits for an entire group of companies. Both individual corporations and trade organizations sometimes try to institute grassroots lobbying by mobilizing customers, employees, and other stakeholders. In the 1990s, there has been a public backlash against lobbyists. Several new laws and regulations have been put into place in an attempt to limit lobbying activities.

7. Companies and trade organizations, as well as other special interest groups, can attempt to influence election outcomes and the consequent public policymaking by forming political action committees (PACs) which are increasingly important. Currently, for a PAC to be legal, the money must be raised from at least fifty volunteer donors and must be given to at least five candidates in the federal election. Each corporation and each union is limited to one PAC. General company funds may not be contributed to a PAC; instead, corporate PACs obtain their funds from executives, employees, and shareholders. PAC money favors incumbent candidates, particularly those who are unopposed.

8. Studies have shown that members of Congress generally vote according to how much PAC money they receive from special interest groups.

9. Campaign reform bills have been introduced in recent years in order to change the political process. There has been little true progress, though.

10. Business can directly affect public opinion, which will then possibly change the voting patterns of specific legislators. Additionally, business can access the public-policy process by supporting pro-business public-interest law firms.
11. Much of the foreign policy of the United States has an impact on the economic well-being of domestic corporations. For example, a trade embargo prevents American corporations from legally trading with companies owned and controlled by certain countries. Currently, there are trade embargoes on Cuba, Iraq, Libya, and North Korea.
12. Domestic producers typically lobby for protection from foreign imports. Domestic companies that export are generally in favor of free trade, because they benefit from increased world trade.
13. Corporate leaders have to decide on a strategy in their attempts to influence public policy. Researchers Carl P. Zeithaml and Gerald D. Keim have developed a five-part framework for a corporate political strategy. It includes (a) a planning phase, (b) an assessment of the planned political activity, (c) the circulation of a document outlining the proposed activity for discussion and prioritization, (d) the determination of a specific strategy by upper management and the implementation of the strategy, and finally (e) evaluation of this political action program.

EXERCISES

1. Keep track of articles in the newspaper that involve potential legislation that would affect business. Write out how you think the proposed legislation will end up either hurting or helping businesses (and which businesses, if the legislation is specific).
2. Reexamine *Exhibit 11–1*, which shows selected models of the policymaking process. Construct the outline of an article you would write supporting one of the five models as being the most appropriate for the American public policymaking process as we approach the year 2000.
3. Assume that you are the head of a cable-modem manufacturing company. (Cable modems, which were only in experimental use as of the mid-1990s, can transmit data extremely rapidly in comparison with the standard modems that people normally use to access the Internet.) Outline the type of public-policy changes you would like to see occur that would benefit your business. Use the two lists presented in this chapter under the heading "Managing Public Policy" (these two lists were developed by the Harvard Business School).
4. Develop your own iron triangle for the Department of Defense (similar to *Exhibit 11–2*). Who are the key participants?
5. You are a lobbyist for an industry group in Washington, D.C. Write down what you would say to convince a group of citizens that your job is actually in the public interest.
6. Reread the five lobbying activities presented in this chapter under the heading "Strategies of Lobbyists." Which activity is the most important, and why?
7. Under what circumstances does a corporation benefit by contributing to a trade organization? Under what circumstances does it *not* benefit from contributing to such an organization?
8. Because of high-speed computers, it is possible for lobbying groups, such as the National Rifle Association, to get numerous members to send specialized letters to members of Congress when a particular public-policy issue is being discussed. Do you think this so-called grass-roots lobbying is effective, even though members of Congress know that the individuals who write the letters or call have been asked to do so by a lobbying group?
9. The 1996 Lobbying Disclosure Act places an annual limit on the value of gifts a lawmaker can receive from any one source. What are some ways that lobbyists may skirt this new law?
10. Because corporations are restricted in how much money they can spend on PACs, corporations are getting their employees and other stakeholders to donate "soft money" to the two major political parties. How can a corporation expect such actions to help it in the long run?
11. Why do corporations give money to candidates of both political parties?
12. Mobil Oil Company publishes an opinion piece regularly in the *Wall Street Journal*. Do you think that the shareholders of Mobil Oil benefit from such publicity? If you knew that each piece costs a total of $1,000, would your answer change? If each op-ed piece cost $50,000, would you give a different answer? Why?
13. Give examples of what specific issues pro-business public-interest law firms might support. How would the outcomes of the particular hypothetical examples you cited affect the business world?
14. Some business leaders contend that by the time the U.S. government allowed American businesses to operate in Vietnam, it was too late. What do these critics mean?
15. Use an arithmetic example to show why a special interest group, such as a labor union, will spend money to get laws passed to restrict imports while at the same time those adversely affected (consumers) will spend no money to fight such legislation.

16. Reexamine *Exhibit 11–7*. Make a flow chart with the five phases described there. Estimate how long it should take a midsize corporation to undertake each phase.

17. You are the head of a committee within your corporation to decide how many corporate PACs to develop and who should get the funds. First decide what business your company is in. Then develop a list of criteria for making decisions about which political candidates will receive the PAC funds.

SELECTED REFERENCES

▶ Biersack, Robert, et al., eds. *Risky Business? PAC Decision Making in Congressional Elections.* Armonk, N.Y.: M. E. Sharpe, 1994.

▶ Davis, Charles E. *The Politics of Hazardous Waste.* Upper Saddle River, N.J.: Prentice Hall, 1993.

▶ Fones-Wolf, Elizabeth A. *Selling Free Enterprise: The Business Assault on Labor and Liberalism, 1945–1960.* Urbana: University of Illinois Press, 1994.

▶ Himmelberg, Robert F., ed. *New Issues in Government-Business Relations since 1964: Consumerist and Safety Regulation, and the Debate over Industrial Policy.* New York: Garland Publishing, 1994.

▶ Holland, Max. *The CEO Goes to Washington.* Knoxville, Tenn.: Whittle Direct Books, 1994.

▶ Martin, Brendan. *In the Public Interests? Privatization and Public Sector Reform.* Atlantic Highlands, N.J.: Zed Books, in association with Public Services International, 1993.

▶ Miller, Roger LeRoy, et al. *The Economics of Public Issues,* 10th ed. New York: HarperCollins, 1996.

▶ Mucciaroni, Gary. *Reversals of Fortune: Public Policy and Private Interests.* Washington, D.C.: Brookings Institution, 1995.

RESOURCES ON THE INTERNET

▼ For a discussion of all aspects of U.S. federal domestic policies, use the Michigan State University gopher:

alt.politics.usa.misc.

and choose

News & Weather; USENET News; alt /;politics/

This service will provide you with information on crime policy; environmental policy; welfare, housing, and education reform; and other policy issues.

▼ The best source of information on public policy on the Internet is probably the Library of Congress. For information on the status of bills being considered in both the House and the Senate, along with a state-by-state listing of congressional members, access the Library of Congress at

http://lcweb.loc.gov./homepage/ lchp.html

For more information on members of Congress, along with the text of the United States Constitution, access the following:

ftp://ftp.halycon.com/pub/activism/

▼ Many lobbying groups and other organizations that try to influence public policy have sites on the Internet. To access the home page to perhaps the most successful and controversial lobbying group, the National Rifle Association (NRA), access the NRA's home page at

http://www.nra.org/

For information on the North America Institute, a think tank that was partially responsible for the text of the North American Free Trade Agreement, access

http://sol.uvic.ca/nami

For information on the League of Women Voters, which is active in a number of public-policy issues that relate specifically to women, access

http://www.oclc.org/VoteSmart/ lwv/lwvhome.htm

Lead . . . or Leave is a political organization dedicated to public-policy issues that reflect the interests of "Generation X." For information on this group, access

http://www.cs.caltech.edu/ ~adam/lead.html

CASE

DWAYNE ANDREAS AND THE ETHANOL QUESTION

Background

Ever since a check for $25,000 from Dwayne O. Andreas turned up in the bank account of one of the Watergate burglars in 1974, the chairman of agricultural giant Archer-Daniels-Midland (ADM) has been recognized as a force in the Washington, D.C., public-policy scene. In the 1970s, Andreas successfully lobbied for quotas on imported sugar, which drove up demand from soft-drink companies for ADM's high-fructose corn syrup. He has also managed to procure millions of dollars in soybean subsidies, which account for half of ADM's revenue. In the 1990s, Andreas again proved his reach as a lobbying force by convincing the Clinton administration to fulfill a federal mandate on clean air by requiring that 10 percent of the gasoline sold in United States by 1996 contain ethanol, a corn-based fuel. ADM is responsible for about 70 percent of the ethanol production in the country.

The Clean Air Act and Oxygenates

The demand for ethanol stems from a provision of the Clean Air Act of 1990 that stipulates that gasoline sold in U.S. cities with the poorest air quality must contain smog-reducing oxygenates to reduce hydrocarbon emissions. The legislation set a January 1, 1996, deadline for the fuel in these cities—which include New York, Los Angeles, and Chicago—to contain 30 percent of this reformulated gasoline. The fuel is designed to decrease tailpipe emissions by increasing the oxygen content of the gasoline. In theory, by introducing extra oxygen into the combustion process, the gasoline content of the fuel mixture is decreased with no effect on the volume of fuel being burned.

Ethanol is only one of the possible oxygenate additives that can be used in this process. The others, methanol and methyl tertiary butyl ether (MTBE), are derived from coal or natural gas. During deliberation on the Clear Air Act, Congress could not decide between the benefits of ethanol, which has a higher oxygen content, and those of methanol, which is more stable and more cost effective. Consequently, the final bill contained a provision for the Environmental Protection Agency (EPA) to make the final decision on which additive was more desirable.

The Costs of Ethanol

Initially, the EPA would not consider ethanol for environmental reasons. Although the oxygenate does improve combustion and reduce carbon monoxide emissions, it also makes gasoline evaporate more quickly, which would *add* to the smog problems it was trying to alleviate, especially during the warm summer months. President George Bush, however, granted a waiver instructing the EPA to allow ethanol to be considered as the additive of choice.

There were, though, other reasons to be wary of ethanol as the nation's preferred oxygenate. Ethanol is the most heavily subsidized energy source in the United States—it receives 54 to 64 cents per gallon and costs American taxpayers $500 million a year. With an ethanol mandate by the year 2000, annual production of the fuel would grow 59 percent, to 2.2 billion gallons, driving the subsidies to approximately $1.3 billion at that time.

Considering the political pressure to reduce the federal budget deficit, many observers were surprised when President Bill Clinton, Bush's successor, continued to support ethanol as the preferred oxygenate. In 1994, Clinton decided that the additive to be used in the reformulated gasoline must come from a "renewable" source. The EPA had determined six months earlier that only ethanol—extracted from corn—met its definition of *renewable*, so the president virtually guaranteed that ethanol would be the chosen oxygenate.

Clinton and ethanol supporters pointed out the benefits of the choice, such as stimulating depressed farming communities and reducing the nation's dependence on foreign oil (which would supposedly have increased with a higher demand for natural-gas–based methanol). The oil industry and environmentalists, however—odd allies, indeed—charged the president with putting special interests ahead of the interests of consumers and the environment. These protests only increased when it became public knowledge that Andreas had contributed $100,000 to co-chair a $2.5 million fund raiser for Clinton's Democratic party three weeks before the EPA made its decision in favor of ethanol.

ADM's Low-Key Lobbying

Executive staff officials claimed that the timing between the fund raiser and the EPA's decision was coincidental, but ADM's low-key lobbying approach seems to be based on encouraging coincidence. The company, which does not hire any registered lobbyists or Washington, D.C., law firms, takes a detached stand on political struggles. During the ethanol-methanol debate, ADM tried to keep a low profile, although it failed in the case of Andreas's involvement with the fund raiser. "Our message to ADM was just try to stay out of it," said Senator Thomas A. Daschle, an ethanol backer. Because of the perception that a decision in favor of ethanol would be another federal subsidy for ADM, Daschle said, "we didn't want people to point to ADM and say [it] was the driving force behind this effort."

Nonetheless, Andreas is known for his behind-the-scenes acumen. Although ADM is based in Decatur, Illinois, the chairman is well known among Washington, D.C., insiders. He is a close friend, for instance, of former Democratic National Committee chairman Robert S. Strauss, who sits on ADM's board of directors and whose law firm represents the company. (Among the guests at a seventy-fifth birthday party Andreas threw for Strauss was First Lady Hillary Rodham Clinton.) When Strauss helped the Clinton administration get approval for the North American Free Trade Agreement (NAFTA), he asked Andreas for assistance. ADM responded with a heavy lobbying campaign for NAFTA. It was Strauss's law partner, Vernon Jordan, a Clinton confidant, who solicited Andreas's $100,000 dinner contribution. "You have to respect Andreas's ability to milk the system," says one rival lobbyist. "He is plugged into Washington in every way."

ADM's Political Contributions

"The system" has also gotten its fair share of "milk" out of ADM, as Andreas has spread the company's political contributions widely. When Bush lost the presidential election of 1992, many industry analysts assumed the favorable reception ADM had received in the White House was finished. After all, during Bush's term (1989–1993), Andreas and his company made over $1 million in "soft money" contributions to Republican sources, making ADM the party's top corporate benefactor. (Soft money cannot be legally spent on federal campaigns, but it can go toward state and local elections and other activities such as voting drives.) Over those four years, the company gave only $362,500 to the Democrats. From Clinton's victory in the fall of 1992 to the spring of 1994, however, that trend reversed: ADM gave $206,500 to Democrats and only $47,500 to Republicans. Andreas gave a personal donation of $50,000 to the Democrats' congressional campaign committee six days before the 1992 elections. The strategy paid off, in part, when an ADM vice president was able to arrange a personal meeting with Energy Secretary Hazel O'Leary to discuss the benefits of ethanol.

Andreas and ADM also make strategic contributions to politicians at other levels. Senators Daschle and Charles E. Grassley, who lobbied the president and his advisors on the popularity of ethanol in farming states, each received $10,000 in contributions from ADM. After Wisconsin governor Tommy Thompson sent a state official to Washington, D.C., to lobby for ethanol, he received a $21,000 campaign contribution from ADM.

Grassroots Opportunities

The other aspect of ADM's low-key lobbying strategy is the backing of grassroots organizations. The company provides 70 to 80 percent of the Renewable Fuels Association's $1.4 million budget, and it has strong ties to the National Corn Growers Association. Both organizations have a strong presence on Capitol Hill. The company also helped organize a group called Agriculture for Clean Air, which ran advertisements in several large publications warning of the health risks of methanol. The costs of the advertisements, more than $200,000, were partly financed by ADM.

One of the ads, reprinted in the *Washington Post*, was the script of a commentary by radio personality Paul Harvey in which Harvey listed the benefits of ethanol over methanol. "A swig of ethanol is no more harmful than a shot of vodka or gin," Harvey said, while implying that inhalation of petroleum-based methanol vapors could lead to blindness or death. Ethanol opponents pointed out that ADM is a national sponsor of Harvey's daily program. The American Petroleum Institute (API), contending that health problems only result from contact with pure methanol and not methanol-based fuel, filed a Federal Trade Commission complaint against Agriculture for Clean Air.

Epilogue

After the EPA's decision in favor of ethanol, Fred Craft, the president of the Oxygenated Fuels Association, called ADM's lobbying effort "a steamroller" that "ran over everybody." Taking another tack, two groups, the API and the National Petroleum Refiners Association, filed a lawsuit challenging the legality of the EPA's role in the ethanol-methanol controversy. In the spring of 1995, a three-judge panel on the federal appeals court in Washington, D.C., ruled that the agency lacks the authority to discriminate between renewable and nonrenewable oxygenates. Ethanol backers insisted that their product still had a competitive advantage in its lower prices, which are a direct result of its

CASE (CONTINUED)

federal tax exemptions. The Wall Street community, however, took notice that ADM's added profits from the EPA mandate—estimated at $100 million a year—were no longer guaranteed. The day after the court decision, ADM's stock dropped 12 cents on the New York Stock Exchange.

Critical Thinking Questions

1. Business is most effective in influencing public policy when its financial goals are in keeping with the political strategies of politicians. This was certainly the case with ADM's efforts regarding ethanol. What qualities of ethanol would make it an important political issue?

2. What does this case say about the relative political power of business stakeholders and environmental interest groups?

3. The practice by Andreas and ADM of giving huge sums of "soft money" to whichever party holds political power in Washington, D.C., is completely legal. Is it completely ethical? Do you agree with reformers who suggest that such practices are paramount to buying influence and should be heavily regulated?

4. Should Andreas's "favors"—such as co-hosting the Clinton fund raiser and lobbying for NAFTA—also be regulated? Or are such activities a legitimate means for business to gain access to the political process?

5. What effect, if any, should the fact that corn production is heavily subsidized have on the decision between ethanol and methanol?

SOURCE: Information from T. Noah and S. Kilman, "Archer, Ethanol Industry Dealt Blow As Court Blocks EPA Gasoline Order," *Wall Street Journal*, May 1, 1995, p. A3; T. Noah, "EPA Came Through for Archer-Daniels-Midland after Andreas's Role at Presidential Dinner," *Wall Street Journal*, July 6, 1994, p. A20; P. H. Stone, "The Big Harvest," *National Journal*, July 30, 1994, p. 1792; N. Haas, "Faust Triumphant," *FW*, December 8, 1992, p. 22; "Ethanol Company Gave to Governor's Campaign," *Chicago Tribune*, January 10, 1994, p. 3; "Reporter Says ADM Takes Subtle 'Grassroots' Turn in Ethanol Lobbying," *Clean Air Network Online Today*, January 19, 1995; and C. Burko, "Court Blocks Ethanol Rule," *Chicago Tribune*, April 29, 1995, p. 1.

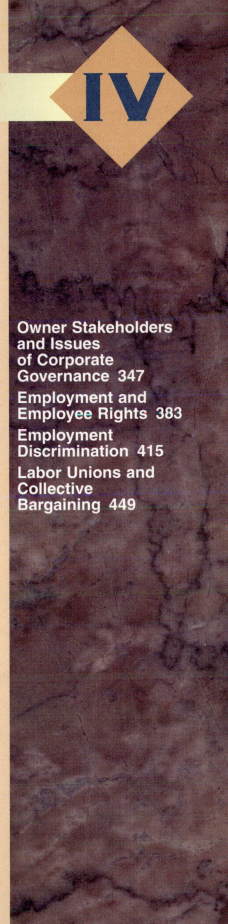

PART IV

INTRINSIC STAKEHOLDERS

CHAPTER 12

OWNER STAKEHOLDERS AND ISSUES OF CORPORATE GOVERNANCE

CHAPTER OUTLINE

- The Structure of Corporate Governance
- Criticisms of Corporate Governance
- Improving Corporate Governance
- Takeovers

INTRODUCTION

Chapter 3 introduced the concept of the *stakeholder* and its importance in the relationship between business and society. Chapter 5 again touched on stakeholders while discussing corporate social responsibility. This chapter and the following three will concentrate on those stakeholders *intrinsic* to the corporate culture; that is, those who function within the daily operations of any business entity. Eventually, the topic will lead us to an in-depth discussion of the status of employees, but we start with the owner stakeholders.

In the early days of American business, one owner stakeholder often had the final say in all managerial decisions; when Henry Ford or John D. Rockefeller said "Jump," as the old military dictum goes, their subordinates only asked "How high?" The modern publicly held corporation, in contrast, has a multitude of decision makers at various layers along the chain of command. Rarely does one individual have the power of a Ford or a Rockefeller.

Management groups and boards of directors have received heavy criticism from shareholders for being more interested in their own financial well-being than that of the corporation, as well as from other stakeholders, who feel themselves marginalized in the corporation's drive to maximize profits. The corporate executives, in return, complain that government regulation and extensive pressures from stakeholders have handicapped their efforts to satisfy the shareholders. Whether or not these complaints are valid, the resulting public squabbles have severely harmed the image of the American corporation: in a 1995 career preferences survey, only 1 percent of 1,000 adult respondents said they would "freely choose" to be corporate managers.[1]

Other observers, instead of seeing the controversy as harmful, treat the changes brought about by the debate as part of a necessary "reinventing" of the corporate structure. They prefer rounds of "downsizing," "reengineering," and takeovers to the more European methods of taxes, regulation, subsidies, and tariffs to restructure the corporation. "Our system is untidy; but it beats the alternative," is how Robert J. Samuelson put it.[2] In this chapter, we take a close look at the decidedly "untidy" system of corporate governance in the United States and investigate some of the ways it is reinventing itself to survive in its ever-changing environment.

THE STRUCTURE OF CORPORATE GOVERNANCE

Simply stated, the people who make up a corporation are its lifeblood—its most valuable and unique resources. The goal of a corporation is to give these employees the opportunity to flourish. In an ultimately efficient corporate system, responsibility is naturally shifted to those best suited to accept it. The groundwork for this efficiency is a basic owner-management structure that is found in most corporations. Understanding this structure is the first step toward understanding corporate governance.

1. K. Labich, "Kissing Off Corporate America," *Fortune*, February 20, 1995, p. 44.
2. R. J. Samuelson, "Reinventing Corporate America," *Newsweek*, July 4, 1994, p. 53.

Corporate Governance Defined

Corporate governance is the term used to describe the manner by which a corporation is controlled and directed in accordance with its goals and corporate culture:

▼ **Simply put, corporate governance refers to how a corporation is governed.**

In the past, the success or failure of corporate governance was primarily measured by profitability. The modern corporation, however, is perceived to have a responsibility to stakeholders that goes beyond profits. Every time a corporation disregards this responsibility, such as when it illegally dumps waste in a local waterway, the validity of corporate governance is brought into question.[3]

Exhibit 12–1 on page 350 displays the model for a corporate governance system. In this model, a corporation is formed through a *charter* issued by the state, which lays down the terms under which the corporation must exist.[4] The hierarchy of the corporation starts with the *shareholders*, who are, under corporate law, the owners. Next comes the *board of directors*, elected by the shareholders; the board in turn hires *management* to oversee the day-to-day operations of the corporation. The importance of *employees* is somewhat belied by their lowly place in the model, but we will give that stakeholder group its due attention in upcoming chapters.

The Nature of the Corporation — Charters

A corporation is a legal entity created and recognized by state law. It can consist of one or more *natural* persons (as opposed to the artificial "person" of the corporation) identified under a common name. A corporation usually has perpetual existence.

The Corporation as a Legal "Person" A corporation is recognized under state and federal laws as a "person," and it enjoys many of the same rights and privileges that U.S. citizens enjoy. A corporation has the same right as a natural person to equal protection of the laws under the Fourteenth Amendment of the U.S Constitution. It has the right of access to the courts as an entity that can sue or be sued. It also has the right of due process before denial of life, liberty, or property, as well as freedom from unreasonable searches and seizures and from double jeopardy.

Under the First Amendment, corporations are entitled to freedom of speech, just as individuals are. This normally includes freedom of commercial speech, or advertising. In addition, corporations may express their political viewpoints on particular issues. The right of corporations to free political speech has been challenged in the past by those who believe that corporations, such as news publishing firms, should give equal space to opposing viewpoints. Recently, however, the United States Supreme Court has made it clear that no such restrictions should be placed on a corporation's freedom of speech.

The Corporate Charter If the corporation is a person, then the state can be considered the corporation's "parent." Any state may issue a certificate of incorporation, known as the **corporate charter.** This charter specifically defines the conditions under which the corporation can function. It delineates the rights and responsibilities of the stockholders,

---

3. W. Boeker and J. Goodstein, "Organizational Performance and Adaptation: Effects of Environment and Performance on Changes in Board Composition," *Academy of Management Journal*, December 1991, p. 805.
4. L. Hanson, "Shareholder Value: Touchstone of Managerial Capitalism," in "Rating the Corporate Governance Compact," *Harvard Business Review*, November–December 1991, p. 142.

▼ **EXHIBIT 12–1
A Model for
Corporate
Governance**

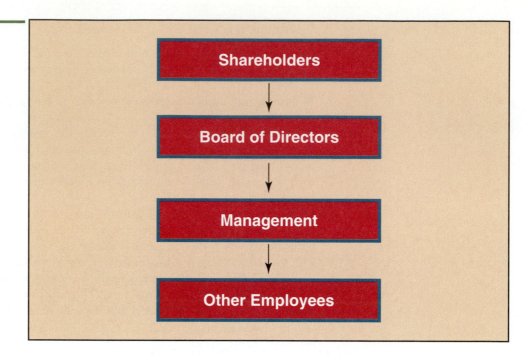

board of directors, and officers. Some charters even set up guidelines for the selling of stock, the election of directors, and annual shareholders' meetings.

The Delaware Phenomenon There are no federal laws that require incorporation in a specific state, so corporations are free to choose the state in which they will incorporate. This buyer's market has led to competition—which sometimes takes extreme forms—among states for the tax revenues of corporate business.

The runaway winner in this competition has been the tiny state of Delaware. Corporate managers obviously lean toward incorporating in the state that places the fewest number of restrictions on business activity, and Delaware has done so to the extent that a disproportionate share of all Fortune 500 corporations are incorporated in the state.

Those states that decide to place restrictive measures on their corporations suffer the consequences. In the first decade of this century, New Jersey had been the leader in offering easy terms for corporations. In 1913, prodded by Governor Woodrow Wilson and his argument that such a pro-business atmosphere was "immoral," the New Jersey legislature decided to increase restrictions on its corporations. The new laws lasted only four years, but by then most of the state's corporations had moved to Delaware.[5]

CORPORATE MANAGEMENT—SHAREHOLDERS

The acquisition of a share of stock makes a person an owner and shareholder in a corporation. As a shareholder, that person acquires certain powers and responsibilities with regard to the corporation.[6] Because these powers and responsibilities tend to be complicated by the demands of corporate governance, the Working Group on Corporate Governance attempted to codify the shareholder's five basic duties:

---

5. J. P. Clarkham, *Keeping Good Company* (Oxford, England: Clarendon Press, 1994), p. 174.
6. B. Baysinger and R. E. Hoskisson, "The Composition of Boards of Directors and Strategic Control: Effects on Corporate Strategy," *Academy of Management Review*, January 1990, p. 72.

1. Institutional shareholders (such as pension plans) of public companies should see themselves as owners, not investors.

2. Shareholders should not be involved in the day-to-day affairs of the company's operations.

3. Shareholders should evaluate the performance of the directors regularly.

4. In evaluating the performance of the directors, the shareholders should be informed.

5. Shareholders should recognize and respect that the primary goal common to all shareholders is the ongoing prosperity of the company.[7]

Institutional versus Individual Shareholders The Working Group on Corporate Governance recognized that its rules could apply only to institutional shareholders, such as pension funds, mutual funds, and insurance companies. These groups hold large blocks of stock and consequently have the power to affect the corporation's governance policies, should they choose to do so. For most of the individual shareholders, even if they had the inclination (which the majority do not), it would be too expensive and time consuming to try to change dramatically the governance of the corporation they partially "own." This is not to say, however, that individual shareholders are completely helpless, as we shall soon see.

Shareholders' Powers As individuals or as a group, shareholders have certain powers under the corporate charter. They must approve fundamental changes in the corporation before those changes can be effected. Hence, shareholders are empowered to amend the articles of incorporation and bylaws, approve a merger or dissolution of the corporation, and approve the sale of all or substantially all of the corporation's assets.

The election or removal of the board of directors can be accomplished by a vote of the shareholders. The first board of directors is either named in the articles of incorporation or chosen by the incorporators to serve until the first shareholders' meeting. From that time on, the selection and retention of directors are exclusively shareholder functions.

Relationship between Shareholders and the Corporation As the Working Group on Corporate Governance noted, shareholders generally have no responsibility for the daily management of a corporation, though they are ultimately responsible for choosing the board of directors. Ordinarily, corporate officers and other employees owe no direct duty to individual stockholders. Their duty is to the corporation as a whole. A director, however, is in a *fiduciary* relationship to the corporation—that is, a relationship based on trust and confidence—and therefore serves the interests of the shareholders as a group.

Shareholders' Forum Economist John Kenneth Galbraith asserted that the annual meeting "of the large American corporation is perhaps our most elaborate exercise in popular illusion."[8] He is not alone in this opinion, but nobody has devised a better way of giving the shareholders a voice in the operation of their company.[9]

By law, these shareholders' meetings must occur at least annually, and additional special meetings can be called to take care of urgent matters. Because it is usually not practical for owners of only a few shares of stock of publicly traded corporations to attend the shareholders' meeting, they normally give third persons a written authorization to vote

---

7. "A New Compact for Owners and Directors," *Harvard Business Review*, July–August 1991, p. 41.
8. Clarkham, *op. cit.*, p. 199.
9. P. B. Firstenberg and B. G. Malkiel, "The Twenty-First Century Boardroom: Who Will Be in Charge?" *Sloan Management Review*, Fall 1994, p. 27.

their shares at the meeting. This authorization, called a **proxy**, is often aggressively solicited by management.

Shareholder Voting For shareholders to act, a minimum number of them (in terms of the number of shares held) must be present at a meeting. The minimum number, called a **quorum,** is generally more than 50 percent. Corporate business matters are presented in the form of **resolutions,** which shareholders vote to approve or disapprove. Some states provide that the unanimous consent of shareholders is a permissible alternative to holding a shareholders' meeting.

At times, a larger-than-majority vote is required either by statute or by the articles of incorporation. The approval of extraordinary corporate matters, such as mergers or consolidations, requires a higher percentage of the representatives of all corporate shares entitled to vote, not just a majority of those present at a particular meeting. (For a summary of the shareholder's role, see *Exhibit 12–2.*)

CORPORATE MANAGEMENT—DIRECTORS

Every corporation is governed by a board of directors. The number of directors, which is subject to statutory limitations, is set forth in the corporation's articles or bylaws. Historically, the minimum number of directors has been three, but today many states permit fewer—even just one.

▼ **EXHIBIT 12–2 The Role of Shareholders**

Element	Description
Shareholders' Powers	Shareholders' powers include approval of all fundamental changes affecting the corporation and election of the board of directors.
Shareholders' Meetings	Shareholders' meetings must occur at least annually; special meetings can be called when necessary. Notice of the time and place of the meeting (and its purpose, if the meeting was specially called) must be sent to shareholders. Voting requirements and procedures are as follows: 1. A minimum number of shareholders (a quorum—generally more than 50 percent of shares held) must be present at a meeting; resolutions are normally passed by majority vote. 2. Voting lists of shareholders on record must be prepared by the corporation prior to each shareholders' meeting. 3. Cumulative voting may or may not be required or permitted so as to give minority shareholders a better chance to be represented on the board of directors. 4. Shareholders' voting agreements to vote their shares together are usually held to be valid and enforceable. 5. A shareholder may appoint a proxy (substitute) to vote his or her shares. 6. A shareholder may enter into a voting trust agreement by which title (record ownership) of his or her shares is given to a trustee, and the trustee votes the shares in accordance with the trust agreement.
Shareholders' Rights	Shareholders have numerous rights, including voting rights, the right to a stock certificate, the right to obtain a dividend (at the discretion of the directors), the right to inspect the corporate records, the right to transfer their shares (this right may be restricted), the right to their shares of corporate assets when the corporation is dissolved, and the right to sue on behalf of the corporation (bring a shareholder's derivative suit) when the directors fail to do so.

Directors' Election and Term of Office After the initial board of directors has been appointed, usually by the incorporators, subsequent directors are elected by a majority vote of the shareholders. The term of office for a director is usually one year—from annual meeting to annual meeting. Longer and staggered terms are permissible under most state statutes. A common practice is to elect one-third of the board members each year for a three-year term. In this way, there is greater management continuity.[10]

Directors' Qualifications and Compensation Few legal qualifications exist for directors. Only a handful of states retain minimum age and residency requirements. A director is sometimes a shareholder, but this is not a necessary qualification unless, of course, statutory provisions or corporate articles or bylaws require ownership.

In the past, boards have been made up primarily of company executives, who were believed to be closest to the daily activities of the business and therefore most qualified to sit on the board. The trend, though, in the 1980s and 1990s has been away from these **inside directors,** who are a part of management, toward **outside directors,** who do not have any management role. This change was spurred by an unusually high incidence of alleged inside director wrongdoing in the late 1970s. Shareholders began to believe that boards needed an outside, and supposedly unbiased, perspective to offset the power of the chair of the board, who often also serves as the company's chief executive officer (CEO).

Compensation for the chair of the board and the CEO is ordinarily specified in the corporate articles or bylaws. Because directors have a fiduciary responsibility to both the shareholders and the corporation, an express agreement or provision for compensation is necessary for them to receive money from the funds that they control or for which they are responsible. Besides annual retainers—which averaged over $30,000 for directors of

10. R. C. Breeden et al., "The Fight for Good Governance," *Harvard Business Review*, January–February 1993, p. 76.

large corporations in 1996—members of the board can also receive per-meeting fees, stock options, stock grants, and pensions. A survey of two hundred companies showed that these benefits combined to give directors at large corporations yearly compensation of approximately $83,000.[11]

Directors' Management Responsibilities Directors are responsible for all policy-making decisions necessary to the management of all corporate affairs. Just as shareholders cannot act individually to bind the corporation, the directors must act as a body in carrying out routine corporate business. One director has one vote, and usually the majority rules.[12]

The general areas of responsibility of the board of directors include the following:

1. Authorization for major corporate policy decisions—for example, the initiation of proceedings for the sale or lease of corporate assets outside the regular course of business, the determination of new product lines, and the overseeing of major contract negotiations and major management-labor negotiations.
2. The appointment, supervision, and removal of corporate officers and other high-level managerial employees and the determination of their compensation.
3. Major financial decisions, such as the declaration and payment of dividends to shareholders or the issuance of authorized shares or bonds.

The Chief Executive Officer Another one of the board's duties is to hire and, by extension, to fire the most visible and controversial cog in the corporate governance machine: the CEO. "When examining corporate governance in the USA, the place to start is not the board but the chief executive officer," claims Jonathan Clarkham, who carried out an extensive survey of corporate governance in five different countries.[13] Noting that in more than three-quarters of American corporations the CEO is also chair of the board of directors, Clarkham concludes:

> The dominance of the CEO as a member of the board (which he always is) is virtually built into the general perception of the status of his position. When he assumes office he inherits a board, but gradually over the years his own power of patronage will affect its composition and this naturally tends to buttress his position. Even if he picks powerful independent CEOs like himself to serve as outside directors, he will know they will be inhibited because they owe their appointments to him. . . . These feelings permeate the board to the point where it is generally considered traitorous for the outside directors to caucus behind the CEO's back, and they seldom do it.[14]

Consequently, although the ideal of corporate governance is a collegiate system in which the board of directors makes policy decisions as a group, in reality the individual CEO usually holds sway over any corporate decisions. Whether or not a shareholder believes this to be a positive trend usually depends on how well his or her stock is performing; shareholders generally do not criticize CEOs who consistently produce profits.

---

11. J. A. Byrne, "How Much Should It Take to Keep the Board on Board?" *Business Week,* April 17, 1995, p. 41.
12. J. W. Lorsch, "Empowering the Board," *Harvard Business Review,* January–February 1995, p. 130.
13. Clarkham, *op. cit.,* p. 182.
14. *Ibid.,* p. 183.

CRITICISMS OF CORPORATE GOVERNANCE

Increasing numbers of large corporations are attempting to reconcile the divisions between managers and owners. Critics of the present system of corporate governance, however, are skeptical that any panacea will emerge. Many observers feel there must be fundamental changes in the way U.S. companies are run in order to create corporations that are more responsive to the needs of their many stakeholders.

THE ELUSIVE QUESTION OF OWNERSHIP

When the Working Group on Corporate Governance urged institutional shareholders to "see themselves as owners, not investors," it was simply restating what has been a cornerstone of the system: shareholders, by virtue of their shares of stock, own part of the company. The fact that the Working Group felt it necessary to echo such a fundamental aspect of corporate governance suggests that the opposite is occurring. Instead of seeing themselves as owners, shareholders consider themselves investors in the process, a perception that places a strain on the legitimacy of the corporate governance system. That is, managers and directors appear able to work without the oversight of the corporation's true owners.

Institutional Investors as Owners In addressing institutional investors as owners, Professor Jay W. Lorsch of the Harvard Business School asks two questions:

1. Can and should institutional investors act as true long-term owners?
2. If they cannot, then to whom and for what should directors be accountable?[15]

The answer to the first question, in Lorsch's opinion, is a resounding no. In direct contrast to the Working Group's assertions that the shareholders' only common goal is "the ongoing prosperity of the company," Lorsch believes the primary responsibility of institutional shareholders "is to their investors and beneficiaries, which can lead to a conflict of interest with their acting as owner."

Lorsch takes the example of the California Public Employees Retirement System (CalPERS), the largest publicly funded retirement system in the United States, and asks whether institutional shareholders are able to act as owners in a practical sense. CalPERS's most substantial single investment is with General Motors—6.6 million shares. Even that impressive number, however, translates into only 0.72 percent of GM's total stock, rendering CalPERS incapable of a "strong voice of ownership" (see *Managing Social Issues—Making a Difference: CalPERS as Shareholder Activist* on page 356). The situation is similar among the balance of U.S. corporations; of the fifty largest U.S. companies, only eight have shareholders that hold 5 percent or more of the available stock. For these reasons, Lorsch concludes that "large institutional funds cannot . . . act as owners, and it is not constructive to pretend that they can."[16]

Other Investors as Owners What about the over forty million individual shareholders not tied to large institutional funds? Is their claim to ownership as tenuous? Although the small investor is an important part of the capitalist landscape, it would be difficult to

---

15. J. W. Lorsch, "Real Ownership Is Impossible," in "Rating the Corporate Governance Compact," *Harvard Business Review*, November–December 1991, p. 139.
16. *Ibid.*, p. 140.

MANAGING SOCIAL ISSUES

MAKING A DIFFERENCE: CalPERS AS SHAREHOLDER ACTIVIST

It is known in business circles as a "Dear CEO" letter, and—like a Dear John letter containing bad news from a former love—corporate executives shudder at the thought of its message. Every year executives from twelve companies receive such a letter from the California Public Employees Retirement System (CalPERS), and all twelve letters deliver essentially the same message: Shape up your corporate governance, or lose CalPERS as an investor.

Activist Beginnings

CalPERS is the single largest public-sector pension fund in the United States; it covers almost 1 million active and retired beneficiaries from about 2,500 employers. The fund's 800 employees manage over $70 billion in assets invested in almost 1,300 companies. CalPERS had not always been involved in shareholder activism, but by the mid-1980s it found that it was one of the biggest owners of companies in the nation. This led the fund's managers to pay closer attention to the activities of executives at firms in which it owned stock. At first, this meant simply objecting when companies used antitakeover strategies like poison pills and greenmail, which hurt shareholders. Eventually, CalPERS's interests spread into basic questions of corporate governance, and it became the most feared and respected shareholder activist in the country.

Stockholders' Responsibility

Dale Hanson, the chief executive of CalPERS, believes that stockholders have a responsibility to ensure that a company they partly own is functioning efficiently. "If we buy an office building and the property manager isn't properly maintaining it, we don't sell the building," he analogizes. "We change the property manager."

CalPERS targets the CEOs and corporate boards for its "hit list" based on the performance of their companies' total shareholder return over a five-year period, compared with the returns from other companies in the same industry. If a firm lags behind its peers, a "Dear CEO" letter goes out to the firm's top executives that asks for a meeting with CalPERS to discuss the company's recent problems. The letter usually focuses on three areas—board composition and practices, CEO compensation, and the formation of shareholder advisory committees.

In the first year of this practice, response was lukewarm. Top executives are not used to being told how to run their companies, and many did not take CalPERS seriously. Dial Corporation refused outright to meet with CalPERS, and several others tried to postpone any meeting indefinitely. The ones who did listen were impressed, however. After seeing representatives from CalPERS, a general counsel from Ryder said they "knew as much about Ryder as we did."

Growing Influence

Ryder and ITT Corporation were the only two companies that met CalPERS's standards after the first year. Displeased by this lack of response from most of the targeted companies, CalPERS decided to become more aggressive. The fund threatened to go public with "hit list" members who refused to alter their corporate governance. It also sponsored shareholder resolutions at offending companies and, as a last resource, used legal measures. In 1990, CalPERS brought legal action against management at Occidental Petroleum for improperly using company assets to build the Armand Hammer Museum of Art in Los Angeles.

The growing power of CalPERS can be traced through its effect on General Motors Corporation. In 1990 Hanson wrote to the CEO, Roger Smith, about the company's performance. Smith, without consulting his board, told the fund to mind its own business. Later that year, when Hanson addressed the same concern to Robert C. Stempel, Smith's successor, Hanson received a message from GM's general counsel agreeing to meet. By 1992, when John F. Smith, Jr., replaced Stempel, GM *called* CalPERS to request a meeting.

For Critical Analysis:

Jay W. Lorsch believes that CalPERS, or any institutional shareholder, is incapable of a "strong voice of leadership" because of low ownership percentages. Do you agree with his statement? Why or why not?

SOURCE: Information from D. Hanson, "Much, Much More Than Investors," *Financial Executive*, March 1, 1993, p. 48; J. H. Dobrzynski, "CalPERS Is Ready to Roar, but Will CEOs Listen?" *Business Week*, March 30, 1992, p. 44; and J. H. Dobrzynski, "Tales from the Boardroom Wars," *Business Week*, June 6, 1994, p. 71.

argue that individual investors have as much stake in the overall well-being of a corporation as do very large investors. Indeed, the fact is that small individual shareholders rarely want to act as owners of large corporations. They normally do not read annual reports or proxy statements or vote for officers, directors, or important corporate business that is presented to them. Instead,

▼ Individual owners of U.S. corporations exercise their influence on the corporations they own in a very efficient and swift manner: if they don't think the corporation is being run the way it should be, they simply sell their shares and buy stock in another corporation.

The small investors who routinely discard information and voting materials about the corporations they own are probably acting rationally; they know they cannot make much difference in the way the corporation is run.

The directors of each corporation are accountable to shareholders. One might ask, however, to which shareholders the directors are accountable. Should corporate directors be worried about investors who are only interested in short-run profits? Alternatively, should corporate directors be beholden to those who are looking to make a good rate of return over the long run? The statement that directors should be accountable to shareholders gives rise to these valid questions, because there are so many types of shareholders with different demands, needs, and desires.

The Director's Accountability   Lorsch's second question asks to whom exactly directors and managers are accountable. Under traditional corporate governance, the answer would be the shareholders, but we have seen that this group is often unwilling or unable to accept the responsibility of ownership. Besides, directors may resent seeing their careful management subverted into short-term gains for opportunistic shareholders.

The question has been further complicated by the continuing trend toward recognizing the rights of stakeholders other than shareholders. Twenty-five states now have laws that allow directors to widen their sphere of decision making to account for the rights of employees, customers, the community, suppliers, lenders, and so on. Although these laws may in a sense give directors more power, they also leave management accountable to diverse stakeholders and compromise the effectiveness of corporate governance.

In fact, at this point, a definitive stakeholder to whom the director is ultimately accountable cannot be pinpointed. Those seemingly in the best position to answer the question—the directors themselves—are increasingly unable to do so. After research that included two thousand questionnaires and nearly a hundred interviews with outside directors, Lorsch was struck "by how perplexed directors are by these changes. . . . [T]hey are unclear about their responsibility to nonownership groups, and they are unsure of the extent to which they should focus on 'the ongoing prosperity of the company.'"[17] As for the traditional owners, the shareholders, Lorsch found directors to be "trapped" between this group's short-term profit interests and the best long-term strategy "for the health of the company."[18]

Some companies, such as Procter & Gamble, have tried to ease this predicament by offering a manager incentives to uphold his or her responsibility to nonownership groups. The company rewards its executives for nonfinancial undertakings, including "a commitment to integrity, doing the right thing, maximizing the development of each individual, developing a diverse organization, and continually improving the environmental quality of our products and operations."[19]

---

17. *Ibid.*, p. 141.
18. J. W. Lorsch, *Pawns or Potentates* (Boston: Harvard Business School Press, 1989), p. 49.
19. M. Baker, "I Feel Your Pain?" *Wall Street Journal*, April 12, 1995, p. R6.

CRITICISM OF THE BOARD

If the shareholders do not take the responsibilities of ownership, some other group or individual will. Often it is the board of directors, under the leadership of a powerful CEO. Many boards do their job—to oversee the smooth and profitable running of the corporation—quite well. Often, however, the board fails to live up to the expectations of the shareholders. Other stakeholders, too, feel free to criticize boards, and this has led to much discussion of what many see to be structural weaknesses in boards of directors.[20] Harry Edelson, who is a managing partner of a venture capital firm and has served on a number of boards, estimates that 10 percent of CEOs are dishonest, 15 percent are incompetent, and 25 percent stay past their prime—hampering their boards accordingly.[21]

A list of similar complaints could take up an entire chapter, so we turn to Murray Weidenbaum, who generalizes criticisms of boards of directors into three useful categories: (1) the board as rubber stamp, (2) the board dominated by the CEO, and (3) the board plagued by conflicts of interest.[22]

The Board as Rubber Stamp Possibly the oldest complaint about boards, dating back to a 1948 study of large companies by R. A. Gordon, is that they may function as mere rubber stamps. Gordon concluded that because directors are usually closer to management than to shareholders, the ratification of management proposals by the board is more often than not treated as a formality. Furthermore, as management often controls the proxy machinery by which directors are elected, the ties between the two entities are further linked.

Companies are beginning to take steps against cronyism in the boardroom. For years, the board at Time Warner was seen as little more than a rubber stamp for Chairman Steven J. Ross. With twenty-one members, many of them hand picked by Ross and provided with relatively high levels of compensation, the board was seen as an industry dinosaur—large and anachronistic. When Ross died in 1993, company executives launched a "house revolution" to revive the board's reputation. In fact, eight members of the board, considered to have been Ross's closest allies, resigned on the day he died. The board of General Motors also had the reputation of signing off automatically on anything the CEO suggested, until a board revolt shattered that notion in 1992 (see *Company Focus: General Motors, Inc.* on pp. 360–61).

The Board Dominated by the CEO A similar complaint, which we touched on earlier in this chapter, is that the board acts as a mere agent of the CEO, unquestioningly following his or her orders.[23] As Weidenbaum adds, "When the same person controls the agenda and conduct of the boardroom proceedings as well as the day-to-day performance of the company, the power of the individual director may indeed become . . . [counterproductive]."[24] The latest figures show that over 80 percent of the largest U.S. corporations have CEOs who also serve as chairs of their boards, so this concern is particularly pressing.

Another effect of this intimate relationship between the CEO and the board is the sabotage of one of the basic tenets of corporate governance: power should be given to those

20. Firstenberg and Malkiel, *op. cit.*, p. 27.
21. H. Edelson, "Dispatch from the Boardroom Trenches," *Wall Street Journal*, February 6, 1995, p. A12.
22. M. Weidenbaum, *The Evolving Corporate Board* (St. Louis: Center for the Study of American Business, Washington University, May 1994), pp. 2–5.
23. G. S. Crystal, "The Baron of the Boardroom," *Business and Society Review*, Summer 1993, p. 43.
24. Weidenbaum, *op. cit.*, p. 3.

who use it wisely and should be taken away from those who do not. The board is given the responsibility of changing leadership when necessary; if board members respond to crises by acting as so many "ornaments on a corporate Christmas tree," as one critic describes board members,[25] ineffective CEOs will more likely than not retain their posts. Furthermore, when board leadership and management leadership rest in the same person, board leadership has a tendency to be slack in its responsibility to reward or penalize management performance.[26]

The Board Plagued with Conflicts of Interest   Corporate directors often have many business affiliations, and they can even sit on the board of more than one corporation. There are certain legal restrictions, however. The Clayton Act, in Section 8, prohibits *interlocking directorates*; that is, it generally prohibits individuals from serving as directors on the board of two or more corporations that operate in direct competition with one another. Furthermore, the fiduciary duty requires directors to make a full disclosure of any potential conflicts of interest that might arise in any corporate transaction.

These legal and ethical restrictions, however, have not stopped outside directors of corporations from engaging in allegedly questionable activities. There have been some cases of outside directors whose decision making seemed to lead toward self-aggrandizement rather than the best interests of the stockholders. The outside directors of Loral Corporation, a producer of radar-warning gear for jet fighters, were sued by Banner Industries, Inc., and their own stockholders after they decided to sell two of the company's divisions to Loral's chairman, Bernard Schwartz. Although Banner had offered $467 million in cash and debt for the divisions, a special committee of outside directors—which included a longtime personal friend of the CEO—decided to accept Schwartz's lower offer of only $455 million in cash and debt. In the stockholder suit, it was pointed out that each member of the special committee owed his position to Schwartz and could clearly be seen to have a conflict of interest.

Another conflict of interest that Weidenbaum points out is that outside directors may have ties to the local community. Outside directors who do business in the area surrounding the corporation can personally benefit from steering corporate funds toward local causes. A company that deals mostly with national and international markets, however, faces this problem to a lesser extent.[27]

THE CONTROVERSY OVER EXECUTIVE PAY

In the late 1930s, taking a hint from President Franklin Delano Roosevelt, who had been railing against the "entrenched greed" of business executives, the Treasury Department released a list of corporate executives who earned an annual salary of more than $15,000. A national outrage ensued. More than half those adults who participated in an opinion poll believed executives were grossly overpaid.[28]

In January 1992 a similar controversy was sparked when President George Bush, on a trade mission to Japan, made the ill-fated political choice to bring twelve leading American CEOs with him. Bush's decision once again focused attention on the pay of American CEOs, especially as compared with CEOs in our economic competitor. The dozen American CEOs averaged $25 million in annual salaries, whereas their Japanese

---

25. Clarkham, *op. cit.*, p. 194.
26. Weidenbaum, *op. cit.*, pp. 3–4.
27. *Ibid.*, p. 5.
28. A. R. Brownstein and M. J. Panner, "Who Should Set CEO Pay? The Press? Congress? Shareholders?" *Harvard Business Review*, May–June 1992, pp. 28–29.

COMPANY FOCUS: GENERAL MOTORS, INC.

THE BOARD REVOLT AT GENERAL MOTORS

What is good for the United States is good for General Motors, and what is good for General Motors is good for the United States. So said GM chairman Charles E. Wilson in 1952, and forty-five years later his words seemed eerily appropriate as the world's largest automobile company experienced a board revolt that shocked executives across the United States.

Financial Troubles at GM

GM slumped into the 1990s; indeed, one observer called the company a "big, lazy, stodgy, sleeping giant." Throughout the previous decade, shareholders had complained continuously about a board of directors that seemed more than willing to go along with a succession of CEO/chairmen who lacked initiative or acumen. The latest chairman and chief executive of this type, Robert C. Stempel, assumed control in 1990, promising to turn things around. Stempel, however, exhibited two of the corporate governance flaws that had been plaguing the company for years: cronyism and inefficiency. He insisted on naming longtime friend and colleague Lloyd Reuss president of the company, despite Reuss's lackluster performance as chief of GM's North American unit since 1986. As an example of Stempel's inefficiency, the divisions within GM that did sell well—notably Saturn, but also Cadillac Seville and Eldorado —were inexplicably hampered by upper management's timid unwillingness to expand production.

GM's performance in 1991 proved to be the Waterloo for both Stempel and the company's outdated system of corporate governance. That year, GM reported a loss of $4.5 billion, the largest such figure in American history. The company was actually $7.1 billion in the red from its North American operations, but that figure was partly offset by success in Europe. In December 1991, as GM's stock dropped to a four-year low of $27, the board called a meeting in which it implored Stempel to move more aggressively toward downsizing. A few days later, Stempel announced the closing of twenty-one plants and the elimination of 74,000 jobs, which pleased the board. The target date of 1996, however, did not please it.

Executive Overhaul

On April 6, 1992, after the company had posted $95 million in losses during the year's first quarter, the board finally lost

counterparts were receiving around $400,000 a year.[29] Coming at a time when Americans were worried about Japan's continuing economic strength, the difference in salaries sparked another round of debate over executive pay.

Whether the numbers are $15,000 or $25 million, executive compensation is one area of corporate governance in which the debate has spread outside board rooms, academic circles, and business journals. Relatively few Americans have ever had to deal with issues of shareholder ownership or board room inefficiency, but most workers have been in a situation in which they feel their superiors are getting paid too much. Consequently, when it is announced that Michael D. Eisner, CEO of the Walt Disney Company, earned $203 million in 1993, the initial reaction of many Americans was a mixture of outrage and disbelief.

Are Executives Paid Too Much? Typically, CEOs receive a base salary, supplemented by some or all of the following:

1. Annual bonuses. The incentive of the annual bonus is based on the corporation's profits.

---

29. D. C. Sales, "Are Top Executives Paid Too Much?" *Business and Society Review,* Summer 1994, p. 18.

COMPANY FOCUS: (CONTINUED)

its patience. Moving forward with a vengeance, the board replaced Stempel as head of its own executive committee with John Smale, a former CEO of Procter & Gamble who had been an outside director at GM. The board also demoted Reuss and Robert O'Connell, the latter another Stempel confidant who had been the company's chief financial officer. After the meeting in which these changes were announced, the board released a statement that read, "Regaining profitability requires a more aggressive management approach to remove excess costs."

The shareholder activists that had been demanding better results exulted over the action. "Significantly, this went beyond Stempel into lower-level managers," said Dale M. Hanson, the chief executive of the $68 billion California Public Employees Retirement System, who had been pushing for a change. Indeed, one auto analyst estimated that GM had 30 to 50 percent too many white-collar employees. "The board is playing a little bit of kick-ass and that's good."

Echoing Hanson, many observers hoped the revolt at GM would inspire similar behavior by other corporate boards of directors. The GM board's action was significant in that it was fueled by discordant shareholders and put into action by outside directors, two groups that are expected to take a more visible role in corporate governance in the future. "If it can happen at GM, it can happen anywhere," remarked one industry expert. "This is truly momentous—it's the culmination of the corporate-governance movement to make outside directors perform," agreed a colleague. The only regret was that the board had not acted earlier—when GM had billions of dollars in reserve—and thus saved the thousands of jobs that would be lost in the company's reorganization.

The New Bottom Line

Shareholders, especially after the bold action of the GM directors, will demand more of boards at poorly performing companies, no matter how large. Boards must learn to act before losses mount as they did at GM; they must not allow traditional boardroom protocol to keep them from replacing inefficient CEOs.

SOURCE: Information from J. B. Treece, "The Board Revolt," *Business Week*, April 20, 1992, p. 30; and J. H. Dobrzynski, "A Wake Up Call for Corporate Boards," *Business Week*, April 20, 1992, p. 35.

2. Restricted stock. Particularly when a corporation is just starting up, important investors, officers, and directors purchase shares at a very low price. They are issued what is known as restricted stock certificates, usually Rule 144 and 144A stock. Typically, the owner of restricted stock has to wait a minimum of two years after the initial public offering of the corporation's shares to the public before selling that stock. Then the owner of the restricted stock is allowed to sell only a certain amount every quarter. Of course, capital gains taxes must be paid on the difference between the usually relatively low purchase price of the restricted stock and the value in the marketplace when it is sold. Frequently, one reads in the financial press that the founders and officers of corporations have decided to sell a small amount of the shares that they own. Normally these are restricted shares.

3. Long-term bonuses. Long-term bonuses, instead of being paid each year, are contingent on the corporation's performance over a longer period of time, usually three to five years.

4. Stock options. Usually as an incentive for employees, particularly officers, to remain loyal to the corporation and to maximize its market value, **stock options** are issued at various times.[30] A stock option typically allows an officer or valued employee of the company

---

30. T. J. Rodgers et al., "Taking Account of Stock Options," *Harvard Business Review*, January–February 1994, p. 27.

to purchase at some later date shares of the company stock (not yet issued to anyone else) at a specified price, usually at the price that exists in the marketplace when the stock options are issued. Consequently, if, say, in five years the shares of stock of a company have gone from $1 to $5, the owner of the stock options can *exercise* them at $1 and then resell them in the marketplace at $5, making a $4-per-share profit. Obviously, if the corporation's shares fall below the exercise price of the stock options, they become worthless. (For a breakdown of executive compensation, see *Exhibit 12–3*.)

These salary supplements can be significant. Eisner's base pay in 1993, for example, was $750,000; the rest came from stock options and other bonuses.[31] Theodore Buyinski, Jr., a consultant for Sibson & Company, calculates that more than 80 percent of U.S. companies use stock compensation to link executive pay to the company's long-term performance[32] (see *Exhibit 12–4* on page 365).

Greaf Crystal, former executive and author of *In Search of Excess: The Overcompensation of American Executives*, warns that soon "CEO pay will be equal to the gross national product of countries."[33] Crystal believes that this "pay-the-moon" attitude is reflected in the gap between the average salaries of the American CEO and the average salaries of the American factory worker—in 1995, the CEO made more than 200 times the annual salary of the factory worker.

According to Crystal, these numbers not only show that CEOs are vastly overpaid but also—despite the link of stock options—accentuate the fact that their compensation is not in line with their companies' performance.

▼ "CEOs get paid hugely in good years," Crystal writes, "and, if not hugely, then merely wonderfully in bad years."[34]

A study conducted by the Institute for Policy Studies in Washington, D.C., backs this assertion: from 1991 to 1994, CEO compensation rose an average of 30 percent at twenty-three of the twenty-seven companies announcing the largest staff reductions over the same time.[35] In 1994, Eastman Kodak's earnings fell below target, yet CEO George Fisher received performance incentives that added $1.7 million to his $2 million base salary.[36]

CEO Reaction to Negative Publicity   Some executives are feeling the pressure of negative publicity and are reacting accordingly. In 1994, Northwest Airlines CEO John H. Dasburg returned a $750,000 bonus after the airline's employees agreed to wage cuts to prevent the company from filing bankruptcy. Although Dasburg, who earned a base salary of $464,000 that year, received the bonus for an effective restructuring of the airline's finances, he felt his actions were necessary to restore trust between management and the workers. "Leadership has a price," he said, "and sometimes it includes my pocketbook."[37]

---

31. D. C. Salas, "Fantasyland Payday for Disney CEO," *Business and Society Review,* Summer 1994, p. 19.
32. Brownstein and Panner, *op. cit.,* p. 31.
33. J. A. Byrne, "That Eye-Popping Executive Pay," *Business Week,* April 25, 1994, p. 53.
34. Brownstein and Panner, *op. cit.,* p. 29.
35. Baker, *op. cit.,* p. R6.
36. W. Bounds, "Kodak's CEO Got $1.7 Million Bonus in 1994 Despite Below-Target Profits," *Wall Street Journal,* March 13, 1995, p. B9.
37. Byrne, *op. cit.,* p. 56.

▼ **EXHIBIT 12–3 Breakdown of Executive Pay in a Typical Year**

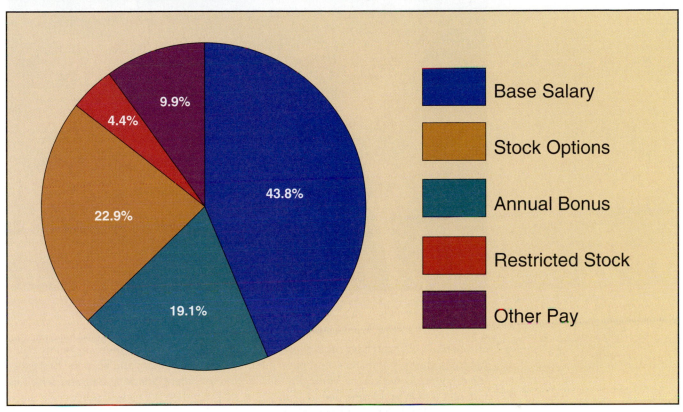

SOURCE: United Shareholders Association.

A poll taken the same year as Dasburg's actions showed that many of his peers might not feel obligated to act accordingly. More than two-thirds of the CEOs who responded to the poll said they felt little or no pressure from outside directors concerning their salaries. Their main complaint, which should not come as a surprise, was that the media had blown the issue of CEO compensation out of proportion. Sixty percent of the respondents criticized the press for its coverage of the issue, and nine out of ten wondered why the same scrutiny was not directed toward high-paid entertainers and athletes.[38]

In Defense of the CEO The populist stance of those who criticize CEO pay has caused a backlash in the business community.[39] Some members of that community say that the key question with regard to corporate governance is not "Are executives paid too much?" but "Are shareholders getting their money's worth from their executives?"[40]

The answer to the latter, in many cases, is yes, followed by the contention that the average American who complains about executive pay does not understand the effect a highly

38. V. Contavespi, "What about Michael Jordan's Pay?" *Fortune*, May 23, 1994, p. 142.
39. C. W. L. Hill and P. Phan, "CEO Tenure as a Determinant of CEO Pay," *Academy of Management Journal*, June 1992, p. 370.
40. Brownstein and Panner, *op. cit.*, p. 29.

Michael Eisner waves to crowds in a celebration at Euro Disney, France.

competent CEO can have on the fortunes of a company.[41] Furthermore, as in any competitive industry, companies must pay a premium salary to acquire and keep the best executive talent. As we saw in *Managing Social Issues: Culture Shock at Ben and Jerry's* in Chapter 5, Ben and Jerry's had to abandon its rule that the CEO could not receive more than seven times the salary of an ice cream scooper in order to lure a chief executive with the skills necessary to run what had become a billion-dollar business. Michael Eisner may have pulled down a 1993 salary comparable to the gross national product of the Caribbean island of Grenada, but in the ten years after he became CEO of Walt Disney, the company's total market value rose from $2.2 billion to $22.7 billion. A shareholder who held $100 worth of stock at the beginning of that period saw his or her holdings jump to $1,640.[42] "The complaints [about CEO pay] aren't coming from institutional investors if the executive has performed," remarked consultant James E. McKinney. In fact, the opposite often occurs: when Coca-Cola CEO Roberto C. Goizueta received a grant of stock worth $81 million, he was given a standing ovation by shareholders at the company's annual meeting.[43]

Defenders of the American CEO also discredit the Japanese example, saying that the different systems of corporate governance in the two countries render such comparisons moot. First of all, Japanese management uses a team approach that downplays the skills of any one individual, such as a CEO. Furthermore, Japanese executives receive benefits that are unavailable—even unthinkable—in the American corporate governance system, including lifetime job security.[44] Even considering these factors, however, the difference in salaries between executives in the two countries is significant.

41. R. V. Whitworth, "Are Executive Pay Scales Off Balance?" *Business and Society Review,* Fall 1991, p. 22.

42. D. C. Salas, "Fantasyland Payday for Disney CEO," p. 19.

43. Byrne, *op. cit.,* p. 56.

44. D. C. Salas, "Are Top Executives Paid Too Much?" p. 18.

Executive	Company	Value of Nonexercised Stock (thousands)
Michael D. Eisner	Walt Disney	$161,376
N. Wayne Huzienga	Blockbuster Entertainment	93,667
Wayne Calloway	PepsiCo	81,283
James L. Donald	DCS Communications	50,731
Sanford I. Weill	Travelers	47,288
Roberto C. Goizueta	Coca-Cola	45,947
Reuben Mark	Colgate-Palmolive	42,584
Harry A. Merlo	Louisiana-Pacific	42,075
Daniel P. Tully	Merrill Lynch	40,453
Gordon M. Binder	Amgen	39,469

SOURCE: *Business Week*, April 25, 1994, p. 57.

IMPROVING CORPORATE GOVERNANCE

Criticism within and outside the business community has led to a number of changes in the corporate governance system—changes that have reached the magnitude of those brought on by deregulation for some companies. Some companies have taken drastic measures, such as forcing executives to purchase a predetermined amount of the firm's stock (see *Managing Social Issues—Ethics and Social Responsibility: Required Executive Stock Ownership* on page 366). Unlike the sudden changes brought on by deregulation, however, reform of corporate governance has taken a rather steady course over the past two decades. Few believe, though, that reform has run its course. If criticism persists, politicians will no doubt feel the pressure to turn their regulatory spotlights more harshly on corporate governance.

IMPROVING PERFORMANCE OF THE BOARD

Many critics of corporate governance seek to abolish the dual position of board chair and CEO. "How can one person who serves as both chairperson and CEO evaluate his or her own performance?" asked a pamphlet from the New York City Employees' Retirement System. Shareholder rights activist A. G. Monks points out that the "only person to whom the [dual title holder] has to speak is his shaving mirror." Although it did not pass, in 1992 Sears, Roebuck & Company faced a shareholders' resolution calling for the permanent split between the two roles on the corporation's board—the first resolution of its kind at any major U.S. company.[45]

Unless every state outlaws the practice, however, probably 80 percent of CEOs will continue to be the chair of the board of directors. There is a straightforward competitive

45. J. S. Lublin, "Shareholders Campaign to Dilute Power of Chief Executives by Splitting Top Jobs," *Wall Street Journal*, April 1, 1992, p. B1.

MANAGING SOCIAL ISSUES

ETHICS AND SOCIAL RESPONSIBILITY: REQUIRED EXECUTIVE STOCK OWNERSHIP

In 1993, Campbell Soup Company announced a stock-ownership plan that required its president and CEO, David Johnson, to hold at least three times his annual base salary in company stock—about $2.2 million worth. Along with Johnson, seventy other senior executives were given less expensive targets to meet. Later that same year, Eastman Kodak Company placed the same requirement on forty of its top managers, prompting Johnson to send a fax to a peer at Kodak. "Welcome to the club," the message read. "The dues are very high."

Why Executive Stock Ownership Works

These "dues" are being paid by more and more top executives across the country, as companies try to get their managers to think more like shareholders. The theory is based on a perception that unlike small-business owners—whose pangs of hunger for profits are kept sharp by constant worry of failure—corporate executives tend to be sated by large salaries that do not hinge on company performance. A 1994 survey by the consulting firm Wyatt Company found that of 105 large companies examined, 11 percent had executive stock-ownership requirements, compared with virtually none five years earlier.

This trend toward required executive stock ownership is making many investors very happy. Sarah Teslick, the executive director of the Council of Institutional Investors, says, "I think my chances are better with [management] owning [substantial amounts of] stock" because then "your life is in fact wrapped up in the company." According to Wyatt Company, this confidence is not misplaced. In the Wyatt survey, companies with above-median stock ownership had an average rate of return 4 percentage points higher than those with below-median stock ownership.

Pros and Cons

Members of management at Continental Bank Corporation, which instituted a required executive stock-ownership plan in 1991, say the policy has dramatically changed their outlook. Joseph V. Thompson, the bank's chief human resources officer, says his $60,000 share purchase "affects me every day, whether I'm buying pencils or putting in merit pay budgets," because it seems as though it is "my money that I'm spending." The company also found a greater willingness among managers to let star performers switch departments for the overall good of the bank. One vice president said she approved the move of a valued staff member, whereas before she owned stock she would have "thrown [herself] in front of a truck and said, 'No.'"

There is some controversy in the business community concerning the practice. For starters, there is the question of the right of individuals to invest their own money as they wish. Then there is the risk a company runs that the value of the stock will plummet, taking management morale along with it. Some observers believe talented managers will opt not to join companies that require stock ownership because of the added risk and expense. Thomas Theobald, Continental's chairman, has a simple response to that criticism. If fellow executives "are not willing to put their money on the line," then "I don't want them standing next to me on the firing line."

For Critical Analysis:

Is it within a company's ethical boundaries to force an executive to own a certain amount of its stock? How would you react to such a directive from a potential employer?

SOURCE: Information from J. S. Lublin, "Buy or Bye: More Companies Force Top Executives to Purchase Large Amounts of Company Stock," *Wall Street Journal*, April 21, 1993, p. R9; and L. Young, "The Owner Mentality," *Wall Street Journal*, April 12, 1995, p. R12.

market reason why we can predict this. Corporations compete for officers and directors. People who have good track records or great potential as the heads of corporations are normally in great demand. Corporations competing for these people's services will typically be forced to give them whatever they desire in order to entice them to become heads of corporations. Normally, aggressive heads of corporations do not want to be told what to do by a board of directors that they do not control. The result is that good CEOs often want to chair the board of directors.

Outside Directors Harold Williams, former chairman of the Securities and Exchange Commission (SEC) and a former CEO himself, believes the ideal board of directors would have only one representative from the company: the chief executive. Every other board member, including the chair, would come from outside the company. Williams sees his plan as solving the problem of conflicts of interest. By excluding lawyers, bankers, or anybody else with an interest in the company, he envisions a board committed to the shareholders' long-term interest without being tied up in the duties of management.[46]

General Motors Corporation went one step further, spelling out the difference between generally accepted outside directors and its truly independent directors. According to GM, an independent director is one who has the following characteristics:

1. Has not been employed by the company in an executive capacity in the past five years.
2. Is not a significant advisor or consultant.
3. Is not affiliated with any of the company's significant customers or suppliers.
4. Does not have significant personal-service contracts with the company.
5. Is not affiliated with any tax-exempt organization that receives significant company contributions.
6. Is not an executive's spouse, parent, sibling, or child.[47]

The company incorporated these definitions in its highly regarded guidelines for corporate governance—known as the company's Magna Carta, after the seventeenth-century British legal charter designed to limit royal power (see *Exhibit 12–5* on page 368).

This emphasis on outside directors has been reflected in the makeup of boards. In 1938, only around 50 percent of industrial corporations had boards with a majority of outside directors; by 1992, the average board had nine outside directors and three inside directors. The same year, eleven major firms had realized Harold Williams's vision of boards in which the only "insider" was the chairperson.[48] How independent, at least by GM's standards, these outside directors really are is another question. Jonathan Clarkham estimates that a "very high proportion" of outside directors—around 90 percent—"are already known to the CEO even if he did not himself put the name forward."[49]

Committees of the Board Another attempt to make the board more independent from the CEO, as well as more responsive to shareholders and other stakeholders alike, is the proliferation of committees within the board. There are many different sorts of committees, so we will concentrate on the ones most integral to the corporate governance system: the **audit committee,** the **compensation committee,** and the **nominating committee.**

Audit Committee By 1996, about 98 percent of companies had audit committees, which are responsible for monitoring the fiscal well-being of the company by overseeing internal

46. Weidenbaum, *op. cit.*, p. 6.
47. "Board Independence Is Hallmark of Good Governance, Veasey Says," BNA's *Corporate Counsel Weekly*, August 20, 1995, p. 2.
48. Weidenbaum, *op. cit.*, p. 10.
49. Clarkham, *op. cit.*, p. 190.

▼ **EXHIBIT 12–5 General Motors' Magna Carta**

The highlights of GM's six-page, twenty-eight-point boardroom code are as follows:

- The board and only the board—not the CEO—can select new members. This proposal is expected to eliminate any question of where the board members' loyalties lie.
- Outside directors will choose a "lead director" in situations where the chairperson and the CEO posts are held by a single person. The lead director will chair at least three "executive sessions" of outside directors a year, to be followed by a discussion with the CEO. Once a year, the outside director will formally evaluate the CEO.
- The board will have a "Director Affairs Committee" with duties including evaluating the board's performance in an annual report to the full board.
- Board members will have "complete access to GM's management."
- GM's outside directors will make all decisions about corporate governance.

  By removing ultimate power from the CEO/chair, GM's Magna Carta (established in 1994) is aimed at ensuring each outside director that he or she is not merely a figurehead but rather an integral part of the company's corporate government. "The difference is night and day," says a member who has been on the board since 1987. "Everyone can speak candidly, there is no sense of not wanting to hear something, and it doesn't matter if it's controversial."

SOURCE: *Business Week,* April 4, 1994, p. 37.

and external audits and scrutinizing other financial indicators. These committees generally have four members and meet three times a year.

The key role of the audit committee is maintaining the integrity of the corporate governance system with regard to the financial systems and controls of the company. The committee provides a link between the board and management, and it should keep the board appraised of the financial situation of the company. In a sense, the audit committee is a preventive body—by keeping close watch on the finances of the company, it should be able to spot approaching trouble and warn the full board to take appropriate evasive steps. In 1978 the New York Stock Exchange made a listing requirement that audit committees be made up of a majority of outside directors, an action repeated by the American Stock Exchange and NASDAQ/NMS. Consequently, about 90 percent of audit committee members are outside directors.

Compensation Committee Judging from the criticism of executive pay discussed earlier, there is some question whether the compensation committee, which is concerned with setting pay for upper management, has improved corporate governance. Compensation committees are marginally larger (with sometimes five directors) and meet more frequently (four times a year) than do audit committees. Also, as with audit committees, they are mostly made up of outside directors. They have one major procedural difference: the CEO often attends compensation committee meetings (this is true for virtually all Fortune 500 companies). Because the CEO has usually in some way been responsible for the board members' being on the board, his or her presence at the meetings may be one reason why CEO pay has continued to escalate. The "back-scratching" nature of many compensation committees is well known.[50]

Obviously, a solution would be to keep the CEO from attending meetings and to require only independent directors on the committee. Because of the controversy, not to mention a number of regulatory attempts to control executive pay (see *Exhibit 12–6*),

50. A. G. Perkins, "Director Compensation: The Growth of Benefits," *Harvard Business Review,* January–February 1995, p. 12.

▼ **EXHIBIT 12–6 Federal Attempts to Regulate Executive Pay**

Regulation	Description
Omnibus Budget Reconciliation Act (or Tax Act) of 1993	The response to a campaign promise by President Bill Clinton, this act created two new individual tax brackets. One of them, referred to as the "millionaires' surtax" (soon to become known as the upper-middle-class surtax), placed a 10 percent tax on income in excess of $250,000. The act also mandated that deductions for nonperformance-related compensation in excess of $1 million are disallowed for publicly traded companies. Furthermore, the maximum annual amount protected from taxation in retirement plans was reduced from $235,000 to $150,000. Along with these provisions to increase an executive's income taxes and reduce the amount of money he or she can keep free from taxes, the act also gave shareholders more power to directly influence executive pay.
Financial Accounting Standards Board (FASB) Stock Option Plan	In 1993, the FASB proposed a ruling that would have required companies to deduct stock options from their earnings. The aim of the proposal was to give companies an incentive to reduce or eliminate large stock options. No final decision has been made on the extent to which the proposal will be adopted.
Securities and Exchange Commission (SEC) Pay Disclosure Requirements	This is the attempt that has received the most criticism from business sources. Implemented in 1992, this law required SEC-registered companies to make public documents that contain detailed information about that company's compensatory plans for the CEO and the four other highest-paid executives earning more than $100,000 a year. Included in this document must be base salary, bonuses, stock options, and other stock awards, as well as any perquisites that reached or exceeded $50,000 during the previous year. The company is also required to disclose its overall performance, to be compared with its compensatory policies, through a performance graph mapping the company's cumulative total shareholder return for a five-year period. In 1993, the SEC revised the rules to require, in addition to those factors already listed, a full explanation of the compensation committee's rationale and policies for compensation and an explanation of how the reported amounts are justified when compared with corporate performance. Businesspersons complain about the amount of employee time and paperwork involved in meeting these regulations, but activists note that the public disclosure is a strong incentive against unfair or unethical compensatory practices.

SOURCE: B. M. Longnecker, "Smart Compensation Programs for Today's Regulatory Environment," *Compensation and Benefits Review,* September 19, 1995, p. 47.

many companies have come up with highly structured formal compensation policies. These policies limit the compensation committee's power in setting executive pay.

Nominating Committee A majority of companies now have nominating committees, whose responsibility is to nominate replacement board members. These committees meet once or twice a year and are made up of one company director and four outside directors. Again, the CEO attends meetings of the nominating committee. A survey by Korn Ferry International in 1992 showed that despite all the outside consultants hired by the nominating committee, the recommendation of the board chairperson (who is, you remember, in most cases the CEO) is the most important nominating factor.[51]

Public-Policy/Public-Issues Committee Another important corporate governance tool is the *public-policy/public-issues committee.* Although only about one-fifth of major

---

51. Clarkham, *op. cit.,* p. 193.

corporations had such committees in the late 1990s, the number is growing. This growth reflects increased concern among executives about the topics addressed by the public-policy/public-issues committee, such as the corporation's effects on the environment, affirmative action, employee health and safety, business ethics, and other social issues.

INCREASED SHAREHOLDER ACTIVISM

Another avenue for improved corporate governance opens up when the shareholders, the owners, become more active in influencing the activities of their corporations. Indeed, an increasing number of shareholder activist groups have started to make themselves heard. After all,

▼ As Nell Minnow, a principal with the group Lens, Inc., says to directors, "If you take our money, you also get our mouth."[52]

Shareholder activism came into prominence in the late sixties and early seventies, particularly during the period of civil rights concerns and the Vietnam War (1963–1975). Perhaps the most impressive example of shareholder activism during that period involved consumer activist Ralph Nader's campaign to reform General Motors. Nader's group was successful in forcing GM to create a public-policy committee of the board of directors, which was composed of five outside directors. The job of GM's public-policy committee was to monitor social performance.

The publicity that Ralph Nader garnered in the field of shareholder activism caused a surge of religious activism with similar targets. In particular, in the 1970s, the Interfaith Center on Corporate Responsibility became a clearinghouse for those concerned with the social impact of corporations.

In the 1980s, institutional investors, particularly pension plans, became very active in fighting what they saw as corporate mismanagement from a social point of view. Then, in 1986, the United Shareholders Association was created to represent the rights of almost fifty million individual U.S. shareholders.

One way that shareholder activism has affected the behavior of corporations is through the required filing of shareholder resolutions at annual meetings. There has been a continuing battle over this issue, as corporations have argued that many of the proposed shareholder resolutions are not relevant and can safely be ignored. The SEC, nonetheless, has often forced corporations to include a wide-ranging number of shareholder-initiated corporate resolutions for voting at annual corporate meetings. A switch in SEC policy in 1994 allowed a number of shareholder proposals to appear in proxy statements (see *Exhibit 12–7*).

Finally, more and more shareholder activist groups are filing lawsuits. These lawsuits may be filed against the corporate directors for mismanaging corporate resources or to redress a wrong suffered by the corporation. Shareholders are permitted to do so "derivatively" in what is known as a **shareholder's derivative suit.** The right of shareholders who bring a derivative action is especially important when the wrong suffered by the corporation results from the actions of corporate directors or officers.

The right of shareholders to sue derivatively on behalf of their corporations was indicated as early as the 1830s. In 1855, the United States Supreme Court upheld a shareholder's right to sue on behalf of a corporation whose officer had paid a tax that the shareholder claimed was unconstitutional. In the second half of the nineteenth century,

---

52. M. J. Verespej, "What's Next for Directors," *Industry Week*, February 21, 1994, p. 11.

▼ **EXHIBIT 12–7 Shareholder Resolutions Offered to Boards in the Mid-1990s**

Corporation	Description of Resolution
PepsiCo, Inc.	Asked the board to adopt a policy making all of PepsiCo's restaurants smoke free by 1995.
Philip Morris Companies	Requested that the company refrain from undermining legislation geared toward restricting smoking in public places and to cease expenditures used for challenging studies on environmental tobacco smoke.
General Electric Company	Asked the board to review subsidiary NBC's implementation of program standards and to issue a report to shareholders regarding violence on NBC programs.
AT&T Company	Sought the creation of a board committee to evaluate the impact on the company of national health-care proposals.
AT&T Company	Requested a company policy to evaluate environmental and human rights impacts of expansion into Mexico.
Amoco Corporation	Sought to have a compensation committee devise a scheme for incentive awards for executives.
Micronics Computers, Inc.	Sought to mandate that the board be denied the right to reduce the price of stock options approved by shareholders.

SOURCE: *BNA Corporate Counsel Weekly,* April 27, 1994, p. 7.

the derivative suit developed more fully. One well-documented lawsuit against corporate directors involved John Van Gorkom, the chairman of the board of Trans Union Corporation. Shareholders sued Van Gorkom for working out a merger agreement in which the company's shares were sold for $55 each, a price allegedly below market value. In *Smith v. Van Gorkom,* a court ruled that directors could be held liable for accepting an offer for the purchase of a corporation because they purportedly failed to investigate the value of the business and whether a higher price could be obtained.

TAKEOVERS

So far in this chapter, we have primarily dealt with the interior workings of the corporate governance system. Now we examine the effects that outside maneuvering can have on a corporation, with the understanding that shareholders, CEOs, and boards of directors are not static entities. They can, and often are, changed or replaced. The key factor in the stability of any participant in corporate governance is *who controls the corporation.*

The control of a corporation may be acquired through a merger, a consolidation, or a purchase of the corporation's assets. The most direct way to acquire the control of a corporation is through a **takeover.**[53] A takeover is accomplished through the purchase of a substantial number of the voting shares of a firm. The majority shareholders can thus control the acquired corporation's assets and dictate its corporate governance. In effecting a takeover, the acquiring firm deals directly with the shareholders of the corporation whose control is being sought.

---

53. H. Ingham, I. Kran, and A. Lovestam, "Mergers and Profitability: A Managerial Success Story?" *Journal of Management Studies,* March 1992, p. 195.

Takeovers are of two types: friendly and hostile. A *friendly takeover* occurs when the management of the firm being acquired welcomes the acquisition. A *hostile takeover,* by contrast, occurs when the management of the firm being acquired opposes the acquisition. In both cases, the individual, group, or firm seeking to take over a target corporation is often referred to as the aggressor.

TAKEOVER TACTICS

A takeover, especially a hostile one, can be a complicated process. Sometimes a takeover may begin as a proposed merger, with a public offer to buy shares from the shareholders of the target corporation. Other times the takeover of a publicly traded corporation may begin with an anonymous purchase of shares on an open stock exchange.

During the "merger mania" that swept Wall Street in the 1980s, corporate takeovers often resembled open warfare:

▼ **Takeover battles were sometimes launched in a manner comparable to an army's surprise invasion of another country.**

Corporate "raiders" went to great lengths to keep from alerting opposing management to the fact that its company was "in play." Decoy raiders were sent, with considerable publicity, to distant cities, for example, while the anonymous masterminds met in seclusion with their investment advisors and lawyers to map out corporate battle plans. Sometimes, dummy corporations would be used to buy shares, with the names of the parties that owned the dummy corporation kept secret. Frequently, smaller blocks of shares would be sold at the same time large blocks were being bought so as to avoid running up the price of stock of the target corporation and alerting others that a takeover attempt was in the making.

The next merger wave, that of the mid-1990s, was characterized, at least by those taking part in it, as being fundamentally different from its predecessor. The 1990s deal makers like to be seen as being driven by the laws of efficiency. On one hand, conglomerates have shown an inclination to reduce the number of suppliers with which they do business, giving those suppliers an incentive to join forces. On the other hand, bigger is seen as stronger; many executives hope mergers lead to a competitive advantage (see the *Case—Analysis of a Takeover: Quaker and Snapple*—at the end of this chapter). An industry watcher commenting on the increase in railroad company mergers in the early 1990s called the actions "the railroads' way of saying that the enemy is not really one another—the enemy is the highway and the truckers."[54]

There are a number of different maneuvers that bring about takeovers, but we concentrate on the three most common: tender offers, beachhead acquisitions, and leveraged buyouts, along with a financial strategy related to takeovers, called greenmail.

Tender Offers Perhaps the least difficult takeover tactic occurs when the acquiring corporation makes a public offer to all the shareholders of a corporation, known as a **tender offer.** The price of the stock in the tender offer is generally higher than the market price of the target stock prior to the announcement of the tender offer. The higher price induces shareholders to tender their shares to the acquiring firm.

The tender offer can be conditional on the receipt of a specified number of outstanding shares by a specific date. The offering corporation can make an *exchange tender offer,*

---

54. J. Greenwald, "Come Together, Right Now," *Time,* August 15, 1994, p. 28.

in which it offers target stockholders its own securities in exchange for their target stock. In a *cash tender offer*, the offering corporation offers the target stockholders cash in exchange for their target stock.

Beachhead Acquisitions and Proxy Fights   An attempted takeover may begin with a gradual accumulation of a target corporation's shares. Having established a *beachhead* (hence the military name **beachhead acquisition**) with a block of shares, the purchaser of the shares may then launch a *proxy fight* for control of the corporation. A **proxy fight** resembles a political campaign in that the individual or group seeking control of the target corporation must secure the proxies of other shareholders.[55] (Remember, a proxy entitles the holder to cast votes on behalf of the party conferring the proxy. A proxy may be obtained for each share that may be voted.) If the voting shares owned and the proxies obtained equal enough votes to outvote all of the other shareholders, effective control of the corporation will have been gained. The controlling group usually exercises authority by using its majority vote to elect a board of directors that supports its views.

Leveraged Buyouts (LBOs)   In the last twenty-five years, a number of corporations have arranged to become privately held through so-called **leveraged buyouts (LBOs).** In an LBO, the management of a corporation (or any other group, but management is usually included) purchases all outstanding corporate stock held by the public and in this way gains control over the corporate enterprise. The LBO is financed by borrowing against the assets of the corporation, which may include real estate or plants and equipment. The borrowing may take the form of the issuance of bonds, a straight bank loan, or a loan from an investment bank.

Because an LBO often results in a high debt load for the corporation, the interest payments on the debt may become so burdensome that the corporation cannot survive. Some corporations have failed to survive following LBOs for this reason, the best known being R. H. Macy & Company. In 1986, CEO Edward Finklestein directed a $3.6 billion LBO in which several hundred Macy managers would become owners of the retail company. Finklestein's strategies to offset the interest payments failed, and by January 1992 the company was forced to apply for bankruptcy protection.[56]

Greenmail   Takeover attempts may prove profitable even when they are unsuccessful. After a takeover attempt is launched—usually beginning with a beachhead acquisition—negotiations may begin between the aggressor and the target's incumbent management. Out of these negotiations may come an agreement in which the target agrees to pay the aggressor a premium (a price above the current market price) for its block of shares. In return, the aggressor agrees to make no further acquisitions of the target's shares for a definite period. The net result of the agreement is that the aggressor abandons any fight for control of the target in return for what is in effect a peace payment. Such payments are referred to as **greenmail.**

As unseemly as greenmail may appear, it is not illegal. It also may be quite profitable—for the aggressor, anyway. T. Boone Pickens and his small firm, Mesa Petroleum Corporation, launched six different takeover attempts between 1982 and 1985. Even though not a single attempt was successful, the firm earned $978 million merely by collecting greenmail. Greenmail may or may not continue to generate such enormous

55. D. Ikenberry and J. Lakonishok, "Corporate Governance through the Proxy Contest: Evidence and Implications," *Journal of Business*, July 1993, p. 405.
56. J. A. Trachtenberg, "Separate Seats at the Parade," *Wall Street Journal*, April 24, 1992, p. A1.

profits. It may eventually be prohibited by legislation. In the meantime, to curb the use of greenmail, Congress has imposed a nondeductible excise tax on the receipt of greenmail payments.

TAKEOVER DEFENSES

As discussed earlier in this chapter, the directors of a corporation owe a fiduciary duty to the stakeholders. In the context of a tender offer, this requires that after full consideration, the directors of the target firm must make a good faith decision as to whether the shareholders' acceptance or rejection of the offer would be most beneficial. In making any recommendation, the directors must fully disclose all *material facts*. A fact is material if there is a substantial likelihood that a reasonable shareholder would consider it important in deciding how to vote. For example, information identifying a good price for stock would be considered material.

Sometimes, a target firm's board of directors sees a tender offer as favorable and recommends to the shareholders that they accept it. Alternatively, to resist a takeover, a target company may make a *self-tender*, which is an offer to acquire stock from its own shareholders and thereby retain corporate control. A target corporation also might resort to one of several other tactics, which are discussed here.

Crown Jewel Defense Virtually every corporation, and certainly every conglomerate (a firm owning two or more unrelated businesses), possesses a variety of assets. Some assets, of course, are more valuable than others. When a corporation is threatened with an imminent takeover, management may seek to prevent it by making the firm less attractive to the aggressor. One way to do this is by selling off the firm's most valuable assets. By selling the valuable assets and retaining the undesirable ones, the firm becomes less of a prize in a potential takeover. This defense is referred to as the **crown jewel defense,** because the firm attempts to avoid a takeover by selling off its most valuable assets—that is, its crown jewels.

Scorched-Earth Tactics In a related defense, the target corporation eliminates its valuable assets and pursues other actions designed to make it less appealing to an aggressor. Using **scorched-earth tactics,** the target firm sells off assets or divisions or takes out loans that it agrees will be paid off in the event of a takeover. These actions make the target less financially attractive to the aggressor, though they may have unwanted—and unhealthy—repercussions (see *Company Focus: Unocal Corporation*).

Poison Pill Defense Another way a firm can make itself less attractive to takeover is by using the **poison pill defense,** which involves the target corporation's issuance to its stockholders shares that may be exchanged for cash in the event of a successful takeover. This not only makes the target less attractive but also has the potential for making the takeover prohibitively expensive for a successful aggressor. On the consummation of the takeover, the management would be forced to redeem for cash those shares issued as part of the poison pill.

Pac-Man Defense Consistent with the belief that the best defense is a good offense, a takeover perhaps can be avoided by the target firm's turning on the acquiring firm and taking it over. In 1982, an attempt by Bendix Corporation to take over Martin Marietta failed spectacularly when the latter announced its intentions to purchase the supposed aggressor. Bendix was forced to strengthen its own defenses with an ill-fated merger with Allied Corporation. Because Martin Marietta's defense involved the prey turning on the predator, the strategy was called the *Pac-Man defense,* after a popular video game of the

COMPANY FOCUS: UNOCAL CORPORATION

THE LONG, SLOW BURN OF SCORCHED EARTH

During the hostile takeover movement of the mid-1980s, T. Boone Pickens was a name that struck fear in the hearts of companies with a strong cash flow and little debt. With hostile takeovers succeeding at an incredible rate—a Wall Street rule of thumb at the time was that only one of every five takeover targets could survive intact—Pickens was the king of the corporate raiders. Starting in 1984, he turned his attention to the oil and gas industry, launching takeover attempts against Gulf Oil Corporation, Philips Petroleum Company, and Unocal Corporation. All three companies managed to fend off his attacks, but in the case of Unocal, the scorched-earth tactics it employed are still plaguing the company more than a decade later.

Pickens's Takeover Attempt

In 1985, Unocal was a prime target for a takeover; the company had high profits and little debt thanks to the fact that it had the lowest cost of finding oil ($6 a barrel) of any major oil company. Consequently, Pickens and his investors gathered together $1.2 billion to purchase a majority of the firm's stock. Pickens always maintained that his takeover attempts were in the best interests of stockholders, whose stocks were undervalued, but court documents concerning the Unocal case belie this contention. Pickens's plans for the firm were to cut spending for exploration and development from $850 million in 1984 to $100 million in 1990. Foreign exploration was to disappear by 1988—it had been $355 million in 1983. The goal of the raiders seemed to be liquidation, not improvement.

Scorched-Earth Tactics

To counter the takeover attempt, Unocal's board decided to inflate the price of its stock, making it too expensive for Pickens. The firm wound up buying back 36 percent of its stock and agreed to spin off 45 percent of its oil and gas reserves to shareholders. The scorched-earth plan succeeded, but Fred Hartley, Unocal's chief executive, admitted that although the firm had won "this war, we were forced to take on over $4 billion in new debt." Actually, the operation required more than $4.5 billion in debt to finance.

Unocal's Costly Victory

Eight years later, Unocal won a $48 million settlement from Mesa, Inc., a company that Pickens chaired, for illegal short-term profit making. The victory was costly in the extreme. After the initial battle, Unocal's debt swelled to nearly $6 billion. Each year since, the company has had to swallow nearly $300 million in additional yearly interest expenses from that debt. At the time Unocal received Mesa's settlement, the firm's debt was at $3.4 billion.

These cash woes severely hampered Unocal's ability to stay competitive in the West Coast gas business. In the 1980s, when oil prices were strong, Unocal was unable to spend the money needed to upgrade service stations. By the 1990s, when oil prices had softened, it was nearly too late. In 1994, Unocal announced a plan to convert about 200 of its 1,240 gas stations in California to sell nongasoline products such as fast food and liquor. The move was seen by many experts as a belated attempt to match the shift to convenience stores that most other large gas companies had made in the 1980s; that shift had allowed them to dominate the market and leave Unocal with only 11 percent of the state's stations. "We didn't move nearly as fast as our competition," admitted Roger Beach, the company's president. "We're just trying to play catch up."

There have been other decade-old repercussions. In 1993, Unocal put $257 million in assets up for sale, realizing about $92 million in pretax gains. The next year, the company agreed to take unsolicited offers for its California gas and oil assets, which industry watchers believe could sell for as much as $700 million. Unocal executives said the profits from such a fire sale would go to the company's overseas operations in the Gulf of Mexico and Thailand. In 1993 these operations—which Pickens intended to liquidate—accounted for more than 70 percent of Unocal's total earnings.

The New Bottom Line

Scorched-earth tactics are often too damaging to the long-term health of a company to be in its best interests. When management senses a hostile takeover attempt, it should strongly consider other strategies, such as those listed in this chapter.

SOURCE: Information from D. Hertzberg, "Borrowing Time," *Wall Street Journal*, September 10, 1985, p. A1; A. Pastzor, "Unocal Hopes Station Overhaul Pumps up Its Fortunes," *Wall Street Journal*, May 13, 1994, p. B4; and N. Byrnes, "Scorched Earth," *FW*, August 2, 1994, p. 32.

time. In employing this strategy, the target firm may utilize any of the takeover tactics described earlier and used by any other aggressor.

White Knight Defense If it is unlikely that the target firm will be able to successfully defend against an imminent takeover, it may still avoid the takeover by undertaking a merger with a third corporation, one that it favors over the aggressor. The target corporation usually searches for and solicits a merger with a third corporation. The third corporation then makes a better (usually higher) tender offer to the target firm's shareholders. The third corporation is seen as having *rescued* the target from a hostile takeover and is referred to as a white knight. Thus, this defense is called the **white knight defense.**

Golden Parachute Although not a takeover defense, the so-called **golden parachute** often comes into play when a company has failed to resist a takeover attempt. The incumbent management more often than not is opposed to the takeover, because top management is often changed after a takeover. One way to appease the top management of a corporation, then, is to provide special termination or retirement benefits that must be paid to the management if it is replaced or "retired" following a takeover. In other words, a departing high-level manager's *parachute* will be *golden* if the manager is forced to "bail out" of the firm after a takeover.

Limitations on Takeover Defenses The ultimate responsibility for deciding whether to accept or resist a takeover attempt rests with the target corporation's board of directors.[57] In making its decision, the board must meet the standards imposed under its fiduciary duty to the corporation's shareholders. Regardless of whether the board decides to accept or resist the takeover attempt, it must meet high standards of loyalty and care. Indeed, because the directors—especially inside directors, who also serve as officers of the target corporation—may fear being replaced after a successful takeover, the degree of scrutiny that a court may use in assessing whether the directors met their standards of loyalty and care in trying to fend off a takeover may be greater than the degree of scrutiny applied to directors who accepted a takeover.

---

57. J. E. Gutknecht and J. B. Keys, "Mergers, Acquisitions, and Takeovers: Maintaining Morale and Protecting Employees," *Academy of Management Executive*, August 1993, p. 26.

THE DELICATE BALANCE

The issue of corporate governance, and even the term itself, is relatively new, and it has attracted widespread interest in the last decade. There has always been a debate in the United States about who controls corporations, but not until recently has the debate been turned into action on the part of those who govern today's corporations. Certainly the controversy over supposed excessive executive pay has been around for a while. Even our tax code has been changed in recent years in an attempt to nudge corporations into offering smaller compensation packages to their executives. Specifically, corporations are unable to write off the excess of executive pay over $1 million per year, unless that excess is based on some type of performance standard. Critics of this legislation point out that no such punishment is made when a corporation has to pay an outside supplier of services large amounts of money. For example, singer Barbra Streisand was paid $20 million to give two concerts in Las Vegas. This $20 million was a legitimate business expense that could be deducted from the hotel-casino's revenues before tax liabilities were calculated. What is the difference, these critics ask, between payment of a superstar in the entertainment and sports world and payment of an executive?

To be sure, government policymakers, as well as corporate leaders, must address the delicate balance between keeping the corporation viable and profitable and satisfying the public's displeasure with many aspects of corporate governance today.

TERMS AND CONCEPTS FOR REVIEW

Audit committee 367
Beachhead acquisition 373
Compensation committee 367
Corporate charter 349
Corporate governance 349
Crown jewel defense 374
Golden parachute 376
Greenmail 373

Inside director 353
Institutional shareholder 351
Leveraged buyout (LBO) 373
Nominating committee 367
Outside director 353
Poison pill defense 374
Proxy 352
Proxy fight 373

Quorum 352
Resolution 352
Scorched-earth tactics 374
Shareholder's derivative suit 370
Stock options 361
Takeover 371
Tender offer 372
White knight defense 376

SUMMARY

1. The term *corporate governance* is used to describe the manner by which a corporation is controlled and directed in accordance with its goals and corporate culture. Corporate governance includes the basic relationship between shareholders and management. A typical model of corporate governance involves shareholders at the top, who direct the board of directors, which chooses upper management, which manages other employees.

2. A corporation is created by an act of the state and usually has perpetual existence. The shareholders elect a board of directors to manage the affairs of the corporation.

3. Shareholders' powers include approval of all fundamental changes affecting the corporation and election of the board of directors.

4. Shareholders' meetings must occur at least annually; special meetings can be called when necessary. Notice of the time and place of the meeting (and its purpose, if it is specially called) must be sent to shareholders. A shareholder may appoint a proxy (substitute) to vote his or her shares.

5. The first board of directors is usually appointed by the incorporators; thereafter, directors are elected by the shareholders. Directors usually serve a one-year term, although the term can be longer.

6. Few qualifications of directors are required; a director can be a shareholder but is not required to be. Compensation is usually specified in the corporate articles or bylaws.

7. Directors' management responsibilities include the following: the authorization of major corporate decisions; the appointment, supervision, and removal of corporate officers and other high-level managerial employees; the determination of employees' compensation; and financial decisions necessary for the management of corporate affairs.

8. Institutional owners, such as pension and mutual funds, even though relatively large, own a relatively minor percentage of the largest U.S. corporations. Consequently, very few institutional owners actively try to influence the activities of corporate boards of directors.

9. Ineffective boards of directors are often dominated by a powerful CEO who has helped pick the board members. These boards may be mere rubber stamps for the CEO. Additionally, corporate directors can have numerous business affiliations that lead to conflicts of interest. Even an outside director may have ties to a local community and therefore have a conflict of interest, certainly with respect to shareholders.

10. There has been controversy over excessive executive pay since the 1930s. Most executives are paid a base salary plus an annual bonus, restricted stock, long-term bonuses, and stock options. Some CEOs have reacted to negative publicity about their high salaries by giving back their bonuses in years during which their corporations have had relatively low profits or suffered losses.

11. Those who are critical of our current system of corporate governance claim that more truly independent outside directors would improve the situation. There is a difference between outside directors and independent outside directors. Those who are independent do not have close ties to the CEO.

12. Within most boards of directors are several important committees, including the audit committee, the compensation committee, the nominating committee, and the public-policy/public-issues committee. For virtually all Fortune 500 companies, the compensation committee consists of outside directors. The CEO, however, is usually part of that committee.

13. Increased shareholder activism has led to numerous public-policy shareholder resolutions being offered to boards in the 1990s. Many boards have fought such shareholder resolutions.

14. If a company chooses to purchase a substantial number of shares of another company's stock, it may make a ten-der offer to all the shareholders of the target corporation. A cash tender offer involves the payment of cash to the target company's shareholders in exchange for their stock, whereas an exchange tender offer involves a swapping of target company stock for stock of the acquiring company.

15. In a leveraged buyout, the purchaser acquires all of the company's outstanding stock. The acquisition is normally financed by borrowing against the assets of the corporation. The borrowing may involve the issuance of bonds, an ordinary bank loan, or a loan from an investment bank. The resulting debt load may be so burdensome, however, that the company is not able to survive in the long run.

16. Companies may employ a variety of takeover defenses to ward off the advances of unwelcome corporate suitors. Takeover defenses include greenmail tactics, the crown jewel defense, scorched-earth tactics, the poison pill defense, the Pac-Man defense, and the white knight defense. In considering whether to oppose an unwelcome takeover attempt, the board of directors must place the stockholders' welfare above any concerns they may have about their own jobs and determine whether the offer is appropriate.

EXERCISES

1. Lucy has acquired one share of common stock of a multimillion-dollar corporation with over 500,000 shareholders. Lucy's ownership is so small that she is questioning what her rights are as a shareholder. For example, she wants to know whether this one share entitles her to attend and vote at shareholders' meetings, inspect the corporate books, and receive yearly dividends. Discuss Lucy's rights in these three matters.

2. What does it mean when we say that a corporation is a legal person?

3. Frank Enterprises, Inc., purchased all the assets of Grosmont Corporation. The directors of both corporations approved the sale, and 80 percent of Grosmont's shareholders approved. The shareholders of Frank Enterprises, however, were never consulted. Some of these shareholders claimed that the purchase was thus invalid. Are they correct? Explain.

4. Reexamine *Exhibit 12–2*. Of the three powers of shareholders, which is most important in your opinion, and why?

5. The chapter described three general areas of responsibility of the board of directors with respect to management. Which of the three is most important, and why?

6. Write a short essay defending the practice of having the CEO be the dominant figure within the board of directors.

7. In *Exhibit 12–1*, shareholders are shown at the top of the corporate organization. How do you defend this positioning of shareholders from the contention by critics of current corporate governance that shareholders have virtually no impact on the way boards of directors act?

8. "Shareholders have the most important power that is available—they can sell their shares when they are dissatisfied with the operation of a corporation. That is all the power they need." Do you agree with this statement? Explain your answer.

9. "Corporate America is now owned by everybody." Does this statement have any validity? If so, why? If not, why not?

10. On average, CEOs are paid more the larger the corporation is. Is there any justification for this practice?

11. Write a scenario for an ideal world in which corporations would be governed exactly the way you think they should be.

12. Shareholder activist groups are increasingly asking boards of directors to introduce resolutions that have little to do with the actual day-to-day operation of corporations. If

you were on a board of directors faced with such a resolution, how would you react, and why?

13. Ten-Four Corporation is a small midwestern business that owns a valuable patent. Ten-Four has approximately 1,000 shareholders with 100,000 authorized and outstanding shares. Bartlett Corporation would like to have use of the patent, but Ten-Four refuses to give Bartlett a license. Bartlett has tried to acquire Ten-Four by purchasing Ten-Four's assets, but Ten-Four's board of directors has refused to approve the acquisition. Ten-Four's shares are selling for $5 per share. Discuss how Bartlett Corporation might proceed to gain the control and use of Ten-Four's patent.

SELECTED REFERENCES

▶ Berenbeim, Ronald E. *Corporate Boards: Improving and Evaluating Performance.* New York: Conference Board, 1994.

▶ Blair, Margaret M. *Ownership and Control: Rethinking Corporate Governance for the Twenty-First Century.* Washington, D.C.: Brookings Institution, 1995.

▶ Eisenberg, Melvin Aron. *The Structure of the Corporation.* Boston: Little, Brown, 1976.

▶ Green, Mark, and Robert Massie, Jr., eds. *The Big Business Reader: Essays on Corporate America.* New York: Pilgrim Press, 1983.

▶ Monks, Robert A. G. *Corporate Governance.* Cambridge, Mass.: Blackwell Publications, 1995.

▶ Prowse, Stephen David. *Corporate Governance in an International Perspective: A Survey of Corporate Control Mechanisms among Large Firms in the United States, the United Kingdom, Japan, and Germany.* Cambridge, Mass.: Blackwell Publications, 1995.

▶ Schwartz, George P. *Shareholder Rebellion: How Investors Are Changing the Way America's Companies Are Run.* Burr Ridge, Ill.: Irwin Professional Publishing, 1995.

▶ Zander, Alvin Frederick. *Making Boards Effective: The Dynamics of Nonprofit Governing Boards.* San Francisco: Jossey-Bass, 1993.

RESOURCES ON THE INTERNET

▼ In the Entrepreneurs' Forum on the commercial service CompuServe you can find answers to questions about incorporating and the like. When on CompuServe, type in

Go usen

From the library menu, choose

Browse

Then select

Legalities

▼ You can also obtain legal advice from the Microsoft Small Business Center if you subscribe to America Online. On that commercial service, the key word is

microsoft

Then click

The Small Business Center

And select

Legal Issues

▼ You can get useful information from the Small Business Administration about financial assistance and related matters from

http://www.sbaonline.sba.gov/

▼ If you want to find out about the benefits of incorporation, you can access the Company Corporation at

http://amber.ora./gnn/bus/ compcorp/index.html

▼ For information on corporate law and the Securities and Exchange Commission, access the Center for Corporate Law at the University of Cincinnati College of Law at

http://www.law.uc.edu/CCL/

▼ If you are interested in learning the inner workings of the stock market without risking any money, the League of American Investors runs an investment game. For information on this activity, access

http://www.goldsword.com/ pc-signs/nvestor/nvestor/html

CASE

ANALYSIS OF A TAKEOVER: QUAKER AND SNAPPLE

Background

Ever since Quaker Oats Company bought Gatorade in 1983 and turned the sports drink into a market dominator, the company has been beset with talk of its imminent takeover. Quaker executives consistently denied the reports. In 1988, dismayed by fluctuating stock prices, the firm went as far as to request an investigation by the Securities and Exchange Commission into rumors that Quaker was in danger of a hostile takeover by Philip Morris Company.

Denials aside, the Chicago-based food company did have the characteristics of an attractive takeover target. With sales of $5.9 billion and a market value of $5 billion, Quaker was small enough to be swept up by a larger company without heavy risk. Gatorade has strong name recognition and would be an asset to any company, whereas Quaker's other product lines—including pet foods, frozen waffles, and cereals—could be sold off to finance acquisition debts. Furthermore, the trend of the 1990s in the food industry has been for large companies to consolidate themselves by buying smaller ones.

It is not surprising that the rumors persisted. In June 1994, Swiss food giant Nestlé SA was supposedly interested in purchasing Quaker; the next month, Philip Morris's name again surfaced as a possible suitor. Finally, Quaker took what it felt to be the best defense against a takeover—it took over a small firm itself. Although Quaker executives insisted that the acquisition of the Snapple Beverage Company was not related to its history of takeover rumors, industry analysts interpreted the move as such. "It was a do-or-die deal," said one. "Quaker had to buy something or they were going to be taken out."381

Benefits of the Takeover

On November 2, 1994, Quaker announced it was going to buy Snapple, the iced tea and fruit drink maker, for $1.7 billion. Quaker locked up the deal by signing a tender agreement with holders of almost two-thirds of Snapple's stock. The new company would be the largest maker of what Quaker's CEO, William Smithburg, calls "good-for-you" beverages in the United States, and the country's third largest nonalcoholic drink producer behind Coca-Cola Company and PepsiCo.

Helping Both Companies

Aside from its takeover protection, industry analysts saw the deal as being necessary for the participants, who were beginning to struggle in areas they had previously dominated. "Both companies needed to get bigger," said analyst Michael Bellis. "The ante is bigger everyday in this industry."

In the 1980s, Quaker enjoyed a near monopoly of the sports drink market, with Gatorade's holding a 95 percent market share. By the end of the decade, however, Coca-Cola and Pepsi were planning competing products, and Quaker executives realized they would need a strategy to continue to prosper in a changing business landscape. In 1990, the company streamlined operations by selling off the Fisher-Price toy business. Fisher-Price had strong brand names and a solid overseas position, but Quaker felt the need to become a "pure food" company in anticipation of future efforts to protect Gatorade. Nonetheless, Coke's PowerAde and Pepsi's AllSport (buoyed by an intense advertising campaign featuring basketball star Shaquille O'Neal) cut Gatorade's market share to 88 percent by 1995, with further erosion predicted.

Snapple was having its own problems competing with Coke and Pepsi. Started in 1972 by three Brooklyn entrepreneurs with their grandmothers' recipe for jam-sweetened tea, Snapple burst on the scene in the late 1980s as a healthful alternative to soft drinks. The company's revenues more than doubled each year from 1989 to 1993, jumping from $23.6 million to $516 million over that time period. Snapple went public in December 1992, and the worth of the company's stock increased from $10 a share to $33 by February 1994.

The fact that Quaker was able to purchase Snapple's stock at $14 a share, however, indicated the company's slowdown by the summer of 1994. Snapple reported a third-quarter-earnings drop of 74 percent just before its takeover by Quaker. Again, industry analysts credited Snapple's sagging fortune to increased competition from Coke, which markets Nestea bottled and canned teas and introduced the fruit drink Fruitopia in 1992. Pepsi's joint venture with Lipton posed additional competition. Whereas sales of Snapple products rose 82 percent during a twelve-week period surveyed in 1994, Lipton ice tea rose 352 percent, and Nestea doubled during the same time.

Combating Coke and Pepsi

Quaker executives planned to combat the challenges from Coke and Pepsi by combining the strengths of their company with those of Snapple. The latter firm expertly advertised itself as the drink of choice for health-conscious baby boomers and captured new markets with innovative flavors such as "Mango Madness" and "Kiwi Strawberry." Quaker's strategies have been considerably less adventurous. "We'll be able to bring a more comprehensive marketing approach to the business," predicted Quaker executive Donald Uzzi. "[Snapple] bring[s] us a move-with-dispatch orientation [and] a more entrepreneurial flair that we think will be healthy for both organizations."

The distribution systems of both brands should have benefited from the takeover. Snapple has an industry-wide reputation for its strength in direct store distribution into the "cold" channel markets, such as street vendors, delicatessens, restaurants, and recreation areas. Gatorade, in contrast, had nearly saturated "warm" channels such as supermarkets. Under Quaker, each brand was supposed to "piggyback" the other into untapped channels. The company also planned to distribute Snapple—which realizes only 1 percent of its sales overseas—outside the United States through Gatorade outlets, which amount to 31 percent of that product's sales. "We expect to create the most innovative distribution system in the beverage industry," said Quaker CEO Smithburg.

The proposed distribution system, along with increased advertising costs to combat Coke and Pepsi, led Quaker executives to look toward spinning off other product lines. By February 1995, the company had sold off its North American and European pet food lines and a Mexican chocolate business, which together netted $1.8 billion.

Reactions of Shareholders and Analysts

Although executives at both companies may have been heartened by the prospects of the takeover, a large group of Snapple shareholders were not as pleased with the deal. In fact, seventeen of them filed separate suits against Snapple in Delaware alleging breach of fiduciary duties with the friendly takeover. Snapple founders Hyman Golden and Leonard Marsh realized $130 million each from the sale, but the shareholders were generally not as fortunate. Most of them paid at least $23 per share of stock, well above the $14-a-share price given to Quaker (which was actually 25 cents below the stock's closing price on the day of the deal). One lawsuit claimed that the takeover was "wrongful, unfair, and

harmful" to Snapple's public stockholders because it denied them the "right to share appropriately" in the company's windfall. Said one financial analyst, "Snapple shareholders should be angry—they got less than they deserve. . . . The owners are bailing out at their expense."

Another group of investors, who had predicted further problems for an independent Snapple, thought the shareholders should be thankful for having gotten $14 per share at that time. Snapple's recent drop-off in both sales and stock had some Quaker shareholders wondering if the company did not pay *too much* for the stock.

There is also the question as to the growth potential of the iced tea market as a whole. Sales of diet soft drinks, which grew sharply in the 1980s on a similar "healthful alternative" theme, leveled off considerably in the 1990s. One industry analyst went so far as to predict that Snapple was "a fully exploited product" and that Quaker's gamble would fail, driving the company's stock price down and leaving it open to the hostile takeover it had been trying to avoid. In fact, in January 1995, two months after the acquisition of Snapple, Quaker's stock prices were again buffeted by a rumor of a hostile takeover, this one from competitor Coca-Cola.

Snapple's Decline

Two years later, many Quaker stakeholders must have been wondering if the acquisition had not been a mistake. At the time of the deal, Quaker stock had been trading at $37 a share. By the summer of 1996, the price was hovering close to $31, and the Snapple brand lost $100 million in 1995. Instead of being infused with Snapple's "entrepreneurial flair," Quaker appears to have stifled the product line with its more conservative corporate culture. For example, before its acquisition, Snapple had been a regular advertiser on radio shows by extreme personalities Rush Limbaugh and Howard Stern. Quaker, feeling that neither show fit with its corporate personality, pulled the ads. The feedback from the two shows' loyal fans was swift and negative.

"The most innovative distribution system in the beverage industry" never came to pass, as Quaker executives and Snapple distributors failed to agree on a distribution plan. Furthermore, an expensive mainstream advertising campaign based on Snapple's goal of being the "No. 3" beverage company behind Coke and Pepsi was pulled after two unproductive months. Snapple executives and employees spent the summer months of 1996 handing out $40 million of free samples in American parks, beaches, and city streets. If this

CASE (CONTINUED)

last-ditch effort to attract new customers fails, many analysts believe Quaker will be forced to divest Snapple.

Critical Thinking Questions

1. Who would benefit from false rumors that Quaker was the imminent target of a hostile takeover?

2. Given our discussion of horizontal mergers in Chapter 8, why do you think the federal antitrust watchdogs paid relatively little attention to Quaker's friendly takeover of Snapple?

3. What Quaker and Snapple shareholder interests were served by the merger? Does this appear to you to be a case in which the interests of improved corporate governance were served?

4. Do the shareholders who filed the complaints have a valid case? Were Snapple's owners acting unethically by selling their company?

5. What lessons concerning the risks of takeovers—be they friendly or hostile—can be learned from Snapple's two-year struggle after its acquisition by Quaker?

SOURCE: Information from P. Gallagher, "Takeover Talks Haunt Quaker," *Advertising Age*, August 8, 1994, p. 10; M. J. McCarthy, "Quaker Oats to Buy Snapple for $1.7 Billion," *Wall Street Journal*, November 3, 1994, pp. A3–A4; J. Liesse, "Quaker Ups the Ante by Buying Snapple," *Advertising Age*, November 7, 1994, p. 4; R. Gibson, "Quaker Oats to Spin Off Fisher-Price Unit," *Wall Street Journal*, April 25, 1990, p. A4; F. Norris, "Big Winners, Big Losers in Snapple's Life Story," *New York Times*, November 3, 1994, p. D1; L. Bird, "Trouble Is Brewing For Snapple As Rivals Fight for Iced Tea Sales," *Wall Street Journal*, June 9, 1994, p. B6; R. Gibson and L. M. Grossman, "Snapple's Lowering of Profit Projection Underscores Continuation of Problems," *Wall Street Journal*, November 7, 1994, p. A4; L. Zinn, "Tea and Synergy?," *Business Week*, December 14, 1994, p. 44; A. Kaplan, "Distribution Shifts Ahead for Gatorade/Snapple," *U.S. Distribution Journal*, December 15, 1994, p. 5; A. Miller, "A Good Deal or Mango Madness?," *Newsweek*, November 14, 1994, p. 50; L. LaFemina, "Snapple's Liquid Assets Slakes Quaker's Thirst," *LI Business News*, November 21, 1994, p. 3; "The Gambler," *Delaney Report*, February 20, 1995; and N. Millman, "New-age Drama: If Quaker Is Achilles on the Beverage Stage, Snapple Is a Natural in Heel's Role," *Chicago Tribune*, August 25, 1996, Sec. 5, pp. 1, 6.

CHAPTER 13

EMPLOYMENT AND EMPLOYEE RIGHTS

Introduction

When Sibi Soroka applied for a security job at an outlet of Target Stores in Walnut Creek, California, he expected to give his prospective employer information about his previous employment experience. What he did not expect was a true-false test in which he was required to field 704 statements, including: "I am very strongly attracted by members of my own sex"; "I have never indulged in unusual sex practices"; "I have had no difficulty starting or holding my urine"; and "I feel sure there is only one true religion."[1]

Feeling that this so-called psychological screening exercise, known as the Rodgers Condensed CPI-MMPI test, was illegal, Soroka and his lawyer brought a class-action suit against Target that charged the company with violating Soroka's right to privacy. A Target spokesperson defended the company's application procedure, saying, "We believe the use of this test as part of the hiring process assisted in evaluating the emotional stability of potential security officer candidates."[2] The California Court of Appeals disagreed and barred Target from continuing to administer the test. Finally, after a lengthy court dispute, the company made a total of $2 million available to Soroka and three hundred other applicants who had taken the test.

In the model for corporate governance (see *Exhibit 12–1* in Chapter 12), the employee is at the bottom. For much of this nation's history, that chart would represent the legal standing of the employee; the award granted to Soroka and his fellow applicants would have been unthinkable. Indeed, prior to the twentieth century, there was little in the way of legislated employee rights. The employee rights movement began during the Great Depression in the 1930s, when the Norris-LaGuardia Act of 1932 permitted employees nationwide to organize. The labor movement in the United States has continued to improve employee rights. In addition, both state and federal legislation concerning the rights of employees have been passed even without strong union influence.

In this chapter, we examine how these **employee rights** have evolved and how their evolution has fundamentally changed the employer-worker—historically known as the master-servant—relationship and the dynamics of the workplace. The chapter is basically separated into two parts. The first discusses the rights employees have come to expect their employers to protect, including the security of their jobs, their privacy, and their safety and health. The second part provides strategies for managers to preserve these employee rights.

Employee Right to Job Security

There is widespread sentiment in the United States that every honest and hard-working citizen should have an inherent right to continuing employment—that unless we perform poorly or break the law, we have a right to keep our jobs. However, until the 1960s there were virtually no legal restrictions on an employer's ability to fire an employee. In the eyes of federal and state courts, although the Constitution protected citizens from the improper use of government power, it did not place the same restrictions on private businesses.

---

1. S. Silverstein, "Target to Pay $2 Million in Testing Case," *Los Angeles Times*, July 10, 1993, p. D1.
2. *Ibid.*

The 1884 case *Payne v. Western* set the legal guidelines for most of the next century; the court ruled that an employer could fire an employee at will "for good cause, for no cause, or even for cause morally wrong, without thereby being guilty of a legal wrong." In fact, in the eyes of the courts, workers could even be fired for refusing to commit an illegal act at the request of their supervisors.[3]

EMPLOYMENT AT WILL

Because most employee-employer relationships have been considered to be "at will" since the 1880s, the termination of that relationship has been governed by the **employment-at-will doctrine.** Under this doctrine, either party may terminate an employment contract at any time for any reason. However, federal statutes later began to modify the doctrine.

At first, the only restriction on employer actions came from the Wagner Act of 1935, which prohibited the firing of an employee for union activity. It was not until the Civil Rights Act of 1964 that the arbitrary power to fire was further weakened, as antidiscrimination policies forced companies to justify some of their employment decisions. The Civil Rights Act was followed by a deluge of laws prohibiting a person's being fired solely on the basis of race, gender, age, religion, sexual orientation, or national origin.

Illegal Firing Despite the laws, the employment-at-will doctrine is still in place. In many states, a employer can still fire an employee without notice for basically any reason (other than race, religion, or gender). The difference is that now there is recourse for the employee who believes he or she has been dismissed for a reason declared to be illegal.[4] According to attorney Barbara Kate Repa, there are three basic legal theories used to challenge the employment-at-will doctrine: breach of good faith and fair dealing, breach of contract, and defamation.[5]

Breach of Good Faith and Fair Dealing The extremely broad theory of breach of good faith and fair dealing is based on the legal principle that an employer has an inherent responsibility to act fairly and in good faith toward his or her employees. Transferring a worker to remote or undesirable locations in order to coerce that worker into quitting is one example of bad faith by an employer. Another example is firing an employee on the basis of trumped-up poor performance reports when the employer's real goal is to replace that employee with someone who will work for lower wages.

Breach of Contract In a situation in which there is a written contract delineating the terms of employment, an employee may turn to the theory of breach of contract in protesting a firing. Written contracts, however, are relatively rare; in most cases the wronged employee has to prove that an *implied* contract has been breached. Some of the factors that Repa thinks should lead an employee to believe that his or her implied employment contract is on solid legal ground include (1) lengthy duration of employment, (2) regular promotions, (3) consistently positive performance reviews, (4) assurances of continued employment, (5) a lack of warning of poor job performance that may lead to a firing, and (6) promises of permanence at the time of hiring.

---

3. S. A. Culbert and J. A. McDonough, "Wrongful Termination and the Reasonable Manager: Balancing Fair Play and Effectiveness," *Sloan Management Review*, Summer 1990, p. 39.

4. J. W. Fenton, Jr., and D. E. Kelley, "Resurrection of an Old but Timely Proposal: Voluntary Arbitration of Employment Discharges," *SAM Advanced Management Journal*, Autumn 1994, p. 10.

5. B. K. Repa, *Your Rights in the Workplace* (Berkeley, Calif.: Nolo Press, 1994), pp. 11/2–11/7.

Defamation Although defamation is not a challenge to a job loss itself, a fired employee may use this theory to protest the manner in which a termination was carried out. The assumption behind charges of defamation is that the method by which an employee was fired damaged that employee's "good name," and therefore made it more difficult for that employee to find employment in the future. To prove defamation, the employee must usually show that the employer made damaging statements about him or her, as well as communicated those feelings to others through either verbal or written means. Often, these damaging statements concern charges that the employee committed a crime, showed incompetence at his or her duties, or was involved with drugs or alcohol. Because employers usually do not put these charges in writing, however, defamation is often difficult to prove.

The Family and Medical Leave Act Until recently, the employment-at-will doctrine also applied to situations in which an employee needed to leave his or her job for family or medical reasons. An employer could fire a worker who needed to take time off to care for a sick relative or newborn baby, and the employee had no recourse.

The Family and Medical Leave Act of 1993 (FMLA) requires employers with fifty or more employees to provide up to twelve weeks of unpaid family or medical leave during any twelve-month period. During the employee's leave, the employer must continue the worker's health-care coverage and guarantee employment in the same position or a comparable position when the employee returns to work. An important exception to the FMLA, however, allows the employer to avoid reinstatement of a *key employee* — defined as an employee whose pay falls within the top 10 percent of the work force.

Generally, family leave may be taken when an employee wishes to care for a newborn baby, an adopted child, or a foster child.[6] Medical leave may be taken when the

6. The foster care must be state sanctioned before such an arrangement falls within the coverage of the FMLA.

employee's spouse, child, or relative has a "serious health condition" requiring care. The FMLA also allows for intermittent leave when it is medically necessary.

Employment Law on the State Level Employment at will is a common law issue, meaning that it is part of the body of legal precedents that the United States inherited from English custom. Common laws are not attributable to the legislature, so the states have the freedom to amend them if they so choose. If a state wishes, it can eradicate some of the uncertainty inherent in employment at will by passing specific laws governing employee rights within its borders. California is particularly active in legislating new employee rights; it has laws on its books specifically outlawing firing based on pregnancy and childbirth, political activity, work-related injury, physical handicap, sexual preference, medical condition, marital status, and refusal to take a lie-detector test.[7] In addition, in 1989, Montana became the first—and so far the only—state to pass "just-cause" legislation, to set guidelines by which employers must prove a legitimate reason for terminating a worker's employment. Eleven other state legislatures have considered similar laws, but so far none have been passed.[8]

PUBLIC-POLICY EXCEPTIONS TO EMPLOYMENT AT WILL

The most widespread common law exception to the employment-at-will doctrine is the public-policy exception. Under this rule, an employer may not fire a worker for reasons that violate a fundamental public policy of the jurisdiction; for example, jury duty. Also, most states have held that firing a worker for refusing to perform an illegal act violates public policy.

Whistleblowing, which we discussed in Chapter 5, occurs when an employee tells a government official, upper-management authorities, or the press that his or her employer is engaged in some unsafe or illegal activity. Employees who expose the wrongdoing of employers often find themselves disciplined or even out of a job. In a few cases, whistleblowers have been protected from wrongful discharge for reasons of public policy. For example, a bank was held to have wrongfully discharged an employee who pressured the employer to comply with state and federal consumer credit laws.

In another case, an at-will employee—a probation officer with the police department in Globe, Arizona—discovered that a man had been arrested for vagrancy under an obsolete statute, had been sentenced to ten days in prison, and had been in jail for twenty-one days. The officer pointed out to a magistrate that this was illegal. The magistrate informed the police chief, the chief fired the officer, and the officer sued the city for wrongful discharge. Holding that the discharge violated public policy, the court said, "So long as employees' actions are not merely private or proprietary, but instead seek to further the public good, the decision to expose illegal or unsafe practices should be encouraged. . . . There is no public policy more important or fundamental than the one favoring the effective protection of the lives, liberty, and property of the people. The officer's successful attempt to free the arrestee from illegal confinement was a refreshing and laudable exercise that should be protected, not punished."[9]

---

7. *Note on Employees' Legal Rights* (Boston: Harvard Business School, 1990), p. 1.
8. G. M. Gomes and J. G. Morgan, "Meeting the Wrongful Discharge Challenge: Legislative Options for Small Business," *Journal of Small Business*, October 1, 1992, p. 96.
9. R. L. Miller and G. A. Jentz, *Business Law Today: Comprehensive Edition*, 3d ed. (St. Paul: West Publishing Co., 1994), p. 901.

Employee Right to Privacy

In recent years, the right to privacy has become a significant issue in the workplace, and in the 1980s the law began to protect the privacy of employees in a number of areas. Employers today have to be careful that certain practices in which they may engage—such as drug testing, the administration of lie-detector tests, or the electronic monitoring of their employees' actions—do not violate the rights of their employees to privacy and personal security.

Drug Testing in the Workplace

Workers whose ability to perform is impaired as a result of drug use or abuse can pose a substantial threat to themselves and the safety of others. For example, certain railway or airline employees may seriously endanger the public safety if they perform their jobs under the influence of alcohol or other drugs. This was the case in New York City in 1991, when an intoxicated subway driver caused an accident that resulted in the deaths of five passengers and injuries to two hundred others. Substance abuse is also costly for employers:

▼ **It is estimated that absenteeism, impaired performance, and accidents resulting from drug and alcohol use by employees cost industries between $50 billion and $100 billion each year.**

In the interest of public safety, as well as out of the desire to reduce unnecessary costs, many employers, including the government, have begun to require that their employees submit to drug testing. By the mid-1990s, a record 87 percent of major companies were testing some of their workers for drug use.[10]

Trade-Offs of Drug Testing   Drug-testing programs involve an obvious trade-off: an individual's right to personal privacy versus the safety of those affected by the individual's actions. This trade-off is particularly marked in the case of drug testing of government employees. Clearly, the government has a duty to protect the public safety. In protecting that safety, however, can the government violate an individual's Fourth Amendment right to be "secure in their persons . . . against unreasonable searches and seizures"? The question, of course, turns on whether drug testing constitutes an "unreasonable" intrusion on the rights of employees to be secure in their persons.

The Fourth Amendment also requires that "no Warrants shall issue, but upon probable cause." In recent years, however, whenever the public safety could be substantially and immediately threatened by employee drug use, the courts have allowed government employers and agencies to undertake drug testing in the absence of probable cause or any evidence that an employee is, in fact, abusing drugs. Thus, the United States Supreme Court upheld a requirement that arms-bearing U.S. customs officers—whose duty is to apprehend illegal drug carriers—be subjected to drug testing.[11] In another case, the testing of train workers following a train accident or other railway mishap was held by the Supreme Court to be a reasonable search and seizure.[12]

---

10. "Good News about Downers," *Journal Of Business Strategy*, May–June 1994, p. 9.
11. *National Treasury Employees Union v. Von Raab* (1989).
12. *Skinner v. Railway Labor Executives Association* (1989).

For employers in the private business community, the guidelines are not as clear. This is because drug testing by private employees is governed mainly by state law, which varies widely. Some states have statutes restricting drug testing; most do not (see *Exhibit 13–1* on pages 390–91). To date, the courts have produced conflicting decisions on when drug testing is permissible and when it constitutes a violation of an employee's or applicant's privacy rights. In some cases, employers are turning to alternative methods to avoid the legal and ethical questions that surround the practice of drug testing (see *Managing Social Issues—Information/Technology: Technological Alternatives to Drug Testing* on page 392).

Effects of Drug Testing Is drug testing having any effect? According to a study done by the American Management Association (AMA) in New York, drug use and drug-related accidents have indeed fallen off. Between 1989 and 1994, the number of companies that conducted random drug tests increased tenfold, and the rate of positive-test results for employees dropped from 8.1 percent to 2.5 percent.[13] Further study by the AMA showed that drug education and awareness programs had a marked effect on abuse. Companies that provided these services to their employees had a ratio of positive to negative drug test results 40 percent lower than companies that did not.[14]

AIDS TESTING

The impact of acquired immune deficiency syndrome (AIDS) on the American workplace has been significant.[15] As in other segments of society, in the business community response to the myths and realities of the disease has been mixed. In the next chapter we discuss issues of discrimination against those with AIDS and the virus that causes it— human immunodeficiency virus (HIV)—but first we look at the phenomenon as a privacy issue. Those who are HIV-positive or have AIDS may find that testing for the virus can lead to situations that not only shatter their privacy but also place a strain on interpersonal relations in the workplace.

As far back as 1987, the Centers for Disease Control rejected a proposal to require AIDS tests for federal employees. In the private sector, companies such as IBM, AT&T, and Johnson & Johnson have endorsed guidelines for AIDS testing that include the following:

1. Employees with AIDS or those who are infected with HIV are entitled to the same rights and opportunities as employees with other serious illnesses.
2. Employment policies should be based on the scientific evidence that people with AIDS or HIV infection do not pose a risk of transmitting the virus through ordinary work contact.
3. Employers have the duty to protect the confidentiality of their employees' medical information.
4. Employers should provide workers with sensitive and timely education about AIDS and its risk reduction in their personal lives.
5. Employers should not require HIV testing as part of general preemployment or workplace physical examinations.[16]

---

13. "Good News about Downers," p. 9.
14. *Ibid.*
15. J. K. Ross III and B. J. Middlebrook, "AIDS Policy in the Work Place: Will You Be Ready?" SAM *Advanced Management Journal*, Winter 1990, p. 37.
16. "AIDS Focus: Employee Rights and On-Site Education," *Bulletin to Management*, March 1988, p. 74.

▼ **EXHIBIT 13–1 State Laws on Drug and Alcohol Testing** Thirty-three states and the District of Columbia have no statutes concerning alcohol and drug testing. The highlights of those that do follow.

State	Testing Law
California	Employers with twenty-five or more employees must reasonably accommodate any employee who enters an alcohol or drug rehabilitation program, unless the employee's current alcohol or drug use prohibits him or her from performing work duties or doing a job safely.
Connecticut	Employers may require a drug or alcohol test when there is a reasonable suspicion that an employee is under the influence and job performance is or could be impaired. Random testing is allowed if the employee works in a dangerous or safety-sensitive occupation, is part of a voluntary employee assistance program, or as authorized by federal law. Job applicants may be tested.
Florida	Employers may test for drugs under a reasonable suspicion that an employee is under the influence. Employees who voluntarily seek treatment cannot be fired, disciplined, or discriminated against, unless they have tested positive or been in treatment in the past.
Georgia	State employees who are involved in dangerous work may be subject to random testing.
Hawaii	Employers may test employees or job applicants as long as the following conditions are met: the employer pays all costs, individuals are given a list of the substances for which they are being tested and a disclosure form for the medicines and legal drugs they are taking, and the results are kept confidential.
Iowa	Employers cannot generally request random drug testing or require drug testing of employees as a condition of employment, preemployment, promotion, or change in employment status. An employer may require a specific employee to be tested if there is reasonable suspicion that he or she is impaired on the job.
Louisiana	Employers may require all applicants and employees to submit to drug testing as long as certain procedural guidelines are met and due regard is given to the subject's privacy.
Maine	Employers may require testing when there is probable cause to believe the subject is impaired. Random testing is permitted when substance abuse might endanger co-workers or the public, or when specified under union contract.

INFORMATION GATHERING AND USE BY EMPLOYERS

We are often told we live in the "Information Age," and in few places is that name more apt than with regard to the dossier that an employer can put together on an employee. The inherent risks in such information gathering to the privacy rights of the employee are widespread and, consequently, the focus of much debate and legislative action.[17]

Background Checks of Prospective Employees With valid reason, the information-gathering process begins before an employee receives his or her first paycheck. After all, an employer would not want someone, for example, with a history of criminal conduct to be hired for a position that required handling large sums of money. Background checks can also minimize potential lawsuits by protecting the employer from being blamed for injuries that may have occurred in an applicant's prior employment. There is a thin line between self-protection and intrusion, however. Alice M. McCarthy, associate counsel with Norrel Services, Inc., identifies three areas in which background checks may constitute an illegal

---

17. T. L. Griffith, "Teaching Big Brother to Be a Team Player: Computer Monitoring and Quality," *Academy of Management Executive*, February 1993, p. 73.

▼ **EXHIBIT 13–1** *continued*

State	Testing Law
Maryland	Employers may require testing of employees, contractors, or other people for job-related reasons for substance abuse as long as procedural guidelines are followed.
Minnesota	Employers may require employees to submit to substance testing if there is a written and posted testing policy and the test is performed by an independent licensed laboratory. Random tests may be given only to employees in "safety-sensitive" positions. Specific employees may be tested if there is reasonable suspicion.
Mississippi	Testing is authorized if it is written and posted, if there is reasonable suspicion, or if it is part of a routine fitness-for-duty examination or part of follow-up to a rehabilitation program. Job applicants may be tested if they are warned when they apply for the job.
Montana	No person may be required to submit to a blood or urine test unless the job involves hazardous work or security, public safety, or fiduciary responsibilities.
Nebraska	Employers may not require testing unless certain screening procedures are met.
Oregon	Employees may not require a Breathalyzer alcohol test unless reasonable suspicion has been established. Employees may be tested for drugs if the laboratory utilized is authorized by the state and certain procedural safeguards are employed.
Rhode Island	Employers may require testing if there is reasonable suspicion, the test sample is provided in private, the testing is part of a rehabilitation program, positive results are confirmed by the most accurate method available, the employee is given reasonable notice that the test will be given, and the employee is given a chance to explain the results.
Vermont	Employers may require employees to be tested if there is probable cause for suspicion and the employee who tests positive is given a chance to participate in a rehabilitation program provided by the employer rather than be fired. Employees who have already participated in rehabilitation and who again test positive may be fired.

invasion of the applicant's privacy: arrest data, credit history, and workers' compensation claims.[18]

Arrest data, including data on motor vehicle arrests and criminal records, can provide employers with information on the applicant. Employers, however, should be aware that there are limits to how they can use this information. Federal laws governing employment opportunity and similar laws in many states prohibit employers from using information found on an applicant's arrest record in the hiring process so long as no conviction occurred.

A credit history search can give an employer some insight into a prospective applicant's reliability, but once again there are limits to how this information may be used. If the determination not to hire someone was made based on credit history, the Fair Credit Reporting Act requires that the company inform the applicant of this development and provide him or her with the same credit report used to make the decision. Some states have their own laws regarding the matter. In New York, for instance, the employer must get permission from the applicant to look into his or her credit history.

18. "Federal, State Law Limit Employers' Freedom to Act on Background Checks of Prospective Employees," *Bureau of National Affairs Conference Report*, June 20, 1994, pp. 12–13.

MANAGING SOCIAL ISSUES

INFORMATION/TECHNOLOGY: TECHNOLOGICAL ALTERNATIVES TO DRUG TESTING

In addition to the many privacy questions that drug testing raises, many businesses also face the question of what the point of their drug-testing policy should be. Is a manager ultimately concerned with the employee's health, or his or her performance? Because of all the problems that accompany drug-testing policies—drug testing is invasive, unreliable, and expensive, and it fosters ill feelings between management and employees—some companies are turning toward technological alternatives. Although these businesses may not know if their employees are abusing drugs, they will know if the workers are functioning competently at their jobs.

Purgatory Resort

"Our industry is moving towards drug testing," says Tammy Fray, human resources director at the Purgatory ski resort in Durango, Colorado. "But we don't feel it addresses the issues of safety. The majority of accidents are caused by stress and fatigue, not substance abuse."

So, while competitors such as the Sun Valley ski resort in Idaho embrace drug testing, Purgatory uses a personal computer (PC)–based screening program called Factor 100. Developed by Performance Factors, a Golden, Colorado, company, Factor 100 allows for the daily testing of employees in safety-sensitive jobs such as ski-lift operations and child care. The employees complete a training program on Factor 100 and then set their own baseline levels of competency on the computer.

Every morning, about 250 of the resort's 700 employees sit down at a PC for the Factor 100 test before beginning work. Each test, which consists of tracking a cursor across the screen, takes less than a minute, and employees have eight chances to meet their baseline scores. If they fail to do so, they are reassigned to less demanding responsibilities or sent home for the day. Fray says employees "overwhelmingly support the idea over random drug testing." Management also likes the idea—the total cost is a fraction of what it would be for a drug-testing apparatus.

Assets Protection

Robert Lubkay, president of Assets Protection, a security company in Penndel, Pennsylvania, was looking for a test "that gives immediate results and gets away from the invasive nature of drug testing." Assets turned to the Essex Corporation of Columbia, Maryland, for Delta-WP. Under the system, supervisors with laptop computers randomly select security guard employees to be tested. The program measures the cognitive skills of the employees by having them analyze images and sequences of numbers or letters; then, like Factor 100, the program compares the results with preset baseline performances.

"It's like a computer game," says Lukbay of Delta-WP. He paid only $3,000 for the software, which is run on three different computers. Lukbay is confident that the testing discourages drug and alcohol abuse, and the on-site nature of the test has made the system a popular one with clients.

For Critical Analysis:

These alternatives bring into question the basic goal of drug testing, which is to measure employee performance, not health. If you, as a manager, knew that an employee was using drugs or alcohol, yet his or her work was not affected, what would you do?

SOURCE: "An Alternative to Drug Testing?" *Inc.*, April 1, 1995, p. 112.

The legality of making an employment decision based on an applicant's prior *workers' compensation* (the state-run worker injury insurance system) claims, McCarthy believes, is largely a matter of degree. That is, if an applicant has filed one claim during the last three years, there are no grounds for refusing to hire him or her. If, however, the applicant has filed nineteen claims in that same time period, then the employer has grounds to investigate whether fraud was involved. McCarthy also notes that because the

Americans with Disabilities Act of 1990 prohibits discrimination against applicants whose workers' compensation claims may represent a disability, it is risky for employers to make employment decisions based solely on such information.

Record Keeping by Employers Employers often keep extensive records concerning numerous aspects of their employees' lives. The records kept by corporations can determine whether an employee is promoted, whether he or she is sold insurance, and so on. From a practical, ethical, and efficiency point of view, corporations should collect only employee information that is absolutely necessary. Moreover, any information collected should be used only for the specific purpose for which it was collected. The practice of using medical data to make decisions about job promotions, for example, is not only unethical, but also could result in legal action by the employee. Additionally, employee records should never be sold to marketing firms or political solicitation firms. Nor should employee records be released to any third party without the employee's explicit written consent. Otherwise, the corporation may find itself the subject of an invasion of privacy lawsuit.[19]

Employers usually are willing to allow employees to see what has been said about them. Generally, employees should have some procedure that enables them to obtain at least a summary of the information that the corporation is maintaining about them (see *Exhibit 13–2* on page 394).

Lie-Detector Tests Until recently, some employers used lie-detector tests (**polygraph tests**) in an attempt to reduce employee theft. A polygraph expert presumably can determine whether a person is lying by examining the polygram (the graphic results of a polygraph test), which shows changes in pulse rate, blood pressure, and other physiological data that occurred while the person was answering the tester's questions. In some cases, polygraph tests were administered to potential employees as a screening device in an attempt to ensure the integrity of the work force.

Many regarded polygraph tests as an invasion of the employee's right to privacy and privilege against self-incrimination. A number of union contracts eventually banned lie-detector tests, and several states passed laws prohibiting employers from requiring prospective employees to undergo such tests. The case against lie-detector tests stemmed partly from concerns about employees' constitutional rights but primarily from the fact that polygraph test results are not 100 percent accurate.

To regulate the use of lie-detector tests, in 1988 Congress passed the Employee Polygraph Protection Act. The act prohibits certain employers from (1) requiring, suggesting, requesting, or causing employees or job applicants to take lie-detector tests; (2) using, accepting, referring to, or asking about the results of lie-detectors tests taken by employees or applicants; and (3) taking or threatening negative employment-related actions against employees or applicants based on the results of lie-detector tests or because they refused to take the tests. Employers exempted from these provisions include federal, state, and local government employers; certain security service firms; and companies manufacturing and distributing controlled substances. Other employers may use polygraph tests when investigating losses attributable to theft, including embezzlement and the theft of trade secrets. In all situations in which lie-detector tests are still permitted, stringent procedural requirements are imposed on employers.

It has been estimated that this act has eliminated 85 percent of lie-detector testing by employers. Although some employers cite the benefits of polygraphs—a more honest

---

19. R. E. Smith, "Corporations That Fail the Fair Hiring Test," *Business and Society Review*, Winter 1994, p. 25.

▼ **EXHIBIT 13–2 Guidelines for Maintaining Personnel Records**

Closely Monitor Legal Developments.
The recent trend toward expanding employee rights in the workplace makes it imperative that employers closely monitor developments at both the state and federal levels.

Organize and Segregate Personnel and Medical Records.
An employer should carefully review its current methods of organizing and maintaining personnel records and should consider organizing its personnel files into the categories discussed below:
- **Medical records.** The Family and Medical Leave Act (FMLA) and the Americans with Disabilities Act (ADA) require that any information collected regarding an employee's medical files be contained on separate forms, be kept in a separate medical file, and be treated as a confidential medical record.
- **Other personnel records.** Employers may also want to consider segregating documents excluded from an employee's access, such as letters of reference, within an employee's personnel file. Records that are personal and unrelated to employee performance should be accessible only to authorized individuals. Records that are related to employee performance should be accessible only to human resources personnel and supervisors or managers to whom the specific employee reports.

Retain Personnel Records for a Reasonable Period of Time.
State laws are limited concerning retention requirements, and federal law generally does not require the retention of personnel files beyond one year after an employee's termination. Even so, employers should consider a five-year retention period because of the risk of potential lawsuits by terminated employees. As a general rule, no personnel records relating to any employee should be destroyed without the approval of counsel while there is a pending or threatened lawsuit from a former employee.

Establish Guidelines and Training for Managers.
Despite differences among state personnel record access laws, an employer should establish some general guidelines concerning personnel records:
- Explain to managers the importance of retaining any relevant records used in employment decisions.
- Require managers to forward such records to a certain source, such as the human resources department, so that a complete personnel file can be maintained for each employee.
- Train managers concerning topics such as the following: (1) the information discussed above; (2) the importance of keeping all personnel information confidential and of strictly limiting disclosures to persons other than the employee to whom the information pertains, except on a "need to know" basis; and (3) the need to strictly limit disclosure of personnel information to third parties outside the company and to persons within the company other than human resources personnel and persons to whom the employee in question reports.

SOURCE: *Employment Law Strategist*, June 1994, p. 3.

workplace, less employee theft, and so on—society clearly felt that the costs required by the practice outweighed those benefits.[20]

MONITORING JOB PERFORMANCE

Another privacy issue arises when employers want to monitor their employees' performance. Employees have no constitutional guaranty against being monitored at the workplace, and many American employers have taken advantage of this loophole. Using the most liberal interpretation of the term "surveillance," as many as 80 percent of American workers in insurance, banking, and telecommunications are subject to surveillance by their employers.[21]

---

20. J. H. Bernardin and D. K. Cooke, "Validity of an Honesty Test in Predicting Theft among Convenience Store Employees," *Academy of Management Journal*, October 1993, p. 1097.
21. "Intrusions in the Workplace," *U.S. News & World Report*, August 8, 1994, p. 18.

Some employers use cameras to watch their workers; others place wiretaps on their phones. The most widespread and controversial means of surveillance, however, is through the computer terminals that have become so commonplace on American work desks. Because of the word *personal* in *personal computers,* many employees believe that the terminals and the information contained within them belong to them and not the company that provides the machine. In reality, a typical firm treats electronic data just as it does paperwork, and believes it has the same right to search a person's computer as it would his or her paper files if the situation called for that particular action.[22]

Many employers feel such monitoring is necessary to ensure high levels of performance—and, in some cases, to prevent theft.[23] Some experts, however, believe that surveillance can create an adverse atmosphere in the workplace that is counterproductive, as workers feel pressured and paranoid and are more likely to suffer from work-related stress[24] (see the *Case—Electronic Banking Systems, Inc., and the "Modern Sweatshop"—* at the end of this chapter). In many situations, employees react by trying to circumvent attempts to monitor them. In companies that assert a right to read employees' computer messages (E-mail), some employees are protecting their own privacy by encrypting those messages[25] (see *Managing Social Issues—Information/Technology: The Challenges of E-Mail* on page 396).

Congress has considered taking legislative measures to find some equilibrium between the rights of employers and employees in matters of surveillance. Two bills introduced in 1993, if passed, would have forced employers to notify all staff members and customers regarding any surveillance activities. The extent to which worker monitoring is allowed would have been based on length of service. Employees could have been monitored randomly and without notice during their first sixty days on the job. Other employees could have been monitored only if given notice of at least twenty-four hours, and those employed with a company for more than five years would be considered exempt from monitoring altogether.[26]

Representative Pat Williams, who sponsored one of the bills in the House of Representatives, argued that U.S. employees were not even given the same consideration as targets of FBI investigations, who are afforded court protection before their phones can be wiretapped.[27] Business leaders countered that such a law would unfairly impose on their right to maintain high productivity and to protect against security risks, and their argument has held sway in Congress: neither bill has passed.

RIGHTS TO HEALTH AND SAFETY

On September 3, 1991, a fire broke out at the Imperial Food Products plant in Hamlet, North Carolina, leaving 25 workers dead and 49 injured. In the aftermath of the tragedy,

---

22. "PCs in Workplace Create Balancing Act for Counsel," *Bureau of National Affairs Conference Report,* June 20, 1994, pp. 13–14.
23. S. L. Robinson, M. S. Kraatz, and D. M. Rousseau, "Changing Obligations and the Psychological Contract: A Longitudinal Study," *Academy of Management Journal,* February 1994, p. 137.
24. B. P. Niehoff and R. H. Moorman, "Justice as a Mediator of the Relationship between Methods of Monitoring and Organizational Citizenship Behavior," *Academy of Management Journal,* June 1993, p. 527.
25. W. M. Bulkeley, "Cipher Probe: Popularity Overseas of Encryption Code Has U.S. Worried" *Wall Street Journal,* April 28, 1994, p. A8.
26. T. Anderson, "Is Electronic Monitoring Getting the Plug Pulled?" *Security Management,* October 1, 1994, p. 73.
27. A. Kaplan, "Privacy Bill Seen as a Threat to Productivity," *U.S. Distribution Journal,* October 15, 1994, p. 12.

⬛ MANAGING SOCIAL ISSUES

INFORMATION/TECHNOLOGY: THE CHALLENGES OF E-MAIL

In 1990, a class-action lawsuit was filed against Epson Corporation concerning the company's electronic mail, or E-mail, privacy policies. Alana Shoars, the company's E-mail system coordinator, claimed she was fired after she complained about management's reading of thousands of supposedly private E-mail messages.

Although the case was still being fought five years later, there is a sense in U.S. corporations that Epson's lawsuit is only a hint of the potentially troubling aspects of E-mail. The computerized message system, which is used by more than thirty million American workers, has been a boon to productivity, as it allows employees to reach one another quickly without leaving their desks or risking a busy phone. The E-mail system also presents a number of problems, however, and managers will need to decide on workplace policies to limit the possibility of lawsuits like Epson's.

Workplace Pitfalls

The primary area of concern for E-mail is, of course, privacy. Many employees have expectations that E-mail messages, just like phone messages or memorandums, will be kept private from all sources except the recipient. Computer systems, however, offer easier methods of monitoring than do telephone messages. Even fairly sophisticated E-mail systems can be broken into, and most businesses do not have sophisticated systems.

There is also the worry of frivolity. Although E-mail is an effective communications tool for business-related messages, it can also be used for idle gossip. E-mail is well adapted for frivolous use, because employees can appear to be working diligently on the computer while in fact they are sending personal messages by E-mail.

Finally, E-mail offers another pathway for harassment. Because E-mail is not a face-to-face form of communication, a harasser can keep his or her identity hidden while sending disturbing messages. Alternatively, because E-mail eliminates tone of voice and facial expressions from its communication, messages can more easily be misconstrued as harassing when that is not the sender's intention.

E-Mail Policy

John H. Shannon and David A. Rosenthal, professors at the W. Paul Stillman School of Business at Seton Hall University in South Orange, New Jersey, believe there are two ways to resolve the E-mail conflict. The first concerns technological innovation, and the second involves a clear company policy concerning the use of the system.

The two most important privacy features, say Shannon and Rosenthal, are passwords and encryption of messages. The benefits of passwords are obvious: not only do they keep unauthorized users out of the system but they also allow messages to be sent to specific recipients with less chance of interception. Through encryption, E-mail users can encode their messages so that only those they intend to read them can do so. The time it would take to translate the coded messages would deter all but the most determined third party readers. Encryption can also discourage harassment, because the harasser would have to be someone with access to the code and thus could be easily identified.

Shannon and Rosenthal believe that any company policy begins with a clear statement of "if and when" management has a right to read the E-mail messages of its employees. The Electronic Mail Association recommends that a number of questions be asked before such a policy is implemented. These questions include the following: Does the policy comply with the law? Does it unnecessarily compromise the interests of the employee, the employer, or a third party? Is the policy workable, and is it likely to be enforced? Finally, has the policy been announced and agreed to by all concerned?

For Critical Analysis:

Some analysts think restricting E-mail to business use would use the system to its best advantage by discouraging employees from engaging in personal message sending. Do you agree? If so, is it acceptable to monitor E-mail messages to ensure that only work-related topics are being discussed? Explain your answer.

SOURCE: J. H. Shannon and D. A. Rosenthal, "Electronic Mail and Privacy: Can the Conflict Be Resolved?" *Business Forum*, Winter–Spring 1993, pp. 31–34.

John Brooks, the state's labor secretary, claimed that a shortage of staff at the state's Occupational Safety and Health Administration (OSHA) left that agency unable to hold his state's businesses to stringent safety standards. With only 27 inspectors at his command, Brooks complained it would take 100 years to inspect the 150,000 plants in North Carolina.[28] Federal officials denied Brooks's charges, but the incident raised questions about the rights of American employees to a safe workplace.

According to the statistics, worker safety in the United States is better today than ever before. Death rates in the workplace peaked in the 1930s, at 40 deaths per 100,000 workers; in the 1990s, that number has dropped by 75 percent.[29] Some insist, however, that the number of workplace deaths is still too high. Many say a lack of government initiative and resources is to blame, a perception that assumes companies are willing to sacrifice employees for lower safety costs.

WORKPLACE SAFETY AND OSHA

At the federal level, the primary legislation for employee health and safety protection is the Occupational Safety and Health Act of 1970. This act was passed to ensure safe and healthful working conditions for practically every employee in the United States. The act requires that businesses be maintained free from recognized hazards.

OSHA Three federal agencies were created to develop and enforce the standards set by the Occupational Safety and Health Act. The Occupational Safety and Health Administration is part of the Department of Labor and has the authority to create and publish standards, make safety inspections, and enforce the act. The National Institute for Occupational Safety and Health is part of the Department of Health and Human Services. Its main duty is to conduct research on safety and health problems and recommend standards for OSHA administrators to adopt. Finally, the Occupational Safety and Health Review Commission is an independent agency set up to handle appeals resulting from actions taken by OSHA administrators.

All employers affecting interstate commerce who have one or more employees are covered by the act. Employees can file complaints of OSHA violations. Under the act, an employer cannot discharge an employee who files a complaint or who, in good faith, refuses to work in a high-risk area (if bodily harm or death might result). Employers with eleven or more employees are required to keep occupational and illness records for each employee. Each record must be kept and updated for a continuous five-year period and made available for inspection when requested by an OSHA inspector. Whenever a work-related injury or disease occurs, employers are required to make reports directly to OSHA. Whenever an employee is killed in a work-related accident, or if five or more employees are hospitalized in one accident, the Department of Labor must be notified within forty-eight hours. If it is not, the company can be fined. Following a fatal accident, a complete inspection of the premises is mandatory.

Restrictions within OSHA As we discussed in Chapter 8, OSHA has taken a great deal of criticism for focusing on minor rules while sometimes overlooking the larger picture of worker safety. For example, in 1993 the agency fined an Idaho plumbing company $8,000 after two of its employees rescued a man who was trapped under a collapsed

---

28. "Of Foam and Fried Chicken," *Economist*, May 2, 1992, p. 31.
29. J. Jefferson, "Dying for Work," *ABA Journal*, January 1993, p. 47.

trench wall. The problem was that neither rescuer had followed OSHA safety regulations by wearing hard hats during the rescue.[30]

Criticism of such incidents is met with insistence that budget cuts have compromised the agency's efficiency and effectiveness. OSHA's operating budget was cut by one-fifth during the Reagan administration, and the number of field inspectors was reduced to 1,200.[31] That translates to a single inspector for thousands of workplaces and hundreds of thousands of workers who may need the agency's attention. Furthermore, because the agency does not have the staff to check each violation, it must make shortsighted, narrow rulings—such as in the Idaho incident—when closer inspection actually is warranted.

OSHA is also limited by the political process needed to pass new safety regulations. For example, in 1975 the agency announced a regulatory blueprint that set safety standards for the nearly two million workers who operate in "confined spaces" such as storage tanks, manholes, and railroad tank cars. The rules took over fifteen years to implement, despite OSHA's own estimate that the standards could have prevented 80 to 90 percent of the deaths and injuries that occur annually in confined spaces.[32]

RIGHT-TO-KNOW LAWS

Over twenty states have passed **right-to-know laws** that require employers to provide employees with information about workplace dangers. In the 1980s, OSHA developed what it called a Hazard Communications Standard. Any manufacturer, whether it be a chemical manufacturer or one that uses chemicals, has to undertake certain steps to comply with the Hazard Communications Standard. For example, it has to keep an up-to-date inventory of hazardous chemicals that are present, as well as maintain "material-safety data sheets" for each chemical. Any containers that have hazardous chemicals must be so labeled, and any workers who are going to be exposed to hazardous chemicals must be trained and provided with appropriate safety equipment.

Despite good intentions, the Hazard Communications Standard has come under criticism. For example,

▼ Because of OSHA regulations, containers of sodium chloride, or table salt, must have labels that read "WARNING: CAUSES IRRITATION. Avoid contact with eyes, skin, or clothing. . . . Wash thoroughly after handling."

Salt handlers are further advised to wear a "respirator, chemical safety goggles, rubber boots, and heavy rubber gloves" when using the substance. Similarly drastic warnings must appear on paraffin (used to make candles) and crystalline silica (found in beach sand), and some feel that because of the overuse of warning labels, workers will ignore warnings on substances that pose a realistic health risk.[33]

SMOKING AT WORK

An issue concerning worker health that has become more salient over the past decade is that of the smoke-free workplace. In the 1980s, many states passed laws limiting or entirely banning smoking in facilities such as restaurants and public office buildings. Much of this legislation was prompted by increasing concerns about the health risks that smoking poses

---

30. M. S. Johncox, "Trench Rescue Draws Fines," *Idaho Statesman,* July 17, 1993, p. 1A.

31. Jefferson, *op. cit.*, p. 49.

32. *Ibid.*

33. M. M. Segal, "Spilled Some Salt? Call OSHA," *Wall Street Journal,* July 9, 1991, p. A16.

to smokers and also to the nonsmokers who breathe exhaled smoke—so-called passive smokers. In 1992, these concerns were substantiated by a study by Stanton Gantz of the University of San Francisco that linked secondhand smoke to the annual deaths of fifty-three thousand Americans from heart disease, lung cancer, and other health problems.[34]

OSHA has remained relatively uninvolved in smoking issues, as the levels of tobacco smoke in a workplace must be exceedingly high for the air quality to fall below federally allowable limits. In 1994, however, a Florida appeals court ruled that sixty thousand flight attendants—who had been exposed to passenger cigarette fumes before Congress banned most in-flight smoking five years earlier—could file a class-action lawsuit against tobacco companies.[35]

To be on the safe side, several businesses decided to control, if not ban, smoking in the workplace. Hallmark Cards, Inc., for example, restricted smoking to separate smoking lounges in 1990 after management discovered that eight out of ten workers did not smoke. Deere & Company went a step further in 1994 by banning smoking completely in offices and company cars.[36]

VIOLENCE IN THE WORKPLACE

In the past, discussion of dangers in the workplace centered almost exclusively around the risks workers faced from machinery and other environmental factors. In the 1990s, however, a disturbing trend emerged that in many ways offsets any safety gains in other areas: workplace violence. In 1993, of the 6,271 American workers killed on the job, 21 percent were the victims of homicide.[37] By the mid-1990s, more than 1,000 workers in the United States were being murdered at work every year.[38] Violence in the workplace has become the most common cause of death for female employees and the third largest cause for men.[39] There are no statistics to reflect threats to workers or violent incidents in which nobody dies, so the homicide numbers reflect only the surface of workplace violence.[40]

Forms of Workplace Violence Workplace violence takes many forms, but experts have identified five basic categories that cover a majority of the incidents:

1. Attacks of emotionally enraged employees on co-workers or employers for personal or business reasons, such as after a layoff.
2. Attacks by an angry spouse or relative who tracks an employee to work in order to attack him or her.
3. Random violence, such as robbery.
4. Violence against law enforcement personnel or other employees in high-risk jobs.
5. Terrorism or hate crimes, such as the bombing of the World Trade Center in New York City in 1994, which killed 6 persons and injured almost 1,000 more, and the similar destruction of the federal building in Oklahoma City, Oklahoma, in 1995, which caused 168 deaths.

---

34. A. Liddle, "Study: Smoke Exposure Endangers Servers," *Nation's Restaurant News*, December 14, 1992, p. 7.
35. "Tobacco Lawsuit," *Wall Street Journal*, March 17, 1994, p. B2.
36. "Proposed Smoking Restrictions Worry Some Businesses; Others Comply Now," *Wall Street Journal*, March 28, 1994, p. A3.
37. "In Brief . . .," *The Bureau of National Affairs Conference Report*, August 17, 1994, p. 7.
38. A. Toufexis, "Workers Who Fight Fire with Fire," *Time*, April 25, 1994, p. 34.
39. "In Brief . . .," *op. cit.* p. 7.
40. F. E. Kuzmits, "Workplace Homicide: Prediction or Prevention," *SAM Advanced Management Journal*, Spring 1992, p. 4.

Violence by Workers Committed against Other Workers The issue of employees who attack co-workers or their employers has assumed a high priority for many experts on worker violence.[41] Forensic psychiatrist Pat Dietz, head of the Threat Assessment Group in Newport Beach, California, claims these actions "run the gamut from anonymous love letters on secretaries' desks to feces smeared on men's rooms' walls to death threats sent to CEOs' homes to workers talking of mass murder and specifying which guns they'll use on which supervisors."[42]

Besides the obvious effect that increased violence in society as a whole has had on individual employees, there are various reasons given for violent outbursts in the workplace. Dennis Johnson, a clinical psychologist, believes part of the answer is that many laid-off or disciplined workers, especially men (who account for almost all incidents of violence), have been made desperate by the prospects of finding "positions with lower pay, fewer benefits and very little job satisfaction."[43] Failed grievance procedures or poorly handled layoffs can also spur employees or former employees to react irrationally.

Philip R. Hyde, a practicing attorney, and Stephen G. White, a psychologist who works with work trauma victims, believe workers who are more likely to commit violent acts have common traits: they are "brooding, mistrustful, obsessional, delusional."[44] Hyde and White, along with many other psychological and business observers, believe the best way to stem workplace violence is to recognize the symptoms of possible offenders before these people take action.[45] Of course, this is not always possible, and in some cases none of the above characteristics are evident before an employee acts violently. Therefore, it is important that corporations keep a watchful staff and a direct line to law enforcement officers, as well as use security measures such as surveillance cameras (recognizing privacy rights, of course) or even security guards, if their budgets allow.

WORKERS' COMPENSATION LAW

Although the specifics can differ from state to state, in general, **workers' compensation** laws establish an administrative procedure for compensating workers injured on the job. Under these laws,

▼ Instead of suing his or her employer, an injured worker files a claim with the administrative agency or board that administers local workers' compensation claims.

These agencies have quasi-judicial powers. All their rulings are subject to review by the courts. In most cases, the right to recover under workers' compensation laws is determined without regard to the existence of negligence or fault in the traditional sense. Rather, it is predicated wholly on the employment relationship and the fact that the injury *arose out of or in the course of normal employment*. A simple, two-pronged test for determining whether an employee can receive workers' compensation consists of the following questions: (1) Was the injury accidental? and (2) Did the injury arise out of or in the course of employment? Intentionally inflicted self-injury, for example, would not be considered

---

41. J. Windau and G. Toscano, "Murder Inc.—Homicide in the American Workplace," *Business and Society Review*, Spring 1994, p. 58.
42. Toufexis, *op. cit.*, p. 36.
43. *Ibid.*
44. P. R. Hyde and S. G. White, "Psychological Profiles of Potentially Violent Offenders," *Employment Law Strategist*, October 1994, p. 5.
45. *Ibid.*

accidental and hence would not be covered under workers' compensation laws. In the past, heart attacks or other medical problems arising out of preexisting diseases or physical conditions were not covered by workers' compensation, but recently some states have allowed financial recovery in these situations.

Basically, employers are under a system of strict liability. Few, if any, defenses exist for them. Therefore, the costs of treating workers' injuries are considered a cost of production and are passed on to consumers. As these costs soar, however, more and more business leaders are arguing that workers' compensation harms a company more than it helps an employee. Today's workers' compensation costs are about $100 billion—triple the total only a decade earlier[46] (see *Company Focus: Steelcase, Inc.* on page 402).

Even if an injury is caused by an employer's negligence, the injured worker normally must accept workers' compensation as the sole remedy. On average, recoveries under these statutes are less than half of what they would be in comparable tort suits in the regular judicial system.[47]

STRATEGIES TO PRESERVE EMPLOYEE RIGHTS

Employers have reacted two different ways to the growth of employee rights. Some companies see any infringement on the employment-at-will doctrine as an affront to the basic principles of employee-employer dealings, and they have taken steps to protect their ability to fire their workers for any reason—or none at all. Sears, Roebuck, for example, requires applicants to sign a form stating that their jobs can be terminated at any time "without just cause."[48] Business groups have lobbied heavily against additional legislation to protect workers' rights and have presented their own bills to limit workers' legal protections with methods such as placing restrictions on the amounts awarded in workers' compensation claims.

Other companies have taken the opposite approach and accepted employee rights as another factor of doing business in today's society. These companies argue that employers and employees ultimately have a symbiotic relationship, and that an environment that benefits one benefits the other. Legal realities have forced this outlook on more than a few companies.

COSTS AND BENEFITS OF PROTECTING EMPLOYEE RIGHTS

The opposition of businesses to workers' rights, like their opposition to many other regulations, has revolved around the criticism that the costs of protecting employees are greater than the benefits. In California, for example, in the mid-1990s businesses paid 52 percent above the national average in workers' compensation costs, and the state's unemployment rate was 2.4 percentage points higher than the national average. These numbers caused Lloyd Aubry, California's director of industrial relations, to complain that "the [state] legislature doesn't make the obvious connection that workers' compensation is a job killer and a barrier to job creation."[49] It is also easy to come up with examples of companies—mostly small ones—that have failed because of excessive worker protection costs.

---

46. W. Cohen, "Sticking It to Business," *U.S. News & World Report*, March 8, 1993, p. 59.
47. R. L. Miller and F. B. Cross, *The Legal and Regulatory Environment Today* (St. Paul: West Publishing Co., 1993), p. 465.
48. *Note on Employees' Legal Rights*, p. 3.
49. Cohen, *op. cit.*, p. 60.

COMPANY FOCUS: STEELCASE, INC.

SAVING ON WORKERS' COMPENSATION

The goal of workers' compensation law is relatively simple: give employees medical care and wage protection benefits while at the same time protecting employers from medical lawsuits. The reality, however, is more complicated—adversarial relationships between workers and management have turned workers' compensation into an expensive headache for many corporations.

While costs for most companies have skyrocketed, furniture manufacturer Steelcase, Inc., has managed to *save* $4 million a year in workers' compensation claims. Through its innovative return-to-work program, the company has managed to restore a key element to the worker-management relationship—trust. The national average cost per workers' compensation claim in 1992 was $7,500; Steelcase paid only $2,500 per claim.

The Steelcase Program

Under Steelcase's program, employees injured while working meet with a company-sponsored physician, who gives a diagnosis and determines when and if they can return to work. The company never requires an employee to return to his or her prior job earlier than the physician suggests. Through a system of job redirection and on-site physician care, however, Steelcase is often able to provide injured employees with some sort of meaningful work.

At the company's Grand Rapids, Michigan, plant, for example, three physicians work on location with the 8,300 employees. At plants with no on-site medical facility, Steelcase hires a physician to visit the work site two or three times a week. These physicians are able to monitor the progress of employees recuperating from workplace injuries and determine when they are ready to come back to work.

Often an employee may be relatively healthy but not able to return to his or her regular job. At Steelcase, the employee will take on "light duty," such as cleaning company uniforms or towels, or sorting work gloves. Outsourcing these jobs could cost Steelcase as much as $400,000 a year, which the company saves on top of its lower workers' compensation costs.

Trust

The company tries to build a relationship of trust between workers and the on-site physicians. Before an injured employee returns to the job, a company employee-relations representative invites him or her to lunch to make sure that the employee does not feel pressured to return.

If an employee does not feel comfortable with the recommendations of the company-sponsored physician, he or she can appeal the case to a medical review board. Few do; more follow the example of Patricia Berens, who developed carpal-tunnel syndrome (a repetitive-motion wrist injury) while making office furniture and was back at the work site cleaning company uniforms five days after surgery for her condition. Berens, who collected full pay while she recuperated, says she returned quickly because "I trust the company's doctor."

The New Bottom Line

Workers' compensation expenses have become a significant cost of doing business for American companies: $100 billion in 1996. In most cases, those costs are driven up by an adversarial relationship between employees and employers. Innovative methods such as the one exemplified by Steelcase, which is based on trust, are reflected in a company's profitability.

SOURCE: Information from "Workers' Compensation Strategy Saves $4 Million Yearly," *Personnel Journal*, January 1993, p. 55; and E. Schine, "Workers' Compensation Goes under the Knife," *Business Week*, October 19, 1992, p. 90.

The Cost of Litigation Some statistical evidence supports the opposite contention— that as far as worker protection is concerned, "an ounce of prevention is worth a pound of cure." For example, not respecting the privacy of its applicants cost Target Stores

$2 million. Procter & Gamble was forced to pay $15.5 million for "defamation of character" to a former employee who had been improperly fired and publicly accused of stealing a $35 telephone.[50]

At the Elgar Corporation, a small San Diego manufacturer of power electronics equipment, a technician went on a rampage several weeks after being laid off and killed two supervisors. The company had to compensate the families of the men who were killed $400,000, and Elgar's workers' compensation expenses have gone up $100,000 annually because of higher insurance premiums.[51] Perhaps Elgar could have prevented the tragedy if it had instituted a program to prevent workplace violence.

Health-Care Costs Until 1994, employer health-care costs, mainly for employee health-care insurance paid for by the employer, rose much faster than inflation virtually every year for three decades. Since 1994, because of managed care, there has been a slight reduction in employer payments for employee health-care costs. Nonetheless, employers continue to feel the need to reduce employee health-care costs and note that the costs have caused them to hire fewer workers than they might have otherwise.

It is obviously in a company's best interests to reduce its health-care costs. In 1994 more than 75 percent of the 1,034 firms surveyed by Hewitt Associates offered "wellness" programs that encouraged employees to stay in better shape—making them less likely to drive up the company's health-care costs.[52] Often these programs feature cash incentives, as well as disincentives, to employees. Dominion Resources, a Virginia utility company, for example, rewards an employee and his or her spouse for healthy checkups with a $480 deduction from the employee's annual premium. On the other side of the spectrum, overweight

50. M. E. Reid, "Words That May Later Haunt You," *Wall Street Journal*, December 20, 1993, p. A10.

51. H. F. Bensimon, "Violence in the Workplace," *Training & Development*, January 1, 1994, p. 26.

52. B. Montague, "Companies Encourage Employees to Get Fit," *USA Today*, international ed., June 20, 1994, p. 12B.

workers at Hershey Foods must pay $30 more per month for health coverage, and smokers on the payroll at Texas oil-drilling equipment maker Baker Hughes find themselves with a $10 monthly charge for their habit.[53] Nike adds a $1,000 deductible to the health-care bills for any accident involving an employee who is drunk, on drugs, or not wearing a seat belt.[54]

Productivity Many of the same strategies used to lower health-care costs also may improve worker productivity.

▼ **Though there is little concrete evidence to support this contention, the idea that a healthy, happy employee is a more productive employee has ingrained itself in many corporate cultures.**

Many corporations are focusing on alleviating stress, which causes approximately one million people each day to call in sick and costs a total of $150 billion each year in loss of productivity and rehiring and retraining of workers, in addition to health-care costs.[55]

Some degree of stress is natural, and even desirable, in the workplace. *Exhibit 13–3* portrays the performance-stress relationship. The vertical axis represents the level of performance, and the horizontal axis shows the amount of stress the employee is experiencing. Where there is no stress, there is often no incentive, leading to a sluggish and even bored employee. When the pressure placed on a worker is too high, he or she will become too irritated, too threatened, or too sick to perform. At an optimum level of stress, the worker reaches maximum productivity. The optimum level of stress for each employee is different and must be ascertained by his or her employer or manager.

Many physicians believe that exercise raises the levels of stress an employee can handle. A study of Union Pacific Railroad workers showed that 80 percent of them felt more productive as a result of the company's exercise program; 75 percent of them felt the activity helped them achieve higher levels of relaxation and concentration at work.[56]

The National Energy Management Institute (NEMI) believes another avenue to improve worker health and productivity is improved air quality in the workplace. The institute, a private operation of the sheet-metal industry and sheet-metal workers' union, believes improved ventilation in 2.3 million American offices could increase the productivity of the country's work force by $54.5 billion a year.[57] The NEMI study was quickly embraced by OSHA, which estimates that 83 percent of worker health complaints are related to air-quality problems.[58] NEMI predicts that net productivity gains per business would outweigh the costs of improving indoor ventilation—about $2,000 a building—sevenfold.

EMPLOYER STRATEGIES FOR JOB SECURITY RIGHTS

The previous section on "The Cost of Litigation" mentioned the former Procter & Gamble employee who was awarded $15.5 million for defamation of character. The charge was brought because the just-fired man's boss had posted on a bulletin board a

53. M. D. Fefer, "Tailored Health Plans Take Off," *Fortune*, June 27, 1994, p. 12.
54. Montague, *op. cit.*
55. R. Carey, "Exercising Your Options," *Sales & Marketing Management*, June 1, 1995, p. 30.
56. *Ibid.*
57. "Better Indoor Quality Could Boost Workers' Productivity," *Contractor*, October 1, 1994, p. 58.
58. K. G. Salwen, "Ban on Smoking Expected to Bring Productivity Gain," *Wall Street Journal*, March 28, 1994, p. A10.

▼ **EXHIBIT 13–3
The Stress Curve**

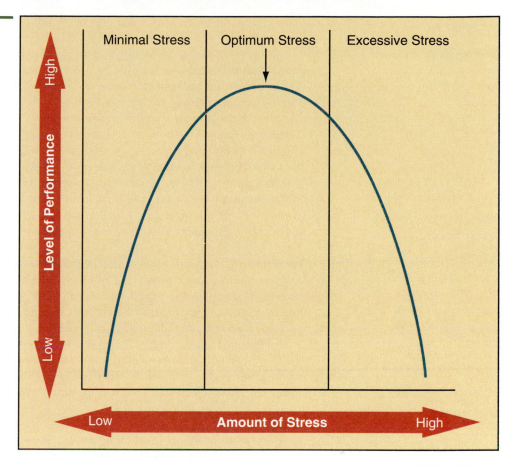

SOURCE: D. Hellriegel et al., *Organizational Behavior*, 6th ed. (St. Paul: West Publishing Co., 1992), p. 293.

note stating that his position had been terminated because of theft of company property. In court, the former employee was able to prove that this notice had ruined his reputation and prevented him for being hired at any of the one hundred jobs for which he subsequently applied.

There is a right and a wrong way to fire an employee. The right way is a process in the corporate culture that begins well before the possibility of a firing even exists.

Communication in the Corporate Culture The first step is protecting against the need for future termination by establishing communication in the workplace. The employer must communicate to the employees what is expected of them and what actions are specifically prohibited. This can be accomplished through written policy statements, job descriptions, and performance reviews. These steps, especially performance reviews, can be particularly helpful if a business is later involved in a wrongful termination suit. If an employer is able to prove that the employee had negative performance reviews, the company becomes less vulnerable to a successful wrongful-termination lawsuit by the employee.

An employer can also communicate standards of conduct by treating all workers equally. If one employee is fired for improperly using business trips to increase his or her frequent flier miles, then the next employee caught doing the same act must receive the same treatment. Handling these employee matters is difficult, and periodic training of managers and supervisors in the area of communicating with employees can be very productive.[59]

Progressive Discipline It would be unwise to assume that even with proper communication from employers, all employees will be suited for their jobs. When it becomes evident to an employer that a worker is not putting forth the performance desired, **progressive discipline** begins. In its simplest sense, progressive discipline consists of "notice to an employee of his or her shortcomings and one or more opportunities to correct them."[60] The first notice should be verbal; in most cases, employees do not want to lose their jobs, and this step should be enough to clear up any problems.

If the unacceptable behavior continues, then written notice should be given to the employee and placed in his or her employment file (a *very* important step if a wrongful-termination suit should occur at a later date). Further actions in progressive discipline may include suspension, probation, fines, transfers, and demotion.

Termination Except in cases of violence, theft, or any other felony or serious violation that an employee may commit on the job, discharge should come only after appropriate progressive disciplinary actions have taken place. In wrongful-termination suits, the employer must make it clear to the court that termination was a last resort forced on the company when all other alternatives had failed.

After termination, as Procter & Gamble learned the hard way, there is one rule: keep quiet. Even an offhand comment to another manager or employee about the fired worker can be construed as defamation. Because the number of defamation suits is growing— more than 25,000 are in state and federal courts at any one time[61]—employers should follow these four steps after termination:

1. Avoid giving references to prospective employers of the fired individual. If pressed, simply provide the dates of employment and refrain from any personal observations.
2. Be absolutely certain about the factual evidence behind the termination, perhaps even going as far as contracting for an independent review of the action.
3. Restrict the number of people informed of the reasons for the termination to those who need to know.
4. Do not use the fired employee as an example to other employees, even if such an action would provide a strong disincentive for others to repeat his or her behavior.[62]

MANAGEMENT STRATEGIES FOR PRIVACY AND SAFETY RIGHTS

Employers must protect the privacy and safety of their employees for both legal and moral reasons. Managers must have well-defined strategies to uphold these employee rights, even in cases where federal, state, or local legislation does not guarantee such treatment.

Employee Privacy Rights and Records Access Legislative regulation of private employer-employee relationships is limited, and only recently have U.S. corporations given much attention to employee privacy rights and records access. Today, however,

59. R. S. Schuler and V. L. Huber, *Personnel and Human Resource Management*, 5th ed. (St. Paul: West Publishing Co., 1993), p. 640.
60. R. H. Baxter, Jr., and T. B. Klein, "Protecting against Exposure," *National Law Journal*, February 28, 1994, p. S2.
61. C. O. Longnecker and F. R. Post, "The Management Termination Trap," *Business Horizons*, May 1, 1994, p. 71.
62. Reid, *op. cit.*

more than 50 percent of major companies have written privacy policies, and around 85 percent have written policies concerning employees' access to records containing information about them.[63] (For an example, see some aspects of the General Foods Privacy Policy in *Exhibit 13–4* on page 408.)

The contentiousness of debate on the privacy issue of drug and alcohol testing also has led many companies to form policies on the matter. Ciba-Geigy Corporation's strategy for dealing with the issue, formulated in 1987 with the help of employee focus groups, proved so sensible that many of its tenets were adopted in the Drug-Free Workplace Act of 1988. Under its policy, the company stated the following:[64]

1. It would encourage employees to ask for help by establishing a positive tone for the company's drug program. Instead of punishment, rehabilitation would be offered.
2. The thrust of the program would be educational; employees and supervisors would be trained to recognize drug problems and understand what to do about them.
3. The company would test an employee only when an incident or behavioral patterns indicated possible drug or alcohol use.

Employee Safety Rights and Workplace Violence The main issue in workplace safety is proper precautionary measures in the work environment. Every workplace, from a construction site to a secretary's desk, has its own dangers and required precautionary measures. Each employer, therefore, is responsible for complete knowledge of the safety risks in the work environment and for eliminating them.

As we have discussed, violence is a relatively new issue in workplace safety. As one manager put it, "People think violence just happens, but violent employees usually provide many clues to supervisors."[65] The first of these clues, or warning signs, is often the following kinds of threats of violence made by an employee: "If he doesn't get off my back, I'm going to kill . . ." or "If I get fired, I'm going to get . . . ."

How should employers react to such threats? Many have a policy of zero tolerance; that is, no employee threat is insignificant enough to go unnoticed or unpunished. Zero tolerance raises problems of workers' rights, however, including the right to be free from harassment. After all, probably millions of such threats are uttered every workweek, but very few are acted on.

Management consultants Hyde and White warn that employers cannot "overreact or underreact" to these threats. They urge companies to give all potential employees a thorough background investigation to check for past criminal or violent behavior (within the limits of the law, as discussed earlier in this chapter).[66]

Instead of ignoring the problem of workplace violence or addressing it on an "ad hoc, piecemeal basis," Hyde and White suggest that all companies start violence management programs, which include three basic ingredients:[67]

1. A statement of intent. The employer should set forth a "strong, unambiguous" statement outlining the company's "intent to act upon and resolve all threats of violence in the workplace."

63. Schuler and Huber, *op. cit.*, p. 643.
64. "Soul Searching at Ciba-Geigy," *HR Reporter*, May 1987, pp. 5–6.
65. "Experts, Urging Watchfulness, Note That Employees Who Turn to Violence Often Provide Clues in Advance," *BNA's Corporate Counsel Weekly*, August 23, 1995, p. 8.
66. P. R. Hyde and S. G. White, "Coping with Workplace Violence," *Employment Law Strategist*, October 1994, pp. 4–5.
67. *Ibid.*, pp. 5–8.

▼ EXHIBIT 13–4 The Four Points of the General Foods (GF) Privacy Policy

Point 1. Employees can review their personnel files only after having given the human resources department advance notice and may review their files only during business hours. Before the employee is given access to his or her files, any information relating to co-workers or GF's activities or plans in such areas as investigations, litigation, and personnel or salary planning must be removed.

Point 2. Because the release of an employee's medical records can lead to problems such as the misinterpretation of health information, GF requires company physicians to make oral reports to workers and send written reports to the worker's personal doctor. Medical reports are not released to third parties unless an employee files an insurance claim.

Point 3. GF will release personnel information in compliance with a subpoena without contesting the request, but it will advise the employee that the information was released, unless prohibited by law to do so.

Point 4. In instances when information is to be released that do not fall under normal procedures, the employee will be notified and given the option of stopping the release. For example, GF was approached by the United Givers Fund, a charity campaign within the company, for payroll records to determine each employee's level of charitable contributions. Employees were notified of this request and given the option of withholding the information from the fund.

SOURCE: R. S. Schuler and V. L. Huber, *Personnel and Human Resource Management,* 5th ed., (St. Paul: West Publishing Co., 1993), p. 643.

2. A responsible committee. The company should have a multidisciplinary program development committee with representatives from the human resources, legal, security, and medical/mental health departments. This committee should be responsible for creating and overseeing the violence management program and should be encouraged to seek outside assistance when the need arises.

3. Education of supervisors. Supervisors should be "given sufficient training to understand the problem [of workplace violence], to recognize psychological profiles and warning signs, and to implement response procedures."

To many employers, the costs of both hiring outside trainers and lost time to their own employees would render such a program too expensive, especially for an event with such a low probability of occurrence. The risks of ignoring the growing problem of workplace violence are great, however. Any instance of workplace violence, much less one that involves homicide, can shatter a harmonious workplace for months, if not years. Employers have a moral obligation to their employees to protect them from any threats, as well as a financial obligation to protect their businesses (or those of other owners) from the loss in productivity and possible lawsuits that inevitably result from an instance of violence.

THE DELICATE BALANCE

Long gone are the days of the employer that could do, say, and act exactly as it wanted, with no legal consequences. U.S. workers have more rights today than ever before. Even though the employment-at-will doctrine still exists, it has been overridden in many instances by federal and state law. Clearly, it is illegal under all circumstances to discriminate against prospective or actual employees on the basis of race, age, sex, religion, ethnic origin, or gender. The law goes further: employees have certain rights to privacy, the ability to take family and medical leave, and so on. Employers now have to maintain the delicate balance between getting the most from their employees in terms of productivity and at the same time protecting their employees' rights to privacy, job security, safety, and the like.

Upper management must take a strategic view of the issue of employee rights. Managers today must be trained in the proper way to deal with many employee problems, including workplace violence, privacy, the safety of working conditions, and stress and other health-care issues.

TERMS AND CONCEPTS FOR REVIEW

Employee rights 384
Employment-at-will doctrine 385

Polygraph tests 393
Progressive discipline 406

Right-to-know law 398
Workers' compensation 400

SUMMARY

1. Most employee-employer relationships are considered to be at will. The employment-at-will doctrine allows either party to terminate an employment agreement at any time for any reason, and until the 1960s there were virtually no legal restrictions on an employer's ability to fire a worker.

2. A fired employee can challenge the employment-at-will doctrine by alleging that (a) there was a breach of good faith and fair dealing by the employer, (b) a breach of contract occurred, or (c) defamation occurred.

3. Subsequent to the federal Family and Medical Leave Act of 1993, employers with fifty or more employees must allow their employees to take up to twelve weeks of family or medical leave during any twelve-month period (without pay).

4. Drug-testing programs by employers involve the trade-off between an individual's right to privacy and the safety of those affected by the individual's actions. The courts have upheld drug testing of federal employees whose actions affect public safety. Within the private sector, the laws vary dramatically across states. According to the American Management Association, drug use and drug-related accidents decrease when employees are routinely tested for drugs.

5. AIDS testing also involves an issue of privacy. Many companies have developed their own guidelines that require them to (a) provide the same rights and opportunities to individuals with AIDS and HIV infection as to employees with other serious illnesses, (b) protect the confidentiality of an employee's medical information, and (c) provide workers with timely education about AIDS.

6. There are three areas in which background checks of prospective employees may constitute an illegal invasion of privacy: arrest data, credit history, and workers' compensation claims.

7. Because of the 1988 Employee Polygraph Protection Act, relatively few companies routinely require their prospective or current employees to take lie-detector tests.

8. The Occupational Safety and Health Administration (part of the Department of Labor) creates and publishes standards, makes safety inspections, and enforces the Occupational Safety and Health Act of 1970. Employers with eleven or more employees must keep occupational and illness records for each employee. These records must be updated regularly and made available for inspection. Today, over twenty states have passed right-to-know laws that require employers to provide employees with information about hazardous chemicals and other workplace dangers. One of the most serious safety problems in the workplace is violence perpetrated by workers on fellow workers.

9. A system of workers' compensation has been set up throughout the United States to administer payments to workers who are injured on the job. Workers who make claims to these systems are then normally prohibited from suing their employers in court. Workers' compensation costs are currently about $100 billion a year.

10. Employers have economic reasons to protect the rights of their employees. If they do so correctly, they will avoid the costs of many kinds of lawsuits, among them defamation of character. Employers that attempt to reduce the

number of medical visits needed by employees through wellness and stress-reduction programs reduce the corporation's health-care costs. Finally, there is some evidence that employers that use a strategy of protecting employee rights have a more productive labor force.

11. There is a right and a wrong way to fire employees. Communication within the corporate culture is necessary so employees know if they are acting improperly. When performance is not adequate, the employer must use progressive discipline. In this system, the first notice is verbal and the next is written. Further action includes probation, transfers, and demotion. An employer that is terminating an employee must act in such a way as to avoid a defamation suit. The employer should do the following: (a) avoid giving references to prospective employers of the fired individual, (b) be certain about the factual evidence behind the termination, (c) restrict the number of people informed of the reasons for the termination, and (d) not use the behavior of the fired employee as a negative example to other employees.

12. An antiviolence management program includes three basic ingredients: a statement of intent, a responsible committee, and the education of supervisors.

EXERCISES

1. What does *employment at will* mean? Make a list of the benefits that today's employees obtain from the laws that prohibit many actions that used to be legal under the employment-at-will doctrine.

2. Reexamine *Exhibit 13–1*. Of the states listed, which one gives employers the most freedom in the drug testing of employees?

3. You are a top-level manager at a major manufacturing plant. You have just discovered by chance that one of your key employees is HIV-positive. What should you do?

4. Under what circumstances would you be able to use arrest-data information when deciding whether or not to hire an applicant?

5. Often when you place orders over the phone for merchandise, ask questions of long-distance telephone companies, and so on, you are told either through a recording or by the operator that your call may be monitored "for quality control." Do you think such monitoring violates your right to privacy as a customer? What about the right to privacy of the employee talking to you? Are there other ways in which employers could monitor employees that seemingly would not violate their right to privacy?

6. OSHA-compliance officers normally have to produce a warrant in order to search facilities for violations of health and safety laws. Nonetheless, very few businesses actually ask for such a warrant. Why not?

7. Write down the profile of an employee who might commit a violent act toward other workers.

8. "An ounce of prevention is worth a pound of cure." Apply this saying to various employee rights by explaining what type of prevention is appropriate to protect each right and how each prevention will save a corporation money in the long run.

9. Make a flow chart of a system of progressive discipline.

10. Robert Adams worked as a delivery-truck driver for George W. Cochran & Company. Adams persistently refused to drive a truck that lacked a required inspection sticker and was subsequently fired as a result of his refusal. Adams was an at-will employee, and Cochran contended that because there was no written employment contract stating otherwise, the company was entitled to discharge Adams at will—that is, for cause or no cause. Adams sought to recover $7,094 in lost wages and $200,000 in damages for the "humiliation, mental anguish, and emotional distress" that he had suffered as a result of being fired from his job. Do you think that Adams was right? Why or why not?

11. Paul Luedtke was employed by Nabors Alaska Drilling, Inc., to work on the company's drilling rigs on Alaska's North Slope. Over the course of this employment, Luedtke was promoted to driller, a position in which he was responsible for overseeing the work of an entire drilling crew. Twice during Luedtke's employment, he was accused of violating company drug and alcohol policies, and he was once disciplined for taking alcohol to the North Slope in contravention of company regulations. Sometime later, Luedtke was ordered to submit to a physical examination, ostensibly to ensure that he met the company's physical standards for work on offshore drilling rigs. As part of the examination, Luedtke's urine was tested for drugs. The results indicated marijuana use, and Luedtke was ordered to submit to and pass two subsequent drug tests before continuing employment with the company. Luedtke refused to comply and was fired. Luedtke brought suit against the company. The Alaska Supreme Court held that the common law of Alaska expressed a public policy of protecting certain "spheres of employee conduct" and "'private' information" from scrutiny by private employers. The court went on to find, however, that the policy did not protect Luedtke, because the drug testing was based on the company's legitimate need to control drug use in the hazardous environment in which Luedtke was employed.

a. The court in this case stated that the public policy of the state protected off-the-job activities and that companies could test employees only at times "contemporaneous with the employee's work time" and only if testing was for the limited purpose of "monitoring drug use that may directly affect employee performance." Is this a fair restriction on employers? Society seeks to protect against racial and other forms of discrimination in the workplace but generally leaves employers free to choose workers on the basis of whatever other criteria they deem fit. Should private employers be free to discharge or not hire workers on the basis of characteristics they find objectionable—such as drug use, for instance—regardless of the relationship between those characteristics and work performance?

b. Even if a worker's off-the-job lifestyle does not "directly affect employee performance," are there other practical considerations that support an employer's wanting to know about certain employee characteristics? Could not certain "private" activities affect a worker's long-term health and life expectancy? This is certainly a practical concern of an employer, if not a moral one. Should any other social goal—the right to privacy, say—take precedence over such practical considerations?

c. Could investigation into the private affairs of an employee be justified as indicating the employee's propensities for other conduct important to the employer? For example, does illegal drug use demonstrate a propensity to break other laws? What about marital infidelity? Are unfaithful spouses likely to be employees who are prone to stealing or embezzling from an employer? In general, how limited should an employee's expectation of privacy be?

12. At an REA Express shipping terminal, a conveyor belt was inoperative because an electrical circuit had shorted out. The manager called a licensed electrical contractor. When the contractor arrived, REA's maintenance supervisor was in the circuit breaker room. The floor was wet, and the maintenance supervisor was using sawdust to try to soak up the water. The licensed electrical contractor was attempting to fix the short circuit while standing on the wet floor, and he was electrocuted. Simultaneously, REA's maintenance supervisor, who was standing on a wooden platform, was burned and knocked unconscious. OSHA sought to fine REA Express $1,000 for failure to furnish a place of employment free from recognized hazards. Do you agree with OSHA's decision? Explain.

13. Denton and Carlo were employed at an appliance plant. Their jobs required them to do occasional maintenance work while standing on a wire mesh twenty feet above the plant floor. Other employees had fallen through the mesh, and one had been killed by the fall. When Denton and Carlo were asked by their supervisor to do work that would likely require them to walk on the mesh, they refused because of their fear of bodily harm or death. Because of their refusal to do the requested work, the two employees were fired from their jobs. Was their discharge wrongful? Explain.

14. Perlman is an employee of Jacobs, Inc., a pea cannery that has a three-story plant. On top of the third story is a flagpole. The company has a set lunch break, during which time the plant is shut down. The employees are not allowed to leave the plant property, and most of them eat their lunch outside on a grassy area. Some employees, however, eat their lunch on top of the roof. Perlman, known as a joker, climbs the flagpole one afternoon to show off. While waving wildly at the other employees, he loses his grip and falls, suffering numerous injuries. Do you think Perlman is entitled to workers' compensation? Explain.

SELECTED REFERENCES

▶ Baird, James. *Public Employee Privacy: A Legal and Practical Guide to Issues Affecting the Workplace*. Chicago: American Bar Association, Section of State and Local Government Law, 1995.

▶ Bendix, Reinhard. *Work and Authority in Industry*. Berkeley: University of California Press, 1974.

▶ Ewing, David W. *Freedom inside the Organization*. New York: McGraw-Hill, 1977.

▶ Finkin, Matthew W. *Privacy in Employment Law*. Washington, D.C.: Bureau of National Affairs, 1995.

▶ Gibson, Mary. *Worker's Rights*. Totowa, N.J.: Rowman & Allenhead, 1983.

▶ Siegel, Richard L. *Employment and Human Rights: The International Dimension*. Philadelphia: University of Pennsylvania Press, 1994.

▶ Walsh, James. *Rightful Termination: Defensive Strategies for Hiring and Firing in the Lawsuit-Happy 90's*. Santa Monica, Calif.: Merritt, 1994.

RESOURCES ON THE INTERNET

▼ The U.S. Department of Labor is on the Internet at
gopher://marvel.loc.gov:70/11/federal/ fedinfo/byagency/executive/labor

You can also access the National Institute for Occupational Safety and Health at
http://www.cdc.gov/niosh/ homepage.html

▼ The Legal Information Institute at Cornell Law School provides introductions to various employment topics at
http://fatty.law.cornell.edu/topics/ topics2.html#employment_law

▼ You can visit the 'Lectric Law Library Web site concerning employment at
http://www.inter=law.com/temp.html

▼ For information on health-care benefits to which employees may have a right, access
http://www.rbvdnr.com/eb/ eb-main.htm

▼ For information on employee privacy rights, you can access the biweekly EPIC Alert at
gopher://cpsr.org/11/cpsr/alert

▼ For advice and information on firings, access When You Have to Let Someone Go at
http://nearnet.gnn.com/gnn/ bus/nolo/letgo.html

▼ For information on the Family and Medical Leave Act, access
http://nearnet/gnn.com/bus/ nolo/work.html

CASE

ELECTRONIC BANKING SYSTEMS, INC., AND THE "MODERN SWEATSHOP"

Background

At Electronic Banking Systems, Inc. (EBS), surveillance dominates the workplace environment. Long lines of work desks face the front, where a manager surveys the room from a raised platform known as "the birdhouse" by employees. Other supervisors are positioned in the back of the room; according to EBS owner Ron Edens, it is easier to watch someone from behind, "because they don't know you're watching." From the ceiling hangs a dark globe, in which cameras are positioned to scan the workers' every move.

For many American workers, this kind of atmosphere is becoming a workplace reality. According to a 1994 survey by the International Labor Organization (ILO), Americans are more likely than any other workers in the industrialized world to be placed under the surveillance of computers, cameras, or listening devices. The ILO, an agency of the United Nations, estimated that twenty million Americans—almost one-sixth of the work force—are subject to some form of electronic monitoring at work. In the telecommunications, insurance, and banking industries, as well as in businesses like EBS, whose employees deal directly with money, the number of watched workers jumps to 80 percent.

For many executives and managers, electronic monitoring is a justifiable tool for improving the productivity of their work force. It is also a valuable security device that severely diminishes the probability of employee theft. Union leaders and worker advocacy groups, however, see in it the emergence of a "modern sweatshop" and claim that constant surveillance causes undue stress and other health problems, in addition to infringing on a worker's right to privacy. At EBS, Edens feels the dominating presence of electronic monitoring does not reflect "a Big Brother attitude" but instead "more of a calming attitude." His employees might not agree.

Lockbox Processing

EBS, based in Hagerstown, Maryland, is one of a growing field of firms that provide a financial service known as lockbox processing. In the interest of saving costs on labor, many businesses, organizations, and charities that once handled their paperwork on-site are outsourcing clerical chores to lockbox processors. EBS, for example, processes donations to groups such as the National Organization for Women, Mothers Against Drunk Driving, Greenpeace, and the Doris Day Animal League.

Edens's self-described "controlled environment" does indeed have the appearance of workers "locked" in a "box" to do their processing duties. Workers in "the cage," as the main room is known, must open and sort the contents of three envelopes a minute. The sorted contents are then sent to the audit department, which computes the collected figures, which are then conveyed to data-entry clerks, who must keep pace with a quota that demands 8,500 lines an hour. If a mistake is made, the computer buzzes and flashes a "check digit error" message onto the screen. "We don't ask these people to think—the machines think for them," says Edens.

The settings are spartan compared with most American work sites. The room is almost silent, as no communication between workers is allowed. Any personal items such as coffee mugs, desk calendars, or family photos are banned from workers' desks. To ensure that none of these various rules are broken, Edens resides in an upstairs office with access to a TV monitor that flashes various images from eight surveillance cameras. "Order and control are everything in this business," he says by way of explanation.

The Modern Sweatshop

EBS is only a single manifestation of a larger trend toward blue-collar work in a white-collar setting. As communities like Hagerstown lose manufacturing employment because of technological improvements or overseas competition, the employment vacuum is filled with lower-paying clerical jobs. EBS is located in a former garment factory, and most of the company's employees are women, just as was the case in the garment-producing sweatshops of the early industrial era.

"The office of the future can look a lot like the office of the past," notes Barbara Garson, who studies trends in workplace conditions. "Modern tools are being used to bring nineteenth century working conditions into the white-collar world." The difference, of course, is that the supervisor with a pocket watch has been replaced with more efficient technology to get the most out of the worker.

The electronically monitored workplace may have other similarities with the sweatshop in the area of health. Whereas industrial revolution sweatshops presented the danger of tuberculosis because of filthy work settings, sparkling clean modern workshops offer their own health risks. In the early 1990s, the

University of Wisconsin's Industrial Engineering Department, in concert with the Communications Workers of America (CWA), released a study that suggested that workers under the scrutiny of electronic monitoring have higher levels of stress-related medical problems. Overall, workers under intense scrutiny reported higher tension, extreme anxiety, depression, anger, and severe fatigue. Furthermore, these workers reported higher instances of wrist, arm, shoulder, neck, and back problems. The catalyst for all these problems was considered by the authors of the study to be higher levels of stress.

Counterproductive Results of Monitoring

Many employee rights advocates believe that producing high levels of stress through employee monitoring is ultimately counterproductive for employers. They argue that electronic monitoring strains worker loyalty to the point at which disdain of omnipresent management negatively affects performance. Because information gathered via surveillance can also be used as ground for dismissal, the employee may spend too much time worrying about mistakes and actually increase the likelihood they will be made. The accumulated pressure, stress, and paranoia does more harm than the monitoring does good.

"I think there is something unhealthy, unsavory about creating a spy society at the workplace," says Louis Gerber, a legislative representative for the CWA. "Companies want to use it as a lever over workers," adds Diana Roose, a research director for the National Organization for Working Women. In fact, the National Labor Relations Board filed a series of complaints against EBS, charging that the company illegally threatened and spied on workers using its cameras.

EBS's Defense to Criticism

EBS settled the issue by reinstating a fired worker, but Edens remains unbowed and calls the charges "noise." He does not deny that the electronic monitoring causes stress but dismisses that fact as "the nature of the beast." Edens also feels that the scope of EBS's services make surveillance a business necessity. The company handles many thousands of dollars a day in cash and checks, and employee knowledge of constant monitoring will discourage any thoughts of theft. Edens also believes that such measures, along with the assembly line aspect of the work, help him win the confidence of clients. "If you're disorderly, [clients] will think you are out of control and things could get lost."

Productivity is another goal of EBS's culture. By monitoring computer activity, Edens is able to keep a daily list of errors made by data processors. If any employee accumulates an unacceptable number of mistakes, the company can take steps to improve his or her job performance. As for charges of his stifling individuality, Edens counters, "I'm paying these people to open envelopes. . . . They don't have to make any decisions."

Critical Thinking Questions

1. Would you resist working for an employer that uses surveillance, even if not to the extent used at EBS?

2. Would you, as a business owner, outsource clerical chores to a lockbox processor? What trade-offs would be involved in such a decision?

3. To those who accuse Edens of being a profit-driven tyrant, what can be said in his defense? Is there any ethical justification to his system?

4. The sweatshops of the early industrial era were outlawed in the United States in part because public outrage over working conditions brought federal intervention. Does the modern sweatshop deserve such regulatory attention? Explain your answer.

5. How does the stress curve shown in *Exhibit 13–3* apply to EBS? Do you think Edens would agree with the basic assumptions of the exhibit?

SOURCE: Information from T. Horwitz, "Mr. Edens Profits from Watching His Workers' Every Move," *Wall Street Journal*, December 1, 1994, p. A9; "Survey: More Employers Snooping," *Phoenix Gazette*, August 2, 1994, p. A2; J. A. Lopez, "When 'Big Brother' Watches, Workers Face Health Risks," *Wall Street Journal*, October 5, 1990, p. A3; and L. S. Kadaba, "The Boss Is Watching," *Dallas Morning News*, October 16, 1993, p. 1C.

CHAPTER 14

EMPLOYMENT DISCRIMINATION

INTRODUCTION

R acial and gender prejudice has been a problem for people throughout history. Only in recent decades have systematic efforts to eliminate discriminatory practices been made through laws such as the Civil Rights Act of 1964. Because a person's ability to make a living depends not only on his or her skills but also on the availability of adequate employment opportunities, policymakers have tried to ensure that all persons have equal access to employment. Despite substantial new legal rights, however, employment discrimination continues to remain a pressing problem for many Americans.[1] Making the situation even more complex is the changing status of whites in the United States. Most studies agree that by 2060, the population of racial minorities will pass that of whites in this country. A marketing firm in Coral Gables, Florida, has even begun to test "Anglos" as a distinct minority group in its market research.[2]

As we saw in Chapter 13, under common law, employment was terminable at will. Any employer could establish all terms and conditions of employment, which meant that employers were free to discriminate on the basis of color, race, religion, nationality, age, or gender. Labor unions were deemed private associations, so they could determine all membership requirements without the oversight of the courts. In the past several decades, however, as a result of judicial decisions, administrative agency actions, and legislation, both employers and unions have been restricted in their ability to discriminate on the basis of race, religion, color, nationality, age, or gender.

More recently, the range of prohibited employment discrimination has expanded to include those treated differently on the job because of their sexual preference, weight, disability, language, and even propensity to smoke. To understand the state of employment discrimination law in the United States, we first discuss what has been the most important statute relating to employment discrimination: Title VII of the Civil Rights Act of 1964 as amended.

TITLE VII OF THE CIVIL RIGHTS ACT OF 1964

Title VII of the Civil Rights Act of 1964 as amended makes it unlawful for employers to discriminate against employees, applicants, and union members on the basis of race, color, national origin, religion, or gender at any stage of employment. A class of persons defined by one or more of these criteria is a *protected class*. Title VII applies to employers with fifteen or more employees, to labor unions with fifteen or more members, to all labor unions that operate hiring halls (to which members go regularly to be rationed jobs as they become available), and to all employment agencies. The 1972 amendments extended coverage to all state and local governments, government agencies, political subdivisions, and departments. A special section forbids discrimination in most federal government employment.

---

1. M. Jaramillo, "Reflections of an Affirmative Action Baby," *Business and Society Review*, Summer 1992, p. 72.
2. "Recognizing Whites as an Ethnic Group, *Wall Street Journal*, June 15, 1994, p. B1.

DISPARATE-TREATMENT DISCRIMINATION

Title VII was intended to put an end to **disparate-treatment discrimination**, which occurs when individuals are intentionally discriminated against on the basis of color, gender, national origin, race, or religion. A plaintiff wishing to establish by circumstantial evidence a *prima facie* case (one that is presumed true until disproved by contrary evidence) of disparate treatment must demonstrate that he or she is a member of a protected class, that he or she applied for and was qualified for the position of employment, that he or she was denied employment, and that the employer continued to seek applicants for the position or hired someone not in a protected class. Note that the employer can defend its decision if it hired a more qualified candidate for the position, as long as that candidate applied for the position when applications were being accepted.

The fact that the plaintiff is able to establish a *prima facie* case merely shifts the burden to the employer to explain that it has a lawful reason for not hiring the applicant. The plaintiff then must prove that the employer's stated reason was a pretext and that the employer was actually guilty of discrimination. A plaintiff with direct evidence of discrimination may forgo this procedure and sue directly.

One significant defense that employers have in some cases of disparate-treatment discrimination involves the **bona fide occupational qualification (BFOQ)** language in Title VII. Under BFOQ, employers can justify discriminatory hiring practices if the job in dispute is "essentially" defined by gender, age, or other criteria. For example, the Atlanta-based Hooters of America, Inc., restaurant chain defended its policy of hiring only female servers and bartenders under BFOQ. "Hiring men to be Hooter Girls," as one restaurant advertisement stated, would compromise the "essence" of the chain and cause undue financial damage. In 1995, the chain refused a settlement offer from the Equal Employment Opportunity Commission (EEOC).[3] Eventually, the EEOC backed off its stance that Hooters should be forced to hire males for server and bartender positions.

DISPARATE-IMPACT DISCRIMINATION

Employers often find it necessary to choose from among a large number of job applicants. Consequently, they often use personnel tests and interviews to screen applicants. Minimum educational requirements are also common. When employer practices, such as those involving educational or job requirements, have a discriminatory effect on a class of people protected under Title VII, **disparate-impact discrimination** results. This type of discrimination, which is perhaps not intended, is distinguished from disparate-treatment discrimination, which is intentional.

Disparate-impact discrimination occurs when, as a result of educational or other job requirements or hiring procedures, an employer's work force does not reflect approximately the same percentages of nonwhites, women, or other protected groups that characterize qualified individuals in the local labor market. If it can be shown that employment practices having a discriminatory effect are not necessary for job performance or for business reasons, the practices will be deemed illegal.

Employers thus are eliminating such practices. The Los Angeles Police Department, for example, no longer uses the scaling of a six-foot wall as part of its entrance requirements for officers and has substituted a more scientific strength test; scaling the wall was difficult for many female applicants, which needlessly impaired their entrance chances.

---

3. J. Hayes, "Hooters Comes Out against EEOC—Sex Bias Suit," *Nation's Restaurant News,* November 27, 1995, p. 3.

Likewise, United Airlines ended a policy that allowed the company to base the employment of flight attendants on weight restrictions.

RACE, COLOR, AND NATIONAL-ORIGIN DISCRIMINATION

If a company's standards or policies for selecting or promoting employees have the effect of discriminating against applicants on the basis of race, color, or national origin and do not have a substantial, demonstrable relationship to qualifications for the job in question, they are illegal. Discrimination in employment conditions and benefits is also illegal. For example,

▼ An employer cannot maintain all-white or all-nonwhite crews for no demonstrable reason, nor can an employer grant higher average Christmas bonuses to whites than to nonwhites.

However, if differences in employment conditions or benefits are related to objective evidence of job performance, they are not relevant to a claim of discrimination. It is up to the employer to demonstrate job relatedness.

SEX DISCRIMINATION IN THE WORKPLACE

In 1923, the leaders of the National Women's Party introduced the Equal Rights Amendment (ERA) to Congress. Feeling that the recently granted right to vote would not be enough to change the status of women in the United States, the party wanted the further protection of the ERA, which states, "Equality of rights under the law shall not be denied or abridged by the United States or by any state on account of sex."

Because of the prevailing views about women in Congress in 1923, the ERA was shelved. The amendment was not approved until 1972, when it was sent to the state legislatures. Any constitutional amendment must be ratified by the legislatures (or conventions) of three-fourths of the states, and although the ERA gained the support of six presidents and both houses of Congress, it was not ratified by the necessary thirty-eight states, and on its 1981 deadline, the amendment failed.

Why is there so much controversy over what appears to be an obvious and seemingly harmless assertion of equal rights between the sexes? Opponents of the ERA, such as the Eagle Forum's Phyllis Schlafly, saw it as a legislative attack against women's traditional role in society. Schlafly saw the ERA as "sexual harassment" directed "by feminists and their federal government allies against the role of motherhood and the role of the dependent wife."[4] Supporters asserted that despite assurances of equality in the Constitution, women continued to lag behind men in employment opportunities, wages, and protection against violence.

SEX DISCRIMINATION AND THE CIVIL RIGHTS ACT OF 1964

Gender was included as a prohibited basis for discrimination in the job market under Title VII of the Civil Rights Act of 1964. Since its enactment, Title VII has been used to strike down so-called protective legislation, which prevents women from undertaking jobs

---

4. P. Schlafly's statement before a Senate labor subcommittee in 1981, quoted in the *Los Angeles Herald Examiner*, April 22, 1981, p. 2.

deemed "too dangerous or strenuous by the state." In practice, such protective legislation often "protected" women from higher-paying jobs. Under the EEOC guidelines, such state statutes may not be used as a defense to a charge of illegal sex discrimination.

Title IX of the Education Act of 1972 complemented Title VII by prohibiting sex discrimination in federally subsidized education programs, including athletics. Because the federal statutes and guidelines have not completely eliminated sex discrimination in the workplace, however, the women's rights movement has continued to work for the passage of the ERA. Furthermore, some of the conditions that led to the necessity for protective legislation in the first place persist to some degree in the workplace. The continuing existence of sexual harassment is one of these problems.

SEXUAL HARASSMENT

In recent years, workers have been given some protection against **sexual harassment** in the workplace under the Title VII provisions against sex discrimination. Under the guidelines of the EEOC set in 1980, all unwelcome sexual advances, requests, or other physical or verbal conduct of a sexual nature constitutes illegal sexual harassment if submission to them is a condition of employment or a basis of pay, promotion, or other employment decisions.[5]

In the intervening years, federal and state courts have defined sexual harassment more specifically:

▼ **In 1986, the United States Supreme Court ruled that a "hostile environment"— tantamount to sexual harassment—exists when actions are taken that unreasonably interfere with an employee's performance or tend to create an intimidating work environment.**

This ruling has led to some decisions by state and federal courts that go beyond the EEOC's initial guidelines. In California, a state court ruled that a nurse had been sexually harassed although she had not actually been touched; the court decided that because a doctor had been grabbing the nurse's co-workers, the workplace environment had been compromised. A federal court in Michigan ruled that a boss had been sexually harassing a female employee by constantly asking her to "do something nice."

The law is not limited to the protection of female employees. In Rhode Island, a federal court ruled that two male employees had been sexually harassed when they were forced to engage in sexual activity with their boss's female secretary or be fired.[6] Cases of same-sex sexual harassment have also begun to appear on the legal landscape, though states have differed in their reactions. In 1993, a Michigan appellate court ruled that the state's civil rights act allowed an employee to sue in response to unwanted homosexual advances from co-workers or supervisors.[7] In a similar case a year later, a Maryland district judge ruled that the Civil Rights Act of 1964 did not allow sexual-harassment claims to be brought against a "supervisor or worker of the same gender."[8]

Many American companies now recognize that sexual harassment affects worker productivity and morale, and that it is in the company's best interests to take steps to deal with

5. K. E. Lewis and P. R. Johnson, "Preventing Sexual Harassment Complaints Based on Hostile Work Environments," SAM *Advanced Management Journal*, Spring 1991, p. 21.
6. A. S. Hayes, "How the Courts Define Harassment," *Wall Street Journal*, October 11, 1994, p. B7.
7. M. P. Norris and M. A. Randon, "Sexual Orientation and the Workplace: Recent Developments in Discrimination and Harassment Law," *Employee Relations Law Journal*, September 22, 1993, pp. 233–246.
8. "Maryland Man Loses Claim of Same-Sex Harassment," *Liability Week*, January 2, 1995, p. 2.

such incidents. Corning, DEC, and Honeywell, for example, have instituted seminars and training programs designed to sensitize workers to the more common forms of sexual harassment. Other companies, such as CBS, periodically post corporate policies regarding sexual harassment to inform employees as to what types of conduct are prohibited. Still others, such as DuPont, have set up hotlines and special offices to handle complaints involving sexual harassment. Most large employers have sexual-harassment policies in place.

"Reasonable Woman" Standard Because the victims of sexual harassment are almost always women, is it valid to consider the question of harassment from the viewpoint of the "reasonable man" or even the "reasonable person"? This is the legal standard generally used to determine whether a person's behavior was appropriate under given circumstances. At least one court, the U.S. Court of Appeals in San Francisco, ruled that whether certain conduct was or was not sexual harassment should be decided using a **"reasonable woman" standard**. The case, *Ellison v. Brady*, was filed by an employee who alleged that a fellow employee's persistent, unwelcome letters and requests for dates had created a hostile working environment. The court held that the plaintiff had established a *prima facie* case because she had made allegations of fact that a reasonable woman would probably consider sufficient to create a hostile working environment.

One problem with the reasonable woman standard, or even the reasonable person standard, is that people often disagree on what is reasonable. For example, some observers complain that sexual-harassment cases often violate the accused person's right to freedom of speech. John Leo, a columnist for *U.S. News & World Report*, adds that many of these cases are characterized by "hair-trigger Puritanism" on the part of the plaintiffs. To prove his point, Leo brings up two examples. The first involves columnist David Nyhan of the *Boston Globe*, who was overheard by a female co-worker as he used a crude synonym for hen-pecked in a conversation about basketball with another *Globe* employee. The woman, insulted by the term, reported Nyhan to their superiors. He was "put through the wringer" and fined $1,250 (which later was rescinded). Leo's second example involves an employee at a TV network who was suspended for displaying a postcard from Paris with a nude photo from the Folies-Bergère, a popular nightclub.[9] Leo's examples are extreme, but they do illustrate the problem of differing perceptions.

Although many corporate managers have become more aware of the extent of sexual harassment in the workplace, companies often find it difficult to determine which types of arguably ambiguous behavior should be punished. Often it is not clear whether a statement is offensive or merely a compliment. Consequently, companies may be inclined to overlook incidents that do not involve blatantly suggestive remarks or conduct. There are concerns that office romances that have fizzled may spark claims of sexual harassment, and that publicizing corporate policies on sexual harassment will merely encourage more people to file questionable claims against the company.

Proof and Damages Although the EEOC receives over twelve thousand sexual-harassment complaints annually, relatively few are prosecuted. Many of these cases come down to the question of who is more believable—the alleged victim or the alleged offender—because there are usually no third party witnesses. Moreover, there is often no written evidence that the statements in question were actually made. This sort of situation may present an insurmountable problem for the victim who must prove that the offensive conduct took place.

---

9. J. Leo, "An Empty Ruling on Harassment," *U.S. News & World Report*, November 29, 1993, p. 20.

The number of sexual-harassment cases that do make it to court is growing, however. There are several reasons for this increase. First of all, women have more confidence in bringing these charges. Furthermore, the Civil Rights Act of 1991 (discussed later in greater detail) allows plaintiffs in sexual-harassment suits to recover both punitive and compensatory damages. These compensatory damages can include not only lost wages but also payment for emotional stress and humiliation.

The next move to clear the way for more sexual-harassment lawsuits was the United States Supreme Court's decision in the 1993 case *Harris v. Forklift Systems*, which made it easier to prove sexual harassment. In the lawsuit, Teresa Harris, a manager at Forklift Systems, an equipment rental company in Nashville, Tennessee, quit her job because of the workplace environment fostered by the company's president, Charles Hardy. According to Harris, Hardy called one employee a "dumb-ass woman," suggested to another that that employee and he "go to a Holiday Inn to negotiate your raise," and asked Harris herself if she had closed a business deal by having sexual relations with the customer.[10]

A lower federal court judge decided that although Hardy's behavior had hardly been desirable, it was not severe enough to seriously affect a female worker's psychological well-being and therefore did not create a "hostile environment." Harris's lawyer appealed, and the Supreme Court agreed to review the question of whether a plaintiff must prove psychological damage to prove sexual harassment.

The Court ruled unanimously in Harris's favor that as long as a work environment can be perceived, and is perceived, as hostile or abusive to a class of people based on gender, then there is no need to prove it is also psychologically harmful to the plaintiff. Although Associate Justice Sandra Day O'Connor wrote in her opinion that *Harris* did not provide "a mathematically precise test," concerns have been expressed that the decision makes it *too* easy to prove sexual harassment by making illegal some kinds of conduct—such as telling crude jokes—that are merely offensive.[11]

CREATING A NONHOSTILE WORK ENVIRONMENT

In light of *Harris*, not to mention some of the high damage awards handed out in other sexual-harassment cases, employers must recognize the importance of creating an appropriate atmosphere at their workplaces. In its guidelines, the Equal Employment Opportunity Commission suggests that "prevention is the best tool for the elimination of sexual harassment [and an] employer should take all steps necessary to prevent" it.[12]

Because of the nature of the problem, however, it is not simple to set up an effective sexual-harassment prevention program. Many companies make the mistake of setting up formal complaint systems in which employees are required to make written statements when they feel they have been harassed. Many victims of harassment, however, hesitate to make formal complaints for a variety of reasons: fear of retaliation by a harassing supervisor, fear of ridicule by co-workers, or embarrassment at broaching a subject that may be perceived as shameful. As Rebecca Thacker, assistant professor of management at the University of Louisville's College of Business and Public Management, says, "A policy that requires passive targets to complain is similar to having no prevention policy at all."[13]

---

10. D. O. Stewart, "Sex, Lies, and the Workplace," *ABA Journal*, April 1994, p. 44.
11. R. G. Silberman, "After Harris, More Questions on Harassment," *Wall Street Journal*, November 17, 1993, p. A20.
12. C. Michelle Kirk, "Supreme Court Issues Ruling on Sexual Harassment," *Business Law Update*, Winter 1994, p. 5.
13. R. A. Thacker, "Innovative Steps to Take in Sexual Harassment Prevention," *Business Horizons*, January–February 1994, p. 29.

A Commitment to Eliminating Sexual Harassment Thacker believes that a critical step in creating a nonhostile environment is conveying a strong message to the employees that sexual harassment will not be tolerated and, just as important, that the rights of those who report being harassed will be protected. She believes every business should have a written sexual-harassment policy that includes the following:[14]

1. Assurances of confidentiality of complaints. Perhaps the most important single step an employer can take is to raise the comfort level of passive victims of sexual harassment.
2. Assurance of a prompt, tactful investigation. If victims do not believe their employers will act quickly and firmly on complaints, they are less likely to file complaints in the first place. In a tactful investigation, at first only the victim and the accused harasser should be involved in discussions of the matter. Ideally, the two parties can settle the dispute in the initial discussions.
3. A guarantee that there will be no retaliation against the victim for presenting a complaint. Again, this gives a victim an incentive to come forward.
4. Standards to discipline proved harassers. A company should have predetermined standards for punishing proved harassers, and the company should rigorously adhere to these guidelines.
5. Visible top management support. Employees need to know that top management perceives sexual harassment as a serious issue. If the company holds training sessions on the subject, top management should make sure that it is represented in order to support the proceedings.
6. Thoroughness in choosing the person who will handle complaints. "He or she should be tactful, kind, warm, and capable of conducting an objective investigation," says Thacker. "If the person who might naturally receive complaints, such as the human resources manager, does not possess these characteristics, then top management should designate someone else who does." This person should be made visible at every opportunity and be presented to other employees as somebody they can trust.

For a simple management checklist concerning sexual harassment, see *Exhibit 14–1*.

The Role of the Manager Thacker also stresses the importance of the manager or supervisor as "the first line of defense" for organizations that want to protect their employees effectively against sexual harassment. Too often, managers have difficulty recognizing that there are two types of sexual harassment: *quid pro quo* harassment and environmental harassment. The obvious one is *quid pro quo* harassment, in which the harasser demands sexual favors in return for benefits or in lieu of punishments of some kind. *Quid pro quo* harassment is blatant, and managers have little trouble recognizing it. Environmental harassment is less clear-cut. Many managers find it hard to believe that a joke, offhand comment, nonverbal behavior, or desk calendar that offends one of their employees can be construed as sexual harassment. "When supervisors observe social-sexual behavior in the workplace," says Thacker, "the appropriate question is whether the target is bothered by it, not whether the supervisor perceives it as sexually harassing."[15] Managers must understand this distinction and use it in the workplace. Rather than directing the interaction between male and female employees in the workplace, they should be alert to any potentially dangerous situations and attempt to diffuse them at the early stages.

---

14. *Ibid.*, p. 30.
15. *Ibid.*, p. 31.

__ **1.** Instruct employees to explicitly ask an offending co-worker, supervisor, or boss to stop any activity that they feel constitutes sexual harassment.

__ **2.** Make it easy and safe for employees to seek help. DuPont, for example, has a twenty-four-hour hot line that offers advice on personal security and sexual harassment. Callers do not need to identify themselves.

__ **3.** Respond immediately, often with a full-fledged investigation, if a victim or witness of harassment lodges an official complaint. If the allegations are substantiated, respond appropriately with actions ranging from warnings to reassignment to job termination.

__ **4.** Create stable work environments and treat all employees with sensitivity and respect. Companies that follow these guidelines typically report fewer cases of sexual harassment.

PREGNANCY DISCRIMINATION

The Pregnancy Discrimination Act of 1978, which amended Title VII, prohibits the discriminatory treatment of employees on the basis of pregnancy. With regard to pregnancy, childbirth, or related medical conditions, women must be treated—for all employment-related purposes, including the receipt of benefits under employee-benefit programs—the same as other persons not so affected but similar in ability to work.

An employer is required to treat an employee who is temporarily unable to perform her job because of a pregnancy-related condition in the same manner as the employer would treat other temporarily disabled employees. The employer must change work assignments, grant paid disability leaves, or grant leaves without pay if that is how the employer would treat other temporarily disabled employees. Policies concerning an employee's return to work, accrual of seniority, pay increases, and so on must also result in equal treatment.

FETAL PROTECTION POLICIES

Most laws mandating that pregnant women be treated the same as other workers are accepted by employers. Many companies, however, have adopted so-called fetal protection policies, which prevent fertile women (who may or may not be pregnant) from working in jobs that could expose them or their unborn children to hazardous substances. Until recently, such policies were regarded as the surest way to avoid later health-related lawsuits by the parent or child. In deciding whether to adopt a fetal protection policy, however, companies were essentially choosing between violating various civil rights laws and facing the prospect of liability in the future.

For many companies, it appeared more prudent to risk discrimination suits than to be accused in front of a jury of causing birth defects in a child. As a result, many companies, including General Motors and DuPont, adopted workplace rules barring fertile women from jobs that involved day-to-day contact with substances that could cause genetic or other kinds of abnormalities in unborn children. Men were not usually affected by these restrictions, even though medical studies have revealed that the male reproductive system can be damaged by prolonged exposure to certain types of materials, such as lead.

One of the most extreme fetal protection policies was adopted in 1982 by Johnson Controls, the biggest U.S. producer of automobile batteries. The Johnson Controls policy required that all women of childbearing age working in jobs that entailed periodic exposure to lead or other hazardous materials prove that they were infertile or else be transferred to other positions. Those women who agreed to be transferred often had to accept

cuts in pay and reduced job responsibilities. At least one woman who refused to accept a safer job agreed to be sterilized. Employees and their union, United Auto Workers, brought a suit against Johnson Controls, claiming that the fetal protection policy violated Title VII.

In 1991, the Supreme Court ruled that the policy was discriminatory: "Women as capable of doing their jobs as their male counterparts may not be forced to choose between having a child and having a job."[16] The Court's rulings paved the way for further lawsuits in the area. In fact, within a year the EEOC filed a suit on behalf of an employee at Sundstrand Corporation who had been reassigned to a low-paying janitorial position because of her pregnancy. The courts have generally struck down such policies as violations of the civil rights laws.

EQUAL PAY FOR EQUAL WORK

One of the main goals of the women's rights movement and the ERA was to resolve the situation that existed in 1923, and still exists to some extent today, which sees males paid different wages than their female counterparts. In 1994, the National Committee on Pay Equity estimated that over a lifetime of work at the same job, women will earn $420,000

16. *United Auto Workers v. Johnson Controls, Inc.*, 111 S.Ct. 1196, 113 L.Ed.2d 158 (1991).

less than men. Along those same lines, college-educated women earn about $10,000 a year less than men with the same education.[17]

Equal Pay Act of 1963 The first attempt to correct this difference came during World War II, when the War Labor Board issued an "equal pay for women" policy. In implementing the policy, the board often evaluated jobs for their comparability and required equal pay for comparable jobs.[18] Supported by the next three presidential administrations, the Equal Pay Act was enacted in 1963 as an amendment to the Fair Labor Standards Act of 1938. Since 1979, it has been administered by the EEOC. Basically, the act prohibits gender-based discrimination in the wages paid for equal work on jobs when their performance requires similar skill, effort, and responsibility. For the equal pay requirements to apply, the employees must work at the same establishment.

The issue of equal pay focuses more on the jobs performed by two employees and whether they are substantially equal than on the equivalence of the employees' skills and training. A wage differential for equal work is justified if it is shown to exist because of (1) seniority, (2) merit, (3) a system that pays according to quality or quantity of production, or (4) any factor other than gender.[19] The courts look on the primary duties of the two jobs. The jobs of a barber and a beautician are considered essentially equal. So, too, are those of a tailor and a seamstress.

Few supporters of the concept of equal pay for equal work look on the Equal Pay Act as a success. As the numbers mentioned above show, on average, women's earnings are still not level with men's. As of the early 1990s, men were consistently earning more than women for the same jobs (see *Exhibit 14–2* on page 426).

Comparable Worth Equal pay laws do not address the issue of **comparable worth**, or pay equity. The notion of comparable worth involves equality in pay not just for different persons holding the same kind of job but for different persons holding different kinds of jobs that require the same degree of education or training. In short,

▼ The comparable worth theory aims to correct the fact that male-dominated jobs still draw higher salaries than female-dominated jobs, even though the former may not require any more expertise or effort than the latter.

In the private sector, the issue of comparable worth often hinges on whether managers believe they have a moral obligation to correct inequities in female-male pay standards. Those who believe they do have this duty must face the fact that their decision may be costly to the firm, because relative pay is determined largely by overall supply and demand in the marketplace. The supply of word processors, for example, is so great relative to the demand that their pay scale is 50 percent lower than that of truck drivers. If an employer adopts a comparable worth standard that requires word processors to be paid only 10 percent less than truck drivers, that employer will face higher costs than competing firms that do not adopt a comparable worth pay scale. These higher costs will result in lower profits, which could jeopardize the firm's financial future.

The Glass Ceiling Pay inequity even exists at the highest levels in U.S. corporations. A survey of 194 mid- to upper-level managers at major U.S. companies by Eckerd College

---

17. J. Mann, "Doing What's Fair on Payday," *Washington Post*, July 15, 1994, p. E3.
18. P. Barnum, R. C. Liden, and N. Ditomaso, "Double Jeopardy for Women and Minorities: Pay Differences with Age," *Academy of Management Journal*, June 1995, p. 863.
19. P. England, *Comparable Worth: Theories and Evidences* (New York: Walter de Gruyter, 1992).

▼ **EXHIBIT 14–2** **Lack of Pay Equity**

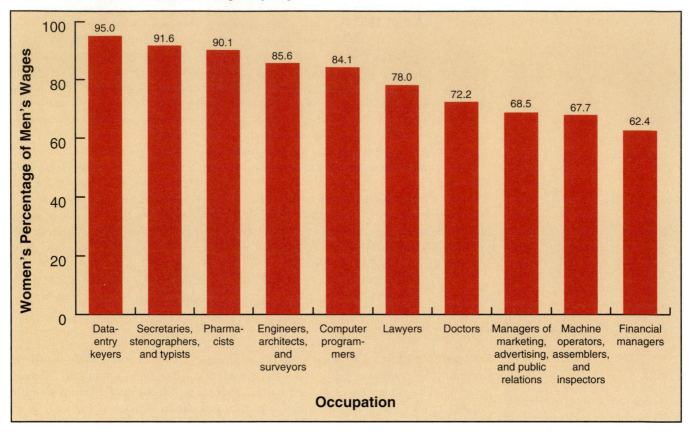

SOURCE: Bureau of Labor Statistics.

economics professor Peter Hammerschmidt found that male managers earned an average salary of $80,722 compared with $65,258 for their female counterparts. Hammerschmidt could account for $3,740 of the difference as legitimate—taking into consideration factors such as length of service—but the remaining gap could be attributed only to the executives' gender.[20]

A closer look at CEO salaries points out another aspect of sex discrimination in the workplace: there are relatively few female CEOs. In 1995, only 13 of the Fortune 500 companies had women in their top five management positions; in other words, women occupy less than 1 percent of the 2,500 top jobs in these firms.[21] This phenomena is partly blamed on the so-called **glass ceiling**, which alludes to an imaginary (though not necessarily imagined) barrier that keeps women from moving to progressively higher positions in a corporation even though they can clearly see the positions to which they aspire.[22]

20. P. Hammerschmidt and B. Osmundsvaag, "The Impact of Leadership Effectiveness Ratings, Personal Characteristics, and Occupations Factors on Male and Female Compensation," presented at the Eastern Economic Meeting, March 1992.

21. "Washington Insider: Women Executives," *Set-Aside Alert,* January 1, 1995.

22. G. N. Powell and D. A. Butterfield, "Investigating the Glass Ceiling Phenomenon—An Empirical Study of Actual Promotions in Top Management," *Academy of Management Journal,* February 1994, p. 68.

There are numerous theories to explain these numbers, all of which begin with the presumption that the corporate world has yet to fully accept women. Sexual harassment in various forms may discourage women from attaining top positions; many women may leave the workplace to start a family, thus effectively stopping their active career progress for a time; and leadership training opportunities may not be extended to women.

Another theory is that the corporate culture at many companies is basically an "old boy's network," and women have yet to break into the club. It is easy to speculate that many top male executives do not want women to attain their level, partly because they fear the greater competition and partly because the men are not sure how to treat women of equal power. Consequently, women often are kept out of the lines of communication with—and do not have the same access to—job-enhancement opportunities. In Scandinavian countries, women were kept out of government and business by the location of important meetings: in the male-only sanctuary of the steam hut, or sauna. The United States and Japan have similar bastions of male business, especially the golf course. In the 1990s, instructional golf classes for businesswomen began to open what had previously been a somewhat closed activity (see *Managing Social Issues—Barriers to Success: The Golf Club* on page 428).

Some companies have made their own efforts to address the existence of the glass ceiling. The international accounting firm Deloitte & Touche offers female employees workshops on gender issues, flexible work arrangement guidelines, and career-planning aids. Both AT&T and Motorola increased the number of women in the upper ranks by offering family leave benefits and adjustable work hours. Most of the significant activity in this area, however, has come through pressure from the federal government. In the Civil Rights Act of 1991, Congress included a provision for the establishment of the Glass Ceiling Commission to study the problem and offer solutions.

Many women are not waiting for government help to smash the glass ceiling. Instead of trying to struggle their way to the top of male-dominated Fortune 500 companies, women are increasingly starting their own businesses. A large percentage of the three million new businesses formed each year in the 1990s have been started by women, and statistics show that two-thirds of the work force in companies started by women are also female.[23] Most of these businesses are in the fields of health care, education, child care, information networks, and beauty products.

DISCRIMINATION AGAINST GAY MEN AND LESBIANS IN THE WORKPLACE

If the issue of women's rights has been controversial, then the issue of gay rights in the United States has been explosive. Starting with the Stonewall riots in New York City in the summer of 1969, gay male and lesbian grassroots political groups have been outspoken and active in trying to reverse the discriminatory practices they have historically faced; the workplace is only one area in which gay men and lesbians have been striving to receive equal treatment.

GAY MALES AND LESBIANS IN THE PRIVATE WORKPLACE

As of 1997, no federal legislation had been passed that specifically outlaws workplace discrimination on the basis of sexual orientation. Eight states (California, Massachusetts,

---

23. A. David Silver, "The New American Hero," *Wall Street Journal*, May 9, 1994, p. A14.

▣ Managing Social Issues

Barriers to Success: The Golf Club

Janet Thompson, vice president of marketing at Mazda Motor of America in Irvine, California, is an avid golfer. It's not all fun and games for Thompson, however, who says she has built strong business ties with many car and truck dealers on the links. "Dealers always have golf outings," she says. "If I wasn't there too, I'd be standing on the sideline missing out."

Many women, like Thompson, are discovering that a smooth golf swing is a necessary business skill. As of the mid-1990s, close to 40 percent of beginning golfers were women, and the overall number of women who play golf has been steadily increasing. By 1992, there were 5.4 million female golfers in the United States, up 600,000 from 5 years earlier. Along the way, however, women are finding that getting onto a golf course can be as difficult as breaking through the glass ceiling.

The Business Sport

According to the nearest estimates, nearly half the women taking up golf are professionals, administrators, or managers. Consequently, organizations such as the Executive Women's Golf League and the Professional Businesswomen's Golf Network are forming chapters across the United States to teach women the ins and outs of "business golf." The former group has grown to more than fifty chapters nationwide. One EWGF member thinks the group's popularity stems from the fact "that more women are in positions where they have sales meetings that include golf. . . . They don't want to embarrass themselves."

Sex Discrimination at Golf Clubs

As important as golf has become to many businesswomen, it is still surprisingly difficult for some of them to make it onto a course. Because federal law does not prohibit sex discrimination (or any other sort of discrimination) by private golf clubs, these institutions have been able to keep women off their courses. Many private courses still have rules designed to keep women from playing golf on Saturday and Sunday mornings—the most popular golfing times of the week. Often, the clubs designate one "Ladies Day" a week to try to compensate for their discriminatory practices. Ladies Day is usually Tuesday, the least popular golfing day of the week.

Such practices not only keep women from playing golf but do not allow them the same business opportunities as men. Some states have taken legal steps to improve the situation. Minnesota denies tax breaks to private golf courses that discriminate against women and minorities. In 1992, Michigan amended its civil rights act to include private clubs under antidiscrimination provisions. The Wisconsin legislature is considering revoking the liquor licenses of private clubs that restrict women from playing on weekends.

For Critical Analysis:

Should the federal law that protects private clubs from setting their own membership policies be reconsidered in light of their discriminatory practices?

SOURCE: Information from "Women's Work Is on the Links," *Fortune*, June 3, 1991, p. 15; "Forging Links among Executive Women," *Working Women*, June 1994, p. 15; B. Kaberline, "Women Stepping Up in Business Are Learning to Step Up to the Tee," *Kansas City Business Journal*, July 16–22, 1993, p. 55; and R. Hillberg, "Restrictions at Private Golf Clubs Are Teeing Off Plenty of Women," *Los Angeles Times*, January 6, 1994, p. A5.

Hawaii, Wisconsin, Vermont, New Jersey, Minnesota, and Connecticut), plus the District of Columbia and more than a hundred cities, do, however, forbid discrimination on that basis. The issue has been an inflammatory one for local communities. In 1992, both Oregon and Colorado considered highly controversial initiatives to deny protected-class status to gay men and lesbians; the ballot measure passed in Colorado (though the amendment was eventually struck down as unconstitutional) and failed in Oregon. Voters from the city of Austin, Texas—considered a liberal college town—overwhelmingly overturned an ordinance granting health insurance to unmarried partners of city employees.

"DON'T ASK, DON'T TELL" POLICY

Despite the protection against discrimination offered by a few state and local governments to gay men and lesbians, it would appear that a *de facto* "don't ask, don't tell" policy exists in many parts of the private sector. It seems that gay males or lesbians usually take a risk in deciding to reveal their sexual orientation at work, and often these individuals must rely on the judicial system for protection if this action causes them to suffer discrimination.

The legal system is not infallible, however. In 1991 a federal judge in Atlanta upheld the firing of attorney Robin Shahar from the Georgia attorney general's office in a case that appeared to many to be discriminatory. Shahar had been offered a position in the state's Department of Law before her employer discovered she planned to take part in a religious wedding ceremony with her lesbian partner. The employer withdrew the job offer, citing worries about how Shahar would affect morale in his office. Judge Richard Freeman decided that Shahar's constitutional rights were outweighed by the employer's concerns for an efficient workplace.[24]

CHANGES IN WORKPLACE ATTITUDES

The overall situation is changing for gay and lesbian employees in the private sector. More than sixty major companies—including Microsoft, Levi Strauss, Starbucks Coffee, and Warner Brothers—offer "domestic partnership" benefits such as health care and bereavement leave to gay and lesbian employees. More than a quarter of the Fortune 500 companies have antidiscrimination policies protecting gay men and lesbians. Furthermore, gay and lesbian employees have formed employee groups at Walt Disney Company, AT&T, Johnson & Johnson, and a number of other companies[25] (see *Company Focus: Intel Corporation* on page 430). Ed Mickens, who publishes a newsletter on gay and lesbian employment issues, hopes that many businesses are coming to understand that policies aimed at improving the status of gay and lesbian employees "increase productivity, loyalty, and improve harmony."[26]

AFFIRMATIVE ACTION

Title VII and equal opportunity regulations were designed to reduce or eliminate discriminatory practices with respect to hiring, retaining, and promoting employees. To put some teeth into the new legislation, President Lyndon B. Johnson (1963–1968) applied the concept of **affirmative action** in 1965. Affirmative action programs attempt to make amends for past patterns of discrimination by giving qualified minorities and women preferential treatment in hiring and promotion.

By the early 1970s, Labor Department regulations imposing numerical employment goals and timetables for affirmative action had been applied to every company that did more than $10,000 worth of business of any sort with the federal government. The courts and the EEOC also required some companies to produce affirmative action plans because of past discrimination.

---

24. W. Lambert, "Georgia Agency Can Bar Lesbian from Employment, Judge Rules," *Wall Street Journal*, October 14, 1993, p. B12.
25. E. Iwata, "Gay Hurdles Ease," *Orange County Register*, February 27, 1995, p. D6.
26. L. F. Kaplan, "Gay Friendly Policies Pay Off," *USA Today*, June 7, 1994, p. 1B.

COMPANY FOCUS: INTEL CORPORATION

INTEL'S GAY AND LESBIAN SUPPORT GROUP

When Liz Parrish, a marketing manager at Intel Corporation's headquarters in Santa Clara, California, returned from the 1993 Gay March on Washington, D.C., she decided to make a difference in the way her employer perceived and treated gay and lesbian employees. Her plan was to create a support group for gay men and lesbians who worked at the computer-chip manufacturing firm. The initial reaction among Intel's management and other employees was not positive. Parrish persevered, however, and in 1995 the company endorsed its first employee group for gay, lesbian, and bisexual workers.

Nationwide Progress

Intel is not alone in adopting a more tolerant stance when it comes to homosexual workers. Over a quarter of the Fortune 500 companies in the United States have antidiscrimination policies that include sexual orientation. About 250 public and private organizations offered full medical benefits to same-sex partners in 1995, up from only five companies six years earlier.

Jeff Howard, of the Northwest Gay, Lesbian, Bisexual, and Transgender Employee Network, attributes this change of attitude in the business community to a growing aggressiveness in gay and lesbian employees. "People can see that we work, pay taxes, and that we will insist on equal rights in all facets of our life, including one of the most important—in the workplace." Noting that Intel had never enjoyed the reputation of being a particularly tolerant firm, Howard added, "When a company as conservative as Intel formally acknowledges their gay and lesbian employees, it indicates that gay issues are being recognized as important in conducting business."

IGLOBE

Intel Gay, Lesbian, or Bisexual Employees (IGLOBE), formed by Parrish in 1993, is the only member group of the Northwest Network with a corporate endorsement. Originally, there was some controversy concerning the $1,000 contribution Intel makes every year toward IGLOBE's activities fund, along with the permission the group received to meet on company property and post fliers on company billboards. Segments of Intel's community balked at the idea of a company-sponsored group whose membership was based solely on sexual orientation.

Parrish counters that heterosexual employees do not realize the degree to which the "straight view" dominates Intel's corporate culture. "People think they don't bring their sexuality into the workplace, but they do—whether they wear their wedding ring or put a photo of their partner on their desk," she says. "It's very uncomfortable to a gay person to dispel that assumption."

Donna Allen Taylor, corporate diversity manager for Intel, was instrumental in convincing management to indorse IGLOBE. Although she would still not describe the company as progressive when it comes to diversity, Taylor calls IGLOBE part of a company effort to get "more sophisticated about building an environment where people can be more effective."

Improving Productivity

Taylor echoes the sentiments of many diversity consultants who believe that antidiscrimination policies help create a productive work force. The reaction of IGLOBE members seems to underline this contention. Sherman Tame, who works in Intel's sales and marketing department, says IGLOBE helps his morale: "When you work in an environment that's pretty stressful and you can't be yourself, it makes [work situations] pretty awkward." He adds, "So this is kind of nice because you realize you're not the only one."

The New Bottom Line

Business activists hope that steps like the one taken by Intel will dispel the notion that antidiscrimination and diversity programs exist for political, not economic, reasons. "These are not radical, left-wing, earth-mama kinds of companies," says one. "These are very sober-eyed businessmen from traditional industries who understand from a strictly bottom line perspective this makes sense."

SOURCE: C. Gonzalez, "Out and About at Intel," *Portland Oregonian*, April 30, 1995, p. F1.

REACTIONS TO AFFIRMATIVE ACTION

By the early 1990s, 5.3 percent of African Americans, 3.2 percent of Hispanics, and 2 percent of Asian Americans held managerial positions, compared with less than 1 percent for each minority before affirmative action programs spread.[27] (For an industry-by-industry breakdown of some of the effects of affirmative action, see *Exhibit 14–3* on page 432.) Affirmative action programs have resulted in much controversy, however, particularly when they result in what is frequently called **reverse discrimination**—discrimination against "majority" workers, such as white males. Opponents of affirmative action often point out that the restrictions placed on white workers are just as discriminatory as the practices that have been applied to minorities in the past.

Affirmative Action and U.S. Corporations In the 1980s, U.S. corporations generally welcomed affirmative action guidelines. In a sense, antibias hiring laws gave companies a blueprint to follow that would assure them protection from discrimination suits. In the 1990s, some businesses around the United States have begun to question the wisdom of the policy.

Part of the reasons for this are purely economic. Many companies are reducing their staffs, which makes it more difficult to reserve certain positions for members of minority groups. On the same principle, a large corporation has many jobs to choose among in complying with federal affirmative action guidelines, but small businesses have fewer options.[28]

Quite obviously, the backlash against affirmative action in business, however, is sparked mainly by the attitudes of employees and employers themselves. After all, many of the 49 percent of Californians who indicated in a 1995 poll by the *Los Angeles Times* that they disapproved of affirmative action programs also go to work and take their opinions with them.[29] An increasing number of white men are bringing up complaints in private meetings with their employers and even at company meetings.[30]

Some businesses have responded to these concerns with unenthusiastic implementation of their affirmative action policies. Out of incompetence or even deliberate action, a few employers do not give the proper support, training, or guidance to new minority employees. This leaves such employees with little hope of success, lessens their self-esteem, and increases tensions in the workplace. Furthermore, some businesses blame their bad decisions in hiring and promotion on a "quota system" imposed by the federal government. In reality, situations in which management and minority groups are partners in creating a better working environment are relatively rare.

Legal Changes in Affirmative Action Political and legal support for affirmative action, like support from the business community, also seems to be eroding in the 1990s, and the consequences for businesses, especially small ones, are far-reaching. In 1995, the Supreme Court ruled five to four that Congress must meet rigorous standards to justify any contracting or hiring practices based on race. In the majority opinion, Justice Sandra Day O'Connor wrote that "strict scrutiny of all government racial classifications is essential" to distinguish between affirmative action programs that redress historical

---

27. C. Yang, "A 'Race-Neutral' Helping Hand?" *Business Week*, February 27, 1995, p. 120.
28. T. Loughran, "Corning Tries to Break the Glass Ceiling: Can Corning Achieve Its Ambitious Affirmative Actions Goals?" *Business and Society Review*, Winter 1991, p. 52.
29. L. Stammer, "Mahony Calls for No Retreat from Affirmative Action Politics," *Wall Street Journal*, June 6, 1995, p. A3.
30. J. Kaufman, "How Workplaces May Look without Affirmative Action," *Wall Street Journal*, March 20, 1995, p. B1.

▼ **EXHIBIT 14–3 Women and Minorities in Management Roles, by Industry**

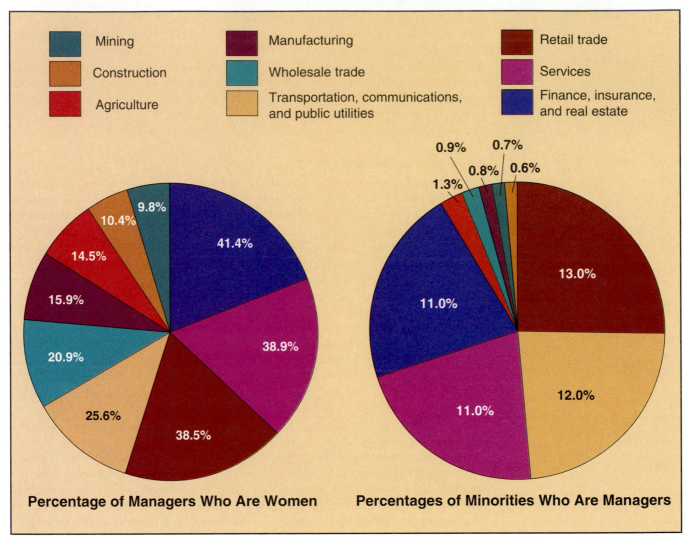

Percentage of Managers Who Are Women

Percentages of Minorities Who Are Managers

SOURCE: Federal Glass Ceiling Commission.

wrongs and programs that "are in fact motivated by illegitimate notions of racial inferiority or simple racial politics"[31] (see *Exhibit 14–4*).

This decision affects hundreds of thousands of businesses. In 1994, the government directed $14.4 billion worth of contracts to minority businesses in keeping with affirmative action policies. The Defense Department alone paid minority firms $6.1 billion for services, and over 100,000 businesses and universities with federal contracts of more than $50,000 are required to have "goals and timetables" for minority hiring.

Randy Pech, a Colorado Springs highway guardrail subcontractor whose lawsuit led to the Supreme Court's decision, challenged a Transportation Department policy that

---

31. P. M. Barrett, "Not Affirmed: Supreme Court Ruling Imperils U.S. Programs of Racial Preference," *Wall Street Journal*, June 13, 1995, p. A1.

▼ **EXHIBIT 14–4**
How the Supreme Court's 1995 Ruling on Federal Preference Programs Could Affect Corporate Affirmative Action Programs

Still Acceptable	• Voluntary hiring and promotion goals for women and minorities.
	• Advertising job openings in publications targeting minorities.
	• Recruiting on predominately minority campuses.
In Question	• Reserving jobs for women and minorities.
	• Special arrangements with recruiters to bring in only minorities.
	• Plans based on federal mandates for aggressive minority

SOURCE: *Business Week,* June 26, 1995, p. 37.

provides incentives to road contractors that give more than 10 percent of their subcontracting work to "disadvantaged firms." Said Pech of the circumstances leading to his suit, "It's not fair when I'm the low bidder." Many owners of small businesses agree with Pech that affirmative action regulations place an unfair burden on their ability to compete. They plan to use the Supreme Court's decision in Pech's case to take similar action.[32]

Alternatives to Affirmative Action Because of the divisive nature of the debate over affirmative action, not to mention the voting power of its opponents, business and government officials are looking for alternatives. One that has been gaining in popularity because of its supposedly race-neutral characteristics is the concept of a **needs-based system** that would redistribute the benefits of affirmative action based on income, or lack thereof, instead of race and gender.

Proponents believe a needs-based system would still benefit minorities, who are statistically poorer than whites, and at the same time take some of the sting out of the debate. Others, however, believe that low-income whites would overwhelm minorities under such a system. In 1993, 20.3 million white households earned under $25,000, compared with 6.7 million black households and 4 million Hispanic households. "You'd have an awful lot of needy whites taking the place of blacks," points out Abigail Thernstrom of the conservative Manhattan Institute for Policy Research.[33]

Echoing another cultural trend of the mid-1990s, Professor Lawrence H. Fuchs of Brandeis University proposes eliminating affirmative action benefits for new immigrants, who he feels have not suffered sufficient discrimination in the United States to warrant protection. Critics of this idea assert that trying to quantify who has suffered more discrimination raises countless practical, if not ethical, questions.

The African American community has responded to the lack of progress made under affirmative action with a stronger commitment to self-help. This attitude can be seen in the growth of historically African American colleges, whose enrollment expanded 25 percent from 1986 to 1992, compared with a 13.8 percent rise over the same period at all U.S. institutions of higher learning.[34] A similar pattern seems to have emerged in the business community. A mid-1990s study of employment patterns among small businesses within twenty-eight large metropolitan areas showed that although more than 93 percent

32. *Ibid.*
33. Yang, *op. cit.*, p. 121.
34. *Ibid.*

of the African American business employers relied on minorities to fill 50 percent or more of their jobs, nearly 60 percent of the nonminority employers had no minority employees.[35]

The most promising alternative action—and the one that relies the least on formal plans or government—will come about of its own volition as the demographic makeup of the American population continues to evolve through diversity.[36]

DIVERSITY

Patricia Fleming, director of affirmative action at Eastman Kodak Company, says, "If affirmative action wasn't legislated, we'd still continue with our goal of building a diverse work force." A closer look at the changing makeup of the U.S. work force helps explain Kodak's goal:

▼ **White men are now a minority in the work force, and 85 percent of new recruits between 1995 and 2000 will be women and nonwhite men.**[37]

Companies with a reputation for producing nonwhite, nonmale managers will have a competitive advantage in recruiting top prospects from the increasingly multicultural pool of prospective managers. Furthermore, minority managers may be more attuned to the needs of minority customers—who are also growing at a proportionally more rapid rate. Companies that do not create a diverse workplace may find themselves severely limited.

---

35. T. Bates, "A New Kind of Business," *Inc.*, July 1, 1994, p. 23.
36. T. R. Roosevelt, Jr., "From Affirmative Action to Affirming Diversity," *Harvard Business Review*, March–April 1990, p. 107.
37. "Affirmative Action: Why Bosses Like It," *Economist*, March 11, 1995, p. 29.

Many companies besides Kodak are stating their commitment to diversity. At AT&T, the corporate education and training center added a course on diversity in response to requests from its business entities. DuPont has instituted programs on career management for minorities, a program specifically for the professional development of women, a course on managing diversity for managers, and a course entitled "Women and Men as Colleagues." At Mobil Corporation, a special executive committee chooses female and minority employees who show potential and moves them from staff positions to higher-paying jobs with more responsibility and better advancement prospects.[38]

Indeed, the question for many businesses is not whether to commit themselves to a culturally diverse work force but how to do so. In some areas, the education system is helping businesses in this effort by providing well-prepared graduates; the American Association of Collegiate Schools of Business recently moved to require diversity training in business administration curricula. The most effective diversity activity, however, is still taking place within the firms themselves (see *Company Focus: US West, Inc.*).

AGE DISCRIMINATION

Affirmative action programs were designed in part to eliminate discrimination based on race or gender. Discrimination, however, may also be based on age. Age discrimination is potentially the most widespread form of discrimination, because anyone—regardless of race or gender—could be a victim at some point. This issue will also become more relevant as the number of persons who are sixty-five years old or older increases in the United States over the next fifty years (see *Exhibit 14–5* on page 437).

The Age Discrimination in Employment Act (ADEA) of 1967, as amended, prohibits employment discrimination on the basis of age against individuals forty to sixty-five years of age. (In 1978, the ceiling was eliminated.) The act was recently amended to prohibit mandatory retirement for nonmanagerial workers. For the act to apply, an employer must have twenty or more employees, and interstate commerce must be affected by the employer's business activities.

The act is similar to Title VII in that it offers protection against both intentional (disparate-treatment) age discrimination and unintentional (disparate-impact) age discrimination. If a plaintiff can prove that his or her age was a determining reason for an employer's treatment, the employer will be held liable under the ADEA unless the allegedly discriminatory practice was due to some legitimate and nondiscriminatory business reason.

CUTTING COSTS

Age discrimination becomes especially tempting to companies when the economic environment forces them to search for ways to trim their payrolls. U.S. corporations let go as many as 1,500 workers a day in the early 1990s.[39] Older, highly paid employees—particularly those who will be retiring in a few years—are often vulnerable to such layoffs, because company managers want to keep younger, lower-paid workers, who are expected to do more work for less money.

---

38. C. Deinard, *Workforce Diversity: Practitioners Responses* (Boston: Harvard University Business School, 1991), pp. 4–6.
39. L. Doup, "Older Workers Fired from Jobs Are Firing Back," *Miami Herald*, August, 29, 1993, p. 4J.

COMPANY FOCUS: US WEST, INC.

MANAGING DIVERSITY AT US WEST

US West achieved a rare distinction in the first half of the 1990s: the telecommunications firm was named one of the sixty best companies in the United States for women employees by *Working Woman*, one of the "fifty best companies for blacks" by *Black Enterprise*, and one of the top twenty companies for Hispanics by *Hispanic Business*. Such accolades reflect a commitment to workplace diversity by US West management.

Pluralism at US West

US West was formed as a "Baby Bell" in 1984 after the breakup of the Bell System. It was in 1977, however, that CEO Jack McAllister introduced "sensitivity training" to the employees at Northwest Bell, as the company was then called. McAllister's strong influence from the top has led to a cultural diversity program—known as *pluralism* in company offices—that covers all the company's hiring practices, as well as all promotions. To ensure that pluralism is taken seriously by managers, US West links compensation for its top employees directly to the level of pluralism in their staffs.

If a deficiency is discovered, the company quickly creates a program to deal with it. In the late 1980s, for example, the firm's human resources department noticed that there was a lack of nonwhite women in director-level positions. US West quickly introduced the Accelerated Development Program for Women of Color. Overall, women hold over 20 percent of the jobs at US West's top salary level, one of the highest percentages in a major U.S. company.

The compensation of managers is also tied to participation in Leading a Diverse Workforce, a company-sponsored three-day diversity training program. On the employee level, the company offers eight different resource groups that provide a forum for different minority groups at US West to communicate with management. These groups, including US West Women, Voice of Many Feathers (for Native American workers), and the Black Employees Association, have a chance each year to meet with more than forty top executives to iron out any differences that may have sprung up in the day-to-day work environment.

A Philosophy, Not a Program

US West applies the same pluralistic standards to companies it does business with, and it has stopped working with employee search firms that do not supply it with a diverse mix of job candidates. To make sure the company maintains its own high standards, each department at US West is subjected to a yearly audit to check that every effort is made to diversify its work force.

Despite the attention US West has received for its policies, Darlene Siedschlaw, the company's director of EEO/affirmative action, says the program has not reached a static phase. She would even disagree that her company has a pluralism *program*, because "a program has a start and a finish." Siedschlaw adds, "What we have is a philosophy called pluralism and what we're trying to do is change the texture of this corporation, and that's ongoing."

The New Bottom Line

For a telephone company like US West, with operations in twenty-seven states and eight countries, work force diversity is a necessity. The closer any company can model the diversity in the workplace to the diversity in the community being served, the stronger that company's economic position can become.

SOURCE: Information from J. Rundles, "US West Drives Progressive Human Resources Policy from the Top Down," *Colorado Business*, July 1, 1991, p. 22; and "US West's Effort to Manage Its Changing Work Force, Which Began in the Mid-1970s, Has Paid Off," *Personnel Journal*, January 1992, p. 57.

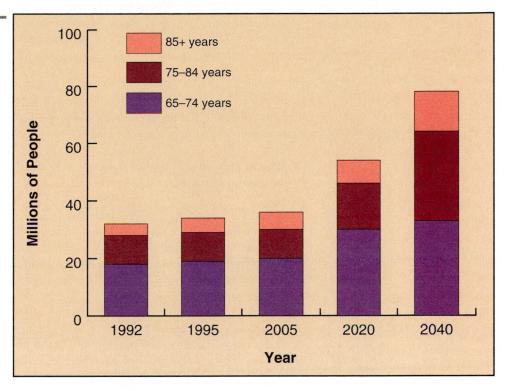

▼ EXHIBIT 14–5 Population Projections: Persons Aged Sixty-Five and Older

SOURCE: U.S. Department of Commerce, *Statistical Abstract of the United States* (Washington, D.C.: U.S. Government Printing Office, 1994).

During the 1993 fiscal year, the Equal Employment Opportunity Commission received 19,884 age discrimination complaints—up 32 percent from four years earlier[40]—even though it prosecutes comparatively few of these cases itself. Most potential plaintiffs must choose between litigating their claims themselves and doing nothing at all.

The number of age discrimination complaints will continue to grow. "It does not take a rocket scientist to realize demographics are going to drive this issue," says Harvard law professor Charles Fried. He adds that although the issue has not "caught the imagination of the academic world in the same way as race and sex discrimination, it is going to be the bread and butter of a lot of lawyers."[41]

AMERICANS WITH DISABILITIES ACT

After Charles H. Wessel was diagnosed with inoperable brain cancer, he found himself, after 30 years in the business, summarily fired from his job as executive director of the Chicago based AIC Security Investigations, Ltd. For most of this nation's history, Wessel would have had no recourse. The passage of the Americans with Disabilities Act (ADA) of 1990, which became effective in 1992, changed that. The ADA grants basic civil rights

---

40. T. J. Lueck, "Job Loss Anger: Age Bias Cases Soar in Region," *New York Times*, December 12, 1993, p. 5.
41. *Ibid.*

protection to an estimated 40 million workers with disabilities, including Wessel, who in 1993 won $572,000 from AIC in the first ruling under the new act.[42]

Wʜᴀᴛ Is ᴀ Dɪsᴀʙɪʟɪᴛʏ?

The relatively new law, like earlier civil rights legislation, was designed to eliminate discriminatory hiring and firing practices that prevent otherwise qualified workers from fully participating in the labor force. In short,

▼ **The ADA is broadly drafted to define a disabled person as a person with a physical or mental impairment that "substantially limits" his or her everyday activities.**

The act defines disability as a "physical or mental impairment that substantially limits one or more of the major life activities of such individuals." In total, the law covers more than nine hundred disabilities, including such physical disabilities as heart disease, cancer, muscular dystrophy, cerebral palsy, paraplegia, and diabetes. A number of people argue that ADA coverage is *too* broad, thus allowing employees to take advantage of the legislation at the private sector's expense.

Especially controversial has been protection of mental disabilities, which are the second and third most common causes of ADA claims (see *Exhibit 14–6*). Given the difficulty the medical community has in defining psychological ailments, it is not surprising that firms, courts, and clinical psychologists are having a difficult time agreeing on what kinds of impairments affect "major life activities." In 1992, an employee who had been fired by Eastman-Kodak Company for insubordination sued the company under the ADA, claiming that his termination was linked to manic depression.[43] (After four years, the case was still in the courts.) In 1995, a former executive at Coca-Cola, Inc., won a $7.1 million jury award from the company for being fired while undergoing treatment for alcoholism (see *Managing Social Issues—Ethics/Social Responsibility: Substance Abuse and the ADA*). Because both depression and alcoholism can be interpreted as mental illnesses under the ADA's broad definition, both lawsuits were legally justified.

▼ **EXHIBIT 14–6**
ADA Claims Received during its First Three Years

Impairment Cited in Claim	Total Number	Percentage of Total
Back injury	8,738	19.4
Neurological	5,354	11.9
Emotion/psychiatric	5,243	11.6
Injury to extremities (arms, legs, etc.)	3,500	7.8
Heart problems	2,700	4.5
Diabetes	1,608	3.6
Substance abuse	1,593	3.5
Total	**45,053**	

SOURCE: Equal Employment Opportunity Commission.

42. C. Yang, "Business Has to Find a New Meaning for 'Fairness,'" *Business Week*, April 12, 1993, p. 72.
43. J. Simmons, "ADA Suit Focuses on Mental Illness," *Cincinnati Business Courier*, May 1, 1995, p. 1.

⑤ MANAGING SOCIAL ISSUES

ETHICS/SOCIAL RESPONSIBILITY: SUBSTANCE ABUSE AND THE ADA

Of all the issues covered under the Americans with Disabilities Act (ADA), the definition of *substantial risk* is one of the most troubling for many business owners. Under the law, employers may reject job applicants or fire employees if their medical conditions pose a "substantial risk" to the health and safety of co-workers or customers. The ADA's definition of risk—the likelihood that an event will occur over a certain period of time—is vague, and employers must be aware of the intricacies of the definition before taking action in instances that concern substance abuse.

Exxon's Substance Abuse Policy

In some cases, risk is obvious. A company can justifiably refuse to hire a blind person for a truck-driving position. With substance abuse, however, which has been defined as an illness under the ADA, risk is not so simple. Sometimes, the determination of risk may even seem contradictory. Following the crash in Alaska of the *Exxon Valdez* oil tanker under the control of a captain who had been drinking on the job, Exxon received a great deal of criticism for not screening employees properly. In response to the negative publicity, the oil company instituted a policy that excluded employees with histories of substance abuse from "safety-sensitive" positions, such as tanker captain. After two Exxon workers were demoted for this reason in June 1995, the Equal Employment Opportunity Commission (EEOC) sued Exxon for not establishing the substantial risk regarding the demotions.

Lawsuit against Coca-Cola

One week after the EEOC's suit against Exxon, a jury awarded Coca-Cola employee Robert Burch a $7.1 million award for alleged discrimination under the ADA. (The ADA limits punitive damages to $300,000, so it was expected that a judge would reduce the actual recovery.) Burch, an executive in the company's fountain division, was fired a month after he informed his boss that he had been diagnosed as an alcoholic and was undergoing treatment. Burch claims that he had been offered two promotions before knowledge of his condition became known. "Basically, they fired me for trying to get help," Burch says.

Coca-Cola denies this charge, insisting that Burch was fired not because he was an alcoholic but because of alleged violent behavior, including making threatening remarks at a colleague's farewell party in September 1993. Three days following that incident, he was admitted to an inpatient treatment program at the Dallas Charter Healthcare Systems. When he was fired two months later, he had outpatient status and had not returned to work. "Employers who have workers with alcohol or drug problems have to give them a chance if they've undergone treatment," said a former assistant general counsel for the EEOC of Burch's case. "An employer simply cannot have a blanket policy that someone with a history of drug abuse or alcoholism should be targeted for dismissal." A lawyer who edits *Disability Law Compliance*, a newsletter, disagrees: "You can't hold alcoholics to a different standard than any other employee. . . . An employer [should not] have to accept disruptive outbursts of anger as a form of reasonable accommodation."

For Critical Analysis:

Do you feel that Exxon is ethically justified in its substance abuse policy? Do you feel that Coca-Cola was ethically justified in firing Burch? How does the EEOC's position on these issues affect employers' attempts to curb workplace violence—such as policies of zero tolerance—which we discussed in Chapter 13?

SOURCE: R. Frank and A. Markels, "Coca-Cola Company Loses ADA Case for Firing Alcoholic in Treatment," *Wall Street Journal*, July 3, 1995, p. B5; and H. M. Sandler, "ADA and Occupational Health: A Status Report," *Occupational Hazards*, October 1, 1993, p. 55.

REASONABLE ACCOMMODATION

The law prohibits employers from refusing to hire persons with disabilities who are otherwise qualified for a particular position. An employer may have to make reasonable accommodation for an applicant with disabilities, such as installing ramps for a wheelchair. The law does not, however, require that unqualified applicants with disabilities be hired.

Because the law does not define what it means by **reasonable accommodation,** small businesses have expressed concern that their responsibility for making the workplace more accessible to employees with disabilities could subject them to potentially staggering costs. To clarify these potential responsibilities of employers, the law provides illustrative examples. Reasonable accommodation might include such things as more flexible working hours, new job assignments, and improved training materials (see the *Case—Marriott: Accommodating Employees with Disabilities*—at the end of this chapter). Employers who do not wish to make these accommodations must demonstrate that they would cause "undue hardship." The law offers no uniform standards for identifying an undue hardship other than saying it is the imposition of a "significant difficulty or expense" on the employer.

The ease with which individual companies can handle such costs varies. Larger companies are better able to handle the costs of complying with the ADA than are smaller ones. Although the costs of implementing the ADA have been vigorously debated, it does appear that the ADA has had a significant impact on the costs incurred by businesses. All new buildings under construction and all existing buildings being renovated, for example, must have elevators if they have three or more stories and 3,000 square feet per floor. Such costs may be offset, however, if these changes help the nation to reduce appreciably the estimated $60 billion it pays in disability benefits each year.

In fact, when business managers complain about the ADA, costs of compliance are usually not the first subject they bring up. The main worry seems to be that workers will use the ADA to avoid working at their potential on the job. Nearly one in every ten ADA complaints concerns mental illness, and mental-health specialists insist that workers suffering from stress or depression should be given less strenuous chores and time off for visits to the doctor. "If every employee escapes the hardest part of the job by claiming stress, we're in trouble," remarks one top management lawyer.[44]

The only category of ADA complaints larger than mental illness is back injuries, which appear in nearly 20 percent of the cases. The law requires that people with back injuries be put on light duty if possible, at the same salary. Proponents of the ADA say this will eventually save companies from workers' compensation claims. As the owner of a forty-five-employee marble production plant asks, however, "What do you do if you're a small company and all the jobs require lifting?"[45]

PREEMPLOYMENT PHYSICALS

Employers can no longer require persons with disabilities to submit to preemployment physicals unless these exams are required of all other applicants. They are also not permitted to ask job applicants about the nature or extent of any known disabilities. Employers can condition an offer of employment on the employee's successfully passing a medical examination. Any resulting disqualifications must result from the discov-

---

44. Yang, "Business Has to Find a New Meaning for 'Fairness.'" p. 72.
45. *Ibid.*

ery of problems that render the applicant unable to perform the job for which he or she was hired.

DANGEROUS WORKERS

An employer may defend a decision not to hire a worker with disabilities if the applicant poses a "direct threat to the health or safety" of his or her co-workers. This danger must be substantial and immediate; it cannot be speculative. A worker who has hallucinations that cause him or her to attack co-workers, for example, would probably be considered such a threat. Any medical diagnosis of the applicant's condition by company experts may be challenged by the applicant. New federal regulations also permit employers to terminate the employment of qualified workers whose disabilities are such that they may pose a danger to their own personal well-being.

REMEDIES

Persons with disabilities who wish to file a claim under the ADA may sue for many of the same remedies contained in Title VII of the Civil Rights Act of 1964. They may seek damages, reinstatement, and back pay. The plaintiff may begin these actions only after pursuing the claim through the Equal Employment Opportunity Commission. Repeat violators may be ordered to pay fines of up to $100,000.

CIVIL RIGHTS ACT OF 1991

The U.S. courts have generally been at the forefront of efforts to expand the legal rights and protections afforded to members of ethnic and racial minorities. During the 1960s and 1970s, the courts interpreted existing laws, such as Title VII, broadly in upholding affirmative action programs that arguably discriminated against white men (called *reverse discrimination*). In the 1980s, however, the courts became increasingly conservative as they reflected a shift throughout society. This judicial conservatism culminated in a series of 1989 rulings by the Supreme Court that, according to civil rights activists, made it much more difficult for plaintiffs to prevail in employment discrimination claims. Because social activists no longer believed that the courts could be counted on to expand existing civil rights protections, they turned to Congress and requested that it in effect overrule the 1989 Supreme Court decisions.

PROTECTION UNDER THE ACT

President George Bush signed the Civil Rights Act of 1991, in effect endorsing Congress's attempt to reverse all or part of the controversial 1989 Supreme Court employment discrimination decisions. The new law altered the civil rights landscape, particularly for women seeking to redress discrimination claims. In particular, the law made it possible for women to obtain more damages for a wide variety of discriminatory practices, including sexual harassment and company rules limiting the jobs available to fertile women.

The legislative reversal of these Supreme Court decisions was seen as a key element in the attempt by the bill's sponsors to bolster the legal protection available to women, minorities, and people faced with age discrimination in the workplace. Although the Civil Rights Act of 1991 does not expressly encourage quotas, it does require companies whose hiring practices may appear to be neutral to demonstrate the necessity of their business practices if they have a "disparate impact" on women and minorities. In other words, an employee no longer has to prove that the challenged employment practices are not a "business necessity." Instead, the *employer* must demonstrate that the particular practices *are* necessary.

For example, a construction company denies Maureen employment because she is under six feet tall. This arguably neutral job requirement has a disparate impact on women, because far more men than women are six feet tall or taller. Under the Civil Rights Act of 1991, the construction company would have to demonstrate that its height requirement was necessary for the successful performance of the job. Simply stated, the Civil Rights Act of 1991 shifted the burden of proof from the *employee* to the *employer*.

DAMAGES

Under the Civil Rights Act of 1991, women and persons with disabilities are permitted to sue employers for increased damages. Before the Civil Rights Act of 1991, only persons filing racial discrimination claims against their employers could recover punitive damages. Note, however, that the sum of the compensatory and punitive damages is limited by the statute to specific amounts against specific employers—ranging from $50,000 against employers with one hundred or fewer employees to $300,000 against employers with more than five hundred employees. Sponsors of the Civil Rights Act of 1991 have indicated that future legislation will be introduced in Congress to remove these damage caps, thus bringing sexual discrimination remedies in line with those available to plaintiffs alleging racial discrimination.

IMPACT OF THE ACT

Because most large companies have already implemented affirmative action hiring programs and configured their staffs to ensure compliance with earlier civil rights laws, the Civil Rights Act of 1991 should not impose enormous new administrative burdens on them. Instead,

▼ **The real impact of the law is likely to be felt among small and midsize businesses having more than fifteen employees.**

These companies are large enough to attract suits by litigants but may be relatively unfamiliar with the procedures that should be implemented to avoid liability for such claims. Because small and midsize firms rarely have the financial resources to engage in protracted suits, they may be tempted to settle most cases out of court. In fact, firms with fewer than fifteen employees may decide not to expand, thereby avoiding potential liability under the law.

THE DELICATE BALANCE

The issue behind all employment discrimination laws, rules, and regulations is individual rights. Nonetheless, on numerous occasions we allow certain individual rights to be compromised because of an overriding group right. The Americans with Disabilities Act does not, for example, require *every* employer to accommodate *every* single person with a disability. Rather, the law allows for *reasonable* accommodation only. After all, many smaller employers would be forced into bankruptcy if they had to spend all their resources accommodating all prospective employees with disabilities.

The delicate balance that corporate leaders must undertake involves this trade-off between what is good for the individual and what is good for the whole organization. Certainly, managers must follow the law. Indeed, management is wise to keep everyone regularly informed about changes in the law with respect to workers' individual rights. At times, though, some employers must decide to take a stand. Because they have a duty to keep the company in business, they cannot give in to the requests of every individual worker simply because of fear of being sued by that worker. Because enough corporate decision makers have chosen to take a stand, there are now some judicial restraints on what many observers feel is an excessive exaggeration of employee rights in the workplace.

TERMS AND CONCEPTS FOR REVIEW

Affirmative action 429
Bona fide occupational
qualification (BFOQ) 417
Comparable worth 425
Disparate-impact discrimination
417

Disparate-treatment
discrimination 417
Glass ceiling 426
Needs-based system 433
Reasonable accommodation 440

"Reasonable woman" standard 420
Reverse discrimination 431
Sexual harassment 419

SUMMARY

1. The Civil Rights Act of 1964 and its amendments make it unlawful for employers to discriminate against employees, applicants, and union members on the basis of race, color, national origin, religion, or gender. The 1972 amendments extended coverage to all state and local governments and their associated agencies and subdivisions.

2. Unlike disparate-treatment discrimination, which involves intentional discrimination against a specific group, disparate-impact discrimination occurs when educational or other job requirements result in an employer's work force not reflecting the same percentages of qualified women, minorities, and other protected groups as are in the local labor market.

3. Sexual-harassment occurs when job opportunities, promotions, and the like are conditioned on sexual favors or when an employee is subjected to sexually offensive conduct by supervisors or co-workers. Many companies are now attempting to combat sexual harassment in the workplace by instituting a variety of affirmative steps, such as seminars and training programs designed to sensitize workers to the more common forms of sexual harassment.

4. Most sexual-harassment complaints filed with the Equal Employment Opportunity Commission (EEOC) are not prosecuted. These cases often come down to a question

of who to believe, because the offensive incidents are usually not witnessed by third parties. This sort of situation may present an insurmountable problem for the victim, who must prove that the offensive conduct actually took place.

5. The Pregnancy Discrimination Act of 1978 prohibits the discriminatory treatment of employees on the basis of pregnancy. Pregnant women must be treated, for employment-related purposes, the same as all other similarly capable persons.

6. Some companies have attempted to avoid possible liability for workplace injuries to unborn children by adopting fetal protection policies. These policies prevent women of childbearing age who are fertile from working in certain jobs that might entail exposure to hazardous chemicals, such as lead. The courts have generally struck down these policies as violations of the civil rights laws.

7. Affirmative action programs attempt to make up for past discriminatory practices by giving qualified minorities and women preferential treatment in hiring and promotion.

8. Discrimination against persons on the basis of age is prohibited by the Age Discrimination in Employment Act of 1967. A plaintiff must prove that his or her age was a determining factor in the employer's discriminatory

treatment. The employer will be held liable unless the practice can be justified by a legitimate and nondiscriminatory business reason.

9. The Americans with Disabilities Act (ADA) of 1990 grants basic civil rights to an estimated forty million workers with disabilities. It requires that employers make reasonable accommodation for employees with disabilities but does not require employers to hire persons with disabilities for jobs if they are not qualified for them.

10. Persons with disabilities who sue their employers under the ADA may seek damages, reinstatement, back pay,

and certain other forms of injunctive relief. Prospective litigants must first pursue their claims through the Equal Employment Opportunity Commission.

11. The Civil Rights Act of 1991 was enacted by Congress to counteract the increasingly conservative nature of the United States Supreme Court. The act requires companies whose hiring practices have a disparate impact on women and minorities to demonstrate the necessity of those practices. Women and persons with disabilities may now sue employers for increased damages.

EXERCISES

1. Make a list of those employees who form part of a protected class according to Title VII of the Civil Rights Act of 1964.

2. What is the difference between disparate-treatment discrimination and disparate-impact discrimination? Is the distinction important? Why or why not?

3. What is the difference between sex discrimination and sexual harassment? Why is the distinction important for an employer to understand?

4. Why has the "reasonable person" standard in the law sometimes been altered to become the "reasonable woman" standard?

5. Review Rebecca Thacker's six suggestions for a company's written sexual-harassment policy presented under the heading "A Commitment to Eliminating Sexual Harassment." If you had to pick which of the six was the most important, which one would you choose, and why?

6. If pregnant employees are exposed to hazards that might produce birth defects, most employers would want to protect themselves from potential lawsuits. The Supreme Court, however, has ruled that "women as capable of doing their jobs as their male counterparts may not be forced to choose between having a child and having a job." What, therefore, can and should an employer do when the employer knows that certain types of jobs could possibly harm a fetus?

7. Even under the Equal Pay Act of 1963, wage differentials between men and women are still allowed. What are the justifiable reasons for wage differentials that do not violate the law?

8. Is there any federal legislation that protects people against workplace discrimination on the basis of sexual orientation? If so, what is it?

9. What is the difference between an affirmative action program and a needs-based system?

10. Discuss the significant provisions of Title VII of the Civil Rights Act of 1964. How have those rights been changed by the Civil Rights Act of 1991?

11. Discuss fully which one or more of the following constitutes a violation of the 1964 Civil Rights Act, Title VII, as amended:
   a. Tennington, Inc., is a consulting firm and has ten employees. These employees travel on consulting jobs in seven states. Tennington has an employment record of hiring only white men.
   b. Novo Films, Inc., is making a film about Africa and needs to employ approximately one hundred extras for this film. Novo advertises in all major newspapers in southern California for the hiring of these extras. The ad states that only African Americans need apply.
   c. Chinawa, a major processor of cheese sold throughout the United States, employs one hundred employees at its principal processing plant. The plant is located in Heartland Corners, a city with a population that is 50 percent white; 25 percent African American; and the balance Hispanic, Asian American, and other minorities. Chinawa requires a high school diploma as a condition of employment for its cleanup crew. Three-fourths of the white population in Heartland Corners completes high school, as compared with only one-fourth of the minority groups. Chinawa has an all-white cleaning crew.

12. Several African American employees of the Connecticut Department of Income Maintenance who sought promotion to supervisory positions took the required written examination but failed to pass it. Of all those who took the examination, 54 percent of the African American employees passed it, whereas nearly 80 percent of the white employees who took the test passed. Following the examination, the state of Connecticut promoted eleven African American employees (representing 23 percent of all African American employees) and thirty-five white employees (representing 14 percent of all white employees). Teal and three other African American employees who failed the test sued the state of Connecticut and the Department of Income Maintenance. The employees

asserted that the written test excluded a disproportionate number of African American employees from promotion to supervisory positions and therefore violated Title VII of the Civil Rights Act. The state argued that because a greater percentage of African American employees had been promoted relative to white employees, the test was not discriminatory. Which side was correct?

13. Milton Kizer began working for Lakeway Resort in 1974; his job was maintaining golf carts. During the next decade, he received positive job evaluations and numerous merit pay raises. He was promoted to the position of supervisor of golf cart maintenance at three courses. Then a new employee, McManus, was placed in charge of the golf courses. McManus demoted Kizer, who was over the age of forty, to running one of the three cart facilities, and also froze his salary indefinitely. McManus demoted five other men over the age of forty as well. Another cart facility was placed under the supervision of Roger Rodeman. Later, the cart facilities for three courses were again consolidated, but Rodeman—not Kizer—was put in charge. At the time, Kizer was in his forties, and Rodeman was in his twenties. Rodeman said that "we are going to have to do away with these . . . old and senile" men. Kizer quit and sued Lakeway for employment discrimination. Should he prevail? Explain why or why not.

SELECTED REFERENCES

▶ Arvey, Richard. *Fairness in Selecting Employees.* Reading, Mass.: Addison-Wesley, 1979.

▶ Bourne, C. J. *Race and Sex Discrimination.* London: Sweet & Maxwell, 1993.

▶ Doyle, Brian John. *Disability, Discrimination, and Equal Opportunities: A Comparative Study of the Employment Rights of Disabled Persons.* New York: Mansell, 1995.

▶ Glazer, Nathan. *Affirmative Discrimination.* New York: Basic Books, 1975.

▶ Gunderson, Morley. *Comparable Worth and Gender Discrimination: An International Perspective.* Geneva: International Labour Office, 1994.

▶ Spiegel, Fredelle Zaiman. *Woman's Wages, Women's Worth: Politics, Religion, and Equity.* New York: Consortium, 1994.

▶ Williams, Martha R. and Marcia L. Russell. *ADA Handbook: Employment and Construction Issues Affecting Your Business.* Chicago: Real Estate Education Co., 1993.

RESOURCES ON THE INTERNET

▼ The most information available about discrimination with respect to disabilities is included in the Americans with Disabilities Act document center at

http://janweb.icdi.wvu.edu./kinder

Additional information on the Americans with Disabilities Act is available from the U.S. Department of Justice, Civil Rights Division, at

gopher://justice2.usdoj.gov/11/crt

▼ For perspectives on sexual harassment court opinions, go to the following Web site:

http://www.vix.com/pub/men/ harass/harass.html

▼ For information on government contracts available to minority-run businesses, you can access Fedix/Molis at

http://web.fie/com

Additional information on these government contracts, as well as a wealth of data on business opportunities for minority businesses, is available from the Minority Information Service (USAID). You can access USAID at

http://web.fie.com/web/fed/aid

CASE

MARRIOTT: ACCOMMODATING EMPLOYEES WITH DISABILITIES

Background

When President George Bush signed the Americans with Disabilities Act (ADA) into law in 1990, the reaction from many businesses was decidedly negative. Prior to the enactment of the legislation in July 1992, Americans with disabilities were protected against discrimination by the Rehabilitation Act of 1973 only in public sector jobs and in jobs offered by companies that had grants or contracts with the federal government. The ADA guaranteed the same protections to applicants at all establishments with more than fifteen employees, and it also required employers to make "reasonable accommodation" for employees with disabilities.

In most cases, reasonable accommodation was translated into structural renovations such as ramps (for wheelchairs), in addition to stairways, bathrooms with wheelchair access, and equipment upgrades. Occasionally, the ADA would be applied in what many saw as extreme situations. In Florida, for example, a strip club was ordered to construct a ramp to its stage when a woman with disabilities applied for a job. Such media reports only served to heighten business anxiety over the unreasonable costs of the act. Many managers, instead of immediately complying with the law, tried to instead prove "undue hardship," a provision under the ADA that exempts a facility if compliance can be proved to be unduly expensive or disruptive.

One of the exceptions has been the Washington, D.C.–based Marriott Corporation, a nationwide hotel operator. Even before the ADA went into effect, Marriott was reaping the benefits of its commitment to hiring employees with disabilities. In today's more regulated environment, the hotel chain offers a model for ADA compliance not just for compliance's sake.

Beyond Government Requirements

For the hotel industry, one of the more significant mandates of the ADA is that businesses must make themselves more accessible to people in wheelchairs. Along with widening doorways to thirty-two inches, remodeling restrooms, and adding ramps to entranceways, compliance also requires level floors and the removal of deep shag carpet. When the Los Angeles Airport Marriott underwent renovations in the early 1990s, its management did not need the government to dictate such features. In fact, the one-thousand–room motel was refitted with twenty-seven wheelchair-accessible sleeping rooms. "It was a business decision [to attract consumers with disabilities]," said the hotel's director of marketing. By 1994, 5 to 8 percent of the motel's convention business came from organizations for persons with disabilities.

Marriott was also ahead of the game in hiring workers with disabilities. When the ADA went into effect in 1992, 9,000 of the more than 200,000 Marriott employees had disabilities. The Chicago Marriott has found particular success in the area; a partnership with the International Association of Machinists Center for Administering Rehabilitating and Employment Services (IAM CARES) has proved fruitful in training and placing job applicants with disabilities.

IAM CARES

IAM CARES, based in Upper Marlboro, Maryland, is an international nonprofit organization that joins with businesses to train and employ people with mental-function disabilities, physical disabilities, learning disabilities, or hearing impairments. Because the ADA does not require that a business hire persons with disabilities—only that it not discriminate in hiring a "qualified person" who can perform the "essential functions" of the job—the goal of IAM CARES is to provide persons with disabilities with the skills to be qualified. Consequently, the organization's job-training program, called the Transitional Employment Program (TEP), addresses the lack of job experience, job skills, and job-seeking skills among persons with disabilities. TEP also aims to change the business community's negative attitude toward hiring these potential workers.

Training and Orientation

The partnership between IAM CARES and the Chicago Marriott began in 1985, and since 1987 the two establishments have been training about thirty individuals with disabilities at the hotel each year. The training sessions last a minimum of six weeks, though many of the trainees stay on site for four to six months in order to gain extra experience.

The Chicago Marriott has an extensive network within its human resources department to help the trainees; about 28 Marriott supervisors and 130 employees take part in TEP as "job-buddies." One full-time and two part-time employees of

CASE (CONTINUED)

IAM CARES work in the hotel's human resources department to acclimate the trainees to the work environment, as well as to help the Marriott staff work successfully with the trainees.

These trainees usually work three hours a day and five days a week in positions in which they do not come in contact with the hotel guests. An emphasis is placed on putting the trainees in group situations, where they can establish teamwork skills. Once they graduate from TEP and are hired by the hotel (as nearly one hundred have been), the employees find themselves in a variety of areas, from cleaning rooms with the housekeeping department to handling light paperwork for human resources.

Once a trainee is hired, he or she enters an orientation program along with other new employees. The Chicago Marriott's human resources management sees this as a critical part of creating a comfortable work environment for the workers with disabilities. "It's a good opportunity for them to meet other people who work in the hotel," says Stacy Cataneo, human resources supervisor for the Chicago Marriott. "I don't want any of them to feel as if they're being separated. I want them to feel like any other employee."

The worry in some industry circles is that supervisors who lack specific training on how to relate to workers with disabilities can impede the process. The Chicago Marriott, however, has not found the need for any formal training program for its supervisors. IAM CARES representatives meet with each supervisor individually to provide information and answer questions, and these representatives are available for consultation at any time. Cataneo has found her management team very willing to work with the trainees. "The supervisors may need a lot of explanation as to what the disability is, but once they understand it, it seems that they're really willing and eager to work [with the employee with disabilities]," she says.

Reaping the Benefits

Chicago Marriott executives bristle at the idea that the entire program is designed for ADA compliance. "It obviously assists us in our compliance obligations, but we were way ahead of the curve in regard to ADA," says the hotel's director of human resources, Byron Peterson. He continues, "ADA is a law. What we're doing is morally and ethically responsible."

Initially, however, there were other considerations besides morals and ethics. When IAM CARES and the Chicago Marriott began the training program, many experts were predicting a severe labor shortage for low-paying service jobs. One study in particular—done by the Hudson Institute, a conservative Washington, D.C., think tank—entitled *Workforce 2000*, predicted that such shortages would be prevalent by the turn of the century.

In addition, food service employers such as McDonald's, Burger King, KFC, Hilton, and Marriott were experiencing turnover rates for hourly jobs as high as 250 to 300 percent at the end of the 1980s. At the time, it seemed wise strategy to develop an alternative labor source.

A labor shortage of that magnitude has not come to pass, however, at least at the Chicago Marriott. In an industry with a 50 percent turnover rate a year, the hotel's rate runs at only 32 percent. The human resources department is having no trouble filling any positions that do open, either; it receives two hundred to four hundred applications a week.

In fact, regulatory and economic considerations do not seem to be driving the Chicago Marriott's efforts to recruit workers with disabilities. As the hotel's human resources team points out, these employees have had a number of positive effects on business operations. First of all, employees with disabilities tend to show refreshing job enthusiasm, along with a propensity for hard work and greater job retention times. Their presence also forces managers and supervisors to develop their management skills, such as patience, listening, training, and communicating. The human resources department has found employees with disabilities to be inspirational for their co-workers, which helps morale and improves teamwork. If nothing else, the hotel benefits from free labor while the trainees are still in TEP.

Marriott Accommodations

Employing persons with disabilities is not easy, however. "It's a lot of work," said a human resources manager. As each employee is unique, it takes a great amount of supervision to keep the program efficient. The reason the Chicago Marriott has been so successful, says an IAM CARES employee, is that the program has been endorsed by each level of the hotel—the CEO, human resources, and the direct supervisors.

Such support leads to changes being made quickly and efficiently when the need arises. A bell station job, for example, was modified for a trainee with a mental disability. Instead of helping guests with their luggage, his job was changed to polishing the bell carts. This worker also had trouble understanding the hotel's time-clock system, so the IAM CARES

CASE (CONTINUED)

staff intervened to help him. Workers in the convention-services department were provided with electronic watches so they would know when to move from task to task.

"People have a tendency to look at limitations [of persons with disabilities]," says an IAM CARES executive. "We're not going to put them in an area in which they are going to fail because they can't accomplish a task. But we're going to look at what they can do and work on their capabilities and functional skills and build on that so they can be as independent as possible."

Critical Thinking Questions

1. Is Marriot a valid example of how the ADA can be incorporated into business operations? In other words, what advantages does a hotel have in complying with the ADA as opposed to other, nonservice-oriented companies?

2. Do you accept the contention that ADA compliance is "morally and ethically" necessary for any business organization?

3. What trade-offs does a firm make in ADA compliance?

4. What risks would a company run in trying to hire workers with mental disabilities without the assistance of a group such as IAM CARES?

5. Is there any ethical dilemma inherent in considering workers with mental disabilities as an alternative work force to help the food service industry deal with a labor shortage?

SOURCE: Information from N. Brumback, "Rising to the Challenged," *Restaurant Businesses*, May 1, 1994, p. 186; M. Bordenaro, "ADA Generates Action—and Confusion," *Building Design & Construction*, February 1, 1992, p. 50; and B. Carlino, "Operators Tap Disabled to Ease Labor Shortage," *Nation's Restaurant News*, March 6, 1989, p. 1.

CHAPTER 15

CHAPTER

LABOR UNIONS AND COLLECTIVE BARGAINING

CHAPTER OUTLINE

Introduction

During a speech, then Secretary of Labor Robert Reich voiced worries that U.S. efforts to stay globally competitive were taking too great a toll on the financial security of the middle class. Reich announced that he was beginning a campaign for what he called a "new social contract" between government, business, and citizens. During this speech to the National Alliance of Business in Dallas, Reich said that he hoped private industry could be persuaded to increase the amount of job training offered to employees in order to upgrade the skills of the U.S. work force.[1]

Reich did not once mention the role organized labor would play in this social contract. That unions would go virtually unmentioned in a speech by a U.S. secretary of labor concerning the situation of American workers shows the weaknesses of organized labor in the mid-1990s.

To be sure, labor unions, as well as the government regulations they have influenced, are still operating in our society, and a business that tries to ignore organized labor does so at its own risk. Both labor unions and businesses still must operate within the confines established by statutes regulating employment and labor relations, and these statutes have far-reaching effects on the rights and liabilities of both employers and employees.

Until the early 1930s, laws at the federal and state levels generally favored management. Unions were discouraged by employers—sometimes forcibly. Early legislation protecting the rights of employees, such as the National War Labor Board, which operated during World War I, was often temporary. Moreover, this type of legislation was frequently restricted to a particular industry. The Railway Labor Act of 1926, for example, required railroad companies and their employees to attempt to make employment agreements through representatives chosen by each side. Beginning in 1932, however, a number of statutes were enacted that greatly increased employees' rights to join unions, to engage in collective bargaining, to receive retirement and income security benefits, to be protected against various discriminatory practices, and to have a safe place to work.

At the heart of labor rights is the right to unionize and bargain with management for improved working conditions, salaries, and benefits. The ultimate weapon of labor is, of course, the strike. Management's ultimate weapon is to move the plant to a less organized, more labor-friendly place—a weapon that has been used during the past twenty-five years.

In this chapter we examine the means by which labor has been a forceful player in the business world and, until the 1960s, the dominant presence in federal workplace regulation. We also examine the present state of organized labor, along with criticisms that unions have become anachronistic and a drag on the global competitiveness of the United States.

Legislation Regulating Unions and Collective Bargaining

Most of the early legislation to protect employees focused on the rights of workers to join unions and to engage in collective bargaining. Until the early 1930s, an employer was free

---

1. F. Swoboda, "Reich, Redefining 'Competitiveness,'" *Washington Post*, September 24, 1994, p. D1.

to establish the terms and conditions of employment. Collective activities by employees, such as participation in unions, were discouraged by employers.

NORRIS-LaGUARDIA ACT

Congress protected peaceful strikes, picketing, and boycotts in 1932 with the Norris-LaGuardia Act. The statute restricted federal courts in their power to issue **injunctions** (orders that a party refrain from doing a particular act) against unions engaged in peaceful strikes. In effect, this act declared a national policy permitting employees to organize.

NATIONAL LABOR RELATIONS ACT

The National Labor Relations Act (NLRA) of 1935 established the rights of employees to engage in **collective bargaining** and to strike. Collective bargaining is the process by which labor and management negotiate the terms and conditions of employment, including wages, benefits, working conditions, and other matters. The act is often referred to as the Wagner Act, because it was sponsored by Senator Robert Wagner.

Bargaining Power   Section 1 of the NLRA justifies the act under the commerce clause of the U.S. Constitution. Section 1 states that unequal bargaining power between employees and employers leads to economic instability, whereas refusals of employers to bargain collectively lead to strikes. These disturbances impede the flow of interstate commerce. The policy of the United States Congress, under the authority granted to it by the commerce clause, is to ensure the free flow of commerce by encouraging collective bargaining and unionization.

The pervading purpose of the NLRA was to protect interstate commerce by securing for employees the rights established by Section 7 of the act: to organize, to bargain collectively through representatives of their own choosing, and to engage in concerted activities for collective bargaining and other purposes. The act specifically defined a number of employer practices as being unfair to labor:

1. Interference with the efforts of employees to form, join, or assist labor organizations or to engage in concerted activities for their mutual aid or protection.
2. An employer's domination of a labor organization or contribution of financial or other support to it.
3. Discrimination in the hiring or awarding of tenure to employees because of union affiliation.
4. Discrimination against employees for filing charges under the act or giving testimony under the act.
5. Refusal to bargain collectively in good faith with the duly designated representative of the employees.

The National Labor Relations Board   Another purpose of the NLRA was to promote fair and just settlements of disputes by peaceful processes and to avoid industrial warfare. The act created the **National Labor Relations Board (NLRB)** to oversee union elections and to prevent employers from engaging in unfair and illegal union activities and unfair labor practices. The board was granted investigatory powers and was authorized to issue and serve complaints against employers in response to employee charges of unfair labor practices. The board was further empowered to issue **cease-and-desist orders**—injunctions against specific actions that could be enforced by a federal court of appeals if necessary—when violations were found.

LABOR-MANAGEMENT RELATIONS ACT

The Labor-Management Relations Act (Taft-Hartley Act) was signed into law by President Harry Truman on June 23, 1947, after being passed by Congress over his veto. Intended to amend the Wagner Act, it contained provisions protecting employers as well as employees. The act was bitterly opposed by organized labor groups. It provided a detailed list of unfair labor activities that unions, as well as management, were now forbidden to practice. Moreover, a free speech amendment allowed employers to propagandize against unions prior to any National Labor Relations Board election.

Closed Shop Made Illegal A **closed shop** is a firm that requires union membership by its workers as a condition of employment. Closed shops were made illegal under the Taft-Hartley Act. The act preserved the legality of the union shop, which does not require membership as a prerequisite for employment but can, and usually does, require that workers join the union after a specified period on the job. The Taft-Hartley Act, however, allowed individual states to pass their own **right-to-work laws**—laws making it illegal for union membership to be required for *continued* employment in any establishment. Thus, union shops are technically illegal in states with right-to-work laws.[2]

Eighty-Day Cooling-Off Period One of the most controversial aspects of the Taft-Hartley Act was the eighty-day cooling-off period—a provision allowing federal courts to issue injunctions against strikes that would create a national emergency. The president of the United States can obtain a court injunction that will last eighty days, and presidents have occasionally used this provision. For example, Dwight Eisenhower applied the eighty-day injunction order to striking steelworkers in 1959, Richard Nixon applied it to striking longshoremen in 1971, and Jimmy Carter applied it to striking coal miners in 1978. In each instance, the president felt that a continued strike by the respective workers would have amounted to a national emergency.

LABOR-MANAGEMENT REPORTING AND DISCLOSURE ACT

Prompted by numerous exposés of union corruption by Congress and the news media, the Labor-Management Reporting and Disclosure Act of 1959 (Landrum-Griffin Act) established an employee bill of rights and reporting requirements for union activities. This act strictly regulates internal union business procedures.

Union elections, for example, are regulated by this act. The act requires that regularly scheduled elections of officers occur and that secret ballots be used. Former convicts and self-proclaimed communists are prohibited from holding union office. (The Supreme Court, however, subsequently declared the act's anticommunist provisions unconstitutional.) Union officials are accountable for union property and funds. Members have the right to attend and to participate in union meetings, to nominate officers, and to vote in most union proceedings. (For a summary of labor laws, see *Exhibit 15–1.*)

FORMING A UNION

Nearly every union begins with a decision by the workers in an organization to form some sort of bargaining unit to negotiate with the employer over the terms and conditions of

---

2. States with right-to-work laws are Alabama, Arizona, Arkansas, Florida, Georgia, Idaho, Iowa, Kansas, Louisiana, Mississippi, Nebraska, Nevada, North Carolina, North Dakota, South Carolina, South Dakota, Tennessee, Texas, Utah, Virginia, and Wyoming.

▼ EXHIBIT 15–1 A Summary of Labor Laws

Legislation	Year	Description
Norris-LaGuardia Act	1932	Extended legal protection to peaceful strikes, picketing, and boycotts. Restricted the power of the courts to issue injunctions against unions engaged in peaceful strikes.
National Labor Relations Act (Wagner Act)	1935	Established the rights of employees to engage in collective bargaining and to strike. Created the National Labor Relations Board (NLRB) to oversee union elections and prevent employers from engaging in unfair labor practices.
Labor-Management Relations Act (Taft-Hartley Act)	1947	Extended to employers protections already enjoyed by employees. Provided a list of prohibited union activities (including secondary boycotts and the use of coercion or discrimination to influence employees' decisions to participate in or refrain from union activities) and allowed employers to propagandize against unions before any NLRB election. Prohibited closed shops (which require that all workers belong to a union as a condition of employment), allowed states to pass right-to-work laws, and provided for an eighty-day cooling-off period.
Labor-Management Reporting and Disclosure Act (Landrum-Griffith Act)	1959	Regulated internal union business procedures and union elections. Imposed restrictions on the types of persons who may serve as union officers and outlawed hot-cargo agreements (in which employers agree not to use, handle, or deal in the non-union-produced goods of other employers).

employment. Because worker support is often not very explicit, however, it may fall to a union representative to determine the extent of support for a union. Union representatives also take the lead in organizing employees when the employees fear that becoming active in union-related activities will adversely affect their jobs.

GAUGING WORKER SUPPORT

The extent to which workers favor the establishment of a union to represent them in collective bargaining negotiations is determined by how many of them sign authorization cards. These cards give an organizer some idea of the number of workers who desire union representation. The cards also indicate whether a union election can be won. If, as a hypothetical example, the International Order of Lumber Cutters (IOLC) union representative manages to obtain authorization cards from a significant percentage of the employees of Northwest Lumber Yard, then the IOLC can ask Northwest to recognize the union. If Northwest refuses to consider that request, the IOLC would then submit the cards, with a petition calling for an election, to the nearest office of the NLRB.

DETERMINING THE APPROPRIATE BARGAINING UNIT

If the NLRB decides that there are enough authorization cards to substantiate the union's claim of worker support (at least 30 percent), then it will examine whether the proposed election will result in the formation of an **appropriate bargaining unit**.[3] The NLRB must consider whether the skills, tasks, and job classifications of the Northwest workers are sufficiently similar so that all the members of the proposed bargaining unit can be adequately

---

3. W. E. Lissy, "New Bargaining Unit Work Relocation Rules (National Labor Relations Board Decision)," *Supervision*, March 1992, p. 20.

served by a single negotiating position. Moreover, the NLRB must verify that the proposed bargaining unit does not include persons who are part of management.

Although the NLRB has jurisdiction over all employers engaged in interstate commerce, it may decline to assert jurisdiction over small businesses whose impact on interstate commerce is negligible. Similarly, the NLRB will not intervene in certain types of labor disputes, such as those involving railway or airline workers, because such matters are covered by other federal labor laws. If the NLRB does decide that the proposed bargaining unit is appropriate, however, then it will order that an election be held.

Conducting a Union Election

The workers will vote using secret ballots to ensure that the election accurately reflects their sentiments. The primary task of the NLRB is to make sure that the election is conducted in a lawful manner and that only those persons who are eligible to vote participate in the election. In our hypothetical example, if these conditions are satisfied and 50 percent plus one of the workers vote in favor of the union, then the NLRB will certify the IOLC as the representative of the Northwest workers for purposes of collective bargaining. If the union does not win the election, however, the union will not be recognized.

Limiting Union Organizers The NLRB is particularly sensitive to efforts by companies to unlawfully impede the efforts of union organizers before an election. Because Northwest's management has a genuine interest in regulating employee conduct in the workplace, it may legally limit union activities, as long as the limitations can be justified by legitimate business considerations. If the IOLC believes that it needs to give Northwest's workers hour-long on-site pep talks every day during business hours to ensure maximum participation in the election, for example, Northwest can lawfully refuse to permit the talks, because such meetings would be too time consuming and would greatly disrupt production. Of course, the workers can meet with the IOLC off-site on their own time as often as they wish.

Northwest's ability to regulate the IOLC's presence on the premises is restricted by the **nondiscrimination rule**. This rule requires that Northwest treat the IOLC the same way it would treat any other entity with regard to on-site contact with workers. Northwest can lawfully prohibit on-site solicitations by any third party. It cannot discriminate against union organizers, however, by refusing them access to workers while permitting other groups to meet with the same workers. Most companies avoid this problem by banning all solicitations and thereby leaving it to the workers and the union to meet on their own time.

The NLRB as Watchdog In our hypothetical example, both the IOLC and Northwest's management can be expected to campaign vigorously prior to the election. Each side's behavior is monitored by the NLRB. The NLRB is particularly sensitive to expressed or implied threats contained in Northwest's communications to its workers, such as statements that the plant might have to close if the union is approved. Moreover, the NLRB will closely monitor any sudden policy changes regarding compensation, hours, or working conditions that Northwest makes before the election. The NLRB does not want workers to be improperly swayed by a last-minute gift from management. Similarly, Northwest cannot question workers about their attitudes toward the union or threaten to fire persons it identifies as union sympathizers.

Although the IOLC is also prohibited from using coercive activities to boost its vote, the NLRB's main focus will be on Northwest, because an employer usually has much more power over workers than does an outside union. Should the NLRB decide that

Northwest engaged in any unfair labor practices to influence the outcome of the election, then the NLRB may invalidate the outcome and certify the union as the appropriate representative, even though it did not obtain a majority of the votes cast (assuming that a majority of the workers had originally signed authorization cards).[4]

COLLECTIVE BARGAINING

If the Northwest employees vote for union representation, the NLRB will certify the union, and the IOLC local office will be authorized to negotiate with Northwest's management on behalf of the workers. This right to act as the **exclusive bargaining agent** for the workers is critical to the continued existence of the union. In short,

▼ The strength of a union is its *collective* force.

If the union could not bargain collectively, then Northwest's management would have little incentive to negotiate with the union. Instead, the company could simply present each worker with a job offer.[5]

The concept of **collective bargaining** is at the heart of the federal labor laws. When a union is officially recognized, it may make a demand to bargain with the employer. The union then sits at the table opposite the representatives of management to negotiate a contract for its workers. The terms of employment that result from the negotiations apply to all workers in the bargaining unit, even those who do not choose to belong to the union. This process is known as collective bargaining. Such bargaining is like most other business negotiations, and each side uses its economic power to pressure or persuade the other side to grant concessions.

Bargaining is a somewhat vague term. Bargaining does not mean that either side must give in on demands. It does mean that a demand must be taken seriously and considered as part of a package to be negotiated. Both sides must bargain in good faith, a concept we will discuss in more detail.

NEGOTIATING TERMS AND CONDITIONS

Once Northwest and the union sit down at the conference table, they must negotiate in good faith and make a reasonable effort to come to an agreement. They are not *obligated* to reach an agreement. Instead, they must approach the negotiations with the idea that an agreement is possible. Thus, Northwest's representatives cannot simply stare across the table in silence, refusing to acknowledge or comment on any of the union's proposals. Similarly, the union cannot insist on a variety of expensive proposals, knowing that Northwest cannot afford them. Both parties may engage in hard bargaining with each other, but the bargaining process itself must be geared to reaching a compromise—not avoiding a compromise.

Federal law requires that wages, hours of work, and certain other conditions of employment be discussed during collective bargaining sessions.[6] Among the mandatory subjects

---

4. R. Hanson, R. I. Porterfield, and K. Ames, "Employee Empowerment at Risk: Effects of Recent NLRB Rulings," *Academy of Management Executive*, May 1995, p. 45.
5. S. L. Thomas and B. L. Wisdom, "Labor Negotiations in the Nineties," *SAM Advanced Management Journal*, Autumn 1993, p. 32.
6. B. S. Klaas, "Determinants of Grievance Activity and the Grievance System's Impact on Employee Behavior: An Integrative Perspective," *Academy of Management Review*, July 1989, p. 445.

are workplace safety, employee discounts, health-care plans, pension funds, and apprentice programs. Other subjects that *may* be lawfully raised include the establishment of college scholarship programs for the children of workers and the adoption of new technologies on the factory floor. Northwest is not obligated to bargain over these nonmandatory issues, but it may choose to discuss certain permitted subjects to obtain concessions from the union on mandatory subjects, such as overtime payments or pension plan benefits.

Some demands are illegal in collective bargaining. Management need not bargain over a provision that would be illegal. Thus, if a union presents a specific demand for **featherbedding** (putting workers in unnecessary jobs) or for an unlawful closed shop, management need not respond to these demands.

Although management need not bargain over a decision to shut down a certain facility, it must bargain over the economic consequences of this decision. Thus, issues such as **severance pay** in the event of plant shutdown or employee rights of transfer to other plants are considered mandatory subjects of collective bargaining. This does not mean that management must provide a severance plan; it only means that such a plan must be a subject of the bargaining.

Collective bargaining limits the managerial discretion of the employer. While bargaining is going on, management may not make unilateral changes in important working conditions, such as wages or hours of employment. These changes must be bargained over. Once bargaining reaches what is considered to be an impasse, management may normally make such unilateral changes. The law also includes an exception permitting unilateral changes in cases of business necessity. (For a comparison of the U.S. system and Germany's mode of bargaining, see *Managing Social Issues—International Issues: Germany's Centralized Bargaining System.*)

GOOD FAITH IN BARGAINING

Labor negotiations are often protracted, contentious affairs in which each side accuses the other of not bargaining in good faith. There is no way to read the minds of the negotiators and determine whether they are indeed making a good faith effort to reach an agreement. Consequently, the NLRB and the courts focus on any observable conduct that shows evidence of a desire or lack of desire on the part of either party to reach an agreement. If Northwest refuses to meet with the IOLC, for example, then the NLRB can properly accuse the company of lacking good faith.

What if Northwest's management still refuses to meet with the union? The union may ask the NLRB to penalize the company for refusing to bargain in good faith. The NLRB will then initiate an unfair labor practice hearing and, if it can be justified by the facts, issue an order that Northwest negotiate in good faith. If Northwest refuses to comply with that order, then the union will have to go to the appropriate federal court and attempt to obtain a court order enforcing the NLRB order. This process could take years. Northwest might find the delay to be advantageous, because it will not be required to negotiate with the union during the appeal. If the federal appellate court issues a ruling three years later threatening to impose sanctions on Northwest, then Northwest can resume negotiations with the union, which may no longer have the enthusiastic backing of its members. Moreover, the company may benefit if the costs of litigating the NLRB decision are less than the costs of entering into a collective bargaining agreement soon after the IOLC is approved. Although most companies are not so resistant, there is always the danger that a newly formed union may be obliterated through litigation with a determinedly antiunion employer.

Although good faith is a matter of subjective intent, a party's actions are used to evaluate the presence or absence of good faith. Obviously, the employer must be willing to

MANAGING SOCIAL ISSUES

INTERNATIONAL ISSUES: GERMANY'S CENTRALIZED BARGAINING SYSTEM

Like other aspects of our economy, the U.S. labor market is based on the assumption of competition. Workers, in a sense, compete for jobs based on the benefit the workers represent to a company compared with the wages they will cost. Collective bargaining protects the rights of employees, but it also allows a company to compete by trying to negotiate lower wages for its workers than do its competitors. Most Americans have come to accept this as a fair arena in which employers and employees can bargain. In Germany, however, such a system would be unthinkable. In fact, Germans have come up with a name for our collective bargaining system: "filthy competition."

Centralized Bargaining

In Germany, the idea that companies would compete on the basis of lower wages is reprehensible. This philosophy is mirrored in the country's labor market, which is predicated on the concept of *centralized* bargaining, or *Mithestimmung*. Under centralized bargaining, employers belong to voluntary industry associations, and employees belong to trade unions. These two entities are responsible for bargaining. Wages and other work issues are determined not for an individual company but across entire industries. For example, a 1994 deal between the industry association Gesamtmetall and the trade union IG Metall—with 3.4 million members, the largest in Western Europe—assured equal wages for employees in the automobile, engineering, shipbuilding, and electronics industries. Within these confines, an individual company may pay wages above the industry level, but not below it.

Benefits for Unions and Business

Employees applaud centralized wage bargaining, of course, because it provides them with high wages. Unions also favor the system, under which they have the power to co-determine wages. Furthermore, German managers are among the biggest supporters of the system. The reason is that strong unions tend to act predictably, which not only saves managers from the worry of wildcat strikes but also eliminates the problems of multiunion firms. In fact, Germany loses fewer work-hours per day to strikes than almost any other industrialized nation. Because unions have nearly as much stake in the health and profitability of entire industries as do the corporations themselves, the unions are much less likely to order their members to do something that would place their own industry in jeopardy.

Problems with *Mithestimmung*

In the 1990s, two developments have threatened *Mithestimmung*: a recession and the incorporation of former Communist and economically weak East Germany into the national fold. The recession had the effect on *Mithestimmung* that many economists would predict: financially weak companies were not allowed to reduce wages to help them keep up with healthier competitors, and they were forced either to leave their employers' associations or go out of business. In 1994, IBM Germany opted out of Gesamtmetall rather than agree to negotiated industry-wide wage increases.

When East Germany and West Germany were reunited in the early 1990s, the leaders did not want to bring the living standards of East Germany up to those in West Germany by fast growth based on low wages. The western unions demanded that eastern wages be brought up to par with western wages by 1994, and the German government agreed. This proved impossible, however, as eastern firms could not afford such high wages. Eventually, an agreement was struck that allowed eastern firms to reduce wages as long as the reduction was approved by the unions.

For Critical Analysis:

What are the reasons why the German labor system, Mithestimmung, *could not be used in the United States?*

SOURCE: "The Perils of Cosy Corporatism," *Economist*, May 21, 1994, pp. 8–10.

meet with union representatives. Excessive delaying tactics may be proof of bad faith, as is insistence on obviously unreasonable contract terms. Suppose that a company makes a single overall contract offer on a "take-it-or-leave-it" basis and refuses to consider modifications of individual terms. This, too, might be considered bad faith in bargaining (see *Exhibit 15–2*).

A party to collective bargaining may be excused from bargaining when the other party commits an unfair labor practice. For example, if a union refuses to bargain in good faith, the employer is normally not required to bargain.

STRIKES

Sometimes a union and an employer may approach the bargaining table in good faith but simply be unable to reach an agreement because of genuine differences of opinion. If there are no visible signs of movement from either party after protracted negotiations, then the parties may have reached an impasse.

There are relatively few options following an impasse. One is mediation, in which both sides call on the services of a neutral third party. This mediator acts as a communicating agent between the parties in the hopes that a fresh perspective on the situation may provide alternative resolutions. Both sides can request aid from the Federal Mediation and Conciliation Service (FMCS), an independent agency of the federal government that was established in 1947. Although no party is required to accede to the suggestions of the FMCS, the agency is often involved in disputes that may have far-reaching effects.

If mediation fails and the parties are truly deadlocked despite lengthy discussions, then the union may call a strike against the employer to apply additional economic pressure. (See *Exhibit 15–3* for a list of major strikes in recent years.) Once the workers approve the plan to go on strike, then their labor services will no longer be available to the employer. Of course, the employer will no longer be obligated to pay the striking workers or provide benefits. Because both sides will initially suffer some economic hardship, some time may elapse before one side's sustainable economic power becomes apparent.

The right to strike is of fundamental importance to the collective bargaining process, for the threat of a strike balances the bargaining power between management and labor. In addition,

▼ The First Amendment to the U.S. Constitution protects all forms of expression, including strikes.

Workers who are not involved in the strike also have the right to refuse to cross a picket line being walked by other employees. If the IOLC pickets Northwest's mill, for example, then the Northwest secretaries affiliated with the Federation of Office Workers (a differ-

▼ **EXHIBIT 15–2 Bad Faith in Bargaining**
A series of court decisions have found the following actions, among others, to constitute bad faith in bargaining:

- Rejecting a proposal without offering a counterproposal.
- Engaging in a campaign among workers to undermine the union.
- Unilaterally changing wages or terms and conditions of employment during the bargaining process.
- Constantly shifting positions on disputed contract terms.
- Sending bargainers who lack authority to commit the company to a contract.

▼ **EXHIBIT 15–3** **Selected Recent Strikes in the United States**

Company Involved	Started	Resolved	Union Involved	Number of Employees Involved	Major Issues of Contention
Boeing Company	October 1995	December 1995	Machinists	32,500	Job security, health-care insurance cost-sharing demands by Boeing, wages
Caterpillar, Inc.	May 1994	Employees returned to work December 1995, but labor issues unresolved	United Auto Workers	8,700	Wage reductions, work schedules, work rules
Detroit News and *Detroit Free Press* (newspapers)	July 1995	Unresolved	Six local unions	2,500	Wages, union control, work rules
PepsiCo	June 1995	August 1995	Teamsters	600	Inadequate health-care and pension benefits
Bridgestone/ Firestone, Inc.	July 1994	May 1995	United Rubber Workers	4,000	Work schedules and medical benefits
Safeway, Inc.	April 1995	April 1995	United Food and Commercial Workers	32,000	Proposed cutbacks in health benefits
Major league baseball	August 1994	Employees returned to work April 1995, but issues unresolved	Baseball player's union	650	A proposed salary cap and the elimination of salary arbitration
General Motors Corporation	January 1995	January 1995	United Auto Workers	6,500	Job security, work schedules, outsourcing, capital improvements
Ryder System, Inc.	September 1995	October 1995	Teamsters	12,000	Job security, wages, benefits

ent union) may refuse to cross the picket line. This refusal to go to work would be viewed as a lawful exercise of free speech (a statement of support for the striking IOLC workers), not as grounds for firing the secretaries.

ILLEGAL STRIKES

An otherwise lawful strike may become illegal because of the conduct of the strikers. Violent strikes (or those with the threat of violence) are illegal. The use of violence against management employees (managers and their assistants) or substitute workers is illegal. Certain forms of massed picketing are also illegal. If the strikers form a massed barrier and deny management or other nonunion workers access to the plant, the strike is illegal. Similarly, sit-down strikes, in which employees simply stay in the plant without working, are illegal.

Secondary Boycotts Strikers are not permitted to engage in **secondary boycotts** by picketing the suppliers or customers of the employer. The rationale for this prohibition is that these suppliers and customers have no dispute with the striking workers and should not be penalized merely because they do business with the employer. The IOLC would commit a secondary boycott if it began picketing the tree farmers from which Northwest purchases the lumber for its mills.

The Landrum-Griffin Act also outlawed **hot-cargo agreements**—agreements in which employers voluntarily agree with unions not to handle, use, or deal in the goods of employers who have nonunionized work forces. Furthermore, striking workers are not permitted to coerce the employer's customers into agreeing not to do business with the employer. The IOLC would be liable if it successfully pressured retailers to stop carrying Northwest's products, thus forming a hot-cargo agreement. If Northwest could no longer find retail outlets for its wood products, then it would be able to sue the union for any damages resulting from the boycott. The union would be allowed to picket the retailers only if the action was limited to notifying customers not to patronize Northwest products because of the ongoing labor dispute.

Wildcat Strikes Unions are often viewed by the public as monolithic entities. It is not uncommon, however, for union members to hold a wide range of views regarding the desirability and necessity of going on strike at any particular time. Union members may be divided into highly vocal competing camps. Some members may favor accepting an employer's latest offer, whereas others may advocate a strike.

A **wildcat strike** occurs when a minority of union members, without the authorization of the union itself, go out on strike against an employer. Because the strike is not authorized, it is illegal. Consequently, wildcat strikers do not enjoy the legal protections afforded to workers who engage in authorized economic strikes. In general, a union is not liable for damages caused by wildcat strikers unless it is contractually obligated in the collective bargaining agreement to pay for damages resulting from such strikes.

HIRING REPLACEMENT WORKERS

If a strike goes on for several weeks and management finds that it is unable to maintain the production schedules needed to fulfill existing orders, it may decide to hire replacement workers to fill the positions vacated by the strikers. (A company could hire replace-

ment workers the first day of the strike, though this is uncommon.) A company may even give the replacement workers permanent positions with the company.

In the 1930s and 1940s strikes were powerful, in part because employers often had difficulty finding trained replacements to keep their businesses running during the strikes. Since the illegal air traffic controller strike in 1981, when President Ronald Reagan successfully hired replacement workers, employers have increasingly used this strategy, with considerable success. Even major league baseball, when struck by its players in 1994, found replacements to play for the professional baseball teams during the next season's spring training. Although some scoffed at the ability of the replacement players, the tactic was in part successful for management, as the strike was called off before the beginning of the 1995 season.

RIGHTS OF STRIKING WORKERS

The rights of strikers after a strike ends are an important consideration. In a typical strike over working conditions, the strikers have no inalienable right to return to their jobs. If satisfactory replacement workers were found, the strikers may find themselves out of work (see *Company Focus: Bridgestone/Firestone, Inc.*). The law does prohibit the employer from discriminating against former strikers, however. Even if the employer fires all the strikers and retains all the replacement workers, former strikers must be given preferential rights to any new vacancies that arise, and they retain their seniority rights.

In a move opposed by most U.S. corporations, President Bill Clinton tried to change this situation in 1995 with an executive order banning the federal government from doing business with companies that hire permanent replacement workers. In explaining the president's move, Secretary of Labor Robert Reich said that replacement workers disabled the collective bargaining process and hurt worker productivity and morale, which in turn damaged the U.S. economy. The U.S. Chamber of Commerce claimed that the directive contradicts labor law and was "a shallow political ploy" to gain labor union support in the 1996 presidential elections.[7] A federal court in 1996 struck down the executive order.

Different rules apply when a union strikes because the employer has engaged in unfair labor practices. If an employer is discriminating against a union's workers, the workers may go out on an unfair-labor-practice strike. An economic strike may also become an unfair-labor-practice strike if the employer refuses to bargain in good faith. In the case of an unfair-labor-practice strike, the employer may still hire replacement workers but must give the strikers their jobs back once the strike is over.

LOCKOUTS

Lockouts are the employer's counterpart to the worker's right to strike. A **lockout** occurs when the employer shuts down to prevent employees from working. Lockouts are usually used when the employer believes that a strike is imminent.

Lockouts may be a legal employer response. In the leading Supreme Court case on the issue, a union and an employer had reached a stalemate in collective bargaining. The employer feared that the union would delay a strike until the busy season and thereby cause the employer to suffer more from the strike. The employer called a lockout before the busy season to deny the union this leverage, and the Supreme Court held that this action was legal.

---

7. A. Q. Nomani, "Clinton Bans Use of Firms That Replace Strikers," *Wall Street Journal*, March 9, 1995, p. A5.

COMPANY FOCUS:
BRIDGESTONE/FIRESTONE, INC.

PERMANENT REPLACEMENT WORKERS AT BRIDGESTONE

When the United Rubber Workers (URW) signed a labor agreement with Goodyear in March 1994, the union hoped it would solve its struggles with Bridgestone/Firestone, Inc., another tire manufacturer with which the union had similar disputes. The tradition of negotiations with tire manufacturers had been one of "pattern" bargaining, in which unions would enforce "master" contracts across different companies in a particular industry. The URW hoped Bridgestone Corporation would pattern its own contract after Goodyear's.

Labor leaders might not have been so optimistic had they known that Bridgestone was stockpiling its product by buying more than 500,000 tires from rival Cooper Tire & Rubber Company. In fact, Bridgestone refused to pattern its bargaining, and it shocked the tire industry, as well as the U.S. government, by hiring 2,300 permanent replacement workers.

Genesis of the Labor Problems

After the Japanese-owned Bridgestone Corporation bought Firestone Tire & Rubber Company in 1988, labor's relationship with the company was positive. In fact, management allowed the URW to represent workers at a new plant without any reservations. In 1992, however, the company had lost $1 billion, and it began looking for ways to increase productivity while cutting costs. Buoyed by the extra inventory of tires, Bridgestone prepared to take a hard-line stance in negotiations to replace its old contract with the URW. The tire company asked for twelve-hour shifts, pay hikes tied to productivity, and a reduction in medical and pension benefits.

Just before the URW's contract with Bridgestone expired, the union signed a deal with Goodyear that called for a 16 percent increase in wages and benefits over three years. Bridgestone rejected the idea of the deal as a blueprint for industry-wide standards and refused to change its demands. On July 12, 1994, consequently, 4,200 union members walked out of five Bridgestone plants.

Hiring Replacement Workers

Bridgestone's half-million tire stockpile, along with production from its nonunion workers, allowed the company to supply its major clients during the early part of the strike. The company, however, was losing, by some estimates, $10 million a month while its union workers were absent. To stem the tide, nearly six months after the beginning of the strike the company hired 2,300 replacement workers, a move that put the manufacturing process at 70 percent of capacity. Initially, the company said the replacements were temporary, but within weeks it announced they were, in fact, permanent.

The move sparked criticism from union leaders and politicians. Clinton used the opportunity to further his campaign for legislation to prevent companies from hiring replacement workers, saying Bridgestone's action "shows exactly why this protection is necessary." Bridgestone, however, argued that the action was legal and that the company was entitled to hire the replacement workers. After forty-six bargaining sessions with the URW, Bridgestone reasoned, the union did not appear to be serious about bargaining. With a conservative U.S. Congress, the president's legislation did not get passed.

The New Bottom Line

Most analysts agree that Bridgestone "won" its battle with the union. With the declining power of labor unions in the modern economy, it is likely that other companies will increasingly consider the option of hiring replacement workers rather than compromise while conducting labor negotiations during which a strike occurs.

SOURCE: Information from S. B. Garland, "Blowup at Bridgestone," *Business Week*, January 30, 1995, p. 30; "Bridgestone/Firestone Hires 2,300 Replacement Workers," *Autoparts Report*, January 18, 1995; B. Koening, "In Strike at Bridgestone/Firestone, It's Obvious Who Won," *Indianapolis Star/Indianapolis News*, June 5, 1995, p. 7; and R. Narisetti, "Bridgestone/Firestone Begins to Hire Permanent Replacements for Strikers," *Wall Street Journal*, January 5, 1995, p. A3.

Some lockouts are illegal, however. An employer may not use its lockout weapon as a tool to break the union and pressure employees into decertification—in effect kicking out the union. Consequently, an employer must show some economic justification for instituting a lockout.

EMPLOYER UNFAIR LABOR PRACTICES

The preceding sections have discussed unfair labor practices during union elections, collective bargaining, and strikes. Many unfair labor practices may occur in yet other employment-related contexts. The most significant of these practices are discussed below.

EMPLOYER REFUSAL TO RECOGNIZE UNIONS AND NEGOTIATE

As already noted, once a union has been certified by the NLRB as the exclusive representative of a bargaining unit, an employer must recognize and bargain in good faith with the union over issues affecting all employees who are within the bargaining unit. Failure to do so is an unfair labor practice. Because the National Labor Relations Act embraces a policy of majority rule, certification of the union as the bargaining unit's representative binds *all* of the employees in that bargaining unit (whether or not they are members of the union).

Certification does not mean, however, that a union will continue indefinitely as the exclusive representative of the bargaining unit. If the union loses the majority support of those it represents, an employer is not obligated to continue recognition of, or negotiation with, the union. As a practical matter, though, a newly elected representative needs time to establish itself among the workers and to begin to formulate and implement its programs. Therefore, as a matter of labor policy, a union is immune from attack by employers and from repudiation by the employees for one year after certification. During this period, it is *presumed* that the union enjoys majority support among the employees; the employer cannot refuse to deal with the union as the employees' exclusive representative, even if the employees have changed their minds and prefer not to be represented by that union.

After one year, an employer may challenge the presumption of majority support for the union if it can show that a majority of employees do not wish to be represented by the union. If the evidence is sufficient to support a *good faith* belief that the union no longer enjoys majority support among the employees, the employer may refuse to continue to recognize and negotiate with the union.

A delicate question arises during a strike in which an employer hires replacement workers. Specifically, should it be assumed that the replacement workers do not support the union? If, in fact, they do not, and if, as a result, the union no longer has majority support, then the employer no longer needs to negotiate with the union.

EMPLOYER INTERFERENCE IN UNION ACTIVITIES

The NLRA declares it to be an unfair labor practice for an employer to interfere with, restrain, or coerce employees in the exercise of their rights to form a union and to bargain collectively. Unlawful employer interference may take a variety of forms. For example,

▼ **Courts have found it an unfair labor practice for an employer to make threats that may interfere with an employee's decision to join a union.**

Even asking employees about their views on the union may be considered coercive. Employees responding to such questioning must be able to remain anonymous and must receive assurances against employer reprisals.

Employers also may not prohibit certain forms of union activity in the workplace. If an employee has a grievance with the company, for example, the employer cannot prevent the union's participation in support of the employee. If an employer has unlawfully interfered with the operation of a union, the NLRB or a reviewing court may issue a cease-and-desist order halting the practice. The company typically is required to post the order on a bulletin board and renounce its past unlawful conduct. To avoid these legal entanglements, some companies prefer to compete with unions by offering employees the same grievance hearing protections as unions offer, without the dues normally paid to unions (see *Company Focus: Coors Brewing Company*).

DISCRIMINATION

The NLRA prohibits employers from discriminating against workers because they are union officers or are otherwise associated with a union. When workers must be laid off, the company is not allowed to consider union participation as a criterion for deciding whom to lay off.

Discriminatory punishment of union members or officers can be difficult to prove, however. A company can claim to have good reasons for its action. The NLRB considers a series of factors in determining whether an action is discriminatory, and thus unlawful. These factors include giving inconsistent reasons for the action, applying rules erratically and more strictly against union members, failing to give an expected warning prior to discharge or other discipline, and acting contrary to worker seniority.[8]

The decision to close a facility is generally within the discretion of management, but even this decision cannot be made with a discriminatory motive. If a company has several facilities and only one is unionized, the company cannot shut down the union plant simply because of the union. The company could shut down the union plant if it were demonstrably less efficient than the other facilities, however.

UNION UNFAIR LABOR PRACTICES

Certain union activities are declared to be unfair labor practices by the Taft-Hartley Act. The secondary boycott, which was previously discussed, is one such unfair labor practice by unions.

Another significant union unfair labor practice is coercion or restraint in regard to an employee's decision to participate in or refrain from union activities. Obviously, it is unlawful for a union to threaten an employee or his or her family with violence for failure to join the union. The law's prohibition includes economic coercion as well. Suppose that a union official declares, "We have a lot of power here; you had better join the union, or you may lose your job." This threat is an unfair labor practice.

The NLRA provides unions with the authority to regulate their own internal affairs, which includes disciplining union members. This discipline cannot be used in an improperly coercive fashion, however. Suppose that a disaffected union member feels that

---

8. B. S. Klaas and A. S. DeNisi, "Managerial Reactions to Employee Dissent: The Impact of Grievance Activity on Performance Ratings," *Academy of Management Journal*, December 1989, p. 705.

COMPANY FOCUS: COORS BREWING COMPANY
IN-HOUSE PEER REVIEW

When labor tried to organize at Coors Brewing Company in the mid-1970s, a popular argument in favor of organization was that unions would give employees of the beer company a means for resolving grievances. The labor leaders had a point. Coors, like any other company without organized employees, risked a large employee-management rift without an effective authoritative voice to solve problems between management and workers. Coors, however, created the Peer Review System, and the unions lost one of their major recruiting tools.

The Peer Review System

Coors's program is based on the concept that workers are willing to keep grievance resolutions in-house—as long as they feel their views are not being ignored or suppressed by management. The Peer Review System guarantees that this will not be the case by allowing employees to bring their complaints before a review board that includes their co-workers.

Under the process, any employee who is not satisfied with the application of a company policy may file an appeal within seven working days of the incident in question. The worker's employee-relations representative then convenes an appeals board by randomly selecting two members of management and three employees from the same job area as the person who feels wronged.

The employee-relations representative next conducts a hearing on the matter, in which the supervisor is usually called to explain the circumstances and reasoning behind his or her disciplinary measure. The applicant is then given the chance to discuss why he or she feels the measure is unfair. Board members can ask questions of both parties and request testimony from witnesses.

After the board has gathered enough information, it convenes to decide, by a majority vote, on one of three possible rulings: to uphold the disciplinary action, to reduce its severity, or to overturn it completely. The board's decision is considered final.

Increased Employee Participation

In most of the cases in which an appeals board is convened, the original action is upheld. In 1992, for example, the boards upheld 58 percent of sixty-five appeals heard, modified 26 percent, and reversed 15 percent. Even though the majority of decisions favor management, Coors employees have accepted the system as fair. "At first, employees' use of the system was low," admits Edward Cruth, an employee-relations manager. "The first few years the system was in existence, less than eight appeals per year were held." Employee satisfaction grew, however, and by the 1990s the company was averaging sixty appeals a year.

The New Bottom Line

Coors found that its Peer Review System not only has diminished employees' incentive to bring lawsuits against the company but also has increased the odds against such cases being successful. In two 1993 cases in which a worker did take the company to court, judges ruled that the in-house appeals process was equal to final and binding arbitration.

SOURCE: D. Anfuso, "Peer Review Wards Off Unions and Lawsuits," *Personnel Journal*, January 1994, p. 64.

the union is no longer providing proper representation for employees and starts a campaign to decertify the union. The union may expel the employee from membership but may not fine or otherwise discipline the worker.

Another significant union unfair labor practice is discrimination:

▼ **A union may not discriminate against workers because they refuse to join a union, except in union shop situations.**

Current federal law also prohibits a union from using its influence to cause an employer to discriminate against workers who refuse to join the union. A union cannot force an employer to deny promotions to workers who fail to join the union.

RIGHTS OF NONUNION EMPLOYEES

Most of labor law involves the formation of unions and associated rights. Nonunion employees also have rights, however. Most workers do not belong to unions, so this issue is important. In fact, by 1997 only 15 percent of the labor force was unionized, down from 30.5 percent in 1968.[9] The NLRA protects concerted employee action, and does not limit its protection to certified unions.

CONCERTED ACTIVITY

Protected concerted action is action taken by employees for their mutual aid regarding wages, hours, or terms and conditions of employment. Even an action by a single employee may be protected concerted activity if that action is taken for the benefit of other employees and if the employee has at least discussed the action with other approving workers. If only a single worker engages in a protest or walkout, the employer will not be liable for an unfair labor practice if it fires the worker unless the employer is aware that this protest or walkout is concerted activity taken with the assent of other workers. Sometimes the mutual interest of other workers should be obvious to the employer, however. Data from the NLRB indicate that a growing number of nonunion employees are challenging employer barriers to their concerted action.

WORKPLACE SAFETY

A common cause for nonunion activity is concern over workplace safety. The federal Labor-Management Relations Act (LMRA) authorizes an employee to walk off the job if he or she has a good faith belief that the working conditions are abnormally dangerous. The employer cannot lawfully discharge the employee under these conditions. To be protected under federal labor law, a safety walkout must be a *concerted* activity. If a single worker walks out over a safety complaint, other workers must be affected by the safety issue for the walkout to be protected under the LMRA.

LABOR UNIONS: PRESENT AND FUTURE

The Great Depression of the 1930s effectively ended a period of public nonsupport for unions, as harsh employment conditions highlighted the need for a change in the adversarial relationship between labor and management. In 1935, the National Labor Relations Act forced business to deal fairly with labor, thereby strengthening unions significantly. The newly powerful unions sought safer working conditions, better benefits, and higher wages for their members, whereas management was assured a stable labor force—if at a greater cost than it would have liked.

---

9. U.S. Department of Labor, Bureau of Labor Statistics.

This truce has lasted more than half a century, a period during which both owners and workers enjoyed the highest profits and standards of living in the world. As the United States faces the challenges of international competition, however, its hegemony has weakened. Part of the blame has fallen on labor unions, which critics say are too rigid to keep up with the speedy decisions corporations must make in this age of technology and fickle consumer tastes.[10] The time for lengthy negotiations over changes in working conditions and workplace environments has passed, say these critics, as has the era of the modern labor union.

To address the problems of the unions, in 1994 President Clinton created a ten-member commission to study labor-management relations in the United States. The findings of the Commission on the Future of Worker-Management Relations were hardly surprising: tensions between the two groups must be lessened if the American workplace is going to remain efficient and globally competitive. "What we want is a new framework for worker-management relations that breaks the stalemate that now exists and holds back innovation and efficiency at the workplace," stated one commission member.[11] It is interesting to note that when the last such presidential commission was formed, during the Great Depression, its suggestions became the basis of modern labor law. Although nobody is proposing that the worldwide economic slowdown of the early 1990s was akin to the situation of the 1920s, it will be interesting to see if we have entered another turning point in the history of organized labor in the United States.

CRITICISMS OF ORGANIZED LABOR

The most persistent criticism of the modern labor system is that it has fallen behind the times—that somehow, labor and its leaders have failed to adjust to the needs of a more diverse work force that is "increasingly temporary or part-time, more educated, and includes more women, minorities and baby boomers."[12]

A study by the International Labor Organization (ILO), an arm of the United Nations, shows that although women now account for 37 percent of all trade union members in the United States, only two of the ninety-five unions in the American Federation of Labor–Congress of Industrial Organizations (AFL-CIO) have female presidents, and the number of women in top national leadership positions has not significantly increased since the mid-1980s.[13] Furthermore, although 23 percent of African American males are union members, few African American men hold positions in labor management.[14]

For many years, organized labor was ahead of its time as it urged companies to provide such benefits as minimum wages and maximum hours, family and medical leave, protection against discrimination, and secure pension and health benefits. Much of labor law, however, seems insufficient in light of the demands of today's workplace and marketplace.

The Action Committees Issue One of the more controversial labor issues of the past decade concerns a ruling the NLRB made in 1992 with regard to Electromation, Inc., a small, nonunion manufacturer of electrical components based in Indiana.[15] Finding itself

---

10. L. Troy, "Big Labor's Big Problems," *Business and Society Review,* Fall 1993, p. 49.
11. L. Uchitelle, "A Call for Easing Labor-Management Tension," *New York Times,* May 30, 1994, p. 17.
12. R. Samborn, "Report: Changed Work Force Leaves Labor Law a Relic," *National Law Journal,* June 13, 1994, p. A16.
13. F. Swoboda, "Women Aspiring to Union Leadership Roles Find Limits There Too," *Washington Post,* February 14, 1993, p. H2.
14. "Demographics of Union Members," *Labor Trends,* March 26, 1994, p. 1.
15. *Electromation, Inc.,* 309 NLRB No. 163 (1992).

in financial difficulty in the late 1980s, the company's management decided to eliminate raises and bonuses based on good attendance. When sixty-eight employees petitioned management to reconsider this policy, the company set up five "action committees" in which employees could discuss the issue with managers. The committees were also designed as a forum for the discussion of other topics, including absenteeism, future wage increases, and the company's smoking policy.

Electromation paid its employees for time spent participating in the action committees, supplied the meeting rooms, and covered the costs of any materials needed. The local Teamsters Union, trying to organize at the company, complained that the committees were unlawful under the Wagner Act, and the NLRB agreed.[16] According to Section 8(a)(2) of the act, it is an unfair labor practice for employers to "dominate or interfere with the formation or administration of any labor organization or contribute financial or other support to it." The law's definition of a *labor organization* includes any "employee representation committee or plan, in which employees participate and [deal] with grievances, labor disputes, wages, rates of pay, hours of employment, or conditions of work."

The NLRB ruled that Electromation had in fact "dominated" these action committees and ordered that they be disbanded. Because more than thirty thousand companies in the United States have some form of employee-involvement programs—patterned after the innovative Japanese "quality circles"—the business community's reaction to the board's ruling was predictable. "The decision puts into question every participation group that companies have put into place the past twenty years," said one observer. "It is an anti-employee decision because it discourages employees from coming forward with ideas and solutions unless they do it through a union"[17] (see *Managing Social Issues—Barriers to Success: Illegal Employee-Management Action Committees*).

Counterproductive Labor Law Jeffrey C. McGuiness, president of the Labor Policy Association, feels many labor laws are not only outdated but actually hurt the employees they are trying to protect. For example, a stipulation in the Fair Labor Standards Act forces a worker who needs only part of a day for personal business to take the whole day off without pay if that worker has already used up his or her leave time. Another Fair Labor Standards Act rule involves "gain-sharing programs," in which employees are paid part of the profits made on the products of their labor. Because labor laws require that all payments made to hourly employees must be figured into the employees' regular hourly rate, an employer wishing to provide any sort of lump sum payment must make "time-consuming calculations" to balance the books. "In large businesses, this is a tremendously burdensome task and, if a mistake is made in the calculation, the employer becomes vulnerable to lawsuits," says McGuiness.[18]

Tʜᴇ Dᴇᴄʟɪɴɪɴɢ Iɴꜰʟᴜᴇɴᴄᴇ ᴏꜰ Uɴɪᴏɴs

Partly because unions are perceived to have anachronistic tendencies, union membership is dropping at a precipitous pace. From 1983 to 1997, it fell to 16.4 million—15 percent of the work force—the lowest union membership level since the Great Depression (see *Exhibit 15–4*). Unions represent only 11 percent of the private sector work force today, a

---

16. "NLRB Decides Labor-Management Committees Case," *Personnel Journal,* February 1993, p. 20.
17. M. A. Verespej, "New Rules on Employee Involvement," *Industry Week,* February 1, 1993, p. 55.
18. J. C. McGuiness, "Outdated Laws Govern Modern Workplace," *National Law Journal,* November 29, 1993, pp. S14–S15.

⧉ MANAGING SOCIAL ISSUES

BARRIERS TO SUCCESS: ILLEGAL EMPLOYEE-MANAGEMENT ACTION COMMITTEES

Coming as it did on the heels of the *Electromation, Inc.,* ruling discussed in this chapter, the decision of the National Labor Relations Board (NLRB) concerning a similar situation at the DuPont Corporation further confused and worried many managers. In 1988, DuPont formed six safety committees that included representatives from both management and labor. The company set up a similar action committee two years later to deal with employee fitness. Like Electromation, DuPont provided funds for all of the safety committees' activities. The company retained veto power over who could serve on the committee and any actions the committee could take, and the company could abolish the program at will.

A Vague Ruling?

As in *Electromation,* the NLRB ruled that DuPont's actions constituted unlawful domination of a labor organization, and the board ordered the seven action committees to disband. In effect, both companies had set up "sham-unions," which the Wagner Act specifically prohibits. Businesses with a cooperative labor-management situation had been watching both the *Electromation* and *DuPont* cases closely for guidance on what the NLRB would consider a lawful action committee. After eighteen months of NLRB deliberations, the corporate community was looking for definitive guidelines on the issue.

The NLRB went to great lengths to assure the business community that its rulings were based only on the merits of the situation at both Electromation and DuPont and did not reflect on employee-management collaborations in general. Instead of reassuring managers, this stance seemed to worry them further. "[A]ll we got was that Electromation violated labor laws and other cases might be different,"

lamented a lawyer from the Labor Policy Association in Washington, D.C. "If they thought employee cooperation was good and legal, they would have come up with a more broad-reaching definition."

Self-Regulating Committees

Labor lawyers say there are some clues about how to avoid having an illegal employee-management action committee:

▶ **Avoid collective bargaining topics.** Electromation's committees discussed employment issues such as wages, hours, and bonuses. Action committees that deal only with quality control are unlikely to draw the interest of the NLRB.

▶ **Avoid management domination.** In the case of both DuPont and Electromation, management clearly dominated the proceedings and had a degree of control over the action committees. Employee-participation programs initiated by employees are more clearly within legal boundaries.

▶ **Work with established unions.** In both cases, the complaints were brought before the NLRB by unions that felt their power had been abrogated. Communication between labor and management during all phases of the establishment of action committees is a necessity.

For Critical Analysis:

Where does the issue of employee rights fit into the debate over action committees? Do you believe that the NLRB was looking out for the best interest of DuPont's employees when it made its decision?

SOURCE: Information from *E. I. du Pont de Nemours and Company,* 311 NLRB No. 88 (1993); "DuPont's Employee Committees Ordered Disbanded," *Personnel Journal,* August 1993, p. 24; and M. A. Verespej, "New Rules on Employee Participation," *Industry Week,* February 1, 1993, p. 56.

number that some experts predict will drop to 4 or 5 percent by the beginning of the next century.[19]

---

19. *Ibid.,* p. 70.

▼ **EXHIBIT 15–4 Union Membership as a Percentage of Nonagricultural Employment from 1830 to Present**

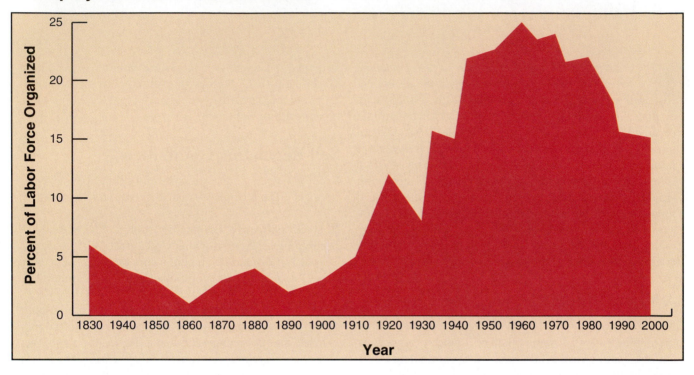

SOURCE: U.S. Department of Labor.

An Economic Theory for Union Decline Leo Troy, a professor of economics at Rutgers University, explains why unionism has declined in one word: *substitution.*[20] Instead of looking at factors such as labor-management hostility or union outdatedness, Troy concentrates on economic theory to show why there are not as many union members now as there were last year, five years ago, or thirty years ago.

"Markets continuously attempt to substitute more efficient, less costly alternatives for the existing arrangements," Troy explains. "This means that competition engages, and attacks any form of noncompetitive behavior, irrespective of its source—business, union, or government."[21] In other words,

▼ Unions add costs to businesses, making them less competitive; eventually, more efficient forms of business (without the burden of union costs) *substitute* themselves for those that are less efficient.

According to Troy, unions were at their strongest point during the 1950s, when the United States enjoyed a *goods-dominated labor market*—a market in which manufactured goods dominated both employment and spending. In other words, until the 1960s, much of American employment and spending was concentrated in the manufacturing sector. Ever

20. L. Troy, *The End of Unionism: A Reappraisal* (St. Louis: Washington University, Center for the Study of American Business, September 1994), pp. 6–10.
21. *Ibid.*, p. 6.

since, the country has been moving more steadily toward a *service-dominated labor market* — a market characterized by relatively fewer workers actually working in factories and most workers providing services. A service-dominated labor market is one in which computer programmers, accountants, attorneys, educators, acoustical engineers, and the like dominate.

Organized unions have always been stronger in goods-dominated labor markets than in service-dominated ones. As the latter kind grows at the expense of the former, the number of nonunion workers in relation to union workers will also grow. The unions associated with goods-intensive industries have disappeared along with the industries themselves; no longer do we hear of the Elastic Goring Workers, Carriage Workers, Sheep Shearers, Broom and Whisk Makers, and so on.

Although Troy concedes that "employer opposition has been a factor in the unraveling" of organized labor, he refuses to see it as the overriding reason. He points out that the labor movement made its greatest gains during the 1930s, when there was also the staunchest, and most violent, resistance from big business. He also brings up the example of the United Auto Workers (UAW), one of the largest unions in the country. In 1969, UAW membership was over 1.4 million, a number that has subsequently been halved. What is the reason for this decline? "Certainly not the opposition of the Big Three automakers. They did not oust UAW members," asserts Troy. "[R]ather the downsizing of their companies reduced employment in the industry, and thereby the membership of the union."[22] As the move toward a service-oriented labor market continues, Troy predicts a continued shrinking of union membership rolls.

Effect of Union Decline on Workers Whatever the reasons for decreased union power, there is ample evidence that it has hurt blue-collar workers in the United States.[23]

---

22. *Ibid.*, pp. 9–10.
23. T. A. Kochan, J. C. Wells, and M. Smith, "Consequences of a Failed IR System: Contract Workers in the Petrochemical Industry," *Sloan Management Review*, Summer 1992, p. 79.

The difficult struggle by union leaders to protect their members is shown by their failure to effectively halt a widespread antiunion firing campaign by business in the 1980s, as well as by the fact that they could not come close to defeating the supposedly antilabor North American Free Trade Agreement (NAFTA) in 1993. Until the 1990–1991 recession, annual pay increases for union members lagged behind those of nonunion workers every year after 1983.[24] In 1988, white-collar males aged twenty-five to sixty-four earned 48 percent more than blue-collar males in the same age bracket, up from 35 percent more in 1979 (see *Exhibit 15–5*). Since 1980, the portion of workers under age sixty-five with employer-paid health care dropped from 63 to 56 percent. Some experts believe these numbers are directly linked to the decline in union power.[25]

Union Response: Merge Organized labor's reaction to its own decline has been less than overwhelming. Elections to form new unions are running at half the pace of the 1970s, at about 3,500 a year. In addition, there were only 31 major strikes in 1995, compared with 187 in 1980—the lowest total in the 50 years the Bureau of Labor Statistics has been keeping such records.[26]

In 1995, however, U.S. unions began to follow a new strategy to counterbalance their weakening influence. That year, the nation's three largest industrial unions—the UAW, the International Association of Machinists, and the United Steelworkers—announced a merger. The goal of the three principals is to consolidate power in a two-million-member superunion that will span a number of different industries and have a more powerful influence on U.S. corporations. Organizers believe that the new union, to be finalized in 2001, will benefit its members in a number of areas. First, it will eliminate the need for the financial resources and energy the three unions now expend in fighting one another during membership drives. It will also add negotiating power to collective bargaining, especially at corporations that now deal with multiple unions. Lobbying power will certainly be enhanced, as will the union's position in aligning itself with unions in Mexico, Asia, and Europe. Observers see this merger, along with another one the same year by the two dominant textile unions, as forerunners of a trend that could reduce the number of American unions from one hundred to just twenty by 2010.[27]

THE FUTURE OF THE LABOR-MANAGEMENT RELATIONSHIP: A PARTNERSHIP?

Critics of union mergers see them as a last gasp of an obsolete institution. Some worry that the mega-unions might cause the widespread hostilities of the earlier part of the century to return. As one observer suggests, the best hope for renewed union success would be "a more collaborative relationship" between labor and management.[28]

This goal may be unrealistic. First, many labor leaders began their careers in the days when management was the inherent enemy and contentious strikes were the only form of negotiation that seemed to work. Second, increased competition in almost every segment of the economy has forced business into strategies that often place management in conflict with union employees. Third, many businesses are finding that they can make unions unnecessary by offering their workers such benefits as productivity bonuses, job

---

24. *Ibid.*, p. 70.
25. *Ibid.*, p. 74.
26. R. L. Rose, "As Caterpillar Lures Picket-Line Crossers, A Striker's Mettle Is Put to a Severe Test," *Wall Street Journal*, July 6, 1994, p. B1; and U.S. Department of Labor.
27. S. B. Garland, "Breath of Fire or Last Gasp?" *Business Week*, August 14, 1995, p. 42.
28. Samborn, *op. cit.*, p. A16.

▼ **EXHIBIT 15–5
Average Hourly Blue-
Collar Wages, 1979 to
Present**

Year	Average Blue-Collar Wages, 1996 Dollars
1979	$14.04
1983	$13.24
1988	$12.66
1992	$12.46
1996	$12.52

SOURCE: *Economic Report to the President,* various issues; and *Economic Indicators,* various issues.

security, and many of the employee rights discussed in Chapter 13 (see the *Case—Xerox: A Model of Management-Labor Cooperation*—at the end of this chapter).

One of the major problems the unions face is that they seem to have lost the support of the American public. A sign of this loss of prestige surfaced during congressional debate over the North American Free Trade Agreement in 1993. In a public opinion poll, 62 percent of all respondents said they disapproved of the way organized labor handled its NAFTA lobbying.[29] (The respondents seemed to be antiunion in principle, because very few of us actually understood the intricacies of the NAFTA debate.) The results of this poll, as well as the constant debate over the desirability of unions, suggest that organized labor has less than a firm foothold in American culture.

An obvious contrast is Europe, where some companies consider unions as partners rather than adversaries, and labor political parties are common. The image of unions rarely suffers the kinds of attack that have become common in the United States. (Of course, many European countries have high rates of unemployment, precarious living standards, and mushrooming national debt, so perhaps such union acceptance is not completely desirable.)

Even considering political bias, few experts believe that American unions should just dissolve. "All across the United States, one sees that workers need to have their economic interests represented in order to be able to bargain with their employers to ensure that they receive the best wages and working conditions," insists Lynn Williams, president of the United Steelworkers of America.[30] "There are always going to be people who take advantage of workers. Unions even that out, to their credit. We need them to level the field between labor and management," echoes Senator Orrin G. Hatch.[31] The challenge for organized labor, as well as for the business interests with which it deals, is to come up with a framework that makes a union an asset rather than a liability in the modern marketplace.

---

29. "U.S. & Mexico Labor Sectors Undergoing Transition after Implementation of North American Free Trade Agreement," *Sourcemex Economy,* February 16, 1994, p. 1.
30. B. Presley Noble, "Reinventing Labor: An Interview with Union President Lynn Williams," *Harvard Business Review,* July–August 1993, p. 121.
31. Bernstein, *op. cit.,* p. 70.

THE DELICATE BALANCE

Although the proportion of the labor force that is unionized has fallen steadily in the past several decades, employers in some industries must still take account of actual or potential union activity. An employer with a nonunionized labor force must rationally respond to the threat of unionization. An employer that attempts to convince its work force not to agree to become unionized must follow rather strict procedures.

A company in which the labor force is already unionized faces a delicate balance between trying to avoid a strike and keeping labor costs low enough to maintain the company's profitability. Both companies and unions certainly have an incentive to reach agreements that do not cause the ultimate bankruptcy of the employers. Companies with unionized labor forces confront another serious question when labor negotiations fail and workers walk out on strike. Should replacements be hired? If so, should they be offered permanent positions? What should the employer do if the strike ends and that employer wants to keep the replacements?

Sometimes employers anticipate a strike. They increase production rates and stockpile higher-than-normal quantities of the goods they produce in order to better weather the strike. Is this an unfair labor practice? Some may say yes, and lawsuits may ensue. The fact is there is no easy way to deal with union questions.

TERMS AND CONCEPTS FOR REVIEW

Appropriate bargaining unit 453
Cease-and-desist order 451
Closed shop 452
Collective bargaining 455
Exclusive bargaining agent 455
Featherbedding 456

Hot-cargo agreement 460
Injunction 451
Lockout 461
National Labor Relations Board (NLRB) 451
Nondiscrimination rule 454

Protected concerted action 466
Right-to-work law 452
Secondary boycott 459
Severance pay 456
Wildcat strike 460

SUMMARY

1. The Norris-LaGuardia Act of 1932 extended legal protection to peaceful strikes, picketing, and boycotts. It also restricted the power of the courts to issue injunctions against unions engaged in peaceful strikes. The National Labor Relations Act of 1935 established the rights of employees to engage in collective bargaining and to strike.

2. The Labor-Management Relations Act of 1947 (Taft-Hartley Act) extended certain protections to employers that were already enjoyed by employees. The act provided a list of activities that unions could not practice and allowed employers to propagandize against unions prior to any National Labor Relations Board (NLRB) election.

3. Closed shops require that all workers belong to a union as a condition of employment. The Taft-Hartley Act made closed shops illegal. Union shops, by contrast, merely require that workers join a union after a specified amount of time on the job. Union shops are legal. Each state is free to determine whether union membership may be required for continued employment in any organization.

4. The Labor-Management Reporting and Disclosure Act of 1959 (the Landrum-Griffin Act) regulates internal union business procedures and union elections. It also imposes certain restrictions on the types of persons who may serve as union officers and outlaws hot-cargo agreements.

5. Before beginning an organization effort, a union will attempt to assess worker support for unionization by obtaining signed authorization cards from the employees. The union can then ask the employer to recognize the union, or it can submit the cards with a petition to the NLRB.

6. In determining whether workers constitute an appropriate bargaining unit, the NLRB will consider whether the skills, tasks, and jobs of the workers are sufficiently similar so that they can all be adequately served by a single negotiating position.

7. During a union election, an employer may legally limit union activities as long as it can offer legitimate business justifications for those limitations. In regulating the union's presence on the business premises, the employer must treat the union in the same way it would treat any other entity having on-site contact with its workers.

8. The NLRB is charged with monitoring union elections. The NLRB is particularly sensitive to any threats in an employer's communications to its workers, such as declarations that a union victory will result in the closing of the plant. The NLRB will also closely monitor sudden policy changes regarding compensation, hours, or working conditions that the employer makes before the election.

9. Once a union is elected, its representatives engage in collective bargaining with the employer. Each side tries to use its economic power to persuade or pressure the other side to grant concessions. Topics such as wages, hours of work, and other conditions of employment must be discussed during collective bargaining sessions. Other topics, such as college scholarships for the children of union members, may also be brought up for consideration. Some demands, such as a demand for featherbedding or for a closed shop, are illegal.

10. If the parties reach an impasse, the union may call a strike against the employer to apply additional economic pressure. During a strike, an employer is no longer obligated to pay union members, and union members are no longer required to show up for work. The right to strike is of fundamental importance to the collective bargaining process, because it is one way in which the union can offset the superior bargaining power possessed by management.

11. Strikers are not permitted to engage in secondary boycotts by picketing the suppliers or customers of an employer. Similarly, striking employees are not permitted to coerce the employer's customers into agreeing not to do business with the employer.

12. A wildcat strike occurs when a minority of union members engage in a strike against the employer without the permission of the union.

13. An employer may hire permanent replacement employees in the event of an economic strike. If the strike is called by the union to protest the employer's unwillingness to engage in good faith negotiations, then the employer must rehire the striking workers after the strike is settled, even if it has since replaced them with other workers.

14. An employer may respond to a threatened employee strike with a lockout, or shutting down the plant altogether to prevent employees from working. Lockouts are used when the employer believes a strike is imminent.

15. Certification by the NLRB means that a union is the exclusive representative of a bargaining unit and that the employer must recognize the union and bargain with it in good faith over issues affecting all employees who are within the bargaining unit. A union's certification may not be challenged for a period of one year to give it time to establish itself.

16. Union unfair labor practices include secondary boycotts, coercing employees to participate in or refrain from union activities, and discriminating against employees who support or refuse to support union activities.

17. Since the 1970s, union membership has declined, except among public sector employees.

EXERCISES

1. Why is a union shop essentially illegal in states that have right-to-work laws?

2. Reread *Exhibit 15–2* on bad faith in bargaining. Write out a hypothetical contract proposal made by management that would be deemed bargaining in bad faith by the National Labor Relations Board.

3. Why are strikers prohibited from engaging in secondary boycotts?

4. In 1995, President Bill Clinton attempted to put into place a legal strategy that would prevent some employers from hiring permanent replacements for striking workers. Given that unions represent a declining share of the American work force (and hence of the population), why do you think Clinton showed such strong support for striking union workers?

5. Suppose that you are working in an organization that is unionized. You would like to get a better deal than your fellow workers, because you believe you are more valuable to your boss. What prevents you from negotiating individually with your boss?

6. Does certification of a union by the National Labor Relations Board mean that the certified union will remain the exclusive representative of the bargaining unit? Why or why not?

7. How does the concept of substitution affect the power of unions today?

8. How might global competition affect the power of unions today?

9. A group of employees at the Briarwood Furniture Company's manufacturing plant were interested in joining a union. A representative of the AFL-CIO told the group that her union was prepared to represent the workers and suggested that the group begin organizing by obtaining authorization cards from the employees. After obtaining 252 authorization cards from among Briarwood's 500 nonmanagement employees, the organizers requested that the company recognize the AFL-CIO as the official representative of the employees. The company refused. Has the company violated federal labor laws? What should the organizers do?

10. The Briarwood Furniture Company, discussed in *Exercise 9*, employs 400 unskilled workers and 100 skilled workers in its plant. The unskilled workers operate the industrial machinery used in processing Briarwood's line of stan-

dardized plastic office furniture. The skilled workers, who work in a separate part of the plant, are experienced artisans who craft Briarwood's line of expensive wood furniture products. Do you see any problems with a single union's representing all the workers at the Briarwood plant? Explain your answer. Would your answers to the preceding problem change if you knew that 51 of the authorization cards had been signed by the skilled workers, with the remainder signed by the unskilled workers?

11. Suppose that the employees of Consolidated Stores are undergoing a unionization campaign. Before the election, management says that the union is unnecessary to protect workers. Management also provides bonuses and wage increases to the workers during this period. The employees reject the union. Union organizers protest that the wage increases during the election campaign unfairly prejudiced the vote. Should these wage increases be regarded as an unfair labor practice? Discuss your answer.

12. SimpCo was engaged in ongoing negotiations over a new labor contract with the union representing the company's employees. As the deadline for expiration of the old labor contract drew near, several employees, who were also active in union activities, were disciplined for being late to work. The union claimed that other employees had not been dealt with as harshly and that

the company was discriminating on the basis of union activity. When the contract negotiations failed and the old contract expired, the union called a strike. The company claimed that the action was an economic strike to press the union's demands for higher wages. The union contended that the action was an unfair-labor-practice strike because of the alleged discrimination. What importance does the distinction have for the striking workers and for the company?

13. The employees of Midland National Life Insurance were engaged in a unionization campaign. To fight the union, Midland distributed campaign literature, including a six-page document distributed the day before the election that described a strike at Meilman Food Company. The document suggested that the Meilman strike had become violent and had caused that plant to shut down. These statements were demonstrably false. In the election, 107 workers cast ballots for the union, and 107 workers voted against the union. The union organizers filed an unfair-labor-practice complaint against Midland with the National Labor Relations Board (NLRB), complaining of the inaccuracy of the campaign literature. How should the NLRB decide this issue? Discuss your answer fully.

SELECTED REFERENCES

▶ Draper, Alan. *Conflict of Interests: Organized Labor and the Civil Rights Movement in the South, 1954–1968.* Ithaca, N.Y.: ILR Press, 1994.

▶ Edwards, Richard. *Contested Terrain: The Transformation of the Workplace in the Twentieth Century.* New York: Basic Books, 1979.

▶ Flanagan, Robert J. *Trade Union Behavior, Pay Bargaining, and Economic Performance.* New York: Oxford University Press, 1993.

▶ Greenstone, J. David. *Labor in American Politics.* New York: Knopf, 1969.

▶ Vigilante, Richard. *Strike: The Daily News War and the Future of American Labor.* New York: Simon & Schuster, 1994.

▶ Walsh, David J. *On Different Plans: An Organizational Analysis of Cooperation and Conflict among Airline Unions.* Ithaca, N.Y.: ILR Press, 1994.

▶ Wolkingson, Benjamin W. *Employment Law: The Workplace Rights of Employees and Employers.* Cambridge, Mass.: Blackwell, 1996.

▶ Zeiger, Robert H. *American Workers, American Unions.* Baltimore: Johns Hopkins University Press, 1995.

RESOURCES ON THE INTERNET

▼ You can find an extensive index of resources on labor law compiled by the Institute of Labor Relations at Cornell University. Go to
  http://www.ilr.cornell.edu/othersites/

▼ The American Federation of Labor–Congress of Industrial Organizations (AFL-CIO) provides policy statements, press releases,

boycott lists, and other information on its operations over the Internet. To access this information, go to
  http://www.aflcio.org/

To access the AFL-CIO's biweekly newsletter on the Internet, go to
  http://www.aflcio.org/newsonline/

RESOURCES ON THE INTERNET (CONTINUED)

▼ The Institute for Global Communications provides an on-line guide to many of the unions in the United States. To access this service, called LaborNet, go to

**http:www.igc.apc.org/labornet/
unions.htlml**

▼ For information on opportunities for employee-employer cooperation, access the following:

http://www.fed.org/fed/

XEROX: A MODEL OF MANAGEMENT-LABOR COOPERATION

Background

Until the 1970s, the Samford, Connecticut–based Xerox Corporation was an unchallenged giant in the photocopying machine industry. The company enjoyed a market share of 80 percent and high profit margins. It was relatively generous in its labor contracts and had a stable relationship with the Amalgamated Clothing and Textile Workers Union (ACTWU).

In the early 1980s, however, increased competition from Japanese firms dropped Xerox's copier market share to less than half, and the company came close to bankruptcy. Management knew that changes needed to be made to affect production, cost, and quality, but it was also aware that such changes could not be made without the full cooperation of employees and, hence, the labor union. Xerox needed to change work rules to allow for greater flexibility and productivity, and the company expected to form a partnership with employees and the union to reach those ends. ACTWU leadership agreed to go along with the changes, but only if its members received job security in return. The resulting management-labor partnership at the company's Webster, New York, facility literally saved Xerox Corporation.

Labor Conditions at Xerox

During the 1950s and 1960s, as Xerox established itself as the dominant photocopier maker in the world, labor negotiations were not a primary worry of company management. Employees received ample wages and benefits, and the company was profitable enough to share its wealth. Furthermore, says Joe Laymon, director of corporate industrial relations for Xerox, "It was relatively easy to pass the additional costs on to customers who didn't have many alternatives in the marketplace."

That *de facto* monopoly situation disappeared in the 1970s, when ultraefficient Japanese companies entered the industry. "The foreign competition was selling products at a price that it cost us to make them," remembers Laymon. "And the products were of outstanding quality. For the first time, the American consumer had a choice, and their choices were based on quality, price, and delivery. In all three of those areas, we tended not to be the best provider." It was not surprising that Xerox's revenues flattened and its costs soared as it tried to stay competitive with the Japanese firms.

Management realized that to regain its market share, the company would have to reduce the cost of doing business while at the same time improving the standards and quality of its product. Top executives saw employee involvement in quality control as critical in reaching these goals, which meant they would need the cooperation of ACTWU, the union that represented four thousand workers in the key areas.

Initially, progress in talks between the two sides was slow. The 1980 ACTWU contract contained a provision that the union "would explore the concept of employee involvement," but it did not contain any substantial concessions. In fact, it specifically prohibited employee-involvement programs that affected wages and work rules. Management, for its part, wanted employee involvement to occur on workers' off-hours, an unacceptable condition to the union.

Cooperation increased over the next few years, as management launched its "Leadership Through Quality" worker training program with the help of ACTWU. When negotiations for the 1983 ACTWU pact began, union officials were more willing to explore creative options. Laymon remembers being told by union officials that if Xerox was serious about getting union members' support for cutting costs, "then take away their biggest fear, which is the loss of employment." Basically, workers needed assurance that any ideas they supported would not eventually leave them unemployed.

The Mexico City Impetus

When the 1983 labor contract was signed, it contained three-year job guaranties. In return, ACTWU members accepted a pay freeze for the first year of the contract, a cut in benefits coverage, and a no-fault absenteeism program that would allow for termination of employment for four non-illness-related absences over a twelve-month period. Xerox was also permitted to hire temporary workers and to use outside sources for any work that could not be performed competitively at the Webster facility.

Initially, union members did not embrace the idea of employee involvement. They generally felt that Xerox's financial difficulties were the fault of management, not of employees, and that the union workers should not have had to give concessions when the company was at fault. As a result, admits ACTWU head Gary Bonadonna, to punish the company, the workers did not involve themselves.

CASE (CONTINUED)

That attitude changed when Xerox announced that because of the Webster plant's high manufacturing costs, it could save $3 million by moving production of the wire harness—the mechanism through which electric currents are delivered through the copier—to its plant outside Mexico City. According to the contract, however, before the company could consider such a move, it had to give the union the opportunity to reduce the costs of the wire-harness operation to keep it in Webster. The company had to cover the financial, engineering, and legal costs for a small management-labor team that had three to seven weeks to make a competitive bid.

For the wire-harness operation, a team of eight individuals, led by a company manager and a union employee and consisting of representatives from both sides, analyzed why manufacturing costs were higher in Webster. Eventually, the team found ways to reduce overtime, redesign factory layout to pare down overhead costs and production inefficiencies, and employ more self-management. The team discovered, for example, that the wire-harness operation was being charged for one-sixth of the company's energy bill although it was responsible for only one-fiftieth of its electricity use. The management-labor cooperation team was also able to find savings in cheaper materials; different training methods; and the purchase of new, more efficient materials. In the end, the team's suggested changes saved Xerox $2.9 million and kept the wire-harness operation from moving to Mexico City. The benefit for ACTWU was that 180 union members kept their jobs.

Focus Factories

The wire-harness success provided the impetus for employee-involvement programs, but in 1990 Xerox management realized that further changes would have to be made. According to Laymon, the company's manufacturing operation had grown large and unmanageable. To study the problem of the need for greater efficiency, he took union representatives on an introductory tour of "focus factories" in Europe, California, and Texas.

A focus factory consists of self-managed cells of workers who produce specific product lines more efficiently than do workers in an assembly line approach. Each cell contains its own finance, engineering, human resources, and quality control staffs, which significantly reduces the number of management personnel and places decision-making responsibility on employees. "These factories were smaller, self-contained, quick-to-respond entities that were more manageable, had higher productivity, better team cohesiveness, and higher quality of work than nonfocus factories," says Laymon. Furthermore, their cost of operations was lower.

Under the latest contract with Xerox, ACTWU officials were under no obligation to begin implementing focus factories until 1992. Union leadership, however, accepted the importance of the new approach for the long-term health of Xerox and allowed for employee movement without regard for seniority in order to staff the new cells. By 1991, a focus team made up of both management and union representatives had created six focus factories used for consumer replacement units, low-volume machines, high-volume machines, components, and color machines.

Xerox executives were pleased with the results. "You get the workers' views and you also get the managers' views in terms of the big picture," says vice president Ron Slahetka. "And when you get both views, you can get more data and can come up with more effective solutions. Also, if everyone's involved, it's easier to implement." Whereas there was once one management-chosen supervisor for every twenty employees at Xerox, now the cells elect their leaders from within the group. This employee-manager helps set schedules, balance overtime pay, order parts, and assign tasks on short- and long-term bases. Consequently, "the teams tend to be more cohesive than they were before," says Laymon.

A Landmark Contract

Xerox management showed its appreciation for the union's willingness to cooperate with a landmark contract in June 1994. Although the company was going through a major restructuring that projected layoffs of more than ten thousand workers nationwide, the four thousand union members were given seven-year job guarantees. In return, the employees would be given no wage increases except quarterly cost-of-living adjustments to keep pace with inflation, and the previous condition concerning the use of outside sources and temporary workers remained in place. Thanks to the spirit of negotiation established between management and labor, the contract talks were remarkably painless. ACTWU had only twelve demands, and management countered with a mere seven requests to change these demands. The talks concluded after just five weeks with a single three-hour meeting.

The cooperation has produced impressive results for Xerox. The focus factories have cut product development costs by 30 percent, improved quality, and increased return on investment by 8 percent, to 14 percent. As a result, the

CASE (CONTINUED)

copier manufacturer became the first American company to win back market share from Japanese competitors without the support of the federal government.

Critical Thinking Questions

1. How does this case underscore the effect that global competition has had on union power in the United States? How did Japan's success in the photocopier market limit ACTWU's bargaining position?

2. How has the existence of less expensive foreign labor further weakened U.S. labor unions? Would Xerox have been ethically justified in moving the wire-harness operation to Mexico City if the ACTWU had not been able to cut costs sufficiently?

3. On what grounds could the ACTWU have challenged the concept of focus factories? Why do you think it did not?

4. What lessons does the Xerox–ACTWU relationship hold for other management-labor partnerships?

SOURCE: D. Anfuso, "Xerox Partners with the Union to Regain Market Share," *Personnel Journal*, August 1994, p. 46.

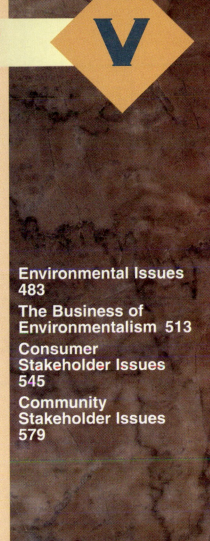

PART V

EXTRINSIC STAKEHOLDERS

CHAPTER 16

ENVIRONMENTAL ISSUES

CHAPTER OUTLINE

Introduction

When the human population was small and dispersed and industry was limited, the earth was relatively unspoiled. Environmental degradation was not a significant problem. As the world has become more populated, urbanized, and industrialized, people have become more concerned about how human beings affect the global ecosystem—our "Spaceship Earth," as the American engineer, architect, and inventor R. Buckminster Fuller (1895–1983) called it. According to some, the generation of waste by society threatens the very existence of human life. Controlling this waste is not without a price, however. For many businesses, the costs are high. Businesses face a constant tension between the desire to increase profits and productivity and the need to improve the quality of the environment.

In this chapter and the next, we discuss this tension and the emergence of environmental protection as a controversial topic in the past few decades. Try to keep in mind, as you contemplate the issues raised in these chapters, that there are no simple answers to environmental problems, despite the many activists, politicians, and business executives who would like to find easy solutions. The environment and our knowledge of it are not static; constant shifts in the ecosystem and in our understanding have a tendency to frustrate even the most carefully crafted environmental plans.

For example, after the oil tanker *Exxon Valdez* spilled eleven million gallons of oil into Prince William Sound, Alaska, Exxon came up with the idea of spraying the beaches and rocks of the sound with warm seawater to wash the oil slick away. This plan won the approval of both the National Oceanic and Atmospheric Administration (NOAA) and the Environmental Protection Agency (EPA). Unfortunately, the warm spray sterilized the rocks and killed off many forms of lower marine life. Furthermore, 90 percent of the sea otters captured and caged for their own protection during the process died of diseases they contracted in captivity. "At the time, it made sense," said Sylvia Earle, chief scientist at NOAA. "[Now we know that] sometimes the best and ironically the most difficult thing to do in the face of an ecological disaster is to do nothing."[1]

Technology can also change environmental policy. Because of the fact that the oil in automobile engines should be changed every 3,000 to 5,000 miles, environmentalists have long pointed out the damage done by the billions of gallons of oil that need to be disposed of every year. Engineers at TF Purliner, Inc., however, have come up with an oil-cleansing system that allows vehicles to travel as many as 250,000 miles without needing an oil change. This process would dramatically change the future of the oil-disposal debate.[2]

The key to keeping a grasp on the changing world of environmental controversy is being well informed on the environmental issues and the federal, state, and local regulations that society has devised to deal with them. This chapter will provide insight into issues such as pollution, recycling, and global environmentalism, as well as discussions of the statutes that regulate these issues.

---

1. H. G. Sparrow, "EcoQuiz II: How Environmentally Correct Can You Get?" *Washington Post*, June 5, 1994, p. C3.
2. "Change Your Oil Every 250,000 Miles," *Business Week*, June 20, 1994, p. 171.

FEDERAL REGULATION OF THE ENVIRONMENT

Congress has passed a number of statutes to control the impact of human activities on the environment. The major federal environmental statutes are listed in *Exhibit 16–1*.

NATIONAL ENVIRONMENTAL POLICY ACT

The National Environmental Policy Act (NEPA) of 1969 imposes environmental responsibilities on all agencies of the federal government by requiring that they consider environmental factors when making significant decisions. Effectively, for every major federal action that significantly affects the quality of the environment, an **environmental impact statement (EIS)** must be prepared. An action qualifies as "major" if it involves a substantial commitment of resources (monetary or otherwise). An action is "federal" if a federal agency has the power to control it. Construction by a private developer of a ski resort on federal land, for example, may require an EIS. So would building or operating a nuclear power plant that requires a federal permit, or constructing a dam as part of a federal project.

An EIS must analyze (1) the impact on the environment that the action will have, (2) any adverse effects to the environment and alternative actions that might be taken, and (3) irreversible effects that the action might cause. If an agency decides that an EIS is unnecessary, it must issue a statement supporting this conclusion. The EIS has become an instrument by which private citizens, consumer interest groups, businesses, and others can challenge federal agency actions on the basis that the actions improperly threaten the environment. Today, much environmental litigation involves disputes with government agencies rather than disputes between private parties.

COMPLEMENTARY FEDERAL LAWS

Other federal laws also require that environmental values be considered in agency decision making. Among the most important of these laws are those that have been enacted to protect fish and wildlife. Under the Fish and Wildlife Coordination Act of 1958, federal agencies proposing to approve the impounding or diversification of the waters of a stream must consult with the Fish and Wildlife Service with a goal of preventing the loss of fish and wildlife resources. Also important is the Endangered Species Act of 1973. Under this act, all federal agencies are required to take steps to ensure that their actions "do not jeopardize the continued existence of endangered species" or the habitat of an endangered species. An action may jeopardize the continued existence of a species if it sets in motion a chain of events that reduces the chances of that species to survive.

ENVIRONMENTAL PROTECTION AGENCY

In 1970, the Environmental Protection Agency (EPA) was formed to coordinate federal environmental responsibilities. The EPA administers most federal environmental policies and statutes. Other federal agencies with authority for regulating specific environmental matters include the Department of the Interior, the Department of Defense, the Department of Labor, the Food and Drug Administration, and the Nuclear Regulatory Commission.

▼ **EXHIBIT 16–1 Major Federal Environmental Legislation**

Regulation	Purpose
1899 Refuse Act	Made it unlawful to dump refuse into navigable waters without a permit. A 1966 court decision made all industrial waters subject to this act.
1948 Federal Water Pollution Control Act	Set standards for the treatment of municipal water waste before discharge. Revisions to this act were passed in 1965 and 1967.
1955 Air Pollution Control Act	Assisted local and state governments in establishing control programs and coordinated research.
1963 Clean Air Act	Controlled air pollution from mobile and stationary sources.
1965 Clean Air Act Amendments	Authorized the establishment of federal standards for automobile exhaust emissions, beginning with 1968 models.
1965 Water Quality Act	Authorized the setting of standards for discharges into water.
1967 Air Quality Act	Established air-quality regions and acceptable regional pollution levels; required local and state governments to implement approved control programs or be subject to federal controls.
1969 National Environmental Policy Act	Established the Council for Environmental Quality (CEQ) for the purpose of coordinating all federal pollution-control programs; authorized the establishment of the Environmental Protection Agency (EPA) to implement CEQ policies.
1970 Clean Air Act Amendments	Authorized the EPA to set national air-pollution standards and restricted the discharge of six major pollutants into the lower atmosphere; required automobile manufacturers to reduce nitrogen oxide, hydrocarbon, and carbon monoxide emissions by 90 percent (in addition to the 1965 requirements) during the 1970s.
1972 Federal Water Pollution Control Act Amendments	Set nationwide water quality goal of restoring polluted waters to swimmable, fishable waters by 1983.
1972 Federal Environmental Pesticide Control Act	Required that all pesticides used in interstate commerce be approved and certified for their stated purpose; required certification that they were harmless to humans, animal life, animal feed, and crops.
1972 Noise Control Act	Required the EPA to establish maximum noise level standards below which no harmful effects occur because of interference with speech or other activity.
1973 Endangered Species Act	Required that all federal agencies take steps to ensure that their actions do not jeopardize the continued existence of endangered species or harm the habitat of an endangered species.
1974 Clean Water Act	Originally called the Safe Drinking Water Act, this law set (for the first time) federal standards for water suppliers serving more than twenty-five people, having more than fifteen service connections, or operating more than sixty days a year.
1976 Conservation and Recovery Act	Encouraged the conservation and recovery of resources; put hazardous waste under government control; prohibited the opening of new dumping sites; required that all existing open dumps be closed or upgraded to sanitary landfills by 1983; set standards for providing technical, financial, and marketing assistance to encourage solid-waste management.
1977 Clean Air Act Amendments	Postponed the deadline for automobile emission requirements.
1980 Comprehensive Environmental Response, Compensation and Liability Act	Established a "Superfund" to clean up toxic waste dumps (this important law is discussed later in the chapter).

▼ **EXHIBIT 16–1** *continued*

1990 Clean Air Act Amendments	Provided for precise formulas for new gasoline to be burned in the smoggiest cities, further reduction in carbon monoxide and other exhaust emissions in certain areas that still have dangerous ozone levels in the year 2003, and a cap on total emissions of sulfur dioxide from electricity plants; placed new restraints on toxic pollutants.
1990 Oil Pollution Act	Established liability for the clean-up of navigable waters after oil-spill disasters.

POLLUTION

The term *pollution* is used quite loosely and can refer to a variety of by-products of human activity. Industrial pollution involves mainly air and water but also can include noise and such concepts as aesthetic pollution (when the appearance of a landscape is altered in a negative way). The government has been responding to pollution problems since before the American Revolution; the Massachusetts Bay Colony issued regulations to try to stop the pollution of Boston Harbor. In the nineteenth century, states passed laws controlling water pollution after scientists and medical researchers convinced most policymakers that dumping sewage into drinking and bathing water caused disease. In the second half of the twentieth century, regulation has become intensely focused on specific forms of pollution, some of which we discuss in the following pages.[3]

AIR POLLUTION

The most important effect of air pollution is its threat to human health (see *Exhibit 16–2* on page 488). A report in the *New England Journal of Medicine* concluded that air pollution, especially from automobile exhaust and smokestacks, can shorten lives by up to two years. The study concentrated on Stubenville, Ohio (the most polluted municipal area observed), and Portage, Wisconsin (the least polluted). Residents of Stubenville were 26 percent more likely than those in Portage to die from lung cancer, lung disease, and heart disease, yet the level of air pollution in Stubenville was within federal limits.[4]

Federal involvement in the air-pollution issue goes back to the 1950s, when Congress authorized funds for air-pollution research.[5] In 1963, the federal government passed the Clean Air Act, the first federal attempt to regulate air pollution. The act focused on multi-state air pollution, authorized the creation of emissions standards, and provided assistance to states. Various amendments, particularly in 1970, 1977, and 1990, strengthened the government's authority to regulate the quality of air.

Motor Vehicles Regulations governing air pollution from automobiles and other mobile sources specify pollution standards and time schedules for clean-up measures. For example, the 1970 Clean Air Act (actually an amendment to the 1963 act) required a 90 percent reduction in the amount of carbon monoxide and hydrocarbons emitted from automobiles by 1975. (This did not happen, however, and the act was amended to extend

---

3. J. A. Savage and J. M. Majot, "Industry Preaches Green but Is Far from Clean," *Business and Society Review*, Spring 1993, p. 10.
4. "Air Pollution Standards May Need Tightening, Study Suggests," *Washington Post*, December 9, 1993, p. A3.
5. D. B. Webster, "The Free Market for Clean Air," *Business and Society Review*, Summer 1994, p. 34.

the deadline to 1983.) An automobile purchased today emits only about 4 percent of the pollutants that a new 1970 model did. Nevertheless, so many more automobiles are being driven today that urban ground-level ozone, which decreased between the late 1970s and the late 1980s, has risen in some cities to former levels. Under the 1990 amendments, automobile manufacturers must cut the exhaust emission of nitrogen oxide from new automobiles by 60 percent and the emission of other pollutants by 35 percent. Beginning in 1994, increasing numbers of new vehicles had to meet these standards. By 1998, all new automobiles will have had to do so.

Stationary Sources   The Clean Air Act also authorizes the EPA to establish air-quality standards for stationary sources (such as electric utilities and manufacturing plants), but

▼ **EXHIBIT 16–2**
Seven Main Classes of Air Pollutants

- *Carbon monoxide* is a colorless, odorless, poisonous gas that can reduce mental performance and result in death if inhaled in sufficient quantities.

- *Sulfur oxides* are acrid, corrosive, poisonous gases that are produced when fuel containing sulfur is burned.

- *Nitrogen oxides* are produced when fuel is burned at very high temperatures. (After being emitted into the atmosphere, sulfur dioxides and nitric oxides convert into sulfates and nitrates and return to the earth as acid rain.)

- *Hydrocarbons* are unburned fuel, an ingredient of smog.

- *Ozone* is smog, a gas that results from the combination of hydrocarbon vapors and nitrogen oxides in the presence of sunlight.

- *Lead* is a metallic chemical element that as an environmental contaminant often occurs as lead oxide aerosol or dust.

- *Particulates* are particles of solid or liquid substances produced by stationary fuel combustion and industrial processes.

it recognizes that the primary responsibility for preventing and controlling air pollution rests with state and local governments. The EPA sets two levels (primary and secondary) of ambient standards—that is, the maximum level of certain pollutants—and the states formulate plans to achieve those standards. The plans are to provide for the attainment of primary standards within three years and secondary standards within a reasonable time. For economic, political, or social reasons, however, the deadlines are often subject to change.[6]

Hazardous air pollutants are those likely to cause an increase in mortality or an irreversible or incapacitating illness. There are 189 hazardous air pollutants, including asbestos, benzene, beryllium, cadmium, mercury, radon, vinyl chloride, and other materials, many of them carcinogenic. These pollutants may also cause neurological and reproductive damage. They are emitted by a variety of business activities, including smelting, dry cleaning, house painting, and commercial baking.

Penalties For violations of emissions limits under the Clean Air Act, the EPA can assess civil penalties of up to $25,000 per day. To penalize companies for whom this amount makes a violation more cost effective than compliance, the EPA can obtain a penalty equal to the violators' economic benefits from noncompliance. Private citizens can also sue violators. Those individuals or corporations who knowingly violate this act may be subject to criminal fines.

WATER POLLUTION

The major sources of water pollution are industrial, municipal, and agricultural. Pollutants entering streams, lakes, and oceans include organic wastes, heated water, sediments from soil run-off, nutrients (such as detergents, fertilizers, and human and animal wastes), toxic chemicals, and other hazardous substances.

Certain types of fish and other aquatic life cannot live in waters in which organic wastes decompose. Heated water speeds the growth of algae and disrupts fish reproduction. The accumulation of sediments and nutrients accelerates the natural process that turns lakes into land. Toxic chemicals and hazardous substances make water and fish unsafe for human consumption, even after the water has been treated or the fish have been cooked. Despite progress made during the 1970s and 1980s, 40 percent of U.S. waterways were still too polluted for fishing or swimming in 1995.[7]

Navigable Waters Federal regulations governing the pollution of water can be traced back to the Rivers and Harbors Act of 1886, as amended in 1899. These regulations required a permit for discharging or depositing refuse in navigable waterways. Once limited to waters actually used for navigation, the term *navigable waters* is today interpreted to include coastal and freshwater wetlands (how the EPA defines *wetlands* will be discussed shortly), as well as intrastate lakes and streams used by intrastate travelers and industries.

In 1972, amendments to the Federal Water Pollution Control Act of 1948 established a new system of goals and standards. These amendments established goals to (1) make waters safe for swimming, (2) protect fish and wildlife, and (3) eliminate the discharge of pollutants into the water. They set forth specific time schedules, which were extended by amendment in 1977 and by the Water Quality Act of 1987. Regulations, for the most part,

---

6. E. Barker, "Du Pont Tries to Clean Up Its Act," *Business and Society Review*, Winter 1992, p. 36.

7. "Congress Wants to Gut Clean Water Act," *Water Tech News*, May 1, 1995, p. 1.

specify that the best available antipollution technology be installed. The 1972 amendments also required municipal and industrial polluters to apply for permits before discharging wastes into navigable waters. As with the Clean Air Act, violators of the Clean Water Act are subject to a variety of civil and criminal penalties, as well as injunctive relief and damages. The polluting party can be required to clean up the pollution or pay for the cost of doing so.

Wetlands   The Clean Water Act prohibits the filling or dredging of **wetlands** unless a permit is obtained from the Army Corps of Engineers. Initially, the EPA defined wetlands as "those areas that are inundated or saturated by surface or groundwater at a frequency and duration sufficient to support, and that under normal circumstances do support, a prevalence of vegetation typically adapted for life in [water] saturated soil conditions." Following President George Bush's promise in 1989 that the country would suffer no "net losses" in wetlands under his administration, however, the definition was expanded to include any land in which water is present within eighteen inches of the surface for one week of the year.

The new definition elicited substantial controversy because of its broad interpretation of what constitutes a wetland that is subject to the regulatory authority of the federal government. The definition covered potholes that fill with water after heavy rains, manmade agricultural ditches, pine forests, and 40 percent of California, which was stricken by a drought at the time of Bush's promise. Thus, businesses and landowners must be very careful about any changes they make on their property. In the early 1990s, as an example, John Pozsgai went to prison for three years for filling a tire dump near Trenton, New Jersey, with topsoil. Because of a small stream that ran on the edge of the land in damp conditions, the property was deemed a wetland, and Pozsgai was found to be in violation of the Clean Water Act.[8]

Drinking Water   Another statute governing water pollution is the Safe Drinking Water Act, later renamed the Clean Water Act. Passed in 1974, this act requires the EPA to set maximum levels for pollutants in public water systems. Operators of public water supply systems must come as close as possible to meeting the EPA's standards by using the best available technology that is economically feasible. The EPA is particularly concerned with contamination from underground sources. Pesticides and wastes leaked from landfills or disposed of in underground injection wells are among the more than two hundred pollutants known to exist in groundwater used for drinking in at least thirty-four states. Many of these substances are associated with cancer and damage to the central nervous system, liver, and kidneys.

Ocean Dumping   The Marine Protection, Research, and Sanctuaries Act of 1972 (popularly known as the Ocean Dumping Act), as amended in 1983, regulates the transportation and dumping of material into ocean waters. It prohibits entirely the ocean dumping of radiological, chemical, and biological warfare agents and high-level radioactive waste. The Ocean Dumping Act also authorizes the designation of marine sanctuaries for "preserving or restoring such areas for their conservation, recreational, ecological, or aesthetic values."

Each violation of any provision may result in a civil penalty of not more than $50,000 or the revocation or suspension of the violator's permit. A knowing violation is a criminal offense that may result in a $50,000 fine, imprisonment for not more than a year, or both.

---

8. M. Fabey, "Many Businesses Say Wetlands Are Overregulated," *Philadelphia Business Journal*, March 30, 1992, p. 1.

Oil Pollution In response to the *Exxon Valdez* disaster in 1989, Congress passed the Oil Pollution Act of 1990. Any onshore or offshore oil facility, oil shipper, vessel owner, or vessel operator that discharges oil into navigable water or onto an adjoining shore may be liable for clean-up costs, as well as damages. The act created a $1 billion oil clean-up and economic compensation fund and decreed that by 2011, oil tankers using U.S. ports must be double hulled to limit the severity of accidental spills.

Technology has provided environmental authorities with an indispensable tool to enforce this act. Called **chemical fingerprinting**, it allows scientists to trace the origins of oil spills by separating and cataloguing specific types of oil products. The Oil Pollution Act, along with the Clean Water Act, metes out harsh penalties to those who damage navigable waters, and chemical fingerprinting should allow the government to assign blame where it is due. Innocent defendants in lawsuits also will benefit; they now have proof and can avoid paying the clean-up costs from oil spills they did not originate.

NOISE POLLUTION

Regulations concerning noise pollution include the Noise Control Act of 1972. This act requires the EPA to establish noise emission standards (maximum noise levels below which no harmful effects occur because of interference with speech or other activity). The standards must be achievable by the best available technology, and they must be economically within reason. The act prohibits, among other things, distributing products whose operation results in noise levels that do not meet the standards. This activity, along with any other activity prohibited under the act, can result in an injunction or whatever other remedy "is necessary to protect the public health and welfare." Illegal product distribution can also result in fines and imprisonment.

The sources of noise pollution are varied and range from motor vehicles and airplanes to chain saws and stereos. In the workplace, the Occupational Safety and Health Administration (OSHA) requires that protection be provided for the ears of workers who are exposed to noise levels of 85 decibels or greater for 8 hours. (For comparison, the decibel level of a lawn mower is between 80 and 96, a motorcycle can reach 110, and a vacuum cleaner hovers between 70 and 85.)[9] Outside the work environment, it often takes legal action to control noise pollution. Despite complaints by nearby residents, for example, the Mission Foods tortilla plant in Los Angeles did not limit the operations of its noisy ovens and deep-fat fryers until the office of the city's attorney charged it with violating noise-pollution laws.

TOXIC CHEMICALS

Originally, most environmental clean-up efforts were directed toward reducing smog and making water safe for fishing and swimming. However, it has become clear that chemicals released into the environment in even relatively small amounts may pose a considerable threat to human life and health. In one year alone, American society produces 300 million tons of toxic waste. Consequently, control of these toxic chemicals has become an important part of environmental law.

Pesticides and Herbicides The first toxic chemicals to receive widespread public attention were pesticides and herbicides. Using these chemicals to kill insects and weeds

---

9. R. S. Bahadori and B. A. Bohne, "Adverse Effects of Noise on Hearing," *American Family Physician*, April 1, 1993, pp. 12–19.

has increased agricultural productivity, but their residue remains in the environment. In some instances, accumulations of this residue have killed animals. Scientists have also identified potential long-term effects that are detrimental to people.

The federal statute regulating pesticides and herbicides is the Federal Insecticide, Fungicide, and Rodenticide Act (FIFRA) of 1947. Under FIFRA, pesticides and herbicides must be (1) registered before they can be sold, (2) certified and used only for approved applications, and (3) used in limited quantities when applied to food crops. If a substance is identified as harmful, the EPA can cancel its registration after a hearing. If the harm is imminent, the EPA can suspend registration pending the hearing. The EPA may also inspect factories in which these chemicals are manufactured.

Other Toxic Substances The first comprehensive law covering toxic substances was the Toxic Substances Control Act, which was passed in 1976. This act regulates chemicals and chemical compounds that are known to be toxic, such as asbestos and polychlorinated biphenyls (PCBs), and investigates any possible harmful effects from new chemical compounds. The regulations authorize the EPA to require that manufacturers, processors, and other organizations planning to use chemicals first determine their effect on human health and the environment. The EPA can regulate substances that potentially pose an imminent hazard or an unreasonable risk of injury to health or the environment. The EPA may require special labeling, limit the use of a substance, set production quotas, or prohibit the use of a substance altogether.

Hazardous Wastes Some industrial, agricultural, and household wastes pose more serious threats. If not properly disposed of, these toxic chemicals may present a substantial danger to human health and the environment. If released into the environment, they may contaminate public drinking water resources.

In 1976, Congress passed the Resource Conservation and Recovery Act (RCRA) in reaction to an ever-increasing concern about the effects of hazardous waste materials on the environment. The RCRA required the EPA to establish regulations to monitor and control hazardous waste disposal and to determine which forms of solid waste should be considered hazardous and thus subject to regulation. Under the authority granted by this act, the EPA has promulgated various technical requirements for limited types of facilities for the storage and treatment of hazardous waste. The EPA also requires all producers of hazardous waste materials to label and properly package any hazardous waste to be transported. Businesses often complain that these hazardous waste regulations are inefficient and result in unacceptable burdens, and there is some momentum toward revamping the rules (see the *Case—The Yorktown Project—*at the end of this chapter).

SUPERFUND

In 1980, Congress passed the Comprehensive Environmental Response, Compensation, and Liability Act (CERCLA), commonly known as **Superfund**. CERCLA provided a $1.6 billion "Superfund," financed by taxes on petroleum products and forty-two chemicals, to provide for the clean-up of hazardous waste that could not be traced to a particular party.[10]

Superfund, as amended in 1986 by the Superfund Amendments and Reauthorization Act (SARA), states that in the event of a real or threatened toxic release from a site, the

---

10. J. A. Hird, *Superfund: The Political Economy of Environmental Risk* (Baltimore: John Hopkins University Press, 1994), pp. 9–10.

EPA can use federal funds to clean up the site and then recover the cost of the clean-up from (1) the person (individual or corporation) who arranged for the waste disposal (such as the generator), (2) the person who transported the wastes to the site, (3) the person who owned or operated the site at the time of the disposal, or (4) the current owner or operator. A person falling into one of these categories is referred to as a **potentially responsible party (PRP).**

Liability under Superfund   The potential Superfund liability to businesses is enormous:

▼   Liability under Superfund is usually "joint and several"—that is, a person who generated only a fraction of the hazardous waste disposed of at the site may nevertheless be liable for *all* of the clean-up costs.

CERCLA authorizes a party who has incurred clean-up costs to bring a "contribution action" against any other person who is liable for a percentage of the costs (see *Company Focus: Paramount Communications, Inc.* on page 494).

Courts often focus on the meaning of the words *owner or operator* to determine who is a PRP. In the past, a parent company has been held liable as an operator for clean-up costs for a chemical spill at a plant owned by its subsidiary. The court pointed out that the parent company controlled the subsidiary's finances, real estate transactions, and a contract with the government, and that the parent company's personnel held most of the subsidiary's officer and director positions. In other cases, courts have held officers and shareholders liable based on their authority to exercise control over their corporations.

Reforming Superfund   When CERCLA came up for renewal in 1994, the difficult job of placating its many critics fell to the Clinton administration. Environmentalists did not think Superfund went far enough and were dissatisfied with its performance record: Since 1981, only 49 of the 1,270 sites the EPA had placed on its Superfund list had been

COMPANY FOCUS: PARAMOUNT COMMUNICATIONS, INC.

SUPERFUND AND CAVEAT EMPTOR

Residents in Palmerton, Pennsylvania, have a soil-contamination problem. Thanks to a 33-ton, 2.5-mile-long, 100-foot-high cinder bank generated by 80 years of zinc-smelting operations, many of the 5,000 people in the city have been forced to retill their lawns to decontaminate the soil. Government regulators are worried that high levels of ground contamination from the zinc smelter could pose a danger to pregnant women and children under six years old. As late as 1993, fires were still burning from the waste site, which was abandoned in 1980.

In 1983, the Environmental Protection Agency (EPA) designated the area a Superfund site, requiring the owner of the land to cover the costs of a clean-up. That would be Horsehead Industries, whose Zinc Corporation of America is still producing zinc by-products at the location. Horsehead, however, bought the property in 1981 from Paramount Communications, Inc. The EPA has designated Paramount a potentially responsible party (PRP), which makes it liable for part of the clean-up bill. Horsehead, claiming that Paramount was not contributing its fair share, hit the giant communications company with a lawsuit. Paramount retorted, in essence, *caveat emptor*—"let the buyer beware."

ment Company, a recycler of zinc-bearing electric arc furnace dust. Since the plot was designated a Superfund site, Horsehead has spent $15 million in clean-up efforts, but the EPA does not believe the area to be up to environmental standards. The federal agency wants Horsehead to cover the cinder bank with three feet of topsoil, which could cost $250 million, or remove the cinder accumulation completely, which would be even more expensive.

Starting in 1991, Horsehead began private negotiations with Paramount to force it to assume more of the financial responsibility for the clean-up. As a PRP, Paramount had a legal, yet vague, accountability for some of the costs. When the two sides could not agree on the amount of Paramount's contribution, Horsehead took the matter to court.

"Our company is not large enough to cover [Paramount's] liability with our funding," said a Horsehead spokesperson. He noted that because Horsehead had conducted no primary zinc operations at the site, it could not be held responsible for the entire clean-up.

"In the 1981 purchase agreement, Horsehead assumed all responsibility for any and all environmental issues relating to the site," Paramount said in a prepared statement. "Now, twelve years later, it is seeking to shift responsibility. We intend to defend the suit vigorously."

Horsehead's Case

Gulf and Western Natural Resources Group, which is now Paramount Communications, purchased the site in 1966 in the acquisition of New Jersey Zinc Company. Throughout the 1970s, New Jersey Zinc was the city of Palmerton's largest employer and taxpayer, but its zinc-smelting process turned the area into a wasteland. Because of zinc fallout, the town's soil was too poisoned to sustain lawns or other greenery.

All smelting was discontinued in 1980, and the next year Horsehead purchased two thousand acres in the area, forty acres of which now house Horsehead Resource Develop-

The New Bottom Line

Unfortunately for Horsehead, when it purchased the Palmerton site, Superfund legislation was in its infancy and not fully understood by many businesses. The episode has been a disaster, costing the company millions of dollars in clean-up and court expenses for its still-unsettled suit against Paramount. Businesses must be absolutely sure that property they buy is environmentally sound, because PRPs are rarely willing to share the costs of clean-up, at least not without a battle.

SOURCE: Information from "Palmerton Gets Much Study, Less Cleanup," *Superfund Week*, December 24, 1993; "Paramount Answers Horsehead," *American Metal Market*, October 26, 1993, p. 6; and "Lead and Zinc Horsehead Sues Paramount over Cleanup Costs," *Hazardous Waste Business*, October 20, 1993, p. 4.

completely cleaned up.[11] The corporate community balked at the huge costs associated with Superfund; businesses and other nonfederal organizations had spent billions of dollars in hazardous waste clean-up since 1981. Economists point out that these burdens are passed on to consumers as a "hidden tax," and that the extra costs are hampering the competitiveness of U.S. companies abroad. Some pragmatists argue that Superfund actually hurts the environment by giving companies an incentive to build new facilities on "greenfields," or pristine land with no possible taint from previous owners (which the present corporations could be liable for), instead of in older urban areas, or "brownfields."

If there is disagreement over Superfund's results, there is little argument over the pressing problem of the government program: liability. Superfund is characterized by litigation; the EPA sues the alleged polluters to collect clean-up costs, and the alleged polluters sue each other in turn for the same reason. Orin Kramer, president of the consulting firm Kramer Associates, and Richard Briffault, professor at the Columbia University School of Law, observe that Superfund has "degenerated into an elaborate and costly game" in which "each player's behavior is driven by the constant need to prepare for litigation against the other players, and where the ultimate goal is not cleaning up hazardous waste but, instead, shifting the costs of clean-up to the other players."[12] A total of almost $15 billion has been spent on litigation costs since Superfund's inception, not to mention the hundreds of thousands of hours spent in court by various government agencies and businesses. In fact, a study by the University of Kentucky estimates that costs for all hazardous waste clean-up programs, including Superfund expenditures, will total more than $750 billion in the thirty-year period between 1990 and 2020 (see *Exhibit 16–3* on page 496).

Other critics protest that the law should not be applied retroactively as defined in the original act, whereby businesses can be held liable for hazardous waste disposal that was legal at the time but is no longer legal. Still others complain about the "deep pocket" tactics of the EPA. These critics say the EPA often finds the potential responsible party with the most funds to cover a clean-up, regardless of whether that party was primarily responsible for the pollution.

In 1994, the Clinton administration proposed a bill to overhaul the system. Under the new plan, Superfund would not be able to be applied retroactively in some cases, and a new, nonjudicial process to assign costs for clean-ups proportionately among the various responsible companies would be set up. Congress was unable to agree on the renewal of Superfund in 1994, partly because of the influence of the insurance lobby—which balked at a provision in the overhaul that would place a ten-year, $8.1 billion tax on those who insured companies against Superfund lawsuits.

POLLUTERS AND PRISON TERMS

In the past, those who were caught violating federal and state environmental laws—particularly those who illegally dumped hazardous wastes—were usually sued in a civil court proceeding or brought before an administrative board. When the government was successful, the defendant would have to pay a fine that often included the cost of cleaning up the dump site, as well as a hefty punitive fee. Concerns that this approach was making it possible for defendants to buy their way out of lawsuits prompted government attorneys in the mid-1980s to begin prosecuting polluters under various criminal statutes. Although nearly one hundred corporate officials have been jailed since this program began, its true value may be as a deterrent.

---

11. M. B. Regan, "Can Clinton Clean Up the Superfund Morass?" *Business Week*, February 14, 1994, p. 41.
12. O. Kramer and R. Briffault, *Cleaning Up Hazardous Waste: Is There Another Way?* (New York: Insurance Information Institute Press, 1993), p. 64.

▼ **EXHIBIT 16–3
Projected Cost of
Hazardous Waste
Clean-Up,
1990–2020**

Program	Spending (In 1990 Dollars in Billions)
Superfund	$152
RCRA Corrective Action[a]	234
Underground storage tanks[b]	67
Department of Defense[c]	30
Department of Energy[c]	240
State and private clean-up[d]	30
Total	**$752**

a. The Environmental Protection Agency (EPA) estimates that 5,700 facilities are subject to the "Corrective Action" provisions of the Resource Conservation and Recovery Act (RCRA). This program requires the EPA to regulate and oversee the clean-up of contamination resulting from past activities at manufacturing and waste management businesses that must obtain RCRA operating permits.
b. This category covers the clean-up costs of those underground storage tanks not covered under Superfund, including gasoline storage tanks at refueling stations.
c. Federal law requires the clean-up of land used or in use by the Department of Defense and the Department of Energy. This includes closed military bases, power plants, and nuclear weapons factories.
d. Non-Superfund site clean-up costs are often covered by state programs or concerned private parties.

SOURCE: University of Kentucky, Waste Management Research Education Institute, 1991.

Law enforcement officials are turning their attention to corporate executives who set and implement illegal waste-disposal policies. The efforts of these officials are being aided by tougher laws, such as the 1990 Clean Air Act Amendments, which greatly increased the number of environmental crimes that can be treated as felonies. So far, persons convicted of criminal violations have not been high-ranking officers of Fortune 500 companies but rather self-employed businesspersons. That these convictions have not involved executives at better-known companies has prompted criticism that the government is concentrating on smaller defendants who lack the resources to contest such claims vigorously.

In any case, the number of lawyers at the Department of Justice who deal with environmental crimes has increased eightfold in ten years. Similarly, the EPA has more than doubled its number of criminal investigators in the past decade. The result has been that in 1990, the Department of Justice brought 134 indictments for civil environmental crimes—three times the number for any year under the Reagan administration, from 1981 to 1989.[13] Even though defense lawyers continue to declare that it is unfair to hold high-ranking corporate officials responsible for the actions of lower-level employees, it may be only a matter of time before major corporations and their officers are criminally prosecuted for environmental law violations.

13. "What Shade of Green?" *Wall Street Journal*, April 2, 1990, p. A20.

RECYCLING

The current environmental movement includes intensive efforts to save scarce resources via recycling. **Recycling** involves taking paper, plastics, glass, and metal products; treating them so that they become raw material; and then using the material to make another product. To this end, many cities have instituted mandatory recycling programs. More and more Americans, however, do not need to be forced to take part in this activity. By the mid-1990s, Americans were recycling about 15 percent of their garbage, compared with 7 percent thirty-five years earlier. Many feel it part of their civic duty to place old newspapers on the side of the road for curbside collecting or to take aluminum cans and plastic containers to recycling depots. Proponents of recycling celebrate the virtues of individual environmental responsibility.[14]

Others, who question the effectiveness of recycling programs, sense the "warm glow of self-righteousness" in the recycling movement.[15] They point out the following:

▼ Although the benefits of recycling—fewer *natural* resources used—are straightforward, the process does not necessarily save *total* resources.

Recycling paper products, for example, may not necessarily save trees in the long run, according to A. Clar Wiseman, an economist for Resources for the Future, in Washington, D.C. He argues that an increase in paper recycling eventually will lead to a reduction in the demand for virgin paper and, thus, in the demand for trees. Because many trees are planted specifically to produce paper, a reduction in the demand for trees will mean that certain land now used to grow trees will be put to other uses. The end result may be smaller, rather than larger, forests. Nonetheless, every ton of recycled paper does save seventeen cubic yards of landfill space in the short run.

THE DEMAND FOR RECYCLED GOODS

In an economic sense, the efficacy of recycling relies on the demand for recycled goods. If there is no market for the recycled materials, then these materials may wind up in landfills anyway, defeating the purpose of the activity. When there is a market for the waste, recycling can be a highly efficient process. Because recycling aluminum uses only 5 percent of the energy needed to create the material from raw bauxite, there is an economic incentive for businesses to buy used soda and beer cans. The results are predictable: in the United States, approximately 55 percent of aluminum cans are recycled, and in Sweden that number jumps to 70 percent.[16]

Aluminum cans, unfortunately, make up a very small amount (1 percent in the United States) of recycled materials. Garden materials and food waste, for example, make up almost a quarter of the total waste in the United States, but they are notoriously difficult and expensive to recycle. Plastic bottles have a similar problem: a single plastic mayonnaise jar may be made up of many different resins that are impossible for an individual to separate for recycling purposes and that are prohibitively expensive for a business to separate.

---

14. F. Cairncross, "How Europe's Companies Reposition to Recycle," *Harvard Business Review*, March–April 1992, p. 34.
15. F. Cairncross, *Costing the Earth* (Boston: Harvard Business School Press, 1991), p. 235.
16. *Ibid.*

SHIFTING THE BURDEN TO BUSINESS

Reduced demand for recycled materials, combined with lower prices for recycled products, has proved financially disastrous for the government agencies responsible for recycling programs. In the mid-1990s, it cost an average of $175 to $200 a ton to collect and process recycled material that could be sold for only about $40.[17] As a result, local politicians who oversee recycling programs are placed in the difficult position of either having to discontinue them and face angered community environmentalists, or take funds from other programs to pay for recycling. How can these government officials solve this dilemma?

Creating Demand In many cases, the government has decided to create a demand for recycled materials through a variety of programs. In a move applauded by environmentalists, ten states now require paper goods, plastic containers, and other products to have a minimum recycled content, which instantly provided a market for recycled materials. Almost thirty states buy recycled paper themselves, paying 5 to 10 percent above the market prices. Other states have tried to give businesses an incentive to foster recycling.[18] In New York and Illinois, for example, businesses are offered low-interest loans and grants to buy recycling machines or to develop recycled products. Many states have followed suit, offering tax credits to businesses that invest in recycling machines.

In 1992, Florida took a forceful step in this direction; Governor Lawton Chiles unveiled a plan that would urge companies to set up joint ventures to buy waste materials from state agencies. The state, in return, would buy back the recycled goods from the same joint ventures. "It's a no-brainer for the companies," said Chiles. "Not too many businesses have got a captive customer. We think we'll create much more demand for products, and that's what's been missing."[19]

Responsible Entity Other environmentalists and politicians feel that programs offering tax breaks or similar incentives to businesses to encourage recycling pamper American corporations. Senator Max Baucus echoed the thoughts of many when he proclaimed, at the Conference of Mayors and the National Association of Counties, "Anyone who sells a product should be responsible for the product when it becomes waste."[20] This line of thinking holds that industry and business create waste and thus, as **responsible entities,** should pay the cost of its recycling or disposal. A program based on Germany's "Ordinance on the Avoidance of Packaging," in which manufacturers and retailers take full legal responsibility for the packaging of products they produce or sell, would certainly shift the costs of recycling from the public to the private sector (see *Managing Social Issues—International Issues: Germany's "Green Dot" Program*). (Remember, though, that business inevitably passes such costs on to the consumer through "hidden taxes.")

TECHNOLOGY AND RECYCLING

Of course, neither the public nor the private sector is enthusiastic about shouldering the costs of recycling. The best hope for severely limiting these costs can be found in technological advances. Frances Cairncross, environmental editor of *The Economist*, uses the

17. C. Boerner and K. Chilton, *Who Is "Responsible" for Garbage?* (St. Louis: Washington University, Center for the Study of American Business, July 1994), p. 2.

18. A. Mitchell and K. Dupre, "The Environmental Movement: A Status Report and Implications for Pricing," *SAM Advanced Management Journal*, Spring 1994, p. 35.

19. L. M. Grossman, "Florida to Buy Back Its Recycled Waste," *Wall Street Journal*, June 19, 1992, p. B1.

20. Boerner and Chilton, *op. cit.*, p. 1.

◪ MANAGING SOCIAL ISSUES

INTERNATIONAL ISSUES: GERMANY'S "GREEN DOT" PROGRAM

No country in the world has taken the concept of "responsible entity" as far as Germany. In June 1991, that country's Parliament approved the "Ordinance on the Avoidance of Packaging Waste," often referred to as the "green dot" program. Proponents of the responsible entity concept point to the overwhelming volume of recycled material collected by German businesses—420,000 metric tons of used plastics alone in 1994. Critics, however, point to the costs of Germany's ordinance, which they say outweigh the benefits.

Three Categories of Packaging

Generally, the legislation required that manufacturers and retailers take full legal responsibility for the packaging of products they produce or sell. The law separates packaging into three categories: (1) transport packaging, or packaging designed to protect goods during the shipping process; (2) secondary packaging, or additional packaging that has the purpose of allowing products to be sold for self-service, preventing theft, or presenting advertising; and (3) sales packaging, or the actual packaging that contains the product before it is consumed, such as a shoe box or candy-bar wrapper. The law provides different recycling procedures for the various kinds of packaging. Transport packaging must be accepted and reused by manufacturers. Distributors and retailers must allow customers to remove secondary packaging at the point of sale for recycling. Retailers must provide bins for customers to return all sales packaging and previously unremoved secondary packaging. Once the system was in place (by 1993), businesses were required to collect 80 percent of all packaging used.

Duales System Deutschland

Because of the high costs to businesses of running recycling programs themselves, German legislators provided a loophole. All businesses that were part of a privately funded packaging collection and recycling program were exempt from the law. Consequently, German companies formed the Duales System Deutschland (DSD), a nonprofit consortium that collects, sorts, and recycles packaging. The six hundred members each pay a fee for the service based on the weight and material content of the packaging. Once membership fees to DSD have been paid, the recycled packaging is stamped with a "green dot," informing DSD's waste haulers that the material is ready for reprocessing.

Benefits and Costs of the Green Dot Program

Germany's consumers reacted enthusiastically to the green dot program. In the first year of the ordinance, packaging consumption was reduced by approximately 500,000 metric tons—4 percent of total annual waste production. The program also has led to an 80 percent reduction in secondary packaging, which environmentalists had criticized long ago as being particularly wasteful.

In a sense, the German people have been too enthusiastic. In 1993, for example, the DSD expected to collect 100,000 tons of plastic packaging. Instead, 800,000 tons were collected, exceeding the nation's recycling capacity by almost 700 percent. This forced the consortium to export its excess supply of packaging to locations ranging from nearby France to distant Southeast Asia.

Export Possibilities

Some environmentalists would like to see similar legislation passed in the United States, but the likelihood is low. Critics question whether American consumers would be willing to support the higher costs that would result from such a program. It is estimated that a family of four in Germany pays an extra $125 a year in hidden taxes for the green dot program. A responsible entity system in the United States, which has three times the population of Germany, would cost at least $8 billion to $9 billion a year.

For Critical Analysis:

The concept of responsible entity assumes that businesses have no incentive to reduce packaging themselves and therefore must be forced to do so by government. Is this a valid assumption? Explain your answer.

SOURCE: C. Boerner and K. Chilton, *Who Is "Responsible" for Garbage?* (St. Louis: Washington University, Center for the Study of American Business, July 1994), pp. 3–9; "Bonn Determined to Amend Packaging Decree, Official Says," *Environmental Watch Western Europe*, April 7, 1995, p. 1; F. Cairncross, "How Europe's Companies Reposition to Recycle," *Harvard Business Review*, March–April 1992, p. 36; and "Germany Rescues Recycler," *Wall Street Journal*, November 1, 1993, p. A12.

example of junk cars in the United States to illustrate how technology has affected the market for recyclables.[21]

In the late 1960s, the practice of dumping old cars in unseemly junkyards had become so widespread that in 1970, President Richard Nixon mentioned the problem in a speech to Congress. Within three years, thanks to two technological advances, the number of junked cars cluttering the landscape had largely diminished. First, a new steel-making process, the electric arc furnace, made it possible to produce steel almost entirely from scrap. Second, the automobile shredder became available. The shredder, which turns an entire car (minus tires, radiator, battery, and gas tank) into baseball-sized pieces of scrap, provided ready fuel for the electric arc furnace. As Cairncross summarizes, "Put the [arc furnaces] and shredders together, and add the boom in demand for steel scrap in 1973–1974, and the market has serendipitously devised a solution to the problem of car junkyards."

There are more recent parallels to the junk car example. In the 1990s, scientists are perfecting a method to convert plastics into crude oil for commercial use. Mendi Taghei, an engineer at the University of Kentucky's Institute for Mining and Minerals, estimates that this method could transform a year's worth of plastic waste into "over 80 million barrels of oil," which comes to about a five days' supply for the United States.[22]

Even the Federal Reserve is getting into the act. In trying to find a way to keep the seven thousand tons of used currency out of landfills each year, the government agency has discovered that because of their long, tough fibers, greenbacks can be used in roofing tiles, particle board, fuel pellets, stationery, packing material, and artwork. In fact, roofing tiles made partially out of old bills and cement in California burn less easily than wooden ones, lessening the hazard to homes from the frequent firestorms in that state.[23]

GLOBAL ENVIRONMENTAL ISSUES

On June 3, 1992, representatives from 178 nations gathered in Rio de Janeiro, Brazil, for an unprecedented international gathering. The topic of discussion was not free trade, currency devaluation, or a military crisis. These representatives met for eleven days that summer to discuss the global environment. In one sense, this Earth Summit, as the event was quickly dubbed, was inevitable. Like free trade, currency devaluation, or a military crisis, the state of the environment is of global importance. Pollution of the oceans and the air, global warming, and rain forest depletion transcend national borders and must be regulated through treaties between and among different countries.[24] At the same time, however, the world of international agreement is complex and unpredictable. At the eleventh hour, it was not even certain that George Bush—president of the country that produces 22 percent of the world's carbon dioxide emissions—would attend.

In the end, Bush did make it to Rio de Janeiro, but only after the other industrialized nations agreed to change the language of a draft treaty on allowable levels of pollution in the atmosphere. In fact, the United States became the scapegoat for environmentalists who did not feel enough was accomplished at the Earth Summit. Bush was an easy target; before the summit, he vowed not to let environmental interests "shut down" U.S. busi-

21. Cairncross, *Costing the Earth*, pp. 236–237.
22. "Forget Recycling, Turn Plastics Back into Oil," *Wall Street Journal*, September 29, 1993, p. B1.
23. C. Sims, "In Recycling Greenbacks, New Meaning for Old Money," *New York Times*, May 22, 1994, p. 1.
24. J. Manakkalathil, "Corporate Social Responsibility in a Globalizing Market," *SAM Advanced Management Journal*, Winter 1995, p. 29.

nesses.[25] Upon returning from Rio, EPA administrator William K. Reilly, angered at what he felt was a lack of commitment from the Bush administration, likened his experience to taking a "bungee jump" in which "someone might cut your line."[26] Critics of the results of the Rio summit accused ubiquitous business interests of sabotage, but in reality the complexities of ecological diplomacy go far deeper than the desires of the executives of U.S. corporations or those of any other country. As we will discuss, the Earth Summit highlighted the difficulties of international agreement on environmental issues while at the same time pointing the way toward international accord on the same issues in the future.

INTERNATIONAL AGREEMENTS AND CONTROVERSIES — GLOBAL WARMING AND BIODIVERSITY

The two most controversial topics at the Earth Summit were climate control and the need to maintain biodiversity, or a variety of living species on earth. As the meeting came to a close, treaties signed by more than a hundred countries on both subjects had to be amended because of demands from the United States. U.S. negotiators agreed to the global warming treaty only after a firm target date for emission reductions had been removed, and they refused to accept the biodiversity agreement altogether. The American contingent also balked at any reference to widespread foreign aid to developing nations for environmental programs, reasoning that American taxpayers would not approve of the idea, especially during a recession.

Global Warming   Many scientists blame what is perceived to be an increase in the average global temperature on the **greenhouse effect**. The phenomenon takes its name from the concept behind a greenhouse, in which sunlight passes through glass and is transferred into heat. The heat naturally rises, but it is trapped by the glass, warming the greenhouse. The water vapor and carbon dioxide in the earth's atmosphere have always produced a greenhouse effect; otherwise, our planet would be as cold and barren as Mars, which lacks a similar atmosphere. The amount of carbon dioxide in the atmosphere, however, has risen from 280 to 340 parts per million in the last century, probably because of the burning of fossil fuels such as coal, oil, and gasoline, as well as the destruction of forests, whose trees absorb carbon dioxide. The higher the concentration of carbon dioxide, the more heat is trapped within the earth's atmosphere; this leads, at least theoretically, to global warming.

In a related concern, scientists are measuring a depletion in the earth's stratosphere of ozone, an oxygen-based gas that blocks the sun's powerful ultraviolet rays. A hole in the ozone layer, measured to be roughly the size of Europe, has opened up over Antarctica and parts of Australia, subjecting that area's animal and plant life to a part of the spectrum that is potentially harmful to them. It appears that the hole is growing; scientists affiliated with the United Nations estimate that it doubled in size from 1994 to 1995.[27] According to Antarctica weather stations, water temperatures around Antarctica have increased approximately two degrees since 1945, when monitoring began, and land temperatures have risen four degrees since the 1950s. Some scientists attribute these increases to the hole in the ozone layer above the continent.[28] The damage is thought to be caused by chlorofluorocarbons (CFCs) used in refrigerators and air-conditioning units.

---

25. J. A. Baden, "Species Preservation without Tears, " *Wall Street Journal*, June 2, 1992, p. A14.
26. M. Weisskopf, "Reilly Faults Summit Preparation," *Washington Post*, August 1, 1992, p. A13.
27. "What's News," *Wall Street Journal*, September 13, 1995, p. A1.
28. "Scientists Wonder If Antarctica's Increasing Ice/Snow Signals Warming," *Global Warming Network Online Today*, May 30, 1995.

The issue of global warming would seem to cry out for an international agreement. All countries are affected by global warming and a hole in the ozone layer, and all countries—though mostly industrialized ones—release some CFCs into the atmosphere and burn fossil fuels. In fact, there had been efforts to address these and other environmental issues on a global scale prior to the Earth Summit (see *Exhibit 16–4*). At the Earth Summit, however, the United States refused to sign the Rio treaty because of its provisions requiring developed countries to share sensitive technical results of environmental research. American pharmaceutical and biotechnology companies were not willing to lose the patent protection that allows them to make research and development efforts profitable.

Furthermore, one segment of the scientific community doubts the validity of the idea of global warming.[29] These scientists point out that over millions of years, the earth's climate has swung wildly between ice ages and periods of warmth with far warmer temperatures, even a couple of centuries ago, than we have today. "It is not possible at this time," cautioned a report drawn up specifically for the Earth Summit, "to attribute all, or even a large part, of the observed global-mean warming to the enhanced greenhouse effect on the basis of the observational data currently available."[30]

Biodiversity Everything depends on everything else. This fact is perhaps most apparent in the plant and animal world. Within every ecosystem, there is a complex interdependence among plant and animal species. If one species of plant or animal is eradicated, there will be a chain reaction. All other elements of the ecosystem will be affected in some way. Certainly, the rise of civilization has affected ecosystems throughout the world. Every time humankind has hunted, fished, grown crops, or raised livestock, it has affected the ecosystem.

Some experts insist that the destruction of different species within the earth's ecosystem may threaten civilization. In other words, the elimination of certain species may in turn create a chain reaction that will ultimately harm us all through, for example, global warming and the elimination of medicines based on tropical plants and animals. Some scientists argue that over a hundred species a day are being eliminated in the world. They argue that human beings are bound to suffer, so the current situation must not be allowed to continue.

Others argue the opposite, however. They point out that on the earth today, less than 0.02 percent of all of the species that have ever existed are now living. Therefore, the history of the earth is one in which some species have died out and new ones have developed.

ENVIRONMENTALISM AND THE DEVELOPING NATIONS

"We are poor countries, and the little we have we will put to alleviate the poverty and despair," said Noah Nkambule, a delegate to the Earth Summit from Swaziland. "But there is now a political commitment to see that development and the environment are taken together."[31] Nkambule's assertion illustrates a basic split between two groups of nations involved in the Earth Summit. On one side are the industrialized countries,

29. A. T. Lawrence, "Global Warming: Are We Entering the Greenhouse Century?" *Business and Society Review*, Fall 1991, p. 69.

30. R. Rensberger, "As Earth Summit Nears, Consensus Still Lacking on Global Warming's Cause," *Washington Post*, May 31, 1992, p. A1.

31. M. Dolan and Rudy Abramson, "Earth Summit Ends on Note of Hope, Not Achievement," *Los Angeles Times*, June 14, 1992, p. A1.

▼ **EXHIBIT 16–4 Selected International Environmental Treaties**

Treaty	Number of Signatories	Provisions
International Convention for the Regulation of Whaling (1946)	37	Initially this treaty was concerned with replenishing the stock of commercially harvested species (that is, it was not established for conservation purposes). It established the International Whaling Commission (IWC) to oversee regulation. Consideration in the 1970s turned to conservation, and in 1982 the convention decided to phase out commercial whaling over a three-year period. The ban became permanent in 1986 and remains so today, though Iceland, Japan, and Norway are seeking IWC approval to resume commercial whaling.
Treaty Banning Nuclear Weapons Tests in the Atmosphere, in Outer Space, and Underwater (1963)	118	The purpose of this treaty was to limit radioactive contamination, particularly through atmospheric dispersion, beyond the jurisdictional boundary of any nation conducting a nuclear weapons test. The treaty banned the above-ground testing of nuclear weapons but does not cover underground testing. Of the signatories, only the United States, France, and the former Soviet Union opposed a complete ban on all forms of testing.
Convention on International Trade in Endangered Species (CITES) (1973)	114	This treaty concerned the overexploitation and extinction of endangered species of animal and plant life through international trade. Trade in certain species was outlawed altogether and was limited for others. Convention members are required to forward annual report and trade records to the World Conservation Union. Now that some species have been saved from extinction, some countries are petitioning for a loosening of the regulations. For example, countries with well-managed elephant populations are requesting a lifting of the trade ban regarding those animals.
Convention for the Conservation of Antarctic Marine Living Resources (CCAMLR) (1980)	27	The CCAMLR concerns the degradation of marine ecosystems surrounding the Antarctic continent and overexploitation of the area's natural resources. CCAMLR established quotas on harvesting commercial species, such as krill, and limited the amount of pollution caused by commercial activities and scientific research. The agreement is legally binding, and signatories are subject to inspections.
Montreal Protocol on Substances That Deplete the Ozone Layer (1990)	93	To halt the depletion of the ozone layer, signatories agreed to a total phaseout of CFCs, halons, and carbon tetrachlorides by 2000. The treaty has been plagued to some extent by disagreements over the extent of the problem and the issue of whether developing nations should be given aid to help meet targets. The declaration to reduce these emissions is nonbinding, and each country has the responsibility of reporting its own levels of emissions.
Biodiversity Convention (1992)	153	The treaty proposes to halt species extinction on a global scale by restricting the development of habitats; providing financial and technological assistance to less developed countries to further conservation efforts; ensuring access to, and sharing of, biological resources; and establishing biotechnology regulations. Much disagreement on the specifics of the treaty was evident at the Rio de Janeiro Summit, and no monitoring arrangements have been established.

SOURCE: L. E. Susskind, *Environmental Diplomacy* (New York: Oxford University Press, 1994), pp. 152–169.

which possess the technology needed to alleviate the environmental problems they have caused over the last century. On the other side are the developing nations, whose increasing populations and industrial growth are the root of increasing ecological harm on both the domestic and global front. Neither side is eager to expend scarce resources to save the environment, and as the developing nations move toward industrialization, global environmental efforts become even more complicated and factional.[32]

Sustainable Development   The model for developing nations is encompassed by the term **sustainable development**, which envisions an accommodation between economic development and environmental protection.[33] As Cairncross of *The Economist* points out, the phrase *sustainable development* has become widely used because it "implies so many different things to different people."[34] That is, sustainable development can be whatever a politician from either an industrialized or a developing nation would like it to be. Cairncross refers to Papua New Guinea's cutting down its forests to finance the education of the country's children as being acceptable under the model of sustainable development. When corporations from the United States and other Western countries consider expanded operations in less developed countries, they often must justify the effect their presence will have on the sustainable development of the area.

When politicians or activists from industrialized countries have a narrower view of what is acceptable as sustainable development, they are often accused by those in developing nations of engaging in environmental imperialism:

▼ To condemn those who clear-cut the rain forests in Brazil or poach elephants in Zimbabwe is to disregard the economic conditions that drive them to do so, the argument goes.

The Victim Pays   The developing nations are starting to realize that the value placed by industrialized nations on a clean environment is a powerful bargaining chip. For example, when forest floor samples taken in 1994 on Mount Moosilauke, New Hampshire, showed traces of the insecticide DDT and industrial chemicals known as PCBs—both banned in the United States since the 1970s—scientists concluded that these substances had traveled to New England through the atmosphere from another country.[35] It would be unlikely that the country, if ever pinpointed, would stop production of the substances just because of U.S. domestic environmental policy. Some form of financial compensation would probably be necessary.

In fact, some developing nations argue that the industrialized nations should pay for a cleaner environment, as well as for biodiversity efforts, within the developing nations: the **"victim pays" principle**. Those who value the biodiversity of developing nations, such as the rain forests in Brazil and the elephant herds in Zimbabwe, do feel "victimized" by the clear-cutting of these rainforests or the slaughtering of the elephants, just to name two examples. Again, the most successful way to protect biodiversity and continue sustainable development is to place an economic value on these natural resources that is equal to or greater than what is realized through their destruction. Thus, environmental groups purchase plots of Brazilian rain forest to save them from destruction and even take part in the

32. D. Vogel et al., "Can Slower Growth Save the World?" *Business and Society Review,* Spring 1993, p. 10.
33. J. Elkington, "Towards the Sustainable Corporation: Win-Win Business Strategies for Sustainable Development," *California Management Review,* Winter 1994, p. 90.
34. Cairncross, *Costing the Earth,* p. 26.
35. L. Rosenthal, "Global Pollution Gnaws into Forest Environment," *Los Angeles Times,* February 27, 1994, p. A24.

▣ MANAGING SOCIAL ISSUES

INTERNATIONAL ISSUES: SAVING THE ELEPHANTS?

In the late 1980s, many of the world's richest countries agreed to uphold a ban on the trade of ivory, and conservationists rejoiced. In one step, a huge percentage of the ivory market had been eliminated—good news for those distressed by the near extinction of the African elephant. Amid the almost universal acclaim for the ban, however, a group of economists took a contrary position. Not only was the ivory trade *not* a major factor in the declining population of the species, they said, but it actually held the key for the species's long-term survival.

Relative Values of the African Elephant

Conservation, in an economic sense, can be reduced to a cost-benefit analysis. If the costs to those doing the conserving are significantly greater than the benefits, then it is unlikely that conservation will take place. Specifically, although the benefits of preserving the African elephant herd may seem obvious to many, the case is not so clear-cut for African governments and, more important, for the people living there.

The affected areas of eastern and southern Africa are characterized by high population growth rates, declining per-capita food production, and some of the highest rates of malnutrition in the world. Because of these concerns, protecting the elephants is often low on the list of priorities for local governments. The cost of this protection, however, is increasing. On one hand, the government of Zimbabwe estimated costs of $200 per square kilometer to protect wild elephants, a figure that would place a total price tag for protecting the animals in Africa at $80 million to $100 million a year. On the other hand, a growing human population has created the demand for more land for living space, crops, and livestock—land that had been the habitat of elephant herds. As is usually the case when humans and wildlife battle for scarce land, the humans have been winning.

Given these factors, a group of economists from the London Environmental Economics Center (LEEC) argue that the ban on ivory may actually *speed* the vanishing of the elephant herds by removing one of the few ways African governments can recover the costs of conservation. If these governments see elephants as valuable national resources, they will have greater incentives to fight off poachers and discourage the overutilization of the elephants' habitat. To fortify their example, the LEEC economists point to the case of

---

seemingly contradictory practice of harvesting elephants to save them (see *Managing Social Issues—International Issues: Saving the Elephants?*).

STATE AND LOCAL REGULATION

Before we close this chapter, which has focused primarily on federal regulation of the environment, we must mention that managers and entrepreneurs also encounter similar, and significant, state and local regulations. States regulate land use under master or comprehensive plans through regional or statewide zoning laws. Many states also regulate the degree to which the environment may be polluted. Thus, for example, even when state zoning laws permit a business's proposed development, the proposal may be altered to lessen the development's impact on the environment. State laws may restrict a business's discharge of chemicals into the air or water. States may also regulate the disposal or recycling of other wastes, including glass, metal, and plastic containers, as well as toxic wastes. Additionally, states may restrict the emissions from motor vehicles.

City, county, and other local governments also control some aspects of the environment. For instance, local zoning laws control some land use. These laws may be designed to inhibit or direct the growth of cities and suburbs or to protect the natural environment. Other aspects of the environment may be subject to local regulations for other reasons.

MANAGING SOCIAL ISSUES: (CONTINUED)

the black rhino, which in 1975 was given protection similar to that now given the elephant and whose numbers had declined by 92 percent fifteen years later.

Sustainable Development

The LEEC economists see the reinvolvement of local people in the "harvesting" of elephants as a further step in protecting the species. In the 1940s and 1950s, game legislation placed ownership of wildlife in the hands of the state, and eventually many Africans came to resent laws that restricted their access to, and hunting in, ancestral lands. As a result, "the incentives for the local population to engage in or assist in poaching increased, while their incentives to cooperate in reducing poaching or aiding conservation efforts decreased."

Some conservationists have claimed that the value of elephants as tourist attractions is enough to justify their protection. However, the government of Botswana conducted a study that showed that an elephant herd that is "cropped" for gains such as tanning hides, meat for crocodile farms, and ivory carving has double the total economic value of a herd completely preserved for tourist enjoyment. In fact, the countries that have been most successful in conserving elephants, such as Botswana, oppose the ban on ivory trade. They argue that their herds were not declining because they were able to pay for conservation efforts by exporting ivory and hides. The LEEC economists support these countries and argue that the control of the ivory trade, instead of its banning, would serve the elephants better in the long run. Otherwise, those conducting illegal trade in ivory will eventually place more value on the elephants than will those protecting them, a potentially disastrous situation for the survival of the species.

For Critical Analysis:

The Organization of Petroleum Exporting Countries (OPEC) is a consortium of oil-producing countries that agrees to consult with one another before changing the prices of their crude oil. What would be the economic and environmental benefits of a similar arrangement among ivory-producing African countries?

SOURCE: F. Cairncross, *Costing the Earth* (Boston: Harvard Business School Press, 1991), pp. 136–141.

Methods of waste and garbage removal and disposal, for example, can have a substantial impact on a community. The appearance of buildings and other structures, including advertising signs and billboards, may affect traffic safety, property values, or local aesthetics. Noise generated by a business or customers may be annoying, damaging, or disruptive to neighbors. The location and condition of parks, streets, and other public uses of land subject to local control affect the environment and can also affect business.

THE DELICATE BALANCE

Considering how long human beings have been living in a civilized fashion in the Western world, concerns about the environment are relatively recent. That does not make these concerns any less important, however. The United States has been among the leaders in passing legislation protecting the environment. Certain leaders in developing countries, however, have contended that we are unrealistic in our demands for environmental policies in these countries. Leaders in developing nations remind us of the time in U.S. history when vast forests were clear-cut to make room for cattle grazing and agricultural production. Developing nations claim that what they are doing today is similar to that period in our own past. They point out that although the United States wants to impose its ecological values elsewhere today,

it did not do so when it was a developing and relatively poor country.

Whether at home or abroad, protecting the environment involves trade-offs. It is virtually impossible to have cleaner air or water without paying for it somehow. Usually people do not see the explicit costs of the cleaner environment, but they pay them nonetheless in terms of a reduced amount of other goods and services consumed. Corporate leaders have both a legal and an ethical obligation for environmentally sensitive production. The delicate balance for them is to fulfill this obligation while also getting goods to the marketplace that are competitively priced. This struggle is even more evident when American businesses face global competition.

TERMS AND CONCEPTS FOR REVIEW

Chemical fingerprinting 491
Environmental impact statement
 (EIS) 485
Greenhouse effect 501

Potentially responsible party (PRP)
 493
Recycling 497
Responsible entity 498

Superfund 492
Sustainable development 504
"Victim pays" principle 504
Wetlands 490

SUMMARY

1. The first American environmental statutes, which predated the Revolutionary War, prohibited such things as polluting Boston Harbor.

2. The National Environmental Policy Act of 1969 requires that federal agencies consider environmental factors when making significant decisions and that an environmental impact statement be prepared in such situations. The Environmental Protection Agency (EPA) was created in 1970 to coordinate federal environmental responsibilities.

3. The Clean Air Act of 1963 represented the first attempt by the federal government to regulate air pollution; it authorized the creation of emission standards and provided assistance to the states. The Clean Air Act authorized the EPA to issue regulations to control pollution from a variety of sources, including electric utilities and motor vehicles.

4. The Clean Water Act of 1972 (which amended the Federal Water Pollution Control Act of 1948) and its amendments set specific time schedules and regulatory standards with regard to water pollution. The act requires that the best available antipollution technology be installed. Similarly, the Safe Drinking Water Act of 1974 authorizes the EPA to set maximum levels for pollutants in public water systems.

5. Pesticides and herbicides were among the first toxic chemicals to receive widespread public attention. Federal law requires that such chemicals be registered before they can be sold, that they be used only for approved applications, and that they be used in limited amounts on food crops. The EPA is authorized to cancel the registration of any substance identified as harmful.

6. The Resource Conservation and Recovery Act (RCRA) of 1976 requires the EPA to establish regulations to monitor and control hazardous waste disposal and to determine which forms of solid waste should be considered hazardous and subject to regulation. In 1980, Congress passed the Comprehensive Environmental Response, Compensation, and Liability Act (CERCLA), commonly known as Superfund, to regulate the clean-up of leaking hazardous waste disposal sites, fund those clean-ups with federal money, and recover the cost of the clean-up efforts from persons (individuals and corporations) responsible for the leak, the waste, or the site.

7. Those caught violating federal and state environmental laws, particularly those who dump hazardous wastes, have usually been sued in a civil court or brought before an administrative agency. The federal government is now prosecuting polluters under various criminal statutes. Most of the businesspersons convicted so far have operated

small businesses; the government does not appear to have been as vigorous about prosecuting executives in major corporations.

8. The current environmental movement includes efforts to save scarce resources by recycling paper, plastics, glass, and metal products. Many cities have instituted mandatory recycling programs. Critics of recycling claim that in some instances, although certain natural resources are preserved, *total* resource use is actually greater because of recycling. In any event, some environmentalists believe that responsible entities should take care of waste from their products. Finally, improved technology may make recycling economically more viable in the future.

9. Global warming is a major issue at the international level. Many experts believe that the earth's ozone layer is being destroyed by our use of CFCs. They have been successful in getting legislation passed in the United States and elsewhere that reduces the use of CFCs and other ozone-destroying chemical compounds. Biodiver-

sity is another global environmental issue. Its champions argue that the rain forests in South America (as just one example) should be protected.

10. Sustainable development is an accommodation between economic development and environmental protection. Although this is a popular concept, it means different things to different people.

11. Some developing nations have argued that the industrialized nations should pay for biodiversity and a cleaner environment within the developing nations. This position has been labeled the "victim pays" principle.

12. States regulate land use under master or comprehensive plans through regional or statewide zoning laws. Many states regulate the pollution activities of businesses by restricting chemical discharges into the air or water and regulating the disposal of toxic wastes. Local regulation of the environment also may be accomplished through zoning laws. Furthermore, municipalities may regulate waste and garbage disposal, the appearance of buildings, and noise levels.

EXERCISES

1. Reexamine *Exhibit 16–1*. Choose the two statutes that you think have created the greatest additional costs for American corporations. Explain why you chose them.

2. Assume that the corporation for which you work is planning to build a plant near a small town in the Rocky Mountains. Make a list of what you would have to do to develop an environmental impact statement if you were asked to do so.

3. Give four examples of how a business might have to change its plans because of the Endangered Species Act.

4. Today's automobile emits only a fraction of the pollutants given off by an automobile in the 1960s. Nonetheless, some cities have just as much air pollution as before. How can you explain this apparent anomaly?

5. Make a list of the groups potentially affected by a manufacturing plant that disposes of its effluent in a river.

6. What are the benefits to Americans of our current wetlands policy? What are the costs?

7. If you were in charge of purchasing an existing plant, including the land on which it was located, what types of action could you take to reduce any exposure to the Comprehensive Environmental Response, Compensation, and Liability Act and its amendments?

8. Some critics of Superfund argue that it has been a failure, because more money has been spent on litigation than on the clean-up of toxic waste sites. Explain how such a situation could have occurred.

9. Develop a short speech on the pros and cons of recycling. Make sure that you explicitly list the *potential* costs and benefits of recycling.

10. International agreements relating to the environment often are ignored by governments. Why?

11. What is your definition of sustainable development?

SELECTED REFERENCES

▶ *Environmental Issues: Energy, Water, Noise, Waste, and Natural Resources.* Washington, D.C.: National Academy Press, 1995.

▶ Jessup, Deborah Hitchcock. *Guide to State Environmental Programs.* 3d ed. Washington, D.C.: Bureau of National Affairs, 1994.

▶ Read, Peter. *Responding to Global Warming: The Technology, Economics, and Politics of Sustainable Energy.* Atlantic Highlands, N.J.: Zed Books, 1994.

▶ Revesz, Richard L., and Richard B. Stewart, eds. *Analyzing Superfund: Economies, Science, and Law.* Washington, D.C.: Resources for the Future, 1995.

◗ Rogers, Michael D., ed. *Business and the Environment.* New York: St. Martin's Press, 1995.

◗ Welford, Richard. *Environmental Strategy and Sustainable Development: The Corporate Challenge for the Twenty-First Century.* New York: Routledge, 1995.

◗ Worobec, Mary Devine, and Girard Ordway. *Toxic Substances Controls Guide.* Washington, D.C.: Bureau of National Affairs, 1989.

RESOURCES ON THE INTERNET

▼ To access the central environmental law and resources part of the World Wide Web virtual library, go directly to
http://www.law.indiana.edu/

▼ For information on the policies and laws of the Environmental Protection Agency, including the full text of standards, guidelines, and regulations, access the following:
http://www.epa.gov/

For similar information on the federal Office of Ocean and Coastal Resource Management, go to
http://wave.nos.noaa.gov/ocrm/

For similar information on the U.S. Fish and Wildlife Services, go to
http://www.fws.gov/

▼ If you are interested in environmental treaties and agreements on an international level, you should go to
gopher:infoserver.ciesin.org:70/11/ catalog/Politics/gc_policy/intl/treaties

▼ You might want to see what is happening at the National Resources Defense Council by accessing the following:
http://www.nrdc.org/nrdc

▼ For a wealth of information on environmental conferences and environmental organizations, access Enviro Orgs at
gopher://envirolink.org:70/ 11/.EnviroOrgs

Similar information is available from GreenGopher at
gopher://ecosys.drdr.Virginia.EDU:70/ 00/library/gen/greengopher/intro

▼ The Global Recycling Network (GRN) is an on-line marketplace set up to provide businesses around the world with possible trading partners for the sale of recyclable goods. To access GRN's massive database, type
http://grn.com:80/grn/

C A S E

THE YORKTOWN PROJECT

Background

Few business-government relationships are more adversarial than those between companies that produce pollutants and the federal agencies that regulate them. When two old friends found themselves on the same airplane flight in 1989, however, one such relationship began to thaw. During the flight, Deborah Sparks, an employee of Amoco Oil Company, and James Lounsbury, who worked for the pollution-control division of the Environmental Protection Agency (EPA), discussed the possibility of an industry-government cooperative project to ease relations between the two sides.

Sparks and Lounsbury took their plans to their respective superiors, but the initial reaction was not positive. Both sides had built up a significant amount of distrust, and even dislike, for one another. Eventually, however, the possible benefits overcame most misgivings. The oil company wanted the possibility of meeting emission standards in the most cost-efficient way, whereas the EPA was interested in changing its regulations to reflect changes in the industry.

The resulting Yorktown Project, the first cooperative study of its kind by a business and a federal agency, proved to be a struggle for both sides. It offered each party valuable insight into how the other operated, however, and in the end it provided a blueprint for more efficient and effective pollution control in the United States.

Early Goals and Misgivings

"It was a hard sell at Amoco," remembers Walter Quanstrom, the company's vice president for environmental affairs. "Lots of people thought opening the gates was stupid," because it would give the EPA access to Amoco's operations and the opportunity to find problems.

Similarly, the idea of working with an oil company was unthinkable in the offices of the EPA. However, Mahesh Podar, a midlevel official at the EPA, had been considering a joint venture with a company to institute a multimedia procedure for emissions permitting. The EPA's single-media permitting system, in which each facility's emission source was tested separately, had come under criticism as being inefficient, and Podar was intrigued with the possibility of testing the spectrum of a plant's emission outlets at one time.

Quanstrom eventually approved the project, and soon teams from Amoco and the EPA were assembling at the oil company's Washington headquarters. Initially, the different cultures clashed. One participant said the first few meetings "were what I envision the Vietnam peace talks were like when they fought over the shape of the table." Amoco executives were still wary of handing over any vital information to "the enemy," and the EPA officials wanted their counterparts to understand that Amoco would be given no preferential treatment. Even the language of the two teams was a barrier. When Amoco representatives discussed RVs, for example, they were speaking of relief valves. An EPA staff member thought the reference was to a recreational vehicle.

Cooperation in Problem Solving

The meetings did not produce anything worthwhile until a specific problem was identified: neither side knew exactly how to measure emissions from Amoco's Yorktown, Virginia, refinery, which had been chosen for the project because of its proximity to Washington, D.C. The EPA is not required to actually test the emissions of the plants it regulates. Instead, it makes sure that companies are equipped with emissions-reducing equipment. If the proper equipment is in place and functioning properly, the reasoning goes, the emissions will be kept to acceptable levels. The regulated industry does not check actual emissions either, focusing more on the equipment rules it must meet.

Both teams agreed that the first step of the $2.3 million project (financed 70 percent by Amoco and 30 percent by the EPA) was to devise a way to measure the actual amount of pollutants given off by the refinery as fumes, fluids, and solid waste. The group decided to take an inventory of toxic emissions from the Yorktown plant during a ten-day period in September 1990, when the refinery was producing gasoline at near-maximum levels. With this goal in mind, Amoco drilled forty wells to test the groundwater around the refinery. The company also put a testing device atop a 130-foot smokestack. The Yorktown Project was specifically looking for the 406 specific emissions regulated under Title III of the Superfund Amendments and Reauthorization Act of 1986 (SARA).

Surprising Results

After four months of analysis, the project yielded some surprising results. Generally, the study showed that the EPA's

SARA Title III surveys of the Yorktown site overestimated the amount of regulated emissions. Specifically, both sides found that their assumptions about individual pollutants at the refinery were seriously flawed.

Yorktown's primary pollutant is benzene, a carcinogenic by-product of gasoline production. Until 1990, Amoco had disposed of benzene-tainted waste water by running it through pipes to an open-air treatment site. In that year, the EPA drafted specific rules to contain benzene. Based on these new regulations, Amoco began building a $41 million enclosed canal and water treatment system to capture the benzene waste—at the same time it was participating in the Yorktown Project.

The 1959 study of benzene emissions on which the EPA had based its guidelines turned out to be unsuitable for the Yorktown plant. The Amoco/EPA study found that fumes and vaporization from the refinery's "dirty water" were twenty times less than the 1959 data would suggest. The more serious benzene emissions came at the company's loading docks, where fuel is pumped into barges for disbursement. Fumes from this procedure amounted to 1.6 million pounds of pollutants released into the atmosphere each year.

The fact that the EPA had no regulations concerning benzene emissions at loading docks proved to some regulators that the agency's checklist approach and outdated assumptions were often flawed. "We didn't know as much as we thought we knew about what is being released to the environment," said the EPA's Podar about the Yorktown Project results.

Conflicting Reports

In early 1991, the work group presented its finding to 120 EPA and Amoco representatives in Williamsburg, Virginia. Many of the participants called the conference an enlightening experience. The EPA's new attitude toward Amoco seemed to be, "Gee, you don't all have horns." The oil company, for its part, realized that "not everybody at EPA was walking around with a pair of handcuffs."

The conference was the high point of the relationship, however. Shortly after it, another division of the EPA hit Amoco with a $5.5 million fine for lead pollution. Amoco employees, as well as some EPA officials, felt that the fine was a "reminder" that the company was not going to receive any special treatment because of the Yorktown Project.

Perhaps more frustrating for the oil company, however, was the fact that it could not put the results of the Yorktown Project to good use. Amoco found that benzene emissions at

the loading docks could be controlled by replacing the existing fuel lines with a special two-nozzle hose. The second nozzle would suck in the benzene fumes, and pipes would transport them to waste sites. The cost of the new device would be $6 million. The EPA–mandated waste water treatment system was costing $41 million to control one-fifth the amount of benzene emissions.

Consequently, in 1992 the company petitioned the EPA for an exemption to the rules that required the more expensive sewer system. Under federal regulations, Amoco pointed out, the company had to pay $2,400 to control each ton of emissions. Using the two-nozzle system, the company could do a 90 percent better job at only $510 a ton.

The EPA refused Amoco's petition on the ground that there was no procedure to waive the existing regulations, even if they were contradicted by the Yorktown Project's findings. Therefore, in 1993 the oil company completed construction of the EPA–mandated sewer system, while five times more waste continued to be emitted at the loading docks. "It's not required to be controlled, so it's not," explained an Amoco manager. Meanwhile, the EPA is working on dock-loading benzene emissions regulations, which Amoco will comply with using the two-nozzle system when required. "There's a disincentive to do something before the regulations are written," says Howard Klee, Amoco's director of regulatory affairs.

The Final Report

When the final report of the Yorktown Project was finished in 1993, it made the general observation that because each plant is different and has different emissions problems, the EPA should concentrate on specifically testing individual sites—such as was done at Amoco-Yorktown—instead of writing broad guidelines for entire industries. Given Amoco's experience with the EPA, the finding may seem ingenuous. After all, what's the use of doing exhaustive self-testing if the EPA does not allow a company to implement its test results?

Ronald Schmitt, director of environmental performance management at Amoco, believes that the Yorktown Project was worthwhile, despite its frustrating results for his employer. He says "a sense of trust" developed between the two sides, as did significant sharing of knowledge. "Each side brings its own perspective and ideas to the table. EPA could not have come up with all those ideas by itself. Amoco could not have come up with all the ideas by itself."

There is also hope that the Yorktown Project will prove that businesses can be trusted—with EPA observance—to devise

CASE (CONTINUED)

pollution-control devices for their own needs. The incentives to do so on both sides are obvious. On one hand, if the EPA had allowed Amoco to change its pollution-control system, the company would have saved millions of dollars. On the other hand, Amoco's improvement would have significantly reduced the amount of pollution in the environment, which is the overall goal of the EPA.

Critical Thinking Questions:

1. What does Amoco's decision to finish construction on the more expensive, higher-polluting waste water treatment system reveal about the incentive to business to follow environmental regulations?

2. Is Amoco behaving ethically by refusing to install the special hose that would halt the emissions of benzene at the loading docks? Do you accept its reasoning in this instance?

3. Was the EPA acting in the best interests of society when it refused Amoco's petition to install the hose system? Do you accept the agency's reasons for refusal?

4. Does it appear that the EPA is placing an "unacceptable" regulatory burden on Amoco?

5. From the information in this case, provide an overview of the cultures at both Amoco and the EPA. Are these cultures necessarily in conflict?

SOURCE: Information from "EPA and Amoco Conduct Study of Virginia Refinery, Learn New Lessons," *Clean Air Network Online Today*, March 30, 1993; C. Solomon, "Clearing the Air: What Really Pollutes?" *Wall Street Journal*, March 29, 1993, p. A1; K. Rademaker, "Pairing Up against Pollution," *Occupational Hazards*, September 1, 1991, p. 145; H. Sharber, "Industries, Government Preparing for Chemical Emergencies," *Business Journal–Richmond*, November 16, 1987, p. 3; S. Paul, "Regulation and the Environment," *Platt's Oilgram News*, July 12, 1993, p. 3; and M. O. Weinstock, "EPA's New Push for Pollution Prevention," *Occupational Hazards*, June 1, 1993, p. 33.

CHAPTER 17

THE BUSINESS OF ENVIRONMENTALISM

INTRODUCTION

Before 1990, American Telephone and Telegraph Company (AT&T) used chloro-fluorocarbons (CFCs) to clean soldering debris and resin from its circuit boards. AT&T did not want to alter this cleaning process, but the Clean Air Act and other legislation required that the corporation reduce the levels of CFCs it released into the atmosphere. In response, AT&T began to install new cleaning equipment that uses solutions similar to household detergents to clean its circuit boards. As a result, cleaning a square foot of board now costs 15 cents, as compared with 25 cents with the CFCs, and AT&T saves $3 million per year.[1]

Such examples please environmentalists such as Vice President Al Gore, who insists that the traditional role of business and environmentalists as competitors rather than collaborators belongs to a bygone era. "[We] can prosper by leading the environmental revolution and producing for the world marketplace the new products and technologies that foster economic progress without environmental destruction," writes Gore in *Earth in the Balance*.[2] In Gore's vision, being "green," or environmentally responsible, is no longer a hindrance to profit-making abilities; it is an opportunity to realize new markets, improve productivity with innovation (as AT&T did), and generate wealth.

Gore's theories have proved profitable for many different companies in the United States and abroad, but it would be a mistake to assume that they always apply. Although there are myriad new business opportunities created by environmental awareness and legislation, there are also many associated costs that business cannot recover easily. Today's business manager must neither blindly embrace environmentalism nor stubbornly resist it, as there are prohibitive costs and penalties in both courses. A manager's success in dealing with environmental challenges instead hinges on his or her ability to respond to them in a cost-efficient manner while at the same time being ethically responsible. As environmental consultants Noah Walley and Bradley Whitehead caution, "As a society, we may rightly choose [environmental] goals despite their costs, but we must do so knowingly. And we must not kid ourselves. Talk is cheap; environmental efforts are not."[3]

This chapter explores the various incentives businesses have to be environmentally friendly, green marketing, environmental management, and other challenges and opportunities for firms with regard to the "silent stakeholder." First, we turn our attention to some of the economic trade-offs involved in being environmentally conscious.

COST-EFFECTIVENESS IN "GREEN" BUSINESS

AT&T was, on a small scale, in what is known as a win-win situation with regard to its CFCs. Other companies have been in this situation on a much larger scale, the prime example being the 3M Corporation. This company has made 2,500 different manufacturing changes since 1975 that have reduced its toxic emissions by one billion pounds and

---

1. A. K. Naj, "Industrial Switch: Some Companies Cut Pollution by Altering Production Methods," *Wall Street Journal*, December 24, 1990, p. A1.
2. A. Gore, *Earth in the Balance* (New York: Houghton Mifflin, 1992), p. 14.
3. N. Walley and B. Whitehead, "It's Not Easy Being Green," *Harvard Business Review*, May–June 1994, p. 47.

saved the company $500 million.[4] Other corporations, however, definitely lose in meeting environmental requirements. Texaco, for example, plans to spend $7 billion annually over a five-year period ending in 2000 on environmental compliance programs that will bring the company little, if any, revenue in return.[5]

These three companies, and any others that expend funds to meet ecological goals, are responding to the fact that society has placed a relatively high value on a more healthful environment. Is the cost worth the price?[6]

PLACING A VALUE ON THE ENVIRONMENT

For those holding Texaco stock, the answer to the above question would probably be a resounding no. As Texaco noted in one of its annual reports, the company has placed a value on protecting the environment for its stakeholders—that value is how much the worth of its shares decreases as a result of the oil company's $7 billion no-return investment. Most of the time, however, it is not so easy to assign a clear monetary value to ecological initiatives.

The problems in placing a value on environmental initiatives are daunting. To start with, many people find it morally reprehensible to place a dollar amount on the life of a tree, a whale, or a human being. For practical purposes, however—such as the settling of lawsuits or policy decisions by a government or business—we often are forced to do so. Even in so doing, we are dealing with things that carry many different types of worth, which makes it difficult to assess their costs.

Consider the minke whale, for example. It has a market value in Japan because of its protein, oil, skin (leather), and medicinal properties. In Norway, whalers can make $2.50 a pound for the meat on a 4,000-pound minke.[7] In contrast, live whales may also have a monetary value based on the fact that some people are willing to spend large sums of money to see one, either in captivity or in the open sea. Two hundred whale-watching boats in California support a $35 million annual business.[8] Finally, a minke whale has a value to those who may never actually see a live one but feel comfort in knowing that they exist; many would feel guilt on behalf of humankind if we managed to render the species extinct.

It may seem impossible to quantify these disparate views of worth, but those who try to do so take one of two basic paths. In the first path, researchers survey people for answers. In the second path, they use the marketplace.

Contingent Valuation The method of surveying a cross-section of individuals to estimate how much society values its natural resources is known as **contingent valuation.** These individuals are asked how much they would be willing to spend to either prevent an ecological disaster or to improve the environment. More and more often, government prosecutors are using these surveys as a means to force polluters to pay for damages that have in the past been unquantifiable, such as the extinction of a species or the destruction of a public beach.

---

4. Naj, *op. cit.*
5. Walley and Whitehead, *op. cit.*, p. 46.
6. C. J. Corbett and L. N. Wassenhove, "The Green Fee: Internalizing and Operationalizing Environmental Issues," *California Management Review,* Fall 1993, p. 116.
7. T. Jones, "Rough Seas for Defiant Whalers," *Los Angeles Times,* July 6, 1993, p. A1.
8. J. Rae-Dupree, "Many Whales to See, but Few at Sea to Watch Them," *Los Angeles Times,* January 23, 1992, p. B3.

The most celebrated example of contingent valuation was conducted by the state of Alaska as part of its lawsuit in the *Exxon Valdez* case. A sampling of 1,400 people from different parts of the United States were asked fifty questions to try to ascertain how much they would be willing to pay to prevent another such disaster. The researchers found, by extrapolating the evidence, that Americans would spend $3 billion to prevent another oil spill in Prince William Sound, even though the vast majority of them had never, and would never, visit the waterway themselves.[9]

Of course, not everybody accepts the premise of contingent valuation. "The whole thing is fundamentally crazy," complains Harvard University economics professor Zvi Grilrich. "Asking a housewife in Raleigh what a seal is worth to her in Alaska doesn't strike me as sensible."[10]

Using the Market Another way to estimate environmental values is to look to the actual market—the real world—to obtain real numbers.[11] On the cost side, for example, the actual damages incurred because of pollution can often be estimated. Consider the case of air pollution. Steel mills may create sulfur oxides in the air that have many effects, including the following: (1) cause buildings to have to be cleaned more often; (2) make people wash their cars more often; and (3) cause increased lung disease and lost workdays. One way to estimate these costs is by a comparison with a similar city without such air pollution. Each of these factors is analyzed, and the difference in cost on an annualized basis is determined. Alternatively, we could estimate the cost of air pollution in the polluted city by comparing its real estate prices with those in the unpolluted city.

Benefits of good environmental practices, however, are often not so easily estimated. Attempts can be made, nonetheless. Consider the example of forested areas. Trees stabilize soil, as well as regulate rainfall run-off. Because of the value of preventing soil erosion, some governments have increased the size of national parks in order to safeguard watersheds. One way to estimate the benefits of such environmental actions is to compare the output from hydroelectric facilities before and after the increase in the size of the watershed. Market prices can be applied to the additional electricity to obtain an estimated value of the benefit of the environmental action.

ENVIRONMENTAL COST-BENEFIT ANALYSES

In Chapter 9, we looked at cost-benefit analyses of regulatory policy in general. Cost-benefit analyses are also an integral part of environmental policy. Most environmental impact statements, as required by the National Environmental Policy Act (discussed in Chapter 16), include one or more cost-benefit analyses to determine the worthiness of a proposed policy or investment. This fact has hardly made them acceptable, however, to all those concerned with the ecosystem.

It is usually far easier to calculate the costs of environmental policy to taxpayers, an individual business, or industry than it is to calculate the benefits of such policies to society as a whole. Consequently, the costs often appear to overwhelm the unquantifiable benefits, a situation that provides ready ammunition to those who feel business is being unfairly burdened by environmental legislation.

---

9. L. Himmelstein and M. B. Regan, "Fresh Ammo for the Eco-Cops," *Business Week*, November 29, 1993, p. 138.

10. *Ibid.*

11. *Ibid.*

Determining Costs and Benefits To illustrate this point, we attempt to do a basic cost-benefit analysis of legislation to protect the California spotted owl in the Sierra Nevada mountain range, which keeps logging companies from cutting down the old-growth forests that are the bird's habitat. The benefit of keeping the trees standing is most obvious to the spotted owl itself, and possibly to the ecosystem of which it is an intricate part. There is further benefit, as we mentioned earlier, to those who enjoy visiting the Sierra Nevada forests and those who simply like knowing that old-growth forests and spotted owls are protected by society.

The costs are also extensive. The U.S. Forest Service predicts that local communities that surround the Sierra Nevadas and rely on the timber industry will lose $176 million in yearly personal income, as employment in the area will drop by one-third to one-half. The lost income from timber manufacturers who could harvest the forest is also immense—easily many millions of dollars. Furthermore, it turns out that by clear-cutting deadwood and dense stands of small trees, the timber companies greatly lessen the risk of large-scale forest fires. Without the services of the timber industry, says one U.S. Forest Service researcher, "We're sitting on dynamite." If the Forest Service cleared out the incendiary growth itself, it would cost taxpayers $100 million every decade.[12]

This cost-benefit analysis attempts to determine the costs to humans of saving the forests, but what about the costs to the ecosystem of the Sierra Nevadas because of the loss of the spotted owl? We know the monetary benefits of harvesting the forests, but what about the intangible benefits of the wilderness? Furthermore, how do we compare the profits to be made by the timber industry with the possible extinction of a species? The answers seem to lie more in the political than in the scientific arena.[13]

A Cost-Benefit Analysis of the 1990 Clean Air Act Politics played a part in the passage of the 1990 Clean Air Act, approved by Republican president George Bush over the protests of conservative elements in his party. These critics decried the costs of the legislation, estimated by some at $40 billion a year for the national economy. Political analysts, however, felt there was no chance the president would have opposed any bill with the words *clean air* in it.

Although it is impossible to calculate the total costs of the legislation and then compare them with the health benefits from cleaner air, individual companies could quantify the results. Three years after passage of the act, the costs of the act to business could be calculated by the "hidden taxes" passed on to consumers.[14] Ford Motor Company, which was required under the law to replace CFCs in its air-conditioning units with less dangerous hydrofluorocarbons, estimates that the price of each of its new cars in 1994 went up $225 because of the legislation. The owner of a dry-cleaning shop in New York City estimated that the price of cleaning a suit went up from $9.50 to $10.50 because he was required to purchase upgraded, environmentally friendly equipment. Drivers in the thirty-six cities targeted by the EPA as having particularly poor air quality paid three to five cents per gallon more for "oxygenated" gas in the winter of 1992–1993.

According to Paul Portney of Resources for the Future, the measurable benefits of the Clean Air Act, based on a reduction in illnesses caused by air pollution, might be $4 billion to $12 billion a year, whereas the costs to businesses and consumers might be

---

12. F. Clifford, "Owl Protection Measures Could Backfire," *Los Angeles Times*, April 18, 1994, p. A4.

13. D. Rogers, "Senate Narrowly Upholds GOP Plan to Speed Timber Salvage of U.S. Lands," *Wall Street Journal*, March 31, 1995, p. A4.

14. T. Noah, "Clear Benefits of Clean Air Act Come at a Cost," *Wall Street Journal*, November 15, 1993, p. B1.

approximately $29 billion to $39 billion a year.[15] Taking another vantage point, Portney predicts the Clean Air Act might prevent five hundred cases of cancer a year. This means that we would be spending approximately $80 million for each cancer case avoided.

As repugnant as the idea might be, society must ask itself if the benefits are worth the costs. How much more would you be willing to spend for a car to ensure that another member of your species does not contract cancer? It is a rhetorical question, but one that nonetheless puts the inherent contradictions and difficulties of cost-benefit analyses in perspective when it comes to the environment.

RISK ASSESSMENT

A cousin of the cost-benefit analysis is **risk assessment** in environmental decision making. Risk assessment is based on the same principle as cost-benefit analyses: the trade-offs between the environment and other factors are used to decide whether a certain policy or legislation is desirable. But instead of quantifying, or trying to quantify, the costs and benefits of a policy, in risk assessment the possibility of worse-case scenarios is measured against the costs of preventing them.

For example, risk assessment has been applied to EPA regulations that concern which chemicals and what quantities can be allowed in various products. Let's say that if a certain chemical is used as a pesticide on a plant, people eating the food product may have an increased probability of contracting cancer of some sort. Normally, the figures are remarkably small, such as one person in twenty million. The cost to society of a regulation on the particular pesticide is then estimated. The estimated cost is divided by the estimated number of lives saved because of the regulation. For some examples of risk assessment, see *Exhibit 17–1*.

Unfortunately, risk assessment has many of the same problems as cost-benefit analysis. As Frances Cairncross, environmental editor of *The Economist*, points out, we are notoriously inconsistent in assessing risk:

> Familiar risks are less frightening than the unfamiliar; visible risks less scary than the invisible sort. People clearly feel more frightened by the remote risk of a large catastrophe than by the greater risk of an equivalent number of deaths spread out over a long period. Hence the greater fear of nuclear power stations than coal-mining facilities, and of aircraft crashes than road accidents. People feel more frightened by risks over which they feel they have no control than by those they inflict on themselves. Hence the greater desire for regulation of pesticide than of alcohol consumption.[16]

Cairncross believes this inconsistency can lead to environmental policies in which risk is misused to the detriment of society. This theory is backed up by studies such as the one carried out by the Harvard School of Public Health's Risk Analysis Center, which found that (1) medical care generally saves lives at less cost than workplace safety or environmental measures, and (2) extravagantly large sums are spent by business and consumers to alleviate relatively minor cancer risks. As one example, the study found that preventing the release of carcinogenic chloroform at pulp mills costs an estimated $99.4 billion for each life saved.[17]

---

15. P. Portney, "Economics and the Clean Air Act," *Journal of Environmental Protections*, Vol. 4, 1990, pp. 173–178.
16. F. Cairncross, *Costing the Earth* (Boston: Harvard Business School Press, 1991), p. 56.
17. D. Stipp, "Prevention May Be Costlier Than a Cure," *Wall Street Journal*, July 6, 1994, p. B1.

▼ **EXHIBIT 17–1**
Risk Assessments of Various Environmental Regulations

Regulation	Cost per Premature Death Averted, in Millions of Dollars
Ban on unvented space heaters	0.1
Trihalomethane drinking water standards	0.2
Ethylene dibromide drinking water standards	5.7
Asbestos exposure limit for workers	8.3
Arsenic emission standards for glass plants	13.5
Hazardous waste listing for sludge from petroleum refining	27.6
Hazardous waste disposal ban	4,190.4
Hazardous waste listing for wood-preserving chemicals	5,700,000.0

SOURCE: Office of Management and Budget.

INCENTIVE STRUCTURES AND THE MARKET FOR CLEAN AIR

From the end of World War II until the beginning of the 1990s, the countries in Eastern Europe, to a large extent, were governed by the politicoeconomic systems of communism and socialism. In these systems, most property was owned by the state, and government bureaucrats were rewarded for productivity and output, not for preserving the environment. In effect, the governments did not take account of the negative externalities that resulted from their actions. The end result was decades of ecological destruction, from 50 percent of the forests in the former Czechoslovakia damaged or dying, to arsenic contamination of the drinking water in southern Hungary, to 40 percent of Poland's children suffering from pollution-related illnesses.

These countries had no incentive structure to encourage their governments to protect the environment. Simply stated, an **incentive structure** is the system of rewards and punishments that individuals or organizations face with respect to their own actions. The incentive structure in communist and socialist Eastern Europe rewarded productivity at the expense of the environment, and the results were predictable.

NEGATIVE INCENTIVES AND THE ENDANGERED SPECIES ACT

Most environmental law is based on providing **negative incentives**, or disincentives, for industry to pollute. If company X is caught illegally contaminating the Colorado River, company X will have to pay a substantial fine. The threat of the fine, it is hoped, is enough of a disincentive to company X that it would not contaminate the river in the first place. Negative incentives are widespread in our society; our justice system is based on them.

Some experts feel that reliance on negative incentives is too prevalent in environmental law, often to the detriment of the environment. When Exxon Corporation offered to pay $100 million in fines as part of a plea bargain in the *Exxon Valdez* oil spill, Judge H. Russel Holland refused. "I'm afraid these signs send the wrong message," said Holland, "which suggests spills are a cost of business [that] can be absorbed."[18]

Similar concerns about the value of negative incentives are often cited with regard to the Endangered Species Act (ESA) of 1973. As you learned in Chapter 16, the ESA requires all federal agencies to take steps to ensure that their actions do not jeopardize the continued existence of endangered species or harm their habitats. The ESA holds that if the habitat of an endangered species coincides with private property, the landowner is severely restricted in the amount of development allowed on that property. Consequently, landowners who discover an endangered species on property they wish to use, sell, or develop do not have much of an incentive to report the species to the government. Instead, the incentive structure dictates that the landowner somehow drive the species off the property or develop the property quickly, before the species is discovered by the government. In some cases, landowners have been known to kill the animal to prevent its detection. This is known as the "shoot, shovel, and shut up" syndrome.[19]

The ESA has in essence made endangered species a liability to landowners, so its effects are in a sense predictable. Businesses are often unable to recover the lost income caused by the ESA while adhering to its requirements (see *Company Focus: Boise Cascade Corporation*). As a consequence, there have been examples of races to develop land against the discovery or new designation of an endangered species.[20]

Another unfortunate side effect of the negative incentives has been a movement of public support away from the endangered species themselves. In the Northwest, where spotted owls have led to the loss of many jobs in the timber industry, bars have signs that read, "If it's a hootin', I'm a shootin'," and locals wear baseball caps with the slogan "Spotted Owl Hunting Club."[21]

Some observers feel that the endangered species themselves might be better served by a change in the incentive structure imposed by the ESA. The legislation of *positive* incentives for landowners to report endangered species might be more effective than the present negative incentive structure.

The government, for example, could guarantee the purchase of endangered species habitats. Alternatively, in a more revolutionary move, the EPA could provide positive incentives by rewarding landowners who preserve the endangered species on their property. The environmental group Defenders of Wildlife has shown that this idea might be feasible through a program to reward ranchers in Montana and Wyoming who help protect wolves. These programs, of course, would not be without costs to taxpayers.

INCENTIVE STRUCTURES AND ELECTRIC AUTOMOBILES

Incentive structures can also be used to predict the actions of consumers. This fact seems to have been overlooked in the debate over the electric automobile.[22] To lower toxic emissions, the California Air Resources Board decreed that 2 percent of all vehicles sold

---

18. A. Sullivan, "Judge Rejects Exxon Alaska-Spill Pact," *Wall Street Journal*, April 25, 1991, p. A3.
19. T. Lambert and R. J. Smith, *The Endangered Species Act: Time for a Change* (St. Louis: Washington University, Center for the Study of American Business, March 1994), p. 34.
20. "New Stiff Penalties for Bird Killers," *Engineering News-Record*, September 24, 1987, p. 14.
21. Lambert and Smith, *op. cit.*, p. 35.
22. M. Tucker, "The Shocking State of Electric Car Technology," *Business and Society Review*, Spring 1995, p. 44.

COMPANY FOCUS: BOISE CASCADE CORPORATION

BOISE CASCADE AND THE TIMBER SHORTFALL

In 1995, Boise Cascade Corporation, along with other major timber companies in the Northwest, was pushing for the passage of salvage lumber legislation that would allow it to harvest forests previously protected by environmental laws. Even as Boise Cascade executives lobbied the president and members of Congress, they knew that a victory would provide only short-term relief. The timber business has been irrevocably changed by what industry leaders call simply "the spotted owl," and Boise Cascade was going to have to find a long-term solution.

The Timber Shortage

"The spotted owl" is code for the Endangered Species Act (ESA) of 1973, which prohibits any destruction of natural resources that would jeopardize the existence of an endangered species. The habitat of the northern spotted owl, along with that of marbled mullets, certain kinds of salmon, and other endangered species, coincides with forests that Boise Cascade and its competitors would like to harvest for timber.

According to industry estimates, restrictions imposed by the ESA have reduced the timber output on protected federal lands in the Northwest from a yearly average of about 8

billion board feet in 1983 to 300 million board feet in the mid-1990s. At that same time, the market quantity demanded of timber in the United States was 16 billion board feet per year.

For the time being, other sources are filling in the gaps. State governments have increased their timber production. Idaho, for example, almost doubled the amount of timber it produced from 1990 to 1992, to more than 270 million board feet. Total state sales from the Northwest are expected to level out at 1 billion board feet by the mid-1990s. Private timber stands have also sharply increased output, to almost 10 billion board feet in 1993. Industry analysts, however, say that growth has been spurred by worry over future environmental laws that would limit a private party's ability to harvest its own property, and that private timber is "being cut at an unsustainable rate."

Alternative Sources

Boise Cascade officials realize that federal timber sales of 8 billion board feet in the Northwest—the yearly average "before the spotted owl"—will not be repeated. The best production projections for the beginning of the next century are between 900 million and 1.7 billion board feet. Even taking into account state and private timber production, this will leave a yearly shortfall of 5.5 billion to 8 billion board feet by 2000.

This prediction caused Dick Parrish, senior vice president of Boise Cascade, and other company officials to tour logging sites in Siberia during the winter of 1995. Between the Ural Mountains and the Pacific Ocean in Russia lie nearly four thousand miles of harvestable timber, more than enough to satisfy the U.S. market. Boise Cascade, however, decided not to invest in logging operations there because of the unwillingness of the Russian government to upgrade operations; some Russian loggers were still using axes instead of chain saws.

There are other alternatives. Domestic wood substitutes include steel, plastics, and engineered wood products, which use half as much wood to obtain the same strength as lumber. Boise Cascade's sales of such products doubled from 1992 to 1994, to more than $82 million. If the Russian government does not bolster its timber capacity, executives expect those sales to rise in the near future.

COMPANY FOCUS: (CONTINUED)

The New Bottom Line

Businesses that deal with environmentally sensitive products are constantly challenged to predict and react to legislative change. These companies must be proactive in creating alternatives to ecologically unfriendly supplies or products.

SOURCE: Information from S. Anderson, "Shrinking Timber Supplies in Idaho Force Companies to Scout Offshore," *Idaho Business Review*, May 22, 1995, p. 1; and S. Anderson, "BC Studies Timber Ties to Siberia," *Idaho Business Review*, May 22, 1995, p. 1.

in the state by 1996 be zero-pollution emission—a number that was to rise to 5 percent by 2001 and to 10 percent by 2003. This prompted, through negative incentives, the Big Three U.S. automakers—General Motors, Ford, and Chrysler—to begin construction of a car that is battery powered.

The automakers balked at the costs of such a project. Chrysler announced that it would be adding a surcharge to its internal combustion engine models in California to cover the added expense of research and development for the electric automobile. By 1994, a prototype of the Ford Ecostar was being tested. Although it met the requirements of the Air Resources Board by being battery powered, it was priced at $105,000, so there is still much work to be done.[23]

At the same time the Big Three were arguing strenuously that the costs of producing zero-emission vehicles outweighed the benefits, Americans were driving more than ever. Since 1970, vehicle miles traveled have increased by over 70 percent, offsetting the reductions in emissions per mile brought about by auto emission standards. The reason is the availability of relatively inexpensive fuel. During the 1980s, the real (inflation-corrected) price of gasoline went down by 50 percent. In the summer of 1996, the average price of a gallon of regular no-lead gasoline was only $1.19 (or, corrected for inflation, about the same as it was in 1950). Furthermore, in the 1990s the market for less fuel efficient vehicles such as pickup trucks, minivans, and four-wheel-drive vehicles was booming, as low fuel prices did not punish consumers for such purchases.

Thus, the alternative of the nonpolluting electric automobile may not be the best solution to air pollution in U.S. cities. In the first place, the electricity that has to be generated to charge the batteries of these automobiles is created by a process that in most cases generates pollution. Therefore, we would simply be substituting pollution at electricity-generating plants for less pollution in the city. Moreover, the disposal of the batteries used in electric automobiles would cause environmental degradation.

Alternative actions to reduce air pollution in American cities might lead to a better solution than the electric car. One way is to reduce the amount of driving. This can be done by imposing higher taxes on gasoline, by charging the full cost of parking on public streets, and so on. At a high enough price per mile driven, people would probably drive fewer miles or use public transportation.

---

23. J. A. Savage, "The Road Warriors: Utilities and Automakers Square Off on Alternative Fuel Vehicles," *Business and Society Review*, Winter 1994, p. 6.

The second way to reduce air pollution is to tax the output of pollution directly. Cars can be monitored based on the amount of pollutants they emit. People could be charged a so-called carbon tax that would be proportional to the amount of pollution they generated; after all, 80 percent of the pollution is generated by 20 percent of the cars (usually older ones that are not kept in proper working order).

THE FREE MARKET FOR CLEAN AIR

If pollutants must be removed, there is an incentive to do so at the beginning of any cleaning process, for the simple reason that this is when the process is the least expensive. Each additional step in the cleaning process becomes more expensive, and the incentive for those footing the bill lessens.

Some observers believe that a relatively new incentive structure—creating a market for pollution—would help curb pollution by U.S. companies:

▼ **While environmentalists tend to insist that the only acceptable level of pollutants is zero, economists point out that it is in society's interests to find tolerable levels of pollution rather than try to eradicate all pollutants, no matter what the cost.**

The Market for Pollution Rights and the Clean Air Act For many years, various levels of government have charged individuals and companies for the right to pollute. Many municipalities allow individuals and businesses to dispose of garbage in the city dump for a fee. In essence, then, governments have created pollution rights. After one of the first federal clean air acts was passed in 1963, the EPA formalized an **offset policy** that required a company wishing to build a plant in an already polluted area to work out a corresponding reduction in pollution at an existing plant. Such arrangements usually involved the buying and selling of so-called pollution rights.

This concept was actually put into law in 1990, when Congress passed an amendment to the Clean Air Act of 1970. This 1990 amendment included the important Title IV, which allows for a market-based approach for controlling the emissions of sulfur dioxide from electrical power plants and other emitting sources. (Sulfur dioxide is a chemical that is thought to be the primary cause of acid rain, which may harm forests, lakes, and other natural resources, particularly in the northeastern United States and Canada.)

Each sulfur-emitting source is allowed to emit a fixed number of tons of sulfur dioxide each year. For example, a generating unit in the Midwest might be allowed to emit 2.6 million tons of sulfur dioxide each year. Once the sulfur dioxide emissions allowances are assigned to each pollution-generating facility, the allowances can be traded among companies rather than used for emissions. Also, allowances can be traded between years using a concept called **emission banking,** in which allowances can be kept on reserve for the future.

Proponents of this system point out that rather than using mandatory pollution-abatement technology or abandoning production completely, polluting firms have the flexibility to reduce pollution any way they want to do so. In the meantime, firms can either sell or buy a limited amount of emissions allowances on the free market. (*Exhibit 17–2* on page 524 shows the estimated trading value of various pollutants.) On March 29, 1993, the EPA conducted the first auction of tradable sulfur dioxide emissions allowances through the Chicago Board of Trade.[24]

---

24. G. Korentz, "Smog Futures Raise a Cloud of Controversy," *Business Week,* April 19, 1993, p. 22.

▼ **EXHIBIT 17–2**
Estimated Trading
Values of Rights to
Pollute

Pollutant	Trading Value (Per Ton)
Sulfur dioxide	$400
Manganese	25 million
Mercury	250 million
Nickel	250 million
Cadmium	250 million
Beryllium	250 million
Arsenic	2.5 billion
Chromium	2.5 billion

SOURCE: R. L. Miller, *Economics Today,* updated 8th ed. (New York: HarperCollins College Publishers, 1996), p. 747.

Opportunities for Environmentalists As would be expected, many environmental groups were not pleased with the idea of trading polluting rights. Greenpeace picketed the first auction in Chicago. A Greenpeace spokesperson likened the selling of allowances to "giving a pack of cigarettes to a man dying of lung cancer."[25]

Other environmental organizations took a different view of the circumstances. The National Healthy Air License Exchange (NHALE) of Cleveland submitted bids for 1,100 units, with the goal of retiring the permits to keep the pollution they represented out of the air. "Historically, environmental groups have been able only to litigate or lobby," remarked David Webster, head of NHALE. "But now we can actually buy pollution rights and let them expire unused, thereby keeping tons of pollution from being released into the atmosphere."[26]

Some sulfur dioxide–emitting corporations have even used this new market for charitable donations; Northwest Utilities donated ten thousand of its allowances to the Lung Association, which promptly retired them.[27] It is interesting to note that this kind of activity, by reducing the total amount of pollution, drives the price of tradable permits up, thereby providing an incentive to firms to reduce pollution more than they normally would.

THE ENVIRONMENTAL CHALLENGE FOR BUSINESS

Environmental awareness in the public—and therefore in the government—periodically surges. The latest wave offers unprecedented challenges as well as opportunities for business. The rapid changes of the last decade, no doubt, unnerve many in the business com-

---

25. *Ibid.*
26. J. Taylor and D. Kansas, "Environmentalists Vie for Right to Pollute," *Wall Street Journal,* March 26, 1993, p. C1.
27. D. B. Webster, "The Free Market for Clean Air," *Business and Society Review,* Summer 1994, p. 36.

munity.[28] Terms such as *offset policy, emission banking,* and *contingent valuation* are vaguely threatening, as is the increased possibility of lawsuits and government fines for environmental mistakes. However,

▼ **Business managers must realize that environmentalism is not a trend. It is rock-solid reality.**

Bjorn Stigson, head of a Swedish engineering firm, summed up the situation with an interesting twist when he remarked, "We treat nature like we treated workers a hundred years ago. We included then no cost for the health and social security of workers in our calculations, and today we include no cost for the health and security of nature."[29] In continuing that thought, Stigson and many others see it as inevitable that corporations will accept the costs of protecting the environment as part of the costs of doing business.[30]

BUSINESS AS VICTIM

The statistics can be alarming: the number of federal environmental acts being enforced has increased from five in 1972 to over forty in the mid-1990s. The number of pages in the *Federal Register* that pertain to environmental legislation has increased by a factor of eight over the same period. As the amount of environmental regulation has risen, so have compliance costs. Since 1972, the total annualized environmental protection costs in the United States have tripled as a percentage of gross domestic product, from 0.88 percent to 2.39 percent.[31]

Many business leaders, on hearing these figures, say they are victims of irrational, unreasonable, and unfair "eco-terrorists."[32] In 1993, when the U.S. Sentencing Commission proposed stricter penalties for environmental crimes based on a formula that combined the severity of the crime with the economic gain of the offending business, representatives of U.S. corporations protested vehemently. Alan Slobodin, a spokesman for the Washington Legal Foundation, said the prosecutions of companies for environmental crimes were "the civil liberties issues of the 1990s."[33]

CONSUMER AND SHAREHOLDER INFLUENCE

Business leaders who are encouraged by such statements should remember that government environmental activism did not spring out of a vacuum. The regulations, for a large part, were based on public opinion.[34] In a survey by Democratic pollsters before the 1994 election, although very few voters named the environment as a *top* priority, only 8 percent believed enough was being done to protect the environment, and 41 percent said environmental laws needed reinforcing.[35]

---

28. K. Dechant and B. Altman, "Environmental Leadership: From Compliance to Competitive Advantage," *Academy of Management Executive,* August 1994, p. 7.
29. Cairncross, *op. cit.,* p. 178.
30. U. Steger, "Corporations Capitalize on Environmentalism," *Business and Society Review,* Fall 1990, p. 72.
31. Walley and Whitehead, *op. cit.,* p. 49.
32. D. Bandow, "Trashing the Economy: How Runaway Environmentalism Is Wrecking America," *Business and Society Review,* Summer 1994, p. 59.
33. "Few Like Pollution Guidelines," *ABA Journal,* June 1993, p. 25.
34. J. H. Cushman, Jr., "Congressional Republicans Take Aim at an Extensive List of Environmental Statutes," *New York Times,* February 22, 1995, p. A9.
35. A. O'Hanlon, "Nov. 8 Had a Green Tint, Wildlife Federation Finds," *Washington Post,* December 24, 1994, p. A4.

Consumer Influence Individual consumers and special interest groups—made up of consumers—have come to believe that they can have an effect on the environmental awareness of the business community. There are several tactics that these consumers can use to influence corporate environmental policies, including using their purchasing power, lobbying, and threatening boycotts or media attention.

In January 1994, a survey by a company that tracks consumer trends, EDK Associates, showed that two-thirds of the consumers polled consciously seek environmentally safe products.[36] Perhaps the most impressive proof is that items such as recycled toilet paper and paper towels are now common on the shelves of large supermarket chains such as Food Lion and Winn-Dixie.[37]

Influential environmental special interest groups spend large amounts of money to influence public policy and the actions of corporations. The Environmental Defense Fund, for example, spent $196,041 in 1993 to lobby on issues such as energy use and climate change. That same year, the Audubon Society earmarked almost $500,000 to protect wildlife and its habitats. The most active environmental interest group is the Sierra Club, which invested $8.79 million in 1993 to influence Congress and state legislatures on pollution prevention and land protection issues.[38]

Numerous boycotts have been used by special interest groups and consumer organizations to highlight unfriendly environmental action by corporations. The most successful may have been a boycott of the H. J. Heinz Company by the Earth Island Institute. Environmentalists wanted the company to discontinue its policy of buying tuna for its Star Kist brand from fishers whose nets also ensnared and killed dolphins. They urged consumers to stop buying Star Kist until Heinz remedied the situation. Although Heinz did not feel the boycott would seriously hurt sales, the negative media attention was

36. "Focus on Environment," *Orange County Register*, July 4, 1994, p. A24.
37. M. Silverstein, "What Does It Mean to Be Green?" *Business and Society Review*, Summer 1993, p. 16.
38. "Rating Environmental Groups," *USA Today*, October 24, 1994, p. 8A.

enough to force the company to take action. In 1990, the company agreed to enact a dolphin protection plan that ensured that the company would purchase tuna only from fishers who used dolphin-safe nets. "The idea that the company could be branded the largest slaughterers of dolphins in the world seemed to us to be dramatically opposed to where the company wanted to position itself as health conscious and caring," said an executive at the Earth Island Institute who explained the decision.[39]

Using the Media To keep the issue of corporate environmentalism in the public eye, many special interest groups annually list the "best" and "worst" companies in regard to environmentalism. The Business Enterprise Trust, Council of Environmental Equality, and Renew America each have awards programs that highlight the most ecologically friendly corporations. Likewise, every year the Council on Economic Priorities lists "environmental offenders." These organizations release their choices with as much media coverage as possible in order to catch the public's attention.

In response to these pressures, U.S. corporations have begun to market products that proclaim their parent company's environmentalism. A consumer walking down a supermarket aisle is informed by packaging that Star Kist tuna is "dolphin friendly," Ultra Purex detergent "cleans without phosphates," and so on. Countless products—including this textbook—announce that they are made with recycled paper or other materials. Green marketing—in which a product's ecologically friendly qualities are its main selling point, even over price—is a growing trend. At times, advertising today often focuses on a product's environmentally friendly characteristics rather than on the product itself.

Tie-ins with the Environment Environmentalism has found its way into other elements of the consumer culture. Visa offers the Co-Op America Visa "affinity" credit card, in which a percentage of each purchase is sent to an affinity group chosen by the cardholder. The environmental groups available to receive affinity funds range from the World Wildlife Fund to the National Wild Turkey Association. Twenty million Americans have these affinity cards, which helped the Audubon Society, for example, earn $100,000 in 1992.[40]

Los Angeles offers its citizens the *Greater Los Angeles Green Pages*, a telephone book for ecologically friendly businesses and resources in the area. Ecotech Autoworks in Northern Virginia offers environmentally sensitive car lubrication, and its owner, Jeff Shumway, has published *The Planet Mechanic's Guide to Environmental Car Care*.

Stockholder Influence through Mutual Funds Chapter 6 discussed ethical investing mutual funds, or mutual funds investing only in companies that conduct business "ethically." There are also a number of environmental mutual funds that invest only in companies with laudable environmental performances. For example, the Investment Strategic Environmental Fund's twenty-two-stock portfolio includes WMX Technologies and United Waste, both committed to the ecological disposal of solid waste; IMCO Recycling, a metals recycler; Wheelbrator Technologies, a developer of waste-to-energy plants; and Englehard, which has unveiled a process in which automobile air conditioners could be made to remove pollutants from the air.

It is important to understand that environmental mutual funds, like ethical investing mutual funds, have not always provided the highest profits. From 1990 to 1994,

39. A. S. Hayes and J. Pereira, "Facing a Boycott, Many Companies Bend," *Wall Street Journal*, November 8, 1990, p. B1.
40. R. Kahlberg, "Color Credit Green," *Los Angeles Times*, December 31, 1992, p. J14.

environmental funds grew at less than 2 percent per year, a dismal performance that analysts blame on their overestimating the effect of the Clean Air and Clean Water Acts. In 1995, however, the trend reversed, with Invesco leading the way by realizing a return of 13.2 percent—far better than many mutual funds.[41] Improved performance by environmental technology companies, especially in the solid waste industry, is given credit for the improvement. The more successful the environmental mutual funds are, the more investors they will attract, and the more influence stockholders will have on the performance of specific businesses with regard to the environment.

CERES and the Valdez Principles The ultimate expression of consumer and stockholder pressure on businesses came directly after the *Exxon Valdez* oil spill.[42] In response to the disaster, the Coalition for Environmentally Responsible Economics (CERES) released the Valdez Principles, a set of guidelines that require corporate cosigners to commit themselves to protecting the environment (see *Exhibit 17–3*). CERES is composed of environmental groups, social investments groups, and other institutional investors that control millions of dollars in investments. "Preserving and protecting the environment is so important and so complex that none of us can do the job alone," said MacAllister Booth, chairman, president, and CEO of Polaroid, Inc., of his company's decision to endorse the principles. "There is much that we can learn from others; as a concerned and knowledgeable company, there is much that we can share with them as well."[43]

After the Valdez Principles were announced in September 1989, CERES began meeting with corporations in order to urge them to sign on. A corporation that chose not to do so left itself open to a negative publicity campaign, including consumer boycotts and shareholder resolutions concerning the company's environmental practices. Thus, it is not surprising that many companies agreed to the Valdez Principles.

NEW OPPORTUNITIES FOR BUSINESS

To counterbalance the costs of new regulations, businesses can take advantage of the new markets created by green consumer demands.[44] The new rules themselves have even created a new market—for products that do less polluting and therefore give businesses that use them a competitive advantage.

The Rewards of Green Technology The accidental spilling by a nearby hospital of several gallons of hazardous formaldehyde was an inspiration of sorts for Randy M. Skalla, vice president of S&S Company of Georgia, a chemical manufacturer. Skalla calculated that hospitals were spending hundreds of thousands of dollars to dispose of used formaldehyde in a safe manner. He decided that S&S would develop a process in which the preservative could be chemically treated so that it could be harmlessly poured down the drain.[45]

Skalla is not the only entrepreneur to follow an environmental technology strategy. Government regulations, and the threat of them, have created a $140 billion environmental business community in the United States that is made up of approximately 45,000

41. E. J. Savitz, "It's Not Easy Being Green," *Barron's,* April 24, 1995, p. 33.

42. I. I. Mitroff, "Crisis Management and Environmentalism: A Natural Fit," *California Management Review,* Winter 1992, p. 101.

43. "Polaroid, Arizona Public Service Company Endorse CERES Principle," *Business and the Environment,* September 1, 1994, p. 1.

44. A. Kleiner, "What Does It Mean to Be Green?" *Harvard Business Review,* July–August 1991, p. 38.

45. J. Carey, "A Green Industrial Policy Takes Root," *Business Week,* July 25, 1994, p. 10.

▼ **EXHIBIT 17–3 The Valdez Principles**

Principle	Purpose
1. Protection of the Biosphere	We will minimize and strive to eliminate the release of any pollutant that may cause environmental damage to the air, water, and earth or its inhabitants. We will safeguard habitants in rivers, lakes, wetlands, coastal zones, and oceans and will minimize contributing to the greenhouse effect, depletion of the ozone layer, acid rain, or smog.
2. Sustainable Use of Natural Resources	We will make sustainable use of renewable natural resources, such as water, soils, and forests. We will conserve nonrenewable natural resources through efficient use and careful planning. We will protect wildlife habitat, open spaces, and wilderness, while preserving biodiversity.
3. Reduction and Disposal of Waste	We will minimize the creation of waste, especially hazardous waste, and wherever possible recycle materials. We will dispose of all wastes through safe and responsible methods.
4. Wise Use of Energy	We will make every effort to use environmentally safe and sustainable energy sources to meet our needs. We will invest in improved energy efficiency and conservation in our operations. We will maximize the energy efficiency of products we produce or sell.
5. Risk Reduction	We will minimize the environmental, health, and safety risks to our employees and the communities in which we operate by employing safe technologies and operating procedures and by being constantly prepared for emergencies.
6. Marketing of Safe Products and Services	We will sell safe products or services that minimize adverse environmental impacts and that are safe as consumers commonly use them. We will inform consumers of the environmental impacts of our products or services.
7. Damage Compensation	We will take responsibility for any harm we cause to the environment by making every effort to fully restore the environment and to compensate those persons who are adversely affected.
8. Disclosure	We will disclose to our employees and to the public incidents relating to our operations that cause environmental harm or pose health or safety hazards. We will disclose potential environmental, health, or safety hazards posed by our operations, and we will not take any action against employees who report any condition that creates a danger to the environment or poses health and safety hazards.
9. Environmental Directors and Managers	We will commit management resources to implement the Valdez Principles, to monitor and report upon our implementation efforts, and to sustain a process to ensure that the Board of Directors and the Chief Executive Officer are kept informed of and are fully responsible for all environmental matters. We will establish a Committee of the Board of Directors with responsibility for environmental affairs. At least one member of the Board of Directors will be a person qualified to represent environmental interests.
10. Assessment and Annual Audit	We will conduct and make public an annual self-evaluation of our progress in implementing these Principles and in complying with all applicable laws and regulations throughout our worldwide operations. We will work toward the timely creation of independent environmental audit procedures which we will complete annually and make available to the public.

SOURCE: Coalition for Environmentally Responsible Economics.

companies.[46] Some, such as S&S, offer the service of minimizing pollution-disposal costs. Others use "green chemistry" to gain market shares. The Danish company Novo Nordisk has obtained more than 50 percent of the world's $1 billion enzyme market by finding harmless natural replacements for synthetic chemicals.

Some companies make a profit by discovering *future* clean-up costs. An entirely new industry that emerged in the 1990s provides the environmental histories of properties that are up for sale. One of the first companies to offer this service, Vista Environmental Information of San Diego, started in 1989 and four years later had annual revenues of $10 million.[47] "Everybody is scared to death of toxic liabilities" under such federal programs as Superfund, says Walter Hang, president of competing Toxic Targeting, Inc. As one banker explained, "You can have an appraisal in front of you that shows a property is worth $1 million, but if it has some sort of environmental contamination, it could be worth nothing."[48]

Finally, some companies, such as Logan Aluminum, use new technology to improve their own environmental records while saving costs at the same time (see *Managing Social Issues—Information/Technology: Constructed Wetlands Wastewater Purification*).

Exporting Environmental Technology The market for exporting environmental technology is growing. Western European countries, such as England, France, and Germany, have been purchasing environmental technology from the United States since the 1970s, but those in the field see an expanding opportunity for the export of this technology to Eastern Europe and Southeast Asia. Nations such as Romania, Bulgaria, and Poland suffered years of environmental neglect under past regimes. Stopping cross-border pollution has become a priority in these countries because of the environmental standards required for entry into the European Union. In Southeast Asia, the economies of countries such as Taiwan and Thailand are growing at rates approaching 10 percent a year, and these nations are producing pollution to match their economic growth. Health concerns for both citizens and tourists have caused these governments to look abroad for assistance.

There have been a number of concerted efforts by the U.S. government and U.S. industry to meet this need. The United States–Asia Environmental Partnership was formed in 1992 to introduce environmental technologies to nearly three dozen Asian countries and territories. That same year, representatives of sixteen American businesses traveled to Eastern Europe to promote exports to that region. Westinghouse Electric Corporation has two significant projects in Eastern Europe: a $10 million effort to start the area's first low-level radioactive waste-processing facility in Sofia, Bulgaria, and a $40 million, four-year contract to build more than thirty thousand containers to store dismantled nuclear weapons in Russia.[49] QED Environmental Systems, Inc., of Ann Arbor, Michigan, is marketing its groundwater sampling pumps in England, Saudi Arabia, Germany, Denmark, Italy, Spain, Ukraine, Taiwan, Australia, and New Zealand.

With the longest history of significant environmental legislation in the world, the United States is in a unique position to profit by spreading its knowledge across the globe.

---

46. *Ibid.*
47. R. G. Blumenthal, "Polluted Sites Are Fertile Ground for Entrepreneurs," *Wall Street Journal*, April 15, 1993, p. B2.
48. *Ibid.*
49. D. Welch, "Environmental Tech Exports Seen as Growth Industry by Local Companies," *Pittsburgh Business Times and Journal*, February 7, 1994, p. 14.

▣ MANAGING SOCIAL ISSUES

INFORMATION/TECHNOLOGY: CONSTRUCTED WETLANDS WASTEWATER PURIFICATION

The Logan Aluminum processing plant in Russellville, Kentucky, had a wastewater problem. Its treatment system could not handle the volume from expansions to the plant, and weaknesses in the system were leading to a build-up of bacteria and mold. This led to a need for constant cleaning, which was an inefficient use of company time and money. To solve this problem, Logan turned to new technology and an age-old natural system that has a bad reputation among many U.S. corporations—wetlands.

Constructing Wetlands

After spending more than two years analyzing their options, engineers at Logan Aluminum decided that a series of constructed wetlands would be the best solution to their wastewater problems. The company spent $1.6 million on wetlands treatment technology, which was implemented in the summer of 1992.

The constructed wetland treatment system is spread over thirty acres of water and ten acres of berms, islands, and other natural buffer zones outside the plant. The system has an overall capacity of 14 million gallons of water, and water depths vary from less than an inch to three feet. Over 144,000 different plants, representing thirteen different species indigenous to the area, have prospered in the system, and cattails have become the dominant plant.

Between 360,000 and 600,000 gallons of wastewater per day are released into the system. The water is pretreated with chemicals to break down various waste solids before it enters the first stage of the system, a 200-foot-long overland flow area. This thin layer of water exposes the wastewater to oxygen and soil, which further break down the solid wastes. The wastewater then empties into two basins and begins a twenty-day meander through the system. During this period, the waste is further decimated by constant exposure to oxygen and filtration through the plant mass and root structures. Finally, the treated wastewater winds up in a two-million-gallon tank for reuse in the aluminum-manufacturing process.

Challenges and Benefits

Harnessing wetlands in this way is not without challenges. "A natural system is not something you can turn off and tweak at will," says Harry Wojner, utilities team leader at Logan. Problems include cold weather, which causes the system to ice over and treatment efficiency to drop, and muskrats, which eat the cattails and burrow into berms.

These are minor inconveniences, however, compared with the benefits of the wetlands project. The system is expected to last thirty years, though it could survive longer. The constructed wetlands also offer low capital investment, savings in operation and maintenance costs, decreased chemical usage, and low energy usage. All things told, the wetlands wastewater purification system is saving the plant more than $500,000 a year.

For Critical Analysis:

What constraints are there for the increased use of wetlands as a filtering system?

SOURCE: B. Gillette, "Constructed Wetlands for Industrial Wastewater," *BioCycle*, November 1994, pp. 80–83.

In the mid-1990s, American environmental technology firms were exporting only about 5 percent of their output, but as the markets abroad continue to expand, so will the export activity.[50]

---

50. M. Dempsey, "Sweeping the World Clean," *Crain's Detroit Business*, May 8, 1995, p. 9.

A Green Industrial Policy

After its initial success, the environmental business slowed down considerably in the mid-1990s.[51] Environmental companies experienced double-digit growth of their revenues in the late 1980s, but their revenues rose by only 3.0 percent in 1996. Such a slowdown is consistent with the evolution of other industries. A new industry typically has a slower rate of growth after its initial spurt, for three reasons. First, all the easy opportunities have been exploited by the early entrants into the industry. Second, increased competition reduces profitability, thereby causing fewer potential entrants to explore the industry. Third, once an industry is established, it attracts the attention of regulators at local, state, and federal levels. Such regulation normally slows its rate of growth.

In 1994, President Bill Clinton and Vice President Al Gore introduced the idea of a green industrial policy in which the federal government would promote the development and distribution of environmental technologies. The Clinton administration planned to eliminate rules that keep new technologies from hitting the market; to boost environmental technology exports; and to loosen regulation in order to allow businesses to test new environmental technology without fear of federal, state, or local retribution. The administration was committed to spending $100 million over two years to promote these goals.

A statewide model for what the federal government envisioned began in 1994, when California started a test and certification program that by-passed many of the former regulations. One of the first five technologies to win state approval that year was the previously mentioned S&S formaldehyde-disposal system. The benefits for Randy Skalla and his company were immediate: on the same day the state announced its intention to certify the S&S product, the giant health-care organization Kaiser-Permanente announced its intention to use the product in all its Northern California facilities. Skalla claimed that the state certification was a critical endorsement and would "open doors as far away as Australia."[52]

Environmental Management

In the spring of 1994, the following sign appeared at New York City's River Café and the Water Club:

> GENERAL ELECTRIC EXECUTIVES ARE NOT WELCOME . . . BECAUSE OF GENERAL ELECTRIC'S FLAGRANT AND PERNICIOUS POLLUTION OF OUR RIVERS AND WATERWAYS—AND THE POISONING OF AMERICA'S #1 GAME FISH—THE STRIPED BASS—AND THE GENERAL POISONING OF THE NEW YORK AREA MARINE ENVIRONMENT.

When asked about the economic impact of this bold statement, Buzzy O'Keefe, the owner of the two establishments, replied, "There are some things more important than business."[53]

What should a manager do when the demands of the environment are at odds with the demands of the profit structure? The answer lies in a still-developing field known gener-

---

51. M. Silverstein, "The Pollution of Environmental Theory; Environmentalism Needs to Get with It," *Business and Society Review*, Summer 1995, p. 62.
52. Carey, *op. cit.*
53. "The High Horse," *New York Times*, April 18, 1994, p. 22A.

ally as **environmental management.** O'Keefe's style of environmental management is not an option most executives could choose, and neither is Skalla's strategy of coming up with a useful product and waiting for government regulators to approve it.

THE TQM APPROACH TO ENVIRONMENTAL MANAGEMENT

Just before the opening of a trial in which ten thousand Alaskan fishers, property owners, and Native Americans were suing Exxon for $1.5 billion in damages and lost income as a result of the *Exxon Valdez* oil spill, John Havelock, who directed a state commission to examine the spill, stated the obvious. "I guess you could say," offered Havelock, "the trial will show that a million dollars in prevention would be better than a billion dollars in court fines."[54]

Havelock's comment struck at the heart of environmental management, the motto of which, if it had one, would be "Plan ahead." As any executive will attest, however, planning ahead is easier said in a boardroom than done in the restrictions of a work environment. Once it is decided that a company must plan ahead, then someone must decide on a plan. One strategic method for doing so involves environmental quality management.

Total Quality Management In *Costing the Earth*, Cairncross promotes the idea of **total quality management (TQM)** in environmental corporate planning.[55] In TQM, all aspects of a product's production and distribution are considered at all times. A Japanese innovation in organizational strategy, TQM became popular in many American corporations in the 1980s because of its commitment to producing high-quality products at low costs instead of sacrificing one for the other. Cairncross believes this strategy can be applied to "cradle-to-grave" environmental management.

Environmental Quality Management The basis of TQM is reflected in Havelock's statement concerning the *Exxon Valdez*: it is less expensive to fix a defect before it leaves the factory floor than afterward. In Cairncross's version, it is less costly to prevent an environmental accident before it has occurred than to clean it up afterward. She argues that the costs of poor environmental quality management are already carried by many companies through damage to their reputations and "sudden" changes in regulations and customer tastes. In light of these often high-priced detriments, companies should aim to minimize the "societal loss" incurred by each of their products.[56]

One such societal loss is customer dissatisfaction; another is the damage done to the environment as a result of the manufacturing and disposal of a product. Indeed, writes Cairncross, "some managers wonder whether traditional definitions of quality that apply to customer satisfaction should be broadened to incorporate environmental criteria and extend to all who are affected by a product from its cradle to its grave." She hints that environmental quality management may require additional personnel and regular environmental audits (see *Managing Social Issues—Making a Difference: The Environmental Audit* on page 534). Cairncross realizes that this is an expensive step but insists that in the end, the investment of time and money will be worthwhile.

54. "Exxon Trial on Oil Spill Starts Monday," *New York Times*, May 1, 1994, p. 33.
55. Cairncross, *op. cit.*, pp. 280–281.
56. D. Bandow, "Eco-Sanity: A Common Sense Guide to Environmentalism," *Business and Society Review*, Summer 1994, p. 59.

MANAGING SOCIAL ISSUES

MAKING A DIFFERENCE: THE ENVIRONMENTAL AUDIT

Despite its name, the environmental audit is much more than a public relations nod to special interest groups. Having a formal process to evaluate the environmental performance of a business could prove invaluable should that business find itself in a legal battle with a regulatory agency. Lawrence D. Kornreich, president of Enviro-Health and Safety Management, has prepared a list of dos and don'ts for companies planning to implement a well-conceived environmental audit.

Dos in an Environmental Audit

▶ **Do commit to corrective action.** If an environmental audit uncovers any defects or deficiencies, the company must be firmly committed to correcting them. If this is not the case, the audit may turn into a liability and could even lead to a civil or criminal action by a regulatory agency or a lawsuit. Corrective action and follow-up are integral to any program.

▶ **Do set specific goals.** Decide whether the audit will be limited to determining the company's regulatory compliance status or if it will go further to increase environmental awareness in the company overall. This needs to be specified so that proper goals can be set for managers.

▶ **Do encourage in-house participation.** Even though an environmental expert should guide the audit team, the company's personnel should be intimately involved in the process. Employees can sharpen their environmental skills and publicize the company's concern for the environment by being involved.

▶ **Do establish an adequate budget.** Make sure that before the auditing process begins, sufficient funds are provided for its development and full implementation.

▶ **Do document fully and adequately.** A key to acceptance of the audit by a regulatory agent or a judge is complete and full documentation of the entire process.

▶ **Do update the program periodically.** It is important that any changes in regulatory law be reflected in ongoing audits. Furthermore, after the first or second audit, it will be expected that improvements will be made in the environmental management of the company according to the findings of the audit.

▶ **Do consider what can be made public.** Companies that subscribe to international standards of environmental performance, such as those of the Coalition for Environmentally Responsible Economics (CERES), are obligated to publicize their audit results. Others should strongly consider doing so, as no company has yet been punished for such an effort, even if the results reflected negatively on the audited firm. In fact, the release of previously "privileged" information has aided the public relations efforts of the companies that released it.

Don'ts in an Environmental Audit

▶ **Don't punish managers for early audit results.** It is important to wait until several audits have been completed before holding managers accountable for audit results. Any problems uncovered may be historical and not the fault of the present manager.

▶ **Don't exclude any facilities.** All warehouses and offices should be audited.

▶ **Don't rely too much on ratings or quantitative summaries.** Putting too much weight on a ratings system, quantitative or not, can defeat the purpose of an audit. Rather, companies should base the success of their programs on meeting specific goals set up during the auditing process.

For Critical Analysis:

What challenges would face small businesses with regard to environmental audits in comparison with large corporations?

SOURCE: L. D. Kornreich, "Planning Tips for Environmental Audits," *Occupational Hazards*, January 1, 1995, p. 65.

LOBBYING

Businesses do not have to wait for government to make regulatory decisions that affect them. As we saw in Chapter 11, businesses can assert their own influence through lobbying. Especially for large companies, lobbying is definitely a key aspect of environmental management.

Environmental lobbying from industry comes under the same scrutiny as other forms of "influence peddling," especially from environmental special interest groups. A writer from the monthly magazine of the Sierra Club described the frustration of trying to speak with his congressional representative: "While you're waiting, the lobbyist for the polluting factory you're trying to shut down strolls in, writes your representative a check for $5,000, and walks out with a wink . . . that's just how Washington works today. And when greenbacks govern, green issues are pushed to the background."[57]

Despite such criticisms, lobbying is a part of the governmental process that businesses cannot afford to ignore. Lobbying can be valuable in dissuading the government from passing certain legislation. An example is the fate of car-pool requirements for certain businesses. As part of the Clean Air Act of 1990, companies in or near large cities with more than a hundred employees have to raise the number of passengers per vehicle that drive to work by 125 percent over four years, starting in November 1994.

Even the most rudimentary cost-benefit analysis on this "employer trip reduction" program showed that it would unduly burden business for a relatively small environmental gain. Because cars are cleaner today, and commuting accounts for a declining share of total vehicle travel—down to one-quarter in 1990 from one-third in 1969—the total reduction in carbon monoxide and ozone-forming hydrocarbons from the program would be less than 3 percent in any single area.[58] The cost of implementing a plan to meet the law's goals, however, would be from $200 to $900 per employee. Furthermore, because company-mandated travel arrangements could be construed as an extension of the workplace, businesses could face litigation over traffic accidents or sexual harassment that took place in the car-pool. There were also many insurance-related issues.[59]

The business community, facing possible fines of $25,000 a day for noncompliance, reacted with a concentrated lobbying effort. When November 1994 came and passed without any compliance to speak of around the country, managers were relieved that the EPA "seemed to be looking the other way."[60]

PUBLIC-INTEREST GROUPS AND GREENWASHING

When environmental public-interest groups were growing in stature and power, industrialists tended to treat them as enemies. This proved to be unwise strategy, as the environmental groups were much more effective at mobilizing public opinion than were the businesses or industries they had targeted.

Consequently, in the late 1980s, business began making an effort to join with these groups rather than fight them. In 1988, the Conservation Law Foundation and the New England Electrical System, a public utility, formed a partnership so successful that it was

57. P. Raber, "Under the Influence," *Sierra*, September–October 1994, p. 26.

58. D. A. Price, "Newest Mandate—Everyone into the Carpool," *Wall Street Journal*, November 8, 1993, p. A14.

59. W. Lambert, "Businesses Must Wean Workers from Their Cars," *Wall Street Journal*, November 4, 1993, p. B1.

60. "EPA's Big Road Test," *Wall Street Journal*, April 6, 1995, p. A14.

extended to twelve retail electrical companies in New England and New York. A break-fast meeting between members of industry, state regulators, and environmental groups in Colorado had evolved by 1991 into the Colorado Pollution Prevention Partnership. Large corporations such as McDonald's Corporation and General Motors Corporation have formed formal alliances with the Environmental Defense Fund (EDF) to reduce waste and toxic emissions (see the *Case—McDonald's Polystyrene Problem—and Its Solution—* at the end of this chapter). Another business-environmentalist alliance is the Great Print-ers Project in the Great Lakes region, which has joined the EDF, the Council of Great Lakes Governors, and the Printing Industries of America to reduce pollution.[61]

Not all environmental groups are pleased with the willingness of certain groups to form alliances with corporations. "Corporations should not have to form alliances to meet their environmental responsibility," says Jerry Leape, director for ocean ecology at Greenpeace USA. "It should be a normal consideration in all business operations."[62] Some critics also point out that corporations that ally themselves with environmental interests sometimes do so because of financial considerations rather than an underlying concern for the environment (see *Company Focus: Louisiana-Pacific Corporation*).

What further worries Leape and other environmentalists is the possibility that environmental groups may tend to ignore a company's infractions if they are getting significant contributions from that corporation. Observers also criticize the practice of **greenwashing**, in which a corporation works with an environmental group to improve its actions and its image while one of its subsidiaries is "building a toxic waste dump or using carcinogens in their manufacturing process."[63]

HAZARDS OF GREEN MARKETING

Earlier we discussed the trend of companies' turning toward green marketing to capitalize on the popularity of the environment with consumers. However,

▼ Managers should not assume that such a strategy has no risks; environmental advertising alone is not likely to attract consumers.

The market research company Roper Starch Worldwide, in a four-year study of green magazine advertisements, found that too many of these ads fail to make the connection between what the company is doing for the environment and how it affects individual consumers. Roper Starch cited a Ford Motors ad declaring "Environmental Responsibility Fuels Our Research," which announced Ford's commitment to meeting California's strict emission standards. The problem, according to Roper Starch researcher Philip W. Sawyer, is that the ad "is all about Ford and not about [the consumer]. Hence, the consumer finds him or herself asking 'What do I get out of this? Nothing.'"[64] (The consumer, however, might get the satisfaction of owning a car with strict emission standards.)

Companies should also avoid making claims for things that turn out to be unfeasible. The public acclaim for recycling, for example, lured many companies into making the mistake of promising more than they could economically provide.[65] In 1989, Larry L.

61. T. A. Hemphill, "Strange Bedfellows Cozy Up for a Clean Environment," *Business and Society Review*, Summer 1994, pp. 38–42.

62. *Ibid.*, p. 44.

63. *Ibid.*

64. K. Goldman, "Survey Addresses a '90s Question: What Will Get a 'Green' Ad Read?" *Wall Street Journal*, April 11, 1994, p. B8.

65. W. W. Wossen and D. Verma, "Balancing Traditional Packaging Functions with the New 'Green' Packaging Concerns," *SAM Advanced Management Journal*, Autumn 1992, p. 15.

COMPANY FOCUS: LOUISIANA-PACIFIC CORPORATION

UNEXPECTED ALLIANCES ON ENVIRONMENTAL ISSUES

Louisiana-Pacific Corporation, one of the largest U.S. paper companies, has had a number of conflicts with environmental groups over issues ranging from toxic waste to timber production. When President Bill Clinton considered issuing an executive order in which the federal government would purchase only chlorine-free paper products, however, Louisiana-Pacific found itself on the same side of the fence as the environmental groups.

Chlorine-Free Paper

The use of chlorine to bleach the pulp used in the production of paper has long been an area of concern for environmentalists. The process results in wastewater emissions of dioxin and other toxic chemicals that cannot be recycled because the chlorinated waste products are too corrosive. Environmentalists would like paper companies to use a more benign bleach, such as hydrogen peroxide, instead of chlorine. The industry contends that such a change in their production process would be too costly.

A notable exception is Louisiana-Pacific. Because of a consent decree the company signed with the Environmental Protection Agency over pollution at its plant in Somoa, California, Louisiana-Pacific is already producing chlorine-free bleached kraft softwood pulp. Although some European firms have embraced the concept, Louisiana-Pacific is the only paper company in the United States with production facilities that use this environmentally friendly, and possibly competitively advantageous, process.

A Pleasant Surprise

"We certainly didn't have anything to do with getting the provision" on chlorine-free paper into the executive order, said a spokesperson from Louisiana-Pacific, but "we were pleasantly surprised to see it there and would love to see it stay." To better the odds of this occurring, Louisiana-Pacific allied itself with environmental groups such as the National Wildlife Fund and the Natural Resources Defense Council in lobbying for the order. Some environmentalists, however, do not like the idea of an alliance with a common enemy. "I'm not exactly comfortable with any policy that would elevate Louisiana-Pacific's current market share," said one of them. The groups in the alliance took a more pragmatic view, saying they would accept any help as long as the end result would improve the environment.

Louisiana-Pacific's industry partners, of course, were not pleased with the situation. A lobbyist for Georgia-Pacific Corporation noted that although Louisiana-Pacific is generally enemy number one for environmental groups, "now they're kissing cousins with Greenpeace."

The New Bottom Line

As we saw in Chapter 9, government regulations can often provide a company with competitive advantages. Louisiana-Pacific enjoys technological superiority over its competitors in this case, and the company would be foolish not to take advantage of its investment—forced though it may have been—in a chlorine-free pulp process.

SOURCE: Information from "Slants and Trends," *Air Water Pollution Report*, September 6, 1993; and T. Noah, "Louisiana-Pacific, Target of Environmentalists, Finds Itself Allied with Them on U.S. Proposal," *Wall Street Journal*, August 24, 1993, p. A14.

Thomas, president of the Society of the Plastics Industry, warned his business partners that "the image of plastics is deteriorating at an alarmingly fast pace" and "we are approaching a 'point of no return.'" Part of the problem was that consumers felt plastics were environmentally unsafe. To change that perception, in 1990 the plastics industry committed $50 million to an advertising and public relations campaign to convince the American public that plastics were recyclable. The industry announced the goal of recycling 25 percent of plastic bottles and containers by 1995.[66] Such claims turned out to be wildly optimistic. "We probably overdid it," said an industry recycling expert. By convincing consumers that plastic recycling was easy and cost effective, the industry found itself with more used plastics than it could handle.

Individual companies have also had to retract marketing promises. When Procter & Gamble Company's disposable diapers were criticized for taking up landfill space, the company began running advertisements that claimed composting could turn fouled Pampers into "a rich soil conditioner." Although this was technically possible, very few facilities could put the process into practice; this fact made the ads, according to the New York attorney general's office, "virtually untrue for most of the nation's consumers."[67] Procter & Gamble discontinued the advertisements, though the company did continue contributing to composting efforts.

---

66. J. Bailey, "Marketers Make Extravagant Promises, Then Begin to Regret Them," *Wall Street Journal,* January 19, 1995, p. A8.
67. *Ibid.*

THE DELICATE BALANCE

If a corporation will be adversely affected by a new environmental law or regulation, and if members of top management believe the new law or regulation will be far more costly than it is worth, the corporation should engage in a serious cost-benefit analysis of the proposed law or regulation. There is a delicate balance here, though, because the public, as well as government officials, will suspect that the corporation has ulterior motives. When corporate leadership firmly believes it is the right action, though, the corporation should follow through with the cost-benefit analysis.

In any event, corporations today may find that they can diversify into the production of products and services that satisfy the environmental needs of other corporations because of existing or future legislation.

TERMS AND CONCEPTS FOR REVIEW

Contingent valuation 515
Emission banking 523
Environmental
  management 533

Greenwashing 536
Incentive structure 519
Negative incentive 519
Offset policy 523

Risk assessment 518
Total quality management (TQM)
  533

SUMMARY

1. One way to place a value on the environment or its destruction is through contingent valuation. In this process, a cross section of individuals are asked how much they would be willing to spend either to prevent an ecological disaster or to improve the environment. Critics of this procedure argue that simply asking what people think something is worth is not the same thing as requiring them to make a payment to back up their opinions. Nonetheless, the EPA usually uses the contingent valuation process when deciding how much to "charge" (fine) polluters.

2. Another way to evaluate environmental values is by using actual market values. If we were able to examine two towns that were exactly the same in all respects except for the amount of air pollution, we could estimate the cost of air pollution by, for example, looking at the decreased real estate values in the polluted town.

3. Most environmental impact statements required by the National Environmental Policy Act require one or more cost-benefit analyses. One problem in doing these analyses is that it is difficult to measure the costs to an ecosystem that stem from the loss of one part of that system. Nonetheless, one researcher claims that the 1990 Clean Air Act will cost between $29 billion and $39 billion a year but will prevent only about five hundred cases of cancer a year—a cost of $70 million for each cancer case avoided.

4. Another type of analysis in environmental decision making involves risk assessment. With risk assessment, the possibility of worst-case scenarios is measured against the costs of preventing them. Risk analysis derives a cost of each premature death averted, which is typically in the millions of dollars.

5. Most environmental legislation sets up a set of negative incentives as part of an overall incentive structure designed to change the behavior of businesses and individuals. Sometimes these negative incentives backfire, as has occurred with the Endangered Species Act. Owners of property who discover endangered species often develop the property quickly before those species can be discovered by federal or state authorities. Consequently, some have argued in favor of a change to positive incentives. An example would be a program that rewards landowners who preserve endangered species on their properties.

6. Subsequent to a 1990 Clean Air Act amendment, there has been an active market for pollution rights, particularly for the rights to disperse sulfur dioxide into the air.

7. Business managers must realize that environmentalism is not just a trend but a rock-solid reality. Total annualized environmental protection costs total about 2.5 percent of the gross domestic product.

8. Consumers can influence corporate environmental policies through purchasing power, lobbying, and threatening boycotts or media attention.

9. Today's supermarkets are lined with packages that inform us that their product is environmentally friendly. This is a direct response to consumer purchasing power. The majority of consumers say they seek environmentally friendly products.

10. The Coalition for Environmentally Responsible Economics (CERES) has released a set of guidelines that require corporate cosigners to commit to the protection of the environment. These Valdez Principles require (a) the protection of the biosphere, (b) the sustainable

use of natural resources, (c) the reduction and disposal of waste, (d) the wide use of energy, (e) risk reduction, (f) marketing of safe products and services, (g) damage compensation, (h) disclosure, (i) environmental directors and managers, and (j) assessment and annual audit.

11. U.S. companies are able to export their environmental technology not only to traditional markets, such as Western Europe, but also to the newly independent nations in Eastern Europe and to the fast-developing nations in Southeast Asia.

12. For many executives, attention to the developing field of administrative theory known as environmental management is mandatory. One approach is total quality management, in which all aspects of a product's production and distribution are considered at all times.

13. Environmental quality management requires a preventive approach to environmental problems rather than a reactive approach. U.S. corporations can influence environmental legislation through lobbying in favor of appropriate legislation and regulation of the environment and against inefficient and ineffective laws.

14. Many major corporations have formed partnerships with environmental groups. Some observers criticize greenwashing, which occurs when corporations work with environmental groups while also creating toxic waste or carcinogens at their plants or subsidiaries.

EXERCISES

1. "Talk is cheap; environmental efforts are not." Is this a fair statement? Back up your answer with specific examples.

2. Why might there be an upward bias in a public opinion survey concerning individuals' perceived value of, say, pristine wilderness areas?

3. Develop an argument in favor of contingent valuation.

4. You have been put in charge of developing an environmental impact statement for a new hydroelectric power plant. In creating the power plant, a new dam will have to be built. Make a list of the benefits of such a plan. Make another list of its costs.

5. How would you argue with someone who stated that it is morally reprehensible to place a dollar amount on the life of a tree, a whale, or a human being?

6. Medical care generally saves lives at less cost than do workplace safety or environmental measures, according to a statement made by the Risk Analysis Center of the Harvard School of Public Health. Explain what this means, and give examples.

7. Make a list with two column headings, "Negative Incentives" and "Positive Incentives." Under the headings write down different environmental policies that generate negative or positive incentives.

8. Why is the electric automobile not really a zero-pollution mode of transportation?

9. Currently, about 2.5 percent of the gross domestic product is devoted to protecting the environment. This exceeds similar ratios anywhere else in the world. Is the United States spending too much on environmental protection? Too little? Support your answer.

10. In what ways can businesses engage in a "win-win" situation in terms of helping the environment?

11. Reexamine *Exhibit 17–3* which gives the Valdez Principles. Pick one principle. Then make a flow chart showing how you would institute this principle in your organization if you were a top-level manager.

12. Does the size of an organization have any impact on whether or not its leadership can implement the Valdez Principles? Explain your answer.

13. How does environmental management fit into the concept of total quality management (TQM)?

14. What are the most important aspects of an environmental audit? Why?

15. At first glance, the practice of greenwashing seems to reflect an internal inconsistency within a corporation. Does it really? Why or why not?

SELECTED REFERENCES

▶ Collins, Denis, and Mark Starik, eds. *Sustaining the Natural Environment: Empirical Studies on the Interface between Nature and Organizations*. Greenwich, Conn.: JAI Press, 1995.

▶ Ditz, Daryl, Janet K. Ranganathan, and Darryl Banks, eds. *Green Ledgers: Case Studies in Corporate Environmental Accounting*. Washington, D.C.: World Resources Institute, 1995.

▶ Ledgerwood, Grant. *Implementing an Environmental Audit: How to Gain a Competitive Advantage Using Quality and Environmental Responsibility*. Burr Ridge, Ill.: Irwin Professional Publishing, 1994.

▶ Roberts, Peter. *Environmentally Sustainable Business: A Local and Regional Perspective*. London: P. Chapman, 1995.

▶ Shrivastava, Paul. *Greening Business: Profiting the Corporation and the Environment*. Cincinnati: Thomas Executive Press, 1996.

▶ Young, Steven Scott. *Environmental Auditing*. Des Plaines, Ill.: Cahners Publishing, 1994.

RESOURCES ON THE INTERNET

▼ Communicopia is an environmental consulting company that provides services to businesses interested in informing the public about their environmentally conscious programs. To access the Communicopia Environmental Research and Communications service, go to

**http://interchange.idc.uvic.ca/
communicopia/**

The Progressive Business Web Pages also provide information on environmentally conscious businesses. To access these pages, go to

http://envirolink.org/products

▼ If you are interested in equipping an office with ecologically friendly materials, ForestSaver is a manufacturer of recycled stationery and office supplies. To learn more about ForestSaver and its products, access the following:

**http://www.nando.net/prof/
eco/forest/html**

TreEco also supplies nontoxic and biodegradable products. This company can be accessed at

http://www.envirolink.org/treeco/

CASE

MCDONALD'S POLYSTYRENE PROBLEM—AND ITS SOLUTION

Background

Ever since McDonald's Corporation began packaging its hamburgers in polystyrene foam miniboxes in the mid-1970s, the fast-food chain has found itself defending the "clamshells" against claims that they were overly harmful to the environment. "We use foam packing for the same reasons that schools, hospitals and other restaurants do," said Shelby Yarbow, senior vice president for environmental affairs at the company. "It keeps our products hot, it keeps them fresh, it's portable, and it's a safe and sanitary way to serve our product." As to charges from environmental groups that the clamshells were ecologically unsavory, McDonald's chief executive officer and president Ed Rensi vowed, "We cannot allow ourselves to be held hostage to self-appointed saviors who are just trying to scare the American public."

One month after Rensi's statement, however, the fast-food chain had allied itself with one of those "self-appointed saviors," the Environmental Defense Fund (EDF), and was announcing a switch from plastic to paper packaging for its hamburgers, breakfast sandwiches, and soft drinks. Although the company's executives defended polystyrene until the very end, the realities of an environmentally conscious market dictated the firm's action. Through a swell of negative publicity, the clamshell had come to symbolize a lack of concern with environmental issues by U.S. corporations. With one-third to three-quarters of consumers making choices based on "green" considerations, McDonald's found itself forced to follow an age-old managerial dictate: "The customer is always right."

The Problem with Polystyrene

Polystyrene has a number of environmental drawbacks, including the fact that it is nonbiodegradable and gives off toxic fumes when incinerated. The biggest problem with the clamshells, however, was that there were so many of them. Serving 7 percent of the U.S. population and operating outlets in fifty-two countries, McDonald's found itself responsible for forty-five million pounds of plastic waste a year. As communities struggled to reduce the amount of garbage in their shrinking landfill space, McDonald's was targeted as a prime waste producer. In fact, local governments in Portland, Oregon, Berkeley, California, and Glen Cove, New York,

banned the plastic material, forcing McDonald's to switch to paper packaging in those areas.

For McDonald's, with its historically strong commitment of corporate giving to children through the Ronald McDonald Houses and the affiliated Ronald McDonald Children's Charities, one aspect of the public backlash was particularly disturbing: young people seemed to be turning against the company. By 1990, there were eight hundred chapters of a student group called Kids Against Pollution, which had been started by a fifth-grade civics class in Closter, New Jersey, to protest the use of polystyrene in the school cafeteria. The student groups mounted a number of initiatives against McDonald's, including a Send-It-Back campaign in which members collected used clamshells and sent them to the company's headquarters in Illinois. One high school student, in a widely publicized incident, demonstrated in front of a New Jersey outlet dressed as "Ronald McToxic" to voice the message "The planet deserves a break today."

McDonald's Response

To counteract this barrage of criticism, McDonald's publicly defended its image as an environmentally friendly entity. The company pointed out that less than 1 percent of the total solid waste in landfills came from polystyrene food packaging. Some analysts likened McDonald's 1989 annual report to an "Audubon Society brochure," as the financial statement was filled with nature pictures, poetry, and quotations from public figures concerning the environment. The firm also released a twenty-page booklet called *McDonald's Packaging: The Facts*, which contained "eye-opening facts" on the ecological desirability of polystyrene—mainly the fact that it was recyclable.

Judging from public response, this defense campaign was a failure. In a 1990 survey by a packaging design company, 60 percent of the respondents believed that plastic packaging was the biggest contributing factor in the nation's solid waste disposal problems. Therefore, McDonald's management tried a new tactic to improve its public image: a $16 million recycling program. Launched in cooperation with the National Polystyrene Recycling company, a consortium of plastic producers, the pilot program provided for the recycling of the plastic foam at 450 New England restaurants.

The plan called for customers, who seemed so eager to recycle and who had become accustomed to disposing of their own trash, to separate that trash into two bins—one for plastic and one for other waste materials. Once recycled, the used clamshells would be shipped to a small, start-up company called Plastics Again and turned into plastic resin pellets, which could be used to make products ranging from videocassettes to food trays.

The Environmental Defense Fund

As McDonald's became more involved in the details of its environmental policy, it became more aware of its shortcomings. "We're good at running restaurants, but we don't know much about the environment," admitted Bob Langert, McDonald's director of environmental affairs. To strengthen these shortcomings, in the summer of 1990 the firm agreed to work in concert with the Environmental Defense Fund (EDF), an environmental organization that had gained public attention in the 1960s by almost single-handedly ending the use of the insecticide DDT in the United States. A task force of four officials from the environmental group and McDonald's was created to consider options for reducing and reusing the fast-food chain's plastic waste.

The benefits for both sides were obvious. McDonald's was gaining the backing of a respected environmental organization, which could silence some of its critics. For its part, the EDF was presented with an opportunity to affect the environmental policies of one of the largest U.S. corporations. There were also risks, however. If the two sides were unable to agree on key issues, the task force "could be an embarrassment," in the words of a McDonald's executive.

Switching from Plastic to Paper

The first major disagreement between the two sides took place almost immediately, when McDonald's told the EDF it planned to expand its polystyrene recycling program to include most of its 8,500 American restaurants. The environmental organization was convinced that the food chain should move to reduce the amount of packaging material used rather than recycling it, and it urged McDonald's to discontinue its use of polystyrene altogether.

Having defended the clamshell for more than fifteen years, many McDonald's executives did not want to abandon the packaging. In truth, however, the recycling program had not been going as planned. To begin with, customers were either unwilling or unable to sort their trash as directed. Plas-

tics Again, as a result, was receiving waste that was covered with food and was therefore unsuitable for economically viable processing. To correct the situation, the food chain's employees would have to sort the trash themselves, a very inefficient use of their time. Furthermore, almost three-fourths of McDonald's products are sold to be taken out of the restaurants, effectively eliminating them from any recycling program.

The company may have been willing to look for solutions to these problems, but after the state of Massachusetts threatened to rescind Plastics Again's tax benefits as a plastic processor, the program lost its economic feasibility. Therefore, one week after McDonald's was scheduled to announce the expansion plans of its recycling program, the company instead proclaimed that the clamshell was going to be phased out in favor of a new Quilt-Rap paper package.

Quilt-Rap: A Healthier Alternative?

Quilt-Rap, developed by James River Corporation of Richmond, Virginia, is composed of a polyethylene quilted inner layer sandwiched between two layers of paper. The EDF approved of the new packaging because it is 70 to 90 percent less bulky than the clamshell (hence taking up less landfill space) and could be shipped using less cardboard packaging. The fact that Quilt-Rap was cheaper to produce was a bonus for McDonald's executives, who were primarily concerned that the new packaging would do the same job of containing heat and controlling condensation as the clamshell.

The switch was not universally applauded. Industry insiders felt that the food chain had "caved in to the environmentalists." Some environmentalists were quick to point out that unlike polystyrene, the paper wrap could not be recycled, and the process by which it is manufactured creates more pollution than does making a clamshell. Hardee's Food Systems, Inc., another fast-food company, announced it would continue using polystyrene packaging for its products and criticized McDonald's new paper wrap as "not environmentally sound" because "reforestation is a major [environmental] concern."

The EDF countered these arguments by pointing out that they all make the assumption that polystyrene is being widely recycled, which it is not. Even assuming that 50 percent of the clamshells were recycled, "and that is bending over backward," said a senior scientist for the EDF, "the paper wrap still produces a better profile than polystyrene . . . in terms of how much waste is going to landfills." The

CASE (CONTINUED)

organization determined that the paper wrap represented an 80 percent reduction in the amount of solid waste generated compared with polystyrene.

McDonald's Last Word

The other primary criticism of the decision centered on the belief that McDonald's was motivated by public relations rather than the environment. In fact, the company's executives did little to dispel that notion. In the official press release announcing the switch to paper wrap, Rensi stated, "Although some scientific studies indicate that foam packaging is environmentally sound, our customers just don't feel good about it. So we're changing." Added Langert, "When they look at [clamshells], our customers just aren't thinking good things."

McDonald's and the EDF didn't stop at polystyrene; they created an action plan that reached almost all areas of the fast-food chain's service, from composting eggshells to ordering the company's suppliers to use corrugated cardboard boxes that contain at least 35 percent recycled product. The partnership appears to have paid off not just for environmental groups but also for McDonald's. In 1993, the former greatest enemy of green groups was the top-rated company in the United States in terms of its environmental reputation among consumers.

Critical Thinking Questions

1. Evaluate McDonald's decision to switch from the polystyrene clamshells to Quilt-Rap. Which stakeholders benefited, and which stakeholders may have been hurt by the decision?

2. Is the customer always right when it comes to environmental issues? If McDonald's felt that the "foam packaging [was] environmentally sound," did it have a responsibility to stay with the clamshell even in the face of public criticism (which may or may not have been justified)?

3. Do you see any ethical problems for either side in the alliance between McDonald's and the EDF?

4. How does this case underscore the strategic drawbacks of recycling?

5. Are businesses generally to be faulted for "caving in to the environmentalists"?

SOURCE: Information from P. S. Gutis, "McDonald's Is Urged to Alter Packaging," *New York Times*, November 11, 1987, p. B2; "McDonald's Flip Flops Again and Ditches Its Clamshell," *Adweek*, November 5, 1990, p. 4; J. Castro, "One Big Mac, Hold the Box," *Time*, June 25, 1990, p. 44; S. M. Livesey, *McDonald's and the Environment*, Harvard Business School Case No. 9-391-108, 1993, pp. 8, 17; "Lever to Use More Recycled Plastics," *New York Times*, August 19, 1990, p. D3; P. Berman, "McDonald's Caves In," *Forbes*, February 4, 1991, p. 73; "Food for Thought," *Economist*, August 29, 1992, p. 64; R. Gutfeld, "Big Mac Joins with Big Critic to Cut Trash," *Wall Street Journal*, August 2, 1990, p. B1; G. C. Lodge and J. F. Rayport, "Knee-deep and Rising: America's Recycling Crisis," *Harvard Business Review*, September–October 1991, p. 131; J. Oleck, "The Great Clamshell Debate," *Restaurant Business*, November 1, 1992, p. 68; "Hardee's, Swiping at Rival, Will Recycle Plastic Foam," *Wall Street Journal*, March 22, 1991, p. B1; McDonald's press release, November 1, 1990; J. Bailey, "Marketers Make Extravagant Promises, Then Begin to Regret Them," *Wall Street Journal*, January 19, 1995, p. A8; and P. Stisser, "A Deeper Shade of Green," *American Demographics*, March 1, 1994, p. 24.

CHAPTER 18

CONSUMER STAKEHOLDER ISSUES

CHAPTER OUTLINE

Introduction

The relationship between merchants and consumers—in a general sense, the basis of all economic activity—has always been an uneasy one. Four centuries ago, the English clergyman and poet George Herbert (1593–1633) commented that "The buyer needs a hundred eyes, the seller not one." Modern consumers express similar sentiments when they say that businesses are "exploiting" them in order to realize a higher profit margin.

In 1962, President John F. Kennedy initiated what became known as "the age of the consumer" when he introduced the Consumer Bill of Rights. Kennedy stated that all consumers should enjoy (1) the right to make an informed choice among products and services in a free market, (2) the right to have accurate and adequate information on which to base purchasing decisions, (3) the right to expect that their health and safety will be protected in the marketplace, and (4) the right to a full and fair hearing in any cases of dissatisfaction.

Sensing the potential for increased regulatory activity in Kennedy's proclamation, many business leaders began to take what one observer called a "rigid posture of opposition" to the idea of consumer rights.[1] In fact, at least one corporation's opposition contributed to the large body of legislation passed to protect the consumer during the 1960s and 1970s. In 1966, General Motors hired private detectives to discredit consumer advocate Ralph Nader. (Nader's *Unsafe at Any Speed* [1965] had linked auto accidents involving the Chevy Corsair, then one of the top-selling cars in the United States, to manufacturer design error.) When Nader made GM's actions known, public backlash was so great that Congress was able to pass a series of safety laws.

Ralph Nader is still pursuing alleged corporate misdeeds more than thirty years later—his complaints caused the recall of the Melitta Aroma Brew automatic drip coffeemaker in 1994. The age of the consumer, however, has faded somewhat. In the 1980s and 1990s, the consumer movement declined because many of its goals had been achieved. For example, both state and federal legislation now regulates how businesses advertise, engage in mail-order and electronic transactions, package and label their products, and so on. In addition, numerous local, state, and federal agencies now exist to aid the consumer in settling grievances.

Another reason for the reduction in consumer activism has been a changed attitude on the part of the corporate community. Businesspersons realize that consumers are stakeholders in the truest sense of the word: a business's very survival depends on how it responds to the needs and complaints of its customers. The most effective management strategy cannot save a faulty product. So while the body of consumer protection law appears necessary to safeguard the interests of consumers, there is an awareness among managers that quality control and improved customer service represent a more profitable and ethical strategy.

Sources of Consumer Protection

Kennedy's Consumer Bill of Rights was a political, not a legal, directive, for it did not have the force of law. During the past thirty years, Congress passed a number of federal laws—

---

1. E. B. Weiss, "Consumerism and Marketing: Part II—From Caveat Emptor to Caveat Vendor," *Advertising Age*, May 15, 1967, p. 93.

such as the Consumer Credit Protection Act (1968) and the Magnuson-Moss Warranty Act (1975)—to provide more explicit direction on the duties of sellers and the rights of consumers. (See *Exhibit 18–1* on page 548 for a list of major federal consumer protection statutes.) In addition, several state legislatures have passed consumer protection statutes. Nearly every department of the federal government has an office of consumer affairs, and most states have one or more such offices to assist consumers. Administrative agencies such as the Federal Trade Commission (FTC) and the Food and Drug Administration (FDA) also provide an important source of consumer protection.

THE FEDERAL TRADE COMMISSION

One of the earliest consumer protection laws was the Federal Trade Commission Act (1914). This act created the Federal Trade Commission (FTC) to carry out the broadly stated goal of preventing unfair and deceptive trade practices. We discussed the FTC's activities with regard to monopolistic and other anticompetitive practices in Chapter 10. In this chapter, we concentrate on the FTC's duties concerning the regulation of consumer information. More specifically, according to the latest *Federal Regulatory Directory*, the responsibilities of the FTC include:

▶ Protection of the public from false and deceptive advertising.
▶ Regulation of the packaging and labeling of consumer products to prevent deception.
▶ Prohibition of credit discrimination on the basis of sex, race, marital status, national origin, age, or receipt of public assistance.
▶ Prohibition of false or malicious practices in door-to-door and mail-order sales.

FTC Regulation of Specific Industries Over the last decade, the FTC has targeted certain practices on an industry-wide basis. Two examples are the used-car and funeral-home industries.

In 1984, the FTC enacted a rule requiring used-car dealers to affix a "Buyer's Guide" label to all cars sold on their lots. The label must include the following: (1) the car's warranty or a statement that the car is being sold "as is," (2) information regarding any service contract or promises being made by the dealer, and (3) a suggestion that the purchaser obtain both an inspection of the car and a written statement of any promises made by the dealer.

Also in 1984, the FTC enacted rules for the funeral-home industry. The rules (1) require that funeral homes provide customers with itemized prices of all charges incurred for a funeral, (2) prohibit funeral homes from requiring specific embalming procedures, and (3) prohibit funeral homes from using specific types of caskets for bodies that are to be cremated.

The Scope of the FTC As with any federal agency, the scope and power of the FTC is linked to the political goals of the executive branch of the federal government. During the 1980s, resources for enforcement of rules on advertising were cut almost 50 percent, and some perceived that the FTC "largely abandoned the regulation of advertising, especially national advertising."[2] This trend was reversed in the 1990s. Business reacted to the shift by taking a more proactive stance to defend against FTC actions. In 1991, the FTC ruled that Kraft General Foods Group could no longer advertise its "Singles" cheese as being high in calcium. Kraft disputed this charge that it had misled consumers by claim-

---

2. R. D. Petty, "Recent Trends in FTC Advertising Enforcement," *Business Law Review*, Vol. 24, 1991, p. 106.

▼ **EXHIBIT 18–1 Federal Consumer Protection Statutes and Rules**

Statute or Agency Rule	Purpose
Advertising	
Federal Trade Commission Act (1914/1938)	Prohibits deceptive and unfair trade practices.
Public Health Cigarette Smoking Act (1970)	Prohibits radio and TV cigarette advertising.
Federal Trade Commission Rules of Negative Options (1973)	Regulate advertising of book and record clubs.
Smokeless Tobacco Health Education Act (1986)	Prohibits radio and TV advertising of smokeless tobacco products; requires special labeling to warn consumers of potential health hazards associated with smokeless tobacco.
Health and Safety	
Pure Food and Drug Act (1906)	Prohibits adulteration and mislabeling of food and drugs sold in interstate commerce.
Meat Inspection Act (1906)	Provides for inspection of meat.
Federal Food, Drug, and Cosmetic Act (1938)	Protects consumers from unsafe food products and from unsafe and/or ineffective drugs (superseded Pure Food and Drug Act of 1906).
Flammable Fabrics Act (1953)	Prohibits the sale of highly flammable clothing.
Poultry Products Inspection Act (1957)	Provides for the inspection of poultry.
Child Protection and Toy Safety Act (1966)	Requires childproof devices and special labeling.
National Traffic and Motor Vehicle Safety Act (1966)	Requires manfacturers to inform new-car dealers of any defects found after manufacture and sale of auto.
Wholesale Meat Act (1967)	Updates Meat Inspection Act of 1906 to provide for stricter standards for plants where red-meat animals are slaughtered.
Consumer Product Safety Act (1972)	Comprehensive scheme of regulation over matters concerning consumer safety. Established the Consumer Product Safety Commission.
Department of Transportation Rule on Passive Restraints in Automobiles (1984)	Requires automatic restraint systems in all new cars sold after September 1, 1990.
Toy Safety Act (1984)	Allows the Consumer Product Safety Commission to quickly recall toys and other articles intended for use by children that present a substantial risk of injury.
Drug-Price Competition and Patent-Term Restoration Act (Generic Drug Act) (1984)	Speeds up and simplifies Food and Drug Administration approval of generic versions of drugs on which patents have expired.
Labeling and Packaging	
Wool Products Labeling Act (1939)	Requires accurate labeling of wool products.
Fur Products Labeling Act (1951)	Prohibits misbranding of fur products.
Textile Fiber Products Identification Act (1958)	Prohibits false labeling and advertising of all textile products under Wool Products Labeling Act and Fur Products Labeling Act.
Hazardous Substances Labeling Act (1960)	Requires warning labels on all items containing dangerous chemicals.
Cigarette Labeling and Advertising Act (1965)	Requires labels warning of possible health hazards.
Child Protection and Toy Safety Act (1966)	Requires childproof devices and special labeling.
Fair Packaging and Labeling Act (1966)	Requires that accurate names, quantities, and weights be given on product labels.
Smokeless Tobacco Health Education Act (1986)	Requires special labeling to warn consumers of potential health hazards associated with smokeless tobacco; prohibits radio and TV advertising of smokeless tobacco products.
Nutrition Labeling and Education Act (1994)	Requires that food labels include nutritional information regarding daily diet allowances and health concerns of consumers; requires that certain terms, such as *light* and *fat-free*, meet federal requirements.

ing that its cheese slices contained a certain amount of calcium. Though Kraft lost the case when a court of appeals ruled that the FTC's action was constitutional, the company set a precedent by presenting a defense based on its own research to counter a government claim.

The FDA and Health Protection

Consumer information law is only one area in which the federal government has imposed extensive regulations. Perhaps even more significant is legislation Congress enacted to ensure the quality of the nation's health. The government's increasing regulation of food through the Food and Drug Administration (FDA) is central to this effort.

The first step toward protecting consumers against adulterated and misbranded food and drug products came in 1906 when Congress passed the Pure Food and Drug Act. In 1938, Congress passed the Federal Food, Drug, and Cosmetic Act to strengthen the protective features of the 1906 legislation. These acts and subsequent amendments established standards for foods, specified safe levels of potentially dangerous food additives, and created classifications of foods and food advertising. The FDA monitors most statutes involving food and drugs.

Seizures and Recalls In cases involving label violations, the FDA issues Warning Letters, formerly called Notices of Adverse Findings and Regulatory Letters. In most instances, the seller only needs to change the labeling to meet federal requirements, and the products may be placed back on the shelves. Sometimes, however, a manufacturer or retailer disputes the FDA's assertions. The agency can then take legal action resulting in an injunction against the manufacturer, seizure of the products, or criminal charges.

In some situations, the FDA feels it must act to protect food consumers. In these instances, the FDA can order seizures of food that it deems adulterated or spoiled because of unsanitary storage or handling. The list of goods seized and destroyed in the early 1990s includes beans contaminated with mammalian urine, vanilla extract containing the poison coumarin, and peppercorns contaminated by *Salmonella* bacteria.[3]

The agency categorizes its recalls based on the degree of hazard. **Class I recalls** involve serious health concerns. In 1994, for example, the FDA ordered a class I recall of Yoder's potato salad after the agency found traces of harmful bacteria in the food product.[4] **Class II recalls** represent health hazards that are not life threatening, while **Class III recalls** may be undertaken when no health hazard exists and the violations concern labeling or manufacturing guidelines.

Tobacco Laws Congress has enacted a number of statutes to protect individuals from harmful products. For example, in response to public concern over the dangers of cigarette smoking, Congress requires warnings to be placed on cigarette and little-cigar packages, as well as on containers of smokeless tobacco. Producers of major cigarette brands must rotate four warning labels on a quarterly basis. Smaller companies may use the four warnings interchangeably on a random basis. Each cautionary notice begins "Surgeon General's Warning" and then states one of the following:

1. Smoking Causes Lung Cancer, Heart Disease, Emphysema, and May Complicate Pregnancy.

---

3. B. T. Hunter, "Some Federal Actions That Protect Our Foods," *Consumers' Research Magazine*, January 1993, p. 8.

4. A. Gasior, "Ohio Company Recalls Potato Salads," *Dayton Daily News*, October 25, 1994, p. 7B.

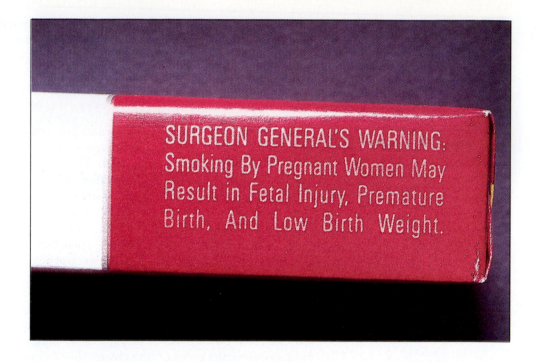

2. Quitting Smoking Now Greatly Reduces Serious Risks to Your Health.
3. Smoking by Pregnant Women May Result in Fetal Injury, Premature Birth, and Low Birth Weight.
4. Cigarette Smoke Contains Carbon Monoxide.

The Smokeless Tobacco Act of 1986 requires producers, packagers, and importers of smokeless tobacco to label their products conspicuously with one of three warnings:

1. WARNING: This product may cause mouth cancer.
2. WARNING: This product may cause gum disease and tooth loss.
3. WARNING: This product is not a safe alternative to cigarettes.

All advertising of tobacco products, except on outdoor billboards, must include these warnings.

THE CONSUMER PRODUCT SAFETY COMMISSION

Government regulation of consumer product safety mirrors the trend toward increased government regulation in the area of public health. Congress began to regulate consumer product safety in 1953 with the enactment of the Flammable Fabrics Act, which prohibits the sale of highly flammable clothing or materials. Between 1953 and 1972, Congress enacted relatively limited legislation to regulate specific classes of products, product design, and product composition, rather than the overall safety of consumer products. Finally, as a result of the 1970 recommendations of the National Commission on Product Safety, the Consumer Product Safety Act was passed in 1972 to protect consumers from unreasonable risk of injury from hazardous products.[5] The act created the Con-

---

5. 15 U.S.C. Sections 2051–2083.

sumer Product Safety Commission (CPSC). The purposes of the CPSC, as stated in the act, are as follows:

1. To protect the public against unreasonable risk of injury associated with consumer products.
2. To assist consumers in evaluating the comparative safety of consumer products.
3. To develop uniform safety standards for consumer products and to minimize conflicting state and local regulations.
4. To promote research and investigation into the causes and prevention of product-related deaths, illnesses, and injuries.

Generally, the Consumer Safety Act authorizes the CPSC to set standards for consumer products and to ban the manufacture and sale of any product deemed potentially hazardous to consumers. The commission also has the authority to remove products from the market if it deems the products imminently hazardous. Furthermore, the CPSC requires manufacturers and retailers to report information about any products already sold or intended for sale that have proved to be hazardous. In addition, the CPSC has the authority to administer other acts relating to product safety, such as the Child Protection and Toy Safety Act, the Hazardous Substances Labeling Act, and the Flammable Fabrics Act.

STATE CONSUMER PROTECTION LAWS

Our primary focus has been on federal legislation. If we failed to mention the state laws affecting consumer transactions, though, our discussion of consumer protection legislation would be incomplete. Although variation among state laws prevents us from making all-encompassing generalizations, we should note that state laws often provide more sweeping and significant protection for the consumer than do federal laws. Thus, a businessperson should consider all aspects of state laws before engaging in business in a particular state. Even remote business connections with a state may bring a transaction within the authority of that state's law. Furthermore, basic principles of contract law allow the contracting parties considerable discretion in choosing which state's laws will govern the terms of their agreement.

Despite variations among states, a common thread runs through most state consumer protection laws. Typically, legislatures direct state consumer protection laws at deceptive trade practices, such as a seller's providing false or misleading information to consumers. As suggested above, some of the legislation is quite broad.[6] A prime example is the Texas Deceptive Trade Practices Act of 1973, which covers a wide range of deceptive advertising practices. Under the Texas law, in 1991, Trans World Airlines (TWA) was charged by the state attorney general with deceiving consumers. A TWA promotion advertised a "drop-everything fare: $219 London" that the state felt was deceptive, because additional fees mentioned only in small print brought the actual price of the round trip to $461. The Texas law also forbids a seller from selling to a buyer anything that the buyer does not need or cannot afford. A Muslim family in Houston used this aspect of the law to seek $600,000 from an On the Border Cafe after discovering that the restaurant's beef tacos contained pork. Because of religious dietary restrictions, the family did not want or need the pork and sought protection under the Trade Practices Act.[7]

---

6. M. Bordwin, "Don't Bad-Mouth Your Competition," *Management Review*, March 1995, p. 45.
7. R. Ruggless, "Muslim Family Sues On the Border Cafes," *Nation's Restaurant News*, March 14, 1994, p. 4.

THE CONSUMER AND ACCESS TO INFORMATION

Acceptance of consumer protection regulation has not been universal. Echoing arguments made by Milton Friedman (see Chapter 6), in 1973, Professor Richard Posner, a proponent of the school of "legal economics," contended that consumer protection is largely a function of the marketplace. Taking the example of misleading advertising, Posner lists four ways the "invisible hand" guards consumer rights:

1. Consumers can easily determine the truthfulness of most advertising.
2. Competitors can expose misleading advertising in their own industries with their own advertising or private lawsuits.
3. The profits of an advertiser that developed a reputation for dishonesty would be negatively affected.
4. Consumers may sue individually or in a class action for breach of contract or fraud.[8]

While each of these points is true, Posner's critics contend that he leaves one important factor out of the equation: information.

▼ **If advertisers do not give consumers complete information, then consumers cannot make informed purchasing decisions.**

Take, for example, two television advertisements run in 1990. In one, a Volvo automobile survives a crash that destroys a competitor's car. In the other, Warner-Lambert touts its product Listerine as a cure for sore throats. If consumers had relied only on the information provided in these commercials to make purchasing choices, they would have been deceived. The Volvo automobile in the ad was reinforced with corrugated steel, while the competitors' product was not; and there is no medical proof that Listerine improves the condition of a sore throat.[9]

Eventually, Posner's market forces would have corrected these deceptions, but at the cost of numerous untreated sore throats and perhaps a few fatal automobile accidents. During the "age of the consumer," American society decided that it did not trust the market or businesses to provide reliable information to consumers. Consequently, it pressured federal and local governments to regulate the flow of information from seller to buyer.

Today, a business that "fakes" an ad may see a negative effect on the bottom line. The FTC forced Volvo and Warner-Lambert to run corrective advertising, which harmed both products in terms of consumer confidence and wasted advertising dollars. As previously noted, the FTC is charged with carrying out the broadly stated goal of protecting the public against unfair and deceptive trade practices. The FTC's jurisdiction extends over the advertising, labeling, and packaging of consumer goods.

DECEPTIVE ADVERTISING

Advertising can have many positive effects for society. It can discourage unwanted or unhealthful behavior, such as drunk driving or child abuse. It can encourage participa-

---

8. R. Posner, *Regulation of Advertising by the FTC* (Washington, D.C.: American Enterprise Institute, 1973), p. 8–9.
9. A. G. Perkins, "Advertising: The Costs of Deception," *Harvard Business Review*, May–June 1994, p. 10.

tion in socially acceptable behavior, such as volunteer work or protecting the environment. It can provide information to help consumers make rational product choices. If the information contained in product advertising is misleading or incorrect, though, the results can be, at worst, dangerous to consumers.[10] It is the responsibility of the FTC to protect consumers against this possibility.

Defining Deceptive Advertising   The FTC defines **deceptive advertising** as advertising that may be interpreted in two or more ways, one of which is false or misleading. False and deceptive statements come in many forms. Deception may arise out of a false statement or claim about a company's own product or a competitor's product. The deception may concern a product's quality, effects, origin, or availability; or it may arise from an omission of important information about the product.

Some advertisements contain "half-truths," meaning that the information presented is true but incomplete, leading consumers to a false conclusion. For example, the makers of Campbell's soups advertised that "most" Campbell's soups are low in fat and cholesterol and thus helpful in fighting heart disease. The ad did not disclose that Campbell's soups are high in sodium and that high-sodium diets may increase the risk of heart disease. The FTC ruled that Campbell's claims were deceptive.

Other ads contain statements not supported by adequate scientific evidence, as was the case with Warner-Lambert's contention that Listerine cures sore throats. Such statements may or may not be considered deceptive. When the claim is incapable of measurement, as in "When you're out of Schlitz, you're out of beer," no problem of deception is perceived by the FTC.

An ad may be deceptive even though it is literally true. An ad for "Teak tables," for example, might represent tables manufactured by a firm named "Teak," and thus the advertiser could claim that the ad was truthful. Nonetheless, the ad would probably be considered deceptive because most consumers would be led to assume that the ad referred to teak wood. As a general rule, the test for a deceptive ad is *whether or not a reasonable consumer would be deceived by the ad.* (For the winners of the Harlan Page Hubbard Lemon Awards for misleading advertisements, see *Exhibit 18–2* on page 554.)

Reasonable Belief   Within the parameters of "reasonable consumer" perception, regulators can accept advertisements that are obviously spoofs, jokes, or exaggerations. When a joking salesperson tells a consumer that his company's cars gets 500 miles to the gallon, a reasonable consumer knows that he is exaggerating as part of the joke. Such claims are known as **puffing**. Advertising that would appear to be based on factual evidence but in fact is untrue, such as in the Kraft example described earlier, is often deemed deceptive.

The FTC draws the line between puffery and deception by assuming that a reasonable consumer—with a reasonable amount of knowledge concerning the product being advertised—should be able to recognize a "puffed" advertisement. Under this standard, the intent of the advertiser is immaterial. In 1984, the FTC stated, "advertising is judged [by] whether it is likely to mislead reasonable consumers; proof of actual deception is not required."[11] Consequently, when California Milk Products claimed in the late 1970s that drinking milk in large quantities was beneficial to all consumers, the FTC ruled that the advertisement was not deceptive even though "all" persons do not benefit from milk intake. The commission ruled that the small percentage of the population that experiences

---

10. *Ibid.*
11. I. L. Preston and J. I. Richard, "A Role for Consumer Belief in FTC and Lanham Act Deceptive Advertising Cases," *American Business Law Journal,* 1993, p. 5.

▼ **EXHIBIT 18–2 The Harlan Page Hubbard Awards for Misleading Advertising**

Harlan Page Hubbard mounted America's first advertising campaign in the 1890s. Each year, the Center for Science in the Public Interest commemorates this event with the Harlan Page Hubbard Lemon Awards for the most unfair, misleading, or irresponsible advertisements of the year. Recently, "lemmies" have gone to:

- **Mitsubishi Motors**, for Galant S automobile leasing commercials that promise in big print "$0 down—$249 a month for 36 months." The total cost of the lease—including the extra charges accrued over the life of the lease—is contained in illegible fine print that scrolls across the bottom of the screen during the thirty-second spot.

- **John Paul Mitchell Systems**, for claiming that its hair products are "cruelty free" because it does not test them on animals, despite the fact that the company's products contain *ingredients* that *have* been tested on animals by suppliers.

- **Hasbro, Inc.**, for deceptively representing in advertisements aimed at children that the "Play-Doh Cookie Lovin' Oven" can bake real cookies when, in fact, it can only heat make-believe cookies made from Play Doh. (The ad shows a young boy eating a cookie and saying "Delicious!")

- **Paddington Importers**, for Malibu Rum ads that encourage heavy, reckless drinking. The ads make light of the effects of drinking binges and hangovers by including statements such as, "You're going to call your boyfriend back home. As soon as you can remember his name. Blame it on Malibu."

- **R. J. Reynolds Tobacco Co.**, for a Winston Select Lights cigarette promotional campaign in which the company mails free cigarettes to smokers and nonsmokers alike. There is no safeguard in the promotion to ensure that those receiving the cigarettes are over twenty-one years old.

- **Ross Products Division of Abbott Laboratories**, for claiming that Ensure, a liquid meal-replacement product, is "the #1 doctor recommended source of nutrition" for healthy adults. In fact, Ensure was originally designed for use in nursing homes and by people who are too sick or weak to eat normal food. By using Ensure, healthy people forego vitamins and minerals only available in real food.

- **The Tennessee Valley Authority**, for implying that TVA-generated electricity is so inexpensive that one can afford to waste it. The ad pictures an empty room with a television set running and states that TVA rates are one-third below the national average, "so it costs you less to watch TV even if no one is watching." In fact, TVA rates are low because they are subsidized by the federal government, meaning taxpayers nationwide are sharing the costs of TVA power.

- **Chrysler Corporation**, for corporate image ads that claim that the company is "working to reduce emissions and improve air quality," even though Chrysler vociferously opposed increases in government fuel efficiency standards, which would reduce air pollution.

SOURCE: Center for Science in the Public Interest, 1995.

ill effects from milk has "learned to associate symptoms [of discomfort] and milk drinking, and to limit their milk intake or avoid milk." In other words, even though the content of the ad was not entirely accurate, a reasonable consumer could make his or her own decision on the benefits of milk.[12] (See *Managing Social Issues—Making a Difference: A War against Puffery.*)

Bait-and-Switch Advertising The FTC's "Guide on Bait Advertising" contains one of the commission's most important rules. The rule prohibits advertisements that specify a very low price for a particular item that will likely be unavailable to the consumer, who will then be encouraged to purchase a more expensive version of the same item. The low price is used as "bait" to lure the customer into the store, and the salesperson (instructed

---

12. *Ibid.*, p. 10.

⊞ MANAGING SOCIAL ISSUES

MAKING A DIFFERENCE: A WAR AGAINST PUFFERY

From time to time, Ivan L. Preston tapes eight hours of television just for the commercials. A professor of advertising at the University of Wisconsin, Preston scours the tape for what he feels to be dubious advertising claims. An example of his findings during one session: AT&T is "the best in the business"; the Sealy Corporation makes "the world's best mattresses"; the Gillette Company's deodorant is "the best a man can get"; BMW is "the ultimate driving machine." To say a product is the best or the ultimate is a factual claim, Professor Preston believes. "It means the competitors aren't as good, and that is a significant matter." He would like the Federal Trade Commission (FTC) to demand stricter substantiation of such advertising than it does presently.

Is "the Best" Really the Best?

The kind of puffery Professor Preston rails against in his book *The Tangled Web They Weave: Truth, Falsity, and Advertising* (University of Wisconsin Press, 1994) is so commonplace that few people give it a second thought. Consumers are used to Bayer's calling itself "the best aspirin" without actually proving that there is a discernible difference between its product and the competitors'. The FTC and the American courts have long considered puffery harmless, an attitude Professor Preston, who also serves as president of the American Academy of Advertising, criticizes.

"Advertising people tend to act like they have a right to say their brand is different," he complains. "I would curtail that right and say that they can say brands are different only when they can prove they really are different." Preston would like to expand the definition of what is deceptive in advertising. He thinks that advertisements should only be

allowed to make claims that give consumers a logical reason to choose one brand over another.

Going Too Far?

Particularly, and dangerously, illogical in Professor Preston's view are cigarette advertisements in magazines. A Marlboro ad that shows two strapping cowboys heading back to the bunkhouse after a long day roping dogies presents, in Professor Preston's opinion, an implicit—and empirically false—claim that smoking is good for one's health. "That little warning in the corner is completely overwhelmed by what's around it," he says.

Professor Preston also has problems with advertising claims that Colgate toothpaste "cleans your breath while it cleans your teeth" (what brand does not?) and that Vic Tanny gyms "shape your life" (no, they shape your muscles). Is the professor taking his views too far?

John F. Canny, vice president of the American Association of Advertising, thinks so. "I would say, come on, Ivan, people know that working out isn't going to shape their life unless they shape their life themselves," Canny says. "At some point, we have to assume that people are pretty smart, and know sales when they see it."

For Critical Analysis:

Professor Preston, in fact, is not always willing to make this assumption. He cites one study that showed consumers preferred to purchase coffee that had been "crystallized" through freeze drying, even after researchers told them the process made no difference in the coffee's taste. Do you think Professor Preston has gone too far, or are his calls to regulate puffery valid?

SOURCE: C. Shea, "One Man's War against 'Puffery,'" *Chronicle of Higher Education*, November 2, 1994, p. A8.

by management) attempts to "switch" the consumer to a more expensive alternative. Consequently, this practice is known as **bait-and-switch advertising**. (See *Exhibit 18–3* to understand what legally constitutes this kind of advertising.)

Prodigy Services Company, which provides access to the Internet and other on-line services, found itself in a bait-and-switch advertising controversy in the early 1990s. In the fall of 1990, Prodigy advertised a flat-rate fee for electronic mail services. Within six

▼ **EXHIBIT 18–3**
Bait-and-Switch
Guidelines

According to the FTC guidelines, bait-and-switch advertising occurs when the seller:

1. Refuses to show the advertised item.

2. Fails to have adequate quantities of it available.

3. Fails to promise to deliver the advertised item within a reasonable time.

4. Discourages employees from selling the item.

SOURCE: E. P. Lazear, "Bait and Switch," *Journal of Political Economy,* August 1995, p. 813.

months, the company had restructured its E-mail fees to charge subscribers twenty-five cents for each message sent above an allotted number of thirty each month. Prodigy explained that it had underestimated the volume of the E-mail and needed to compensate by limiting the service. Unsatisfied, one Prodigy customer filed a class-action suit charging bait-and-switch advertising. Prodigy suffered as thousands of angry consumers switched to other on-line service providers.[13]

FTC Actions against Deceptive Advertising The FTC receives complaints from many sources, including competitors of alleged violators, consumers, consumer organizations, trade associations, Better Business Bureaus, government organizations, and state and local officials. If enough consumers complain and the criticisms are widespread, the FTC investigates the problem. After the investigation, if the FTC believes that a given advertisement is unfair or deceptive, it drafts a formal complaint, which is sent to the alleged offender.

The company may agree to settle the complaint without further proceedings. If the company does not agree to settle the complaint, the FTC can conduct a hearing—similar to a trial—before an administrative law judge (ALJ) in which the company can defend its actions. If the FTC succeeds in proving that an advertisement is unfair or deceptive, the agency usually issues a **cease-and-desist order** requiring that the challenged advertising be stopped. The FTC may also impose a sanction known as **counteradvertising** by requiring the company to advertise anew—in print, on radio, and on television—to inform the public about earlier misinformation.

If the ALJ rules against a company, the company can appeal to the full FTC. The agency's commissioners listen to the parties' arguments and may uphold, modify, or reverse the ALJ's decision. If the commission rules against a company, the company can appeal the FTC's decision to a federal appeals court. Most federal courts recognize that the FTC, because it deals continually with such cases, is often in a better position than the courts to determine when a practice is deceptive within the meaning of the law. Therefore, prolonged legal battles in this arena are uncommon.

In one typical ten-year period, the commission had only twelve decisions taken to appeals courts and won eleven of them. The FTC settles nearly 80 percent of its advertising cases during the investigative stage or in the process of litigation.[14] Furthermore, the FTC quietly closes numerous investigations owing to lack of evidence or other mitigating circumstances. A quick survey of the FTC's public record in the mid-1990s showed a number of closed actions, from an investigation of Colgate Palmolive's claim that its

---

13. N. Welch, "Subscriber Lawsuit Hits Prodigy Advertising," *MacWEEK,* April 2, 1991, p. 28.
14. Preston and Richard, *op. cit.*, p. 107.

toothpaste prevented cavities to an inspection of American Food's claims that its Pam cooking spray was "natural."[15]

Deceptive Advertising and Damages The late 1980s saw a development in deceptive advertising cases that advertisers would ignore at their peril. In the past, the FTC resolved most false advertising cases with an order to cease the advertising in question. Thanks to two court cases and the Trademark Law Revision Act, courts are more inclined to award damages in false advertising cases.

In the 1986 case *U-Haul International Inc. v. Jartran, Inc.*, U-Haul was able to prove that a competitor, Jartran, had run **comparative advertisements** that falsely stated that its rates were significantly lower than those of U-Haul. The court not only agreed with U-Haul but awarded that company damages, based on the following factors:

1. U-Haul's gross revenue for the period in which Jartran ran the false ads was $49 million less than projected.
2. U-Haul expended $13.6 million in advertising costs to counteract Jartran's campaign.
3. Jartran secured approximately 10 percent of the truck and trailer rental market during the period in question.
4. Jartran expended approximately $6 million to carry out the false advertising.

Adding the $13.6 million spent by U-Haul for counteractive advertising to the $6 million spent by Jartran, the court awarded the plaintiff $20 million in damages.

In 1989, a federal district court established similar reasoning when it awarded Alpo Petfoods more than $10 million in damages as a result of a deceptive advertising campaign by Ralston Purina Company. Ralston claimed in its campaign that its products helped reduce hip dysplasia in dogs, an assertion the courts found to be scientifically unproved. The court awarded Alpo compensation for the market share the deceptive advertising had allowed Purina to gain.[16]

Finally, in the eyes of many legal experts, the Trademark Law Revision Act, which went into effect in November 1989, provides statutory authority for the award of damages in false advertising suits.

▼ **The act not only prohibits advertisers from misrepresenting their own products but prevents them from misrepresenting "another person's goods, services, or commercial activities."[17]**

Not all comparative advertising disputes end up in court. When two corporations dominate an industry, they often find themselves using negative advertising to discredit each other rather than positive advertising to spotlight their own advantages for the consumer.[18] Consumers have seen this scenario played out with Visa and American Express credit cards, Pepsi and Coca-Cola soft drinks, and AT&T and MCI long-distance phone services. While a corporation may feel the need to defend itself against negative advertising with commercial attacks of its own, marketing managers should be aware that such campaigns may be counterproductive when it comes to consumer response. (See *Company Focus: AT&T and MCI* on page 558.)

---

15. "Closed Investigations," *FTC Watch*, May 22, 1995, p. 1.
16. *Alpo Petfoods, Inc. v. Ralston Purina Co.*, 1989.
17. J. A. Tratchenberg, "New Law Adds Risk to Comparative Ads," *Wall Street Journal*, June 1, 1989, p. B6.
18. Bordwin, *op. cit.*

COMPANY FOCUS: AT&T AND MCI
THE DANGERS OF COMPARATIVE ADVERTISING

The dangers inherent in comparative advertising are not only legal; companies that promote themselves by "bashing" the competition run the risk of alienating consumers in the process. Some marketing analysts believe consumers regard two companies trading negative advertisements "the same as looking at a car wreck—you slow down to see the mess, but you don't really pay attention to what's going on." If this is indeed the case, then long-distance telephone rivals AT&T and MCI have wasted millions of dollars in a high-stakes, low-impact advertising battle.

The Battle for Customers

In 1989, MCI ran a series of advertisements claiming that "every week 100,000 AT&T customers switch to MCI." AT&T retaliated with its own comparative campaign, including one ad that stated that the "MCI fax network transmits one unreadable page out of every twelve." MCI called its competitor's ads "factually sleazy," and the first battle for long-distance superiority since the breakup of AT&T's monopoly five years earlier was joined in earnest.

In 1992, the stakes rose when nearly eight million customers converted to MCI as their long-distance carrier, a majority of them from AT&T. Analysts attributed this success in part to MCI's successful "Family and Friends" marketing campaign, which offered discounts on frequent calls. They also blamed AT&T for ignoring one of the cardinal rules of comparative advertising: consumers love underdogs. "By naming us, AT&T has made this a two-horse race," said an MCI marketing director. "They are Goliath taking on David."

AT&T responded to MCI's success by highlighting MCI's alleged propensity for network failures in the winter of 1992 and the spring of 1993, even though AT&T's chairman had told reporters that his firm was "too classy" to do so. The smaller company responded with ads questioning its rival's research, saying, "When it comes to reliability, AT&T is either practicing deception or is lousy at math."

Two years later, AT&T grabbed 1.1 million customers from MCI on the strength of its "True Friends" campaign.

The centerpiece of the marketing effort was a 30 percent discount for new consumers for the first six months—in December 1994 alone, 300,000 customers made the switch. MCI tried to stem the flow with a series of "Shame on you, AT&T" ads claiming that the savings promised on the "True Friends" ads "just don't ring true." When that failed, MCI was forced to offer a 6 percent discount on AT&T's rates—just enough, according to analysts, to stabilize the company's declining market share without triggering another rate cut from its competitor.

What the Customers Think

There is a growing suspicion among marketing experts that these figures prove that, as any economist would tell you, customers flock to lower prices when the service is basically equal. Many believe that the AT&T–MCI battles have, far from building the consumer loyalty that companies crave, created a special class of customers called "spinners." Spinners take advantage of the fare wars by jumping from one company to another as the rates drop. Some spinners may change long-distance carriers as frequently as every three months.

There is also a sense that consumers are tiring of the war dance. "Our research shows consumers don't want to be a pawn in the fight," says the president of a New York advertising agency. "They feel the companies are not interested in them and only want to make a sale."

The New Bottom Line

In the modern remote-control climate, comparative advertising may be expecting too much attention from the viewer. "Marketers who use [comparative ads] are operating on the assumption that everyone is listening to every word they're saying," says one analyst. "But for the consumers who may not be glued to the set, there will be a dilution of the message." In fact, in one recent survey of 1,000 long-distance customers, more than half of AT&T's subscribers thought the name of their calling package was "Family and Friends."

SOURCE: Information from G. Koprowski, "Theories of Negativity," *Brandweek*, February 20, 1995, p. 22; M.E. Thyfault, "MCI Sues AT&T, Alleges Deceptive Ads," *MIS Week*, October 16, 1989, p. 13; "AT&T '800' Attack Ad Claims MCI Is More Outage Prone," *Report on AT&T*, December 7, 1992; "MCI Dubs AT&T Claims 'Hogwash,'" *Report on AT&T*, April 26, 1993; and M. Lewyn, "MCI: A Smaller Family and Fewer Friends," *Business Week*, February 6, 1995, p. 147.

LABELING AND PACKAGING LAWS

Just as laws place broad restrictions on advertising, a number of federal and state laws deal with the information given on labels and packages. The laws promote the disclosure of accurate information about the product and require warnings about possible dangers from use or misuse.

In general, labels must be accurate. Furthermore, they must use words that are understood by the ordinary consumer. For example, a company cannot follow the lead of turn-of-the-century labelers who included mandatory information on their packages in a foreign language. In a more commonplace example, a cereal manufacturer cannot label a box of cereal "giant" if its labeling would exaggerate the amount of cereal contained in the box.

In some instances, labels must specify the raw materials used in products, such as the percentage of nylon, cotton, or other fibers used in a garment. In other instances, as we saw with cigarette packages, the product must carry a warning. Managers in some industries must also be aware that consumers expect labeling of certain products, such as those containing genetically engineered materials, even if the FDA does not require it. (See the *Case—Fear of Science: Monsanto and the Bovine Growth Hormone*—at the end of this chapter.)

Early Mandatory and Voluntary Legislation An especially important law to come out of the "age of the consumer" is the Fair Packaging and Labeling Act of 1966, which requires that products have labels that identify the product, the net quantity of the contents and the quantity of servings, the manufacturer, and the packager or distributor. Eight years later, the FDA and the U.S. Department of Agriculture established voluntary nutritional labeling guidelines, requiring only that nutrition information be provided on the labels of products that contain additional nutritional claims such as "healthy" or "low sodium." The food industry initially opposed the nutrition label but gradually came to accept it and even use it as an advertising tool.

The Nutrition Labeling and Education Act The next significant change in food labeling laws came twenty years later, with the Nutrition Labeling and Education Act of 1994. Congress designed this legislation to give consumers more information on how individual foods fit into their overall daily diets. The latest labeling regulations include the following requirements:

1. The labels of almost all food must include nutritional information.
2. Labels must include information on how the food fits into a recommended daily diet.
3. Labels must include information on the amount per serving of saturated fat, cholesterol, dietary fiber, and other nutrients that are deemed to be of concern to health-conscious consumers.
4. Terms used to describe a food's nutrient content—such as light, fat-free, and low-calorie—must meet federal requirements to assure they mean the same on all labels that use them.
5. Health claims about the relationship between a nutrient or food and a disease are allowed for the first time, as long as the claims are scientifically viable.[19]

The new labeling laws reflect the FDA's belief that consumers are now making purchasing decisions based not only on a food's price and taste but also on its nutritional

---

19. P. Kurtzweil, "Good Reading for Good Eating," *FDA Consumer*, May 1993, p. 7–8.

value. Before this period, the food industry recognized this fact and began placing health claims on its labels. On the one hand, the claims were positive because consumers were getting more information. On the other hand, many felt the industry was taking advantage of the health-conscious consumer by making claims that were deceptive or, at a minimum, exaggerated. In the 1980s, for example, oat bran became popular among many consumers because of its high fiber content, especially after some studies linked high-fiber diets to reduced cancer risks. Consequently, a number of products, notably breakfast cereals, added negligible amounts of the fiber and boldly—and truthfully—scrawled "Contains oat bran!" on the box.[20]

The 1994 regulations forbid such labeling practices; "significant amounts" of oat bran—or any other item—must be used in a product for it to be listed on a label. The FDA also placed strict requirements on the use of the term *healthy* on any label. To make that claim, a food must be low in fat and saturated fat, contain limited amounts of cholesterol and sodium, and have at least 10 percent of the Daily Value of vitamin A or C or of iron, calcium, protein, or fiber.[21] (See *Exhibit 18–4* for a closer look at the latest labeling requirements.)

Among the products exempt from mandatory labeling are plain coffee and tea, certain spices, flavorings, and other foodstuffs that contain no significant nutrients; ready-to-eat food prepared on-site; and bulk food that is not resold. Also, food produced by small businesses—defined as those with gross food sales of less than $50,000 a year, total sales of less than $500,000, or fewer than 50 employees—need not carry the nutritional labels. The FDA estimates that those food processors to whom the regulations do apply will spend between $1.4 billion and $2.3 billion over twenty years complying with the laws. The hoped-for benefits for consumers include lower rates of heart disease, cancer, osteoporosis, obesity, high blood pressure, and allergic reactions to food.[22]

ISSUES OF PRODUCT LIABILITY

One of Richard Posner's market factors that provide consumer protection is the right of consumers to "sue individually or in a class action for breach of contract or fraud." In the context of packaging and labeling, this implies that if a product is incorrectly labeled and therefore causes harm to a consumer, the buyer has legal recourse. Generally, manufacturers and sellers of goods can be held liable to consumers, users, and bystanders (people in the vicinity of the product) for physical harm or property damage that is caused by the goods. This is called **product liability.**

Debates over product liability moved from legal reviews to the front and editorial pages of major news outlets in the early 1990s, thanks to a series of spectacular jury awards of punitive damages, most notably $2.7 million to a woman who spilled McDonald's coffee in her lap while driving and burned herself. (**Punitive damages** are designed to punish and deter wrongdoing; by comparison, **compensatory damages** are awarded to cover direct losses and costs.) These punitive damages—later reduced to $480,000 by a judge—shocked and dismayed many observers. As a result, a question with a familiar theme was raised in the business and legal communities: Do the costs of product liability to businesses outweigh the benefits for consumer protection?

---

20. S. McCollum, "Nothing but the Truth?" *Scholastic Update*, May 7, 1993, p. 19.
21. "Defining 'Healthy,'" *FDA Consumer*, September 1994, p. 4.
22. Kurtzweil, *op. cit.*, p. 13.

▼ **EXHIBIT 18–4**
A Label for Lowfat
Chocolate Milk
(1% Milkfat)

The Serving Size reflects the amount most people eat. Similar foods have comparable Serving Sizes. ➤

The label now includes how many of the total calories come from fat. ➤

The Percent Daily Values indicate the amount of each nutrient contained in the food in relation to the amount of each nutrient needed per day. ➤

Vitamin A, Vitamin C, calcium, and iron are the only vitamins and minerals that must be listed. Any others are added voluntarily by the company. ➤

An addition on some labels is the listing of approximately how many calories are in one gram of fat, carbohydrates, and protein. ➤

Nutrition Facts

Serving Size 8 fl. oz. (240 ml)
Servings Per Container 1

Amount Per Serving

Calories 160   Calories from Fat 20

% Daily Value*

Total Fat 2.5 g	**4%**
Saturated Fat 1.5 g	**8%**
Cholesterol 5 mg	**2%**
Sodium 150 mg	**6%**
Total Carbohydrate 26 g	**9%**
Dietary Fiber 0 g	**0%**
Sugars 23 g	

Protein 8 g

Vitamin A 15 %	•	Vitamin C	4%
Calcium 30%	•	Iron	4%

*Percent Daily Values are based on a 2,000 calorie diet. Your daily values may be higher or lower depending on your calorie needs:

		Calories	2,000	2,500
Total Fat	Less than		65 g	80 g
Sat Fat	Less than		20 g	25 g
Cholesterol	Less than		300 mg	300 mg
Sodium	Less than		2,400 mg	2,400 mg
Total Carbohydrate			300 g	375 g
Dietary Fiber			25 g	30 g

Calories per gram:
Fat 9   •   Carbohydrates 4   •   Protein 4

SOURCE: Dairy Council of Wisconsin.

WARRANTY LAW

In part, product liability has its basis in **warranty law.** Most goods are covered by some type of warranty designed to protect consumers. The concept of warranty is based on the seller's assurance to the buyer that the goods will meet certain standards. Because a warranty imposes a duty on the seller, a breach of warranty is a breach of the seller's promise.

The **Uniform Commercial Code (UCC)**—a set of rules that govern commercial transactions in all states—designates the types of warranties that can arise in a contract for the sale of goods. These include express and implied warranties.

Express Warranties An **express warranty** is an affirmation of fact or a promise offered expressly by the seller. A seller can create an express warranty by making a representation concerning the quality, condition, description, or performance potential of goods at such a time that the buyer could have relied on the representation when he or she agreed to the contract. These representations may be written or oral. A salesperson's statement to a potential buyer that a car is new is an example of an express warranty.

Implied Warranties An **implied warranty of merchantability** assures that goods are "reasonably fit for ordinary purposes for which such goods are used" and arises automatically in a sale of goods by a merchant who deals in such goods. In simpler terms, the implied warranty of merchantability means that what you buy is supposed to work: a copy machine is supposed to make copies, a flea collar is supposed to keep fleas off pets, and so on. If the copy machine does not copy, or the flea collar does not drive away fleas, the consumer is entitled to a replacement or a refund.

An **implied warranty of fitness for a particular purpose** arises when any seller—merchant or nonmerchant—knows the particular purpose for which a buyer will use the goods and knows that the buyer is relying on the seller's skill and judgment to select suitable goods. If the seller does not know how the consumer plans to use the product, then an implied warranty may not exist. For example, say you purchase formatted floppy disks that are compatible with IBM computers but not with the Macintosh laptop you own. If you did not inform the seller that you needed a Macintosh-compatible product, the seller is not obligated to refund or replace your purchase.

Consumers, purchasers, and even users of goods can generally recover *from any seller* those losses resulting from breach of express and implied warranties. A manufacturer is a seller. Therefore, a person who purchases goods from a retailer can recover from the retailer or the manufacturer (or both) if the goods are not merchantable. Thus, a product purchaser may sue not only the firm from which he or she purchases a product but also a third party—the manufacturer of the product—in product liability.

PRODUCT LIABILITY BASED ON NEGLIGENCE

Legally, **negligence** relates to the duty one individual owes another. In a court case, four elements make up the definition of negligence:

1. The actor (that is, the defendant) had a duty of care to another (that is, the plaintiff).
2. The actor breached that duty.
3. The breach of the duty was the cause of the plaintiff's injury.
4. Injury to the plaintiff's person or property resulted from the negligence.

A plaintiff must prove all four elements in order to recover an award from the actor.

In nonlegal terms, negligence is the failure to exercise the degree of care that a reasonable, prudent person would have exercised under the circumstances. This concept is known as due care.

▼ If a seller fails to exercise reasonable care and an injury results, the seller may be sued for negligence. Thus, a manufacturer must exercise "due care" to make a product safe.

Due care must be exercised in designing the product, in selecting the material, in using the appropriate production process, in assembling and testing the product, and in placing adequate warnings on the label informing the users of dangers of which an ordinary person might not be aware. The duty to exercise due care also extends to the inspection and testing of any purchased products that are used in the final product sold by the manufacturer. The failure to exercise due care is negligence.

Violation of Statutory Duty Simply stated, a manufacturer is liable for its failure to exercise due care to any person who sustains an injury proximately (substantially) caused by a negligently made (defective) product. Furthermore, a manufacturer can be held in violation of statutory duty if it fails to live up to federal, state, or local laws.

Suppose, for example, that Jason Manufacturing Company produces pipe fittings *specifically* for use in the construction of houses in Monroe County. The fittings do not comply with county building codes. A pipe fitting bursts in one home, allowing hot water to spray on the homeowner. The homeowner can bring a negligence action for personal damages on the ground that failure to comply with the building codes is an automatic breach of the manufacturer's duty to exercise reasonable care. In fact, in 1994, DuPont, Hoescht Celanese, and Shell Oil agreed to fix faulty polybutylene pipes installed in approximately six million American homes in the 1970s. The pipes failed prematurely after reacting to high levels of chlorine in the water.

Defenses to Negligence Any manufacturer, seller, or processor who can prove that due care was used in the manufacture of its product may have an appropriate defense against a negligence suit, because a failure to exercise due care is one of the major elements of negligence.

But there are other defenses, and their use and application vary from state to state. One legal protection afforded to manufacturers in many states is the tying of the breach (the failure to exercise reasonable care) to the injury. Numerous events, involving different people, may take place between the time a product is manufactured and the time of its use. If any of these events can be shown to have caused or contributed to the injury, the manufacturer can claim, on the basis of this intervening cause, that it has no liability.

One other defense is **contributory negligence**. For example, assume that the manufacturer of an industrial grinder states in its instructions that the grinder's operator should wear safety goggles. The owner of a machine-tool repair shop purchases a grinder, has her employees read the manufacturer's instructions, and reminds them to wear safety goggles when they use the machine. Employee Joe Kidd chooses to ignore the warnings. As Kidd begins to use the grinder to sharpen a saw blade's cutting edge, a tiny spark of hot metal flies into his right eye, causing loss of the eye. Kidd files suit, claiming that the manufacturer was negligent in failing to warn that the grinder might throw off hot metal sparks. The defendant-manufacturer claims that Kidd knew he was supposed to wear goggles and that his failure to wear the goggles was the proximate (substantial) cause of the injury. Kidd's own negligent actions contributed to his accident.

If a plaintiff misuses a product or fails to make a reasonable effort to preserve his or her own welfare, the manufacturer or seller may claim contributory negligence—that is, that the plaintiff contributed to causing the injuries. The claim is that the plaintiff's negligence offsets the negligence of the manufacturer or seller.

THE DOCTRINE OF STRICT LIABILITY

Under the doctrine of **strict liability**, in certain circumstances, parties are liable for the results of their acts regardless of their intentions or their exercise of reasonable care. For example, a company that uses dynamite to blast for a road is strictly liable for any damages that it causes, even if its takes reasonable and prudent precautions to prevent such damages. In essence, the blasting company becomes liable for any personal injuries it causes and thus is liable for damages regardless of fault.

Currently, strict liability is imposed by law as a matter of public policy, based on a threefold assumption:

1. Consumers should be protected against unsafe products.
2. Manufacturers and distributors should not escape liability for faulty products simply because they did not have direct dealings with the ultimate users of those products.
3. Manufacturers and sellers of products are in a better position to bear the costs associated with injuries caused by their products—costs they can ultimately pass on to all consumers in the form of higher prices.

Requirements of Strict Liability Just because a person is injured by a product does not mean he or she will automatically successfully be able to sue the manufacturer of the product. Only under specific circumstances does the injured person have a *cause of action*. A cause of action exists only if the following six basic requirements of strict product liability are met:

1. The defendant must sell the product in a defective condition.

2. The defendant must normally be engaged in the business of selling that product.

3. The product must be unreasonably dangerous to the user or consumer because of its defective condition. (This element is no longer required in some states—for example, California.)

4. The plaintiff must incur physical harm to self or property from use or consumption of the product.

5. The defective condition must be the proximate (substantial) cause of the injury or damage.

6. The product must not have been substantially changed from the time it was sold to the time the injury was sustained.

Thus, in a strict liability action against a manufacturer or seller, the plaintiff does not have to show why or how the product was defective. The plaintiff does, however, have to show that at the time the injury was sustained, the condition of the product was essentially the same as it was when it left the hands of the manufacturer or seller.

The plaintiff normally must also show that the product was so defective as to be unreasonably dangerous. A court may consider a product so defective as to be unreasonably dangerous if either (1) it was dangerous beyond the expectation of the ordinary consumer or (2) a less dangerous alternative was economically feasible for the manufacturer, but the manufacturer failed to produce it.

Under the feasible-alternative approach, courts consider a product's utility and desirability, the probability of injury from the product's use, and the viability of eliminating the danger without appreciably impairing the product's function or making the product too expensive. For example, people often hit themselves on a thumb or other finger when pounding nails with a hammer, but a court would consider that hammers are very useful. Reasoning that there is no way to avoid injuries without making the product useless and that the danger is obvious to users, a court normally would not find a hammer to be unreasonably dangerous and would not hold a supplier of hammers liable.

Some products are safe when used as their manufacturers and distributors intend but not safe when used in other ways. Manufacturers are generally required to expect reasonably foreseeable misuses and to design products that are either safe when misused or marketed with some protective device—for example, a childproof cap on a bottle of pain reliever. (For a comparison of negligence and strict liability, see *Exhibit 18–5* on page 566.)

Defenses to Strict Liability Frequently, negligent misconduct or misuse of the product by the harmed person or a third party combines with the product's defect to cause damage or injury. If the misconduct or misuse can be charged to a claimant (the person claiming the injury), a number of defenses can be used to reduce that claimant's recovery award or bar it altogether. Some of these defenses are discussed below.

Assumption of Risk A defense that can be used in an action based on strict liability is **assumption of risk.** For such a defense to be established, the defendant must show the following:

1. The plaintiff voluntarily engaged in the risk while realizing the potential dangers.

2. The plaintiff knew and appreciated the risk caused by the defect.

3. The plaintiff's decision to undertake the known risk was unreasonable.

Product Misuse Similar to the defense of voluntary assumption of risk is that of misuse of the product. Here, the injured party does not know that the product is dangerous for a

▼ **EXHIBIT 18–5 Comparison of Negligence and Strict Liability in the Area of Product Liability**

Theory	Negligence	Strict Liability
Applicability	All products.	Products dangerously defective in design or manufacture.
Basic test	Considering all the circumstances, was reasonable care exercised?	Is there a defect that makes the product unreasonably dangerous?
Elements	1. Duty of care. 2. Breach of duty. 3. Breach causes injury or damage.	1. Unreasonably dangerous defect. 2. Defect causes injury or damage.
Defenses	1. Exercise of reasonable care. 2. Intervening or superseding event caused injury or damage. 3. Claimant unreasonably assumed risk. 4. Claimant was also negligent.	1. Defect did not exist when product was in defendant's hands. 2. Claimant misused product in an unforeseeable way. 3. Claimant unreasonably assumed risk. 4. Claimant was also negligent.

particular use, but that use is not the one for which the product was designed. This defense has been severely limited by the courts, however. Even if the injured party does not know about the inherent danger of using the product the wrong way, if the misuse is foreseeable, the seller must take measures to guard against it.

Comparative Negligence Recent developments in the area of comparative negligence— liability is shared proportionately by all persons who acted negligently, including the injured party—also are affecting the doctrine of strict liability. Whereas previously the plaintiff's conduct was not a defense in strict liability cases, today a growing number of jurisdictions consider the negligent or intentional actions of the plaintiff in the apportionment of liability and damages. This "comparing" of the plaintiff's conduct with the defendant's strict liability results in an application of the doctrine of comparative negligence. Thus, for example, failure to take precautions against a known defect will reduce a plaintiff's recovery. The majority of states have adopted this doctrine, either legislatively or though court decisions.

PRODUCT-LIABILITY REFORM

The doctrine of comparative negligence has not satisfied many members of the business community, who feel that damage awards have gotten out of hand. Business lobbying groups have been pushing Congress to reform the product-liability litigation process.[23] Opponents of these groups maintain that large damage awards in product-liability cases are necessary to protect consumers.

The Complaints of the Business Community One of the main complaints of the business community is that the goal of large damage awards has evolved into not only punishing the defendant but also "sending a message" to any other manufacturers or sellers who may place their products' buyers in a similar situation. The instructions given to the jury by the judge in at least fifteen states urge jurors to award damages "which will serve to punish the defendant and to deter others from the commission of like offenses." The

---

23. T. D. McCann, "Win the Legal Battle, Lose the Public War," *Management Review*, August 1994, p. 43.

president of the California Trial Lawyers Association calls large damage awards a way "to deter despicable acts by corporate America."[24]

This line of thinking has been obvious among juries that have been involved in particularly large awards. An Arizona jury ordered a Phoenix bowling alley to pay $5.8 million to the estate of a woman killed in an automobile accident by a drunk man because the bowling alley had served the man too many beers. The intent of the verdict was "to send a clear warning to Arizona tavern operators about the legal perils of serving drinks to intoxicated persons." In the McDonald's coffee case mentioned earlier, the message was, in the words of one juror, "the coffee's too hot out there."[25]

Not surprisingly, business has been quick to criticize this particular trend. In a poll conducted by *Nation's Business*, 94 percent of the small-business owners polled said they believed current product-liability laws encourage too many lawsuits against makers and sellers of products. Eighty-two percent of the respondents also said that liability laws deter production of beneficial goods and services because the laws increase insurance costs.[26]

There is factual evidence that product-liability cases have surged in the 1990s. From 2,393 such cases in 1975, the number rose to 8,026 in 1983 and to 18,959 in 1993.[27] The National Association of Insurance Commissioners places the annual cost to American businesses of product-liability cases at $4 billion.[28]

In Defense of Strict Product Liability Consumer advocates retort that despite the publicity garnered by huge awards, such cases are the exception rather than the rule. Product-liability cases make up only 0.36 percent of all lawsuits, according to the National Center for State Courts.[29] A study conducted by RAND, a nonprofit research institute in Santa Monica, California, revealed that just one in fifty persons injured by a product outside of the workplace makes any type of compensatory claim, and only 1 percent hire lawyers. Deborah Hensler, who headed the RAND study, says the data show that "most of us, if we drove through McDonald's and burned ourselves on a cup of coffee, would say, 'Why was I trying to drink my coffee while I was driving? I should have known better.'"[30]

The benefit of this litigation, claim many consumer advocates, is that it keeps unsafe products off the market.[31] Furthermore, business should worry about making its products safe, not changing the law. As one expert pointed out, had the Exxon Corporation not opposed regulations mandating stronger hulls on its tankers, it might have avoided the *Valdez* oil spill and the billion-dollar damage award that resulted from it.[32]

MANAGING CONSUMER RIGHTS— PRODUCT QUALITY CONTROL

In 1994, Joel J. Davis, an associate professor in the School of Communication at San Diego State University, conducted a revealing, and somewhat disturbing, survey of business

24. A. Kozinski, "The Case of Punitive Damages v. Democracy," *Wall Street Journal*, January 19, 1995, p. A16.
25. *Ibid.*
26. "Readers' Views on Liability Reform," *Nation's Business*, July 1994, p. 85.
27. P. Mergenbagen, "Product Liability? Who Sues?" *American Demographics*, June 1, 1995, p. 48.
28. R. Kuttner, "Phony Litigation 'Crisis,'" *Washington Post*, June 24, 1994, p. A27.
29. R. Kuttner, "The Trumped Up Case against Damage Awards," *Business Week*, March 20, 1995, p. 22.
30. Mergenbagen, *op. cit.*
31. Kuttner, *op. cit.*
32. J. J. Davis, "Federal and State Regulation of Environmental Marketing: A Manager's Guide," *SAM Advanced Management Journal*, Summer 1994, p. 36.

managers' attitudes toward providing consumers with more information.[33] Davis presented 206 advertising professionals with five different decision-making situations. The point of the study was to determine which of the following factors most influenced managers in their evaluation: ethics, legal considerations, business considerations, or anticipated approval of management/peers. Here is a typical situation offered the participants:

> Your client says that she wants the advertising to say that the product is "new and improved." The product, a shampoo, has been improved chemically (higher-grade chemicals are now being used), but these changes are very unlikely to make the product perform any better than the original version. You must decide whether or not to recommend making the claim.

Davis found that the law guided almost half of the advertising professionals, with ethical considerations a distant second. The trend *against* considering "the social good" in business was even more pronounced among the younger survey participants, leading Davis to bemoan the quality of ethics instruction in American business schools and liberal arts colleges.

Does Davis make a reasonable argument? Can we expect ethical considerations to dominate the "ad game," or any medium in which business imparts information to customers? The cynical answer is no, with Davis's survey results coming as no surprise. But taking into consideration the idea of the consumer as stakeholder, not to mention the rising levels of sophistication among buyers over the past thirty years, we might conclude that managers who emphasize legality above all other considerations do so at their own risk.

▼ **More and more businesspeople are concluding that addressing the needs of consumers leads to a healthier corporate environment.**

This attitude has manifested itself in the product quality control movement.

THE PRODUCT QUALITY CONTROL MOVEMENT

An integral part of total quality management (TQM), discussed in Chapter 17, is improving the quality of the final product.[34] In a sense, TQM was forced upon corporate America by consumer demand for **quality control**. During the 1970s and 1980s, the perception among many American consumers was that quality was lacking in American goods and services, especially when compared with goods and services offered by Japanese manufacturers.

In 1987, sixty-five leaders in the fields of business, labor, government, and academia gathered under the auspices of the American Assembly of Collegiate Schools of Business to discuss U.S. struggles in the global marketplace. This gathering's final report stressed the importance of quality in the competitive equation: "This does not mean quality merely to specifications, but quality that improves constantly, quality that is characterized by constant innovations that create a loyal customer. It means achieving this attitude from top to bottom, from the board room to the factory floor."[35]

33. J. J. Davis, "Ethics in Advertising Decision Making: Implications for Reducing the Incidence of Deceptive Advertising," *Journal of Consumer Affairs*, Winter 1994, pp. 380–401.

34. R. W. Grant, R. Shani, and R. Krishnan, "TQM's Challenge to Management Theory and Practice," *Sloan Management Review*, Winter 1994, p. 25.

35. M. K. Starr, ed., *Global Competitiveness: Getting the U.S. Back on Track* (New York: W. W. Norton and Company, 1988), p. 307.

▼ **EXHIBIT 18–6**
The Top-Down
Control Cycle

Phase I:	Ownership/executives make decisions based on financial/accounting information.
Phase II:	Ownership empowers top management to plan strategy based on financial/accounting information.
Phase III:	Top management passes instructions to the work force.
Phase IV:	The work force attempts to produce results that meet expectations of ownership based on financial/accounting information.

SOURCE: Adapted from J. S. Harrison and C. H. St. John, *Strategic Management of Organizations and Stakeholders* (St. Paul: West Publishing Company, 1994), pp. 64–66.

BOTTOM-UP EMPOWERMENT

The first step in quality control is to place the consumer stakeholder (buyer) at the top of the corporate "food chain"—that is, assume that the well-being of the buyer is the most important consideration in the business process. In contrast, in the past the most often cited model for corporate America has been the **top-down control cycle.** (See *Exhibit 18–6.*) In this model, because control information resides with an organization's top management, top executives possess the power to control organizational processes.[36] Mid-level managers use information to provide subordinates with instructions concerning the goals of top executives. The entire process is geared toward satisfying upper-level management—not consumers.

In contrast, the **bottom-up empowerment cycle** makes customer satisfaction an organization's top priority. This model assumes that the consumer has knowledge, and therefore power, through increasingly available information about products, services, and prices. A key factor in bottom-up empowerment is a feedback system that allows management and workers to make necessary adjustments by monitoring consumer trends. For example, Ito-Yokado Company, which manages 7-Eleven stores in Japan, controls each level of the selling process: product mix, manufacturing schedule, and delivery of supplies. Through computerization, the instant a customer purchases a soft drink or can of beer, that information is sent to the bottler or brewery, and production and delivery systems are immediately adjusted to reflect consumers' tastes and needed supplies.[37] (For another example of bottom-up empowerment, see *Company Focus: Tom's of Maine.*)

QUALITY IMPROVEMENT STRATEGIES

Most companies realize that even if sales are strong for a time, poor quality will eventually cause consumers to turn away from a given product or brand.[38] The academic and business communities have offered a number of strategies for improving product quality. The Ford Motor Company, considered a leader in quality improvement programs, relies on a variety of points to guide its strategy. These points follow the philosophy of W. Edwards Deming, one of the fathers of quality control, and include

---

36. R. J. Clinton, S. Williamson, and A. L. Bethke, "Implementing Total Quality Management: The Role of Human Resource Management," *SAM Advanced Management Journal* (Spring 1994), p. 10.
37. P. Drucker, "The Economy's Power Shift," *Wall Street Journal*, September 24, 1992, p. A16.
38. L. B. Swartz and M. T. Knapp, "Designing Environmental and Consumer Safe Products for the 21st Century," *SAM Advanced Management Journal*, Summer 1994, p. 32.

COMPANY FOCUS: TOM'S OF MAINE
A CONSUMER POWER PLAY

For Tom's of Maine, the change seemed natural. The $20 million personal hygiene products manufacturer had built a loyal customer base with its blend of corporate environmentalism and "green" goods. So when the company reformulated its deodorants and antiperspirants, eliminating petroleum in favor of a glycerin base and adding lichen, it appeared in keeping with the shared values of the corporation and its external stakeholders. After shipping the new product, however, Tom's offices were flooded with complaints—for all its environmental advantages, in about half the cases, the new deodorant did not work.

A Question of Trust

Deodorant sales, previously healthy, dropped precipitously. Market studies conducted by Tom's revealed a split among those who purchased the product: half loved it, half hated it. For an organization whose corporate culture was in large part based on its relationship with loyal customers, the experience was disturbing. "It's a question of fundamental trust," said Tom Chappell, the company's founder.

Consequently, six months after releasing the new deodorant, Tom's withdrew it and switched back to the petroleum-based formula, absorbing $375,000 in recall costs. Those approximately two thousand customers who had written the company to complain about the reformulation received letters of explanation and high-value deodorant coupons, which were also inserted in the packaging of Tom's toothpaste. The reintroduction was also supported by $2 rebate coupons offered at retail outlets—a huge savings, considering that the product sells for around $4.

Winning Back Customers

The recall was not popular with retailers, who had to adjust their stock for the second time in half a year. It probably won more loyalty from Tom's customers, though. The "new" old formula received a 95 percent positive rating from a test group of the same people who had complained about the reformulation. Tom's further cemented its core values in its disposal of the reformulated product. As a massive landfill contribution was clearly unacceptable, Tom's donated the deodorants to Second Harvest, a charitable group that serves homeless shelters.

"We learned that Tom's can't just reformulate and put a sticker on something," said Kate Shisler, the company's vice president of marketing. "Mistakes will happen, but we found that if you respect your consumer's intelligence and respond openly and honestly, you can turn a negative into a positive."

The New Bottom Line

Especially for small businesses like Tom's of Maine, bottom-up empowerment is a crucial aspect of marketing. In a sense, the company allowed its customers to provide the strategy for handling a product problem that could easily have turned into an image problem.

SOURCE: T. Lefton, "Tom's Cleans Up Deodorant after Formula Change Goofs," *Brandweek*, May 17, 1993, p. 18.

▶ Creating consistency and continuity of purpose in the corporate culture.

▶ Refusing to allow commonly accepted levels of delay in the manufacturing process for defective material and worker mistakes.

▶ Eliminating the need for and dependence on mass inspection.

▶ Reducing the number of suppliers. The major consideration in buying should be statistical evidence of consistent high quality, not just the lowest price.

▶ Focusing supervision on helping people do a better job; providing the tools and techniques to encourage pride in work.

▶ Eliminating the use of numerical goals, slogans, and posters for employees.

▶ Instituting a vigorous program of education and training to keep management and employees abreast of developments in methods and technologies.[39]

Some firms believe that quality control deserves the constant attention of a full-time staff and have dedicated resources to special departments that deal with customers' concerns. These departments include *consumer affairs offices* and *product-safety offices*. Companies that direct resources in this manner have a step up on the competition when it comes to strategic management, the subject of Chapters 20 to 22.

---

39. R. S. Schuler and V. L. Huber, *Personnel and Human Resource Management*, 5th ed. (St. Paul: West Publishing Company, 1993), pp. 558–559.

T<small>HE</small> D<small>ELICATE</small> B<small>ALANCE</small>

Some say that the ultimate stakeholder in all of corporate activity is the consumer. It is consumers, after all, who "vote" in the marketplace with their dollars. Even in monopoly situations, consumers typically do not have to purchase a fixed amount of the monopolist's product. In the more common situation in which numerous competing products and services exist, consumer dollars flow naturally to the "best buys" just as water flows downhill. This view of the marketplace argues that management should seek to satisfy consumer wants in an optimal way, which does not necessarily mean the cheapest way. Higher-price products that offer more durability or other positive attributes can and do become successful.

Managers in charge of advertising are usually reminded by the marketplace that promising consumers more than they actually get will be punished. Indeed, a big advertising campaign about a product that does not work or is not desired simply cements in consumers' minds that the manufacturer is not to be trusted. So advertisers face a delicate balance— grab the consumers' attention and make sure the product is well known and understood, but at the same time don't oversell attributes that do not exist.

T<small>ERMS</small> <small>AND</small> C<small>ONCEPTS</small> <small>FOR</small> R<small>EVIEW</small>

Assumption of risk 565
Bait-and-switch advertising 555
Bottom-up empowerment cycle 569
Cease-and-desist order 556
Class I recall 549
Class II recall 549
Class III recall 549
Comparative advertisements 556
Compensatory damages 560

Contributory negligence 563
Counteradvertising 556
Deceptive advertising 553
Express warranty 562
Implied warranty of fitness for a
  particular purpose 562
Implied warranty of merchantability
  562
Negligence 562

Product liability 560
Puffing 553
Punitive damages 560
Quality control 568
Strict liability 564
Top-down control cycle 569
Uniform Commercial Code (UCC)
  562
Warranty law 562

S<small>UMMARY</small>

1. The Federal Trade Commission (FTC) targets sales practices in specific industries. It requires used-car dealers to affix "Buyer's Guide" labels to all cars sold on their lots. The label must state, for example, whether the car is being sold under warranty. The FTC has also targeted the sales practices of the funeral industry and now requires that customers be provided with itemized lists of charges for all expenses incurred for a funeral, among other things.

2. In 1906, Congress passed the Pure Food and Drug Act, the first law designed to regulate the quality of food and drugs. To strengthen the act, the Federal Food, Drug, and Cosmetic Act was passed in 1938. The law now sets limits on the amounts of potentially dangerous food additives that may be used and specifies the tests that must be passed before drugs can be marketed.

3. The Consumer Product Safety Commission (CPSC) was created in 1972 to protect the public against unreasonable risks of injury from consumer products and to develop uniform safety standards for consumer products while minimizing conflicting state and local regulations. The CPSC was authorized to ban the manufacture and

sale of any product deemed to be potentially hazardous to consumers.

4. An opponent of consumer protection laws, Richard Posner, believes that the marketplace guards consumer rights because (a) consumers can determine the truthfulness of most advertising; (b) competitors will expose misleading advertising; (c) advertisers that develop reputations for dishonesty will be punished in the marketplace with lower profits; and (d) consumers can sue for breach of contract or fraud.

5. There is no single legal definition of deceptive advertising. The Federal Trade Commission defines it as advertising that may be interpreted in two or more ways, one of which is false or misleading. The test for a deceptive ad is whether or not a reasonable consumer would be deceived by it. Deceptive advertising regulation is not applied to puffing—obvious exaggeration.

6. Bait-and-switch advertising occurs when the seller (a) refuses to show the advertised item, (b) fails to have adequate quantities available, (c) fails to promise to deliver the advertised item within a reasonable time, or (d) discourages employees from selling the item. Bait-

and-switch advertising is normally against FTC rules. The FTC can issue a cease-and-desist order requiring that the challenged advertising be stopped. Occasionally it can order that counteradvertisements be made.

7. Many federal and state labeling and packaging laws have been passed to ensure that consumers are provided with accurate information or warnings about products or their misuse. These laws deal with a variety of products, including foods, flammable fabrics, cosmetics, cigarettes, and fur products. Labels must be accurate and use words as they are ordinarily understood by consumers.

8. The Nutrition Labeling and Education Act of 1994 requires, among other things, that: (a) food labels include information on how the food fits into a recommended daily diet; (b) food labels include information on saturated fat, cholesterol, and dietary fiber; and (c) terms such as *lite* and *fat-free* meet federal requirements.

9. Under product-liability laws, manufacturers and sellers can be held liable to consumers, users, and bystanders for harm caused by the products sold by the manufacturers and sellers.

10. A manufacturer must exercise due care in the design and manufacture of its products. This duty of care may also involve affixing appropriate warning labels to the product and inspecting and testing component parts or the final product itself.

11. An injured person's suit against the manufacturer of a defective product will not be dismissed merely because there was no contract between the plaintiff and the defendant-manufacturer. Plaintiffs can generally recover damages from any sellers, including third parties such as manufacturers, of defective products. Manufacturers of foods, cosmetics, drugs, toxic substances, and flammable materials are subject to numerous federal and state consumer protection laws.

12. Any manufacturer that can prove that it used due care in the manufacture of its products may have a valid defense against a negligence suit, because the failure to exercise due care is one of the major elements of negligence. A manufacturer may defend itself by asserting that the plaintiff was also negligent or that the plaintiff assumed the risk of injury.

13. Under the doctrine of strict liability, parties may be held liable for the results of their acts regardless of whether they exercised reasonable care or were at fault.

14. The doctrine of strict liability is grounded on the assumptions that (a) consumers should be protected against unsafe products; (b) manufacturers and distributors should not escape liability for defective products simply because of an absence of direct dealings with the ultimate users of the products; and (c) manufacturers and sellers are in a better position than consumers to bear the costs associated with injuries caused by their products.

15. A plaintiff may pursue a claim under a theory of strict liability if he or she can show that (a) the defendant sold the product in a defective condition; (b) the defendant normally sells the product in question; (c) the product is unreasonably dangerous owing to its defective condition; (d) the plaintiff incurred physical harm to self or property from using or consuming the product; (e) the defective condition was the proximate cause of the injury or damage; and (f) the product was not significantly altered from the time it was sold to the time of the injury.

16. A court may consider a product unreasonably dangerous if the product is dangerous beyond the expectations of the ordinary consumer or if a less dangerous alternative was economically feasible for the manufacturer and the manufacturer failed to provide it.

17. If negligent misconduct or misuse of a product by an injured individual causes damage or injury, it may be a defense to the individual's suit on the basis of strict liability. Assumption of risk can also be used as a defense in a strict liability suit.

18. One way to avoid product-liability claims is to engage in total quality management, focusing on quality control. This management technique is said to follow from the bottom-up empowerment cycle, which makes customer satisfaction the corporation's top priority.

EXERCISES

1. Reexamine the Consumer Bill of Rights promulgated in 1962 by President John F. Kennedy (at the opening of this chapter). After each "right," make a list of how that right is currently being enjoyed by American consumers.

2. Reexamine *Exhibit 18–1*, which lists federal consumer protection statutes and their purposes. Make a list of which statutes you were aware of before reading that exhibit. Alongside each one, indicate how you came to know the statute existed. (For example, if you sold a car, you had to sign a statement about the accuracy of its odometer reading.)

3. "The regulation of tobacco product advertising has had no effect." Do you agree or disagree with this statement? Justify your answer.

4. Reread Posner's list of four ways the marketplace guards consumer rights in the section entitled "The Consumer

and Access to Information." Write a statement for each point indicating whether you agree or disagree with Posner and why. Finally, consider your answers for all four points and determine whether or not you agree with Posner.

5. "Because most manufacturers and sellers depend on repeat customers as well as word-of-mouth advertising, laws against deceptive advertising are not very important." Write a short speech disagreeing with this position.

6. How would you draw the line between puffing, which is not illegal, and deceptive advertising, which is?

7. Why is bait-and-switch advertising not a viable long-run marketing technique for a corporation that wishes to stay in business?

8. As a research project, find six examples of FTC counter-advertising sanctions.

9. Why do so few of the FTC's decisions about advertising end up in a federal court of appeals?

10. In what ways might the 1994 Nutrition Labeling and Education Act help consumers?

11. List examples of how an implied warranty of fitness for a particular purpose was implicit in some purchases you made in the past few years.

12. Assume you manufacture snowboards. A user of one of your boards recently hurt herself. She is suing you. What arguments might you use to defend your company?

13. The doctrine of strict liability seems to mean that no matter what happens, if you are liable under the doctrine as a manufacturer or seller, you have to pay damages. Are there any defenses to strict liability? If so, what are they?

14. What is the relationship between the current concern about excessive product-liability awards and total quality management?

15. "The top-down control cycle was always a fiction. How could any corporation exist if it catered to the demands of top management, unless those demands were consistent with what the consumer wanted and with what competitors were doing?" Is this an accurate statement? Explain your answer. How does it fit in with the bottom-up empowerment cycle?

SELECTED REFERENCES

▶ Hinton, Tom. *Customer-Focused Quality: What to Do on Monday Morning*. Englewood Cliffs, N.J.: Prentice Hall, 1994.

▶ Magat, Wesley A. *Information Approaches to Regulation*. Cambridge, Mass.: MIT Press, 1992.

▶ Miller, R. L. *Economics Issues for Consumers*, 8th ed. St. Paul: West Publishing Company, 1997.

▶ Miller, R. L., and Jentz, G. A. *Business Law Today*, 4th ed. St. Paul: West Publishing Company, 1997 (Ch. 31).

▶ Neeley, Richard. *The Product Liability Mess: How Business Can Be Rescued from the Politics of State Courts*. New York: Free Press, 1988.

▶ Nordenberg, Tamar. *Recalls: FDA, Industry Cooperate to Protect Consumers*. Rockville, Md.: U.S. Department of Health and Human Services, Public Health Service, Food and Drug Administration, 1996.

▶ Rothschild, D. "The Magnuson-Moss Warranty Act: Does It Balance Warrantor and Consumer Interests?" *George Washington University Law Review*, Vol. 44 (1976).

▶ Stapleton, Jane. *Product Liability*. Boston: Butterworths, 1994.

RESOURCES ON THE INTERNET

▼ If you subscribe to the commercial service CompuServe, you have access to its Consumer Forum. Once on CompuServe, type in

Go legal

Then select

Consumer Forum

From the Library Menu, choose
Browse

▼ The Alexander law firm offers consumer law articles at

**http://tsw.ingress.com/tsw/talf/
talf.html**

▼ The Nolo Press, which is also available on the commercial services America Online and CompuServe, has a section called Money and Consumer Matters. You can access it at
http://gnn.com/gnn/bus/nolo/

RESOURCES ON THE INTERNET (CONTINUED)

▼ For a full listing of legal and historical resources available on-line concerning consumer issues, go to Citizen Rights at
**gopher://una.hh.lib.umich.edu:70/00/
inetdirsstacks/citizens:bachpfaff**

The gopher address is
una.hh.lib.umich.edu

Once you are in that gopher address, select
inetdirsstacks

Then select
Citizens' Rights; M. Plaff, D. Bachman

▼ The goal of the Better Business Bureau (BBB) is to provide information to consumers so they can make informed buying decisions. To access the BBB's home page, go to
http://www.igc.apc.org:80/cbbb/

▼ ConsumerLine is a consumer education resource offering publications of the Federal Trade Commission on a range of consumer issues. To access ConsumerLine, go to
**gopher://consumer.ftc.gov:2416/
11/ConsumerLine**

▼ The U.S. Consumer Product Safety Commission (CPSC) works to maintain and ensure the safety of consumer products in the United States. To access the CPSC, go to
gopher://cpsc.gov/

▼ The Consumer Law Page provides links to a number of articles on topics of interest to consumers. To access this page, go to
**http://starbase.ingress.com/
tsw/talf/txt/intro.html**

CASE

FEAR OF SCIENCE: MONSANTO AND THE BOVINE GROWTH HORMONE

Background

On November 5, 1993, the Food and Drug Administration (FDA) approved a drug called Posilac, the trade name for bovine somatropin (BST). Posilac is given to cows to increase milk output by supplementing a hormone produced naturally in the pituitary gland. Monsanto Company, of St. Louis, exclusive manufacturer of BST, immediately began an extensive marketing campaign for its product. The firm offered a package including a "how-to" videotape and other Posilac information material to 105,000 commercial dairy farmers. To counteract claims that BST was harmful to cows, Monsanto also offered a $150 voucher toward veterinarian consultation, which was ultimately accepted by 15,000 farmers.

Many of Posilac's potential dairy-farmer customers had worries beyond the effect of the hormone on their cows. Would consumers ultimately accept this application of genetic engineering—a relatively new field—to their food? "To me, consumer perception of a product will determine whether or not it will sell," said James Goodman, a dairy farmer from Wisconsin. "This perception, whether based on scientific fact or on personal opinions, will ultimately make a consumer buy or reject a product." Leonard Southwell, president of Prairie Farms Dairy in Illinois, echoed these sentiments, warning that "there's got to be a lot more consumer education done . . . in order to get public acceptance."

These two farmers proved better marketing forecasters than the managers at Monsanto. The company found little resistance to BST in the regulatory community. Ultimately, the firm's hopes of realizing the projected $100 million to $200 million in annual BST sales rested in consumer perception and acceptance of genetic engineering of milk. And despite a great deal of scientific data indicating that the milk from cows on Posilac is safe, many people—Monsanto learned—do not like the idea of someone "messing" with their food.

Monsanto and Bovine Somatropin

Primarily a petrochemical company for most of its history, in the 1980s Monsanto shifted focus, investing approximately $1 billion in biotechnology. The firm hoped to manufacture, among other things, genetically enhanced tomato plants that would secrete their own insecticides and a hormone that would make pigs yield leaner pork. The first product out of the company's labs was BST.

In 1985, Monsanto received approval from the FDA to test the product on the open market. Approval was granted after the federal agency determined that milk from BST-supplemented cows was virtually the same in taste, smell, and nutritional value as milk from other cows. Over the next five years, milk from more than 11,000 test cows—amounting to less than 1 percent of the total supply—was sold by BST users on the U.S. market.

An Unwilling Public

Controversy surrounded BST from the beginning. Industry experts noted that American farmers were already producing *too much* milk—better breeding and nutrition had tripled the yearly milk output per cow from 1950 to 1992. In fact, to cap a milk glut in 1986, the federal government paid dairy farmers $1 billion to hold down production by, among other methods, slaughtering cattle. Small-dairy producers complained that the hormone would disproportionately favor their large competitors, who could increase output at a lower per-cow cost. Animal health advocates noted that use of BST in the testing stage led to increased instances of mastitis, an udder infection. This raised the possibility that residue from the antibiotics used to treat mastitis could taint the animals' milk.

But more harmful to Monsanto interests than pressure from small-farmer interest groups or unsubstantiated medical worries was a sign posted in 1994 outside the principal's office at Belvedere Elementary School in Fairfax, Virginia. The sign, stating that "the milk served in Fairfax County public schools . . . does *not* contain the growth hormone BST," represented a consumer backlash against the product. Market studies showed that the idea of a hormone additive associated with milk simply repelled many Americans, who saw biotechnology companies as the "archvillains of the food world."

Individual consumers were eloquent in their mistrust of Monsanto and BST. "I have nothing to gain from this, and the chemical companies have a lot to gain," said one. "I'm not willing to risk my family's health. Milk is something that shouldn't be tampered with."

Monsanto's Strategy

In the face of this negative reaction, Monsanto's plan was to try to convince the scientific and medical community—not milk drinkers themselves—of BST's safety. The Animal

Health Group, a pro-BST lobbying organization, distributed 16,000 pamphlets extolling the drug to doctors and health professionals and only 50 to consumer groups.

The strategy backfired. Recognizing consumers' negative response to genetic engineering of food, retail organizations began to promote the fact that their dairy products were BST free. As early as 1989, Kraft USA announced that it would not purchase milk products from dairy farmers who used BST. Chains such as 7-Eleven, Giant, Shoprite, and Pathmark moved to procure legal assurance from their supply dairies that no BST was involved in milk production. Ben and Jerry's ice cream company labeled its cartons with an advisory that it used only milk and cream from dairies that did not use the hormone.

Although Monsanto spent almost two years trying to convince Kraft of the safety of the product, marketing concerns overrode any scientific proof. "This is a market associated with small children," said Gregory Stoh, Kraft's vice president in charge of refrigerated products. "It's very sensitive." Not even FDA approval could change the conglomerate's policy. "We're going to follow our consumers' concerns on this," said Stoh.

BST Labeling

Proponents of BST and the benefits of genetically engineered foods in general criticized the media and special interest groups for feeding misinformation to the public. On May 19, 1994, for example, the CBS news show "48 Hours" featured a former FDA researcher who claimed the agency was mistaken in its approval of BST and a General Accounting Office employee who said no concrete proof existed that the hormone was safe for cows or humans. The Consumer Policy Institute (CPI) produced a report in 1990 claiming that the FDA erred in allowing "tainted" milk to go on the market. The Foundation on Economic Trends (FET) filed a lawsuit charging the U.S. Department of Agriculture's National Dairy Research Board with "serious and gross violations of federal law governing the promotion of new products."

Once it became evident that the FDA was not going to abandon the bovine growth hormone, CPI, FET, and other opponents pushed for required labeling of products from BST-influenced cows. "Given the potential adverse economic consequences and the concern about increased antibiotic residues, consumers have—at the very least—the right to know whether their milk comes from cows treated with" the drug, said David C. Berliner, assistant director of

the Consumers Union. A Monsanto executive countered that as BST has no effect on milk composition, labeling the product would "create a distinction where no difference exists" and would consequently "be useless at best and misleading at worst."

Court Rulings

After lengthy hearings, the FDA agreed with Monsanto, deciding that the public's right to know did not apply in a situation where, in a sense, there was nothing to know. The agency ruled that individual states could allow voluntary labeling, and the legislatures of Minnesota, Wisconsin, and Maine passed such laws.

The FDA ruling did not save Monsanto from further legal battles concerning the drug. In the spring of 1994, the company filed suit against Swiss Valley Farms Company of Iowa and the Pure Milk and Ice Cream Company of Texas. The two companies had created marketing campaigns around the fact that their products did not come from animals treated with the synthetic hormone. Monsanto charged that the tactics misled consumers by insinuating that BST had a negative effect on dairy products. More legal activity was spurred in 1994 when Vermont passed a law—upheld a year later by a federal appeals court—requiring label identification of milk products from cows treated with BST.

Learning Consumer Trends

A year after final FDA approval, 350 of the country's 1,700 dairy cooperatives and 2,000 supermarket chains continued to boycott the hormone. But Monsanto executives say the company has learned valuable lessons from the BST controversy—lessons it can apply to the marketing of genetically engineered food products in the future.

Karen Marshall, the company's manager of public relations, believes the company should have taken a more straightforward approach. Instead of trying to convince the medical community of BST's safety, Monsanto should have gone directly to consumers and established that the hormone affected only milk production—not milk itself. She also believes the company should have made more of an effort to learn about the dairy industry. "Today, if you have any responsibility at any level of food production, you need to accept that you are in the food industry."

Dr. David F. Kowalcyzk, director of regulatory affairs for Monsanto's animal science division, points out that the firm

CASE (CONTINUED)

did not appreciate America's fear of science. "New technologies should be positioned as evolutionary, not revolutionary," he says. "The public is scared of revolutions. We were just throwing gasoline on the fire."

Critical Thinking Questions

1. Do manufacturers and retailers have an ethical responsibility to label products from cows treated with BST or any other controversial substance—even if such actions are not required by the government?

2. Do you agree with Monsanto that labeling BST-linked products would "create a distinction where no difference exists" and would consequently "be useless at best and mis-

leading at worst"? Was Monsanto ethically justified in its legal efforts to block such labeling efforts?

3. What does this case reveal about corporate values versus public values?

4. Consider the argument that the FDA should have rejected BST because too much milk is already being produced in the United States. Is this a valid reason to keep factors that improve output off the market? How about small-dairy producers' complaint that BST production would favor larger competitors? Is that a valid reason to limit BST?

5. Even Monsanto insiders admit that mistakes were made in introducing BST. In retrospect, how could the company have better presented BST to suppliers, retailers, and consumers?

SOURCE: Information from B. J. Feber, "Monsanto Has Its Wonder Hormone. Can It Sell It?" *New York Times*, March 12, 1995, p. 8; "Despite Assurances, BST Safety Concerns Prompt Threats," *Food Chemical News*, May 17, 1993; J. I. Dwyer, "Monsanto Rides Herd on Cow Hormone," *St. Louis Business Journal*, May 15, 1989, p. 1B; R. Koenig, "Tricky Roll-Out: Rich in New Products, Monsanto Must Only Get Them on Market," *Wall Street Journal*, May 18, 1990, p. A1; S. Kilman, "Growing Pains: Genetic Engineering's Biggest Impact May Eventually Be in Agriculture," *Wall Street Journal*, May 20, 1994, p. R7; C. McCarthy, "Monsanto's Cash Cow Trips Milk Alarm," *Washington Post*, March 1, 1994, p. D20; B. Richards, "Sour Reception Greets Milk Hormone," *Wall Street Journal*, September 15, 1989, p. B1; E. Johnson, "Consumers Vent Their Udder Dismay on Milk Hormone," *Vancouver Sun*, July 10, 1995, p. B2; "News Show Questions Safety of Produce, BGH in Milk," *Food Chemical News*, May 23, 1994; "FDA Urged to Reconsider Bovine Growth Hormone Policy," *Chemical Marketing Reporter*, December 3, 1990, p. 5; "Letters to the Editor: rbGH-Treated Milk Should be Labeled," *Wall Street Journal*, August 19, 1994, p. A11; D. Gershon, "Monsanto Sues over BST," *Nature*, March 31, 1994, p. 384; R. Steyer, "Court OK's Vermont Law Requiring BST Milk Label," *St. Louis Post-Dispatch*, September 6, 1995, p. C1; P. Chatterjee, "Environment: New Butter Faces Fear of Cancer, Gigantism," *Inter Press Service*, August 18, 1995; "BST Promotion Curbs Seen Helpful to Monsanto," *Food Chemical News*, April 4, 1994; and "Some 13,000 U.S. Dairy Producers Have Tried BST," *Food Chemical News*, January 30, 1995, p. 2.

CHAPTER 19

COMMUNITY STAKEHOLDER ISSUES

INTRODUCTION

I n 1995, at the request of the federal Department of Education, the U.S. Census Bureau conducted a survey of managers at 3,347 companies. The results seemed to show that the business community was dissatisfied with the American education system. The managers questioned estimated that one out of every five U.S. employees was not proficient at his or her job. Furthermore, these managers ranked teacher recommendations at the bottom of eleven criteria used for hiring, and grades placed ninth. "There is a disconnection" between employees and educators, said Peter Cappelli, a professor of management at Pennsylvania's Wharton School and one of the project's principal researchers. The survey and focus groups showed, according to Cappelli, that "employers don't work with schools and have a prejudice against them."[1]

For many members of the educational establishment, this attitude calls to mind the old joke, "everybody complains about the weather, but nobody does anything about it." They point out the folly of not taking an interest in a student's skills until that student makes his or her way through the employer's door and then grumbling that the work force is ill prepared for the demands of modern employment.[2] G. Alfred Hess, Jr., executive director of the Chicago Panel of School Policy, calls corporations "two-tongued mammoths" that speak of social obligations to public education while at the same time fighting tax increases to increase funding for education.[3]

THE COMMUNITY AS STAKEHOLDER

These attitudes concerning education go to the heart of the issue of the community as a stakeholder of business. There is no question that the actions of business have an impact on any community. On the positive side, a business can improve the quality of life in a community by making a profit, hiring employees, and contributing funds in the areas of education, social and health-related services, culture and the arts, and other activities. A company can also send its employees into the community to perform a variety of volunteer activities. In contrast, throughout this textbook, you have learned about ways in which business can negatively affect a community: pollution of the environment, discrimination against members of the community, disrespect for employee rights, exploitation of consumers, and so on.

The question we address in this chapter is: *Why should a corporation treat the community as a stakeholder?* Earlier, we discussed the ethical reasons for doing so, but ethical considerations never completely add up in bottom-line equations. Consequently, we focus on two practical reasons why the well-being of the community is a concern for the corporation:

1. There is a *symbiotic* relationship between business and its community. In other words, what benefits one often benefits the other. To take the example of education, if business

---

1. J. J. Fialka, "Employers Give Schools Low Grade on Job Preparation," *Wall Street Journal*, February 21, 1995, p. A13.
2. R. Riley, S. Feldman, S. Sa, B. S. Cooper, D. W. Wyllie, T. Kolderie, H. Decker, G. A. Hess, Jr., A. Tucker, and B. Avashi, "Educating the Workforce of the Future," *Harvard Business Review*, March–April 1994, p. 39.
3. G. A. Hess, Jr., "Educating the Workforce of the Future," *Harvard Business Review*, March–April 1994, pp. 46–47.

could help to improve the schools that feed students into employment ranks, it would find itself with a more productive, more efficient work force. Note that this symbiotic relationship includes not only local, city, and state communities but the global community. If a company harms the environment in which it does business, it will eventually suffer— even if that environment happens to be halfway around the world.

2. Long-term business success is often directly related to community stakeholder satisfaction. The modern consumer is aware of a wide variety of corporate actions, including the corporation's treatment of community stakeholders. A company's image among consumers can benefit from charitable activity within its community. Likewise, harmful activity can result in consumer disdain and brand abandonment.

Still, many businesspeople take a cautionary tone when it comes to adding the community to their ever-growing list of stakeholders.[4] "I think there are unrealistic expectations . . . in regard to what it is possible for business to do," says James A. Joseph, president of the Council on Foundations. "Corporations spend less than $5 billion a year on social programs," he notes. "Obviously, this cannot be an alternative to the social role of governments (which spend several hundred billion dollars each year)."[5]

CORPORATE PHILANTHROPY

"I think the notion that business is here to serve [stockholders] first, foremost, and always is nonsense," contends James E. Burke, former CEO of Johnson & Johnson. "Most corporate leaders recognize that in the long run if you are not responsive to those people who are dependent on you as an institution, then you are going to fail."[6] While Burke's views are widely repeated in the corporate community, debate over just who these "dependents" are, and what the best method is to be "responsive" to them, is considerable.

THE CHANGING TIDES OF CORPORATE PHILANTHROPY

Before the twentieth century, Burke would not have found much agreement. The emphasis in the early industrial period was on *individual* philanthropy, rather than corporate charity. Industrial giants such as Rockefeller, Carnegie, Vanderbilt, and Morgan, following the path of *noblesse oblige* (the idea that generous behavior is the responsibility of those of high birth)—used profits to sponsor and support the well-being of universities, libraries, community recreation centers, and the like, but a clear distinction was made: these were personal funds, not corporate profits. Carnegie specifically identified philanthropy as the *duty* of the rich person, who is called on to consider all extra revenues that come to him or her simply as trust funds to be administered in the manner which, in his or her judgment, is best calculated to produce the most beneficial results for the community.

Corporate Giving and World War II By the 1920s, these attitudes had changed, as an increased focus on workers' rights led businesses to show more concern for their employees' well-being outside the workplace. Companies such as AT&T, Procter & Gamble, and

---

4. R. C. Pozen, "Institutional Investors: The Reluctant Activists," *Harvard Business Review*, January–February 1992, p. 140.
5. D. Cordtz, "Corporate Citizenship: No More Soft Touches," *FW*, May 29, 1990, p. 30.
6. *Ibid.*

General Electric were noted for providing funds for local charities as well as for the well-being of their employees.

The national prosperity that followed World War II dampened the ardor for charitable giving in the business community somewhat. With a growing welfare state, new taxes, and increased government involvement in social programs, business had less incentive to act as community caregiver. Furthermore, consumers demanded that corporations focus on providing goods for purchase.

From Enlightened Self-Interest to Private Initiatives Business's attitude reversed itself once again, to a certain extent, during the 1960s, when racial unrest brought the nation's attention to the deteriorating conditions of many of America's inner cities.

▼ Businesses began to realize the direct effect society's ailments could have on the bottom line, and this period saw an increase in enlightened self-interest—the concept that business could help the community while helping itself.[7]

The most obvious manifestation of this idea was a movement within the insurance industry. Spurred into action by the multiple and expensive claims that followed outbreaks of civil unrest in the 1960s, a group of industry leaders banded together and sponsored a $2 billion effort to invest in inner cities. The effort resulted in the Center for Corporate Public Involvement, an organization that monitors community activity within the insurance industry.

The pendulum swung again in the early 1970s, when business entered what one observer called its "benign neglect" period, once again allowing government to shoulder the entire burden of social spending. As this did not mesh with his campaign promises to cut federal spending, in the early 1980s President Ronald Reagan issued an appeal for "private initiatives" to deal with society's problems. The response was marked by a campaign for businesses to form "2 percent clubs"—in other words, to give 2 percent of pre-tax profits back to the community.

By 1985, the business community had mobilized to the point at which the average contributions from all companies was almost at the 2 percent level.[8] These levels have stayed relatively stable through the 1990s. Nevertheless, the philosophy of corporate giving has again undergone a change, as we shall see.

ARGUMENTS AGAINST CORPORATE GIVING

Throughout the various stages of corporate commitment to philanthropy, the argument against such activity has remained basically the same: the business of business is business. The corporation contributes to the community by providing jobs to its citizens, tax dollars to its public facilities, and products for its households. In fact, the corporation does a disservice to the community when it engages in philanthropy, because those funds must be made up in lower dividends to shareholders (members of the community) and higher prices for consumers (also members of the community).

Menlo F. Smith, chairman of the Sunmark Capital Corporation in St. Louis, echoes values commonly held in the nineteenth century when he argues, "I cannot be considered a benefactor if I take funds from a corporation with which I might be associated and

---

7. B. Ettorre, "Charity Begins at Home," *Management Review*, February 1995, p. 34.
8. Cordtz, *op. cit.*

devote them to purposes that I think are important." Such an activity makes a manager not a benefactor, according to Smith, but "an expropriator."[9]

Also, if shareholders wish to be philanthropic, they are free to do so by sharing their dividends and/or stock price gains from the corporation. Shareholders invest in a corporation for economic gain—they should be free to designate which charities should benefit from that gain and not allow the corporation to make that decision.

STRATEGIC PHILANTHROPY

As suggested earlier, the philosophy of corporate philanthropy underwent a change in the early 1990s, though not necessarily along the lines that Menlo Smith, much less Milton Friedman and his intellectual supporters, would have liked. It seems as though corporate America is just now heeding the words of Carnegie, who warned, "It is more difficult to give money away intelligently than it is to earn it in the first place." Though corporations are giving somewhat less money in the mid-1990s than in 1985, they are pledging more human resources to the act of giving than before. Gone are the days of "checkbook philanthropy," or indiscriminate giving to large programs such as the United Way.

This attitude has given way to **strategic philanthropy**, in which philanthropic efforts are focused on the greatest benefit for the corporation. No longer can companies afford to look on their philanthropic activities as lying outside the spectrum of profit making; donations must be handled as a business.[10]

Trends toward Strategic Philanthropy The impetus toward using philanthropy as a means to further corporate strategic goals came from several sources. First, the 1986 Tax Reform Act lowered the top corporate tax rate from 46 percent to 34 percent, which effectively increased the costs of giving pretax dollars to charity. Second, the wave of mergers and acquisitions in the 1980s and 1990s left many conglomerates with mountains of debt, which tended to discourage indiscriminate philanthropy. Third, the recession of 1990–1991 had a similar tightening effect on the funds available for giving.[11] Fourth, companies began to notice the consequences of poorly conceived philanthropic activities.

AT&T became the "poster child" for mismanaged philanthropy in 1990 when it decided to end a twenty-five-year association with the Planned Parenthood Federation of America. The decision was made in response to a threat by the Christian Action Council (CAC) that it would boycott AT&T if the communications giant continued to support Planned Parenthood, which at that time actively supported a pro-choice position. "Eighty percent of the decision to stop funding Planned Parenthood was based on its ever increasing political nature, and its increasing attention to a very divisive issue [abortion rights]," said an AT&T spokesperson.[12]

AT&T badly bungled the move. The company informed Planned Parenthood and the CAC of its decision at precisely the same time, leaving the latter to celebrate with a victorious press release and placing the former in the uncomfortable position of having to defend itself when it was hardly aware of why the decision had been made. Planned Parenthood responded by running an extensive ad campaign denouncing AT&T for "corporate cowardice." As a result, many customers who supported Planned

9. M. F. Smith, "Should Corporations Be Charitable?" *Business and Society Review,* Spring 1994, p. 20.

10. A. Reder, "The Wide World of Corporate Philanthropy," *Business and Society Review,* Winter 1995, p. 36.

11. B. C. O'Hare, "Good Deeds Are Good Business," *American Demographics,* September 1, 1991, p. 38.

12. M. Zetlin, "Companies Find Profit in Corporate Giving," *Management Review,* December 1, 1990, pp. 10–12.

Parenthood switched long-distance phone carriers, a group of angry shareholders donated $100,000 of AT&T stock to Planned Parenthood, and the company's headquarters was swamped with cut-up AT&T phone cards.[13] AT&T is not the only company to disassociate itself from Planned Parenthood because of the controversial abortion issue, but "even if AT&T made the right [business] decision," one observer noted, "it was interpreted as being unduly influenced by some customers and stockholders."[14] (See *Company Focus: Pioneer Hi-Bred International, Inc.*)

Managing Corporate Contributions In order to avoid fiascoes like the one experienced by AT&T, many companies have professionalized their philanthropic activity. Some companies have subjected all giving to cost-benefit analyses in order to determine the long-term return on the programs. In the late 1980s, Shell Oil took the unusual step of assigning vice presidents to oversee its various social planning areas and making these executives responsible for the ultimate performance of those areas.[15]

Assigning specific managers to oversee philanthropy is only one of the steps suggested by Richard I. Morris and Daniel A. Beiderman. Morris, president of the Grace Foundation, and Beiderman, an executive heavily involved with not-for-profit organizations, have established a number of guidelines for managers to follow to "determine how well your company gives its money away and how it could do better"—that is, how effectively it is engaging in strategic philanthropy.

1. **Align gifts with the company's products and goals.** Corporations often shy away from making grants that could be seen as furthering their self-interest. Morris and Biederman dismiss this fear and champion the notion of enlightened self-interest. On a practical level, matching the interest of the company with the goals of the charitable organization often provides a more substantial partnership, as employees' expertise can be matched to the charity's needs.

Along these lines, in the early 1990s the Eastman Kodak Company redefined its giving from "nice to do" to "need to do." It directed its philanthropic energies to universities that are near its Rochester, New York, headquarters and that offer courses in chemical and electrical engineering, computer science, and physics. Not coincidentally, these are the skills needed by employees at Kodak. Essie L. Calhoun, director of community relations and contributions at the company, says the company is also making sure the charitable organizations themselves are well run. (This concern became prominent after the United Way scandal of the early 1990s, when executives from that charitable organization were indicted on seventy-one counts, including conspiracy, money laundering, and filing false tax returns.) "As more of us look at better management of resources, this gets to be critical with grant recipients," she says.[16] Obviously, Kodak is better prepared to assess the efficiency of a chemical engineering educational program than one dealing with, say, AIDS research.

2. **Put some distance between the corporate contributions effort and the CEO.** Although some CEOs may have the expertise to guide a company's charitable efforts, most do not. Separating the CEO from the process is beneficial because it removes any suspicion that the corporation's giving is being dictated by "personal whim." It also protects those charities that may not have friends in high places. Furthermore, a CEO may

---

13. G. E. David, "Of Grants and Grief," *FW*, August 3, 1993, p. 64.
14. Zetlin, *op. cit.*
15. T. S. Meson and D. J. Tilson, "Corporate Philanthropy: A Strategic Approach to the Bottom Line," *California Management Review*, Winter 1987, p. 59.
16. Ettore, *op. cit.*

COMPANY FOCUS: PIONEER HI-BRED INTERNATIONAL, INC.

ISSUES TERRORISM

In its Planned Parenthood controversy, AT&T was the target of the Christian Action Council (CAC), an organization with ample resources to pressure a large corporation. But Pioneer Hi-Bred International Inc., the world's largest seed company, was driven to make a similar decision based on the actions of a single individual, raising the question of the best way to respond to "issues terrorism."

Dorr's Pressure

In the spring of 1992, former banker Paul Dorr of Ocheyedan, Iowa, began distributing handbills entitled "Is Pioneer Hi-Bred pro-abortion?" to Midwest farmers. "The record is clear," the handbills read. "Pioneer's long commitment to superior genetics has served other purposes than just those of seed corn—that is, the coercive control of the human existence. If you are an employee or dealer for Pioneer and cherish innocent human life, you need to seriously reflect on where the fruits of your labors are going."

According to Dorr, Iowa's "catastrophic depopulation trend" was the impetus for his actions. "I knew it was not all out-migration," he said. Dorr also pointed out that the heirs of Pioneer founder Henry A. Wallace, who served as vice president under Franklin Roosevelt and ran for president in 1948, are long-time supporters of family planning. Dorr not only handed his notices to farmers in the Ocheyedan area but distributed them in Sunday school classes and used six phones and a fax machine to spread the message.

Pioneer's Decision

As far as Pioneer executives were concerned, their $25,000 grant to Planned Parenthood was in no way "pro-abortion." In fact, the money went to rural clinics that were primary health-care facilities for many farm women and performed low-cost Pap smears, breast cancer exams, and other cancer exams. Company representatives had a number of meetings with Dorr to try to explain these facts, but Dorr refused to stop his campaign.

"We were blackmailed," said Pioneer chairman and president Thomas N. Urban. Nonetheless, Pioneer gave in to Dorr's request and canceled the grant, because "you can't put your core business at risk." Urban says his sales force—made up primarily of farmers—was also a factor in the decision. "It became very clear to us that whatever our individual positions were, we couldn't ask [salespeople] to carry a particular belief system with them when they knocked" on their neighbors' doors, he explained.

A spot check by the *Wall Street Journal* showed that Dorr was having little effect on Pioneer's sales. After questioning a dozen of the company's sales representatives and district sales managers in Iowa, the company reported only one instance of business lost because of the Planned Parenthood grant. In fact, one customer threatened to cancel an order for seed *because* of the discontinuation of the Planned Parenthood grant. As for Dorr, he refused to call off his boycott push: "I think Pioneer is trying to shake us off by making this announcement. They have no credibility with me."

The New Bottom Line

"I'm a firm believer that corporations have a responsibility to respond to social needs," said Urban, but they "get in trouble when they become advocates for a particular position." But it appears in this instance that Pioneer stopped its grant to Planned Parenthood based on rumors of trouble rather than the reality. Because of the risk of backlash, companies should take steps to assure themselves that their core stakeholders are against a specific philanthropic activity before stopping it. In this case, perhaps a public relations message outlining the actual uses of the Planned Parenthood grant would have been sufficient.

SOURCE: R. Gibson, "Boycott Drive against Pioneer Hi-Bred Shows Perils of Corporate Philanthropy," *Wall Street Journal*, June 10, 1992, p. B1.

be exposed to pitches for funds at dinner parties and business meetings, which hardly tends to favor a balanced exchange of information.

This is not to say that CEOs should be unaware of the activities of their companies' charitable wings. Grant proposals should cross the chief executive's desk for final approval, because he or she may ultimately have to defend the donations to shareholders, single-issue lobbies, or an inquisitive press. The ideal situation is an aware but relatively uninvolved CEO.

3. Pick a line manager to give company money away. A common mistake is for a company to choose an executive with public relations or personnel experience (an executive in a so-called staff position) to head its contribution efforts. According to Morris and Beiderman, no other policy does so much damage to good corporate philanthropy. They believe an operating manager from one of the company's profit-making divisions (a manager in a line position) is the ideal person to head a contributions program, because they believe line managers are better attuned to bottom-line concerns. The problem is that many executives have yet to view their companies' grants as *investments*—although such an outlook is critical in today's philanthropic environment. Morris and Beiderman point out that the ability to analyze a profit-and-loss statement gives business managers a greater ability to make proper decisions about grant proposals. For example, a ballet troupe applying for a corporate grant will often submit a proposal that assumes a full house for every performance. A philanthropic manager with no bottom-line experience may not even think to question such an assumption.

4. Set a long-term budget for contributions. Very simply, long-term budgets allow for long-term planning, which allows managers to implement the kind of creative, innovative philanthropic partnerships that are the most desirable. They also provide stability to the grant recipient.

5. Expect and prepare for opposition. At the least, companies can expect to be called on to explain and defend donation choices at shareholders' meetings. At most, they may face attacks from single-issue pressure groups. They must prepare for these eventualities by constantly reassessing the reasons for their grants. By doing so, they will also be more likely to question philanthropic policies that may have grown stale or counterproductive.

CAUSE-RELATED MARKETING

One overriding problem that many executives and managers have with strategic philanthropy in general and enlightened self-interest in particular involves the profit motive: it is virtually impossible to determine just how much the strategy is helping the bottom line. It is very difficult, for example, to carry out a cost-benefit analysis on a donation to a local library. Yet the pressure for large corporations to engage in philanthropic activities is great.

How can companies reconcile the vague benefits of corporate giving with the realities of the new business environment? Many companies reason that by linking their contributions to marketing decisions, they can forge a more stable link between "doing good" and "making money." The resulting phenomenon is known as **cause-related marketing,** in which a company ties the sale of a product or service to a philanthropic cause. This facet of strategic philanthropy has brought corporate America some spectacular successes and consequently has become popular in the business community. But some observers question whether cause-related marketing is ultimately effective.

Company Examples The first widely recognized cause-related marketing campaign was run by American Express (Amex) in 1983. The credit-card company spent $4 million to advertise its plan to donate one cent of each American Express card transaction to the restoration of the Statue of Liberty. In addition, the company would donate one dollar for

▼ **EXHIBIT 19–1**
**Examples of
Cause-Related
Marketing**

Company	Cause
• Sears, Roebuck & Company	In 1984, the giant retailer hired pop star Phil Collins to appear in its advertisements and sponsored his forty-city concert tour, with a goal of raising more than $1 million for services to help America's homeless.
• Dannon	The yogurt producer launched a line of products for children, called Dannon Danimals, featuring containers decorated with wild animals. The National Wildlife Federation receives 1.5 percent of the price of each container sold.
• Jardines' Gourmet Fat-Free Crackers	The Texas-based snack company donates 10 percent of its net profits to the National Coalition against Domestic Violence.
• Micrografix	The software developer in Richardson, Texas, began an industry-wide "chili cook-off" to benefit the National Center for Missing and Exploited Children. More than sixty sponsors from the software community, including IBM, have contributed to the campaign.
• Fresh Choice	A family restaurant chain with locations in California, Washington, and Texas, Fresh Choice ties school fund raisers to the opening of new sites. A few months before a restaurant opens its doors, the company selects local schools to host pre-opening parties. Students sell tickets to the events, raising an average of $2,700 for their schools.

SOURCE: Information from "Advertising: Cause-Related Cautions, Success Stories,"*Marketing to Women*, March 1, 1995, p.2; and "Cause-Related Marketing: What Works," *Inc.*, August 1, 1994, p. 102.

every new customer application. The campaign raised $1.7 million in tax-deductible funds for the statue's restoration. At the same time, Amex card usage increased 28 percent, and applications jumped 45 percent.

Since this initial success, American Express has mounted about fifty cause-related marketing campaigns, including a "Charge Against Hunger" effort in 1993 that raised $5 million for soup kitchens and other hunger-fighting campaigns.[17] This strategy compelled its competitor Visa to offer customers the Working Assets card, which, according to promotional material, "is the first credit card that works for peace, human rights, and the environment—at no cost to you." Visa promised to contribute two dollars for every new cardholder and five cents each time the Working Assets Card was used.[18] This sort of bottom-line philanthropy has spread well beyond the credit-card industry. See *Exhibit 19–1* for a sampling of some other cause-related marketers.

17. P. Sweeney, "Corporate Giving Goes Creative," *New York Times*, May 15, 1994, p. 6.
18. P. Ceasar, "Cause-Related Marketing: The New Face of Corporate Philanthropy," *Business and Society Review*, Fall 1986, p. 18.

Passion Branding The 1990s have seen an offshoot of cause-related marketing known as **passion branding**. With passion branding, executives and managers take the idea of cause-related marketing a step further by attempting to indelibly associate the fundamental personality of their company with the cause or causes. The marketing plan of Ryka, a footwear company in Noorwood, Massachusetts, has, for example, used images of rape and domestic violence to sell its products. The firm donates 7 percent of its pretax profits to causes that combat violence against women (well above the generally applauded 2 percent), and a company-supported foundation produces advertising that focuses on the issue.

Marketing experts believe that companies such as Ryka, The Body Shop, Ben & Jerry's, and Working Assets Phone Service can tap into a small but loyal segment of consumers who will become "passionate" customers if they identify strongly with the company's cause. "You can measure the success of [passion branding] by looking at traditional sales figures," says David Alder of Cone Communication, a Boston-based advertising firm. Cone points to Ben & Jerry's, whose sales have gone "through the roof" thanks to linking its product with environmental issues, and Ryka footwear, with an average annual growth of 50 percent.[19]

Consumer Response and "Causeploitation" Both cause-related marketing and passion branding are based on the assumption that consumers will react positively to a company's association with a social cause. In describing Sears, Roebuck's decision to link itself to Phil Collins and the homeless—neither of which would seem to have a natural tie-in to the retail business—the company's marketing chief, John H. Costello, says, "We think it will reinforce the idea that Sears is the most compelling place to shop."[20] (Again, see *Exhibit 19–1*.)

Is this a valid assumption? The issue seems to rest on the highly subjective issue of sincerity. In an environment filled with cynicism about the motives of business, consumers may simply assume a company is exploiting a cause for its own profit. If this "causeploitation" is suspected, then cause-related marketing will not likely be effective.

Obviously, it is difficult for managers to determine strategy by attempting to predict what consumers will accept as sincere social awareness and what the public will perceive as exploitation of a cause for profit. Carol Cone, director of Cone/Coughlin Communication, believes the key to the strategy is matching a company's causes to its consumers. This process involves four steps:

1. Establish the company's values.
2. Consider the product's, service's, or brand's image.
3. Overlay the result to identify target customers, psychographics, and age.
4. Ensure that the resulting campaign is presented in such a way that the social motives of the company are stressed above profit motives.[21] (See the *Case—Avon's Cause-Related Marketing Crusade*—at the end of this chapter.)

The Cause-Related Marketing Trap The problem for managers is that the results of cause-related marketing are rarely self-evident. Sears, Roebuck, for example, will have a difficult task in detailing the effects of its campaign for the homeless, especially because the retail outlet has no history of connection with that particular area of social service.

---

19. "Reaching the Passionate Consumer," *American Demographics*, November 1993, pp. 26–27.
20. G. Smith and R. Stodghill, II "Are Good Causes Good Marketing?" *Business Week*, March 21, 1994, p. 64.
21. "If You're Not Committed, Don't Bother," *American Demographics*, December 1994, p. 16.

Furthermore, managers should not assume that support for a cause is comparable to more traditional reasons for consumer brand name loyalty. In a 1993 survey by Roper Starch Worldwide, even though 66 percent of the respondents claimed they were likely to switch brands if another company supported a cause that was important to them, only 12 percent described helping a cause as one of the most important factors in their purchase decisions. Of much more consequence was past experience with a brand (71 percent), price (62 percent), the company's reputation for quality (56 percent), and word-of-mouth recommendations (31 percent). More than half of the 1,981 consumers (58 percent) believed that cause marketing is "just for show to improve the company's image."[22]

As Harvard business professor Stephen A. Greyser warns, "Why should a person switch toothpaste just because you're giving a few pennies to a charity when the real reason you buy toothpaste is to fight cavities?"[23]

▼ The lesson appears to be that cause-related marketing, and strategic philanthropy as a whole, can only be an important *part* of good management. It should not be relied on to the exclusion of other aspects of the process.

WHERE COMPANIES DIRECT THEIR CHARITABLE DOLLARS

Reasons do exist for charitable giving besides cause-related marketing or "aligning gifts with products and goals." A number of companies practice altruism for altruism's sake, giving with little or no consideration to self-interest. There are directors and CEOs who have personal commitments to causes, as Carnegie and Rockefeller did, and contribute accordingly. Pressure from industry peers, employees, or consumers can also influence philanthropic traits. In some cases, the principle of pluralism—assuring that government is not the sole provider for social causes—is at the core of contributions.

Nevertheless, strategic philanthropy seems to play a clear role in the decisions corporations make today about what charitable causes to support. *Exhibit 19–2* on page 590 shows the four general categories that attract the majority of corporate charitable dollars: (1) education, (2) health and human services, (3) culture and the arts, and (4) civic and community activities. As we shall see, contributions in these areas often serve the corporation's interest as well as the interests of society.

EDUCATION

Education has historically received the highest percentage of corporate contributions, but the thinking behind such contributions may be changing. As we suggested in the chapter's opening paragraphs, corporate America perceives a gap between the education that America's businesses would like the work force to be receiving and that which students are actually receiving. The nature of work has shifted from the agricultural, mechanical base of past years to work of a more service-oriented technological and technical nature. Many businesses are finding that their fresh recruits do not have the basic skills to cope. This can lead to extra operating costs, some of which can be considerable. Motorola, for example, screens up to fifteen applicants for every employee it hires, even though the

---

22. Smith and Stodghill, *op. cit.*
23. *Ibid.*

▼ **EXHIBIT 19–2 Distribution of Corporate Charitable Giving**

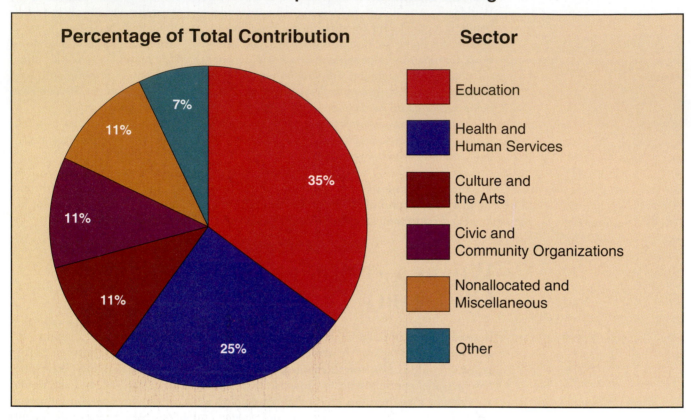

Percentage of Total Contribution

Sector

- Education
- Health and Human Services
- Culture and the Arts
- Civic and Community Organizations
- Nonallocated and Miscellaneous
- Other

35% — 25% — 11% — 11% — 11% — 7%

SOURCE: The Conference Board.

company is looking for seventh-grade reading and ninth-grade math skills. Motorola must then spend an average of $250 per employee to train its workers in quality control processes. IBM will spend approximately 17 percent of its annual $60 billion in total revenues on training and education.[24]

Educational shortcomings among American workers are presumably not the result of a lack of support from the U.S. government—in fact, in 1997, the federal government is estimated to spend $55 billion on education funding. That leaves two fundamental questions for business concerning the nation's educational system: (1) To what extent should it become involved in the process of educating American students? (2) What strategy would best serve business and the national community? When some industries are turning away one out of every three job applicants for lack of basic reading and math skills,[25] the idea that business must become involved seems to be a given.

The Partnership Approach The business community's recognition of its need to be involved is reflected in one of the most telling statistics concerning its philanthropic activities. Since the days of Carnegie and the dawn of corporate philanthropy, private universities and other forms of higher education have received the bulk of charitable funds for

24. A. Tucker, "Educating the Workforce of the Future," *Harvard Business Review*, March–April 1994, pp. 49–50.
25. T. Segal, "When Johnny's Whole Family Can't Read," *Business Week*, July 7, 1992, p. 68.

AutoZone P.I.E. Coordinators Eric Walls (front) and Noel Nabors teach high school students how to use the new cash registers that AutoZone donated to their retail/business class.

educational purposes. In the 1990s, however, corporations have been looking to make an impact earlier in a student's life. (See *Managing Social Issues—Forging New Alliances: Aiding Education with Cause-Related Marketing* on page 592.) With a strong majority— around 75 percent[26]—of high school students unable or unwilling to finish four years of college, the future work force is not being molded in the halls of higher learning. The U.S. Labor Department predicts that by 2005, only one-fifth of American workers may have a college degree.[27] Consequently, through partnership ventures and attempts at school reform, business efforts have increasingly turned to lower levels of education—elementary through high school.

The Corporation-Education "Merger" Not surprisingly, many businesspeople approach the education system as they would a business problem. Hence, terms such as *incentive, merger, partnership,* and *TQM* have found their way into the language of education reform. Ted Kolderie, for example, urges a rearrangement of the incentive systems for teachers. According to Kolderie, a senior associate at the Center for Policy Studies in St. Paul, Minnesota, to improve the quality of education, "we will have to rearrange the system so that teachers benefit directly from improvements in student performance and productivity."

In an effort to provide students in Tucson, Arizona, with job skills, Autozone, a Fortune 500 company, formed a partnership, called a "merger" in promotional materials, with a local high school in 1988. The program, called "Partners In Education" (P.I.E.), targets "educationally fragile" students who are either economically or educationally disadvantaged and provides its young participants with a "classroom" set up like an Autozone store. In this environment, students are taught skills applicable to Autozone or a similar business, along with such basic tasks as how to fill out a job application and

26. R. Riley, "Educating the Workforce of the Future," *Harvard Business Review,* March–April 1994, p. 40.
27. J. Spiers, "Why the Income Gap Won't Go Away," *Fortune,* December 11, 1995, p. 65.

Managing Social Issues

Forging New Alliances: Aiding Education with Cause-Related Marketing

The classroom is a highly sought-after platform for cause-related marketing campaigns. Its appeal to business is easy to understand; education is a low-risk area for corporate involvement, being free of many of the controversies that other social areas—such as AIDS research and the environment—may carry. The difficulty in forming business-and-education partnerships, however, lies in the details. Few marketing staffs are qualified to create an educational program that just happens to prominently display the corporate logo. For this reason, many organizations find themselves using the services of companies such as the Mazer Corporation, a provider of sponsored educational materials.

Mazer and NAM

The Dayton-based company has seen its fortunes rise in the 1990s, in direct correlation with corporate America's increased interest in cause-related marketing. "We've been doing this type of thing for twenty years, and there's always been interest," said Don Laclede, Mazer's director of educational services. "But it's only in the last five years that [this strategy] has really moved into the corporate marketing arena."

Mazer designs national and regional educational programs for its clients, including corporations, associations, and government agencies. These programs are provided free to schools. In 1994, for example, the National Association of Manufacturers (NAM) sought out Mazer's services. Concerned with America's declining reputation as a producer of high-quality goods, NAM wanted to create a program that interested the country's students in the manufacturing field. Mazer designed a classroom exercise that gave students the opportunity to play the roles of senior vice presidents by solving a number of manufacturing problems. To sell the program to teachers, Mazer distributed a folder entitled "Made in America: Manufacturing in Action" to every high school in the country. The folder included a teacher's guide, a wall chart, student handouts, and a set of problem cards, all introducing students to a career in manufacturing.

Business-and-Education Partnerships

The goal of the company is to make its materials serve a purpose beyond the marketing goals of its clients. In this vein, some of Mazer's successful campaigns include:

▶ "Teaching Economics in American History," a high school economics program sponsored by Exxon.
▶ "Go for Fit," a fitness and nutrition program for teenagers, jointly sponsored by the U.S. Olympic Committee and Coca-Cola, featuring world-class athletes.
▶ "Total Health," a program on nutrition, exercise, and health developed for high school students under a grant from NutraSweet.
▶ "The Great Face Case," a software program on skin care for high school students sponsored by Richardson-Vicks.
▶ "Genetics: Investigating the Mosaic of Life," a series of lessons that teaches students the basics of genetics, sponsored by Hoffman-La Roche.

In each case, Mazer makes sure that the advertising message is subordinate to the educational message; usually, a small corporate logo or one of the sponsor's products is discreetly placed in the educational materials. A poster on good nutrition sponsored by IronKids, for example, features a bag of groceries containing a loaf of IronKids bread. "Teachers are a very intelligent group," says Laclede. "They know marketing, and they know curriculum enhancement, and they're not at all adverse to throwing marketing in the trash."

Some critics of commercializing the classroom do not think teachers should be put in a position to make such decisions. Marianne Manilov, a co-director of the nonprofit group Unplug, asks "if [corporations] want to help education, why don't they give money to build schools instead?"

For Critical Analysis:

Do you agree with Manilov? Many teachers have hesitated to accept corporate-sponsored materials. Why would they do so, and how can companies such as Mazer overcome this attitude?

SOURCE: Information from J. DeBrosse, "Sponsored Education Marketers Target U.S. Classrooms," *Dayton Daily News*, November 6, 1994, p. G1; and S. A. Ryan, "Education: Companies Teach All Sorts of Lessons with Educational Tools They Give Away," *Wall Street Journal*, April 19, 1994, p. B1.

present a résumé. Autozone provides financial and in-kind gifts, and its employees volunteer as teachers, guest lecturers, and consultants. The company also rewards performance; student who receive A's or have perfect attendance in the program receive awards ranging from T-shirts and backpacks to televisions and stereos. The "senior of the year" is presented with a $500 savings bond.

The merger has proceeded to the point where, as program developer Mary Hinson boasts, some of its graduates have gone on to management positions at higher salaries than their high school teachers. As of 1994, more than twenty students of "Autozone Marketing" had been hired by the company, a clear payoff of enlightened self-interest.[28]

In-House Education The idea of enlightened self-interest with regard to partnerships between business and education has its critics. In some instances, the difference between goal-oriented corporations and bureaucratically organized school systems has created problems. Furthermore, in speaking out against a California Business Roundtable plan to link educational initiatives to levels set by the state's business community, an educational writer, J. A. Savage, expressed another concern: that institutions that presently teach children to think would be forced to teach them to work. "If adopted," warned Savage, "this plan would mean that those who believe learning is valuable in and of itself will have been silenced in favor of economic development."[29]

Many members of the business community believe that the existing educational system should not be the focal point of their efforts, for a number of reasons. First, academic performance has, at least statistically, not fallen off dramatically in the past few decades. What has changed are the demands of the workplace. Second, because of population growth trends, fewer young people are entering the work force than during the heyday of the Baby Boomer generation. Third, and perhaps most important, nearly three-fourths of the people who will be at work in the first decade of the twenty-first century are already on the job. The conclusion: if managers are worried about the education of the work force, they must be prepared to train the workers they already have.[30]

An Example: IBM and Keyboards Supporting this argument is the experience of an IBM plant in Austin, Texas, that produces keyboards for personal computers. In the mid-1980s, IBM's engineers pointed out that the company could save $60 million by buying keyboards of equal quality from overseas manufacturers. Because of its labor policy, IBM gave the Texas plant the opportunity to save itself—if it could cut $60 million in costs.

The managers planned to rescue the facility by completely overhauling its organizational structure. They reorganized production line workers into multifunctional teams, in the process redefining the plant's job-classification structure. Eventually, every manufacturing worker would have much broader responsibilities and better career prospects.

The managers found they had to invest in improving the basic skills of their workers, some of whom had to learn to read and do basic math before they could take part in the restructuring. Five percent of the workers' payroll went into improving such skills, along with training in more technical areas. By 1990, the plant's cost gap had sufficiently closed,

28. M. Hinson, "A Corporate-Education Merger Creates a Winning Team," *Vocational Education Journal*, May, 1995, pp. 33–34.

29. J. A. Savage, "Is California Handing Over Its Schools to Business?" *Business and Society Review*, Summer 1994, p. 12.

30. N. Stone, "Does Business Have Any Business in Education?" *Harvard Business Review*, March–April 1994, pp. 46–52.

the quality of its product had improved fivefold, productivity had jumped 200 percent, and a new product had been introduced.[31]

Literacy Programs That some IBM employees needed basic training in reading should come as no surprise. This would be true for employees of most companies. It is estimated that over 20 million adults in the United States are illiterate. Managers must not only be aware of the problem of illiteracy but also plan a strategy on how to deal with it in their workplaces.

In 1993, the Work in America Institute suggested that companies set up a **job-linked literacy program (JLLP)** to help employees gain skills needed to advance in their jobs while at the same time providing a more skilled work force. Corporations interested in forming a JLLP should:

▶ Provide trainees with support services such as tutoring, counseling, help with family and personal problems, and paid time for learning.
▶ Make sure that any training is clearly and quickly applicable to each individual's job.
▶ Involve any relevant unions in the process.
▶ Reward increased skills acquired through the training process with appropriate monetary or career advances.

Proponents of JLLPs believe that the programs pay for themselves with increases in quality and customer satisfaction; reduced turnover and therefore reduced recruiting costs; and improved efficiency through heightened employee morale, loyalty, and motivation.[32]

HEALTH AND HUMAN SERVICES

Debate over a national health-care system in the early 1990s inspired many companies to contribute to the health and welfare of community citizens as well as their education. For example, in 1995, Blue Cross and Blue Shield of Michigan pledged more than $250,000 to provide health-care coverage for the state's uninsured children.[33]

The largest share of corporate philanthropy to health and human services is donated to and distributed by federated giving programs such as the United Way. In fact, the huge amounts given to these programs are the reason almost a quarter of total corporate donations involve health and human services. Furthermore, the causes targeted by these drives, such as cancer research and heart disease prevention, are usually quite popular with the population at large. By allying themselves with these causes through the federated programs, businesses can place themselves in a positive light while participating in consolidated efforts already supported by the community.

When a company desires more direct involvement with a health-and-welfare cause (and therefore greater recognition for its involvement), it often turns to sponsorship of a fund-raising event. For example, Safeway food stores have sponsored the annual Easter Seals campaign to help pay for medical research; and IGA grocery stores, along with many other businesses, sponsor the Special Olympics. The popularity of sponsoring five- and ten-kilometer foot races for health-related causes such as research to find a cure for

---

31. *America's Choice: High Skills or Low Wages* (Rochester, N.Y.: National Center on Education and Community, 1990).
32. "The Benefits of Job-Linked Literacy Programs," *Training & Development*, September 1993, pp. 12–13.
33. M. Dempsey, "Money Isn't a Given: Businesses Show Charity in New Ways," *Crain's Detroit Business*, December 18, 1995, p. 8.

breast cancer or multiple sclerosis is spreading through the corporate world. Such events have several benefits: raising money for a worthy cause, promoting general fitness in the community, and getting the company's name out to the public in a favorable context. Companies can also focus on local concerns by raising money for community hospitals, providing new facilities and equipment for those key institutions.

While supporting cancer research or the local children's hospital is a relatively safe strategy, health-related giving in other areas can bring difficulties. As we saw with AT&T and its giving to Planned Parenthood, support of a controversial subject brings with it the possibility of public relations challenges and, in the worst case, boycotts. Such concerns need not relegate a corporation to the "safe" issues, however. Both Levi Strauss and Metropolitan Life contribute nearly $1 million each year to AIDS education and support services, and such support has become an important part of the companies' corporate culture and public image.

CULTURE AND THE ARTS

Compared with areas such as education and public health, culture and the arts are often an afterthought. When there are "more important" problems to be solved, why should the business community get involved in the arts? One business writer, Robert C. Solomon, puts forth the following arguments in favor of such involvement: (1) the "finer things" that culture and the arts have to offer are "an essential part of business ethics," and (2) "supporting culture is the obligation of those who can."[34] As attractive as such thinking may be in the ideal, it is doubtful that either argument would hold much sway in the board room of a company operating under the economic pressures of the 1990s.

---

34. R. C. Solomon, *The New World of Business* (Lanham, Md.: Littlefield Adams Quality Paperbacks, 1993), pp. 278–279.

The Game of Corporate Arts Giving Taking a more pragmatic view, Jeffrey S. Kimpton, director of institutional education for the Yamaha Corporation, likens corporate philanthropy in the cultural arena to a facetious board game entitled "Finding Corporate Support." The participants in this game are the givers, who provide corporate support for the arts, and the seekers, who are in constant need of funds. "The challenge of the game," says Kimpton, "is for the seekers, who usually need and ask for more money each time they get a turn . . . to obtain from the givers, who are forced to play the game with a dwindling supply of dollars." The game, adds Kimpton, is rarely much fun, because of the pressure on the seekers to obtain funds and the fact that the number of givers who are willing to play is declining.[35]

With his game analogy, Kimpton tries to show those seeking grants that they can no longer expect corporations to give to the arts "because they can." He specifically warns applicants that they will have to present potential corporate benefactors with opportunities for *directed* giving, as opposed to donations with "no strings attached."

An example of relatively undirected, though cause-related, marketing in the arts is provided by American Express. During a three-month period in 1981, the company donated two cents to the San Francisco Arts Festival each time customers used an American Express card.[36] As Kimpton suggests, such relatively low-key marketing strategies are being replaced by a more direct approach. Guests at a recent gala evening of the Handel and Haydn Society in Boston passed Chrysler luxury cars in the entranceway to the concert hall and found promotional material about the automobiles waiting on their seats. Afterward, patrons received videotapes of Chrysler's latest lines, as the automobile manufacturer had access to the society's mailing list. For Chrysler, sponsorship of the event went far beyond the reward of choice seats for company executives; it was a chance to expose its product to a high-income clientele.[37]

Arts Giving With respect to arts donations, according to Stephanie French, too many businesspeople see arts programs as "a distraction from the 'real' business of making money." French, vice president of cultural affairs at Philip Morris, credits her corporation's creative program of cultural giving with helping it grow into the "world's largest consumer packaged products company." Philip Morris specifically tailors its funding of cultural events to emphasize diversity and innovation within its own corporate culture and attract new audiences among highly brand-loyal tobacco products users. French contrasts the goals of Philip Morris with those of companies such as Texaco, whose product is not easily differentiated from other brands of gasoline by consumers. Texaco's arts program "built a corporate culture based on quality—democratically available to everyone through sponsorship of opera broadcasts."

French suggests that managers direct funding for the arts to communities in which the company is established. This allows employees to benefit from the philanthropy and also is practical for communicating with grant recipients. She also stresses that "funding on an immediate, local scale can create strong ties between the company and the community."[38] (For a complete list of French's suggestions, see *Exhibit 19–3.*)

---

35. J. S. Kimpton, "Forum on Corporations and Arts Education," *Arts Education Policy Review,* March–April 1993, pp. 19–20.

36. T. S. Mescon and D. J. Tilson, "Corporate Philanthropy: A Strategic Approach to the Bottom Line," *California Management Review,* Winter 1987, p. 56.

37. Sweeney, *op. cit.*

38. S. French, "The Corporate Art of Giving to the Arts," *Public Relations Quarterly,* Fall 1991, pp. 25–27.

▼ **EXHIBIT 19–3**
Do's and Don'ts for Arts Funding Directors

Do
1. Develop objectives that match the corporation's business—for instance, reaching employees or a group of consumers.
2. Identify your stakeholders both inside and outside the company, and be sure to communicate your purposes and goals to them.
3. Use follow-up reports to show those inside the company what your arts programs have accomplished and how those accomplishments are in the best interests of the company.
4. Build support for the arts program throughout the ranks of the organization, not just from top directors or executives.
5. Remember at all times and when making any decision that your program must benefit your company's various stakeholders.
Don't
1. Let your program be operated at the whim of a single executive or management clique.
2. Insist on complete independence and authority in funding decisions; such absolute power can only breed resentment among some stakeholders.
3. Design your program to promote your own image outside the company—or else that is where you may soon find yourself.

SOURCE: S. French, "The Corporate Art of Giving to the Arts," *Public Relations Quarterly*, Fall 1991, pp. 25–27.

COMMUNITY INVOLVEMENT

At first, it may seem surprising that the fourth major area of charitable giving, civic and community involvement, garners a relatively small percentage of total corporate contributions. The numbers seem to raise the question, "Why isn't corporate America more involved with its communities?" However, as is often the case, statistics do not reveal the entire truth of corporate civic and community involvement. The economic pressures already mentioned have given many companies an incentive to vary their philanthropy to include forms other than monetary giving. Statistics do not measure the nonfinancial aspects of civic and community giving that are becoming a crucial part of corporate philanthropy.

Alternative Forms of Philanthropy   To give an example, IBM lost $5 billion in 1992. Not surprisingly, its giving decreased 12 percent that year from two years earlier. IBM did, however, supplement its lower volume of giving with the donation of $39.3 million worth of computers and other products,[39] known as **in-kind gifts**. Another important cost-effective form of philanthropy is the **employee giving campaign**, in which a company offers its workers the opportunity to give through means such as payroll deductions, benefit events, matching donations, and other activities.

▼ By staying in touch with the specific needs of the community, a company can be relatively conservative with direct contributions and still have an effective philanthropic program.

39. Sweeney, *op. cit.*

In 1992, Atlanta-based Home Depot, a do-it-yourself home furnishings company, gave less than 1 percent of its pretax income to charities. When Hurricane Andrew devastated Dade County, Florida, that same year, however, the company not only provided shelter for a hundred employees who had lost homes but organized hurricane relief teams to provide for the rest of the community. In total, Home Depot sent fifteen truckloads of food, diapers, cooking equipment, clothes, and other supplies to hurricane victims.[40]

In most cases, the needs of the community are not quite so obvious. It is the responsibility of the company to keep abreast of community issues in order to maximize the effectiveness of its community involvement. In 1994, the manager of a New York Foot Locker store instituted a "Shoes for Guns" program that provided a hundred-dollar gift certificate for every gun turned in to a local police precinct. Such a program would make little sense in a low-crime suburban area; but for the high-crime neighborhood that included that Foot Locker outlet, it was appropriate.[41]

Of course, most companies already have an in-house community relations force: their employees.

Volunteer Programs As companies are becoming more goal oriented with their philanthropy, they are also mining a valuable source of community outreach: volunteerism.[42] (See *Company Focus: United Parcel Service of America.*) One of the most far-reaching volunteer programs has been instituted at Eastman-Kodak Company. In addition to donating money, Kodak also offers its employees as paid volunteers to programs such as Dollars for Doers and the Kodak Learning Challenge. Under the first program, employees can request small grants of up to $500 from the company for a specific charitable activity, such as taking a group of Boy Scouts on a hike or purchasing space heaters for a homeless shelter. The second program involves seven hundred employees who tutor children in the Rochester, New York, area in mathematics and science. These volunteers are called "technocrats" and receive normal pay from Kodak for the time they spend in the classroom each week.[43]

Junius Davidson, manager of community affairs for Schering-Plough Health Care Products in Memphis, Tennessee, lists the benefits of a **corporate volunteer council (CVC)**—a partnership between corporate volunteers, social interest groups, community leaders, and local government agencies. In a CVC, such as the one that has been set up in Memphis, these groups coordinate their efforts for the most effective and efficient use of volunteer time. Davidson believes CVCs can eliminate a persistent problem that faces charities looking for corporate volunteers by allowing them to access a single source instead of making thirty or forty separate requests for help.[44]

Community Involvement in the Inner City: A Special Concern After an initial wave of attempts to change the declining state of America's cities in the 1960s, during the 1970s and 1980s business seemed to give up on trying to solve the cities' problems. When a corporation did venture into the community, it did so with the idea that its experts would talk and the citizens would listen and follow suggestions. When that did not take place,

40. A. Reder, *op. cit.*, p. 40.

41. R. Wilner, "Foot Locker Offer Aids War on Guns," *Footwear News*, January 3, 1994, p. 2.

42. C. Romano, "Pressed to Service, Corporate Volunteer Programs Are a Way to Service a Business's Community As Well As Boost the Morale of Employee Volunteers," *Management Review*, June 1994, p. 37.

43. B. Ettorre, *op. cit.*, p. 34.

44. J. Davidson, "The Case for Corporate Cooperation in Community Affairs," *Business and Society Review*, Summer 1994, pp. 29–30.

COMPANY FOCUS: UNITED PARCEL SERVICE OF AMERICA

UPS DELIVERS COMMUNITY SERVICE

For years, the belief that business has a moral obligation to the community inspired corporate community service. Thus, even if community service did not serve a "business purpose," it was still worthwhile for humanitarian reasons. Clearly, however, a new rationale has emerged: that an organization can help the community while at the same time helping itself. The dual rewards of community service are the backbone of the Urban Internship Program of United Parcel Service (UPS). The program offers aid to inner-city citizens while enhancing the management skills of participating employees.

Gaining New Skills

The internship, which UPS has sponsored since 1968, sends managers on a month-long, paid assignment to participate in a specific project in support of a nonprofit organization, such as Holy Angels Parish in Chicago or Henry Street Settlement in New York. Working either in pairs or in a group, managers may assist in a homeless shelter, an inner-city school, or a drug rehabilitation center. To ensure that the experience is a fruitful one, the managers stay on-site or nearby, making only one visit home two weeks into the program. On completing the internship, managers make a presentation on what they have learned to their co-workers and staffs.

Over the years, UPS has discovered that the program enhances management skills such as those involving human interaction and problem solving. Most managers, at some point in their careers, get in a "rut." They find themselves making the same decisions about the same problems over and over. When a UPS manager who is comfortable dealing with route problems or lost packages suddenly finds himself

or herself counseling a junior high student with an abusive father, that manager's horizons are bound to expand. "We believe that through the [internship program] our managers will gain an invaluable experience that will influence not only their lives, but also the lives of the many people they will deal with throughout their careers at UPS," says the company's CEO, Kent C. Nelson.

Added Value and Expansion

The value of the program goes beyond enhancing management skills, as Bob Lane discovered in 1990, when he spent a month working with local agencies in the Mexican-American community in McAllen, Texas. "The good feeling I have is knowing that I did help in at least some way," Lane says of the experience.

The internship program, which began in Pittsburgh, has expanded to cover other cities, such as New York, Chicago, Oakland, San Antonio, Atlanta, Indianapolis, Chattanooga, and Montgomery. Managers consider the assignment an honor. Although the criteria for selection vary, participants must be respected leaders within their own work groups before being allowed to face the challenges of the inner city.

The New Bottom Line

Programs such as the one devised by UPS provide an important feedback mechanism from the community to the company as well as helping to embed the idea of a moral obligation to perform community service in a corporate culture. They also have the practical goal of increasing the skills of managers, who receive insight and understanding that they can apply to on-the-job decision making.

SOURCE: "Urban Interns Gain New Perspectives," *Personnel Journal*, January 1993, p. 62.

says Charles R. Stephens of the Center on Philanthropy, the corporations said, "This is too overwhelming; we'll just move out."[45]

The South Central Los Angeles riots of 1992, in which rioters destroyed thousands of buildings, marked a change in the attitude of at least some businesses. The problems of crime and illiteracy had become so great that corporate America could no longer ignore them. Indeed, companies from Xerox to J. C. Penney are now helping to rebuild neighborhoods in partnership with local citizens.

Corporate involvement in the community usually takes one of three paths:

1. Direct involvement. At the beginning of the 1990s, thirty-five companies, including AT&T, Prudential, Xerox, and J. C. Penney, invested $77 million to construct 2,000 units of low-cost housing nationwide.[46] Other companies, including Hallmark and General Mills, have donated funds to rebuild neighborhoods and schools and reduce crime. A long-term commitment in such cases is crucial.

2. Partnership with community groups. This strategy has the benefit of allowing the company to concentrate on its field of knowledge, while relying on the community groups to ensure that the company's involvement is what the citizens actually want. For example, San Antonio's United Service Automobile Association (USAA), an insurance and financial services company, donated funds to Neighborhood Housing Services of San Antonio (NHS), a nonprofit community group. Although a USAA assistant vice president is the chairperson of NHS, the agenda is set by the community. "The residents let us know what they need," says an NHS board member. "They are the experts in their neighborhood."

3. Community intermediaries. In some instances, companies feel most comfortable investing through entities that funnel private funds to areas of need in the community. The danger of this tactic is that by adding a layer of bureaucracy to the community involvement process, it may have the effect of stagnating instead of encouraging progress.[47]

To be sure, public relations plays a role in such efforts. But many companies are finding that helping to rebuild inner cities has economic benefits that go beyond even strategic philanthropy. In 1990, Pathmark opened a supermarket in the Central Ward of Newark, New Jersey—the first national chain to locate there since riots wracked the area more than twenty-three years earlier. Pathmark's weekly sales volume in the Central Ward is as high as $700,000, comparable with receipts in other, more affluent neighborhoods.[48]

PLANT CLOSINGS AND DOWNSIZING

The relationship between a corporation and its community is not always so positive. In some cases, decisions by company executives can have a widely felt negative impact on the community. In other cases, the natural course of business can have similar effects. When Whitehall Laboratories closed its doors in November 1991, the effects in Elkhart, Indiana, went far beyond the unemployment rate, which rose from 6.2 percent to 7 percent in the month following the shutdown. Arrests for assault and battery jumped 33 percent, reports of mental depression rose 184 percent, and calls to the local suicide hot line

45. M. Galen, "How Business Is Linking Hands in the Inner Cities," *Business Week*, September 26, 1994, p. 81.
46. Cordtz, *op. cit.*
47. Galen, *op. cit.*
48. S. Bennett, "Making It Work in the Inner City," *Progressive Grocer*, November 1, 1991, p. 22.

▼ **EXHIBIT 19–4 Downsizing in the 1990s: Eleven Major Layoffs**

Company	Date	Layoffs
AT&T	January 1996	40,000
Chemical/Chase Manhattan	August 1995	12,000
Digital Equipment	May 1994	20,000
Nynex	January 1994	16,800
GTE Corporation	January 1994	17,000
Delta Air Lines	April 1994	15,000
Philip Morris	November 1993	14,000
IBM	July 1993	60,000
Boeing	February 1993	28,000
Sears, Roebuck & Company	January 1993	50,000
General Motors	December 1991	74,000

SOURCE: *Newsweek,* February 26, 1996, pp. 44–48.

increased by almost 30 percent. The feeling in the city was that Whitehall, by relocating its plant to Puerto Rico, had betrayed the community.[49]

The experience of the eight hundred Elkhart residents who made up the Whitehall work force is hardly unique. Plant closings and layoffs are a given in a capitalist system. There is a sense, however, that the 1990s have been a particularly stressful time for employees and the communities in which they live. As we discussed in detail in Chapter 7, global competition has forced many companies to relocate abroad in search of lower labor costs. Technology has allowed companies to replace outmoded factories with more efficient ones that require fewer human hands to operate. The search for efficiency has also led to the paring down of work forces at an unprecedented rate: in the first quarter of 1994, for example, America's employers were announcing an average of 3,106 layoffs each day (but less than 1,000 per day in 1996).[50] (For a list of eleven major staff cutbacks in the 1990s, see *Exhibit 19–4.*)

In the past, some corporations showed little concern for community stakeholders when it came to closing down a plant or engaging in a round of layoffs. Workers were employed at the will of the employer, and concern for a worker's well-being ended with the paycheck. As the perception of employee rights has evolved, however, so has the notion that business should assist its displaced workers.

LEGAL PROTECTIONS FOR DISPLACED WORKERS

As we noted in Chapter 13, the American legal system has tended to respect the sanctity of the at-will employment relationship.[51] Consequently, any overview of legal protection

49. K. Kelly, "A 'Living Hell' in Indiana," *Business Week,* March 9, 1992, p. 33.
50. J. A. Bryne, "The Pain of Downsizing," *Business Week,* May 9, 1994, p. 61.
51. A. A. Colia, G. Kourpias, and S. C. Gault, "Should There Be National Standards for Employer/Employee Relations?" *Business and Society Review,* Summer 1995, p. 30.

for workers caught in plant closings or other massive layoffs begins with the Worker Adjustment and Retraining Notification Act.

The Worker Adjustment and Retraining Notification Act (WARN) Although labor unions and employee rights advocates had long pushed for legislation that would force employers to give workers significant notification before massive layoffs, it was not until 1988 that the Worker Adjustment and Training Notification Act (WARN) was passed. WARN went into effect in 1989. The legislation generally requires that certain employers give advance notice—usually sixty days—before undertaking an action that results in a large-scale employment loss.

Not every action of this sort triggers WARN's protection. Under the law, notice is only required in the event of a "plant closing" or "massive layoff." A plant closing occurs when a single site of employment, a facility, or an "operating unit" within a facility is permanently or temporarily shut down, resulting in the loss of fifty or more employees over a thirty-day period. A massive layoff results from a thirty-day work force reduction that affects

1. At least five hundred full-time employees; or
2. Thirty-three percent of the full-time employees at an employment site but no less than fifty employees.

Like many federal regulations, WARN is designed not to affect small businesses negatively. Therefore, the law only applies to companies with one hundred or more employees (or their equivalent, including part-time workers). Part-time employees are defined as those who work an average of less than twenty hours per week or have been employed for fewer than six of the twelve months preceding the need for WARN notice.

The Effectiveness of WARN The legislation does have a number of exceptions. A "faltering business" exception allows a company to give less than sixty days' notice if it is actively seeking financial capital or new contracts to avoid the shutdown or massive layoff. This exemption addresses the fear of many managers that the sixty-day notification law reduces worker incentive to perform satisfactorily during a time when the company may be struggling for survival. Furthermore, a company is relieved of WARN obligations if the plant closing or mass layoff results from "unforseeable business circumstances"—that is, sudden, dramatic, or unexpected actions or conditions beyond the company's control.

As these exceptions are rather general, many businesses have managed to skirt WARN requirements. Of the seven thousand plant closures and mass layoffs that occurred in 1990 and 1991, according to the General Accounting Office (GAO), over half of the workers affected were not given *any* advance notice, much less sixty days' worth.[52] Of those companies that did notify their workers of impending unemployment, 29 percent failed to give two months' notice.[53] Such statistics have given some members of Congress an incentive to try to restructure WARN to offer more protection, but these efforts have not yet been successful.

Community Actions Another legal challenge to plant closings has come from the communities themselves. After General Motors announced the closing of a plant in

---

52. "Dislocated Workers," *General Accounting Office Reports and Testimony*, February 1, 1993.
53. K. G. Salwen, "Most Firms Fail to Warn Workers of Plant Closings," *Wall Street Journal*, February 23, 1993, p. A2.

Ypsilanti, Michigan, for relocation to Arlington, Texas, in 1992, the city filed suit against the automobile manufacturer, charging breach of oral contract. Ypsilanti's lawyers contended that GM had received tax breaks from the city on $250 million in investments from 1984 to 1988 on the understanding that the concessions would keep the Willow Run assembly plant, and its 4,014 jobs, within the community.

For its part, GM argued that it could not have foreseen the economic conditions that forced the relocation when it asked for the tax breaks. Although Ypsilanti prevailed in a lower-court ruling, a Michigan appeals court ruled that a company has the right to move freely and that the company cannot contract the right away. Though it is of little consolation to Ypsilanti, municipalities have learned other ways to persuade companies to stay within city limits. The most effective of these methods is to impose "penalties for early withdrawal." Perhaps shaken by GM's treatment of its predecessor, Arlington signed a ten-year contract with the company. Under the contract, the city can recover all the abated taxes already given if GM closes its plant during that period.[54]

BUSINESS'S RESPONSIBILITY TO DISPLACED WORKERS

The legal protection for displaced workers is limited. In most cases, if laid-off employees are to find any relief, it will have to come from the company that has just terminated their employment. Before we discuss various ways in which business can perform this most valuable community service, we should note that it will be difficult for managers to find any direct bottom-line benefits in this strategy.[55] The same financial difficulties that prompted the plant closing or layoffs are a major deterrent to committing extra funds to released employees.

▼ In the end, enlightened executives and managers will make the effort to "do the right thing" not because of financial considerations but because it is the right thing.

Job Sharing and Early Retirement The first option management can consider is, of course, to somehow keep the plant running or minimize the layoffs. At the end of Chapter 15, in the *Case—Xerox: A Model of Management-Labor Cooperation*, we saw how cooperation between the Amalgamated Clothing and Textile Workers Union and Xerox management saved a photocopier manufacturing plant in Samford, Connecticut. Other options include initiating a **job-sharing program**, under which a number of jobs are saved by decreasing the work hours and pay of a larger number of employees. This has the potential benefit of also increasing productivity, as each employee works more concentrated hours. A drawback is that companies base most employee benefits on number of employees and not on hours per week of work or salary. If a company is considering layoffs as a way to reduce benefit costs, then a job-sharing program may not be practical.

Some companies soften the blow of layoffs through an **early retirement program**, which offers workers with long service monetary incentives to take early retirement. Such incentives may include pension payments before the age of sixty-two, when Social Security benefits commence, company-paid health and life insurance, and generous

54. K. Miller and E. Felsenthal, "GM Can't Be Forced to Keep Plant Open," *Wall Street Journal*, August 5, 1993, p. B8.

55. R. E. Parker, "Why Temporary Workers Have Become a Permanent Fixture," *Business and Society Review*, Fall 1994, p. 36.

▼ **EXHIBIT 19–5 Six Steps for Management during a Plant Closing**

Steps	Ethical Actions
1. Announce the closing early.	In the case of the Chicago plants, Leaf North American announced the closings three years in advance. While Van Buren–Jordan realizes such early warning is not always possible, she stresses the importance of an early announcement in allowing both the employee and the employer to prepare for the future. This is especially true for unskilled workers, who usually need more time to find new jobs. An early announcement also improves the performance of the targeted employees because they feel they have been treated fairly by management.
2. Communicate with employees.	Remember that people are losing their jobs. Ensure that the inevitable questions and concerns of employees are met quickly and honestly. Not only will this make the transitional period easier for the employees, but it will also keep morale—and productivity—relatively stable.
3. Emphasize teamwork.	Closing an operation or making a significant layoff necessitates an efficient working relationship between corporate executives, managers, and outside consultants. Teamwork is critical to avoid mistakes.
4. Train and provide services.	The most effective way to help employees is through training and outplacement services. Keeping these activities on-site ensures higher levels of participation and success. Leaf North American offered on-site programs that included training for the General Equivalency Diploma (GED) and English as a second language (ESL), skills training in high-growth fields, and support services such as sustenance allowances, transportation, and day care.
5. Hire an outplacement consultant.	Leaf North American employed the services of the Derson Group Ltd., which provided information about public and private education and training programs. Even if the company cannot afford to directly employ an outplacement firm, it should at least consult one to learn the do's and don'ts of the process.
6. Keep accurate employee records.	Accurate records ensure that departing employees receive compensation and benefits as well as protecting the company in the case of government investigation or private lawsuits.

SOURCE: S. Van Buren–Johnson, "Three-Year Plan Eases the Pain of Plant Closings," *Personnel Journal,* April 1993, p. 66.

severance pay. A company may also maintain its current retirement program and simply lower the age of retirement.[56]

Key Steps in Providing for Displaced Workers In many cases, an employer cannot avoid a plant closing or mass layoff. This can be a traumatic experience for both sides in the employee-employer relationship. The employer often feels a strong sense of failure and loss, both financial and personal. The employee loses wages, security, and a workplace culture that may have played an important role in his or her social life. In order to fulfill a responsibility to displaced workers, many large companies have outplacement centers, which may offer computerized job banks, on-site counseling, a reference library, and office space for conducting a job hunt.

Not all companies have the resources to house and staff an outplacement center. There are other, similar alternatives, however. Susan Van Buren–Jordan, human resources man-

---

56. R. S. Schuler and V. L. Huber, *Personnel and Human Resource Management,* 5th ed. (St. Paul: West Publishing Company, 1993), p. 646.

ager for Leaf North American, a confectionery manufacturer, had to oversee the closing of the company's two Chicago plants in 1993. Her experience led her to specify six steps she feels are necessary when displacing workers, which are detailed in *Exhibit 19–5.*

Executives and managers should be prepared for the costs of ethical actions in such situations. When Stroh Brewery Company decided to close a seventy-year-old brewery in 1985, the company spent about $1.5 million on a program similar to that advocated by Van Buren–Johnson of Leaf North American. That amounted to $2,000 spent for each unemployed worker. As one executive commented, "considering the shattering impact that job loss can have on a person and his or her family, that seems like a small price to pay to do the outplacement job right."[57]

---

57. D. S. Perkins, "What Can CEOs Do for Displaced Workers?" *Harvard Business Review,* November–December 1987, p. 93.

THE DELICATE BALANCE

While there are critics of the stakeholder view of corporate social responsibility, business leaders cannot realistically ignore the community in which they find themselves. Consequently, corporate strategic philanthropy is as important today as ever, perhaps even more so. Whether because of enlightened self-interest or simply because of an ethical commitment to the community, a corporate leader must continuously seek ways to engage in philanthropic endeavors that simultaneously help the community and the corporation's bottom line. This may mean taking time to develop a strategic philanthropic program—time that some managers may believe could be better spent in cutting costs or developing new products. The delicate balance exists here, though, because a narrow focus on the bottom line may end up costing the corporation more in the future if it has to take on activist groups in the community that decide the corporation's activities are inappropriate. Moreover, philanthropic actions that promote public education may ultimately lead to higher profits in the future because of a better trained work force.

TERMS AND CONCEPTS FOR REVIEW

Cause-related marketing 586
Corporate volunteer council
  (CVC) 598
Early retirement program 603

Employee giving campaign 597
In-kind gifts 597
Job-linked literacy program
  (JLLP) 594

Job-sharing program 603
Passion branding 588
Strategic philanthropy 583

SUMMARY

1. The corporation must treat the community as a stakeholder because (a) there is a symbiotic relationship between business and its community and (b) there is often a direct relation between business success and community stakeholder satisfaction.

2. Strategic philanthropy is a new way to view gift giving within the community. It involves using philanthropic efforts as a means to further corporate strategic goals.

3. Guidelines for strategic philanthropy include: (a) aligning corporate gifts with the corporation's products and goals; (b) putting some distance between the corporate contributions effort and the CEO; (c) picking a line manager to be responsible for corporate gift giving; (d) setting a long-term budget for contributions; and (e) expecting and preparing for opposition, either from shareholders or from special interest groups in the community.

4. One type of strategic philanthropy involves cause-related marketing, through which companies attempt to create a stable link between "doing good" and "making money."

5. An offshoot of cause-related marketing is passion branding, in which the fundamental personality of a corporation is linked permanently with a cause or causes, such as a reduction in domestic violence or the protection of the rain forest. One way to link a company's causes to the consumer is by: (a) establishing the company's values, (b) considering the product's image, (c) overlaying the result to identified target customers, and (d) ensuring that the resulting campaign is presented so that the social motives of the company are stressed above the profit motive.

6. As of the mid-1990s, education receives 35 percent of corporate charitable contributions; health and human services, 25 percent; culture and the arts, 11 percent; civic and community organizations, 11 percent; and others, 18 percent.

7. Corporations use several approaches in contributing to education, including: (a) the partnership approach, (b) the corporation-education "merger," and (c) in-house education for existing workers. Additionally, some corporations have started job-linked literacy programs.

8. In addition to money, corporations can give away some of their products as in-kind gifts. Companies can offer employees employee giving campaigns, in which workers have the opportunity to give through payroll deductions and other means. Finally, corporations can pay for time that employees spend in volunteer programs.

9. Legal protection for some workers who lose their jobs because of plant closings or massive layoffs is afforded by the Worker Adjustment and Retraining Notification Act of 1988. In general, certain large employers are supposed to give sixty-days' advance notice before undertaking an action that results in a large-scale employment loss. However, because of exceptions to the law, many workers involved in plant closings or mass layoffs are given little or no advance notice.

10. Businesses that feel responsible to potentially displaced workers can: (a) try to keep the plant running or minimize the layoffs, (b) institute a job-sharing program, or (c) offer early retirement programs.

EXERCISES

1. Explain what it means to say that there is a symbiotic relationship between business and its community.
2. What basic conflict might exist between corporations and community stakeholders?
3. Why do you think that the philosophy of corporate philanthropy changed from *noblesse oblige* during the era of Rockefeller and Carnegie to enlightened self-interest and strategic philanthropy?
4. Analyze the arguments *against* corporate giving. Point out where you agree or disagree with these arguments.
5. The text described one group's negative reaction to AT&T's contribution to Planned Parenthood. Outline a strategy that AT&T could have utilized to avoid this negative publicity.
6. One of the ways to engage in strategic philanthropy is to align the corporation's gifts with the corporation's products. Give additional examples of how this could be done.
7. Why, according to Morris and Beiderman, is it important to pick a line manager who manages corporate gift giving?
8. One of Morris and Biederman's rules for strategic philanthropy involves expecting and preparing for opposition. Pick two gift-giving strategies and write down examples of potential opposition to those strategies.
9. Reexamine *Exhibit 19–1*, which lists some cause-related marketing campaigns. Before looking at that exhibit, had you ever heard of such campaigns? If so, explain how.
10. Find examples of passion branding besides Ryka, The Body Shop, Ben & Jerry's, and Working Assets Phone Service.
11. Imagine that you are in charge of strategic marketing for a large manufacturing concern that produces preconstructed frames for average-priced houses. Develop a strategy that would allow you to match your marketing with a particular cause. What would an appropriate cause be, and how could you guide your company in using that cause?
12. Why do you think so much more corporate gift giving involves education than civic and community activities?
13. Which is the most effective way to help education: the partnership approach, the corporation-education merger, or in-house education? Defend your answer.
14. How can gift giving to the arts specifically help a corporation's bottom line?
15. Suppose you are in charge of developing a plan by which your corporation will allow employees to engage in volunteer programs in the community during work hours. List what programs you will target and whether you will pay for the time employees spend off the job in volunteer activities.
16. Does a corporation have a duty to the community to minimize the costs to employees of plant closings? Justify your answer.
17. Are job-sharing programs an effective way to reduce the number of layoffs? Why or why not?
18. Reexamine *Exhibit 19–5*, which gives six steps management can use during a plant closing. State which steps you consider most important, and why.

SELECTED REFERENCES

▶ Bruder-Mattson, Robert J. *Finding the Right Corporate Dollars for Your Charity.* New York: Garland, 1993.

▶ Cascio, Wayne F. *Guide to Responsible Restructuring.* Washington, D.C.: U.S. Department of Labor, Office of the American Workplace, 1995.

▶ Logan, David. *Community Involvement of Foreign-Owned Companies.* New York: Conference Board, 1994.

▶ Neiheisel, Steven R. *Corporate Strategy and the Politics of Goodwill: A Political Analysis of Corporate Philanthropy in America.* New York: P. Lang, 1994.

▶ Wild, Cathleen. *Corporate Volunteer Programs: Benefits to Business.* New York: Conference Board, 1993.

RESOURCES ON THE INTERNET

▼ The Sales and Marketing Exchange (SME) offers information on marketing techniques, including techniques for cause-related marketing. To access SME, go to

http://sme.com/default.html

▼ Information on nonprofit and charitable organizations on the Internet can be found at the Internet Non-Profit Center. To access this information, go to

http://human.com/inc/index.html

or

gopher://gopher.human.com/11/inc

For another source of American charities, go to

http://www.charities.org/charity.html

▼ The *Philanthropy Journal* is a publication that deals with news, announcements, and connections for nonprofit and volunteer organizations. To access this journal's Internet pages, go to

http://www.nando.net/philant/ philant.html

Also, go to

http://www.contact.org

CASE

AVON'S CAUSE-RELATED MARKETING CRUSADE

Background

Selling lipstick and eyeshadow door to door, the Avon lady is an enduring piece of America's past. By the 1980s, however, it looked as if Avon might not be part of the country's future. With net income falling, the giant beauty products company attempted to diversify into the health-care industry and suffered serious losses. In its weakened state, Avon was the target of four takeover attempts, including one by rival Mary Kay.

The effectiveness of Avon's method of direct selling, which sent 400,000 sales representatives to households across the nation to sell products to the American housewife, also raised questions. First, many American women were no longer at home, having entered the workplace. Second, employment opportunities for women had expanded greatly, leaving fewer interested in traditional women's work—such as selling cosmetics door to door. Finally, technological innovations such as television shopping networks and the Internet were cutting down on the need for personal sales.

But by the mid-1990s, Avon's profits were up, and the company's sales force had actually increased to 450,000. Avon's reinvigoration has been attributed in part to its success in the field of cause-related marketing. In October 1993, the company initiated a five- year Breast Cancer Awareness Crusade that has been lauded as a model of corporate enlightened self-interest.

Misguided Diversification

In the 1980s, questions about Avon's viability came from internal as well as external sources. Company executives saw net income drop from $472 million in 1980 to $187 million in 1985 and concluded that Avon could not survive on its beauty products line. Consequently, using cash from Avon's core direct-selling business, Avon made the decision to diversify into the health-care industry.

That corporate-level decision proved ill fated. In 1984, for example, Avon acquired Foster Home Health Care for stock valued at more than $205 million. Two years later, a change in federal regulations restricted Medicare reimbursements for home health care, leaving Foster—which sold home services such as respiratory therapy and oxygen equipment—at a distinct competitive disadvantage. "We were delivering products and services which we subsequently discovered we weren't going to get paid for," said an Avon spokesperson.

In 1988, Avon sold Foster and its two other health care divisions, Mediplex Group and Retirement Inns of America, at large losses.

Direct Sales Rebound

The company attributes its turnaround to the efforts of James E. Preston, an Avon executive in the company's direct-selling division. In 1985, Preston embarked on a series of "pep rallies" in thirty-three cities for 56,000 sales representatives. He encouraged new sales strategies, including the selling of Avon products in the workplace by representatives who had other jobs. Lunch breaks, for example, could be used to sell to co-workers.

By 1987, profits from U.S. direct-sales operations had increased to $157 million, up almost 60 percent from the time of Preston's national tour, and the resulting cash flow had begun to help Avon recover from its diversification debts. Hailing Preston as a savior, the board of directors rewarded him with the CEO post in January 1989.

Part of Preston's master plan was to change the marketing strategy of Avon. "We don't want to [just] build transactions, we want to build relationships," he said in an interview. "Today's working woman has more needs and less time in which to fulfill them. If we can provide her with services no one else can match, that's also customer value." He left the details of creating relationships with loyal consumers to Joanne Mazurki, Avon's director of worldwide communications.

Building a Relationship with Customers

Avon had attempted a cause-related marketing venture in the 1980s, with results similar to those of its diversification efforts. Attracted to the idea of connecting the hundredth anniversary of the Statue of Liberty with Avon's hundredth year of operation, the company linked the sales of some of its products to the restoration of the statue. The problem, according to Mazurki, was that "we found our customers didn't relate much to the statue."

In 1993, Preston gave Mazurki seven months to construct a marketing program to which Avon's customers would relate. Remembering the Statue of Liberty debacle, and aware that the great majority of Avon's sales representatives and customers are women, Preston wanted to link the company's name to "a women's issue or a family issue." Mazurki said she was guided in her decision-making process by the knowledge that "consumers will choose to buy from a company that stands for something and services their needs, and our customer's needs are more than just lipstick."

Mazurki's research drew her to the issue of breast cancer awareness. Breast cancer claimed almost 45,000 lives in 1993, making it the number-one health concern of women in the United States. In the statistics, Mazurki saw what she believed to be an area in which Avon could help: early detection, which significantly improves a victim's chances of survival. Almost 60 percent of women do not follow the guidelines for early detection, and Mazurki felt education and access to testing were "underfunded" by business and the government.

Avon's Competitive Advantage

To be sure, breast cancer awareness was not being completely ignored by corporate America. In fact, Avon competitors Estee Lauder and Revlon raised money for the issue, and pink ribbons—based on the red ribbons used to symbolize AIDS awareness—were becoming ubiquitous in the beauty products and modeling industries.

But Mazurki felt Avon had a competitive advantage that could help its brand name become synonymous with breast cancer awareness: the direct-selling system. So when the company's Breast Cancer Awareness Crusade began in October 1993, it relied to a large extent on the sales representatives. The salespeople attended a number of seminars on breast cancer and the importance of detecting the disease in its early stages and then went out to spread the word among customers. In the first year, the representatives raised $7 million for a charitable fund, the Avon Breast Health Access Fund, through the sale of pink breast cancer awareness pins.

The representatives distribute informational brochures featuring "ten facts every women should know about breast cancer." The company estimates that the program helps educate around 40 million women a year about the disease. Preston and Mazurki attribute the success of the program to the intimate relationship between sales representatives and customers. When the salesperson "begins to talk to a customer about something like this, suddenly there's a linkage and a bonding between them," says Avon's CEO. "The fact that our business is not one big business, but thousands of small ones, makes for very personal relationships," echoes Mazurki.

The company continued to stress awareness by underwriting a Public Broadcasting Service special entitled "The Breast Care Test" and cosponsoring an ABC special hosted by reporter Linda Ellerbee—a survivor of breast cancer—entitled "The Other Epidemic." (Avon used the ABC program to introduce an advertising campaign focusing on breast cancer awareness.) Building on the success of the pink pin sales, in 1995 Avon introduced a pink pen for its representatives to offer, with proceeds also going to its charitable fund. With every three-dollar purchase of a pink pen, customers were provided with a "Take the Pledge" pamphlet detailing three steps women can take for early breast cancer detection.

Dissenting Voices

Avon's intense participation, and that of numerous other companies, in the cause of breast cancer awareness has raised some questions in the health-care community. Why, for example, is breast cancer receiving so much more attention from corporations than AIDS? Besides the obvious reason that AIDS is considered more controversial and therefore more frightening to corporations, a cause-related marketing analyst thinks breast cancer is more attractive because early detection can lead to a "happy ending." "Ultimately, AIDS very much means death, doesn't it?" she asks. "When you look at a marketing overlay, you'd rather associate yourself with something positive."

Perhaps evoking a cynical, or "causeploitative," view, the *Cosmetic Insiders' Report* declared at one point that Avon had edged ahead of Estee Lauder and Revlon in "the breast cancer awareness race." Said one breast cancer fund raiser, "I wish more companies put more money into research and weren't quite so concerned about their corporate image."

Critical Thinking Questions

1. What corporate values do you believe Avon has established with promulgating the Breast Cancer Awareness Crusade?

2. Do you think Avon is placing enough emphasis on the social motives behind its campaign, as opposed to the economic motives?

3. Do you have any ethical or moral qualms concerning the campaign? For instance, do you agree with the criticism that Avon should simply contribute money to breast cancer research without engaging in a publicity campaign? Do you believe that Avon's salespersons should use the breast cancer issue as a means to "bond" with potential consumers?

CASE (CONTINUED)

4. Does Avon's failure with its Statue of Liberty campaign reinforce the assumptions of causeploitation?

5. What is your response to the cause-related marketing prospects of AIDS research discussed in this case?

SOURCE: Information from W. Konrad, "The Problems at Avon Are More Than Skin Deep," *Business Week*, June 20, 1988, p. 49; K. Slater, "Avon to Sell Health Unit, Take a Charge," *Wall Street Journal*, January 19, 1988, p. 14; A. Rothman, "For James Preston, It's Still Avon Calling," *Wall Street Journal*, December 9, 1988, p. B12; M. H. Peak, "Avon's Calling: Now a Full-Service Resource for Women," *Management Review*, February 1, 1993, p. 30; F. Warner, "Choose Your Partners," *Mediaweek*, October 17, 1994, p. S16; N. Arnott, "Marketing with a Passion," *Sales & Marketing Management*, January 1, 1994, p. 64; F. Gibb, "Avon: Cause Marketing," *Sales & Marketing Management*, September 1, 1994, p. 85; S. L. Hwang, "Linking Products to Breast Cancer Fights Helps Firms Bond with Their Customers," *Wall Street Journal*, September 21, 1993, p. B1; R. Carter, "Avon Leads Corporate Drive against Breast Cancer," *Cincinnati Enquirer*, October 4, 1995, p. C1; and "Avon Edges Ahead in Breast Cancer Awareness Race," *Cosmetic Insiders' Report*, December 13, 1993, p. 1.

PART VI

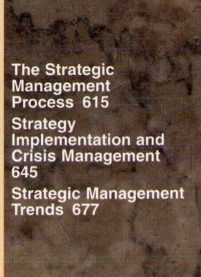

STRATEGIC MANAGEMENT

CHAPTER 20

THE STRATEGIC MANAGEMENT PROCESS

CHAPTER OUTLINE

- The Evolution of Strategic Management
- Analyzing the External and Internal Environments
- Strategy Development: Corporate Missions and Goals
- Strategy Formulation

INTRODUCTION

To understand management, we must first understand three skills managers must possess. The first, technical skills, involve "being able to perform the mechanics of a particular job." The second, human relations skills, involve "understanding people and being able to work well with them." The third, conceptual skills, involve the ability to see the "big picture" (to use a term that has become popular in the 1990s) by "understanding the relationship of the parts of a business to one another and the business as a whole."[1]

The focus of the final three chapters of this textbook is "big picture," or strategic, management. Jefferey S. Harrison and Caron H. St. John define **strategic management** as "the process through which organizations analyze and learn from their internal and external environments, establish long- and short-term goals, create strategies that are intended to help achieve established goals, and execute those strategies, all in an effort to satisfy key organizational stakeholders."[2]

For our purposes, the final concept in Harrison and St. John's definition is critical, for it expands the boundaries of management strategy beyond satisfying a few *shareholders*—the owners of the business—to satisfying the organization's and society's many *stakeholders*. This textbook is largely concerned with analysis of these stakeholders and their relationship with the business community and individual corporations. In this context, we examine how the organization operates as an integrated and interrelated whole and how the organization's values and strategies are influenced by both the internal and external environment.[3]

THE EVOLUTION OF STRATEGIC MANAGEMENT

American executives and managers have always tried to exert a certain amount of control over the business environment. But until the 1970s, their attention was focused mainly on controlling internal aspects of that environment.[4] The general assumption was that if upper management kept tight control over an efficient infrastructure, the external stakeholders would recognize a company's achievements and reward it with profits.

In the 1960s and 1970s, however, the dominance of the United States and its industries in the global market began to decline.

▼ One of the theories for the cause of this decline centered around American managers' short-sighted obsession with efficiency—completely ignoring the external environment at the expense of internal concerns.

To be truly efficient, many business theorists argue, a company has to take into account external environments as well as internal environments.

---

1. L. W. Rue and L. L. Byars, *Management: Skills and Application,* 7th ed. (Chicago: Irwin, 1995), p. 242.
2. J. S. Harrison and C. H. St. John, *Strategic Management of Organizations and Stakeholders* (St. Paul: West Publishing Company, 1994), p. 1042.
3. A. Campbell, M. Goold, and M. Alexander, "Corporate Strategy: The Quest for Parenting," *Harvard Business Review,* March–April 1995, p. 120.
4. F. Mueller, "Teams between Hierarchy and Commitment: Change Strategies and the Internal Environment," *Journal of Management Studies,* May 1994, p. 383.

Business schools began to reflect these new strategies in the 1970s with a new course called Business Policy. This course relied on case studies to introduce students to real-world business situations and challenges. The students were expected to integrate materials from functional disciplines such as finance, accounting, personnel, and operation strategy, which they learned independently, and apply this knowledge to case studies. Eventually, the American Assembly of Collegiate Schools of Business (AACSB) made Business Strategy and Policy a part of the required curriculum in accredited business schools.[5]

MANAGING UNCERTAINTY

As the stature of the strategy/policy approach to business programs began to grow in the academic world, its tenets began to take hold in the business community. The competitiveness problems of U.S. business led to a rise in the number of consulting firms hired to overhaul management strategies. The consultants in these firms adapted many of the lessons they had learned in business school to their clients, and the notion that companies needed to look outward to solve their problems gained more influence. A conference was held at the University of Pittsburgh in which fourteen research papers were commissioned to define this field of policy-driven strategy and give it direction for the future. This conference is often identified by management experts as the official birthplace of strategic management.

To its proponents, strategic management works because it is proactive rather than reactive. It became a given in many business and academic circles that companies fail as a result of change: they either fail to respond to changes in their environment or fail to create them.[6] Strategic management, with its emphasis on constant monitoring of the external environment, gives business an "ear to the ground" so it will be prepared for change. In other words, strategic management allows a company to manage uncertainty.

THE PITFALLS OF STRATEGIC MANAGEMENT

If you find the idea of managing uncertainty self-contradictory, you are not alone. Some management experts caution against relying too much on strategic management for that very reason—uncertainty is by definition unmanageable.[7] Therefore, strategic management can at times offer a false sense of security.

One business writer, Henry Mintzberg, sees strategic management as an extension of human nature: managers, along with the rest of us, feel more comfortable in situations they feel they can control (even if that control is illusory). A manager who has established long- and short-term goals and created strategies to help achieve these goals feels as though he or she is in control of the business situation. Planning boosts our confidence by making us feel more in command.

Thus, the primary pitfall of strategic management is that the plan itself becomes more important than how it applies to the external environment.

---

5. K. F. Skousen and D. P. Bertelsen, "A Look at Change in Management Education," *SAM Advanced Management Journal*, Winter 1994, p. 13.

6. P. Buhler, "Strategic Management: A Process for Supervisors Organizationwide," *Supervision*, March 1, 1994, p. 7.

7. R. Boscheck, "Competitive Advantage: Superior Offer or Unfair Dominance?" *California Management Review*, Fall 1994, p. 132.

▼ When unexpected external forces ruin what seemed to be a perfectly sound piece
of strategic management, the tendency among many managers is to blame the
situation instead of the plan.

Not only is this reasoning false—managers should always expect the unexpected—it is
also counterproductive. If a manager places the blame on "bad luck," he or she is also
unlikely to revise the initial plan to guard against the likelihood of such bad luck occurring again.

For this reason, Mintzberg stresses the importance of *vision* and *learning* in the strategic management process. A visionary approach to management offers broad outlines of a
strategy, while leaving the specific details to be worked out on a case-by-case basis.
Accordingly, "when the unexpected happens, assuming the vision is sufficiently robust,
the organization can adapt—it learns."[8] When the vision is not sufficient, managers need
to experiment and learn how to change the vision to be better prepared for environmental changes in the future. "If you have no vision, but only formal plans," warns Mintzberg,
"then every unpredicted change in the environment makes you feel like your sky is
falling."[9]

As we explore the practical aspects of strategic management in the next three chapters,
starting with the process of analyzing external and internal environments, keep Mintzberg's
warning in mind. The best strategies are those which are flexible enough to change, given
a changing business environment.

A<small>NALYZING THE</small> E<small>XTERNAL AND</small> I<small>NTERNAL</small> E<small>NVIRONMENTS</small>

According to some researchers, firms pass through four distinct stages as part of strategic
management, as dictated by increasing size, diversity, and environmental complexity:

▶ **Phase 1:** *Basic financial planning.* In this first phase, organizations focus on internal
goals such as meeting budgets and developing financial plans.
▶ **Phase 2:** *Forecast-based planning.* After solidifying initial financial health, organizations look outward to the external environment to predict trends and developments that
may affect them in the future.
▶ **Phase 3:** *Externally oriented planning.* After forecasting, organizations begin to think
strategically by devising strategies in response to changing markets and the actions of
competitors.
▶ **Phase 4:** *Strategic management.* In this final phase, organizations use infrastructural
resources to develop sustainable competitive advantages and "create the future."[10]

A firm normally first responds to its environment and then tries to control its environment. **Adaptation** is the phase in which the company is primarily reacting to its environment, while **enactment** is the phase in which the firm is concerned with controlling the
environment to make it more conducive to profit.

---

8. H. Mintzberg, *The Rise and Fall of Strategic Planning* (New York: Free Press, 1994), pp. 209–210.
9. *Ibid.*
10. F. W. Gluck, S. P. Kaufman, and A. S. Walleck, "Strategic Management for Competitive Advantage,"
Harvard Business Review, July–August 1980, pp. 154–161.

▼ **A key element in successful adaptation is understanding.**

A firm and its top management must have knowledge of the current situation in both the external and internal environments to make good decisions. To gain this knowledge, executives must take the first step in strategic management: scanning to determine the organization's strengths, weaknesses, opportunities, and threats.

STRENGTHS, WEAKNESSES, OPPORTUNITIES, AND THREATS (SWOTs)

Traditionally, a company has scanned only its business operations for strengths, weaknesses, opportunities, and threats (SWOTs). Because we take a stakeholder view of strategic management, however, we will relate SWOTs to stakeholder analysis. For example, when consumer tastes change, **opportunities**—or alternatives for improving the scope and profit of business—are opened for business in the form of new markets. As we have seen, stakeholders can offer a wide variety of opportunities for firms, from the environmental group that provides a new means to control pollution to the special interest group that influences social trends and changes the competitive landscape.

Similarly, stakeholder groups can represent **threats**, or factors that block a firm in its strategy goals. Threats can appear from special interest groups in the form of boycotts, negative publicity, or a push for restrictive government regulation. Other threats we have discussed in this textbook include workplace violence, environmental degradation, unethical employees, and inefficient corporate governance. How managers react to these threats can be just as important to the health of a corporation as how they take advantage of opportunities.

In calculating its organizational **strengths** and **weaknesses**, a company must be aware of what it does and does not do well. In many cases, a company's strength gives it a distinct advantage over its competitors. An example is Louisiana-Pacific's ability to manufacturer paper without using chlorine bleach (described in *Corporate Focus: Louisiana-Pacific Corporation*, later in this chapter). The firm lobbied the government to pass environmental legislation to limit the use of chlorine, playing to its own strengths. Conversely, a weakness, such as not having the capability to produce paper products without using chlorine, leads to a strategic disadvantage. Obviously, a company's success will be determined in large measure by how it emphasizes its strengths and compensates for its weaknesses.

Throughout this textbook, we have determined a firm's environment to be those organizations, individuals, and entities (such as the community) that are significantly influenced by or that have an impact on that firm. Also, we have divided these stakeholders into two groups—external and internal. The initial SWOT analysis concerns itself with these two groups, and we will quickly review external and internal stakeholders for the purposes of strategic management.

THE EXTERNAL ENVIRONMENT

The external environment can be divided into the **operating environment** and the **remote environment**.

The Operating Environment The operating environment consists of those stakeholders with which organizations interact on a fairly regular basis but over which they have no direct control. These stakeholders include:

1. Customers. The most important external stakeholders are customers, for a business ultimately relies on their patronage for survival. One of the earliest insights of the strategic management movement was that American industries were suffering because they were not giving enough attention to high-quality, low-cost, and efficient service—all of which consumers demanded. As we shall see in the next chapter, a key component of strategic management is the ability to predict trends in consumers' tastes.

2. Suppliers. Under some circumstances, suppliers can dramatically affect the SWOTs of a firm. When there are only a few suppliers for a raw material that is in great demand, the manufacturers that require that raw material are in a position of weakness with regard to the suppliers. When there are no substitutes for a product or service, suppliers again have the advantage. When the strength of suppliers is great, the strategic manager must give these stakeholders high priority in decision making. For example, consider construction company X, which has a contract to build an office building in Burns, Oregon. Assume there is only one supplier of glass windows in Burns—Burns Glass—and the nearest competing glass supplier is located 131 miles away in Bend, Oregon. Burns Glass is in a position of strength, and company X must be sensitive in its dealings with the glass supplier. If company X were operating in Portland, Oregon, with dozens of glass suppliers, it would not have to be as concerned with suppliers' demands.

3. Existing competitors. Of course, a company must be aware of the strategies of competitors, as the strategic management of one firm affects competing firms. In particular, individual corporations in industries experiencing slow growth or having little product differentiation are under pressure to gain customers through strategic management. Therefore, firms must be aware of the actions of their closest competitors. Accordingly, many firms engage in **competitive benchmarking**, in which they base their performance goals on the standards set by the most successful performers in their industry. (See *Managing Social Issues—Small Business/Entrepreneurial: Benchmarking.*)

4. Potential competitors and entrance barriers. A potential competitor is not necessarily a stakeholder but still must be accounted for as a threat to the firm, as new competitors may drive down prices and profits. Although it is difficult to determine when a

New computer companies may experience great difficulties in entering the communications industry due to economies of scale, capital requirements, and product differentiation.

⬚ MANAGING SOCIAL ISSUES

SMALL BUSINESS/ENTREPRENEURIAL: BENCHMARKING

Why benchmark? "When major decisions are being made, if we don't ask ourselves who else is good at this and how they handle it, we are potentially missing something very substantial," says one benchmarking expert, Robert Camp. "If you don't learn from others, how are you going to grow and improve your business?"

Why refuse to benchmark? According to a 1992 survey, the International Benchmarking Clearinghouse (IBC) found the average annual investment in the process was $1,227,754 per member, with an average cost per benchmarking study of $67,657. Most small businesses simply do not believe they can afford these kinds of costs and so dismiss the idea. But the IBC's figures represent the costs for large companies with benchmarking staffs. Less expensive benchmarking options exist for limited budgets.

Sources of Benchmarking Information

Business professors refer to benchmarking as a science, but the operator of a small business should not think of it as rocket science. Most aspects of the process can be self-taught, and a valuable primer is Camp's book, *Benchmarking.*

Before carrying out a benchmarking strategy, small businesses should check with a number of inexpensive external information services to avoid redundancies. The first step should be to access the Industrial Technology Institute (ITI) Performance Benchmarking Service database, funded by the U.S. Department of Commerce. Nearly one thousand manufacturers with fewer than five hundred employees contribute information on their production facilities to this database, and the ITI collects and tabulates forty key performance measures—from value added per employee to warranty costs as a percent of sales—for quick reference. To take part in this process, small manufacturers contact the ITI directly, complete a performance benchmarking questionnaire concerning their own processes, and receive a twenty-five-page report comparing their results with those of other companies in their industries. The cost is $495.

Firms can also receive free benchmarking reports from any of the regional manufacturing technology centers funded by the National Institute of Standards and Technology. For an annual membership fee of $6,000, companies can become members of the IBC, which (plus extra costs for specific studies) provides on-line, industry-wide access to benchmarking information.

For Critical Analysis:

In 1994, the Industrial Technology Institute of Ann Arbor, Michigan, conducted a survey in which manufacturers were asked to rank themselves within their industries. Fifty percent of the respondents placed themselves within the top 10 percent of their fields, 75 percent felt they were in the top quarter, and 98 percent placed themselves in the upper 50 percent. What do these percentages indicate about the respondents, and how does benchmarking apply to this line of thinking?

SOURCE: Information from T. B. Kinni, "Best Practices Revealed," *Industry Week,* December 5, 1994, p. 30; and T. B. Kinni, "Measuring Up," *Industry Week,* December 5, 1994, pp. 27–28.

---

specific potential competitor may become an actual competitor, a company can protect itself in general against possible new rivals with a number of entry barriers.[11] Entry barriers may involve economies of scale, capital requirements, government policy, or product differentiation.

▶ *Economies of scale* exist when it is more efficient to produce a product in large amounts at a large plant. When economies of scale exist, such as in the petroleum industry, it is

---

11. M. W. Hordes, J. A. Clancy, and J. Baddaley, "A Primer for Global Start-Ups," *Academy of Management Executive,* May 1995, p. 7.

simply too expensive for a small company to produce enough of the product to make entry into the industry worthwhile.

▶ *Capital requirements*, also known as start-up costs, are linked with economies of scale. Large capital requirements, such as those in the auto industry, can keep small companies from entering an industry.

▶ *Government policy*. As we discussed in Chapter 9, in certain cases, government regulation can be a *de facto* entry barrier.

▶ *Product differentiation*. In many cases, established firms have built up such a strong customer base over a long period of time that any potential customer would have to have enormous resources to compete. There have been, for example, relatively few successful challenges to Coca-Cola and Pepsi's dominance of the soft-drink market in the past thirty years.

5. Indirect competitors or substitutes. Managers should note, however, that although no soft-drink companies have successfully challenged Coke and Pepsi, the explosive popularity of bottled iced-tea products such as those marketed by Snapple in the early 1990s did offer customers a substitute for carbonated drinks. Firms must be aware of indirect competitors and use forecasting to determine the possibility of threats. Indirect competitors can also highlight opportunities, however, as both Coca-Cola and Pepsi used their distribution strength to produce their own iced-tea products.

Other stakeholders that make up the operating environment include government agencies and administrators, politicians, local communities, unions, and activist or special interest groups. (For an overview of the various stakeholder groups and their relevance to strategic management, see *Exhibit 20–1.*)

The Remote Environment When the Federal Reserve Board (the Fed) raised interest rates in 1994, Orange County had to pay higher interest rates on its loans than it was earning on its investments. The county treasurer's office and Merrill Lynch had no control over the Fed's actions and could only react to a change in the remote environment. Even more so than with the operating environment, the remote environment is basically free from the influence of any individual business entity. In fact, a corporation is often at the mercy of social issues, the global economy, legal and political developments, and technological innovation. Over the course of this textbook, we have seen many cases in which legal or social pressures force business to react to issues such as pollution, AIDS, and declining educational quality. Global economic factors such as foreign exchange rates, inflation, and trade imbalances have had major effects on the profitability of multinational and domestic companies. Technological innovations can change the face of an industry practically overnight, as was the case with Microsoft's Windows 95 and the computer industry in the mid-1990s.

THE INTERNAL ENVIRONMENT

There are three key overlapping groups in the internal environment—managers, owners, and employees. Chapter 12 was dedicated to analysis of owner stakeholders, and Chapters 13 and 14 addressed the issue of employee stakeholders. Let us now turn to manager stakeholders and examine their primary role in the internal environment: that of decision maker.

Managers in the Strategic Management Process As the decision makers, managers generally determine the path a firm takes in its strategic operations. Often, a manager

▼ **EXHIBIT 20–1　Stakeholders and Strategic Management**

Stakeholder	Needs/Demands	Strategies for Dealing with Demands	Common Goals	Strategies for Meeting Common Goals
Customers	Excellent products and services, product safety and low prices, many choices, truth in advertising	Compliance within rational limits, recognition of trade-offs, development of new customers and markets, fostering of demand	Excellent products and services, product safety	Direct contact with customers and assimilation of customer feedback through surveys and response cards, involvement of customers with design teams and product testing
Competitors	Truth in advertising and all public communications, a profitable share of the market, acceptable levels of competition/price cutting	Competitive tactics such as product and service differentiation, benchmarking, mergers	Continued growth of industry demand, less government regulation, new products and services, low cost of supplies and labor	*Keirestu* (see page 300), joint ventures, collective lobbying efforts, industry-wide panels to deal with labor problems, mergers
Government Agencies/ Administrators	The public good, including employment, safe workplace and products, preservation of environment, philanthropy; tax revenues; favorable trade conditions	Formation of department to deal with legal, tax, and government regulatory issues; individual and collective lobbying efforts; philanthropic giving to charitable and educational oganizations; self-regulation; proactive environmental programs; political action committees (PACs)	Favorable environment for conducting domestic and international trade, stable market and healthy economy, advancement of knowledge through research, mutually beneficial rules and regulations	Joint government/ business consortia on trade and competitiveness, jointly sponsored research programs, joint ventures on social problems such as illiteracy and crime, use of government resources such as the Small Business Administration, joint panels on product and workplace safety
Local Communities	Employment, strong local economy, philanthropy and taxes, preservation of the environment	Involvement in community service and politics, purchase of local supplies and services, employment of local workers, donations to local charities	Well-trained work force and livable community	Social partnerships such as task forces to work on employment issues, urban renewal efforts, employee training programs, employment of community members such as persons with disabilities

(Continued)

▼ **EXHIBIT 20–1** *continued*

Stakeholder	Needs/Demands	Strategies for Dealing with Demands	Common Goals	Strategies for Meeting Common Goals
Activist Groups	Different with each group, from protection of civil liberties to protection of the environment	Conformance within rational boundaries, not sacrificing other goals for activist issues; seeking counsel when making decisions; public relations efforts to offset negative publicity; financial donations	Different with each group, from protection of civil liberties to protection of the environment	Joint research projects and consortia, appointment of activist group members to board of directors
Unions/Employees	Higher wages and better benefits, workplace safety, job security, fair treatment	Professional union negotiators; labor leaders on board of directors; in some cases, elimination of labor union	Motivated and productive work force, growth in revenues, workplace safety	Mutually satisfactory (win-win) labor contracts, contract clauses that link pay to performance, profit sharing, joint committees on safety and other issues
Shareholder Owners	Good corporate governance that results in positive return on investment	Successful balance of short-term goals of investors with needs and demands of other stakeholder groups, trade-offs between social goals and fiscal responsibilities	A profitable business	High-quality management decisions leading to high profits and low risk

SOURCE: Adapted from J. S. Harrison and C. H. St. John, *Strategic Management of Organizations and Stakeholders* (St. Paul: West Publishing Company, 1994), pp. 64–66.

makes a decision based on his or her personal analysis of a situation. From time to time, a crisis or some other environmental factor, such as a sharp decrease in sales, makes the need for a decision obvious. In the stakeholder analysis of strategic management, we know there is another spur to decision making—pressure from one or more groups of stakeholders.

Once a need for action has been established, the manager must clearly define the problem he or she is about to address. In this process, the manager often turns to internal stakeholders such as other managers or the CEO for help. External stakeholders such as community groups are also contacted at times for advice. The larger the decision—that is, the more resources involved—the more likely a manager is to consult with internal or external stakeholders.

Cognitive Bias in Decision Making Earlier, we discussed how a manager's ethical makeup affects his or her decisions. Remember, each individual manager's cognitive base, consisting of his or her mental abilities, knowledge, and ethical makeup, is the platform on which decisions are built. Because, like everyone else, they suffer from cognitive overload—too much information and too many stimuli—managers often practice selective perception in making decisions. That is, they choose only certain inputs on which to base a decision. This selective process is known as **cognitive bias**—the tendency of all managers to lean toward decisions based on subjective rather than objective opinion.

Cognitive bias does not necessarily result in poor decision making, as a bias may come from a reasonable assumption. But it is doubtful that cognitive bias will lead to effective decision making in the long run. In many cases, cognitive bias is based on past experiences, which may not hold up in a changing decision-making environment. Furthermore, biases tend to reduce a manager's decision-making efforts; the bias provides an easy answer, and the manager usually does not search for better solutions. (See *Exhibit 20–2* on page 626 for common forms of cognitive bias in strategic decision making.)

INFORMATION MANAGEMENT

One way to reduce the chance of cognitive overload is to delegate responsibility for information management, the process of scanning the operating and remote environments. To a certain extent, the delegation occurs naturally within a corporation. Marketing departments track consumer tastes; sales departments manage direct interaction with customers; human resource departments deal with employee rights issues and stay informed about union activities; and public relations departments manage media relations, special interest groups, and other representatives of the general public. The question for executives is: How can we assimilate this wealth of information and use it in the best interests of the corporation?

Environmental Scanning Personnel Many companies are deciding that stakeholder analysis has become sufficiently important to warrant its own high-level manager.[12] Sometimes called the **chief information officer (CIO)**, this executive helps "determine what information is critical for management decision making, what kinds of information-based links to customers and suppliers can and should be forged, and how information technology can be incorporated into marketing, manufacturing, and virtually every other facet of the company."[13]

Another reaction to the need for information management is the formation of environmental scanning units. These small groups of employees are held responsible for specific stakeholder analysis roles. One type of environmental scanning unit, a *public-policy* scanning unit, studies the environment for emerging issues that may signal widespread shifts. For example, a public-policy team might determine to what extent greater public scrutiny of sexual harassment should dictate a firm's own policy on the issue. In contrast, a *function-oriented* scanning unit concentrates on the activities of a specific function of the corporation, such as marketing or product development. For example, technologists predict that the average viewer will have a choice of more than five hundred television channels in the first decade of the next century. A function-oriented marketing team would examine the advertising possibilities and limitations of such a situation.

Business Intelligence All the information gathered from scanning and analyzing the environment can be classified as a firm's collective business intelligence.[14]

---

12. A. F. Hagen and S. G. Amin, "Corporate Executive and Environmental Scanning Activities: An Empirical Investigation," *SAM Advanced Management Journal*, Spring 1995, p. 41.
13. A. B. Glou, "Do You Need a CIO?" *Inc.*, September 12, 1995, p. 23.
14. Harrison and St. John, *op. cit.*, p. 104.

▼ **EXHIBIT 20–2** **Common Forms of Cognitive Bias in Strategic Decision Making**

Cognitive Bias	Behavior
1. Hindsight	When managers recall earlier decisions, their recollection is distorted by knowledge of the end result. Using hindsight, a manager may accept a certain strategy because it worked once in the past and disregard another strategy because it did not. This bias can reduce the consideration of alternatives in some situations and prevent learning in others.
2. Illusion of control	Managers often feel they have a greater measure of control over a situation than they do. For example, a manager might believe he or she knows how a certain employee will act in a given situation, which may not be the case.
3. Pygmalion effect	Managers are biased by their expectations. If a manager expects a certain product to sell at high levels, he or she is more likely to interpret sales figures favorably.
4. Causal attribution	Managers necessarily assign responsibility for the outcome of strategies or decisions. A manager may assign such responsibility to the wrong set of factors. For example, a manager may blame poor sales of a product on the advertising department instead of poor product design.
5. Stereotyping	Managers may assign characteristics to individuals because of personal bias. For example, a manager may think that because all Chinese are hard workers, a particular Chinese employee will necessarily be a hard worker. Negative stereotyping is common and, of course, discriminatory.
6. Perceptual defense	If managers find information unsatisfactory or threatening, they tend to alter their perception of it. For example, if a manager receives a report from an employee detailing losses in the company's German division, the manager may blame the individual who furnished the report rather than examining the factors behind the poor business performance.
7. Escalating commitment	Once a manager has made a commitment to a strategy, he or she tends to be hesitant to drop or change it. Even if a parts plant is proving unprofitable, the manager who decided to build the plant might decide to commit more resources to it rather than sell it off, though the latter decision might be in the best interests of the organization.

SOURCE: Adapted from J. S. Harrison and C. H. St. John, *Strategic Management of Organizations and Stakeholders* (St. Paul: West Publishing Company, 1994), p. 81.

▼ Every firm has some level of business intelligence, but just how "smart" a firm becomes depends wholly on the resources it is willing to devote to stakeholder analysis.

Business intelligence units in an organization act primarily as information sources to support the strategic management processes of the organization. The cliché "knowledge is power" applies to strategic management, and the more knowledge a company possesses, the more power it will have to make appropriate decisions. Business intelligence alone, however, does not ensure a healthy strategic management process. An effective strategy development process is needed to channel knowledge in the proper direction.

STRATEGY DEVELOPMENT: CORPORATE MISSIONS AND GOALS

In a sense, the move toward strategic management is a move toward a more aggressive style of strategy development. The traditional process for developing strategy relies heavily on analysis of SWOTs and an approach that is called **environmental determinism.** Environmental determinism is environmentally derived and necessarily reactive (in contrast to strategic choice, which is managerially derived and proactive). Using environmental determinism, managers formulate strategy by choosing the path that will best fit environmental, technical, and human forces and resources at any particular time. This traditional view of development also lends itself to **deliberate strategy**, in which managers respond to changes in the internal and external environment by pursuing a preconceived strategic course.

Nobody can predict *all* of the environmental changes that will affect a business, however, and it is foolhardy to make decisions based on general strategies that may not fit a specific challenge. Strategic management finds its strength in the realization that strategy development is not an exact science. Going back to Mintzberg's idea of vision and learning, strategic management lends itself to **emergent strategy**, in which managers learn what to do in a certain situation by trial and error.[15]

The consensus among managerial experts is that it is best to combine a degree of emergent strategy with a degree of deliberate strategy. In other words, make plans, but be flexible enough to abandon them if the situation calls for innovation.

A SENSE OF MISSION

Even emergent strategy must be enacted within certain boundaries. The firm's missions and goals create these boundaries. A firm's sense of mission encompasses both the external and the internal environments.

▼   **The company's mission should provide a clear purpose for executives, managers, and employees and communicate to external stakeholders such as consumers and special interest groups the underlying values of an organization.**

A company's mission should also reflect the constant feedback that business intelligence can provide on the changing needs and wants of internal and external stakeholders.

The Ashridge Mission Model   After intensive research on various management strategies, the Ashridge Strategic Management Centre in London, England, identified four key elements of an effective corporate mission: purpose, strategy, values, and behavior.

1. Purpose. For whose benefit does the organization exist? Answering this question is the central issue in identifying the organization's purpose. The purpose of a company could be to make the highest possible profits for shareholders, to create interesting and fulfilling employment for its workers, and/or to provide its customers with high-quality and long-lasting products.

The idea of purpose can lend itself to a certain amount of idealism on the part of a corporation. The Japanese company Matsushita Electric has the philosophy: "The happiness of man is built on material affluence and mental stability. To serve the foundation of happiness through making man's life affluent with an inexpensive and inexhaustible supply of necessities, like water flowing from a tap, is the duty of the manufacturer. Profit comes in compensation for contribution to society." The purpose statement of the pharmaceutical company Merck is briefer but just as grand: "We are in the business of preserving and

---

15. Harrison and St. John, *op. cit.*, p. 114.

improving life."[16] We may at first wonder what such lofty goals have to do with operating a business, but in fact they fit well into strategic management. Both Matsushita and Merck have stated the purpose of benefiting external stakeholders—consumers, the community, society in general—with their products and have also reasserted their capitalist purpose through terms such as *profit* and *business*. These purposes may seem broad, even vague, but they do provide a framework in which strategy can be learned and developed.

2. Strategy. The strategy aspect of the Ashridge Mission Model relates to how a firm will execute its purpose in competition with other organizations. If, for example, a rug-cleaning company has a strategy based on service, it may produce a statement that says the company will clean any rug within a given geographical area within forty-eight hours of receiving a job order. (As we will see later in this chapter, strategic management lends itself to fairly specific strategy formulations.)

3. Values. The values aspect of the model addresses how a firm will achieve its purposes for the benefit of its internal stakeholders. In many cases, an organization attracts employees not because of its strategies, goals, or product but because of its culture. A clear definition of values gives managers and employees a sense not of what their business is but of how their business will be undertaken.

4. Behavior. This final aspect of the mission model is in a sense the end product of the other three. Purpose, strategy, and values combine to dictate the behavior of an organization's work force. The ultimate mission of strategic management should be to align purpose and strategy based on a set of values concerning treatment of the environment that can be shared by internal stakeholders—in other words, to give employees at every level of the organization a set of shared values to guide their behavior. For example, the Scottish engineering company BBA has delineated a set of behavior standards that strongly complement its purpose, strategy, and values. These standards include the following:

- ▶ "Budgets are personal commitments made by management to their superiors, subordinates, shareholders, and their self-respect."
- ▶ "The Victorian work ethic is not an antique."
- ▶ "Go home tired."[17]

These statements give a clear picture of the behavior expected from BBA's employees.

MISSION STATEMENTS AND GOALS

We have been discussing organizations' *sense* of mission, but a shared sense of mission may be too vague to serve as the basis for strategy. Consequently, many businesses provide mission statements and operating goals as benchmarks in the strategic management process.[18]

Mission Statements Mission statements have been called the "operational, ethical, and financial guiding lights of companies." At worst, a mission statement is merely a motto or a slogan; at best, the statement articulates "the goals, dreams, behavior, culture, and strategies" of a company "more than any other document."[19]

16. A. Campbell, "The Power of Mission: Aligning Strategy and Culture," *Planning Review*, September 1, 1992, p. 10.

17. Campbell, *op. cit.*

18. P. Drucker, "The Theory of Business," *Harvard Business Review*, September–October 1994, p. 11.

19. P. Jones and L. Kahaner, *Say It and Live It: The 50 Corporate Mission Statements That Hit the Mark* (New York: Currency/Doubleday, 1995), p. ix.

Though the basic goal of corporations is to make a profit, mission statements usually concentrate on the culture of a particular company. In J. M. Smucker Company's *Basic Beliefs*, for example, financial considerations are not explicitly mentioned until well into the document. (See *Exhibit 20–3* on page 630.) Tim Smucker, chairman of the company, says the values inherent in this mission statement have been handed down from his great-grandfather J. M. Smucker, who believed that "whatsoever a man soweth, that shall he also reap." It follows that the goals spelled out under "quality" do not refer only to products and manufacturing but to marketing efforts, personnel, and "our relationships with each other." Though he thinks it would profit the company's bottom line, Smucker refuses to advertise on television game shows or soap operas, because he does not find them in keeping with the high quality of the organization's culture: "Quality comes first. Sales growth and earnings will follow."[20]

Mission statements are not, however, above the fray of stakeholder conflict. A company cannot support a worthy goal in a mission statement and expect to escape the wrath of interest groups or employees if the statement is not carried out to the letter. J. M. Smucker's *Basic Beliefs* promise that the company "will be fair with our employees and maintain an environment that encourages personal responsibility." This may sound harmless, but under certain circumstances, it could be seen as constituting a contractual obligation on the company's part. In some cases, a jury or judge will have to decide how binding a mission statement is. (See *Company Focus: Johnson & Johnson* on page 631.)

Operating Goals Whereas a mission statement provides broad guidelines, **operating goals** are more specific. They usually refer to precise objectives that are to be met at different levels of the organization. Furthermore, whereas mission statements are "for the ages," operating goals usually are to be met within a certain time period.

---

20. *Ibid.*, pp. 209–211.

▼ **EXHIBIT 20–3** **J. M. Smucker Company's** *Basic Beliefs*

Basic Beliefs are an expression of the Company's values and principles that guide strategic behavior and direction. The Basic Beliefs are deeply rooted in the philosophy and heritage of the Company's founder.

In 1897, the Smucker Company was formed by a dedicated, honest, forward looking businessman, J. M. Smucker. Because he made a quality product, sold it at a fair price, and followed sound policies, this Company prospered. Today, we who inherit the Smucker name and the Smucker tradition of successful business operations base present policies on these time-honored principles. We interpret them in terms of modern corporate thinking, to be the guideposts of our operations. They are as follows:

Quality

Quality applies to our products, our manufacturing methods, our marketing efforts, our people, and our relationships with each other. We will only produce and sell products that enhance quality of life and well-being. These will be the highest quality products offered in our respective markets because Smucker's growth and business success have been built on quality. We will continuously look for ways to achieve daily improvements that will, over time, result in consistently superior products and performance. At Smucker's, quality comes first. Sales growth and earnings will follow.

People

We will be fair with our employees and maintain an environment that encourages personal responsibility. In return, we expect our employees to be responsible for not only their individual jobs, but for the Company as a whole. We will seek employees who are committed to preserving and enhancing the values and principles inherent in our Basic Beliefs through their own actions. We firmly believe that:

- Highest quality people produce the highest quality products and service.
- Highest business ethics require the highest personal ethics.
- Responsible people produce exceptional results.

Ethics

The same, strong ethical values on which our company was founded and has grown are ingrained in our management team today. This style of management is the standard by which we conduct our business, as well as ourselves. We accept nothing less regardless of the circumstances. Therefore, we will maintain the highest standards of ethics with our shareholders, customers, suppliers, employees, and communities where we work.

Growth

Along with day-to-day operations, we are also concerned with the potential of our Company. Growing is reaching for that potential whether it be in the development of new products and new markets, the discovery of new manufacturing or management techniques, or the personal growth and development of our people and their ideas. We are committed to a strong balanced growth that will protect or enhance our consumer franchise within prudent financial parameters. We want to provide a fair return for our stockholders on their investment in us.

Independence

We have a strong commitment to stewardship of the Smucker name and heritage. We remain an independent company because of our desire and motivation to control our own direction and succeed on our own. We strive to be an example of a company which is successful by operating under these Beliefs within the free enterprise system.

These Basic Beliefs regarding quality, people, ethics, growth, and independence have served as a strong foundation in our history. They will continue to be the basis for future strategy, plans, and achievements.

SOURCE: J. M. Smucker Company.

Johnson&Johnson

COMPANY FOCUS: JOHNSON & JOHNSON
READING INTO A MISSION STATEMENT

A criticism of mission statements is that they are vague, bland documents filled with buzzwords such as *empowerment* and *mentoring*. One author, researching a book on mission statements, said he read almost a thousand corporate creeds and only smiled once—when a monopoly utility expressed its desire to be a "utility of choice." Unintended irony aside, critics say mission statements can be summed up in one word: boring. Johnson & Johnson (J&J), however, may have wished its mission statement had been a bit more vague after being hit with a wrongful termination suit because of it.

Tripodi's Complaint

Dr. Daniel Tripodi spent five years as director of biotechnology for J&J before transferring in 1988 to a subsidiary, Therakos, Inc., in West Chester, New Jersey, for a two-year post as vice president for research and development of a new product, Centrinet. The device performs a process called photopheresis that exposes a patient's white blood cell samples to ultraviolet light before returning the blood into the patient. The intent is that the treated cells will induce remission of cancers, infections, and autoimmune diseases.

Tripodi wanted to conduct clinical trials for Centrinet before seeking its approval by the U.S. Food and Drug Administration (FDA). The existing test results did not convince Tripodi that the device was entirely safe. Therakos's president, John MacLean, disagreed. After Tripodi went to MacLean's superiors with his concerns about sending "inadequate and misleading" test results to the FDA, McLean fired him.

The Jury's Decision

In a $3.2 million wrongful termination lawsuit, Tripodi highlighted two sections of J&J's fifty-one-year-old corporate mission statement. One section asserts that employees "must feel free to make suggestions and complaints," and the other says they "must have a sense of security in their jobs." Tripodi and his lawyer contended that the credo is a contract that protected him from termination under the circumstances presented. J&J's defense team said the company fired the doctor because he sowed dissension and missed deadlines, and J&J's lawyers asserted that the corporate mission statement was a philosophy, not a binding contract.

Given the contents of the mission statement, in 1994, a jury awarded Tripodi $434,000 on the ground that J&J had improperly terminated him.

The New Bottom Line

Three months later, a federal judge set aside the jury verdict. The judge ruled that a mission statement lists "general policies or goals" that are "aspirational rather than contractual." Nonetheless, some employment lawyers have said that J&J's corporate credo was a wrongful termination lawsuit waiting to happen. In today's litigious society, corporations must make sure that their mission statements reflect the organization's overall culture without making what could be construed as specific promises about employment terms or other subjects.

SOURCE: Information from A. Farnham, "Brushing Up Your Vision Thing," *Fortune*, May 1, 1995, p. 129; J. George, "Jury Awards Doctor $430,000; Finds His Firing Was Unjustified," *Philadelphia Business Journal*, December 9, 1994, p. 7; "J&J: Tripped by Its Own Credo," *Business Week*, November 21, 1994, p. 6; and J. Weber, "Corporate Credos: Vows That Aren't," *Business Week*, February 20, 1995, p. 8.

There are two primary approaches to goal setting: bottom up and top down. "Bottom" and "top" refer to the basic levels that make up the decision-making structure of an organization. These levels are (1) the corporate level, in which decisions are made on what business areas the organization will enter; (2) the business level, in which decisions focus on how to compete in those areas; and (3) the functional level, in which decisions are made on how an organization's different functional areas should work together. In the **bottom-up approach**, the executives in functional areas establish goals, which then form the basis for the business-level goals, which are in turn summed up to form corporate-level goals. In the **top-down approach**, the ideas flow in the opposite direction, with corporate-level goals being passed down to the business level and then the functional level.

The recent trend in management circles has been to discredit the command-and-control aspects of the top-down approach in favor of the empowerment and cooperation inherent in the bottom-up style. Success stories such as that of the motorcycle manufacturer Harley Davidson (H-D) certainly support this trend.

After losing significant market share in the 1970s to higher-quality, lower-cost Japanese motorcycles, H-D adjusted its operating goals to respond to consumer demand. In spite of the rebellious image associated with motorcycle riders, H-D found that its average owner was male, married, and thirty-eight years old with a college or technical school degree and an annual salary of $42,700. Furthermore, a Harley rider was concerned, almost obsessively, with quality. The company tightened its quality control to the extent that, in 1992, one buyer was told his motorcycle would be delivered late because its gas tank had to be repainted six times before its color and sheen were acceptable. H-D also sponsors the 200,000-member Harley Owners Group (HOG) and holds a number of annual HOG events that celebrate the Harley culture. The events augment a close-to-the-customer marketing philosophy by creating opportunities for direct customer feedback.

Furthermore, H-D has instituted a popular system of employee empowerment that uses rewards. Once a year, an employee may purchase a motorcycle, pay for it, turn in the receipt, and be reimbursed for 20 percent of the bill. The result is that any employee, from line worker to executive manager, can drive and test the product for however long he or she pleases, sell it, and then buy another. Employees consider this the gemstone of their benefits package, and the company gains a built-in quality control system based on personal ownership.[21] The company's motorcycle segment has been producing at full capacity since the mid-1980s, with sales reaching $427 million by the third quarter of 1995.[22]

The Management of Operating Goals In a sense, operating goals are the building blocks with which the ideas found in the mission statement are constructed. Whereas a mission statement can provide internal stakeholders with ideals that crystallize the organization's values, operating goals provide specific guidance. In this context, Harrison and St. John believe operating goals should have the following characteristics:[23]

1. They are realistic. Employees know their own limits. If goals are set too high, employees tend to become discouraged before even beginning a task, and results suffer.

2. They are high enough to be motivating. At the same time, goals must be set high enough to challenge employees. If goals are set too low, they will be achieved quickly and employees may pursue their own interests on company time.

---

21. H. Allen, "Sweet Ride to Success," *Corporate Report Wisconsin*, December 1, 1993.
22. *Wall Street Journal*, October 11, 1995, p. B6.
23. Harrison and St. John, *op. cit.*, pp. 131–132.

3. They are specific. Managers should divide broad goals into narrower goals, with the process repeating itself through specific departments, units, and individuals. Goals that do not set forth specific responsibilities are less likely to be met effectively.

4. They are measurable. Similarly, a goal that is unmeasurable will be difficult to meet. "The plant will be productive" is not a measurable goal; "the plant will produce one thousand carburetors a day" is. Furthermore, once measurable goals are met, they can be raised.

5. They are understood by all affected employees. Obviously, an unclear goal is less likely to be met than one that is readily understood. Effective communication is critical.

6. They cover a specific time period. The pressure of time limits can provide a focus for employees' efforts, whereas an open-ended operational strategy may lead to poor focus. It should be remembered, however, that the line between constructive pressure and too much pressure, leading to stress, is thin.

7. They are set through a participative process. All the above steps may be ineffective if the managers and employees involved in meeting the goals are not involved in setting them. Participation often leads to commitment.

8. Continual feedback is part of the process. If goals are set and then forgotten, the process will quickly break down. Both positive and negative sanctions should reinforce the goal-setting process.

STRATEGY FORMULATION

Once a mission has been decided on and operating goals have been set, a plan of action is needed to move the organization toward those specific goals and ultimately toward the overall mission.[24] This plan of action is strategy, and next we look at strategy formulation on two different levels: the corporate level and the business level.

CORPORATE-LEVEL STRATEGY FORMULATION

In Chapter 10, we discussed some of the processes that firms employ as they engage in **corporate-level strategy formulation,** such as mergers, takeovers, and joint ventures. At this point, we concentrate on the content of corporate-level strategies and the decisions high-level managers must make regarding which areas of business the corporation will enter. (See the *Case—The Corporate-Level Strategy of Toys "Я" Us*—at the end of this chapter.)

As shown in *Exhibit 20–4* on page 634, internal and external stakeholders and the remote environment play an important role in corporate-level strategy formulation.

▼ Corporate-level managers should not only be aware of the concerns of stakeholders but should encourage the suggestions of customers, unions, special interest groups, and other stakeholder groups.

Keeping in mind the importance of environment, corporate missions, and corporate goals, we next examine three broad corporate-level strategies: concentration, vertical integration, and diversification.[25]

---

24. E. K. Valentin, "Anatomy of a Fatal Business Strategy," *Journal of Management Studies,* May 1994, p. 359.
25. Harrison and St. John, *op. cit.,* pp. 181–194.

▼ **EXHIBIT 20–4 Influences on Corporate-Level Strategy**

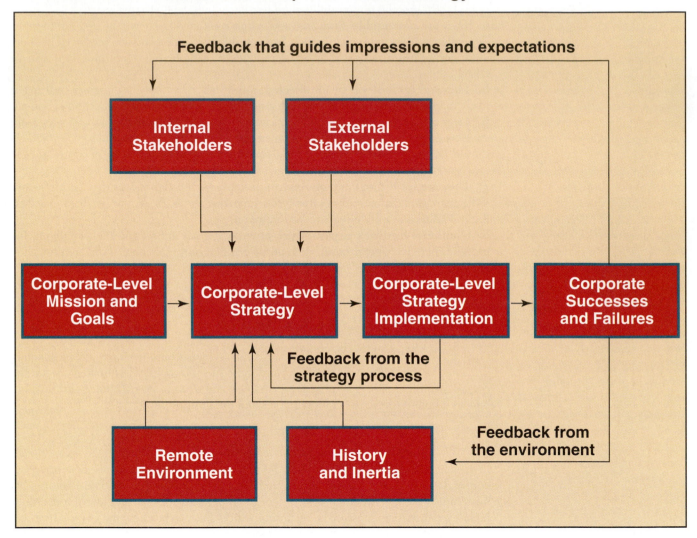

SOURCE: J. S. Harrison and C. H. St. John, *Strategic Management of Organizations and Stakeholders* (St. Paul: West Publishing Company, 1994), p. 176.

Concentration The simplest corporate-level strategy is **concentration,** which is followed by major corporations from Pizza Hut (owned by PepsiCo) to American Airlines to McDonald's. Using concentration strategy, a firm develops a single product or small group of products in a specific market, and all the resources of the firm are concentrated in that area. The benefits of this approach are readily apparent. Because top executives and managers are dealing with a specialized product or service, they should have in-depth knowledge of that product or service, which reduces the possibility of strategic error. By concentrating on doing one thing well, a firm has a better chance of creating a sustainable competitive advantage in that field. Specialization also means the firm is dealing with a narrowed scope of internal and external stakeholders, lessening the chances for misunderstanding between the firm and its stakeholders.

If the benefits of concentration strategy are apparent, so are its shortcomings. By concentrating all the firm's resources in one area, the firm is vulnerable to the possibility of a hostile environment. The airline industry is a good example, as major carriers such as Pan American and Eastern failed to survive the turbulence that followed deregulation. Technological innovation also poses a threat. If the principal product of a company becomes obsolete, the company will have to turn to other strategies to survive. This threat is obviously greater to Apple Computers than to McDonald's, however.

Vertical Integration To ensure against the weaknesses inherent in concentration strategy, many companies use vertical integration to expand their core business forward or backward in the industry supply chain.[26] Although vertical integration can raise questions of competitive fairness (see Chapter 12), many firms employ the strategy to solidify business operations.

A company decides whether to vertically integrate by comparing the cost of purchasing a product or service on the open market with the cost of manufacturing the product or providing the service itself. If a firm can purchase the needed goods and services from an outside source without allocating an inordinate amount of financial and personnel resources, then the firm should do so. If those costs become too high, however, vertical integration is desirable. An electric utility may decide that it will be better off if it buys a coal company to provide its generators with fuel. In contrast, a car manufacturer may decide it is better to buy its spark plugs from an outside source.

Diversification The ultimate defense against "putting all your eggs in one basket," from a corporate-level strategy point of view, is **diversification**, or becoming involved in a variety of business interests across one or more industries. The primary benefit of diversification is risk reduction, as a firm's resources are spread out over a number of dissimilar businesses. Corporations also use diversification to generate cash in one area for use in another. For example, Microsoft's core business was originally computer operating systems. Then the company diversified into business application software, followed by a move into consumer software. Later, Microsoft diversified into services related to the Internet.

BUSINESS-LEVEL STRATEGY FORMULATION

Once a corporate-level strategy has been decided on, managers move to the next step: **business-level strategy formulation**, which focuses on how a business will compete in its chosen field or product market.[27] (For an example of business-level strategy decisions, see *Company Focus: Apple Computers* on page 636.) Once Sears, Roebuck and Company had decided to enter the highly competitive credit-card industry with the Discover Card, it had to formulate a business-level strategy to compete with American Express, MasterCard, Visa, and the other credit-card companies.

The Value Discipline Approach to Business-Level Strategy Formulation It would be impossible to outline the perfect business-level strategy, for every situation has its own unique opportunities and pitfalls.[28] Management consultants Michael Tracy and Fred Wiersema, however, believe they have established a generic business-level strategy based on *value disciplines*—always focusing on giving better value to the customer.[29]

26. R. A. D'Aveni and D. J. Ravenscraft, "Economies of Integration versus Bureaucracy Costs: Does Vertical Integration Improve Performance?" *Academy of Management Journal*, October 1994, p. 1167.
27. W. Q. Judge, Jr., and H. Krishnan, "An Empirical Investigation of the Scope of a Firm's Enterprise Strategy," *Business and Society*, August 1994, p. 167.
28. Drucker, *op. cit.*
29. M. Tracy and F. Wiersema, "How Market Leaders Keep Their Edge," *Fortune*, February 6, 1995, pp. 88–98.

COMPANY FOCUS: APPLE COMPUTERS
APPLE'S BUSINESS-LEVEL STRATEGY

Ever since Apple Computers' beginnings in 1976, the company's business-level strategy was to stay one step ahead of the competition in innovation and user friendliness. When pushed by other manufacturers, Apple responded. In the mid-1980s, IBM captured 90 percent of the market with its own personal computer. Apple answered with the successful Macintosh model. But as 1990 came to an end, the ground-breaking company found itself in deep financial trouble. Apple's market share had dropped to well under 10 percent, and company executives struggled to formulate a strategy for survival.

A Changing Market Environment

In 1986, Apple made the decision to deemphasize its personal computers and concentrate on the growing market for office systems. This led the company to build more powerful, and more expensive, models, ranging up to the $10,000 Macintosh IIFX. Initially, the strategy proved successful, as the high-end, high-margin products drove sales from $1.9 billion in 1986 to $5.3 billion in 1989.

But by the winter of 1990, the personal computer industry had dramatically changed, leaving Apple with a worldwide market share of only 7.3 percent. Manufacturers of IBM–compatible units, which account for almost 90 percent of global sales of PCs, struggled with each other in a price war. While good news for consumers, it was disastrous for Apple, which continued to produce its high-end Macintoshes. The price differential made Apple's financial woes inevitable—a Mac with color monitor, significant memory, and hard disk then cost $5,000, as much as two of the IBM–compatible machines. Individuals, schools, and small businesses began deserting Macs for the cheaper

computers, and even large businesses complained that the product was too expensive. Furthermore, Apple would not allow Mac "clones" to use its resident software, keeping a monopoly (and supposedly bigger profits) for itself.

Apple's Low-Cost Line

Because Apple's corporate culture had always sacrificed cost to creativity and innovation, the company would have to change its strategy drastically to compete in the new personal computer market. As it had no choice, that is exactly what it did. In the fall of 1990, the company announced three inexpensive new product lines, with prices ranging from one-fifth to one-half the prices of previous models. The company was betting that a higher volume of sales would offset lower profit margins, a 180-degree shift in strategy. To reach a wider range of customers, Apple signed an agreement with Sears to sell its products at the retail giant's office centers. The company's new advertising campaign noted, "What was affordable by the few becomes available for the many."

The New Bottom Line

Apple built its reputation and its bottom line on a business-level strategy that emphasized high quality, user friendliness, and leading-edge technology. Changes in Apple's external environment, along with its own decision not to license clones, however, resulted in a significantly lower market share. Hard market reality led the company to adjust its traditional strategy to include a lower-priced line of computers and, in 1995, to allow some cloning of its product.

SOURCE: Information from B. Freedman, "Apple to Sell Macs through Sears Stores," *PC Week*, April 13, 1992, p. 149; C. Humphrey, "Cultural Changes Needed to Make Apple's New Strategy Work," *PC Week*, October 22, 1990, p. 155; J. S Harrison and C. H. St. John, *Strategic Management of Organizations and Stakeholders* (St. Paul: West Publishing Company, 1994), p. 142; and B. R. Schlender, "Yet Another Strategy for Apple," *Fortune*, October 22, 1990, pp. 81–87.

Tracy and Wiersema urge firms to begin their business-level strategy formulation by recognizing one basic characteristic of customer stakeholders: they want more of the things they value. "If they value low cost, they want it lower. If they value convenience or speed when they buy, they want it easier or faster. If they want state-of-the-art design, they want to see that art pushed forward. If they need expert advice, they want companies to give them more depth, more time, and more of a feeling that they're the only customer."

By raising the level of value that it offers customers, a firm can also place pressure on its competitors to match the changes or be left behind. Tracy and Wiersema warn, however, that a firm cannot be all things to all consumers and may go bankrupt trying. A firm is better served by concentrating on a specific value discipline on which to stake its reputation for the long term. Tracy and Wiersema identify three distinct value disciplines that consumers respond to and offer them as goals for a firm's business-level strategy formulation. They are operational excellence, product leadership, and customer intimacy.

1. Operational excellence. Companies that focus on operational excellence are not product or service innovators, but they do offer a combination of quality, price, and ease of purchase. They offer consumers a simple yet effective guaranty of low-price, hassle-free shopping. In recent years, PriceCostco, the chain of warehouse club stores, has been extremely successful stressing operational excellence. A PriceCostco outlet does not offer a particularly wide variety of products—only 3,500 items, versus 50,000 or more in competing department stores. But the company's rigorous process of evaluating leading brands essentially promises the consumer that the best buying choice has already been made. The specificity of brands allows PriceCostco to buy its products in larger quantities and at lower costs—savings that are passed on to the consumer. The company also has a computerized product movement system that tracks how well various items sell, and these data are used to optimize floor space usage. For the consumer, PriceCostco has created an almost hassle-free shopping experience at prices that are often very low.

2. Product leadership. Companies that concentrate on product leadership aim to offer their customers the best product on the market. Though such firms cannot ignore price and customer service, they will keep their customers as long as they innovate enough to continue to offer the best product. Tracy and Wiersema believe such companies must have three characteristics. First, they must be creative, in order to find new ideas in the internal and external environments. Second, they must commercialize their ideas quickly, which means efficient production and management processes that are engineered for speed. Third, they must understand that they are their own most important competitor. If a company focusing on product leadership cannot continually top its own product, then it is not likely to be able to stay ahead of external competitors.

3. Customer intimacy. When a firm decides on the customer intimacy strategy, it emphasizes the individual over the market. The firm specializes in cultivating relationships by satisfying the unique needs of the customer. The challenge for this firm is to constantly tailor its products and services to customer expectations. In return, the firm relies on—in fact, requires—consumer loyalty. The long-distance carrier Cable & Wireless, for example, knew that it could not compete on the basis of price with AT&T, MCI, and Sprint, so it chose the strategy of customer intimacy to differentiate itself from its larger competitors. Cable & Wireless forms "partnerships" with its customers, mostly small- to medium-sized businesses. The firm's salespeople act, in effect, as telecommunication managers for customers, providing integrated planning and technical support. Cable & Wireless offers specialized services that appeal to specific market segments, such as the legal profession. The firm developed technology to track and segment the billing of calls linked to client accounts, a tool of great service to lawyers. "We want to sell products that fit the legal industry like a glove," says a Cable & Wireless executive.

The Delicate Balance

"Nothing is certain." While this truism certainly applies to businesses, it does not rule out the need for strategic planning. Managers can always, at a minimum, delineate several possible courses of action, each of which depends on different possible outcomes. The *proactive* manager still must choose among a limited number of strategies for his or her group or the corporation as a whole. In so doing, the manager must take account of external factors that may change over time. Managers face the delicate balance of planning for uncertainty while at the same time making sure that managerial resources are not overused in this process. In effect, managers must use a cost-benefit analysis to determine how far they should go in strategic planning. At any point in time, a response must be made even if it involves inaction—for inaction involves an opportunity cost to the corporation, too.

Terms and Concepts for Review

Adaptation 618
Bottom-up approach 632
Business-level strategy
  formulation 635
Chief information officer
  (CIO) 625
Cognitive bias 625
Competitive benchmarking 620
Concentration 634

Corporate-level strategy
  formulation 633
Deliberate strategy 627
Diversification 635
Emergent strategy 627
Enactment 618
Environmental determinism 627
Operating environment 619
Operating goals 629

Opportunities 619
Remote environment 619
Strategic management 616
Strengths 619
Threats 619
Top-down approach 632
Weaknesses 619

Summary

1. Strategic management can be defined as the process through which organizations analyze and learn from their internal and external environments, establish long- and short-term goals, create strategies that are intended to help achieve established goals, and execute those strategies, all in an effort to satisfy key organizational stakeholders.

2. Throughout the entire strategic management process, managers should keep in mind that plans are the means to reaching a business goal and not the goal itself. Therefore, managers must have the vision to understand that a changing business environment often forces readjustment of even the best-constructed strategies. Furthermore, managers must learn from these changes when they do occur.

3. Some researchers believe that firms pass through four distinct stages in the planning process: (a) basic financial planning, (b) forecast-based planning, (c) externally oriented planning, and (d) strategic management. The final stage allows the corporation to develop sustainable competitive advantages.

4. Adaptation occurs when a firm responds to its environment; enactment occurs when it tries to control its environment. In order to adapt, management must attempt to understand both the internal and the external environments.

5. We can combine a stakeholder view of strategic management with an assessment of environmental strengths, weaknesses, opportunities, and threats (SWOTs). When consumer tastes change, for example, new opportunities emerge. When stakeholder groups can block a firm's strategic goals, threats emerge.

6. The operating environment consists of stakeholders with which an organization interacts on a regular basis but over which it has no control. These include customers, suppliers, existing competitors, potential competitors, and indirect competitors.

7. With respect to existing competitors, some organizations engage in competitive benchmarking in order to measure their performance standards against those of their competitors.

8. Barriers to entry include: (a) economies of scale, (b) large capital requirements, (c) government policy, and (d) product differentiation.

9. The internal environment consists of managers, owners, and employees.

10. Managers may have a cognitive bias if they lean toward making decisions based on subjective rather than objective criteria.

11. Some organizations have a high-level manager with the title of chief information officer (CIO). One of the jobs of this executive is to engage in environmental scan-

ning—to recognize and predict changes in the environment. The result of scanning and analysis is business intelligence.

12. Traditionally, strategy development has relied heavily on environmental determinism, which is a reactive approach. The traditional view also lends itself to deliberate strategy, in which managers respond to changes in the environment by pursuing a preconceived strategic course. In contrast, strategic management lends itself to an emergent strategy, in which managers learn what to do by trial and error.

13. Organizations typically develop a statement of mission. In order to do so, they need to clearly identify four key elements: (a) purpose, (b) strategy, (c) values, and (d) behavior.

14. Operating goals can be developed by use of the bottom-up approach or the top-down approach. Recently, the command-and-control aspects of the top-down approach have been discredited in favor of empowerment and cooperation inherent in the bottom-up style.

15. Operating goals should: (a) be realistic, (b) be high enough to be motivating, (c) be specific, (d) be measurable, (e) be understood by all affected employees, (f) cover a specific time period, (g) be set through a participative process, and (h) involve continual feedback.

16. At the corporate level, management strategies may involve: (a) concentration through acquisition or merger, (b) vertical integration, or (c) diversification.

17. Business-level strategy formulation focuses on how a business will compete in its chosen field or product market. The value discipline approach to business-level strategy formulation emphasizes raising the level of value offered to customers. Three key value disciplines are: (a) operational excellence, (b) product leadership, and (c) customer intimacy.

EXERCISES

1. How can an organization manage uncertainty?
2. List some of the pitfalls of strategic management.
3. What is the distinction between external and internal environments?
4. Using a hypothetical firm, show how it passes through four distinct stages in the planning process, as described in the section "Analyzing the External and Internal Environments."
5. Why is understanding a key element in adaptation?
6. Assume that you are in charge of product development for a major consumer products manufacturer. List examples of strengths, weaknesses, opportunities, and threats (SWOTs) that might affect your company.
7. The operating environment includes potential competitors. How can a corporation take account of this aspect of the operating environment?
8. Go back to the list of barriers to entry found under the heading "Potential Competitors and Entrance Barriers." Which of them do you think is most important for a corporation? Why?
9. What does it mean to say that managers may have cognitive bias in decision making?
10. Reexamine *Exhibit 20–2*. Which of the common forms of cognitive bias do you think are most prevalent in corporations today? Explain your answer.
11. Under what circumstances, and for what type of organization, would you argue in favor of creating the position of chief information officer? Why?
12. Does every organization need a mission statement? Why or why not?
13. Review the behavior standards set out by the Scottish engineering company BBA under the heading "A Sense of Mission." Create a similar set of standards for a hypothetical company for which you are a manager.
14. Why do operating goals have to be measurable? Make a list of operating goals that are not measurable. Then make a list of operating goals that are.
15. How do corporate-level and business-level strategies differ?
16. Could diversification negatively affect a corporation's bottom line? How?

SELECTED REFERENCES

▶ Burke, Gerard, and Joe Peppard, eds. *Examining Business Process Re-engineering: Current Perspectives and Research Directions.* London: Kogan Page, 1995.

▶ Estabrooks, Maurice. *Electronic Technology, Corporate Strategy, and World Transformation.* Westport, Conn.: Quorum Books, 1995.

▶ Galbraith, Jay R. *Designing Organizations: An Executive Briefing on Strategy, Structure, and Process.* San Francisco: Jossey-Bass, 1995.

▶ Georgantzas, Nicholas C. *Scenario-Driven Planning: Learning to Manage Strategic Uncertainty.* Westport, Conn.: Quorum Books, 1995.

▶ Graham, John W. *Mission Statement: A Guide to the Corporate and Nonprofit Sectors.* New York: Garland, 1994.

RESOURCES ON THE INTERNET

▼ The Journal of Economics and Management Strategy (JEMS) is a quarterly journal edited by economists and management strategy experts. JEMS's on-line service provides a forum for interaction and research on management strategies. To access the JEMS home page, go to

gopher://gopher.enews.com:70/11/ business/pubs/business/jems

▼ The Academy of Management provides a wealth of information on management strategies. To access the Academy of Management Online, go to

http://hsb.baylor.edu/html/fuller/ am/am_home.htm

▼ For still more information on management ideas and information, access the Management Archive at

gopher://ursus.jun.alaska.edu/

▼ Mantis Consultants, Ltd., offers a number of services, including case studies, to help businesses better understand strategic management. To access this company's home page, go to

http://ftp.mantis.co/uk

▼ The site of the Graduate School of Management at Macqaurie University in Australia has valuable research information on management issues. To access this site, go to

gopher://gsmgopher.gsm.mq.edu.au/

▼ The Management Science Program at the University of Tennessee also provides information on management science at

http://northstar/bus.utk/ edu/mgmtsci/

CASE

THE CORPORATE-LEVEL STRATEGY OF TOYS "Я" US

Background

In 1948, Charles Lazarus began selling baby furniture in the back of his father's Washington, D.C., bicycle repair shop, located below the apartment where the Lazarus family lived. Within a few months, and in response to customer requests, he added a few toys to his line of baby furniture. Before long, he realized parents who bought toys returned for more toys—but parents who bought furniture rarely came back. "When I realized that toys broke," he said, "I knew it was a good business." Soon his entire business was focused on toys.

By 1988, Lazarus had proved that toys were indeed a "good business." That year Toys "Я" Us, the company he founded in the bicycle repair shop, had $3.14 billion in sales and operated 313 stores in the United States and 37 in foreign countries. In fact, Toys "Я" Us was the largest toy retailer in the world.

CEO Lazarus has consistently been the motivating force behind the growth of Toys "Я" Us (TRU). His vision is for TRU to become the McDonald's of toy retailing. "We don't have golden arches, but we're getting there."

The Toy Industry in the 1980s

The U.S. toy industry saw the best of times and the worst of times during the decade of the eighties. Between 1980 and 1984, sales growth in the toy industry, fueled by electronic games and Cabbage Patch Kids, was very strong. Including electronic games, sales growth in those years exceeded 18 percent per year. In 1984 and 1985, however, interest in electronic games fell sharply. This trend, combined with a dearth of blockbuster new toys of the caliber of Cabbage Patch Kids and Trivial Pursuit, resulted in relatively flat sales for the industry from 1985 to 1987.

During the slow-growth years, many toy manufacturers suffered financially. Several companies posted losses in 1986 and 1987, and two large companies—Coleco and World of Wonder were forced into Chapter 11 bankruptcy. By 1988, the industry had turned toward cost control. Hasbro and Mattel closed facilities to reduce overhead costs, and Tonka shifted much of its production to contract vendors in the Far East.

Another industry trend in the 1980s saw toy stores, particularly toy supermarkets like TRU, make major inroads into the retail toy market. In 1982, such outlets accounted for 19 percent of total toy sales. By 1987, the number had grown to 39 percent.

Although all categories of retailers compete with one another, they use different approaches to appeal to customers. The national toy chains offer a large selection at low prices with a minimum level of in-store service. Discount stores frequently offer similar low prices with minimal service, but their selection is not as extensive as that of the toy chains. Small independent toy stores provide personalized service and specialty items but ask higher prices. The larger department stores compete on the basis of convenience—the customer can purchase toys while shopping for other items.

Industry Trends

Some demographic and industry trends that are expected to continue to influence demand for toys in the 1990s are:

- *Number of children.* The number of households headed by people aged 35 to 44 grew by 38 percent from 1980 to 1988. Since the late 1970s, many of these members of the baby boom generation, who delayed having children while in their twenties, started having babies. This trend should slow down by the end of 1990s, as the baby bust generation moves into the childbearing years, replacing the baby boomers.
- *More money to spend on toys.* Many parents are having children after their households have been formed and careers have been established, so family incomes are higher. In many families, both parents are employed full time. The higher family incomes mean there is more money for discretionary items such as toys.
- *Broader market appeal of toy stores.* The toy market has joined with the video game and home electronics markets to form a broader category of "toys." The objective is to appeal to the teen and young adult market segment and draw this new group of buyers into toy stores.
- *Licensing.* Licensing, or basing a product on a motion picture, television program, or comic strip character, acceler-

ated in importance in the early 1980s and is expected to continue to play an important role in sales.

TRU Retailing Operations

The aim of TRU is to be the customer's only place of purchase for toys and related products. Management says it is proud that TRU attracts the least affluent purchasers because of the everyday discount prices and also attracts the most affluent purchasers because of the extensive product selection. In order to provide total service to all customer segments, the company maintains tight operating procedures and a strong customer orientation.

According to Charles Lazarus, "Nothing is done in the stores." What he means is that all buying and pricing decisions are made at corporate headquarters in Rochelle Park, New Jersey. The corporate buying and pricing decisions are made using an elaborate computerized inventory control system where sales by item and sales by store are monitored daily. Those actual sales numbers are compared with forecasts, and when substantial differences exist, the slow items are marked down to get them out of stores and the fast-selling items are reordered in large quantities.

The TRU stores are regionally clustered, with a warehouse within driving distance of every store. The company also owns a fleet of trucks to support its warehousing operations. These regional warehouses allow TRU to keep the stores well stocked and make it possible for TRU to order large quantities of merchandise early in the year, when manufacturers are eager to ship. Since most manufacturers defer payment for twelve months on shipments made in the months following Christmas, TRU is able to defer payment on about two-thirds of its inventory each year. TRU's competitors typically buy closer to Christmas, when buying terms are tighter.

All TRU stores have the same layout, with the same items arranged on exactly the same shelves—according to blueprints sent from the corporate office. Each store is jointly managed by a merchandise manager and an operations manager. The merchandise manager has full responsibility for the merchandise effort in the store: content, stock level, and display. The operations manager is responsible for the building, personnel, cash control, customer service, and everything else that is not directly related to the merchandise. Area supervisors oversee the total operations of three or four stores in a given area, and area general managers are responsible for the performance and profitability of all the TRU stores in a given region.

TRU Marketing

Each TRU store carries over 18,000 items. Although toys represent by far the majority of the items stocked, other products include baby furniture, diapers, and children's clothing. The feeling at TRU is that the parent will go to the store to buy a necessity and will leave with at least one toy purchase.

The product line at TRU includes home computers and software as well as traditional toys. This serves to broaden the company's customer base to include teenagers and adults. According to company statistics, products for these "older children" account for more than 15 percent of sales. TRU strongly feels this is not a change in its basic business—computers and software are toys for adults. This strategy also encourages year-round buying at its stores by not concentrating sales at holidays.

TRU has a strong policy of offering year-round discount prices. Because TRU buys most of its merchandise during the off-season, when manufacturers are offering discounts, the company is able to pass the discounts on to the customer. TRU has a policy of not having store sales. Individual items are marked down if they are not selling, but TRU does not have sales that are category-wide or storewide.

Virtually all TRU stores are located on an important traffic artery leading to a major shopping mall. A location of this type serves two purposes: it allows TRU to attract mall patrons without paying high mall rents, and it gives TRU the space to do business the way it wants to—as a large "supermarket" for toys, complete with grocery-type shopping carts.

Other customer conveniences include stock availability and the return policy. Product availability is virtually guaranteed. Because of extensive inventory monitoring and attention to customer buying habits, TRU rarely has "stock outs." Also, TRU boasts a liberal return policy. The company claims it will accept all returns with no questions asked—even if a toy with no defects is broken by a child after several months of play.

TRU does no national advertising. Before entering a new region, TRU promotes the opening of new stores through heavy television and newspaper advertising. Once the stores are open, TRU may continue very limited television and newspaper advertising.

TRU Expansion

TRU pursues a corporate objective of 18 percent expansion of retail space each year. In order to meet this objective, it opens nearly forty new stores a year in the United States.

CASE (CONTINUED)

Each expansion is made as a total entry into a new region. First, TRU builds a warehouse, then it clusters several stores within one day's driving distance of the warehouse. Typically, the warehouse and stores are up and running within the same fiscal year, and in time for the December holiday season.

In addition to domestic expansion, TRU is embarking on a plan of growth in the large non-U.S. toy market. The first Canadian and European stores were opened in late 1984. At the end of the 1980s, TRU operated over fifty stores in Canada, Europe, and the Far East.

TRU's only venture outside of toy retailing has been into children's clothing. The corporate objective in creating Kids "Я" Us was to "provide one-stop shopping with an overwhelming selection of first quality, designer, and brand name children's clothing in the season's latest styles at everyday prices. . . . We have taken the knowledge and systems we have refined for our toy stores over the past thirty years and applied some of these principles to our Kids "Я" Us stores."

In 1983, TRU opened its first two Kids "Я" Us stores in the New York area. By the beginning of the 1990s, more than a hundred such stores were operating. Some observers felt TRU would meet more resilient competition in children's

clothing than it did in toys. Department and discount stores make more money on children's clothing than they do on toys and are not willing to give up that market easily. Some department store managers feel the purchase of children's clothing sets a family's buying pattern for years—so the implication of losing the children's department as a way to draw in families goes beyond the immediate loss of profits in those areas.

Critical Thinking Questions

1. Summarize the corporate-level strategy of Toys "Я" Us.

2. How could the toy industry trends listed in the case affect this corporate-level strategy?

3. Does Toys "Я" Us follow a bottom-up approach or a top-down approach? Why do you feel its approach is appropriate?

4. Discuss the corporate-level strategies of concentration, vertical integration, and diversification as they apply to Toys "Я" Us.

5. Which stakeholder group does Toys "Я" Us seem to focus on the most? Describe the strategy with regard to these stakeholders, compared with the strategies of its competitors.

SOURCE: Adapted from Caron H. St. John, Alan N. Hoffman, and Hugh M. O'Neill, in *The Strategic Management Casebook and Skill Builder* (St. Paul: West Publishing Company, 1993), pp. 484–495. Information from S. P. Sherman, "Where the Dollars 'Я'", *Fortune*, June 1, 1981, pp. 45–47; D. Fesperman, "Toys "Я" Us Is a Giant in Kids' Business," *Miami Herald*, November 22, 1982; M. B. Exstein, "Toys "Я" Us," *Shearson Lehman Hutton Investment Analysis*, August 19, 1988; and "Kids "Я" Us—The Children's Clothing Stores Both Parents and Kids Will Choose," press release from Toys "Я" Us, July 1983.

CHAPTER 21

STRATEGY IMPLEMENTATION AND CRISIS MANAGEMENT

CHAPTER OUTLINE

▶ Strategy Implementation
▶ Strategic Control
▶ Issues Management
▶ Crisis Management

INTRODUCTION

On paper, General Electric does an exemplary job of gearing strategic management to the internal and external environments. The conglomerate has one of the most lauded codes of corporate ethics in the business world. GE's 1990 annual report boasted that the customer's vision of his or her needs and the company's view had "become identical, and every effort of every man and woman in the company is focused on satisfying those needs" and furthermore that "everybody [in the company] is an environmentalist." GE's widely respected CEO, Jack Welch, is constant in his focus on the company's integrity.

Yet the last decade has seen an apparent real-world divergence from these written missions and goals. From 1990 to 1994, GE paid fines or settlement fees in sixteen cases of abuse, fraud, and waste in government contracting, continuing a trend from 1985, when the firm pleaded guilty to fraud charges stemming from overcharging the Air Force on a missile contract. The company has been named a potentially responsible party in regard to seventy-two Superfund environmental clean-up sites. In 1993, NBC News, a division of GE, issued an on-air apology to General Motors for staging a misleading simulated crash test of a pickup truck. Finally, in 1994, Kidder, Peabody & Company, another GE holding, fired its government bond trader for fabricating $350 million in trading profits.[1]

GE's troubles point to a key principle of strategic management: mission statements are not enough. For that reason, we must concern ourselves not only with strategy formulation but also with strategy implementation. This chapter discusses strategy implementation, its potential pitfalls, and the various controls that managers can use to keep vision in tune with reality.[2] It also describes two aspects of emergent strategy known as issues management and crisis management.

STRATEGY IMPLEMENTATION

Following strategy formulation, the next logical step in strategic management is **strategy implementation**, or laying out the specific details of how to put a chosen strategy in place. Strategy is implemented via structure, culture, leadership, and reward systems. Many business strategy experts consider implementation the most important step of the strategic management process, for inspired action can often overcome ordinary or even incomplete planning.[3]

Furthermore, an otherwise brilliant plan can be sabotaged by poor implementation. An example involves People Express, an airline started by Donald Burr after the deregulation of the airline industry in 1978. People Express formulated a strategy based on low-cost commuting: the company purchased secondhand aircraft, negotiated inexpensive terminal leases, and encouraged high employee productivity with pay based on profit-sharing plans. Company pilots logged longer hours than pilots of competing airlines. Initially, the strategy was successful. But as People Express prospered, it lost sight of its

---

1. T. P. Pare, "Jack Welch's Nightmare on Wall Street," *Fortune*, September 5, 1994, pp. 40–48; and N. Byrnes, "The Smoke at General Electric," *FW*, August 16, 1994, p. 32.
2. G. Hamel and C. K. Prahalad, "Competing for the Future: What Drives Your Company's Agenda: Your Competitor's View of the Future or Your Own?" *Harvard Business Review*, July–August 1994, p. 122.
3. J. T. Gilbert, "Faster [Newer] Is Not a Strategy," *SAM Advanced Management Journal*, March–April 1994, p. 21.

original plans and tried to compete with its larger industry mates. The company came into direct competition with established airlines by undertaking longer routes, contracting for more expensive terminal space, and purchasing new aircraft at market prices. People Express also began to hire more employees, effectively destroying the profit-sharing process that had led to high worker productivity in earlier days. In the end, the airline did not have the extensive reservation systems and customer service infrastructure to justify the abandonment of its initial plan. Eventually, a competitor purchased the company. People Express had formulated an effective plan based on an environmental analysis that revealed that consumers would be willing to accept no-frills service for lower prices. The problem? The airline failed to implement its strategy on a functional level.[4]

FUNCTIONAL STRATEGIES

In Chapter 20, we discussed corporate-level and business-level strategies. We now turn our attention to functional strategies. All companies have an organizational structure that provides for task assignments, the division of employees into operating groups or departments, and communication among these groups or departments. The collective patterns of decisions and actions taken in this organizational framework are known as **functional strategies**; they allow the organization to function on a day-to-day basis. The two primary functional strategies are marketing strategy and operations strategy, with other significant planning revolving around research and development, information systems, human resources, and finances.[5] A manager must understand the intricacies of each level of functional strategy and their interdependence with each other as well as with business-level and corporate-level strategies.

Marketing Strategy In strategic management, an organization's interaction with external stakeholders such as consumers and the community is critical. On a functional level, the firm's marketing division has this responsibility. Marketing employees are responsible for stakeholder analysis, which ultimately determines "what the people want." **Marketing strategy** evolves from the cumulative pattern of decisions made by the employees who interact with consumers.

In any organization, the marketing strategy has one straightforward, ultimate goal—to support growth. Within this broad assignment, marketing must make a number of complex strategy decisions: identification of new customer and product opportunities, linkage of pricing and customer service policies with the proper consumer groups, creation of advertising and promotional programs, and development of distribution channels that best serve the goals of the organization. The implementation of a marketing strategy relies on a thorough understanding of stakeholder needs. The success of marketing tools such as advertisements and price discounts are directly related to acceptance by the external environment.[6]

Operations Strategy Ultimately, marketing strategy is only as effective as the products and services the organization produces. **Operations strategy**—the organization's plan for designing and managing the process by which its goods and services are offered to customers—is therefore a vital part of the strategic management process.

---

4. J. S. Harrison and C. H. St. John, *Strategic Management of Organizations and Stakeholders* (St. Paul: West Publishing Company, 1994), p. 240.

5. Harrison and St. John, *op. cit.*, pp. 244–255.

6. J. S. Goodwin and C. J. Elliot, "Exporting Services: Developing a Strategic Framework," SAM *Advanced Management Journal*, Winter 1995, p. 21.

Until the Japanese emphasis on quality caused American businesses to rethink their relationship with consumers, the predominant operations strategy seemed to be, "We made it, it's up to marketing to sell it." At present, most operations managers realize that their strategy is not simply to provide marketing with a product or service but to manage the resources of the firm in a way that makes the product or service competitive in the marketplace. To do so, an operations strategy must ultimately be based on the wants and desires of the consumer—high quality, prompt delivery, and reasonable prices.

Operations managers must be aware of other stakeholders as well, because of the effect those stakeholders can have on customer satisfaction. Employees demand decent wages and benefits and a safe working environment; communities demand stable employment for their citizens and limited negative externalities such as pollution; owner stakeholders are continually looking at the bottom line.

▼ Operations managers must be aware of the interdependencies among various stakeholder groups and how these links affect strategic management.

A new product may be of high value to consumer stakeholders, but its production may necessitate a new labor contract or cause the firm to create pollution in the community. Managers must weigh the costs of these consequences against the benefits of the new product line.

Other Functional Strategies To support marketing and operations strategies, firms must also formulate strategies in other areas. In order to develop more effective products and applications of their products, companies must have a **research and development strategy.** The banking industry, for example, reacted to growing consumer demand for efficient and easy-to-use service by developing automated teller machines (ATMs). Research and development strategy is in many ways linked with **information systems strategy,** which dictates how an organization uses information technology to facilitate business activities. Over the past decade, computer technology has revolutionized the

flow of information in both the internal and external environments. Many firms use information systems to their competitive advantage. For example, PriceCostco and other companies scan sales data by product in order to determine trends and patterns in customer buying behavior.

If information systems strategy seems to change every few years because of technological innovations, **human resources strategy** relies on concepts that are relatively stable—assignment of specific tasks to specific employees, training, and creation of incentives through rewards and benefits. In many cases, the human resources department is the link between management and employees and between management and certain external stakeholders, such as labor unions and government regulators. As we discussed earlier, the efforts undertaken by human resources departments are critical in issues such as workplace violence and plant closings.

Another functional strategy is **financial strategy**, which has the goal of assuring that an organization will have the proper capital structure and the funds it needs to implement growth and competitive strategies. Financial managers make decisions on how funds will be allocated among various internal stakeholder groups—marketing, operations, R&D, and even employees. Financial managers must also decide whether or not to sacrifice the short-term goals of shareholders, who want a quick return on their investments, for the long-term goals of other stakeholders, which may include long-term job security for employees or expensive air-quality control technology for the community.

THE RELATIONSHIP OF STRUCTURE AND STRATEGY

The manner in which an organization divides its activities and employees into specialized departments or groups is called its *formal structure*. Obviously, each of the functional strategies discussed has a place in the formal structure of an organization. One of the first researchers to recognize the structure-strategy relationship was Alfred Chandler, who argued that a firm's structure should be organized to support the intended strategy of the firm.[7] A number of different structures can be used to implement strategy:

1. The *functional structure* is most closely tied to functional strategies. Organizations that are functionally structured usually have departments for marketing, operations, R&D, and finance. Here, by creating a centralized and highly specified structure, the organization aims to maximize internal efficiency and the specific expertise of employees.

2. The *product or market group structure* focuses on the outputs of the organization rather than on the internal processes that produce the outputs. A computer company might, for example, develop its structure around specific customer groups such as home users, business users, and academic users.

3. In a *project matrix structure*, elements of the functional and product/market structures are combined. This type of structure is most common in highly competitive environments in which internal stakeholders must be interdependent in order to react to diverse and fluctuating external stakeholder demands. The ideal project matrix structure allows a flexible use of people and equipment within a centralized command system. The danger of the project matrix structure is that "too many bosses" will lead to slow decision-making processes, which add to administrative costs.

4. The *network structure*, also known as the "spider's web" structure, is highly decentralized and organized around customer groups or geographical regions. In this web of independent units, little or no hierarchy exists, and information sharing links most units. A

7. A. D. Chandler, *Strategy and Structure: Chapters in the History of American Industrial Enterprise* (Cambridge, Mass.: MIT Press, 1962).

▼ **EXHIBIT 21–1**
Four Corporate
Orientations

1. The *craftsperson* organization is one in which employees are passionately dedicated to quality. In this corporate culture, organizational pride is primarily driven by the high quality of goods and services produced.

2. The *builder* organization is primarily a risk-taking culture in which the organization rewards managers and employees for producing growth, new acquisitions, and new market niches.

3. The *pioneer* organization builds its business by being the leader in its particular industry or field.

4. The *salesperson* organization prides itself on excellent marketing strategies, which include the creation of successful brand names and distribution channels. This corporate culture encourages aggressive advertising and innovative packaging.

SOURCE: D. Miller, *The Icarus Paradox* (New York: Harper Business, 1990).

common example of a network structure can be found in most universities, in which departments are independent of one another and the university president and board of trustees serve an advisory function.[8]

CULTURE AND STRATEGY IMPLEMENTATION

An issue with regard to formal structure is how well it allows the organization to align itself with its environment—to *fit* its environment. In part, managers can achieve fit by implementing one of the four structures listed above. For example, a home-construction company may implement a project matrix structure by giving individual work teams autonomy at various work sites. Instead of waiting for instructions from a central headquarters, these work teams would be more efficient making decisions themselves. This would help the company fit in the construction industry.

But, as any manager can tell you, strategy implementation requires more than devising a plan and assuming employees will follow it. Perhaps in the example from the paragraph above, some employees would take advantage of this freedom by working fewer hours or loosening quality controls. A key part of fit is corporate culture, or the shared values of an organization's employees. As you already know, an organization's culture embodies "how things are done" and in many cases is as important in the achievement of a company's goals as formal structure. In his book *The Icarus Paradox*, Danny Miller identifies four corporate orientations that he believes enhance the strategic management process: craftpersons, builders, pioneers, and salespersons. These orientations are discussed in *Exhibit 21–1*.

Even with high-performance corporate cultures, however, organizations can lose sight of their environments. When this happens, craftspersons can become *tinkerers*, and their obsessive quest for perfection will lead to products that are overengineered and consequently overpriced. When builders lose sight of market constraints, they become *imperialists* and neglect core businesses for unrelated ones. Pioneers that pursue technology for technology's sake and lose sight of consumer tastes evolve into *escapists*. And salespersons that become so confident in their marketing abilities that they lose sight of the quality of their merchandise are labeled *drifters*.[9]

8. Harrison and St. John, *op. cit.*, pp. 260–266.
9. D. Miller, *The Icarus Paradox* (New York: Harper Business, 1990).

How does a company make sure the strategies it has formulated are carried out in the implementation process? The various means are grouped under the blanket term *strategic control.*

STRATEGIC CONTROL

For our purposes, **strategic control** refers to the safeguards built into the strategic management process to ensure that an organization achieves its mission and goals. From the corporate-level perspective, a strategic control system should support managers in assessing the relevance of the organization's strategy to its progress in the accomplishment of its goals. Under this very broad description, we can identify a number of different control structures. Basically, corporations establish control systems to motivate and evaluate—that is, motivate employees to follow the established strategy and evaluate both employee performance and the strategy itself. Here, we examine two types of control relevant to stakeholder analysis: feedforward control and feedback control.[10]

FEEDFORWARD CONTROL

In a **feedforward control system,** a manager must anticipate changes in the internal and external environments based on analysis of inputs from stakeholders and the remote environment. Such systems are based on the assumption that as the environment changes—influenced by economic, social, legal, political, and technological forces—each individual business organization must adjust accordingly.

One sort of feedforward control device involves premise control. Managers base missions, goals, and strategies on analysis of an organization not only with regard to its own capabilities but also its external environment. When a sports equipment manufacturer decides how many tennis racquets to produce in a given fiscal year, for example, it forms a number of *premises,* or assumptions, concerning the demand for the product. As another example, when a company makes a decision about debt restructuring, it must predict future interest rate changes. Under one set of premises, the company will issue a series of short-term bonds. Under another set of premises, it will issue some short-term bonds and some long-term bonds.

Executives need **premise control** to make such decisions. A premise control system evaluates whether the information used to establish missions, goals, and strategies is still valid given the current internal and external environments. (We discuss specific premise control systems later in this chapter.)

FEEDBACK CONTROL

Feedback control systems provide managers with information concerning the outcome of organizational activities that are essential to meeting goals. In this process, managers usually set specific objectives whereby these activities will be achieved within a certain time frame and then measure the actual feedback against the targeted performance levels. If the objectives are met, the strategy is performing properly. If not, the managers must use information feedback to decide why it is not and make appropriate strategy adjustments.

An example might be a professional baseball team that sets an operating target of 2 million attendance, give or take 50,000 fans. If, at the end of the baseball season, only 1.5

10. Harrison and St. John, *op. cit.,* pp. 312–320.

million fans have passed through the stadium turnstiles, the organization will set in motion a feedback control process to determine why the target was not met. After doing some research, the team's marketing staff might find that many fans feel the general atmosphere at the stadium does not lend itself to family entertainment. With this information, the team owners may decide to limit the sale of beer in the stadium and therefore diminish the influence of drunken fans. (Of course, the team owners will then also have to consider the number of customers they might lose because of these restrictions.)

Feedback control systems are useful because they create specific targets that clearly establish employee goals. A common feedback control system is a budget, which clearly delineates for employees the boundaries within which they can allocate the organization's finances.

OTHER STRATEGIC CONTROLS

The strategic control measures we have discussed so far can best be described as *output-based* control systems. They measure a company's performance, or output, and the control mechanism is primarily one of response. Output-based controls have several drawbacks. Performance is often difficult to quantify, responsibility is often difficult to assign, and controls, such as social audits, can be prohibitively expensive. Consequently, organizations often seek less formal controls to supplement or take the place of output-based controls. These less formal controls can be described as *behavioral* controls, because the systems focus not on outcomes but on the behavior of individuals within the organization. Behavioral controls include clan control, bureaucratic control, and the human resources system.[11]

Clan Control Previously, we discussed the socialization process companies use to introduce individuals to the values of the corporate culture. In terms of control systems, this is

---

11. Harrison and St. John, *op. cit.*, p. 325.

known as **clan control**. In clan control, the work unit establishes certain standards/norms, monitors conformity, and takes action when social deviations occur.[12] In the United States, clan control is most common in smaller or family-run organizations. These small organizations consist of only a few employees who generally know each other well.

Bureaucratic Control Under a **bureaucratic control system**, rules, policies, and procedures guide the behavior of organizational members. For example, chain stores and franchises use a bureaucratic control system, requiring each store to comply with specific operational parameters. Thus, a consumer who walks into a Starbuck's coffee shop will see virtually the same things whether the shop is in San Francisco or Washington, D.C.

Human Resources Systems When a company turns to its human resources system for control, it is essentially following a course of strategic hiring and training. In doing so, it tailors the work force specifically to its mission and goals. For example, a firm that wants to increase its technical expertise can instruct its human resources department to hire technically proficient workers, or train current employees in the desired technical fields, or both. The human resources department can also offer rewards to employees who embody corporate values. Rewards can take the form of bonuses or promotions or extra vacation time and often provide incentives to other employees to follow their colleagues' example.

ISSUES MANAGEMENT

A special type of control closely linked to feedforward control is **issues management**. In the context of strategic management, issues management is the process that allows organizations to know and understand their environments.[13] Another definition refers to issues management as a "management process whose goal is to help preserve markets, reduce risk, create opportunities, and manage image as an organizational asset."[14]

When the term *issues management* became part of the business lexicon in the mid-1970s, the process was seen primarily as a tool for expanding the role of public relations beyond media relations and product publicity.[15] W. Howard Chase, a public relations practitioner who is given credit for coining the term, saw issues management as a strategy to help corporations avoid spending large sums of "clean-up money" on the social issues that began affecting the business community in the 1960s and 1970s.[16] As the process evolved in the 1990s, many executives came to consider issues management as a problem-solving function critical to the success and, in some cases, survival of a business entity.[17]

Before we examine the key issues in the process, we should note that the term *issues management* may be somewhat misleading. Many of the issues tackled under the name

12. R. F. Lusch and B. J. Jaworski, "Management Controls, Role Stress, and Retail Store Manager Performance," *Journal of Retailing*, December 22, 1991, p. 397.

13. M. M. Lauzen, "Public Relations Practitioner Role Enactment in Issues Management," *Journalism Quarterly*, Summer 1994, p. 356.

14. K. Tucker and B. Trumpfheller, "Managing Issues Acts As Bridge to Strategic Planning," *Public Relations Journal*, November 1993, p. 38.

15. K. F. Slousen and D. P. Bertelsen, "A Look at Change in Management Education," *SAM Advanced Management Journal*, Winter 1994, p. 21.

16. Tucker and Trumpfheller, *op. cit.*

17. R. W. Easley, W. O. Bearden, and J. E. Teel, "Testing Predictions Derived from Inoculation Theory and the Effectiveness of Self-Disclosure Communications Strategies," *Journal of Business Research*, October 1995, p. 93.

issues management cannot be managed by a single company or even an industry. A more accurate name for the process might be *issues influence*.

EARLY IDENTIFICATION OF KEY ISSUES

A popular analogy compares issues management to a radar system that forewarns executives and managers of issues that may affect the organization in the future. If managers can anticipate trends and changes in the external environment, they should have a wider range of appropriate decision-making alternatives.[18]

A few years ago, for example, issues analysts for the dairy industry identified a growing concern among health-care professionals about levels of iodine, an additive to livestock feed, in dairy products. These analysts also discovered that a major medical organization was preparing a position paper on the iodine issue for publication in a professional journal. The article would have been a public relations disaster for dairy companies, as it was going to suggest that dairy products contained unhealthful levels of iodine. In a proactive move, producers removed iodine livestock feed from the market, resulting in a 50 percent reduction of iodine in dairy foods. The producers shared the results with the medical association planning to publish the position paper. Faced with the new data, the group withdrew its article.

Obviously, then, the earlier management identifies an issue, the more options the organization has to incorporate that knowledge into its strategic planning.[19] If the dairy industry had discovered the position paper on iodine the day before it was to be published, the industry would not have had time to take actions that disarmed the article's assertions.

Environmental Scanning Collectively, the methods used to identify environmental issues are known as **environmental scanning** (discussed in Chapter 20). Sources for scanning the external environment include industry and academic journals, trade books, and the news media. Companies are also finding that dominant or reoccurring themes in movies, novels, and television programs can help them identify important trends in popular culture. In addition, "surfing" the Internet has proved to be a valuable tool for gauging public opinion. Some companies provide information scanning services for others, but because these services may cost upwards of $50,000 a year, many firms do not have the budget to outsource issues identification.

Brainstorming Issues can also be identified in brainstorming sessions among midlevel and upper management. Two issues management specialists, Kerry Tucker and Bill Trumpfheller, suggest that managers begin the process by separating potential issues into five broad categories: economics, social trends, the government, technology, and the competition. Then managers should ask the following questions:

1. What changes do we project in each category in the next three to five years?
2. What trends are likely to affect the organization?
3. What specific events are likely to affect the organization?[20]

18. K. M. Sutcliffe, "What Executives Notice: Accurate Perceptions in Top Management Trams," *Academy of Management Journal*, October 1994, p. 1360.
19. A. F. Hagen and S. G. Amin, "Corporate Executive and Environmental Scanning Activities: An Empirical Investigation," *SAM Advanced Management Journal*, Spring 1995, p. 41.
20. Tucker and Trumpfheller, *op. cit.*

These questions will raise a number of potential issues, probably many more than the company has the time or money to follow closely. Limited resources inevitably prohibit managing all potential emerging issues. To warrant close consideration, therefore, an issue must be identified as one that will have some measurable impact on the organization. For best results, managers should choose the three or four issues that they believe will have the highest measurable impact on the organization and place all others, so to speak, on the back burner. Once these priorities have been established, managers can decide how each issue is likely to affect the company's strategic systems, such as marketing. (See *Managing Social Issues—Multicultural/Tolerance: Magic Johnson versus the Advertising Industry* on page 656.)

ISSUE URGENCY

Once the key issues have been identified, managers must analyze the issues so that the appropriate information can be incorporated into the strategic planning process.[21]

▼ **An important aspect of issues analysis is calculating each issue's urgency. By determining how urgently a corporation needs to respond, a manager can more efficiently apply resources to issues management.**

When, for example, PriceCostco was planning to open a store in downtown Portland, Oregon, the company needed to identify issues of immediate community concern. Once upper management recognized these issues, the discount warehouse chain moved to address them. (See *Exhibit 21–2* on page 657.)

Two steps used to calculate issue urgency are: (1) evaluating the issue's impact on the bottom line, and (2) estimating the issue's probability of occurrence within a specific period of time.[22]

Evaluating the Degree of Impact The greater the impact an issue is expected to have on an organization's bottom line, the more urgent that issue will be. Sometimes, evaluating the degree of impact is relatively simple. If a paper manufacturer's issues analysts determine that environmental special interest groups are pushing the government to ban the use of chlorine bleach in the pulp process—and that paper manufacturer has not incorporated chlorine-free production technology in its plants—then the company is facing an urgent, even critical, issue.

Sometimes, however, evaluating an issue's impact is less straightforward. Issues can have an indirect impact on an organization's bottom line, and a company must use a degree of foresight in analysis. As an example, consider Atlantic Richfield Oil Company's reaction to Ronald Reagan's election to the presidency in 1980. Most business executives were pleased at the thought of Reagan occupying the Oval Office, presiding over a conservative, pro-business federal government. Issues analysts at Atlantic Richfield, however, saw a harmful side effect of Reagan's election. Predicting that the new administration would embark on a series of budget cuts, these analysts surmised that states would have to make up the resulting lost federal revenue by increasing taxes on local businesses. And Atlantic Richfield, a profitable oil company operating in twenty-eight states, would be a prime target.

---

21. K. Roth, "Managing International Interdependence: CEO Characteristics in a Resource-Based Framework," *Academy of Management Journal*, February 1995, p. 200.
22. M. Meng, "Early Identification Aids Issues Management," *Public Relations Journal*, March 1992, pp. 22–24.

MANAGING SOCIAL ISSUES

MULTICULTURAL/TOLERANCE: MAGIC JOHNSON VERSUS THE ADVERTISING INDUSTRY

On November 7, 1991, Earvin "Magic" Johnson announced his retirement from professional basketball on the advice of his physician; he had tested positive for HIV, the virus that causes AIDS. The news sent shock waves not only through the athletic world but also through corporate America. Besides being one of the most celebrated basketball players in the sport's history, the Los Angeles Lakers guard was one of the most successful marketing celebrities of all time. It was estimated that in 1991 alone, Johnson earned $12 million endorsing products for Converse, Spalding, Pepsi-Cola, Kentucky Fried Chicken, Nestlé's Crunch, and Nintendo. These organizations, and any others considering the future use of Johnson in this role, had to analyze the external environment to determine whether someone who had contracted one of the most feared and stigmatized of all diseases could still be an effective marketing force.

No Guidelines for Advertisers

In the past, organizations have seldom hesitated to drop celebrities from commercials in the wake of negative publicity. But Johnson's situation was more challenging. A number of questions surrounded Johnson's health. For example, would it deteriorate to the point where he would not be able to meet commitments? Furthermore, in efforts to warn others about the dangers of contracting the disease, Johnson admitted to a lifestyle that hardly fit the clean-cut image advertising executives covet. Finally, lurking beneath the situation's surface was the long-standing fear of advertisers to be associated with anything having to do with homosexuality—and in the minds of many, AIDS is a homosexual disease. "There's no road map, no playbook, no guidelines," said a Pepsi spokesperson about the dilemma.

Initially, support for Johnson was so overwhelming that, in the words of one analyst, "even if advertisers were inclined to drop [Johnson], I'm sure they've assessed the general public's reaction and would be terrified to do so." When the vice president of the advertising agency Jordan, McGrath, Case & Taylor advised its client Nestlé to "disassociate" itself from Johnson because "we have a lot of people in this country with a lot of prejudice about AIDS," the chocolate manufacturer issued a press release saying his comments were "not authorized."

Industry analysts openly wondered whether corporations would stand by Johnson in the long run, however. Even supporting him in a goodwill roll such as an ambassador for "safe sex" had the downside of associating the organization with teenage sex or widespread condom use. Any company that took the lead in such areas "has to understand that it will be shot with arrows," said one advertising executive. "It will take a lot of guts for an advertiser to brave the reaction in Peoria," warned another. "And unfortunately, not too many companies have that kind of courage."

Hero No More

Despite assurances that Johnson would not be abandoned, these predictions held true. Nestlé, for example, scrapped a series of candy bar ads that it had filmed with the basketball player and decided not to work with him in the future. A Nestlé spokesperson said the Crunch ads, "where the product is hero, were inappropriate." In the two months following his retirement, only Converse announced any plans for an advertising campaign that featured Johnson. When he briefly considered returning to the National Basketball Association in 1992, only Pepsi decided to bring Johnson back to the commercial spotlight. And Pepsi's "We Believe in Magic" campaign was not a product commercial *per se*, as it did not show Johnson drinking Pepsi.

For Critical Analysis:

One sports marketing expert estimates that infection with the HIV virus ultimately cost Johnson $25 million in endorsement contracts. Has issues management "cost" Johnson these endorsements in any sense? Explain your answer.

SOURCE: Information from J. Lipman, "Advertisers Support Johnson As Educator," *Wall Street Journal*, November 11, 1991, p. B1; E. Kiersh, "Disappearing Act?" *Adweek*, November 18, 1991, p. 22; J. Lipman, " 'Magic' Johnson's Ads for Pepsi Will Come Back with Him," *Wall Street Journal*, October 2, 1992, p. B12; and B. Horovitz, "Sidelined Sponsors Reconsider Magic Johnson Ads," *Los Angeles Times*, December 28, 1991, p. 1.

▼ **EXHIBIT 21–2
PriceCostco Issues
Management in
Portland, Oregon**

WHY A DOWNTOWN PORTLAND COSTCO MAKES SENSE—THE CONDENSED VERSION:

- Brings 175 good inner-city jobs and new revenues to Portland

- Cost savings for 50,000+ city residents & small businesses

- Eliminates 600,000+ miles of traffic *monthly*

- Traffic impact less than feared (actually makes NW Yeon safer)

- No Govt. subsidies (in fact, returns $1.9 million to community)

- Helps nearly 100 local companies who supply Costco

- Saves/Restores historic U.S. Steel warehouse

- City and State agree road system can safely handle traffic

- Majority of businesses and residents support it

- Only practical site available in city. If not here, where?

SOURCE: PriceCostco, Inc. Reprinted with permission.

Subsequently, many states did aim new tax legislation at oil companies—at times, up to ten such bills a week were introduced. Atlantic Richfield, however, had already identified the side effects of Reagan's budget cuts as an issue of some urgency, so the company had prepared a lobbying campaign to combat the state tax bills. In a majority of cases, the campaigns were successful.

Estimating the Probability of Occurrence Atlantic Richfield was able to successfully apply the precepts of strategic issues management because it was confident of the high probability that the states would attempt to levy new taxes. How was the company able to make this accurate prediction? In assessing issues, analysts strive to identify what pattern an issue is following or to forecast what pattern that issue may follow. The term "pattern" can be frustrating; some patterns are easier to predict than others. A timber company that decides to harvest old-growth forest, for example, can be certain that this act will draw criticism from environmental groups. A company that devises a new logo that some offbeat consumer group later declares is the disguised sign of Satan will of course be completely taken off guard.

Generally, however, the operating environment follows a historical pattern in reacting to an issue. When a state government loses a source of revenue, for instance, the state has few options for recouping that income. As Atlantic Richfield correctly surmised, raising state taxes on oil companies is one of them. Thus, it behooves a corporation to take the time and effort necessary to gather strategic information about external forces that may impact the company once a particular important decision is made or when there is an obviously important event external to the corporation that has occurred. The goal should be to take as much of the guesswork as possible out of estimating the probability of something occurring.

MESSAGE FORMULATION

Once a company has analyzed an issue, it must formulate a message in which its position or interests regarding the issue may be communicated to internal and external stakeholders.

In Chapter 11, we discussed how business can influence public policy; the message formulation step of issues management relates to much of what was discussed there. Of particular importance is the identification of **priority publics**, those groups or individuals in the environment that can most help or hinder an organization in attempting to influence an issue.

One element in message formulation is to determine the political and social risks of taking a position on a given issue. In 1992, Levi Strauss revoked its contributions to the Boy Scouts of America because of that organization's refusal to allow homosexuals or atheists to serve as scoutmasters. The company received a great deal of criticism for this stance, but it had determined that the move was in keeping with the values of its priority publics. Many organizations, fearing the backlash from conservative and religious interest groups, would not have made the same choice as Levi Strauss.

A firm must answer four key questions in establishing priority publics with regard to its position on a given issue:

1. Who in the environment makes the decisions on this issue?
2. What segments of the environment are likely to support the organization's position?
3. What segments of the environment are likely to oppose the organization's position?
4. What segment can the organization successfully target to make the biggest difference in advancing the organization's position?[23]

Essentially, the final question concerns finding allies among opinion leaders in the community—politicians, special interest groups, members of the media, and so on. Given that many of these opinion leaders will also be eager to find corporate backing, the challenge for an issues manager is to decide with which ones the company should align itself. The strategy for choosing public allies is relatively simple: decide whom the public trusts on the issue, decide who has the greatest credibility to advance the organization's position on the issue, and then approach the individual and/or group to see if a working relationship is possible.[24]

ISSUES MANAGEMENT AND STRATEGIC PLANNING

Issues management is a tool not only for avoiding negative consequences but also for spotlighting positive opportunities. McDonald/Richards Model Agency, for example, noted U.S. society's growing acceptance of and comfort level with Americans with disabilities and capitalized on the trend. In 1992, the firm employed two models with disabilities; by 1994, the number had risen to fifty, and clients included Macy's, Hecht's, Dayton-Hudson, Target, and Kmart.[25] That same year, Coca-Cola used its issues analysis of American teenagers to design and market a new brand of soft drink called OK Soda. (See *Company Focus—Coca-Cola Company.*)

CRISIS MANAGEMENT

Issues management implies a relatively long process in which the corporation has the luxury of studying the internal and external environments and forecasting possible trends

---

23. Tucker and Trumpfheller, *op. cit.*, p. 37.
24. M. Davids, "Lean and Green," *Journal of Business Strategy*, March–April 1994, p. 18.
25. "Sitting Pretty in a Wheelchair," *Business Week*, July 18, 1994, p. 8.

COMPANY FOCUS: COCA-COLA COMPANY

ISSUE BRANDING: OK SODA

The purchasing power of the American teenager is, in a word, awesome. In a given year, twelve- to twenty-year-olds in the United States spend more than $100 billion on food, clothing, videos, and other items. Of that total, more than $3 billion goes toward soft drinks, providing corporations such as Coca-Cola ample incentive to capture the teen market. Besides expendable income, however, American teens seem to share another trait, bred from thousands of hours being bombarded by advertisements—deep cynicism about messages that come from big business. Coca-Cola feels it has overcome this mistrust of corporate America with OK Soda, which it hopes will be the choice of a skeptical generation.

Analysis of the Teenage Mind

OK Soda, released in 1994, is the culmination of years of marketing studies, including the two-year Global Teenager program, which employed the services of the Massachusetts Institute of Technology. The research confirmed that age-old adolescent anxieties are being exacerbated with modern worries about violence and AIDS to create a crop of teenagers with diminished expectations. "Economic prosperity is less available to them than it was for their parents," notes Brian Langham, manager of special projects for Coke's marketing division. "Even traditional rites of passage, such as sex, are fraught with life-or-death consequences."

Consequently, the company decided, OK soda would have to address the concerns of teenagers without exploiting them too obviously. That led to an exaggeratedly self-conscious advertising campaign targeted at "people who watch 'Beavis and Butt-head' and the 'Partridge Family' in the same half hour [on television]," according to Sergio Zyman, Coke's head of global marketing. The campaign includes a national hotline (1-800-I-FEEL-OK) that allows callers to hear prerecorded messages or speak their own minds about anything, including the soft drink. Some of the messages are planted by Coke's marketers, including one

from an Arkansas teen who says, "I started drinking OK two days after my boyfriend and I broke up, and ever since I started drinking it, bad things happen to him. He even broke his leg. That's pretty good." Another marketing ploy is a series of chain letters sent to teens to ask them to spread the "feeling of OK-ness" to six friends.

"OK-ness" As Marketing

The packaging of OK Soda downplays the traditional colorful, upbeat soft-drink designs. The aluminum cans come in four different designs, each of them black-on-gray and dreary. One design underscores loss of individuality by obscuring a teen's face with the bar code. Others are scrawled with messages such as "What is the point of OK? Well, what's the point of anything?" and "OK emphatically rejects anything that is not OK, and fully supports anything that is."

The transparency of these messages *is* the message. "OK-ness is part of a marketing ploy," says Zyman, "and our audience knows that; they're in on the joke." Initial reviews of OK Soda, while supporting Coke's hopes that teens will "get the joke," were less positive toward the mildly fruity, mildly peppery taste of the product. One real caller to the hot line said, "this stuff tastes like crap."

The New Bottom Line

Coca-Cola integrated issues management and marketing to create a product based solely on analysis of a certain segment of the external environment: teenagers. As creative a marketing approach as this may have been, in the end OK Soda did not find a market. The main reason for the product's failure seems not to have been in its marketing but in its taste: the sentiment noted in this feature's last line was shared by a majority of the target market. No amount of issues management or awareness can supersede the golden rule of marketing—consumers have to like the product in order to be convinced to buy it.

SOURCE: Information from J. Greenwald, "Will Teens Buy It?" *Time*, May 30, 1994, p. 51; L. M. Grossman, "Coke Hopes 'OK,' New Drink, Will Be Toast of Teen," *Wall Street Journal*, April 21, 1994, p. B7; and L. Jabbonsky, "OK for Whom?" *Beverage World*, May 1, 1994, p. 6.

▼ **EXHIBIT 21–3 General Types of Business Crises**

• major product defects	• boycotts	• major computer breakdowns
• major plant/equipment defects	• false rumors, slander	• on site/off-site product tampering
• executive kidnappings	• on-site/off-site sabotage	• terrorism
• major industrial accidents	• sexual harassment	• hostile takeovers
• recalls	• bribery, price fixing	
• illegal/unethical employee practices	• poor or faulty operator training	

SOURCE: I. L. Mitroff, "Crisis Management: Cutting through the Confusion," *Sloan Management Review,* Winter, 1988, p. 15.

that may affect it.[26] As any manager employed by Tylenol, Perrier, or Exxon can attest, the environment does not always allow this luxury. In some circumstances—when someone laces one of its products with poison or when one of its oil tankers runs aground—a firm finds itself forced into **crisis management.** A crisis can be characterized, in a business context, as a low-probability, high-consequence event that threatens the operation of an organization. Crisis management, then, involves strategic techniques for reducing the adverse effects of such events on the organization through planning, risk identification, loss mitigation, legal compliance, and management accountability. (For a list of some crisis events, see *Exhibit 21–3.*)

One of the goals of issues management is to avoid the need for crisis management. Environmental groups had been urging Exxon to take steps—strengthening the hulls of tankers and preparing quick-strike cleanup teams—that could have prevented or lessened the damage of the *Exxon Valdez* disaster. The oil company, however, was not responsive to its external stakeholders. The firm's response to the crisis ultimately damaged both the firm's credibility and its bottom line.

In a sense, to start a discussion of crisis management with the *Exxon Valdez* oil spill is misleading. Too many managers make the mistake of only considering crisis management in the wake of a major incident such as the *Exxon Valdez* spill or the bombing of the Murrah federal building in Oklahoma City in 1995. Often, crises result from a number of less dramatic situations, such as erosion of positive public perception, sudden market shifts, product failures, top management successions, cash shortages, and sudden shifts in government regulation or policy.[27]

Failure to plan for the occurrence of crises—whether the event makes the front page or the business page—leaves an organization vulnerable. In 1993, the University of Southern California Center for Crisis Management conducted studies on crisis response and identified four basic characteristics of the crisis-prone organization:

1. If the organization has any crisis preparation, that preparation is limited to a few specific types of crises and is too fragmented to be effective.

2. The organization focuses on single aspects of the crisis, and then only after it has occurred.

---

26. N. R. Augustine, "Managing the Crisis You Tried to Prevent," *Harvard Business Review,* November–December 1995, p. 147.

27. J. B. Kaufman, I. F. Kesner, and T. L. Hazen, "The Myth of Full Disclosure: A Look at Organizational Communications during Crises," *Business Horizons,* July–August 1994, p. 29.

▼ **EXHIBIT 21–4**
The Phases of
Crisis Management

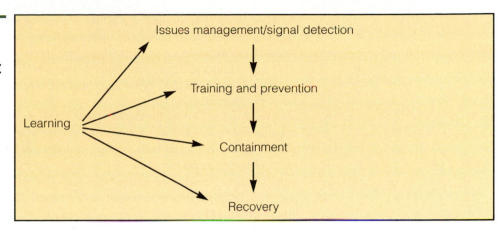

SOURCE: I. L. Mitroff, "Crisis Management: Cutting through the Confusion," *Sloan Management Review*, Winter, 1988, p. 10.

3. The organization's management only considers technical factors (as opposed to social or human factors) in the cause or prevention of crises.
4. The organization's management considers few, if any, stakeholders explicitly.

Because crisis situations differ, there are no ironclad rules for crisis management, and organizations in crisis do a great deal of learning during the crisis situation. *Exhibit 21–4* shows the five phases of crisis management identified by Professor Ian I. Mitroff of the University of Southern California. Note that learning is part of each of the other phases — a fact to remember as we examine various theories of the best ways to prepare for the worst.

PREPARATION FOR CRISES

Organizations that do not get involved in crisis management until the crisis is on them will spend most of their energy (and money) in the containment and recovery stages of *Exhibit 21–4*. A better strategy is to focus on *signal detection* and to prepare for crises. For many organizations, the first step is to develop and maintain a crisis management team. The second step is to train the team to deal effectively with a range of crises.

Training in Crisis Management In staffing a crisis management team, the organization should choose members representing all its divisions. Each member should have specific duties to perform and have the ability to execute those duties under pressure.

▼ The difficulty in crisis management training is that it is almost impossible to reproduce the pressure of a real crisis situation with a simulation, though many organizations have tried.

As simulations can be a prohibitively expensive method of crisis management training, many corporations rely on discussion-based, or "tabletop," activities to prepare their staffs for crises. Most tabletop crisis management exercises take place in a small-group setting, with participants sitting around a table and discussing how they would react to hypothetical situations. Beth A. Loewendick of the Washington, D.C.–based Corporate Response Group has identified four basic steps in creating a tabletop exercise: designing, developing, conducting, and evaluating.

1. Designing. The design of a tabletop exercise revolves around two key factors: the organization members chosen by upper management to participate and the specific risks and vulnerabilities faced by the company or industry engaged in the training. Crisis management training designers must specify the objectives of the sessions: What do we want to define, solve, and test? What aspects of our response capabilities do we want to place under a microscope?

2. Developing. During the development stage, trainers create specific scenarios that will provide the basis for discussion during the exercise. It should be possible to reasonably predict events that could have significant short- and long-term effects on the organization. After choosing a specific crisis, or crises, trainers must decide who would be involved in responding to the situation in the internal and external environments. They must also predict in what forms the crisis would manifest itself. Would it be a physical crisis, such as a fire or product tampering resulting in death and injuries, or would it be an economic crisis, such as a stock market crash or a hostile takeover? The exercise scenarios should be realistic and challenging for participants and should force them to consider critical issues and their roles in responding to the events both as individuals and as a group.

3. Conducting. The exercise itself should last from two to eight hours, beginning with an introduction to the crisis scenario. Participants could receive this information in written form or, if the organization has the resources, in a more realistic form, such as a video clip of simulated media coverage of an incident. Participants could receive information about the crisis event in time-based pieces, or "moves," to simulate reaction to a situation as it evolves.

As information is produced, participants discuss possible responses based on the organization's goals and resources. In this stage, a "devil's advocate" role-player can question any decision made by the trainees and force them to consider the numerous factors in crisis management.

4. Evaluating. In many cases, evaluation is a self-explanatory process, as a well-run tabletop exercise should point out any obvious weaknesses in an organization's crisis management capabilities. Companies often hire a professional evaluator to monitor the tabletop exercise and to make recommendations based on what he or she has observed.[28]

Reputation Management Many public relations experts believe that an organization needs to supplement crisis management teams with an ongoing strategy of **reputation management**. This aspect of crisis management is based on the notion that an organization must continually build a "reservoir of goodwill" with both internal and external stakeholders in preparation for a crisis.[29]

▼ A stakeholder that has a strong relationship with an organization is much less likely to take a combative stance against that organization in the event of a crisis.

When, for example, an employee is killed in a workplace accident, the crisis management process will most likely involve the union. If, on the one hand, the employer excluded the union from workplace safety discussions, the union's leadership will likely be publicly critical of the organization. If, on the other hand, the employer involved union leaders in workplace safety considerations, the union will be more apt to help the company figure out what went wrong rather than placing blame.

---

28. B. A. Loewendick, "Laying Your Crisis on the Table," *Training & Development*, November 1993, p. 15.
29. M. R. Hyman and A. A. Blum, "'Just' Companies Don't Fail: The Making of the Ethical Corporation," *Business and Society Review*, Spring 1995, p. 48.

We have already discussed most of the stakeholder groups with which this "reservoir of goodwill" must be established—unions, consumers, employees, the government, and so on. Reputation management underscores the importance of the media in acting as an information link between an organization and these stakeholders. "Perception is truth," according to one reputation management expert, Bill Patterson, "and, even though most executives don't like it, the media establishes the perception of your organization."[30]

Media scrutiny of business crises has exploded in the 1990s. As Patterson notes: "Most medium- and large-market TV news departments now have special teams to dig into consumer complaints and expose business foul-ups. They salivate over stories such as the Sears auto repair fiasco, the Dow Corning silicone breast implant nightmare, and the false syringe-in-the-Pepsi-can reports. Just listen to the 10-second news 'teasers' that run before the evening news and you will get a feel for the new media focus on the business scandal."[31]

Consequently, it is more important than ever before for organizations to have good relations with the media, meaning that reporters trust the information sources within the organization and turn to those sources for details during a crisis. (For a media relations checklist, see *Exhibit 21–5* on page 664.) Many public relations experts believe Pepsi was able to survive the aforementioned syringe scare because of its long-standing commitment to reputation management.

THE CONTAINMENT PROCESS

Once a crisis occurs, the focus of crisis management quickly turns to limiting the damage it causes. A critical element of this containment process is communication with external and internal stakeholders. In this regard, honesty is generally accepted as the best policy. "When the unexpected happens, be sure to apply the cardinal rule of crisis communications: Tell it all and tell it fast."[32]

The only problem with this rule of thumb is that a cynical American public does not always believe corporate spokespeople, even when they are telling the truth. Recently, Porter/Novelli, a New York public relations firm, conducted a survey to determine how the public reacts to the information given by corporations during a crisis. The findings were as follows:

▶ 19 percent of those questioned believe companies are totally truthful in a crisis situation.
▶ 75 percent say companies refuse to take responsibility for crises.
▶ 57 percent believe companies withhold negative information or lie following a crisis.
▶ 65 percent believe that when a company declines to comment, that means the company is guilty of wrongdoing.

Significantly, almost every respondent (95 percent) said he or she is more offended by a company's lying about a crisis than by the crisis itself.[33] This suggests that the manner in which a company discloses information goes a long way toward determining the success of crisis management policy.

---

30. B. Patterson, "Crises Impact on Reputation Management," *Public Relations Journal*, November 1993, p. 47.
31. *Ibid.*
32. B. Dilenschneider and R. Hyde, "Crisis Communications: Planning for the Unplanned," *Business Horizons*, January–February 1985, p. 35.
33. "In a Crisis, What You Say Isn't Always What the Public Hears," *Public Relations Journal*, September 1993, pp. 10–11.

▼ EXHIBIT 21–5 Media Relations Checklist: Ten Points to Remember When Dealing with the Media in a Crisis Situation

1. Prepare a one-page media crisis plan that delineates how your organization will handle the news media during the first hours of a crisis situation. Use the plan as the backbone of your activities during a crisis, and be sure to share the plan with co-employees.

2. Name a company spokesperson and a back-up to deal directly with the media during the crisis. Only one story must come from the company, and that story must remain consistent. By having a single spokesperson, you avoid the possibility that several versions of your story will reach media outlets.

3. Brainstorm about possible crises. Pick ten truly horrible events that could place your organization in a crisis situation, and decide how you would deal with the media in each case.

4. Face the media quickly and openly. Do not hide out. This may be a time when you do not want to deal with the media, but being candid and open are very important in the resolution of the crisis in the public's mind.

5. Have a team of fact gatherers made up of personnel different from those dealing directly with the media. Up-to-date information is critical.

6. Respond to every media question, no matter how tiresome or obvious. If the media outlet does not receive an answer from you, it will turn elsewhere, and the result might be harmful to the organization. Return calls to radio first, then television, then newspapers, because it is in that order that the news of the crisis will be reported to the community.

7. Never lie—not even one little "white lie." The media are quite effective in finding out lies, and a lie can severely damage you and your company's relationship with the media and the community.

8. Don't babble. Don't volunteer negative information; do not ramble on, saying more than you need to. The media will generally be negative enough without aid from the company.

9. Never go "off the record." Do not speculate. Keep safely within the facts.

10. Don't use business jargon to reporters. Keep your words basic. While it may be tempting to intellectualize with reporters hanging on your every word, resist temptation. Remember that the media represent a means of communicating with a public that will generally react negatively to such jargon.

SOURCE: B. Patterson, *Public Relations Journal,* November 1993, p. 48.

The Need for Full Disclosure Those who believe that an organization should "tell it all and tell it fast" make three basic assumptions about crisis situations: (1) credibility with stakeholders is the most important asset of an organization; (2) given today's media scrutiny, all the facts will come out eventually; and (3) a company is more likely to be forgiven if it makes a full disclosure.[34] (See the *Case—Intel Pentium—A Crisis of Management*—at the end of this chapter.)

The first assumption is an argument against one of the main reasons a company withholds information in the first place: worry over possible lawsuits. A report by *Fortune* magazine concluded that "in many crisis situations, potential legal liability may be trivial compared with the risk of alienating . . . customers, employees, or regulators."[35] Because company lawyers worry about short-term litigation possibilities, they may blind themselves to the long-term effects of withholding information.

---

34. Kaufman, Kesner, and Hazen, *op. cit.*, pp. 30–31.
35. "Smart Ways to Handle the Press," *Fortune,* June 19, 1989, pp. 69–75.

All three assumptions rest on the belief that both internal and external stakeholders form a relationship with a company.

▼ **When a company either withholds information or relays faulty information, the result is that "instead of viewing the firm as an ally undergoing difficulty, [stakeholders] develop an adversarial relationship which may prove devastating in the long run."[36]**

There are examples of both the good done by full disclosure and the harm done by other methods. In 1981, in the first week after poisoned Tylenol tablets caused seven deaths, nine out of ten Americans were aware of the story. In response, Tylenol's manufacturer, Johnson & Johnson, immediately pulled the product from the shelves and established a toll-free consumer information hotline. The company placed full-page ads in major newspapers across the country, produced a number of videotapes and 450,000 electronic messages for the medical community, and answered all letters concerning the issue. In addition, a sixty-second television spot describing the situation and outlining the company's reaction was seen in 85 percent of American households an average of 2.5 times during that first week. Instead of hiding from the crisis, Johnson & Johnson executives made themselves available to television shows such as *60 Minutes* and *Nightline* and publications such as the *Wall Street Journal* and *Business Week*. Within three years of the crisis, Tylenol had regained 98 percent of its market share.

In contrast, A. H. Robins seemed to ignore problems with its intrauterine contraceptive device, the Dalkon Shield. From 1970 to 1975, over 4.5 million of these devices were implanted in women, even though infections caused by the Dalkon Shield had resulted in miscarriages, sterility, and death from the very beginning. A. H. Robins never ordered a recall of the Dalkon Shield. In fact, the company never publicly acknowledged any problem with its product and continued to aggressively market the device. By the early 1980s, victims had filed 12,000 claims against the company. With no reservoir of goodwill to survive the charges, A. H. Robins filed for bankruptcy in 1985.[37]

Arguments against Full Disclosure Although the policy of full and immediate disclosure has many proponents, some crisis management experts warn managers against seeing it as the solution in every instance. One point often made is that the public does not know about the incidents in which organizations have successfully withheld information, kept a crisis internal, and avoided public exposure.

Incidents have occurred, however, in which full disclosure seems to have hurt a company. In the 1970s, in defending itself against charges of a design flaw in its Pinto automobile, the Ford Motor Company made public a cost-benefit analysis approximating the costs of deaths ($200,000 per person) and of injuries ($67,000 per person). The result was a public relations nightmare, as the public vilified the organization for seeming to have little regard for the value of human life.

Furthermore, when employees speak out following a crisis, the risk of litigation increases. As mentioned, many lawyers operate under the assumption that plaintiffs will use anything said by the organization against it and that disclosures could provide the impetus for further lawsuits. The possibility also exists that in disclosing too soon a company will react without knowing all the facts. "If you say something before you really know

---

36. Kaufman, Kesner, and Hazen, *op.cit.*, p. 30.
37. *Ibid.*, pp. 31–33.

the facts, you are speculating. If it is subsequently wrong, you are a liar," notes Warren Anderson, former CEO of Union Carbide.[38]

Deciding Whether to Disclose How can a manager decide whether full disclosure is the best policy? Crisis analysts Jeffrey B. Kaufmann, Idalene F. Kesner, and Thomas Lee Hazen have devised five questions that should provide managers with some guidance.

1. *Could nondisclosure be fatal or lead to further injury?* "Fatal" refers to both people and the company. If nondisclosure poses any risk to the lives, safety, and health of employees or any other stakeholders, then it is an unacceptable policy. Furthermore, if the crisis can be regarded in any way as a "time bomb" that, if detonated, could destroy the company, full disclosure is the only choice.

2. *Is the organization the victim or the culprit?* If, as was the case with Johnson & Johnson and the Tylenol-tampering crisis, the company is the victim, it is obviously easier from a public relations standpoint to justify full disclosure. If, however, the crisis resulted from internal mismanagement, then the possibility for lawsuits raises the risks of full disclosure. It should be noted, however, that even if a company is at risk, partial or dishonest disclosure can be more costly than telling the truth. When an unusually high number of accidents involving Audi cars became apparent in the early 1980s, the German auto manufacturer blamed them on driver error. Only under mounting pressure from the National Highway Safety Administration did the company admit the possibility that its 1986 Audi 5000 series had technical defects that caused sudden, unintended acceleration. Finally, the model was recalled.

Besides the costs of recalling the automobiles, Audi's questionable crisis management had two serious repercussions: (1) two hundred lawsuits, which wound up costing the company millions of dollars, and (2) a damaged reputation, which proved disastrous for U.S. sales. In 1985, Audi of America sold 74,241 units in the country; by 1992, sales were just over 14,000.[39] Eventually, the company was able to prove that nothing was ever wrong with the car. That proof came too late, however.

3. *Are the fictions surrounding the crisis worse than the facts?* The power of rumor can destroy a company, and sometimes full disclosure is the best self-defense against falsehoods perpetrated by the media or an external stakeholder. The danger of releasing only partial information to rebut rumor should also be recognized. In the wave of publicity surrounding Dow Corning breast implants and breast cancer, two women performed surgery on themselves to remove their implants—incidents the company might have been able to prevent with a stronger information campaign. Sometimes, the rumors that lead to a crisis are completely untrue, in which case a company must aggressively campaign to discredit them. (See *Company Focus: Procter & Gamble Company*.)

4. *Can the organization afford to respond to the crisis?* The recall and reintroduction of Tylenol cost Johnson & Johnson $250 million. Many companies cannot afford such large expenditures and must therefore consider the bottom line in weighing full disclosure. Remember, however, that the first important question concerns safety risks, which outweigh any financial considerations.

5. *Can the organization afford* not *to respond?* This question deals with reputation management, mostly applicable to firms that produce more than one product. For example, a drug manufacturer whose pain-relieving pill is associated with harmful side effects may

38. *Ibid.*, p. 34.
39. K. Goldman, "Audi of America Puts Account, Held by Needham, Up for Review," *Wall Street Journal*, March 24, 1993, p. B6.

COMPANY FOCUS: PROCTER & GAMBLE COMPANY
THE DEVIL IN THE P&G TRADEMARK

A bizarre example of crisis management involves a persistent rumor that links Procter & Gamble Company and devil worship. Since 1980, the rumor has spread that the conglomerate's trademark is a satanic symbol and that the president of P&G made a deal with the devil in which he agreed to donate a large portion of the company's profits to the church of Satan in return for financial success. P&G has filed fifteen lawsuits, the latest one in 1995, to quell the rumors, and its public relations department has devoted significant resources to the issue. Some crisis management experts question if P&G is not, in effect, keeping the gossip alive by responding to it, but the company continues to treat the rumor as a serious threat to its reputation.

Trademark Problems

The P&G trademark was first used in the 1850s. Over the next thirty years, the logo evolved into a half moon in the shape of an elderly bearded man and thirteen stars, to honor the thirteen original colonies. The trademark was copyrighted in that form in 1882 and remained unchanged for more than a century.

The basic rumor claims this logo includes a ram's horn and three sets of stars that can be connected to form the number 666, a Biblical reference to Satan. The rumor also claims that the satanic connection has been discussed on television shows such as *60 Minutes*, *Merv Griffin*, and *Donahue*. In 1990, a flyer surfaced in Nashville, Tennessee, reading: "Recently, on the *Merv Griffin Show*, a group of cultists were featured, among them the owner of Proctor [*sic*] & Gamble Corp. He said that as long as the gays and other cults have come out of the closet, he was doing the same. He said that he had told Satan that if he (Satan) would help him prosper, then he would give his heart and soul to him. He gave Satan all the credit for his riches." The flyer went on to list P&G products such as Crest, Tide, Ivory Soap, Oil of Olay, and Crisco, urging Christians to boycott these items.

P&G Strikes Back

To combat these "totally ludicrous" rumors, P&G's public relations department sent "truth packets" to hundreds of churches, schools, newspapers, and radio stations in states where the rumors had cropped up. These packets included letters from evangelists Billy Graham and Jerry Falwell giving P&G a clean bill of moral health and messages from the producers of the *Phil Donahue Show* and the *Merv Griffin Show* saying that no one had ever appeared on their sets speaking of deals between P&G and the devil. To ensure that the logo could not be misconstrued, in 1991 the company made changes to avoid the perception that anything in the logo represented sixes.

P&G's legal department has also become involved in fighting the rumors. In 1982, the company filed federal lawsuits in Florida, Georgia, New Mexico, and Tennessee against individuals—including a minister and a schoolteacher—spreading "false and malicious statements about the company and calling for boycotts." After a five-year period in which the rumors seemed to disappear, in the summer of 1995, P&G sued Randy L. Haugen, an independent Amway distributor, for leaving a message on the company's voice mail system repeating the *Phil Donahue Show* story. It was the sixth such lawsuit involving an Amway distributor, even though Amway has continually stated that it does not "condone the spreading of false and malicious" rumors against P&G.

The New Bottom Line

A few years after the stories about P&G and the devil first appeared, Advertising Age *conducted a survey in which one-third of the consumers who responded said they had heard of the rumors and, of those, only 3 percent said they believed them. Nonetheless, P&G feels justified in its aggressive tactics to dispel the story. Boycotts often fester over a long period of time, and with the growing popularity of information technology such as the Internet, negative information about a company can spread quickly.*

SOURCE: Information from M. J. Austin and L. Brumfield, "P&G's Run-in with the Devil," *Business and Society Review*, Summer 1991, pp. 16, 18; A. Swasy, "P&G Once More Has a Devil of a Time with the Firm's Logo," *Wall Street Journal*, March 26, 1990, p. B3; and Z. Schiller, "P&G Is Still Having a Devil of a Time," *Business Week*, September 11, 1995, p. 46.

find that its other product lines suffer from association. In this case, it would seem that full disclosure of steps taken to reduce the side effects of the pain-relieving drug is needed to reassure the consumer about the entire product spectrum.[40]

DECISION MAKING IN THE CRISIS SITUATION

Whether or not to disclose all the facts is only one of the decisions that must be made in a crisis situation. While we could not possibly cover, or even predict, all possible decisions, we can examine decision-making patterns. The one constant in crisis decision making is pressure resulting from: (1) the need to react quickly; (2) the intense scrutiny of the media, public interest groups, and other external stakeholders; and (3) the threat of negative consequences resulting from poor decision making. Because of this pressure, even a decision maker who performs very well in normal conditions may struggle in a crisis situation.[41]

In crisis situations, decision makers tend to choose among four maladaptive strategies and one adaptive strategy. The four maladaptive strategies are (1) unconflicted inertia, (2) unconflicted change, (3) defense avoidance, and (4) hypervigilance. These are labeled maladaptive because they do not enable the decision maker to "discover the best means for escaping danger." The adaptive strategy—the vigilant approach—gives a company the best chance to survive the crisis situation with minimum damage.[42]

The specifics of the maladaptive decision-making strategies are as follows:

1. *Unconflicted inertia* results when decision makers determine that initial signs of a crisis do not warrant any action. This is a failure in issues management as well as crisis management, for it suggests a misreading of the business environment. The inertia often results in varying states of unpreparedness when the actual crisis hits.

2. *Unconflicted change* occurs when a decision maker "wears blinders." That is, one solution to the problem is selected by management, and all other options are ignored. Unconflicted change is often the result of choosing the first possible solution, or the easiest, which results in the feeling that "nothing more needs to be done." There are two obvious pitfalls to this approach. First, the most easily adopted solution to a crisis may not be the best one. Second, if and when the initial solution fails, the decision maker is left without a better back-up.

3. *Defense avoidance* occurs when the decision maker copes with the crisis by avoiding all signs that point to future anxiety or to other unpleasant emotional reactions. The decision maker ignores the crisis by turning his or her attention to other, less critical situations, thereby trading anxiety for the safety of easy action. The decision maker avoids initial stress but almost certainly ensures greater stress in the future.

4. *Hypervigilance*, possibly the worst of the maladaptive strategies, involves an overreaction to the crisis in which the decision maker changes solutions too quickly. Eventually, this path leads to crisis management that alters direction at every new development, leaving the organization with little or no coherent strategy. One factor leading to hypervigilance is fear, shame, or guilt on the part of the decision maker at the outcome of the crisis situation and the desire on his or her part to "make up" for the damage caused by the sit-

40. *Ibid.*, pp. 35–38.
41. D. E. Williams and B. A. Olaniran, "Exxon's Decision-Making Flaws: The Hypervigilant Response to the Valdez Grounding," *Public Relations Review*, Spring 1994, p. 8.
42. I. L. Janis and L. Mann, *Decision Making: A Psychological Analysis of Conflict, Choice, and Commitment* (New York: Free Press, 1977), pp. 64–65.

uation. Time pressure can also increase hypervigilance, as the decision maker "grasps at straws" to find a quick solution.

The adaptive strategy is referred to as *vigilant* decision making. The vigilant decision maker recognizes and understands the importance of an impending crisis, is confident that thorough analysis will point to the best possible course of action, and does not allow time pressures to force decisions that he or she knows are unwise.[43]

THE RECOVERY PROCESS

If a company can survive the economic consequences of a crisis—lawsuits, government fines, and so on—it moves into the *recovery* stage of crisis management. In crisis situations precipitated by company wrongdoing, the recovery stage is fundamentally a public relations process and involves three strategies: (1) attempting to present a convincing and plausible description of the situation that offsets accepted, negative versions; (2) attempting to diffuse the anger and hostility directed at the company because of the crisis; and (3) attempting to disassociate the organization from the wrongdoing. The primary way in which the company carries out these strategies is by issuing an *apologia*. Although it may contain an apology, an apologia has broader goals in that it is a defense that "seeks to present a compelling, counterdescription of organizational actions." The hope is that "once key publics understand a corporation's explanation, then they will be unable to condemn the corporation."[44]

Lee Iacocca, at that time the chairman of Chrysler, used the apologia strategy in the late 1980s after a disclosure that company executives had driven over 60,000 automobiles with unhooked odometers before selling them as new. One executive drove an unused car home in a rainstorm, hit a mud puddle, and flipped the automobile on its side. After $950 in repairs, the car was sold as new. Some of the cars had been driven more than 400 miles before being sold.

Following severe public criticism, Iacocca tried to rename the practice "a testing program." He took out an advertisement in major newspapers that read: "Testing cars is a good idea. Disconnecting odometers is a lousy idea. That's a mistake we won't make again at Chrysler." By labeling what had happened "a mistake," Iacocca tried to neutralize the ethical implications of the practice by implying that it represented a momentary lack of judgment that may, in fact, have been unintentional.[45] Perhaps Iacocca's apologia would have been easier to accept had his company not fought efforts by federal inspectors to identify the used automobiles.

---

43. Williams and Olaniran, *op. cit.*, pp. 8–10.
44. K. M. Hearit, "Apologies and Public Relations Crises at Chrysler, Toshiba, and Volvo," *Public Relations Review*, Summer 1994, p. 115.
45. *Ibid.*, pp. 113–116.

THE DELICATE BALANCE

Perhaps the most visible and important implementation of strategy for an organization occurs when a crisis crops up. Some crises have meant the death of an organization because they were not anticipated or were improperly handled once they occurred. Consequently, many corporate strategists call for crisis preparation well in advance of an actual emergency. The delicate balance here, though, involves the management resources required to engage in crisis preparation. So-called tabletop crisis exercises have their place, but perhaps not if they are done so frequently and take up so much time that management loses substantial work time elsewhere. Another delicate balance must be found when a crisis actually happens. Whereas, as we have noted, full disclosure can save a company and partial or dishonest disclosure can cause its downfall, we can only speculate about instances in which nondisclosure has been successful. Hence, "telling everything" to the public may not always be in the best interest of the organization.

TERMS AND CONCEPTS FOR REVIEW

Bureaucratic control system 653
Clan control 653
Crisis management 660
Environmental scanning 654
Feedback control systems 651
Feedforward control system 651
Financial strategy 649

Functional strategies 647
Human resources strategy 649
Information systems strategy 648
Issues management 653
Marketing strategy 647
Operations strategy 647
Premise control 651

Priority publics 658
Reputation management 662
Research and development strategy 648
Strategic control 651
Strategy implementation 646

SUMMARY

1. Strategy is implemented through structure, culture, leadership, and reward systems. Implementation is a key step in the strategic management process, for the best strategy can be sabotaged by poor implementation.

2. The two primary functional strategies are marketing strategy and operations strategy. The marketing strategy supports growth and evolves from the cumulative pattern of decisions made by employees who interact with customers. The operations strategy is the organization's plan for designing and managing the process by which its goods and services are offered to customers.

3. Other functional strategies include strategies for research and development, information systems, human resources, and finance.

4. Four types of structures can be used to implement functional strategies: (a) functional, (b) product or market group, (c) project matrix, and (d) network.

5. According to Danny Miller, the strategic management process is enhanced by four high-performance corporate cultures: (a) craftsperson, (b) builder, (c) pioneer, and (d) salesperson.

6. A strategic control system must support managers in assessing the relevance of the organization's strategy to its progress in the accomplishment of its goals. In a feedforward control system, managers anticipate changes in the external and internal environments based on analysis of inputs from stakeholders and the remote environment. In a feedback control system, managers set objectives whereby specific organizational activities are to be achieved within a given time frame. They then measure the actual feedback against the targeted performance levels.

7. Issues management allows organizations to know and understand their environments. To identify key environmental issues before crises occur, organizations engage in environmental scanning.

8. An important aspect of issues analysis is calculating each issue's urgency so that the organization knows when and how quickly it must respond.

9. In formulating a message regarding its position on an issue, an organization must identify its priority publics—those groups or individuals that can most help or hinder attempts to influence the issue. To identify priority publics, the firm must ask: (a) Who in the environment makes the decisions on this issue? (b) What segments are likely to support the organization's position? (c) What segments are likely to oppose it? (d) What segment can be successfully targeted to make the biggest difference in advancing the organization's position?

10. Crisis management may involve such crises as major product defects, major industrial accidents, false rumors, boycotts, and terrorism. Its aim is to reduce the adverse

effects of such events on the organization through planning, risk identification, loss mitigation, legal compliance, and management accountability.

11. Crisis preparation is the best path for most organizations to take in attempting to manage crises. This may involve developing, maintaining, and training a crisis team.

12. Organizations that engage in reputation management typically can handle crises better than those that do not. Strong relationships with stakeholders may reduce the chance that those stakeholders will take a combative stance against the organization in the event of a crisis.

13. When a crisis does occur, full disclosure is often the best policy. Organizations can ask five questions before deciding whether to make full disclosure: (a) Could nondisclosure be fatal or lead to further injury? (b) Is the organization the victim or the culprit? (c) Are the fictions surrounding the crisis worse than the facts? (d) Can the organization afford to respond to the crisis? (e) Can the organization afford *not* to respond?

14. Some maladaptive decision-making strategies in the face of a crisis are: (a) unconflicted inertia, (b) unconflicted change, (c) defense avoidance, and (d) hypervigilance. An adaptive strategy is vigilant decision making.

EXERCISES

1. What is the distinction between a marketing strategy and an operations strategy? Why must the two be intimately linked?

2. Draw a chart with circles and arrows that shows interdependencies among various stakeholder groups. State in writing how these interdependencies affect strategic management.

3. "Given the explosion in telecommunications, information system strategy has become paramount in any organization." Do you agree with this statement? Explain your answer.

4. How does the formal structure of an organization relate to its management strategy?

5. Under the heading "The Relationship of Structure and Strategy," four types of structures were described. What type (or types) of company might find the functional structure most suitable? The product or market group structure? The project matrix structure? The network structure?

6. *Exhibit 21–1* described four corporate orientations, the craftsperson, the builder, the pioneer, and the salesperson. For each orientation, give an example of a corporation that you think is described by that orientation.

7. How do feedforward and feedback control systems differ? Is there any way to use them in conjunction with each other? Explain.

8. Why do you think clan control is more effective in small U.S. organizations than in large ones?

9. List various ways in which you would go about your job if its main purpose was environmental scanning.

10. Assume that you are working for a corporation that makes ladders. You have just been informed that a consumer advocacy group is going to publish the results of a study it recently conducted concerning the use of ladders. You have been told that the results indicate that people who spend a lot of time standing on ladders are more likely to suffer strokes. How should you react to this information? What course of action would you recommend to your organization? Explain your answers.

11. For the question above, identify the priority publics for your organization.

12. Review the list given in *Exhibit 21–3* concerning the general types of business crises. Reorder that list according to which crises are the most detrimental to an organization. Be prepared to defend your rankings.

13. In *Exhibit 21–4*, an arrow points from "Learning" to each of the phases of crisis management. Why?

14. What arguments can you give against using tabletop crisis management exercises in an organization?

15. List the steps involved in reputation management.

16. Do you agree with all of the points in the checklist in *Exhibit 21–5*? Why or why not?

17. Why is the containment process also called damage control?

18. A hundred years ago, large business organizations presumably did not feel the need to make full disclosure when a crisis hit. Why do you think modern large-scale organizations feel compelled to disclose so much? What has changed?

19. Give an example of a crisis situation in which an organization cannot afford to respond.

20. Defense avoidance was listed as a maladaptive decision-making strategy in a time of crisis. Give examples of other times when defense avoidance might occur in a manager's life.

SELECTED REFERENCES

▶ Haigh, David. *Strategic Control of Marketing Finance.* London: Financial Times, Pitman, 1994.

▶ Myers, Kenneth N. *Total Contingency Planning for Disasters: Managing Risk—Minimizing Losses—Ensuring Business Continuity.* New York: Wiley, 1993.

▶ Simons, Robert. *Levers of Control: How Managers Use Innovative Control Systems to Drive Strategic Renewal.* Boston: Harvard Business School Press, 1995.

▶ Stoffels, John D. *Strategic Issues Management: A Comprehensive Guide to Environmental Scanning.* New York: Pergamon Press, 1994.

▶ Walker, Warren E. *The Use of Scenarios and Gaming in Crisis Management Planning and Training.* Santa Monica, Calif.: RAND, 1995.

RESOURCES ON THE INTERNET

▼ The United States Small Business Administration (SBA) helps entrepreneurs and others in small businesses to understand the strategies needed to succeed. SBA's site gives contact information for SBA offices across the United States. To access it, go to

http://sbaonline.sba.gov/

or

gopher://www/sbaonline.sba.gov/

or

ftp://www.sbaobline.sba.gov/

▼ ISX Corporation creates advanced technology systems to help businesses implement strategies. To access ISX's information network, go to

http://isx.com/

For more general information on technology that can help business operations, access Macmillan Publications' Information SuperLibrary at

http://www.mcp.com/

▼ The Centre for Management of Technology and Entrepreneurship is involved in research concerning the use of technology in business-level decisions. To access its site, go to

http://www.ie.utoronto.ca/CMTE/ cmteintr.html

CASE

INTEL PENTIUM—A CRISIS OF MANAGEMENT

Background

In 1994, Thomas Nicely, a math professor at Lynchberg College in Virginia, was engaged in theoretical math analysis when he noticed his personal computer was repeating an error at the ninth decimal place. On October 24, Nicely called Intel Corporation, manufacturer of the Pentium chip microprocessor that controlled his computer, and reported the problem. Intel acknowledged that the chip had a flaw that affected its ability to do certain division equations and told Nicely they had been investigating the problem since early summer.

Not satisfied with Intel's response, Nicely sent an E-mail message to various colleagues, warning them of the "bug." Within a week, news of the flaw had spread across the Internet. Within two weeks, Intel—which dominates the global market for PC chips with a market share of more than 80 percent—faced a major public relations crisis as industry insiders, consumers, and the media expressed outrage at its "cover-up" and subsequent treatment of the flaw. The company's stock dropped 5 percent, and some of its largest customers threatened to look elsewhere for their microprocessors.

In spite of this reaction, the Pentium bug did not represent a rare occurrence; flaws are common in new microprocessors. "We've never had a chip without one," says Intel's CEO, Andrew Grove. In fact, the company's two previous generations of chips—the 386 and 486—were more flawed than the Pentium. What was it about this situation that made Intel, in the words of one observer, "the Exxon of the chip industry"?

Breakthrough Marketing

The roots of Intel's crisis management problems can be found in the company's ground-breaking marketing strategy. Microchips are considered highly technical components of more interest to manufacturers than consumers and have traditionally been marketed as such. But in 1994, Intel launched a $150 million advertising campaign that took two unprecedented steps. First, the company advertised its own name with the far-reaching "Intel Inside" campaign. Second, the company promoted the Pentium chip as an improvement over its own 486 product. The basis of both strategies was to ensure that the growing numbers of beginning computer users would associate Intel with reliability and high performance standards. As one of the advertisements claimed, "with Intel inside, you know you've got . . . unparalleled quality."

While the marketing campaign served to give Intel brand name recognition unmatched in the microprocessor industry, it also left the company open to crisis possibilities that had not existed when few consumers knew who made the parts in their personal computers. Because of Intel's new visibility, when Professor Nicely broadcast Pentium's flaw over the Internet, it became a newsworthy item, as would a crisis at Coca-Cola or General Motors.

Flawed Strategy

Although Intel had been aware of the flaw before Nicely's telephone call, the company had decided that the chance that the flaw would cause a problem—once per nine billion random calculations, according to an internal study—was so slim that no public announcement was necessary. Once the story broke, Intel's response continued to be dominated by the assertion that the odds against the flaw's causing problems were astronomical. The company refused to provide replacement chips unless customers could prove they routinely engaged in the complex equations that the bug would affect. When critics questioned Intel's assessment of the risk factor, Grove responded, "If you know where a meteor will land, you can go there and get hit." That line typified what many felt to be Intel's arrogant attitude concerning the Pentium affair.

Crisis management analysts interpreted this initial response as the action of a company unprepared for the public relations demands of the new consumer market it had cultivated. Intel was focusing on the reality of the problem by insisting that it was highly unlikely that a user would be affected by the flaw. But as Arnold Hubermen, a crisis management expert, pointed out, "We're not talking reality. We're talking marketing." And a rule of marketing is that "consumers expect that with a computer, like any product, if there is a problem you take it in," noted Michael Slater, publisher of the *Microprocessor Report*. Intel was urged to conduct a recall with the goal of restoring consumer goodwill, as the General Motors Corporation had done when it sent thousands of Saturn automobiles to be destroyed because of corroded engines.

The company, however continued to ignore marketing wisdom and treated the crisis as an engineering problem.

CASE (CONTINUED)

"We broke it down into small parts; that was comforting," admitted Paul Otelli, Intel's senior vice president for worldwide sales. Confident that ordinary users would accept the explanation that they would not be affected by the flaw, Intel executives limited their crisis management to daily meetings in which customer complaints were addressed on a case-by-case basis.

Continuing Problems

This reactive strategy proved untenable as the crisis built momentum. On December 12, 1994, IBM announced it would stop all shipments of its personal computers that contained Pentium chips. IBM claimed Intel had underrepresented the risk of problems; using its own methods, IBM estimated that a user could experience an error once every twenty-four days, instead of once every twenty-seven years, as Intel had claimed. Intel executives, and many industry analysts, dismissed IBM's move as an attempt to improve the sales of its own microprocessors, but the damage had been done. The Pentium flaw made its way back to the front pages, and Intel's stock dropped another 6.5 percent.

Around the time of IBM's announcement, Intel yet again displayed its lack of marketing savvy when it announced that it had "fixed" the flaw. In engineering jargon, this means that the company had begun the lengthy process of moving a new Pentium chip into production. But the mass media interpreted "fixed" to mean the company had stopped shipping the flawed chip, which would not be the case for months.

The miscommunication brought the company in for another round of negative publicity. Many critics expressed their views over the Internet: "If they want their chips to be used in critical applications (as they obviously do), they have a responsibility to notify users when problems like these are discovered—and take their lumps if necessary. It's a responsibility that the manufacturers simply must assume voluntarily. If they don't, legislation should be enacted that requires it—as was done with the auto manufacturers."

Intel's Recall

Finally, on December 21, seven weeks after the crisis broke, Intel decided to replace the flawed chips. The company ran a full-page ad in major newspapers that day, apologizing for its "handling of the recently publicized Pentium processor flaw." Though the ad restated Intel's belief that the flaw was "an extremely minor problem," it recognized that many

"users have concerns" and offered an updated version of the Pentium chip, free of charge, for any consumer who requested one.

The response to the "better-late-than-never" announcement was immediate and positive. Within a day, Intel's stock had risen $3.4375 a share. In January 1995, the company made two key announcements: (1) it would take a $475 million pre-tax charge to cover the costs of replacing flawed chips, and (2) in the future, it would broadcast news of chip imperfections and allow the market to decide whether they were relevant or not. A crisis management expert called the latter announcement "a magnificent step." Consumers seemed to share this reaction and rewarded Intel with record sales of $3.55 billion for the first quarter of 1995.

New Industry Trends in Crisis Management

The general opinion is that if Intel had announced the flaw, explained the low probability of its occurrence, and offered free replacements immediately on discovery in the early summer, the company could have avoided the negative publicity and saved itself the replacement costs. (As it turned out, only about 10 percent of owners requested and received a new chip.)

The lessons of the Pentium crisis were not lost on the rest of the computer industry. In the spring of 1995, when a bug turned up in Intuit's MacInTax program, the company immediately offered to replace disks on request for the software company's 1.65 million customers—even though the bug affected fewer than 1 percent of them. When a similar glitch appeared in 10 percent of Compaq Computer Corporation's LTE Elite notebooks in Europe, the company decided to recall all units. Both companies were lauded for their honesty and suffered relatively minor economic damage, at least when compared with Intel. It seems that when it comes to crisis management, as one expert remarked, "the public loves a confessed sinner."

Critical Thinking Questions

1. Earlier in this chapter, we listed three assumptions concerning crisis situations: (a) credibility with stakeholders is the most important asset of an organization; (b) given today's media scrutiny, all the facts will come out eventually; and (c) a company is more likely to be forgiven if it makes a full disclosure. Evaluate Intel's performance with regard to each point.

2. How does the Intel crisis underscore the effect technological advances such as the Internet have on crisis management? Did the company underestimate this aspect of the remote environment?

3. Is it possible to explain Intel's response to this situation as a failure in communications between business-level strat-

egy—in this case marketing—and the crisis management team? Explain your answer.

4. Evaluate the learning process that occurred during the crisis and its end result not only for Intel but for the microchip industry.

SOURCE: Information from J. Kim, "Intel Puts Chips on the Table," *USA Today*, December 21, 1994, pp. B1–B2; "Intel's Chip of Worms," *Economist*, December 17, 1994, p. 65; J. Charlton and S. K. Yoder, "Humble Pie: Intel to Replace Its Pentium Chips," *Wall Street Journal*, December 21, 1994, p. B1; R. D. Hof, "The Education of Andrew Grove," *Business Week*, January 16, 1995, p. 61; B. Johnson, "Should Pentium Chips Be Recalled by Intel?" *Advertising Age*, December 12, 1994, p. 58; J. Markoff, "Intel's Crash Course on Consumers," *New York Times*, December 21, 1994, pp. C1–C6; I. Sager, "Bare Knuckles at Big Blue," *Business Week*, December 26, 1994, pp. 60–62; "Internet Voices," *Computerworld*, December 5, 1994, p. 14; Advertisement, *USA Today*, December 21, 1994, p. 9A; B. Johnson, "Will '95 Be the Year of the Pentium?" *Advertising Age*, January 30, 1995, p. 23; T. Quinlan, "Intel Recovers from Pentium Woes with Record Profits," *Infoworld*, April 24, 1995, p. 12; D. Foust, "Good Instincts at Intuit," *Business Week*, March 27, 1995, p. 36; and S. McCartney, "Compaq Recalling Notebook Computer from Dealers in Europe to Repair Bugs," *Wall Street Journal Europe*, December 22, 1994, p. B8.

CHAPTER 22

STRATEGIC MANAGEMENT TRENDS

CHAPTER OUTLINE

- Global Strategic Management
- Strategic Management of Information Technology
- Technology and the New Workplace
- Managing the New Networks

Iɴᴛʀᴏᴅᴜᴄᴛɪᴏɴ

Every generation of managers and entrepreneurs has to deal with a continually changing business environment.[1] Changes in social mores, changes in technology, changes in local, federal, and global politics—all contribute to the dynamic nature of the business world. It is not an exaggeration to say that the managers heading into the business world in the last years of the twentieth century face a period of change unmatched since the industrial revolution of the 1880s, when the United States began the shift from an agrarian to an industrial society. (See *Exhibit 22–1* for some predictions on how this period of change will manifest itself. Many of the ideas in this exhibit will be discussed at some point in this chapter.) The 1990s ushered in a technological revolution, popularly known as the Information Age, that has dramatically altered the business landscape, not to mention the role of the manager.

For an example, we need look no further than the field of crisis management. In 1995, the Royal Dutch/Shell Group faced a crisis management challenge surrounding the oil company's decision to sink the Brent Spar oil rig in the North Sea. Environmental groups immediately launched a response that included support from German chancellor Helmut Kohl, European trade unions, and even branches of the Protestant Church.[2] A boycott of Shell stations on the European continent was devastating—Deutsche Shell reported that sales had dropped 20 to 30 percent in the first week after the decision to sink the rig had been announced. Members of the environmental group Greenpeace, armed with satellite communication and video equipment for worldwide transmission, occupied the Brent Spar for three weeks as it motored toward its final destination. The camera's eye caught images of protesters and journalists being bullied and harassed by Shell employees—including an incident in which a Greenpeace helicopter was blasted with high-power water cannons—and beamed them around the world.

Although the incidents received little attention from the British press or citizenry, in whose waters the rig was to be sunk, the reaction in the rest of Europe finally convinced Shell to abandon plans to dispose of the Brent Spar in that manner. Ironically, Shell had the backing of many scientists when it claimed that death at sea was the most environmentally friendly demise for the obsolete Brent Spar; in fact, within months, Greenpeace formally apologized for its misguided environmental stance concerning the matter. Faced with a global boycott, however, Shell made a decision based on the realities of public perception rather than on the realities of science.[3]

The lesson of the Brent Spar is that environmental stakeholders were more effective at dispensing information than was Shell, even though the company had the facts on its side.[4] In fact,

---

1. S. Ghoshal and C. A. Bartlett, "Changing the Role of Top Management: Beyond Structure to Processes," *Harvard Business Review,* January–February 1995, p. 86.

2. C. Rohwedder and P. Gumbel, "Green and Gold: Shell Abandons Plans for Scuttling Oil Rig under Protest," *Wall Street Journal,* June 21, 1995, p. A1.

3. B. Bahree, K. Pope, and A. Sullivan, "Giant Outsmarted: How Greenpeace Sank Shell's Plan to Dump Big Oil Rig in Atlantic," *Wall Street Journal,* July 7, 1995, p. A1.

4. M. L. Markus and M. Keil, "If We Build It, They Will Come: Designing Information Systems That People Want to Use," *Sloan Management Review,* Summer 1994, p. 11.

▼ **EXHIBIT 22–1
Predictions for the
Information Age**

- Violence, traffic gridlock, and other societal problems, combined with new telecommuting technologies, will reinforce trends toward "cocooning" and "burrowing." Home and catalogue shopping, home banking, home working, home entertainment, home health care, and home schooling will increase.

- Telecommuting technologies will reinforce and accelerate the movement of people and enterprises from the center to the periphery. More people will live in edge cities and in small-town and rural settings.

- Two-way, interactive technologies—the personal computer and the television—will improve the quality of life by expanding cultural opportunities. When given a choice, many people will choose interactive media over television watching.

- Voice-activated E-mail, video recorders, word processors, and other innovations will make telecommuting easy for corporations to manage.

- Distributed work will result in decreased demand for downtown office space.

- Companies will create "enterprise networks"—virtual organizations that link people in widely scattered locations around shared missions and common tasks. Work will move electronically to different time zones every eight hours, providing customer access on a twenty-four-hour basis.

- Leadership will favor persons skilled in symbol manipulation (for example, those with skills in journalism, public relations, acting, and advertising). Historically, leaders were skilled in violence (for example, military leaders). The industrial revolution produced leaders skilled in finance and negotiation (for example, bankers, lawyers, and accountants).

- Just-in-time learning will increase the effectiveness of educational delivery. Home schooling and parental control of education will grow.

SOURCE: *Forbes*, July 17, 1995, p. 32.

▼ The strategic management of information is going to be the primary challenge of the turn-of-the-century manager, not only in the realm of public relations but also in every aspect of decision making on a functional, business, and corporate level.

Business has responded; from 1990 to 1996, U.S. industry spent more on computer and communications equipment than on all other capital equipment combined (all the machinery needed for manufacturing, mining, agriculture, construction, and so on).[5]

As society changes in the Information Age, so will business. The United States leads the world in developing, applying, and exporting technology. This technology, however, is fundamentally altering the business of doing business.[6] In this final chapter, we examine some of the trends of the Information Age and try to predict the effect of these trends on strategic management.

---

5. J. Huey, "Waking Up to the New Economy," *Fortune*, June 27, 1994, p. 36; and U.S. Department of Commerce.

6. L. Brown and H. Pattinson, "Information Technology and Telecommunications: Impacts on Strategic Alliance Formation and Management," *Management Decision*, July 1995, p. 41.

GLOBAL STRATEGIC MANAGEMENT

Previous chapters have made numerous references to the globalization of the business community. We discussed the financial and ethical challenges of multinational corporations, the role of regulation in international business, and the responsibility of a corporation to oversee stakeholders from the governmental level to the community level. One factor of globalization that has not been discussed is global strategic management, or the application of strategic management methods to international business. Because a major component of strategic management is the analysis of the external environment, global strategic management by definition relies on analysis of the global environment—a daunting task for any corporation[7] (as the executives at the Royal Dutch/Shell Group discovered).

Recognizing the need for a framework for global strategic management, the World Future Society has sponsored a project called World 2000. The project takes into consideration such global environment–altering events as the collapse of communism, the unification of Europe, the information revolution, and the environmental ethic, and aims to create a global strategic management process that encompasses what it calls the "revolutionary" changes that will shape the twenty-first century.[8] Project organizers concentrated on reconciling the dominant contradiction of a truly global economy: the unification of markets and communications is often offset by vast differences in cultures, local issues, and values.

The goal of World 2000 has been to develop a global strategic plan following the logic of a typical strategic plan. Consequently, the first step of the process was identifying the dominant trends in the global environment.

THE "SUPERTRENDS" OF GLOBAL ISSUES MANAGEMENT

The global environment encompasses thousands of trends at any one time, and World 2000 could not hope to delineate every one of them. The organizers concentrated on nine "supertrends," which they believe summarize the major features of the global environment. Any organization planning to compete on a global level should be aware of the following trends and how they will affect specific business activities.

A Stable Population of 10 Billion to 14 Billion By 1997, the world's population was 5.5 billion and was growing at a rate of almost 90 million a year. Predictions place the total population at somewhere between 10 billion and 14 billion people by the middle of the next century, at which time the levels should stabilize. About 95 percent of this growth will occur in less developed countries, and it is believed that as these countries industrialize in the next fifty years, their population growth rate will drop proportionately.

Industrial Output Increased by a Factor of 5 to 10 As the rest of the world, especially the population centers of Asia, industrializes to reach the standard of living of North America, Europe, and Japan, the aggregate level of material consumption, or industrial output, should increase by a factor of 5 to 10. Hence, all product and service markets will grow dramatically, too.

---

7. S. A. Stumpf, M. A. Watson, and H. Rustogi, "Leadership in a Global Village: Creating Practice Field to Develop Learning Organizations," *Journal of Management Development*, November 1994, p. 16.
8. W. E. Halal, "Global Strategic Management in a New World Order," *Business Horizons*, November 1, 1993, p. 5.

The Wiring of the Globe Information technology (IT) will continue to influence governments, restructure corporations, and create world networks. World 2000 predicts that eventually this "revolution" will wire the earth with a single communications network, a central nervous system for the entire globe.

The High-Tech Revolution The IT revolution brings with it the acceleration of technical advances to create breakthroughs available on a global scale. Some of the areas in which this trend will be felt in the next few decades include the mapping of DNA, robotics, sustainable "green technology," genetic therapy, automated transportation, and virtual reality.

Global Integration Thanks again to IT, the globe is becoming integrated into a single community connected by common communications systems and a shared international culture. Eventually, this trend may lead to universal systems of open trade, global banking, common currency, and even some form of world governance.

Diversity and Complexity The great paradox of the twenty-first century is that global integration will be accompanied by disintegration into a highly diverse system. Ethnic enclaves, such as those seen in the former republics of the Soviet Union, will strive for autonomy. Within established nations, groups will form pockets of self-governing subcultures, and society will splinter accordingly.

A Universal Standard of Freedom The recognition of human rights and freedom should continue to spread around the globe, with ebbs and flows along the way. For the first time in modern history, a majority of nations have political democracy and free market systems, and that number should grow until freedom becomes accepted as the norm, with authoritarian systems being the exception.

Continued Crime, Terrorism, and War The traumatic upheaval caused by the trend toward diversity and complexity is likely to produce dissatisfied groups and nations, which

will resort to an age-old variety of crimes, terrorism, and limited wars to try to gain satisfaction. The threat of global war and nuclear holocaust, however, should decrease.

Transcendent Values As people's economic desires become satisfied, they will strive for a quality of life beyond the one provided by material possessions. Self-fulfillment, art, spirituality, and other higher-order values will be a growing focus. Some feel that technology will replace spirituality, but others point out that human beings seem to need to balance both these factors. As the philosopher André Malraux predicted, the twenty-first century may be the century of religion (see *Managing Social Issues—Multicultural/Tolerance: Spirituality in the Workplace*).

IMPEDIMENTS TO THE SUPERTRENDS

The supertrends recognized by World 2000 are general, and some—such as global integration, a universal standard of freedom, and transcendent values—may seem a bit idealistic. The organizers of World 2000 realize that the "maturation" process they have mapped out is not without its roadblocks. Specifically, they identified five obstacles to be overcome in their global strategic plan.

Organizing Global Chaos There is a great deal of resistance to the idea of a global order as individual peoples protect their national characteristics. Fragmented economic and political systems, in many cases, remain unchanged from the industrial past. Trade barriers, fluctuating currency rates, and communications problems continue to exist. The leap to some sort of world order will need to overcome much natural resistance before economic dealings can be organized on a worldwide scale.

Reconciling Economic Interests The perfect market system has yet to emerge. Japan's industrial policy has produced efficiency, but its market system apparently falters in many areas of competition. The capitalism advanced by the United States produces a high standard of living, but it appears to have conflicts between business and government, labor and management, private and public sectors, and domestic and foreign trade. Global organization apparently awaits a model based on free markets that can reconcile these different market systems into a stronger whole (if that is possible).

Achieving Sustainable Development The present conflict between economic growth and environmental protection needs to be resolved. The predicted fivefold to tenfold increase in industrial output would seem to be incompatible with the stress that many of the world's ecological systems are already suffering. Because most of the growth in the next century will occur in developing countries, which are striving for Western affluence at a great cost to their natural environments, achieving sustainable development remains a challenge for business and government.

Managing Complexity A glance at any newspaper shows that the institutions of the twentieth century are proving to be incapable of solving today's complex problems, let alone those of the twenty-first century. Much of the world's disorder results from an inability to respond to the diversity of individual and community challenges. This failure was responsible for the downfall of communism in many parts of the globe, and it is straining society in the West. Conglomerate corporations are struggling to serve myriad market niches and stakeholder demands. Both business and government face a constant struggle in dealing with the intricacies of education, poverty, crime, and other social problems.

▣ MANAGING SOCIAL ISSUES

MULTICULTURAL/TOLERANCE: SPIRITUALITY IN THE WORKPLACE

The wonders of information technology are highly extolled by most in the business community, but some companies are noticing that automation has its downside. With telecommuting and virtual offices, the workplace relationships that have traditionally given employees a sense of community on the job have disappeared. Furthermore, modern technology has allowed many firms to increase efficiency through downsizing and reengineering, which often leaves some surviving employees with a low sense of morale, not to mention a realization that they too are expendable. Lacking a motivation for their jobs beyond a paycheck, many employees are asking, "Why am I doing this? Why do I feel so unfulfilled?"

A Growing Trend

To answer these questions, many corporations are turning toward spirituality as a management tool to motivate employees and recreate a sense of mission in the workplace. Lotus Development Corporation, for example, has created a "soul" committee to supervise the company's performance with regard to its core values. The soul committee has a stated goal of incorporating technology into the corporate culture without dehumanizing the organization. In 1995, Boeing's president, Phillip M. Conduit, hired Seattle poet David Whyte to speak to managers three days each month as part of a training program. Rather than lecture, Whyte reads poetry and tells stories. Whyte often uses a Native American tale about being lost in the woods; it contains the following lines: "Stand still. The trees are ahead and bushes beside you/Are not lost/Wherever you are is called here." Through this tale Whyte attempts to help managers become more creative in problem solving by reexamining the dynamics of change both at work and in their personal lives.

Spiritual Motivations

Since 1990, AT&T has sent hundreds of managers to Transpective Business Consulting in Woburn, Massachusetts. For $1,650 per person, the managers are able to spend three days with seminar leader Philip Massarsky writing, reading poetry, and watching videos with the goal of being more effective leaders through a better understanding of their own and their employees' emotional needs. At the end of the session, Massarsky has participants formulate written plans to help them transfer their core values to management practice. After six weeks, the managers return to Massarsky and discuss their progress. According to one AT&T executive, employees find a marked change for the better in many managers who have been to Woburn.

Some companies concentrate on the intrinsic value of their services to inspire employees. The medical device maker Medtronic, for example, sees its "mission" as restoring people to full health, and it motivates workers by stressing that they are "doing good" at their jobs.

For Critical Analysis:

Some critics of the workplace spirituality movement believe such motivational methods blur the distinction between employees' personal and work lives—and take advantage of them. "I worry that companies will make spirit the program of the month and use it to manipulate people," said one critic. What do you feel are the dangers, if any, of the trend toward increased spirituality in the workplace?

SOURCE: M. Galen, "Companies Hit the Road Less Traveled," *Business Week*, June 5, 1995, pp. 82–85.

Dealing with the Developing versus Developed Nations Gap The disparity between the wealth of developing nations and the developed nations shows little signs of lessening. Average income in the developed countries is six times that in the developing countries, which means that three-quarters of the people on earth are living far below the standards of the remaining quarter. This disparity impedes cooperation on such global issues as nuclear weapons containment, terrorism, and the environment, and it will certainly slow down the move toward a fully integrated global economy.

STRATEGIES BASED ON THE GLOBAL PERSPECTIVE

It would be an oversimplification to think that these obstacles to a global strategic plan could be overcome by some master plan fueled by the technological revolution.[9] An analysis of the environment, however, can clarify the direction that businesses and governments need to take to alleviate some of these problems. *Exhibit 22–2* lists what is necessary for a shift in global perspective. The following five subsections give strategies for realizing that new perspective.

Disseminate Advanced Technology to Unify the Globe The World 2000 researchers saw in the fall of the Soviet Union and the Eastern Bloc countries proof of the new role of technology in the world. Television, radio, facsimile machines, video technology, and satellite capabilities "armed" the citizens in these states with the knowledge they needed to overthrow their governments.

Ideally, technology equals information, and information equals freedom. In the World 2000 strategy, IT would be diffused by corporations selling sophisticated products abroad, individuals sharing technical knowledge, and governments supporting joint research and development programs. Especially important is the export of technology to developing countries in order to help speed their modernization process. Any arrangement that does emerge will have a technological foundation. The sooner that foundation is in place, the sooner a global community will be a reality.

Integrate Business and Society As this textbook has shown, the interests of business and society can no longer be separated. When this fact is interpreted as an opportunity for competitive advantage instead of a cost-ineffective burden, then businesses can act as stewards instead of managers. The result, according to World 2000, would be collaborative economic relationships between business and the world community that would vitalize society.

Create a Symbiotic Society-Environment Interface World 2000 recommends a "symbiotic society-environment interface," or the integration of ecological concerns into economic and social life. Sustainable development could be used to increase economic efficiency, develop renewable energy, reforest denuded lands, recycle waste, and improve pollution controls. Rather than use regulation, which relies on negative sanctions, the social costs of externalities such as pollution should be internalized through taxes and credits to guide practical economic choices.

Decentralize Institutions Most major institutions would need to be restructured to adapt to an IT–based global community, and the focus of the new institutions should be decentralization. Many businesses are finding that decentralized networks of small, autonomous units are much more efficient in dealing with the complexities of the modern marketplace. Governments, feeling the pressure of limited budgets and public demands, are also turning toward decentralization. The state of Wisconsin, for example, is experimenting with the introduction of market competition into the public school system; the state is placing control of the schools in the hands of teachers, parents, and local citizens instead of state administrative boards.

The result of decentralization would be the restructuring of authority relationships. Under a decentralized system,

---

9. R. Boscheck, "Competitive Advantages: Superior Offer or Unfair Dominance?" *California Management Review*, Fall 1994, p. 132.

▼ **EXHIBIT 22–2
The Transition to a
New Global
Perspective**

Entities Undergoing Change	Old Perspective	New Perspective
Technology base	Physical technology	Information technology
Economy	Capital centered	Human centered
Frontier of progress	Material growth	Sustainable development
Institutions	Hierarchical	Decentralized
Working relationships	Conflict	Cooperation

SOURCE: World 2000.

▼ The strength of an organization would be its ability to harness the diversity of thought and values among its members.

The decentralization of authority would empower people to think for themselves and thus lead to a self-organizing system of management in which institutions provided umbrellas of support. Whereas the old economy rewarded tightly run hierarchical organizations, the new economy would reward loosely knit weblike organizations without any real chain of command.

Foster Collaborative International Alliances A knowledge-based society fosters cooperation, for as all schoolchildren know, two heads are better than one. In the past, collaborative alliances between governments were concentrated on military strengths. World 2000's final strategy would be to foster collaborative international alliances. IT has already made knowledge sharing the most powerful force in world affairs. Strategic collaboration has led to alliances between business and government, competing nations, corporations, and interest groups—not because of altruism but rather because of enlightened self-interest. In the North American Free Trade Agreement, for example, Mexico gains capital, jobs, and knowledge, whereas the United States gains access to markets and less costly labor.

The binding theme of World 2000's global strategic management plan is that "change is the sum of countless small human actions that collectively produce social transformation." Of what practical use is this idea to a manager in the field, who is more concerned with his or her employees and business-level decision-making challenges than with the spread of information technology to less developed countries? The concepts discussed in World 2000's global plan are indeed relevant, because global strategic management is closely linked to the strategic management of information, a reality for all members of the business community.

STRATEGIC MANAGEMENT OF INFORMATION TECHNOLOGY

"The next ten years are already invented—and the tools are here," says Daniel Burrus, author of *Technotrends: How to Use Technology to Go beyond Your Competition*. "The challenge is to use technology in new ways, not old ways," believes Burrus, who says that few companies are meeting this challenge; too many are using the tools of tomorrow with the thinking of yesterday. As an example, he offers Kodak and its Photo CD, a new technology that replaces chemical imaging with digital imaging. The company's television ad campaign promoted the product by showing a family looking at photographs on a television. "Big deal. Who cares?" comments Burrus. "The new technology is a hindrance in that context—it's easier to flip in an album to the shot you want than to go through a linear program looking for it." He believes Kodak should have concentrated on the new possibilities offered by the Photo CD, such as colorizing black-and-white photos and manipulating images.[10]

Burrus holds up entertainer Natalie Cole as a model for businesspeople. In 1991, Cole used technology to sing a duet with the digitized voice and image of her late father, Nat King Cole. "Natalie Cole is not a scientist. . . . She's a dreamer—a kid who grew up dreaming she would one day sing 'Unforgettable' with her dad," says Burrus. "She has redefined her role as an entertainer. She has accomplished an idealistic and until now impossible goal—and she's made a lot of money doing it."

Dynamically Stable Organizations

Creative entrepreneurs are finding ways to use information technology to reach their goals—and make profits. Management expert Andrew C. Boynton says flexibility is the key to their success. In today's ultracompetitive environment, organizations that are able to respond quickly to changing—and sometimes unpredictable—market conditions, consumer demands, technologies, government regulations, and other stakeholder pressures will ultimately be the most successful. Boynton believes that managers must strive to create organizations that are solidly flexible, or **dynamically stable**—in other words, "organizations capable of serving the widest range of customers and changing product demands [dynamic], while building on long-term process capabilities and the collective knowledge of the organization [stable]."[11]

The key to creating a dynamically stable firm is the management of technology, and Boynton offers three different types of information systems that provide the means to this end—systems of scope, vertical systems, and horizontal systems (see *Exhibit* 22–3). As each system is discussed in the following pages, remember that they are not mutually exclusive. Like the other strategic management plans offered in this textbook, they should be regarded by the manager as groups of suggestions from which each individual can choose the ones appropriate to his or her organization.[12]

Systems of Scope

The ability of management to harness an organization's knowledge base is a critical tool for quick and flexible market response. No matter how efficient an organization is in areas such as the design, manufacture, and marketing of its products, it will suffer if knowledge sharing within the corporate structure is inadequate. For example, managers within the product design department must be able to tap the knowledge of the marketing staff to learn of product trends.[13] Marketing departments must be able to access information on

10. B. Voss, "Shake, Rattle & Roll," *Journal of Business Strategy*, January–February 1994, p. 40.

11. A. C. Boynton, "Achieving Dynamic Stability through Information Technology," *California Management Review*, Winter 1993, p. 58.

12. D. Getz, "Beating the Odds," *Journal of Business Strategy*, July–August 1995, p. 20.

13. B. Voss and S. M. Freeman, "A New Spring for Manufacturing," *Journal of Business Strategy*, January–February 1994, p. 54.

▼ **EXHIBIT 22–3 An Overview of Systems of Scope, Vertical Systems, and Horizontal Systems**

Type of System	Description	Requirements
Systems of Scope (a system of "knowing")	Information systems that allow process and product managers to rapidly develop, gather, store, and disseminate information about markets, products, or process capabilities across all boundaries. Systems of scope are designed to maintain stable, permanent reservoirs and conduits of knowledge about internal capabilities or experiences, as well as the capabilities of competitors. They are designed to be dynamically responsive for managers who have a need to know and must be able to access firmwide knowledge in response to local, fast-changing business environments.	• Need to reach all managers in order to provide the necessary information to build or use organizational know-how and process capabilities. • Must be fast and able to reach instantaneously into all areas of the firm. • Should be open to self-design and a wide variety of information requirements.
Vertical Systems (a system of "knowing")	Information systems that allow an organization to rapidly acquire, store, and provide access to real-time information about market change, product change, and process use and allocation.	• Should not reach all managers—just senior managers involved in resource allocation decisions for products. • Should not allow for self-design. A vertical system should have a very specific design—one that is tapped into, and that collects specific information on, product movement and process use and one that analyzes specifically for product/process evaluation and optimization.
Horizontal Systems (a system of "doing")	Cross-functional or cross-organizational information processing systems that are flexible, reusable, modular, general purpose, and open to links with other platforms that exist inside or outside the organization. Horizontal systems cut laterally across functions and departments so that process capabilities can be combined and recombined to support rapid and flexible product and service delivery. Horizontal systems coordinate, control, and integrate information and technologies across different	• Must be designed specifically with change in mind—changing product specifications, customer requirements, and service needs. Attention to open architecture, modularity, flexibility, reusability, and other capabilities that allow future change are essential within the design process of horizontal systems.

SOURCE: A. C. Boynton, "Achieving Dynamic Stability through Information Technology," *California Management Review*, Winter 1993, p. 63.

competing product lines, especially in multinational corporations for which trends may vary from country to country. Managers in the manufacturing area must have information on production capacity within an organization's factories to avoid investment in duplicate resources.

According to Boynton, the question is, How does a firm "develop, collect, store, and disseminate firm-wide knowledge in order to assure that important questions involving information that already exists somewhere in the organization get answered in a timely, efficient manner?" The answer, also according to Boynton, is **systems of scope**, or "information systems that allow managers within the organization to rapidly develop, gather, store, and disseminate information across all boundaries about markets, products, or process capabilities."[14]

Systems of Scope and Product Management Managers involved in product design and manufacturing face double pressures: to anticipate market changes and to respond to those changes quickly enough to capture (or recapture) market shares. Systems of scope can provide information not only about markets and products but also about the resources within an organization to meet product demands. Take, for example, DuPont Company, which integrated its mainframe and minicomputers in the mid-1990s. Prior to the installment of this system of scope, if a DuPont salesperson in Germany wanted to sell gaskets to an automobile company, he or she was forced to find the parts in a German inventory catalogue. With the new system in place, however, at the touch of a button the salesperson will have access to information not only on German gaskets but also on all related products, even those under production, throughout DuPont's global network. The salesperson can now offer his or her customer a much wider variety of choices and possibilities than was previously possible.

The salesperson not only offers products to customers but also gains information through feedback on what products a customer desires. Thus, product managers must have a means to deliver this information to those managers involved in the process of product design. Companies are using systems of scope to make this information transfer more efficient. Before developing a central database, for example, process managers at Digital Equipment Corporation were forced to rely on inefficient and expensive methods of information sharing, such as meetings and trips abroad. Consequently, process managers often did not know what was happening in the other branches of the organization. With the new technology, managers have access to a pool of information about product requirements and process capabilities within the entire organization; this allows managers to move more quickly and confidently in production processes.

Requirements for Systems of Scope For a system of scope to be worthwhile, it must meet certain design requirements. First, according to Boynton, the system of scope must be available to all managers. The premise of a system of scope is that the knowledge base of each "cog" in the organizational "machine" is a valuable resource that can be accessed by other cogs. Each manager who is unable to access the information shared by his or her colleagues or who is unable to share his or her knowledge with the rest of the organization is a wasted resource.

Second, a worthwhile system of scope is expeditious. Traditional forms of delivering information—from ships and planes to the telephone to modern conveniences such as the fax machine and overnight mail—are simply not efficient enough for a system that needs to rely on immediate access. Firms must use IT to allow immediate, simple communication with electronic mail, as well as complex communication sharing through electronic databases that store large reservoirs of information that can be easily accessed.

Third, the system of scope should increase opportunities for creativity and self-design among managers. Information technology that allows immediate knowledge transfer is wasted if managers are shackled with traditional decision-making controls.

Finally, the system of scope must be able to tap into information outside the organization, as well as internal information. IT that can meet this need is being produced rapidly. In 1995, for example, the Market Vision Corporation produced an application package that allows users to access events-oriented, real-time dynamic interactivity over

---

14. Boynton, *op. cit.*, pp. 64–65.

the Internet. In other words, traders and other interested businesspeople will be able to integrate market information, such as stock prices, dividends, and corporate actions, with desktop programs to recalculate portfolio values or manipulate data in spreadsheets almost immediately.[15]

VERTICAL SYSTEMS

Besides maintaining systems of scope, which provide for information sharing within the organization, a dynamically stable firm needs to maintain real-time information about market response to products and services, as well as about production capabilities and schedules. The firm also must be able to integrate this information so managers making corporate and business decisions can assess information on product demand and production capabilities. The information technology that allows a corporation to meet these requirements manifests itself in **vertical systems.**[16] In many aspects, vertical systems are similar to the strategic control systems we examined earlier; however, with their technological advantage, vertical systems are much more effective in allowing competent decision making in the face of rapidly changing products and services.

Application of Vertical Systems The premise of a vertical system is that senior managers will be able to track product performance in order to make decisions concerning that product's future. The retailer Kmart, for example, invested $300 million in fifty thousand bar code scanners for its cash registers nationwide. Not only did this reduce the time cashiers needed to record sales by one-fourth; it also provided a vertical information system. Information from the scanner is transferred by a local area network to a computer in the back of each store, which then keeps track of sales and inventory. Nine times a day, this computer sends recorded data to Kmart's headquarters in Troy, Michigan, via private satellite. By the next morning, the company's product managers in every corner of the country can view national sales data from the day before.[17]

Requirements for Vertical Systems Although both systems of scope and vertical systems have the goal of increasing the flow of information, the two systems have different requirements. Systems of scope should be available to all managers, but vertical systems should reach only those senior managers involved with resource allocation. Furthermore,

▼ Vertical systems should not allow for self-design. They should provide the framework for a very specific design that collects predetermined information on product movement and market acceptance.

HORIZONTAL SYSTEMS

Both systems of scope and vertical systems deal with gathering and disseminating certain types of information. Boynton believes the dynamically stable firm also needs a system that "coordinates, controls, and integrates information and technologies across different boundaries." He labels these cross-functional or cross-organizational information-processing

---

15. "Internet Access," *Edge Work-Group Computing Report*, July 24, 1995, p. 1.

16. Boynton, *op. cit.*, pp. 66–67.

17. W. J. Cook and W. Cohen, "25 Breakthroughs That Are Changing the Way We Live and Work," *U.S. News & World Report*, May 2, 1994, pp. 46–47.

capabilities **horizontal systems**.[18] In a horizontal system, functions and departments are developed laterally to strengthen an organization's ability to support rapid and flexible product and service delivery.

Data Centered Architecture Boynton says that Corning, Inc., one of the world's leading fiber-optics manufacturers, has an exemplary horizontal system. Fiber optics uses glass fibers that allow for communications through light rather than electricity. This technology revolutionized the telecommunications industry during the 1980s, as long-distance telephone companies such as MCI and AT&T began building fiber-optic networks. Corning was running at peak efficiency by the middle of the decade, but by 1990, the company found itself struggling to meet demand. The original long-distance market, which required a relatively simple form of fiber optics, had been saturated. Corning's customers were demanding more complex fibers at lower cost with faster delivery, and the company's manufacturing and information systems were fighting to meet this new requirement efficiently.

One of the main problems was a "stovepipe" information infrastructure that kept potentially useful information from being shared horizontally across production-stage departments. Spurred by the threat of losing consumers to more flexible competitors, in the early 1990s Corning invested in a multimillion-dollar information system called the Flexible Manufacturing System (FMS). Designed with an emphasis on improving versatility, the FMS aimed to link planning, scheduling, operations management, and strategic control through information technology.

Corning called this new information structure Data Centered Architecture, referring to its ability to build connective links between the fundamental elements of information that the organization uses to operate—orders, products, design procedures, and equipment. The Data Centered Architecture serves as an information resource that is accessible from any computer system in the organization. It will provide on-demand information for orders and cost tracking for manufacturing processes. Furthermore, the trend in fiber-optics manufacturing is toward being able to personalize a product to meet individual customer needs. By allowing the proper department of Corning to learn of these customized needs early in the manufacturing process, FMS provides the speed and flexibility that should allow the company to reestablish its dominant position in the field.

Requirements for Horizontal Systems Boynton warns that a horizontal information system should do more than simply "reengineer" existing modes of communication across the spectrum of the organization. Reengineering might focus on a single specific product, which would provide a competitive advantage in the short term through increased speed of production and distribution but would provide little advantage for the long term. Horizontal systems should be constructed on the premise that product specifications and market demands will change, and reengineering an existing information system will only lock the organization into old ways of managing the business. In short,

▼ In a dynamically stable firm, horizontal systems must be designed specifically to allow for change—the only constant in a market. They must provide for changes in customer demands, service needs, and product specifications.

---

18. Boynton, *op. cit.*, pp. 67–70.

Corning planned its horizontal system with this in mind; its Data Centered Architecture represents a stable infrastructure (architecture) that provides support for a dynamic flow of information (data centered) that dictates the direction of the production process.

INFORMATION TECHNOLOGY AND "FIT"

The decision for senior managers is not whether their organizations should employ an information technology system but what kind of system should be put in place.[19] Competitive pressure dictates that the organization that ignores technology does so at its own peril, and the key challenge is to find the information system that will "fit," or be suitable for, the other elements within the firm. The fit is not fixed; constant technological improvements force organizations to upgrade continually to stay ahead of, or merely keep even with, the competition.[20]

Moore's law, a theory devised more than thirty years ago by scientist Gordon Moore, states that the power and complexity of the silicon chip—the basis for information storing in computers—doubles every eighteen months. Moore's law proved to be relatively accurate: by the end of 1995, Intel Corporation was squeezing six million components into a single microprocessor chip.[21] Managers should heed Moore's law, because it underlines a truth of information technology: next year's model will always be better.

Information Technology as a Strategic Weapon During the Persian Gulf War in early 1991, as most of the American people marveled at the technological feats being performed daily on CNN, U.S. technology experts were not impressed. In Northern California's Silicon Valley, the heartland of American technological innovation, the running joke was that the military's state-of-the-art technology was already five years behind. The reason the United States was able to prevail, according to one technologist, was that "the stuff the Russians had supplied the Iraqis was twenty years behind."[22]

The analogy may disturb those who do not like to equate business activity with warfare, but technology can be just as effective a weapon for a business as it can be for a military organization. Companies that take advantage of the Internet, for example, are expanding their market possibilities beyond the reach of competitors who do not (see *Managing Social Issues—Information/Technology: The Internet as a Business Tool* on page 692).

Organizations can also gain an advantage by internal technology upgrades. United Services Automobile Association (USAA) has become the fifth largest U.S. car insurer—and one of the country's largest direct-marketing companies—through the strategic use of technology. USAA uses more toll-free phone lines than any other company in its industry and has used its advanced information system to reduce paperwork and improve efficiency. Almost all the insurance company's sales are transacted over the phone. When a potential customer calls USAA's headquarters in San Antonio, Texas, a service representative fills out a form on a computer screen, and a policy is sent out that night. In case of an accident, a USAA adjuster on the scene enters a damage report into a laptop computer, which feeds the information to a commercial database via a cellular phone to confirm the prices of parts and repair rates. A USAA spokesman boasts that this process shaves days off the claims process, which results in lower costs and satisfied customers. Furthermore,

---

19. M. Davids, "See How They Run," *Journal of Business Strategy*, January–February 1994, p. 24.
20. M. Cook, "Get Back to Basics," *Computerworld*, March 28, 1994, p. 61.
21. R. Lenzner, "The Reluctant Entrepreneur," *Forbes*, September 11, 1995, p. 162.
22. G. Golzen, "Real Task for Virtual Companies," *European*, June 24–30, 1994, p. 31.

MANAGING SOCIAL ISSUES

INFORMATION/TECHNOLOGY: THE INTERNET AS A BUSINESS TOOL

The use of the Internet is expanding exponentially, but many businesses are not taking advantage of it. As of 1996, only about a third of all businesses had on-line capabilities. Many of the businesses that are involved with the Internet set up cyberspace sites on the World Wide Web, the fastest-growing section of the Internet. There are a number of business opportunities on-line, a few of which are detailed in this feature, along with some companies that have used this new technology to their advantage.

The On-Line Storefront

Businesses that set up sites on the World Wide Web have the same advantage as the businessperson who sets up shop on Main Street: easy access by consumers. Any user with Web software and a business's Web address can access that "store" and browse through its merchandise. The San Jose, California–based mail-order company Hello Direct, Inc., has placed much of its catalogue on the Web and uses a toll-free number to take orders. Each month since November 1994, Internet shoppers have looked at an average of 4,500 screens of information, resulting in as many as 400 inquiries. Sales from Internet users still account for only a fraction of Hello Direct's total sales, but an executive for the company sees that percentage rising: "As the cost of postage and paper goes up, [this could] be a way to reach the consumer that's more cost effective."

Cybermalls

As in an actual mall, groups of businesses that set up in "cybermalls" at a single Web address can offer their wares to a group of consumers attracted by convenience and choice. Hawaii's Best Espresso Company was being pinched by the high rent and overhead expenses of its store on the island of Maui, so it paid a local Internet provider $1,000 to develop a "storefront" describing the firm's wide variety of exotic coffee beans. For a few hundred dollars each, the store joined six cybermalls, including Downtown Anywhere and Planet-Hawaii. In a short time, Hawaii's Best was getting a thousand visits by Web shoppers each day and was taking $15,000 a month in orders.

Mass Marketing

The Internet is host to thousands of public electronic bulletin boards called newsgroups, which cover areas of interest for specific groups ranging from Miami Dolphins fans to mountain biking enthusiasts to insurance salespeople. Although some newsgroups prohibit commercial activity (check the newsgroup's rules for this "netiquette"), many allow users to post a note about a business at the minimal cost of on-line time, usually about $2 an hour.

The twelve-employee Harvard Business Service, Inc. (HBS), a registered agent in Delaware that provides organizations with incorporation services and assists them in finding venture capital, posts advertisements on newsgroups and "surfs" the Internet for potential customers. Setting up the technology for the operation cost $60,000, with additional monthly on-line costs of about $300, but the company's volume doubled in the first year of use. "The Internet is a way to reach millions of people, and it's very cost effective," says HBS's vice president of marketing. "I don't know how we ever did things before."

Direct Marketing

In the "snail mail" world, as regular postal service is called by Internet users, direct marketing is prohibitively expensive for most businesses. On the Internet, however, companies can reach a large number of addresses for a relatively minor cost. The adventure travel company Mountain Travel-Sobeck (MTS) publishes "Hot News," a weekly on-line newsletter that describes the adventure trips available from MTS guides all over the globe to 77,000 people every month. "Can you imagine [the cost] if we tried to mail these every week?" asks MTS's founder. "I just push one button, and 'Hot News' goes to everybody." The company's business increased 37 percent in one year on the Internet.

For Critical Analysis:

To date, relatively few companies have made significant profits from selling on the Internet. Why must businesses nonetheless take a serious interest in this technology?

SOURCE: R. Weston, "Five Ways to Do Business on the Internet," *Inc.*, September 12, 1995, p. 75.

thanks to the automation, USAA employs only one-half to two-thirds as many employees as its competitors of comparable size.[23]

American Airlines has also used technology as a means of obtaining a competitive advantage; in fact, the organization has been called a database company that also owns and operates its own airline. American's SABRE reservation system is used by 26,000 subscribers in seventy countries to process 500,000 passenger transactions per day. This database also performs the key task of flight scheduling, which allows the computer to adjust for disruptions caused by delays in individual flights. If, for example, a connector flight from Boston to Chicago is canceled because of technical difficulties, SABRE automatically corrects for the problem by adjusting crew assignments, food delivery, passenger transfers, and other elements accordingly. This leads to more satisfied customers and keeps minor inconveniences from turning into scheduling disasters.[24]

Information Technology and "Refit" To companies like USAA and American Airlines, technology is a weapon; for others, it has been a savior. In some cases, environmental analysis leads to a frightening forecast: no matter what strategy an organization follows, changes in society have rendered its products and services unwanted, unnecessary, or obsolete. This has been the case with many of the firms that make up the defense and publishing industries.

Defense Industry For decades, most defense companies relied on one very wealthy customer—the federal government—as a constant source of revenue and profit. In the early 1990s, however, the end of the Cold War, combined with the politicization of the American budget deficit, led to a sharp reduction in defense spending. The message for the defense industry was clear: diversify or die.

These companies had the major advantage of being on the cutting edge of technology; their challenge was to find applications for this technology outside of weapons development and national security. The Lockheed Martin Corporation, for example, is now using its advanced computer systems to catalogue payments for illegal parking fines in Los Angeles, Boston, and smaller cities. The manufacturer of the Trident missile and the Stealth bomber is helping states recover delinquent child-support payments. The same artificial intelligence software that helped develop the Star Wars defense system is now being used to link various motor vehicle departments.

Publishing Industry Will consumers ever forgo the pleasure of curling up with a good book? For years, traditional publishers have resolutely believed they would not, and they tried their best to ignore the ramifications of technological innovation. Books on hard disc, and especially interactive CD-ROMs, however, are changing the face of the publishing industry. Until recently, said one industry insider, "traditional publishers didn't know or didn't want to know about CD-ROM. But things are changing so fast that while some may still not know about it, almost all are getting involved."[25] The question in the publishing industry has changed from "Why should we?" to "When can we, and how?"

At first, it seemed that traditional publishers were willing to let technological organizations such as Microsoft, Apple Computers, and Sony dominate the digital publishing field. With CD-ROMs in twenty million homes in 1996, however, the medium could no longer be ignored. At Penguin USA, for example, the subsidiary rights department was

---

23. Cook and Cohen, *op. cit.*, p. 46.
24. *Ibid.*, p. 47.
25. Davids, *op.cit.*, pp. 25–31.

fielding so many calls from CD-ROM specialty companies looking to license Penguin books for their products that the firm decided to start its own electronic publishing department. Some traditional publishers also are joining multimedia packagers. Random House, which has published its unabridged *American English Dictionary* on CD-ROM, has formed a joint venture with software publisher Brøderbund. The two companies will spin off Brøderbund's Living Books children's multimedia series and move Random House's children's titles onto CD-ROM.

Many publishers sense that they have just begun to scratch the surface of what will be a huge new market. CD-ROM offers the possibility of interactive fiction, and the new market for "hyperfiction" will certainly grow. Writers are starting to see the potential for their work that goes beyond the printed page. As people become more experienced with expressing themselves this way, their work will no doubt be more sophisticated. Thanks to CD-ROM technology, a new art form is in the works.

Technology and the New Workplace

Not everybody is excited about the prospects of new technology. In his book *The End of Work*, author Jeremy Rifkin predicts that one day, developed countries will have no need for workers. Rifkin estimates that three out of every four workers in industrialized countries perform simple repetitive tasks that can easily be automated: telephone operators can be replaced by voice-recognizing computers, bank tellers by cash-dispensing machines, and postal workers by address-reading machines, to name only a few.[26]

Rifkin is not the first to predict the job-killing effects of technology. In the early nineteenth century, the Luddites destroyed labor-saving textile machinery that was taking their jobs. Karl Marx predicted that factory owners would create a vast army of unemployed people by investing in machinery. In the late 1940s, computer pioneer Nobert Weiner believed that this new technology would increase the unemployed to numbers far larger than even those of the Great Depression.[27]

For almost as long as people have predicted that technology destroys jobs, economists have been arguing the opposite—that technology creates more jobs than it destroys. So far, the economists have been right. Over the past two hundred years, tens of millions of jobs have been made obsolete through technology, yet the total number of jobs has grown almost continuously. The reason, as economists point out, is that humans have unlimited desires. New technologies create new products and services that people did not even know they wanted. For example, fifty years ago, who could have predicted the widespread use of computers? Today, however, that industry has created, and continues to create, millions of new jobs around the world.

Technology inarguably changes the nature of jobs and is doing so at the present moment:

▼ The traditional workplace where the average worker spends at least forty hours a week at a desk or workstation is being replaced by the "wired" workplace, which allows for more fluidity both in worker movement and worker responsibility.[28]

---

26. J. Rifkin, *The End of Work: The Decline of the Global Labor Force and the Dawn of the Post-Market Era* (New York: Tarcher/Putnam, 1995), p. 241.
27. "A World without Jobs?" *Economist*, February 11, 1995, p. 21.
28. E. Davis, "Have Modem, Won't Travel," *Management Review*, April 1995, p. 7.

Managing such a workplace offers a new set of challenges—challenges that may change the very definition of the traditional manager.

GAZELLES AND THE VIRTUAL COMPANY

In 1994, economist David Birch uncovered some interesting statistics concerning the American economy. He found that over the previous five years, 70 percent of the U.S. economic growth had come from only 3 percent of all firms. Birch labeled these companies **gazelles,** in recognition of their ability to do things faster, better, and less expensively than the competition. In financial terms, a gazelle is a company that has doubled its size since the start of the decade; this translates into an average growth rate of at least 20 percent a year throughout the recession years of the early 1990s. Gazelles are spread across a number of industries.

Gazelles are also defined by their innovative use of new technology and new forms of corporate organization. They recognize a market niche that is not being filled and use technology to fill that niche quickly. Molten Metal Technologies, for example, has created a chemical process that not only neutralizes industrial wastes by submerging them in vats of hot metal but also transforms those wastes into salable by-products such as hydrogen gas, nickel, and ceramic abrasives.[29]

For management consultants such as Tom Peters, gazelles present a natural progression toward the **virtual company**. In his book *Crazy Times Call for Crazy Organizations,* Peters describes *de facto* virtual companies as entities that only come into existence to "exploit a particular market opening." Once the market opening closes or the virtual company has realized the maximum profits available, the organization dissolves, never to appear again in exactly the same form. Peters points out that construction companies are basically virtual in their practice. They pull in contractors and building professionals when there is a project to be completed, and when the project is finished, the construction team dissolves.

Another characteristic of the virtual company is its use of **temporary workers**, contingency workers whose employment depends on the short-term, or even daily, needs of management (see *Company Focus: Manpower, Inc.* on page 696). The temporary service industry in the United States grew over 400 percent between 1982 and 1996, to over two million workers, while the total number of jobs in the economy rose 28 percent.

Business executives value the practice of hiring part-time workers because it gives organizations greater flexibility to react to market changes. Many labor experts, however, see the practice as an example of corporate greed. Part-time and temporary workers earn about 60 percent and 77 percent, respectively, of full-time permanent workers' hourly wages. Furthermore, temporary workers are not as well protected by federal labor laws against discrimination, sexual harassment, and hazardous working conditions. (*Exhibit 22–4* on page 697 shows the meteoric rise in the use of temporary workers over a recent sixteen-year period.)

Temporary work "is a very big problem in America," claims one union leader. "Corporations are trying to create a disposable work force with low wages and no benefits."[30] The rise of virtual companies assures the increased use of temporary workers and other kinds of part-time workers, but society may not allow organizations to continue to reap such advantages from these workers. New laws, for example, may force employers to offer benefits on a prorated basis to those employees who do not work full-time.

---

29. S. Pearlstein, "A Leap into Economic Change," *Washington Post National Weekly Edition*, July 18–24, 1994, p. 6.
30. S. Collins, "The New Migrant Workers," *U.S. News and World Report*, July 4, 1994, p. 53.

COMPANY FOCUS: MANPOWER, INC.
THE GROWING MARKET FOR TEMPORARY EMPLOYEES

What is the second largest employer in the United States, following only the federal government? Chances are you have never heard of the organization unless you happen to be one of the millions of Americans unable or unwilling to find a permanent job—or a senior executive of a large corporation. Nonetheless, Manpower, Inc., employed about 750,000 workers in 1995, more than IBM and AT&T combined. And that number was up 43 percent from three years earlier, proving the company's proficiency in the growth market of providing temporary employees.

Work Force Strategy

Until the late 1980s, companies used temporary employees only in extreme situations—during an emergency work overload; in the peak season; or when a permanent employee was not working because of vacation, illness, or some other circumstance. By the mid-1990s, however, temporary workers were part of a manager's work force strategy, says Manpower CEO Mitchell Fromstein: "They plan the use of temporary workers on a continuing basis to get the flexibility in labor costs."

In 1994, Mellon Bank Corporation found itself in a situation typical of Manpower's recent large clients. The Pittsburgh-based banking firm needed more than a thousand part-time employees for its locations across the United States. Mellon had two obvious options: (1) find and train the workers itself at a relatively high cost for employees who would probably not be with the company more than a month, or (2) continue the current system of drawing workers from more than a hundred temporary worker agencies nationwide. The banking corporation, however, decided to give Manpower an exclusive contract to recruit, train, and place the workers. Not only did Manpower eliminate Mellon's personnel decisions but also the banking corporation estimates an annual savings of $3 million to $5 million as compared with other options.

Efficiency First

Manpower's success goes beyond simply meeting the growing demand for temporary workers in today's economy. The company's corporate strategy is based on the efficiency of a well-run fast-food chain. Indeed, Manpower's Milwaukee headquarters controls the more than nine hundred branch offices of the organization as if they were part of a fast-food chain; assessment, training, and hiring are standardized, as is the physical layout of each office. Fromstein claims his company can establish a new office in ten days for only $200,000. "We're more efficient and economical because we have to be," he says.

Manpower also ensures that its clients will get well-qualified temporary workers. Those who will be taking word-processing assignments must be proficient at forty-three specific skills before accepting a job. An advanced word-processing operator has forty-two additional skills. Manpower has been so successful at developing its programs that companies have hired the agency to train their permanent workers. This competitive advantage has also allowed Manpower to corner the market on the growing number of companies that rely on a single temporary agency for all their needs. Half the organization's clients have this type of relationship with Manpower, which often leads to increased use of temporary employees.

The New Bottom Line

Managers should not expect a temporary work force to be a contented one. Manpower CEO Fromstein estimates that two-thirds of his temporary workers would rather be working elsewhere, with full-time salaries and full benefits. The realities of the marketplace and the growing trend toward virtual companies, however, demand that temporary workers be seen as a low-cost alternative for certain low-skill-level and technical positions.

SOURCE: Information from T. D. Schellhardt, "Manpower's Business Booms as Companies Use More Temps," *Wall Street Journal*, February 3, 1995, p. B6D; R. L. Rose, "Thriving Manpower Mixes Hiring, Hamburger Wisdom," *Wall Street Journal*, June 24, 1994, p. B3; and D. L. Boroughs, "Business Gives in to Temptation," *U.S. News & World Report*, July 4, 1994, pp. 56–57; plus authors' estimates.

▼ **EXHIBIT 22–4 Percentage Increase of Work Categories from 1970 to Present**

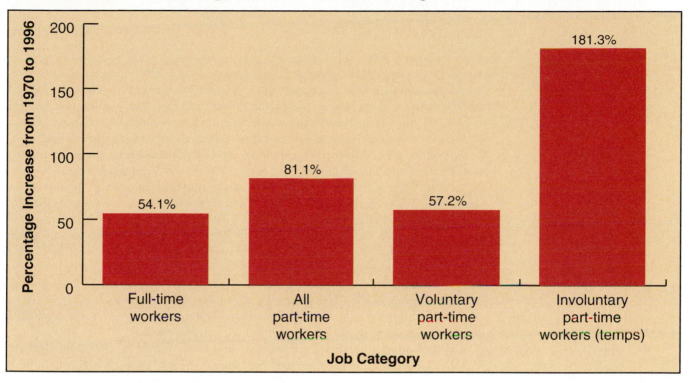

SOURCE: U.S. Department of Labor, Employee Benefit Research Institute.

THE VIRTUAL OFFICE

The **virtual office** is spreading rapidly across the business landscape. There is no specific definition of the virtual office, but it is characterized by a lack of permanent structures for employees[31] (see the *Case—Chait/Day: Building a Virtual Company*—at the end of this chapter). Instead of having an assigned space in which most of his or her work is done, an employee in a virtual office either shares work space with colleagues or spends a great deal of time working elsewhere. One of France's largest management consultant firms, Brossard Consultants, took a step toward the virtual office in the early 1990s when it moved its headquarters to smaller spaces on the outskirts of Paris. To encourage employees to work away from the office, the company refused to assign each person a work space. Instead, two-thirds of the employees were given a cupboard space in which to store their personal belongings and a choice of "community offices" to be used when the need arose.[32]

Brossard's strategy underscores one of the economic motivations for virtual offices: smaller office spaces lead to lower overhead costs. In 1995, the average Fortune 500 company had 25 percent of its assets tied up in real estate holdings. In the early 1990s,

---

31. J. T. C. Tend, V. Grover, and K. D. Fielder, "Business Process Reengineering: Charting a Strategic Path for the Information Age," *California Management Review*, Spring 1994, p. 9.
32. S. Shellenbarger, "Burnout, Low Morale Vex Mobile Office," *Wall Street Journal Europe*, August 18, 1994, p. 4.

corporate giants such as IBM, General Electric, Eastman Kodak, AT&T, and Mobil saved at least $100 million each by reducing space costs.

TELECOMMUTING

With traditional offices shrinking and in some cases disappearing, where will employees function? Some, as noted above, will be squeezed into smaller workplaces. Others will spend much of their time at a client's place of business or, with the technology of cellular telephones and fax machines, working out of their cars. Many more, however, will respond to space pressures by switching to electronic substitutes (fax machines, E-mail, and modems) for the daily trip into the office, called telework or **telecommuting.**

Telecommuters fulfill their conventional job commitments from home or a nearby work center without physically traveling to a central office. The idea first began to develop in the late 1960s and 1970s as environmentalists lamented the air and noise pollution caused by millions of Americans driving to and from work five days a week. As the practice has grown, other benefits have emerged. First, telework saves time; the average commuter in American metropolitan areas spends more than seventy minutes in transit daily. Second, it saves money each week on gasoline and parking. Third, it can save families. As both parents increasingly find themselves in the work force, the pressure to maintain a career and a family has increased. Telework allows one or both parents to work from the home and consequently spend more time with their children and each other. Managers are also finding that telecommuting employees are, on the average, more productive. (*Exhibit 22–5* shows some of the benefits of the virtual workplace.)

Charlie Grantham, founder and president of the Institute for the Study of Distributed Work, in Oakland, California, sees another beneficiary of telecommuting: communities. Since the beginning of the Industrial Age, workers have been forced to leave rural areas for the population centers because most jobs were located there. Telework could reverse this trend. "In the future, communities will once again become known for the work that

▼ **EXHIBIT 22–5 Benefits of Telecommuting**

Fortune 500 companies with telecommuting arrangements were surveyed on the productivity of, and customer response to, such arrangements. The results follow.

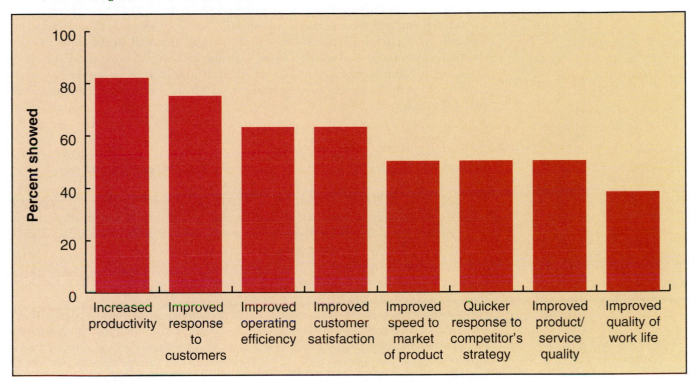

SOURCE: *Personnel Journal,* September 1994, p. 71; and the Center for Workforce Effectiveness.

they do," predicts Grantham. "The word spreads, people start to migrate, and a community grows up around a common interest in a special type of work."[33]

Recognizing this possibility, the French government, in connection with France Telecom, has committed approximately 400 million francs (about $80 million) to setting up telecommuting programs in southern France. The hope is that young people with computer skills and training living in rural areas will have the incentive to avoid already overcrowded metropolitan areas. Similarly, Australia, with its vast stretches of outback, has invested in **telecottages**. A small facility with multiple telephone lines, personal computers, copiers, fax machines, and other equipment, the telecottage provides training for local people in information processing jobs. Because most of the jobs in the country originate in distant cities, these telecottages will be integral in preserving Australia's rural communities.

MANAGING THE NEW NETWORKS

With the revolution in information technology has come what many experts believe to be a revolution in management. James Champy, co-author of *Re-Engineering the Corporation,*

---

33. R. Moskowitz, "Telecommuting: Bringing the Work Home," *Hemispheres,* April 1994, pp. 33–36.

states that managers "must engage in Emersonian thinking—profoundly questioning everything that they do."[34] Bill Raduchel, chief information officer for Sun Microsystems, calls E-mail "a major cultural event—it changes the way you run the organization."[35]

Champy and Raduchel are referring to the evolution of the network in modern business. Networks "connect people to people and people to data." They have always existed in organizations; traditional networks included the "old-boy network," the numerous contacts that led each individual to his or her job, and the "informal organization" of intercorporate relationships that usually proved to be the backbone of most decision making. These old networks were inherently hierarchical; that is, information would move from employees to middle management to upper management, or visa versa, through established channels.

THE END OF HIERARCHY

In a "wired" company, hierarchy is not only useless but also counterproductive:

▼ **Tools such as E-mail, teleconferencing, and group software allow employees to share information without having to go through established channels. If a company resolutely sticks to a chain of command, it erases the benefits of the technology by harnessing the flow of information.**

We have already discussed how information systems save time, provide links across functional boundaries, and provide access to market indicators. All these benefits, however, will be wasted if managers cannot adapt to the new technology. They must recognize that a strict, traditional hierarchy, with its emphasis on planning and control, is antithetical to the free flow of information that improved computer networks offer. This fact is recognized at Hewlett-Packard Corporation (H-P), a large computer and printer manufacturer. H-P's chief information officer says, "With the ability to share information broadly and fully without filtering it through a hierarchy, we can manage the way we always wanted to."[36]

The scope of H-P's information system is huge. Each month the company's 97,000 employees exchange 20 million E-mail messages, share 3 billion characters of data, and perform more than 250,000 electronic transactions with suppliers and customers. The benefits of this massive information infrastructure are readily apparent in the company's customer-response network, made up of a staff of 1,900 technicians. When a customer reports a problem through a phone call or electronic message, the information is automatically sent to operators at one of four international hubs, who type the information into a database.

From the database, the problem is transported to one of twenty-seven centers, where it is studied by a team specializing in the problem area. Each center is connected to the others by a master database, and whenever an employee works on a file, it is updated immediately—and the information is available for any technician. Consequently, if the first center in California cannot solve a particular problem, the file moves on to the next center, possibly in Australia, for scrutiny by a different crew.

The immediacy of this system leaves little room for traditional management. The network runs on its own initiative; any managerial control would only slow it down. "I look out of my office, and often none of my people are there," says John Karlsten, who man-

---

34. H. Lancaster, "Managers Beware: You're Not Ready for Tomorrow's Job," *Wall Street Journal*, January 24, 1995, p. B1.
35. T. A. Stewart, "Managing in a Wired Company," *Fortune*, July 11, 1994, p. 44.
36. *Ibid.*, p. 46.

ages two customer-response teams. Although his office is in Mountain View, California, one of his response teams works out of Sacramento, and many of his employees telecommute from home. Karlsten's management duties are limited to choosing and training employees, setting overall guidelines, and measuring customer satisfaction. In a sense, he is "managing blind," and he admits, "it's not entirely comfortable."[37]

Managers are by no means powerless in a wired organization. They still hire and fire, and they make decisions on how to allocate resources.[38] As Karlsten is learning, however, the whole point behind information technology is to give power to the individual, not the manager. Recognizing this, in 1994 Pitney Bowes presented its employees with the following Freedom of Information Act:

> Know ye by these present that as a member in good standing of the Pitney Bowes Shipping and Weighting Systems organization, you have the inalienable right to whatever information you need to do your job.[39]

THE END OF MANAGEMENT?

Some business experts have concluded that "management theory is dead, and technology killed it."[40] Many of the management strategies discussed in the past three chapters are coming under heavy criticism. The concept of benchmarking, for example, has been criticized as putting a damper on competitiveness. "Yesterday's thinking is helping to ruin the U.S. economy," states one observer. "If you do what your competition is doing, you're [finished.] Your application of technology should be to do what they're not doing."[41]

In the new, technologically superior environment, according to another management critic, "the pace of business has become too fast for theorizers to get a bead on it. What happens is this: A new generation of computers, networks, and software is released. Within weeks customers are implementing them, often in ways unimagined by the vendors. As it happens, some companies harness the digital powers well, some don't. . . . Winning companies no longer pay much heed to organizational theory. Instead, they just dive in, using technology to stimulate, rapidly prototype, de-layer, and establish feedback loops."[42]

The problem with the idea that management is dead is that it ignores the stakeholder influence in today's business community.[43] Society will not allow an organization to "just dive in." The splash may soak employees, the community, the environment, and all the other stakeholders we have discussed in this textbook. If technology has not killed management, however, it has mortally wounded its traditional precepts. From the sweatshop to the assembly line to the electronic eye, the role of management has been to accomplish goals by minimizing the idiosyncrasies of human behavior. Today's best managers encourage some of those idiosyncrasies and harness them to help accomplish the corporation's goals. Instead of micromanaging each employee's job, the manager should provide a general goal—along with the needed tools—and let the workers micromanage themselves to attain that goal.

37. *Ibid.*
38. J. R. Dixon, P. Arnold, J. Keinke, J. S. Kim, and P. Mulligan, "Business Process Reengineering: Improving in Strategic Directions," *California Management Review*, Summer 1994, p. 93.
39. Stewart, *op. cit.*, p. 50.
40. R. Karlgaard, "Management Theory Is in Trouble," *Forbes*, June 6, 1994, p. 8.
41. Voss, *op. cit.*, p. 41.
42. Karlgaard, *op. cit.*
43. T. Kiely, "Reengineering: It Doesn't Have to Be All or Nothing," *Harvard Business Review*, November–December 1995, p. 16.

THE DELICATE BALANCE

Corporate management must try to plan for the future while at the same time taking advantage of today's advances in technology. Changes do not happen overnight. Although there has been an explosion in the use of the Internet, for example, by the late 1990s very few companies had actually made any profits on their ventures in cyberspace. The delicate balance for management involves taking advantage of new business opportunities while at the same time not forsaking the steady profits from solid businesses that will continue long into the future.

Observers of the early computer revolution, for example, predicted that every household would be using computers by 1990. Even in the mid-1990s, a significant fraction of American households still had no computer (and many of the existing computers were used only for games). Most households have videocassette recorders today, but that level was reached over more than a decade. Certainly most or all American homes will someday have regular modems and phone lines, satellite dish hookups, or cable modems. That does not mean, however, that current management has to devote all its resources to figuring out how to tap that market. Many so-called low-tech companies are still making solid returns for their investors. The manager of today should avoid focusing exclusively on the future.

TERMS AND CONCEPTS FOR REVIEW

Dynamically stable 686
Gazelle 695
Horizontal system 690
Moore's law 691

Systems of scope 687
Telecommuting 698
Telecottage 699
Temporary worker 695

Vertical system 689
Virtual company 695
Virtual office 697

SUMMARY

1. The challenge of today's manager is the strategic management of information, not just in the realm of public relations but also in every aspect of corporate-level decision making.

2. According to the World Future Society's project World 2000, there are nine "supertrends" that we can expect: (a) a stable population of 10 billion to 14 billion by the middle of the next century; (b) during the same time, an increase in industrial output to 5 to 10 times what it is today; (c) the wiring of the globe; (d) a high-tech revolution; (e) global integration; (f) diversity and complexity; (g) a universal standard of freedom; (h) continued crime, terrorism, and war; and (i) transcendent values (including self-fulfillment and spirituality).

3. The impediments to these supertrends are (a) organizing global chaos, (b) reconciling economic interests, (c) achieving sustainable development, (d) managing complexity, and (e) alleviating the developing versus developed country gap.

4. The new strategies that are based on a global perspective are the following: (a) disseminate advanced technology to unify the globe, (b) integrate business and society, (c) create a symbiotic society-environment interface, (d) decentralize institutions to empower individuals, and (e) foster collaborative international alliances.

5. Managers today must strive to create organizations that are dynamically stable (solidly flexible). An organization must develop long-term process capabilities while also being able to serve the widest range of customers and changing product demands. To be dynamically stable, a firm must have three different types of information systems: systems of scope, vertical systems, and horizontal systems.

6. A system of scope is a system of knowing. It allows process and product managers to rapidly develop, gather, store, and disseminate information about markets, products, or process capabilities. To be effective, a system of scope must reach all managers and be fast.

7. Vertical systems also are systems of knowing. They allow an organization to rapidly acquire, store, and provide access to real-time information about market and product changes. Vertical systems should reach only those senior managers involved in resource allocation decisions.

8. Horizontal systems are systems of doing. They cut across functions and departments so that process capabilities can be combined and recombined to support rapid and flexible product delivery. They must be designed with change in mind.

9. Information technology can be used as a strategic (aggressive) weapon. Sometimes internal technology adjustments or upgrades will be sufficient.

10. Information technology can prevent a firm from going out of business, notably in the defense, biotechnology, and publishing industries.

11. Although predictions that technology would eliminate jobs have been around as long as automation and technology have, the data dispute these ideas. In spite of rapid innovations in technology—specifically since the advent of the computer—tens of millions of jobs have been added, not only in the United States but also elsewhere. It appears that as long as humans have unlimited desires, technology can create things people demand. Thus, there probably will always be an expanding labor market.

12. Companies that can do things faster, better, and less expensively than the competition have been labeled *gazelles*. One economist found that in recent times, 70 percent of U.S. economic growth has been generated by only 3 percent of all firms. The pattern of a gazelle is to recognize a market niche that is not being filled, use technology to fill it quickly, and then go on to a new opportunity.

13. Virtual companies are entities that come into the marketplace to exploit a particular market opening. Virtual companies may use various subcontractors and temporary workers. Sometimes virtual companies use what is known as the virtual office, which is characterized by a lack of permanent structures for employees.

14. Along with the telecommunications revolution has come the increased use of telecommuting, in which employees can fulfill their job commitments either from home or a nearby work center without physically traveling to a central office.

15. Changes in the corporate landscape may be resulting in new types of networks that have no hierarchy similar to a standard organizational chart within a corporation. Networks that use E-mail, teleconferencing, and group software allow employees to share information without having to go through established channels. These changes may mean not only the end of hierarchy but also the end of management as we know it.

EXERCISES

1. Reread *Exhibit 22–1*. In your opinion, which predictions will actually come true? Explain your answer. For each prediction you think will come true, write down some of the resulting changes that will affect the management of today's corporations.

2. Some argue that the idea of the "wiring" of the globe is misnamed because of the coming age of digital transmission satellites. What is at issue here? Is the issue just semantic?

3. If the trend toward a universal standard of freedom, as outlined by World 2000, is fulfilled, how will it affect the ethical issues that face today's global corporation?

4. The final supertrend identified by World 2000 involves transcendent values. Write a statement explaining what you think that term means. If this trend is accurate, how will it affect the corporation?

5. Review the impediments to the supertrends. Which one do you think will prove to be the most important obstacle? Justify your answer.

6. According to *Exhibit 22–2*, based on the World 2000 report, working relationships will change from those of conflict to those of cooperation. List the ways in which this might occur.

7. "Information equals freedom." Explain this statement.

8. Give examples of a reactive strategy to the challenge of ever-changing information technology. Give an example of a proactive strategy to this same challenge.

9. The term *dynamically stable* seems to contain a contradiction. *Stability* implies no change, but the word *dynamic* implies change. How do you explain this seeming contradiction?

10. Vertical systems were defined in the chapter as information systems that allow an organization to rapidly acquire, store, and provide access to real-time information about market and product changes. One of the requirements of a vertical system that was explained in *Exhibit 22–3* and in the text was that the information should not reach all managers. Given that information dissemination technology has made the process so inexpensive, why shouldn't a corporation disseminate information to everybody and let individuals decide whether they should use the new information? What costs and benefits are there in so doing?

11. Why shouldn't vertical systems allow for self-design?

12. What is the only true constant in a market?

13. "The weapons used today are always from the last war that we fought." How does this assertion fit in with what was said in the chapter about the Persian Gulf War in early 1991? If this assertion is true, is there any way that the military could change the situation?

14. You are the head of product development at a major publishing firm. You have just read yet another review about an interactive CD-ROM novel. Your boss is pressing you to "do something." What should you do, and why? List the steps in a strategy that you might devise to determine what you should do. Describe your strategy as

either reactive or proactive. Indicate how you could evaluate the effectiveness of your strategy at specific points in time after it was implemented.

15. Why haven't technological improvements created massive unemployment?

16. What is the difference between a virtual company and a virtual office?

17. *Company Focus: Manpower, Inc.*, stated that the company has about 750,000 workers on its payroll. Does this mean that from that company alone, at any point in time, 750,000 temporary employees are working? Why or why not?

18. Many of the benefits of telecommuting have been outlined by the press and by management surveys. This trend also has costs, however. Make a list of the costs of the trend toward telecommuting.

19. The end of this chapter has a discussion on managing new networks. One of the traditional networks is the "old-boy network." What does that commonly used term mean? What are the benefits of using the old-boy network?

20. Write an outline of a short speech on the following subject: "Are we seeing the end of management?"

SELECTED REFERENCES

▶ Leonard-Barton, Dorothy. *Wellsprings of Knowledge: Building and Sustaining the Sources of Innovation*. Boston: Harvard Business School Press, 1995.

▶ McKenney, James L. *Waves of Change: Business Evolution through Information Technology*. Boston: Harvard Business School Press, 1995.

▶ Nelson, Carl A. *Managing Globally: A Complete Guide to Competing Worldwide*. Burr Ridge, Ill.: Irwin Professional Publishing, 1994.

▶ Samli, A. Coskun. *International Consumer Behavior: Its Impact on Marketing Strategy Development*. Westport, Conn.: Quorum Books, 1995.

▶ Welford, Richard. *Environmental Strategy and Sustainable Development: The Corporate Challenge for the Twenty-First Century*. New York: Routledge, 1995.

RESOURCES ON THE INTERNET

▼ The Internet Business Journal is a monthly on-line magazine that provides information for companies wishing to use the Internet as part of their operations. To access this magazine, go to

    gopher://gopher.fonorola.net/11/ Internet%20Business%20Journal

or

    ftp://ftp.fonorola.net/ Internet%20Business%20Journal

▼ The World Bank is an international organization that attempts to give economic assistance to developing countries. For information on how the World Bank is trying to reduce the developed versus developing country gap discussed in the chapter, access the following:

    http://www.worldbank.org.html/ extdr/about.html

or

    http://www.worldbank.org.html.extpb/ Publications.html

▼ As you will see in the *Case* at the end of this chapter, the advertising company Chiat/Day has been a forerunner in creating the virtual office. For information on Chiat/Day's technological ideas, go to

    http://chiatday.com/factory/

▼ For more information on possible tools for the virtual office, access the Small Business Resource Center at

    http://www.webcom./~seaquest/

CASE

CHIAT/DAY: BUILDING A VIRTUAL COMPANY

Background

The idea came to Jay Chiat, chairman of Chiat/Day Advertising (C/D), while he was skiing in Telluride, Colorado. He and his staff were considering a makeover for the $900 million, 700-employee advertising agency, and Chiat was musing over the nature of the traditional office. On the slopes, he realized that the office was a place "where we store stuff, shuffle paper, and return calls." His train of thought continued: "But you can solve problems in the shower or anywhere else. And now that the technology exists to work from anywhere, the real question is, can we use it without being dehumanized in the process?"

By the summer of 1993, C/D announced plans to remake its Venice, California, and New York City headquarters into virtual offices in which employees would be freed by technology from the traditional concepts of the workplace. Skeptics labeled this plan an attempt at a positive image for the staff reductions made necessary by the agency's loss of the $90 million American Express account the previous year. An unhappy employee called the new offices "an exercise in reducing overhead by calling it a virtual office."

Lee Clow, the agency's chief creative officer, admits that the move could be perceived as being on "the cutting edge of stupidity." Ultimately, however, the virtual office offers a new model for business as a bureaucracy-free zone, says Clow. Employees are given the opportunity to respond as a large team to a client such as Nissan or as a smaller, three-person team for Coca-Cola. C/D's virtual offices are "based on the idea that if you change the workplace and you change the way people work, the next thing you'll change is the way they think," says Clow.

The Iconoclast of the Industry

Since the company was started by Chiat in the late 1960s, C/D has been considered the iconoclast of the advertising industry. The agency is responsible for some of the most memorable campaigns in television advertising history, including the Energizer Bunny and the "U.B.U." ads for Reebok International. C/D created perhaps the most famous commercial of all time, the Super Bowl halftime "1984" spot that introduced the Macintosh computer by showing a lone, female long-distance runner shattering an Orwellian conformist setting. *Advertising Age* named C/D the Agency of the Decade for the 1980s.

C/D's creativity has been reflected not only in its ad campaigns but also in its vision for the identity of the advertising agency. In the 1970s, Chiat replaced offices at C/D with simple, open, standard-sized cubicles to eliminate the culture of closed-door office politics. In 1983, it was the first ad agency to abandon its typewriters in favor of Apple Macintosh computers. Even before virtualization, C/D's Venice office had a wide corridor called Main Street, in the middle of which was parked a vintage red Datsun with a surfboard in the back seat, as Chiat tried to battle what he felt to be the stifling atmosphere of most office environments.

The University Model

In his virtual offices, Chiat has replaced the cubicles with common areas and technically sophisticated meeting, editing, and screening rooms. He wants to relieve his staff of the constraints of the nine-to-five workday, which he considers to be a distasteful leftover from the Industrial Age. Chiat saw three problems with the old system: it was organized around rigid departments, it was management centered, and it was internally driven—"three elements of a not very flexible organization."

Chiat disagrees with characterizations of the virtual office as one that simply allows employees to work at home. He sees it going beyond that to create what amounts to an "idea factory." Chiat compares the traditional workplace to a grammar school, in which employees feel they must be "in class" for a specific number of hours each day, and "attendance matters almost as much as anything else." His idea factory is based on a university model in which "people gather, they get assignments, they go off and do them. . . . They don't have to stay in class to get their work done."

Team Architecture

Chiat's vision for an effective virtual office relies on two prerequisites: proper design and advanced technology. C/D's approach to the first need was a remodeling strategy called "team architecture," in which the 125,000 square feet of space at the Venice office was subdivided by activity instead of by conference rooms and cubicles. Employees are funneled into work spaces assigned to clients and projects rather than to individuals. Creative teams congregate in "living rooms," where they can exchange ideas on couches and work on laptop computers. Small stations equipped with computers—called "drinking fountains"—are scattered throughout the building, allowing employees to receive their E-mail messages quickly or work on an idea. Large project spaces for specific clients are also part of the team architecture, though they are regarded with suspicion by upper management because of a tendency to become "homerooms."

Following the university theme, Chiat also created the Student Union, a huge open area complete with televisions showing CNN, MTV, and ESPN; vending machines; cappuccino machines; backgammon tables; pool tables; and punching bags. The Student Union also features an outdoor deck and snack bar. "This is a place to go and mix it up, or have informal meetings," says one C/D executive. "If you're one of those people who, in college, couldn't study unless the radio was blaring, this is the place to go."

Technological Innovations

Within the context of team architecture, technology holds the virtual office together. A communications system that allows remote, dial-up access to all the functions traditionally performed at a stationary office desk is an absolute necessity, along with a phone system that allows employees to receive calls "wherever they might be—either remote from the corporate facility, or anywhere in it."

For these services, C/D turned to the Freset Business Wireless Telephone System from Ericcson Business Networks in Cypress, California. Armed with the Freset, a pocket-sized wireless telephone, "our staff is empowered with all the serviceability and functionality that they have come to expect from telephones, but with the added liberation and spontaneity of 'hallway conversations,'" says a C/D manager. No longer are staff members confined to their offices while waiting for an important telephone call or playing "phone tag."

Staff members are assigned virtual telephone numbers, which allow them to choose the workstations at which they want their phones to ring and for what time span. This flexibility, notes a C/D manager, allows employees to accommodate their work habits to their clients' schedules. "While not a strict rule, staff members used to have a tendency to schedule their days conventionally, between nine and five, rather than around their clients who may be working in different time zones. But now, clients can easily reach staff wherever they are, and whatever the time."

The communications system is supplemented with a Macintosh-based computer network with interactive software that was designed in-house. All documents and information relevant to C/D are kept in the computer system. Employees have their own personal electronic files in the network and can access the agency's body of collective intelligence and its accounts from any workstation.

Changes in Management Theory

The changes have also had a profound effect on management theory at C/D. "Management can't control this," says one agency executive of the virtual office. "I find the more control you put on this idea, the more you start looking exactly like what you had before." One of the goals of the new virtual office design is to transform C/D into a meritocracy, in which employees are judged solely on output. Most managers are not worried that their employees will be less productive without constant supervision. In fact, the work ethic at C/D is so strong that the company has been nicknamed "Chiat Night and Day" for the long hours put in by workers. The challenge is to convince employees to use their time more efficiently. "I'm trying to make sure people understand that if [you] walk in the room with a great idea, but I haven't seen you in a week, you win. But if you've been here every day but you don't have any ideas, you lose," says Clow.

Employee Reaction

The virtual reengineering has not been a minor investment for C/D. Chiat estimates that the costs of the new technology come close to $8 million. The Venice office is using a third less office space than before, however, which offsets some of the overhead.

Although efficiency cannot be measured in strict financial terms, C/D believes it increases in the virtual office. Karen Knowles, an assistant producer, found that to be the case the first time she experienced the work of a virtual team:

> One of [Knowles's] teams, the Nissan regional group, had to pull together a major presentation for the client on short order. "Normally, it would have taken us three days," she says. "We all gathered in the project room, we all had our computers set up, we all had our phones. We were in one place at one time and all of our brains were there. We put together the presentation in two hours. I couldn't believe it. . . ." Specifically, the art director was creating

titles and supers on a Quadra, the copywriter was preparing the script on his PowerBook, and Knowles was pulling images off the printer used to make storyboards.

Employee reaction has not been universally positive, however. From force of habit, many C/D employees—like employees at any company—had become attached to their work cubicles as a place to keep their personal items. Staff members no longer had such a place, and this turned out to be emotionally disconcerting. For one employee, the lockers that C/D provided to replace cubicles showed that the company "no longer thinks about people. It thinks about its culture with no regard to how it affects the staff." Managing director Bob Kuperman realizes that the alterations will discourage many employees, and he expects C/D to lose staff at all levels because of the changes. As a result, C/D plans to look for more independent people and self-starters as future employees.

What Clients Think

No matter how well the technology works or how much employees get behind the idea, the virtual office will ultimately be measured according to whether clients approve of it, or at least approve of its result. "Whether [he or she] thinks it's a good idea or a lousy idea, any advertiser looking at this has to be thinking, 'Is it going to help me sell more widgets?'" says one consultant.

It would seem that C/D made the proper decision. After a slump in the early 1990s that left the company in heavy debt, 1994 saw the C/D Venice office capture more than $100 million in new accounts, including Jack in the Box, L.A. Gear, Quaker State, and AirTouch Communications. In 1995, the company obtained the $50 million Sony PlayStation campaign, one of the biggest West Coast accounts of the decade. That same year, C/D won the prestigious assignment of producing the first branding campaign for America Online (AOL), a leading computer on-line service in the United States. C/D's virtual offices led AOL executives to believe that the ad agency would have a solid understanding of its business.

Epilogue

In 1995, Chiat/Day agreed to be acquired by the Omnicom Group and merged with TBWA Advertising to form TBWA Chiat/Day. In the process, TBWA is closing its work spaces and moving into C/D's new offices in New York City. "We'll become virtual too," said Bill Tragos, the founder of TBWA.

Critical Thinking Questions

1. Would you prefer to work or manage in a virtual office such as Chiat/Day's or in a traditional office?

2. According to one employee, the virtual office shows that C/D "no longer thinks about people. It thinks about its culture with no regard to how it affects the staff." Do you find this criticism valid? How can a company considering a virtual office avoid sending this kind of message to employees?

3. What are the drawbacks of giving employees the freedom to, among other things, work at home? How can these drawbacks be controlled or avoided?

4. Does the virtual office as predicted by C/D benefit society as a whole? Describe the ways in which it does and the ways in which it does not.

5. How does C/D's virtual office fortify the "end of management" arguments discussed at the end of this chapter?

SOURCE: Information from R. Rapaport, "Jay Chiat Tears Down the Walls," *Forbes*, October 25, 1993, pp. 26–28; S. Kindel, "This Virtual Office Is Virtually Successful," *Sales & Marketing Management*, December 1, 1994, p. 35; B. Sharkey, "Going Virtual," *Adweek*, May 16, 1994; "Virtual Office Runs on Telecommunications," *Managing Office Technology*, June 1, 1994, p. 57; Y. Gault, "Struggling Chiat Bets on Rearranging Furniture," *Crain's New York Business*, August 30, 1993, p. 4; M. McCarthy, "Chiat/Day, Venice: West Agency of the Year," *Adweek Western Advertising News*, March 20, 1995, p. 34; C. Taylor, "Chiat/Day Set to Win AOL Branding Project," *Adweek Eastern Edition*, June 5, 1995, p. 5; and K. Goldman, "Chiat/Day Reaches Pact to Merge with Omnicom's TBWA Agency," *Wall Street Journal*, February 1, 1995, p. B5.

GLOSSARY

A

Adaptation The process in strategic management of responding to the environment.

Adjudication The act of rendering a judicial decision. In administrative process, the proceeding in which an administrative law judge hears and decides on issues that arise when an administrative agency charges a person or a firm with violating a law or regulation enforced by the agency.

Administrative law judge (ALJ) One who presides over an administrative agency hearing and has the power to administer oaths, take testimony, rule on questions of evidence, and make determinations of fact.

Administrative process The procedure used by administrative agencies in the administration of the law. This process includes the rulemaking, enforcement, and adjudication operations of the agency involved, supplemented by broad investigative powers.

Affirmative action Job-hiring policies that allow special considerations for traditionally disadvantaged groups (such as women or racial minorities) in an effort to overcome the present effects of past discrimination.

Antitrust laws The body of federal and state laws protecting commerce from unlawful restraints, price discrimination, price fixing, and monopolies. The principal federal antitrust statutes are the Sherman Act (1890), the Clayton Act (1914), and the Federal Trade Commission Act (1914).

Appropriate bargaining unit A designation based on job duties, skill levels, and so on, of the proper entity that should be covered by a collective bargaining agreement.

Arbitration The settling of a dispute by submitting it to a disinterested third party (other than a court), who renders a legally binding decision.

Assumption of risk A doctrine whereby a plaintiff may not recover for injuries or damages suffered from risks of which he or she knows and to which he or she assents. A defense against negligence that can be used when the plaintiff has knowledge of and appreciates a danger and voluntarily exposes himself or herself to that danger.

Audit committee A committee, usually made of up four members of a corporation's board of directors, that is responsible for monitoring the fiscal well-being of the corporation.

Authorization card A card signed by an employee that gives a union permission to act on his or her behalf in negotiations with management once a majority of the employees have signed the cards.

B

Bait-and-switch advertising Advertising a product at a very attractive price (the "bait") and then informing the consumer, once he or she is in the store, that the advertised product is either not available or is of poor quality; the customer is then urged to purchase ("switched" to) a more expensive item.

Beachhead acquisition During an attempted takeover, the acquiring corporation may gradually accumulate a large number of the target corporation's shares. Having established a "beachhead," the acquiring company is in position to, if necessary, initiate a proxy fight.

Board of directors Every corporation is governed by a board of directors, the number of which is set forth in the corporation's articles of incorporation or bylaws. These directors decide on corporate policy and appoint corporate managers to manage the day-to-day affairs of the firm.

Bona fide occupational qualification (BFOQ) Under Title VII of the Civil Rights Act of 1964, identifiable characteristics reasonably necessary to the normal operation of a particular business. These characteristics can include gender, national origin, and religion, but not race.

Bottom-up approach A strategic planning method in which goal setting begins at the functional level, leading to business-level goals for the various divisions that are combined to form corporate-level goals.

Bottom-up empowerment cycle A management process in which those at the bottom, such as customers and lower-level employees, create the goals that are pushed up through the organization.

Boycott An organized refusal by consumers to buy specific goods, usually in protest against certain conditions of production or manufacturing.

Bureaucratic control system Rules, policies, guidelines, and procedures that guide the behavior of organizational members.

Business ethics Ethics in a business context; a consensus of what constitutes right and wrong behavior in the world of business and the application of moral principles to situations that arise in a business setting.

Business-level strategy formulation Decisions made by management concerning how organizations will compete in the areas they have selected.

C

Capital All manufactured resources, including buildings, equipment, machines, and improvements to land that is used for production.

Capitalism An economic system in which the individuals own the factors of production and have the right to use those resources in any way they choose within the limits of the law (also called a *market system* or a *free enterprise system*).

Capture hypothesis A theory of regulatory behavior that predicts that the regulators will eventually be captured by the special interests of the industry being regulated.

Cartel An association of producers in an industry that agree to set common prices and output quotas to prevent competition.

Categorical imperative A concept developed by the philosopher Immanuel Kant as an ethical guideline for behavior. In deciding whether an action is right or wrong, or desirable or undesirable, a person should evaluate the action in terms of what would happen if everybody else in the same situation, or category, acted the same way.

Cause-related marketing A marketing concept in which the business ties some or even all of its marketing efforts to a specific cause, such as the Special Olympics or the Amazonian rain forest. Typically, the purchase of the business's products is tied to a small sum of money being donated to the specified cause.

Cease-and-desist order An administrative or judicial order prohibiting a person or business firm from conducting activities that an agency or a court has deemed illegal.

Charity principle The precept that those individuals or groups in society who are financially secure have a moral duty to provide aid and support to those individuals and groups who are not financially secure.

Chemical fingerprinting A process that allows scientists to trace the origins of oil spills. This process allows government agencies to determine which private sources are responsible, and liable, for damaging the environment.

Chief executive officer (CEO) The highest-ranking officer in a corporation, with primary responsibility for determining the corporation's strategic direction.

Chief information officer (CIO) A corporate executive who is given the responsibility of deciding how the corporation can better implement information technology in meeting its operating goals.

Clan control The socialization processes that dictate the type of behavior appropriate in the organization.

Class I recall A recall action initiated by the Food and Drug Administration when a food or drug product presents a life-threatening health risk to consumers.

Class II recall A recall action initiated by the Food and Drug Administration when a food or drug product presents a health risk that is not life threatening to consumers.

Class III recall A recall action initiated by the Food and Drug Administration when a food or drug product does not present a health risk to consumers, but violates labeling or manufacturing laws.

Closed shop A firm that requires union membership of its workers as a condition of employment. Closed shops were made illegal under the Taft-Hartley Act.

Code of ethics A written set of guidelines that provides employees with general knowledge of the ethical standards of the corporation.

Cognitive bias The tendency of managers to make decisions based on cognitive (perceived) rather than objective factors in the operating environment. Cognitive bias does not necessarily result in poor decision making, as the bias may come from a reasonable assumption on the manager's part.

Cognitive dissonance In the context of ethical decision making, occurs when one's moral beliefs and one's actions are opposed or inconsistent.

Cognitive overload In the context of ethical decision making, occurs when managers are exposed to more stimuli than they can effectively process.

Collective bargaining The process by which labor and management negotiate the terms and conditions of employment, including such things as hours and workplace conditions.

Commerce clause The section of the Constitution that grants Congress the power to regulate trade among the states and with foreign countries.

Common law That body of law developed from custom or judicial decision in English and U.S. courts, not attributable to a legislature.

Communism Economic and political system based on the theories of Karl Marx. In such a system, the entire economy is based on collective ownership and government control of property and the means of production. Individuals are expected to contribute to the economy according to their ability and are given income according to their needs. Also an economic and political system implemented in countries such as Cuba, China, and, until recently, the Soviet Union, in which the state controls the production and distribution of goods and the government is directed by a single authoritarian leader or political party.

Comparable worth The comparable worth doctrine supports the belief that women should receive the same wages as men if the levels of skill and responsibility in their jobs are equal or equivalent.

Comparative advertisements Advertisements in which the advertising firm compares its products favorably with the same products of another firm. This style of advertising may be considerd deceptive by courts if the advertising company misrepresents its own goods, services, or commercial activities or those of the named competitor.

Comparative advantage Also known as competitive advantage, the ability to produce at lower cost compared to other producers, whether they are countries, firms, or individuals.

Comparative negligence A theory in tort law under which the liability for injuries resulting from negligent acts is shared by all persons who were guilty of negligence (including the injured party), on the basis of each person's proportionate carelessness.

Compensation committee A committee, generally made up of five members of a corporation's board of directors, that is concerned with determining compensation for the corporation's upper management.

Compensatory damages A money award equivalent to the actual value of injuries or damages sustained by the aggrieved party.

Competitive benchmarking A process in which management uses the successful practices of competitors in setting targets to encourage improvement in its own company's performance.

Concentration strategy A corporate-level strategy in which management concentrates on producing a single product or service or a small group of products or services. This strategy is based on the belief that concentration will necessarily allow for more effective use of resources.

Conglomerate merger A merger between firms that do not compete with each other because they are in different markets (as opposed to horizontal and vertical mergers).

Constant dollars Dollars expressed in terms of real purchasing power using a particular year as the base or standard of comparison, in contrast to current dollars.

Consumer law Statutes, agency rules, and judicial decisions protecting consumers of goods and services from dangerous manufacturing techniques, mislabeling, unfair credit practices, deceptive advertising, and so on. Consumer laws provide remedies and protections that are not ordinarily available to merchants or to businesses.

Contingent valuation A process that attempts to determine the value placed by the public on seemingly unquantifiable natural resources. Contingent valuation relies on the surveying of a cross-section of individuals to acertain the monetary value of, for example, saving a species from extinction.

Contract A set of promises constituting an agreement between parties, giving each a legal duty to the other and also the right to seek a remedy for the breach of the promises/duties owed to each. The elements of an enforceable contract are competent parties, a proper legal purpose, consideration (an exchange of promises/duties), and mutuality of agreement and obligation.

Contributory negligence A theory in tort law under which a complaining party's own negligence contributed to or caused his or her injuries. Contributory negligence is an absolute bar to recovery in some jurisdictions.

Conviction The outcome of a criminal trial in which the defendant has been found guilty of the crime charged and on which sentencing, or punishment, is based.

Corporate charter The document issued by a state official (usually the secretary of state) granting a corporation legal existence and the right to function.

Corporate culture The distinctive manner by which different corporations expose employees to values and norms of acceptable and appropriate behavior.

Corporate governance The manner by which a corporation is controlled and managed in accordance with its goals and corporate culture; how a corporation is governed.

Corporate-level strategy formulation Decisions made by management in selecting the business areas in which the organization will compete.

Corporate social responsibility The concept that corporations can and should act ethically and be accountable to society for their actions.

Corporate raiders People or firms that specialize in seeking out corporations that are potential targets for takeovers.

Corporate volunteer council (CVC) A partnership between corporate volunteers, community leaders, and local government agencies. The goal of a CVC is to link community needs with available corporate volunteers in an efficient manner.

Corporation A legal entity created under the authority of the laws of a state. The entity is distinct from its shareholders/ owners.

Cost-benefit analysis A way to reach decisions in which the costs of a given action are compared with the benefits of the action.

Counteradvertising New advertising that is undertaken pursuant to a Federal Trade Commission order for the purpose of correcting earlier false claims that were made about a product.

Crisis management The strategic decisions made by management before, during, and after an organizational crisis.

Cross-subsidization The selling of a product or service in one market below cost, the losses being compensated for by selling the same product or service in another market at above marginal cost.

Crown jewel defense Efforts of a target company to make itself less attractive to a raider by selling off its most valuable asset (the "crown jewel").

Cultural distance In the context of an employee relocated to a foreign country, the psychological and sociological distance between the society of the employee's home country and his or her new living environment.

D

Damages Money sought as a remedy for a breach of contract or for a tortious act.

Deceptive advertising Advertising that misleads consumers, either by making unjustified claims concerning a product's performance or by omitting a material fact concerning the product's composition or performance.

Defendant One against whom a lawsuit is brought; the accused person in a criminal proceeding.

Defense That which a defendant offers and alleges in an action or suit as a reason why the plaintiff should not recover or establish what he or she seeks.

Delegation doctrine According to this doctrine, Article I, Sections 1 and 8 of the U.S. Constitution have been construed by the courts as granting Congress the power to establish administrative agencies that can create rules for implementing administrative law.

Deliberate strategy A strategy in which managers, having already planned an intentional strategic course, respond to changes in the internal and external environment according to that strategic course.

Denteological perspective A theory that the ethical worth of a decision rests on the intent of the decision maker rather than on the actual outcome of the decision.

Deregulation The removal of regulatory restraints; the opposite of regulation.

Direct costs of regulation Those costs to a company that are directly caused by efforts to conform to regulatory law.

Derivative suit A suit by a shareholder to enforce a corporate cause of action against a third person.

Disparate-impact discrimination In an employment context, discrimination that results from certain employer practices or procedures that, although not discriminatory on their faces, have a discriminatory effect. For example, a requirement that all employees have high school diplomas is not necessarily discriminatory, but it may have the effect of discriminating against minority groups.

Disparate-treatment discrimination In an employment context, intentional discrimination against individuals on the basis of color, gender, national origin, race, religion, age, or disability.

Diversification The corporate-level strategy of developing the skills and production knowledge necessary to compete in new markets. The primary goal of diversification is risk reduction, as a firm's resources are spread over a number of dissimilar businesses.

Diversity In the corporate context, the changing racial and cultural makeup of the work force.

Diversity management The strategy of managing a culturally diverse work force with minimum losses and eventual gains in efficiency and productivity.

Divestiture The act of selling one or more of a company's parts, such as a subsidiary or plant; often mandated by courts in merger or monopolization cases.

Dividend Portion of a corporation's profits paid to its owners (shareholders).

Doctrine of the mean According to Aristotle, the most desired state of moral existence was in the mean, or middle, of behavior. For example, courage is the ideal mean between cowardice and foolhardiness.

Doctrine of vicarious liability A doctrine that places legal responsibility on one person for the acts of another.

Downsizing Measures taken by corporations to sell business units or reduce the number of employees with the ultimate goal of increasing profits.

Dumping Selling goods in a foreign country at a price below the price charged for the same goods in the domestic market.

Dynamically stable An organizational condition that should be the goal of managers. The organization should have the capacity to serve a wide range of changing consumer demands (thus being dynamic), while at the same time creating long-term processing capabilities and storing knowledge of the internal and external environments (thus being stable).

E

Early retirement program An alternative to layoffs during periods of corporate downsizing in which the corporation offers employees with lengthy periods of service incentives to take early retirement.

Economic regulation Regulation that is typically intended to control the prices that regulated industries are allowed to charge. For example, various public utility commissions throughout the United States regulate the rates of electrical utility companies and telephone operating companies.

Economic strike A strike called by a union to pressure an employer to make concessions on hours, wages, or other terms of employment.

Efficiency The situation in which a given output is produced at minimum cost. Alternatively, the case in which a given level of input is used to produce the maximum output possible.

Eighty-day cooling-off period A provision in the Taft-Hartley Act that allows federal courts to issue injunctions against strikes that might create a national emergency.

Eminent domain The power of a government to take land for public use from private citizens for just compensation.

Emergent strategy A strategy not planned or intended, but which occurs naturally from a procession of managerial decisions.

Emission banking A policy which gives companies a certain number of pollution allowances each year. In this system, a business may decide to not pollute as much in any given year, thereby "banking" its allowances for future use.

Employee giving campaign An alternative to direct corporate philanthropy in which a company provides its employees with the opportunity to contribute to charity campaigns funded by payroll deductions, benefit events, matching donations, or direct donations.

Employee rights Rights for employees such as protection from unsafe working conditions and privacy that have evolved through a combination of regulatory laws, labor union activity, and corporate social responsibility.

Employment-at-will doctrine A common law doctrine under which employer-employee contracts are considered to be "at will"— that is, either party may terminate an employment contract at any time and for any reason, unless the contract specifies otherwise. Although several states still adhere to the employment-at-will doctrine, exceptions are frequently made on the basis of an implied employment contract or public policy.

Employment discrimination Treating employees or job applicants unequally on the basis of race, sex, nationality, religion, or age; prohibited by Title VII of the Civil Rights Act of 1964 as amended.

Enabling legislation Statutes enacted by Congress that authorize the creation of an administrative agency and specify the name, composition, and powers of the agency being created.

Enacted values The values reflected in the actions of the corporation and its employees.

Enactment The managerial effort to control the operating environment to make it less averse and more conducive to the company's success.

Enlightened capitalism An envisioned capitalist economic system in business that is concerned with the effects of its activities on the well-being of society, and makes strategic decisions with society's well-being in mind.

Enlightened self-interest The insertion of corporate social responsibility into the profit motive of a corporation. A company will make a decision that benefits society while also increasing its profits.

Entrepreneur One who initiates and assumes the financial risks of a new enterprise and who undertakes to provide or control its management.

Environmental determinism A traditional form of management strategy in which managers formulate strategy by reacting to changes in the operating environment as those changes occur.

Environmental impact statement (EIS) A statement mandated by the Environmental Policy Act that must show the costs and benefits of federal actions that could significantly affect the quality of the environment.

Environmental law All statutory, regulatory, and common law relating to the protection of the environment.

Environmental management A more traditional approach to strategic management in which a strategy is chosen that will best fit environmental, technical, and social forces at a particular point in time.

Environmental scanning Various systems within the organization for detecting changes in the external environment that require management to make organizational changes.

Espoused values The values of a corporation as articulated through pronouncements from management and in codified form, such as codes of ethics and mission statements.

Ethical investing mutual fund A mutual fund is a specific type of investment company that continually buys or sells to investors shares of ownership in a portfolio. An ethical investing mutual fund will only conduct business with corporations it has deemed ethically responsible.

Ethical norms Inputs from various sources—including family and friends, the local community, national beliefs, religious beliefs, corporate culture, and the law—that inform an individual's ethical decision-making process.

Ethical relativism In the context of ethical decision making in a global environment, the question of whether ethical principles should be defined only by what one particular society or individual considers to be ethical at any given moment. Global managers must understand that the ethics of their home societies do not necessarily correspond with the ethical beliefs of foreign communities.

Ethics Moral principles and values applied to social behavior.

Ethics codes Formal codes of corporate conduct that spell out the way in which its employees are expected to act in any given situation. Such codes may make very general statements; others may be quite detailed, such as specifing that all merchandise buyers are prohibited from accepting any gifts from vendors.

Ethnocentrism The assumption that the morals of a manager's home country are superior to, and should be promoted over, those of a foreign country.

Exclusive bargaining agent The party, usually a union, given the right to act as the only representative of labor in negotiations with management.

Exclusive distributorship A distributorship in which the seller and distributor of the seller's products agree that the distributor has the exclusive right to distribute the seller's products in a certain geographic area.

Exclusive-dealing contract An agreement under which a producer of goods agrees to sell its goods exclusively through one distributor.

Executive agency An administrative agency (or subagency) within a cabinet department of the executive branch of the government.

Export To sell products to buyers located in other countries.

Express warranty A promise, ancillary to an underlying sales agreement, that is included in the written or oral terms of the sales agreement under which the promisor assures the quality, description, or performance of the goods.

F

Featherbedding A requirement that more workers be employed to do a particular job than are actually needed.

Federal Reserve System A network of twelve central banks headed by a board of governors, with the advice of the Federal Advisory Council and the Federal Open Market Committee, to give the United States an elastic currency, supervise and regulate banking activity, and facilitate the flow and discounting of commercial paper. All national banks and state-chartered banks that voluntarily join the system are members.

Feedback control system A system that gathers information concerning the outcome of organizational activities. This information is then employed to assess the progress of the organization in meeting its goals.

Feedforward control system A system that analyzes inputs from stakeholders and the remote environment. These inputs are used by management to anticipate changes in the internal and external environments of the organization.

Financial strategy A plan to provide the organization with the proper capital structure and funds it will need achieve growth in the industry in which the company competes.

Fleet mileage standards Average per-mile gas consumption standards that are imposed by the federal government on the various automobile manufacturing companies. That is to say, the miles per gallon results for each of the models sold in any given year are averaged to see if they meet the required standards.

Foreign Corrupt Practices Act (FCPA) Passed in 1977, the FCPA prohibits American firms from using bribery to secure advantageous international trade contracts. The FCPA also requires that all companies keep accurate and fair records of business interactions involving foreign interests.

Fraud Any misrepresentation, either by misstatement or omission of a material fact, knowingly made with the intention of deceiving another and on which a reasonable person would and does rely to his or her detriment.

Functional strategies The sum of decisions made and actions taken by management and other employees that implement the growth and competitive strategies of the corporation.

G

Gazelles Companies characterized by an ability to react to market conditions more quickly and effectively than their competitors. Gazelles are also defined by their innovative use of new technology and new forms of corporate organization.

Geocentricism Concentration on the global ramifications of ethical and strategic corporate decisions.

Glass ceiling A perceived barrier that keeps women from progressing upward in the corporate hierarchy.

Global corporation An updated term for the more commonly used "multinational corporation." A corporation with factors of production, labor, and/or consumer markets in more than two countries.

Global sourcing The location of various factors in the manufacturing process in foreign countries, usually for the express purpose of lowering production costs. For example, a U.S. automobile manufacturer may have its brake parts manufactured in Mexico.

Golden parachute A guaranty to the existing managers of a firm that if they are ousted as a result of a takeover, they will receive large severance payments.

Grassroots lobbying Lobbying efforts conducted by organizations or individuals not part of the professional lobbying industry.

Greenhouse effect The trapping of heat inside the earth's atmosphere, which is a result of pollution caused by the burning of fossil fuels and the emission of carbon dioxide.

Greenmail Payment by a target firm of a substantial premium for shares held by a corporate raider in return for the raider's agreement to cease attempts at a takeover.

Greenwashing A situation in which a corporation is cooperating with an environmental special interest group in one specific area while harming the environment in another specific area.

Group boycott The refusal to deal with a particular person or firm by a group of competitors, prohibited under the Sherman Act.

H

Hearing A proceeding, less formal than a trial, in which definite issues are considered, parties are allowed to present their cases in a meaningful manner, witnesses are heard, and evidence is presented.

Horizontal merger A merger between two businesses or persons competing in the marketplace.

Horizontal restraint Any agreement that in some way restrains competition between rival firms competing in the same market. Price fixing is an example of a horizontal restraint on competition.

Horizontal system Any system of organization operation that basically puts all workers on an equal level in terms of, at a minimum, the ability to communicate with each other. Within a horizontal management arrangement, a "lower-level" employee does not have to necessarily go through his or her immediate manager when he or she has an idea, but can talk specifically to most managers and other executives, no matter how senior they are.

Host government The government of the foreign country in which a particular multinational business has factors of production, labor, or consumer markets.

Hot-cargo agreements An agreement in which employers voluntarily agree with unions not to handle, use, or deal in non-union-produced goods of other employers. A type of secondary boycott specifically prohibited by the Landrum-Griffin Act of 1959.

Human resources strategy A strategy that specifies how an organization will recruit, hire, train, and compensate its employees. This strategy must fit within the goals of the organization as a whole.

I

Implied warranty A warranty that the law implies through either the situation of the parties or the nature of the transaction.

Implied warranty of fitness for a particular purpose A presumed promise made by a merchant seller of goods that the goods are fit for the particular purpose for which the buyer will use the goods. The seller must know the buyer's purpose and know that the buyer is relying on the seller's skill and judgment to select suitable goods.

Implied warranty of *merchantability* A presumed promise by a merchant seller of goods that the goods are reasonably fit for the general purpose for which they are sold, are properly packaged and labeled, and are of proper quality.

Incentive structure The motivational rewards and costs that individuals face in any given situation. Each economic system has its own incentive structure. The incentive structure is different under a system of private property than under a system of government-owned property, for example.

Indictment A charge or written accusation, issued by a grand jury, that a named peson has committed a crime.

Indirect costs of regulation Those costs to a company that are indirectly caused by efforts to conform to regulatory law. Such costs are often called "hidden." For example, the price for new homes may be affected by a regulatory law that requires insulation in the attic. The price of each home will be inflated due to the costs of adding the insulation.

Induced costs of regulation Economic costs of regulation that are not directly covered by business or indirectly covered by consumers, but that are nonetheless a result of regulatory law; for example, the increased health costs of a company due to increased employee stress resulting from government regulations.

Industrial policy Regulatory and other legislative actions taken by the federal government to influence or control the competitive conditions in a particular market or industry.

Informal rulemaking A procedure in agency rulemaking that requires (1) notice; (2) opportunity for comment; and (3) a general statement of the basis for, and purpose of, the proposed rule. Also referred to as notice-and-comment rulemaking.

Information systems strategy The use of information technology to shape and meet a corporation's operating goals.

Initial order In the context of administrative law, an agency's disposition in a matter other than a rulemaking. An administrative law judge's initial order becomes final unless it is appealed.

Injunction An order to a specific person or corporation, directing that person or corporation to do or to refrain from doing a particular act.

In-kind gifts An alternative method of corporate philanthropy in which the corporation donates products that it produces—such as IBM donating computers—instead of cash to charitable foundations.

Inside directors Members of a corporation's board of directors who are also part of that corporation's management team.

Institutional shareholders Organizational entities, such as pension plans, that own large blocks of shares in a corporation. Institutional shareholding organizations have their own directors and management structure to oversee the organization's shares.

Intellectual property rights   The right of the owners of property resulting from intellectual, creative processes—the products of an individual's mind.

Interest   The payment for current rather than future command over resources; the cost of borrowing money.

Interest group   An organized group of individuals sharing common objectives who actively attempt to influence policy through lobbying, the publication of public opinion polls, and other methods.

Interlocking directorate   Persons who serve simultaneously on the boards of two or more corporations (not including banks, banking associations, trust companies, and common carriers), at least one of which is engaged in commerce that has capital, surplus, and undivided profits totaling more than $1 million.

International law   The law that governs relations among nations. International customs and treaties are generally considered to be two of the most important sources of international law.

Interpretative rules   Administrative agency rules that are simply statements and opinions issued by an agency explaining how the agency interprets and intends to apply the statutes it enforces. Such rules are not automatically binding on private individuals or organizations.

Iron triangle   Term used for a three-way alliance between legislators, bureaucrats, and interest groups to make or preserve policies that benefit their respective individual interests.

Issues management   In the context of strategic management, a process that is based on organizational knowledge of its operating environment. In other words, this strategy allows management to preserve markets, reduce risk, create opportunities, and control public relations by understanding the issues that are important to society as a whole.

J

Job-linked literacy programs (JLLP)   Programs established by corporations to help their employees gain literacy skills needed to benefit both the employee and the corporation.

Job-sharing program   An alternative to layoffs during periods of corporate downsizing; a program designed to decrease the work and pay of all employees so that the corporation will not have to completely eliminate any employment positions.

Joint venture   A joint undertaking of a specific commercial enterprise by an association of persons. A joint venture is normally not a legal entity and is treated like a partnership for federal income tax purposes.

Jurisdiction   The authority of a court to hear and decide a specific action.

Justice   What is fair according to the prevailing laws and standards of a particular society, within that society.

L

Labor unions   Worker organizations that usually seek to secure economic improvements for their members; they also seek to improve safety, health, and obtain other benefits for their members.

Laissez faire   A doctrine advocating government restraint in the regulation of business.

Law of agency   The law that governs the relationship between principles and agents (such as between employers and employees). Such law defines the rights and duties of each principle and each agent.

Law of demand   There is a negative, or inverse, relationship between the price of any good or service and the quantity demanded, holding other factors constant. This economic law requires that as the price of goods and services rise, the quantity demanded of those goods and services will fall.

Law of diminishing marginal returns   The principle that as more of any good or service is consumed, its extra benefit declines. Otherwise stated, there are smaller and smaller increases on total utility from the consumption of a good or service as more is consumed during a given time period. In the context of social regulation, the law refers to reduction of societal benefit for every extra dollar spent on the regulation.

Law of supply   There is a positive relationship between the price of any good or service and the quantity producers will supply. This economic law states that as the price of goods and services goes up, so does the quantity supplied. As these prices go down, so does the quantity supplied.

Legislative rules   Administrative agency rules that carry the same weight as congressionally enacted statutes.

Leveraged buyout (LBO)   A corporate takeover financed by loans secured by the acquired corporation's assets or by the issuance of corporate bonds, resulting in a high debt load for the corporation.

Liability   Any actual or potential legal obligation, duty, debt, or responsibility.

Lobbying   All the efforts by individuals or organizations to affect the passage, defeat, or contents of legislation. The term comes from the lobby of the legislature itself, where petitioners used to corner legislators and speak about their concerns.

Lockout   The closing of a plant to employees by an employer to gain leverage in collective bargaining negotiations.

M

Market   An abstract concept concerning all of the arrangements that individuals have for exchanging with one another. Thus, we can speak of the labor market, the automobile market, and the credit market.

Market concentration   A situation that exists when a small number of firms share the market for a particular good or service. For example, if the four largest grocery stores in Chicago accounted for 80 percent of all retail food sales, the market clearly would be concentrated in those four stores.

Market power   The power of a firm to control the market for its product. A monopoly has the greatest degree of market power.

Marketing strategy   A strategy to promote, price, and distribute the products and services of an organization. This strategy also applies to the identification and service of consumer groups.

Maximum profits The profit which a corporation can make in the short term by making business decisions that disregard the effects of those decisions on the well-being of society.

Merger A contractual process by which one corporation (the surviving corporation) acquires all the assets and liabilities of another corporation (the merged corporation). The shareholders of the merged corporation receive either payment for their shares or shares in the surviving corporation.

Minimum wage The lowest wage, either by government regulation or union contract, that an employer must pay an hourly worker.

Monopolization The possession of monopoly power in the relevant market and the willful acquisition or maintenance of that power, as distinguished from growth or development as a consequence of a superior product, business acumen, or historic accident. A violation of Section 2 of the Sherman Act requires that both of these elements be established.

Monopoly An industry or company that has total control over the sale of a product or service and does not face competition.

Monopoly power An extreme amount of market power.

Moore's Law Devised by scientist Gordon Moore, a theory that the power and complexity of the silicon computer chip will double every eighteen months.

Morals Societal rules or guidelines that determine what is right and wrong conduct for individuals and organizations.

Most-favored-nation status (MFN) A status granted in an international treaty by a provision stating that the citizens of the contracting nations may enjoy the privileges accord by either party to citizens of the most favored nations. Generally, most-favored-nation clauses are designed to establish equality of international agreement in regard to imports or exports.

Multinational companies Those organizations that have business operations in many countries, although one country may be considered the "headquarters" of such a company.

Multinational corporation (MNC) A corporation with factors of production, labor, and/or consumer markets in more than two countries.

Mutual fund A specific type of investment company that continually buys or sells to investors shares of ownership in a portfolio.

N

National Labor Relations Board (NLRB) Created by the National Labor Relations Act of 1935, the NLRB was created to oversee union elections and to prevent employers from engaging in unfair and illegal union activities and unfair labor practices. The board has investigatory powers and can issue and service complaints against employers in response to employee charges of unfair labor practices.

Natural monopoly A monopoly that arises from the peculiar production characteristics in an industry. It usually arises when one firm can produce at a lower average cost than can be achieved by multiple firms.

Needs-based system An alternative to affirmative action, which would redistribute the benefits of affirmative action based on an individual's lack of income rather than the individual's race and gender.

Negative externality A situation in which a private cost or benefit diverges from a social cost or benefit; a situation in which the costs or benefits of an action are not fully borne by the two parties engaged in exchange or by an individual engaging in an activity using scarce resources.

Negative incentive A type of incentive that causes people to react in a certain way because of the threat of punishment, either in the form of fines, lost business, lost income, jail sentences, etc. To be contrasted with a positive incentive, such as higher profits, greater prestige in the community, etc.

Negligence The failure to exercise the standard of care that a reasonable person would exercise in similar circumstances.

Noblesse oblige A moral, as opposed to legal, obligation of society's most wealthy citizens—nobles, in the past—to redistribute their income among the poor members of society.

Nominating committee A committee, generally comprised of five members of the corporation's board of directors, whose responsibility is to choose nominees for vacancies on the corporation's board of directors.

Nondiscrimination rule A requirement that an employer treat a union soliciting employee votes in a representation election the same way that the employer would treat any other entity with regard to on-site contact with employees.

Notice of Proposed Rulemaking A notice published (in the Federal Register) by an administrative agency describing a proposed rule. The notice must give the time and place for which agency proceedings on the proposed rule will be held, a description of the nature of the proceedings, the legal authority for the proceedings (which is usually the agency's enabling legislation), and the terms of the proposed rule or the subject matter of the proposed rule.

O

"Obscene" profits The popular opinion that an individual or corporation can enjoy profits so great that the measures used to gain these profits harm society as a whole.

Offset policy A policy requiring one company wishing to build a plant that would pollute to work out an offsetting reduction in pollution at some other plant in a specific geographic area.

Operating environment The sum of an organization's external stakeholders. These stakeholders include competitors, customers, suppliers, financial sources, venture partners, special interest groups, unions, and government agencies.

Operating goals Specific objectives an organization requires its managers to meet within certain time periods.

Operations strategy A strategy to design and manage the procedures needed to generate the organization's products and services.

Opportunities Changing circumstances which provide companies with alternatives to improve their scope and profit.

Opportunity cost The highest-valued, next best alternative that must be sacrificed in order to attain something or satisfy a want.

Optimum profits A satisfactory level of profit realized by a corporation that bases its business and corporate-level decisions, to a certain extent, on the well-being of society.

Organizational crisis A situation that threatens high-priority organizational goals, causes employee time to be diverted from day-to-day activities, and contains an element of surprise.

Outside directors Members of a corporation's board of directors who do not have any other role within the corporation's management structure.

P

Pac-Man defense An aggressive defense to an attempted takeover in which the target corporation attempts its own takeover of the acquiring corporation; named after the Atari video game.

Pareto optimality A microeconomic theory that refers to a condition in which the scarce resources of society are being used so efficiently by the producing firms, and the goods and services are being distributed so effectively by the competitive markets, that it would be impossible to make any single person better off without harming some other person.

Partnership An association of two or more persons to carry on, as co-owners, a business for profit.

Passion branding A marketing strategy in which the corporation links its fundamental personality and culture with a social cause or causes. This strategy relies on the passion of a sufficient number of consumers with regard to the same social cause or causes.

Patent A government grant that gives an inventor the exclusive right or privilege to make, use, or sell his or her invention for a limited time period. The word patent usually refers to some invention and designates either the instrument by which the patent's rights are evidence or the patent itself.

Paternalism When one person or organization asserts that it knows what is best for another person or group of people. In the context of global decision making, also exists when one country, or interest group, assumes that it has higher ethical standards than another, and tries to assert these ethical standards on the second country or group.

Per se violation A type of anticompetitive agreement—such as a price-fixing agreement—that is considered to be so injurious to the public that there is no need to determine whether it actually injures market competition; rather, it is in itself (*per se*) a violation of the Sherman Act.

Picket line One or more employees present at the entrance to an employer's business to publicize a labor dispute or to influence employees or members of the public to withhold their services or business.

Plaintiff One who initiates a lawsuit.

Pluralism A situation in any given society in which members of minority groups maintain traditions independent of the majority.

Poison pill defense In general, any maneuver by the management of a firm targeted for takeover that makes the firm either unattractive to a potential raider or prohibitively expensive.

Political action committee (PAC) A committee that is established by and represents the interests of corporations, labor unions, or special interest groups. PACs raise money and give donations to campaigns on behalf of the groups they represent.

Polygraph A lie-detector test that employers use to ascertain the honesty of employees. Congress has passed laws restricting an employer's ability to use polygraphs in many situations.

Potentially responsible party (PRP) A liable party under the Comprehensive Environmental Response, Compensation, and Liability Act (CERCLA), or Superfund. A person who generated the hazardous waste, operated or owned a waste site at the time of disposal, or currently owns or operates a site may be responsible for some or all of the clean-up costs involved in removing the hazardous chemicals.

Predatory pricing The pricing of a product below cost with the intent to drive competitors out of the market.

Precedent A court decision that furnishes an example or authority for deciding subsequent cases in which identical or similar facts are presented.

Premise control A system that allows managers to ascertain whether the information used to determine strategies and goals is still valid given possible changes in the company's current internal and external environments.

Price discrimination A seller's setting of prices in such a way that two competing buyers pay two different prices for an identical product or service.

Price-fixing agreement An anticompetitive agreement between competitors to fix, or render uniform, the prices at which they will sell their products or services.

Principle of rights The principle that there is no justification for an action that harms an individual, even if that action benefits society as a whole. The principle of rights underlies civil rights, privacy rights, fetal rights, and rights for senior citizens, disabled persons, animals, children, women, and gay and lesbian persons.

Priority publics Those individuals or groups who can most help or hinder a corporation's attempts to influence its operating environment.

Privatization The replacement of products and services paid for by the government with those supplied by private firms.

Privity of contract Because a contract is a private agreement between the parties who have entered into it, it is fitting that these parties alone should have rights and liabilities under the contract. This is referred to as privity of contract, and it establishes the basic concept that third parties have no rights in contracts to which they are not parties.

Product liability The legal liability of manufacturers and sellers to buyers, users, and bystanders for injuries or damages suffered because of defects in goods purchased. Liability arises when a product has a defective condition that makes it unreasonably dangerous to the user or consumer.

Product misuse A defense against product liability that may be raised when the plaintiff used a product in a manner not intended by the manufacturer. If the misuse is reasonably foreseeable, the seller will not escape liability unless measures were taken to guard against the harm that could result from the misuse.

Progressive discipline A process for disciplining employees that begins with a verbal communication to the employee that management is not satisfied with his or her job performance. Further steps in the process include written notice to the same effect, suspension, probation, fines, transfers, demotion, and, finally, termination.

Property rights   The rights of an owner to use and to exchange his or her property.

Protected class   A class of persons with identifiable characteristics who historically have been victimized by discriminatory treatment for certain purposes. Depending on the context, these characteristics include age, color, gender, national origin, race, and religion.

Protected concerted action   The action taken by employees for their mutual benefit regarding wages, hours, or terms and conditions of employment. An action by a single employee may be protected by the courts if that action is taken for the benefit of other employees. Corporations cannot discipline an employee or group of employees for taking a protected concerted action.

Proxy   In corporation law, a written agreement between a stockholder and another under which the stockholder authorizes the other to vote the stockholder's shares in a certain manner.

Proxy fight   During a takeover attempt, the acquiring corporation, having already purchased a number of the target corporation's shares, tries to secure the proxies of other shareholders. In most cases, if the combination of its own shares and proxies constitute a majority vote, the acquiring corporation will gain control of the corporation.

Public interest   The best interests of the community or the national good.

Public policy   What government decides to do or not to do.

Puffing   The act of a salesperson making exaggerated claims concerning the quality of the goods offered. Such claims involve opinions rather than facts and are not considered to be legally binding promises or warranties.

Punitive damages   Compensation in excess of actual or consequential damages. They are awarded in order to punish the wrongdoer and usually will be awarded only in cases involving willful or malicious misconduct.

Q

Quality circle   An arrangement in which workers and management form teams that make decisions about methods of work, pay, etc. in order to increase productivity.

Quality control   A bottom-up approach that focuses on providing high-quality products for consumers. Sometimes, quality control can lead to a competitive disadvantage in areas such as cost of product and speed of service.

Quorum   The number of members of a decision-making body that must be present before business may be validly transacted.

Quota   A rule enforced by the government that states that a certain number of jobs, promotions, or other types of selections must be given to members of certain groups.

R

Reasonable accommodation   The Americans with Disabilities Act (ADA) of 1992 requires that businesses make some reasonable accommodations for a disabled job applicant. Reasonable accommodations might include such things as more flexible working hours, new job assignments, and improved training materials.

Reasonable person standard   The standard of behavior expected of a hypothetical "reasonable person." The standard against which negligence is measured and that must be observed to avoid liability for negligence.

"Reasonable woman" standard   An alternative to the reasonable person standard with regard to determining whether or not sexual harassment has taken place. Some courts have decided that sexual harassment should be based not on how a reasonable person defines an action as being sexually offensive or creating a hostile workplace, but on how a "reasonable woman" would make that definition

Recycling   The reuse of raw materials derived from manufactured products.

Regulation   A government's direct influence on the social and economic activity of a society through its ability to pass laws and make rules.

Remote environment   The context in which the organization and its operating environment exist.

Reputations management   An aspect of crisis management which focuses on prevention. Reputations management is based on the belief that an organization must build a reservoir of goodwill with stakeholders in preparation for a crisis. The goodwill may lessen the damage done to the organization in any given crisis.

Reregulation   The reimposition of regulatory apparatus in an industry that has been deregulated. Reregulation may include new limits on price increases and on who may enter the industry.

Research and development strategy   A strategy that guides the basic research efforts of the organization, as well as its development of more effective and efficient applications, processes, and products.

Resolutions   Corporate business matters that shareholders vote to approve or disapprove.

Responsible entity   The theory that industries and businesses that create waste should be forced by government to pay the costs of recycling or disposing of that waste.

Responsiveness   Term favored by some over corporate social responsibility. Notes an action-oriented environment of corporate social responsiveness in which business actually responds to the needs of society, rather than only being obligated to respond to the needs of society.

Restraint on trade   Any conspiracy or combination that unlawfully eliminates competition or facilitates the creation of a monopoly or monopoly pricing.

Reverse discrimination   A controversial side effect of affirmative action programs, which some people believe cause discrimination against "majority" workers, such as white males.

Right-to-know laws   State laws that require employers to provide employees with information about possible workplace dangers due to chemical emissions and other health hazards.

Right-to-work laws   State laws generally providing that employees are not required to join a union as a condition of receiving or retaining employment.

Risk assessment   Instead of trying to quantify the costs and benefits of a regulation, in this method the possibility of worst-case scenarios is measured against the costs of preventing them.

Rule of reason   A test by which a court balances the reason (such as economic efficiency) for an agreement against its potentially anti-competitive effects. In antitrust legislation, many practices are analyzed under the rule of reason.

Rulemaking   The actions undertaken by administrative agencies when formally adopting new regulations or amending old ones. Under the Administrative Procedures Act, rulemaking includes notifying the public of proposed rules or changes and receiving and considering the public's comments.

S

Scorched-earth tactics   A defense to an attempted takeover attempt in which the target corporation sells off its assets or divisions or takes out loans that it agrees to repay in the event of a takeover, thus making itself less financially attractive to an acquiring corporation.

Searches and seizures   The searching or taking into custody of persons or private property by the government. The Fourth Amendment prohibits unreasonable and unwarranted searches and seizures. In the context of administrative law, administrative agencies may undertake searches and seizures to gather information and necessary evidence to prove that a regulation has been violated.

Secondary boycott   A union's refusal to work for, purchase from, or handle the products of a secondary employer, with whom the union has no dispute, with the object of forcing the employer to stop doing business with the primary employer, with whom the union has a labor dispute.

Self-regulation   Instead of waiting for a government agency to regulate an industry or firm, that industry or firm determines society's requirements and takes the responsibility of implementing obvious regulations itself. For example, the motion picture industry sets its own standards for violent and sexual content in films.

Services   Things purchased by consumers that do not have physical characteristics. Examples of services are actions provided by doctors, lawyers, dentists, waiters and waitresses, repair personnel, educators, and so on.

Severance pay   Funds in excess of normal wages or salary paid to an employee on the termination of his or her employment with a company.

Sexual harassment   In the employment context, hiring or granting job promotions or other benefits in return for sexual favors, or language or conduct that is so sexually offensive that it creates a hostile working environment.

Shareholder   The entity that owns a share of stock, or legal claim to a share of a corporation's future profits. The ownership of common stock comes with certain voting rights regarding major policy decisions of the corporation; the ownership of preferred stock gives the owner preferential treatment in the payment of dividends.

Shareholder's derivative suit   A suit by a shareholder to force a corporate cause of action for a wrong suffered by the corporation committed by a third person.

Short-term profits   Those profits that occur within a specific short period, typically a quarter, or at most, a year.

Social audit   An internal process in which a corporation measures its performance with regard to its corporate social responsibilities.

Social contract   An implied contract between business and society, in which society provides business with an environment in which to make profits as long as business does not engage in activity harmful to society.

Social costs   The costs borne by society whenever a resource use—such as the logging of a forest—occurs.

Social ethic   An expression of the dominant ethical values, or shared beliefs, of society in general or a specific community.

Socialism   An economic system in which the state owns the major share of productive resources, except labor. Socialism also usually involves the redistribution of income.

Socialization   The steps through which an individual is indoctrinated with the values, abilities, and expected behaviors of a corporate culture.

Social regulation   Regulation that is focused on the impact of production on the environment and society, the working conditions under which goods and services are produced, and sometimes the physical attributes of goods. The aim of social regulation is a better quality of life for all through a less polluted environment, better working conditions, and safer and better products.

Stakeholder analysis   The process of identifying and prioritizing the key stakeholders of a corporation, assessing their needs, collecting input from them, and integrating this input into the strategic management process.

Stakeholder concept   A view of corporate social responsibility according to which corporations have duties to all who have a "stake" in the corporation, including shareholders, employees, customers, lenders, suppliers, the community, the environment, and others affected by corporate decision making.

Stakeholder management   The process by which a business communicates, negotiates, and carries out relationships with various stakeholder groups.

Statute   A written law enacted by the legislature under constitutional authority declaring something, prohibiting something, or commanding that something be so.

Stock   In corporate law, a stock is an equity or ownership interest in a corporation, measured in units of shares.

Stock option   A stock option typically allows an officer or valued employee of the corporation to purchase at some later date shares in the company stock at a specific price, usually the price that exists when the stock options are issued.

Strategic control   The ongoing processes of evaluating and updating the missions, goals, and strategies of a corporation.

Strategic management   The process through which organizations analyze and learn from their internal and external environments, establish long- and short-term goals, create strategies that are intended to help achieve established goals, and execute those strategies, all in an effort to satisfy key organizational stakeholders.

Strategic philanthropy   The inclusion of a corporation's philanthropic activities into that corporation's profit-making strategies and goals.

Strategy implementation   The process through which a chosen strategy is implemented within an organization. Strategy is implemented via various structural, cultural, leadership, and reward systems.

Strength   A competitive advantage that an organization holds with regard to other companies in its industry or field.

Strict liability   Liability regardless of fault. In tort law, strict liability is imposed on a merchant who introduces into commerce a good that is unreasonably dangerous when in a defective condition.

Subpoena   A legal writ that requires a person to give testimony in court.

Subsidy   A payment to a producer from the government, usually in the form of a cash grant, but also in the form of protective taxation.

Substitutes   Two goods are substitutes when either one can be used for consumption—for example, coffee and tea. The more you buy of one, the less you buy of another. For substitutes, the change in price of one causes a shift in demand for the other in the same direction as the price change.

Superfund   The commonly known name for the Comprehensive Environmental Response, Compensation, and Liability Act, passed by Congress in 1980. The basic purpose of Superfund, which was amended in 1986 by the Superfund Amendments and Reauthorization Act, is to regulate the clean-up of leaking hazardous waste disposal sites. A special federal fund was created for the purpose.

Sustainable development   A model for the multinational corporation's activities in a developing nation. The model envisions a continuous series of compromises between the profit-making goals of the multinational corporation and the protection of the developing nation's natural environment.

Systems of scope   Information systems that allow managers to rapidly develop, gather, store, and disseminate information throughout the organization.

T

Takeover   The purchase of a firm by another entity. The takeover is considered "hostile" if the purchase is opposed by the target's firm's current management, sometimes because it appears likely that the managers will lose their jobs if the takeover is successful.

Target corporation   The acquired corporation in a corporate takeover; a corporation to whose shareholders a tender offer is submitted.

Tariff   A tax on imported goods.

Telecommuting   The act of using technology to fulfill conventional job commitments from a home or nearby work center without physically traveling to a central office.

Telecottage   A facility with multiple telephone lines, personal computers, and other technological innovations that provides training for residents of rural areas who may not be able to receive the job training that is available in urban areas.

Teleological perspective   A theory that the ethical worth of a decision rests on its outcome rather than on the intent of the decision maker.

Temporary workers   Also known as "temps"; contingency workers whose employment depends on the short-term, even daily, needs of management.

Tender offer   A timely offer or expression of willingness to pay a debt or perform an obligation. During the takeover process, the acquiring corporation often makes a tender offer to all the shareholders of the target corporaton. The price of the stock in the ten-

der offer is generally higher than the market price of the target stock, and acts as an incentive for shareholders of the target firm to tender their shares to the acquiring firm.

Theory of public choice   A model used to predict the actions of administrative agencies. The model assumes that regulators act so as to maximize their own welfare.

Threat   An impediment to the mission and/or goals of an organization.

Top-down approach   A method for setting operating goals in which the corporate level determines and then dictates what lower-level goals should be.

Top-down control cycle   A management system in which upper-level executives first establish the operating goals of the entity, which then dictate what lower-level goals should be.

Tort   Civil (as opposed to criminal) wrongs not arising from a breach of contract. A breach of a legal duty owed by the defendant to the plaintiff; the breach must be the proximate cause of the harm done to the plaintiff.

Total quality management (TQM)   A management philosophy that emphasizes total customer satisfaction and superior quality of goods and services through the implementation of TQM principles in all parts of the organization.

Toxic waste   Hazardous, poisonous substances regulated by such laws as the Comprehensive Environmental Response, Compensation, and Liability Act.

Trade embargo   A foreign policy tool used by a federal government to punish another country for perceived wrongdoing. A trade embargo allows for no or limited imports and exports between the two nations.

Trade-off   A desired result that one must sacrifice (trade off) to obtain another, equally desired result.

Trade organization   A special interest group whose members are all in the same business, such as publishers, software developers, etc. Such organizations attempt to further the interest of their members by effective lobbying and other activities.

Treaty   An agreement, or compact, formed between two independent nations.

Trust   A form of business organization somewhat similar to a corporation. Originally, the trust was a device by which several corporations that were engaged in the same general line of business combined for their mutual advantage to eliminate competition and control the market for their products.

Tying arrangement   An agreement between a buyer and a seller under which the buyer of a specific product or service is obligated to purchase additional products or services from the seller.

Type I error   An error made as the result of a decision or an action.

Type II error   An error made as the result of a failure to make a decision or take action.

U

Unemployment   The total number of adults (aged sixteen years or older) who are willing and able to work and who are actively looking for work but have not found a job.

Uniform Commercial Code (UCC) An agreement adopted by all states, the District of Columbia, and the Virgin Islands. The UCC facilitates commerce among the states by providing a uniform, yet flexible set of rules governing commerical transactions. The UCC assures businesspersons that their cotnracts, if validly entered into, will be enforced.

Union shop A place of employment in which all workers, once employed, must become union members within a specified period of time as a condition of their employment.

Unreasonably dangerous In product liability, defective to the point of threatening a consumer's health and safety. A product will be considered unreasonably dangerous if it is dangerous beyond the expectation of the ordinary consumer or if a less dangerous alternative was economically feasible for the manufacturer, but the manufacturer failed to produce it.

Utilitarianism An approach to ethical reasoning in which ethically correct behavior is not related to any absolute ethical or moral values but to an evaluation of the consequences of a given action on those who will be affected by it. In utilitarian reasoning, a "good" decision is one that results in the greatest good for the greatest number of people affected by the decision.

V

Values The belief that a specific mode of conduct is personally or socially preferable to the opposite mode of conduct.

Vertical merger A combining of two firms, one of which purchases goods for resale from the other.

Vertical restraint Any agreement restraining competition that is made between firms at different levels in the same chain of production or distribution of an item.

Vertical system The typical organizational structure within which there is a definite hierarchy of command.

Victim pays principle A situation in which a developed nation offers financial or other incentives to a developing nation in order to persuade that developing nation to discontinue an activity considered harmful, such as harvesting rain forests.

Virtual office A workplace setting in which traditional limitations of time and space have been replaced by technologically driven freedoms. For example, instead of having assigned office space in which to do most of his or her work, an employee shares work space with colleagues or works outside of the office.

Virtual company A corporate organization that exists for a short period of time, usually to exploit conditions in the operating environment which may be ephemeral.

W

Warranty law The body of law that holds sellers responsible for any real or implied contractual obligations they have with consumers.

Weaknesses Competitive disadvantages that an organization suffers with regard to other companies in its industry or field.

Wetland Area of land designated by government agencies (such as the Army Corp of Engineers or the Environmental Protection Agency) as a protected area that supports wildlife and that therefore cannot be filled in or dredged by private contractors or parties.

Whistleblowing Telling the government or the press that one's employer is engaged in some unsafe or illegal activity.

White knight defense A defense to a takeover attempt in which a target corporation solicits a merger with a third party, resulting in a better tender offer to the target's shareholders than the offer made by the acquiring corporation.

Wildcat strike A strike that is not authorized by the union that ordinarily represents the striking employees.

Workers' compensation State statutes establishing an administrative procedure for compensating workers' injuries that arise out of, or in the course of, their employment, regardless of fault. Instead of suing the employer, an injured worker files a claim with the administrative agency or board that administers the local workers' compensation claims.

Wrongful discharge An employer's termination of an employee's employment in violation of common law principles or statutory law that protects a specific class of employees.

INDEX

PHOTO CREDITS